D. Seltzer
Cambridge, Mass.,

February 1957.

THE POEMS OF
JOHN DRYDEN

Edited with an Introduction and
Textual Notes by

JOHN SARGEAUNT

GEOFFREY CUMBERLEGE
OXFORD UNIVERSITY PRESS
London   New York   Toronto

JOHN DRYDEN

Born, Aldwinkle All Saints, Northamptonshire
                             about 9 August 1631
Died, Gerrard Street, Soho, London   .   1 May 1700

*This edition of 'The Poems of John Dryden' edited by John
Sargeaunt, was first published in 1910 and reprinted in 1913,
1925, 1929, 1935, 1946, and 1948.*

CONTENTS

CONTENTS

TRANSLATIONS

INTRODUCTION

THE text of Dryden's poems as printed in England, whether in his own time or after his death, has never been in a satisfactory state. There is no edition wholly free from errors, and most editions contain many gross blunders. Only one of the editors has really collated the original editions, and even he seems not always to have compared Dryden's translations with the original works.

Badly as Dryden's editors have served him, the author himself is not wholly blameless. It was his misfortune that he could not always see his works through the press. Thus he was in Wiltshire while *Annus Mirabilis* was printing, and before his return the book had come out and some copies had been sold. The list of errata, for which he found room on a fly-leaf, was so hurriedly made that itself is full of false references. But errors were more often due to Dryden's fault than to his misfortune. That he could be careful in correcting the press he showed in the case of the *Epistle to John Driden*, a work for which he had a special affection, as the child of his old age and the encomium of his ancient race. But the last of his publications, the very volume which contains this epistle, has, in other poems, some glaring errors of the press. Some of these, and others in other works, were silently corrected in subsequent editions. It needed no Bentley to detect the husband of Eurydice in a line which Dryden allowed to appear in this form :

> Had Orphans sung it in the neather Sphere.

But there are cases in which the true reading may reasonably be a matter of doubt. Thus in *Eleonora* the original text gives:

> And some descending Courtier from above
> Had giv'n her timely warning to remove.

The word ' Courtier ', or, as Dryden would have said, the word of ' Courtier ', was changed by Broughton into ' Courier ', and Todd denounced the original reading as ' a laughable error of the press '. The original reading is defended by Christie and Dr. Saintsbury, and there is something to be said on either side. In *Palamon and Arcite* a line in the original appeared as

> Rich Tap'stry spread the Streets and Flowers the Pots adorn.

The earlier editors changed ' Pots ' into ' Posts ', and, although Dr. Saintsbury prefers the original reading, the passage cited in my note seems to show that they were right.

Many of the poems were republished soon after Dryden's death, some in a collection and some in volumes of Miscellanies. Jacob Tonson, who had succeeded Herringman as Dryden's publisher, was also the publisher of these early posthumous editions. Whom he employed to see the books through the press does not appear. The work was not well done, and some of the corruptions which were then allowed to defile the text have appeared in every later edition. The first editor with a name was Thomas Broughton, who published two incomplete collections, one in 1741, the other in 1743. Broughton introduced new errors, and some of these have held their ground in the published texts. In 1760 four volumes of the poems appeared under the editorship of Samuel Derrick. Derrick, who in his poetical character is the louse of Johnson's famous epigram, as an editor is styled by Dr. Saintsbury ' the accursed '. What right Dr. Saintsbury had to throw this stone will appear hereafter. That Derrick deserved it is unhappily true. In his edition the game of corruption went merrily on. Not satisfied with accidental errors, Derrick took upon himself to alter Dryden's text, and always altered it for the worse. From his volumes other editions were printed, and in spite of the boasts of later editors, some of his abominations are still printed as the genuine work of Dryden.

In 1808 appeared Walter Scott's complete edition of the works of Dryden. It was unfortunate that the great poet and man of letters hardly suspected the existence of corruption in the text. It is astonishing that he should have passed many passages which on the face of them did not make sense. Nor was there much improvement in the Wartons' edition of 1811. To one of the poems in it were appended some notes by Todd, a textual critic of some capacity, who corrected a few, but only a few, of Derrick's mistakes. Mitford's Aldine edition of 1832 is bad, and was hardly made better by Mr. Richard Hooper, who claims to have revised it in 1866 and again in 1891. Mr. Richard Bell's edition, which appeared in 1854, was quite in Derrick's manner, and added many fresh errors to a corrupt text. And so the melancholy tale goes on.

The first, and, down to the present century, the only serious attempt to present a correct text was made by William Dougal Christie. His edition, which does not contain the translations from Greek and Latin poets, appeared in 1870. Christie had zeal and industry, and was a man of undoubted ability. He was at the pains to consult and in some cases to collate the original editions. That his collation was not as complete or as accurate as he implies is evident from the errors which he allowed to stand in his text. In fact, some evil spirit seems to have dogged the steps of Dryden's editors, and may well raise apprehension in one who ventures to add himself to their number. Some of the blunders in Christie's text are so absurd, so ruinous to sense, that it is hard to see how he passed them even without a collation, and inconceivable that he could have left them if once a collation had called his attention to them. As an editor he had two faults : he was not sure in judgement, and he seems to have had no ear. When Dryden wrote

> If they, through Sickness, seldom did appear,
> Pity the Virgins of each Theatre !

Christie remarks that ' Theatre ' was pronounced with the *a* long. When Dryden wrote

> An Universal Metempsuchosis,

Christie gives a stress both to the penultimate and to the antepenultimate of the last word in the line. From a line in *The Wife of Bath's Tale*,

> But, not to hold our Proffer in Scorn,

a syllable has undoubtedly dropt out. Christie filled the gap with a word which gives no sense. This lack of judgement sometimes makes it doubtful whether he carelessly followed an error of his predecessors, or actually misunderstood his text. An example may be found in the line from *Cymon and Iphigenia* which is cited below. Christie's want of ear, very manifest in his notes, made him overlook some errors which would certainly have roused Dryden's indignation.

Scott's edition was republished in 1883 and the following years as revised and corrected by Dr. George Saintsbury. However well Dr. Saintsbury may have deserved of Dryden in other respects, it must be regretfully declared that his work on the text was worse than useless. It is true that in some of the poems his text is a great improvement on Scott's, but the improvement is due, not to Dr. Saintsbury, but to Christie. Dr. Saintsbury acknowledges to some extent his obligation to his predecessor, but he claims to have made a collation of the original editions. It is unfortunate that he should have used a phrase which well might be, and actually has been, misunderstood. He has been taken to mean that he had throughout collated his text with the original editions. This was not the case. It must be clear to one who really has made the collation that Dr. Saintsbury cannot have meant more than that he had verified the corrections which Christie mentioned in his notes. It follows that, where Scott and Christie agree in an error, that error, however monstrous and palpable, is usually reproduced by Dr. Saintsbury. A few instances will suffice. In Stanza 23 of *Annus Mirabilis*, Dryden wrote and printed :

> So reverently Men quit the open air,
> When Thunder speaks the angry Gods abroad.

This remained the text in both the editions published in Dryden's lifetime. After his death the first word of the second line was corrupted into ' Where ', much to the detriment of the text, and ' Where ' it remained for two hundred years. It is ' Where ' in Christie's text, and consequently it is ' Where ' in Dr. Saintsbury's. The error was the more unpardonable that Dryden was proud enough of his simile to reproduce it in his contemporary play of *The Maiden Queen*:

> As, when it thunders,
> Men reverently quit the open air
> Because the angry gods are then abroad.

Here Dr. Saintsbury prints his text correctly with no corruption of ' then ' into ' there '. The same poem presents us with an error infinitely worse. In Stanza 224, Dryden, after picturing the ghosts of traitors as descending from London Bridge and dancing round the Fire of London, goes on thus :

> Our Guardian Angel saw them where he sate
> Above the Palace of our slumbring King.

In the Miscellany Poems, published after Dryden's death, ' he ' was turned into ' they ', and this piece of egregious nonsense figures in all subsequent English editions, even in Christie's and consequently in Dr. Saintsbury's. It appears even where special care should have been taken to secure sense, in Mr. Humphry Ward's *English Poets*. The editors did not stay to ask themselves why the ghosts should have mounted to the roof of Whitehall, how they could dance in a place so unfit for the exercise, or by what supernatural duplicity they could at the same moment sit on the ridge of the Palace and dance round the Fire.

Another curious error may be quoted from *Cymon and Iphigenia*. The poet, in describing the effect of Love upon one whom he calls a ' Man-Beast ', a human being

> Above, but just above, the Brutal kind,

declares that

> Love made an active Progress through his Mind,
> The dusky Parts he clear'd, the gross refin'd,
> The drowsy wak'd ; and as he went impress'd
> The Maker's Image on the human Beast.

So the lines appear in the first and only contemporary edition. The last word was afterwards corrupted into ' Breast '. This piece of nonsense with its absurd suggestion of tattooing is printed in Christie's text and consequently in Dr. Saintsbury's.

Since Christie did not print Dryden's translations from the ancient poets, Dr. Saintsbury had here no help from his predecessors. He does indeed remark that liberties have been taken with the text and implies that he has taken pains ' to note them singly '. That he has done so I cannot perceive except in one instance, and even there he leaves the error in his text. Of the errors which he has not corrected some are very unfortunate. Thus Ovid has a passage which Dryden correctly rendered :

> Nor cou'd thy Form, O *Cyllarus*, foreslow
> Thy Fate ; (if Form to Monsters Men allow.)

The regret that qualities, mental or physical, do not save one from death is a commonplace of ancient poetry. Yet here the editors unanimously change ' foreslow ' into ' foreshow '. What sense the lines might then have would certainly not have been known to Dryden or to Ovid. In one of the versions from Lucretius there is a line which points the contrast between the brief life of Homer and the eternity of his *Iliad*. As Dryden wrote and printed it, the line ran :

> Th' immortal Work remains, the mortal author 's gone.

Will it be believed that the English editors print ' immortal ' instead of ' mortal ' ?

Since the English editors have ignored Dryden's own texts, it can hardly be expected that they should have consulted the originals of his translations. Nor have they. They have so changed the text as to display their ignorance both of their poet and of his authorities. Dryden translated the Twenty-ninth Ode of the Third Book of Horace, and prefixt to it the correct title. His English editors, one and all, change 'third' into 'first'. One only remarks that 'first' ought to be third, and even he leaves the error in his text because he supposed it was Dryden's.

When Juvenal wrote

> veniet cum signatoribus auspex,

and Dryden wrote and printed

> The Publick Notaries and *Auspex* wait,

the English editors print 'Haruspex', an emendation which makes the scansion harsh in Dryden and impossible in Juvenal. They seem to have desired to display their learning, since at a Roman marriage in Juvenal's time the augur did not use birds for divination. But their learning goes astray, for, as often happens, the old name outlived the change.

Occasionally Dr. Saintsbury following Scott, who himself followed a bad text, has printed a reading other than Christie's. His variations are sometimes for the worse. Thus in the second part of *Absalom and Achitophel*, when Monmouth suggests that Shaftesbury's motives are self-interested, the Earl replies in effect that, if this be so, there is all the more reason why Monmouth should trust him, since his interest lies all in Monmouth's advancement.

> Royal Youth, fix here,
> Let Int'rest be the Star by which I Steer.
> Hence to repose your Trust in Me was wise,
> Whose Int'rest most in your Advancement lies.

The lines may be Tate's but were at least passed by Dryden. Here it is plain that 'let' is used in the sense of 'assume'. An edition published after the deaths of both authors changed 'I' into 'you', taking 'let' in a hortative sense. This illogical reading is deliberately preferred by Dr. Saintsbury.

In some forms used by Dryden his editors have made changes without system and without justification. He uses according to the sense and the sound either 'them' or ''em'. The latter has sometimes been allowed to stand, and has sometimes been altered. It may be that Dryden was not always careful in his use, but there are clear cases where his choice was deliberate. He was doubtless not aware that the two words are etymologically different, but his choice must be respected. A line in the *Epistle to John Driden* is thus printed by most editors :

> Who, while thou shar'st their lustre, lend'st them thine.

This is not what Dryden wrote, nor could he have been guilty of such a cacophony. Again, he chose to write ' ev'n ', but Mr. Hooper invariably prints ' e'en '.

These restorations of the text are such as Dryden's editors might with reasonable industry have succeeded in making. There is, however, one problem of which they never suspected the existence. My friend, Mr. Henry B. Wheatley, discovered that what profess to be copies of the first edition of *Absalom and Achitophel* differ from one another. His discovery led me to the solution of a point which had much puzzled me. In Stanza 105 of *Annus Mirabilis*, the copy of the first edition which I first collated gave a text which has escaped the notice of all editors. An examination of other copies showed me why, for these copies did not give it. Moreover, these copies had a list of errata which the other had not. What must have happened is this. When Dryden came back from Wiltshire after the publication of the poem, he saw for himself, or was told by others, that his lines would give great offence and might even be accused of blasphemy. In those copies which had not been sold he was at the charge of cancelling a sheet in order to give an inoffensive version of the lines. Observing that there was a blank page at the end of the Preface, he printed on it a list of such errors as ' by mistaken words have corrupted ' the text. Something of the same kind must have happened in the case of other poems, but it is obviously impossible to collate all existing copies.

After the copy of the present text, together with the first draft of this Introduction, was in the hands of the press, there appeared at Cambridge, Massachusetts, the first scholarly edition of the poems. The editor, Dr. George Noyes, has made a complete collation of the original texts, and has removed by far the larger number of the defacing errors. Most of the cases in which he has overlooked an error are of small importance, as when in the line

> What is't to thee if he neglect thy Urn ?

he prints ' neglects ' for ' neglect ', or when in the line

> The Fiend, thy Sire, has sent thee from below,

he prints 'hath' for 'has'. There are, however, cases in which he has followed our predecessors in altering the original text without, as it seems to me, just cause. It may be that this deviation has not been intentional. Thus, when Dryden printed

> Not all the Wealth of Eastern Kings, said she,
> Have Pow'r to part my plighted Love and me :

the Cambridge editor prints 'Has' for 'Have'. Here the assumption of a misprint seems highly improbable. The irregular construction, called by Dr. Abbott 'the confusion of proximity', is common and natural. It is paralleled by the taunt thrown at Antony by Cassius in Shakespeare's play :

> The posture of your blows are yet unknown.

Another case in which a misprint has been unduly assumed occurs in *Baucis and Philemon* :

> Heav'ns Pow'r is infinite : Earth, Air, and Sea,
> The Manufacture Mass, the making Pow'r obey.

The change of 'Manufacture' into 'Manufactur'd' may seem plausible, but before it can be accepted there must be some evidence that the verb or participle was used precisely in this sense. The *New English Dictionary* supplies no such evidence. The verb was new in Dryden's time, but the noun had been in use for some time, and sometimes had the sense, now obsolete, of handicraft. Its attributive use in the present passage may be harsh, but it can be justified by analogy, and in all probability the original text is right.

Again, there are instances in the Translations where a reference to the translated work shows that the editor's silent alterations of the original text are mistaken. Thus when Dryden printed

> More grateful to the sight than goodly Planes,

a reference to Ovid's 'platano conspectior alta' shows that the alteration of 'Planes' into 'plains' is a clear error. Nor is it easy to see what sense the Cambridge editor attaches to a passage in Persius when in Dryden's

> There boast thy Horse's Trappings, and thy own :

he substitutes 'Their' for 'There'. This line is, as it happens, given correctly in most of the English editions.

In the matter of spelling the Cambridge editor has occasionally introduced forms for which I find no warrant in the original texts. Thus he prints ' color'd ' where the original gives ' colour'd '. Moreover, he seems to have made insufficient allowance for Dryden's love of his own Northamptonshire speech. In some cases his alterations obscure the rhyme. Thus when Dryden printed

> A Tuft of Daisies on a flow'ry Lay
> They saw, and thitherward they bent their way :

there can be no justification for changing ' Lay ' into ' lea ', though it is only natives who know that the word is still ' lay ', not ' lea ', in Dryden's own village. Again, such a form as ' smoother'd ' should not be ejected in favour of ' smother'd '. Yet again it is not easy to see why such phonetic forms as ' pact ' and ' tane ' should give way to ' pack'd ' and ' ta'en ', the latter a bad representative of a monosyllable. I should add that on the other hand in finally revising the text, I have seen reason to abandon some original readings which I once thought capable of defence, and that I have occasionally corrected an error which I had at first overlooked.

The matter of spelling opens a difficult question. It must be admitted that Dryden was neither careful nor consistent. We cannot always tell whether the spelling was his own or his printer's. We may fairly ascribe to him certain letters which indicate a pronunciation. Usually he wrote ' salvage ' rather than ' savage ', with a sound in the first syllable such as we give to ' calves '. It is not likely that here he was under Italian influence, for this would imply a theory, and of theory he was clearly guiltless. He wrote ' agen ' when he wished to pronounce the word as we do, but, if he desired the diphthong, as poets sometimes do, he wrote ' again '. Christie regarded some of Dryden's spellings as repulsive, for instance, ' eugh ' for ' yew ' and ' ghess ' for ' guess ', though the form ' ghess ' is more phonetic than our own. Dr. Saintsbury modernizes the spelling unless there be strong reason to the contrary, and sometimes when there is. Thus on the line

> The Theatres are Berries for the Fair

he complains that Scott has obscured the sense for modern readers by printing ' berries ', which is Dryden's word, and himself prints ' burrows '. This is worse than obscuring the sense, it is corrupting it. The word 'berry' does not mean a burrow, but a collection of burrows or warren. It still has that sense in Dryden's own county, and in this place is a much more appropriate word. This, at any rate, is not one of those modernizings of which, according to Dr. Saintsbury, Dryden would have approved. That he would have approved of some cannot in face of the Preface to the *Fables* lightly be denied. Still, it must be remembered that a pious adherence to Dryden's wishes is not always possible. It would, in face of the same Preface, have prevented Dr. Saintsbury from republishing some of the Plays. The reader is entitled to know what Dryden passed in the press. Moreover, with a simplified spelling, some of his forms may return into use. Some of them are more rational and phonetic than our own. We write 'her sex's arts', thus pretending to have dropt a vowel which we in fact pronounce. Dryden's 'her Sexes Arts' is better, but he does not always observe this use. Nor does he always keep such better spellings as 'woolf', 'mold', 'sute', 'scepter', 'sheckle'. His 'indew'd' is nearer to speech than our 'endued'. It is true that some of his spellings leave the sense ambiguous, but here editors have not always improved matters by making a choice. Thus Dryden printed

'Old as I am, for Ladies Love unfit.

Here Warton printed 'Ladies'' and Christie 'Lady's'. Since Dryden undoubtedly had in mind a line of Horace, it is certain that here Christie is wrong, but there are cases where there well may be a doubt. Again, Dryden sometimes uses the apostrophe not only in the genitive singular but also, where it is etymologically no less correct, in the nominative plural. He writes it especially in words that end in 'a', whether English or foreign. Thus we have 'Sea's', 'Epocha's', and 'Idea's', all as nominatives. There seems no valid reason for altering these forms. There is certainly none where the changed spelling obscures a rhyme or a scansion. In the Epilogue to *Tyrannick Love*, the editors make Dryden rhyme 'slattern' with 'Catherine', though he printed neither of these words in this form. In this edition no spelling has been altered except in the case of undoubted misprints, nor then without a note.

Most editors have taken on themselves to correct Dryden's Greek, changing for instance his εὕρεκα into ηὕρηκα. But with this form the line will not, as we pronounce Greek, scan as Dryden scanned it. The truth is that Dryden's master, the great Busby,

mistook, like some good people of our own times, the mark of
accent for a mark of stress.   Like a modern Greek, and unlike
an ancient Greek, he made no difference in pronunciation between
εὕρεκα and ηὕρηκα.   In proper names Dryden is not consistent in
his use, falling sometimes under the influence of Latin.   On the
line

But Iphigenia is the Ladies care

Dr. Saintsbury has a note to express his hope that Dryden did not
scan the name as Iphigenïa, and adds that ' it is not impossible '.
Clearly the implication is that Dryden was guilty of a false
quantity.   That he did so scan the name is not only possible but
certain, but his fault was no mistake of the quantity, but adherence
to a mistaken theory.   It is characteristic of the want of thought
displayed by Dryden's editors that they should either never have
noticed that he said Cleomēnes and Hippodamïa, or else not have
asked themselves why he did so.   And so the poor poet has
to answer for his editors' errors as well as for his own.   Thus he
wrote and printed :

Aëtions Heir, who on the Woody Plain
Of Hippoplacus did in Thebe reign,

but Dr. Saintsbury takes on himself to print ' Ætion's ', saying
in a note that ' Aetion's ' would be a better form, but that
Dryden probably meant to write ' Ætion's '.   But, if Dryden
meant what is wrong, why was he at the pains to print what is
right ?   Why should a false diphthong be foisted on him, when he
took trouble to print the mark of diaeresis ?   It is true that
Dryden's Greek was not unexceptionable.   His ' Hippoplacus '
involves no less than three errors.   His editors by printing
' Hypoplacus ' get rid of one, and seem to show that they have
not noticed the other two.   One cannot blame an editor who
changes Dryden's ' Caledonian ' into ' Calydonian ', but if in an
incorrect text of Ovid Dryden found ' Alyxothoe ', there seems
no reason for printing the correct form.   Dryden wrote, as he
had a right to do, ' Perithous,' a form of as sound Latin as the
' Pirithous ', upon which his editors insist.   On his faults in this
kind his editors have been severe, but, as they have failed to
perceive some of them, they have turned their barbs against
themselves.   When Dryden erred not from the acceptance of
a wrong theory, nor, if that be an error, from the desire to put
his Greek names into an English dress, but from sheer ignorance,

his editors for the same reason have failed to correct him. There is an ugly and glaring example in his quotation of the first line of the *Iliad*. He wrote μήνιν, and μήνιν it is in all the editions. He would not mind much if his errors were pointed out to him, but he would rather his editors corrected him when he was wrong than when he was not.

Again, most editors have robbed Dryden of his italics. His employment of them, apart from the habitual use in proper names, is not perhaps always happy, but the reader should be allowed to know what he printed. His italics are used sometimes for emphasis, sometimes to show, as in the case of *Omen* and *Parterre*, that a word was not fully naturalized. There is an interesting and exceptional case in *Palamon and Arcite*, where he wrote

A Virgin-Widow and a *Mourning Bride*.

The English editors print without capitals or italics. It might be thought that they had never heard of Congreve. At any rate, they deprive the dramatist of the compliment which Dryden meant to pay him. It may be that as literature the line is better without the allusion, but, as Dr. Saintsbury, better in his theory than in his practice, once remarks, we are entitled 'to read what Dryden wrote and not what some forgotten pedant thought that Dryden should have written'. Of Dryden's poems some few of those which were prefixed to plays or other works were printed in italics. In this case the italicized words, if we may so call them, were printed in the roman type.

Again, Dryden is entitled to his marks of elision. Dr. Saintsbury drops them on the ground that they are 'a conventional form, now disused, of indicating what Dryden calls "synalaepha", and not affecting the actual scansion'. But it is pretty clear that, unlike Milton, and probably unlike the ancient Greeks, Dryden actually did in speech drop the elided vowel. Dr. Saintsbury holds that 'slurring, not elision, is proper to English'. That may be so, but, if so, Dryden did what is not proper to English, and the reader is entitled to know what Dryden wrote, and not what Dr. Saintsbury thinks that 'Dryden should have written'.

In the matter of punctuation Dryden was often very careless, though it is clear that he was by no means indifferent. Of the first edition of *Annus Mirabilis*, he complains that false stops 'confounded the sense'. Of another poem he complained that the printer had served him ill, and to the printer he seems often

to have left his punctuation, the more that he was often pressed
for time in correcting the press.   To find his principles of punctuation we must take some work to which he gave special care.   Such
a work is the *Epistle to John Driden*, of which he was greatly but
not unduly proud.   A comparison of the text below, with other
editions, or with modern usage, will show what Dryden meant his
stops to convey.   If no poet in the highest sense of the word, he
was at least a surpassing rhetorician, and his stops are a guide
to reading aloud.   They may not mark the logical divisions of
a sentence, but they do indicate the places where a skilful reader
would choose to pause.   Thus in the third line Christie prints :

> Who, studying peace and shunning civil rage,

whereas Dryden printed :

> Who studying Peace, and shunning Civil Rage,

where the comma, if not logical, is the reader's guide.   **Again,**
where Christie gives

> Even then industrious of the common good ;

Dryden has

> Ev'n then, industrious of the Common Good ;

where the comma marks an emphasis and a consequent pause.
Where there is evidence of careless proof-reading the stops in this
edition have been altered, but not without a note.

In any case Dryden's English editors are the last people who
can quarrel with the punctuation in this volume.   Again and
again they have so altered Dryden's stops as to deprive his lines
of all sense.   The opening lines of the Prologue to *Tyrannick
Love* present us with an admirable contrast, and were printed by
Dryden almost as we should print them to-day.   The sole difference is the use of two parenthesis marks for two commas.   As
the editors print them they appear thus :

> Self-love, which, never rightly understood,
> Makes poets still conclude their plays are good,
> And malice in all critics reigns so high,
> That for small errors they the whole decry.

In this form the lines have neither construction nor sense.   ' Self-
love ' is a subject without a verb, and ' understood ' is a participle

without a meaning. Mr. Hooper and Dr. Saintsbury, even Christie no less, have not seen that ' understood ' is a verb. ' The printer,' said Dryden on one occasion, ' is a beast.' To what would he have compared the editor ? The printer, poor soul, had Dryden's handwriting to wrestle with, yet in this and in many other instances the printer was right until the editor came with his ineradicable predilection for absolute nonsense.

The English editors of Dryden, except Christie, who did not cover the whole ground, even of the poems, have always begun at the wrong end. Eager to annotate and criticize their author, they have been at no pains to ascertain what their author wrote. It follows that some of their efforts have been sadly beside the mark. Thus Scott wrote and Dr. Saintsbury repeated a note on a line in one of the translations from Horace, which, being based upon a false reading, is absolutely mistaken. Again, in one of the versions from Ovid, Scott, by accidentally omitting a line, has given cause to some amusing or exasperating futility. Dr. Saintsbury, instead of referring to the original text, assumes that Scott's was right, and finding a line with none to rhyme with it resorts to misplaced and impossible conjectures. He even complains that Dryden's version is so free that the original gives no help. This is not the fact, nor near the fact. Ovid's lines are

> Et secum tenui suspirans murmura dicat,
> Ut puto, non poteras ipsa referre vicem.
> Tum de te narret, tum persuadentia verba
> Addat, et insano iuret amore mori.

In Dr. Saintsbury's text this is represented by

> And sighing make his mistress understand
> She has the means of vengeance in her hand ;
> And swear thou languishest and diest for her.

It needs little scholarship to see that the English, which is at least as close as is usual in Dryden's version, has no representative of the third line in the Latin. The two phrases of that line are well represented by the line which Dr. Saintsbury omits,

> Then naming thee thy humble suit prefer.

It would be hard to name a more serious fault in a textual critic than that which Dr. Saintsbury has here committed.

Another case where a misprint has led to misplaced annotation

and false emendations occurs in *Mac Flecknoe*, l. 185. Christie
prints :

> But so transfused as oil on waters flow,

and repeats this as the reading of 'all the early editions'. He
defends the false grammar on the strange ground that 'the verb
is made plural following the plural noun'. Earlier editors
changed the text to 'oil and water', and some later ones, accepting Christie's report, have printed this impossible alteration. But
Christie's report is not true. The first edition gives

> But so transfus'd as Oyls on Waters flow,

and this is the only reading that gives any sense.

That the present text should be wholly free from errors is more
than can be hoped, but it is at least more correct than any
printed in our own country. It does not contain Dryden's
translations from Virgil, which are long enough for a separate
volume. For another reason it excludes one version from
Theocritus and one from Lucretius. Nor has room been found
for a few poems which have at various times without authority
or probability been attributed to Dryden. On the other hand,
it has been thought well to reprint such of the songs in the plays
as could be detached from their context.

My best thanks are due to my friend, Mr. Henry B. Wheatley,
for the loan of first editions and for generous help on the biblio-
graphy, and to the Secretaries of the Clarendon Press, the Reader,
and the Printers, who have done their best to save me from errors.
Such errors as remain must be ascribed to me alone.

The notes are intended to record, with defined exceptions,
the cases in which this text differs from the original editions.
The exceptions are indisputable misprints, such as ' pobability '
for ' probability ', though some of these have been recorded, false
stops, where the printer, not the author, was clearly in fault, and
false capitals in the same case.

WESTMINSTER, 1910.

A POEM

UPON THE

DEATH

OF

His Late Highness,

OLIVER,

Lord Protector

OF

ENGLAND, SCOTLAND, & IRELAND.

Written by Mr. Dryden.

LONDON,

Printed for *William Wilson* ; and are to be sold in
Well-Yard, near *Little St. Bartholomew's*
Hospital. 1659.

HEROICK STANZA'S,

CONSECRATED TO THE MEMORY OF
HIS HIGHNESS,

OLIVER,

LATE LORD PROTECTOR
OF THIS
COMMONWEALTH, &c.

WRITTEN AFTER THE CELEBRATING OF HIS FUNERAL.

1

AND now 'tis time ; for their officious haste,
  Who would before have born him to the
    Sky,
Like eager *Romans* e'er all Rites were past,
  Did let too soon the sacred Eagle fly.

2

Though our best Notes are Treason to his
    Fame,
  Join'd with the loud Applause of publick
    Voice,
Since Heaven, what Praise we offer to his
    Name,
  Hath render'd too Authentick by its
    Choice.

3

Though in his Praise no Arts can liberal be,
  Since they, whose Muses have the highest
    flown,
Add not to his Immortal Memory ;
  But do an Act of Friendship to their own.

4

Yet 'tis our Duty and our Interest too,
  Such Monuments as we can build, to raise ;
Lest all the World prevent what we shou'd do,
  And claim a Title in him by their Praise.

5

How shall I then begin, or where conclude,
  To draw a Fame so truly Circular ?
For in a Round, what Order can be shew'd,
  Where all the Parts so equal perfect are ?

6

His Grandeur he derived from Heav'n alone,
  For he was great, e'er Fortune made him so ;
And Wars, like Mists that rise against the Sun,
  Made him but greater seem, not greater
    grow.

7

No borrow'd Bays his Temples did adorn,
  But to our Crown he did fresh Jewels
    bring ;
Nor was his Vertue poison'd, soon as born,
  With the too early Thoughts of being
    King.

8

Fortune (that easie Mistress of the Young,
  But to her ancient Servants coy and hard)
Him, at that Age, her Favourites ranked
    among,
  When she her best-lov'd *Pompey* did dis-
    card.

9

He, private, marked the Faults of others
    Sway,
  And set as Sea-marks for himself to shun ;
Not like rash Monarchs, who their Youth
    betray
  By Acts their Age too late wou'd wish un-
    done.

10

And yet Dominion was not his Design ;
  We owe that Blessing not to him, but
    Heav'n,
Which to fair Acts unsought Rewards did join,
  Rewards that less to him, than us, were
    giv'n.

T xt from the original edition of 1659.

11

Our former Chiefs, like Sticklers of the War,
  First sought t' inflame the Parties, then to
    poise :
The Quarrel lov'd, but did the Cause abhor,
  And did not strike to hurt, but make a noise.

12

War, our Consumption, was their gainful
  Trade ;
  We inward bled, whilst they prolong'd our
    Pain ;
He fought to end our Fighting, and assay'd
  To stench the Blood by breathing of the
    Vein.

13

Swift and resistless through the Land he
  pass'd,
  Like that bold *Greek*, who did the East
    subdue ;
And made to Battels such Heroick Haste,
  As if on Wings of Victory he flew.

14

He fought, secure of Fortune, as of fame ;
  Till by new Maps, the Island might be
    shown,
Of Conquests, which he strew'd where-e'er
  he came,
  Thick as the *Galaxy* with Stars is sown.

15

His palms, tho under Weights they did not
  stand,
  Still thriv'd ; no Winter could his Laurels
    fade :
Heaven in his Portraict shew'd a Work-man's
  Hand
  And drew it perfect, yet without a Shade.

16

Peace was the Prize of all his Toil and Care,
  Which War had banish'd and did now
    restore :
Bolognia's walls thus mounted in the Air,
  To seat themselves more surely than before.

17

Her Safety, rescued *Ireland*, to him owes ;
  And treacherous *Scotland*, to no Int'rest
    true,
Yet bless'd that Fate which did his Arms
  dispose,
  Her Land to civilize, as to subdue.

14.4 is] are *1659*.
16.3 *Bolognia's*] Dryden's spelling of Bologna.

18

Nor was he like those Stars which only shine,
  When to pale Mariners they Storms por-
    tend :
He had his calmer Influence, and his Mien
  Did Love and Majesty together blend.

19

Tis true, his Count'nance did imprint an Awe,
  And naturally all Souls to his did bow ;
As Wands of Divination downward draw,
  And point to Beds where Sov'raign Gold
    doth grow.

20

When, past all Off'rings to *Pheretrian Jove*,
  He *Mars* depos'd and Arms to Gowns
    made yield,
Successful Counsels did him soon approve
  As fit for close Intrigues as open Field.

21

To suppliant *Holland* he vouchsaf'd a Peace,
  Our once bold Rival in the *British* Main,
Now tamely glad her unjust Claim to cease,
  And buy our Friendship with her Idol,
    Gain.

22

Fame of th' asserted Sea, through *Europe*
  blown,
  Made *France* and *Spain* ambitious of his
    Love ;
Each knew that Side must conquer, he wou'd
  own ;
  And for him fiercely, as for Empire, strove.

23

No sooner was the *French*-Man's Cause em-
  brac'd,
  Than the light *Monsieur* the grave *Don*
    out-weigh'd :
His Fortune turn'd the Scale where-e'er
  'twas cast,
  Tho' *Indian* mines were in the other laid.

24

When absent, yet we conquer'd in his Right ;
  For tho' some meaner Artist's Skill were
    shown,
In mingling Colours, or in placing Light,
  Yet still the fair Designment was his own.

25

For from all Tempers he cou'd Service draw
  The worth of each, with its Alloy, he knew;
And, as the Confident of Nature, saw
  How she Complections did divide and brew

26

Or he their single Vertues did survey,
  By Intuition, in his own large Breast,
Where all the rich *Idea's* of them lay,
  That were the Rule and Measure to the rest.

27

When such Heroick Vertue Heaven sets out,
  The Stars, like Commons, sullenly obey ;
Because it drains them, when it comes about ;
  And therefore is a Tax they seldom pay.

28

From this high Spring, our Foreign Con-
    quests flow,
  Which yet more glorious Triumphs do
    portend ;
Since their Commencement to his Arms they
    owe,
  If Springs as high as Fountains may ascend.

29

He made us Free-men of the Continent,
  Whom Nature did like Captives treat
    before ;
To nobler Preys the *English* Lion sent,
  And taught him first in *Belgian* Walks to
    roar.

30

That old unquestion'd Pirate of the Land,
  Proud *Rome*, with Dread the Fate of *Dun-
    kirk* heard ;
And trembling, wish'd behind more *Alps* to
    stand,
  Although an *Alexander* were her Guard.

31

By his Command we boldly cross'd the Line
  And bravely fought where Southern Stars
    arise ;
We trac'd the far-fetched Gold unto the Mine,
  And that which brib'd our Fathers, made
    our Prize.

32

Such was our Prince, yet own'd a Soul above
  The highest Acts it could produce to show :
Thus poor Mechanick Arts in Publick move,
  Whilst the deep Secrets beyond Practice
    go.

33

Nor dy'd he when his Ebbing Fame went
    less,
  But when fresh Laurels courted him to
    live :
He seem'd but to prevent some new Success,
  As if above what Triumphs Earth could
    give.

34

His latest Victories still thickest came,
  As near the Centre, Motion does increase ;
Till he, press'd down by his own weighty
    Name,
  Did, like the Vestal, under Spoils decease.

35

But first, the Ocean, as a tribute, sent
  That Giant-Prince of all her Watry Herd ;
And th' Isle, when her protecting *Genius*
    went,
  Upon his Obsequies loud Sighs conferr'd.

36

No Civil Broils have since his Death arose,
  But Faction now, by Habit, does obey ;
And Wars have that Respect for his Repose,
  As winds for *Halcyons* when they breed at
    Sea.

37

His Ashes in a Peaceful Urn shall rest,
  His Name a great Example stands to
    show,
How strangely high Endeavours may be
    bless'd,
  Where Piety and Valour jointly go.

Astræa Redux.

A

POEM

On the Happy

Reſtoration & Return

Of His Sacred Majeſty

Charles the Second.

By *JOHN DRIDEN.*

Jam Redit & Virgo, Redeunt Saturnia Regna. Virgil.

June 19th

LONDON,

Printed by *J. M.* for *Henry Herringman*, and are to be ſold at
his Shop, at the *Blew-Anchor*, in the lower Walk of the New-
Exchange, 1 6 6 0. *June 19*

ASTRÆA REDUX.

A POEM

On the Happy

Restoration and Return.

Of His Sacred Majesty

Charles the Second.

By JOHN DRIDEN.

Jam redit & Virgo, redeunt Saturnia Regna. Virgil.

LONDON,

Printed for *Henry Herringman*, and sold by *Jacob Tonson* at the *Judges-Head* in *Chancery-lane*. 1688

Aſtræa Redux.

A

POEM

On the Happy Reſtoration and Return of His
Sacred MAJESTY
Charles the Second.

Now with a general Peace the World was
  blest,
While Ours, a World divided from the rest,
A dreadful Quiet felt, and worser far
Than Armes, a sullen Interval of War :
Thus, when black Clouds draw down the
  lab'ring Skies,
Ere yet abroad the winged Thunder flies,
An horrid Stillness first invades the ear,
And in that silence We the Tempest fear.
Th' ambitious *Swede* like restless Billows tost
On this hand gaining what on that he lost,
Though in his life he Blood and Ruine
  breath'd,   11
To his now guideless Kingdom Peace be-
  queath'd ;   [Fate,
And Heaven, that seem'd regardless of our
For *France* and *Spain* did Miracles create,
Such mortal Quarrels to compose in Peace
As Nature bred and Int'rest did encrease.
We sigh'd to hear the fair *Iberian* Bride
Must grow a Lilie to the Lilies side,   [bed
While Our cross Stars deny'd us *Charles* his
Whom Our first Flames and Virgin Love did
  wed.   20
For his long absence Church and State did
  groan ;   [Throne :
Madness the Pulpit, Faction seiz'd the
Experienc'd Age in deep despair was lost
To see the Rebel thrive, the Loyal crost :
Youth that with Joys had unacquainted been
Envy'd gray hairs that once good Days had
  seen :   [content,
We thought our Sires, not with their own
Had ere we came to age our Portion spent.
Nor could our Nobles hope their bold Attempt
Who ruined Crowns would Coronets exempt :
For when by their designing Leaders taught
To strike at Pow'r which for themselves they
  sought,   32

The vulgar gull'd into Rebellion, arm'd,
Their blood to action by the Prize was
  warm'd ;
The Sacred Purple then and Scarlet Gown,
Like sanguine Dye, to Elephants was shewn.
Thus when the bold *Typhoeus* scal'd the Sky
And forc'd great *Jove* from his own Heaven
  to fly,
(What King, what Crown from Treasons
  reach is free,
If *Jove* and *Heaven* can violated be ?),   40
The lesser Gods that shar'd his prosp'rous
  State
All suffer'd in the Exil'd Thunderer's Fate.
The Rabble now such Freedom did enjoy,
As Winds at Sea, that use it to destroy :
Blind as the *Cyclops*, and as wild as he,
They own'd a lawless savage Libertie,
Like that our painted Ancestors so priz'd
Ere Empire's Arts their Breasts had Civiliz'd.
How Great were then Our *Charles* his woes,
  who thus
Was forc'd to suffer for Himself and us ! 50
He toss'd by fate, and hurried up and down,
Heir to his Fathers Sorrows, with his Crown,
Could taste no sweets of Youths desired Age,
But found his Life too true a Pilgrimage.
Unconquer'd yet in that forlorn Estate,
His Manly Courage overcame his Fate.
His Wounds he took like *Romans* on his
  Breast,
Which by his Vertue were with Laurels drest.
As Souls reach Heav'n, while yet in Bodies
  pent,
So did he live above his Banishment. 60
That Sun, which we beheld with couz'ned eyes
Within the Water, mov'd along the Skies.
How easie 'tis when Destiny proves kind,
With full spread Sails to run before the Wind,
But those that 'gainst stiff Gales laveering go
Must be at once resolv'd and skilful too.

Text from the second edition, 1688. The first
edition was in 1660.

46 savage] salvage *1660*.

He would not like soft *Otho* hope prevent,
But stay'd and suffer'd Fortune to repent.
These Virtues *Galba* in a Stranger sought ;
And *Piso* to Adopted Empire brought.   70
How shall I then my doubtful Thoughts
    express
That must his Suff'rings both regret and bless !
For when his early Valour Heav'n had crost,
And all at *Worc'ster* but the honour lost,
Forc'd into exile from his rightful Throne,
He made all Countries where he came his own,
And viewing Monarchs secret Arts of sway
A Royal Factor for their Kingdoms lay.
Thus banish'd *David* spent abroad his time,
When to be Gods Anointed was his Crime, 80
And when restor'd, made his proud Neigh-
    bours rue   [drew :
Those choise Remarks he from his Travels
Nor is he only by Afflictions shown
To conquer others Realms, but rule his own:
Recov'ring hardly what he lost before,
His Right indears it much, his Purchase more.
Inur'd to suffer ere he came to raign,
No rash procedure will his Actions stain.
To bus'ness ripened by digestive thought,
His future rule is into Method brought : 90
As they who first Proportion understand,
With easie Practice reach a Master's hand.
Well might the Ancient Poets then confer
On Night, the honour'd name of *Counseller*,
Since struck with rayes of prosp'rous Fortune
    blind,
We Light alone in dark Afflictions find.
In such adversities to Scepters train'd,
The name of *Great* his famous Grandsire
    gain'd :
Who yet a King alone in Name and Right,
With hunger, cold and angry *Jove* did fight ;
Shock'd by a Covenanting Leagues vast
    Pow'rs,   101
As holy and as Catholick as ours : [known
Till Fortunes fruitless spight had made it
Her blows not shook but riveted his Throne.
Some lazy Ages, lost in Sleep and Ease
No action leave to busie Chronicles ;
Such, whose supine felicity but makes
In story *Casmes*, in *Epoche's* mistakes ;
O're whom *Time* gently shakes his wings of
    Down,   109
Till with his silent Sickle they are mown :
Such is not *Charles* his too too active age,
Which govern'd by the wild distemper'd rage

Of some black Star infecting all the Skies,
Made him at his own cost like *Adam* wise.
Tremble ye Nations who secure before,
Laught at those Arms that 'gainst our selves
    we bore ;
Rous'd by the lash of his own stubborn Tail,
Our Lion now will foreign Foes assail.
With *Alga* who the sacred Altar strows ?
To all the Sea-Gods *Charles* an Offering owes;
A Bull to thee *Portunus* shall be slain   121
A Lamb to you the Tempests of the Main :
For those loud Storms that did against him
    rore
Have cast his shipwrack'd Vessel on the shore.
Yet, as wise Artists mix their Colours so
That by degrees they from each other go,
Black steals unheeded from the neighb'ring
    white
Without offending the well couz'ned sight,
So on us stole our blessed change ; while we
Th' effect did feel but scarce the manner see.
Frosts that constrain the ground, and birth
    deny   131
To Flow'rs that in its womb expecting lie,
Do seldom their usurping Pow'r withdraw,
But raging Floods persue their hasty Thaw :
Our Thaw was mild, the Cold not chas'd away,
But lost in kindly heat of lengthned day.
Heav'n would no bargain for its Blessings
    drive,
But what we could not pay for, freely give.
The Prince of Peace would, like himself, confer
A Gift unhop'd without the price of war. 140
Yet, as he knew his Blessings worth, took care
That we should know it by repeated Pray'r,
Which storm'd the skies and ravish'd *Charles*
    from thence,
As Heav'n itself is took by violence.
Booth's forward Valour only serv'd to shew
He durst that duty pay we all did owe :
Th' Attempt was fair ; but Heav'n's prefixed
    hour
Not come ; so like the watchful Travellor,
That by the Moons mistaken light did rise,
Lay down again and clos'd his weary eyes.
'Twas MONK, whom Providence design'd
    to loose   151
Those real bonds false Freedom did impose.
The blessed Saints that watch'd this turning
    Scene
Did from their Stars with joyful wonder lean,

---

108 *Casmes*] Chasmes *1660.*

148 Travellor] Travellour *1660.*
151 MONK] MONCK *1660.*

To see small Clues draw vastest weights along,
Not in their bulk but in their order strong.
Thus Pencils can by one slight touch restore
Smiles to that changed face that wept before.
With ease such fond *Chymæra's* we persue
As Fancy frames for Fancy to subdue ; 160
But when ourselves to action we betake,
It shuns the Mint, like Gold that Chymists make :
How hard was then his Task, at once to be,
What in the body natural we see ;
Mans Architect distinctly did ordain
The charge of Muscles, Nerves, and of the Brain.
Through viewless Conduits Spirits to dispense,
The Springs of Motion from the Seat of Sense.
'Twas not the hasty product of a day,
But the well ripened Fruit of wise delay. 170
He like a patient Angler er'e he stroak,
Would let them play a while upon the hook.
Our healthful food the Stomach labours thus,
At first embracing what it strait doth crush.
Wise Leeches will not vain Receipts obtrude,
While growing Pains pronounce the Humors crude ;
Deaf to complaints they wait upon the Ill,
Till some safe *Crisis* authorize their Skill.
Nor could his Acts too close a Vizard wear
To scape their Eyes whom Guilt had taught to fear, 180
And guard with caution that polluted nest,
Whence Legion twice before was dispossest.
Once Sacred house, which when they entr'd in,
They thought the place could sanctifie a sin;
Like those that vainly hop'd kind Heav'n would wink,
While to excess on Martyrs Tombs they drink.
And as devouter *Turks* first warn their Souls
To part, before they taste forbidden Bowls,
So these when their black Crimes they went about,
First timely charm'd their useless Conscience out. 190
Religions Name against it self was made :
The Shadow serv'd the Substance to invade :
Like Zealous Missions they did Care pretend
Of Souls in shew, but made the Gold their end.
The incensed Powr's beheld with scorn from high
An Heaven so far distant from the Sky,

Which durst, with horses hoofs that beat the Ground
And Martial Brass bely the Thunders Sound.
'Twas hence at length just Vengeance thought it fit 199
To speed their Ruin by their impious wit.
Thus *Sforza* curs'd with a too fertile brain,
Lost by his wiles the Pow'r his Wit did gain.
Henceforth their Fogue must spend at lesser rate,
Than in its flames to wrap a Nations Fate.
Suffer'd to live, they are like *Helots* set
A virtuous Shame within us to beget.
For by example most we sinn'd before 207
And glass-like clearness mixt with frailty bore,
But since, reform'd by what we did amiss,
We by our suff'rings learn to prize our bliss.
Like early Lovers, whose unpractis'd hearts
Were long the May-game of malicious arts,
When once they find their Jealousies were vain,
With double heat renew their Fires again.
'Twas this produc'd the Joy, that hurried o're
Such swarms of *English* to the Neighb'ring shore
To fetch that Prize, by which *Batavia* made
So rich amends for our impoverish'd Trade.
Oh had you seen from *Schevelines* barren Shore,
(Crowded with troops, and barren now no more,) 220
Afflicted *Holland* to his Farewel bring
True sorrow, *Holland* to regret a King ;
While waiting him his Royal Fleet did ride,
And willing Winds to their lowr'd Sails denied. [out,
The wavering Streamers, Flags, and Standart
The merry Seamens rude but chearful Shout ;
And last the Cannons voice that shook the ⎫
  Skies, ⎪
And, as it fares in sudden Extasies, 228 ⎬
At once bereft us both of Ears and Eyes. ⎭
The *Naseby* now no longer *Englands* shame,
But better to be lost in *Charles* his name
(Like some unequal Bride in nobler sheets)
Receives her Lord : The joyful *London* meets
The Princely *York*, himself alone a freight ;
The *Swift-sure* groans beneath great *Glouc's-*
ters weight. [these,
Secure as when the *Halcyon* breeds, with
He that was born to drown might cross the Seas.
Heav'n could not own a Providence, and take
The wealth three Nations ventur'd at a stake.

The same indulgence *Charles* his Voyage
    bless'd,   240
Which in his right had Miracles confess'd.
The Winds that never Moderation knew,
Afraid to blow too much, too faintly blew ;
Or out of breath with joy could not enlarge
Their straightned Lungs, or conscious of
    their Charge.
The British *Amphitryte* smooth and clear
In richer Azure never did appear ;
Proud her returning Prince to entertain
With the submitted Fasces of the Main.

    And welcom now (*Great Monarch*) to your
    own ;   250
Behold th' approaching Cliffes of *Albion* ;
It is no longer Motion cheats your view,
As you meet it, the Land approacheth you.
The Land returns, and in the white it wears
The marks of Penitence and Sorrow bears.
But you, whose Goodness your Descent doth
    show,
Your Heav'nly Parentage and Earthly too ;
By that same mildness which your Fathers
    Crown
Before did ravish, shall secure your own.
Not ty'd to rules of Policy, you find   260
Revenge less sweet than a forgiving mind.
Thus, when th' Almighty would to *Moses* give
A sight of all he could behold and live ;
A voice before his Entry did proclaim
Long-Suffring, Goodness, Mercy in his
    Name.   [Cause,
Your Pow'r to Justice doth submit your
Your Goodness only is above the Laws ;
Whose rigid Letter, while pronounc'd by you,
Is softer made. So winds that tempests brew
When through Arabian Groves they take
    their flight   270
Made wanton with rich Odours, lose their
    spight.
And as those Lees, that trouble it, refine
The agitated Soul of Generous Wine,
So tears of Joy for your returning spilt,
Work out and expiate our former Guilt.
Methinks I see those Crowds on *Dover's*
    Strand,
Who in their haste to welcom you to Land
Choak'd up the Beach with their still growing
    store,
And made a wilder Torrent on the Shore :
While, spurr'd with eager thoughts of past
    Delight,   280

Those who had seen you court a second sight;
Preventing still your Steps and making hast
To meet you often whereso-e're you past.
How shall I speak of that triumphant Day
When you renew'd the expiring Pomp of
    May !
(A month that owns an Interest in your
    Name :
You and the Flow'rs are its peculiar Claim.)
That Star, that at your Birth shone out so
    bright,
It stain'd the duller Suns Meridian light,
Did once again its potent Fires renew,   290
Guiding our Eyes to find and worship you.
    And now times whiter Series is begun,
Which in soft Centuries shall smoothly run ;
Those Clouds that overcast your Morn shall
    fly,
Dispell'd to farthest corners of the Sky.
Our nation, with united Int'rest blest,
Not now content to poize, shall sway, the rest.
Abroad your Empire shall no Limits know,
But like the Sea in boundless Circles flow.
Your much lov'd Fleet shall with a wide
    Command   300
Besiege the petty Monarchs of the Land :
And as Old Time his Off-spring swallow'd
    down,
Our Ocean in its depths all Seas shall drown.
Their wealthy Trade from Pyrate's Rapine
    free,
Our Merchants shall no more Advent'rers be :
Nor in the farthest East those Dangers fear
Which humble *Holland* must dissemble here.
Spain to your gift alone her *Indies* owes ;
For what the Pow'rful takes not he bestows.
And *France* that did an Exiles presence Fear
May justly apprehend you still too near.   311
At home the hateful names of Parties cease
And factious Souls are weary'd into peace.
The discontented now are only they
Whose Crimes before did your Just Cause
    betray :
Of those your Edicts some reclaim from sins,
But most your Life and Blest Example wins.
Oh happy Prince whom Heav'n hath taught
    the way   318
By paying Vows to have more Vows to pay !
Oh Happy Age ! Oh times like those alone,
By Fate reserv'd for great *Augustus* throne !
When the joint growth of Arms and Arts
    foreshew
The World a Monarch, and that Monarch *You.*

TO HIS SACRED

MAIESTY,

A

PANEGYRICK

ON HIS

CORONATION.

BY JOHN DRYDEN.

LONDON,

Printed for *Henry Herringman* , at the *Anchor* on the Lower walk in the
New Exchange. 1661.

TO HIS SACRED MAJESTY,

A PANEGYRICK ON HIS CORONATION.

1661.

In that wild Deluge where the world was
    drownd,
When life and sin one common Tombe had
    found,
The first small prospect of a rising hill
With various notes of Joy the Ark did fill:
Yet when that flood in its own depths was
    drown'd,
It left behind it false and slipp'ry ground,
And the more solemn pomp was still deferr'd
Till new-born Nature in fresh looks appear'd;
Thus (Royall Sir,) to see you landed here
Was cause enough of triumph for a year :
Nor would your care those glorious joyes
    repeat   11
Till they at once might be secure and great :
Till your kind beams by their continu'd stay
Had warm'd the ground and call'd the
    Damps away.
Such vapours, while your pow'rful Influence
    dries,
Then soonest vanish when they highest rise.
Had greater hast these sacred rights pre-
    par'd,
Some guilty Moneths had in your Triumphs
    shar'd :
But this untainted year is all your own,
Your glory's may without our crimes be
    shown.   20
We had not yet exhausted all our store,
When you refresh'd our joyes by adding more:
As Heav'n, of old, dispenc'd Cœlestial dew,
You gave us Manna and still give us new.
Now our sad ruines are remov'd from sight,
The Season too comes fraught with new
    delight ;
Time seems not now beneath his years to
    stoop,
Nor doe his wings with sickly feathers
    droop :
Soft western winds waft o're the gaudy
    spring,
And open'd Scenes of flow'rs and blossoms
    bring   30
To grace this happy day, while you appear
Not King of us alone but of the year.

Text from the original edition, 1661.

All eyes you draw, and with the eyes the
    heart,
Of your own pomp your self the greatest part :
Loud shouts the Nations happiness proclaim,
And Heav'n this day is feasted with your
    Name.
Your Cavalcade the fair Spectators view,
From their high standings, yet look up to you.
From your brave train each singles out
    a Prey
And longs to date a Conquest from your day.
Now charg'd with blessings while you seek
    repose,   41
Officious slumbers haste your eyes to close ;
And glorious dreams stand ready to restore
The pleasing shapes of all you saw before.
Next to the sacred Temple you are led,
Where waits a Crown for your more sacred
    Head :
How justly from the Church that Crown is
    due,
Preserv'd from ruine and restor'd by you !
The gratefull quire their harmony employ
Not to make greater, but more solemn joy.
Wrapt soft and warm your Name is sent on
    high,   51
As flames do on the wings of Incense fly :
Musique herself is lost, in vain she brings
Her choisest notes to praise the best of
    Kings :
Her melting strains in you a tombe have
    found
And lye like Bees in their own sweetnesse
    drowned.
He that brought peace and discord could
    attone,
His Name is Musick of itself alone.
Now while the sacred oyl anoints your head,
And fragrant scents, begun from you, are
    spread   60
Through the large Dome, the peoples joyful
    Sound
Sent back, is still preserv'd in hallow'd
    ground :
Which in one blessing mixt descends on you,
As heightned spirits fall in richer dew.
Not that our wishes do increase your store,
Full of your self, you can admit no more :

We add not to your glory, but employ
Our time like Angels in expressing Joy
Nor is it duty or our hopes alone
Create that joy, but full fruition :   70
We know those blessings which we must
    possesse
And judge of future by past happinesse,
No promise can oblige a Prince so much
Still to be good, as long to have been such.
A noble Emulation heats your breast,
And your own fame now robbs you of your
    rest :
Good actions still must be maintain'd with
    good,
As bodies nourish'd with resembling food.
You have already quench'd sedition's brand ;
And zeal (which burnt it) only warms the
    Land.   80
The jealous Sects, that dare not trust their
    cause
So farre from their own will as to the Laws,
You for their Umpire and their Synod take,
And their appeal alone to *Cæsar* make.
Kind Heav'n so rare a temper did provide
That guilt repenting might in it confide
Among our crimes oblivion may be set,
But 'tis our Kings perfection to forget.
Virtues unknown to these rough Northern
    climes
From milder heav'ns you bring, without
    their crimes.   90
Your calmnesse does no after Storms provide
Nor seeming patience mortal anger hide.
When Empire first from families did spring,
Then every Father govern'd as a King ;
But you that are a Soveraign Prince, allay
Imperial pow'r with your paternal sway.
From those great cares when ease your soul
    unbends,
Your Pleasures are design'd to noble ends :
Born to command the Mistress of the Seas,
Your Thoughts themselves in that blue
    Empire please.   100
Hither in Summer ev'nings you repair
To take the fraischeur of the purer air :
Undaunted here you ride when Winter raves,
With *Cæsars* heart that rose above the waves.
More I could sing, but fear my Numbers
    stays ;
No Loyal Subject dares that courage praise.

In stately Frigats most delight you find,
Where well-drawn Battels fire your martial
    mind.
What to your cares we owe is learnt from
    hence,
When ev'n your pleasures serve for our
    defence.   110
Beyond your Court flows in the admitted tide,
Where in new depths the wond'ring fishes
    glide :
Here in a Royal bed the waters sleep,
When tir'd at Sea within this bay they
    creep.
Here the mistrustfull foul no harm suspects,
So safe are all things which our King pro-
    tects.
From your lov'd *Thames* a blessing yet is due,
Second alone to that it brought in you ;
A Queen, from whose chast womb, ordain'd
    by Fate,   119
The souls of Kings unborn for bodies wait.
It was your Love before made discord cease ;
Your love is destined to your Countries
    peace.
Both *Indies* (Rivalls in your bed) provide
With Gold or Jewels to adorn your bride.
This to a mighty King presents rich ore
While that with Incense does a God implore.
Two Kingdoms wait your Doom ; and, as
    you choose,
This must receive a Crown or that must
    loose.
Thus from your Royal Oke, like *Jove's* of old,
Are Answers sought, and Destinies fore-told :
Propitious Oracles are beg'd with Vows 131
And Crowns that grow upon the sacred
    boughs.
Your Subjects, while you weigh the Nations
    fate,
Suspend to both their doubtfull love or hate :
Choose only, (Sir,) that so they may possesse
With their own peace their Childrens happi-
    nesse.

---

119 from] *Some editors give* near. *It is clear
that ed. 1 is right, since doubtless Dryden had in
mind Virgil, Æneid* vi. 713 sqq.

122 Your] Your your *1661*, a misprint.

133 Nations] *Most editors give* Nation's, *but
Christie gives* Nations'. *The word is probably
genitive plural.*

To my Lord CHANCELLOR,

presented on New-Years-Day, 1662.

MY LORD,
WHILE flattering Crowds officiously appear
To give themselves, not you, an happy Year,
And by the Greatness of their Presents prove
How much they hope, but not how well they
    love,
The *Muses*, who your early Courtship boast,
Though now your Flames are with their
    Beauty lost,
Yet watch their Time, that, if you have
    forgot
They were your Mistresses, the world may not:
Decay'd by Time and Wars, they only prove
Their former Beauty by your former Love,
And now present, as Ancient Ladies do   11
That courted long at length are forc'd to woo.
For still they look on you with such kind
    Eyes
As those that see the Church's Sovereign rise,
From their own Order chose, in whose high
    State
They think themselves the second Choise of
    Fate.
When our great Monarch into Exile went,
Wit and Religion suffer'd Banishment.
Thus once, when *Troy* was wrapt in Fire and
    Smoke,
The helpless Gods their burning Shrines for-
    sook ;   20
They with the vanquished Prince and Party
    go
And leave their Temples empty to the Foe.
At length the Muses stand restor'd again
To that great Charge which Nature did
    ordain,
And their lov'd Druids seem reviv'd by Fate,
While you dispense the Laws and guide the
    State.
The Nation's Soul, our Monarch, does dis-
    pense
Through you to us his vital Influence ;
You are the Channel where those Spirits flow
And work them higher as to us they go.   30
    In open Prospect nothing bounds our Eye
Until the Earth seems join'd unto the Sky :
So in this Hemisphere our utmost View
Is only bounded by our King and you.

Text from the original edition, 1662, which
seems to lack a title-page.

Our Sight is limited where you are join'd
And beyond that no farther Heav'n can find.
So well your Virtues do with his agree
That, though your Orbs of different Great-
    ness be,
Yet both are for each other's use dispos'd,
His to enclose, and yours to be enclos'd : 40
Nor could another in your Room have been,
Except an Emptiness had come between.
Well may he then to you his Cares impart
And share his Burden where he shares his
    Heart.
In you his Sleep still wakes ; his pleasures find
Their Share of Business in your labouring
    Mind.
So, when the weary Sun his Place resigns,
He leaves his Light and by Reflection shines.
    Justice, that sits and frowns where publick
    Laws
Exclude soft Mercy from a private Cause, 50
In your Tribunal most herself does please ;
There only smiles because she lives at Ease,
And, like young *David*, finds her Strength the
    more   [wore.
When disencumber'd from those Arms she
Heaven would your Royal Master should
    exceed
Most in that Virtue, which we most did need;
And his mild Father, who too late did find
All Mercy vain but what with Pow'r was
    join'd,
His fatal Goodness left to fitter Times,
Not to increase but to absolve our Crimes :
But when the Heir of this vast Treasure
    knew   61
How large a Legacy was left to you,
Too great for any Subject to retain,
He wisely tied it to the Crown again :
Yet, passing through your Hands, it gathers
    more,
As Streams through Mines bear Tincture of
    their Ore.
While Emp'rick Politicians use Deceit,
Hide what they give and cure but by a Cheat,
You boldly show that Skill which they pre-
    tend
And work by Means as noble as your End :
Which should you veil, we might unwind the
    Clue   71
As Men do Nature, till we came to you.

And as the *Indies* were not found before
Those rich Perfumes which from the happy
   Shore
The Winds upon their balmy Wings convey'd,
Whose guilty Sweetness first their world
   betray'd,
So by your Counsels we are brought to view
A rich and undiscover'd World in you.
By you our Monarch does that Fame assure
Which Kings must have, or cannot live
   secure :   80
For prosperous Princes gain the Subjects
   Heart,
Who love that Praise in which themselves
   have part.
By you he fits those Subjects to obey,
As Heaven's Eternal Monarch does convey
His Pow'r unseen, and Man to his Designs
By his bright Ministers, the Stars, inclines.
   Our setting Sun from his declining Seat
Shot Beams of Kindness on you, not of Heat:
And, when his Love was bounded in a few 89
That were unhappy that they might be true,
Made you the Favourite of his last sad Times,
That is, a Sufferer in his Subjects' Crimes :
Thus those first Favours you receiv'd were
   sent,
Like Heaven's Rewards, in earthly Punish-
   ment.
Yet Fortune, conscious of your Destiny,
Even then took Care to lay you softly by,
And wrapt your Fate among her precious
   Things,
Kept fresh to be unfolded with your Kings.
Shown all at once, you dazzled so our Eyes
As new-born *Pallas* did the Gods surprise ;
When, springing forth from *Jove's* new-
   closing Wound,   101
She struck the warlike Spear into the Ground ;
Which sprouting Leaves did suddenly enclose,
And peaceful Olives shaded as they rose.
   How strangely active are the Arts of Peace,
Whose restless Motions less than War's do
   cease !   [Noise,
Peace is not freed from Labour, but from
And War more Force, but not more Pains
   employs.
Such is the mighty Swiftness of your Mind
That, like the Earth's, it leaves our Sense
   behind,   110
While you so smoothly turn and roll our
   Sphere
That rapid Motion does but Rest appear.

For as in Nature's Swiftness, with the Throng
Of flying Orbs while ours is borne along,
All seems at rest to the deluded Eye,
Mov'd by the Soul of the same Harmony,
So, carried on by your unwearied Care,
We rest in Peace and yet in Motion share.
Let Envy then those Crimes within you see
From which the happy never must be free ;
Envy that does with Misery reside,   121
The Joy and the Revenge of ruin'd Pride.
Think it not hard, if at so cheap a Rate
You can secure the Constancy of Fate,
Whose kindness sent what does their Malice
   seem
By lesser ills the greater to redeem ;
Nor can we this weak Shower a Tempest call,
But Drops of Heat that in the Sunshine fall.
You have already wearied Fortune so, 129
She cannot farther be your Friend or Foe ;
But sits all breathless, and admires to feel
A Fate so weighty that it stops her Wheel.
In all things else above our humble Fate,
Your equal Mind yet swells not into State,
But like some Mountain in those happy Isles,
Where in perpetual Spring young Nature
   smiles,
Your Greatness shows ; no horror to affright,
But Trees for Shade and Flowers to court
   the Sight ;
Sometimes the Hill submits itself a while
In small Descents, which do its Height
   beguile ;   140
And sometimes mounts, but so as Billows
   play,
Whose rise not hinders but makes short our
   way.
Your Brow, which does no fear of Thunder
   know,
Sees rolling Tempests vainly beat below ;
And, like *Olympus'* Top, the Impression
   wears
Of Love and Friendship writ in former Years.
Yet, unimpair'd with Labours or with Time,
Your Age but seems to a new Youth to climb,
(Thus heavenly Bodies do our Time beget
And measure Change, but share no part of it.)
And still it shall without a Weight increase,
Like this New-year, whose Motions never
   cease ;   152
For since the glorious Course you have begun
Is led by *Charles*, as that is by the Sun,
It must both weightless and immortal prove,
Because the Centre of it is above.

ANNVS MIRABILIS:

The Year of

WONDERS,

1 6 6 6.

AN HISTORICAL

POEM:

CONTAINING

The Progress and various Successes of our Naval War with *Holland*, under the Conduct of His Highness Prince RUPERT, and His Grace the Duke of ALBEMARL. ↑

And describing

THE FIRE
OF
LONDON.

By JOHN DRYDEN, Esq;

Multum interest res poscat, an homines latius imperare velint.
Trajan. Imperator. ad Plin.

Urbs antiqua ruit, multos dominata per annos   Virg

London, Printed for *Henry Herringman*, at the *Anchor* in the Lower Walk of the *New Exchange.* 1667.

[Title-page of Second Edition.]

ANNUS MIRABILIS.

The YEAR of

WONDERS,

M. DC. LXVI.

AN

Historical Poem.

ALSO

A *POEM* on the Happy RESTORATION and RETURN of
His Late *Sacred* MAJESTY

Charles the Second.

LIKEWISE

A PANEGYRICK on His *CORONATION.*

TOGETHER

WITH a POEM to MY LORD CHANCELLOR
Presented on *New-Years-Day.* 1662.

By *JOHN DRYDEN*, Esq;

LONDON, Printed for *Henry Herringman*, and sold by
Jacob Tonson at the *Judges-Head* in *Chancery-Lane.* 1688

TO THE
METROPOLIS
OF
GREAT BRITAIN
The most renowned and late flourishing
City of London,
in its
REPRESENTATIVES
The LORD MAYOR and Court of ALDERMEN,
10   the SHERIFFS and COMMON COUNCIL of it.

As perhaps I am the first who ever presented a work of this nature to the Metropolis of
any Nation, so is it likewise consonant to Justice, that he who was to give the first Example
of such a Dedication should begin it with that City, which has set a pattern to all others
of true Loyalty, invincible Courage, and unshaken Constancy. Other Cities have been
prais'd for the same Virtues, but I am much deceiv'd if any have so dearly purchas'd
their Reputation; their Fame has been won them by cheaper trials than an expensive,
though necessary, War, a consuming Pestilence, and a more consuming Fire. To submit
yourselves with that humility to the Judgments of Heaven, and at the same time to
raise yourselves with that vigour above all human Enemies; to be combated at once from
20 above and from below, to be struck down and to triumph; I know not whether such
Trials have been ever parallel'd in any Nation, the resolution and successes of them never
can be. Never had Prince or People more mutual reason to love each other, if suffering
for each other can indear affection. You have come together a pair of matchless Lovers,
through many difficulties; He, through a long Exile, various traverses of Fortune, and
the interposition of many Rivals, who violently ravish'd and withheld You from Him:
and certainly you have had your share in sufferings. But Providence has cast upon you
want of Trade, that you might appear bountiful to your Country's necessities; and the
rest of your afflictions are not more the effects of God's Displeasure (frequent examples
of them having been in the Reign of the most excellent Princes) than occasions for the
30 manifesting of your Christian and Civil virtues. To you, therefore, this *Year of Wonders*
is justly dedicated, because you have made it so. You, who are to stand a wonder to
all Years and Ages, and who have built yourselves an Immortal Monument on your own
Ruins. You are now a *Phœnix* in her ashes, and, as far as Humanity can approach,
a great Emblem of the suffering Deity. But Heaven never made so much Piety and
Virtue, to leave it miserable. I have heard indeed of some virtuous Persons who have
ended unfortunately, but never of any virtuous Nation: Providence is engaged too
deeply, when the Cause becomes so general. And I cannot imagine it has resolved the
ruin of that People at home, which it has blessed abroad with such Successes. I am,
therefore, to conclude that your Sufferings are at an end, and that one part of my Poem
40 has not been more an History of your destruction, than the other a Prophecy of your
restoration. The accomplishment of which happiness, as it is the wish of all true *Englishmen*, so is by none more passionately desired than by
The greatest of Your Admirers,
and most humble of your Servants,
JOHN DRYDEN.

AN
ACCOUNT
OF THE
ENSUING POEM,
IN
A LETTER
TO THE HONOURABLE
Sʳ ROBERT HOWARD.

SIR,

I am so many ways obliged to you and so little able to return your Favours that, like 10
those who owe too much, I can only live by getting farther into your debt. You have not only
been careful of my Fortune, which was the effect of your Nobleness, but you have been solicitous
of my Reputation, which is that of your Kindness. It is not long since I gave you the trouble
of perusing a Play for me, and now, instead of an Acknowledgment, I have given you a greater
in the Correction of a Poem. But since you are to bear this Persecution, I will at least give
you the encouragement of a Martyr, you could never suffer in a nobler cause. For I have
chosen the most heroick Subject which any Poet could desire : I have taken upon me to describe
the motives, the beginning, progress, and successes of a most just and necessary War ; in it
the care, management, and prudence of our King ; the conduct and valour of a Royal Admiral
and of two incomparable Generals ; the invincible courage of our Captains and Seamen, and 20
three glorious Victories, the result of all. After this, I have in the Fire the most deplorable,
but withal the greatest Argument that can be imagined ; the destruction being so swift, so
sudden, so vast and miserable, as nothing can parallel in Story. The former part of this
Poem, relating to the War, is but a due expiation for my not serving my King and Country
in it. All Gentlemen are almost obliged to it : and I know no reason we should give that
advantage to the Commonalty of England, to be foremost in brave actions, which the noblesse
of France would never suffer in their Peasants. I should not have written this but to a Person
who has been ever forward to appear in all Employments, whither his Honour and Generosity
have called him. The latter part of my Poem, which describes the Fire, I owe, first, to the
Piety and Fatherly Affection of our Monarch to his suffering Subjects ; and, in the second 30
place, to the Courage, Loyalty, and Magnanimity of the City ; both which were so conspicuous
that I have wanted words to celebrate them as they deserve. I have called my Poem Historical,
not Epick, *though both the Actions and Actors are as much Heroick as any Poem can contain.*
But since the Action is not properly one, nor that accomplish'd in the last successes, I have
judg'd it too bold a title for a few Stanza's, which are little more in number than a single Iliad
or the longest of the Æneids. *For this reason (I mean not of length, but broken action, ti'd*
too severely to the laws of History) I am apt to agree with those who rank Lucan *rather among*
Historians in Verse than Epique poets ; in whose room, if I am not deceived, Silius Italicus,
though a worse Writer, may more justly be admitted. I have chosen to write my poem in
quatrains or stanza's of four in alternate rhyme, because I have ever judg'd them more noble 40
and of greater dignity both for the Sound and Number than any other Verse in use amongst
us ; in which I am sure I have your approbation. The learned Languages have certainly
a great advantage of us in not being tied to the slavery of any Rhyme, and were less constrained

*in the quantity of every syllable, which they might vary with Spondæes or Dactiles, besides
so many other helps of Grammatical Figures for the lengthening or abbreviation of them,
than the Modern are in the close of that one Syllable, which often confines, and more often
corrupts, the sense of all the rest. But in this necessity of our Rhymes, I have always found
the couplet verse most easy (though not so proper for this occasion), for there the work is sooner
at an end, every two lines concluding the labour of the Poet : but in* Quatrains *he is to carry
it farther on ; and not only so, but to bear along in his head the troublesome sense of four
lines together. For those who write correctly in this kind must needs acknowledge that the
last line of the* Stanza *is to be considered in the composition of the first. Neither can we give*
10 *ourselves the liberty of making any part of a Verse for the sake of Rhyme, or concluding with
a word which is not currant English, or using the variety of Female Rhymes ; all which
our Fathers practised. And for the Female Rhymes, they are still in use amongst other Nations:
with the* Italian *in every line, with the* Spaniard *promiscuously, with the* French *alternately,
as those who have read the* Alarique, *the* Pucelle, *or any of their latter Poems, will agree with me.
And besides this, they write in* Alexandrins *or Verses of six feet, such as, amongst us, is the
old Translation of* Homer *by* Chapman *; All which by lengthening of their Chain makes the
sphere of their activity the larger. I have dwelt too long upon the choice of my* Stanza, *which
you may remember is much better defended in the Preface to* Gondibert *; and therefore I will
hasten to acquaint you with my endeavours in the writing. In general I will only say I have*
20 *never yet seen the description of any Naval Fight in the proper terms which are used at Sea; and
if there be any such in another Language, as that of* Lucan *in the third of his* Pharsalia, *yet
I could not prevail myself of it in the* English *; the terms of Art in every Tongue bearing
more of the Idiom of it than any other words. We hear, indeed, among our Poets, of the
Thundring of Guns, the Smoke, the Disorder and the Slaughter ; but all these are common
notions. And certainly as those who, in a Logical dispute, keep in general terms, would hide
a fallacy, so those who do it in any Poetical description would veil their Ignorance.*

Descriptas servare vices, operumque colores,
Cur ego, si nequeo ignoroque, Poeta salutor ?

For my own part, if I had little knowledge of the Sea, yet I have thought it no shame to learn :
30 *and if I have made some few mistakes, 'tis only, as you can bear me witness, because I have
wanted opportunity to correct them ; the whole Poem being first written, and now sent you from
a place where I have not so much as the converse of any* Sea-man. *Yet though the trouble I had
in writing it was great, it was more than recompens'd by the pleasure ; I found myself so
warm in celebrating the Praises of Military men, two such especially as the* Prince *and* General,
*that it is no wonder if they inspired me with thoughts above my ordinary level. And I am
well satisfied, that as they are incomparably the best subject I have ever had, excepting only
the* Royal Family, *so also that this I have written of them is much better than what I have
performed on any other. I have been forc'd to help out other Arguments ; but this has been
bountiful to me : they have been low and barren of praise, and I have exalted them and made*
40 *them fruitful : but here—*Omnia sponte suâ reddit justissima tellus. *I have had a large,
a fair, and a pleasant field ; so fertile, that, without my cultivating, it has given me two Harvests
in a Summer, and in both oppressed the reaper. All other greatness in Subjects is only counterfeit, it will not endure the test of danger ; the greatness of arms is only real : other greatness
burdens a Nation with its weight, this supports it with its strength. And as it is the happiness
of the Age, so is it the peculiar goodness of the best of Kings, that we may praise his Subjects
without offending him : Doubtless it proceeds from a just confidence of his own Virtue, which
the lustre of no other can be so great as to darken in him ; for the Good or the Valiant are
never safely praised under a bad or a degenerate Prince. But to return from this digression
to a farther account of my Poem, I must crave leave to tell you, that, as I have endeavoured*
50 *to adorn it with noble thoughts, so much more to express those thoughts with elocution. The
Composition of all Poems is or ought to be of wit ; and wit in the Poet, or wit writing (if you*

*will give me leave to use a School distinction), is no other than the faculty of imagination in
the Writer ; which, like a nimble Spaniel, beats over and ranges through the field of Memory,
till it springs the Quarry it hunted after ; or, without metaphor, which searches over all the
Memory for the Species or Ideas of those things which it designs to represent. Wit written,
is that which is well defin'd, the happy result of Thought, or product of Imagination. But
to proceed from wit in the general notion of it to the proper wit of an Heroique or Historical
Poem ; I judge it chiefly to consist in the delightful imaging of Persons, Actions, Passions,
or Things. 'Tis not the jerk or sting of an Epigram, nor the seeming contradiction of a poor
Antithesis (the delight of an ill-judging Audience in a Play of Rhyme), nor the gingle of a more
poor Paranomasia ; neither is it so much the morality of a grave Sentence, affected by Lucan,* 10
*but more sparingly used by Virgil ; but it is some lively and apt description, dressed in such
colours of speech, that it sets before your eyes the absent object, as perfectly and more delightfully
than nature. So then, the first happiness of the Poet's Imagination is properly Invention, or
finding of the thought ; the second is Fancy, or the variation, deriving or moulding of that
thought as the Judgment represents it proper to the subject ; the third is Elocution, or the Art of
clothing and adorning that thought so found and varied, in apt, significant and sounding
words : The quickness of the Imagination is seen in the Invention, the fertility in the Fancy,
and the accuracy in the Expression. For the two first of these, Ovid is famous amongst the
poets, for the later Virgil. Ovid images more often the movements and affections of the mind,
either combating between two contrary passions, or extreamly discompos'd by one : his words* 20
*therefore are the least part of his care ; for he pictures Nature in disorder, with which the
study and choice of words is inconsistent. This is the proper wit of Dialogue or Discourse,
and, consequently, of the Drama, where all that is said is to be suppos'd the effect of sudden
thought ; which, though it excludes not the quickness of Wit in repartees, yet admits not a too
curious election of words, too frequent allusions, or use of Tropes, or, in fine, anything that
shows remoteness of thought, or labour, in the Writer. On the other side, Virgil speaks not so
often to us in the person of another, like Ovid, but in his own, he relates almost all things as
from himself, and thereby gains more liberty than the other, to express his thoughts with all
the graces of elocution, to write more figuratively, and to confess as well the labour as the force
of his Imagination. Though he describes his Dido well and naturally, in the violence of her* 30
*Passions, yet he must yield in that to the Myrrha, the Biblis, the Althæa of Ovid ; for as great
an admirer of him as I am, I must acknowledge that, if I see not more of their souls than I see
of Dido's, at least I have a greater concernment for them : And that convinces me that Ovid
has touched those tender strokes more delicately than Virgil could. But when Action or Persons
are to be described, when any such Image is to be set before us, how bold, how masterly are
the strokes of Virgil ! We see the objects he represents us within their native figures, in their
proper motions ; but so we see them, as our own eyes could never have beheld them, so beautiful
in themselves. We see the Soul of the Poet, like that universal one of which he speaks, informing
and moving through all his Pictures, Totamque infusa per artus Mens agitat molem et magno
se corpore miscet ; we behold him embellishing his Images, as he makes Venus breathing* 40
beauty upon her son Æneas.

lumenque juventæ
Purpureum, et lætos oculis afflârat honores :
Quale manus addunt Ebori decus, aut ubi flavo
Argentum, Pariusve lapis circundatur auro.

    *See his Tempest, his Funeral Sports, his Combat of Turnus and Æneas, and in his Georgicks,
which I esteem the Divinest part of all his writings, the Plague, the Country, the Battel of
Bulls, the labour of the Bees, and those many other excellent Images of Nature, most of which
are neither great in themselves nor have any natural ornament to bear them up : But the words
wherewith he describes them are so excellent, that it might be well appli'd to him which was said* 50
*by Ovid, Materiam superabat opus : The very Sound of his Words has often somewhat that
is connatural to the subject ; and, while we read him, we sit, as in a Play, beholding the Scenes*

*of what he represents. To perform this, he made frequent use of Tropes, which you know change
the nature of a known word, by applying it to some other signification ; and this is it which
Horace means in his Epistle to the Pisos :*

> Dixeris egregie, notum si callida verbum
> Reddiderit junctura novum.

*But I am sensible I have presum'd too far to entertain you with a rude discourse of that
Art which you both know so well, and put into practice with so much happiness. Yet before
I leave Virgil, I must own the vanity to tell you, and by you the world, that he has been my
Master in this Poem : I have followed him everywhere, I know not with what success, but I am*
10 *sure with diligence enough : My Images are many of them copied from him, and the rest are
imitations of him. My Expressions also are as near as the Idioms of the two Languages would
admit of in translation. And this, Sir, I have done with that boldness, for which I will stand
accomptable to any of our little Criticks, who, perhaps, are not better acquainted with him
than I am. Upon your first perusal of this Poem, you have taken notice of some words which
I have innovated (if it be too bold for me to say refin'd) upon his Latin ; which, as I offer not
to introduce into English prose, so I hope they are neither improper nor altogether unelegant
in Verse ; and, in this, Horace will again defend me.*

> Et nova, fictaque nuper, habebunt verba fidem, si
> Græco fonte cadant, parcè detorta.

20 *The inference is exceeding plain ; for if a Roman Poet might have liberty to coin a word,
supposing only that it was derived from the Greek, was put into a Latin termination, and
that he used this liberty but seldom, and with modesty : How much more justly may I challenge
that priviledge to do it with the same prerequisits, from the best and most judicious of Latin
Writers ? In some places, where either the Fancy, or the Words, were his or any others, I have
noted it in the Margin, that I might not seem a Plagiary ; in others I have neglected it, to avoid
as well tediousness as the affectation of doing it too often. Such descriptions or images, well
wrought, which I promise not for mine, are, as I have said, the adequate delight of heroick
Poesie ; for they beget admiration, which is its proper object ; as the Images of the Burlesque,
which is contrary to this, by the same reason beget laughter ; for the one shows Nature beautified,*
30 *as in the Picture of a fair Woman, which we all admire ; the other shows her deformed, as
in that of a Lazar, or of a Fool with distorted face and antique gestures, at which we cannot
forbear to laugh, because it is a deviation from Nature. But though the same Images serve
equally for the Epique Poesie, and for the historique and panegyrique, which are branches
of it, yet a several sort of Sculpture is to be used in them : If some of them are to be like those
of Juvenal, Stantes in curribus Æmiliani, Heroes drawn in their triumphal Chariots and in
their full proportion ; others are to be like that of Virgil, Spirantia mollius æra : there is
somewhat more of softness and tenderness to be shown in them. You will soon find I write
not this without concern. Some, who have seen a paper of Verses which I wrote last year to
her Highness the Dutches, have accus'd them of that only thing I could defend in them ; they*
40 *have said, I did humi serpere, that I wanted not only height of Fancy, but dignity of Words
to set it off ; I might well answer with that of Horace, Nunc non erat his locus, I knew I
address'd them to a Lady, and accordingly I affected the softness of expression and the smoothness of measure, rather than the height of thought ; and in what I did endeavour, it is no vanity
to say, I have succeeded. I detest arrogance ; but there is some difference betwixt that and
a just defence. But I will not farther bribe your candor, or the Readers. I leave them to speak
for me ; and, if they can, to make out that character, not pretending to a greater, which I have
given them.*

Verses to Her Highness the DUTCHES *on the*
Memorable Victory gained by the DUKE *against*
the Hollanders, June *the* 3ᵈ 1665. *And*
on Her Journey afterwards into the North.

MADAM,
WHEN for our sakes your *Heroe* you resign'd
To swelling Seas and every faithless wind ;
When you releas'd his Courage and set free
A Valour fatal to the Enemy,
You lodg'd your Countries cares within your
    breast,
(The mansion where soft love should only
    rest :)
And e're our Foes abroad were overcome,
The noblest conquest you had gain'd at
    home.
Ah, what concerns did both your Souls
    divide !
Your Honour gave us what your Love deni'd:
And 'twas for him much easier to subdue   11
Those Foes he fought with, than to part from
    you.
That glorious day, which two such Navies
    saw
As each, unmatch'd, might to the world give
    Law,
Neptune, yet doubtful whom he should obey,
Held to them both the Trident of the Sea :
The Winds were hush'd, the Waves in ranks
    were cast,
As awfully as when God's People past :
Those, yet uncertain on whose Sails to blow,
These, where the wealth of Nations ought
    to flow.   20
Then with the Duke your Highness rul'd
    the day :
While all the Brave did his Command obey,
The Fair and Pious under you did pray.
How pow'rful are chast Vows ! the Wind
    and Tyde
You brib'd to combat on the *English* side.
Thus to your much loved Lord you did
    convey
An unknown succour, sent the nearest way.

New vigour to his wearied arms you brought
(So *Moses* was upheld while *Israel* fought.)
While, from afar, we heard the Cannon
    play,   30
Like distant Thunder on a shiny day.
For absent Friends we were asham'd to fear,
When we consider'd what you ventur'd there.
Ships, Men and Arms our Country might
    restore,
But such a Leader could supply no more.
With generous thoughts of Conquest he did
    burn,
Yet fought not more to vanquish than return.
Fortune and Victory he did persue
To bring them as his Slaves, to wait on you :
Thus Beauty ravish'd the rewards of Fame
And the Fair triumph'd when the Brave
    o'recame.   41
Then, as you meant to spread another way
By Land your Conquests far as his by Sea,
Leaving our Southern Clime, you march'd
    along
The stubborn North, ten thousand *Cupid's*
    strong.
Like Commons the Nobility resort,
In crowding heaps, to fill your moving Court:
To welcome your approach the Vulgar run,
Like some new Envoy from the distant Sun,
And Country Beauties by their Lovers go, 50
Blessing themselves, and wondring at the
    show.
So, when the New-born *Phœnix* first is seen,
Her feather'd Subjects all adore their Queen,
And, while She makes her Progress through
    the East,
From every Grove her numerous Train's
    increast :
Each Poet of the air her Glory sings,
And round him the pleas'd Audience clap
    their Wings.

And now, Sir, 'tis time I should relieve you from the tedious length of this account. You
have better and more profitable employment for your hours, and I wrong the Publick to detain
you longer. In conclusion, I must leave my Poem to you with all its faults, which I hope
to find fewer in the Printing by your emendations. I know you are not of the number of those.

of whom the younger Pliny *speaks ;* Nec sunt parum multi, qui carpere amicos suos judicium vocant ; *I am rather too secure of you on that side. Your candor in pardoning my Errors may make you more remiss in correcting them ; if you will not withal consider that they come into the world with your approbation, and through your hands. I beg from you the greatest favour you can confer upon an absent person, since I repose upon your management what is dearest to me, my Fame and Reputation ; and, therefore, I hope it will stir you up to make my Poem fairer by many of your blots. If not, you know the story of the Gamster who married the rich Man's Daughter and, when her Father denied the Portion, Christened all the Children by his Sirname, that, if in conclusion they must beg, they should do so by one Name as well*
10 *as by the other. But since the reproach of my faults will light on you, 'tis but reason I should do you that justice to the Readers to let them know, that, if there be anything tolerable in this Poem, they owe the Argument to your choice, the Writing to your encouragement, the Correction to your judgment, and the Care of it to your friendship, to which he must ever acknowledge himself to owe all things, who is,*

Sir,

The most Obedient and most
Faithful of your Servants,

JOHN DRYDEN.

From Charlton, *in*
Wiltshire, *Nov.*
10, 1666.

ANNUS MIRABILIS:

THE YEAR OF WONDERS,

M DC LXVI.

1

IN thriving Arts long time had *Holland* grown,
Crouching at home, and cruel when abroad :
Scarce leaving us the means to claim our own ;
Our King they courted, and our Merchants aw'd.

2

Trade, which like Blood should circularly flow,
Stopp'd in their Channels, found its Freedom lost :
Thither the Wealth of all the World did go,
And seem'd but Shipwrack'd on so base a Coast.

3

For them alone the Heav'ns had kindly heat ;
[a] In Eastern Quarries ripening precious Dew :
For them the Idumæan Balm did sweat,
And in hot Ceilon Spicy Forrests grew.

4

The Sun but seem'd the Lab'rer of their Year ;
[b] Each waxing Moon supplied her watry store,
To swell those Tides, which from the Line did bear
Their brim-full Vessels to the *Belg'an* shore.

Text from the second edition, 1688, except where noted. In the first edition, 1667, some faults 'escaped the press'. The readings of the first edition are given wherever there was a deliberate change. The current texts have bad errors in 23.4 and 224.1. No editor seems to have observed the earliest text of 105.

---

[a] *In Eastern Quarries,* &c. Precious Stones at first are dew, condens'd, and harden'd by the warmth of the Sun, or subterranean Fires.
[b] *Each waxing,* &c. According to their opinion, who think that great heap of Waters under the Line is depressed into Tides by the Moon toward the Poles.

4.2 waxing] wexing *1667*.

5

Thus, mighty in her Ships, stood *Carthage*
    long,
And swept the Riches of the world from far,
Yet stoop'd to *Rome*, less wealthy, but more
    strong :
And this may prove our second Punick War.

6

What peace can be, where both to one pre-
    tend ?
(But they more diligent, and we more strong)
Or if a peace, it soon must have an end ;
For they would grow too pow'rful were it
    long.

7

Behold two nations then, ingag'd so far,
That each seven years the Fit must shake
    each Land ;
Where *France* will side to weaken us by
    War,
Who only can his vast Designs withstand.

8

See how he feeds th' *Iberian* [c] with delays,
To render us his timely Friendship vain ;
And, while his secret soul on *Flanders* preys,
He rocks the Cradle of the babe of *Spain*.

9

Such deep designs of Empire does he lay
O're them, whose Cause he seems to take in
    hand :
And, prudently would make them Lords at
    Sea,
To whom with ease he can give Laws by
    Land.

10

This saw our King ; and long within his
    breast
His pensive counsels ballanc'd too and fro ;
He griev'd the Land he freed should be
    oppress'd,
And he less for it than Usurpers do.

11

His gen'rous mind the fair *Ideas* drew
Of Fame and Honor, which in dangers lay ;
Where wealth, like Fruit on precipices, grew,
Not to be gather'd but by Birds of prey.

12

The Loss and Gain each fatally were great ;
And still his Subjects call'd aloud for War :
But peaceful Kings, o're martial people set,
Each other's poize and counter-ballance are.

13

He, first, survey'd the Charge with careful
    eyes,
Which none but mighty Monarchs could
    maintain ;
Yet judg'd, like vapours that from Limbecks
    rise,
It would in richer showers descend again.

14

At length resolv'd t' assert the watry Ball,
He in himself did whole Armado's bring :
Him aged Sea-men might their Master call,
And choose for General were he not their
    King.

15

It seems as every Ship their Sovereign knows,
His awful Summons they so soon obey ;
So hear the skaly herd when [d] *Proteus* blows,
And so to Pasture follow through the Sea.

16

To see this Fleet upon the Ocean move,
Angels drew wide the Curtains of the Skies :
And Heav'n, as if there wanted Lights above,
For Tapers made two glaring Comets rise.

17

Whether they unctuous Exhalations are,
Fir'd by the Sun, or seeming so alone ;
Or each some more remote and slippery
    Star,
Which loses footing when to Mortals shown.

18

Or one that bright companion of the Sun,
Whose glorious aspect seal'd our new-born
    King ;
And now, a round of greater years begun,
New influence from his walks of light did
    bring.

[d] *when* Proteus *blows*, or Cœruleus Proteus
immania ponti armenta, & magnas pascit sub
gurgite phocas. *Virg.*

14.3 Him] Him, *1667 and 1688.*

[c] *th'* Iberian. *The* Spaniard.

19

Victorious *York* did first, with fam'd success,
To his known valour make the *Dutch* give place :
Thus Heav'n our Monarch's fortune did confess,
Beginning conquest from his Royal Race.

20

But since it was decreed, Auspicious King,
In *Britains* right that thou shouldst wed the Main,
Heav'n, as a gage, would cast some precious thing,
And therefore doom'd that *Lawson* should be slain.

21

Lawson amongst the formost met his fate,
Whom Sea-green *Syrens* from the Rocks lament :
Thus as an off'ring for the *Grecian* state,
He first was kill'd who first to Battel went.

22

Their Chief † blown up in air, not waves expir'd,
To which his pride presum'd to give the Law ;
The *Dutch* confess'd Heav'n present, and retir'd,
And all was *Britain* the wide Ocean saw.

23

To nearest Ports their shatter'd Ships repair,
Where by our dreadful Canon they lay aw'd :
So reverently Men quit the open air,
When Thunder speaks the angry Gods abroad.

24

And now approach'd their Fleet from *India*, fraught
With all the riches of the rising Sun : *The attempt at Berghen.*
And precious Sand from ᵉSouthern Climates brought,
(The fatal Regions where the War begun.)

† *The admiral of* Holland.
ᵉ *Southern Climates,* Guinny.

23.4 When] *The editors wrongly give* Where

25

Like hunted *Castors*, conscious of their Store,
Their way-laid wealth to *Norways* coasts they bring :
There first the North's cold bosome spices bore,
And Winter brooded on the Eastern Spring.

26

By the rich scent we found our perfum'd Prey,
Which flanck'd with Rocks, did close in covert lie ;
And round about their murdering Canon lay,
At once to threaten and invite the Eye.

27

Fiercer than Canon, and than Rocks more hard,
The English undertake th' unequal War :
Seven Ships alone, by which the Port is barr'd,
Besiege the *Indies*, and all *Denmark* dare.

28

These fight like Husbands, but like Lovers those :
These fain would keep, and those more fain enjoy :
And to such height their frantick Passion grows,
That what both love, both hazard to destroy.

29

Amidst whole heaps of Spices lights a Ball,
And now their Odours arm'd against them flie :
Some preciously by shatter'd Porc'lain fall,
And some by Aromatick Splinters die.

30

And though by Tempests of the Prize bereft,
In Heavens inclemency some ease we find ;
Our foes we vanquish'd by our valour left,
And only yielded to the Seas and Wind.

31

Nor wholly lost we so deserv'd a prey ;
For storms, repenting, part of it restor'd :
Which, as a tribute from the Baltick Sea,
The British Ocean sent her mighty Lord.

27.2 undertake] undertook *1667.*

32

Go, Mortals, now, and vex yourselves in vain
For Wealth, which so uncertainly must come:
When what was brought so far, and with
      such pain
Was onely kept to lose it nearer home.

33

The Son, who twice three months on th'
      Ocean tost,
Prepar'd to tell what he had pass'd before,
Now sees in *English* Ships the *Holland* coast,
And parents Arms, in vain, stretcht from
      the shore.

34

This careful Husband had been long away,
Whom his chaste Wife and little Children
      mourn ;
Who on their fingers learn'd to tell the day
On which their Father promis'd to return.

35

*Such are the proud Designs of human kind,
And so we suffer Shipwrack every where !
Alas ! what port can such a Pilot find,
Who in the night of Fate must blindly steer.

36

The undistinguish'd Seeds of Good and Ill,
Heaven, in his bosom, from our knowledge
      hides ;
And draws them in contempt of human skill,
Which oft, for friends, mistaken foes pro-
      vides.

37

Let *Munsters* Prelate ever be accurst,
In whom we seek the g*German* Faith in
      vain :
Alas, that he should teach the *English* first,
That Fraud and Avarice in the Church could
      reign !

38

Happy who never trust a Strangers will,
Whose Friendship's in his Interest under-
      stood !
Since Money giv'n but tempts him to be ill,
When pow'r is too remote to make him good.

f *Such are*, &c. from Petronius. Si bene cal-
culum ponas. ubique fit naufragium.
g *The* German *faith*] Tacitus saith of them,
Nullos mortalium fide aut armis ante Germanos
esse.

39

Till now, alone the Mighty Nations strove ;
The rest, at gaze, without the Lists
      did stand :   *War de-*
And threatning *France*, plac'd like *clared by*
      a painted *Jove*,   *France.*
Kept idle Thunder in his lifted hand.

40

That Eunuch Guardian of rich *Hollands*
      trade,
Who envies us what he wants pow'r t' enjoy ;
Whose noiseful valour does no Foe invade,
And weak assistance will his Friends destroy.

41

Offended that we fought without his leave,
He takes this time his secret Hate to
      show :
Which *Charles* does with a mind so calm
      receive,
As one that neither seeks, nor shuns his Foe.

42

With *France*, to aid the *Dutch*, the *Danes*
      unite,
France as their Tyrant, *Denmark* as their
      slave.
But when with one three Nations join to
      fight,
They silently confess that one more brave.

43

Lewis had chas'd the *English* from his shore ;
But *Charles* the *French* as Subjects does
      invite :
Would Heav'n for each some *Solomon* restore,
Who, by their mercy, may decide their right.

44

Were Subjects so but only by their choice,
And not from Birth did forc'd Dominion
      take,
Our Prince alone would have the publique
      voice ;
And all his Neighbours Realms would desarts
      make.

45

He without fear a dangerous War pursues,
Which without rashness he began before.
As Honour made him first the danger choose,
So still he makes it good on virtues score.

46

The doubled charge his Subjects love sup-
    plies,
Who, in that bounty, to themselves are kind :
So glad Egyptians see their *Nilus* rise,
And in his plenty their abundance find.

47

With equal pow'r he does two Chiefs create,
Two such, as each seem'd
    worthiest when alone ;   *Prince* Ru-
Each able to sustain a Nations   pert and
    fate,   *Duke* Albe-
Since both had found a greater   marl *sent*
    in their own.   *to sea.*

48

Both great in Courage, Conduct and in
    Fame,
Yet neither envious of the other's Praise ;
Their Duty, Faith, and Int'rest too the same,
Like mighty Partners equally they raise.

49

The Prince long time had courted Fortune's
    love,
But once possess'd did absolutely reign ;
Thus with their *Amazons* the *Heroes* strove,
And conquer'd first those Beauties they
    would gain.

50

The Duke beheld, like *Scipio*, with disdain,
That *Carthage* which he ruin'd, rise once
    more ;
And shook aloft the Fasces of the Main,
To fright those Slaves with what they felt
    before.

51

Together to the watry Camp they haste,
Whom Matrons passing to their children
    shew :
Infants first vows for them to Heav'n are
    cast,
And future [h] people bless them as they go.

52

With them no riotous pomp, nor *Asian* train,
T' infect a Navy with their gaudy fears :
To make slow fights, and victories but vain ;
But war, severely, like it self, appears.

---

[h] *future people*] Examina infantium futurusque
populus. Plin. Jun. in Pan. ad Traj.

53

Diffusive of themselves, where e're they pass,
They make that warmth in others they
    expect ;
Their Valour works like Bodies on a glass,
And does its Image on their men project.

54

Our Fleet divides, and straight the *Dutch*
    appear,
In number, and a fam'd Com-   *Duke of*
    mander, bold :   *Albemarl's*
The Narrow Seas can scarce   *Battel, first*
    their Navy bear   *day.*
Or crowded Vessels can their Soldiers hold.

55

The Duke, less numerous, but in Courage
    more,
On wings of all the winds to Combat flies ;
His murdering Guns a loud Defiance roar,
And bloody Crosses on his Flag-staffs rise.

56

Both furl their Sails, and strip them for the
    Fight,
Their folded Sheets dismiss the useless Air :
[i] Th' *Elean* plains could boast no nobler
    sight,
When struggling Champions did their Bodies
    bare.

57

Born each by other in a distant Line,
The Sea-built Forts in dreadful order move :
So vast the noise, as if not Fleets did join,
[k] But lands unfixt, and floating Nations
    strove.

58

Now pass'd, on either side they nimbly tack,
Both strive to intercept and guide the wind :
And, in its eye, more closely they come back,
To finish all the Deaths they left behind.

59

On high-rais'd Decks the haughty *Belgians*
    ride,
Beneath whose shade our humble Frigats go :
Such port the *Elephant* bears, and so defi'd
By the *Rhinocero's* her unequal foe.

---

[i] *Th'* Elean, &c. *Where the Olympick Games
were celebrated.*

[k] *lands unfix'd, from* Virgil : Credas innare
revulsas Cycladas, &c.

60

And as the Built, so different is the Fight ;
Their mounting Shot is on our Sails design'd:
Deep in their Hulls our deadly Bullets light,
And through the yielding Planks a passage
   find.

61

Our dreaded Admiral from far they threat,
Whose batter'd Rigging their whole war
   receives ;
All bare, like some old Oak which Tempests
   beat,
He stands, and sees below his scatter'd leaves.

62

Heroes of old, when wounded, Shelter sought ;
But he, who meets all Danger with disdain,
Ev'n in their Face his Ship to Anchor
   brought,
And Steeple-high stood propt upon the Main.

63

At this excess of Courage all amaz'd,
The foremost of his Foes a while withdraw :
With such respect in enter'd *Rome* they gaz'd,
Who on high Chairs the God-like Fathers saw.

64

And now, as where *Patroclus* Body lay,
Here *Trojan* Chiefs advanc'd, and there the
   Greek :
Ours o're the Duke their pious wings display,
And theirs the noblest Spoils of *Britain* seek.

65

Mean time his busie Mariners he hasts,
His shatter'd Sails with Rigging to restore,
And willing Pines ascend his broken Masts,
Whose lofty heads rise higher than before.

66

Streight to the *Dutch* he turns his dreadful
   Prow,
More fierce th' important Quarrel to decide :
Like Swans, in long array his vessels shew,
Whose creasts, advancing, do the waves
   divide.

67

They charge, recharge, and all along the Sea
They drive, and squander the huge *Belgian*
   Fleet ;
Berkley alone, who nearest Danger lay,
Did a like Fate with lost *Creusa* meet.

68

The night comes on, we eager to persue
The Combat still, and they asham d to leave :
Till the last streaks of dying day withdrew,
And doubtful Moon-light did our rage de-
   ceive.

69

In th' *English* fleet each Ship resounds with
   Joy,
And loud applause of their great Leader's
   Fame :
In fiery dreams the *Dutch* they still destroy,
And slumbring, smile at the imagin'd Flame.

70

Not so the *Holland* fleet, who tired and done,
Stretch'd on their Decks like weary Oxen lie :
Faint Sweats all down their mighty Members
   run ;
(Vast bulks which little Souls but ill supply.)

71

In Dreams they fearful Precipices tread :
Or, shipwrack'd, labour to some distant shore ;
Or in dark Churches walk among the Dead ;
They wake with horror and dare sleep no
   more.

72

The Morn they look on with unwilling eyes
Till from their Main-top joyful
   news they hear   *Second*
Of Ships, which by their mould   *days*
   bring new Supplies,   *Battel.*
And in their colours *Belgian* Lions bear.

73

Our watchful General had discern'd from far
This mighty succour, which made glad the
   Foe :
He sigh'd, but, like a Father of the War,
[1] His face spake hope, while deep his Sorrows
   flow

74

His wounded men he first sends off to shore,
(Never, till now, unwilling to obey.)
They, not their wounds but want of Strength
   deplore,
And think them happy who with him can
   stay.

[1] *His face*, &c. Spem vultu simulat, premit
altum corde dolorem. *Virg.*

67.3 who *etc.*] not making equal way *1667.*

69.2 Leader's] *1667* : Lead'rs *1688.*

75

Then to the rest, Rejoyce (said he) to-day ;
In you the fortune of *Great Britain* lies :
Among so brave a people, you are they
Whom Heav'n has chose to fight for such
    a Prize.

76

If number *English* courages could quell,
We should at first have shun'd, not met
    our Foes :
Whose numerous Sails the fearful only tell ;
Courage from hearts, and not from numbers,
    grows.

77

He said ; nor needed more to say : with
    hast
To their known Stations chearfully they go ;
And all at once, disdaining to be last,
Solicite every Gale to meet the Foe.

78

Nor did th' incourag'd *Belgians* long delay,
But, bold in others, not themselves, they
    stood :
So thick, our Navy scarce could sheer their
    way,
But seem'd to wander in a moving wood

79

Our little Fleet was now ingag'd so far,
That, like the Sword-fish in the Whale, they
    fought.
The Combat only seem'd a Civil War,
Till through their Bowels we our Passage
    wrought.

80

Never had Valour, no not ours, before,
Done ought like this upon the Land or
    Main :
Where not to be o'rcome was to do more
Than all the Conquests former Kings did
    gain.

81

The mighty ghosts of our great *Harries* rose,
And armed *Edwards* look'd with anxious
    eyes,
To see this Fleet among unequal Foes,
By which fate promis'd them their *Charles*
    should rise.

82

Mean time the *Belgians* tack upon our Reer,
And raking Chase-guns through our Sterns
    they send ;
Close by, their fire-ships, like *Jackals*, appear,
Who on their Lions for the Prey attend.

83

Silent in smoke of Cannons they come on
(Such Vapours once did fiery *Cacus* hide.)
In these the height of pleas'd Revenge is
    shewn,
Who burn contented by anothers side.

84

Sometimes from fighting Squadrons of each
    Fleet,
(Deceiv'd themselves, or to preserve some
    Friend,)
Two grappling *Ætna's* on the Ocean meet,
And *English* Fires with *Belgian* Flames con-
    tend.

85

Now, at each tack, our little Fleet grows less ;
And, like maim'd Fowl, swim lagging on the
    Main ;
Their greater loss their Numbers scarce con-
    fess,
While they lose cheaper than the *English*
    gain.

86

Have you not seen, when, whistled from the
    Fist,
Some Falcon stoops at what her Eye design'd,
And, with her eagerness, the quarry miss'd,
Streight flies at check, and clips it down
    the Wind ?

87

The dastard Crow that to the Wood made
    wing,
And sees the Groves no shelter can afford,
With her loud Kaws her Craven kind does
    bring,
Who, safe in numbers, cuff the noble Bird.

88

Among the *Dutch* thus *Albemarl* did fare :
He could not conquer, and disdain'd to flie ;
Past hope of safety, 'twas his latest care,
Like falling *Cæsar*, decently to die.

78.3 sheer] *1667* : steer *1688. Probably a mis-*
print.

83.1 Cannons] *The editors give* Cannon
86.4 Wind ?] Wind. *1667 and 1688.*

89

Yet Pity did his manly Spirit move,
To see those perish who so well had fought ;
And, generously, with his despair he strove,
Resolv'd to live till he their safety wrought.

90

Let other Muses write his prosp'rous fate,
Of conquer'd Nations tell, and Kings restor'd:
But mine shall sing of his eclips'd estate,
Which, like the Sun's, more wonders does afford.

91

He drew his mighty Frigats all before,
On which the Foe his fruitless Force employes :
His weak ones deep into his Reer he bore
Remote from Guns, as Sick-men from the noise.

92

His fiery Canon did their passage guide,
And following Smoke obscur'd them from the Foe :
Thus *Israel*, safe from the *Egyptian's* pride,
By flaming Pillars, and by Clouds did go.

93

Elsewhere the *Belgian* force we did defeat,
But here our Courages did theirs subdue :
So *Xenophon* once led that fam'd Retreat,
Which first the *Asian* Empire overthrew.

94

The Foe approach'd, and one, for his bold Sin,
Was sunk, (as he that touch'd the Ark was slain :)
The wild Waves master'd him and suck'd him in,
And smiling *Eddies* dimpled on the Main.

95

This seen, the rest at awful distance stood ;
As if they had been there as Servants set,
To stay, or to go on, as he thought good,
And not persue, but wait on his Retreat.

96

So *Lybian* Huntsmen on some Sandy plain,
From shady coverts rouz'd, the Lion chace :
The Kingly beast roars out with loud disdain,
[m]And slowly moves, unknowing to give place.

97

But if some one approach to dare his Force,
He swings his Tail, and swiftly turns him round :
With one Paw seizes on his trembling Horse,
And with the other tears him to the ground.

98

Amidst these Toils succeeds the balmy night ;
Now hissing waters the quench'd Guns restore ;
[n]And weary waves, withdrawing from the Fight,
Lie lull'd and panting on the silent Shore.

99

The Moon shone clear on the becalmed floud,
Where, while her beams like glittering silver play,
Upon the Deck our careful General stood,
And deeply mus'd on the [o] succeeding day.

100

That happy Sun, said he, will rise again,
Who twice victorious did our Navy see :
And I alone must view him rise in vain,
Without one ray of all his Star for me.

101

Yet like an *English* Gen'ral will I die,
And all the Ocean make my spatious grave :
Women and Cowards on the Land may lie,
The Sea's a Tomb that's proper for the Brave.

102

Restless he pass'd the remnants of the Night,
Till the fresh Air proclaim'd the Morning nigh :
And burning Ships, the Martyrs of the Fight,
With paler fires beheld the Eastern sky.

103

But now, his Stores of Ammunition spent,
His naked Valour is his only guard ; *Third day.*
Rare Thunders are from his dumb Cannon sent,
And solitary Guns are scarcely heard.

[m] *The Simile is* Virgil's : Vestigia retro improperata refert, &c.

91.4 from the noise] are from noise *1667.*
96.1 *Lybian*] *The editors correct to* Libyan

[n] *weary waves,* from Statius Sylv.
Nec trucibus fluviis idem sonus : Occidit horror æquoris, et terris maria acclinata quiescunt.
[o] The third of June, *famous for two former Victories.*

104

Thus far had Fortune pow'r, here forc'd to
    stay,
Nor longer durst with Virtue be at strife :
This, as a Ransom, *Albemarl* did pay
For all the Glories of so great a Life.

105

For now brave *Rupert* from afar appears,
Whose waving Streamers the glad General
    knows :
With full-spread Sails his eager Navy steers,
And every Ship in swift proportion grows.

106

The anxious Prince had heard the Cannon
    long,
And from that length of time dire *Omens* drew
Of *English* over-match'd, and *Dutch* too
    strong,
Who never fought three days but to persue.

107

Then, as an eagle, (who, with pious care,
Was beating widely on the wing for prey,)
To her now silent *Eiry* does repair,
And finds her callow Infants forc'd away.

108

Stung with her Love, she stoops upon the
    Plain,
The broken Air loud whistling as she flies :
She stops, and listens, and shoots forth again,
And guides her Pinions by her Young ones
    cries.

109

With such kind passion hasts the Prince to
    fight,
And spreads his flying Canvass to the sound ;
Him, whom no danger, were he there could
    fright,
Now, absent, every little noise can wound.

110

As in a drought the thirsty Creatures cry,
And gape upon the gather'd Clouds for Rain ;
And first the Martlet meets it in the Sky,
And, with wet wings, joys all the feather'd
    Train.

105 *The text of 1688 is that of later copies of
1667. The earliest copies of 1667 have*

For now brave *Rupert's* Navy did appear,
    Whose waving streamers from afar he knows :
As in his fate something divine there were
    Who dead and buried the third day arose.

111

With such glad hearts did our despairing Men
Salute the appearance of the Princes Fleet ;
And each ambitiously would claim the Ken,
That with first eyes did distant safety meet.

112

The *Dutch*, who came like greedy Hinds
    before,
To reap the harvest their ripe Ears did yield ;
Now look like those, when rowling Thunders
    roar,
And sheets of Lightning blast the standing
    Field.

113

Full in the Princes Passage, hills of Sand
And dang'rous Flats in secret Ambush lay,
Where the false tides skim o'er the cover'd
    Land,
And Sea-men with dissembled Depths betray.

114

The wily *Dutch*, who, like fall'n-Angels,
    fear'd
This new *Messia's* coming, there did wait,
And round the verge their braving Vessels
    steer'd,
To tempt his Courage with so fair a Bait.

115

But he, unmov'd, contemns their idle threat,
Secure of fame when e're he please to fight :
His cold Experience tempers all his heat,
And inbred worth doth boasting Valour
    slight.

116

Heroick Virtue did his Actions guide,
And he the substance not th' appearance
    chose :
To rescue one such Friend he took more
    pride,
Than to destroy whole Thousands of such
    Foes.

117

But when approach'd, in strict Embraces
    bound,
Rupert and *Albemarl* together grow :
He joys to have his Friend in safety found,
Which he to none but to that Friend would
    owe.

115.4 doth] does *1667*.

118

The chearful Soldiers, with new stores suppli'd,
Now long to execute their spleenful Will ;
And, in revenge for those three days they
tri'd,
Wish one, like *Joshuah's*, when the Sun stood
still.

119

Thus re-inforc'd, against the adverse Fleet,
Still doubling ours, brave *Rupert*
leads the way ;   *Fourth*
With the first blushes of the Morn *days*
they meet,   *Battel.*
And bring night back upon the new-born
day.

120

His presence soon blows up the kindling
Fight.
And his loud Guns speak thick like angry
men :
It seem'd as Slaughter had been breath'd all
night,
And Death new pointed his dull Dart agen.

121

The *Dutch* too well his mighty Conduct
knew,
And matchless Courage since the former
Fight !
Whose Navy like a stiff-stretch'd cord did
show,
Till he bore in, and bent them into flight.

122

The wind he shares, while half their Fleet
offends
His open side, and high above him shews,
Upon the rest at pleasure he descends,
And, doubly harm'd, he double harms
bestows.

123

Behind, the Gen'ral mends his weary Pace,
And sullenly to his Revenge he sails :
ᴾ So glides some trodden Serpent on the
Grass,
And long behind his wounded Volume trails.

124

Th' increasing Sound is born to either shore,
And for their stakes the throwing Nations
fear :
Their Passion, double with the Cannons roar,
And with warm wishes each Man combats
there.

125

Pli'd thick and close as when the Fight begun,
Their huge unwieldy Navy wasts away ;
So sicken waning Moons too near the Sun,
And blunt their Crescents on the edge of day.

126

And now reduc'd on equal terms to fight,
Their Ships like wasted Patrimonies show ;
Where the thin scatt'ring Trees admit the
light,
And shun each others Shadows as they grow.

127

The warlike Prince had sever'd from the rest
Two giant Ships, the pride of all the Main ;
Which, with his one, so vigorously he press'd,
And flew so home they could not rise again.

128

Already batter'd, by his Lee they lay,
In vain upon the passing Winds they call :
The passing Winds through their torn Can-
vass play,
And flagging Sails on heartless Sailors fall.

129

Their open'd sides receive a gloomy light,
Dreadful as day let in to shades below :
Without, grim death rides bare-fac'd in their
sight,
And urges ent'ring billows as they flow.

130

When one dire shot, the last they could supply,
Close by the board the Prince's Main-mast
bore :
All three now, helpless, by each other lie,
And this offends not, and those fear no more.

131

So have I seen some fearful Hare maintain
A Course, till tir'd before the Dog she lay,
Who, stretch'd behind her, pants upon the
Plain,
Past pow'r to kill as she to get away.

ᴾ *So glides*, &c. *from* Virgil: Quum medii nexus
extremæque agmina caudæ solvuntur, tardosque
trahit sinus ultimus orbes, &c.

124.3 Passion] *Some editors give* Passions

DR.   C

132

With his loll'd tongue he faintly licks his
    Prey,
His warm breath blows her flix up as she lies ;
She, trembling, creeps upon the ground away,
And looks back to him with beseeching eyes.

133

The Prince unjustly does his Stars accuse,
Which hinder'd him to push his Fortune on ;
For what they to his Courage did refuse,
By mortal Valour never must be done.

134

This lucky hour the wise *Batavian* takes,
And warns his tatter'd Fleet to follow home :
Proud to have so got off with equal stakes,
q Where 'twas a Triumph not to be o're-come.

135

The General's force, as kept alive by fight,
Now, not oppos'd, no longer can persue :
Lasting till Heav'n had done his courage
    right ;
When he had conquer'd he his Weakness
    knew.

136

He casts a Frown on the departing Foe,
And sighs to see him quit the watry Field :
His stern fix'd eyes no satisfaction shew,
For all the glories which the Fight did yield.

137

Though, as when Fiends did Miracles avow,
He stands confess'd e'en by the boastful
    Dutch,
He only does his Conquest disavow,
And thinks too little what they found too
    much.

138

Return'd, he with the Fleet resolv'd to stay ;
No tender thoughts of Home his heart divide;
Domestick Joys and Cares he puts away ;
For Realms are households which the Great
    must guide.

139

As those who unripe veins in Mines explore,
On the rich bed again the warm Turf lay,
Till time digests the yet imperfect Ore,
And know it will be Gold another day :

140

So looks our Monarch on this early Fight,
Th' essay and rudiments of great Success,
Which all-maturing time must bring to Light,
While he, like Heav'n, does each days labour
    bless.

141

Heav'n ended not the first or second day,
Yet each was perfect to the work design'd :
God and Kings work, when they their work
    survey,
And passive aptness in all Subjects find.

142

In burden'd Vessels first, with speedy care,   *His*
His plenteous Stores do season'd   *Majesty*
    Timber send   *repairs*
Thither the brawny Carpenters   *the Fleet.*
    repair,
And as the Surgeons of maim'd Ships
    attend.

143

With Cord and Canvass from rich *Hamburgh*
    sent,
His Navies molted wings he imps once more ;
Tall *Norway* Fir, their Masts in Battel spent,
And *English* Oak sprung Leaks and Planks
    restore.

144

All hands employ'd r the Royal work grows
    warm :
Like labouring Bees on a long Summers day,
Some sound the Trumpet for the rest to
    swarm,
And some on bells of tasted Lillies play.

145

With glewy wax some new Foundations lay
Of Virgin-combs, which from the Roof are
    hung :
Some arm'd within doors, upon Duty stay
Or tend the Sick, or educate the Young.

146

So here some pick out Bullets from the side,
Some drive old Okum through each Seam
    and Rift :
Their left-hand does the Calking-iron guide,
The ratling Mallet with the right they lift.

---

r   Fervet opus : *the same similitude in* Virgil.

142.4 Surgeons] Chyrurg'ons *1667*.
145.1 Foundations] Foundation *1667*.
146.1 side] sides *1667 and 1688*.

---

q   **From Horace :**   quos opimus
    Fallere & effugere est-triumphus.

147

With boiling Pitch another near at hand,
(From friendly *Sweden* brought) the seams
    instops :
Which well paid o'r, the salt-Sea waves with-
    stand,
And shake them from the rising Beak in
    drops.

148

Some the gall'd Ropes with dawby Marling
    bind,
Or sear-cloth Masts with strong Tarpawling
    coats :
To try new Shrouds one mounts into the
    wind,
And one, below, their Ease or Stifness notes.

149

Our careful Monarch stands in Person by,
His new-cast Cannons Firmness to explore :
The strength of big-corn'd Powder loves to
    try,
And Ball and Cartrage sorts for every bore.

150

Each day brings fresh supplies of Arms and
    Men,
And Ships which all last Winter were
    abroad :
And such as fitted since the Fight had
    been,
Or new from Stocks were fall'n into Road.

151

The goodly *London* in her gallant Trim,
(The *Phœnix* daughter of the
    vanish'd old :)   Loyal
Like a rich Bride does to the   *London*
    Ocean swim,   *described.*
And on her shadow rides in Floating-gold.

152

Her Flag aloft spread ruffling to the Wind,
And sanguine Streamers seem the Floud to
    fire :
The Weaver charm'd with what his Loom
    design'd,
Goes on to Sea, and knows not to retire.

153

With roomy Decks, her Guns of mighty
    strength,
Whose low-laid Mouths each mounting
    Billow laves :
Deep in her Draught, and warlike in her
    Length,
She seems a Sea-wasp flying on the Waves.

154

This martial Present, piously design'd,
The Loyal City give their best-lov'd King :
And with a Bounty ample as the wind,
Built, fitted and maintain'd to aid him bring.

155

By viewing Nature, Nature's Hand-maid
    Art   *Digression*
Makes mighty things from small *concerning*
    beginnings grow :   *Shipping*
Thus Fishes first to Shipping did *and Naviga-*
    impart,   *tion.*
Their Tail the Rudder, and their Head the
    Prow.

156

Some Log, perhaps, upon the waters swam,
An useless drift, which rudely cut within,
And, hollow'd, first a floating Trough became
And cross some Riv'let Passage did begin.

157

In shipping such as this, the *Irish Kern*,
And untaught *Indian*, on the Stream did
    glide :
Ere sharp-keel'd Boats to stem the Floud did
    learn,
Or fin-like Oars did spread from either side.

158

Add but a sail, and *Saturn* so appear'd,
When from lost Empire he to Exile went,
And with the Golden age to *Tyber* steer'd,
Where Coin and first Commerce he did
    invent.

159

Rude as their Ships was Navigation, then ;
No useful Compass or Meridian known ;
Coasting, they kept the Land within their
    ken,
And knew no North but when the Pole-star
    shone.

147.4 shake] shakes *1667 and 1688.*
150.4 Road] *Some editors wrongly give the*
Road

160

Of all who since have used the open Sea,
Than the bold *English* none more Fame have
    won ;
s Beyond the Year, and out of Heav'n's
    high-way,
They make discoveries where they see no Sun.

161

But what so long in vain, and yet unknown,
By poor man-kinds benighted Wit is sought,
Shall in this Age to *Britain* first be shewn,
And hence be to admiring Nations taught.

162

The Ebbs of Tides and their mysterious Flow,
We, as Arts Elements shall understand,
And as by Line upon the Ocean go,
Whose Paths shall be familiar as the Land.

163

t Instructed ships shall sail to quick Com-
    merce,
By which remotest Regions are alli'd ;
Which makes one City of the Universe ;
Where some may gain, and all may be sup-
    pli'd.

164

Then we upon our Globes last verge shall go,
And view the Ocean leaning on the Sky :
From thence our rolling Neighbours we shall
    know,
And on the Lunar world securely pry.

165

This I fore-tel from your auspicious Care,
Who great in search of God and
    Nature grow ;   *Apostrophe*
Who best your wise Creator's   *to the Royal*
    Praise declare,   *Society.*
Since best to praise his works is best to know.

166

O truly Royal ! who behold the Law,
And rule of Beings in your Makers mind :
And thence, like Limbecks, rich Idea's draw,
To fit the levell'd use of Human-kind.

167

But first the toils of War we must endure,
And from th' injurious *Dutch* redeem the Seas,
War makes the valiant of his right secure,
And gives up Fraud to be chastis'd with ease.

168

Already were the *Belgians* on our Coast,
Whose Fleet more mighty every day became
By late success, which they did falsely boast,
And now by first appearing seem'd to claim.

169

Designing, Subtil, Diligent, and Close,
They knew to manage War with wise delay :
Yet all those arts their Vanity did cross,
And, by their pride, their prudence did
    betray.

170

Nor staid the *English* long : But well sup-
    pli'd,
Appear as numerous as th' insulting Foe :
The Combat now by Courage must be
    tri'd,
And the Success the braver Nation shew.

171

There was the *Plimouth* Squadron new come
    in,
Which in the Streights last Winter was
    abroad ;
Which twice on *Biscay's* working-Bay had
    been,
And on the Mid-land sea the *French* had
    aw'd.

172

Old expert *Allen*, Loyal all along,
Fam'd for his action on the *Smirna* fleet :
And *Holmes*, whose name shall live in Epick
    Song,
While Musick Numbers, or while Verse has
    Feet.

173

Holmes, the *Achates* of the Gen'ral's Fight ;
Who first bewitch'd our eyes with *Guinny*
    gold :
As once old *Cato* in the *Roman's* sight
The tempting Fruits of *Africk* did unfold.

174

With him went *Sprag*, as bountiful as brave,
Whom his high Courage to command had
    brought :
Harman, who did the twice fir'd *Harry* save,
And in his burning ship undaunted fought.

---

s Extra anni solisque vias. *Virg.*
t By a more exact *measure* of Longitude.

171.1 new] *1667* : now *1688. Probably a misprint.*

175

Young *Hollis* on a *Muse* by *Mars* begot,
Born, *Cæsar*-like, to write and act great
    Deeds :
Impatient to revenge his fatal Shot,
His right hand doubly to his left succeeds.

176

Thousands were there in darker fame that
    dwell,
Whose Deeds some nobler Poem shall adorn :
And though to me unknown, they, sure,
    fought well,
Whom *Rupert* led, and who were *British* born.

177

Of every size an hundred fighting Sail,
So vast the Navy now at Anchor rides,
That underneath it the press'd Waters fail,
And, with its weight, it shoulders off the
    Tides.

178

Now Anchors weigh'd, the Sea-men shout
    so shrill,
That Heav'n, and Earth, and the wide Ocean
    rings :
A Breeze from Westward waits their Sails to
    fill,
And rests, in those high beds, his downy
    Wings.

179

The wary *Dutch* this gathering storm fore-
    saw,
And durst not bide it on the *English*-coast :
Behind their treacherous Shallows they with-
    draw,
And there lay Snares to catch the *British*
    Host.

180

So the false Spider, when her Nets are spread,
Deep ambush'd in her silent Den does lie :
And feels, far off, the trembling of her
    thread,
Whose filmy Cord should bind the struggling
    Fly.

181

Then, if at last she find him fast beset,
She issues forth, and runs along her Loom :
She joys to touch the Captive in her Net,
And drag the little Wretch in triumph
    home.

182

The *Belgians* hop'd that, with disorder'd
    haste,
Our deep-cut Keels upon the Sands might
    run :
Or, if with caution leisurely were past,
Their numerous Gross might charge us one
    by one.

183

But with a Fore-wind pushing them above,
And swelling Tide that heav'd them from
    below,
O'er the blind Flats our warlike Squadrons
    move,
And, with spread Sails, to welcom Battel go.

184

It seem'd as there the *British Neptune*
    stood,
With all his hosts of Waters at Command,
Beneath them to submit th' officious Floud ;
ᵘAnd, with his Trident, shov'd them off the
    Sand.

185

To the pale Foes they suddenly draw near,
And summon them to unexpected Fight ;
They start like Murderers when Ghosts
    appear,
And draw their Curtains in the dead of night.

186

Now Van to Van the foremost Squadrons
    meet,
The midmost Battels hastning up   *Second*
    behind :   *Battel.*
Who view, far off, the storm of falling Sleet;
And hear their Thunder ratling in the wind.

187

At length the adverse Admirals appear ;
(The two bold Champions of each Countries
    right)
Their Eyes describe the lists as they come
    near,
And draw the lines of Death before they fight.

ᵘ Levat ipse tridenti & vastas aperit Syrtes.
Virg.

184.2 hosts] host *1667*.
186.2 hastning] hasting *1667*.

188

The distance judg'd for Shot of every size,
The Linstocks touch, the pond'rous Ball
  expires :
The vigorous Sea-man every Port-hole plies,
And adds his heart to every Gun he fires.

189

Fierce was the Fight on the proud *Belgians*
  side,
For Honour, which they seldom sought
  before :
But now they by their own vain Boasts were
  ti'd
And forc'd, at least in show, to prize it more.

190

But sharp remembrance on the *English*
  part
And shame of being match'd by such a
  Foe,
Rouze conscious Virtue up in every heart,
ᵂAnd seeming to be stronger makes them so.

191

Nor long the *Belgians* could that Fleet sus-
  tain,
Which did two Gen'rals fates, and *Cæsar's*
  bear :
Each several Ship a Victory did gain,
As *Rupert* or as *Albemarl* were there.

192

Their batter'd Admiral too soon withdrew,
Unthank'd by ours for his unfinish'd Fight ;
But he the Minds of his *Dutch* Masters knew,
Who call'd that providence which we call'd
  flight.

193

Never did Men more joyfully obey,
Or sooner understood the sign to flie :
With such alacrity they bore away,
As if to praise them All the States stood by.

194

O famous leader of the *Belgian* fleet,
Thy Monument inscrib'd such praise shall
  wear,
As *Varro* timely flying once did meet,
Because he did not of his *Rome* despair.

195

Behold that Navy, which a while before
Provok'd the tardy *English* close to Fight ;
Now draw their beaten Vessels close to
  shore,
As Larks lie dar'd to shun the Hobbies flight.

196

Who e're would *English* Monuments survey,
In other Records may our Courage know :
But let them hide the Story of this day,
Whose Fame was blemish'd by too base
  a Foe.

197

Or if too busily they will enquire
Into a Victory which we disdain :
Then let them know, the *Belgians* did
  retire
ˣ Before the Patron Saint of injur'd *Spain.*

198

Repenting *England* this revengeful day
To *Philip's* Manes ʸ did an offering bring
England, which first, by leading them astray,
Hatch'd up Rebellion to destroy her King.

199

Our Fathers bent their baneful industry,
To check a Monarchy that slowly grew ;
But did not *France* or *Holland's* Fate fore-
  see,
Whose rising Pow'r to swift Dominion flew.

200

In fortunes Empire blindly thus we go,
And wander after pathless Destiny ;
Whose dark resorts since Prudence cannot
  know,
In vain it would provide for what shall be.

201

But what e're *English* to the bless'd shall go,
And the fourth *Harry* or first *Orange* meet ;
Find him disowning of a *Burbon* foe,
And him detesting a *Batavian* Fleet.

ˣ *Patron Saint* : St. James, *on whose day this
Victory was gain'd.*
ʸ Philip's *Manes* : Philip *the Second of* Spain,
against whom the Hollanders *rebelling, were
aided by* Queen Elizabeth.

ᵂ Possunt, quia posse videntur. *Virg.*

195.2 Fight] the Fight *1667.*

202

Now on their Coasts our conquering Navy
    rides,
Way-lays their Merchants, and their Land
    besets;
Each day new Wealth without their Care
    provides;
They lie asleep with Prizes in their Nets.

203

So, close behind some Promontory lie
The huge Leviathans t' attend their Prey;
And give no Chace, but swallow in the
    Frie,
Which through their gaping Jaws mistake
    the way.

204

Nor was this all: In Ports and Roads remote,
Destructive Fires among whole
    Fleets we send;   *Burning of*
Triumphant Flames upon the   *the fleet in*
    Water flote,   *the Vly by*
And out-bound Ships at home   *Sir Robert*
    their Voyage end.   *Holmes.*

205

Those various Squadrons, variously design'd
Each Vessel fraighted with a several
    Load,
Each Squadron waiting for a several wind,
All find but one, to burn them in the Road.

206

Some bound for *Guinny*, golden Sand to find,
Bore all the Gauds the simple Natives
    wear:
Some for the pride of *Turkish* Courts design'd,
For folded *Turbants* finest *Holland* bear.

207

Some *English* wool, vex'd in a *Belgian* Loom,
And into Cloth of spungy softness made,
Did into *France* or colder *Denmark* doom,
To ruine with worse ware our staple Trade.

208

Our greedy Sea-men rummage every hold,
Smile on the Booty of each wealthier Chest;
And, as the Priests who with their Gods
    make bold,
Take what they like, and sacrifice the rest.

209

But, ah! how unsincere are all our Joys!
Which, sent from Heav'n, like
    Lightning, make no stay: *Transit to*
Their palling Taste the Journeys   *the Fire of*
    Length destroys,   *London.*
Or Grief, sent post, o'retakes them on the
    way.

210

Swell'd with our late Successes on the Foe,
Which *France* and *Holland* wanted power
    to cross,
We urge an unseen Fate to lay us low,
And feed their envious Eyes with *English*
    loss.

211

Each Element his dread Command obeys,
Who makes or ruines with a Smile or Frown:
Who as by one he did our Nation raise,
So now, he with another pulls us down.

212

Yet *London*, Empress of the Northern Clime,
By an high Fate thou greatly didst expire:
*Great as the Worlds, which, at the death
    of time,
Must fall, and rise a nobler frame by fire.

213

As when some dire Usurper Heav'n provides
To scourge his Country with a lawless sway:
His birth perhaps some petty Village hides,
And sets his Cradle out of Fortune's way.

214

Till fully ripe his swelling Fate breaks out,
And hurries him to mighty Mischiefs on:
His Prince, surpriz'd at first, no ill could
    doubt,
And wants the pow'r to meet it when 'tis
    known.

215

Such was the Rise of this prodigious fire,
Which in mean Buildings first obscurely bred,
From thence did soon to open Streets aspire,
And straight to Palaces and Temples spread.

216

The diligence of Trades and noiseful Gain,
And luxury, more late, asleep were laid:
All was the nights, and in her silent reign
No sound the rest of Nature did invade.

206.4 *Turbants*] Turbans *1667.*
207.2 made,] made: *1667 and 1688.*

ᶻ Quum mare, quum tellus, correptaque **regia**
cœli, ardeat, &c. *Ovid.*

217

In this deep quiet, from what scource un-
known,
Those seeds of Fire their fatal Birth disclose ;
And first, few scatt'ring Sparks about were
blown,
Big with the flames that to our Ruin rose.

218

Then, in some close-pent Room it crept
along,
And, smouldring as it went, in silence fed ;
Till th' infant Monster, with devouring
strong,
Walk'd boldly upright with exalted head.

219

Now like some rich or mighty Murderer,
Too great for Prison, which he breaks with
Gold,
Who fresher for new Mischiefs does appear
And dares the World to tax him with the old :

220

So scapes th' insulting Fire his narrow Jail
And makes small out-lets into open air :
There the fierce Winds his tender Force assail,
And beat him down-ward to his first repair.

221

ᵃ The Winds, like crafty Courtezans, with-
held
His Flames from burning, but to blow them
more :
And every fresh attempt he is repell'd
With faint Denials, weaker than before.

222

And now, no longer letted of his Prey,
He leaps up at it with inrag'd desire :
O'relooks the Neighbours with a wide survey,
And nods at every House his threatning Fire.

223

The Ghosts of Traitors from the *Bridge*
descend,
With bold Fanatick Spectres to rejoyce :
About the fire into a Dance they bend,
And sing their Sabbath Notes with feeble
voice.

ᵃ *like crafty*, &c., Hæc arte tractabat cupidum
virum, ut illius animum inopia accenderet.

221 note. *Some editors correct the misquota-
tion.*

224

Our Guardian Angel saw them where he sate
Above the Palace of our slumbring King ;
He sigh'd, abandoning his charge to Fate,
And, drooping, oft lookt back upon the wing.

225

At length the crackling noise and dreadful
blaze
Call'd up some waking Lover to the sight ;
And long it was ere he the rest could raise,
Whose heavy Eye-lids yet were full of Night.

226

The next to Danger, hot persu'd by Fate,
Half-cloth'd, half-naked, hastily retire :
And frighted Mothers strike their Breasts,
too late,
For helpless Infants left amidst the Fire.

227

Their Cries soon waken all the Dwellers near ;
Now murmuring Noises rise in every Street ;
The more remote run stumbling with their
fear,
And, in the dark, Men justle as they meet.

228

So weary Bees in little Cells repose ;
But if Night-robbers lift the well-stor'd Hive,
An humming through their waxen City
grows,
And out upon each others wings they drive.

229

Now Streets grow throng'd and busie as by
day :
Some run for Buckets to the hallow'd Quire :
Some cut the Pipes, and some the Engines
play ;
And some more bold mount Ladders to the
fire.

230

In vain : For from the East a *Belgian* wind
His hostile Breath through the dry Rafters
sent ;
The Flames impell'd soon left their Foes
behind
And forward, with a wanton fury went.

224.1 he] *By a most thoughtless error all English editors give* they

231

A Key of Fire ran all along the Shore,
b And lighten'd all the River with a blaze:
The waken'd Tides began again to roar,
And wond'ring Fish in shining waters gaze.

232

Old Father Thames rais'd up his reverend head,
But fear'd the fate of *Simoeis* would return:
Deep in his *Ooze* he sought his sedgy Bed,
And shrunk his Waters back into his Urn.

233

The Fire, mean time walks in a broader gross;
To either hand his Wings he opens wide:
He wades the Streets, and streight he reaches cross,
And plays his longing Flames on th' other side.

234

At first they warm, then scorch, and then they take;
Now with long Necks from side to side they feed:
At length, grown strong, their Mother-fire forsake,
And a new Colony of Flames succeed.

235

To every nobler Portion of the Town
The curling Billows roll their restless Tide:
In parties now they straggle up and down,
As Armies, unoppos'd, for Prey divide.

236

One mighty Squadron with a Side-wind sped,
Through narrow Lanes his cumber'd Fire does haste:
By pow'rful charms of Gold and Silver led,
The *Lombard* Banquers and the *Change* to waste.

237

Another backward to the *Tow'r* would go,
And slowly eats his way against the Wind:
But the main body of the marching Foe
Against th' Imperial Palace is design'd.

b Sigæa igni freta lata relucent. *Virg.*

235.3 straggle] *1667*: struggle *1688. A mis-print.*

238

Now Day appears, and with the day the King,
Whose early Care had robb'd him of his rest:
Far off the Cracks of Falling houses ring,
And Shrieks of Subjects pierce his tender Breast.

239

Near as he draws, thick harbingers of Smoke
With gloomy Pillars cover all the place:
Whose little intervals of Night are broke
By Sparks, that drive against his Sacred Face.

240

More than his Guards his Sorrows made him known,
And pious Tears, which down his Cheeks did show'r:
The Wretched in his Grief forgot their own;
(So much the Pity of a King has pow'r.)

241

He wept the Flames of what he lov'd so well
And what so well had merited his love:
For never Prince in Grace did more excel,
Or Royal City more in Duty strove.

242

Nor with an idle Care did he behold:
(Subjects may grieve, but Monarchs must redress;)
He chears the Fearful and commends the Bold,
And makes Despairers hope for good Success.

243

Himself directs what first is to be done,
And orders all the Succours which they bring:
The Helpful and the Good about him run,
And form an Army worthy such a King.

244

He sees the dire Contagion spread so fast
That where it seizes, all Relief is vain:
And therefore must unwillingly lay waste
That Country, which would, else, the Foe maintain.

245

The Powder blows up all before the Fire:
Th' amazed flames stand gather'd on a heap;
And from the precipices-brink retire,
Afraid to venture on so large a leap.

238.3 Falling houses] *1667*: Falling houses *1688.*

246

Thus fighting Fires a while themselves con-
sume,
But streight like *Turks*, forc'd on to win or
die,
They first lay tender Bridges of their fume,
And o're the Breach in unctuous vapours flie.

247

Part stays for Passage, 'till a gust of wind
Ships o're their Forces in a shining Sheet :
Part, creeping under ground, their Journey
blind,
And, climbing from below, their Fellows
meet.

248

Thus to some desert Plain, or old Wood-side,
Dire Night-hags come from far to dance their
round :
And o're broad rivers, on their Fiends, they
ride,
Or sweep in Clouds above the blasted ground.

249

No help avails : for, *Hydra*-like, the Fire
Lifts up his Hundred heads to aim his way :
And scarce the wealthy can one half retire,
Before he rushes in to share the Prey.

250

The Rich grow suppliant, and the Poor grow
proud :
Those offer mighty gain, and these ask more ;
So void of pity is th' ignoble Crowd,
When others Ruin may increase their Store.

251

As those who live by Shores with joy behold
Some wealthy Vessel split or stranded nigh ;
And from the Rocks leap down for ship-
wrack'd Gold,
And seek the Tempest which the others flie :

252

So these but wait the Owners last despair,
And what's permitted to the flames invade :
Ev'n from their Jaws they hungry morsels
tear,
And, on their backs, the Spoils of *Vulcan*
lade.

246.2 die,] die : *1667 and 1688.*
251.4 Tempest] *1667* : Tempests *1688. A misprint.*

253

The days were all in this lost labour spent ;
And when the weary King gave place to
Night,
His Beams he to his Royal Brother lent,
And so shone still in his reflective Light.

254

Night came, but without darkness or repose,
A dismal Picture of the gen'ral Doom ;
Where Souls distracted when the Trumpet
blows,
And half unready with their Bodies come.

255

Those who have Homes, when Home they
do repair,
To a last Lodging call their wand'ring
Friends :
Their short uneasie Sleeps are broke with
Care,
To look how near their own Destruction
tends.

256

Those who have none, sit round where once
it was,
And with full Eyes each wonted Room
require :
Haunting the yet warm Ashes of the place,
As murder'd Men walk where they did expire.

257

Some stir up Coals, and watch the Vestal fire,
Others in vain from sight of Ruin run ;
And, while through burning Lab'rinths they
retire,
With loathing Eyes repeat what they would
shun.

258

The most in Feilds like herded Beasts lie
down,
To Dews obnoxious on the grassie Floor ;
And while their Babes in Sleep their Sorrows
drown,
Sad Parents watch the remnants of their
Store.

259

While by the Motion of the Flames they guess
What Streets are burning now, and what
are near,
An infant waking to the Paps would press,
And meets, instead of Milk, a falling Tear.

260

No thought can ease them but their Sove-
    reign's Care,
Whose Praise th' afflicted as their Comfort
    sing ;
Ev'n those, whom Want might drive to just
    despair,
Think Life a Blessing under such a King.

261

Mean time he sadly suffers in their Grief,
Out-weeps an Hermite, and out-praysa Saint:
All the long night he studies their relief,
How they may be suppli'd, and he may
    want.

262

O God, said he, thou Patron of my Days,
Guide of my Youth in Exile and
    Distress !   *King's
Who me unfriended brought'st   Prayer.*
    by wondrous ways,
The Kingdom of my Fathers to possess :

263

Be thou my Judge, with what unwearied
    Care
I since have labour'd for my People's good ;
To bind the Bruises of a Civil War,
And stop the Issues of their wasting Blood.

264

Thou, who hast taught me to forgive the Ill,
And recompense, as Friends, the Good mis-
    led :
If Mercy be a Precept of thy Will,
Return that Mercy on thy Servants head.

265

Or, if my heedless Youth has stept astray,
Too soon forgetful of thy gracious hand ;
On me alone thy just Displeasure lay,
But take thy Judgments from this mourning
    Land.

266

We all have sinn'd, and thou hast laid us low,
As humble Earth from whence at first we
    came :
Like flying Shades before the Clouds we
    shew,
And shrink like Parchment in consuming
    Flame.

267

O let it be enough what thou hast done ;
When spotted Deaths ran arm'd thro' every
    Street,
With poison'd Darts which not the Good
    could shun,
The Speedy could out-flie, or Valiant meet.

268

The living few, and frequent Funerals then,
Proclaim'd thy Wrath on this forsaken place :
And now those few, who are return'd agen,
Thy searching Judgments to their dwellings
    trace.

269

O pass not, Lord, an absolute Decree,
Or bind thy Sentence unconditional :
But in thy Sentence our Remorse foresee,
And, in that foresight, this thy Doom recall.

270

Thy Threatings, Lord, as thine thou maist
    revoke :
But, if immutable and fix'd they stand,
Continue still thy self to give the stroke,
And let not Foreign-foes oppress Thy Land.

271

Th' Eternal heard, and from the Heav'nly
    Quire
Chose out the Cherub with the flaming
    Sword :
And bad him swiftly drive th' approaching
    Fire
From where our Naval Magazins were stor'd.

272

The blessed Minister his Wings displai'd,
And like a shooting Star he cleft the night ;
He charg'd the Flames, and those that dis-
    obey'd
He lash'd to duty with his Sword of light.

273

The fugitive Flames, chastis'd, went forth
    to prey
On pious Structures, by our Fathers rear'd ;
By which to Heav'n they did affect the way,
Ere Faith in Church-men without Works
    was heard.

270.1 Threatings] threatnings *1667*.

274

The wanting Orphans saw with watry Eyes
Their Founders Charity in Dust laid low,
And sent to God their ever-answer'd cries,
(For he protects the Poor, who made them so.)

275

Nor could thy Fabrick, *Paul's*, defend thee
long,
Though thou wert Sacred to thy Makers
praise:
Though made Immortal by a Poet's Song,
And Poets Songs the *Theban* walls could
raise.

276

The daring Flames peep't in, and saw from
far
The awful Beauties of the Sacred Quire:
But, since it was prophan'd by Civil War,
Heav'n thought it fit to have it purg'd by fire.

277

Now down the narrow Streets it swiftly
came,
And, widely opening, did on both sides prey:
This benefit we sadly owe the Flame,
If only Ruin must enlarge our way.

278

And now four days the Sun had seen our
Woes;
Four nights the Moon beheld th' incessant
fire;
It seem'd as if the Stars more sickly rose,
And farther from the feav'rish North retire.

279

In th' Empyrean Heav'n (the Bless'd abode,)
The Thrones and the Dominions prostrate lie.
Not daring to behold their angry God:
And an hush'd silence damps the tuneful Sky.

280

At length th' Almighty cast a pitying Eye,
And Mercy softly touch'd his melting Breast:
He saw the Towns one half in Rubbish lie,
And eager flames drive on to storm the rest.

281

An hollow chrystal Pyramid he takes,
In firmamental Waters dipt above;
Of it a broad Extinguisher he makes
And hoods the Flames that to their quarry
strove.

282

The vanquish'd Fires withdraw from every
place,
Or, full with feeding, sink into a sleep:
Each household Genius shows again his face,
And, from the hearths, the little Lares creep.

283

Our King this more than natural change
beholds;
With sober Joy his heart and eyes abound:
To the All-good his lifted hands he folds,
And thanks him low on his redeemed ground.

284

As when sharp Frosts had long constrain'd
the earth,
A kindly Thaw unlocks it with mild Rain,
And first the tender Blade peeps up to birth,
And streight the Green fields laugh with
promis'd grain:

285

By such degrees the spreading Gladness grew
In every heart, which Fear had froze before:
The standing Streets with so much joy they
view,
That with less grief the Perish'd they deplore.

286

The Father of the People open'd wide
His Stores, and all the Poor with Plenty fed:
Thus God's Anointed God's own place sup-
pli'd,
And fill'd the Empty with his daily Bread.

287

This Royal bounty brought its own Reward,
And, in their Minds, so deep did print the
sense;
That if their Ruins sadly they regard,
Tis but with fear the sight might drive him
thence.

288

But so may he live long, that Town to sway,
Which by his Auspice they will
nobler make,   *Cities re-*
As he will hatch their Ashes by   *quest to the*
his stay,   *King not to*
And not their humble Ruins   *leave them.*
now forsake.

289

They have not lost their Loyalty by Fire;
Nor is their Courage or their Wealth so low,
That from his Wars they poorly would retire,
Or beg the Pity of a vanquish'd Foe.

274.2 Dust] the Dust *1667*.
280.4 drive] give *1667*.

284.2 mild] *Editors till Christie give* cold

290

Not with more Constancy the *Jews* of old,
By *Cyrus* from rewarded Exile sent,
Their Royal City did in Dust behold,
Or with more vigour to rebuild it went.

291

The utmost Malice of their Stars is past,
And two dire Comets, which have scourg'd
the Town
In their own Plague and Fire have breath'd
their last,
Or, dimly, in their sinking sockets frown.

292

Now frequent Trines the happier lights
among,
And high rais'd *Jove* from his dark Prison
freed,
(Those Weights took off that on his Planet
hung,)
Will gloriously the new-laid Works succeed.

293

Me-thinks already, from this Chymick flame,
I see a city of more precious mold :
Rich as the town which gives the *c Indies*
name,
With Silver pav'd, and all divine with Gold.

294

Already lbouring with a mighty fate,
She shakes the Rubbish from her mounting
Brow,
And seems to have renew'd her Charters date,
Which Heav'n will to the death of time
allow.

295

More great than human now, and more
d August,
New deified she from her Fires does rise :
Her widening Streets on new Foundations
trust,
And, opening, into larger parts she flies.

296

Before, she like some Shepherdess did shew,
Who sate to bathe her by a River's side ;
Not answering to her fame, but rude and low,
Nor taught the beauteous Arts of Modern
pride.

c Mexico.
d Augusta, *the old name of* London.

292.4 Works] *1688* : Work *1667.*

297

Now, like a Maiden Queen, she will behold,
From her high Turrets, hourly Sutors come :
The East with Incense, and the West with
Gold,
Will stand, like Suppliants, to receive her
Doom.

298

The silver *Thames,* her own domestick Floud,
Shall bear her Vessels, like a sweeping Train,
And often wind (as of his Mistress proud,)
With longing eyes to meet her Face again.

299

The wealthy *Tagus,* and the wealthier *Rhine,*
The glory of their Towns no more shall boast,
And *Sein,* that would with *Belgian* Rivers
join,
Shall find her Lustre stain'd, and Traffick
lost.

300

The vent'rous Merchant who design'd more
far,
And touches on our hospitable Shore,
Charm'd with the Splendour of this Northern
Star,
Shall here unlade him, and depart no more.

301

Our pow'rful Navy shall no longer meet,
The wealth of *France* or *Holland* to invade :
The beauty of this Town without a Fleet,
From all the World shall vindicate her Trade.

302

And, while this fam'd Emporium we prepare,
The *British* Ocean shall such Triumphs boast,
That those, who now disdain our Trade to
share,
Shall rob like Pyrats on our wealthy Coast.

303

Already we have conquer'd half the War,
And the less dang'rous part is left behind :
Our Trouble now is but to make them dare,
And not so great to Vanquish as to Find.

304

Thus to the Eastern wealth through Storms
we go,
But now, the Cape once doubled, fear no
more :
A constant Trade-wind will securely blow,
And gently lay us on the Spicy shore,

ABSALOM

AND

ACHITOPHEL.

A

POEM.

---------*Si Propiùs stes*
Te Capiet Magis---------

LONDON,
Printed for *J. T.* and are to be Sold by *W. Davis* in
Amen-Corner, 1681.

ABSALOM
AND
ACHITOPHEL.

A
POEM.

--------*Si Propiùs ſtes*
Te Capiet Magis---------

The Second Edition ; Augmented and Reviſed.

LONDON,

Printed for *J. T.* and are to be Sold by
W. Davis in *Amen-Corner,* 1681.

TO THE
READER.

'Tis not my intention to make an Apology for my Poem : Some will think it needs no Excuse, and others will receive none. The Design, I am sure, is honest : but he who draws his Pen for one Party must expect to make Enemies of the other. For Wit and Fool are Consequents of Whig and Tory : and every man is a Knave or an Ass to the contrary side. There's a Treasury of Merits in the Phanatick Church as well as in the Papist, and a Penny-worth to be had of Saintship, Honesty, and Poetry, for the Leud, the Factious, and the Block-heads : But the longest Chapter in Deuteronomy has not Curses enough for an Anti-Broming-

10 ham. My Comfort is, their manifest Prejudice to my Cause, will render their Judgment of less Authority against me. Yet if a Poem have a Genius, it will force its own reception in the World. For there's a sweetness in good Verse, which Tickles even while it Hurts : And, no man can be heartily angry with him, who pleases him against his will. The Commendation of Adversaries, is the greatest Triumph of a Writer ; because it never comes unless Extorted. But I can be satisfied on more easy terms : If I happen to please the more Moderate sort, I shall be sure of an honest Party ; and, in all probability, of the best Judges ; for the least Concern'd are commonly the least Corrupt : And, I confess, I have laid in for those, by rebating the Satyre (where Justice would allow it), from carrying too sharp an Edge. They, who can Criticize so weakly, as to imagine I have done my Worst, may be Convinc'd at their own Cost

20 that I can write Severely, with more ease, than I can Gently. I have but laugh'd at some mens Follies, when I coud have declaim'd against their Vices ; and, other mens Vertues I have commended as freely as I have tax'd their Crimes. And now, if you are a Malicious Reader, I expect you should return upon me that I affect to be thought more Impartial than I am. But if men are not to be judg'd by their Professions, God forgive you Common-wealths-men, for professing so plausibly for the Government. You cannot be so Unconscionable, as to charge me for not Subscribing of my Name ; for that woud reflect too grosly upon your own Party, who never dare, though they have the advantage of a Jury to secure them. If you like not my Poem, the fault may possibly be in my Writing : (though 'tis hard for an Author to judge against himself ;) But, more probably, 'tis in your Morals, which cannot bear the

30 truth of it. The Violent on both sides will condemn the Character of Absalom, as either too favourably or too hardly drawn. But they are not the Violent whom I desire to please. The fault, on the right hand, is to Extenuate, Palliate, and Indulge ; and, to confess freely, I have endeavoured to commit it. Besides the respect which I owe his Birth, I have a greater for his Heroick Vertues ; and, David himself, coud not be more tender of the Young-man's Life, than I woud be of his Reputation. But, since the most excellent Natures are always the most easy and, as being such, are the soonest perverted by ill Counsels, especially when baited with Fame and Glory, 'tis no more a wonder that he withstood not the temptations of Achitophel, than it was for Adam not to have resisted the two Devils, the Serpent and the Woman. The conclusion of the Story, I purposely forbore to prosecute ; because, I could not obtain from my self to

40 show Absalom Unfortunate. The Frame of it was cut out but for a Picture to the Waste ; and if the Draught be so far true, 'tis as much as I design'd.

Were I the Inventor, who am only the Historian, I shoud certainly conclude the Piece, with the Reconcilement of Absalom to David. And, who knows but this may come to pass ? Things were not brought to an Extremity where I left the Story : There seems yet to be room left for a Composure ; hereafter, there may only be for Pity. I have not so much as an un-charitable Wish against Achitophel, but am content to be Accus'd of a good natur'd Errour ;

The first edition and the second were both of 1681. The text is from the latter, except as noted. The current texts have several serious errors.

16 probability] ed. 1 : pobability ed. 2.
42 only] ed. 1 : onely ed. 2.

and to hope with Órigen, *that the Devil himself may, at last, be sav'd. For which reason, in this* Poem, *he is neither brought to set his House in order, nor to dispose of his Person afterwards, as he in wisdom shall think fit. God is infinitely merciful; and his Vicegerent is only not so, because he is not Infinite.*

The true end of Satyre *is the amendment of Vices by correction. And he who writes Honestly, is no more an Enemy to the Offender than the Physician to the Patient, when he prescribes harsh Remedies to an inveterate Disease : for those, are only in order to prevent the Chyrurgeon's work of an* Ense rescindendum, *which I wish not to my very Enemies. To conclude all, If the Body Politique have any Analogy to the Natural, in my weak judgment, an Act of* Oblivion *were as necessary in a Hot, Distempered State, as an* Opiate *woud be in a Raging Fever.* 10

ABSALOM

AND

ACHITOPHEL.

A POEM.

IN pious times, e'r Priest-craft did begin,
Before *Polygamy* was made a Sin ;
When Man on many multipli'd his kind,
E'r one to one was cursedly confin'd,
When Nature prompted and no Law deni'd
Promiscuous Use of Concubine and Bride ;
Then *Israel's* Monarch, after Heavens own
    heart,
His vigorous warmth did, variously, impart
To Wives and Slaves : And, wide as his Command,
Scatter'd his Maker's Image through the
    Land. 10
Michal, of Royal Blood, the Crown did wear,
A soil ungrateful to the Tiller's care :
Not so the rest ; for several Mothers bore
To God-like *David* several sons before.
But since like Slaves his Bed they did ascend,
No True Succession could their Seed attend.
Of all this Numerous Progeny was none
So Beautiful so Brave as *Absalon* :
Whether, inspird by some diviner Lust,
His father got him with a greater Gust, 20
Or that his Conscious Destiny made way
By manly Beauty to Imperial Sway.
Early in Foreign Fields he won Renown
With Kings and States allied to *Israel's*
    Crown :

In Peace the thoughts of War he coud re-
    move
And seem'd as he were onely born for Love.
What e'r he did was done with so much ease,
In him alone, 'twas Natural to please ;
His motions all accompanied with grace ;
And *Paradise* was open'd in his face. 30
With secret Joy, indulgent *David* view'd
His Youthful Image in his Son renew'd ;
To all his wishes Nothing he deni'd
And made the Charming *Annabel* his Bride.
What faults he had (for who from faults is
    free ?)
His father coud not or he woud not see.
Some warm excesses, which the Law forbore,
Were constru'd Youth that purg'd by boil-
    ing o'r :
And *Amnon's* Murther, by a specious Name,
Was call'd a Just Revenge for injur'd Fame.
Thus Prais'd and Lov'd, the Noble Youth
    remain'd, 41
While *David*, undisturb'd, in *Sion* reign'd.
But Life can never be sincerely blest :
Heav'n punishes the bad, and proves the
    best.
The *Jews*, a Headstrong, Moody, Murm'ring
    race
As ever tri'd th' extent and stretch of grace ;
God's pamper'd People, whom, debauch'd
    with ease,
No King could govern nor no God could
    please ;

TO THE READER 4 *only*] ed. 1 : *onely* ed. 2.
  10 *Fever*] ed. 1 : *Feavour* ed. 2.
19 by] with *ed. 1*.

(Gods they had tri'd of every shape and
     size
That God-smiths could produce or Priests
     devise :)   50
These *Adam*-wits, too fortunately free,
Began to dream they wanted liberty ;
And when no rule, no president was found
Of men, by Laws less circumscrib'd and
     bound ;
They led their wild desires to Woods and
     Caves ;
And thought that all but Savages were
     Slaves.
They who, when *Saul* was dead, without a
     blow
Made foolish *Ishbosheth* the Crown forgo ;
Who banisht *David* did from *Hebron* bring,
And, with a General shout, proclaim'd him
     King :   60
Those very *Jews* who at their very best
Their Humour more than Loyalty exprest,
Now wondred why so long they had obey'd
An Idol-Monarch which their hands had
     made ;
Thought they might ruine him they could
     create
Or melt him to that Golden Calf, a State.
But these were random Bolts : No form'd
     Design
Nor Interest made the Factious Croud to
     join :
The sober part of *Israel*, free from stain,
Well knew the value of a peaceful reign ; 70
And, looking backward with a wise afright,
Saw Seams of wounds, dishonest to the
     sight :
In contemplation of whose ugly Scars,
They curst the memory of Civil Wars.
The moderate sort of Men, thus qualifi'd,
Inclin'd the Ballance to the better side ;
And *David's* mildness manag'd it so well,
The bad found no occasion to Rebel.
But, when to Sin our byast Nature leans,
The careful Devil is still at hand with means ;
And providently Pimps for ill desires :   81
The Good Old Cause, reviv'd, a Plot requires,
Plots, true or false, are necessary things,
To raise up Common-wealths and ruin Kings.

Th' inhabitants of old *Jerusalem*,
Were *Jebusites* ; the Town so call'd from
     them ;
And their's the Native right——

But when the chosen People grew more
     strong,
The rightful cause at length became the
     wrong ;
And every loss the men of *Jebus* bore,   90
They still were thought God's enemies the
     more.
Thus, worn and weaken'd, well or ill content,
Submit they must to *David's* Government :
Impoverish't and depriv'd of all Command,
Their Taxes doubled as they lost their Land ;
And, what was harder yet to flesh and blood,
Their Gods disgrac'd, and burnt like common
     Wood.
This set the Heathen Priesthood in a flame,
For Priests of all Religions are the same :
Of whatsoe'er descent their Godhead be,   100
Stock, Stone, or other homely Pedigree,
In his defence his Servants are as bold,
As if he had been born of beaten Gold.
The *Jewish Rabbins*, though their Enemies,
In this conclude them honest men and wise :
For 'twas their duty, all the Learned think,
T' espouse his Cause by whom they eat and
     drink.
From hence began that Plot, the Nations
     Curse,
Bad in itself, but represented worse,   109
Rais'd in extremes, and in extremes decri'd,
With Oaths affirm'd, with dying Vows deni'd,
Not weigh'd or winnow'd by the Multitude,
But swallow'd in the Mass, unchewed and
     crude.
Some Truth there was, but dashed and
     brew'd with Lies :
To please the Fools, and puzzle all the Wise.
Succeeding Times did equal Folly call
Believing nothing or believing all.
The *Egyptian* Rites the *Jebusites* embrac'd,
Where Gods were recommended by their
     taste.
Such sav'ry Deities must needs be good 120
As serv'd at once for Worship and for
     Food.
By force they could not Introduce these
     Gods,
For Ten to One in former days was odds.
So Fraud was us'd, (the Sacrificers Trade,)
Fools are more hard to Conquer than Per-
     suade.

92 and] *Scott, Saintsbury, and others absurdly
give* or
     121 As] And *ed. 1.*

Their busie Teachers mingled with the *Jews*
And rak'd for Converts even the Court and
Stews:
Which *Hebrew* Priests the more unkindly
took,
Because the Fleece accompanies the Flock.
Some thought they God's Anointed meant to
slay 130
By Guns, invented since full many a day:
Our Author swears it not; but who can
know
How far the Devil and *Jebusites* may go?
This Plot, which fail'd for want of common
Sense,
Had yet a deep and dangerous Consequence;
For as, when raging Fevers boil the Blood
The standing Lake soon floats into a Floud;
And ev'ry hostile Humour which before
Slept quiet in its Channels bubbles o're:
So, several Factions from this first Ferment
Work up to Foam, and threat the Govern-
ment. 141
Some by their Friends, more by themselves
thought wise,
Oppos'd the Pow'r to which they could not
rise.
Some had in Courts been Great and, thrown
from thence,
Like Fiends were hardened in Impenitence.
Some, by their Monarch's fatal mercy grown,
From Pardon'd Rebels, Kinsmen to the
Throne
Were raised in Pow'r and Publick Office
high;
Strong Bands, if Bands ungrateful men coud
tie.
Of these the false *Achitophel* was first, 150
A Name to all succeeding Ages curst.
For close Designs and crooked Counsels fit,
Sagacious, Bold, and Turbulent of wit,
Restless, unfixt in Principles and Place,
In Pow'r unpleased, impatient of Disgrace;
A fiery Soul, which working out its way,⎞
Fretted the Pigmy Body to decay: ⎬
And o'r informed the Tenement of Clay. ⎠
A daring Pilot in extremity;
Pleas'd with the Danger, when the Waves
went high 160
He sought the Storms; but, for a Calm unfit,
Would Steer too nigh the Sands to boast his
Wit.

Great Wits are sure to Madness near alli'd
And thin Partitions do their Bounds divide;
Else, why should he, with Wealth and
Honour blest,
Refuse his Age the needful hours of Rest?
Punish a Body which he coud not please,
Bankrupt of Life, yet Prodigal of Ease?
And all to leave what with his Toil he won
To that unfeather'd two-legg'd thing, a
Son: 170
Got, while his Soul did huddled Notions trie;
And born a shapeless Lump, like Anarchy.
In Friendship false, implacable in Hate,
Resolv'd to Ruine or to Rule the State;
To Compass this the Triple Bond he broke;⎞
The Pillars of the Publick Safety shook, ⎬
And fitted *Israel* for a Foreign Yoke; ⎠
Then, seiz'd with Fear, yet still affecting
Fame,
Usurp'd a Patriot's All-attoning Name.
So easie still it proves in Factious Times 180
With publick Zeal to cancel private Crimes:
How safe is Treason and how sacred ill,
Where none can sin against the Peoples Will,
Where Crouds can wink; and no offence be
known,
Since in anothers guilt they find their own,
Yet, Fame deserv'd, no Enemy can grudge;
The Statesman we abhor, but praise the
Judge.
In *Israels* courts ne'er sat an *Abbethdin*
With more discerning Eyes or Hands more
clean,
Unbrib'd, unsought, the Wretched to re-
dress; 190
Swift of Dispatch and easie of Access.
Oh, had he been content to serve the Crown
With Vertues onely proper to the Gown,
Or had the rankness of the Soil been freed
From Cockle that opprest the Noble Seed,
David for him his tuneful Harp had strung,
And Heav'n had wanted one Immortal Song.
But wild Ambition loves to slide, not stand,
And Fortunes Ice prefers to Vertues Land.
Achitophel, grown weary to possess 200
A lawful Fame, and lazie Happiness,
Disdain'd the Golden Fruit to gather free
And lent the Crowd his Arm to shake the
Tree.
Now, manifest of Crimes, contriv'd long since,
He stood at bold Defiance with his Prince:

152 Counsels] Counsel *ed. 1.*
154 Principles] Principle *ed. 1.*

179 Usurp'd] Assum'd *ed. 1.*
180-91 *Not in ed. 1.*

Held up the Buckler of the Peoples Cause
Against the Crown ; and sculk'd behind the
    Laws.
The wish'd occasion of the Plot he takes ;
Some Circumstances finds, but more he
    makes.
By buzzing Emissaries, fills the ears   210
Of listening Crouds, with Jealousies and Fears
Of Arbitrary Counsels brought to light,
And proves the King himself a *Jebusite*.
Weak Arguments ! which yet he knew full
    well,
Were strong with People easie to Rebel.
For, govern'd by the *Moon*, the giddy *Jews*
Tread the same Track when she the Prime
    renews :
And once in twenty Years, their Scribes
    record,
By natural Instinct they change their Lord.
Achitophel still wants a Chief, and none 220
Was found so fit as Warlike *Absalon* :
Not, that he wish'd his Greatness to create,
(For Polititians neither love nor hate :)
But, for he knew his Title not allow'd,
Would keep him still depending on the Croud,
That Kingly pow'r, thus ebbing out, might be
Drawn to the Dregs of a Democracie.
Him he attempts with studied Arts to please
And sheds his Venome in such words as
    these.

Auspicioùs Prince ! at whose Nativity 230
Some Royal Planet rul'd the Southern Sky ;
Thy longing Countries Darling and Desire,
Their cloudy Pillar, and their guardian Fire,
Their second *Moses*, whose extended Wand
Divides the Seas and shows the promis'd
    Land,
Whose dawning Day, in every distant Age,
Has exercised the Sacred Prophets rage,
The Peoples Pray'r, the glad Diviners
    Theam,
The Young mens Vision and the Old mens
    Dream !
Thee, *Saviour*, Thee the Nations Vows con-
    fess ;   240
And, never satisfi'd with seeing, bless :
Swift, unbespoken Pomps, thy steps pro-
    claim,
And stammering Babes are taught to lisp thy
    Name.

How long wilt thou the general Joy detain ;
Starve, and defraud the People of thy
    Reign ?
Content ingloriously to pass thy days,
Like one of Vertues Fools that Feeds on
    Praise ?
Till thy fresh Glories, which now shine so
    bright,
Grow Stale and Tarnish with our dayly sight.
Believe me, Royal Youth, thy Fruit must be
Or gather'd Ripe, or rot upon the Tree. 251
Heav'n has to all allotted, soon or late,
Some lucky Revolution of their Fate :
Whose Motions, if we watch and guide with
    Skill,
(For humane Good depends on humane
    Will,)
Our Fortune rolls as from a smooth Descent
And, from the first impression, takes the
    Bent ;
But, if unseiz'd, she glides away like wind ;
And leaves repenting Folly far behind.
Now, now she meets you with a glorious
    prize   260
And spreads her Locks before her as she
    flies.
Had thus Old *David*, from whose Loins you
    spring,
Not dar'd, when Fortune call'd him, to be
    King,
At *Gath* an Exile he might still remain,
And Heavens Anointing Oil had been in vain.
Let his successful Youth your hopes engage,
But shun th' example of Declining Age.
Behold him setting in his Western Skies,
The Shadows lengthening as the Vapours
    rise.   269
He is not now, as when, on *Jordan's* Sand,
The Joyful People throng'd to see him Land,
Cov'ring the *Beach* and blackning all the
    Strand :
But like the Prince of Angels, from his height,
Comes tumbling downward with diminish'd
    light :
Betray'd by one poor Plot to publick Scorn,
(Our onely blessing since his curst Return,)
Those heaps of People which one Sheaf did
    bind,
Blown off and scatter'd by a puff of Wind.
What strength can he to your Designs
    oppose,
Naked of Friends, and round beset with
    Foes ?   280

235 Divides] Shuts up *ed. 1.*

If *Pharaoh's* doubtful succour he should use,
A Foreign Aid would more incense the *Jews* :
Proud *Egypt* woud dissembled Friendship
bring ;
Foment the War, but not support the King ;
Nor woud the Royal Party e'r unite
With *Pharaoh's* arms t' assist the *Jebusite* ;
Or if they shoud, their Interest soon would
break,
And, with such odious Aid, make *David*
weak.
All sorts of men, by my successful Arts
Abhorring Kings, estrange their altered
Hearts   290
From *David's* Rule : And'tis the general Cry,
Religion, Common-wealth, and Liberty.
If you, as Champion of the Publique Good,
Add to their Arms a Chief of Royal Blood ;
What may not *Israel* hope, and what Ap-
plause
Might such a General gain by such a Cause ?
Not barren Praise alone, that Gaudy Flow'r,
Fair onely to the sight, but solid Pow'r :
And Nobler is a limited Command,   299
Giv'n by the Love of all your Native Land,
Than a Successive Title, Long, and Dark,
Drawn from the Mouldy Rolls of *Noah's* ark.

What cannot Praise effect in Mighty
Minds,
When Flattery Sooths and when Ambition
Blinds !
Desire of Pow'r, on Earth a Vitious Weed,
Yet, sprung from High is of Cœlestial Seed ;
In God 'tis Glory : And when Men Aspire,
'Tis but a Spark too much of Heavenly Fire.
Th' Ambitious Youth, too Covetous of Fame,
Too full of Angels Metal in his Frame,   310
Unwarily was led from Vertues ways,
Made Drunk with Honour, and debauch'd
with Praise.
Half loath and half consenting to the Ill,
(For Loyal Blood within him strugled still,)
He thus repli'd—And what Pretence have I
To take up Arms for Publick Liberty ?
My Father Governs with unquestion'd Right;
The Faiths Defender and Mankinds Delight,
Good, Gracious, Just, observant of the Laws;
And Heav'n by Wonders has espous'd his
Cause.   320
Whom has he Wrong'd in all his Peaceful
Reign ?
Who sues for Justice to his Throne in Vain ?

What Millions has he pardoned of his Foes
Whom Just Revenge did to his Wrath expose ?
Mild, Easie, Humble, Studious of our Good,
Enclin'd to Mercy, and averse from Blood.
If Mildness Ill with Stubborn *Israel* Suit,
His Crime is God's beloved Attribute.
What could he gain, his People to Betray
Or change his Right, for Arbitrary Sway ?
Let Haughty *Pharaoh* Curse with such a
Reign   331
His Fruitful *Nile*, and Yoak a Servile Train.
If *David's* Rule *Jerusalem* Displease,
The *Dog-star* heats their Brains to this
Disease.
Why then should I, Encouraging the Bad,
Turn Rebel and run Popularly Mad ?
Were he a Tyrant who, by Lawless Might,
Opprest the *Jews* and rais'd the *Jebusite*,
Well might I Mourn ; but Nature's holy
Bands
Would Curb my Spirits, and Restrain my
Hands ;   340
The People might assert their Liberty ;
But what was Right in them, were Crime in
me.
His Favour leaves me nothing to require ;
Prevents my Wishes and out-runs Desire.
What more can I expect while *David* lives ?
All but his Kingly Diadem he gives :
And that : But there he paus'd ; then Sigh-
ing, said,
Is Justly destin'd for a Worthier head.
For when my Father from his Toyls shall
Rest   349
And late Augment the Number of the Blest :
His Lawful Issue shall the Throne ascend,
Or the *Collat'ral* Line, where that shall end.
His Brother, though Opprest with Vulgar
Spight,
Yet Dauntless and Secure of Native Right,
Of every Royal Vertue stands possest ;
Still Dear to all the Bravest and the Best.
His Courage Foes, his Friends his Truth
Proclaim ;
His Loyalty the King, the World his Fame.
His Mercy ev'n th' Offending Croud will
find,
For sure he comes of a Forgiving Kind. 360
Why shoud I then Repine at Heavens Decree
Which gives me no Pretence to Royalty ?
Yet oh that Fate, Propitiously Inclin'd,
Had rais'd my Birth, or had debas'd my
Mind ;

To my large Soul, not all her Treasure lent,
And then betrai'd it to a mean Descent.
I find, I find my mounting Spirits Bold,
And *David's* part disdains my Mothers Mold.
Why am I scanted by a Niggard Birth? 369
My soul Disclaims the Kindred of her Earth:
And, made for Empire, Whispers me within;
Desire of Greatness is a God-like Sin.

Him Staggering so when Hells dire Agent
    found,
While fainting Vertue scarce maintain'd her
    Ground,
He pours fresh Forces in, and thus Replies:
Th' eternal God, Supreamly Good and
    Wise,
Imparts not these Prodigious Gifts in vain;
What Wonders are Reserv'd to bless your
    Reign?
Against your will your Arguments have
    shown,   379
Such Vertue's only giv'n to guide a Throne.
Not that your Father's Mildness I contemn,
But manly Force becomes the Diadem.
'Tis true he grants the People all they crave;
And more perhaps than Subjects ought to
    have:
For Lavish Grants suppose a Monarch tame
And more his Goodness than his Wit pro-
    claim.
But when should People strive their Bonds
    to break,
If not when Kings are Negligent or Weak?
Let him give on till he can give no more,
The thrifty Sanhedrin shall keep him poor:
And every Sheckle which he can receive 391
Shall cost a Limb of his Prerogative.
To ply him with new Plots shall be my care;
Or plunge him deep in some Expensive War;
Which, when his Treasure can no more
    supply,
He must, with the Remains of Kingship, buy.
His faithful Friends our Jealousies and Fears
Call *Jebusites*; and *Pharaoh's* Pensioners,
Whom, when our Fury from his Aid has torn,
He shall be naked left to publick Scorn. 400
The next Successor, whom I fear and hate,
My Arts have made obnoxious to the State;
Turn'd all his Vertues to his Overthrow,
And gain'd our Elders to pronounce a Foe.
His Right, for Sums of necessary Gold,
Shall first be Pawn'd, and afterwards be
    Sold:

Till time shall Ever-wanting *David* draw,
To pass your doubtful Title into Law.
If not; the People have a Right Supreme
To make their Kings; for Kings are made
    for them.   410
All Empire is no more than Pow'r in Trust,
Which, when resum'd, can be no longer Just.
Succession, for the general Good design'd,
In its own wrong a Nation cannot bind:
If altering that, the People can relieve,
Better one suffer, than a Nation grieve.
The *Jews* well know their pow'r: e'r *Saul*
    they chose
God was their King, and God they durst
    Depose.
Urge now your Piety, your Filial Name,
A Father's Right and Fear of future Fame;
The Publick Good, that Universal Call, 421
To which even Heav'n submitted, answers
    all.
Nor let his Love enchant your generous
    Mind;
'Tis Natures trick to propagate her Kind.
Our fond Begetters, who would never die,
Love but themselves in their Posterity.
Or let his Kindness by th' Effects be tried
Or let him lay his vain Pretence aside.
God said he loved your Father; coud he
    bring
A better Proof than to anoint him King? 430
It surely shew'd, He lov'd the Shepherd well
Who gave so fair a Flock as *Israel*.
Would *David* have you thought his Darling
    Son?
What means he then, to Alienate the Crown?
The name of Godly he may blush to bear:
'Tis after Gods own heart to Cheat his
    Heir.
He to his Brother gives Supreme Command;
To you a Legacie of Barren Land:
Perhaps th' old Harp on which he thrums
    his Lays:
Or some dull *Hebrew* Ballad in your Praise.
Then the next Heir, a Prince, Severe and
    Wise,   441
Already looks on you with Jealous Eyes,
Sees through the thin Disguises of your Arts,
And marks your Progress in the Peoples
    Hearts.

---

416 Nation] Million *ed. 1.*
436 'Tis] *Derrick and others absurdly give*
Is't

Though now his mighty Soul its Grief con-
    tains ;
He meditates Revenge who least Complains.
And like a Lion, Slumb'ring in the way,
Or Sleep dissembling, while he waits his
    Prey,
His fearless Foes within his Distance draws,
Constrains his Roaring, and Contracts his
    Paws :   450
Till at the last, his time for Fury found,
He shoots with sudden Vengeance from the
    Ground :
The Prostrate Vulgar, passes o'r and Spares ;
But with a Lordly Rage, his Hunters tears ;
Your Case no tame Expedients will afford ;
Resolve on Death, or Conquest by the Sword,
Which for no less a Stake than Life, you
    Draw,
And Self-defence is Natures Eldest Law.
Leave the warm People no Considering time ;
For then Rebellion may be thought a Crime.
Prevail your self of what Occasion gives, 461
But trie your Title while your Father lives ;
And, that your Arms may have a fair Pre-
    tence,
Proclaim, you take them in the King's
    Defence ;
Whose Sacred Life each minute woud Ex-
    pose,
To Plots, from seeming Friends and secret
    Foes.
And who can sound the depth of *David's*
    Soul ?
Perhaps his fear, his kindness may Controul.
He fears his Brother, though he loves his
    Son,
For plighted Vows too late to be undone. 470
If so, by Force he wishes to be gain'd,
Like Womens Leachery to seem Constrain'd :
Doubt not ; but, when he most affects the
    Frown,
Commit a pleasing Rape upon the Crown.
Secure his Person to secure your Cause ;
They who possess the Prince, possess the
    Laws.

He said, And this Advice above the rest
With *Absalom's* Mild Nature suited best ;
Unblamed of Life (Ambition set aside,)
Not stain'd with Cruelty, nor puft with pride.

How happy had he been, if Destiny   481
Had higher placed his Birth, or not so high !
His Kingly Vertues might have claim'd a
    Throne
And blest all other Countries but his own :
But charming Greatness, since so few refuse ;
'Tis Juster to Lament him, than Accuse.
Strong were his hopes a Rival to remove,
With Blandishments to gain the publick
    Love,
To Head the Faction while their Zeal was hot,
And Popularly Prosecute the Plot.   490
To farther this, *Achitophel* Unites
The Malecontents of all the Israelites :
Whose differing Parties he could wisely Join
For several Ends, to serve the same
    Design.
The Best, and of the Princes some were such,
Who thought the pow'r of Monarchy too
    much :
Mistaken Men, and Patriots in their Hearts ;
Not Wicked, but seduc'd by Impious Arts.
By these the Springs of Property were bent,
And wound so high, they Crack'd the
    Government.   500
The next for Interest sought t' embroil the
    State,
To sell their Duty at a dearer rate ;
And make their *Jewish* Markets of the
    Throne ;
Pretending Publick Good, to serve their own.
Others thought Kings an useless heavy Load,
Who Cost too much, and did too little Good.
These were for laying Honest *David* by
On Principles of pure good Husbandry.
With them join'd all th' Haranguers of the
    Throng
That thought to get Preferment by the
    Tongue.   510
Who follow next, a double danger bring,
Not onely hating *David*, but the King ;
The *Solymæan* Rout ; well Vers'd of old
In Godly Faction, and in Treason bold ;
Cowring and Quaking at a Conqu'ror's
    Sword,
But Lofty to a Lawful Prince Restored ;
Saw with Disdain an *Ethnick* Plot begun
And Scorned by *Jebusites* to be Out-done.
Hot *Levites* Headed these ; who pul'd before
From th' *Ark*, which in the Judges days they
    bore,   520
Resum'd their Cant, and with a Zealous Crie
Pursu'd their old belov'd Theocracie.

---

461 Prevail] *Derrick and others wrongly give*
Avail

Where Sanhedrin and Priest enslav'd the
    Nation
And justifi'd their Spoils by Inspiration :
For who so fit for Reign as *Aaron's* Race,
If once Dominion they could found in Grace ?
These led the Pack ; though not of surest
    scent,
Yet deepest mouth'd against the Govern-
    ment.
A numerous Host of dreaming Saints suc-
    ceed :
Of the true old Enthusiastick Breed :   530
'Gainst Form and Order they their Pow'r
    imploy.
Nothing to Build, and all things to Destroy.
But far more numerous was the Herd of such,
Who think too little, and who talk too much.
These, out of meer instinct, they knew not
    why,
Adored their Fathers' God, and Property :
And, by the same blind Benefit of Fate,
The Devil and the *Jebusite* did hate :
Born to be sav'd, even in their own despight ;
Because they could not help believing right.
Such were the Tools ; but a whole Hydra
    more   541
Remains, of sprouting heads too long to score.
Some of their Chiefs were Princes of the Land ;
In the first Rank of these did *Zimri* stand :
A man so various, that he seem'd to be
Not one, but all Mankind's Epitome.
Stiff in Opinions, always in the wrong ;
Was Every thing by starts, and Nothing long :
But, in the course of one revolving Moon,
Was Chymist, Fidler, States-man, and
    Buffoon ;   550
Then all for Women, Painting, Rhiming,
    Drinking,
Besides ten thousand Freaks that died in
    thinking.
Blest Madman, who coud every hour employ,
With something New to wish, or to enjoy !
Railing and praising were his usual Theams ;
And both (to shew his Judgment) in Extreams :
So over Violent, or over Civil,
That every Man, with him, was God or Devil.
In squandring Wealth was his peculiar Art :
Nothing went unrewarded, but Desert. 560
Begger'd by fools, whom still he found too
    late :

He had his Jest, and they had his Estate.
He laugh'd himself from Court ; then sought
    Relief
By forming Parties, but could ne'r be Chief :
For, spight of him, the weight of Business fell
On *Absalom* and wise *Achitophel* :
Thus wicked but in Will, of Means bereft,
He left not Faction, but of that was left.
    Titles and Names 'twere tedious to Re-
    herse
Of Lords, below the Dignity of Verse. 570
Wits, Warriors, Commonwealths-men were
    the best :
Kind Husbands and meer Nobles all the rest
And, therefore in the name of Dulness, be
The well-hung *Balaam* and cold *Caleb* free ;
And Canting *Nadab* let Oblivion damn,
Who made new Porridge for the Paschal
    Lamb.
Let Friendships holy Band some Names
    assure,
Some their own Worth, and some let Scorn
    secure.
Nor shall the Rascal Rabble here have Place,
Whom Kings no Titles gave, and God no
    Grace :   580
Not Bull-fac'd *Jonas*, who coud Statutes draw
To mean Rebellion, and make Treason Law.
But he, though bad, is follow'd by a worse,
The Wretch, who Heav'ns Anointed dar'd
    to Curse.
Shimei, whose Youth did early Promise bring
Of Zeal to God, and Hatred to his King ;
Did wisely from Expensive Sins refrain,
And never broke the Sabbath, but for Gain :
Nor ever was he known an Oath to vent,
Or Curse, unless against the Government.
Thus, heaping Wealth, by the most ready
    way   591
Among the *Jews*, which was to Cheat and
    Pray ;
The City, to reward his pious Hate
Against his Master, chose him Magistrate :
His Hand a Vare of Justice did uphold ;
His Neck was loaded with a Chain of Gold.
During his Office, Treason was no Crime.
The Sons of *Belial* had a Glorious Time :
For *Shimei*, though not prodigal of pelf, 599
Yet lov'd his wicked Neighbour as himself :

---

585 Youth did early Promise] early Youth did
Promise *ed. 1.*
595 Vare] *Derrick, Scott, and others wrongly
give* Vase

525 for] *ed. 1 :* to *ed. 2.*
542 long] *ed. 3 :* long, *edd. 1 and 2.*

When two or three were gather'd to declaim
Against the Monarch of *Jerusalem*,
Shimei was always in the midst of them.
And, if they Curst the King when he was by,
Woud rather Curse, than break good Company.
If any durst his Factious Friends accuse,
He pact a jury of dissenting *Jews* :
Whose fellow-feeling, in the godly Cause
Would free the suff'ring Saint from Humane
    Laws. 609
For Laws are onely made to Punish those
Who serve the King, and to protect his Foes.
If any leisure time he had from Pow'r,
(Because 'tis Sin to misimploy an hour ;)
His bus'ness was by Writing to persuade
That kings were Useless, and a Clog to Trade :
And that his noble Stile he might refine,
No *Rechabite* more shund the fumes of Wine.
Chaste were his Cellars ; and his Shrieval
    Board
The Grossness of a City Feast abhor'd :
His Cooks, with long disuse, their Trade
    forgot ; 620
Cool was his Kitchin, though his Brains
    were hot.
Such frugal Vertue Malice may accuse ;
But sure 'twas necessary to the *Jews* :
For Towns once burnt, such Magistrates
    require
As dare not tempt Gods Providence by Fire.
With Spiritual Food he fed his Servants well,
But free from Flesh that made the *Jews* rebel :
And *Moses's* Laws he held in more account,
For forty days of Fasting in the Mount.
To speak the rest, who better are forgot, 630
Would tire a well-breath'd Witness of the
    Plot :
Yet, *Corah*, thou shalt from Oblivion pass ;
Erect thy self thou Monumental Brass :
High as the Serpent of thy Metal made,
While Nations stand secure beneath thy
    shade.
What though his Birth were base, yet
    Comets rise
From Earthy Vapours, e'r they shine in Skies.
Prodigious Actions may as well be done
By Weaver's issue as by Prince's son.
This Arch-Attestor for the Publick Good 640
By that one Deed enobles all his Bloud.
Who ever ask'd the Witnesses high race
Whose Oath with Martyrdom did *Stephen*
    grace ?

Ours was a *Levite*, and as times went then,
His tribe were God-almighties Gentlemen.
Sunk were his Eyes, his Voice was harsh and
    loud,
Sure signs he neither Cholerick was, nor
    Proud :
His long Chin prov'd his Wit ; his Saint-like
    Grace
A Church Vermilion, and a *Moses's* Face.
His Memory, miraculously great, 650
Coud Plots, exceeding mans belief, repeat ;
Which, therefore cannot be accounted Lies,
For humane Wit coud never such devise.
Some future Truths are mingled in his Book ;
But where the Witness fail'd, the Prophet
    spoke :
Some things like Visionary flights appear ;
The Spirit caught him up, the Lord knows
    where :
And gave him his *Rabinical* degree,
Unknown to Foreign University.
His Judgment yet his Mem'ry did excel, 660
Which piec'd his wondrous Evidence so well :
And suited to the temper of the Times ;
Then groaning under *Jebusitick* Crimes.
Let *Israels* foes suspect his Heav'nly call,
And rashly judge his Writ Apocryphal ;
Our Laws for such affronts have Forfeits
    made :
He takes his Life, who takes away his Trade.
Were I myself in Witness *Corah's* place,
The Wretch who did me such a dire disgrace
Should whet my memory, though once forgot,
To make him an Appendix of my Plot. 671
His Zeal to Heav'n, made him his Prince
    despise,
And load his Person with indignities :
But Zeal peculiar priviledge affords,
Indulging latitude to deeds and words :
And *Corah* might for *Agag's* murther call,
In terms as course as *Samuel* us'd to *Saul*.
What others in his Evidence did join,
(The best that coud be had for love or coin,)
In *Corah's* own predicament will fall 680
For *Witness* is a Common Name to all.

Surrounded thus with Friends of every
    sort,
Deluded *Absalom* forsakes the Court :
Impatient of high hopes, urg'd with renown,
And Fir'd with near possession of a Crown.
The admiring Croud are dazled with surprize
And on his goodly person feed their eyes :

His joy conceal'd, he sets himself to show ;
On each side bowing popularly low :
His looks, his gestures, and his words he
    frames   690
And with familiar ease repeats their Names.
Thus, form'd by Nature, furnished out with
    Arts,
He glides unfelt into their secret hearts :
Then with a kind compassionating look,
And sighs, bespeaking pity e'r he spoke,
Few words he said, but easie those and fit,
More slow than Hybla drops, and far more
    sweet.
    I mourn, my Country-men, your lost
    Estate,
Though far unable to prevent your Fate :
Behold a Banish'd man, for your dear cause
Expos'd a prey to Arbitrary Laws !   701
Yet oh ! that I alone coud be undone,
Cut off from Empire, and no more a Son !
Now all your Liberties a spoil are made ;⎫
Egypt and *Tyrus* intercept your Trade, ⎬
And *Jebusites* your Sacred Rites invade. ⎭
My Father, whom with reverence yet I name,
Charm'd into Ease, is careless of his Fame :
And, brib'd with petty sums of Foreign Gold,
Is grown in *Bathsheba's* Embraces old : 710
Exalts his Enemies, his Friends destroys,
And all his pow'r against himself imploys.
He gives, and let him give my right away;
But why should he his own and yours betray?
He onely, he can make the Nation bleed,
And he alone from my revenge is freed.
Take then my tears (with that he wiped his
    Eyes)
'Tis all the Aid my present pow'r supplies :
No Court-Informer can these Arms accuse ;
These Arms may Sons against their Fathers
    use ;   720
And, 'tis my wish, the next Successor's reign
May make no other *Israelite* complain.

    Youth, Beauty, Graceful Action seldom
    fail :
But Common Interest always will prevail :
And pity never Ceases to be shown
To him, who makes the Peoples wrongs his
    own.
The Croud, (that still believe their Kings
    oppress,)
With lifted hands their young *Messiah* bless :

Who now begins his Progress to ordain
With Chariots, Horsemen, and a num'rous
    train ;   730
From East to West his Glories he displays :
And, like the Sun, the Promis'd Land sur-
    veys.
Fame runs before him as the Morning-Star,
And shouts of Joy salute him from afar :
Each house receives him as a Guardian God ;
And Consecrates the Place of his abode :
But hospitable Treats did most commend
Wise *Issachar*, his wealthy Western Friend.
This moving Court that caught the Peoples
    Eyes,
And seem'd but Pomp, did other Ends
    disguise :   740
Achitophel had form'd it, with intent
To sound the depths, and fathom where it
    went,
The Peoples hearts distinguish Friends from
    Foes ;
And trie their strength before they came to
    Blows.
Yet all was colour'd with a smooth pretence
Of specious love, and duty to their Prince.
Religion, and Redress of Grievances,
Two names, that always cheat and always
    please,
Are often urg'd ; and good King *David's* life
Endanger'd by a Brother and a Wife.   750
Thus, in a Pageant Shew, a Plot is made ;
And Peace it self is War in Masquerade.
Oh foolish *Israel* ! never warn'd by Ill :
Still the same Bait, and circumvented still ! –
Did ever men forsake their present ease,
In midst of health imagine a Disease ;
Take pains Contingent mischiefs to foresee,
Make Heirs for Monarchs, and for God
    decree ?
What shall we think ! Can People give away
Both for themselves and Sons their Native
    sway ?   760
Then they are left Defenceless, to the Sword
Of each unbounded, Arbitrary Lord :
And Laws are vain, by which we Right enjoy,
If Kings unquestion'd can those Laws de-
    stroy.
Yet if the Croud be Judge of Fit and Just,
And Kings are onely Officers in Trust,
Then this resuming Cov'nant was declar'd
When Kings were made, or is for ever bar'd :

---

    688 His joy conceal'd] Dissembling Joy *ed. 1.* | 742 depths] depth *ed. 1.*

If those who gave the Scepter, coud not tie
By their own Deed their own Posterity, 770
How then coud *Adam* bind his future Race ?
How coud his Forfeit on Mankind take place ?
Or how coud heavenly Justice damn us all
Who ne'r consented to our Fathers Fall ?
Then Kings are Slaves to those whom they command,
And Tenants to their Peoples pleasure stand.
Add that the Pow'r, for Property allow'd,
Is mischievously seated in the Croud ;
For who can be secure of private Right,
If Sovereign Sway may be dissolv'd by Might ? 780
Nor is the Peoples Judgment always true :
The Most may err as grosly as the Few.
And faultless Kings run down, by Common Cry,
For Vice, Oppression, and for Tyranny.
What Standard is there in a fickle rout,
Which, flowing to the Mark, runs faster out ?
Nor onely crouds, but Sanhedrins may be
Infected with this publick Lunacy :
And Share the madness of Rebellious Times,
To Murther Monarchs for Imagin'd crimes.
If they may Give and Take when e'r they please, 791
Not Kings alone, (the Godheads Images,)
But Government it self at length must fall
To Natures state, where all have Right to all.
Yet, grant our Lords the People, Kings can make,
What prudent men a setled Throne woud shake ?
For whatsoe'r their Sufferings were before,
That Change they Covet makes them suffer more.
All other Errors but disturb a State ;
But Innovation is the Blow of Fate. 800
If ancient Fabricks nod, and threat to fall,
To Patch the Flaws, and Buttress up the Wall,
Thus far 'tis Duty ; but here fix the Mark :
For all beyond it is to touch our Ark.
To change Foundations, cast the Frame anew,
Is work for Rebels who base Ends pursue :

777 Add that the Pow'r] That Pow'r which is *ed. 1.*
802 the Flaws] *Many editors give* their Flaws
804 our] *Many editors give* the

At once Divine and Humane Laws controul,
And mend the Parts by ruine of the Whole.
The tamp'ring World is subject to this Curse,
To Physick their Disease into a Worse. 810

Now what Relief can Righteous *David* bring ?
How Fatal 'tis to be too good a King !
Friends he has few, so high the madness grows ;
Who dare be such, must be the People's Foes :
Yet some there were ev'n in the worst of days ;
Some let me name, and Naming is to praise.

In this short File *Barzillai* first appears ;
Barzillai crown'd with Honour and with Years :
Long since, the rising Rebels he withstood
In Regions Waste, beyond the *Jordans* Flood :
Unfortunately Brave to buoy the State ; 821
But sinking underneath his Master's Fate :
In Exile with his God-like Prince he Mourn'd,
For him he Suffer'd, and with him Return'd.
The Court he practis'd, not the Courtier's Art :
Large was his Wealth, but larger was his Heart :
Which, well the Noblest Objects knew to chuse,
The Fighting Warriour, and Recording Muse.
His Bed coud once a Fruitful Issue boast :
Now more than half a Father's Name is lost.
His Eldest Hope, with every Grace adorn'd,
By me (so Heav'n will have it) always Mourn'd
And always honour'd, snatch'd in manhoods prime
B' unequal Fates and Providences crime :
Yet not before the Goal of Honour won, }
All Parts fulfill'd of Subject and of Son ; }
Swift was the Race, but short the Time to run. }
Oh Narrow Circle, but of Pow'r Divine,
Scanted in Space, but perfect in thy Line !
By Sea, by Land, thy Matchless Worth was known ; 840
Arms thy Delight, and War was all thy Own :
Thy force, Infus'd, the fainting *Tyrians* prop'd ;
And haughty *Pharaoh* found his Fortune stop'd.

Oh Ancient Honour, Oh unconquered Hand,
Whom Foes unpunish'd never coud with-
 stand !
But *Israel* was unworthy of thy Name :
Short is the date of all Immoderate Fame.
It looks as Heav'n our Ruine had design'd,
And durst not trust thy Fortune and thy
 Mind.
Now, free from Earth, thy disencumbred
 Soul   850
Mounts up, and leaves behind the Clouds
 and Starry Pole :
From thence thy kindred Legions maist thou
 bring,
To aid the Guardian Angel of thy King.
Here stop my Muse, here cease thy painful
 flight ;
No pinions can pursue Immortal height :
Tell good *Barzillai* thou canst sing no more,
And tell thy Soul she should have fled before ;
Or fled she with his life, and left this Verse
To hang on her departed Patron's Herse ?
Now take thy steepy flight from Heav'n,
 and see   860
If thou canst find on Earth another *He* ;
Another he would be too hard to find ;
See then whom thou canst see not far be-
 hind.
Zadock the priest, whom, shunning Pow'r and
 Place,
His lowly mind advanc'd to *David's* Grace :
With him the *Sagan* of *Jerusalem*,
Of hospitable Soul and noble Stem ;
Him of the Western dome, whose weighty
 sense
Flows in fit words and heavenly eloquence.
The Prophets Sons, by such Example led,
To Learning and to Loyalty were bred : 871
For *Colleges* on bounteous Kings depend,
And never Rebel was to Arts a Friend.
To these succeed the Pillars of the Laws,
Who best coud plead, and best can judge
 a Cause.
Next them a train of Loyal Peers ascend :
Sharp judging *Adriel*, the Muses Friend,
Himself a Muse :—In Sanhedrins debate
True to his Prince, but not a Slave of State.
Whom *David's* love with Honours did adorn,
That from his disobedient Son were torn. 881

Jotham of piercing Wit and pregnant
 Thought,
Endew'd by nature and by learning taught
To move Assemblies, who but onely tri'd
The worse a while, then chose the better
 side ;
Nor chose alone, but turned the Balance too ;
So much the weight of one brave man can do.
Hushai the friend of *David* in distress,
In publick storms of manly stedfastness; 889
By Foreign Treaties he inform'd his Youth ;
And join'd Experience to his Native Truth.
His frugal care suppli'd the wanting Throne ;
Frugal for that, but bounteous of his own :
'Tis easie Conduct when Exchequers flow ;
But hard the task to manage well the low :
For Sovereign Power is too deprest or high,
When Kings are forced to sell, or Crouds to
 buy.
Indulge one labour more, my weary Muse,
For *Amiel* ; who can *Amiel's* praise refuse ?
Of ancient race by birth, but nobler yet 900
In his own worth, and without Title great :
The Sanhedrin long time as Chief he rul'd,
Their Reason guided, and their Passion
 cool d :
So dextrous was he in the Crown's defence,
So form'd to speak a Loyal Nations Sense,
That, as their Band was *Israels* Tribes in
 small,
So fit was he to represent them all.
Now rasher Charioteers the Seat ascend,
Whose loose Carriers his steady Skill com-
 mend :
They, like th' unequal Ruler of the Day, 910
Misguide the Seasons, and mistake the Way;
While he withdrawn at their mad Labour
 smiles
And safe enjoys the Sabbath of his Toils.

 These were the chief ; a small but faith-⎫
 ful Band   ⎬
Of Worthies in the Breach who dar'd to stand⎭
And tempt th' united Fury of the Land.
With grief they view'd such powerful Engines
 bent
To batter down the lawful Government.
A numerous Faction with pretended frights,
In Sanhedrins to plume the Regal Rights. 920
The true Successor from the Court removed :
The plot, by hireling Witnesses improv'd.

---

846 thy] *Many editors give* his
  Name] Birth *ed. 1.*
847 Fame] Worth *ed. 1.*
875 can] *Many editors absurdly give* could

882 piercing] ready *ed. 1.*

These Ills they saw, and, as their Duty
  bound,
They shew'd the King the danger of the
  Wound :
That no Concessions from the Throne woud
  please ;
But Lenitives fomented the Disease ;
That *Absalom*, ambitious of the Crown,
Was made theLure to draw the People down:
That false *Achitophel's* pernitious Hate
Had turn'd the Plot to ruine Church and
  State ;   930
The Council violent, the Rabble worse :
That *Shimei* taught *Jerusalem* to Curse.

With all these loads of Injuries opprest,
And long revolving in his careful Brest
Th' event of things ; at last his patience tir'd,
Thus from his Royal Throne, by Heav'n
  inspir'd,
The God-like *David* spoke ; with awful fear
His Train their Maker in their Master hear.

Thus long have I by Native Mercy sway'd,
My Wrongs dissembl'd, my Revenge delay'd;
So willing to forgive th' Offending Age ;   941
So much the Father did the King asswage.
But now so far my Clemency they slight,
Th' Offenders question my Forgiving Right.
That one was made for many, they contend ;
But 'tis to Rule, for that's a Monarch's End.
They call my tenderness of Blood, my Fear,
Though Manly tempers can the longest bear.
Yet since they will divert my Native course,
'Tis time to show I am not Good by Force.
Those heap'd Affronts that haughty Subjects
  bring,   951
Are burdens for a Camel, not a King :
Kings are the publick Pillars of the State,
Born to sustain and prop theNations weight:
If my young *Sampson* will pretend a Call
To shake the Column, let him share the Fall :
But oh that yet he woud repent and live !
How easie 'tis for Parents to forgive !
With how few Tears a Pardon might be won
From Nature, pleading for a Darling Son !
Poor pitied youth, by my Paternal care,   961
Rais'd up to all the Height his Frame coud
  bear :
Had God ordain'd his Fate for Empire born,
He woud have giv'n his Soul another turn :

Gull'd with a Patriot's name, whose Modern
  sense
Is one that woud by Law supplant his
  Prince:
The Peoples Brave, the Politicians Tool ;
Never was Patriot yet, but was a Fool.
Whence comes it that Religion and the Laws
Should more be *Absalom's* than *David's*
  Cause ?   970
His old Instructor, e'r he lost his Place,
Was never thought indu'd with so much
  Grace.
Good heav'ns, how Faction can a Patriot
  Paint !
My Rebel ever proves my Peoples Saint :
Woud *They* impose an Heir upon the Throne ?
Let Sanhedrins be taught to give their Own.
A king's at least a part of Government ;
And mine as requisite as their Consent :
Without my leave a future King to choose,
Infers a Right the present to Depose: 980
True, they petition me t' approve their
  Choice :
But *Esau's* Hands suit ill with *Jacob's* Voice.
My Pious Subjects for my Safety pray,
Which to Secure, they take my Pow'r away.
From Plots and Treasons Heav'n preserve
  my Years,
But save me most from my Petitioners.
Unsatiate as the barren Womb or Grave ;
God cannot Grant so much as they can Crave.
What then is left but with a Jealous Eye
To guard the Small remains of Royalty ?   990
The Law shall still direct my peaceful Sway,
And the same Law teach Rebels to obey :
Votes shall no more Established Pow'r con-
  troul,
Such Votes as make a Part exceed the Whole :
No groundless Clamours shall my Friends
  remove
Nor Crouds have pow'r to Punish e'r they
  Prove ;
For Gods and God-like kings their Care
  express,
Still to defend their Servants in distress.
Oh that my Pow'r to Saving were confin'd : ⎞
Why am I forc'd, like Heav'n, against my ⎟
  mind,   1000 ⎟
To make Examples of another Kind?   ⎠
Must I at length the Sword of Justice draw ?
Oh curst Effects of necessary Law !

How ill my Fear they by my Mercy scan,
Beware the Fury of a Patient Man.
Law they require, let Law then shew her
    Face ;
They could not be content to look on
    Grace,   1007
Her hinder parts, but with a daring Eye
To tempt the terror of her Front, and Die.
By their own Arts 'tis Righteously decreed,
Those dire Artificers of Death shall bleed.
Against themselves their Witnesses will
    Swear,
Till, Viper-like, their Mother Plot they tear,
And suck for Nutriment that bloudy gore
Which was their Principle of Life before.
Their *Belial* with their *Belzebub* will fight ;
Thus on my Foes, my Foes shall do me Right.

1007 Grace,] *Some editors omit the comma and thereby destroy the sense.*

Nor doubt th' event ; for Factious crouds
    engage
In their first Onset, all their Brutal Rage ;
Then let 'em take an unresisted Course ;
Retire and Traverse, and Delude their
    Force :   1021
But when they stand all Breathless, urge
    the fight,
And rise upon 'em with redoubled might :
For Lawful Pow'r is still Superiour found,
When long driv'n back, at length it stands
    the ground.

  He said. Th' Almighty, nodding, gave
    consent ;
And peals of Thunder shook the Firmament.
Henceforth a Series of new time began,   1028
The mighty Years in long Procession ran :
Once more the God-like *David* was Restor'd,
And willing Nations knew their Lawful Lord.

THE

SECOND PART

OF

ABSALOM

AND

ACHITOPHEL.

A
POEM.

——*Si Quis tamen Hæc quoque, Si Quis*
Captus Amore Leget——————

LONDON.
Printed for *Jacob Tonson*, at the *Judges Head* in
Chancery-Lane, near *Fleet-Street*. 1682.

ABSALOM AND ACHITOPHEL.

THE SECOND PART.

Since Men, like Beasts, each others Prey
 were made,
Since Trade began, and Priesthood grew a
 Trade,
Since Realms were form'd, none sure so curst
 as those
That madly their own Happiness oppose ;
There Heaven itself, and Godlike Kings, in
 vain
Showr down the *Manna* of a gentle Reign ;
While pamper'd Crowds to mad Sedition run,
And Monarchs by Indulgence are undone.
Thus *David's* Goodness was e'en fatal grown,
While wealthy Faction aw'd the wanting
 Throne. 10
For now their Sov'reign's Orders to contemn
Was held the Charter of *Jerusalem* ;
His Rights t' invade, his Tributes to refuse,
A Privilege peculiar to the *Jews* ;
As if from Heav'nly Call this Licence fell
And *Jacob's* seed were chosen to rebell !

Achitophel with triumph sees his Crimes
Thus suited to the madness of the Times ;
And *Absalom,* to make his hopes succeed,
Of Flatteries Charms no longer stands in
 need ; 20
While fond of Change, though ne'er so dearly
 bought,
Our Tribes out-strip the Youth's Ambitious
 Thought ;
His swiftest Hopes with swifter Homage
 meet,
And crowd their servile Necks beneath his
 Feet.
Thus to his aid while pressing Tides repair,
He mounts and spreads his Streamers in the
 Air.

The Charms of Empire might his Youth
 mis-lead,
But what can our besotted *Israel* plead ?
Sway'd by a Monarch, whose serene Com-
 mand
Seems half the Blessing of our promis'd
 Land. 30
Whose onely Grievance is excess of Ease,
Freedome our Pain, and Plenty our Disease !
Yet since all Folly wou'd lay claim to Sense,
And Wickedness ne'er wanted a Pretence,
With Arguments they'd make their Treason
 good
And righteous *David's* self with Slandersload:
That Arts of foreign Sway he did affect,
And guilty *Jebusites* from Law protect,
Whose very Chiefs, convict, were never freed,
Nay, we have seen their Sacrificers bleed !
Accusers Infamy is urg'd in vain, 41
While in the bounds of Sense they did con-
 tain,
But soon they launcht into th' unfathom'd
 Tide
And in the Depths they knew disdain'd to
 Ride ;
For probable Discoveries to dispence
Was thought below a pentioned Evidence ;
Mere Truth was dull, nor suited with the port
Of pamper'd *Corah,* when advanc't to Court.
No less than Wonders now they will impose
And Projects void of Grace or Sense disclose.
Such was the Charge on pious *Michal*
 brought, 51
Michal, that ne'er was cruel e'en in thought,
The best of Queens, and most obedient Wife,
Impeach'd of curst Designs on *David's* Life !
His Life, the Theam of her eternal Pray'r,
'Tis scarce so much his Guardian Angels Care.
Not Summer Morns such Mildness can dis-
 close,
The *Hermon* Lilly nor the *Sharon* Rose.
Neglecting each vain Pomp of Majesty,
Transported *Michal* feeds her thoughts on
 high. 60

Part II. Text from the original edition, 1682.
Most of this part is by Nahum Tate. The only
part known to be Dryden's is ll. 310-509. In the
second edition, 1716, there are some changes which
may have been made by Tate who died the year
before.

9 Goodness was e'en] Clemency was *1716.*
20 Flatteries] Flattering *1716.*

33 since] *The editors give as*

She lives with Angels, and as Angels do,
Quits Heav'n sometimes to bless the world
Below,
Where cherisht by her Bounties plenteous
Spring,
Reviving Widows smile, and Orphans sing.
Oh! when rebellious *Israel's* Crimes at
height
Are threatned with her Lord's approaching
Fate,
The Piety of *Michal* then remain
In Heav'ns Remembrance, and prolong his
Reign.

Less Desolation did the Pest pursue
That from *Dan's* limits to *Beersheba* slew, 70
Less fatal the repeated Wars of *Tyre*,
And less *Jerusalem's* avenging Fire.
With gentler terrour these our State o'erran,
Than since our Evidencing Days began!
On every Cheek a pale Confusion sat,
Continu'd Fear beyond the worst of Fate!
Trust was no more, Art, Science useless
made,
All occupations lost but *Corah's* Trade.
Mean while a Guard on modest *Corah* wait,
If not for safety needfull yet for State. 80
Well might he deem each Peer and Prince
his Slave:
And Lord it o'er the Tribes which he could
save:
E'en Vice in him was Vertue—what sad Fate,
But for his Honesty had seiz'd our State?
And with what Tyranny had we been curst,
Had *Corah* never proved a Villain first?
T' have told his knowledge of th' Intrigue
in gross
Had been alas to our Deponent's loss:
The travell'd Levite had th' Experience got
To husband well, and make the best of 's
Plot; 90
And therefore like an Evidence of skill,
With wise Reserves secur'd his Pension
still;
Nor quite of future Pow'r himself bereft,
But Limbo's large for unbelievers left.
For now his Writ such Reverence had got,
'Twas worse than Plotting to suspect his
Plot.
Some were so well convinc't, they made no
doubt,
Themselves to help the founder'd Swearers
out.

Some had their Sense impos'd on by their
Fear,
But more for Int'rest sake believe and swear:
E'en to that height with some the Frenzy
grew, 101
They rag'd to find their danger not prove
true.

Yet, than all these a viler Crew remain,
Who with *Achitophel* the Cry maintain;
Not urg'd by Fear, nor through misguided
Sense,
(Blind Zeal, and starving need had some
Pretence)
But for the *Good Old Cause*, that did excite
Th' Original Rebells Wiles, Revenge and
Spight,
These raise the Plot to have the Scandal
thrown
Upon the bright Successor of the Crown,
Whose Vertue with such wrongs they had
pursu'd 111
As seem'd all hope of pardon to exclude.
Thus, while on private Ends their Zeal is
built
The cheated Crowd applaud and share their
Guilt.

Such Practices as These, too gross to lye
Long unobserv'd by each discerning Eye,
The more judicious *Israelites* Unspell'd,
Though still the Charm the giddy Rabble
held.
Ev'n *Absalom* amid the dazling Beams 119
Of Empire, and ambitions flattering Dreams,
Perceives the Plot (too foul to be excus'd)
To aid Designs, no less pernicious, us'd.
And (Filial Sense yet striving in his Breast)
Thus to *Achitophel* his Doubts exprest.

Why are my Thoughts upon a Crown
employ'd,
Which once obtain'd, can be but half En-
joy'd?
Not so when Virtue did my Arms require,
And to my Father's Wars I flew Intirc.
My Regal Pow'r how will my Foes resent,
When I my Self have scarce my own Con-
sent? 130
Give me a Son's unblemish't Truth again
Or quench the Sparks of Duty that remain.

---

118 held.] *1716*: held, *1682*.

How slight to force a Throne that Legions
  guard
The Task to me; to prove Unjust, how
  hard!
And if th' imagined Guilt thus wound my
  Thought,
What will it, when the tragick Scene is
  wrought?
Dire War must first be conjur'd from below,
The Realm we'd Rule we first must Over-
  throw.
And when the Civil Furies are on wing
That blind and undistinguish't Slaughters ⎫
  fling,   140 ⎬
Who knows what impious chance may   ⎭
  reach the King?
Oh! rather let me perish in the strife,
Than have my Crown the Price of *David's*
  Life!
Or if the Tempest of the War he stand,
In Peace, some vile officious Villain's hand
His Soul's anointed Temple may invade,
Or, prest by clamorous Crowds, my Self be
  made
His murtherer; rebellious Crowds, whose
  Guilt
Shall dread his vengeance till his Bloud be
  spilt.
Which if my filial Tenderness oppose, 150
Since to the Empire by their Arms I rose,
Those very Arms on Me shall be employ'd,
A new Usurper Crown'd, and I Destroyed:
The same Pretence of Publick Good will hold ⎫
And new *Achitophels* be found, as bold   ⎬
To urge the needfull Change, perhaps the   ⎭
  Old.

  He said. The statesman with a Smile
    replies,
(A smile that did his rising Spleen disguise.)
My thoughts presum'd our labours at an
  End,   159
And are we still with Conscience to contend?
Whose Want in Kings, as needfull is allow'd
As 'tis for them to find it in the Crowd.
Far in the doubtfull Passage you are gone,
And onely can be Safe by pressing on.
The Crowns true Heir, a Prince severe, and
  wise,
Has view'd your Motions long with Jealous
  Eyes:

Your Persons Charms, your more prevailing
  Arts,
And marked your Progress in the Peoples
  Hearts,
Whose Patience is th' effect of stinted Pow'r,
But treasures Vengeance for the fatal hour.
And if remote the Perill He can bring, 171
Your Present Danger's greater from the
  King.
Let not a Parent's name deceive your Sense,
Nor trust the Father in a Jealous Prince!
Your trivial Faults if he could so resent,
To doom you little less than Banishment,
What rage must your Presumption Since
  inspire,
Against his Orders your Return from *Tyre*?
Nor onely so, but with a Pomp more high
And open Court of Popularity,   180
The Factious Tribes—And this Reproof from
  Thee?
(The Prince replies) O Statesman's winding
  Skill,
They first Condemn that first Advis'd the Ill!
Illustrious Youth (returned *Achitophel*)
Misconstrue not the Words that mean you
  well.
The Course you steer I worthy Blame con-
  clude,
But 'tis because you leave it Unpersu'd.
A Monarch's Crown with Fate surrounded
  lyes,
Who reach, lay hold on Death that miss the
  Prize.
Did you for this expose yourself to Show,
And to the Crowd bow popularly low? 191
For this your Glorious Progress next ordain,
With Chariots, Horsemen, and a numerous
  Train,
With Fame before you like the Morning
  Starr,
And Shouts of Joy saluting from afarr?
Oh from the Heights you've reached but
  take a View,
Scarce leading *Lucifer* cou'd fall like you!
And must I here my Shipwrackt Arts be-
  moan?
Have I for this so oft made *Israel* groan!
Your single interest with the Nation weigh'd,
And turned the Scale where your Desires
  were laid?   201

Ev'n when at Helm a Course so dang'rous mov'd,
To Land your Hopes, as my Removal prov'd.

I not dispute (the Royal youth replys)
The known Perfection of your Policies,
Nor in *Achitophel* yet grudge, or blame,
The Priviledge that Statesmen ever claim ;
Who private Interest never yet persu'd,
But still pretended 'twas for Others good :
What Polititian yet e'er scap't his Fate 210
Who saving his own Neck not sav'd the State ?
From hence on ev'ry hum'urous Wind that veer'd
With shifted Sayls a sev'ral Course you Steer'd.
What Form of Sway did *David* e'er persue
That seem'd like Absolute but sprung from You ?
Who at your instance quasht each penal Law,
That kept dissenting factious *Jews* in awe ;
And who suspends fixt Laws, may abrogate,
That done, form New, and so enslave the State.
Ev'n Property, whose Champion now you stand, 220
And seem for this the Idol of the Land,
Did ne'er sustain such Violence before
As when your Counsel shut the Royal Store ;
Advice, that Ruine to whole Tribes procur'd,
But secret kept till your own Banks secur'd.
Recount with this the tripple Cov'nant broke,
And *Israel* fitted for a Foreign Yoke,
Nor here your Counsels fatal Progress staid,
But sent our levied Pow'rs to *Pharaoh's* Aid.
Hence *Tyre* and *Israel*, low in Ruins laid,
And *Egypt*, once their Scorn, their common Terrour made. 231
Ev'n yet of such a Season we can dream,
When Royal Rights you made your darling Theam.
For Pow'r unlimited could Reasons draw,
And place Prerogative above the Law ;
Which on your fall from Office grew Unjust,
The Laws made King, the King a Slave in Trust ;
Whom with State-craft, to Int'rest onely True,
You now Accuse of ills contriv'd by You.

To this Hell's Agent—Royal Youth fix here, 240
Let Int'rest be the Star by which I Steer.
Hence to repose your Trust in Me was wise,
Whose Int'rest most in your Advancement lies.
A Tye so firm as always will avail
When Friendship, Nature and Religion fail ;
On ours the Safety of the Crowd depends,
Secure the Crowd and we obtain our Ends,
Whom I will cause so far our Guilt to share
Till they are made our Champions by their Fear.
What Opposition can your Rival bring, 250
While Sanhedrims are Jealous of the King ?
His strength as yet in *David's* Friendship lies,
And what can *David's* Self without supplies ?
Who with Exclusive Bills must now dispence,
Debar the Heir, or Starve in his Defence.
Conditions which our Elders ne'er will quit
And *David's* Justice never can admit.
Or forc't by Wants his Brother to betray,
To your Ambition next he clears the Way ;
For if Succession once to Nought they bring
Their next Advance removes the present King : 261
Persisting else his Senates to dissolve
In equal Hazzard shall his Reign involve.
Our Tribes, whom *Pharaoh's* Pow'r so much Alarms,
Shall rise without their Prince t' oppose his Arms ;
Nor boots it on what Cause at first they Joyn,
Their Troops once up, are Tools for our Design.
At least such subtle Covenants shall be made,
Till peace it self is War in Masquerade.
Associations of Mysterious Sense, 270
Against, but seeming for the King's Defence :
Ev'n on their Courts of Justice Fetters draw,
And from our Agents Muzzle up their Law.
By which, a Conquest if we fail to make,
'Tis a drawn Game at worst, and we secure our Stake.

He said, and for the dire Success depends
On various Sects, by common Guilt made Friends.
Whose Heads, though ne'er so diff'ring in their Creed,
I' th' point of Treason yet were well Agreed.

---

214 Form of] *Derrick and others give* from a

241 I Steer] you steer *1716, a false and feeble reading which Dr. Saintsbury prefers.*

'Mongst these, Extorting *Ishban* first appears,
Persu'd b' a meagre Troop of Bankrupt
 Heirs. 281
Blest times when *Ishban*, He whose Occupa-
 tion
So long has been to Cheat, Reformes the
 Nation !
Ishban of Conscience suited to his Trade,
As good a Saint as Usurer e'er made.
Yet *Mammon* has not so engrost him quite
But *Belial* lays as large a Claim of Spight ;
Who, for those Pardons from his Prince he
 draws
Returns Reproaches, and cries up the Cause.
That Year in which the City he did sway,
He left Rebellion in a hopefull way ; 291
Yet his Ambition once was found so bold
To offer Talents of Extorted Gold ;
Could *David's* Wants have So been brib'd to
 shame
And scandalize our Peerage with his Name ;
For which, his dear Sedition he'd forswear,
And e'en turn Loyal, to be made a Peer.
Next him, let Railing *Rabsheka* have place,
So full of Zeal He has no need of grace ; 299
A Saint that can both Flesh and Spirit use,
Alike haunt Conventicles and the Stews :
Of whom the Question difficult appears,
If most i' th' Preachers or the Bawds arrears.
What Caution cou'd appear too much in Him
That keeps the Treasure of *Jerusalem* !
Let *David's* Brother but approach the Town,
Double our guards, He cries, *We are undone*.
Protesting that He dares not Sleep in 's Bed,
*Lest he shou'd rise next Morn without his
 Head.* 309

Next these, a Troop of buisy Spirits press,
Of little Fortunes and of Conscience Less ;
With them the Tribe, whose Luxury had
 drain'd
Their Banks, in former Sequestrations gain'd :
Who Rich and Great by past Rebellions
 grew,
And long to fish the troubled Waves anew.
Some future Hopes, some present Payment
 draws,
To Sell their Conscience and espouse the
 Cause, 317
Such Stipends those vile Hirelings best befit,
Priests without Grace, and Poets without wit,

Shall that false *Hebronite* escape our Curse,
Judas that keeps the Rebells Pension-Purse ;
Judas that pays the Treason-writers Fee,
Judas that well deserves his Namesake's
 Tree ;
Who at *Jerusalem's* own Gates Erects
His College for a Nursery of Sects.
Young Prophets with an early Care secures,
And with the Dung of his own Arts manures.
What have the Men of *Hebron* here to doe ?
What part in *Israels* promis'd Land have
 you ?
Here *Phaleg* the Lay *Hebronite* is come, 330
Cause like the rest he could not live at
 Home ;
Who from his own Possessions cou'd not
 drain
An *Omer* even of *Hebronitish* Grain,
Here Struts it like a Patriot, and talks high
Of Injur'd Subjects, alter'd Property :
An Emblem of that buzzing Insect Just,
That mounts the Wheell, and thinks she
 raises Dust.
Can dry Bones Live ? or *Skeletons* produce
The Vital Warmth of Cuckoldizing Juice ?
Slim *Phaleg* cou'd, and at the Table fed, 340
Return'd the gratefull product to the Bed.
A Waiting-man to Trav'ling Nobles chose,
He, his own Laws wou'd Sawcily impose ;
Till Bastinado'd back again he went,
To Learn those Manners he to Teach was
 sent.
Chastiz'd, he ought to have retreated Home,
But He reads politicks to *Absalom*.
For never *Hebronite*, though Kickt and
 Scorn'd,
To his own Country willingly return'd.
—But leaving famish'd *Phaleg* to be fed 350
And to talk Treason for his daily Bread,
Let *Hebron*, nay let Hell produce a Man
So made for Mischief as *Ben Jochanan*,
A *Jew* of humble Parentage was He,
By Trade a Levite, though of low Degree :
His Pride no higher than the Desk aspir'd,
But for the Drudgery of Priests was hir'd
To Reade and Pray in Linen Ephod brave,
And pick up single Sheckles from the Grave.
Married at last, and finding Charge come
 faster, 360
He cou'd not live by God, but chang'd his
 Master :

315 Waves] Streams *1716*.

360 and] but *1716*.

Inspir'd by Want, was made a Factious Tool,
They Got a Villain, and we lost a Fool.
Still Violent, whatever Cause he took,
But most against the Party he forsook,
For Renegadoes, who ne'er turn by halves,
Are bound in Conscience to be double
  Knaves.
So this Prose-Prophet took most monstrous
  Pains,
To let his Masters see he earn'd his Gains. 369
But as the Dev'l ows all his Imps a Shame,
He chose th' *Apostate* for his proper Theme ;
With little Pains he made the Picture true,
And from Reflexion took the Rogue he
  drew.
A wondrous Work, to prove the *Jewish*
  nation
In every Age a Murmuring Generation ;
To trace 'em from their Infancy of Sinning,
And shew 'em Factious from their First
  Beginning ;
To prove they cou'd Rebell, and Rail, and
  Mock,
Much to the Credit of the Chosen Flock ;
A strong Authority which must Convince,
That Saints own no Allegiance to their
  Prince.   381
As 'tis a Leading-Card to make a Whore,
To prove her Mother had turn'd up before.
But tell me, did the Drunken Patriarch Bless
The Son that shew'd his Father's Nakedness?
Such Thanks the present Church thy Pen
  will give,
Which proves Rebellion was so Primitive.
Must Ancient Failings be Examples made,
Then Murtherers from *Cain* may learn their
  Trade.
As thou the Heathen and the Saint hast
  drawn,   390
Methinks th' Apostate was the better man :
And thy hot *Father* (waving my respect)
Not of a mother church but of a Sect.
And Such he needs must be of thy Inditing,
This Comes of drinking Asses milk and
  writing,
If *Balack* should be cal'd to leave his
  place,
(As Profit is the loudest call of Grace,) 397
His Temple, dispossessed of one, would be
Replenish'd with seven Devils more by thee.

Levi, thou art a load, I'll lay thee down,
And shew Rebellion bare, without a Gown ;
Poor Slaves in metre, dull and adle-pated,
Who Rhime below ev'n *David's* Psalms
  translated.
Some in my Speedy pace I must outrun,
As lame *Mephibosheth* the Wisard's Son ;
To make quick way I'll Leap o'er heavy
  blocks,
Shun rotten *Uzza* as I woud the Pox ;
And hasten *Og* and *Doeg* to rehearse,
Two Fools that Crutch their Feeble sense
  on Verse,
Who by my Muse, to all succeeding times
Shall live in spight of their own Dogrell
  Rhimes.   411
Doeg, though without knowing how or
  why,
Made still a blund'ring kind of Melody ;
Spurd boldly on, and Dash'd through Thick
  and Thin,
Through Sense and Non-sense, never out
  nor in ;
Free from all meaning, whether good or
  bad,
And in one word, Heroically mad,
He was too warm on Picking work to dwell,
But Faggotted his Notions as they fell,
And, if they Rhim'd and Rattl'd, all was
  well.   420
Spightfull he is not, though he wrote a Satyr,
For still there goes some *thinking* to ill-
  Nature :
He needs no more than Birds and Beasts
  to think,
All his occasions are to eat and drink.
If he call Rogue and Rascal from a Garrat,
He means you no more Mischief than a Parat :
The words for Friend and Foe alike were
  made,
To Fetter 'em in Verse is all his Trade.
For Almonds he'll cry Whore to his own
  Mother :
And call young *Absalom* King *David's*
  Brother.   430
Let him be Gallows-Free by my consent,
And nothing suffer, since he nothing meant :
Hanging Supposes humane Soul and reason,
This Animal's below committing Treason
Shall he be hang'd who never cou'd Rebell ?
That's a preferment for *Achitophel*.
The Woman that Committed Buggary,
Was rightly Sentenc'd by the Law to die ;

384 Patriarch] *1716* : Patriot *1682*. *A mis-print*.

But 'twas hard Fate that to the Gallows led
The Dog that never heard the Statute read.
Railing in other Men may be a crime, 441
But ought to pass for mere instinct in him ;
Instinct he follows and no farther knows,
For to write Verse with him is to *Transprose.*
'Twere pity treason at his Door to lay
Who *makes Heaven's gate a Lock to its own
    Key :*
Let him rayl on, let his invective muse
Have four and Twenty letters to abuse,
Which if he Jumbles to one line of Sense,
Indict him of a Capital Offence.   450
In Fire-works give him leave to vent his
    spight,
Those are the only Serpents he can write ;
The height of his ambition is we know
But to be Master of a Puppet-show ;
On that one Stage his works may yet appear,
And a months Harvest keeps him all the
    Year.

Now stop your noses, Readers, all and
    some,
For here's a tun of Midnight work to come,
Og from a Treason Tavern rowling home.
Round as a Globe, and Liquored ev'ry
    chink,   460
Goodly and Great he Sayls behind his Link ;
With all this Bulk there's nothing lost in *Og*,
For ev'ry inch that is not Fool is Rogue :
A Monstrous mass of foul corrupted matter,
As all the Devils had spew'd to make the
    batter.
When wine has given him courage to Blas-
    pheme,
He curses God, but God before Curst him ;
And if man cou'd have reason, none has
    more,
That made his Paunch so rich and him so
    poor.
With wealth he was not trusted, for Heav'n
    knew   470
What 'twas of Old to pamper up a *Jew* ;
To what would he on Quail and Pheasant
    swell,
That ev'n on Tripe and Carrion cou'd rebell ?
But though Heaven made him poor, (with
    rev'rence speaking,)
He never was a Poet of God's making ;
The Midwife laid her hand on his Thick
    Skull,
With this Prophetick blessing—*Be thou Dull;*

Drink, Swear, and Roar, forbear no lew'd
    delight
Fit for thy Bulk, doe anything but write.
Thou art of lasting Make, like thoughtless
    men,   480
A strong Nativity—but for the Pen ;
Eat Opium, mingle Arsenick in thy Drink,
Still thou mayst live, avoiding Pen and Ink.
I see, I see, 'tis Counsell given in vain,
For Treason botcht in Rhime will be thy
    bane ;
Rhime is the Rock on which thou art to
    wreck,
'Tis fatal to thy Fame and to thy Neck.
Why should thy Metre good King *David* blast?
A Psalm of his will Surely be thy last.
Dar'st thou presume in verse to meet thy foes,
Thou whom the Penny Pamphlet foil'd in
    prose ?   491
Doeg, whom God for Mankinds mirth has
    made,
O'er-tops thy tallent in thy very Trade ;
Doeg to thee, thy paintings are so Course,
A Poet is, though he's the Poets Horse.
A Double Noose thou on thy Neck dost pull
For Writing Treason and for Writing dull ;
To die for Faction is a common Evil,
But to be hang'd for Non-sense is the Devil.
Hadst thou the Glories of thy King exprest,
Thy praises had been Satyr at the best ; 501
But thou in Clumsy verse, unlickt, unpointed,
Hast Shamefully defi'd the Lord's Anointed :
I will not rake the Dunghill of thy Crimes,
For who would reade thy Life that reads thy
    rhimes ?
But of King *David's* Foes be this the Doom,
May all be like the Young-man *Absalom* ;
And for my Foes may this their Blessing be,
To talk like *Doeg* and to Write like Thee.

Achitophel each Rank, Degree, and Age
For various Ends neglects not to Engage,
The Wise and Rich for Purse and Counsell
    brought,   512
The Fools and Beggars for their Number
    sought :
Who yet not onely on the Town depends,
For Ev'n in Court the Faction had its
    Friends.
These thought the Places they possest too
    small,
And in their Hearts wisht Court and King
    to fall :

Whose Names the Muse, disdaining, holds
i' th' dark,
Thrust in the Villain Herd without a Mark ;
With Parasites and Libell-spawning Imps,
Intriguing Fopps, dull Jesters, and worse
Pimps.   521
Disdain the Rascal Rabble to persue,
Their Sett Caballs are yet a viler Crew ;
See where involv'd in Common Smoak they
sit ;
Some for our Mirth, some for our Satyr fit ;
These Gloomy, Thoughtfull and on Mischief
bent,
While those for mere good Fellowship fre-
quent
Th' appointed Clubb can let Sedition pass,
Sense, Non-sence, anything t' employ the
Glass ;
And who believe in their dull honest Hearts,
The Rest talk Treason but to show their
Parts ;   531
Who ne'er had Wit or Will for Mischief yet,
But pleased to be reputed of a Set.

But in the Sacred Annals of our Plot,
Industrions AROD never be forgot :
The Labours of this Midnight-Magistrate,
May vie with *Corah's* to preserve the State ;
In search of Arms, He failed not to lay hold
On War's most powerfull dang'rous Weapon,
GOLD.   539
And last, to take from *Jebusites*, all odds,
Their Altars pillaged, stole their very Gods.
Oft wou'd he Cry, when Treasure he sur-
priz'd,
'Tis Baalish *Gold in* David's *Coyn Disguiz'd.*
Which to his House with *richer Relicts* came
While Lumber Idols onely fed the Flame :
For our wise Rabble ne'er took pains t'
inquire,
What 'twas he burnt, so 't made a rousing
Fire.
With which our Elder was enricht no more
Than False *Gehazi* with the *Syrian's* Store ;
So Poor, that when our Choosing-Tribes were
met,   550
Even for his Stinking Votes He ran in Debt ;
For Meat the Wicked, and, as Authours
think,
The Saints He Choused for His Electing
Drink ;
Thus, ev'ry Shift and subtle Method past,
And All to be no *Zaken* at the Last.

Now, rais'd on *Tyre's* sad Ruines, *Pharaoh's*
Pride
Soar'd high, his Legions threatning far and
wide ;
As when a battring Storm ingendred high,
By Winds upheld, hangs hov'ring in the
Skye,
Is gaz'd upon by ev'ry trembling Swain, 560
This for his Vineyard fears, and that his
Grain,
For blooming Plants and Flow'rs new Open-
ing, These
For Lambs ean'd lately, and far-lab'ring
Bees ;
To Guard his Stock each to the Gods does call,
Uncertain where the Fire-charg'd Clouds will
Fall :
Even so the doubtfull Nations watch his
Arms,
With Terrour each expecting his Alarms.
Where, *Judah*, where was now thy Lyons
Roar ?
Thou onely cou'dst the Captive Lands restore ;
But Thou, with inbred Broils and Faction
prest,   570
From *Egypt* needst a Guardian with the
Rest.
Thy Prince from Sanhedrims no Trust
allow'd,
Too much the Representers of the Crow'd,
Who for their own Defence give no Supply
But what the Crowns Prerogatives must buy :
As if their Monarch's Rights to violate,
More needfull were than to preserve the
State !
From present Dangers they divert their Care,
And all their Fears are of the Royal Heir ;
Whom now the reigning Malice of his Foes
Unjudged wou'd Sentence and e'er Crown'd,
Depose :   581
Religion the Pretence, but their Decree
To barr his Reign, whate'er his Faith shall
be !
By Sanhedrims, and clam'rous Crowds, thus
prest
What passions rent the Righteous *David's*
Breast ?
Who knows not how t' oppose or to comply,
Unjust to Grant and dangerous to Deny !
How near in this dark Juncture *Israel's* Fate,
Whose Peace one sole Expedient could create,

563 ean'd] yean'd *1716.*

Which yet th' extremest Virtue did require,
Ev'n of that Prince whose Downfall they
   conspire !   591
His Absence *David* does with Tears advise,
T' appease their Rage, Undaunted He Com-
   plies ;
Thus is who, prodigal of Bloud, and Ease,
A Royal Life expos'd to Winds and Seas,
At once contending with the Waves and
   Fire,
And heading Danger in the Wars of *Tyre*,
Inglorious now forsakes his Native Sand
And, like an Exile, quits the promis'd Land !
Our Monarch scarce from pressing Tears
   refrains,   600
And painfully his Royal State maintains.
Who, now embracing on th' extremest Shore.
Almost Revokes what he Injoyn'd before :
Concludes at last more Trust to be allow'd
To Storms and Seas than to the raging
   Crow'd !
Forbear, rash Muse, the parting Scene to
   draw,
With Silence charm'd as deep as theirs that
   saw !
Not onely our attending Nobles weep,
But hardy Saylers swell with Tears the
   Deep !
The Tyde restrained her Course, and more
   amaz'd,   610
The Twyn Stars on the Royal Brothers gaz'd ;
While this sole Fear——
Does Trouble to our suff'ring Heroe bring,
Lest next the Popular Rage oppress the King.
Thus parting, each for th' Others Danger
   griev'd,
The Shore the King, and Seas the Prince
   receiv'd.
Go injur'd Heroe, while propitious Gales,
Soft as thy Consorts breath, inspire thy
   Sails ;
Well may She trust her Beauties on a Flood,
Where thy Triumphant Fleets so oft have
   rode !   620
Safe on thy Breast reclin'd, her Rest be deep,
Rockt like a *Nereid* by the waves asleep ;
While happiest Dreams her Fancy entertain,
And to *Elysian Fields* convert the Main !
Go injur'd Heroe, while the shores of *Tyre*,
At thy Approach so Silent shall admire,
Who on thy Thunder still their thoughts
   imploy,
And greet thy Landing with a trembling Joy.

On Heroes thus the Prophet's Fate is
   thrown,   629
Admir'd by ev'ry Nation but their Own ;
Yet while our factious *Jews* his Worth
   deny,
Their Aking Conscience gives their Tongue
   the Lye.
Ev'n in the worst of Men the noblest Parts
Confess him, and he Triumphs in their
   Hearts,
Whom to his King the best Respects com-
   mend
Of Subject, Souldier, Kinsman, Prince and
   Friend ;
All Sacred Names of most divine Esteem,
And to Perfection all sustained by Him,
Wise, Just and Constant, Courtly without
   Art,
Swift to discern and to reward Desert ; 640
No Hour of His in fruitless Ease destroy'd,
But on the noblest Subjects still employed ;
Whose steddy Soul ne'er learnt to Separate
Between his Monarch's Int'rest and the
   State,
But heaps those Blessings on the Royal
   Head,
Which He well knows must be on Subjects
   shed.

On what Pretence cou'd then the Vulgar
   Rage
Against his Worth, and native Rights en-
   gage ?
Religious Fears their Argument are made,
Religious Fears his Sacred Rights invade !
Of future Superstition They complain 651
And *Jebusitic* Worship in his Reign ;
With such Alarms his Foes the Crowd
   deceive,
With Dangers fright, which not Themselves
   believe.

Since nothing can our Sacred Rites remove,
Whate'er the Faith of the Successour prove,
Our *Jews* their Ark shall undisturb'd retain,
At least while their Religion is their Gain,
Who know by old Experience *Baal's* Com-
   mands
Not onely claim'd their Conscience but their
   Lands ;   660
They grutch God's Tythes, how therefore
   shall they yield
An Idol full possession of the Field ?

Grant such a Prince enthron'd, we must confess
The People's Suff'rings than that Monarch's less,
Who must to hard Conditions still be bound
And for his Quiet with the Crowd compound;
Or shou'd his thoughts to Tyranny incline,
Where are the means to compass the design ?
Our Crowns Revenues are too short a Store,
And Jealous Sanedrims would give no more !
As vain our Fears of *Egypt's* potent Aid ;
Not so has *Pharoah* learnt Ambition's Trade,
Nor ever with such Measures can comply 673
As Shock the common Rules of Policy ;
None dread like Him the growth of *Israel's* King,
And He alone sufficient Aids can bring ;
Who knows that Prince to *Egypt* can give Law
That on our Stubborn Tribes his Yoak cou'd draw.
At such profound Expense He has not stood,
Nor dy'd for this his Hands so deep in blood ;
Wou'd nere through Wrong and Right his Progress take,   681
Grudge his own Rest, and keep the World awake,
To fix a Lawless Prince on *Judah's* Throne,
First to Invade our Rights, and then his Own ;
His dear-gain'd Conquests cheaply to despoil,
And Reap the Harvest of his Crimes and Toil.
We grant his Wealth Vast as our Ocean's Sand
And Curse its Fatal Influence on our Land,
Which our Brib'd *Jews* so num'rously partake
That ev'n an Host his Pensioners wou'd make ;   690
From these Deceivers our Divisions spring,
Our Weakness, and the Growth of *Egypt's* King :
These with pretended Friendship to the State
Our Crowd's Suspition of their Prince Create,
Both pleas'd and frightened with the specious Cry,
To Guard their Sacred Rights and Property ;
To Ruin, thus, the Chosen Flock are Sold,
While Wolves are tane for Guardians of the Fold ;
Seduc'd by these, we groundlessly complain,
And loath the Manna of a gentle Reign : 700

Thus our Fore-fathers crooked Paths are trod,
We trust our Prince, no more than They their God.
But all in vain our Reasoning Prophets Preach,
To those whom sad Experience ne're could Teach,
Who can commence new Broils in Bleeding Scars
And fresh Remembrance of Intestine Wars ;
When the same Houshold Mortal Foes did yeild,
And Brothers stain'd with Brothers Blood the Feild ;
When Sons Curst Steel the Fathers Gore did Stain,
And Mothers Mourn'd for Sons by Fathers Slain !   710
When thick, as *Egypt's* Locusts on the Sand,
Our Tribes lay Slaughter'd through the promis'd Land,
Whose few Survivers with worse Fate remain,
To drag the Bondage of a Tyrants Reign :
Which Scene of Woes, unknowing We renew,
And madly, ev'n those ills we Fear, persue ;
While *Pharoah* laughs at our Domestick Broils
And safely crowds his Tents with Nations Spoils.
Yet our fierce Sanedrim in restless Rage,
Against our absent Heroe still engage,   720
And chiefly urge, (such did their frenzy prove),
The only Suit their Prince forbids to move,
Which till obtain'd, they cease Affairs of State,
And real Dangers wave, for groundless Hate.
Long *Davids* patience waits relief to bring,
With all th' Indulgence of a lawful King,
Expecting till the troubled Waves wou'd cease,
But found the raging Billows still increase.
The Crowd, whose Insolence Forbearance swells,   729
While he forgives too far, almost Rebels.
At last his deep Resentments silence broke,
Th' imperial Palace shook, while thus He spoke,
   Then Justice wake, and Rigour take her time,
For Lo ! Our Mercy is become our Crime.
While haulting Punishment her stroke delays,
Our Sov'reign Right, Heav'ns Sacred Trust, decays ;

For whose support ev'n Subjects Interest
    calls,
Wo! to that Kingdom where the Monarch
    Falls.
That Prince who yields the least of Regal
    Sway,
So far his Peoples Freedom does Betray. 740
Right lives by Law, and Law subsists by
    Pow'r;
Disarm the Shepherd, Wolves the Flock
    devour.
Hard Lot of Empire o're a stubborn Race,
Which Heav'n it Self in vain has try'd with
    Grace!
When will our Reasons long-charm'd Eyes
    unclose,
And *Israel* judge between her Friends and
    Foes?
When shall we see expir'd Deceivers Sway,
And credit what our God and Monarchs say?
Dissembled Patriots bribed with *Egypts*
    Gold   749
Even Sanedrims in blind Obedience hold;
Those Patriots Falshood in their Actions see,
And judge by the pernicious Fruit the Tree;
If ought for which so loudly they declaim
Religion, Laws, and Freedom, were their Aim;
Our senates in due Methods they had led,
T' avoid those Mischeifs which they seem'd
    to dread;
But first e're yet they propt the sinking State,
T' impeach and charge, as urg'd by private
    Hate;
Proves that they ne're beleiv'd the Fears
    they prest,   759
But Barb'rously destroy'd the Nations Rest!
O! Whither will ungovern'd Senates drive,
And to what Bounds licentious Votes arrive?
When their Injustice We are prest to share,
The Monarch urg'd t' exclude the lawful
    Heir;
Are princes thus distinguish'd from the
    Crowd,
And this the Priviledge of Royal Blood?
But grant we shou'd Confirm the Wrongs
    they press,
His Sufferings yet were than the Peoples less;
Condemn'd for Life the Murd'ring Sword to
    weild,   769
And on their Heirs entail a Bloody Feild.
Thus madly their own Freedom they betray,
And for th' Oppression which they fear,
    make way;

Succession fixt by Heav'n the Kingdoms Bar,
Which once dissolv'd, admits the Flood of
    War;
Wast, Rapine, Spoil, without th'Assault begin,
And our mad Tribes Supplant the Fence
    within.
Since then their Good they will not under-
    stand,
'Tis time to take the Monarchs Power in
    Hand;
Authority, and Force to joyn with Skill,
And save the Lunaticks against their Will.
The same rough Means that swage the
    Crowd, appease   781
Our senates raging with the Crowds Disease.
Henceforth unbiass'd Measures let 'em draw
From no false Gloss, but Genuine text of
    Law;
Nor urge those Crimes upon Religions score
Themselves so much, in Jebusites abhor.
Whom Laws convict (and only they) shall
    Bleed,
Nor Pharisees by Pharisees be Freed.
Impartial Justice from our Throne shall
    shou'r,
All shall have Right, and We our Sov'reign
    Pow'r.   790
  He said, th' Attendants heard with awful
    Joy,
And glad Presages their fixt Thoughts em-
    ploy;
From *Hebron* now the Suffering Heir Re-
    turn'd,
A Realm that long with Civil Discord
    Mourn'd;
Till his Approach, like some Arriving God,
Compos'd, and heal'd the place of his Aboad;
The Deluge checkt that to *Judea* spread,
And stopt Sedition at the Fountain's Head.
Thus in forgiving *David's* Paths he drives,
And, chas'd from *Israel*, *Israels* Peace con-
    trives.   800
The Feild confest his Pow'r in Arms before,
And Seas proclaim'd his Tryumphs to the
    Shore;
As nobly has his Sway in *Hebron* shown,
How fit t' inherit Godlike *Davids* Throne.
Through *Sion's*-Streets his glad Arrivals
    spread
And Conscious Faction shrinks her snaky
    head;

---

804 Throne.] *1716*: Throne? *1682*.

His Train their Sufferings think o'repaid, to see
The Crowds Applause with Vertue once agree.
Success charms All, but Zeal for Worth distrest
A Virtue proper to the Brave and Best; 810
'Mongst whom was *Jothran, Jothran* always bent
To serve the Crown and Loyal by Descent.
Whose Constancy so Firm, and Conduct Just,
Deserv'd at once Two Royal Masters Trust ;
Who *Tyre's* proud Arms had Manfully withstood
On Seas, and gather'd Lawrels from the Flood ;
Of Learning yet no Portion was deny'd,
Friend to the Muses, and the Muses Pride.
Nor can *Benaiah's* Worth forgotten lie,
Of steddy Soul when Publick Storms were high ; 820
Whose Conduct, while the *Moor* fierce Onsets made,
Secur'd at once our Honour and our Trade.
Such were the Chiefs, who most his Suff'rings mourn'd,
And viewd with silent Joy the Prince return'd ;
While those that sought his Absence to Betray,
Press first their Nauseous False Respects to pay ;
Him still th' officious Hypocrites Molest,
And with malicious Duty break his Rest.
While real Transports thus his Friends Employ, 829
And Foes are Loud in their dissembled Joy,
His Tryumphs so resounded far and near,
Mist not his Young Ambitious Rival's Ear ;
And as when joyful Hunters clam'rous Train,
Some Slumbring Lion Wakes in *Moab's* Plain,
Who oft had forc'd the bold Assailants yeild,
And scatter'd his Persuers through the Feild,
Disdaining, furls his Main, and tears the Ground,
His Eyes enflaming all the Desart Round,
With Roar of Seas directs his Chasers Way,
Provokes from far, and dares them to the Fray ; 840
Such Rage storm'd now in *Absalom's* fierce Breast,
Such Indignation his Fir'd Eyes Confest ;

Where now was the Instructer of his Pride ?
Slept the Old Pilot in so rough a Tide ?
Whose Wiles had from the happy Shore betray'd,
And thus on Shelves the cred'lous Youth convey'd ;
In deep revolving Thoughts He weighs his State,
Secure of Craft, nor doubts to baffle Fate,
At least, if his storm'd Bark must go adrift,
To baulk his Charge and for himself to shift,
In which his dextrous Wit had oft been shown, 851
And in the wreck of Kingdoms sav'd his own ;
But now with more than Common Danger prest,
Of various Resolutions stands possest,
Perceives the Crowds unstable Zeal decay,
Least their Recanting Chief the Cause betray,
Who on a Father's Grace his Hopes may ground,
And for his Pardon with their Heads compound.
Him therefore, e're his Fortune slip her Time,
The Statesman Plots t' engage in some bold Crime 860
Past Pardon, whether to Attempt his Bed,
Or Threat with open Arms the Royal Head
Or other daring Method, and Unjust,
That may secure him in the Peoples Trust.
But failing thus t' ensnare him, nor secure
How long his foil'd Ambition may endure,
Plots next to lay him by, as past his Date,
And try some new Pretenders luckier Fate ;
Whose Hopes with equal Toil he wou'd persue,
Nor cares what Claimer's Crownd, except the True. 870
Wake *Absalom,* approaching Ruin shun,
And see, O see, for whom thou art Undone !
How are thy Honours, and thy Fame betray'd,
The Property of desp'rate Villains made !
Lost Pow'r and Conscious Fears their Crimes Create,
And Guilt in them was little less than Fate ;
But why shou'dst Thou, from ev'ry Grievance free,
Forsake thy Vineyards for their Stormy Sea?

---

864 secure] confirm *1716.*
874 made !] *1716* : made ? *1682.*

For Thee did *Canaan's* Milk and Honey flow,
Love drest thy Bow'rs and Lawrels sought
   thy Brow,   880
Preferment, Wealth and Pow'r thy Vassals
   were,
And of a Monarch all things but the Care.
Oh shou'd our Crimes, again, that Curse
   draw down,
And Rebel-Arms once more attempt the
   Crown,
Sure Ruin waits unhappy *Absalon,*
Alike by Conquest or Defeat undone ;
Who cou'd relentless see such Youth and
   Charms,
Expire with wretched Fate in Impious
   Armes ?
A Prince so form'd with Earth's, and
   Heaven's Applause,
To Tryumph ore Crown'd Heads in *David's*
   Cause :   890
Or grant him Victor, still his Hopes must fail,
Who, Conquering, wou'd not for himself pre-
   vail ;
The Faction whom He trusts for future
   Sway,
Him and the Publique wou'd alike Betray ;
Amongst themselves divide the Captive
   State,
And found their *Hydra*-Empire in his Fate !
Thus having beat the Clouds with painful
   Flight,
The pitty'd Youth with Scepters in his Sight;
(So have their Cruel Politicks Decreed,)
Must by that Crew that made him Guilty,
   Bleed.   900
For cou'd their Pride brook any Prince's
   Sway,
Whom but mild *David* would they choose
   t' Obey ?
Who once at such a gentle Reign Repine,
The Fall of Monarchy it self Design ;
From Hate to That their Reformations
   spring,
And *David* not their Grievance, but the
   King.
Seiz'd now with pannick Fear the Faction
   lies,
Least this clear Truth strike *Absaloms*
   charm'd Eyes ;
Least He perceive, from long Enchantment
   free,
What all, beside the flatter'd Youth, must
   see   910

But whate're doubts his troubled Bosome
   swell,
Fair Carriage still became *Achitophel.*
Who now an envious Festival enstalls,
And to survey their Strength the Faction
   calls,
Which Fraud, Religious Worship too must
   Guild ;
But oh how weakly does Sedition Build !
For Lo ! the Royal Mandate issues Forth,
Dashing at once their Treason, Zeal, and
   Mirth !
So have I seen disastrous Chance Invade,
Where careful Emmits had their Forrage
   laid,   920
Whether fierce *Vulcan's* rage the Furzy Plain
Had seiz'd, Engendred by some careless
   Swain ;
Or swelling *Neptune* lawless Inroads made
And to their Cell of Store his Flood convey'd;
The Common-Wealth broke up distracted go,
And in wild Hast their loaded Mates o're-
   throw :
Ev'n so our scatter'd Guests confus'dly meet,
With Boil'd, Bak'd, Roast, all Justling in
   the Street ;
Dejected all, and rufully dismaid,   929
For *Sheckle* without Treat, or Treason paid.

Seditions dark Eclipse now fainter shows,
More bright each Hour the Royal Plannet
   grows,
Of Force the Clouds of Envy to disperse,
In kind Conjunction of Assisting Stars.
Here lab'ring Muse those Glorious Chiefs
   relate
That turned the doubtful Scale of *David's*
   Fate ;
The rest of that Illustrious Band rehearse,
Immortalliz'd in Lawrell'd *Asaph's* Verse :
Hard task ! yet will not I thy Flight recall,
View Heav'n, and then enjoy thy glorious
   Fall.   940
First Write *Bezaliel,* whose Illustrious
   Name
Forestals our Praise, and gives his Poet
   Fame.
The *Kenites* Rocky Province his Command,
A barren Limb of Fertile *Canaans* Land ;
Which for its gen'rous Natives yet cou'd be
Held Worthy such a President as He !

916 **Build !]** *1716* : Build ? *1682.*

Bezaliel with each Grace, and Virtue Fraught,
Serene his Looks, Serene his Life and
    Thought,
On whom so largely Nature heapt her Store,
There scarce remain'd for Arts to give him
    more !   950
To Aid the Crown and State his greatest
    Zeal,
His Second Care that Service to Conceal ;
Of Dues Observant, Firm in ev'ry Trust,
And to the Needy always more than Just.
Who Truth from specious falsehood can
    divide,
Has all the Gown-mens Skill without their
    Pride ;
Thus crown'd with worth from heights of
    honor won,
Sees all his Glories copied in his Son,
Whose forward Fame should every Muse
    Engage :
Whose Youth boasts skill denied to others
    Age.   960
Men, Manners, Language, Books of noblest
    kind
Already are the Conquest of his Mind.
Whose Loyalty before it's Date was prime,
Nor waited the dull course of rowling Time :
The Monster *Faction* early he dismaid,
And *David's* Cause long since confest his
    Aid.
  Brave *Abdael* o're the Prophets' School
    was plac'd ;
Abdael, with all his Father's Virtue grac'd ;
A Heroe, who, while Stars look'd wondring
    down,
Without one *Hebrew's* Bloud restor'd the
    Crown.   970
That praise was His ; what therefore did
    remain
For following Chiefs, but boldly to maintain
That Crown restor'd ? and in this Rank of
    Fame,
Brave *Abdael* with the First a place must
    claim.
Proceed, illustrious, happy, Chief, proceed,
Foreseize the Garlands for thy Brow decreed,
While th' inspir'd Tribe attend with noblest
    strein
To Register the Glories thou shalt gain :

---

953 in] to *1716.*
967 Prophets'] *1716* : Prophet's *1682.*
973 restor'd ?] *1716* : restor'd ; *1682.*

For sure, the Dew shall *Gilboah's* Hills for-
    sake,
And *Jordan* mix his Stream with *Sodom's*
    Lake ;   980
Or Seas retir'd their Secret stores disclose,
And to the Sun their scaly Brood expose,
Or swell'd above the Clifts, their Billows
    raise,
Before the Muses leave their Patron's Praise.
  Eliab our Next labour do's invite,
And hard the Task to do *Eliab* right :
Long with the royal Wanderer he rovd,
And firm in all the Turns of Fortune prov'd !
Such ancient Service and Desert so large,
Well claim'd the Royal Household for his
    Charge.   990
His Age with only one mild Heiress blest,
In all the Bloom of smiling Nature drest,
And blest again to see his Flow'r ally'd
To *David's* Stock, and made young *Othniel's*
    Bride !
The bright Restorer of his Father's Youth,
Devoted to a Son's and Subject's Truth :
Resolv'd to bear that prize of Duty home,
So bravely sought (while sought) by *Absalom.*
Ah Prince ! th' illustrious Planet of thy
    Birth,
And thy more powerful Virtue guard thy
    worth ;   1000
That no *Achitophel* thy Ruine boast ;
Israel too much in one such Wreck has
    lost.
  Ev'n Envy must consent to *Helon's* Worth,
Whose Soul (tho' *Egypt* glories in his Birth)
Cou'd for our Captive-Ark its Zeal retain,
And *Pharoah's* Altars in their Pomp disdain :
To slight his Gods was small ; with nobler
    pride,
He all th' Allurements of his Court defi'd.
Whom Profit nor Example cou'd betray
But *Israel's* friend, and true to *David's*
    Sway.   1010
What acts of favour in his Province fall
On Merit he confers, and Freely all.
  Our List of Nobles next let *Amri* Grace,
Whose Merits claim'd the *Abethdins* high
    place ;
Who, with a Loyalty that did excel,
Brought all th' endowments of *Achitophel.*
Sincere was *Amri,* and not only knew,
But *Israel's* Sanctions into practice drew ;
Our Laws, that did a boundless Ocean seem,
Were coasted all, and fathom'd all by Him.

No *Rabbin* speaks like him their mystick
    Sense,   1021
So just, and with such Charms of Eloquence :
To whom the double Blessing does belong,
With *Mose's* Inspiration *Aaron's* Tongue.
    Than *Sheva*, none more loyal Zeal have
        shown,
Wakeful as *Judah's* Lion for the Crown.
Who for that Cause still combats in his Age,
For which his Youth with danger did engage.
In vain our factious Priests the Cant revive ;
In vain seditious Scribes with Libels strive
T' enflame the Crow'd, while He with watch-
    ful Eye   1031
Observes, and shoots their Treasons as They
    fly ;
Their weekly Frauds his keen Replies detect,
He undeceives more fast than they infect.
So *Moses*, when the Pest on *Legions* prey'd,
Advanced his Signal and the Plague was
    stay'd.
    Once more my fainting Muse thy Pinnions
        try,
And Strengths exhausted store let *Love*
    supply.
What Tribute *Asaph* shall we render Thee ?
We'll crown thee with a Wreath from thy
    own Tree !   1040
Thy Lawrel Grove no Envye's flash can blast.
The Song of *Asaph* shall for ever last !
With wonder late Posterity shall dwell
On *Absalom*, and false *Achitophel* :
Thy streins shall be our slumbring Prophets
    dream,
And, when our *Sion* Virgins sing their Theam,
Our *Jubilees* shall with thy Verse be grac't,
The Song of *Asaph* shall for ever last !
How fierce his Satyr loos'd, restrain'd, how
    tame
How tender of th' offending *Young man's*
    Fame !   1050
How well his worth, and brave Adventures
    still'd,
Just to his Vertues, to his Error mild.
No Page of thine that fears the strictest
    view,
But teems with just Reproof, or Praise, as
    due ;
Not *Eden* cou'd a fairer Prospect yield,
All *Paradise* without one barren Field :
Whose Wit the Censure of his Foes has
    past,
The Song of *Asaph* shall for ever last !

What Praise for such rich Strains shall we
    allow ?
What just Rewards the grateful Crown
    bestow ?   1060
While Bees in Flow'rs rejoyce, and Flow'rs
    in Dew,
While Stars and Fountains to their Course
    are true ;
While *Judah's* Throne and *Sion's* Rock stand
    fast,
The Song of *Asaph* and the Fame shall last.

    Still *Hebron's* honour'd happy Soil Retains
Our Royal Heroes beauteous dear remains ;
Who now sails off, with Winds nor Wishes
    slack,
To bring his Suff'rings bright Companion
    back,
But e're such Transport can our sense em-
    ploy   1069
A bitter grief must poyson half our Joy ;
Nor can our Coasts restor'd those Blessings
    see
Without a Bribe to envious Destiny !
Curs'd *Sodom's* Doom for ever fix the Tyde,
Where, by inglorious Chance, the Valiant
    dy'd.
Give not insulting *Askalon* to know,
Nor let *Gath's* Daughters triumph in our
    Woe !
No Sailer with the News swell *Egypt's* Pride
By what inglorious Fate our Valiant dy'd !
Weep, *Arnon* ! *Jordan* weep thy fountains
    dry   1079
While *Sion's* Rock dissolves for a supply !
Calm were the Elements, Night's silence
    deep,
The Waves scarce murm'ring, and the Winds
    asleep ;
Yet Fate for Ruine takes so still an hour,
And treacherous Sands the Princely Barque
    devour ;
Then Death unworthy seiz'd a gen'rous Race,
To Virtues scandal, and the Stars disgrace !
Oh ! had th' Indulgent Pow'rs vouchsaf't
    to yield,
Instead of faithless Shelves, a listed Field ;
A listed Field of Heav'ns and *David's*
    Foes,
Fierce as the Troops that did his Youth
    oppose,   1090
Each Life had on his slaughter'd heap retir'd,
Not Tamely, and Unconqu'ring thus expir'd:

But Destiny is now their only Foe,
And dying, even o're that they tryumph too ;
With loud last Breaths their Master's Scape
   applaud,
Of whom kind Force cou'd scarce the Fates
   defraud ;
Who for such Followers lost, O matchless
   mind !
At his own Safety now almost repin'd !
Say Royal Sir, by all your Fame in Arms,
Your Praise in Peace, and by *Urania's*
   Charms ;   1100
If all your Suff'rings past so nearly prest,
Or pierct with half so painful Grief your
   Breast ?
Thus some Diviner Muse her *Heroe* forms,
Not sooth'd with soft Delights, but tost in
   storms.
Not stretched on Roses in the Myrtle Grove,
Nor Crowns his Days with Mirth, his Nights
   with Love
But far remov'd in Thundring Camps is
   found,
His Slumbers short, his Bed the herbless
   Ground :
In Tasks of Danger always seen the First,
Feeds from the Hedge, and slakes with Ice
   his Thirst.   1110
Long must his Patience strive with Fortunes
   Rage,
And long, opposing Gods themselves engage,
Must see his Country Flame, his Friends
   destroy'd,
Before the promis'd Empire be enjoy'd,
Such Toil of Fate must build a Man of Fame,
And such, to *Israel's* Crown, the God-like
   David came.

What suddain Beams dispel the Clouds so
   fast !
Whose drenching Rains laid all our Vine-
   yards waste ?   1118
The Spring so far behind her Course delay'd
On th' Instant is in all her Bloom array'd ;
The Winds breathe low, the Element serene,
Yet mark what Motion in the Waves is seen !
Thronging and busie as *Hyblæan* Swarms,
Or stragled Souldiers Summon'd to their
   Arms.
See where the Princely Barque in loosest
   Pride,
With all her Guardian Fleet, Adorns the
   Tide !
High on her Deck the Royal Lovers stand,
Our Crimes to Pardon e're they toucht our
   Land.
Welcome to *Israel* and to *David's* Breast !
Here all your Toils, here all your Suff'rings
   rest.   1130

   This year did *Ziloah* Rule *Jerusalem,*
And boldly all Sedition's Syrges stem,
How e're incumbred with a viler Pair
Than *Ziph* or *Shimei,* to assist the Chair ;
Yet *Ziloah's* loyal Labours so prevail'd
That Faction at the next Election Fail'd,
When ev'n the common Cry did Justice
   Sound,
And Merrit by the Multitude was Crown'd :
With *David* then was *Israel's* peace restor'd,
Crowds Mourn'd their Errour and Obey'd
   their Lord.   1140

1132 Syrges] Syrtes *1716. This is a false correction. The original reading is right, the later
spelling being* Surges

KEY TO BOTH PARTS OF ABSALOM AND ACHITOPHEL.

(*From Vol. II. of* MISCELLANY POEMS, *edition of* 1716.)

Abethdin.	.	Lord Chancellor.	*Ishban* . .	Sir R. Clayton.
Abdael . .	Duke of Albemarle.		*Israel* . .	England.
Absalom. .	Duke of Monmouth.		*Issachar* .	T. Thin, Esq.
Achitophel .	Lord Shaftesbury.		*Jebusites* .	Papists.
Adriel . .	Earl of Mulgrave.		*Jerusalem* .	London.
Agag . .	Sir Edmund Berry Godfrey.		*Jonas* . .	Sir W. Jones.
Amiel . .	Mr. Seymour, Speaker.		*Jotham* . .	Marquis of Halifax.
Amri .	Lord Chancellor Finch.		*Jothran* . .	Lord Dartmouth.
Annabel .	Duchess of Monmouth.		*Judas* . .	Ferguson
Arod . . .	Sir W. Waller.		*Mephibosheth*	Pordage.
Asaph . .	Mr. Dryden.		*Michal* . .	Queen Katharine.
Balaam . .	Earl of Huntingdon.		*Nadab* . .	Lord Howard of Escrick.
Balak . .	Burnet.		*Og* . . .	Shadwell.
Barzillai .	Duke of Ormond.		*Othniel* .	Duke of Grafton.
Bathsheba .	Duchess of Portsmouth.		*Pharaoh* .	French King.
Benaiah . .	General Sackville.		*Phaleg* . .	Forbes.
Ben Jochanan	Johnson.		*Rabshakeh* .	Sir Thomas Player.
Bezaliel .	Duke of Beaufort.		*Sagan of Jeru-salem* . .	} Bishop of London.
Caleb. . .	Lord Grey.		*Sanhedrim* .	Parliament.
Corah . .	Dr. Oates.		*Saul* . . .	Oliver.
David . .	King Charles II.		*Sheva* . .	Sir R. L'Estrange.
Doeg . . .	Settle.		*Shimei* . .	Sheriff Bethel.
Egypt . .	France.		*Solymean Rout*	London Rebels.
Eliab . .	Earl of Arlington.		*Tyre* . .	Holland.
Ethnic Plot .	Popish Plot.		*Uzza* . .	J. H.
Hebrew Priests	} Church of England Ministers.		*Western Dome*	Dolben.
Hebron . .	Scotland.		*Zadoch* . .	Archbishop Sancroft.
Helon . .	Lord Feversham.		*Zaken* . .	Parliament-man.
Hushai . .	Earl of Rochester, Hyde.		*Ziloah* . .	Sir J. Moor.
Ishbosheth .	Richard Cromwell.		*Zimri* . .	Duke of Buckingham.

The Medall.

A

SATYRE

AGAINST

SEDITION

By the Authour of *Absalom* and *Achitophel.*

Per Graiûm populos, mediæque per Elidis Urbem
Ibat ovans; Divumque sibi poscebat Honores.

LONDON,
Printed for *Jacob Tonson* at the *Judge's Head* in
Chancery-lane, near *Fleet-street.* 1682.

EPISTLE TO THE WHIGS.

For to whom can I dedicate this Poem, *with so much justice, as to you? 'Tis the representation of your own Heroe : 'tis the Picture drawn at length, which you admire and prize so much in little. None of your Ornaments are wanting ; neither the landscap of the Tower, nor the Rising Sun, nor the* Anno Domini *of your New Sovereign's Coronation. This must needs be a gratefull undertaking to your whole Party : especially to those who have not been so happy as to purchase the Original. I hear the* Graver *has made a good Market of it : all his Kings are bought up already ; or the value of the remainder so inhanc'd, that many a poor* Polander *who would be glad to worship the Image is not able to go to the cost of him : But*
10 *must be content to see him here. I must confess I am no great artist; but Signpost painting will serve the turn to remember a Friend by, especially when better is not to be had. Yet for your comfort the lineaments are true ; and though he sate not five times to me, as he did to* B., *yet I have consulted History, as the* Italian *Painters do, when they would draw a* Nero *or a* Caligula *; though they have not seen the Man, they can help their Imagination by a Statue of him, and find out the Colouring from* Suetonius *and* Tacitus. *Truth is, you might have spar'd one side of your Medall : the Head wou'd be seen to more advantage, if it were plac'd on a Spike of the Tower ; a little nearer to the Sun. Which wou'd then break out to better purpose. You tell us in your Preface to the* No-Protestant Plot, *that you shall be forc'd hereafter to leave off your Modesty : I suppose you mean that little which is left you ;*
20 *for it was worn to rags when you put out this Medall. Never was there practis'd such a piece of notorious Impudence in the face of an Establish'd Government. I believe, when he is dead, you will wear him in Thumb-Rings, as the* Turks *did* Scanderbeg *; as if there were virtue in his Bones to preserve you against Monarchy. Yet all this while you pretend not onely zeal for the Publick good ; but a due veneration for the person of the King. But all men who can see an inch before them, may easily detect those gross fallacies. That it is necessary for men in your circumstances to pretend both, is granted you ; for without them there could be no ground to raise a Faction. But I would ask you one civil question, what right has any man among you, or any Association of men,* (to come nearer to you,) *who out of Parliament cannot be consider'd in a publick Capacity, to meet, as you daily doe, in Factious Clubs, to vilify*
30 *the Government in your Discourses and to libel it in all your Writings? Who made you Judges in* Israel? *or how is it consistent with your Zeal of the publick Welfare to promote Sedition? Does your definition of loyal, which is to serve the King according to the Laws, allow you the licence of traducing the Executive Power with which you own he is invested? You complain that his Majesty has lost the love and confidence of his People ; and by your very urging it you endeavour what in you lies, to make him lose them. All good Subjects abhor the thought of Arbitrary Power, whether it be in one or many : if you were the Patriots you would seem, you would not at this rate incense the Multitude to assume it ; for no sober man can fear it, either from the King's Disposition, or his Practice, or even, where you would odiously lay it, from his Ministers. Give us leave to enjoy the Government and the benefit of laws under*
40 *which we were born, and which we desire to transmit to our Posterity. You are not the Trustees of the Publick liberty : and if you have not right to petition in a Crowd, much less have you to intermeddle in the management of Affairs, or to arraign what you do not like : which in effect is everything that is done by the King and Council. Can you imagine that any reasonable man will believe you respect the person of his Majesty, when 'tis apparent that your Seditious Pamphlets are stuff'd with particular Reflexions on him? If you have the confidence to deny this, 'tis easy to be evinc'd from a thousand Passages, which I onely forbear to quote, because I desire they should die and be forgotten. I have perus'd many of your Papers : and to show you that I have, the third part of your* No-Protestant Plot *is much of it stolen, from your dead Authour's Pamphlet, called the* Growth of Popery, *as manifestly as* Milton's *defence of*

the English *People is from* Buchanan, *de Jure regni apud Scotos, or your First Covenant and new Association, from the holy League of the* French Guisards. *Any one who reads* Davila *may trace your Practices all along. There were the same pretences for Reformation, and Loyalty, the same Aspersions of the King, and the same grounds of a Rebellion. I know not whether you will take the Historian's word, who says it was reported that* Poltrot, *a* Hugonot, *murthered* Francis, *Duke of* Guise, *by the instigations of* Theodore Beza : *or that it was a* Hugonot *Minister, otherwise call'd a* Presbyterian *(for our Church abhors so devilish a Tenent) who first writ a Treatise of the lawfulness of deposing and murthering kings of a different Perswasion in Religion : But I am able to prove from the doctrine of* Calvin, *and Principles of* Buchanan, *that they set the People above the Magistrate ; which if I mistake not, is your* 10 *own Fundamental, and which carries your Loyalty no farther than your liking. When a vote of the House of Commons goes on your side, you are as ready to observe it as if it were pass'd into a Law : But when you are pinch'd with any former, and yet unrepealed* Act of Parliament, *you declare that, in same cases, you will not be oblig'd by it. The Passage is in the same third part of the* No-Protestant Plot ; *and is too plain to be denied. The late Copy of your intended Association you neither wholly justify nor condemn ; But, as the Papists, when they are unoppos'd, fly out into all the Pageantry's of Worship ; but in times of War, when they are hard press'd by Arguments, lie close intrench'd behind the* Council of Trent ; *So, now, when your Affairs are in a low condition, you dare not pretend that to be a legal Combination, but whensoever you are afloat, I doubt not but it will be maintain'd and justify'd to purpose.* 20 *For indeed there is nothing to defend it but the Sword : 'tis the proper time to say anything, when men have all things in their power.*

In the mean time, you wou'd fain be nibbling at a parallel betwixt this Association and that in the time of Queen Elizabeth. *But there is this small difference betwixt them, that the ends of the one are directly opposite to the other : one with the Queen's approbation and conjunction, as head of it ; the other, without either the consent, or knowledge of the King, against whose Authority it is manifestly designed. Therefore, you doe well to have recourse to your last Evasion, that it was contriv'd by your Enemies, and shuffled into the Papers that were seiz'd ; which yet you see the nation is not so easy to believe as your own Jury ; But the matter is not difficult, to find twelve men in* New-gate, *who would acquit a Malefactour.* 30

I have one onely favour to desire of you at parting, that when you think of answering this Poem, you wou'd employ the same Pens against it who have combated with so much success against Absalom *and* Achitophel : *for then you may assure yourselves of a clear Victory, without the least reply. Raile at me abundantly ; and, not to break a Custome, doe it without wit : By this method you will gain a considerable point, which is wholly to wave the answer of my Arguments. Never own the botome of your Principles, for fear they should be Treason. Fall severely on the miscarriages of Government : for, if scandal be not allow'd, you are no freeborn subjects. If God has not bless'd you with the Talent of Rhiming, make use of my poor Stock and wellcome : let your Verses run upon my feet ; and for the utmost refuge of notorious* Block-heads, *reduc'd to the last extremity of sense, turn my own lines upon me ; and, in utter* 40 *despaire of your own Satyre, make me Satyrize my self. Some of you have been driven to this Bay already ; But above all the rest commend me to the* Non-conformist Parson, *who writ the* Whip *and* Key. *I am afraid it is not read so much as the Piece deserves, because the bookseller is every week crying help at the end of his* Gazette, *to get it off. You see I am charitable enough to doe him a kindness, that it may be publish'd as well as printed ; and that so much skill in* Hebrew *Derivations may not lie for Wast-paper in the Shop. Yet I half suspect he went no farther for his learning, than the Index of* Hebrew *Names and Etymologies, which is printed at the end of some* English *Bibles. If* Achitophel *signify the Brother of a Fool, the Authour of that Poem will pass with his Readers for the next of kin. And perhaps 'tis the Relation that makes the kindness. Whatever the Verses are, buy 'em up I beseech you out* 50 *of pity ; for I hear the Conventicle is shut up, and the Brother of* Achitophel *out of service.*

---

9 *and Principles of* Buchanan] The editors give *and the principles of* Buchanan

Now Footmen, you know, have the generosity to make a Purse for a Member of their Society, who has had his Livery pull'd over his Ears ; and even Protestant Socks are bought up among you, out of veneration to the name. A Dissenter in Poetry from Sense and English will make as good a Protestant Rhymer, as a Dissenter from the Church of England *a Protestant Parson. Besides, if you encourage a young Beginner, who knows but he may elevate his stile a little above the vulgar epithets of prophane and sawcy* Jack, *and Atheistick Scribler, with which he treats me, when the fit of Enthusiasm is strong upon him : by which well-mannered and charitable Expressions I was certain of his Sect, before I knew his name. What would you have more of a man ? he has damn'd me in your Cause from* Genesis *to the* Revelations :*
10 *And has half the Texts of both the* Testaments *against me, if you will be so civil to your selves as to take him for your Interpreter ; and not to take them for* Irish *Witnesses. After all, perhaps you will tell me, that you retain'd him onely for the opening of your Cause, and that your main Lawyer is yet behind. Now if it so happen he meet with no more reply than his Predecessours, you may either conclude that I trust to the goodness of my Cause, or fear my Adversary, or disdain him, or what you please, for the short on't is, 'tis indifferent to your humble servant, whatever your Party says or thinks of him.*

THE MEDALL.

A SATYRE AGAINST SEDITION.

OF all our Antick Sights and Pageantry
Which *English* Idiots run in crowds to see,
The *Polish Medal* bears the prize alone : ⎫
A Monster, more the Favourite of the Town ⎬
Than either Fairs or Theatres have shown. ⎭
Never did Art so well with Nature strive,
Nor ever Idol seem'd so much alive ;
So like the Man ; so golden to the sight,
So base within, so counterfeit and light.
One side is fill'd with Title and with Face ; 10
And, lest the King shou'd want a regal Place,
On the reverse, a Tow'r the Town surveys,
O'er which our mounting Sun his beams displays.
The Word, pronounc'd aloud by Shrieval voice,
Lætamur, which in Polish is rejoyce,
The Day, Month, Year, to the great Act are join'd,
And a new Canting Holiday design'd.
Five daies he sate for every cast and look ;
Four more than God to finish *Adam* took.
But who can tell what Essence angels are 20
Or how long Heav'n was making *Lucifer* ?

Oh, cou'd the Style that copy'd every grace
And plough'd such furrows for an Eunuch face,
Cou'd it have formed his ever-changing Will,
The various Piece had tir'd the Graver's Skill !
A Martial Heroe first, with early care
Blown, like a Pigmee by the Winds, to war.
A beardless Chief, a Rebel e'er a Man,
(So young his hatred to his Prince began.)
Next this, (How wildly will Ambition steer !)
A Vermin wriggling in th' Usurper's ear, 31
Bart'ring his venal wit for sums of gold,
He cast himself into the Saint-like mould ;
Groan'd, sigh'd, and pray'd, while Godliness was gain,
The lowest Bag-pipe of the Squeaking train.
But, as 'tis hard to cheat a Juggler's Eyes,
His open lewdness he cou'd ne'er disguise.
There split the Saint : for Hypocritique Zeal
Allows no Sins but those it can conceal.
Whoring to Scandal gives too large a scope ;
Saints must not trade ; but they may interlope. 41
Th' ungodly Principle was all the same ;
But a gross Cheat betrays his Partner's Game.
Besides, their pace was formal, grave, and slack ;

Text from the second edition, 1683, except as noted. The first edition was of 1682.
7 alive. *1682*: alive? *1683*.
21 *Lucifer* ?] *1682*: *Lucifer* ! *1683*.

His nimble Wit out-ran the heavy Pack.
Yet still he found his Fortune at a stay,
Whole droves of Blockheads choaking up his
    way ;
They took, but not rewarded, his advice ;
Villain and Wit exact a double price.
Pow'r was his aym ; but, thrown from that
    pretence, 50
The Wretch turned loyal in his own defence,
And Malice reconciled him to his Prince.
Him, in the anguish of his Soul he serv'd ;
Rewarded faster still than he deserv'd.
Behold him, now exalted into trust ;
His Counsels oft convenient, seldom just ;
Ev'n in the most sincere advice he gave
He had a grudging still to be a Knave.
The Frauds he learnt in his Fanatique years
Made him uneasie in his lawfull gears. 60
At best as little honest as he cou'd :
And, like white Witches, mischievously good.
To his first byass, longingly he leans ;
And _rather_ would be great by wicked means.
Thus fram'd for ill, he loos'd our Triple hold ;
(Advice unsafe, precipitous, and bold.)
From hence those tears ! that _Ilium_ of our
    woe !
Who helps a pow'rful Friend fore-arms a foe.
What wonder if the Waves prevail so far,
When He cut down the Banks that made the
    bar ? 70
Seas follow but their Nature to invade ;
But he by Art our native Strength betray'd.
So _Sampson_ to his Foe his force confest,
And, to be shorn, lay slumb'ring on her breast.
But, when this fatal Counsel, found too late,
Expos'd its Authour to the publique hate ;
When his just Sovereign, by no impious way,
Cou'd be seduced to Arbitrary sway ;
Forsaken of that hope, he shifts the sayle ;
Drives down the Current with a pop'lar gale ;
And shows the Fiend confess'd without a
    vail. 81
He preaches to the Crowd that Pow'r is lent,
But not convey'd to Kingly Government ;
That Claimes successive bear no binding force;
That Coronation Oaths are things of course ;
Maintains the Multitude can never err ;
And sets the People in the Papal Chair.
The reason's obvious ; _Int'rest never lyes ;_
The most have still their Int'rest in their
    eyes ;
The pow'r is always theirs, and pow'r is ever
    wise. 90

Almighty crowd, thou shorten'st all dispute ;
Power is thy Essence ; Wit thy Attribute !
Nor Faith nor Reason make thee at a stay,
Thou leapst o'er all Eternal truths in thy
    Pindarique way !
Athens, no doubt, did righteously decide,
When _Phocion_ and when _Socrates_ were try'd ;
As righteously they did those dooms repent ;
Still they were wise, whatever way they
    went.
Crowds err not, though to both extremes
    they run ;
To kill the Father and recall the son. 100
Some think the Fools were most as times
    went then,
But now the World's o'er stock'd with pru-
    dent men.
The common Cry is ev'n Religion's Test ;
The _Turk's_ is, at _Constantinople_, best,
Idols in _India_, Popery at _Rome_,
And our own Worship onely true at home,
And true, but for the time, 'tis hard to
    know
How long we please it shall continue so ;
This side to-day, and that to-morrow burns ;
So all are God a'mighties in their turns. 110
A Tempting Doctrine, plausible and new ;
What Fools our Fathers were, if this be
    true !
Who, to destroy the seeds of Civil War,
Inherent right in Monarchs did declare :
And, that a lawfull Pow'r might never cease,
Secur'd Succession, to secure our Peace.
Thus Property and Sovereign Sway, at last
In equal Balances were justly cast :
But this new _Jehu_ spurs the hot mouth'd
    horse ;
Instructs the Beast to know his native force : 121
To take the Bit between his teeth and fly
To the next headlong Steep of Anarchy.
Too happy _England_, if our good we knew ;
Wou'd we possess the freedom we pursue !
The lavish Government can give no more ;
Yet we repine ; and plenty makes us poor.
God try'd us once ; our Rebel-fathers fought ;
He glutted 'em with all the Pow'r they
    sought,
Till, master'd by their own usurping Brave,
The free-born Subject sunk into a Slave. 130
We loath our Manna, and we long for
    Quails ;
Ah, what is man, when his own wish pre-
    vails !

How rash, how swift to plunge himself in ill ;
Proud of his Pow'r and boundless in his Will !
That Kings can doe no wrong we must believe ;
None can they do, and must they all receive ?
Help Heav'n ! or sadly we shall see an hour,
When neither wrong nor right are in their
    pow'r !
Already they have lost their best defence,
The benefit of Laws which they dispence. 140
No justice to their righteous Cause allow'd ;
But baffled by an Arbitrary Crowd ;
And Medalls grav'd, their Conquest to record,
The Stamp and Coyn of their adopted Lord.

The Man who laugh'd but once, to see an
    Ass
Mumbling to make the cross-grained Thistles
    pass,
Might laugh again, to see a Jury chaw
The prickles of unpalatable Law.
The Witnesses that, Leech-like, liv'd on
    bloud,
Sucking for them were med'cinally good ; 150
But, when they fasten'd on *their* fester'd ⎫
    Sore,   ⎪
Then *Justice* and Religion they forswore, ⎬
Their Maiden Oaths debauch'd into a Whore. ⎭
Thus Men are rais'd by Factions and decry'd;
And Rogue and Saint distinguish'd by their
    Side.
They rack ev'n Scripture to confess their
    Cause ;
And plead a Call to preach in spight of Laws.
But that's no news to the poor injur'd Page,
It has been us'd as ill in every Age ;
And is constrain'd, with patience, all to
    take ;   160
For what defence can Greek and Hebrew
    make ?
Happy who can this talking Trumpet seize ;
They make it speak whatever Sense they
    please !
'Twas fram'd at first our Oracle t' enquire ; ⎫
But Since our Sects in prophecy grow higher, ⎬
The Text inspires not them ; but they the   ⎪
    Text inspire.   ⎭

London, thou great *Emporium* of our Isle,
O, thou too bounteous, thou too fruitfull
    Nile !
How shall I praise or curse to thy desert !
Or separate thy sound, from thy corrupted
    part !   170

I call'd thee *Nile* ; the parallel will stand :
Thy tydes of Wealth o'erflow the fatten'd
    Land ;
Yet Monsters from thy large increase we find
Engender'd on the Slyme thou leav'st behind.
Sedition has not wholly seiz'd on thee,
Thy nobler Parts are from infection free.
Of *Israel's* Tribes thou hast a numerous
    band ;
But still the *Canaanite* is in the Land.
Thy military Chiefs are brave and true,
Nor are thy disinchanted Burghers few. 180
The Head is loyal which thy Heart com-
    mands,
But what's a Head with two such gouty
    Hands ?
The wise and wealthy love the surest way ;
And are content to thrive and to obey.
But Wisedom is to Sloath too great a Slave ;
None are so busy as the Fool and Knave.
Those let me curse ; what vengeance will
    they urge,
Whose Ordures neither Plague nor Fire can
    purge ;
Nor sharp experience can to duty bring,
Nor angry Heaven nor a forgiving King ! 190
In Gospel phrase their Chapmen they betray;
Their Shops are Dens, the Buyer is their
    Prey.
The Knack of Trades is living on the Spoil ;
They boast e'en when each other they beguile.
Customs to steal is such a trivial thing,
That 'tis their Charter to defraud their King.
All hands unite of every jarring Sect ;
They cheat the Country first, and then infect.
They, for God's Cause their Monarchs dare
    dethrone,
And they'll be sure to make his Cause their
    own.   200
Whether the plotting Jesuite lay'd the plan
Of murth'ring Kings, or the *French* Puritan,
Our Sacrilegious Sects their guides outgo ;
And Kings and Kingly Pow'r would murther
    too.

    What means their Trait'rous Combination
        less,
Too plain t'evade, too shamefull to confess ?
But Treason is not own'd when 'tis descry'd;
Successfull Crimes alone are justify'd.
The Men, who no Conspiracy wou'd find,
Who doubts but, had it taken, they had
    join'd ?   210

Join'd in a mutual Cov'nant of defence ;
At first without, at last against their Prince ?
If Sovereign Right by Sovereign Pow'r they
    scan,
The same bold Maxime holds in God and
    Man:
God were not safe ; his Thunder cou'd they
    shun
He shou'd be forc'd to crown another Son.
Thus, when the Heir was from the Vineyard
    thrown,
The rich Possession was the Murth'rers own.
In vain to Sophistry they have recourse ; ⎫
By proving theirs no Plot they prove 'tis ⎬
    worse, 220 ⎪
Unmask'd Rebellion, and audacious Force, ⎭
Which, though not Actual, yet all Eyes may
    see
'Tis working, in th' immediate Pow'r to be ;
For from pretended Grievances they rise,
First to dislike, and after to despise ;
Then, *Cyclop*-like, in humane Flesh to deal,
Chop up a Minister at every meal ;
Perhaps not wholly to melt down the King ;
But clip his regal rights within the Ring.
From thence t' assume the pow'r of Peace
    and War ; 230
And ease him by degrees of publique Care.
Yet, to consult his Dignity and Fame, ⎫
He shou'd have leave to exercise the Name, ⎬
And hold the Cards while Commons play'd ⎪
    the game. ⎭
For what can Pow'r give more than Food
    and Drink,
To live at ease, and not be bound to think ?
These are the cooler methods of their Crime,
But their hot Zealots think 'tis loss of time :
On utmost bounds of Loyalty they stand, ⎫
And grin and whet like a *Croatian* band; 240 ⎬
That waits impatient for the last Command. ⎭
Thus Out-laws open Villainy maintain ;
They steal not, but in Squadrons scoure the
    Plain ;
And, if their Pow'r the Passengers subdue ;
The Most have right, the wrong is in the Few.
Such impious Axiomes foolishly they show ;
For in some Soils Republicks will not grow :
Our Temp'rate Isle will no extremes sustain
Of pop'lar Sway or Arbitrary Reign :
But slides between them both into the best ;
Secure in freedom, in a Monarch blest. 251

And though the Climate, vex't with various
    Winds,
Works through our yielding Bodies, on our
    Minds,
The wholesome Tempest purges what it
    breeds ;
To recommend the Calmness that succeeds.

But thou, the Pander of the Peoples hearts,
(O crooked Soul and Serpentine in Arts ;)
Whose blandishments a Loyal Land have
    whor'd,
And broke the Bonds she plighted to her
    Lord ; 259
What Curses on thy blasted Name will fall! ⎫
Which Age to Age their Legacy shall call ; ⎬
For all must curse the Woes that must ⎪
    descend on all. ⎭
Religion thou hast none : thy *Mercury*
Has pass'd through every Sect, or theirs
    through Thee.
But what thou giv'st, that Venom still
    remains ;
And the pox'd Nation feels Thee in their
    Brains.
What else inspires the Tongues & swells the
    Breasts
Of all thy bellowing Renegado Priests,
That preach up thee for God ; dispence thy
    Laws ;
And with thy Stumm ferment their fainting
    Cause ? 270
Fresh Fumes of Madness raise ; and toile and
    sweat,
To make the formidable Cripple great.
Yet, shou'd thy Crimes succeed, shou'd law-
    less Powr
Compass those Ends thy greedy Hopes
    devour,
Thy Canting Friends thy Mortal Foes wou'd
    be,
Thy God and Theirs will never long agree ;
For thine, (if thou hast any,) must be one
That lets the World and Humane Kind
    alone ;
A jolly God that passes hours too well
To promise Heav'n, or threaten us with
    Hell. 280
That unconcern'd can at Rebellion sit ;
And wink at Crimes he did himself commit.
A Tyrant theirs ; the Heav'n their Priest-
    hood paints
A Conventicle of gloomy sullen Saints ;

---

237 their] *1682* : the *1683.*

A Heav'n, like *Bedlam*, slovenly and sad,
Fore-doomed for Souls with false Religion
    mad.
Without a Vision Poets can fore-show
What all but Fools by common Sense may
    know:
If true Succession from our Isle should fail,
And Crowds profane with impious Arms
    prevail,   290
Not thou nor those thy Factious Arts ingage ⎤
Shall reap that Harvest of Rebellious Rage, ⎬
With which thou flatter'st thy decrepit Age. ⎦
The swelling Poison of the sev'ral Sects,
Which, wanting vent, the Nations Health
    infects
Shall burst its Bag; and fighting out their
    way,
The various Venoms on each other prey.
The *Presbyter*, puft up with spiritual Pride,
Shall on the Necks of the lewd Nobles
    ride:
His Brethren damn, the Civil Pow'r defy; 300
And parcel out Republique Prelacy.
But short shall be his Reign; his rigid Yoke
And Tyrant Pow'r will puny Sects provoke,
And Frogs, and Toads, and all the Tadpole
    Train
Will croak to Heav'n for help from this
    devouring Crane.

The Cut-throat sword and clamorous Gown
    shall jar
In sharing their ill-gotten Spoils of War;
Chiefs shall be grudg'd the part which they ⎤
    pretend,   ⎥
Lords envy Lords, and Friends with every ⎬
    Friend   ⎥
About their impious Merit shall con- ⎦
    tend.   310
The surly Commons shall respect deny;
And justle Peerage out with Property
Their Gen'ral either shall his Trust betray
And force the Crowd to Arbitrary sway;
Or they suspecting his ambitious Aim, ⎤
In hate of Kings shall cast anew the ⎬
    Frame;   ⎥
And thrust out *Collatine* that bore their ⎦
    Name.

Thus in-born broils the Factions would ⎤
    ingage;   318 ⎬
Or Wars of Exil'd Heirs, or Foreign Rage, ⎦
Till halting Vengeance overtook our Age:
And our wild Labours, wearied into Rest,
Reclin'd us on a rightfull Monarch s Breast.

Pudet hæc opprobria, vobis
Et dici potuisse, et non potuisse refelli.

Mac Flecknoe.

OR A

SATYI

UPON THE

TRUE-BLEW-PROTESTAI

POET, T.

By the Author of

ABSALOM & ACHITOPHE

LONDON,

Printed for *D. Green*, 1682.

MAC FLECKNOE.

ALL humane things are subject to decay,
And, when Fate summons, Monarchs must obey:
This *Fleckno* found, who, like *Augustus*, young
Was call'd to Empire and had govern'd long:
In Prose and Verse was own'd, without dispute
Through all the realms of Non-sense, absolute.
This aged Prince now flourishing in Peace,
And blest with issue of a large increase,
Worn out with business, did at length debate
To settle the Succession of the State ;   10
And pond'ring which of all his Sons was fit
To Reign, and wage immortal War with Wit,
Cry'd, 'tis resolv'd ; for Nature pleads that He
Should onely rule, who most resembles me :
Sh—— alone my perfect image bears,
Mature in dullness from his tender years ;
Sh—— alone of all my Sons is he
Who stands confirm'd in full stupidity.
The rest to some faint meaning make pretence,
But *Sh*—— never deviates into sense.   20
Some Beams of Wit on other souls may fall,
Strike through and make a lucid intervall ;
But *Sh*——'s genuine night admits no ray,
His rising Fogs prevail upon the Day :
Besides, his goodly Fabrick fills the eye
And seems design'd for thoughtless Majesty :
Thoughtless as Monarch Oakes that shade the plain,
And, spread in solemn state, supinely reign.
Heywood and *Shirley* were but Types of thee,
Thou last great Prophet of Tautology :   30
Even I, a dunce of more renown than they,
Was sent before but to prepare thy way :
And coarsely clad in *Norwich* Drugget came
To teach the Nations in thy greater name.

My warbling Lute, the Lute I whilom strung,
When to King *John* of *Portugal* I sung,
Was but the prelude to that glorious day,
When thou on silver *Thames* did'st cut thy way,
With well tim'd oars before the Royal Barge,
Swelled with the Pride of thy Celestial charge ;   40
And, big with Hymn, Commander of an Host,
The like was ne'er in *Epsom* blankets tost.
Methinks I see the new *Arion* Sail,
The Lute still trembling underneath thy nail.
At thy well sharpned thumb from Shore to Shore
The Treble squeaks for fear, the Bases roar :
Echoes from Pissing-Ally, *Sh*—— call,
And *Sh*—— they resound from *A*—— *Hall*.
About thy boat the little Fishes throng,
As at the Morning Toast that Floats along. 50
Sometimes, as Prince of thy Harmonious band,
Thou wield'st thy Papers in thy threshing hand.
St. *André's* feet ne'er kept more equal time,
Not ev'n the feet of thy own *Psyche's* rhime :
Though they in number as in sense excell,
So just, so like tautology they fell
That, pale with envy, *Singleton* forswore ⎫
The Lute and Sword which he in Triumph ⎬
   bore,   ⎪
And vow'd he ne'er would act *Villerius* ⎭
   more.
Here stopt the good old Syre ; and wept for joy,   60
In silent raptures of the hopefull boy.
All Arguments, but most his Plays, persuade
That for anointed dulness he was made
   Close to the Walls which fair *Augusta* bind,
(The fair *Augusta* much to fears inclin'd)
An ancient fabrick raised t' inform the sight,
There stood of yore, and *Barbican* it hight :

Text from the second and corrected edition, 1684. The first, 1682, has several errors of the press. There is at Lambeth Palace a manuscript of the poem, which Todd collated. It is of no authority and most of its variants are manifestly wrong. One of them has by inadvertence been admitted into the texts of Scott, Christie, and Saintsbury.

15 *Sh*—] *Here and throughout the editors print* Shadwell   Shad— *1682.*

48 *A*—] Aston *1682.*
50 And gently waft the over all along. *1682.*

A watch Tower once, but now, so Fate
   ordains,
Of all the Pile an empty name remains.
From its old Ruins Brothel-houses rise,   70
Scenes of lewd loves, and of polluted joys,
Where their vast Courts the Mother-Strum-
   pets keep,
And, undisturb'd by Watch, in silence sleep.
Near these a Nursery erects its head,
Where Queens are formed, and future Hero's
   bred ;
Where unfledged Actors learn to laugh and
   cry,
Where infant Punks their tender voices try,
And little *Maximins* the Gods defy.
Great *Fletcher* never treads in Buskins here,
Nor greater *Johnson* dares in Socks appear.
But gentle *Simkin* just reception finds   81
Amidst this Monument of vanisht minds ;
Pure Clinches, the suburbian Muse affords ;
And *Panton* waging harmless war with words.
Here *Flecknoe*, as a place to Fame well
   known,
Ambitiously design'd his *Sh*——'s throne.
For ancient *Decker* prophesi'd long since,
That in this Pile should Reign a mighty
   Prince,
Born for a scourge of Wit, and flayle of
   Sense,
To whom true dulness should some *Psyches*
   owe,   90
But Worlds of *Misers* from his pen should
   flow ;
Humorists and Hypocrites it should produce,
Whole *Raymond* Families and Tribes of
   Bruce.
   Now Empress Fame had publisht the
   renown
Of *Sh*——'s Coronation through the Town.
Rows'd by report of Fame, the Nations meet,
From near *Bun-Hill* and distant *Watling-
   street.*
No *Persian* Carpets spread th' imperial way,
But scatter'd Limbs of mangled Poets lay ;
From dusty shops neglected Authors come,
Martyrs of Pies and Reliques of the Bum. 101
Much *Heywood*, *Shirley*, *Ogleby* there lay,
But loads of *Sh*—— almost choakt the way.
Bilk't *Stationers* for Yeomen stood prepar'd
And *H*—— was Captain of the Guard.

The hoary Prince in Majesty appear'd,
High on a Throne of his own Labours rear'd.
At his right hand our young *Ascanius* sat
Rome's other hope and Pillar of the State.
His Brows thick fogs, instead of glories,
   grace,   110
And lambent dullness plaid around his face.
As *Hannibal* did to the Altars come,
Swore by his Syre a mortal Foe to *Rome* ;
So *Sh*——swore, nor should his Vow bee vain,
That he till Death true dullness would main-
   tain ;
And, in his father's Right, and Realms
   defence,
Ne'er to have Peace with Wit, nor truce with
   Sense.
The King himself the sacred Unction made,
As King by Office, and as Priest by Trade :
In his sinister hand, instead of Ball,   120
He placed a mighty Mug of potent Ale ;
Love's Kingdom to his right he did convey,
At once his Sceptre and his rule of Sway ;
Whose righteous Lore the Prince had prac-
   tis'd young
And from whose Loyns recorded *Psyche*
   sprung.
His temples, last, with Poppies were o'er-
   spread,
That nodding seem'd to consecrate his head :
Just at that point of time, if Fame not lye,
On his left hand twelve reverend *Owls* did fly.
So *Romulus*, 'tis sung, by *Tyber's Brook*, 130
Presage of Sway from twice six Vultures
   took.
Th' admiring throng loud acclamations make
And Omens of his future Empire take.
The Syre then shook the honours of his head,
And from his brows damps of oblivion shed
Full on the filial dullness : long he stood,
Repelling from his Breast the raging God ;
At length burst out in this prophetick mood :
   Heavens bless my Son, from *Ireland* let
   him reign
To far *Barbadoes* on the Western main ;   140
Of his Dominion may no end be known,
And greater than his Father's be his Throne.
Beyond loves Kingdom let him stretch his
   Pen ;
He paused, and all the people cry'd *Amen.*

Then thus continued he, my son, advance
Still in new Impudence, new Ignorance.
Success let others teach, learn thou from me
Pangs without birth, and fruitless Industry.
Let *Virtuoso's* in five years be Writ ;
Yet not one thought accuse thy toyl of
    Wit.   150
Let gentle *George* in triumph tread the stage,
Make *Dorimant* betray, and *Loveit* rage ;
Let *Cully, Cockwood, Fopling*, charm the Pit,
And in their folly show the Writers wit.
Yet still thy fools shall stand in thy defence
And justifie their Author's want of sense.
Let 'em be all by thy own model made
Of dulness and desire no foreign aid,
That they to future ages may be known,
Not Copies drawn, but Issue of thy own. 160
Nay let thy men of wit too be the same,
All full of thee, and differing but in name ;
But let no alien *S—dl—y* interpose
To lard with wit thy hungry *Epsom* prose.
And when false flowers of *Rhetorick* thou
    would'st cull,
Trust Nature, do not labour to be dull ;
But write thy best, and top ; and in each
    line
Sir *Formal's* oratory will be thine.
Sir *Formal*, though unsought, attends thy
    quill,
And does thy *Northern Dedications* fill. 170
Nor let false friends seduce thy mind to
    fame,
By arrogating *Johnson's* Hostile name.
Let Father *Flecknoe* fire thy mind with praise
And Uncle *Ogleby* thy envy raise.
Thou art my blood, where *Johnson* has no
    part :
What share have we in Nature or in Art ?
Where did his wit on learning fix a brand
And rail at Arts he did not understand ?
Where made he love in Prince *Nicander's*
    vein,
Or swept the dust in *Psyche's* humble strain ?
Where sold he Bargains, Whip-stich, kiss
    my Arse,   181
Promis'd a Play and dwindled to a Farce ?

When did his Muse from *Fletcher* scenes
    purloin,
As thou whole *Eth'ridg* dost transfuse to
    thine ?
But so transfused as Oyls on waters flow,
His always floats above, thine sinks below.
This is thy Province, this thy wondrous way,
New Humours to invent for each new Play :
This is that boasted Byas of thy mind,
By which one way, to dullness, 'tis inclined,
Which makes thy writings lean on one side
    still,   191
And, in all changes, that way bends thy will.
Nor let thy mountain belly make pretence
Of likeness ; thine's a tympany of sense.
A Tun of Man in thy large Bulk is writ,
But sure thou 'rt but a Kilderkin of wit.
Like mine thy gentle numbers feebly creep ;
Thy Tragick Muse gives smiles, thy Comick
    sleep.
With whate'er gall thou settst thy self to
    write,
Thy inoffensive Satyrs never bite.   200
In thy fellonious heart though Venom lies,
It does but touch thy *Irish* pen, and dyes.
Thy Genius calls thee not to purchase fame
In keen Iambicks, but mild Anagram :
Leave writing Plays, and chuse for thy
    command
Some peacefull Province in Acrostick Land.
There thou maist wings display, and Altars
    raise,
And torture one poor word Ten thousand
    ways ;
Or, if thou would'st thy diff'rent talents suit,
Set thy own Songs, and sing them to thy lute.
He said, but his last words were scarcely
    heard,   211
For *Bruce* and *Longvil* had a *Trap* prepar'd,
And down they sent the yet declaiming
    Bard.
Sinking he left his Drugget robe behind,
Borne upwards by a subterranean wind.
The Mantle fell to the young Prophet's part
With double portion of his Father's Art.

---

163 *S-dl-y*] *The editors print* Sedley

185 Oyls] *1682.* Oyl *1684 and editors.*
215 a] A *1684.*

RELIGIO LAICI

OR A

Laymans Faith.

A

POEM.

Written by Mr. *DRYDEN*.

Ornari res ipsa negat ; contenta doceri.

LONDON,

Printed for *Jacob Tonson* at the *Judge's Head* in
Chancery-lane, near *Fleet-street*. 1682.

THE PREFACE.

A POEM with so bold a Title, and a Name prefix'd from which the handling of so serious a Subject wou'd not be expected, may reasonably oblige the Author to say somewhat in defence both of himself, and of his undertaking. In the first place, if it be objected to me that, being a *Layman*, I ought not to have concern'd myself with Speculations which belong to the Profession of *Divinity*, I cou'd answer that perhaps Laymen, with equal advantages of Parts and Knowledge, are not the most incompetent Judges of Sacred things ; But in the due sense of my own weakness and want of Learning, I plead not this : I pretend not to make myself a Judge of Faith in others, but onely to make a Con-
10 fession of my own ; I lay no unhallow'd hand upon the Ark, but wait on it with the Reverence that becomes me at a distance : In the next place I will ingenuously confess, that the helps I have us'd in this small Treatise, were many of them taken from the works of our own Reverend Divines of the Church of England ; so that the Weapons with which I Combat Irreligion are already Consecrated, though I suppose they may be taken down as lawfully as the Sword of *Goliah* was by *David*, when they are to be employed for the common Cause, against the Enemies of Piety. I intend not by this to intitle them to any of my errours, which yet I hope are only those of Charity to Mankind ; and such as my *own* Charity has caus'd me to commit, that of *others* may more easily excuse. Being naturally inclin'd to Scepticism in Philosophy, I have no reason to impose my Opinions, in a Subject
20 which is above it : but whatever they are, I submit them with all reverence to my Mother Church, accounting them no further mine, than as they are Authoriz'd, or at least, uncon-demn'd by her. And, indeed, to secure my self on this side, I have us'd the necessary Precaution of showing this Paper, before it was Publish'd, to a judicious and learned Friend, a Man indefatigably zealous in the service of the Church and State : and whose Writings, have highly deserv'd of both. He was pleas'd to approve the body of the Dis-course, and I hope he is more my Friend than to do it out of Complaisance ; 'Tis true he had too good a tast to like it all ; and amongst some other faults recommended to my second view, which I have written perhaps too boldly on St. *Athanasius*, which he advis'd me wholy to omit. I am sensible enough that I had done more *prudently* to have followed
30 his opinion ; But then I could not have satisfied myself that I had done honestly not to have written what was my own. It has always been my *thought*, that Heathens who never did, nor without Miracle cou'd, hear of the name of Christ, were yet in a possibility of Salvation. Neither will it enter easily into my belief, that before the coming of our Saviour, the whole World, excepting only the Jewish Nation, shou'd lye under the inevitable necessity of everlasting Punishment, for want of that Revelation, which was confin'd to so small a spot of ground as that of *Palestine*. Among the Sons of *Noah* we read of one onely who was accurs'd ; and if a blessing in the ripeness of time was reserv'd for *Japhet* (of whose Progeny we are,) it seems unaccountable to me, why so many Generations of the same Offspring as preceeded our Saviour in the Flesh should be all involv'd in one common
40 condemnation, and yet that their Posterity should be Intitled to the hopes of Salvation : as if a Bill of Exclusion had passed only on the Fathers, which debar'd not the Sons from their Succession. Or that so many Ages had been *deliver'd over* to Hell, and so many *reserv'd* for Heaven, and that the Devil had the first choice, and God the next. Truly I am apt to think, that the revealed Religion which was taught by *Noah* to all his Sons, might continue for some Ages in the whole Posterity. That afterwards it was included wholly in the Family of *Sem* is manifest : but when the Progenies of *Cham* and *Japhet* swarm'd into Colonies, and those Colonies were subdivided into many others, in process of time their Decendants lost by little and little the Primitive and Purer Rites of Divine Worship, retaining onely the notion of one Deity ; to which succeeding Generations

added others: (for Men took their Degrees in those Ages from Conquerours to Gods.) Revelation being thus Eclips'd to almost all Mankind, the Light of Nature as the next in Dignity was substituted; and that is it which St. *Paul* concludes to be the Rule of the Heathens; and by which they are hereafter to be judg'd. If my supposition be true, then the consequence which I have assum'd in my Poem may be also true; namely, that Deism, or the Principles of Natural Worship, are onely the faint remnants or dying flames of reveal'd Religion in the Posterity of *Noah*: and that our Modern Philosophers, nay and some of our Philosophising Divines have too much exalted the faculties of our Souls, when they have maintain'd that by their force, mankind has been able to find out that there is one Supream Agent or Intellectual Being which we call God: that Praise and 10 Prayer are his due Worship; and the rest of those deducements, which I am confident are the remote effects of Revelation, and unatainable by our Discourse, I mean as simply considered, and without the benefit of Divine Illumination. So that we have not lifted up our selves to God by the weak Pinions of our Reason, but he has been pleas'd to descend to us: and what *Socrates* said of him, what *Plato* writ, and the rest of the Heathen Philosophers of several Nations, is all no more than the Twilight of Revelation, after the Sun of it was set in the Race of *Noah*. That there is some thing above us, some Principle of *motion*, our Reason can apprehend, though it cannot discover what it is by its own Vertue. And indeed, 'tis very improbable, that we, who by the strength of our faculties cannot enter into the knowledg of any *Beeing*, not so much as of our *own*, should be able to find 20 out by them that Supream Nature, which we cannot otherwise define than by saying it is Infinite; as if Infinite were definable, or Infinity a Subject for our narrow understanding. They who wou'd prove Religion by Reason, do but weaken the cause which they endeavour to support: 'tis to take away the Pillars from our Faith, and to prop it only with a twig: 'tis to design a Tower like that of *Babel*, which, if it were possible (as it is not) to reach heaven, would come to nothing by the confusion of the Workmen. For every man is Building a several way; impotently conceipted of his own Model, and his own Materials: Reason is always striving, and always at a loss; and of necessity it must so come to pass, while 'tis exercis'd about that which is not its proper object. Let us be content at last, to know God, by his own methods; at least, so much of him, as he is pleas'd to reveal to 30 us in the sacred Scriptures; to apprehend them to be the word of God, is all our Reason has to do; for all beyond it is the work of Faith, which is the Seal of Heaven impress'd upon our humane understanding.

And now for what concerns the Holy Bishop *Athanasius*, the Preface of whose Creed seems inconsistent with my opinion; which is, That Heathens may possibly be sav'd; in the first place, I desire it may be consider'd that it is the Preface onely, not the Creed it self, which, (till I am better informed) is of too hard a digestion for my Charity. 'Tis not that I am ignorant how many several Texts of Scripture seemingly support that Cause; but neither am I ignorant how all those Texts may receive a kinder, and more mollified Interpretation. Every man who is read in Church History, knows that Belief 40 was drawn up after a long contestation with *Arrius* concerning the Divinity of our Blessed Saviour, and his being one Substance with the Father; and that, thus compil'd, it was sent abroad among the Christian Churches, as a kind of Test, which whosoever took, was look'd on as an Orthodox Believer. 'Tis manifest from hence, that the Heathen part of the Empire was not concerned in it: for its business was not to distinguish betwixt Pagans and Christians, but betwixt Hereticks and true Believers. This, well consider'd, takes off the heavy weight of Censure, which I wou'd willingly avoid from so venerable a Man; for if this Proportion, *whosoever will be saved*, be restrain'd onely to those to whom it was intended, and for whom it was compos'd, I mean the Christians, then the Anathema, reaches not the Heathens, who had never heard of Christ and were nothing 50 interested in that dispute. After all, I am far from blaming even that Prefatory addition to the Creed, and as far from cavilling at the continuation of it in the Liturgy of the Church, where on the days appointed, 'tis publickly read: for I suppose there is the same

reason for it now, in opposition to the Socinians, as there was then against the Arrians ; the
one being a Heresy, which seems to have been refin'd out of the other ; and with how
much more plausibility of Reason it combats our Religion, with so much more caution
to be avoided : and therefore the prudence of our Church is to be commended, which
has interposed her Authority for the recommendation of this Creed. Yet to such as are
grounded in the true belief, those explanatory Creeds, the *Nicene* and this of *Athanasius*,
might perhaps be spar'd : for what is supernatural will always be a mystery in spight
of Exposition : and for my own part the plain Apostles Creed, is most sutable to my
weak understanding ; as the simplest diet is the most easy of Digestion.

10   I have dwelt longer on this Subject than I intended ; and longer than perhaps I ought :
for having laid down, as my Foundation, that the Scripture is a Rule ; that in all things
needfull to Salvation it is clear, sufficient, and ordain'd by God Almighty for that purpose,
I have left my self no right to interpret obscure places, such as concern the possibility of
eternal happiness to Heathens : because whatsoever is obscure is concluded not necessary
to be known.

But, by asserting the Scripture to be the Canon of our Faith, I have unavoidably created
to my self two sorts of Enemies : The Papists indeed, more directly, because they have
kept the Scripture from us, what they cou'd ; and have reserved to themselves a right
of Interpreting what they have deliver'd under the pretence of Infallibility : and the
20 Fanaticks more collaterally, because they have assum'd what amounts to an Infallibility
in the private Spirit : and have detorted those Texts of Scripture, which are not necessary
to Salvation, to the damnable uses of Sedition, disturbance and destruction of the Civil
Government. To begin with the Papists, and to speak freely, I think them the less
dangerous, (at least in appearance) to our present State ; for not onely the Penal Laws
are in force against them, and their number is contemptible ; but also their Peerage and
Commons are excluded from Parliaments, and consequently those Laws in no probability
of being Repeal'd. A General and Uninterrupted Plot of their Clergy, ever since the
Reformation, I suppose all Protestants believe ; for 'tis not reasonable to think but that
so many of their Orders, as were outed from their fat possessions, wou'd endeavour
30 a reentrance against those whom they account Hereticks. As for the late design, Mr. *Cole-*
mans Letters, for ought I know are the best Evidence ; and what they discover, without
wyre-drawing their Sense or malicious Glosses, all Men of reason conclude credible. If
there be anything more than this requir'd of me, I must believe it as well as I am able,
in spight of the Witnesses, and out of a decent conformity to the Votes of Parliament : for
I suppose the Fanaticks will not allow the private Spirit in this Case : Here the Infallibility is at least in one part of the Government ; and our understandings as well as our
wills are represented. But to return to the Roman Catholicks, how can we be secure from
the practice of Jesuited Papists in that Religion ? For not two or three of that Order,
as some of them would impose upon us, but almost the whole Body of them are of opinion,
40 that their Infallible Master has a right over Kings, not onely in Spirituals but Temporals.
Not to name *Mariana, Bellarmine, Emanuel Sa, Molina, Santarel, Simancha,* and at least
twenty others of Foreign Countries ; we can produce of our own Nation, *Campian,* and
Doleman or *Parsons,* besides many are nam'd whom I have not read, who all of them
attest this Doctrine, that the Pope can depose and give away the Right of any Sovereign
Prince, *si vel paulum deflexerit,* if he shall never so little Warpe : but if he once comes
to be Excommunicated, then the Bond of obedience is taken off from Subjects ; and
they may and ought to drive him like another *Nebuchadnezzar, ex hominum Christianorum
Dominatu,* from exercising Dominion over Christians : and to this they are bound by
virtue of Divine Precept, and by all the tyes of Conscience, under no less Penalty than
50 Damnation. If they answer me (as a Learned Priest has lately written,) that this Doctrine
of the Jesuits is not *de fide,* and that consequently they are not oblig'd by it, they must
pardon me, if I think they have said nothing to the purpose ; for 'tis a Maxim in their
Church, where Points of Faith are not decided, and that Doctors are of contrary opinions,

they may follow which part they please ; but more safely the most receiv'd and most Authoriz'd. And their champion *Bellarmine* has told the World, in his Apology, that the King of *England* is a vassal to the Pope, *ratione directi Domini*, and that he holds in Villanage of his Roman Landlord. Which is no new claim put in for *England*. Our chronicles are his Authentique Witnesses, that King *John* was depos'd by the same plea, and *Philip Augustus* admitted Tenant. And which makes the more for *Bellarmine*, the French King was again ejected when our King submitted to the Church, and the Crown receiv'd under the sordid Condition of a Vassalage.

'Tis not sufficient for the more moderate and well-meaning Papists (of which I doubt not there are many) to produce the Evidences of their Loyalty to the late King, and to 10 declare their Innocency in this Plot ; I will grant their behaviour in the first, to have been as loyal and as brave as they desire ; and will be willing to hold them excus'd as to the second (I mean when it comes to my turn, and after my betters ; for 'tis a madness to be sober alone, while the Nation continues Drunk :) but that saying of their Father *Cres*: is still running in my head, that they may be dispens'd with in their Obedience to an Heretick Prince, while the necessity of the times shall oblige them to it : (for that (as another of them tells us,) is only the effect of Christian Prudence) but when once they shall get power to shake him off, an Heretick is no lawful King, and consequently to rise against him is no Rebellion. I should be glad therefore, that they wou'd follow the advice which was charitably given them by a Reverend Prelate of our Church ; namely, that 20 they would joyn in a publick Act of disowning and detesting those Jesuitick Principles ; and subscribe to all Doctrines which deny the Popes Authority of Deposing Kings, and releasing Subjects from their Oath of Allegiance : to which I shou'd think they might easily be induced, if it be true that this present Pope has condemn'd the doctrine of King-killing (a thesis of the Jesuites) amongst others *ex Cathedra* (as they call it) or in open consistory.

Leaving them, therefore, in so fair a way (if they please themselves) of satisfying all reasonable Men of their sincerity and good meaning to the Government, I shall make bold to consider that other extream of our Religion, I mean the Fanaticks, or Schismaticks, of the English Church. Since the Bible has been Translated into our Tongue, they have 30 us'd it so, as if their business was not to be sav'd, but to be damn'd by its Contents. If we consider onely them, better had it been for the English Nation that it had still remained in the original Greek and Hebrew, or at least in the honest Latine of St. *Jerome*, than that several Texts in it, should have been prevaricated to the destruction of that Government which put it into so ungrateful hands.

How many Heresies the first translation of *Tyndal* produced in few years, let my Lord *Herbert's* History of *Henry* the Eighth inform you ; Insomuch that for the gross errours in it, and the great mischiefs it occasion'd, a Sentence pass'd on the first Edition of the Bible, too shameful almost to be repeated. After the short reign of *Edward* the Sixth (who had continued to carry on the Reformation on other principles than it was begun) 40 every one knows that not onely the chief promoters of that work, but many others, whose Consciences wou'd not dispence with Popery, were forc'd, for fear of persecution, to change Climates : from whence returning at the beginning of Queen *Elizabeth's* reign, many of them who had been in *France*, and at *Geneva*, brought back the rigid opinions and imperious discipline of *Calvin*, to graffe upon our Reformation. Which, though they cunningly conceal'd at first, (as well knowing how nauseously that Drug wou'd go down in a lawfull Monarchy which was prescrib'd for a rebellious Common-wealth) yet they always kept it in reserve, and were never wanting to themselves, either in Court or Parliament, when either they had any prospect of a numerous Party of Fanatique Members in the one, or the encouragement of any Favourite in the other, whose Covetousness was gaping at the 50 Patrimony of the Church. They who will consult the Works of our venerable *Hooker*, or the account of his Life, or more particularly the Letter written to him on this Subject, by *George Cranmer*, may see by what gradations they proceeded ; from the dislike of Cap and

DR. E

Surplice, the very next step was Admonitions to the Parliament against the whole Government Ecclesiastical ; then came out Volumes in English and Latin in defence of their Tenets : and immediately, practices were set on foot to erect their Discipline without Authority. Those not succeeding, Satyrc and Rayling was the next : and *Martin Marprelate* (the *Marvel* of those times) was the first Presbyterian Scribler who sanctify'd Libels and Scurrility to the use of the Good Old Cause. Which been was done, (says my Authour,) upon this account ; that (their serious Treatises having been fully answered and refuted) they might compass by rayling what they had lost by reasoning ; and, when their Cause was sunk in Court and Parliament, they might at least hedge in a stake amongst the Rabble ;
10 for to their ignorance all things are Wit which are abusive ; but if Church and State were made the Theme, then the Doctoral Degree of Wit was to be taken at *Billingsgate* : even the most Saintlike of the Party, though they durst not, excuse this contempt and villifying of the Government, yet were pleas'd, and grind at it with a pious smile ; and call'd it a judgment of God against the Hierarchy. Thus Sectaries, we may see, were born with teeth, foul-mouthed and scurrilous from their Infancy : and if Spiritual Pride, Venome, Violence, Contempt of Superiours, and Slander had been the marks of Orthodox Belief ; the Presbytery and the rest of our Schismaticks, which are their Spawn, were always the most visible Church in the Christian World.

'Tis true, the Government was too strong at that time for a Rebellion ; but to shew
20 what proficiency they had made in *Calvin's* School, even *Then* their mouths water'd at it : for two of their gifted Brotherhood (*Hacket* and *Coppinger*) as the Story tells us, got up into a Pease-Cart, and harangued the People, to dispose them to an insurrection and to establish their Discipline by force ; so that, however it comes about, that now they celebrate Queen *Elizabeth's* Birth-night, as that of their Saint and Patroness, yet then they were for doing the work of the Lord by Arms against her ; and in all probability they wanted but a Fanatique Lord Mayor and two Sheriffs of their Party to have compass'd it.

Our venerable *Hooker*, after many Admonitions which he had given them, toward the end of his Preface breaks out into this Prophetick speech. "*There is in every one*
"*of these Considerations most just cause to fear, lest our hastiness to embrace a thing of so*
30 "*perilous Consequence*, (meaning the Presbyterian discipline) *should cause Posterity to*
"*feel those Evils which as yet are more easy for us to prevent, than they would be for them*
"*to remedy.*"

How fatally this *Cassandra* has foretold, we know too well by sad experience : the Seeds were sown in the time of Queen *Elizabeth*, the bloudy Harvest ripened in the Reign of King *Charles* the Martyr : and, because all the Sheaves could not be carried off without shedding some of the loose Grains, another Crop is too like to follow ; nay, I fear 'tis unavoidable, if the Conventiclers be permitted still to scatter.

A man may be suffer'd to quote an Adversary to our Religion, when he speaks Truth : And 'tis the observation of *Meimbourg* in his History of Calvinism, that, where-ever that
40 Discipline was planted and embrac'd, Rebellion, Civil War, and Misery attended it. And how indeed should it happen otherwise ? Reformation of Church and State has always been the ground of our Divisions in *England*. While we were Papists, our Holy Father rid us by pretending authority out of the Scriptures to depose Princes, when we shook off his Authority, the Sectaries furnish'd themselves with the same Weapons ; and out of the same Magazine, the Bible. So that the Scriptures, which are in themselves the greatest security of Governours, as commanding express obedience to them, are now turned to their destruction ; and never since the Reformation, has there wanted a Text of their interpreting to authorize a Rebel. And 'tis to be noted by the way, that the Doctrines of King-killing and Deposing, which have been taken up onely by the worst Party of
50 the Papists, the most frontless Flatterers of the Pope's Authority, have been espous'd, defended, and are still maintain'd by the whole Body of Nonconformists and Republicans. 'Tis but dubbing themselves the People of God, which 'tis the interest of their Preachers to tell them they are, and their own interest to believe ; and, after that, they cannot dip

into the Bible, but one Text or another will turn up for their purpose : If they are under Persecution (as they call it,) then that is a mark of their Election ; if they flourish, then God works Miracles for their Deliverance, and the Saints are to possess the earth.

They may think themselves to be too roughly handled in this Paper ; but I who know best how far I could have gone on this Subject, must be bold to tell them they are spar'd : though at the same time I am not ignorant that they interpret the mildness of a Writer to them, as they do the mercy of the Government ; in the one they think it Fear, and conclude it Weakness in the other. The best way for them to confute me, is, as I before advised the Papists, to disclaim their Principles, and renounce their Practices. We shall all be glad to think them true Englishmen, when they obey the King, and true Protestants, 10 when they conform to the Church Discipline.

It remains that I acquaint the Reader, that the Verses were written for an ingenious young Gentleman, my Friend, upon his Translation of *The Critical History of the Old Testament*, composed by the learned Father *Simon* : The Verses therefore are address'd to the Translatour of that Work, and the style of them is, what it ought to be, Epistolary.

If any one be so lamentable a Critique as to require the Smoothness, the Numbers, and the Turn of Heroique Poetry in this Poem ; I must tell him, that, if he has not read *Horace*, I have studied him, and hope the style of his Epistles is not ill imitated here. The Expressions of a Poem designed purely for Instruction ought to be Plain and Natural, and yet Majestic : for here the Poet is presumed to be a kind of Law-giver, and those three qualities 20 which I have nam'd are proper to the Legislative style. The Florid, Elevated, and Figurative way is for the Passions ; for Love and Hatred, Fear and Anger, are begotten in the Soul by shewing their Objects out of their true proportion ; either greater than the Life, or less ; but Instruction is to be given by shewing them what they naturally are. A Man is to be cheated into Passion, but to be reason'd into Truth.

RELIGIO LAICI.

DIM, as the borrow'd beams of Moon and
 Stars
To *lonely*, *weary*, *wandring* Travellers
Is *Reason* to the *Soul* : And as on high
Those rowling Fires *discover* but the Sky
Not light us *here* ; So *Reason's* glimmering)
 Ray
Was lent, not to *assure* our *doubtfull* way, }
But *guide* us upward to a *better Day*.)
And as those nightly Tapers disappear
When Day's bright Lord ascends our Hemi-
 sphere ;
So pale grows *Reason* at *Religions* sight ; 10
So *dyes*, and so *dissolves* in *Supernatural
 Light*.
Some few, whose Lamp shone brighter, have
 been led
From Cause to Cause to *Natures* secret head ;
And found that *one first principle* must be ;
But *what*, or *who*, that UNIVERSAL HE ;

Text from the original edition of 1682.

Whether some *Soul* incompassing this Ball,
Unmade, unmov'd ; yet *making, moving All* ;
Or *Atom's*, interfering Dance
Leapt into *Form* (the Noble work of *Chance*,)
Or this great *All* was from *Eternity* ; 20
Not ev'n the *Stagirite* himself could see ; }
And *Epicurus Guess'd* as well as He.)
As *blindly grop'd* they for a *future State*,
As *rashly Judg'd* of *Providence* and *Fate* :
But least of all could their En-   *Opinions*
 deavours find   *of the*
What most concern'd the good of   *several*
 Humane kind :   *sects of*
For *Happiness* was never to be   *Philoso-*
 found ;   *phers con-*
But vanish'd from 'em, like En-   *cerning*
 chanted ground.   *the* Sum-
One thought *Content* the Good to   *mum Bo-*
 be enjoyed :   *num.*
This, every little *Accident* destroyed : 30
The *wiser Madmen* did for *Vertue* toyl,
A Thorny, or at best a barren Soil :

In *Pleasure* some their glutton Souls would
   steep,
But found their Line too short, the Well
   too deep,
And leaky Vessels which no *Bliss* cou'd
   keep.
Thus, *anxious Thoughts* in *endless Circles* roul,
Without a *Centre* where to fix the *Soul* :
In this wilde Maze their vain Endeavours
   end :
How can the *less* the *Greater* comprehend ?
Or *finite Reason* reach *Infinity* ?   40
For what cou'd *Fathom* GOD were *more* than
   He.

   The *Deist* thinks he stands on firmer
      ground,
Cries εὕρεκα : the mighty Secret's   *Systeme*
   found :   *of Deism.*
God is that *Spring* of *Good* ; *Supreme* and
   Best,
We, made to *serve*, and in that Service *blest* ;
If so, some *Rules* of Worship must be given,
Distributed alike to all by Heaven :
Else *God* were *partial*, and to *some* deny'd
The Means His Justice shou'd for *all* provide.
This *general Worship* is to PRAISE, and PRAY :
One part to *borrow* Blessings, one to *pay* : 51
And when frail Nature slides into *Offence*,
The *Sacrifice* for *Crimes* is *Penitence*.
Yet, since th' Effects of Providence, we find
Are variously dispensed to Humane kind ;
That *Vice Triumphs* and *Vertue suffers* here,
(A Brand that Sovereign justice cannot
   bear ;)
Our Reason prompts us to a *future* State,
The *last Appeal* from *Fortune*, and from *Fate*,
Where God's all-righteous ways will be
   declar'd,   60
The *Bad* meet *Punishment*, the *Good*, *Reward*.

   Thus Man by his own strength to Heaven
      wou'd soar :
And wou'd not be Obliged to   *Of Reveal'd*
   God for more.   *Religion.*
Vain, wretched Creature, how art thou
   misled
To think thy Wit these God-like notions
   bred !
These Truths are not the product of thy
   Mind,
But dropt from Heaven, and of a Nobler
   kind.

Reveal'd Religion first inform'd thy sight,
And *Reason* saw not till *Faith* sprung the
   Light.
Hence all thy *Natural Worship* takes the
   Source :   70
'Tis *Revelation* what thou thinkst *Discourse*.
Else how com'st *Thou* to see these truths so
   clear,
Which so obscure to *Heathens* did appear ?
Not *Plato* these, nor *Aristotle* found.
Nor He whose wisedom *Oracles*   *Socrates.*
   renown'd.
Hast thou a Wit so deep, or so sublime,
Or canst thou lower dive, or higher climb ?
Canst *Thou*, by *Reason*, more of *God-head*
   know
Than *Plutarch*, *Seneca*, or *Cicero* ?
Those Gyant Wits, in happyer Ages born, 80
(When *Arms*, and *Arts* did *Greece* and *Rome*
   adorn,)
Knew no such *Systeme* : no such Piles cou'd
   raise
Of *Natural Worship*, built on *Pray'r* and
   Praise,
To One sole GOD :
Nor had Remorse, to Expiate Sin, prescribe :
But slew their fellow Creatures for a Bribe :
The guiltless *Victim* groan'd for their Offence ;
And *Cruelty* and *Blood*, was *Penitence*.
If *Sheep* and *Oxen* cou'd Attone for Men
Ah ! at how cheap a rate the *Rich* might
   Sin !   90
And great Oppressours might Heavens
   Wrath beguile
By offering his own Creatures for a Spoil !

   Dar'st thou, poor Worm, offend *Infinity* ?
And must the Terms of Peace be given by
   Thee ?
Then *Thou* art *Justice* in the *last Appeal* ;
Thy easie God instructs *Thee* to *rebell* :
And, like a King remote, and weak, must
   take
What Satisfaction *Thou* art pleased to make.

   But if there be a *Pow'r* too *Just*, and
      strong
To wink at *Crimes* and bear unpunish'd
   Wrong ;   100
Look humbly upward, see his Will disclose
The *Forfeit* first, and then the *Fine* impose
A *Mulct thy* poverty cou'd never pay
Had not *Eternal Wisedom* found the way

And with Cœlestial Wealth supply'd thy
   Store ;
His Justice makes the *Fine, his Mercy* quits
   the *Score.*
See God descending in thy Humane Frame ;
Th' *offended,* suffering in th' *Offenders* name :
All thy Misdeeds to Him imputed see,
And all his Righteousness devolv'd on thee.

   For granting we have Sin'd, and that th'
      offence   111
Of *Man,* is made against *Omnipotence,*
Some Price, that bears *proportion,* must be
   paid
And *Infinite* with *Infinite* be weigh'd.
See then the *Deist lost* : *Remorse* for *Vice*
Not paid, or *paid,* inadequate in price :
What farther means can *Reason* now direct,
Or what Relief from *humane Wit* expect ?
That shews us *sick* ; and sadly are we sure
Still to be *Sick,* till *Heav'n* reveal the
   Cure :   120
If then *Heaven's Will* must needs be under-
   stood,
(Which must, if we want *Cure,* and *Heaven*
   be *Good,*)
Let all Records of *Will reveal'd* be shown ;)
With *Scripture,* all in equal ballance thrown, }
And *our one Sacred Book* will be *That one.*)

   Proof needs not here ; for whether we
     compare
That Impious, Idle, Superstitious Ware
Of *Rites,Lustrations,Offerings,*(which before,
In various Ages, various Countries bore,)
With *Christian Faith and Vertues,* we shall
   find   130
None answ'ring the great ends of humane
   kind,
But *This one rule of Life* ; That shews us
   best
How *God* may be *appeas'd,* and *mortals* blest.
Whether from length of *Time* its worth we
   draw,
The *World* is scarce more *Ancient* than the
   Law :
Heav'ns early Care prescrib'd for every Age ;
First, in the *Soul,* and after, in the *Page.*
Or, whether more abstractedly we look,
Or on the *Writers,* or the *written* Book,
Whence, but from *Heav'n* cou'd men, un-
   skill'd in Arts,   140
In several Ages born, in several parts,

Weave such *agreeing Truths* ? or *how* or *why*
Shou'd *all* conspire to cheat us with a *Lye* ?
Unask'd their *Pains, ungratefull* their *Advice,*
Starving their *Gain* and *Martyrdom* their
   Price.

   If on the Book itself we cast our view,
Concurrent Heathens prove the Story *True* :
The *Doctrine, Miracles* ; which must con-
   vince,
For *Heav'n* in *Them* appeals to *humane*
   Sense ;
And though they *prove* not, they *Confirm*
   the Cause,   150
When what is *Taught* agrees with *Natures*
   Laws.

   Then for the *Style, Majestick* and *Divine,*
It speaks no less than God in every Line ;
Commanding words ; whose *Force* is still the
   same
As the first *Fiat* that produc'd our Frame.
All Faiths *beside,* or did by *Arms* ascend ;
Or *Sense* indulg'd has made *Mankind* their
   Friend ;
This *onely* Doctrine does our *Lusts* oppose :
Unfed by Natures Soil, in which it grows ;
Cross to our *Interests,* curbing Sense and
   Sin ;   160
Oppress'd without, and undermin'd within,
It thrives through pain ; its own Tormen-
   tours tires ;
And with a stubborn patience still aspires.
To what can *Reason* such Effects assign,
Transcending *Nature,* but to *Laws Divine* ?
Which in that Sacred Volume are contain'd ;
Sufficient, clear, and for that use ordained.

   But stay : the *Deist* here will urge anew,
No *Supernatural Worship* can be   *Objection of*
   True :   *the Deist.*
Because a *general Law* is that alone   170
Which must to *all* and every *where* be known:
A *Style* so large as not *this* Book can claim,
Nor aught that bears *reveal'd* Religions
   Name.
'Tis said the sound of a *Messiah's Birth*
Is gone through all the habitable Earth :
But still that Text must be confin'd alone
To what was *Then* inhabited, and known :
And what Provision could from *thence* accrue
To *Indian* Souls, and Worlds discovered
   New ?

In other parts it helps, that Ages past,   180
The Scriptures there were *known*, and were
    imbrac'd,
Till Sin spread once again the Shades of
    Night :
What's that to these who never *saw* the Light ?

Of all Objections this indeed is   *The objec-*
    chief   *tion an-*
To startle Reason, stagger frail   *swered.*
    Belief :
We grant, 'tis true, that Heav'n from
    humane Sense
Has hid the secret paths of *Providence* ;
But *boundless Wisedom, boundless Mercy,*
    may
Find ev'n for those *be-wildred* Souls, a *way* :
If from his *Nature Foes* may Pity claim,   190
Much more may *Strangers* who ne'er heard
    his *Name*.
And though *no Name* be for *Salvation* known,
But that of His *Eternal Sons* alone ;
Who knows how far transcending Goodness
    can
Extend the *Merits* of *that Son* to *Man* ?
Who knows what *Reasons* may his *Mercy*
    lead ;
Or *Ignorance invincible* may plead ?
Not onely *Charity* bids hope the *best,*
But *more* the great Apostle has exprest : 199
That, if the Gentiles, (whom no Law inspir'd,)
By Nature did what was by *Law required,*
They, who the written Rule had never known,
Were to themselves both Rule and Law alone :
To Natures plain indictment they shall plead ;
And, by their Conscience, be condemn'd or
    freed.
Most Righteous Doom ! because a *Rule*
    reveal'd
Is *none* to *Those,* from whom it was *con-*
    ceal'd.
Then those who follow'd *Reasons* Dictates
    right ;
Liv'd up, and lifted high their *Natural Light* ;
With *Socrates* may see their Maker's Face,
While Thousand *Rubrick-Martyrs* want a
    place.   211

Nor does it baulk my Charity to find
Th' *Egyptian* Bishop of another mind :

---

193 *Sons*] *This is genitive singular.* Scott
wrongly wished to read Son

For, though his *Creed Eternal Truth* contains,
'Tis hard for *Man* to doom to *endless pains*
All who believ'd not all, his Zeal requir'd ;
Unless he first cou'd prove he was inspir'd.
Then let us either think he meant to say
This Faith, where *publish'd,* was the onely
    way ;
Or else conclude that, *Arius* to confute,   220
The good old Man, too eager in dispute,
Flew high ; and, as his *Christian* Fury rose,
Damn'd all for *Hereticks* who durst *oppose.*

Thus far my Charity this path has
    try'd,   *Digression*
(A much unskilfull, but well   *to the Trans-*
    meaning guide :)   *latour of*
Yet what they are, even these   *Father* Si-
    crude thoughts were bred   mon's *Cri-*
By reading that, which better   *tical History*
    thou hast read,   *of the Old*
Thy Matchless Author's work :   *Testament.*
    which thou,
    my Friend,
By well translating better dost commend :
Those youthfull hours, which of thy Equals
    most   230
In *Toys* have *squander'd,* or in Vice have *lost,*
Those hours hast thou to Nobler use
    employ'd ;
And the severe Delights of Truth enjoy'd.
Witness this weighty Book, in which appears
The crabbed Toil of many thoughtfull
    years,
Spent by thy Authour in the Sifting Care
Of *Rabbins*' old Sophisticated Ware
From Gold Divine, which he who well can
    sort
May afterwards make *Algebra* a Sport.
A Treasure which, if *Country-Curates* buy, 240
They *Junius,* and *Tremellius* may defy :
Save pains in various readings, and Transla-
    tions,
And without *Hebrew* make most learn'd
    quotations.
A Work so full with various Learning fraught,
So nicely pondred, yet so strongly wrought,
As Natures height and Arts last hand
    requir'd :
As much as Man cou'd compass, uninspir'd.
Where we may see what *Errours* have been
    made
Both in the *Copiers* and *Translaters Trade* :
How *Jewish,* *Popish,* Interests have prevail'd,
And where *Infallibility* has *fail'd.*   251

For some, who have his secret meaning ghes'd,
Have found our Authour not too much a Priest ;
For *Fashion-sake* he seems to have recourse
To *Pope*, and *Councils*, and *Traditions* force:
But he that *old* Traditions cou'd subdue,
Cou'd not but find the weakness of the *New* :
If *Scripture*, though deriv'd from *heav'nly birth*,
Has been but carelessly preserved on *Earth* ;
If *God's own People*, who of *God* before   260
Knew what we know, and had been promis'd more,
In fuller Terms of Heaven's assisting Care,
And who did neither *Time*, nor *Study* spare
To keep this Book *untainted, unperplext* ;
Let in gross *Errours* to corrupt the *Text*,
Omitted *paragraphs*, embroyl'd the *Sense*,
With vain *Traditions* stopt the gaping Fence,
Which every common hand pull'd up with ease :
What Safety from such *brushwood-helps* as these ?
If *written words* from time are not secur'd, 270
How can we think have *oral Sounds* endur'd ?
Which *thus* transmitted, if *one* Mouth has fail'd,
Immortal Lyes on *Ages* are intail'd ;
And that some such have been, is prov'd too plain ;
If we consider *Interest, Church,* and *Gain.*

Oh but, says one, *Tradition* set aside, *(Of the Infallibility of Tradition in General.)*
Where can we hope for an *un-erring Guid* ?
For since th' *original* Scripture has been lost,
All Copies *disagreeing, maim'd* the *most,*
Or *Christian Faith* can have no *certain* ground   280
Or *Truth* in *Church Tradition* must be found.

Such an *Omniscient* Church we wish indeed ;
'Twere worth *Both Testaments*, and cast in the *Creed* :
But if *this Mother* be a *Guid* so sure
As can all doubts resolve, all *truth* secure,
Then her *Infallibility*, as well
Where Copies are *corrupt*, or *lame*, can tell ;

Restore *lost Canon* with as little pains,
As *truly explicate* what still *remains* :   289
Which yet no *Council* dare *pretend* to doe ;
Unless like *Esdras*, they could *write* it new :
Strange Confidence, still to *interpret* true,
Yet not be sure that all they have explain'd,
Is in the blest *Original* contain'd.
More Safe, and much more modest 'tis to say
God wou'd not leave Mankind without a way :
And that the *Scriptures*, though not *every where*
Free from Corruption, or intire, or clear,
Are uncorrupt, sufficient, clear, intire,
In all things which our needfull *Faith* require.   300
If *others* in the *same Glass better* see,
'Tis for *Themselves* they look, but not for *me* :
For MY Salvation must its Doom receive
Not from what OTHERS, but what *I* believe.

Must *all Tradition* then be set aside ? *(Objection in behalf of Tradition ; urg'd by Father Simon.)*
This to affirm were Ignorance or Pride.
Are there not many points, some needfull sure
To saving Faith, that Scripture leaves obscure ?
Which every Sect will wrest a several way
(For what *one* Sect interprets, *all* Sects *may* :)
We hold, and say we prove from Scripture plain,   311
That *Christ* is GOD ; the bold *Socinian*
From the *same* Scripture urges he's but MAN.
Now what Appeal can end th' important Suit ;
Both parts *talk* loudly, but the *Rule* is *mute*.

Shall I speak plain, and in a Nation free
Assume an honest *Layman's Liberty* ?
I think (according to my little Skill,)
To my own Mother-Church submitting still)
That many have been sav'd, and many may,
Who never heard this Question brought in play.   321
Th' *unletter'd* Christian, who believes in *gross*,
Plods on to *Heaven* and ne'er is at a loss :
For the *Streight-gate* would be made *streighter* yet,
Were *none* admitted there but men of *Wit*.
The few, by Nature form'd, with Learning fraught,
Born to instruct, as others to be taught.

Must Study well the Sacred Page ; and see
Which Doctrine, this, or that, does best
agree
With the whole *Tenour* of the Work Divine :
And plainlyest points to Heaven's reveal'd
Design : 331
Which Exposition flows from *genuine Sense* ;
And which is *forc'd* by *Wit* and *Eloquence.*
Not that Traditions parts are useless here :
When general, old, disinteress'd and clear :
That Ancient Fathers thus expound the Page
Gives *Truth* the reverend Majesty of *Age,*
Confirms its force by biding every *Test* ;
For best *Authority's,* next *Rules,* are best.
And still the nearer to the Spring we go 340
More limpid, more unsoyl'd, the Waters flow.
Thus, *first Traditions* were a proof alone ;
Cou'd we be *certain* such they *were,* so
known :
But since some Flaws in long descent may be,
They make not *Truth* but *Probability.*
Even *Arius* and *Pelagius* durst provoke
To what the *Centuries preceding* spoke.
Such difference is there in an oft-told Tale :
But Truth by its own Sinews will prevail.
Tradition written therefore more commends
Authority, than what from *Voice* descends :
And this, as perfect as its kind can be, 352
Rouls down to us the Sacred History :
Which, from the *Universal Church* receiv'd,
Is *try'd,* and *after* for its *self* believed.

The partial *Papists* wou'd infer from
hence,
Their Church, in last resort,   *The Second*
shou'd Judge the *Sense.*   *Objection.*
But first they would assume,
with wondrous Art,   *Answer*
Themselves to be the *whole,*   *to the*
who are but *part*   *Objection.*
Of that vast Frame, the Church ; yet grant
they were   360
The handers down, can they from thence
infer
A right t' interpret ? or wou'd they alone
Who brought the Present claim it for their
own ?
The *Book's* a *Common Largess* to *Mankind* ;
Not more for *them* than *every* Man design'd ;
The *welcome News* is in the *Letter* found ;
The *Carrier's* not Commission'd to *expound.*
It *speaks* it *Self,* and what it does contain,
In all things *needfull* to be *known,* is *plain.*

In times o'ergrown with Rust and
Ignorance, 370
A gainfull Trade their Clergy did advance :
When want of Learning kept the *Laymen*
low,
And none but *Priests* were *Authoriz'd* to
know ;
When what small Knowledge was, in them
did dwell ;
And he a *God* who cou'd but *Reade* or *Spell* ;
Then *Mother Church* did mightily prevail :
She parcel'd out the Bible by *retail* :
But still *expounded* what She *sold* or *gave* ;
To keep it in *her Power* to *Damn* and *Save* :
Scripture was *scarce,* and as the Market went,
Poor *Laymen* took *Salvation* on *Content* ; 381
As needy men take Money, good or bad :
God's Word they had not, but the *Priests*
they had.
Yet, whate'er *false Conveyances* they made,
The *Lawyer* still was *certain* to be paid.
In those dark times they learn'd their knack
so well,
That by long use they grew *Infallible* :
At last, a knowing Age began t' enquire
If *they* the *Book,* or *That* did *them* inspire :
And, making narrower search they found,
thô' late, 390
That what they thought the *Priest's* was
Their Estate,
Taught by the *Will produc'd,* (the written
Word,)
How long they had been *cheated* on *Record.*
Then, every man who saw the title fair,
Claim'd a Child's part, and put in for a Share :
Consulted Soberly his private good ;
And sav'd himself as cheap as e'er he cou'd.

'Tis true, my Friend, (and far be Flattery
hence)
This good had full as bad a Consequence :
The Book thus put in every vulgar hand, 400
Which each presum'd he best cou'd under-
stand,
The *Common Rule* was made the *common*
Prey ;
And at the mercy of the *Rabble* lay.
The tender Page with horney Fists was
gaul'd ;
And he was gifted most that loudest baul'd ;
The *Spirit* gave the *Doctoral Degree,*
And every member of a *Company*
Was of *his* Trade and of the *Bible free.*

Plain *Truths* enough for needfull *use* they
   found ;   409
But men wou'd still be itching to *expound* ;
Each was ambitious of th' obscurest place,
No measure ta'n from *Knowledge*, all from
   GRACE.
Study and *Pains* were now no more their
   Care ;
Texts were explain'd by *Fasting* and by
   Prayer :
This was the Fruit the *private Spirit* brought ;
Occasion'd by *great Zeal* and *little Thought*.
While Crouds unlearn'd, with rude Devotion
   warm,
About the Sacred Viands buz and swarm,
The *Fly-blown Text* creates a *crawling Brood* ;
And turns to *Maggots* what was meant for
   Food.   420
A Thousand daily Sects rise up, and dye ;
A Thousand more the perish'd Race supply :
So all we make of Heavens discover'd Will
Is, not to have it, or to use it ill.
The Danger's much the same ; on several
   Shelves
If *others* wreck *us* or *we* wreck our *selves*.

   What then remains, but, waving each
   Extreme,
The Tides of Ignorance, and Pride to stem ?
Neither so rich a Treasure to forgo ;
Nor proudly seek beyond our pow'r to know :

Faith is not built on disquisitions vain ; 431
The things we *must* believe, are *few* and
   plain :
But since men *will* believe more than they
   need ;
And every man will make *himself* a Creed,
In doubtfull questions 'tis the safest way
To learn what unsuspected Ancients say :
For 'tis not likely *we* should higher Soar
In search of Heav'n than *all the Church before* :
Nor can we be deceiv'd, unless we see
The *Scripture* and the *Fathers disagree.*   410
If after all, they stand suspected still,
(For no man's Faith depends upon his Will ;)
'Tis some Relief, that points not clearly
   known,
Without much hazard may be let alone :
And after hearing what our Church can say,
If still our Reason runs another way,
That private Reason 'tis more Just to curb,
Than by Disputes the publick Peace disturb.
For points obscure are of small use to learn :
But *Common quiet* is *Mankind's concern.* 450

   Thus have I made my own Opinions clear :
Yet neither Praise expect, not Censure fear :
And this unpolish'd, rugged Verse I chose ;
As fittest for Discourse, and nearest prose :
For while from *Sacred Truth* I do not swerve,
Tom Sternhold's or *Tom Sha—ll's Rhimes*
   will serve.

FINIS.

[Title-page of Original Edition.]

THRENODIA AUGUSTALIS:

A

Funeral-Pindarique

POEM

Sacred to the Happy Memory

OF

King CHARLES II

By *JOHN DRYDEN*,

Servant to His late MAJESTY, and to the Present KING.

Fortunati Ambo, si quid mea Carmina possunt,
Nulla dies unquam memori vos eximet ævo!

London, Printed for *Jacob Tonson*, at the *Judge's Head* in *Chancery-lane*, near *Fleet-street*, 1685. 9. *March*.

THRENODIA AUGUSTALIS

A

FUNERAL PINDARIQUE

POEM

Sacred to the Happy Memory

OF

KING CHARLES II.

I

THUS long my Grief has kept me dumb :
Sure there's a Lethargy in mighty Woe,
Tears stand congeal'd, and cannot flow ;
And the sad Soul retires into her inmost Room :
Tears, for a Stroke foreseen, afford Relief ;
But, unprovided for a sudden Blow,
Like *Niobe* we Marble grow ;
And Petrifie with Grief.
Our *British* Heav'n was all Serene,
No threatning Cloud was nigh,   10
Not the least wrinkle to deform the Sky ;
We liv'd as unconcern'd and happily
As the first Age in Natures golden Scene ;
Supine amidst our flowing Store,
We slept securely, and we dreamt of more :
When suddenly the Thunder-clap was heard,
It took us unprepar'd and out of guard,
Already lost before we fear'd.
Th' amazing News of *Charles* at once were spread,
At once the general Voice declar'd,   20
Our Gracious Prince was dead.
No Sickness known before, no slow Disease,
To soften Grief by Just Degrees ;
But, like an Hurricane on Indian seas,
The Tempest rose ;
An unexpected Burst of Woes :
With scarce a breathing space betwixt,
This *Now* becalm'd, and perishing the next.
As if great *Atlas* from his Height

Shou'd sink beneath his heavenly Weight, 30
And, with a mighty Flaw, the flaming Wall
   (As once it shall)
Shou'd gape immense, and rushing down,
   o'erwhelm this neather Ball ;
So swift and so surprizing was our fear ;
Our *Atlas* fell indeed; But *Hercules* was near.

II

His Pious Brother, sure the best
   Who ever bore that Name,
Was newly risen from his Rest,
   And, with a fervent Flame,
His usual morning Vows had just addrest 40
For his dear Sovereign's Health ;
   And hop'd to have 'em heard,
   In long increase of years,
In Honour, Fame, and Wealth :
Guiltless of Greatness, thus he always pray'd,
Nor knew nor wisht those Vows he made
On his own head shou'd be repay'd.
Soon as th' ill-omen'd Rumour reacht his Ear,
   (Ill news is wing'd with Fate and flies apace)
Who can describe th' Amazement in his Face !   50
Horrour in all his Pomp was there,
Mute and magnificent, without a Tear :
And then the *Hero* first was seen to fear.
Half unarray'd he ran to his Relief,
So hasty and so artless was his Grief :
Approaching Greatness met him with her Charms
   Of Power and future State ;
But looked so ghastly in a Brother's Fate,
   He shook her from his Armes.

Text from the second edition, 1685. The first was of the same year.

Arriv'd within the mournfull Room, he saw
  A wild Distraction, void of Awe,   61
And arbitrary Grief unbounded by a Law.
  God's Image, God's Anointed, lay
    Without Motion, Pulse or Breath,
    A senseless Lump of sacred Clay,
    An Image, now, of Death.
Amidst his sad Attendants' Grones and
    Cryes,
  The Lines of that ador'd, forgiving Face,
Distorted from their native grace ;   69
An Iron Slumber sat on his Majestick Eyes.
The Pious Duke——forbear, audacious Muse,
No Terms thy feeble Art can use
Are able to adorn so vast a Woe :
The grief of all the rest like subject-grief did
    show,
  His like a sovereign did transcend ;
No Wife, no Brother such a Grief cou'd know,
  Nor any name, but Friend.

III

O wondrous Changes of a fatal Scene,
  Still varying to the last !
Heav'n, though its hard Decree was past,
Seem'd pointing to a gracious Turn agen : 81
  And Death's up-lifted Arme arrested in its
    hast.
Heav'n half repented of the doom,
And almost griev'd it had foreseen,
  What by Foresight it will'd eternally to
    come.
    Mercy above did hourly plead
      For her Resemblance here below ;
    And mild Forgiveness intercede
    To stop the coming Blow.
New Miracles approach'd th' Etherial Throne,
Such as his wondrous Life had oft and lately
    known,   91
And urg'd that still they might be shown.
  On Earth his Pious Brother pray'd and
    vow'd.
    Renouncing Greatness at so dear a rate,
  Himself defending what he cou'd
    From all the Glories of his future Fate.
With him th' innumerable Croud
  Of armed Prayers
Knock'd at the Gates of Heav'n, and knock'd
    aloud ;
  The first well-meaning rude Petitioners.
All for his Life assayl'd the Throne,   101
All wou'd have brib'd the Skyes by offring
  up their own.

So great a Throng not Heav'n it self cou'd
    bar ;
'Twas almost born by force, as in the Giants
    War.
The Pray'rs, at least, for his Reprieve were
    heard ;
His Death, like *Hezekiah's*, was deferr'd :
  Against the Sun the Shadow went ;
  Five days, those five Degrees, were lent,
To form our Patience and prepare th' Event.
The second Causes took the swift Command,
The med'cinal Head, the ready Hand,   111
All eager to perform their Part,
All but Eternal Doom was conquer'd by their
    Art :
Once more the fleeting Soul came back
  T' inspire the mortal Frame,
And in the Body took a doubtfull Stand,
  Doubtfull and hov'ring, like expiring
    Flame,
That mounts and falls by turns, and trembles
    o'er the Brand.

IV

The joyful short-liv'd news soon spread
    around,
Took the same Train, the same impetuous
    bound :   120
The drooping Town in smiles again was drest,
  Gladness in every Face exprest,
  Their eyes before their Tongues confest.
Men met each other with erected look,
  The steps were higher that they took ;
Friends to congratulate their friends made
    haste ;
And long inveterate Foes saluted as they
    past :
Above the rest Heroick *James* appear'd
Exalted more, because he more had fear'd :
His manly heart, whose Noble pride   130
    Was still above
    Dissembled hate or varnisht love,
Its more than common transport cou'd not
    hide ;
But like an Eagre * rode in triumph o're the
    tide.

---

  * *An* Eagre *is a Tyde swelling above another
Tyde, which I have my self observ'd on the
River Trent.*

---

126 Friends to congratulate their friends] **Each**
to congratulate his friend *ed. 1.*

Thus, in alternate Course
  The Tyrant passions, hope and fear,
  Did in extreams appear,
And flasht upon the Soul with equal force.
Thus, at half Ebb, a rowling Sea
  Returns, and wins upon the shoar ; 140
  The wat'ry Herd, affrighted at the roar,
Rest on their Fins a while, and stay,
Then backward take their wondring way ;
The Prophet wonders more than they,
  At Prodigies but rarely seen before,
And cries a *King* must fall, or Kingdoms
    change their sway.
Such were our counter-tydes at land, and so
  Presaging of the fatal blow,
  In their prodigious Ebb and flow.
The Royal Soul, that, like the labouring
    Moon, 150
By Charms of Art was hurried down,
Forc'd with regret to leave her Native
    Sphear,
Came but a while on liking here :
Soon weary of the painful strife,
And made but faint Essays of Life :
    An Evening light
    Soon shut in Night ;
A strong distemper, and a weak relief,
Short intervals of joy, and long returns of
    grief.

V

The Sons of Art all Med'cines try'd, 160
And every Noble remedy applied,
With emulation each essay'd
His utmost skill, nay more they pray'd :
Never was losing game with better conduct
    plaid.
Death never won a stake with greater toyl,
Nor e're was Fate so near a foil :
But, like a fortress on a Rock,
Th' impregnable Disease their vain attempts
    did mock ;
They min'd it near, they batter'd from a far
With all the Cannon of the Med'cinal War ;
No gentle means could be essay'd, 171
'Twas beyond parly when the siege was laid :
The extreamest ways they first ordain,
Prescribing such intolerable pain
As none but *Cæsar* could sustain ;
Undaunted *Cæsar* underwent
The malice of their Art, nor bent
Beneath what e're their pious rigour cou'd
    invent.

In five such days he suffer'd more
Than any suffer'd in his reign before ; 180
More, infinitely more than he
Against the worst of Rebels cou'd decree,
A Traytor, or twice pardon'd Enemy.
Now Art was tir'd without success,
No Racks could make the stubborn malady
    confess.
  The vain *Insurancers* of life,
And He who most perform'd and promis'd
    less,
Even *Short* himself forsook the unequal
    strife.
Death and despair was in their looks,
No longer they consult their memories or
    books ; 190
Like helpless friends, who view from shoar
The labouring Ship and hear the tempest roar,
  So stood they with their arms across ;
Not to assist ; but to deplore
    Th' inevitable loss.

VI

Death was denounc'd ; that frightful sound
  Which even the best can hardly bear ;
  He took the Summons void of fear ;
And, unconcern'dly, cast his eyes around ;
  As if to find and dare the griesly Chal-
    lenger. 200
What death cou'd do he lately try'd,
When in four days he more then dy'd.
The same assurance all his words did grace ;
The same Majestick mildness held its place,
Nor lost the Monarch in his dying face.
Intrepid, pious, merciful, and brave,
He lookt as when he conquer'd and forgave.

VII

As if some Angel had been sent
To lengthen out his Government,
And to foretel as many years again, 210
As he had number'd in his happy reign,
So chearfully he took the doom
  Of his departing breath ;
  Nor shrunk, nor stept aside for death
  But, with unalter'd pace, kept on ;
Providing for events to come,
  When he resigned the Throne.
Still he maintained his Kingly State ;
And grew familiar with his fate.
Kind, good and gracious to the last, 220
On all he lov'd before his dying beams he
    cast

Oh truly good and truly great,
For glorious as he rose benignly so he set !
All that on earth he held most dear
He recommended to his Care,
 To whom both heav'n
 The right had giv'n,
And his own Love bequeath'd supream command :
He took and prest that ever loyal hand,
Which cou'd in Peace secure his Reign, 230
Which cou'd in wars his Pow'r maintain,
That hand on which no plighted vows were ever vain.
Well for so great a trust, he chose
 A Prince who never disobey'd :
 Not when the most severe commands were laid ;
 Nor want, nor Exile with his duty weigh'd:
A Prince on whom (if Heav'n its Eyes cou'd close)
The Welfare of the World it safely might repose.

VIII

That King who liv'd to Gods own heart,
 Yet less serenely died than he ; 240
Charles left behind no harsh decree
For Schoolmen with laborious art
 To salve from cruelty :
Those, for whom love cou'd no excuses frame,
He graciously forgot to name.
Thus far my Muse, though rudely, has design'd
Some faint resemblance of his Godlike mind :
But neither Pen nor Pencil can express
 The parting Brothers *tenderness* : 249
Though thats a term too mean and low ;
(The blest above a kinder word may know :)
 But what they did, and what they said,
The Monarch who triumphant went,
 The Militant who staid,
Like Painters, when their heigthning arts are spent,
I cast into a shade.
 That all-forgiving King,
  The type of him above,
 That inexhausted spring
  Of clemency and Love ; 260
Himself to his next self accus'd,
And ask'd that Pardon which he ne're refus'd :
For faults not his, for guilt and Crimes
Of Godless men, and of Rebellious times :

For an hard Exile, kindly meant,
When his ungrateful Country sent
 Their best *Camillus* into banishment :
And forc'd their Sov'raign's Act, they could not his consent.
Oh how much rather had that injur'd Chief
 Repeated all his sufferings past, 270
 Then hear a pardon beg'd at last,
Which given cou'd give the dying no relief :
He bent, he sunk beneath his grief :
His dauntless heart wou'd fain have held
From weeping, but his eyes rebell'd.
Perhaps the Godlike Heroe in his breast
 Disdain'd, or was asham'd to show
 So weak, so womanish a woe,
Which yet the Brother and the Freind so plenteously confest.

IX

Amidst that silent show'r, the Royal mind
 An Easy passage found, 281
And left its sacred earth behind :
 Nor murm'ring groan exprest, nor labouring sound,
 Nor any least tumultuous breath ;
Calm was his life, and quiet was his death.
Soft as those gentle whispers were,
In which th' Almighty did appear ;
By the still Voice, the Prophet knew him there.
That Peace which made thy Prosperous Reign to shine,
That Peace thou leav'st to thy Imperial Line, 290
That Peace, oh happy Shade, be ever thine !

X

For all those Joys thy Restauration brought,
For all the Miracles it wrought,
 For all the healing Balm thy Mercy pour'd
Into the Nations bleeding Wound,
And Care that after kept it sound,
 For numerous Blessings yearly shouer'd,
And Property with Plenty crown'd ;
For Freedom, still maintain'd alive,
Freedom which in no other Land will thrive,
Freedom an *English* Subject's sole Prerogative, 301
Without whose Charms ev'n Peace would be
But a dull, quiet Slavery :

---

288 Voice] Sound *ed. 1.*

For these and more, accept our Pious
      Praise ;
  'Tis all the Subsidy
  The present Age can raise,
  The rest is charg'd on late Posterity.
    Posterity is charg'd the more,
    Because the large abounding store
To them and to their Heirs, is still entail'd
      by thee.   310
  Succession of a long descent,
Which Chast'ly in the Chanells ran,
And from our Demi-gods began,
  Equal almost to Time in its extent,
Through Hazzards numberless and great,
  Thou hast deriv'd this mighty Blessing
      down,
    And fixt the fairest Gemm that decks th'
      Imperial Crown :
Not Faction, when it shook thy Regal Seat,
Not senates, insolently loud,
(Those Ecchoes of a thoughtless Croud,) 320
Not Foreign or Domestick Treachery,
Could Warp thy Soul to their Unjust Decree.
So much thy Foes thy manly Mind mistook,
Who judg'd it by the Mildness of thy look :
Like a well-temper'd Sword, it bent at
      will ;
But kept the Native toughness of the Steel.

XI

Be true, O *Clio*, to thy Hero's name !
  But draw him strictly so   328
  That all who view, the Piece may know,
He needs no Trappings of fictitious Fame :
The Load's too weighty ; Thou may'st chuse
Some Parts of Praise, and some refuse ;
Write, that his Annals may be thought more
    lavish than the Muse.
In scanty Truth thou hast confin'd
The Vertues of a Royal Mind,
Forgiving, bounteous, humble, just and
    kind :
His Conversation, Wit, and Parts,
His Knowledge in the Noblest, useful Arts,
Were such Dead Authors could not give ;
But habitudes of those who live ;   340
Who, lighting him, did greater lights receive :
He drain'd from all, and all they knew ;
His Apprehension quick, his Judgment
    true :
That the most Learn'd, with shame, confess
His Knowledge more, his Reading only less.

XII

Amidst the peaceful Triumphs of his Reign,
  What wonder if the kindly beams he shed
Reviv'd the drooping Arts again,
  If Science rais'd her Head,
  And soft Humanity that from Rebellion
    fled ;   350
Our Isle, indeed, too fruitful was before ;
  But all uncultivated lay
  Out of the *Solar* walk and Heavens high
    way ;
With rank *Geneva* Weeds run o're,
And Cockle, at the best, amidst the Corn it
    bore :
The Royal Husbandman appear'd,
  And Plough'd and Sow'd and Till'd,
The Thorns he rooted out, the Rubbish
    clear'd,
  And blest th' obedient Field.
When, straight, a double Harvest rose,   360
Such as the swarthy Indian mowes ;
Or happier Climates near the Line,
Or Paradise manur'd, and drest by hands
    Divine.

XIII

As when the New-born Phœnix takes his
    way,
  His rich Paternal Regions to Survey,
  Of airy Choristers a numerous Train
Attends his wondrous Progress o're the
    Plain ;
So, rising from his Fathers Urn,
So Glorious did our *Charles* return ;
  Th' officious Muses came along,   370
A gay Harmonious Quire, like Angels ever
    Young ;
(The Muse that mourns him now his happy
    Triumph sung.)
Even *they* cou'd thrive in his Auspicious
    reign ;
  And such a plenteous Crop they bore,
Of purest and well winow'd Grain
  As *Britain* never knew before.
Tho little was their Hire, and light their
    Gain,
Yet somewhat to their share he threw ;
Fed from his hand, they sung and flew,
Like Birds of Paradise that liv'd on morning
    dew.   380

---

371 Quire, like] Quire of *ed. 1.*

Oh never let their Lays his Name forget !
The Pension of a Prince's Praise is great.
Live then, thou great Encourager of Arts,
Live ever in our Thankful Hearts ;
Live blest Above, almost invok'd Below ;
Live and receive this Pious Vow,
Our Patron once, our Guardian Angel now.
Thou *Fabius* of a sinking State,
Who didst by wise delays, divert our Fate,
When Faction like a Tempest rose   390
In Death's most hideous form,
Then, Art to Rage thou didst oppose,
To weather out the Storm :
Not quitting thy Supream command,
Thou heldst the Rudder with a steady hand,
Till safely on the Shore the Bark did land :
The Bark that all our Blessings brought,
Charg'd with thy Self and *James*, a doubly
   Royal fraught.

XIV

Oh frail Estate of Humane things,
  And slippery hopes below !   400
  Now to our Cost your Emptiness we know,
  (For 'tis a Lesson dearly bought)
  Assurance here is never to be sought.
The Best, and best belov'd of kings,
And best deserving to be so,
  When scarce he had escap'd the fatal blow
  Of Faction and Conspiracy,
Death did his promis'd hopes destroy :
He toyl'd, He gain'd, but liv'd not to enjoy.
What mists of Providence are these   410
  Through which we cannot see !
  So Saints, by supernatural Pow'r set free,
Are left at last in Martyrdom to dye ;
Such is the end of oft repeated Miracles.
Forgive me, Heav'n, that Impious thought,
'Twas Grief for *Charles* to Madness wrought,
  That Questioned thy Supream Decree !
Thou didst his gracious Reign Prolong,
Even in thy Saints and Angels wrong,
  His Fellow Citizens of Immortality :   420
For Twelve long years of Exile, born,
Twice Twelve we number'd since his blest
  Return :
So strictly wer't thou Just to pay,
Even to the driblet of a day.
Yet still we murmur, and Complain
The Quails and Manna shou'd no longer rain :
Those Miracles 'twas needless to renew ;
The Chosen Flock has now the Promis'd
  Land in view.

XV

A Warlike Prince ascends the Regal State,
A Prince, long exercis'd by Fate :   430
Long may he keep, tho he obtains it late.
Heroes, in Heaven's peculiar Mold are
  cast,
They and their Poets are not formed in
  hast ;
Man was the first in God's design, and Man
  was made the last.
False Heroes made by Flattery so,
Heav'n can strike out, like Sparkles, at
  a blow ;
But e're a Prince is to Perfection brought,
He costs Omnipotence a second thought.
    With Toyl and Sweat,   439
  With hardning Cold, and forming Heat,
  The Cyclops did their strokes repeat,
Before th' impenetrable Shield was wrought.
It looks as if the Maker wou'd not own
  The Noble work for his,
Before 'twas try'd and found a Masterpiece.

XVI

  View then a *Monarch* ripen'd for a Throne
Alcides thus his race began,
O're Infancy he swiftly ran ;
The future God, at first was more than
  Man :
Dangers and Toils, and *Juno's* Hate,   450
Even o're his Cradle lay in wait ;
  And there he grappled first with Fate :
In his young Hands the hissing Snakes he
  prest,
So early was the Deity confest ;
  Thus, by degrees, he rose to *Jove's* Im-
   perial Seat ;
  Thus difficulties prove a Soul legitimately
   great.
Like his, our Hero's Infancy was try'd ;
Betimes the Furies did their Snakes pro-
  vide ;
And, to his Infant Arms oppose
His Father's Rebels, and his Brother's
  Foes ;   460
The more opprest the higher still he rose.
  Those were the Preludes of his Fate,
  That form'd his Manhood, to subdue
The *Hydra* of the many-headed, hissing
  Crew.

XVII

As after *Numa's* peaceful Reign
 The Martial *Ancus* did the Scepter
    wield,
Furbish'd the rusty Sword again,
 Resum'd the long forgotten Shield,
 And led the *Latins* to the dusty Field ;
So *James* the drowsy *Genius* wakes 470
 Of *Britain* long entranc'd in Charms,
 Restiff and slumbring on its Arms :
'Tis rows'd, & with a new strung Nerve the
  Spear already shakes.
No neighing of the Warriour Steeds,
No Drum, or louder Trumpet, needs
T' inspire the Coward, warm the Cold,
His Voice, his sole Appearance makes 'em
  bold.
Gaul and *Batavia* dread th' impending
  blow ;
Too well the Vigour of that Arm they know ;
They lick the dust, and Crouch beneath their
  fatal Foe. 480
Long may they fear this awful Prince,
 And not Provoke his lingring Sword ;
Peace is their only sure Defence,
 Their best Security his Word :
In all the Changes of his doubtful State,
His Truth, like Heav'ns, was kept inviolate,
For him to Promise is to make it Fate.
His *Valour* can Triumph o're Land and Main;
With broken Oaths his Fame he will not
  stain ;
With Conquest basely bought, and with
 Inglorious gain. 490

XVIII

For once, O Heav'n, unfold thy Adamantine
  Book ;
 And let his wondring *Senate* see,
 If not thy firm Immutable Decree,
 At least the second Page of strong con-
   tingency ;
 Such as consists with wills, Originally free :
Let them, with glad amazement, look
 On what their happiness may be :
Let them not still be obstinately blind,
Still to divert the Good thou hast design'd,
 Or with Malignant penury, 500
To sterve the Royal Vertues of his Mind.
Faith is a Christian's and a Subject's Test,
Oh give them to believe, and they are surely
  blest !
 They do ; and, with a distant view, I see
 Th' amended Vows of English Loyalty ;
 And all beyond that Object, there appears
The long Retinue of a Prosperous Reign,
 A Series of Successful years,
In orderly Array, a Martial, manly Train.
Behold ev'n to remoter Shores, 510
A Conquering Navy proudly spread ;
 The British Cannon formidably roars,
While starting from his Oozy Bed,
Th' asserted Ocean rears his reverend Head ;
To View and Recognize his ancient Lord
  again :
 And, with a willing hand, restores
  The *Fasces* of the main.

---

494 strong] great *ed. 1.*

FINIS.

THE
HIND
AND THE
PANTHER.
A
POEM,

In Three Parts.

——— *Antiquam exquirite matrem.*
Et vera, incessu, patuit Dea. ——— } Virg.

LONDON,
Printed for *Jacob Tonson*, at the *Judges Head* in
Chancery Lane near *Fleetstreet*, 1687.

TO THE
READER.

The nation is in too high a Ferment, for me to expect either fair War or even so much as fair Quarter from a Reader of the opposite Party. All Men are engag'd either on this side or that : and tho' Conscience is the common Word which is given by both, yet if a Writer fall among Enemies and cannot give the Marks of Their Conscience, he is knock'd down before the Reasons of his own are heard. A Preface, therefore, which is but a bespeaking of Favour, is altogether useless. What I desire the Reader should know concerning me, he will find in the Body of the Poem, if he have but the patience to peruse it. Only this Advertisement let him 10 *take before hand, which relates to the Merits of the Cause. No general Characters of Parties (call 'em either Sects or Churches) can be so fully and exactly drawn as to comprehend all the several Members of 'em ; at least all such as are receiv'd under that Denomination. For example : there are some of the Church by Law established who envy not Liberty of Conscience to Dissenters ; as being well satisfied that, according to their own Principles, they ought not to persecute them. Yet these, by reason of their fewness, I could not distinguish from the Numbers of the rest, with whom they are Embodied in one common Name : On the other side there are many of our Sects, and more indeed than I could reasonably have hop'd, who have withdrawn themselves from the Communion of the* Panther ; *and embrac'd this Gracious Indulgence of His Majesty in point of Toleration. But neither to the one nor the other of these is this Satyr any way intended :* 20 *'tis aim'd only at the refractory and disobedient on either side. For those who are come over to the Royal Party are consequently suppos'd to be out of Gunshot. Our physicians have observ'd, that in Process of Time, some Diseases have abated of their Virulence and have in a manner worn out their Malignity, so as to be no longer Mortal : and why may not I suppose the same concerning some of those who have formerly been Enemies to Kingly Government as well as Catholick Religion ? I hope they have now another Notion of both, as having found by Comfortable Experience that the doctrine of Persecution is far from being an Article of our Faith.*

'Tis not for any Private Man to Censure the Proceedings of a Foreign Prince ; but without suspicion of Flattery I may praise our own, who has taken contrary Measures, and those 30 *more suitable to the Spirit of Christianity. Some of the Dissenters, in their Addresses to His Majesty, have said that he has restor'd God to his Empire over Conscience : I Confess I dare not stretch the Figure to so great a boldness ; but I may safely say, that Conscience is the Royalty and Prerogative of every Private man. He is absolute in his own Breast, and accountable to no Earthly Power for that which passes only betwixt God and Him. Those who are driven into the Fold are, generally speaking, rather made Hypocrites than Converts.*

This Indulgence being granted to all the Sects, it ought in reason to be expected that they should both receive it, and receive it thankfully. For at this time of day to refuse the Benefit and adhere to those whom they have esteemed their Persecutors, what is it else, but publickly 40 *to own that they suffer'd not before for Conscience sake, but only out of Pride and Obstinacy to separate from a Church for those Impositions which they now judge may be lawfully obey'd ? After they have so long contended for their Classical Ordination (not to speak of Rites and Ceremonies) will they at length submit to an Episcopal ? If they can go so far out of Complaisance to their old Enemies, methinks a little reason should perswade 'em to take another step, and see whether that wou'd lead 'em.*

Of the receiving this Toleration thankfully, I shall say no more, than that they ought, and I doubt not they will consider from what hands they receiv'd it. 'Tis not from a Cyrus, *a Heathen*

Prince and a Foreigner, but from a Christian King, their Native Sovereign, who expects a Return in Specie *from them; that the Kindness which He has graciously shown them, may be retaliated on those of his own perswasion.*

As for the Poem in general, I will only thus far satisfie the Reader: *that it was neither impos'd on me nor so much as the Subject given me by any man. It was written during the last Winter and the beginning of this Spring; though with long interruptions of ill health and other hindrances. About a Fortnight before I had finish'd it, His Majesties Declaration for Liberty of Conscience came abroad: which if I had so soon expected, I might have spar'd myself the labour of writing many things which are contained in the third part of it. But I was always in some hope that the Church of* England *might have been persuaded to have* 10 *taken off the* Penal Lawes *and the* Test, *which was one Design of the Poem, when I propos'd to myself the writing of it.*

'Tis evident that some part of it was only occasional, and not first intended. I mean that defence of my self, to which every honest man is bound, when he is injuriously attacqu'd in Print: and I refer my Self to the judgment of those who have read the Answer *to the Defence of the late Kings Papers, and that of the Dutchess (in which last I was concerned) how charitably I have been represented there. I am now inform'd both of the Author and Supervisers of his Pamphlet, and will reply, when I think he can affront me: for I am of* Socrate's *Opinion, that all Creatures cannot. In the mean time let him consider whether he deserv'd not* 20 *a more severe reprehension then I gave him formerly; for using so little respect to the Memory of those whom he pretended to answer: and at his leisure look out for some Original Treatise of Humility, written by any Protestant in English, (I believe I may say in any other Tongue :) for the magnified Piece of* Duncomb *on that subject, which either he must mean, or none, and with which another of his Fellows has upbraided me, was Translated from the Spanish of* Rodriguez: *though with the omission of the* 17th, *the* 24th, *the* 25th, *and the last Chapter, which will be found in comparing of the Books.*

He would have insinuated to the world, that Her late Highness died not a Roman Catholick; he declares himself to be now satisfied to the contrary; in which he has given up the Cause: for matter of Fact was the Principal Debate betwixt us. In the mean time, he would dispute the Motives of her Change; how preposterously, let all men judge, when he seem'd to deny 30 *the Subject of the Controversy, the Change itself. And because I would not take up this ridiculous Challenge, he tells the World I cannot argue: but he may as well infer that a Catholic cannot fast because he will not take up the cudgels against* Mrs. James *to confute the Protestant Religion.*

I have but one word more to say concerning the Poem as such, and abstracting from the Matters, either Religious or Civil, which are handled in it. The first Part, consisting most in general Characters and Narration, I have endeavour'd to raise, and give it the Majestic Turn of Herolc Poesie. The second *being Matter of Dispute, and chiefly concerning Church Authority, I was obliged to make as plain and perspicuous as possibly I cou'd: yet not wholly neglecting the Numbers, though I had not frequent occasions for the Magnificence of Verse. The* third, 40 *which has more of the Nature of Domestick Conversation, is, or ought to be more free and familiar than the two former.*

There are in it two Episodes *or Fables, which are interwoven with the main Design; so that they are properly parts of it, though they are also distinct Stories of themselves. In both of these I have made use of the Common Places of* Satyr, *whether true or false, which are urg'd by the Members of the one Church against the other. At which I hope no reader of either party will be scandaliz'd, because they are not of my invention: but as old, to my knowledge, as the Times of* Boccace *and* Chawcer *on the one side, and as those of the Reformation on the other.*

THE HIND AND THE PANTHER.

A Milk white *Hind*, immortal and unchang'd,
Fed on the lawns and in the forest rang'd ;
Without unspotted, innocent within,
She fear'd no danger, for she knew no sin.
Yet had she oft been chas'd with horns and
   hounds
And Scythian shafts ; and many winged
   wounds
Aim'd at her Heart ; was often forc'd to fly,
And doom'd to death, though fated not to dy.
   Not so her young ; for their unequal line
Was Heroe's make, half humane, half divine.
Their earthly mold obnoxious was to fate,   11
Th' immortal part assum'd immortal state.
Of these a slaughtered army lay in bloud,
Extended o'er the *Caledonian* wood,
Their native walk ; whose vocal bloud arose
And cry'd for pardon on their perjur'd foes ;
Their fate was fruitful, and the sanguin seed,
Endu'd with souls, encreas'd the sacred
   breed.
So Captive *Israel* multiply'd in chains,
A numerous Exile ; and enjoy'd her pains.
With grief and gladness mixt, their mother
   view'd   21
Her martyr'd offspring, and their race
   renew'd ;
Their corps to perish, but their kind to last,
So much the deathless plant the dying fruit
   surpass'd.
   Panting and pensive now she ranged alone,
And wander'd in the kingdoms once Her own.
The common Hunt, though from their rage
   restrain'd
By sov'reign power, her company disdain'd :
Grin'd as They pass'd, and with a glaring eye
Gave gloomy signs of secret enmity.   30
'Tis true, she bounded by, and trip'd so light,
They had not time to take a steady sight,
For truth has such a face and such a meen
As to be lov'd needs only to be seen.
   The bloudy *Bear*, an *Independent* beast,
Unlick'd to form, in groans her hate ex-
   press'd.

Among the timorous kind the *Quaking Hare*
Profess'd neutrality, but would not swear.
Next her, the *Buffoon Ape*, as Atheists use,
Mimick'd all Sects and had his own to chuse :
Still when the Lyon look'd, his knees he bent,
And pay'd at Church a Courtier's Comple-
   ment.   42
The bristl'd *Baptist Boar*, impure as He,
(But whitn'd with the foam of sanctity)
With fat pollutions fill'd the sacred place
And mountains levell'd in his furious race,
So first rebellion founded was in grace.
But, since the mighty ravage which he made
In *German* Forests, had his guilt betray'd,
With broken tusks, and with a borrow'd
   name,   50
He shun'd the vengeance, and concealed the
   shame ;
So lurk'd in Sects unseen. With greater guile
False *Reynard* fed on consecrated spoil ;
The graceless beast by *Athanasius* first
Was chased from *Nice* ; then by *Socinus*
   nurs'd.
His impious race their blasphemy renew'd,
And natures King through nature's opticks
   view'd.
Revers'd they view'd him lessen'd to their
   eye,
Nor in an Infant could a God descry :   59
New swarming Sects to this obliquely tend
Hence they began, and here they all will end.
   What weight of ancient witness can pre-
      vail,
If private reason hold the publick scale ?
But, gratious God, how well dost thou provide
For erring judgments an unerring Guide !
Thy throne is darkness in th' abyss of light,
A blaze of glory that forbids the sight ;
O teach me to believe Thee thus conceal'd,
And search no farther than Thy self reveal'd ;
But her alone for my Directour take   70
Whom Thou hast promis'd never to forsake !
My thoughtless youth was wing'd with vain
   desires,
My manhood, long misled by wandring fires,
Follow'd false lights ; and when their glimps
   was gone,
My pride struck out new sparkles of her own.

Text from the second edition, 1687, except for
a few corrections of the stops, where the first
edition, which was of the same year, is right, and
for a few corrections noted.

Such was I, such by nature still I am,
Be Thine the glory and be mine the shame.
Good life be now my task : my doubts are
    done,
(What more could fright my faith, than
    Three in One ?)
Can I believe eternal God could lye   80
Disguis'd in mortal mold and infancy ?
That the great Maker of the world could dye?
And after that, trust my imperfect sense
Which calls in question his omnipotence ?
Can I my reason to my faith compell,
And shall my sight, and touch, and taste
    rebell ?
Superiour faculties are set aside,
Shall their subservient organs be my guide ?
Then let the moon usurp the rule of day,   89
And winking tapers shew the sun his way ;
For what my senses can themselves perceive
I need no revelation to believe.
Can they, who say the Host should be
    descry'd
By sense, define a body glorify'd ?
Impassible, and penetrating parts ?
Let them declare by what mysterious arts
He shot that body through th' opposing
    might
Of bolts and barrs impervious to the light,
And stood before his train confess'd in
    open sight.
    For since thus wondrously he pass'd, 'tis
        plain   100
One single place two bodies did contain,
And sure the same Omnipotence as well
Can make one body in more places dwell.
Let reason then at Her own quarry fly,
But how can finite grasp Infinity ?
    'Tis urg'd again, that faith did first com-
        mence
By miracles, which are appeals to sense,
And thence concluded that our sense must be
The motive still of credibility.
For latter ages must on former wait,   110
And what began belief, must propagate.
    But winnow well this thought, and you
        shall find,
'Tis light as chaff that flies before the wind.
Were all those wonders wrought by pow'r
    divine
As means or ends of some more deep design ?
Most sure as means, whose end was this
    alone,
To prove the god-head of th' eternal Son.

God thus asserted : man is to believe
Beyond what Sense and Reason can con-
    ceive.
And for mysterious things of faith rely   120
On the Proponent, heaven's authority.
If then our faith we for our guide admit,
Vain is the farther search of human wit,
As when the building gains a surer stay,
We take th' unuseful scaffolding away :
Reason by sense no more can understand,
The game is play'd into another hand.
Why chuse we then like Bilanders to creep
Along the coast, and land in view to keep,
When safely we may launch into the
    deep ?   130
In the same vessel which our Saviour bore
Himself the pilot, let us leave the shoar,
And with a better guide a better world
    explore.
Could He his god-head veil with flesh and
    bloud
And not veil these again to be our food ?
His grace in both is equal in extent ;
The first affords us life, the second nourish-
    ment.
And if he can, why all this frantick pain
To construe what his clearest words con-
    tain,
And make a riddle what He made so
    plain ?   140
To take up half on trust, and half to try,
Name it not faith, but bungling biggottry.
Both knave and fool the Merchant we may
    call
To pay great summs and to compound the
    small.
For who wou'd break with heav'n, and
    wou'd not break for all ?
Rest then, my soul, from endless anguish
    freed ;
Nor sciences thy guide, nor sense thy creed.
Faith is the best ensurer of thy bliss ;
The Bank above must fail before the venture
    miss.
But heav'n and heav'n-born faith are far
    from Thee,   150
Thou first Apostate to Divinity.
Unkennel'd range in thy Polonian Plains ;
A fiercer foe the insatiate Wolf remains.
    Too boastful Britain please thyself no
        more,
That beasts of prey are banish'd from thy
    shoar ;

The *Bear*, the *Boar*, and every salvage name,
Wild in effect, though in appearance tame,
Lay waste thy woods, destroy thy blissfull
   bow'r,
And, muzl'd though they seem, the mutes
   devour.
More haughty than the rest, the *wolfish*
   race   160
Appear with belly Gaunt and famish'd
   face :
Never was so deform'd a beast of Grace.
His ragged tail betwixt his leggs he wears
Close clap'd for shame, but his rough crest
   he rears,
And pricks up his predestinating ears.
His wild disorder'd walk, his hagger'd eyes,
Did all the bestial citizens surprize.
Though fear'd and hated, yet he ruled awhile,
As Captain or Companion of the spoil.   169
Full many a year his hatefull head had been
For tribute paid, nor since in *Cambria* seen :
The last of all the Litter scap'd by chance,
And from *Geneva* first infested *France*.
Some Authors thus his Pedigree will trace,
But others write him of an upstart Race :
Because of *Wickliff's* Brood no mark he
   brings
But his innate Antipathy to Kings.
These last deduce him from th' *Helvetian*
   kind   178
Who near the *Leman lake* his Consort lin'd.
That fi'ry *Zuynglius* first th' Affection bred,
And meagre *Calvin* blest the Nuptial Bed.
In *Israel* some believe him whelp'd long since,
When the proud *Sanhedrim* op-
   press'd the Prince,   *Vid. Pref.*
Or, since he will be *Jew*, derive *to* Heyl.
   him higher,   *Hist. of*
When *Corah* with his Brethren   *Presb.*
   did conspire,
From *Moyses* Hand the Sov'reign sway to
   wrest,
And *Aaron* of his Ephod to devest :
Till opening Earth made way for all to pass,
And cou'd not bear the Burd'n of a *class*.
The *Fox* and he came shuffl'd in the Dark,
If ever they were stow'd in *Noah's* Ark : 191
Perhaps not made ; for all their barking train
The Dog (a common species) will contain.
And some wild currs, who from their
   masters ran,
Abhorring the supremacy of man,
In woods and caves the rebel-race began.

O happy pair, how well have you encreas'd,
What ills in Church and State have you
   redress'd !
With Teeth untry'd and rudiments of Claws,
Your first essay was on your native Laws :
Those having torn with Ease and trampl'd
   down,   201
Your Fangs you fasten'd on the miter'd
   Crown,
And freed from God and Monarchy your
   Town.
What though your native kennel still be
   small
Bounded betwixt a Puddle and a Wall,
Yet your Victorious Colonies are sent
Where the North Ocean girds the Continent.
Quickned with fire below, your Monsters
   Breed,
In Fenny *Holland* and in fruitful *Tweed*.
And like the first the last effects to be   210
Drawn to the dreggs of a Democracy.
As, where in Fields the fairy rounds are
   seen,
A rank sow'r herbage rises on the Green ;
So, springing where these mid-night Elves
   advance,
Rebellion Prints the Foot-steps of the Dance.
Such are their Doctrines, such contempt
   they show
To Heaven above, and to their Prince
   below,
As none but Traytors and Blasphemers
   know.
God, like the Tyrant of the Skies is plac'd,
And Kings, like slaves, beneath the Crowd
   debas'd.   220
So fulsome is their food that Flocks refuse
To bite ; and only Dogs for Physick use.
As, where the Lightning runs along the
   Ground,
No husbandry can heal the blasting Wound,
Nor bladed Grass nor bearded Corn succeeds,
But Scales of Scurf, and Putrefaction breeds :
Such Warrs, such Waste, such fiery tracks of
   Dearth
Their Zeal has left, and such a teemless
   Earth.
But as the Poisons of the deadliest kind
Are to their own unhappy Coasts confin'd,
As only *Indian* Shades of sight deprive, 231
And Magick Plants will but in *Colchos* thrive ;
So Presby'try and Pestilential Zeal
Can only flourish in a Common-weal.

From *Celtique* Woods is chased the *wolfish*
Crew ;
But ah ! some Pity e'en to Brutes is due,
Their native Walks, methinks, they might
enjoy,
Curb'd of their native Malice to destroy.
Of all the Tyrannies on humane kind   239
The worst is that which Persecutes the mind.
Let us but weigh at what offence we strike,
'Tis but because we cannot think alike.
In punishing of this, we overthrow
The Laws of Nations and of Nature too
Beasts are the Subjects of Tyrannick sway,
Where still the stronger on the weaker Prey.
Man only of a softer mold is made ;
Not for his Fellows ruine, but their Aid.
Created kind, beneficent and free,
The noble Image of the Deity.   250
  One Portion of informing Fire was giv'n
To Brutes, the Inferiour Family of Heav'n :
The Smith Divine, as with a careless Beat,
Struck out the mute Creation at a Heat :
But when arriv'd at last to humane Race,
The Godhead took a deep consid'ring space :
And, to distinguish Man from all the rest,
Unlock'd the sacred Treasures of his Breast :
And Mercy mixt with reason did impart,
One to his Head, the other to his Heart :
Reason to Rule, but Mercy to forgive : 261
The first is Law, the last Prerogative.
And like his Mind his outward form
  appear'd
When issuing Naked to the wondring
  Herd,
He charm'd their Eyes, and for they lov'd
  they fear'd.
Not arm'd with horns of arbitrary might,
Or Claws to seize their furry spoils in Fight,
Or with increase of Feet t' o'ertake 'em in
  their flight.
Of easie shape, and pliant ev'ry way,
Confessing still the softness of his Clay,
And kind as Kings upon their Coronation-
  day :   271
With open Hands, and with extended space
Of Arms to satisfy a large embrace.
Thus kneaded up with Milk, the new made
  Man
His Kingdom o'er his Kindred world began :
Till Knowledg mis-apply'd, mis-understood,
And pride of Empire sour'd his Balmy Blood.
Then, first rebelling, his own stamp he coins ;
The Murth'rer *Cain* was latent in his Loins ;

And Blood began its first and loudest Cry
For diff'ring worship of the Deity.   281
Thus persecution rose, and farther Space
Produc'd the mighty hunter of his Race.
Not so the blessed *Pan* his flock encreased,
Content to fold 'em from the famish'd Beast :
Mild were his laws ; the Sheep and harmless
  Hind
Were never of the persecuting kind.
Such pity now the pious Pastor shows,
Such mercy from the *British* Lyon flows,
That both provide protection for their
  foes.   290
Oh happy Regions, *Italy* and *Spain*,
Which never did those monsters entertain !
The *Wolfe*, the *Bear*, the *Boar*, can there
  advance
No native claim of just inheritance.
And self preserving laws, severe in show,
May guard their fences from th' invading foe.
Where birth has plac'd 'em, let 'em safely
  share
The common benefit of vital air ;
Themselves unharmful, let them live un-
  harm'd ;
Their jaws disabl'd, and their claws disarm'd:
Here, only in nocturnal howlings bold, 301
They dare not seize the Hind nor leap the
  fold.
More pow'rful, and as vigilant as they,
The *Lyon* awfully forbids the prey.
Their rage repress'd, though pinch'd with
  famine sore,
They stand aloof, and tremble at his roar ;
Much is their hunger, but their fear is
  more.
  These are the chief ; to number o'er the
  rest
And stand, like *Adam*, naming ev'ry beast,
Were weary work ; nor will the Muse des-
  cribe   310
A slimy-born and sun-begotten Tribe :
Who, far from steeples and their sacred sound,
In fields their sullen conventicles found :
These gross, half animated lumps I leave ;
Nor can I think what thoughts they can
  conceive.
But if they think at all, 'tis sure no high'r
Than matter, put in motion, may aspire.
Souls that can scarce ferment their mass
  of clay ;
So drossy, so divisible are They,   319
As wou'd but serve pure bodies for allay :

Such souls as *Shards* produce, such beetle
   things
As only buz to heaven with ev'ning wings ;
Strike in the dark, offending but by chance,
Such are the blind-fold blows of ignorance.
They know not beings, and but hate a name,
To them the *Hind* and *Panther* are the same.
  The *Panther* sure the noblest, next the
   Hind,   327
And fairest creature of the spotted kind :
Oh, could her in-born stains be wash'd away,
She were too good to be a beast of Prey !
How can I praise, or blame, and not offend,
Or how divide the frailty from the friend ?
Her faults and vertues lye so mix'd, that she
Nor wholly stands condemn'd nor wholly free.
Then, like her injured *Lyon*, let me speak,
He cannot bend her, and he would not break.
Unkind already, and estrang'd in part,
The *Wolfe* begins to share her wandring
  heart.
Though unpolluted yet with actual ill,
She half commits, who sins but in Her
  will.   340
If, as our dreaming *Platonists* report,
There could be spirits of a middle sort,
Too black for heav'n, and yet too white for
  hell,
Who just dropt half-way done, nor lower fell;
So pois'd, so gently she descends from high,
It seems a soft dismission from the skie.
Her house not ancient, whatsoe'er pretence
Her clergy Heraulds make in her defence.
A second century not half-way run
Since the new honours of her blood begun.
A *Lyon* old, obscene, and furious made 351
By lust, compress'd her mother in a shade.
Then by a left-hand marr'age weds the Dame,
Covering adult'ry with a specious name :
So schism begot ; and sacrilege and she,
A well-match'd pair, got graceless heresie.
God's and Kings rebels have the same good
  cause,
To trample down divine and humane laws :
Both would be call'd Reformers, and their
  hate,
Alike destructive both to Church and State :
The fruit proclaims the plant ; a lawless
  Prince   361
By luxury reform'd incontinence,
By ruins, charity ; by riots abstinence.

Confessions, fasts and penance set aside ;
Oh with what ease we follow such a guide !
Where souls are starv'd and senses grati-
  fy'd !
Where marr'age pleasures midnight pray'r
  supply,
And mattin bells (a melancholy cry)
Are tun'd to merrier notes, *encrease and*
  multiply.
Religion shows a Rosie colour'd face, 370
Not hatter'd out with drudging works of
  grace ;
A down-hill Reformation rolls apace.
What flesh and blood wou'd croud the
  narrow gate,
Or, till they waste their pamper'd paunches,
  wait ?
All wou'd be happy at the cheapest rate.
  Though our lean faith these rigid laws has
  giv'n,
The full fed *Musulman* goes fat to heav'n ;
For his *Arabian* Prophet with delights
Of sense, allur'd his eastern Proselytes.
The jolly *Luther*, reading him, began 380
T' interpret Scriptures by his *Alcoran* ;
To grub the thorns beneath our tender feet
And make the paths of *Paradise* more sweet :
Bethought him of a wife, e'er half way gone,
(For 'twas uneasie travailing alone,)
And in this masquerade of mirth and love,
Mistook the bliss of heav'n for *Bacchanals*
  above.
Sure he presum'd of praise, who came to
  stock
Th' etherial pastures with so fair a flock ;
Burnish'd, and bat'ning on their food, to
  show   390
The diligence of carefull herds below.
  Our *Panther*, though like these she chang'd
  her head,
Yet, as the mistress of a monarch's bed,
Her front erect with majesty she bore,
The Crozier wielded and the Miter wore.
Her upper part of decent discipline
Shew'd affectation of an ancient line :
And fathers, councils, church and church's
  head,
Were on her reverend *Phylacteries* read.
But what disgrac'd and disavow'd the rest
Was *Calvin's* brand, that stigmatiz'd the
  beast.   401
Thus, like a creature of a double kind,
In her own labyrinth she lives confin'd.

---

344 done] *i.e.* down, *which the editors give.*

To foreign lands no sound of Her is come,
Humbly content to be despis'd at home.
Such is her faith, where good cannot be had,
At least she leaves the refuse of the bad.
Nice in her choice of ill, though not of
    best,
And least deform'd, because reform'd the
    least.
In doubtful points betwixt her diff'ring
    friends, 410
Where one for substance, one for sign con-
    tends,
Their contradicting terms she strives to joyn
Sign shall be substance, substance shall be
    sign.
A real presence all her sons allow,
And yet 'tis flat Idolatry to bow,
Because the God-head's there they know
    not how.
Her Novices are taught that bread and
    wine
Are but the visible and outward sign, 418
Receiv'd by those who in communion joyn.
But th' inward grace or the thing signify'd,
His blood and body who to save us dy'd,
The faithful this thing signify'd receive.
What is't those faithful then partake or
    leave ?
For what is signify'd and understood,
Is, by her own confession, flesh and blood.
Then, by the same acknowledgment, we
    know
They take the sign, and take the substance
    too.
The lit'ral sense is hard to flesh and blood,
But nonsense never can be understood.
    Her wild belief on ev'ry wave is tost, 430
But sure no Church can better morals boast.
True to her King her principles are found ;
Oh that her practice were but half so sound !
Stedfast in various turns of state she stood,
And seal'd her vow'd affection with her
    blood;
Nor will I meanly tax her constancy,
That int'rest or obligement made the tye,
(Bound to the fate of murdr'd Monarchy :)
(Before the sounding Ax so falls the Vine,
Whose tender branches round the Poplar
    twine.) 440
She chose her ruin, and resign'd her life,
In death undaunted as an *Indian* wife :
A rare example : But some souls we see
Grow hard, and stiffen with adversity :

Yet these by fortunes favours are undone,
Resolv'd into a baser form they run,
And bore the wind, but cannot bear the
    sun.
Let this be natures frailty or her fate,
Or *Isgrim's** counsel, her new chosen   * *The*
    mate ;   *Wolfe.*
Still she's the fairest of the fallen
    Crew, 450
No mother more indulgent but the true.
    Fierce to her foes, yet fears her force to try,
Because she wants innate auctority ;
For how can she constrain them to obey
Who has her self cast off the lawful sway ?
Rebellion equals all, and those who toil
In common theft, will share the common
    spoil.
Let her produce the title and the right
Against her old superiours first to fight ;
If she reform by Text, ev'n that's as plain
For her own Rebels to reform again. 461
As long as words a diff'rent sense will bear,
And each may be his own Interpreter,
Our ai'ry faith will no foundation find
The word's a weathercock for ev'ry wind :
The *Bear*, the *Fox*, the *Wolfe* by turns prevail,
The most in pow'r supplies the present gale.
The wretched *Panther* crys aloud for aid
To church and councils, whom she first
    betray'd ; 469
No help from Fathers or traditions train
Those ancient guides she taught us to disdain.
And by that scripture which she once abus'd
To Reformation, stands herself accus'd.
What bills for breach of laws can she prefer,
Expounding which she owns her self may err ?
And, after all her winding ways are try'd,
If doubts arise, she slips herself aside
And leaves the private conscience for the
    guide.
If then that conscience set th' offender free,
It bars her claim to church auctority. 480
How can she censure, or what crime pretend,
But Scripture may be constru'd to defend ?
Ev'n those whom for rebellion she transmits
To civil pow'r, her doctrine first acquits ;
Because no disobedience can ensue,
Where no submission to a Judge is due ;
Each judging for himself, by her consent,
Whom thus absolv'd she sends to punish-
    ment.
Suppose the Magistrate revenge her cause,
'Tis only for transgressing humane laws. 490

How answ'ring to its end a church is made,
Whose pow'r is but to counsel and perswade?
O solid rock, on which secure she stands!
Eternal house, not built with mortal hands!
Oh sure defence against th' infernal gate,
A patent during pleasure of the state!
  Thus is the *Panther* neither lov'd nor
    fear'd,
A mere mock Queen of a divided Herd;
Whom soon by lawful pow'r she might con-
    troll,
Her self a part submitted to the whole. 500
Then, as the Moon who first receives the light
By which she makes our nether regions bright,
So might she shine, reflecting from afar
The rays she borrowed from a better Star:
Big with the beams which from her mother
    flow
And reigning o'er the rising tides below:
Now, mixing with a salvage croud, she goes,
And meanly flatters her invet'rate foes,
Rul'd while she rules, and losing ev'ry hour
Her wretched remnants of precarious pow'r.
  One evening, while the cooler shade she
    sought,   511
Revolving many a melancholy thought,
Alone she walk'd, and look'd around in vain,
With ruful visage for her vanish'd train:
None of her sylvan subjects made their court;
Leveés and coucheés pass'd without resort.
So hardly can Usurpers manage well
Those whom they first instructed to rebel:
More liberty begets desire of more,
The hunger still encreases with the store.
Without respect they brush'd along the
    wood,   521
Each in his clan, and fill'd with loathsome
    food,
Ask'd no permission to the neighb'ring
    flood.
The *Panther*, full of inward discontent,
Since they wou'd goe, before 'em wisely went:
Supplying want of pow'r by drinking first,
As if she gave 'em leave to quench their
    thirst.
  Among the rest, the *Hind*, with fearful face
Beheld from far the common wat'ring-place,
Nor durst approach; till with an awful
    roar   530
The sovereign *Lyon* bad her fear no more.
Encourag'd thus, she brought her younglings
    nigh,
Watching the motions of her Patron's eye,

And drank a sober draught; the rest amaz'd
Stood mutely still, and on the stranger gaz'd:
Survey'd her part by part, and sought to
    find
The ten-horn'd monster in the harmless
    Hind,
Such as the *Wolfe* and *Panther* had design'd:
They thought at first they dream'd, for 'twas
    offence   539
With them, to question certitude of sense,
Their guide in faith; but nearer when
    they drew,
And had the faultless object full in view,
Lord, how they all admir'd her heav'nly
    hiew!
Some, who before her fellowship disdain'd,
Scarce, and but scarce, from inborn rage
    restrain'd,
Now frisk'd about her and old kindred
    feign'd.
Whether for love or int'rest, every sect
Of all the salvage nation shew'd respect:
The Vice-roy *Panther* could not awe the
    herd,   549
The more the company the less they fear'd.
The surly *Wolfe* with secret envy burst,
Yet cou'd not howl, the *Hind* had seen
    him first:
But what he durst not speak, the *Panther*
    durst.
  For when the herd suffis'd, did late repair
To ferney heaths and to their forest lare,
She made a mannerly excuse to stay,
Proffering the *Hind* to wait her half the way:
That since the Skie was clear, an hour of talk
Might help her to beguile the tedious walk.
With much good-will the motion was em-
    brac'd,   560
To chat a while on their adventures pass'd:
Nor had the grateful *Hind* so soon forgot
Her friend and fellow-suff'rer in the plot.
Yet wondring how of late she grew estrang'd,
Her forehead cloudy and her count'nance
    chang'd,
She thought this hour th' occasion would
    present
To learn her secret cause of discontent,
Which, well she hop'd, might be with ease
    redress d,
Considering Her a well-bred civil beast,
And more a Gentlewoman than the rest. 570
After some common talk what rumours ran,
The Lady of the spotted-muff began.

THE HIND AND THE PANTHER.

The Second Part.

DAME, said the *Panther*, times are mended well
Since late among the *Philistines* you fell.
The Toils were pitch'd, a spacious tract of ground
With expert Huntsmen was encompass'd round ;
The Enclosure narrow'd ; the sagacious pow'r
Of Hounds, and Death drew nearer, ev'ry Hour.
'Tis true, the younger *Lyon* scap'd the snare,
But all your priestly Calves lay strugling there ;
As sacrifices on their Altars laid ;   9⎫
While you their careful mother wisely fled ⎬
Not trusting destiny to save your head.   ⎭
For, whate'er Promises you have apply'd ⎫
To your unfailing Church, the surer side ⎬
Is four fair Leggs in danger to provide.   ⎭
And whate'er tales of *Peter's* Chair you tell, ⎫
Yet, saving Reverence of the Miracle, ⎬
The better luck was yours to 'scape so well. ⎭
    As I remember, said the sober *Hind*,
Those Toils were for your own dear self design'd,   19
As well as me ; and with the self same throw, ⎫
To catch the Quarry and the Vermin too, ⎬
(Forgive the sland'rous Tongues that call'd you so.)   ⎭
Howe'er you take it now, the common Cry
Then ran you down for your rank Loyalty ;
Besides, in Popery they thought you nurst,
(As evil tongues will ever speak the worst,)
Because some forms, and ceremonies some
You kept, and stood in the main question dumb.
Dumb you were born indeed ; but thinking long
The *Test*, it seems, at last has loos'd your tongue.   30
And, to explain what your forefathers meant,
By real presence in the Sacrament,
(After long fencing push'd against a wall,) ⎫
Your *salvo* comes, that he's not there at all : ⎬
There chang'd your faith, and what may change may fall.   ⎭
Who can believe what varies every day,
Nor ever was, nor will be at a stay ?
    Tortures may force the tongue untruths to tell,
And I ne'er own'd my self infallible,
Reply'd the *Panther* ; grant such Presence were,   40
Yet in your sense I never own'd it there.
A real *vertue* we by faith receive,
And that we in the sacrament believe.
    Then, said the *Hind*, as you the matter state,
Not only *Jesuits* can equivocate ;
For *real*, as you now the Word expound,
From Solid Substance dwindles to a Sound.
Methinks an *Esop's* fable you repeat ;
You know who took the Shadow for the Meat ;
Your Churchs substance thus you change at will,   50
And yet retain your former figure still.
I freely grant you spoke to save your Life,
For then you lay beneath the Butchers Knife.
Long time you fought, redoubl'd Batt'ry bore,
But, after all, against your self you swore ;
Your former self, for ev'ry Hour your form
Is chop'd and chang'd, like Winds before a Storm.
Thus Fear and Int'rest will prevail with some,
For all have not the Gift of Martyrdom.
    The *Panther* grin'd at this, and thus reply'd ;   60
That men may err was never yet deny'd.
But, if that common principle be true,
The *Cannon*, Dame, is level'd full at you.
But, shunning long disputes, I fain wou'd see
That wond'rous Wight, infallibility.
Is he from Heav'n this mighty Champion come
Or lodg'd below in subterranean *Rome* ?
First, seat him somewhere, and derive his Race,
Or else conclude that nothing has no place.

---

63 Cannon] *Warton, Scott, and others give* Canon

* Highly complicated double satire : this is the voice of the Hind

Suppose, (though I disown it,) said the
　　Hind,　　　　　　　　　　　　　　70
The certain Mansion were not yet assign'd,
The doubtful residence no proof can bring
Against the plain existence of the thing.
Because *Philosophers* may disagree,
If sight b' emission or reception be,
Shall it be thence infer'd I do not see ?
But you require an Answer positive,
Which yet, when I demand, you dare not
　　give ;
For Fallacies in Universals live.
I then affirm that this unfailing guide　　80
In Pope and gen'ral Councils must reside ;
Both lawful, both combin'd ; what one
　　decrees
By numerous Votes, the other Ratifies :
On this undoubted Sense the Church relies.
'Tis true some Doctors in a scantier space,
I mean in each apart contract the Place.
Some, who to greater length extend the
　　Line,
The Churches after acceptation join.
This last Circumference appears too wide,
The Church diffus'd is by the Council ty'd ;
As members by their Representatives　　91
Oblig'd to Laws which Prince and Senate
　　gives :
Thus some contract, and some enlarge the
　　space
In Pope and Council who denies the place,
Assisted from above with God's unfailing
　　grace ?
Those Canons all the needful points contain ;
Their sense so obvious, and their words so
　, plain,
That no disputes about the doubtful Text
Have, hitherto, the lab'ring world perplex'd :
If any shou'd in after times appear,　　100
New Councils must be call'd, to make the
　　meaning clear.
Because in them the pow'r supreme resides ;
And all the promises are to the Guides.
This may be taught with sound and safe
　　Defence :
But mark how sandy is your own pretence,
Who, setting Councils, Pope, and Church
　　aside,
Are ev'ry Man his own presuming Guide.
The sacred Books, you say, are full and plain,
And ev'ry needful point of Truth contain ;
All who can read, Interpreters may be :　110
Thus though your several Churches disagree,

Yet ev'ry Saint has to himself alone
The Secret of this Philosophick Stone.
These Principles your jarring Sects unite,
When diff'ring Doctors and Disciples fight.
Though *Luther*, *Zuinglius*, *Calvin*, holy
　　Chiefs,
Have made a Battel Royal of Beliefs ;
Or like wild Horses sev'ral ways have whirl'd
The tortur'd Text about the Christian
　　World ;
Each *Jehu* lashing on with furious force, 120
That *Turk* or *Jew* cou'd not have us'd it
　　worse.
No matter what dissension leaders make
Where ev'ry private man may save a stake :
Rul'd by the Scripture and his own advice,
Each has a blind by-path to Paradise ;
Where driving in a Circle slow or fast,
Opposing Sects are sure to meet at last.
A wondrous charity you have in Store
For all reform'd to pass the narrow Door :
So much, that *Mahomet* had scarcely more.
For he, kind Prophet, was for damning
　　none,　　　　　　　　　　　　　　131
But *Christ* and *Moyses* were to save their
　　own :
Himself was to secure his chosen race,
Though reason good for *Turks* to take the
　　place,
And he allow'd to be the better man
In virtue of his holier *Alcoran*.
　　True, said the *Panther*, I shall ne'er deny
My Breth'ren may be sav'd as well as I :
Though *Huguenots* contemn our ordination,
Succession, ministerial vocation,　　140
And *Luther*, more mistaking what he read,
Misjoins the sacred Body with the Bread ;
Yet, *Lady*, still remember I maintain
The Word in needfull points is only plain.
　　Needless or needful I not now contend,
For still you have a loophole for a friend,
(Rejoyn'd the Matron) but the rule you lay
Has led whole flocks and leads them still
　　astray
In weighty points, and full damnation's
　　way.
For did not *Arius* first, *Socinus* now　150
The Son's eternal god-head disavow,
And did not these by Gospel Texts alone
Condemn our doctrine, and maintain their
　　own ?
Have not all hereticks the same pretence,
To plead the Scriptures in their own defence ?

How did the *Nicene* council then decide
That strong debate, was it by Scripture
   try'd ?
No sure to those the Rebel would not yield,
Squadrons of Texts he marshal'd in the field ;
That was but civil war, an equal set,   160
Where Piles with piles, and Eagles Eagles
   met.
With Texts point-blank and plain he fac'd
   the Foe :
And did not *Sathan* tempt our Saviour so ?
The good old Bishops took a simpler way,
Each ask'd but what he heard his Father say,
Or how he was instructed in his youth,
And by tradition's force upheld the truth.
  The *Panther* smil'd at this, and when, said
   she,
Were those first Councils disallow'd by me ?
Or where did I at sure tradition strike,   170
Provided still it were Apostolick ?
Friend, said the *Hind*, you quit your former
   ground,
Where all your faith you did on Scripture
   found,
Now, 'tis tradition joined with holy writ ;
But thus your memory betrays your wit.
No, said the *Panther*, for in that I view
When your tradition's forg'd, and when 'tis
   true.
I set 'em by the rule, and as they square)
Or deviate from undoubted doctrine there, }
This Oral fiction, that old Faith declare. 180)
(*Hind*.) The Council steered, it seems, a
   diff'rent course,
They try'd the Scripture by tradition's force ;
But you tradition by the Scripture try ;)
Pursu'd, by sects, from this to that you fly, }
Nor dare on one foundation to rely.)
The Word is then depos'd, and in this view
You rule the Scripture, not the Scripture you.
Thus said the *Dame*, and, smiling, thus pur-
   su'd,
I see tradition then is disallow'd,
When not evinc'd by Scripture to be true,
And Scripture, as interpreted by you.   191
But here you tread upon unfaithfull ground ;
Unless you cou'd infallibly expound.
Which you reject as odious Popery,
And throw that doctrine back with scorn
   on me.

<hr>

158 those] *Broughton, Scott, and others give*
that

Suppose we on things traditive divide,
And both appeal to Scripture to decide ;
By various texts we both uphold our claim
Nay, often ground our titles on the same :
After long labour lost, and times expence,
Both grant the words and quarrel for the
   sense.   201
Thus all disputes for ever must depend ;
For no dumb rule can controversies end.
Thus when you said tradition must be try'd
By Sacred Writ, whose sense your selves
   decide,
You said no more, but that your selves
   must be
The judges of the Scripture sense, not we.
Against our church tradition you declare,
And yet your Clerks would sit in *Moyses*
   chair :   209
At least 'tis prov'd against your argument,
The rule is far from plain, where all dissent.
  If not by Scriptures, how can we be sure,
(Replied the *Panther*) what tradition's pure ?
For you may palm upon us new for old,
All, as they say, that glitters is not gold.
  How but by following her, reply'd the
   dame,
To whom deriv'd from sire to son they came ;
Where ev'ry age do's on another move,
And trusts no farther than the next above ;
Where all the rounds like *Jacob's* ladder
   rise,   220
The lowest hid in earth, the topmost in the
   skyes ?
  Sternly the salvage did her answer mark,
Her glowing eye-balls glitt'ring in the dark,
And said but this, since lucre was your
   trade,
Succeeding times such dreadfull gaps have
   made
'Tis dangerous climbing : to your sons and
   you
I leave the ladder, and its omen too.
  (*Hind*.) The *Panther's* breath was ever
   fam'd for sweet,
But from the *Wolf* such wishes oft I meet :
You learn'd this language from the blatant
   beast,   230
Or rather did not speak, but were possess'd.
As for your answer, 'tis but barely urg'd ;
You must evince tradition to be forg'd ;
Produce plain proofs ; unblemished authors
   use
As ancient as those ages they accuse ;

Till when 'tis not sufficient to defame :
An old possession stands, till Elder quitts
    the claim.
Then for our int'rest, which is nam'd alone
To load with envy, we retort your own.
For when traditions in your faces fly,   240
Resolving not to yield, you must decry :
As when the cause goes hard, the guilty man
Excepts, and thins his jury all he can ;
So when you stand of other aid bereft,
You to the twelve Apostles would be left.
Your friend the *Wolfe* did with more craft
    provide
To set those toys traditions quite aside :
And *Fathers* too, unless when reason spent
He cites 'em but sometimes for ornament.
But, Madam *Panther*, you, though more
    sincere,   250
Are not so wise as your Adulterer :
The private spirit is a better blind
Than all the dodging tricks your authours
    find.
For they who left the Scripture to the ⎫
    crowd,   ⎬
Each for his own peculiar judge allow'd ; ⎪
The way to please 'em was to make 'em ⎭
    proud.
Thus with full sails they ran upon the shelf ;
Who cou'd suspect a couzenage from him-
    self ?
On his own reason safer 'tis to stand,
Than be deceiv'd and damn'd at second
    hand.   260
But you who *Fathers* and traditions take
And garble some, and some you quite forsake,
Pretending church auctority to fix,
And yet some grains of private spirit mix,
Are like a *Mule* made up of diff'ring seed,
And that's the reason why you never breed ;
At least not propagate your kind abroad,
For home-dissenters are by statutes aw'd.
And yet they grow upon you ev'ry day, ⎫
While you (to speak the best) are at a stay, ⎬
For sects that are extremes, abhor a ⎭
    middle way.   271
Like tricks of state, to stop a raging flood, ⎫
Or mollify a mad-brain'd Senate's mood : ⎬
Of all expedients never one was good. ⎭
Well may they argue, (nor can you deny,)
If we must fix on church auctority,
Best on the best, the fountain, not the
    flood,
That must be better still, if this be good.

Shall she command who has herself rebell'd ?
Is *Antichrist* by *Antichrist* expell'd ?   280
Did we a lawfull tyranny displace,
To set aloft a bastard of the race ?
Why all these wars to win the Book, if we ⎫
Must not interpret for our selves, but she ? ⎬
Either be wholly slaves or wholly free. ⎭
For *purging* fires traditions must not fight ;
But they must prove Episcopacy's right :
Thus those led horses are from service freed ;
You never mount 'em but in time of need.
Like mercenary's, hir'd for home defence,
They will not serve against their native
    Prince.   291
Against domestick foes of *Hierarchy*
These are drawn forth, to make fanaticks fly ;
But, when they see their country-men at ⎫
    hand.   ⎪
Marching against 'em under church-com- ⎬
    mand,   ⎪
Streight they forsake their colours and dis- ⎭
    band.
    Thus she, nor cou'd the *Panther* well
    enlarge ;
With weak defence against so strong a charge;
But said, for what did Christ his Word
    provide,
If still his church must want a living
    guide ?   300
And if all saving doctrines are not there,
Or sacred Pen-men could not make 'em clear,
From after-ages we should hope in vain
For truths, which men inspir'd, cou'd not
    explain.
    Before the Word was written, said the
    Hind,
Our Saviour preached his Faith to humane
    kind ;
From his Apostles the first age receiv'd   307
Eternal truth, and what they taught, believ'd.
Thus by tradition faith was planted first ;
Succeeding flocks succeeding Pastours nurs'd.
This was the way our wise Redeemer chose, ⎫
(Who sure could all things for the best ⎪
    dispose,)   ⎬
To fence his fold from their encroaching ⎪
    foes. ⎭
He cou'd have writ himself, but well foresaw
Th' event would be like that of *Moyses* law ;
Some difference wou'd arise, some doubts
    remain,
Like those which yet the jarring *Jews* main-
    tain.

No written laws can be so plain, so pure,
But wit may gloss and malice may obscure ;
Not those indited by his first command, 320
A Prophet grav'd the text, an Angel held
    his hand.
<u>Thus faith was e'er the written word ap-
    pear'd,
And men believ'd, not what they read, but
    heard.</u>
But since the Apostles cou'd not be confin'd
To these, or those, but severally design'd
Their large commission round the world to
    blow,
To spread their faith they spread their
    labours too.
Yet still their absent flock their pains did
    share ;
They hearken'd still, for love produces care.
And as mistakes arose, or discords fell, 330
Or bold seducers taught 'em to rebel,
As charity grew cold or faction hot,
Or long neglect their lessons had forgot,
For all their wants they wisely did provide,
And preaching by Epistles was supply'd :
So, great Physicians cannot all attend,
But some they visit and to some they send.
Yet all those letters were not writ to all,
Nor first intended, but occasional
Their absent sermons ; nor if they contain
All needfull doctrines, are those doctrines
    plain.   341
Clearness by frequent preaching must be
    wrought ;
They writ but seldom, but they daily taught.
And what one Saint has said of holy *Paul*,
He darkly writ, is true apply'd to all.
For this obscurity cou'd heav'n provide ⎫
More prudently than by a living guide, ⎬
As doubts arose, the difference to decide ? ⎭
A guide was therefore needfull, therefore
    made ;
And, if appointed, sure to be obey'd.   350
Thus, with due reverence to th' Apostles
    writ,
By which my sons are taught, to which, I
    submit,
I think, those truths their sacred works
    contain
The church alone can certainly explain ;
That following ages, leaning on the past,
May rest upon the Primitive at last.
Nor would I thence the word no rule infer,
But none without the church interpreter ;

Because, as I have urg'd before, 'tis mute,
And is it self the subject of dispute.   360
But what th' Apostles their successors ⎫
    taught,   ⎮
They to the next, from them to us is ⎬
    brought,   ⎮
Th' undoubted sense which is in Scripture ⎭
    sought.
From hence the Church is arm'd, when ⎫
    errours rise,   ⎮
To stop their entrance, and prevent sur- ⎬
    prise ;   ⎮
And safe entrench'd within, her foes with- ⎭
    out defies.
By these all festring sores her counsels ⎫
    heal,   ⎮
Which time or has disclos'd or shall ⎬
    reveal,   ⎮
For discord cannot end without a last ⎭
    appeal.
Nor can a council national decide,   370 ⎫
But with subordination to her Guide, ⎬
(I wish the cause were on that issue try'd.) ⎭
Much less the scripture ; for suppose debate
Betwixt pretenders to a fair estate,
Bequeath'd by some Legator's last intent ;
(Such is our dying Saviour's Testament :)
The will is prov'd, is open'd, and is read ;
The doubtfull heirs their diff'ring titles plead :
All vouch the words their int'rest to main-
    tain,
And each pretends by those his cause is
    plain.   380
Shall then the testament award the right ?
No, that's the *Hungary* for which they fight ;
The field of battel, subject of debate ;
The thing contended for, the fair estate.
The sense is intricate, 'tis onely clear
What vowels and what consonants are there.
Therefore 'tis plain, its meaning must be try'd
Before some judge appointed to decide.
    Suppose, (the fair Apostate said,) I grant,
The faithfull flock some living guide should
    want,   390
Your arguments an endless chase persue : ⎫
Produce this vaunted Leader to our view, ⎬
This mighty *Moyses* of the chosen crew. ⎭
    The Dame, who saw her fainting foe retir'd, ⎫
With force renew'd, to victory aspired ; ⎮
(And looking upward to her kindred sky, ⎬
As once our Saviour own'd his Deity, ⎮
Pronounc'd his words—*she whom ye seek* ⎮
    am I.)   ⎭

Nor less amazed this voice the *Panther* heard
Than were those *Jews* to hear a god declar'd.
Then thus the matron modestly renew'd ;
Let all your prophets and their sects be
   view'd,   402
And see to which of 'em your selves think fit
The conduct of your conscience to submit :
Each Proselyte would vote his Doctor best,
With absolute exclusion to the rest :
Thus wou'd your *Polish* Diet disagree,
And end, as it began, in Anarchy ;
Your self the fairest for election stand,
Because you seem crown-gen'ral of the land ;
But soon against your superstitious lawn 411
Some Presbyterian Sabre wou'd be drawn :
In your establish'd laws of sov'raignty   ⎫
The rest some fundamental flaw wou'd see, ⎬
And call Rebellion gospel-liberty.   ⎭
To church-decrees your articles require
Submission modify'd, if not entire ;
Homage deny'd, to censures you proceed ;
But when *Curtana* will not doe the deed,
You lay that pointless clergy-weapon by, 420
And to the laws, your sword of justice fly.
Now this your sects the more unkindly take,
(Those prying varlets hit the blots you make)
Because some ancient friends of yours declare,
Your onely rule of faith the Scriptures are,
Interpreted, by men of judgment sound,
Which ev'ry sect will for themselves expound:
Nor think less rev'rence to their doctours due
For sound interpretation, than to you.
If then, by able heads, are understood   430
Your brother prophets, who reform'd abroad;
Those able heads expound a wiser way,
That their own sheep their shepherd shou'd
   obey.
But if you mean your selves are onely ⎫
   sound,   ⎪
That doctrine turns the reformation   ⎬
   round,   ⎪
And all the rest are false reformers found. ⎭
Because in sundry Points you stand alone, ⎫
Not in Communion join'd with any one ; ⎬
And therefore must be all the Church, or ⎪
   none.   ⎭
Then, till you have agreed whose judge is
   best,   440
Against this forc'd submission they protest :
While *sound* and *sound* a different sense
   explains,
Both play at hard-head till they break their
   brains :

And from their Chairs each other's force
   defy,
While unregarded thunders vainly fly.
I pass the rest, because your Church alone
Of all Usurpers best cou'd fill the Throne.
But neither you, nor any sect beside   ⎫
For this high office can be qualify'd   ⎪
With necessary Gifts requir'd in such a ⎬
   Guide.   450 ⎪
For that which must direct the whole ⎫
   must be   ⎪
Bounc. in one Bond of Faith and Unity : ⎬
But all your sev'ral Churches disagree. ⎭
The *Consubstantiating* Church and Priest
Refuse Communion to the *Calvinist* ;
The *French* reform'd, from Preaching you ⎫
   restrain,   ⎪
Because you judge their Ordination vain ; ⎬
And so they judge of yours, but Donors ⎪
   must ordain.   ⎭
In short, in Doctrine, or in Discipline 459
Not one reform'd, can with another join :
But all from each, as from Damnation fly ;
No Union they pretend, but in *Non-Popery*.
Nor, should their Members in a Synod meet,
Cou'd any Church presume to mount the
   Seat
Above the rest, their discords to decide ;
None wou'd obey, but each would be the
   Guide :
And face to face dissensions would encrease ;
For only distance now preserves the Peace.
All in their Turns accusers and accus'd,
Babel was never half so much confus'd. 470
What one can plead, the rest can plead as ⎫
   well ;   ⎪
For amongst equals lies no last appeal, ⎬
And all confess themselves are fallible. ⎭
Now, since you grant some necessary Guide,
All who can err are justly laid aside :
Because a trust so sacred to confer   ⎫
Shows want of such a sure Interpreter, ⎬
And how can he be needful who can err ? ⎭
Then granting that unerring guide we want,
That such there is you stand obliged to
   grant :   480
Our Saviour else were wanting to supply
Our needs and obviate that Necessity.
It then remains that Church can only be
The guide which owns unfailing certainty ;
Or else you slip your hold, and change your
   side,
Relapsing from a necessary Guide.

But this annex'd Condition of the Crown,
Immunity from Errours, you disown,
Here then you shrink, and lay your weak
    pretensions down.
For petty Royalties you raise debate ;   490
But this unfailing Universal State
You shun : nor dare succeed to such a
    glorious weight.
And for that cause those Promises detest
With which our Saviour did his Church
    invest :
But strive t' evade, and fear to find 'em true,
As conscious they were never meant to you :
All which the mother church asserts her own,
And with unrivall'd claim ascends the throne.
So when of old th' Almighty Father sate
In Council, to redeem our ruin'd state, 500
Millions of millions, at a distance round,
Silent the sacred Consistory crown'd,
To hear what mercy mixt with Justice
    cou'd propound.
All prompt with eager pity, to fulfil
The full extent of their Creatour's will :
But when the stern conditions were declar'd,
A mournful whisper through the host was
    heard,
And the whole hierarchy, with heads hung
    down,
Submissively declin'd the pondrous proffer'd
    crown.   509
Then, not till then, th' eternal Son from high
Rose in the strength of all the Deity ;
Stood forth t' accept the terms, and
    underwent
A weight which all the frame of heav'n
    had bent,
Nor he Himself cou'd bear, but as omni-
    potent.
Now, to remove the least remaining doubt,
That even the blear-ey'd sects may find her
    out,
Behold what heavenly rays adorn her brows,
What from his Wardrobe her belov'd allows
To deck the wedding-day of his unspotted
    spouse.   519
Behold what marks of Majesty she brings ;
Richer than antient heirs of Eastern kings :
Her right hand holds the sceptre and the
    keys,
To show whom she commands, and who
    obeys :
With these to bind or set the sinner free,
With that t' assert spiritual Royalty.

One in herself, not rent by
    Schism, but sound,   *Marks of the Catholick Church from the Nicene Creed.*
Entire, one solid shining Diamond,
Not Sparkles shattered into Sects
    like you,
One is the Church, and must be
    to be true :
One central principle of unity.   530
As undivided, so from errours free,
As one in faith, so one in sanctity.
Thus she, and none but she, th' insulting
    Rage
Of Hereticks oppos'd from Age to Age :
Still when the Giant-brood invades her
    Throne,
She stoops from Heav'n and meets 'em
    half way down,
And with paternal Thunder vindicates her
    Crown.
But like *Egyptian* Sorcerers you stand,
And vainly lift aloft your Magick Wand
To sweep away the Swarms of Vermin
    from the Land.   540
You cou'd like them, with like infernal
    Force
Produce the Plague, but not arrest the
    Course.
But when the Boils and Botches, with dis-
    grace
And publick Scandal sat upon the Face,
Themselves attack'd, the *Magi* strove no
    more,
They saw God's Finger, and their Fate
    deplore ;
Themselves they cou'd not Cure of the
    dishonest sore.
    Thus one, thus pure, behold her largely
    spread
Like the fair Ocean from her Mother-Bed ;
From East to West triumphantly she rides,
All Shoars are water'd by her wealthy
    Tides.   551
The Gospel-sound, diffus'd from Pole to
    Pole,
Where winds can carry and where waves can
    roll.
The self same doctrin of the Sacred Page
Convey'd to ev'ry clime, in ev'ry age.
    Here let my sorrow give my satyr place,
To raise new blushes on my *British* race ;

543 Botches] *Editors till Christie wrongly give*
Blotches

Our sayling Ships like common shoars we
   use,
And through our distant Colonies diffuse
The draughts of Dungeons and the stench
   of stews,   560
Wnom, when their home-bred honesty is lost,
We disembogue on some far *Indian* coast ;
Thieves Pandars, Palliards, sins of ev'ry sort ;
Those are the manufactures we export ;
And these the *Missioners* our zeal has
   made :
For, with my Countrey's pardon be it said,
Religion is the least of all our trade.

   Yet some improve their traffick more than
   we,
For they on gain, their only God, rely :
And set a publick price on piety.   570
Industrious of the needle and the chart,
They run full sail to their *Japponian* Mart ;
Prevention fear, and prodigal of fame
Sell all of Christian to the very name ;
Nor leave enough of that to hide their
   naked shame.

   Thus of three marks, which in the Creed
   we view,
Not one of all can be apply'd to you :
Much less the fourth ; in vain alas you seek
Th' ambitious title of Apostolick :   579
God-like descent ! 'tis well your bloud can be
Prov'd noble in the third or fourth degree :
For all of ancient that you had before,
(I mean what is not borrow'd from our
   store)
Was Errour fulminated o'er and o'er.
Old Heresies condemned in ages past,
By care and time recover'd from the blast.
'Tis said with ease, but never can be prov'd,
The church her old foundations has remov'd,
And built new doctrines on unstable sands :
Judge that, ye winds and rains ; you prov'd
   her, yet she stands.   590
Those ancient doctrines charg'd on her for
   new,
Shew when, and how, and from what hands
   they grew.
We claim no pow'r, when Heresies grow bold,
To coin new faith, but still declare the old.
How else cou'd that obscene disease be
   purg'd
When controverted texts are vainly urg'd ?
To prove tradition new, there's somewhat
   more
Requir'd, than saying, 'twas not us'd before.

Those monumental arms are never stirr'd,
Till Schism or Heresie call down *Goliah's*
   sword.   600
  Thus, what you call corruptions, are in
   truth,
The first plantations of the gospel's youth,
Old standard faith : but cast your eyes
   again,
And view those errours which new sects
   maintain,
Or which of old disturb'd the churches
   peaceful reign ;
And we can point each period of the time,
When they began, and who begot the crime ;
Can calculate how long the eclipse endur'd,
Who interpos'd, what digits were obscur'd :
Of all which are already pass'd away,   610
We know the rise, the progress and decay.

  Despair at our foundations then to strike,
Till you can prove your faith Apostolick ;
A limpid stream drawn from the native
   source ;
Succession lawfull in a lineal course.
Prove any Church, oppos'd to this our head,
So one, so pure, so unconfin'dly spread,
Under one chief of the spiritual state,
The members all combin'd, and all sub-
   ordinate.
Show such a seamless coat, from schism so
   free,   620
In no communion joined with heresie :
If such a one you find, let truth prevail :
Till when, your weights will in the balance
   fail :
A church unprincipl'd kicks up the scale.

  But if you cannot think (nor sure you can
Suppose in God what were unjust in man,)
That he, the fountain of eternal grace,
Should suffer falsehood for so long a space
To banish truth and to usurp her place ;
That seav'n successive ages should be lost
And preach damnation at their proper
   cost ;   631
That all your erring ancestours should die
Drown'd in the Abyss of deep Idolatry ;
If piety forbid such thoughts to rise,
Awake, and open your unwilling eyes :
God has left nothing for each age undone,
From this to that wherein he sent his Son :
Then think but well of him, and half your
   work is done.

─────────────────────

630 seav'n] nine *ed.* 2.

See how his Church, adorn'd with ev'ry grace,
With open arms, a kind forgiving face, 640
Stands ready to prevent her long-lost sons embrace.

Not more did *Joseph* o'er his brethren weep,
Nor less himself cou'd from discovery keep,
When in the crowd of suppliants they were seen,
And in their crew his best-beloved *Benjamin*.

That pious *Joseph* in the church behold,   *The renunciation of the Benedictines to the Abby Lands.*
To feed your famine, and refuse your gold ;
The *Joseph* you exil'd, the *Joseph* whom you sold.

Thus, while with heav'nly charity she spoke, 649
A streaming blaze the silent shadows broke ;
Shot from the skyes; a cheerful azure light;
The birds obscene to forests wing'd their flight,
And gaping graves receiv'd the wand'ring guilty spright.

Such were the pleasing triumphs of the sky
For *James* his late nocturnal victory ;
The pledge of his Almighty patron's love,
The fire-works which his angel made above.

I saw myself the lambent easie light   *Poeta loquitur.*
Gild the brown horrour and dispell the night ;
The messenger with speed the tidings bore ;
News which three lab'ring nations did restore ; 661
But heav'ns own *Nuntius* was arrived before.

By this the *Hind* had reached her lonely cell,
And vapours rose, and dews unwholesome fell,
When she, by frequent observation wise,
As one who long on heav'n had fix'd her eyes,
Discern'd a change of weather in the skyes.

The Western borders were with crimson spread,
The moon descending look'd all flaming red ;
She thought good manners bound her to invite 670
The stranger Dame to be her guest that night.

'Tis true, coarse dyet and a short repast,
(She said) were weak inducements to the tast
Of one so nicely bred, and so unus'd to fast;
But what plain fare her cottage cou'd afford,
A hearty welcome at a homely board
Was freely hers ; and to supply the rest,
An honest meaning, and an open breast.
Last, with content of mind, the poor man's Wealth ;
A grace-cup to their common Patron's health. 680

This she desired her to accept, and stay,
For fear she might be wilder'd in her way,
Because she wanted an unerring guide.
And then the dew-drops on her silken hide
Her tender constitution did declare,
Too Lady-like a long fatigue to bear,
And rough inclemencies of raw nocturnal air.
But most she fear'd that, travelling so late,
Some evil-minded beasts might lye in wait,
And without witness wreak their hidden hate. 690

The *Panther*, though she lent a listening ear,
Had more of *Lyon* in her than to fear :
Yet wisely weighing, since she had to deal
With many foes, their numbers might prevail,
Returned her all the thanks she could afford ;
And took her friendly hostess at her word,
Who ent'ring first her lowly roof, (a shed
With hoary moss and winding Ivy spread,
Honest enough to hide an humble Hermit's head,)
Thus graciously bespoke her welcome guest:
So might these walls, with your fair presence blest, 701
Become your dwelling-place of everlasting rest,
Not for a night, or quick revolving year,
Welcome an owner, not a sojourner.
This peaceful Seat my poverty secures,
War seldom enters but where wealth allures
Nor yet despise it, for this poor aboad
Has oft receiv'd and yet receives a god ;
A god, victorious of the stygian race,
Here laid his sacred limbs, and sanctified the place. 710

This mean retreat did mighty *Pan* contain;
Be emulous of him, and pomp disdain,
And dare not to debase your soul to gain.
  The silent stranger stood amaz'd to see
Contempt of wealth, and wilfull poverty :
And, though ill habits are not soon con-
    troll'd,
A while suspended her desire of gold.

But civilly drew in her sharpn'd paws,
Not violating hospitable laws,
And pacify'd her tail and lick'd her frothy
    jaws.   720
  The *Hind* did first her country Cates
    provide ;
Then couch'd her self securely by her
    side.

THE HIND AND THE PANTHER.

The Third Part.

MUCH malice mingl'd with a little wit
Perhaps may censure this mysterious writ :
Because the Muse has peopl'd *Caledon*
With *Panthers*, *Bears* and *Wolves*, and
    beasts unknown,
As if we were not stock'd with monsters of
    our own.
Let *Æsop* answer, who has set to view,
Such kinds as *Greece* and *Phrygia* never
    knew ;
And mother *Hubbard* in her homely dress
Has sharply blam'd a *British Lioness*,
That *Queen*, whose feast the factious rabble
    keep,   10
Expos'd obscenely naked and a-sleep.
Led by those great examples, may not I
The wanted organs of their words supply ?
If men transact like brutes, 'tis equal then
For brutes to claim the privilege of men.
  Others our *Hind* of folly will endite,
To entertain a dang'rous guest by night.
Let those remember, that she cannot dye
Till rolling time is lost in round eternity ;
Nor need she fear the *Panther*, though un-
    tam'd,   20
Because the *Lyon's* peace was now proclaim'd;
The wary salvage would not give offence,
To forfeit the protection of her *Prince* ;
But watch'd the time her vengeance to
    compleat,
When all her furry sons in frequent Senate
    met.
Mean while she quench'd her fury at the floud
And with a Lenten sallad cool'd her bloud.
Their commons, though but course, were
    nothing scant,
Nor did their minds an equal banquet want.

For now the *Hind*, whose noble nature
    strove   30
T' express her plain simplicity of love,
Did all the honours of her house so well,
No sharp debates disturb'd the friendly meal.
She turn'd the talk, avoiding that extreme,
To common dangers past, a sadly pleasing
    theam ;
Remembering ev'ry storm which toss'd the
    state,
When both were objects of the publick hate,
And drop'd a tear betwixt for her own
    children's fate.
  Nor fail'd she then a full review to make
Of what the *Panther* suffer'd for her sake. 40
Her lost esteem, her truth, her loyal care,
Her faith unshaken to an exil'd Heir,
Her strength t' endure, her courage to defy,
Her choice of honourable infamy.
On these prolixly thankfull, she enlarg'd,
Then with acknowledgments her self she
    charg'd :
For friendship of it self, an holy tye,
Is made more sacred by adversity.
Now should they part, malicious tongues
    wou'd say,
They met like chance companions on the
    way,   50
Whom mutual fear of robbers had possess'd ;
While danger lasted, kindness was profess'd ;
But that once o'er, the short-liv'd union ends,
The road divides, and there divide the friends.
  The *Panther* nodded when her speech was
    done,
And thanked her coldly in a hollow tone.
But said, her gratitude had gone too far
For common offices of Christian care.

If to the lawfull Heir she had been true,
She paid but *Cæsar* what was *Cæsar's* due. 60
I might, she added, with like praise describe
Your suff'ring sons, and so return your
    bribe ;
But incense from my hands is poorly priz'd,
For gifts are scorn'd where givers are despis'd.
I serv'd a turn, and then was cast away ; ⎫
You, like the gawdy fly, your wings display, ⎬
And sip the sweets, and bask in your Great ⎪
    Patron's day. ⎭

  This heard, the *Matron* was not slow to
    find
What sort of malady had seiz'd her mind :
Disdain, with gnawing envy, fell despight, 70
And canker'd malice stood in open sight :
Ambition, int'rest, pride without controul,
And jealousie, the jaundice of the soul ;
Revenge, the bloudy minister of ill,
With all the lean tormenters of the will.
'Twas easie now to guess from whence arose
Her new made union with her ancient foes.
Her forc'd civilities, her faint embrace,
Affected kindness with an alter'd face :
Yet durst she not too deeply probe the
    wound, 80
As hoping still the nobler parts were sound ;
But strove with Anodynes t' asswage the
    smart,
And mildly thus her med'cine did impart.
  Complaints of Lovers help to ease their
    pain ;
It shows a Rest of kindness to complain,
A friendship loth to quit its former hold,
And conscious merit may be justly bold.
But much more just your jealousie would
    show,
If others good were injury to you :
Witness ye heav'ns how I rejoice to see 90
Rewarded worth, and rising loyalty.
Your Warrior Offspring that upheld the
    crown,
The scarlet honours of your peacefull gown,
Are the most pleasing objects I can find,
Charms to my sight, and cordials to my
    mind :
When vertue spooms before a prosperous
    gale,
My heaving wishes help to fill the sail ;
And if my pray'rs for all the brave were
    heard,
Cæsar should still have such, and such should
    still reward.

  The labour'd earth your pains have sow'd
    and till'd : 100
'Tis just you reap the product of the field.
Yours be the harvest, 'tis the beggars gain
To glean the fallings of the loaded wain.
Such scatter'd ears as are not worth your ⎫
    care, ⎪
Your charity for alms may safely spare, ⎬
And alms are but the vehicles of pray'r. ⎭
My daily bread is litt'rally implor'd,
I have no barns nor granaries to hoard ;
If *Cæsar* to his own his hand extends, ⎫
Say which of yours his charity offends: 110 ⎬
You know, he largely gives, to more than ⎪
    are his friends. ⎭
Are you defrauded when he feeds the poor ?
Our mite decreases nothing of your store ;
I am but few, and by your fare you see
My crying sins are not of luxury.
Some juster motive sure your mind with- ⎫
    draws, ⎪
And makes you break our friendships holy ⎬
    laws, ⎪
For barefac'd envy is too base a cause. ⎭
  Show more occasion for your discontent ;
Your love, the *Wolf*, wou'd help you to in-
    vent. 120
Some *German* quarrel, or, as times go now,
Some *French*, where force is uppermost, will
    doe.
When at the fountains head, as merit ought
To claim the place, you take a swilling
    draught,
How easie 'tis an envious eye to throw
And tax the sheep for troubling streams
    below ;
Or call her, (when no farther cause you
    find,)
An enemy profess'd of all your kind !
But then, perhaps, the wicked world wou'd
    think
The *Wolf* design'd to eat as well as drink. 130
  This last allusion gaul'd the *Panther* more,
Because indeed it rubb'd upon the sore.
Yet seem'd she not to winch, though
    shrewdly pain'd :
But thus her Passive character maintain'd.
  I never grudg'd, whate'er my foes report,
Your flaunting fortune in the *Lyon's* court.
You have your day, or you are much bely'd,
But I am always on the suff'ring side :
You know my doctrine, and I need not say
I will not, but I cannot disobey. 140

On this firm principle I ever stood :
He of my sons who fails to make it good,
By one rebellious act renounces to my
    bloud.
    Ah, said the *Hind*, how many sons have
    you
Who call you mother, whom you never knew!
But most of them who that relation plead
Are such ungratious youths as wish you dead.
They gape at rich revenues which you hold
And fain would nible at your grandame gold
Enquire into your years, and laugh to find ;
Your crazy temper shows you much declin'd.
Were you not dim, and doted, you might see
A pack of cheats that claim a pedigree,   152
No more of kin to you, than you to me.
Do you not know that for a little coin
Heralds can foist a name into the line ?
They ask you blessing but for what you have,
But once possess'd of what with care you
    save,
The wanton boyes wou'd piss upon your
    grave.
    Your sons of Latitude that court your
    grace,   160
Though most resembling you in form and
    face,
Are far the worst of your pretended race.
And, but I blush your honesty to blot :
Pray God you prove 'em lawfully begot :
For, in some *Popish* libells I have read,
The *Wolf* has been too busie in your bed ;
At least their hinder parts, the belly-piece,
The paunch, and all that *Scorpio* claims are
    his.
Their malice too a sore suspicion brings ;
For though they dare not bark, they snarl at
    kings ;   170
Nor blame 'em for intruding in your line,
Fat Bishopricks are still of right divine.
    Think you your new *French* Proselytes are
    come
To starve abroad, because they starv'd at
    home ?
Your benefices twinckl'd from afar,
They found the new *Messiah* by the star :
Those *Swisses* fight on any side for pay,
And 'tis the living that conforms, not they.
Mark with what management their tribes
    divide,
Some stick to you, and some to t'other side
That many churches may for many mouths
    provide.   181

More vacant pulpits wou'd more converts
    make ;
All wou'd have Latitude enough to take ;
The rest unbenefic'd, your sects maintain
For ordinations without cures are vain,
And chamber practice is a silent gain.
Your sons of breadth at home, are much like
    these,
Their soft and yielding metals run with
    ease ;
They melt, and take the figure of the mould :
But harden, and preserve it best in gold. 190
    Your *Delphick* sword, the *Panther* then
    reply'd,
Is double-edg'd, and cuts on either side.
Some sons of mine, who bear upon their
    shield,
Three steeples Argent in a sable field,
Have sharply tax'd your converts, who unfed
Have follow'd you for miracles of bread ;
Such who themselves of no religion are,
Allur'd with gain, for any will declare.
Bare lyes with bold assertions they can face,
But dint of argument is out of place.   200
The grim Logician puts 'em in a fright,
'Tis easier far to flourish than to fight.
Thus, our eighth *Henry's* marriage they
    defame ;
They say the schism of beds began the
    game,
Divorcing from the *Church* to wed the
    Dame.
Though largely prov'd, and by himself pro-
    fess'd
That conscience, conscience would not let
    him rest :
I mean, not till possess'd of her he lov'd,
And old, uncharming *Catherine* was remov'd.
For sundry years before did he complain, 210
And told his ghostly Confessour his pain.
With the same impudence, without a ground,
They say, that look the reformation round,
No *Treatise of Humility* is found.
But if none were, the Gospel does not
    want,
Our *Saviour* preach'd it, and I hope you
    grant,
The Sermon in the mount was *Protestant* :
    No doubt, reply'd the *Hind*, as sure as all
The writings of Saint *Peter* and Saint *Paul*.
On that decision let it stand or fall.   220
Now for my converts, who you say unfed
Have follow'd me for miracles of bread.

Judge not by hear-say, but observe at least,
If since their change, their loaves have been
   increast.
The *Lyon* buyes no Converts, if he did,
Beasts wou'd be sold as fast as he cou'd bid.
Tax those of int'rest who conform for gain,
Or stay the market of another reign.
Your broad-way sons wou'd never be too nice
To close with *Calvin*, if he paid their price ;
But, rais'd three steeples high'r, wou'd change
   their note,   231
And quit the Cassock for the Canting-coat.
Now, if you damn this censure, as too bold,
Judge by your selves, and think not others
   sold.
   Mean-time my sons accus'd, by fames
   report
Pay small attendance at the *Lyon's* court,
Nor rise with early crowds, nor flatter late,
(For silently they beg who daily wait.)
Preferment is bestow'd that comes unsought,
Attendance is a bribe, and then 'tis bought.
How they shou'd speed, their fortune is
   untry'd,   241
For not to ask, is not to be denied.
For what they have their *God* and *King* they
   bless,
And hope they shou'd not murmur, had they
   less.
But if reduc'd subsistence to implore,
In common prudence they wou'd pass your
   door.
Unpitty'd *Hudibrass*, your Champion friend,
Has shown how far your charities extend.
This lasting verse shall on his tomb be
   read,
He sham'd you living, and upbraids you dead.
   With odious *Atheist* names you load your
   foes,   251
Your lib'ral *Clergy* why did I expose ?
It never fails in charities like those.
In climes where true religion is profess'd,
That imputation were no laughing jest,
But *Imprimatur*, with a Chaplain's name,
Is here sufficient licence to defame.
What wonder is't that black detraction
   thrives ?
The Homicide of names is less than lives,
And yet the perjur'd murtherer sur-
   vives.   260
   This said, she paus'd a little, and sup-
   press'd
The boiling indignation of her breast ;

She knew the vertue of her blade, nor wou'd
Pollute her satyr with ignoble bloud :
Her panting foes she saw before her lye,
And back she drew the shining weapon dry
So when the gen'rous *Lyon* has in sight
His equal match, he rouses for the fight ;
But when his foe lyes prostrate on the plain,
He sheathes his paws, uncurls his angry
   mane ;   270
And, pleas'd with bloudless honours of the
   day,
Walks over and disdains th' inglorious Prey.
So *JAMES*, if great with less we may compare,
Arrests his rowling thunder-bolts in air ;
And grants ungratefull friends a lengthn'd
   space,
T' implore the remnants of long suff'ring
   grace.
   This breathing-time the *Matron* took ; and
   then,
Resum'd the thrid of her discourse agen.
Be vengeance wholly left to pow'rs divine,
And let heav'n judge betwixt your sons and
   mine :   280
If joyes hereafter must be purchas'd here
With loss of all that mortals hold so dear,
Then welcome infamy and publick shame,
And, last, a long farewell to worldly fame.
'Tis said with ease, but oh, how hardly try'd ⎱
By haughty souls to humane honour ty'd ! ⎰
O sharp convulsive pangs of agonizing pride !
Down then, thou rebell, never more to rise, ⎱
And what thou didst and dost so dearly   ⎰
   prize,
That fame, that darling fame, make that
   thy sacrifice.   290
'Tis nothing thou hast giv'n ; then add thy
   tears
For a long race of unrepenting years
'Tis nothing yet ; yet all thou hast to give :
Then add those *may-be* years thou hast to
   live.
Yet nothing still : then poor, and naked ⎱
   come,   ⎰
Thy father will receive his unthrift home,
And thy blest Saviour's bloud discharge the
   mighty sum.
   Thus (she pursu'd) I discipline a son
Whose uncheck'd fury to revenge wou'd run :
He champs the bit, impatient of his loss, 300
And starts a-side and flounders at the cross.
Instruct him better, gracious God, to know,
As thine is vengeance, so forgiveness too ;

That, suff'ring from ill tongues he bears no
   more
Than what his Sovereign bears, and what his
   Saviour bore.
  It now remains for you to school your child,
And ask why *God's* anointed he revil'd ;
A *King* and *Princess* dead! did *Shimei* worse?
The curser's punishment should fright the
   curse :   309
Your son was warn'd, and wisely gave it o're,
But he who councell'd him has paid the
   score :
The heavy malice cou'd no higher tend,
But woe to him on whom the weights
   descend :
So to permitted ills the *Dæmon* flys :
His rage is aim'd at him who rules the skyes ;
Constrain'd to quit his cause, no succour
   found,
The foe discharges ev'ry Tyre around,
In clouds of smoke abandoning the fight,
But his own thund'ring peals proclaim his
   flight.
  In *Henry's* change his charge as ill
   succeeds ;   320
To that long story little answer needs,
Confront but *Henry's* words with *Henry's*
   deeds.
Were space allow'd, with ease it might be
   prov'd,
What springs his blessed reformation mov'd.
The dire effects appear'd in open sight,
Which from the cause, he calls a distant
   flight
And yet no larger leap than from the sun
   to light.
  Now last, your sons a double *Pæan* sound,
A *Treatise of Humility* is found.
'Tis found, but better had it ne'er been
   sought   330
Than thus in Protestant procession brought.
The fam'd original through *Spain* is known,
Rodriguez work, my celebrated son,
Which yours by ill-translating made his own ;
Conceal'd its authour, and usurp'd the name,
The basest and ignoblest theft of fame.
My Altars kindl'd first that living coal ;
Restore, or practice better what you stole :
That vertue could this humble verse inspire,
'Tis all the restitution I require.   340
  Glad was the *Panther* that the charge was
   clos'd,
And none of all her fav'rite sons expos'd.

For laws of arms permit each injur'd man
To make himself a saver where he can.
Perhaps the plunder'd merchant cannot tell
The names of Pirates in whose hands he
   fell :
But at the den of thieves he justly flies,
And ev'ry *Algerine* is lawfull prize.
No private person in the foes estate   349
Can plead exemption from the publick fate.
Yet Christian laws allow not such redress ;
Then let the greater supersede the less.
But let th' Abbetors of the *Panther's* crime
Learn to make fairer wars another time.
Some characters may sure be found to write
Among her sons ; for 'tis no common sight,
A spotted Dam, and all her offspring white.
  The *Salvage*, though she saw her plea con-
   troll'd,
Yet wou'd not wholly seem to quit her
   hold,
But offer'd fairly to compound the strife; 360
And judge conversion by the convert's life.
'Tis true, she said, I think it somewhat
   strange
So few shou'd follow profitable change ;
For present joys are more to flesh and bloud
Than a dull prospect of a distant good.
'Twas well alluded by a son of mine,
(I hope to quote him is not to purloin ;)
Two magnets, heav'n and earth, allure to
   bliss ;
The larger loadstone that, the nearer this :
The weak attraction of the greater fails, 370
We nodd a-while, but neighbourhood pre-
   vails :
But when the greater proves the nearer too,
I wonder more your converts come so slow.
Methinks in those who firm with me remain,
It shows a nobler principle than gain.
  Your inf'rence wou'd be strong (the *Hind*
   reply'd)
If yours were in effect the suff'ring side ;
Your clergy sons their own in peace possess,
Nor are their prospects in reversion less.
My Proselytes are struck with awfull dread,
Your bloudy Comet-laws hang blazing o're
   their head.   381
The respite they enjoy but onely lent,
The best they have to hope, protracted
   punishment.
Be judge your self, if int'rest may prevail,
Which motives, yours or mine. will turn the
   scale.

While pride and pomp allure, and plenteous
    ease,
That is, till man's predominant passions
    cease,
Admire no longer at my slow encrease.
    By education most have been misled ;   389
So they believe, because they so were bred.
The *Priest* continues what the nurse began,
And thus the child imposes on the man.
The rest I nam'd before, nor need repeat ;
But int'rest is the most prevailing cheat,
The sly seducer both of age and youth ;
They study that, and think they study truth:
When int'rest fortifies an argument,
Weak reason serves to gain the wills assent ;
For souls, already warp'd, receive an easie
    bent.   399
    Add long prescription of establish'd laws,
And picque of honour to maintain a cause,
And shame of change, and fear of future ill,
And Zeal, the blind conductor of the will ;
And chief among the still mistaking crowd,
The fame of teachers obstinate and proud,
And, more than all, the private Judge
    allowed.
Disdain of Fathers which the daunce began,
And lust, uncertain whose the narrower
    span,
The clown unread, and half-read gentleman.
    To this the *Panther*, with a scornfull smile :
Yet still you travail with unwearied toil,   411
And range around the realm without con-
    troll
Among my sons for proselytes to prole,
And here and there you snap some silly soul.
You hinted fears of future change in state,
Pray heav'n you did not prophesie your fate ;
Perhaps you think your time of triumph
    near,
But may mistake the season of the year ;
The *Swallows* fortune gives you cause to
    fear.
    For charity (reply'd the *Matron*) tell   420
What sad mischance those pretty birds befell.
Nay, no mischance, (the salvage Dame
    reply'd,)
But want of wit in their unerring guide,
And eager haste and gaudy hopes and
    giddy pride.
Yet, wishing timely warning may prevail,
Make you the moral, and I'll tell the tale.
    The *Swallow*, privileg'd above the rest
Of all the birds as man's familiar guest,

Pursues the Sun in summer brisk and bold,
But wisely shuns the persecuting cold :   430
Is well to chancels and to chimnies known,
Though 'tis not thought she feeds on smoak
    alone.
From hence she has been held of heav'nly
    line,
Endu'd with particles of soul divine.
This merry Chorister had long possess'd
Her summer seat, and feather'd well her
    nest :
Till frowning skys began to change their
    chear,
And time turn'd up the wrong side of the
    year ;
The shedding trees began the ground to strow
With yellow leaves, and bitter blasts to blow.
Sad auguries of winter thence she drew,   441
Which by instinct, or Prophecy, she knew :
When prudence warn'd her to remove be-
    times,
And seek a better heav'n and warmer clymes.
    Her sons were summon'd on a steeples
    height,
And, call'd in common council, vote a flight ;
The day was nam'd, the next that shou'd
    be fair,
All to the gen'ral rendezvous repair,
They try their flutt'ring wings and trust
    themselves in air.   449
But whether upward to the moon they go,
Or dream the winter out in caves below,
Or hawk at flies elsewhere, concerns not us
    to know.
    Southwards, you may be sure, they bent
    their flight,
And harbour'd in a hollow rock at night ;
Next morn they rose, and set up ev'ry sail ;
The wind was fair, but blew a *mackrel* gale :
The sickly young sat shiv'ring on the shoar,
Abhorr'd salt-water never seen before,
And pray'd their tender mothers to delay
The passage, and expect a fairer day.   460
    With these the *Martyn* readily concurr'd,
A church-begot and church-believing bird ;
Of little body, but of lofty mind,
Round belly'd, for a dignity design'd,
And much a dunce, as *Martyns* are by kind.
Yet often quoted Canon-laws and *Code*
And Fathers which he never understood,
But little learning needs in noble bloud.
For, sooth to say, the *Swallow* brought him in,
Her household Chaplain, and her next of kin.

In Superstition silly to excess,   471
And casting Schemes, by planetary guess :
In fine, shortwing'd, unfit himself to fly,
His fear foretold foul-weather in the sky.
  Besides, a *Raven* from a withered Oak,
Left of their lodging, was observed to croke.
That omen lik'd him not, so his advice
Was present safety, bought at any price :
(A seeming pious care that covered cowar-
    dise.)
To strengthen this, he told a boding dream,
Of rising waters and a troubl'd stream,   481
Sure signs of anguish, dangers, and distress,
With something more, not lawfull to express :
By which he slyly seemed to intimate
Some secret revelation of their fate.
For he concluded, once upon a time,
He found a leaf inscrib'd with sacred rime,
Whose antique characters did well denote
The *Sibyl's* hand of the *Cumæan* Grott :
The mad divineress had plainly writ,   490
A time should come (but many ages yet,)
In which, sinister destinies ordain,
A *Dame* should drown with all her feather'd
    train,
And seas from thence be called the *Cheli-*
    donian main.
At this, some shook for fear, the more devout
Arose, and bless'd themselves from head to
    foot.
  'Tis true, some stagers of the wiser sort
Made all these idle wonderments their sport
They said, their onely danger was delay,
And he who heard what ev'ry fool cou'd
    say,
Would never fix his thoughts, but trim his
    time away.   501
The passage yet was good ; the wind, 'tis
    true,
Was somewhat high, but that was nothing
    new,
Nor more than usual *Equinoxes* blew.
The Sun (already from the scales declin'd)
Gave little hopes of better days behind,
But change from bad to worse of weather
    and of wind.
Nor need they fear the dampness of the Sky
Should flag their wings, and hinder them
    to fly,
'Twas onely water thrown on sails too dry.
But, least of all, *Philosophy* presumes   511
Of truth in dreams, from melancholy fumes ;
Perhaps the *Martyn*, hous'd in holy ground,

Might think of Ghosts that walk their mid-
    night round,
Till grosser atoms tumbling in the stream
Of fancy, madly met and clubb'd into a
    dream.
As little weight his vain presages bear,
Of ill effect to such alone who fear.
Most prophecies are of a piece with these,
Each *Nostradamus* can foretell with ease :   520
Not naming persons, and confounding times,
One casual truth supports a thousand lying
    rimes.
  Th' advice was true, but fear had seized
    the most,
And all good counsel is on cowards lost.
The question crudely put, to shun delay,
'Twas carried by the *major* part to stay.
  His point thus gained, Sir *Martyn* dated
    thence
His pow'r, and from a Priest became a Prince.
He order'd all things with a busie care,
And cells, and refectories did prepare,   530
And large provisions laid of winter fare.
But now and then let fall a word or two
Of hope, that heav'n some miracle might
    show,
And, for their sakes the sun should back-
    ward go ;
Against the laws of nature upward climb,
And, mounted on the *Ram*, renew the prime :
For which two proofs in Sacred story lay,
Of *Ahaz* dial and of *Joshuah's* day.
In expectation of such times as these
A chapel hous'd 'em, truly called of ease :   540
For *Martyn* much devotion did not ask,
They pray'd sometimes, and that was all
    their task.
  It happen'd (as beyond the reach of wit
Blind prophecies may have a lucky hit)
That this accomplish'd, or at least in part,
Gave great repute to their new *Merlin's* art.
Some *Swifts, the Gyants of the
    Swallow kind,
Large limb'd, stout-hearted,
    but of stupid mind,
(For *Swisses*, or for *Gibeonites*
    design'd,)
          **Otherwise call'd* martlets.
These Lubbers, peeping through a broken
    pane,   550
To suck fresh air, survey'd the neighbouring
    plain ;
And saw (but scarcely could believe their eyes)
New Blossoms flourish and new flow'rs arise ;

As God had been abroad, and walking there
Had left his foot-steps and reform'd the year:
The sunny hills from far were seen to glow
With glittering beams, and in the meads
   below
The burnish'd brooks appear'd with liquid
   gold to flow.
At last they heard the foolish *Cuckow* sing,
Whose note proclaim'd the holy-day of
   spring.   560
   No longer doubting, all prepare to fly
And repossess their patrimonial sky.
The *Priest* before 'em did his wings display;
And that good omens might attend their
   way,
As luck wou'd have it, 'twas St. *Martyn's*
   day.
   Who but the *Swallow* now triumphsalone?
The Canopy of heaven is all her own ;
Her youthfull offspring to their haunts re-
   pair ;   568
And glide along in glades, and skim in air,
And dip for insects in the purling springs,
And stoop on rivers to refresh their wings.
Their mothers think a fair provision made,
That ev'ry son can live upon his trade,
And now the carefull charge is off their hands.
Look out for husbands and new nuptial
   bands :
The youthfull widow longs to be supply'd ;
But first the lover is by Lawyers ty'd
To settle jointure-chimneys on the bride.
So thick they couple, in so short a space,
That *Martyns* marr'age offerings rise apace ;
Their ancient houses, running to decay,   581
Are furbish'd up and cemented with clay ;
They teem already ; stores of eggs are laid,
And brooding mothers call *Lucina's* aid.
Fame spreads the news, and foreign fowls
   appear
In flocks to greet the new returning year,
To bless the founder, and partake the cheer.
   And now 'twas time (so fast their numbers
   rise)
To plant abroad, and people colonies ;
The youth drawn forth, as *Martyn* had
   desir'd   590
(For so their cruel destiny requir'd)
Were sent far off on an ill fated day ;
The rest wou'd need conduct 'em on their
   way,
And *Martyn* went, because he fear'd alone
   to stay.

So long they flew with inconsiderate haste,
That now their afternoon began to waste ;
And, what was ominous, that very morn
The Sun was entr'd into *Capricorn* ;
Which, by their bad Astronomers account,
That week the virgin balance shou'd re-
   mount ;   600
An infant moon eclips'd him in his way,
And hid the small remainders of his day :
The crowd amaz'd pursued no certain mark ;
But birds met birds, and justled in the dark;
Few mind the publick in a Panick fright ;
And fear increas'd the horrour of the night.
Night came, but unattended with repose ;
Alone she came, no sleep their eyes to close,
Alone, and black she came, no friendly stars
   arose.
   What shou'd they doe, beset with
   dangers round,   610
No neighbouring Dorp, no lodging to be
   found,
But bleaky plains, and bare unhospitable
   ground ?
The latter brood, who just began to fly,
Sick-feathered and unpractis'd in the sky,
For succour to their helpless mother call,
She spread her wings ; some few beneath
   'em craul,
She spread 'em wider yet, but cou'd not
   cover all.
T' augment their woes, the winds began to
   move
Debate in air, for empty fields above,
Till *Boreas* got the skyes, and poured
   amain   620
His ratling hail-stones mix'd with snow and
   rain.
   The joyless morning late arose, and found
A dreadfull desolation reign a-round,
Some buried in the Snow, some frozen to
   the ground :
The rest were strugling still with death, and
   lay
The *Crows* and *Ravens* rights, an undefended
   prey ;
Excepting *Martyn's* race, for they and he
Had gain'd the shelter of a hollow tree,
But soon discover'd by a sturdy clown,
He headed all the rabble of a town,   630
And finished 'em with bats, or poll'd 'em
   down.

---

603 crowd] crow'd *1687*.

Martyn himself was caught a-live, and try'd
For treas'nous crimes, because the laws
  provide
No *Martyn* there in winter shall abide.
High on an Oak which never leaf shall bear,
He breath'd his last, exposed to open air,
And there his corps, unbless'd, is hanging
  still,
To show the change of winds with his pro-
  phetick bill.
  The patience of the *Hind* did almost fail,
For well she mark'd the malice of the tale :
Which Ribbald art their church to *Luther*
  owes,   641
In malice it began, by malice grows,
He sowed the *Serpent's* teeth, an iron-
  harvest rose.
But most in *Martyn's* character and fate,
She saw her slander'd sons, the *Panther's*
  hate,
The people's rage, the persecuting state :
Then said, I take th' advice in friendly part,
You clear your conscience, or at least your
  heart :
Perhaps you fail'd in your fore-seeing skill,
For *Swallows* are unlucky birds to kill : 650
As for my sons, the family is bless'd,
Whose every child is equal to the rest :
No church reform'd can boast a blameless
  line :
Such *Martyns* build in yours, and more than
  mine :
Or else an old fanatick Author lyes,
Who summ'd their Scandals up by Centuries.
But through your parable I plainly see
The bloudy laws, the crowds barbarity :
The sun-shine that offends the purblind sight,
Had some their wishes, it wou'd soon be
  night.   660
Mistake me not, the charge concerns not you,
Your sons are male-contents, but yet are true.
As far as non-resistance makes 'em so,
But that's a word of neutral sense you know,
A passive term, which no relief will bring,
But trims betwixt a rebell and a king.
  Rest well assured, the *Pardelis* reply'd,
My sons wou'd all support the regal side,
Though heav'n forbid the cause by battel
  should be try'd.
  The Matron answered with a loud Amen,
And thus pursu'd her argument agen.   671

If, as you say, and as I hope no less,
Your sons will practise what your self
  profess,
What angry pow'r prevents our present
  peace ?
The *Lyon*, studious of our common good,
Desires (and Kings desires are ill withstood)
To join our Nations in a lasting love ;
The barrs betwixt are easie to remove,
For sanguinary laws were never made
  above.
If you condemn that Prince of Tyranny 680
Whose mandate forced your *Gallick* friends
  to fly,
Make not a worse example of your own,
Or cease to rail at causeless rigour shown,
And let the guiltless person throw the stone.
His blunted sword, your suff'ring brother-
  hood
Have seldom felt, he stops it short of bloud :
But you have ground the persecuting knife
And set it to a razor edge on life.
Curs'd be the wit which cruelty refines
Or to his father's rod the *Scorpion* joins ;
Your finger is more gross than the great
  Monarch's loins.   691
But you perhaps remove that bloudy note,
And stick it on the first Reformers coat.
Oh let their crime in long oblivion sleep,
'Twas theirs indeed to make, 'tis yours to
  keep.
Unjust, or just, is all the question now,
'Tis plain, that not repealing you allow.
  To name the Test wou'd put you in a rage ;
You charge not that on any former age,
But smile to think how innocent you stand
Arm'd by a weapon put into your hand. 701
Yet still remember that you weild a sword
Forg'd by your foes against your Sovereign
  Lord.
Designed to hew th' imperial Cedar down,
Defraud Succession and dis-heir the Crown.
T' abhor the makers, and their laws approve,
Is to hate Traytors and the treason love :
What means it else, which now your children
  say,
We made it not, nor will we take away ?
  Suppose some great Oppressor had by
  slight   710
Of law, disseis'd your brother of his right,
Your common sire surrendring in a fright ;
Would you to that unrighteous title stand,
Left by the villain's will to heir the land ?

More just was *Judas*, who his Saviour sold ;
The sacrilegious bribe he cou'd not hold,
Nor hang in peace, before he rendr'd back
    the gold.
What more could you have done than now
    you doe,
Had *Oates* and *Bedlow*, and their Plot been
    true ?
Some specious reasons for those wrongs
    were found ;   720
The dire Magicians threw their mists
    around,
And wise men walk'd as on enchanted
    ground.
But now when time has made th' imposture
    plain,
(Late though he follow'd truth, & limping
    held her train,)
What new delusion charms your cheated
    eyes again ?
The painted Harlot might a while bewitch,
But why the Hag uncas'd and all obscene
    with itch ?
    The first Reformers were a modest race ;
Our Peers possessed in peace their native
    place :
And when rebellious arms o'returned the
    state   730
They suffer'd onely in the common fate ;
But now the Sov'reign mounts the regal chair
And mitr'd seats are full, yet *David's* bench
    is bare :
Your answer is, they were not dispossess'd,
They need but rub their mettle on the Test
To prove their ore : 'twere well if gold
    alone
Were touch'd and try'd on your discerning
    stone ;
But that unfaithfull Test unfound will pass
The dross of Atheists and sectarian brass :
As if the experiment were made to hold 740
For base productions, and reject the gold :
Thus men ungodded may to places rise,
And sects may be preferr'd without disguise :
No danger to the church or state from
    these ;
The Papist onely has his Writ of ease.
No gainfull office gives him the pretence
To grind the Subject or defraud the Prince.
Wrong conscience, or no conscience may
    deserve
To thrive, but ours alone is privileg'd to
    sterve.

    Still thank your selves, you cry, your noble
    race   750
We banish not, but they forsake the place.
Our doors are open: true, but e'er they come
You toss your censing Test and fume the
    room ;
As if 'twere *Toby's* rival to expell,
And fright the fiend who could not bear the
    smell.
    To this the *Panther* sharply had reply'd ;
But, having gain'd a Verdict on her side,
She wisely gave the loser leave to chide ;
Well satisfied to have the But and peace,
And for the Plaintiff's cause she car'd the
    less,   760
Because she su'd *in formâ Pauperis ;*
Yet thought it decent something shou'd be
    said,
For secret guilt by silence is betray'd :
So neither granted all, nor much deny'd,
But answer'd with a yawning kind of pride.
    Methinks such terms of proferr'd peace
    you bring,
As once *Æneas* to th' *Italian* King :
By long possession all the land is mine,
You strangers come with your intruding
    line
To share my sceptre, which you call to join.
You plead like him an ancient Pedigree, 771
And claim a peacefull seat by fates decree.
In ready pomp your Sacrificer stands,
To unite the *Trojan* and the *Latin* bands,
And that the league more firmly may be ty'd,
Demand the fair *Lavinia* for your bride.
Thus plausibly you veil th' intended wrong,
But still you bring your exil'd gods along ;
And will endeavour in succeeding space,
Those household Poppits on our hearths to
    place.   780
Perhaps some barb'rous laws have been pre-
    ferr'd ;
I spake against the *Test*, but was not heard.
These to rescind and Peerage to restore
My gracious Sov'reign wou'd my vote
    implore :
I owe him much, but owe my conscience
    more.
    Conscience is then your Plea, replied the
    Dame,
Which well-informed will ever be the same.

759 But] *Christie prints* butt. *Of course the
word is a substantive.*

But yours is much of the *Camelion* hue,
To change the dye with ev'ry diff'rent view.
When first the *Lyon* sat with awfull sway, 790
Your conscience taught you duty to obey ;
He might have had your Statutes and your
    Test ;
No conscience but of subjects was profess'd.
He found your temper, and no farther
    try'd,
But on that broken reed your church rely'd.
In vain the sects assay'd their utmost art, ⎫
With offered treasures to espouse their part, ⎬
Their treasures were a bribe too mean to ⎭
    move his heart.
But when by long experience you had proov'd,
How far he cou'd forgive, how well he lov'd ;
A goodness that excell'd his godlike race, 801
And onely short of heav'ns unbounded grace:
A floud of mercy that o'erflowed our Isle,
Calm in the rise, and fruitfull as the *Nile*,
Forgetting whence your *Ægypt* was supply'd,
You thought your Sov'reign bound to send
    the tide ;
Nor upward look'd on that immortal spring,
But vainly deem'd, he durst not be a king :
Then conscience, unrestrain'd by fear, began
To stretch her limits, and extend the span,
Did his indulgence as her gift dispose,   811
And made a wise Alliance with her foes.
Can conscience own th' associating name, ⎫
And raise no blushes to conceal her shame? ⎬
For sure she has been thought a bashfull ⎭
    Dame.
But if the cause by battel should be try'd, ⎫
You grant she must espouse the regal side : ⎬
O *Proteus* Conscience, never to be ty'd ! ⎭
What *Phœbus* from the *Tripod* shall disclose,
Which are in last resort, your friends or
    foes ?   820
Homer, who learn'd the language of the sky,
The seeming *Gordian* knot wou'd soon unty ;
Immortal pow'rs the term of conscience
    know,
But int'rest is her name with men below.
   Conscience or int'rest be 't, or both in one ;
(The *Panther* answered in a surly tone,)
The first commands me to maintain the
    Crown,
The last forbids to throw my barriers down.
Our penal laws no sons of yours admit, 829
Our *Test* excludes your Tribe from benefit.
These are my banks your ocean to withstand,
Which proudly rising overlooks the land :

And once let in, with unresisted sway
Wou'd sweep the Pastors and their flocks
    away.
Think not my judgment leads me to comply
With laws unjust, but hard necessity :
Imperious need which cannot be withstood
Makes ill authentick, for a greater good.
Possess your soul with patience, and attend :
A more auspicious Planet may ascend ; 840
Good fortune may present some happier
    time,
With means to cancel my unwilling crime ;
(Unwilling, witness all ye Pow'rs above)
To mend my errours and redeem your love :
That little space you safely may allow,
Your all-dispensing pow'r protects you now.
   Hold, said the *Hind*, 'tis needless to ex-
    plain :
You would *postpone* me to another reign :
Till when you are content to be unjust,
Your part is to possess, and mine to trust. 850
A fair exchange propos'd of future chance,
For present profit and inheritance :
Few words will serve to finish our dispute,
Who will not now repeal wou'd persecute ;
To ripen green revenge your hopes attend,
Wishing that happier Planet wou'd ascend :
For shame let Conscience be your Plea no ⎫
    more,   ⎪
To will hereafter proves she might before ; ⎬
But she's a Bawd to gain, and holds the ⎪
    Door.   859 ⎭
   Your care about your Banks, infers a fear
Of threatning Floods and Inundations near ;
If so, a just Reprise would only be
Of what the Land usurped upon the Sea ;
And all your Jealousies but serve to show
Your Ground is, like your Neighbour-Nation,
    low.
T' intrench in what you grant unrighteous
    Laws
Is to distrust the justice of your Cause ;
And argues that the true religion lyes
In those weak Adversaries you despise.
   Tyrannick force is that which least you
    fear,   870
The sound is frightfull in a Christian's ear :
Avert it, Heav'n ; nor let that Plague be
    sent
To us from the dispeopled Continent.
   But Piety commands me to refrain ;
Those Pray'rs are needless in this Monarch's
    Reign.

Behold ! how he protects your Friends
  opprest,
Receives the Banish'd, succours the Dis-
  tress'd :
Behold, for you may read an honest open
  breast.
He stands in Day-light, and disdains to
  hide
An Act to which by Honour he is ty'd, 880
A generous, laudable, and Kingly Pride.
Your Test he would repeal, his Peers restore,
This when he says he means, he means no
  more.
Well, said the Panther, I believe him just,
And yet——
          And yet, 'tis but because you must,
You would be trusted, but you would not
  trust.
The *Hind* thus briefly ; and disdained t'
  inlarge
On Pow'r of Kings, and their Superiour charge,
As Heav'ns Trustees before the People's
  choice :
Tho' sure the *Panther* did not much
  rejoyce   890
To hear those *Echo's* given of her once Loyal
  voice.
  The *Matron* woo'd her Kindness to the last,
But cou'd not win ; her hour of Grace was
  past.
Whom, thus persisting, when she could not
  bring
To leave the *Woolf* and to believe her King,
She gave Her up, and fairly wished her Joy
Of her late Treaty with her new Ally :
Which well she hop'd wou'd more successfull
  prove,
Than was the *Pigeons* and the *Buzzards* love.
The *Panther* ask'd what concord there cou'd
  be   900
Betwixt two kinds whose Natures disagree ?
The *Dame* reply'd, 'Tis sung in ev'ry Street,
The common chat of Gossips when they
  meet :
But, since unheard by you, 'tis worth your
  while
To take a wholesome Tale, though told in
  homely stile.
  A plain good Man, whose Name is under-
  stood,
(So few deserve the name of Plain and Good)
Of three fair lineal Lordships stood possess'd,
And liv'd, as reason was, upon the best.

Inur'd to hardships from his early Youth, 910
Much had he done and suffered for his
  truth :
At Land, and Sea, in many a doubtfull
  Fight,
Was never known a more advent'rous
  Knight,
Who oftner drew his Sword, and always for
  the right.
  As fortune wou'd (his fortune came tho' late)
He took Possession of his just Estate ;
Nor rack'd his Tenants with increase of Rent,
Nor liv'd too sparing, nor too largely spent ;
But overlook'd his *Hinds*, their Pay was just
And ready, for he scorn'd to go on trust : 920
Slow to resolve, but in performance quick ;
So true, that he was awkward at a trick.
For little Souls on little shifts rely,
And coward Arts of mean Expedients try :
The noble Mind will dare do anything but
  lye.
False friends, (his deadliest foes,) could find
  no way
But shows of honest bluntness, to betray ;
That unsuspected plainness he believ'd ;
He looked into Himself, and was deceiv'd.
Some lucky Planet sure attends his Birth, 930
Or Heav'n would make a Miracle on Earth ;
For prosp'rous Honesty is seldom seen
To bear so dead a weight, and yet to win ;
It looks as Fate with Nature's Law would
  strive,
To show Plain-dealing once an age may
  thrive :
And, when so tough a frame she could not
  bend,
Exceeded her Commission to befriend.
  This gratefull man, as Heaven encreas'd
  his Store,
Gave *God* again, and daily fed his Poor ;
His House with all convenience was pur-
  vey'd ;   940
The rest he found, but rais'd the Fabrick
  where he pray'd ;
And in that Sacred Place his beauteous Wife
Employ'd Her happiest hours of Holy Life.
  Nor did their Alms extend to those alone
Whom common Faith more strictly made
  their own ;
A sort of *Doves* were hous'd too near their
  Hall,
Who cross the Proverb, and abound with
  Gall.

Tho' some, 'tis true, are passively inclin'd,
The greater Part degenerate from their kind ;
Voracious Birds, that hotly Bill and breed,
And largely drink, because on Salt they feed.
Small Gain from them their Bounteous
  Owner draws ;   952
Yet, bound by Promise, he supports their
  Cause,
As Corporations priviledg'd by Laws.
  That House, which harbour to their kind
  affords,
Was built, long since, God knows, for better
  Birds ;
But flutt'ring there, they nestle near the
  Throne,
And lodge in Habitations not their own,
By their high Crops, and Corny Gizzards
  known.
Like *Harpy's*, they could scent a plenteous
  board ;   960
Then, to be sure, they never fail'd their
  Lord.
The rest was form, and bare Attendance paid,
They drunk, and eat, and grudgingly obey'd.
The more they fed, they raven'd still for
  more,
They drain'd from *Dan*, and left *Beersheba*
  poor ;
All this they had by Law, and none repin'd,
The pref'rence was but due to *Levi's* Kind,
But when some Lay-preferment fell by
  chance
The Gourmands made it their Inheritance.
When once possess'd they never quit their
  Claim,   970
For then 'tis sanctify'd to Heav'ns high
  Name ;
And Hallow'd thus, they cannot give Con-
  sent.
The Gift should be prophan'd by Worldly
  management.
  Their Flesh was never to the Table served ;
Tho' 'tis not thence inferr'd the Birds
  were starv'd ;
But that their Master did not like the
  Food,
As rank, and breeding Melancholy Blood.
Nor did it with His Gracious Nature suite,
Ev'n though they were not Doves, to perse-
  cute :
Yet He refused, (nor could they take Offence)
Their Glutton Kind should teach him absti-
  nence.   981

Nor Consecrated Grain their Wheat he
  thought,
Which, new from treading, in their Bills they
  brought :
But left his Hinds, each in his Private Pow'r,
That those who like the Bran might leave the
  Flow'r.
He for himself, and not for others chose,
Nor would He be impos'd on, nor impose ;
But in their Faces His Devotion paid,
And Sacrifice with Solemn Rites was made,
And Sacred Incense on his Altars laid.   990
  Besides these jolly Birds, whose Crops
  impure
Repaid their Commons with their Salt
  Manure,
Another Farm he had behind his House,
Not overstock't, but barely for his use ;
Wherein his poor Domestick poultry Fed
And from His Pious Hands received their
  Bread.
Our pamper'd Pigeons with malignant Eyes
Beheld these Inmates and their Nurseries :
Tho' hard their fare, at Ev'ning and at
  Morn,
A Cruise of Water and an Ear of Corn, 1000
Yet still they grudg'd that Modicum, and
  thought
A Sheaf in ev'ry single Grain was brought ;
Fain would they filch that little Food away,
While unrestrain'd those happy Gluttons
  prey.
And much they griev'd to see so nigh their
  Hall
The Bird that warned St. *Peter* of his Fall ;
That he should raise his miter'd Crest on
  high,
And clap his Wings and call his Family
To Sacred Rites ; and vex th' Etherial
  Pow'rs   1009
With midnight Mattins at uncivil Hours :
Nay more, his quiet Neighbours should
  molest,
Just in the sweetness of their Morning rest.
  Beast of a bird, supinely when he might
Lye snugg and sleep, to rise before the
  light :
What if his dull Forefathers used that cry,
Cou'd he not let a Bad Example dye ?
The World was fallen into an easier way ;
This Age knew better, than to Fast and Pray.
Good Sense in Sacred Worship would appear
So to begin, as they might end the year, 1020

Such feats in former times had wrought the
    falls
Of crowing Chanticleers in Cloyster'd Walls.
Expell'd for this and for their Lands, they
    fled ;
And Sister Partlet, with her hooded head
Was hooted hence, because she would not
    pray a-Bed.
The way to win the restiff World to God
Was to lay by the Disciplining Rod,
Unnatural Fasts, and Foreign Forms of
    Pray'r ;
Religion frights us with a meen severe.
'Tis Prudence to reform her into Ease, 1030
And put Her in Undress, to make Her pleas ;
A lively Faith will bear aloft the Mind
And leave the Luggage of Good Works
    behind.
  Such Doctrines in the Pigeon-house were
    taught ;
You need not ask how wondrously they
    wrought ;
But sure the common Cry was all for these,
Whose Life, and Precept both encourag'd
    Ease.
Yet fearing those alluring Baits might fail,
And Holy Deeds o're all their Arts prevail,
(For Vice, tho' frontless and of harden'd Face,
Is daunted at the sight of awfull Grace,)
An hideous Figure of their Foes they drew
Nor Lines, nor Looks, nor Shades, nor
    Colours true ;   1043
And this Grotesque design, expos'd to
    Publick view.
One would have thought it some Ægyptian
    Piece,
With Garden-Gods, and barking Deities,
More thick than *Ptolomey* has stuck the
    Skies.
All so perverse a Draught, so far unlike,
It was no Libell where it meant to strike :
Yet still the daubing pleas'd, and Great and
    Small   1050
To view the Monster crowded Pigeon-hall.
There Chanticleer was drawn upon his knees,
Adoring Shrines, and Stocks of Sainted Trees;
And by him a mishapen, ugly Race ;
The curse of God was seen on ev'ry face.
No *Holland* emblem could that Malice mend,
But still the worse the look the fitter for a
    Fiend.

The Master of the Farm, displeas'd to find
So much of Rancour in so mild a kind,
Enquir'd into the Cause, and came to know,
The Passive Church had struck the foremost
    blow :   1061
With groundless Fears, and Jealousies
    possest,
As if this troublesome intruding Guest
Would drive the Birds of *Venus* from their
    Nest.
A Deed his inborn Equity abhorr'd,
But Int'rest will not trust, tho God should
    plight his Word.
A Law, the Source of many Future harms,
Had banish'd all the Poultry from the Farms ;
With loss of Life, if any should be found 1069
To crow or peck on this forbidden Ground.
That Bloody Statute chiefly was design'd
For *Chanticleer* the white, of Clergy kind ;
But after-malice did not long forget
The Lay that wore the Robe and Coronet.
For them, for their Inferiours and Allyes,
Their Foes a deadly *Shibboleth* devise :
By which unrighteously it was decreed,
That none to Trust, or Profit should succeed,
Who would not swallow first a poysonous
    wicked Weed ;   1079
Or that to which old *Socrates* was curs't,
Or Henbane-Juice to swell 'em till they burst.
The Patron (as in reason) thought it hard
To see this Inquisition in his Yard,
By which the Soveraign was of Subjects
    use debarred.
  All gentle means he try'd, which might
    withdraw
Th' Effects of so unnatural a Law :
But still the Dove-house obstinately stood
Deaf to their own, and to their Neighbours
    good :
And which was worse, (if any worse could be)
Repented of their boasted Loyalty :   1090
Now made the Champions of a cruel Cause,
And drunk with Fumes of Popular Applause ;
For those whom God to ruine has design'd,
He sits for Fate, and first destroys their Mind.
  New Doubts indeed they daily strove to
    raise,
Suggested Dangers, interpos'd Delays ;
And Emissary Pigeons had in store,
Such as the *Meccan* Prophet us'd of yore,
To whisper Counsels in their Patrons Ear ;
And veil'd their false Advice with Zealous
    Fear.   1100

* cp. Pope. ME IV
"somit w? the majesty pleasure, to be seen"

148   THE HIND AND THE PANTHER.

The Master smiled to see 'em work in vain,
To wear him out and make an idle reign :
He saw, but suffer'd their Protractive Arts,
And strove by mildness to reduce their
      Hearts ;
But they abused that Grace to make Allyes ⎫
And fondly clos'd with former Enemies ;   ⎬
For fools are double Fools, endeav'ring to ⎭
      be wise.
    After a grave Consult what course were
      best,
One, more mature in Folly than the rest,
Stood up, and told 'em with his head aside,
That desp'rate Cures must be to desp'rate
      Ills apply'd :   1111
And therefore, since their main impending
      fear
Was from th' encreasing race of *Chanticleer* :
Some Potent Bird of Prey they ought to
      find,
A Foe profess'd to him and all his kind :
Some haggar'd *Hawk*, who had her eyry nigh,
Well pounc'd to fasten, and well wing'd to fly ;
One they might trust, their common wrongs
      to wreak :
The *Musquet*, and the *Coystrel* were too weak,
Too fierce the *Falcon*, but, above the rest,
The noble *Buzzard* ever pleas'd me best ; 1121
Of small Renown, 'tis true ; for, not to lye,
We call him but a *Hawk* by courtesie.
I know he haunts the *Pigeon*-house and
      Farm,
And more, in time of War has done us harm ;
But all his hate on trivial Points depends,
Give up our Forms, and we shall soon be
      friends.
For *Pigeons* flesh he seems not much to care ;
Cram'd *Chickens* are a more delicious fare ;
On this high Potentate, without delay,   1130
I wish you would conferr the Sovereign sway ;
Petition him t' accept the Government,
And let a splendid Embassy be sent.
    This pithy speech prevail'd ; and all
      agreed,
Old Enmity's forgot, the *Buzzard* should
      succeed.
    Their welcom Suit was granted soon as
      heard,
His Lodgings furnish'd, and a Train prepar'd,
With *B's* upon their Breast, appointed for
      his Guard.   1138
He came, and Crown'd with great Solemnity,
God save King *Buzzard*, was the gen'rall cry.

A Portly Prince, and goodly to the sight,
He seem'd a Son of *Anach* for his height :
Like those whom stature did to Crowns
      prefer ;
Black-brow'd and bluff, like *Homer's Jupiter* ;
Broad-backed and Brawny built for Loves
      delight,
A Prophet form'd to make a female Proselyte.
A Theologue more by need, than genial bent,
By Breeding sharp, by Nature confident,
Int'rest in all his Actions was discern'd ;
More learn'd than Honest, more a Wit than
      learn'd.   1150
Or forc'd by Fear, or by his Profit led,
Or both conjoyn'd, his Native clime he fled :
But brought the Vertues of his Heav'n
      along ;
A fair Behaviour, and a fluent Tongue.
And yet with all his Arts he could not thrive ;
The must unlucky Parasite alive.
Loud Praises to prepare his Paths he sent, ✳
And then himself pursu'd his Compliment !
But, by reverse of Fortune chac'd away,
His Gifts no longer than their Author stay ;
He shakes the Dust against th' ungrateful
      race,   1161
And leaves the stench of Ordures in the
      place.
Oft has he flatter'd, and blasphem'd the
      same,
For in his Rage, he spares no Sov'rains name :
The Hero, and the Tyrant change their style
By the same measure that they frown or
      smile ;
When well receiv'd by hospitable Foes,
The kindness he returns, is to expose :
For Courtesies, tho' undeserv'd and great, ⎫
No gratitude in Fellon-minds beget ;   1170 ⎬
As tribute to his Wit, the churl receives the ⎭
      treat.
His praise of Foes is venomously Nice,   ⎫
So touch'd, it turns a Vertue to a Vice :   ⎬
A Greek, and bountiful forewarns us twice.
Sev'n sacraments he wisely do's disown,
Because he knows Confession stands for
      one ;
Where sins to sacred silence are convey'd,
And not for Fear, or Love, to be betray'd :
But he, uncall'd, his Patron to controul,
Divulg'd the secret whispers of his Soul ; 1180
Stood forth th' accusing Sathan of his
      Crimes,
And offerd to the *Moloch* of the Times.

cp. Mac Flecknoe
Dunciad

Poem suddenly comes alive. (handwritten)

Prompt to assayle, and careless of defence,
Invulnerable in his Impudence,
He dares the World, and, eager of a name,
He thrusts about, and justles into fame.
Frontless and Satyr-proof, he scowr's the
    streets,   1187
And runs an *Indian* muck at all he meets.
So fond of loud Report, that not to miss
Of being known (his last and utmost bliss)
He rather would be known, for what he is.
  Such was and is the Captain of the test,
Tho' half his Vertues are not here express't;
The modesty of Fame conceals the rest.
The spleenful *Pigeons* never could create
A Prince more proper to revenge their
    hate ;
Indeed, more proper to revenge, than save ;
A King, whom in his wrath, th' Almighty
    gave :
For all the Grace the Landlord had allow'd
But made the *Buzzard* and the *Pigeons*
    proud,   1200
Gave time to fix their Friends, and to seduce
    the Crowd.
They long their Fellow-Subjects to inthrall,
Their Patrons promise into question call,
And vainly think he meant to make 'em
    Lords of all.
  False Fears their Leaders fail'd not to
    suggest,
As if the *Doves* were to be dispossess't ;
Nor Sighs nor Groans nor gogling Eyes did
    want,
For now the *Pigeons* too had learned to
    Cant.
The House of Pray'r is stock'd with large
    encrease ;
Nor Doors, nor Windows can contain the
    Press :   1210
For Birds of ev'ry feather fill th' abode ;
Ev'n Atheists out of envy own a God :
And, reeking from the Stews, Adult'rers
    come,
Like *Goths* and *Vandals* to demolish *Rome.*
That Conscience, which to all their Crimes
    was mute,
Now calls aloud, and cryes to Persecute.
No rigour of the Laws to be releas'd,
And much the less, because it was their
    Lords request :
They thought it great their Sov'rain to
    controul,
And nam'd their Pride, Nobility of Soul. 1220

'Tis true, the *Pigeons* and their Prince
    Elect
Were short of Pow'r their purpose to effect :
But with their quills, did all the hurt they
    cou'd,
And cuff'd the tender *Chickens* from their
    food :
And much the *Buzzard* in their Cause did
    stir,
Tho' naming not the Patron, to infer,
With all respect, He was a gross Idolater.
  But when th' Imperial owner did espy
That thus they turn'd his Grace to villany,
Not suff'ring wrath to discompose his
    mind,   1230
He strove a temper for th' extreams to find,
So to be just, as he might still be kind.
Then, all maturely weigh'd, pronounc'd a
    Doom
Of Sacred Strength for ev'ry Age to come.
By this the Doves their Wealth and State
    possess,
No Rights infring'd, but Licence to oppress :
Such Pow'r have they as Factious Lawyers
    long
To Crowns ascrib'd, that Kings can do no
    wrong.
But, since his own Domestick Birds have
    try'd   1239
The dire Effects of their destructive Pride,
He deems that Proof a Measure to the rest,
Concluding well within his Kingly Breast
His Fowl of Nature too unjustly were
    opprest.
He therefore makes all Birds of ev'ry Sect
Free of his Farm, with promise to respect
Their sev'ral Kinds alike, and equally pro-
    tect.
His Gracious Edict the same Franchise
    yields
To all the wild Encrease of Woods and
    Fields,
And who in Rocks aloof, and who in Steeples
    builds.
To *Crows* the like Impartial Grace affords,
And *Choughs* and *Daws*, and such Republick
    Birds :   1251
Secur'd with ample Priviledge to feed,
Each has his District, and his Bounds de-
    creed :
Combin'd in common Int'rest with his
    own,
But not to pass the Pigeons *Rubicon.*

Here ends the Reign of this pretended
Dove;
All Prophecies accomplish'd from above,
For *Shiloh* comes the Scepter to remove.
Reduc'd from Her Imperial High Abode,
Like *Dyonysius* to a private Rod,   1260
The Passive Church, that with pretended
Grace
Did Her distinctive Mark in duty place,
Now Touch'd, Reviles her Maker to his Face.
   What after happen'd is not hard to guess;
The small Beginnings had a large Encrease,
And Arts and Wealth succeed (the secret
spoils of Peace.)
'Tis said the Doves repented, tho' too late
Become the Smiths of their own Foolish Fate:
Nor did their Owner hasten their ill hour:
But, sunk in Credit, they decreas'd in Pow'r:
Like Snows in warmth that mildly pass away,
Dissolving in the Silence of Decay.   1172
   The *Buzzard*, not content with equal place,
Invites the feather'd *Nimrods* of his Race,
To hide the thinness of their Flock from
Sight,
And all together make a seeming, goodly
Flight:
But each have sep'rate Interests of their own;
Two *Czars*, are one too many for a throne.

Nor can th' usurper long abstain from Food,
Already he has tasted Pigeons Blood: 1280
And may be tempted to his former fare,
When this Indulgent Lord shall late to
Heav'n repair.
Bare benting times, and moulting Months
may come,
When lagging late, they cannot reach their
home:
Or Rent in schism, (for so their Fate decrees,)
Like the Tumultuous Colledge of the Bees;
They fight their Quarrel, by themselves
opprest;
The Tyrant smiles below, and waits the
falling feast.
   Thus did the gentle *Hind* her fable end,
Nor would the *Panther* blame it, nor com-
mend;   1290
But, with affected Yawnings at the close,
Seem'd to require her natural repose.
For now the streaky light began to peep;
And setting stars admonish'd both to sleep.
The Dame withdrew, and wishing to her
Guest
The peace of Heav'n, betook her self to
rest.
Ten thousand Angels on her slumbers waite
With glorious Visions of her future state.

FINIS.

Britannia Rediviva:

A POEM

ON THE

BIRTH

OF THE

PRINCE.

Written by Mr. *DRYDEN.*

Dii Patrii Indigetes, & Romule, Vestáque Mater,
Quæ Tuscum Tiberim, & Romana Palatia servas,
Hunc saltem everso Puerum *succurrere sæclo*
Ne prohibete. satis jampridem sanguine nostro
Laomedonteæ luimus Perjuria Trojæ.
Virg. Georg. 1.

LONDON,

Printed for *J. Tonson,* at the *Judges-Head* in
Chancery-Lane, near *Fleet-street.* 1688

BRITANNIA REDIVIVA,

A

POEM

ON THE

PRINCE

Born on the 10th of *June*, 1688.

OUR Vows are heard betimes ! and Heaven
    takes care
To grant, before we can conclude the Pray'r :
Preventing angels met it half the way,
And sent us back to Praise, who came to
    Pray.
   Just on the Day, when the high mounted
    Sun
Did farthest in his Northern Progress run,
He bended forward and ev'n stretched the
    Sphere
Beyond the limits of the lengthen'd year ;
To view a Brighter Sun in *Britaine* Born ;⎫
That was the Bus'ness of his longest Morn,⎬
The Glorious Object seen, t'was time to ⎪
    turn.   11⎭
   Departing Spring cou'd only stay to⎫
    shed ⎬
Her bloomy beauties on the Genial Bed, ⎪
But left the manly Summer in her sted, ⎭
With timely Fruit the longing Land to chear
And to fulfill the promise of the year.
Betwixt two Seasons comes th' Auspicious
    Heir,
This Age to blossom, and the next to bear.
   [a] Last solemn Sabbath saw the Church
    attend,
The Paraclete in fiery Pomp descend ;   20
But when his wondrous [b] Octave rowl'd again,
He brought a Royal Infant in his Train,
So great a Blessing to so good a King
None but th' Eternal Comforter cou'd bring.
   Or did the Mighty Trinity conspire,
As once, in Council to Create our Sire ?

It seems as if they sent the New-Born Guest
To wait on the Procession of their feast ;
And on their Sacred Anniverse decree'd   29
To stamp their Image on the promis'd Seed.
Three Realms united, and on One bestow'd
An Emblem of their Mystick Union show'd :
The Mighty Trine the Triple Empire shar'd,
As every Person wou'd have One to guard.
   Hail, son of Pray'rs ! by holy Violence
Drawn down from Heav'n ; but long be
    banish'd thence,
And late to thy Paternal Skyes retire :
To mend our Crimes whole Ages wou'd
    require,
To change th' inveterate habit of our Sins,
And finish what thy Godlike Sire begins. 40
Kind Heav'n, to make us *English-Men* again,
No less can give us than a Patriarchs Reign.
   The Sacred Cradle to your Charge receive
Ye Seraphs, and by turns the Guard relieve ;
Thy Father's Angel and Thy Father joyn
To keep Possession, and secure the Line ;
But long defer the Honours of thy Fate,
Great may they be like his, like his be late,
That *James* this running Century may view,
And give his Son an Auspice to the New. 50
   Our wants exact at least that moderate⎫
    stay : ⎪
For see the [c] Dragon winged on his way, ⎬
To watch the [d] Travail and devour the ⎪
    Prey. ⎭
Or, if Allusions may not rise so high, ⎫
Thus, when *Alcides* rais'd his Infant Cry, ⎬
The Snakes besieg'd his Young Divinity : ⎭

But vainly with their forked Tongues they threat ;
For Opposition makes a Heroe Great.
To needful Succour all the good will run :
And *Jove* assert the Godhead of his Son. 60
O still repining at your present state,
Grudging your selves the Benefits of Fate,
Look up, and read in Characters of Light
A Blessing sent you in your own Despight.
The Manna falls, yet that Cœlestial Bread
Like *Jews* you munch, and murmure while you feed.
May not your Fortune be like theirs, Exil'd,
Yet forty Years to wander in the Wild :
Or if it be, may *Moses* live at least   69
To lead you to the Verge of promis'd Rest !
Tho' Poets are not Prophets, to foreknow
What Plants will take the Blite, and what will grow,
By tracing Heav'n his Footsteps may be found ;
Behold ! how awfully He walks the round !
God is abroad, and, wondrous in his ways,
The Rise of Empires, and their Fall surveys ;
More (might I say) than with an usual eye, ⎫
He sees his bleeding Church in Ruine lye, ⎬
And hears the Souls of Saints beneath his ⎭
    Altar cry.
Already has He lifted high, the [e] Sign,   80
Which Crown'd the Conquering Arms of *Constantine* :
The [f] Moon grows pale at that presaging sight,
And half her Train of Stars have lost their Light.
  Behold another [g] *Sylvester*, to bless
The Sacred Standard, and secure Success ;
Large of his Treasures, of a Soul so great
As fills and crowds his Universal Seat.
  Now view at home a [h] second *Constantine* ;
(The former too, was of the *Brittish* line)
Has not his healing Balm your Breaches clos'd,   90
Whose Exile many sought, and few oppos'd ?
Or did not Heav'n by its Eternal Doom
Permit those Evils, that this Good might come ?

So manifest, that ev'n the Moon-ey'd Sects
See *Whom* and *What* this Providence protects.
Methinks, had we within our Minds no more
Than that One Shipwrack on the Fatal [i] Ore,
That only thought may make us think again,
What Wonders God reserves for such a Reign.
To dream that Chance his Preservation wrought,   100
Were to think *Noah* was preserv'd for nought ;
Or the surviving Eight were not design'd
To people Earth, and to restore their Kind.
  When humbly on the Royal Babe we gaze,
The Manly Lines of a Majestick face
Give awful joy : 'Tis Paradise to look
On the fair Frontispiece of Nature's Book ;
If the first opening Page so charms the sight,
Think how th' unfolded Volume will delight !
See how the Venerable Infant lyes   110
In early Pomp ; how through the Mother's Eyes
The Father's Soul with an undaunted view
Looks out, and takes our Homage as his due.
See on his future Subjects how He smiles,
Nor meanly flatters, nor with craft beguiles ;
But with an open face, as on his Throne,
Assures our Birthrights and assumes his own.
  Born in broad Day-light, that th' ungrateful Rout
May find no room for a remaining doubt :
Truth, which it self is light, does darkness shun,   120
And the true Eaglet safely dares the Sun.
  [k] Fain wou'd the Fiends have made a dubious birth,
Loth to confess the Godhead cloathed in Earth.
But sickned after all their baffled lyes,
To find an Heir apparent of the Skyes :
Abandon'd to despair, still may they grudge,
And, owning not the Saviour, prove the Judge.
  Not Great [l] *Æneas* stood in plainer Day,
When, the dark mantling Mist dissolv'd away,   129
He to the *Tyrians* shew'd his sudden face,
Shining with all his Goddess Mother's Grace :

---

[e] *The Cross.*
[f] *The Crescent, which the* Turks *bear for their Arms.*
[g] *The Pope in the time of* Constantine *the Great, alluding to the present Pope.*
[h] K. James *the Second.*

[i] *The Lemmon Ore.*
[k] *Alluding to the Temptations in the Wilderness.*
[l] Virg. *Æneid.* 1.

100 wrought,] wrought ; *1688.*

For She her self had made his Count'nance
  bright,
Breath'd honour on his eyes, and her own
  Purple Light.
If our Victorious ^m *Edward*, as they say,
Gave *Wales* a Prince on that Propitious
  Day,
Why may not Years revolving with his Fate
Produce his Like, but with a longer Date ?
One who may carry to a distant shore
The Terrour that his Fam'd Forefather
  bore.
But why shou'd *James* or his Young Hero
  stay　　　　　　　　　　　　140
For slight Presages of a Name or Day ?
We need no *Edward's* Fortune to adorn
That happy moment when our Prince was
  born :
Our Prince adorns his Day, and Ages hence
Shall wish his Birth-day for some future
  Prince.
  ⁿ Great *Michael*, Prince of all th' Ætherial
  Hosts,
And what e're In-born Saints our *Britain*
  boasts ;
And thou, th' ^o adopted Patron of our Isle,
With chearful Aspects on this Infant smile :
The Pledge of Heav'n, which dropping from
  above　　　　　　　　　　　150
Secures our Bliss and reconciles his Love.
  Enough of Ills our dire Rebellion wrought,
When, to the Dregs, we drank the bitter
  draught ;
Then airy Atoms did in Plagues conspire, ⎞
Nor did th' avenging Angel yet retire,   ⎬
But purg'd our still encreasing Crimes ⎠
  with Fire.
Then perjur'd Plots, the still impending
  Test,
And worse ; but Charity conceals the Rest :
Here stop the Current of the sanguine flood ;
Require not, Gracious God, thy Martyrs
  Blood ;　　　　　　　　　　　160
But let their dying pangs, their living toyl,
Spread a Rich harvest through their Native
  Soil :
A Harvest ripening for another Reign,
Of which this Royal Babe may reap the
  Grain.

Enough of Early Saints one womb has
  giv'n ;
Enough encreas'd the Family of Heav'n :
Let them for his and our Attonement go ;
And Reigning blest above, leave him to
  Rule below.
  Enough already has the Year foreslow'd
His wonted Course, the Seas have overflow'd,
The Meads were floated with a weeping
  Spring,　　　　　　　　　　　171
And frighten'd birds in Woods forgot to
  sing ;
The Strong-limb'd Steed beneath his harness
  faints,
And the same shiv'ring sweat his Lord
  attaints.
When will the Minister of Wrath give o're ?
Behold him ; at ^p *Araunah's* threshing-floor.
He stops, and seems to sheathe his flaming
  brand ;
Pleas'd with burnt Incense, from our *David's*
  hand.
David has bought the *Jebusites* abode,
And rais'd an Altar to the Living God.　180
Heav'n, to reward him, make his Joys ⎞
  sincere ;   ⎟
No future Ills, nor Accidents appear   ⎬
To sully and pollute the Sacred Infants ⎟
  Year.   ⎠
Five Months to Discord and Debate were
  giv'n :
He sanctifies the yet remaining Sev'n.
Sabbath of Months ! henceforth in Him be
  blest,
And prelude to the Realms perpetual Rest !
  Let his Baptismal Drops for us attone ;
Lustrations for ^q Offences not his own.
Let Conscience, which is Int'rest ill disguis'd,
In the same Font be cleans'd, and all the
  Land Baptiz'd.　　　　　　　　191
  ^r Un-nam'd as yet ; at least unknown to
  Fame :
Is there a strife in Heav'n about his
  Name ?
Where every Famous Predecessour vies,
And makes a Faction for it in the Skies ?

---

^m Edw. *the black Prince, Born on Trinity-*
Sunday.
ⁿ *The Motto of the Poem explain'd.*
^o *St.* George.

^p *Alluding to the passage in 1 Book of Kings,*
Ch. 24. v. 20th.
^q *Original Sin.*
^r *The Prince Christen'd, but not nam'd.*

169 foreslow'd] *Some editions absurdly give*
foreshow'd

Or must it be reserv'd to thought alone ?
Such was the Sacred [s] *Tetragrammaton.*
Things worthy silence must not be reveal'd :
Thus the true Name of [t] *Rome* was kept
   conceal'd,   199
To shun the Spells, and Sorceries of those
Who durst her Infant Majesty oppose.
But when his tender strength in time shall
   rise
To dare ill Tongues, and fascinating eyes ;
This Isle, which hides the little Thund'rer's
   Fame,
Shall be too narrow to contain his Name :
Th' Artillery of Heav'n shall make him
   known ;
[u] *Crete* could not hold the God, when *Jove*
   was grown.
  As *Joves* [x] Increase, who from his Brain
   was born,
Whom Arms and Arts did equally adorn,
Free of the Breast was bred, whose milky
   taste   210
Minerva's Name to *Venus* had debas'd ;
So this Imperial Babe rejects the Food
That mixes Monarchs with *Plebeian* blood :
Food that his inborn Courage might con-
   troul,
Extinguish all the Father in his Soul,
And for his *Estian* Race, and *Saxon* Strain,
Might re-produce some second *Richard's*
   Reign.
Mildness he shares from both his Parents
   blood :
But Kings too tame are despicably good :
Be this the Mixture of this Regal Child, 220
By Nature Manly, but by Virtue Mild.
  Thus far the Furious Transport of the
   News
Had to Prophetick Madness fir'd the
   Muse ;
Madness ungovernable, uninspir'd,
Swift to foretel whatever she desir'd ;
Was it for me the dark Abyss to tread,
And read the Book which Angels cannot
   read ?

How was I punish'd when the [y] sudden blast
The Face of Heav'n and our young Sun
   o'recast !
Fame, the swift Ill, encreasing as she rowl'd,
Disease, Despair, and Death at three reprises
   told :   231
At three insulting strides she stalk'd the
   Town,
And, like Contagion, struck the Loyal down.
Down fell the winnow'd Wheat ; but
   mounted high,
The Whirl-wind bore the Chaff, and hid the
   Sky.
Here black Rebellion shooting from below, ⎫
(As Earth's [z] Gigantick brood by moments ⎪
   grow)   ⎬
And here the Sons of God are petrify'd ⎪
   with Woe :   ⎭
An *Appoplex* of Grief ! so low were driv'n
The Saints, as hardly to defend their Heav'n.
  As, when pent Vapours run their hollow
   round,   241
Earth-quakes, which are Convulsions of the
   ground,
Break bellowing forth, and no Confinement
   brook,
Till the Third settles what the Former
   shook ;
Such heavings had our Souls ; till, slow and
   late,
Our life with his return'd, and Faith prevail'd
   on Fate.
By Prayers the mighty *Blessing* was im-
   plor'd,
To Pray'rs was granted, and by Pray'rs
   restor'd.   248
So e're the [a] *Shunamite* a Son conceiv'd,
The Prophet promis'd, and the Wife believ'd ;
A Son was sent, the Son so much desir'd,
But soon upon the Mother's Knees expir'd.
The troubled Seer approach'd the mournful
   Door,
Ran, prayed, and sent his Past'ral-Staff
   before,
Then stretch'd his Limbs upon the Child,
   and mourn'd,
Till Warmth, and breath, and a new Soul
   return'd.

---

[s] Jehovah, *or the name of God unlawful to be
pronounc'd by the* Jews.
[t] *Some Authors say, that the true name of*
Rome *was kept a secret ;* ne hostes incantamentis
Deos elicerent.
[u] Candie *where* Jupiter *was born and bred
secretly.*
[x] Pallas, *or* Minerva ; *said by the Poets, to have
been bred up by hand.*

[y] *The sudden false Report of the Prince's
Death.*
[z] *Those Gyants are feign'd to have grown
15 Ells every day.*
[a] *In the second Book of* Kings, *chap.* 4th.

Thus Mercy stretches out her hand, and
  saves
Desponding *Peter* sinking in the Waves.
  As when a sudden Storm of Hail and Rain
Beats to the ground the yet unbearded
  Grain.   260
Think not the hopes of Harvest are destroy'd
On the flat Field, and on the naked void ;
The light unloaded stem, from tempestfree'd,
Will raise the youthful honours of his head ;
And, soon restor'd by native vigour, bear
The timely product of the bounteous Year.
  Nor yet conclude all fiery *Trials* past,
For Heav'n will exercise us to the last ;
Sometimes will check us in our full carreer,
With doubtful blessings, and with mingled
  fear ;   270
That, still depending on his daily Grace,
His every mercy for an alms may pass ;
With sparing hands will Dyet us to good ;
Preventing Surfeits of our pampered blood.
So feeds the Mother-bird her craving young
With little Morsels, and delays 'em long.
  True, this last blessing was a Royal Feast,
But where's the Wedding Garment on the
  Guest ?
Our Manners, as Religion were a Dream,
Are such as teach the Nations to *Blaspheme*.
In Lusts we wallow, and with Pride we
  swell,   281
And Injuries, with Injuries repell ;
Prompt to Revenge, not daring to forgive,
Our Lives unteach the Doctrine we believe ;
Thus *Israel* Sind, impenitently hard,
And vainly thought the [b] present Ark their
  Guard ;
But when the haughty *Philistims* appear, ⎫
They fled abandoned to their Foes and   ⎪
  fear ;   ⎬
Their God was absent, though his Ark   ⎪
  was there.   ⎭
Ah ! lest our Crimes shou'd snatch this
  Pledge away,   290
And make our Joys the blessing of a day !
For we have sin'd him hence, and that he
  lives.
God to his promise, not our practice, gives.
Our Crimes wou'd soon weigh down the
  guilty Scale,
But *James*, and *Mary*, and the Church pre-
  vail.

[b] Sam. 4th. v. 10th.

Nor [c] *Amaleck* can rout the *Chosen Bands*,
While *Hur* and *Aaron* hold up *Moses* hands.
  By living well, let us secure his days ;
Mod'rate in hopes, and humble in our ways.
No force the Free-born Spirit can constrain,
But Charity, and great Examples gain. 301
Forgiveness is our thanks, for such a day ;
'Tis Godlike God in his own Coyn to pay.
  But you, Propitious Queen, translated ⎫
  here   ⎪
From your mild Heav'n to rule our rugged ⎬
  Sphere,   ⎪
Beyond the Sunny walks and circling Year. ⎭
You, who your Native Clymate have bereft
Of all the Virtues, and the Vices left ;
Whom Piety, and Beauty make their boast,
Though Beautiful is well in Pious lost ; 310
So lost as Star-light is dissolv'd away,
And melts into the brightness of the day,
Or Gold about the Regal Diadem,
Lost to improve the lustre of the Gem.
What can we add to your Triumphant Day ?
Let the Great Gift the beautious Giver pay ;
For shou'd our thanks awake the rising ⎫
  Sun,   ⎪
And lengthen, as his latest shadows run , ⎬
That, tho' the longest day, wou'd soon,   ⎪
  too soon, be done.   ⎭
Let Angels voices with their harps conspire,
But keep th' auspicious Infant from the
  Quire ;   321
Late let him sing above, and let us know
No sweeter Musick than his Cryes below.
  Nor can I wish to you, Great Monarch,
  more
Than such an annual Income to your store ;
The Day which gave this *Unit*, did not
  shine
For a less Omen, than to fill the *Trine*.
After a *Prince*, an *Admiral* beget,
The Royal Sov'raign wants an Anchor yet.
Our Isle has younger Titles still in store, ⎫
And when th' exhausted Land can yield   ⎪
  no more,   331 ⎬
Your Line can force them from a Foreign ⎪
  shore.   ⎭
  The Name of Great your Martial mind
  will suit ;
But Justice is your Darling Attribute :

[c] Exod. 17. v. 8th.

320 voices] voices, *1688*.
334 Justice] Justice, *1688*.

Of all the *Greeks*, 'twas but [d] one *Hero's* due,
And, in him, *Plutarch* Prophecy'd of you.
A Prince's favours but on few can fall,
But Justice is a Virtue shar'd by all.
  Some Kings the name of Conq'rors have
    assum'd,   339
Some to be Great, some to be Gods presum'd;
But boundless pow'r and arbitrary Lust
Made Tyrants still abhor the Name of Just ;
They shun'd the praise this Godlike Virtue
    gives,
And fear'd a Title that reproach'd their
    Lives.
  The Pow'r from which all Kings derive
    their state,
Whom they pretend, at least, to imitate,
Is equal both to punish and reward ;

For few wou'd love their God, unless they
    fear'd.   ·
  Resistless Force and Immortality
Make but a Lame, Imperfect Deity ;   350
Tempests have force unbounded to destroy,
And Deathless Being ev'n the Damn'd enjoy,
And yet Heav'ns Attributes both last and
    first,
One without life, and one with life accurst ;
But Justice is Heav'ns self, so strictly He
That cou'd it fail, the God-head cou'd not be.
This Virtue is your own ; but Life and State
Are One to Fortune subject, One to Fate :
Equal to all, you justly frown or smile,   ⎫
Nor Hopes, nor Fears your steady Hand   ⎬
    beguile ;   360 ⎪
Your self our Ballance hold, the Worlds   ⎭
    our Isle.

---

[d] Aristides, *see his Life in* Plutarch.

361 Worlds] Worlds, *1688*.

EPISTLES AND COMPLIMENTARY ADDRESSES.

TO JOHN HODDESDON,

ON HIS DIVINE EPIGRAMS.

THOU hast inspired me with thy soul, and I,
Who ne're before could ken of poetry,
Am grown so good proficient I can lend
A line in commendation of my friend ;
Yet 'tis but of the second hand ; if ought
There be in this, 'tis from thy fancy brought.
Good thief who dar'st Prometheus-like
    aspire,
And fill thy poems with Celestiall fire,
Enliven'd by these sparks divine, their
    rayes
Adde a bright lustre to thy crown of bayes.
Young eaglet, who thy nest thus soon for-
    sook,   11
So lofty and divine a course hast took
As all admire, before the down begin
To peep, as yet, upon thy smoother Chin ;

And, making heaven thy aim, hast had the
    grace
To look the sunne of righteousnesse ith' face.
What may we hope, if thou go'st on thus fast!
Scriptures at first, Enthusiasmes at last !
Thou hast commenc'd, betimes, a saint : go
    on,
Mingling Diviner streams with Helicon, 20
That they who view what Epigrams here be,
May learn to make like, in just praise of thee.
Reader, I've done, nor longer will withhold
Thy greedy eyes ; looking on this pure gold
Thou'lt know adult'rate copper, which, like
    this,
Will onely serve to be a foil to his.

         J. DRYDEN, of Trin. C.

To my Honored Friend SIR ROBERT HOWARD
On his Excellent Poems.

As there is Musick uninform'd by Art
In those wild Notes, which with a merry heart
The Birds in unfrequented shades expresse,
Who better taught at home, yet please us
    lesse :
So in your Verse, a native sweetnesse dwells,
Which shames Composure, and its Art excells.
Singing no more can your soft numbers grace,
Then Paint adds charms unto a beauteous
    Face.
Yet as when mighty Rivers gently creep,
Their even calmnesse does suppose them
    deep,   10
Such is your Muse : no Metaphor swell'd high
With dangerous boldnesse lifts her to the sky;
Those mounting Fancies, when they fall again,
Shew sand and dirt at bottom do remain.
So firm a strength and yet withall so sweet,
Did never but in *Sampson's* Riddle meet.

'Tis strange each line so great a weight
    should bear,
And yet no signe of toil, no sweat appear.
Either your Art hides Art, as Stoicks feign
Then least to feel, when most they suffer pain ;
And we, dull souls, admire but cannot see 21
What hidden springs within the Engine be
Or 'tis some happiness that still pursues
Each act and motion of your gracefull Muse.
Or is it Fortune's work, that in your head
The curious * Net that is for   { * *Rete*
    fancies spread,   { *Mirabile.*
Lets through its Meshes every
    meaner thought
While rich Idea's there are only caught ?
Sure that's not all ; this is a piece too fair
To be the child of Chance, and not of Care.

TO JOHN HODDESDON. Text from the original
prefixt to Hoddesdon's *Sion and Parnassus*, 1650.
16 ith'] *Editors wrongly give* i' the *or in the*

TO SIR ROBERT HOWARD. Text from the
original of 1661.
8 Then] *The editors change the spelling to* Than
27 Lets] Let's *1661.*
28 caught ?] caught. *1661.*

No Atoms casually together hurl'd   31
Could e're produce so beautifull a world.
Nor dare I such a doctrine here admit,
As would destroy the providence of wit.
'Tis your strong Genius then which does not
    feel
Those weights would make a weaker spirit reel.
To carry weight and run so lightly too
Is what alone your *Pegasus* can do.
Great *Hercules* himself could ne're do more,
Than not to feel those Heav'ns and Gods
    he bore.   40
Your easier odes, which for delight were
    penn'd,
Yet our instruction make their second end ;
We're both enrich'd and pleas'd, like them
    that woo
At once a Beauty and a Fortune too.
Of Morall Knowledge Poesie was Queen,
And still she might, had wanton wits not
    been ;
Who like ill Guardians liv'd themselves at
    large,
And, not content with that, debauch'd their
    charge.
Like some brave Captain, your successful Pen
Restores the Exil'd to her Crown again ; 50
And gives us hope that having seen the days
When nothing flourish'd but Fanatique Bays,
All will at length in this opinion rest,
" A sober Prince's Government is best.
This is not all ; your Art the way has found
To make improvement of the richest ground,
That soil which those immortal Lawrells bore,
That once the sacred *Maro's* temples wore.
Elisa's griefs, are so expresst by you,
They are too eloquent to have been true. 60
Had she so spoke, *Æneas* had obey'd
What *Dido* rather then what *Jove* had said.
If future Rites can give a Ghost repose,
Your Muse so justly had discharged those,
Elisa's shade may now its wandring cease,
And claim a title to the fields of peace.
But if Æneas be oblig'd, no lesse
Your kindnesse great *Achilles* doth confesse,
Who, dress'd by *Statius* in too bold a look,
Did ill become those Virgin's Robes he took.

To understand how much we owe to you,   71
We must your Numbers with your Author's
    view :
Then we shall see his work was lamely rough,
Each figure stiff, as if design'd in buffe :
His colours laid so thick on every place,
As onely shew'd the paint, but hid the face.
But as in Perspective we Beauties see,
Which in the glasse, not in the Picture, be ;
So here our sight obligeingly mistakes
That wealth, which his your bounty onely
    makes.   80
Thus vulgar dishes are by Cooks disguis'd,
More for their dressing than their substance
    priz'd.
Your curious *Notes so search into   [*Annota-
    that Age,   } tions on
When all was fable but the sacred   (Statius.
    Page,
That, since in that dark night we needs
    must stray,
We are at least misled in pleasant way.
But what we most admire, your Verse no lesse
The Prophet than the Poet doth confess.
Ere our weak eyes discern'd th' doubtfull
    streak
Of light, you saw great *Charles* his morning
    break.   90
So skilfull Sea-men ken th' Land from far,
Which shows like mists to the dul Passenger.
To *Charls* your Muse first pays her dutious
    love,
As still the Antients did begin from *Jove*
With *Monck* you end, whose name preserv'd
    shall be,
As *Rome* recorded * *Rufus* memory,
Who thought it greater honour   ⎧ * Hic situs est
    to obey   ⎪ *Rufus* qui
His Countrey's interest, than   ⎪ pulso vindice
    the world to sway.   ⎬ quondam
But to write worthy things of   ⎪ Imperium
    worthy men,   ⎪ asseruit non
Is the peculiar talent of your   ⎩ sibi sed Patriæ.
    Pen :   100
Yet let me take your Mantle up, and I
Will venture in your right to prophesy.
    " This Work, by merit first of Fame secure,
" Is likewise happy in its Geniture :
" For, since 'tis born when *Charls* ascends th'
    Throne,
" It shares at once his Fortune and its own.

JOHN DRIDEN.

---

40 Gods] gods *1661*.
56 improvement] *The editors wrongly give*
the improvement
62 then] *The editors change the spelling to*
than
70 Virgin's] *The editors wrongly give* Virgin

To my Honour'd Friend Dr. Charleton, *on his learned and useful Works; and more particularly this of* Stone-heng, *by him Restored to the true Founders.*

THe longest Tyranny that ever sway'd
Was that wherein our Ancestors betray'd
Their free-born *Reason* to the *Stagirite*,
And made his Torch their universal Light.
So *Truth*, while onely one suppli'd the State,
Grew scarce, and dear, and yet sophisticate,
Until 'twas bought, like Emp'rique Wares,
    or Charms,
Hard words seal'd up with *Aristotle's* Armes.
Columbus was the first that shook his Throne;
And found a *Temp'rate* in a *Torrid* Zone,   10
The fevrish aire fann'd by a cooling breez,
The fruitful Vales set round with shady
    Trees;
And guiltless *Men*, who danc'd away their
    time,
Fresh as their *Groves* and *Happy* as their
    Clime.
Had we still paid that homage to a *Name*,
Which only *God* and *Nature* justly claim,
The *Western* Seas had been our utmost bound,
Where *Poets* still might dream the *Sun* was
    drown'd:
And all the *Starrs*, that shine in *Southern*
    Skies,   19
Had been admir'd by none but *Salvage* Eyes.
Among th' *Assertors* of free Reason's claim,
Th' *English* are not the least in Worth, or
    Fame.
The World to *Bacon* does not onely owe
Its *present* Knowledge, but its *future* too.
Gilbert shall live, till *Lode-stones* cease to draw
Or *British* Fleets the boundless Ocean awe.
And noble *Boyle*, not less in *Nature* seen,
Than his great *Brother* read in *States* and *Men.*
The *Circling* streams, once thought but pools,
    of blood
(Whether Life's fewel or the Bodie's food)

From dark Oblivion *Harvey's* name shall
    save;
While *Ent* keeps all the honour that he gave.
Nor are *You*, Learned Friend, the least
    renown'd;
Whose Fame, not circumscrib'd with *English*
    ground,
Flies like the nimble journeys of the Light;
And is, like that, unspent too in its flight.
Whatever *Truths* have been, by *Art*, or *Chance*,
Redeem'd from *Error*, or from *Ignorance*,
Thin in their *Authors*, (like rich veins of Ore)
Your Works unite, and still discover more.
Such is the healing virtue of Your Pen,   41
To perfect Cures on *Books*, as well as *Men.*
Nor is This Work the least: You well may
    give
To *Men* new vigour, who make *Stones* to live.
Through You the DANES (their short Do-
    minion lost)
A longer Conquest than the *Saxons* boast.
STONE-HENG, once thought a *Temple*, You
    have found
A *Throne* where Kings, our Earthly Gods,
    were Crown'd.
Where by their wondring Subjects They
    were seen,
Joy'd with their Stature and their Princely
    meen.   50
Our *Soveraign* here above the rest might
    stand;
And here be chose again to rule the Land.
These Ruines sheltered once *His* Sacred
    Head,
Then when from Wor'ster's fatal Field *He*
    fled;
Watch'd by the Genius of this Royal place,
And mighty Visions of the Danish Race,
His *Refuge* then was for a *Temple* shown:
But, *He* Restor'd, 'tis now become a *Throne*.

                      JOHN DRIDEN.

TO DR. CHARLETON. Text from the original prefixt to Charleton's *Chorea Gigantum*, 1663.
   6 sophisticate;] sophisticate. *1663.*
   7 Until 'twas] *Derrick and others nonsensically give* Still it was
   22 Th' *English* are] *Tonson in 1704 printed*
Our Nation's
   28 *Brother*] *Christie, Saintsbury, and others
print a comma after this word and so give
another and wholly false sense.*

   39 of] *Christie wrongly gives* in
   50 Joy'd with] *Scott reports the reading of the
first edition to be* Chose by   *The British
Museum copy has* Joy'd with
   54 Then when] *Tonson in 1704 printed* When he
from Wor'ster's fatal battle fled

TO THE | LADY CASTLEMAINE, |

upon | Her incouraging his first Play.

As *Seamen,* Shipwrack'd on some happy
 Shore,
Discover Wealth in Lands unknown before,
And, what their *Art* had labour'd long in vain
By their Misfortunes happily obtain,
So my much envy'd Muse, by storms long
 tost,
Is thrown upon your hospitable Coast,
And finds more favour by her ill success,
Than she cou'd hope for by her Happiness.
Once *Cato's* Vertue did the Gods oppose,
While they the Victor, He the Vanquish'd
 chose :   10
But you have done what *Cato* cou'd not do,
To chuse the Vanquish'd, and restore him
 too.
Let others still Triumph, and gain their
 Cause
By their Deserts or by the *World's Applause* ;
Let merit Crowns, and Justice Lawrels give,
But let me happy by your Pity live.
True Poets empty Fame and Praise despise ;
Fame is the Trumpet, but your Smile the
 Prize :
You sit above, and see vain Men below
Contend, for what you only can bestow ; 20
But those great actions others do by chance,
Are, like your *Beauty,* your *Inheritance* :
So great a Soul, such sweetness join'd in one,
Cou'd only spring from Noble *Grandison* :
You, like the Stars, not by Reflection bright,
Are born to your own Heav'n, and your own
 light ;

Like them are good, but from a *Nobler* Cause,
From your own Knowledge, not from
 Nature's Laws.
Your Pow'r you never use but for Defence,
To guard your own, or others' Innocence :
Your Foes are such as they, not you, have
 made,   31
And Vertue may repel, tho' not invade.
Such Courage did the *Ancient heroes* show,
Who, when they might prevent, wou'd wait
 the blow ;
With such assurance as they meant to say,
We will o'recome, but scorn the safest way.
What further fear of danger can there be ?
Beauty, which captives all things, sets me
 free.
Posterity will judge by my success
I had the *Grecian* Poet's happiness,   40
Who, waving plots, found out a better way ;
Some God descended and preserv'd the
 Play.
When first the Triumphs of your Sex were
 sung
By those old Poets, *Beauty* was but young,
And few admired the native Red and White,
Till Poets dress'd them up, to charm the
 sight ;
So *Beauty* took on trust, and did engage
For Sums of Praises till she came to *Age.*
But this long growing Debt to Poetry 49
You justly (Madam) have discharg'd to me,
When your *Applause* and *Favour* did infuse
New life to my condemn'd and dying Muse.

To Mr. Lee, *on his* Alexander.

THE Blast of common Censure cou'd I fear,
Before your Play my Name shou'd not
 appear ;
For 'twill be thought, and with some colour
 too,
I pay the Bribe I first receiv'd from You :
That mutual Vouchers for our Fame we
 stand,
To play the Game into each other's Hand ;

And as cheap Pen'orths to our selves afford
As *Bessus,* and the Brothers of the Sword.
Such Libels private Men may well endure,
When *States,* and *Kings* themselves are not
 secure :   10
For ill Men, conscious of their inward
 guilt,
Think the best Actions on By-ends are built,

TO THE LADY CASTLEMAINE.   Text from the *Miscellanies* of 1693.

To MR. LEE.   Text from the original prefixt to Lee's tragedy of *The Rival Queens,* 1677, republished in 1694.

DR.   G

And yet my silence had not scap'd their
    spight,
Then envy had not suffer'd me to write,
For, since I cou'd not Ignorance pretend,
Such worth I must or envy or commend.
So many *Candidates* there stand for Wit,
A place in Court is scarce so hard to get ;
In vain they crowd each other at the Door ;
For ev'n Reversions are all beg'd before :   20
Desert, how known so e're, is long delay'd ;
And, then too, *Fools* and *Knaves* are better
    payd.
Yet, as some Actions bear so great a Name
That Courts themselves are just, for fear of
    Shame :
So has the mighty Merit of your Play
Extorted praise, and forc'd it self a Way.
'Tis here, as 'tis at Sea ; who farthest goes,
Or dares the most, makes all the rest his
    Foes ;
Yet when some Virtue much out-grows the
    rest,
It shoots too fast, and high, to be opprest ;
As his Heroic worth struck Envy dumb,   31
Who took the *Dutchman*, and who cut the
    Boom :
Such praise is yours, while you the Passions
    move,
That 'tis no longer feign'd ; 'tis real Love :

Where Nature Triumphs over wretched
    Art ;
We only warm the Head, but you the Heart,
Alwayes you warm ! and if the rising Year,
As in hot Regions, bring the Sun too near,
'Tis but to make your Fragrant Spices blow,
Which in our colder Climates will not
    grow.   40
They only think you animate your Theme
With too much Fire, who are themselves all
    Phle'me :
Prizes wou'd be for Lags of slowest pace,
Were Cripples made the Judges of the
    Race.
Despise those Drones, who praise while they
    accuse
The too much vigour of your youthful Muse :
That humble Stile which they their Virtue
    make
Is in your pow'r ; you need but stoop and
    take.
Your beauteous Images must be allow'd
By all, but some vile Poets of the Crowd.   50
But how shou'd any Sign-post-dawber know
The worth of *Titian*, or of *Angelo* ?
Hard Features every Bungler can command ;
To draw true Beauty shews a Masters Hand.

JOHN DRYDEN.

To the | *Earl of* Roscomon, *on his Excellent Essay on* Translated Verse.

WHether the fruitful *Nile*, or *Tyrian* Shore
The seeds of Arts and Infant Science bore,
'Tis sure the noble Plant translated, first
Advanced its head in Grecian Gardens nurst.
The *Grecians* added Verse, their tuneful
    Tongue
Made Nature first and Nature's God their
    song.
Nor stopt Translation here : For conquering
    Rome
With *Grecian* Spoils brought *Grecian* Num-
    bers home ;

Enrich'd by those *Athenian* Muses more
Than all the vanquish'd World cou'd yield
    before.   10
Till barb'rous Nations and more barb'rous
    Times
Debas'd the majesty of Verse to Rhymes ;
Those rude at first : a kind of hobbling Prose :
That limp'd along and tinckl'd in the close :
But *Italy*, reviving from the trance
Of *Vandal*, *Goth*, and *Monkish* ignorance,

TO THE EARL OF ROSCOMON. Text from the
original prefixt to Roscomon's *Essay on Translated Verse*, 1684.
  3 Plant translated, first] Plant, translated
first ; *1684*.

TO MR. LEE.
  30 opprest] exprest *1694* : supprest *Scott*.

With pauses, cadence, and well-vowell'd
    Words,
And all the Graces a good Ear affords,
Made Rhyme an Art : and *Dante's* polish'd
    page
Restor'd a silver, not a golden Age :   20
Then *Petrarch* follow'd, and in him we see, ⎫
What Rhyme improv'd in all its height ⎪
    can be ;   ⎬
At best a pleasing Sound, and fair bar- ⎪
    barity.:   ⎭
The *French* pursu'd their steps ; and *Brit-
    tain,* last
In Manly sweetness all the rest surpass'd.
The Wit of *Greece,* the Gravity of *Rome,*
Appear exalted in the *Brittish* Loome ;
The Muses Empire is restor'd agen,
In *Charles* his reign, and by *Roscomon's* Pen.
Yet modestly he does his Work survey   30
And calls a finish'd Poem an ESSAY ;
For all the needful Rules are scatter'd here; ⎫
Truth smoothly told, and pleasantly ⎪
    severe ;   ⎬
(So well is Art disguis'd, for Nature to ⎪
    appeare.)   ⎭
Nor need those Rules to give Translation
    light ;
His own example is a flame so bright ;
That he, who but arrives to copy well,
Unguided will advance ; unknowing will
    excel.
Scarce his own *Horace* cou'd such Rules
    ordain ;
Or his own *Virgil* sing a nobler strain.   40
How much in him may rising *Ireland* boast,
How much in gaining him has *Britain* lost !
Their Island in revenge has ours reclaim'd,
The more instructed we, the more we still
    are sham'd.
'Tis well for us his generous bloud did flow,
Deriv'd from *British* Channels long ago ;
That here his conquering ancestors were
    nurst,
And *Ireland* but translated *England* first :
By this Reprisal we regain our right ;
Else must the two contending Nations fight

A nobler quarrel for his Native earth,   51
Than what divided *Greece* for *Homer's*
    birth.
To what perfection will our Tongue arrive,
How will Invention and Translation thrive
When Authors nobly born will bear their
    part,
And not disdain th' inglorious praise of Art !
Great Generals thus descending from com-
    mand,
With their own toil provoke the Souldiers
    hand.
How will sweet *Ovid's* Ghost he pleas'd to
    hear   59
His Fame augmented by a *Brittish*   *The*
    Peer,   *Earl of*
How he embellishes His *Helen's*   *Mulgrave.*
    loves,
Outdoes his softness, and his sense improves ?
When these translate, and teach Translators
    too,
Nor Firstling Kid nor any vulgar vow ⎫
Shou'd at *Apollo's* grateful Altar stand ; ⎪
Roscomon writes, to that auspicious hand, ⎬
Muse feed the Bull that spurns the yellow ⎪
    sand.   ⎭
Roscomon, whom both Court and Camps
    commend,
True to his Prince and faithful to his
    friend ;   69
Roscomon first in Fields of honour known, ⎫
First in the peaceful Triumphs of the ⎬
    Gown ;   ⎪
Who both *Minerva's* justly makes his own. ⎭
Now let the few belov'd by *Jove,* and
    they
Whom infus'd *Titan* form'd of better Clay,
On equal terms with ancient Wit ingage,
Nor mighty *Homer* fear, nor sacred *Virgil's*
    page ;
Our *English* Palace opens wide in state ;
And without stooping they may pass the
    Gate.

JOHN DRYDEN.

---

47 were] was *1684. Dryden writing to Tonson
pointed out the misprint.*

60 a *Brittish*] *Some editions wrongly give* an
English
65 Shou'd] Thou'd *1684.*
70 Fields] *Christie and others wrongly give*
field

TO MY FRIEND MR. NORTHLEIGH,
AUTHOR OF THE PARALLEL,
ON HIS TRIUMPH OF THE BRITISH MONARCHY.

So *Joseph*, yet a Youth, expounded well
The boding Dream, and did th' Event fore-
  tell,
Judg'd by the past, and drew the Parallel.
Thus early *Solomon* the truth explored,
The Right awarded, and the Babe restor'd.
Thus *Daniel*, ere to Prophecy he grew,
The perjur'd Presbyters did first subdue,
And freed *Susanna* from the canting Crew.

Well may our Monarchy Triumphant stand,
While warlike *James* protects both Sea and
  Land;   10
And, under Covert of his sev'nfold Shield,
Thou sendst thy Shafts to scour the distant
  Field.
By law thy pow'rful Pen has set us free;
Thou studiest that, and that may study
  thee.

To my Ingenious Friend | Henry Higden, Esq.; | on his translation of the | Tenth SATYR | of | JUVENAL.

THE *Grecian* Wits, who *Satyr* first began,
Were Pleasant *Pasquins* on the Life of
  Man;
At Mighty Villains, who the State opprest,
They durst not Rail perhaps; they
  Laugh'd at least,
And turn'd 'em out of Office with a Jest.
No Fool could peep abroad, but ready
  stand
The *Drolls* to clap a *Bauble* in his hand:
Wise *Legislators* never yet could draw
A *Fop*, within the Reach of *Common-Law*;
For Posture, Dress, Grimace, and Affectation,
Tho' *Foes* to *Sence*, are Harmless to the
  Nation.   11
Our last Redress is Dint of *Verse* to try,
And *Satyr* is our *Court* of *Chancery*.
This Way took *Horace* to reform an Age,
Not Bad enough to need an Author's
  Rage:
But Yours,* who liv'd in more   * Juvenal.
  degen'rate Times,
Was forc'd to fasten Deep, and worry
  Crimes:
Yet You, my Friend, have temper'd him so
  well,
You make him Smile in spight of all his
  Zeal:
An Art peculiar to your Self alone,   20
To joyn the Vertues of Two stiles in One.

Oh! were your Author's Principle re-
  ceiv'd,
Half of the lab'ring World wou'd be
  reliev'd;
For not to Wish, is not to be deceiv'd!
Revenge wou'd into *Charity* be chang'd,
Because it costs too Dear to be *Reveng'd*:
It costs our *Quiet* and *Content of Mind*;
And when 'tis compass'd leaves a Sting
  behind.
Suppose I had the better End o' th' Staff,
Why should I help th' ill-natur'd World to
  laugh?   30
'Tis all alike to them who gets the Day;
They Love the Spight and Mischief of the
  Fray.
No; I have Cur'd my Self of that *Disease*,
Nor will I be provok'd, but when I please:
But let me half that *Cure* to You restore;
You gave the *Salve*, I laid it to the Sore.
  Our kind Relief against a Rainy Day,
Beyond a Tavern, or a tedious Play;
We take your Book, and laugh our Spleen
  away,
If all your *Tribe*, (too studious of *Debate*) 40
Wou'd cease false Hopes and Titles to create,
Led by the *Rare Example* you begun,
Clyents wou'd fail and *Lawyers* be undone.

JOHN DRYDEN.

TO MR. NORTHLEIGH. Text from the original, prefixt to John Northleigh's *The Triumph of Our Monarchy*, 1685. (I depend for the collation on another hand.)

TO HENRY HIGDEN. Text from the original, prefixt to Higden's Translation of Juvenal's Tenth Satire, 1687.

4 Rail perhaps;] Rail; perhaps, *1687*.
Laugh'd] *Many editors wrongly give* lash'd

A LETTER TO SIR GEORGE ETHEREGE.

To you who live in chill Degree,
As Map informs, of Fifty three,
And do not much for Cold atone
By bringing thither Fifty one,
Methinks all Climes shou'd be alike,
From Tropick even to Pole Artique ;
Since you have such a Constitution
As nowhere suffers Diminution.
You can be old in grave Debate,
And young in Love-affairs of State :   10
And both to Wives and Husbands show
The Vigour of a Plenipo.
Like mighty Missioner you come
Ad Partes Infidelium ;
A Work of wondrous Merit sure,
So far to go, so much t' indure ;
And all to Preach to *German* Dame,
Where Sound of *Cupid* never came.
Less had you done, had you been sent
As far as *Drake* or *Pinto* went,   20
For Cloves or Nutmegs to the line *a*,
Or e'en for Oranges to *China* ;
That had indeed been Charity, ⎫
Where Love-sick Ladies helpless lye, ⎬
Chapt, and for want of Liquor dry. ⎭
But you have made your Zeal appear
Within the Circle of the *Bear*.
What Region of the Earth's so dull,
That is not of your Labours full ?
Triptolemus, so sung the Nine,   30
Strew'd Plenty from his Cart Divine.
But spite of all these Fable-Makers,
He never sow'd on *Almain* Acres :
No, that was left by Fate's Decree
To be perform'd and sung by thee.
Thou break'st thro' Forms with as much ease
As the *French* King thro' Articles.
In grand Affairs thy Days are spent, ⎫
In waging weighty Complement ⎬
With such as monarchs represent. ⎭   40

They who such vast Fatigues attend,
Want some soft Minutes to unbend,
To show the World that now and then
Great Ministers are mortal Men.
Then *Rhenish* Rummers walk the Round,
In Bumpers ev'ry King is crown'd,
Besides three Holy miter'd Hectors,
And the whole College of Electors,
No Health of Potentate is sunk
That pays to make his Envoy drunk.   50
These *Dutch* Delights I mention'd last,
Suit not I know your *English* taste :
For Wine to leave a Whore or Play
Was ne'er your Excellency's way.
Nor need this Title give Offence,
For here you were your Excellence ;
For Gaming, Writing, Speaking, Keeping,
His Excellence for all but Sleeping.
Now if you tope in form, and treat, ⎫
'Tis the sour Sauce to the sweet Meat, ⎬   60
The fine you pay for being great. ⎭
Nay, here's a harder Imposition,
Which is indeed the Court's Petition,
That setting worldly Pomp aside,
Which Poet has at Font deny'd,
You wou'd be pleased in humble way
To write a Trifle call'd a Play.
This truly is a Degradation, ⎫
But wou'd oblige the Crown and Nation ⎬
Next to your wise Negotiation. ⎭   70
If you pretend, as well you may, ⎫
Your high Degree, your friends will say, ⎬
The Duke *St. Agnon* made a play. ⎭
If *Gallick* Wit convince you scarce,
His Grace of *Bucks* has made a Farce ;
And you, whose Comick Wit is Terse all,
Can hardly fall below Rehearsal.
Then finish what you have began,
But scribble faster if you can :
For yet no *George*, to our discerning,   80
Has writ without a ten Years Warning.

To SIR GEORGE ETHEREGE. Text from the *Miscellanies* of several dates.

TO MR. SOUTHERN;

ON HIS COMEDY, CALL'D THE WIVES EXCUSE.

SURE there's a Fate in Plays; and 'tis in vain
To write, while these malignant Planets Reign.
Some very foolish Influence rules the Pit,
Not always kind to Sence, or just to Wit.
And whilst it lasts, let Buffoonry succeed
To make us laugh; for never was more need.
Farce in it self is of a nasty scent,
But the gain smells not of the Excrement.
The *Spanish* nymph, a Wit and Beauty too,
With all her Charms bore but a single show :   10
But let a Monster *Muscovite* appear,
He draws a crowded Audience round the Year.
May be thou hast not pleas'd the Box and Pit,
Yet those who blame thy Tale, commend thy Wit ;
So *Terence* Plotted, but so *Terence* writ.

Like his, thy Thoughts are true, thy Language clean ;
Ev'n Lewdness is made Moral, in thy Scene.
The Hearers may for want of *Nokes* repine,
But rest secure, the Readers will be thine.
Nor was thy Labour'd Drama damn'd or hiss'd,   20
But with a kind Civility dismiss'd ;
With such good manners, as the * Wife did use,   *The Wife in the play,
Who, not accepting, did but just refuse.   Mrs. *Friendall.*
There was a glance at parting ; such a look
As bids thee not give o're, for one rebuke ;
But if thou wou'dst be seen as well as read ;
Copy one living Author and one dead :
The Standard of thy Style, let *Etherege* be ;
For Wit, th' Immortal Spring of *Wycherly.*
Learn, after both, to draw some just Design,
And the next Age will learn to Copy thine.

JOHN DRYDEN.

TO MY DEAR FRIEND, MR. CONGREVE,

ON HIS COMEDY CALLED THE DOUBLE-DEALER.

WELL then, the promis'd Hour is come at last ;
The present Age of Wit obscures the past :
Strong were our Syres, and as they fought they Writ,
Conqu'ring with Force of Arms and Dint of Wit :
Theirs was the Giant Race before the Flood ;
And thus, when *Charles* Return'd, our Empire stood.
Like *Janus*, he the stubborn Soil manur'd,
With Rules of Husbandry the Rankness cur'd :
Tam'd us to Manners, when the Stage was rude,
And boistrous *English* Wit with Art indu'd.

Our Age was cultivated thus at length,   11
But what we gain'd in Skill we lost in Strength.
Our Builders were with Want of Genius curst ;
The second Temple was not like the first ;
Till you, the best *Vitruvius*, come at length
Our Beauties equal, but excel our Strength.
Firm *Dorique* Pillars found Your solid Base,
The fair *Corinthian* crowns the higher Space ;
Thus all below is Strength, and all above is Grace.
In easie Dialogue is *Fletcher's* Praise :   20
He mov'd the Mind, but had no Pow'r to raise

To MR. SOUTHERN. Text from the original prefixt to the play, 1692.
21 Civility] Civility, *1692.*

To MR. CONGREVE. Text from the original published with the play, 1694.
5 Race] Race, *1694.*
10 Wit] Wit, *1694.*
21 no] *The editors give* not

Great *Johnson* did by Strength of Judgment please,
Yet, doubling *Fletcher's* Force, he wants his Ease.
In diff'ring Talents both adorn'd their Age,
One for the Study, t'other for the Stage.
But both to *Congreve* justly shall submit,
One match'd in Judgment, both o'er-match'd in Wit.
In Him all Beauties of this Age we see,
Etherege his Courtship, *Southern's* Purity,
The Satyre, Wit, and Strength of Manly *Wycherly*.   30
All this in blooming Youth you have Atchiev'd;
Nor are your foil'd Contemporaries griev'd;
So much the Sweetness of your Manners move,
We cannot Envy you, because we Love.
Fabius might joy in *Scipio*, when he saw
A Beardless Consul made against the Law,
And join his Suffrage to the Votes of *Rome*,
Though he with *Hannibal* was overcome.
Thus old *Romano* bow'd to *Raphael's* Fame,
And Scholar to the Youth he taught, became.
   O that your Brows my Lawrel had sustain'd,   41
Well had I been depos'd, if you had reign'd!
The Father had descended for the Son,
For only You are lineal to the Throne.
Thus, when the State one *Edward* did depose,
A greater *Edward* in his Room arose:
But now, not I, but Poetry is curst;
For *Tom* the Second reigns like *Tom* the First.
But let 'em not mistake my Patron's Part
Nor call his Charity their own Desert.   50

Yet this I Prophesie; Thou shalt be seen,
(Tho' with some short Parenthesis between :)
High on the Throne of Wit; and, seated there,
Nor mine (that's little) but thy Lawrel wear,
Thy first Attempt an early Promise made;
That early Promise this has more than paid.
So bold, yet so judiciously you dare,
That your least Praise, is to be Regular.
Time, Place, and Action may with Pains be wrought,
But Genius must be born, and never can be taught.   60
This is Your Portion, this Your Native Store:
Heav'n, that but once was Prodigal before,
To *Shakespear* gave as much; she cou'd not give him more.
   Maintain your Post: that's all the Fame you need;
For 'tis impossible you shou'd proceed.
Already I am worn with Cares and Age,
And just abandoning th' ungrateful Stage:
Unprofitably kept at Heav'n's Expence,
I live a Rent-charge on his Providence:
But You, whom ev'ry Muse and Grace adorn,
Whom I foresee to better Fortune born,   71
Be kind to my Remains; and oh defend,
Against your Judgment, your departed Friend!
Let not th' insulting Foe my Fame pursue;
But shade those Lawrels which descend to You:
And take for Tribute what these Lines express;
You merit more; nor cou'd my Love do less.

John Dryden.

TO SIR GODFREY KNELLER,

PRINCIPAL PAINTER TO HIS MAJESTY.

ONCE I beheld the fairest of her Kind,
(And still the sweet Idea charms my Mind :)
True, she was dumb; for Nature gaz'd so long,
Pleas'd with her Work, that she forgot her Tongue,

But, smiling, said, She still shall gain the Prize;
I only have transferr'd it to her Eyes.
Such are thy Pictures, *Kneller*, Such thy Skill,
That Nature seems obedient to thy Will;
Comes out, and meets thy Pencil in the Draught,
Lives there, and wants but words to speak her thought.   10

TO SIR GODFREY KNELLER. Text from the *Miscellanies*, 1694.

At least thy Pictures look a Voice ; and we
Imagine Sounds, deceiv'd to that degree,
We think 'tis somewhat more than just to
    see.
  Shadows are but Privations of the Light ;
Yet, when we walk, they shoot before the
    Sight,
With us approach, retire, arise, and fall,
Nothing themselves, and yet expressing all.
Such are thy Pieces, imitating Life
So near, they almost conquer'd in the strife ;
And from their animated Canvass came,   20
Demanding Souls ; and loosened from the
    Frame.
  Prometheus, were he here, wou'd cast away
His *Adam,* and refuse a Soul to Clay,
And either wou'd thy Noble Work Inspire
Or think it warm enough without his Fire.
  But vulgar Hands may vulgar Likeness
    raise ;
This is the least Attendant on thy Praise :
From hence the Rudiments of Art began ;
A Coal, or Chalk, first imitated Man :
Perhaps, the Shadow, taken on a Wall,   30
Gave out-lines to the rude Original ;
Ere Canvass yet was strain'd : before the
    Grace
Of blended Colours found their use and
    place :
Or Cypress Tablets first receiv'd a Face.
  By slow degrees the Godlike Art advanc'd;
As man grew polish'd, Picture was inhanc'd :
Greece added Posture, Shade, and Perspec-
    tive,
And then the Mimick Piece began to Live.
Yet Perspective was lame, no distance
    true,
But all came forward in one common View :
No point of Light was known, no bounds
    of Art ;   41
When Light was there, it knew not to depart,
But glaring on remoter Objects play'd ;
Not languish'd and insensibly decay'd.
  Rome rais'd not Art, but barely kept alive,
And with Old *Greece* unequally did strive :
Till *Goths,* and *Vandals,* a rude *Northern* race,
Did all the matchless Monuments deface.
Then all the Muses in one ruine lye,
And Rhyme began t' enervate Poetry.   50
Thus, in a stupid Military State,
The Pen and Pencil find an equal Fate.
Flat Faces, such as wou'd disgrace a Skreen,
Such as in *Bantam's* Embassy were seen,

Unrais'd, unrounded, were the rude delight
Of Brutal Nations only born to Fight.
  Long time the Sister Arts, in Iron Sleep,
A heavy Sabbath did supinely keep ;
At length, in *Raphael's* Age, at once they
    rise,
Stretch all their Limbs and open all their
    Eyes.   60
  Thence rose the *Roman* and the *Lombard*
    Line ;
One colour'd best, and one did best design.
Raphael's, like *Homer's,* was the Nobler
    part,
But *Titian's* Painting looked like *Virgil's*
    Art.
  Thy Genius gives thee both ; where true
    Design,
Postures unforc'd, and lively Colours joyn,
Likeness is ever there ; but still the best,
Like proper Thoughts in lofty Language
    drest,
Where Light, to Shades descending, plays,
    not strives,
Dyes by degrees, and by degrees revives. 70
Of various Parts a perfect whole is wrought ;
Thy Pictures think, and we Divine their
    Thought.
  *Shakespear, thy Gift, I   *Shakespear's
    place before my Sight ;   *Picture
With awe I ask his Blessing   *drawn by
    e're I write ;   *Sir Godfrey
With Rev'rence look on his   *Kneller, and
    Majestick Face ;   *given to the
Proud to be less, but of his Godlike Race.   *Author.
His Soul Inspires me, while thy Praise I
    write,
And I like *Teucer,* under *Ajax* Fight ;
Bids thee thro' me, be bold ; with dauntless
    breast
Contemn the bad and Emulate the best. 80
Like his, thy Criticks in th' attempt are
    lost :
When most they rail, know then they envy
    most.
In vain they snarl a-loof ; a noisie Crowd,
Like Womens Anger, impotent and loud.
While they their barren Industry deplore,
Pass on secure, and mind the Goal before.
Old as she is, my Muse shall march behind
Bear off the Blast, and intercept the Wind.
Our Arts are Sisters, though not Twins in
    Birth,   8
For Hymns were sung in *Edens* happy Earth

By the first Pair ; while *Eve* was yet a Saint ;
Before she fell with Pride and learn'd to
paint.
Forgive th' Allusion ; 'twas not meant to
bite ;
But Satire will have Room, where e're I write.
For oh, the Painter Muse, though last in
place,
Has seiz'd the Blessing first, like *Jacob's*
Race.
Apelles Art an *Alexander* found,   ⎫
And *Raphael* did with *Leo's* Gold abound,   ⎬
But *Homer* was with barren Lawrel   ⎭
crown'd.
Thou hadst thy *Charles* a while, and so had I, 101
But pass we that unpleasing Image by.
Rich in thy self, and of thy self Divine,
All Pilgrims come and offer at thy Shrine.
A graceful Truth thy Pencil can Command ;
The Fair themselves go mended from thy
Hand.
Likeness appears in every Lineament ;
But Likeness in thy Work is Eloquent.
Though Nature there her true Resemblance
bears,
A nobler Beauty in thy Piece appears.
So warm thy Work, so glows the gen'rous
Frame,   110
Flesh looks less living in the Lovely Dame.
Thou paint'st as we describe, improving ⎫
still,   ⎬
When on wild Nature we ingraft our Skill,   ⎪
But not creating Beauties at our Will.   ⎭
Some other Hand perhaps may reach a
Face ;
But none like thee a finish'd Figure place : ⎫
None of this Age, for that's enough for thee, ⎬
The first of these Inferiour Times to be ;   ⎭
Not to contend with Heroes Memory.
Due Honours to those mighty Names we
grant,   120
But Shrubs may live beneath the lofty Plant ;
Sons may succeed their greater Parents gone ;
Such is thy Lott ; and such I wish my own.
But Poets are confin'd in Narr'wer space,
To speak the Language of their Native
Place ;
The Painter widely stretches his Command ;
Thy Pencil speaks the Tongue of ev'ry Land.

From hence, my Friend, all Climates are
your own,
Nor can you forfeit, for you hold of none.
All Nations all Immunities will give   130 ⎫
To make you theirs, where e're you please ⎬
to live ;   ⎪
And not sev'n Cities, but the World, wou'd ⎪
strive.   ⎭
Sure some propitious Planet then did smile
When first you were conducted to this Isle ;
(Our Genius brought you here, t' inlarge our
Fame)
(For your good Stars are ev'ry where the
same.)
Thy matchless Hand, of ev'ry Region free,
Adopts our Climate, not our Climate thee.
* Great *Rome* and *Venice*
early did impart   *He travell'd*
To thee th' Examples of their   *very young*
wondrous Art.   *into* Italy.
Those Masters, then but seen, not under-
stood,   141
With generous Emulation fir'd thy Blood ;
For what in Nature's Dawn the Child admir'd,
The Youth endeavour'd, and the Man ac-
quir'd.
That yet thou hast not reach'd their high
Degree,
Seems only wanting to this Age, not thee.
Thy Genius, bounded by the Times, like ⎫
mine,   ⎬
Drudges on petty Draughts, nor dare   ⎪
design   ⎪
A more exalted Work, and more Divine.   ⎭
For what a Song or senceless Opera   150
Is to the living Labour of a Play,
Or what a Play to *Virgil's* Work wou'd be,
Such is a single Piece to History.
But we, who Life bestow, our selves must
live :
Kings cannot Reign unless their Subjects
give ;
And they who pay the Taxes bear the
Rule :
Thus thou, sometimes, art forc'd to draw
a Fool :
But so his Follies in thy Posture sink,
The senceless Ideot seems at last to think.
Good Heav'n ! that Sots and Knaves
shou'd be so vain,   160
To wish their vile Resemblance may remain !
And stand recorded at their own Request,
To future Days, a Libel or a Jeast.

91–94] *Omitted by Tonson, 1701.*
95 For] But *1701.*
115–123] *Omitted by Tonson, 1701.*

Mean time while just Incouragement you want,
You only Paint to Live, not Live to Paint.
  Else shou'd we see your noble Pencil trace
Our Unities of Action, Time, and Place ;
A Whole compos'd of Parts, and those the best,
With ev'ry various Character exprest ;
Heroes at large, and at a nearer View ; 170
Less, and at distance, an Ignobler Crew ;
While all the Figures in one Action joyn,
As tending to Compleat the main Design.

More cannot be by Mortal Art exprest ;
But venerable Age shall add the rest.
For Time shall with his ready Pencil stand ;
Retouch your Figures with his ripening Hand,
Mellow your Colours, and imbrown the Teint,
Add every Grace, which Time alone can grant ;   179
To future Ages shall your Fame convey ;
And give more Beauties, than he takes away.

TO MR. GRANVILLE,

ON HIS EXCELLENT TRAGEDY, CALLED HEROICK LOVE.

Auspicious Poet, wert thou not my Friend,
How could I envy, what I must commend !
But since 'tis Natures Law in Love and Wit,
That Youth shou'd reign and with'ring Age submit,
With less regret those Lawrels I resign,
Which dying on my Brows, revive on thine.
With better Grace an Ancient Chief may yield
The long contended Honours of the Field
Than venture all his Fortune at a Cast,
And fight, like *Hannibal*, to lose at last.   10
Young Princes Obstinate to win the Prize,
Thô Yearly beaten, Yearly yet they rise :
Old Monarchs though successful, still in Doubt,
Catch at a Peace ; and wisely turn Devout.
Thine be the Lawrel then ; thy blooming Age
Can best, if any can, support the Stage :
Which so declines, that shortly we may see
Players and Plays reduc'd to second Infancy :
Sharp to the World, but thoughtless of Renown,
They Plot not on the Stage, but on the Town,   20
And, in Despair their Empty Pit to fill,
Set up some Foreign Monster in a Bill :

Thus they jog on; still tricking, never thriving ;
And Murd'ring Plays, which they miscal Reviving.
Our Sense is Nonsense, through their Pipes convey'd ;
Scarce can a Poet know the Play He made,
'Tis so disguis'd in Death : nor thinks 'tis He
That suffers in the Mangled Tragedy.
Thus *Itys* first was kill'd, and after dress'd
For his own Sire, the Chief Invited Guest.
I say not this of thy successful Scenes ;   31
Where thine was all the Glory, theirs the Gains.
With length of Time, much Judgment, and more Toil,
Not ill they Acted, what they cou'd not spoil.
Their Setting Sun still shoots a Glim'ring Ray,
Like Ancient *Rome*, Majestick in Decay ;
And better gleanings their worn Soil can boast,
Than the Crab-Vintage of the Neighb'ring Coast.
This difference yet the judging World will see ;
Thou Copiest *Homer*, and they Copy thee. 40

JOHN DRYDEN.

To Mr. Granville. Text from the original published with the play, 1698.

30 Sire,] Sire *1698*.

[TO PETER ANTONY MOTTEUX,

ON HIS TRAGEDY, CALLED BEAUTY IN DISTRESS.]

To my Friend, the AUTHOR.

'TIS hard, my Friend, to write in such an Age
As damns not only Poets, but the Stage.
That sacred art, by Heav'n itself infus'd,
Which *Moses, David, Salomon* have us'd,
Is now to be no more : The Muses' Foes
Wou'd sink their Maker's Praises into Prose.
Were they content to prune the lavish Vine
Of straggling Branches, and improve the
    Wine,
Who but a mad Man wou'd his Faults
    defend ? 9
All wou'd submit, for all but Fools will mend.
But, when to common sense they give the
    Lie,
And turn distorted Words to Blasphemy,
They give the Scandal ; and the Wise discern
Their Glosses teach an Age, too apt to
    learn.
What I have loosly, or profanely writ,
Let them to Fires (their due desert) commit :
Nor, when accus'd by me, let *them* complain :
Their Faults, and not their Function, I
    arraign.
Rebellion, worse than Witchcraft, they
    pursu'd :
The Pulpit preach'd the Crime, the People
    ru'd. 20
The Stage was silenc'd ; for the Saints wou'd
    see
In fields perform'd their plotted Tragedy.
But let us first reform : and then so live,
That we may teach our Teachers to forgive.
Our Desk be plac'd below their lofty Chairs,
Ours be the Practice, as the Precept theirs.
The moral Part at least we may divide,
Humility reward and punish Pride ;
Ambition, Int'rest, Avarice, accuse ;
These are the Province of the Tragic Muse.

These hast thou chosen ; and the public
    Voice 31
Has equall'd thy Performance with thy
    choice.
Time, Action, Place, are so preserv'd by \
    thee \
That ev'n *Corneille* might with Envy see /
Th' Alliance of his tripled Unity.
Thy Incidents, perhaps, too thick are sown ;
But so much Plenty is thy Fault alone :
At least but two, can that good Crime
    commit,
Thou in Design, and *Wycherley* in Wit
Let thine own *Gauls* condemn thee, if they
    dare ; 40
Contented to be thinly regular.
Born there, but not for them, our fruitful
    Soil
With more Increase rewards thy happy Toil.
Their Tongue, infeebl'd, is refin'd so much ;
That like pure Gold, it bends at ev'ry Touch :
Our sturdy *Teuton* yet will Art obey,
More fit for manly Thought, and strengthen'd
    with Allay.
But whence art thou inspir'd, and Thou
    alone,
To flourish in an Idiom, not thy own ?
It moves our Wonder, that a foreign Guest
Shou'd overmatch the most, and match the
    best. 51
In underpraising thy Deserts, I wrong ;
Here, find the first deficience of our Tongue :
Words, once my stock, are wanting to com-
    mend
So Great a Poet and so Good a Friend.

JOHN DRYDEN.

To PETER ANTONY MOTTEUX. Text from the
original, prefixed to the play, 1698.
9 Faults] *Many edd. wrongly give* Thoughts

44 so] *Many edd. wrongly give* too
45 That] *Many edd. wrongly give* And
These false readings are all in Christie's text
but not in Dr. Saintsbury's.

TO MY | HONOUR'D KINSMAN, | JOHN DRIDEN, |

OF | CHESTERTON, | IN THE | COUNTY OF HUNTINGDON, ESQUIRE.

How Blessed is He, who leads a Country Life,
Unvex'd with anxious Cares, and void of Strife !
Who studying Peace, and shunning Civil Rage,
Enjoy'd his Youth, and now enjoys his Age :
All who deserve his Love, he makes his own ;
And, to be lov'd himself, needs only to be known.
  Just, Good, and Wise, contending Neighbours come
From your Award to wait their final Doom ;
And, Foes before, return in Friendship home.   9
Without their Cost, you terminate the Cause;
And save th' Expence of long Litigious Laws:
Where Suits are travers'd ; and so little won,
That he who conquers, is but last undone :
  Such are not your Decrees ; but so design'd,
The Sanction leaves a lasting Peace behind;
Like your own Soul, Serene ; a Pattern of your Mind.
  Promoting Concord, and composing Strife,
Lord of your self, uncumber'd with a Wife ;
Where, for a Year, a Month, perhaps a Night,
Long Penitence succeeds a short Delight : 20
Minds are so hardly match'd, that ev'n the first,
Though pair'd by Heav'n, in Paradise, were curs'd.
For Man and Woman, though in one they grow,
Yet, first or last, return again to Two.
He to God's Image, She to His was made ;
So, farther from the Fount, the Stream at random stray'd.
  How cou'd He stand, when, put to double Pain,
He must a Weaker than himself sustain !
Each might have stood perhaps ; but each alone ;   29
Two Wrestlers help to pull each other down.

Not that my Verse wou'd blemish all the Fair ;
But yet, if *some* be Bad, 'tis Wisdom to beware ;
And better shun the Bait, than struggle in the Snare.
Thus have you shunn'd, and shun the married State,
Trusting as little as you can to Fate.
  No porter guards the Passage of your Door ;
T' admit the Wealthy, and exclude the Poor :
For God, who gave the Riches, gave the Heart
To sanctifie the Whole, by giving Part:
Heav'n, who foresaw the Will, the Means has wrought,   40
And to the Second Son, a Blessing brought :
The First-begotten had his Father's Share,
But you, like *Jacob*, are *Rebecca's* Heir.
  So may your Stores, and fruitful Fields increase ;
And ever be you bless'd, who live to bless.
As *Ceres* sow'd where e'er her Chariot flew ;
As Heav'n in Desarts rain'd the Bread of Dew,
So free to Many, to Relations most,
You feed with Manna your own *Israel*-Host.
  With Crowds attended of your ancient Race,   50
You seek the Champian-Sports, or Sylvan-Chace :
With well-breath'd Beagles, you surround the Wood,
Ev'n then, industrious of the Common Good :
And often have you brought the wily Fox
To suffer for the Firstlings of the Flocks ;
Chas'd ev'n amid the Folds ; and made to bleed,
Like Felons, where they did the murd'rous Deed.
This fiery Game, your active Youth maintain'd :
Not yet, by years extinguish'd, though restrain'd :

To JOHN DRIDEN.   Text from the original and only contemporary edition, 1700.
8 Award] Award, *1700.*

You season still with Sports your serious
Hours ; 60
For Age but tastes of Pleasures, Youth
devours.
The Hare, in Pastures or in Plains is found,
Emblem of Humane Life, who runs the
Round ;
And, after all his wand'ring Ways are done, ⎫
His Circle fills, and ends where he begun, ⎬
Just as the Setting meets the Rising Sun. ⎭
   Thus Princes ease their Cares: But
happier he,
Who seeks not Pleasure thro' Necessity,
Than such as once on slipp'ry Thrones were
plac'd,
And chasing, sigh to think themselves are
chas'd. 70
   So liv'd our Sires, e'er Doctors learn'd to
kill,
And multiply'd with theirs, the Weekly Bill :
The first Physicians by Debauch were made :
Excess began, and Sloth sustains the Trade.
Pity the gen'rous Kind their Cares bestow
To search forbidden Truths; (a Sin to know:)
To which, if Humane Science cou'd attain,
The Doom of Death, pronounc'd by God,
were vain.
In vain the Leech wou'd interpose Delay ;
Fate fastens first, and vindicates the Prey. 80
What Help from Arts Endeavours can we ⎫
have ! ⎪
Guibbons but guesses, nor is sure to save : ⎬
But *Maurus* sweeps whole Parishes, and ⎪
Peoples ev'ry Grave, ⎭
And no more Mercy to Mankind will use,
Than when he robb'd and murder'd *Maro's*
Muse.
Wou'dst thou be soon dispatch'd, and perish
whole ?
Trust *Maurus* with thy Life, and M—lb—rn
with thy Soul.
By Chace our long-liv'd Fathers earned their
Food ;
Toil strung the Nerves, and purifi'd the
Blood :
But we, their Sons, a pamper'd Race of Men,
Are dwindl'd down to threescore Years and
ten. 91
Better to hunt in Fields, for Health un-
bought,
Than fee the Doctor for a nauseous Draught.
The Wise, for Cure, on Exercise depend ;
God never made his Work, for Man to mend.

   The Tree of Knowledge, once in *Eden*
plac'd,
Was easie found, but was forbid the Taste :
O, had our Grandsire walk'd without his Wife,
He first had sought the better Plant of Life !
Now, both are lost : Yet, wandring in the
dark, 100
Physicians for the Tree have found the Bark
They, lab'ring for Relief of Humane Kind, ⎫
With sharpen'd sight some Remedies may ⎬
find ; ⎪
Th' Apothecary-Train is wholly blind. ⎭
From Files, a Random *Recipe* they take,
And Many Deaths of One Prescription make.
Garth, gen'rous as his Muse, prescribes and
gives ;
The Shop-man sells ; and by Destruction
lives :
Ungrateful Tribe ! who, like the Viper's
Brood,
From Med'cine issuing, suck their Mother's
Blood ! 110
Let These obey ; and let the Learn'd pre-
scribe ;
That Men may die, without a double Bribe :
Let Them, but under their Superiours, kill ;
When Doctors first have sign'd the bloody
Bill :
He scapes the best, who Nature to repair,
Draws Phisick from the Fields, in Draughts
of Vital Air.
   You hoard not Health, for your own
private use,
But on the Publick spend the rich Produce.
When, often urg'd, unwilling to be Great,
Your Country calls you from your lov'd
Retreat, 120
And sends to Senates, charg'd with Common
Care,
Which none more shuns ; and none can
better bear.
Where cou'd they find another form'd so fit,
To poise, with solid Sense, a spritely Wit !
Were these both wanting, (as they both
abound)
Where cou'd so firm Integrity be found ?
   Well-born and Wealthy ; wanting no
Support,
You steer betwixt the Country and the
Court :
Nor gratifie whate'er the Great desire,
Nor grudging give, what Publick Needs
require. 130

Part must be left, a Fund when Foes invade ;
And Part employ'd to roll the Watry Trade ;
Ev'n *Canaans* happy Land, when worn with
    Toil,
Requir'd a Sabbath-Year, to mend the
    meagre Soil.
    Good senators, (and such are you,) so
        give,
That Kings may be supply'd, the People
    thrive ;
And He, when Want requires, is truly Wise,
Who slights not Foreign Aids nor over-
    buys ;
But, on our Native Strength, in time of
    need, relies.
Munster was bought, we boast not the
    Success ;   140
Who fights for Gain, for greater, makes his
    Peace.
    Our Foes, compell'd by Need have Peace
        embrac'd :
The Peace both Parties want, is like to
    last :
Which, if secure, securely we may trade ;
Or, not secure, shou'd never have been made.
Safe in our selves, while on our selves we
    stand,
The Sea is ours, and that defends the
    Land.
Be, then, the Naval Stores the Nations
    Care,
New Ships to build, and batter'd to repair.
    Observe the War in ev'ry Annual Course ;
What has been done, was done with *British*
    Force.   151
Namur Subdu'd, is *England's* Palm alone ;
The Rest Besieged ; but we Constrain'd the
    Town :
We saw th' Event that follow'd our Success ;
France, though pretending Arms, pursu'd
    the Peace ;
Oblig'd, by one sole Treaty, to restore
What Twenty Years of War had won before.
Enough for *Europe* has our *Albion* fought :
Let us enjoy the Peace our Blood has bought.
When once the *Persian* King was put to
    Flight,   160
The weary *Macedons* refus'd to fight :
Themselves their own Mortality confess'd ;
And left the son of *Jove*, to quarrel for the
    rest.

Ev'n Victors are by Victories undone ;
Thus *Hannibal*, with Foreign Laurels won,
To *Carthage* was recall'd, too late to keep
    his own.
While sore of Battel, while our Wounds are
    green,
Why shou'd we tempt the doubtful Dye
    agen ?
In Wars renew'd, uncertain of success,
Sure of a Share, as Umpires of the Peace. 170
    A Patriot, both the King and Country
        serves ;
Prerogative, and Privilege preserves :
Of Each, our Laws the certain Limit
    show ;
One must not ebb, nor t' other overflow : .
Betwixt the Prince and Parliament we
    stand ;
The Barriers of the State on either Hand :
May neither overflow, for then they drown
    the Land.
When both are full, they feed our bless'd
    Abode ;
Like those, that water'd once, the Paradise
    of God.
    Some Overpoise of Sway, by Turns they
        share ;   180
In Peace the People, and the Prince in War :
Consuls of mod'rate Pow'r in Calms were
    made ;
When the *Gauls* came, one sole Dictator
    sway'd.
    Patriots, in Peace, assert the Peoples
        Right,
With noble Stubbornness resisting Might :
No Lawless Mandates from the Court receive,
Nor lend by Force ; but in a Body give.
Such was your gen'rous Grandsire ; free to
    grant
In Parliaments, that weigh'd their Prince's
    Want :
But so tenacious of the Common Cause, 190
As not to lend the King against his Laws.
And, in a lothsom Dungeon doom'd to lie,
In Bonds retain'd his Birthright Liberty,
And shamed Oppression, till it set him free.
    O true Descendent of a Patriot Line,
Who, while thou shar'st their Lustre, lend'st
    'em thine,
Vouchsafe this Picture of thy Soul to see ;
Tis so far Good as it resembles thee :
The Beauties to th' Original I owe ;   199
Which, when I miss, my own Defects I show.

135 are] *Editors till Christie wrongly gave as*

Nor think the Kindred-Muses thy Disgrace ;
A poet is not born in ev'ry Race.
Two of a House, few Ages can afford ;
One to perform, another to record.
Praise-worthy Actions are by thee embrac'd ;
And 'tis my Praise, to make thy Praises last.

For ev'n when Death dissolves our Humane Frame,
The Soul returns to Heav'n, from whence it came ;
Earth keeps the Body, Verse preserves the Fame.

ELEGIES AND EPITAPHS.

UPON THE DEATH OF THE LORD HASTINGS.

Must Noble *Hastings* Immaturely die,
(The Honour of his ancient Family ?)
Beauty and Learning thus together meet,
To bring a *Winding* for a *Wedding-sheet* ?
Must *Vertue* prove *Death's* Harbinger ? Must She,
With him expiring, feel Mortality ?
Is *Death* (Sin's wages) Grace's now ? shall Art
Make us more Learned, only to depart ?
If Merit be Disease, if Vertue Death ;   9
To be Good, Not to be, who'd then bequeath
Himself to Discipline ? Who'd not esteem
Labour a Crime, Study self-murther deem ?
Our *Noble Youth* now have pretence to be
Dunces securely, Ign'rant healthfully.
Rare Linguist ! whose Worth speaks it self ; whose Praise,
Though not his Own, all *Tongues* Besides do raise :
Then Whom Great *Alexander* may seem less,
Who conquer'd Men, but not their Languages.
In his Mouth Nations speak ; his Tongue might be
Interpreter to *Greece, France, Italy*.   20
His native Soyl was the four parts o' th' Earth ;
All *Europe* was too narrow for his Birth.

A young Apostle ; and (with rev'rence may
I speak 'it) inspir'd with gift of Tongues, as They.
Nature gave him, a Childe, what Men in vain
Oft strive, by Art though further'd, to obtain.
His body was an Orb, his sublime Soul
Did move on Vertue's and on Learning's pole :
Whose Reg'lar Motions better to our view,
Then *Archimedes* Sphere, the Heavens did shew.   30
Graces and Vertues, Languages and Arts,
Beauty and Learning, fill'd up all the parts.
Heav'ns Gifts, which do, like falling Stars, appear
Scatter'd in Others ; all, as in their Sphear,
Were fix'd and conglobate in's Soul, and thence
Shone th'row his Body with sweet Influence ;
Letting their Glories so on each Limb fall,
The whole Frame render'd was Celestial.
Come, learned *Ptolomy*, and tryal make,
If thou this Hero's Altitude canst take ;   40
But that transcends thy skill ; thrice happie all,
Could we but prove thus Astronomical.
Liv'd *Tycho* now, struck with this Ray, (which shone
More bright i' th' Morn then others Beam at Noon)
He'd take his *Astrolabe*, and seek out here
What new Star 't was did gild our Hemisphere.

Upon the Death of the Lord Hastings. Text from the original in *Lachrymae Musarum*, 1650. The text has never been correctly reprinted in England.

19 speak] *English editors give* spake *This reading makes the passage easier, but it is not likely to be right.*

24 'it] *English editors give* it *Perhaps* 't *should be read.*
35 fix'd and] *Editors till Christie wrongly omit* and

Replenish'd then with such rare Gifts as
    these,
Where was room left for such a Foul Disease?
The Nations sin hath drawn that Veil which
    shrouds
Our Day-spring in so sad benighting Clouds.
Heaven would no longer trust its Pledge ;
    but thus   51
Recall'd it ; rapt its *Ganymede* from us.
Was there no milder way but the Small
    Pox,
The very filth'ness of *Pandora's* Box ?
So many Spots, like *næves*, our *Venus* soil ?
One Jewel set off with so many a Foil ?
Blisters with pride swell'd, which th'row's
    flesh did sprout
Like Rose-buds, stuck i' th' Lilly-skin about.
Each little Pimple had a Tear in it,
To wail the fault its rising did commit :   60
Who, Rebel-like, with their own Lord at
    strife,
Thus made an Insurrection 'gainst his
    Life.
Or were these Gems sent to adorn his Skin,
The Cab'net of a richer Soul within ?
No Comet need foretel his Change drew on,
Whose Corps might seem a *Constellation*.
O had he di'd of old, how great a strife
Had been, who from his Death should draw
    their Life ?
Who should by one rich draught become
    whate'er
Seneca, Cato, Numa, Cæsar, were :   70
Learn'd, Vertuous, Pious, Great, and have
    by this
An Universal *Metempsuchosis*.
Must all these ag'd Sires in one Funeral
Expire ? All die in one so young, so small ?
Who, had he liv'd his life out, his great
    Fame
Had swoln 'bove any *Greek* or *Romane* name?
But hasty Winter, with one blast, hath
    brought
The hopes of Autumn, Summer, Spring, to
    nought.

Thus fades the Oak i' th' sprig, i' th' blade
    the Corn ;
Thus, without Young, this *Phœnix* dies, new
    born.   80
Must then old three-legg'd gray-beards, with
    their Gout,
Catarrhs, Rheums, Aches, live three Ages
    out ?
Times Offal, onely fit for th' Hospital,
Or t' hang an Antiquaries room withal ;
Must Drunkards, Lechers, spent with Sin-
    ning, live
With such helps as Broths, Possits, Physick
    give ?
None live but such as should die ? Shall we
    meet
With none but Ghostly Fathers in the
    Street ?
Grief makes me rail ; Sorrow will force its
    way ;
And Show'rs of Tears, Tempestuous Sighs
    best lay.   90
The Tongue may fail ; but over-flowing
    Eyes
Will weep out lasting streams of *Elegies*.
  But thou, O *Virgin-widow*, left alone,
Now thy Beloved, Heaven-ravisht *Spouse* is
    gone,
(Whose skilful Sire in vain strove to apply
Med'cines, when thy Balm was no remedy)
With greater than *Platonick* love, O wed
His Soul, tho' not his Body, to thy Bed :
Let that make thee a Mother ; bring thou
    forth   99
Th' *Ideas* of his Vertue, Knowledge, Worth ;
Transcribe th' Original in new Copies : give
Hastings o' th' better part : so shall he
    live
In's Nobler Half ; and the great Grandsire be
Of an Heroick Divine Progenie :
An Issue which t' Eternity shall last,
Yet but th' Irradiations which he cast.
Erect no *Mausolœums* : for his best
Monument is his Spouses Marble brest.

---

55 our *Venus*] *Derrick and others wrongly
give* on Venus'

84 t' hang an] *Editors till Christie wrongly*
to hang *Christie prints* to hang an
room] *English editors wrongly give* rooms

ON THE MONUMENT OF THE MARQUIS OF WINCHESTER.

HE who in impious times untainted stood
And midst rebellion durst be just and
good,
Whose arms asserted, and whose sufferings
more
Confirm'd the cause for which he fought
before,
Rests here, rewarded by an heavenly prince
For what his earthly could not recompense.
Pray, reader, that such times no more
appear;
Or, if they happen, learn true honour
here.

Ark of thy age's faith and loyalty,
Which, to preserve them, Heaven confin'd
in thee.   10
Few subjects could a king like thine deserve;
And fewer such a king so well could serve.
Blest king, blest subject, whose exalted
state
By sufferings rose and gave the law to
fate!
Such souls are rare, but mighty patterns
given
To earth were meant for ornaments to
Heav'n.

EPITAPH ON SIR PALMES FAIRBORNE'S TOMB,

IN WESTMINSTER ABBEY.

YE Sacred Relicks which your Marble
keep,
Here, undisturb'd by Wars, in quiet
sleep:
Discharge the trust, which (when it was
below)
Fairborne's undaunted soul did undergo:
And be the Towns Palladium from the
foe.
Alive and dead these Walls he will defend:
Great Actions great Examples must attend.
The Candian Siege his early Valour knew;
Where Turkish Blood did his young hands
imbrew:
From thence returning with deserv'd Ap-
plause,   10
Against the Moors his well-flesh'd Sword
he draws;
The same the Courage, and the same the
Cause.

His Youth and Age, his Life and Death com-
bine:
As in some great and regular design,
All of a Piece, throughout, and all Divine
Still nearer heaven, his Vertues shone more
bright,
Like rising flames expanding in their height;
The Martyrs Glory Crown'd the Soldier's
Fight.
More bravely Brittish General never fell,
Nor General's death was e're reveng'd so well;
Which his pleas'd Eyes beheld before their
close,
Follow'd by thousand Victims of his Foes.
To his lamented loss for time to come,
His pious Widow consecrates this Tomb.

ON THE MONUMENT OF THE MARQUIS OF
WINCHESTER. Text from Pope's *Miscellanies*,
1712.

EPITAPH ON SIR PALMES FAIRBORNE'S TOMB.
Text from the *Miscellanies* of 1693.
4 undaunted] *This was the word in the first
sketch on the stone in Westminster Abbey, but
when the letters were cut it was changed to
disdaunted. The stone has some mistakes,*
Balladium *for* Palladium *and others.*
16 Vertues] *Some edd. wrongly give* Virtue
23 time] *Some edd. wrongly give* times

TO THE MEMORY OF MR. OLDHAM.

FAREWELL, too little and too lately known,
Whom I began to think and call my own :
For sure our Souls were near alli'd, and thine
Cast in the same poetick mold with mine.
One common Note on either Lyre did strike,
And Knaves and Fools we both abhorr'd
    alike.
To the same Goal did both our Studies drive :
The last set out the soonest did arrive.
Thus *Nisus* fell upon the slippery place,
Whilst his young Friend perform'd and won
    the Race.   10
O early ripe ! to thy abundant Store
What could advancing Age have added more?
It might (what Nature never gives the Young)
Have taught the Numbers of thy Native
    Tongue.

But Satire needs not those, and Wit will
    shine
Through the harsh Cadence of a rugged Line.
A noble Error, and but seldom made,
When Poets are by too much force betray'd.
Thy gen'rous Fruits, though gather'd ere
    their prime,
Still shew'd a Quickness ; and maturing
    Time   20
But mellows what we write to the dull Sweets
    of Rhyme.
Once more, hail, and farewell ! farewell, thou
    young,
But ah ! too short, *Marcellus* of our Tongue !
Thy Brows with Ivy and with Laurels bound ;
But Fate and gloomy Night encompass thee
    around.

TO THE PIOUS MEMORY OF THE ACCOMPLISHT YOUNG LADY

MRS. ANNE KILLIGREW,

EXCELLENT IN THE TWO SISTER-ARTS OF POESIE AND PAINTING.

AN ODE.

I

THOU youngest Virgin-Daughter of the
    Skies,
Made in the last Promotion of the *Blest* ;
Whose Palms, new pluckt from Paradise,
In spreading *Branches* more sublimely rise,
    Rich with Immortal Green above the rest :
Whether, adopted to some Neighbouring
    Star,
Thou rol'st above us in thy wand'ring Race,
    Or, in Procession fixt and regular,
Mov'd with the Heavens Majestick pace ;
    Or, call'd to more Superiour *Bliss*,   10
Thou tread'st, with Seraphims, the vast
    Abyss :
Whatever happy region is thy place,

Cease thy Celestial Song a little space ;
(Thou wilt have time enough for Hymns
    Divine,
Since Heav'ns Eternal Year is thine.)
Hear then a Mortal Muse thy praise rehearse
    In no ignoble Verse ;
But such as thy own voice did practise
    here,
When thy first Fruits of Poesie were
    given,
To make thyself a welcome Inmate there ; 20
    While yet a young Probationer,
    And Candidate of Heav'n.

TO THE MEMORY OF MR. OLDHAM. Text
from the original, 1684. (I owe the collation to
another hand.)

TO THE MEMORY OF MRS. KILLIGREW. Text
from the second edition, 1693. The date is given
wrongly by Christie. The variants below are
from the original edition as prefixt to Mrs.
Killigrew's Poems.
    3 Palms] Palmes *1686*
    12 is] be *1686*.

2

If by Traduction came thy Mind,
Our Wonder is the less to find
A Soul so charming from a Stock so good ;
Thy Father was transfus'd into thy *Blood* :
So wert thou born into the tuneful strain,
(An early, rich, and inexhausted Vein.)
But if thy *Præ-existing* Soul
Was form'd, at first, with Myriads more, 30
It did through all the Mighty Poets
  roul
Who *Greek* or *Latine* Laurels wore,
And was that *Sappho* last, which once it was
  before.
If so, then cease thy flight, *O Heav'n-born
  Mind* !
Thou hast no *Dross* to purge from thy Rich
  Ore :
Nor can thy Soul a fairer Mansion find ⎫
Than was the *Beauteous* Frame she left ⎬
  behind : ⎭
Return, to fill or mend the Quire of thy
  Celestial kind.

3

May we presume to say, that at thy
  Birth,
New joy was sprung in HEAV'N as well as
  here on *Earth* ?   40
For sure the Milder Planets did combine ⎫
On thy *Auspicious* Horoscope to shine, ⎬
And ev'n the most Malicious were in Trine. ⎭
Thy *Brother-Angels* at thy *Birth*
Strung each his Lyre, and tun'd it high,
  That all the People of the Skie
Might know a Poetess was born on Earth.
  And then if ever, Mortal Ears
  Had heard the Musick of the Spheres !
  And if no clust'ring Swarm of *Bees*   50
On thy sweet Mouth distill'd their golden
  Dew,
  'Twas that, such vulgar Miracles
  Heav'n had not Leasure to renew :
For all the *Blest* Fraternity of Love
Solemniz'd there thy *Birth*, and kept thy
  Holyday above.

4

O Gracious God ! How far have we
Prophan'd thy Heav'nly Gift of Poesy !
Made prostitute and profligate the Muse,
Debas'd to each obscene and impious
  use,
Whose Harmony was first ordain'd
  Above,   60
For Tongues of *Angels* and for *Hymns* of
  Love !
Oh wretched We ! why were we hurry'd
  down
  This lubrique and adult'rate age,
  (Nay, added fat Pollutions of our own)
  T' increase the steaming Ordures of the
  Stage ?
What can we say t' excuse our *Second
  Fall* ?
Let this thy *Vestal,* Heav'n, atone for all :
  Her *Arethusian* Stream remains unsoil'd,
Unmixt with Forreign Filth and undefil'd,
Her Wit was more than Man, her Innocence
  a Child.   70

5

Art she had none, yet wanted none,
  For Nature did that Want supply :
So rich in Treasures of her Own,
  She might our boasted Stores defy :
Such Noble Vigour did her Verse adorn,
That it seem'd borrow'd, where 'twas only
  born.
Her Morals too were in her *Bosom* bred
  By great Examples daily fed,
What in the best of *Books*, her Father's Life,
  she read.
And to be read her self she need not fear ;
  Each Test, and ev'ry Light, her Muse will
  bear,   81
Though *Epictetus* with his Lamp were there.
  Ev'n Love (for Love sometimes her Muse
  exprest),
Was but a Lambent-flame which play'd
  about her *Breast* :
  Light as the Vapours of a Morning Dream,
So cold herself, whilst she such Warmth
  exprest,
  'Twas *Cupid* bathing in *Diana's* Stream.

---

26 *Blood*] Blood *1686.*
29 Præ-existing] Præexisting *1686.   Editors
give* pre-existing
44 *Brother-Angels*] Brother-Angels *1686.*

67 atone] attone *1686.*
77 *Bosom*] Bosome *1686.*
84 *Breast*] Brest *1686.*

6

Born to the Spacious Empire of the Nine,
One wou'd have thought, she should have
    been content
To manage well that Mighty Government; 90
But what can young ambitious Souls confine?
    To the next Realm she stretcht her Sway, ⎫
    For *Painture* near adjoyning lay,   ⎬
    A plenteous Province, and alluring Prey. ⎭
A *Chamber of Dependences* was fram'd,
(As Conquerors will never want Pretence,
    When arm'd, to justifie th' Offence),
And the whole Fief, in right of Poetry she
    claim'd.
The Country open lay without Defence ;
For Poets frequent In-rodes there had made,
    And perfectly cou'd represent   101
The Shape, the Face, with ev'ry Linea-
    ment ;
And all the large Demains which the Dumb-
    sister sway'd ;
    All bow'd beneath her Government,
    Receiv'd in Triumph wheresoe're she went.
Her Pencil drew whate're her Soul design'd
And oft the *happy Draught* surpass'd the
    Image in her *Mind*.
The *Sylvan* Scenes of Herds and Flocks
And fruitful Plains and barren Rocks,
Of shallow *Brooks* that flow'd so clear, 110
The bottom did the top appear ;
Of deeper too and ampler Floods
Which as in Mirrors, shew'd the Woods ;
Of lofty Trees, with Sacred Shades
And Perspectives of pleasant Glades,
Where Nymphs of brightest Form appear, ⎫
And shaggy Satyrs standing near,   ⎬
Which them at once admire and fear. ⎭
The Ruines too of some Majestick Piece,
Boasting the Pow'r of ancient *Rome* or
    Greece,   120
Whose Statues, Freezes, Columns, broken
    lie,
And, tho' defac'd, the Wonder of the Eye ;
What *Nature*, *Art*, bold *Fiction*, e're durst
    frame,
Her forming Hand gave Feature to the
    Name.

So strange a Concourse ne're was seen
    before,
But when the peopl'd *Ark* the whole Creation
    bore.

7

The Scene then chang'd ; with bold
    Erected Look
Our Martial King the sight with Reverence
    strook :
For, not content t' express his Outward
    Part,   129
Her hand call'd out the Image of his Heart,
His Warlike Mind, his Soul devoid of Fear, ⎫
His High-designing *Thoughts* were figurd' ⎬
    there,   ⎪
As when, by Magick, Ghosts are made ⎭
    appear.
Our Phenix queen was portrai'd too so
    bright,
Beauty alone cou'd *Beauty* take so right :
Her Dress, her Shape, her matchless Grace,
Were all observ'd, as well as heav'nly Face.
With such a Peerless Majesty she stands,
As in that Day she took the Crown from
    Sacred hands :
Before a Train of Heroins was seen,   140
In *Beauty* foremost, as in Rank, the Queen !
    Thus nothing to her Genius was deny'd,
But like a *Ball* of Fire, the farther thrown,
Still with a greater *Blaze* she shone,
    And her bright Soul broke out on ev'ry
    side.
What next she had design'd, Heaven only
    knows :
To such Immod'rate Growth her Conquest
    rose
That Fate alone its Progress cou'd oppose.

8

Now all those Charms, that blooming Grace,
The well-proportion'd Shape and beauteous
    Face,   150
Shall never more be seen by Mortal Eyes ;
In Earth the much-lamented Virgin lies !

---

93 near] neer *1686*.
112 Floods] Flouds *1686*.
117 near] neer *1686*.
122 defac'd] defac't *1686*.   Eye] Eie *1686*.
124 Feature to] Shape unto *1686*.

130 sqq. *These lines as printed in 1686 ran :*
As in that Day she took from Sacred hands
The Crown ; 'mong num'rous Heroins was seen,
More yet in Beauty, than in Rank, the Queen !
Saintsbury wrongly gives 'mongst *for* 'mong
149 Charms] Charmes *1686*.

Not Wit nor Piety cou'd Fate prevent ;
Nor was the cruel *Destiny* content
To finish all the Murder at a blow,
To sweep at once her *Life* and *Beauty*
   too ;
But, like a hardn'd Fellon, took a pride
  To work more Mischievously slow,
And plunder'd first, and then destroy'd.
O double Sacriledge on things Divine, 160
To rob the Relique, and deface the Shrine !
  But thus *Orinda* dy'd :
Heav'n, by the same Disease, did both
   translate,
As equal were their Souls, so equal was their
   fate.

9

Mean time, her *Warlike Brother* on the
   Seas
His waving Streamers to the Winds dis-
   plays,
And vows for his Return, with vain Devotion,
   pays.
  Ah, Generous Youth ! that Wish for-
   bear,
  The Winds too soon will waft thee here !
Slack all thy Sails, and fear to come, 170
Alas, thou know'st not, thou art wreck'd at
   home !
No more shalt thou behold thy Sister's
   Face,
Thou hast already had her last Embrace.

But look aloft, and if thou ken'st from far,
Among the *Pleiad's*, a New-kindl'd star,
If any sparkles, than the rest, more bright,
'Tis she that shines in that propitious Light.

10

When in mid-Air the Golden Trump shall
   sound,
  To raise the Nations under ground ;
  When in the Valley of *Jehosaphat* 180
The Judging God shall close the book of
   Fate ;
  And there the last *Assizes* keep
  For those who Wake and those who Sleep ;
  When ratling *Bones* together fly
  From the four Corners of the Skie,
When Sinews o're the Skeletons are spread,
Those cloath'd with Flesh, and Life inspires
   the Dead ;
The Sacred Poets first shall hear the Sound, ⎫
And formost from the Tomb shall bound : ⎪
For they are cover'd with the lightest ⎬
   ground ; 190 ⎭
And streight, with in-born Vigour, on the
   Wing,
Like mounting Larks, to the New Morning
   sing.
There *Thou*, sweet Saint, before the Quire
   shalt go,
As Harbinger of Heav'n, the Way to show,
The Way which thou so well hast learn'd
   below.

UPON THE DEATH OF THE VISCOUNT
OF DUNDEE.

OH Last and Best of *Scots* ! who did'st
  maintain
Thy Country's Freedom from a Foreign
  Reign ;
New People fill the Land, now thou art gone,
New Gods the Temples, and new Kings the
  Throne.

Scotland and Thee did each in other live,
Nor wou'dst thou her, nor cou'd she thee
  survive.
Farewel ! who living didst support the
  State,
And coud'st not fall but with thy Country's
  Fate

---

170 Sails] Sailes *1686.*
178 Air] Aire *1686.*
192 Larks] Larkes *1686.*

UPON THE DEATH OF THE VISCOUNT OF
DUNDEE. Text of 1704.

EPITAPH ON THE LADY WHITMORE.

FAIR, Kind, and True, a Treasure each
    alone,
A Wife, a Mistress, and a Friend in one,
Rest in this Tomb, rais'd at thy Husband's
    cost,
Here sadly summing, what he had, and
    lost.

EPITAPH ON THE LADY WHITMORE. Text
from the Monument in Twickenham Church.

Come Virgins, ere in equal Bands ye join,
Come first and offer at her Sacred Shrine ;
Pray but for half the Vertues of this
    Wife,
Compound for all the rest with longer
    Life ;
And wish your Vows, like hers, may be re-
    turn'd,
So Lov'd when Living, and when Dead so
    Mourn'd.   10

6ᵈ

Eleonora:

A PANEGYRICAL

POEM:

Dedicated to the

MEMORY

Of the Late

COUNTESS

OF

ABINGDON.

Highly Comending her.

Written by Mr. D R Y D E N.

——*Superas evadere ad auras,*
Hoc opus, hic labor est. Pauci, quos æquus amavit
Juppiter, aut ardens evexit ad æthera virtus;
Diis geniti potuere. Virgil Æneid. I. 6.

LONDON:

Printed for *Jacob Tonson,* at the *Judges Head* in *Chancery-Lane,* near *Fleetstreet.* 1692. 7. March.

Where compleat Sets of Mr. *Dryden's* Works are Sold: The Plays being put in the order they were Written.

TO THE

RIGHT HONOURABLE

THE

EARL OF ABINGDON, &c.

My Lord,—The Commands, with which You honour'd me some Months ago are now per-
form'd : they had been sooner ; but betwixt ill health, some business, and many troubles, I was
forc'd to deferr them till this time. Ovid, going to his Banishment, and writing from on
Shipbord to his Friends, excus'd the Faults of his Poetry by his Misfortunes ; and told them
that good Verses never flow, but from a serene and compos'd Spirit. Wit, which is a kind
10 *of Mercury with Wings fasten'd to his Head and Heels, can fly but slowly in a damp air.*
I therefore chose rather to Obey You late than ill : if at least I am capable of writing anything,
at any time, which is worthy Your Perusal and Your Patronage. I cannot say that I have
escap'd from a Shipwreck ; but have only gain'd a Rock by hard swimming ; where I may
pant a while and gather breath : For the Doctors give me a sad assurance that my Disease
never took its leave of any man but with a purpose to return. However, my Lord, I have
laid hold on the Interval, and menag'd the small Stock which Age has left me to the best
advantage, in performing this inconsiderable service to my Ladies memory. We who are
Priests of Apollo have not the Inspiration when we please ; but must wait until the God comes
rushing on us, and invades us with a fury, which we are not able to resist : which gives us
20 *double strength while the Fit continues, and leaves us languishing and spent, at its departure.*
Let me not seem to boast ; my Lord ; for I have really felt it on this Occasion and prophecy'd
beyond my natural power. Let me add and hope to be believ'd, that the Excellency of the
Subject contributed much to the Happiness of the Execution : And that the weight of thirty
Years was taken off me, while I was writing. I swom with the Tyde, and the water under
me was buoyant. The Reader will easily observe, that I was transported, by the multitude
and variety of my Similitudes, which are generally the product of a luxuriant Fancy ; and
the wantonness of Wit. Had I call'd in my Judgment to my assistance, I had certainly
retrench'd many of them. But I defend them not ; let them pass for beautiful faults amongst
the better sort of Critiques : For the whole Poem, though written in that which they call Heroique
30 *Verse, is of the Pindarique nature, as well in the Thought as the Expression ; and, as such,*
requires the same grains of allowance for it. It was intended, as Your Lordship sees in the
Title, not for an Elegie, but a Panegyrique. A kind of Apotheosis, indeed ; if a Heathen
Word may be applyed to a Christian use. And on all Occasions of Praise, if we take the
Ancients for our Patterns, we are bound by Prescription to employ the magnificence of Words,
and the force of Figures, to adorn the sublimity of Thoughts. Isocrates *amongst the Grecian*
Orators, and Cicero, *and the younger* Pliny, *amongst the* Romans, *have left us their Precedents*
for our security : For I think I need not mention the inimitable Pindar, *who stretches on these*
Pinnions out of sight, and is carried upward, as it were, into another World.

This, at least, my Lord, I may justly plead, that if I have not perform'd so well as I think
40 *I have, yet I have us'd my best endeavours to excel my self. One Disadvantage I have had,*
which is, never to have known, or seen my Lady : And to draw the Lineaments of her Mind,
from the Description which I have receiv'd from others, is for a Painter to set himself at work
without the living Original before him. Which the more beautiful it is, will be so much the
more difficult for him to conceive ; when he has only a relation given him of such and such
Features by an Acquaintance or a Friend ; without the Nice Touches, which give the best
Resemblance, and make the Graces of the Picture. Every Artist is apt enough to flatter himself

---

10 *slowly*] slowly, *1692.*

(and I amongst the rest) that their own ocular Observations would have discover'd more perfections, at least others, than have been deliver'd to them: Though I have receiv'd mine from the best hands, that is, from Persons who neither want a just Understanding of my Lady's Worth, nor a due Veneration for her Memory.

Doctor Donn *the greatest Wit, though not the best Poet, of our Nation, acknowledges that he had never seen Mrs.* Drury, *whom he has made immortal in his admirable Anniversaries; I have had the same fortune; though I have not succeeded to the same Genius. However, I have followed his footsteps in the Design of his Panegyrick, which was to raise an Emulation in the living, to Copy out the Example of the dead. And therefore it was, that I once intended to have call'd this poem, The Pattern: And though, on a second consideration, I chang'd* 10 *the Title into the Name of that Illustrious Person, yet the Design continues, and* Eleonora *is still the Pattern of Charity, Devotion, and Humility; of the best Wife, the best Mother, and the best of Friends.*

And now, my Lord, though I have endeavour'd to answer Your Commands, yet I cou'd not answer it to the World nor to my Conscience, if I gave not Your Lordship my Testimony of being the best Husband now living: I say my Testimony only: For the praise of it, is given You by Your self. They who despise the Rules of Virtue both in their Practice and their Morals, will think this a very trivial Commendation. But I think it the peculiar happiness of the Countess of Abingdon, *to have been so truly lov'd by you, while she was living, and so gratefully honour'd, after she was dead. Few there are who have either had, or cou'd have* 20 *such a loss; and yet fewer who carried their Love and Constancy beyond the Grave. The exteriors of Mourning, a decent Funeral, and black Habits, are the usual stints of Common Husbands: and perhaps their Wives deserve no better than to be mourn'd with Hypocrisie, and forgot with ease. But You have distinguish'd Yourself from ordinary Lovers, by a real and lasting grief for the Deceas'd, And by endeavouring to raise for her the most durable Monument, which is that of Verse. And so it wou'd have proved, if the Workman had been equal to the Work; and Your Choice of the Artificer as happy as Your Design. Yet, as* Phidias, *when he had made the Statue of* Minerva, *cou'd not forbear to ingrave his own Name, as Author of the Piece: so give me leave to hope, that, by subscribing mine to this Poem, I may live by the Goddess, and transmit my Name to Posterity by the memory of Hers. 'Tis* 30 *no flattery to assure Your Lordship, that she is remember'd in the present Age, by all who have had the Honour of her Conversation and Acquaintance; and that I have never been in any Company since the news of her death was first brought me, where they have not extoll'd her Virtues; and even spoken the same things of her in Prose which I have done in Verse.*

I therefore think myself oblig'd to thank Your Lordship for the Commission which You have given me: How I have acquitted my self of it, must be left to the Opinion of the World, in spite of any Protestation, which I can enter against the present Age, as Incompetent, or Corrupt Judges. For my Comfort, they are but Englishmen, and, as such, if they Think Ill of me to Day, they are inconstant enough to Think Well of me to Morrow. And, after all, I have not much to thank my Fortune that I was born amongst them. The Good of both 40 *Sexes are so few, in England, that they stand like Exceptions against General Rules: And though one of them has deserv'd a greater Commendation, than I cou'd give her, they have taken care, that I shou'd not tire my Pen, with frequent exercise on the like Subject; that Praises, like Taxes, should be appropriated; and left almost as Individual as the Person. They say, my Talent is Satyre: if it be so, 'tis a fruitful Age; and there is an extraordinary Crop to gather. But a single hand is insufficient for such a Harvest: They have sown the Dragons Teeth themselves; and it is but just they shou'd reap each other in Lampoons. You, my Lord, who have the Character of Honour, though 'tis not my happiness to know You, may stand aside with the small Remainders of the English Nobility, truly such, and, unhurt your selves, behold the mad Combat. If I have pleas'd You and some few others, I have obtain'd my* 50 *end. You see I have disabled my self, like an Elected Speaker of the House; yet, like him,*

I have undertaken the Charge, and find the Burden sufficiently recompenc'd by the Honour.
Be pleas'd to accept of these my Unworthy Labours, this Paper Monument ; and let her
Pious Memory, which I am sure is Sacred to You, not only plead the Pardon of my many
Faults, but gain me Your Protection, which is ambitiously sought by,

My LORD,

Your Lordship's

Most Obedient Servant,

John Dryden.

ELEONORA :

A | PANEGYRICAL POEM.

Dedicated to the | MEMORY | OF THE | Late Countess of ABINGDON.

As, when some Great and Gracious Monarch
    dies,   *The*
Soft whispers, first, and mournful   *Intro-*
    Murmurs rise   *duction.*
Among the sad Attendants ; then, the sound
Soon gathers voice, and spreads the news
    around,
Through Town and Country, till the dreadful
    blast
Is blown to distant Colonies at last ;
Who, then perhaps, were off'ring Vows in vain,
For his long life and for his happy Reign :
So slowly, by degrees, unwilling Fame ⎫
Did Matchless *Eleonora's* fate proclaim, 10 ⎬
Till publick as the loss the news became. ⎭
    The Nation felt it, in th' extremest parts,
With eyes o'reflowing and with bleeding
    hearts :
But most the Poor, whom daily she sup-
    ply'd ;
Beginning to be such, but when   *Of her*
    she dy'd.   *Charity.*
For, while she liv'd, they slept in peace, by
    night ;
Secure of bread, as of returning light,
And, with such firm dependence on the Day,
That need grew pamper'd ; and forgot to
    pray :
So sure the Dole, so ready at their call, 20
They stood prepar'd to see the Manna fall.
    Such Multitudes she fed, she cloath'd, she
    nurst,
That she, her self, might fear her wanting
    first.

Of her Five Talents, other five she made ;
Heav'n, that had largely giv'n, was largely
    pay'd ;
And, in few lives, in wondrous few, we find
A Fortune better fitted to the Mind.
Nor did her Alms from Ostentation fall,
Or proud desire of Praise ; the Soul gave all :
Unbrib'd it gave ; or, if a bribe appear, 30
No less than Heav'n ; to heap huge treasures,
    there.
    Want passed for Merit, at her open door :
Heav'n saw, he safely might increase his Poor,
And trust their Sustenance with her so well
As not to be at charge of Miracle.
None cou'd be needy, whom she saw, or
    knew ;
All, in the compass of her Sphear, she drew :
He who cou'd touch her Garment, was as
    sure,
As the first Christians of th' Apostles cure.
The distant heard, by fame, her pious deeds ;
And laid her up, for their extremest needs ;
A future Cordial for a fainting Mind ;   42
For, what was ne're refus'd, all hop'd to find,
Each in his turn: The Rich might freely come,
As to a Friend ; but to the Poor, 'twas Home.
As to some Holy House th' Afflicted came ; ⎫
The Hunger-starv'd, the Naked, and the ⎬
    Lame ;   ⎭
Want and Diseases fled before her Name. ⎭
For zeal like hers, her Servants were too ⎫
    slow ;   ⎬
She was the first, where need requir'd, ⎬
    to go,   50 ⎬
Her self the Foundress, and Attendant too. ⎭

ELEONORA. Text from the original edition,
1692, except as noted.

27 Fortune] Fortune, *1692.*

Sure she had Guests sometimes to enter-
tain,
Guests in disguise, of her Great Master's
Train :
Her Lord himself might come, for ought we
know ;
Since in a Servant's form he liv'd below ;
Beneath her Roof, he might be pleased to
stay :
Or some benighted Angel, in his way
Might ease his Wings ; and seeing Heav'n
appear
In its best work of Mercy, think it there,
Where all the deeds of Charity and Love 60
Were in as constant Method, as above,
All carry'd on ; all of a piece with theirs ; }
As free her Alms, as diligent her cares ;
As loud her Praises, and as warm her
Pray'rs.
   Yet was she not profuse ; but fear'd to
wast,
And wisely manag'd, that the   *Of her
stock might last ;   prudent
That all might be supply'd ; and manage-
she not grieve   ment.*
When crowds appear'd, she had not to
relieve.
Which to prevent, she still increas'd her
store ;
Laid up, and spar'd, that she might give
the more :   70
So *Pharaoh,* or some Greater king than he,
Provided for the sev'nth Necessity :
Taught from above, his Magazines to frame ;
That Famine was prevented e're it came.
Thus Heav'n, though All-sufficient, shows
a thrift
In his Oeconomy, and bounds his gift :
Creating for our Day, one single Light ;
And his Reflection too supplies the Night :
Perhaps a thousand other Worlds, that lye
Remote from us, and latent in the Sky, 80
Are lighten'd by his Beams, and kindly
nurst ;
Of which our Earthly Dunghil is the
worst.
   Now, as all Vertues keep the middle
line,
Yet somewhat more to one extreme incline,
Such was her Soul ; abhorring Avarice,
Bounteous, but, almost bounteous to a Vice :
Had she giv'n more, it had Profusion been,
And turn'd the excess of Goodness, into Sin.

These Vertues rais'd her Fabrick to the
Sky ;
For that which is next Heav'n,   *Of her
is Charity.   Humility.*
But, as high Turrets for their Ay'ry steep 91
Require Foundations, in proportion deep :
And lofty Cedars as far upward shoot
As to the neather Heav'ns they drive the
root ;
So low did her secure Foundation lye,
She was not Humble, but Humility.
Scarcely she knew that she was great, or }
fair,
Or wise, beyond what other Women are, }
Or, which is better, knew ; but never durst }
compare.
For to be conscious of what all admire, 100
And not be vain, advances Vertue high'r :
But still she found, or rather thought she
found,
Her own worth wanting, others' to abound:
Ascrib'd above their due to ev'ry one,
Unjust and scanty to her self alone.
   Such her Devotion was, as might give
rules
Of Speculation, to disputing   *Of her
Schools ;   Piety.*
And teach us equally the Scales to hold
Betwixt the two Extremes of hot and cold
That pious heat may mod'rately prevail, 110
And we be warm'd, but not be scorch'd with
zeal.
Business might shorten, not disturb her
Pray'r ;
Heav'n had the best, if not the greater share.
An Active life long Oraisons forbids ;
Yet still she pray'd, for still she pray'd by
deeds.
   Her ev'ry day was Sabbath ; Only free
From hours of Pray'r, for hours of Charity.
Such as the Jews from servile toil releast ;
Where works of Mercy were a part of rest :
Such as blest Angels exercise above, 120
Vary'd with Sacred Hymns, and Acts of
Love ;
Such Sabbaths as that one she now enjoys ;
Ev'n that perpetual one, which she employs,
(For such vicissitudes in Heav'n there are)
In Praise alternate, and alternate Pray'r.

---

93 Cedars as far] Cedars, as far, *1692.*
100 conscious] consc'ious *1692.*
114 life] life, *1692.*

All this she practis'd here ; that when she
   sprung
Amidst the Quires, at the first sight she
   sung.
Sung, and was sung her self, in Angels Lays ;
For praising her, they did her Maker praise.
All Offices of Heav'n so well she knew,   130
Before she came, that nothing there was
   new ;
And she was so familiarly receiv'd,
As one returning, not as one arriv'd.
   Muse, down again precipitate thy flight ;
For how can Mortal Eyes sustain
      Immortal Light !   *Of her*
But as the Sun in Water we can   *various*
      bear,   *Vertues.*
Yet not the Sun, but his Reflection there,
So let us view her here, in what she was,
And take her Image in this watry Glass :
Yet look not ev'ry Lineament to see ;   140
Some will be cast in shades ; and some
   will be
So lamely drawn, you scarcely know, 'tis
   she.
For where such various Vertues we recite,
'Tis like the Milky-Way, all over bright,
But sown so thick with Stars, 'tis undis-
   tinguish'd light.
   Her Vertue, not her Vertues let us call ;
For one Heroick comprehends 'em all :
One, as a Constellation is but one ;
Though 'tis a Train of Stars, that, rolling on,
Rise in their turn, and in the Zodiack run,
Ever in Motion; now 'tis Faith ascends,   151
Now Hope, now Charity, that upward
   tends,
And downwards with diffusive Good, de-
   scends.
   As in Perfumes compos'd with Art and
      Cost,
'Tis hard to say what Scent is uppermost ;
Nor this part Musk or Civet can we call,
Or Amber, but a rich Result of all ;
So, she was all a Sweet ; whose ev'ry part,
In due proportion mix'd, proclaim'd the
   Maker's Art.
No single Virtue we cou'd most commend,
Whether the Wife, the Mother, or the
   Friend ;   161
For she was all, in that supreme degree,
That, as no one prevail'd, so all was she.
The sev'ral parts lay hidden in the Piece ;
Th' Occasion but exerted that, or this.

A Wife as tender, and as true withall,
As the first Woman was, before
   her fall :   *Of her*
Made for the Man, of whom she *Conjugal*
   was a part ;   *Virtues.*
Made, to attract his Eyes, and keep his Heart,
A second *Eve*, but by no crime accurst ;   170
As beauteous, not as brittle as the first.
Had she been first, still Paradise had bin,
And Death had found no entrance by her sin.
So she not only had preserv'd from ill
Her Sex and ours, but liv'd their Pattern still.
   Love and Obedience to her Lord she bore,
She much obey'd him, but she lov'd him
   more.
Not aw'd to Duty by superior sway ;
But taught by his Indulgence to obey.
Thus we love God as Author of our good ;
So Subjects love just Kings, or so they
   shou'd.   181
Nor was it with Ingratitude return'd ;
In equal Fires the blissful Couple burn'd :
One Joy possess'd 'em both, and in one
      Grier they mourn'd.
His Passion still improv'd : he lov'd so fast
As if he fear'd each day wou'd be her last.
Too true a Prophet to foresee the Fate
That shou'd so soon divide their happy
      State :
When he to Heav'n entirely must restore
That Love, that Heart, where he went halves
   before.   190
Yet as the Soul is all in ev'ry part,
So God and He, might each have all her
   Heart.
   So had her Children too ; for Charity
Was not more fruitful, or more
   kind than she :   *Of her*
Each under other by degrees they *love to her*
   grew ;   *Children.*
A goodly Perspective of distant view.
Anchises look'd not with so pleas'd a face
In numb'ring o'er his future *Roman* Race,
And Marshalling the Heroes of his name,
As, in their Order, next to light they came ;
Nor *Cybele* with half so kind an Eye,   201
Survey'd her Sons and Daughters of the
   Skie.
Proud, shall I say, of her immortal Fruit,
As far as Pride with Heav'nly Minds may
   suit.

----

204 Heav'nly] Heav'enly *1692*.

Her pious love excell'd to all she bore ;
New Objects only multiply'd it   *Her care*
      more.   *of their*
And as the Chosen found the   *Educa-*
      perly Grain   *tion.*
As much as ev'ry Vessel could contain ;
As in the Blissful Vision each shall share, ⎫
As much of Glory, as his soul can bear ; 210 ⎬
So did she love, and so dispense her Care. ⎭
Her eldest thus, by consequence, was best ;
As longer cultivated than the rest :
The Babe had all that Infant care beguiles,
And early knew his Mother in her smiles :
But when dilated Organs let in day
To the young Soul, and gave it room to play,
At his first aptness, the Maternal Love
Those Rudiments of Reason did improve :
The tender Age was pliant to command ; 220
Like Wax it yielded to the forming hand :
True to th' Artificer, the labour'd Mind
With ease was pious, generous, just and
      kind;
Soft for Impression, from the first, prepar'd,
Till Vertue, with long exercise, grew hard ;
With ev'ry Act confirm'd ; and made, at last
So durable, as not to be effac'd,
It turned to Habit; and, from Vices free,
Goodness resolv'd into Necessity.
      Thus fix'd she Virtue's Image, that's her
      own,   230
Till the whole Mother in the Children shone;
For that was their perfection : she was such,
They never cou'd express her Mind too much,
So unexhausted her Perfections were,
That, for more Children, she had more to
      spare ;
For Souls unborn, whom her untimely death
Depriv'd of Bodies and of mortal breath :
And (cou'd they take th' Impressions of her
      Mind)
Enough still left to sanctifie her kind. 239
      Then wonder not to see this Soul extend
The bounds, and seek some other   *Of her*
      self, a Friend :   *Friend-*
As swelling Seas to gentle Rivers   *ship.*
      glide,
To seek repose, and empty out the Tyde ;
So this full Soul, in narrow limits pent,
Unable to contain her, sought a vent,
To issue out, and in some friendly breast
Discharge her Treasures, and securely rest :
T' unbosom all the secrets of her Heart,
Take good advice, but better to impart. 249

For 'tis the bliss of Friendship's holy state ⎫
To mix their Minds, and to communicate ; ⎬
Though Bodies cannot, Souls can pene- ⎭
      trate.
Fixt to her choice ; inviolably true ;
And wisely chusing, for she chose but few.
Some she must have ; but in no one cou'd
      find
A Tally fitted for so large a Mind.
      The Souls of Friends like Kings in Progress
      are ;
Still in their own, though from the Pallace
      far :
Thus her Friend's Heart her Country Dwell-
      ing was,
A sweet Retirement to a courser place : 260
Where Pomp and Ceremonies enter'd not ;
Where Greatness was shut out, and Buis'ness
      well forgot.
This is th' imperfect draught ; but short ⎫
      as far   ⎬
As the true height and bigness of a Star ⎭
Exceeds the Measures of th' Astronomer.
She shines above, we know, but in what
      place,
How near the Throne, and Heav'ns Imperial
      Face,
By our weak Opticks is but vainly ghest ;
Distance and Altitude conceal the rest. 269
      Tho all these rare Endowments of the
      Mind
Were in a narrow space of life   *Reflections*
      confin'd ;   *on the*
The Figure was with full Perfec-   *shortness*
      tion crown'd ;   *of her life.*
Though not so large an Orb, as truly round.
      As when in glory, through the publick
      place,
The Spoils of conquer'd Nations were to pass,
And but one Day for Triumph was allowed,
The Consul was constrain'd his Pomp to
      crowd ;
And so the swift Procession hurry'd on,
That all, though not distinctly, might be
      shown :   279
So, in the straiten'd bounds of life confin'd,
She gave but glimpses of her glorious Mind
And multitudes of Vertues pass'd along,
Each pressing foremost in the mighty throng;
Ambitious to be seen, and then make room,
For greater Multitudes that were to come.
      Yet unemploy'd no Minute slipt away ;
Moments were precious in so short a stay

The haste of Heav'n to have her was so great
That some were single Acts, though each compleat ;
But ev'ry Act stood ready to repeat. 290
Her fellow Saints with busie care, will look
For her blest Name in Fate's eternal Book ;
And, pleas'd to be outdone, with joy will see
Numberless Vertues, endless Charity ;
But more will wonder at so short an Age
To find a Blank beyond the thirti'th Page ;
And with a pious fear begin to doubt
The Piece imperfect, and the rest torn out.
But 'twas her Saviour's time ; and, cou'd there be
A Copy near th' Original, 'twas she. *She dy'd in her thirty third year.*
    As precious Gums are not for lasting fire,
They but perfume the Temple, and expire,
So was she soon exhal'd ; and vanish'd hence ; 303
A short sweet Odour, of a vast expence.
She vanish'd, we can scarcely say she dy'd ;
For but a Now, did Heav'n and Earth divide :
She pass'd serenely with a single breath,
This moment perfect health, the next was death.
One sigh, did her eternal Bliss assure ; *The manner of her death.*
So little Penance needs, when Souls are almost pure. 310
As gentle Dreams our waking Thoughts pursue ;
Or, one Dream pass'd, we slide into a new ;
(So close they follow, such wild Order keep,
We think our selves awake, and are asleep :)
So softly death succeeded life, in her ;
She did but dream of Heav'n, and she was there.
    No Pains she suffer'd, nor expir'd with Noise ;
Her Soul was whisper'd out, with God's still Voice ;
As an old Friend is beckon'd to a Feast,
And treated like a long familiar Guest ; 320

He took her as he found ; but found her so,
As one in hourly readiness to go. *Her preparedness to dye.*
Ev'n on that day, in all her Trim prepar'd ;
As early notice she from Heav'n had heard,
And some descending Courier, from above
Had giv'n her timely warning to remove :
Or counsell'd her to dress the nuptial Room ;
For on that Night the Bridegroom was to come. *She dy'd on Whitsunday night.*
He kept his hour, and found her where she lay
Cloath'd all in white, the Liv'ry of the Day : 330
Scarce had she sinn'd in thought, or word, or act ;
Unless Omissions were to pass for fact :
That hardly Death a Consequence cou'd draw,
To make her liable to Nature's Law.
And that she dy'd, we only have to show,
The mortal part of her she left below :
The rest (so smooth, so suddenly she went)
Looked like Translation, through the Firmament ;
Or like the fiery Carr, on the third Errand sent. 339
    O happy Soul ! if thou canst view from high
Where thou art all Intelligence, all Eye, *Apostrophe to her Soul.*
If looking up to God, or down to us,
Thou find'st that any way be pervious,
Survey the ruines of thy House, and see
Thy widow'd, and thy Orphan Family ;
Look on thy tender Pledges left behind ;
And, if thou canst a vacant Minute find
From Heav'nly Joys, that Interval afford
To thy sad Children and thy mourning Lord. 349
See how they grieve, mistaken in their love,
And shed a beam of Comfort from above ;
Give 'em, as much as mortal Eyes can bear,
A transient view of thy full glories there ;
That they with mod'rate sorrow may sustain
And mollifie their Losses, in thy Gain.
Or else divide the grief, for such thou wert,
That should not all Relations bear a part,
It were enough to break a single heart.

Let this suffice : Nor thou, great Saint, refuse *Epiphonema : or close of the Poem.*
This humble Tribute of no vulgar Muse :
Who, not by Cares, or Wants, or Age deprest, 361
Stems a wild Deluge with a dauntless brest :
And dares to sing thy Praises, in a Clime
Where Vice triumphs and Vertue is a Crime :
Where even to draw the Picture of thy Mind,
Is Satyr on the most of Humane Kind :
Take it, while yet 'tis Praise ; before my rage
Unsafely just, break loose on this bad Age ;

So bad, that thou thy self had'st no defence
From Vice, but barely by departing hence.
Be what, and where thou art : To wish thy place, 371
Were in the best, Presumption, more than grace.
Thy Reliques (such thy Works of Mercy are)
Have, in this Poem, been my holy care.
As Earth thy Body keeps, thy Soul the Sky, ⎫
So shall this Verse preserve thy Memory ; ⎬
For thou shalt make it live, because it ⎭
sings of thee.

FINIS.

ON THE DEATH OF MR. PURCELL.

1

MARK how the Lark and Linnet sing,
  With rival Notes
They strain their warbling Throats
  To welcome in the Spring.
  But in the close of night,
When *Philomel* begins her Heav'nly Lay,
  They cease their mutual spight,
  Drink in her Musick with delight,
And list'ning and silent, and silent and
    list'ning, and list'ning and silent
    obey.

2

So ceas'd the rival Crew, when Purcell came, 10
They Sung no more, or only Sung his Fame.
  Struck dumb, they all admir'd
  The godlike man,
  Alas, too soon retir'd,
  As He too late began.

We beg not Hell our *Orpheus* to restore ;
  Had He been there,
  Their Sovereigns fear
  Had sent Him back before. 19
The pow'r of Harmony too well they knew ;
He long e'er this had Tun'd their jarring Sphere,
  And left no Hell below.

3

The Heav'nly Quire, who heard his Notes from high,
Let down the Scale of Musick from the Sky :
  They handed him along,
And all the way He taught, and all the way they Sung.
Ye Brethren of the *Lyre* and tunefull Voice,
Lament his lott : but at your own rejoyce.
Now live secure, and linger out your days,
The Gods are pleas'd alone with *Purcell's* Layes, 30
  Nor know to mend their Choice.

---

369 defence] defence, *1692.*
ON THE DEATH OF MR. PURCELL. Text from the original of 1696. *In the words printed with the music Dr. Blow impudently altered* godlike *into* matchless *and* their jarring Sphere *into* the jarring Spheres.
6 Lay] lay *1696.*
9 *This line has never been correctly reprinted*

in England. Editors till Christie gave And list'ning silently obey. *Christie professed to* 'restore' *the line, but by twice omitting the word* and *gave a wrong and uneuphonic line. Dr Sainsbury copies Christie.*
12 admir'd] admir'd the godlike man *1696.*
16 Hell] Hell, *1696.*
30 Layes] Layes *1696.*

THE MONUMENT OF A FAIR MAIDEN LADY,

WHO DY'D AT BATH, AND IS THERE INTERR'D.

BELOW this Marble Monument is laid
All that Heav'n wants of this Celestial Maid.
Preserve, O sacred Tomb, thy Trust con-
    sign'd:
The Mold was made on purpose for the
    Mind:
And she wou'd lose, if at the latter Day
One Atom cou'd be mix'd, of other clay.
Such were the Features of her heavenly
    Face;
Her Limbs were form'd with such harmonious
    Grace,
So faultless was the Frame, as if the Whole
Had been an Emanation of the Soul;   10
Which her own inward Symmetry reveal'd;
And like a Picture shone, in Glass anneal'd
Or like the Sun eclips'd, with shaded Light:
Too piercing, else, to be sustain'd by
    Sight.
Each Thought was visible that rowl'd within:
As through a Crystal Case, the figur'd Hours
    are seen.
And Heav'n did this transparent Veil pro-
    vide,
Because she had no guilty Thought to hide.

All white, a Virgin-Saint, she sought the
    Skies:
For Marriage, tho' it sullies not, it dies.   20
High tho' her Wit, yet humble was her
    Mind;
As if she cou'd not, or she wou'd not find
How much her Worth transcended all her
    Kind.
Yet she had learn'd so much of Heav'n below,
That, when arriv'd, she scarce had more to
    know:
But only to refresh the former Hint;
And read her Maker in a fairer Print.
So Pious, as she had no time to spare,
For human Thoughts, but was confin'd to
    Pray'r.
Yet in such Charities she pass'd the Day,   30
'Twas wondrous how she found an Hour to
    Pray.
A Soul so calm, it knew not Ebbs or Flows,
Which Passion cou'd but curl; not discom-
    pose.
A Female Softness, with a manly Mind;
A Daughter duteous, and a Sister kind:
In Sickness patient; and in Death resign'd.

ON THE DEATH OF AMYNTAS.

A PASTORAL ELEGY.

'TWAS on a Joyless and a Gloomy Morn,
Wet was the Grass, and hung with Pearls
    the Thorn,
When *Damon*, who design'd to pass the Day
With Hounds and Horns, and chase the
    flying Prey,
Rose early from his Bed; but soon he
    found
The Welkin pitch'd with sullen Clouds
    around,
An Eastern Wind, and Dew upon the
    Ground.

Thus while he stood, and sighing did survey
The Fields, and curs'd th' ill Omens of the
    Day,
He saw *Menalcas* come with heavy pace;   10
Wet were his Eyes, and chearless was his
    Face:
He wrung his Hands, distracted with his Care,
And sent his Voice before him from afar.
Return, he cry'd, return unhappy Swain,
The spungy Clouds are fill'd with gath'ring
    Rain:

THE MONUMENT OF A FAIR MAIDEN LADY.
Text from the edition of 1700. The variants
below are from the monument in the Abbey
Church at Bath as reported by Christie.
  6 of] with
 18 Thought] thoughts

 28 as] that.
 29 was] seem'd
   In 6 with *gives a wrong sense, and in 18*
thoughts *is false grammar. In 29* seem'd *may
be right: at any rate it gives better sense.*
  ON THE DEATH OF AMYNTAS Text from the
Miscellanies, 1704.

The Promise of the Day not only crossed,
But ev'n the Spring, the Spring it self is
   lost.
Amyntas—Oh ! he cou'd not speak the rest,
Nor needed, for presaging *Damon* guess'd.
Equal with Heav'n young *Damon* loved the
   Boy ;   20
The boast of Nature, both his Parents Joy.
His graceful Form revolving in his Mind ;
So great a Genius, and a Soul so kind,
Gave sad assurance that his Fears were
   true ;
Too well the Envy of the Gods he knew :
For when their Gifts too lavishly are plac'd,
Soon they repent, and will not make them
   last.
For, sure, it was too bountiful a Dole,
The Mother's Features, and the Father's
   Soul.
Then thus he cry'd, The Morn bespoke the
   News,   30
The Morning did her chearful Light diffuse,
But see how suddenly she changed her
   Face,
And brought on Clouds and Rains, the
   Day's disgrace :
Just such, *Amyntas*, was thy promis'd
   Race.
What Charms adorn'd thy Youth where
   Nature smil'd,
And more than Man was giv'n us in a Child.
His Infancy was ripe : a Soul sublime
In Years so tender that prevented time ;
Heav'n gave him all at once ; then
   snatch'd away,
E're Mortals all his Beauties cou'd survey,
Just like the Flow'r that buds and withers
   in a day.   41

MENALCAS.

The Mother Lovely, tho' with Grief opprest,
Reclin'd his dying Head upon her Breast.
The mournful Family stood all around ;
One Groan was heard, one Universal Sound:
All were in Floods of Tears and endless
   Sorrow drown'd.
So dire a Sadness sate on ev'ry Look,
Ev'n Death repented he had giv'n the
   Stroke.

He griev'd his fatal Work had been ordain'd,
But promis'd length of Life to those who
   yet remain'd.   50
The Mother's and her Eldest Daughters
   Grace,
It seems had brib'd him to prolong their
   space.
The Father bore it with undaunted Soul,
Like one who durst his Destiny controul :
Yet with becoming Grief he bore his part,
Resign'd his Son, but not resign'd his Heart.
Patient as *Job* ; and may he live to see,
Like him, a new increasing Family !

DAMON.

Such is my Wish, and such my Prophesie.
For yet, my Friend, the Beauteous Mold
   remains,   60
Long may she exercise her fruitful Pains :
But, ah ! with better hap, and bring a Race
More lasting, and endu'd with equal Grace :
Equal she may, but farther none can go ;
For he was all that was exact below.

MENALCAS.

Damon, behold yon breaking Purple Cloud ;
Hear'st thou not Hymns and Songs Divinely
   loud ?
There mounts *Amyntas* ; the young Cherubs
   play
About their Godlike Mate, and Sing him on
   his way.
He cleaves the liquid Air, behold, he
   Flies,   70
And every Moment gains upon the Skies :
The new come Guest admires th' Ætherial
   State,
The *Saphyr* Portal, and the *Golden* Gate ;
And now admitted in the shining Throng,
He shows the Passport which he brought
   along.
His Passport is his Innocence and Grace,
Well known to all the Natives of the Place.
Now Sing, yee joyful Angels, and admire
Your Brother's Voice that comes to mend
   your Quire :
Sing you, while endless Tears our Eyes
   bestow ;   80
For like *Amyntas* none is left below.

DR.   B

ON THE DEATH OF A VERY YOUNG GENTLEMAN.

HE who cou'd view the Book of Destiny,
And read whatever there was writ of thee,
O *Charming Youth*, in the first op'ning Page,
So many Graces in so green an Age,
Such Wit, such Modesty, such strength of
  Mind,
A Soul at once so manly and so kind,
Wou'd wonder, when he turned the Volume
  o're,
And after some few Leaves shou'd find no
  more,
Nought but a blank remain, a dead void
  space,
A step of Life that promised such a Race. 10
We must not, dare not think, that Heav'n
  began
A Child, and cou'd not finish him a Man:
Reflecting what a mighty Store was laid
Of rich Materials, and a Model made :
The Cost already furnished ; so bestow'd,
As more was never to one Soul allow'd :
Yet after this profusion spent in vain,
Nothing but mould'ring Ashes to remain,
I guess not, lest I split upon the Shelf,
Yet, durst I guess, Heav'n kept it for him-
  self :   20
And giving us the use, did soon recal,
E're we cou'd spare, the mighty Principal.
  Thus then he disappear'd, was rarify'd,
For 'tis improper Speech to say he dy'd :
He was exhal'd : His great Creator drew
His Spirit, as the Sun the Morning Dew.
'Tis Sin produces Death ; and he had none,
But the Taint *Adam* left on ev'ry Son.

He added not, he was so pure, so good,
'Twas but th' Original forfeit of his Blood ;
And that so little, that the River ran   31
More clear than the corrupted Fount began.
Nothing remained of the first muddy Clay,
The length of Course had wash'd it in the
  way :
So deep, and yet so clear, we might behold
The Gravel bottom, and that bottom Gold.
  As such we lov'd, admir'd, almost ador'd,
Gave all the Tribute Mortals could afford,
Perhaps we gave so much, the Pow'rs above
Grew angry at our superstitious Love :   40
For when we more than Human Homage pay,
The charming Cause is justly snatched away.
  Thus was the Crime not his, but ours ⎫
    alone ;   ⎪
  And yet we murmur that he went so soon, ⎬
  Though Miracles are short and rarely shown. ⎭
    Hear then, yee mournful Parents, and
      divide
That Love in many which in one was ty'd.
That individual Blessing is no more,
But multiply'd in your remaining store.
The Flame's dispersed, but does not all
  expire :   50
The Sparkles blaze, though not the Globe of
  Fire.
Love him by Parts in all your num'rous
  Race,
And from those Parts form one collected
  Grace ;
Then, when you have refin'd to that degree,
Imagine all in one, and think that one is He.

UPON YOUNG MR. ROGERS

OF GLOUCESTERSHIRE.

OF gentle Blood, his Parents only Treasure,
Their lasting Sorrow and their vanish'd
  Pleasure,
Adorn'd with Features, Virtues, Wit, and
  Grace,
A large Provision for so short a Race :

More mod'rate Gifts might have prolong'd
  his Date,
Too early fitted for a better State :
But, knowing Heav'n his Home, to shun
  Delay
He leap'd o'er Age, and took the shortest Way.

ON THE DEATH OF A VERY YOUNG GENTLE-
MAN. Text from the *Miscellanies*, 1704.

UPON YOUNG MR. ROGERS. Text from the
Miscellanies, 1704.

ON MRS. MARGARET PASTON,

OF BARNINGHAM, IN NORFOLK.

So fair, so young, so innocent, so sweet,
So ripe a Judgment, and so rare a Wit,
Require at least an Age in one to meet.
In her they met; but long they could not stay,
'Twas Gold too fine to fix without Allay.

Heav'n's Image was in her so well ex-
prest,
Her very sight upbraided all the rest ;
Too justly ravish'd from an Age like this,
Now she is gone, the World is of a Piece.

EPITAPH ON A NEPHEW

IN CATWORTH CHURCH, HUNTINGDONSHIRE.

STAY, Stranger, stay, and drop one Tear ;
She allways weeps that layd him here ;
And will do till her Race is run :
His Father's fifth, her only Son.

SONGS, ODES, AND LYRICAL PIECES.

THE TEARS OF AMYNTA FOR THE DEATH OF DAMON

SONG.

1

On a Bank, beside a Willow,
Heav'n her Cov'ring, Earth her Pillow,
Sad *Amynta* sigh'd alone ;
From the chearless dawn of Morning
Till the Dews of Night returning,
Singing thus she made her mone :
    Hope is banish'd,
    Joys are vanish'd,
Damon, my belov'd, is gone !

2

Time, I dare thee to discover
Such a Youth, and such a Lover ;
Oh, so true, so kind was he !
Damon was the pride of Nature,
Charming in his every Feature ;

Damon liv'd alone for me :
    Melting Kisses,
    Murmuring Blisses ;
Who so liv'd and lov'd as we !

3

Never shall we curse the Morning,
Never bless the Night returning,
Sweet Embraces to restore :
Never shall we both ly dying,
Nature failing, love supplying
All the Joys he drain'd before.
    Death come end me
    To befriend me ;
Love and *Damon* are no more.

ON MRS. MARGARET PASTON. Text from
Pope's *Miscellanies*, 1712.

EPITAPH ON A NEPHEW. Text as reported
from the Monument.
THE TEARS OF AMYNTA. Text from the
Miscellany Poems, 1684.

SONG.

I.

SYlvia the fair, in the bloom of Fifteen
Felt an innocent warmth, as she lay on the
    green ;
She had heard of a pleasure, and something
    she guest
By the towzing and tumbling and touching
    her Breast :
She saw the men eager, but was at a loss,
What they meant by their sighing and kissing
    so close ;
    By their praying and whining,
    And clasping and twining,
    And panting and wishing,
    And sighing and kissing,
    And sighing and kissing so close.

II.

Ah she cry'd, ah for a languishing Maid
In a Country of Christians to die without
    aid !
Not a Whig, or a Tory, or Trimmer at
    least,
Or a Protestant Parson or Catholick Priest,

To instruct a young Virgin that is at a loss
What they meant by their sighing and
    kissing so close ;
    By their praying and whining,
    And clasping and twining,
    And panting and wishing,
    And sighing and kissing,
    And sighing and kissing so close.

III.

Cupid in Shape of a Swayn did appear,
He saw the sad wound, and in pity drew near,
Then show'd her his Arrow, and bid her not
    fear,
For the pain was no more than a Maiden may
    bear ;
When the balm was infus'd, she was not at
    a loss
What they meant by their sighing and
    kissing so close ;
    By their praying and whining,
    And clasping and twining,
    And panting and wishing,
    And sighing and kissing,
    And sighing and kissing so close.

A SONG FOR ST. CECILIA'S DAY.

NOVEMBER 22, 1687.

1

FROM Harmony, from heav'nly Harmony
    This universal Frame began ;
  When Nature underneath a heap
    Of jarring Atomes lay,
  And cou'd not heave her Head,
The tuneful Voice was heard from high,
    Arise, ye more than dead.
Then cold and hot and moist and dry
  In order to their Stations leap,
    And MUSICK'S pow'r obey.
From Harmony, from heavenly Harmony
    This universal Frame began :
    From Harmony to Harmony
Through all the Compass of the Notes it ran,
The Diapason closing full in Man

2

What Passion cannot MUSICK raise and
    quell ?
  When *Jubal* struck the corded Shell,
  His listening Brethren stood around,
    And, wond'ring, on their Faces fell
To worship that Celestial Sound :
Less than a God they thought there could
    not dwell
    Within the hollow of that Shell,
    That spoke so sweetly, and so well.
What Passion cannot MUSICK raise and
    quell ?

SONG. Text from the *Miscellany Poems*, 1685.

SONG FOR ST. CECILIA'S DAY. Text from the original of 1687.

3

The TRUMPETS loud Clangor
   Excites us to Arms
   With shrill Notes of Anger
   And mortal Alarms.
The double double double beat
   Of the thund'ring DRUM
   Cryes, heark the Foes come ;
Charge, Charge, 'tis too late to retreat.

4

The soft complaining FLUTE
   In dying Notes discovers
   The Woes of hopeless Lovers,
Whose Dirge is whisper'd by the warbling
   LUTE.

5

Sharp VIOLINS proclaim
Their jealous Pangs and Desperation,
Fury, frantick Indignation,
Depth of Pains and Height of Passion,
   For the fair, disdainful Dame.

6

But oh ! what Art can teach
What human Voice can reach

   The sacred ORGANS Praise ?
Notes inspiring holy Love,
Notes that wing their heavenly Ways
   To mend the Choires above.

7

Orpheus cou'd lead the savage race,
And Trees unrooted left their Place,
   Sequacious of the Lyre ;
But bright CECILIA rais'd the Wonder
      high'r :
When to her Organ vocal Breath was
      given,
An Angel heard, and straight appear'd
      Mistaking Earth for Heav'n.

Grand CHORUS.

As from the Pow'r of Sacred Lays
   The Spheres began to move,
And sung the great Creator's Praise
   To all the bless'd above ;
So, when the last and dreadful Hour
This crumbling Pageant shall devour,
The TRUMPET shall be heard on high,
The dead shall live, the living die,
And MUSICK shall untune the Sky.

THE LADY'S SONG.

I

A QUIRE of bright Beauties in Spring did
   appear,
To chuse a *May*-lady to govern the Year ;
All the Nymphs were in White, and the
   Shepherds in Green,
The Garland was giv'n, and *Phillis* was
   Queen ;
But *Phillis* refus'd it, and sighing did
   say,
I'll not wear a Garland while *Pan* is away.

II

While *Pan*, and fair *Syrinx*, are fled from our
   Shore,
The Graces are banish'd, and Love is no
   more :

THE LADY'S SONG.   Text from the *Miscellany
Poems*, 1704.

The soft God of Pleasure that warm'd our
   Desires
Has broken his Bow, and extinguish'd his
   Fires,
And vows that himself, and his Mother, will
   mourn,
Till *Pan* and fair *Syrinx* in Triumph return.

III

Forbear your Addresses, and Court us no
   more,
For we will perform what the Deity swore :
But, if you dare think of deserving our
   Charms,
Away with your Sheephooks, and take to
   your Arms ;
Then Lawrels and Myrtles your Brows shall
   adorn,
When *Pan*, and his Son, and fair *Syrinx*
   return.

A SONG TO A FAIR YOUNG LADY

GOING OUT OF TOWN IN THE SPRING.

1

ASK not the Cause, why sullen Spring
  So long delays her flow'rs to bear ;
Why warbling Birds forget to sing,
  And Winter Storms invert the Year ?
Chloris is gone ; and Fate provides
To make it *Spring*, where she resides.

2

Chloris is gone, the Cruel Fair ;
  She cast not back a pitying Eye :
But left her Lover in Despair,
  To sigh, to languish, and to die :
Ah, how can those fair Eyes endure
To give the wounds they will not cure !

3

Great God of Love, why hast thou made
  A Face that can all Hearts command,
That all Religions can invade,
  And change the Laws of ev'ry Land ?
Where thou hadst plac'd such Pow'r before,
Thou shou'dst have made her Mercy more.

4

When *Chloris* to the Temple comes,
  Adoring Crowds before her Fall ;
She can restore the Dead from Tombs,
  And every Life but mine recall.
I only am by Love design'd
To be the Victim for Mankind.

ALEXANDER'S FEAST; |

OR, THE | POWER OF MUSIQUE. |

AN ODE | IN HONOUR OF | ST. CECILIA'S DAY: 1697.

I

'Twas at the Royal Feast, for *Persia* won,
  By *Philip's* Warlike Son :
    Aloft in awful State
    The God-like Heroe sate
    On his Imperial Throne ;
His valiant Peers were plac'd around ;
Their Brows with Roses and with Myrtles
    bound.
  (So should Desert in Arms be Crown'd :)
The lovely *Thais* by his side,
Sate like a blooming *Eastern* Bride   10
In Flow'r of Youth and Beauty's Pride.
    Happy, happy, happy Pair !
      None but the Brave,
      None but the Brave,
  None but the Brave deserves the Fair.

CHORUS.

  Happy, happy, happy Pair !
    None but the Brave,
    None but the Brave,
  None but the Brave deserves the Fair.

II

    Timotheus plac'd on high   20
      Amid the tuneful Quire,
With flying Fingers touch'd the Lyre:
  The trembling Notes ascend the Sky,
    And Heav'nly Joys inspire.
The Song began from *Jove* ;
Who left his blissful Seats above,
(Such is the Pow'r of mighty Love.)
A Dragon's fiery Form bely'd the God :
Sublime on Radiant Spires He rode,
  When He to fair *Olympia* press'd :   30
  And while He sought her snowy Breast :
Then, round her slender Waist he curl'd,
And stamp'd an Image of himself, a Sov'-
    raign of the World.
The list'ning crowd admire the lofty
    Sound,
A present Deity, they shout around :
A present Deity, the vaulted Roofs re-
    bound.

A SONG TO A FAIR YOUNG LADY. Text from
the *Miscellany Poems*, 1704.

ALEXANDER'S FEAST. Text from the edition
of 1700.
29 Spires] *Scott wrongly gives* Spheres

With ravish'd Ears
The Monarch hears,
Assumes the God,
Affects to nod,
And seems to shake the Spheres.

CHORUS.

With ravish'd Ears
The Monarch hears,
Assumes the God,
Affects to nod,
And seems to shake the Spheres.

III.

The Praise of *Bacchus* then the sweet
    Musician sung,
Of *Bacchus* ever Fair, and ever Young:
The jolly God in Triumph comes ;
Sound the Trumpets ; beat the Drums ;
Flush'd with a purple Grace   51
He shows his honest Face :
Now give the Hautboys breath ; He comes,
    He comes.
Bacchus ever Fair and Young
    Drinking Joys did first ordain ;
Bacchus Blessings are a Treasure ;
Drinking is the Soldiers Pleasure ;
    Rich the Treasure ;
    Sweet the Pleasure ;
Sweet is Pleasure after Pain.   60

CHORUS.

Bacchus Blessings are a Treasure,
Drinking is the Soldier's Pleasure ;
    Rich the Treasure,
    Sweet the Pleasure,
Sweet is Pleasure after Pain.

IV.

Sooth'd with the Sound the King grew
    vain ;
Fought all his Battails o'er again ;
And thrice He routed all his Foes, and thrice
    he slew the slain.
The Master saw the Madness rise,
His glowing Cheeks, his ardent Eyes ;   70
And while He Heav'n and Earth defy'd,
Chang'd his Hand, and check'd his Pride.
He chose a Mournful Muse,
    Soft Pity to infuse ;
He sung *Darius* Great and Good,
    By too severe a Fate,
Fallen, fallen, fallen, fallen,
    Fallen from his high Estate,
And weltring in his Blood :

Deserted at his utmost Need   80
By those his former Bounty fed ;
On the bare Earth expos'd He lies,
With not a Friend to close his Eyes.
With down-cast Looks the joyless Victor
    sate,
Revolving in his alter'd Soul
    The various Turns of Chance below ;
And, now and then, a Sigh he stole,
    And Tears began to flow.

CHORUS.

Revolving in his alter'd Soul
    The various Turns of Chance below ;
And, now and then, a Sigh he stole,   91
    And Tears began to flow.

V.

The Mighty Master smil'd to see
That Love was in the next Degree ;
'Twas but a Kindred-Sound to move,
For Pity melts the Mind to Love.
    Softly sweet, in *Lydian* Measures,
    Soon he sooth'd his Soul to Pleasures.
War, he sung, is Toil and Trouble ;
Honour but an empty Bubble.   100
    Never ending, still beginning,
Fighting still, and still destroying,
    If the World be worth thy Winning,
Think, O think, it worth Enjoying.
    Lovely *Thais* sits beside thee,
    Take the Good the Gods provide thee.
The Many rend the Skies, with loud
    applause ;
So Love was Crown'd, but Musique won the
    Cause.
The Prince, unable to conceal his Pain,
    Gaz'd on the Fair   110
    Who caus'd his Care,
And sigh'd and look'd, sigh'd and look'd,
Sigh'd and look'd, and sigh'd again :
At length, with Love and Wine at once
    oppress'd,
The vanquish'd Victor sunk upon her Breast.

CHORUS.

The Prince, unable to conceal his Pain,
    Gaz'd on the fair
    Who caus'd his Care,
    And sigh'd and look'd, sigh'd and look'd,
    Sigh'd and look'd, and sigh'd again ;   120
At length, with Love and Wine at once
    oppress'd,
The vanquish'd Victor sunk upon her Breast.

VI.

Now strike the Golden Lyre again ;
A lowder yet, and yet a lowder Strain.
Break his Bands of Sleep asunder,
And rouze him, like a rattling Peal of
    Thunder.
    Hark, hark, the horrid Sound
    Has rais'd up his Head ;
    As awak'd from the Dead,
    And amaz'd, he stares around.   130
Revenge, revenge, *Timotheus* cries,
    See the Furies arise !
    See the Snakes that they rear,
    How they hiss in their Hair,
    And the Sparkles that flash from their
    Eyes !
    Behold a ghastly Band,
    Each a Torch in his Hand !
Those are *Grecian* Ghosts, that in Battail
    were slain,
    And unbury'd remain
    Inglorious on the Plain :   140
    Give the Vengeance due
    To the Valiant Crew.
Behold how they toss their Torches on high,
    How they point to the *Persian* Abodes,
And glitt'ring Temples of their Hostile Gods.
The Princes applaud with a furious Joy ;
And the King seized a Flambeau with Zeal
    to destroy ;
    Thais led the Way,
    To light him to his Prey,
And, like another *Hellen*, fir'd another *Troy*.

CHORUS.

And the King seiz'd a Flambeau with Zeal to
    destroy ;   151

    Thais *led the Way,*
    To light him to his Prey,
And, like another Hellen, *fir'd another Troy.*

VII.

    Thus long ago,
'Ere heaving Bellows learn'd to blow,
    While Organs yet were mute,
    Timotheus, to his breathing Flute
    And sounding Lyre,
Cou'd swell the Soul to rage, or kindle soft
    Desire.   160
At last Divine *Cecilia* came,
    Inventress of the Vocal Frame ;
The sweet Enthusiast, from her Sacred
    Store,
Enlarg'd the former narrow Bounds,
And added Length to solemn Sounds,
With Nature's Mother-Wit, and Arts un-
    known before.
Let old *Timotheus* yield the Prize,
    Or both divide the Crown :
He rais'd a Mortal to the Skies ;
    She drew an Angel down.   170

GRAND CHORUS.

At last Divine Cecilia *came,*
    Inventress of the Vocal Frame ;
The sweet Enthusiast, from her Sacred Store,
    Enlarg'd the former narrow Bounds,
    And added Length to solemn Sounds,
With Nature's Mother-Wit, and Arts un-
    known before.
Let old Timotheus *yield the Prize,*
    Or both divide the Crown :
He rais'd a Mortal to the Skies ;
    She drew an Angel down.   180

A SONG.

1

Go tell *Amynta*, gentle Swain,
I wou'd not die, nor dare complain,
Thy tuneful Voice with numbers joyn,
Thy words will more prevail than mine.
To Souls oppress'd, and dumb with grief,
The Gods ordain this kind releif ;
That Musick shou'd in sounds convey
What dying Lovers dare not say.

2

A Sigh or Tear perhaps she'll give,
But love on pitty cannot live.
Tell her that Hearts for Hearts were made,
And love with love is only paid.
Tell her my pains so fast encrease,
That soon they will be past redress ;
But ah ! the Wretch, that speechless lyes,
Attends but Death to close his Eyes.

A Song. Text from the *Miscellany Poems*, 1685. | Christie wrongly assigned the first edition to 1701.

RONDELAY.

1

CHLOE found *Amyntas* lying,
　All in Tears, upon the Plain,
Sighing to himself, and crying,
　Wretched I, to love in vain !
Kiss me, Dear, before my dying ;
　Kiss me once, and ease my pain.

2

Sighing to himself, and crying,
　Wretched I, to love in vain !
Ever scorning, and denying
　To reward your faithful Swain
Kiss me, Dear, before my dying ;
　Kiss me once, and ease my pain !

3

Ever scorning, and denying
　To reward your faithful Swain.
Chloe, laughing at his crying,
　Told him, that he lov'd in vain :
Kiss me, dear, before my dying ;
　Kiss me once, and ease my pain !

4

Chloe, laughing at his crying,
　Told him that he lov'd in vain ;
But repenting, and complying,
　When he kiss'd, she kiss'd again :
Kiss'd him up, before his dying ;
　Kiss'd him up, and eas'd his pain.

THE FAIR STRANGER

A SONG.

1

HAPPY and free, securely blest,
No Beauty could disturb my Rest ;
My am'rous Heart was in Despair,
To find a new victorious Fair :

2

Till you, descending on our Plains,
With foreign Force renew my Chains ;
Where now you rule without Controul,
The mighty Sov'reign of my Soul.

3

Your Smiles have more of conqu'ring Charm
Than all your Native Country's Arms :
Their Troops we can expel with Ease,
Who vanquish only when we please.

4

But in your Eyes, oh, there's the Spell !
Who can see them, and not rebel ?
You make us Captives by your Stay,
Yet kill us if you go away.

A SONG.

I

FAIR, sweet and young, receive a prize
Reserv'd for your Victorious Eyes :
From Crowds, whom at your Feet you see,
O pity, and distinguish me ;
As I from thousand Beauties more
Distinguish you, and only you adore.

II

Your Face for Conquest was design'd,
Your ev'ry Motion charms my Mind ;
Angels, when you your Silence break,
Forget their Hymns to hear you speak ;
But when at once they hear and view,
Are loath to mount, and long to stay with
　you.

III

No Graces can your Form improve,
But all are lost, unless you love ;
While that sweet Passion you disdain,
Your Veil and Beauty are in vain.
In pity then prevent my Fate,
For after dying all Reprieves too late.

RONDELAY. Text from the *Miscellany Poems*,
1693.

THE FAIR STRANGER.   Text from *A New
Miscellany*, 1701.
A SONG.   Text from the *Miscellany Poems*,
1704.

A SONG.

High State and Honours to others impart,
    But give me your Heart :
That Treasure, that Treasure alone,
    I beg for my own.
So gentle a Love, so fervent a Fire,
    My Soul does inspire.
That Treasure, that Treasure alone,
    I beg for my own.

Your Love let me crave,
    Give me in Possessing   10

So matchless a Blessing ;
That Empire is all I wou'd have.

Love's my Petition,
All my Ambition ;
If e'er you discover
So faithful a Lover,
So real a Flame,
I'll die, I'll die,
So give up my Game.

THE SECULAR MASQUE.

Enter JANUS.

Janus. Chronos, Chronos, mend thy Pace :
    An hundred Times the rowling Sun
    Around the Radiant Belt has run
        In his revolving Race.
    Behold, behold, the Goal in sight ;
    Spread thy Fans, and wing thy flight.

Enter CHRONOS, *with a Scythe in his Hand
    and a great Globe on his Back, which he
    sets down at his entrance.*

Chronos. Weary, weary of my weight,
    Let me, let me drop my Freight,
    And leave the World behind.
        I could not bear,   10
        Another Year,
    The Load of Human-kind.

Enter MOMUS, *Laughing.*

Momus. Ha ! ha ! ha ! Ha ! ha ! ha ! well
        hast thou done
    To lay down thy Pack,
    And lighten thy Back.
    The World was a Fool, e'er since it begun,
    And since neither *Janus,* nor *Chronos,*
        nor I
        Can hinder the Crimes
        Or mend the bad Times,
    'Tis better to Laugh than to Cry.   20

Co. of all 3. *'Tis better to Laugh than to Cry.*

Janus. Since *Momus* comes to laugh below,
    Old Time begin the Show,
    That he may see, in every Scene,
    What Changes in this Age have been.

Chronos. Then Goddess of the Silver Bow
        begin.
            Horns, or Hunting-Musique within.

Enter DIANA.

Diana. With Horns and with Hounds I
        waken the Day,
    And hye to my Woodland walks away :
    I tuck up my Robe, and am buskined soon,
    And tye to my Forehead a wexing Moon.
    I course the fleet Stagg, unkennel the Fox,
    And chase the wild Goats or'e summets of
        Rocks,   32
    With shouting and hooting we pierce thro'
        the Sky ;
    And Eccho turns Hunter, and doubles the
        Cry.

Cho. of all. *With shouting and hooting we
        pierce through the Skie,
    And Eccho turns Hunter, and doubles the
        Cry.*

Janus. Then our Age was in it's Prime :
Chronos. Free from Rage.
Diana.   And free from Crime.
Momus. A very Merry, Dancing, Drinking,
    Laughing, Quaffing, and unthinking Time.

Cho. of all. *Then our Age was in it's Prime,
    Free from Rage, and free from Crime,* 42
    *A very Merry, Dancing, Drinking,
    Laughing, Quaffing, and unthinking Time.*
        {*Dance of* Diana's *attendants.*

THE SECULAR MASQUE. Text from the
original but posthumous edition of 1700, except
as noted.

A SONG. Text from the *Miscellany Poems*, 1704.

Enter MARS.

Mars. Inspire the Vocal Brass, Inspire ;
The World is past its Infant Age :
    Arms and Honour,
    Arms and Honour,
Set the Martial Mind on Fire,
And kindle Manly Rage.   50
    Mars has lookt the Sky to Red ;
And Peace, the Lazy Good, is fled.
Plenty, Peace, and Pleasure fly ;
    The Sprightly Green
In Woodland-Walks no more is seen ;
The Sprightly Green has drunk the *Tyrian*
    Dye.

Cho. of all. *Plenty, Peace,* &c.

Mars. Sound the Trumpet, Beat the Drum ;
    Through all the World around,
    Sound a Reveille, Sound, Sound,   60
The Warrior God is come.

Cho. of all. *Sound the Trumpet,* &c.

Momus. Thy Sword within the Scabbard
    keep,
    And let Mankind agree ;
Better the World were fast asleep,
    Than kept awake by Thee.
The Fools are only thinner,
    With all our Cost and Care ;
But neither side a winner,
    For Things are as they were.   70

Cho. of all. *The Fools are only,* &c.

Enter VENUS.

Venus. Calms appear, when Storms are past ;
Love will have his Hour at last :

Nature is my kindly Care ;
Mars destroys, and I repair ;
Take me, take me, while you may,
Venus comes not ev'ry Day.

Cho. of all. *Take her, take her,* &c.

Chronos. The World was then so light,
    I scarcely felt the Weight ;   80
    Joy rul'd the Day, and Love the
    Night.
But since the Queen of Pleasure left the
    Ground,
    I faint, I lag,
    And feebly drag
The pond'rous Orb around.

Momus. All, all of a piece throughout :
    Pointing   } Thy Chase had a Beast
    to *Diana.* }   in View ;
    to *Mars.*   Thy Wars brought
                     nothing about ;
    to *Venus.*   Thy Lovers were all
                     untrue.

Janus. 'Tis well an Old Age is out.   90

Chro. And time to begin a New.

Cho. of all. *All, all of a piece throughout :*
    Thy Chase had a Beast in View ;
    Thy Wars brought nothing about ;
    Thy Lovers were all untrue.
    'Tis well an Old Age is out,
    And time to begin a New.
    Dance of Huntsmen, Nymphs,
    Warriours, and Lovers.

FINIS

SONG

Of a *Scholar* and his *Mistress,* who, being Cross'd by their Friends, fell Mad
for one another ; and now first meet in *Bedlam.*

[*Musick within.*]
[*The Lovers enter at Opposite Doors, each
held by a Keeper.*]

Phillis. Look, look, I see—I see my Love
    appear :
    'Tis he—'Tis he alone ;
    For like him there is none :
'Tis the dear, dear Man, 'tis thee, Dear.

Amyntas. Hark ! the Winds War ;
    The foamy Waves roar ;
    I see a Ship afar,
Tossing and Tossing, and making to the
    Shoar :
    But what's that I View,
    So Radiant of Hue,   10

---

55 Woodland] *Woodland 1700.*

SONG OF A SCHOLAR AND HIS MISTRESS. Text
from the original but posthumous edition of 1700,
except as noted
3 For like him] For, like him, *1700.*

St. *Hermo*, St. *Hermo*, that sits upon the
    Sails ?
    Ah ! No, no, no.
St. *Hermo* never, never shone so bright ;
'Tis *Phillis*, only *Phillis* can shoot so fair
    a Light ;
'Tis *Phillis*, 'tis *Phillis* that saves the Ship
    alone,
For all the Winds are hushed, and the
    Storm is overblown.

Phillis. Let me go, let me run, let me fly to
    his Arms.

Amyntas. If all the Fates combine,
    And all the Furies join,
I'll force my way to *Phillis*, and break
    through the Charms.   20

    [*Here they break from their
    Keepers; run to each other,
    and embrace.*]

Phillis. Shall I Marry the Man I love ?
    And shall I conclude my Pains ?
Now blest be the Powers above,
    I feel the Blood bound in my Veins ;
With a lively Leap it began to move,
    And the Vapours leave my Brains.

Amyntas. Body join'd to Body, and Heart
    join'd to Heart ;
    To make sure of the Cure ;
Go call the Man in Black, to mumble o're
    his part.

Phillis. But suppose he should stay . . .

Amyntas. At worst, if he delay ;
    'Tis a Work must be done ;
We'll borrow but a Day,
    And the better the sooner begun.

    CHORUS of Both.
At worst, if he delay, &c.
    [*They run out together hand in hand.*

PROLOGUES AND EPILOGUES.

PROLOGUE AND EPILOGUE TO THE WILD GALLANT.

PROLOGUE.

Is it not strange to hear a Poet say,
He comes to ask you how you like the Play ?
You have not seen it yet ! alas 'tis true ;
But now your Love and Hatred judge, not
    You.
And cruel Factions (brib'd by Interest) come,
Not to weigh Merit, but to give their Doome.
Our Poet, therefore, jealous of th' Event,
And (though much Boldness takes) not
    confident,
Has sent me whither you, Fair ladies, too
Sometimes upon as small Occasions goe, 10
And from this Scheme, drawn for the Hour
    and Day,
Bid me inquire the Fortune of his Play.
    *The curtain drawn discovers two Astrologers;
    The Prologue is presented to them.*
  1 *Astrol. reads.* A figure of the heavenly
Bodies in their several Apartments, Feb. the

5th, half an hour after three after Noon,
from whence you are to judge the success
of a new play, called *the Wild Gallant*.
  2 *Astrol.* Who must judge of it, we or
these gentlemen ? We'll not meddle with
it ; so tell your poet. Here are, in this
House, the ablest Mathematicians in *Europe*
for his purpose.   22
They will resolve the Question, e'r they
    part.
  1 *Ast.* Yet let us judge it by the Rules of Art :
First *Jupiter*, the Ascendants Lord dis-
    grac'd,
In the twelfth House and near grim *Saturn*
    plac'd,
Denote short life unto the Play :—
  2 *Ast.*   — *Jove* yet,
In his apartment *Sagitary*, set
Under his own Roof, cannot take much
    Wrong.
  1 *Ast.* Why then the Life's not very short,
    nor long ;   30

SONG OF A SCHOLAR, ETC. 13 *Hermo* never]
Hermo, Never *1700*. 20 Charms] Charm *1700*.

PROLOGUES AND EPILOGUES. Texts from the
original editions.
THE WILD GALLANT, 1663.

2 *Ast.* The Luck not very good, nor very ill ;
Prolo. That is to say, 'tis as 'tis taken still.
1 *Ast.* But, brother, *Ptolomy* the learned says,
'Tis the fifth House from whence we judge
of Plays.
Venus, the Lady of that House, I find
Is *Peregrine* ; your Play is ill design'd ;
It should have been but one continued
Song,
Or at the least a Dance of 3 hours long.
2 *Ast.* But yet the greatest Mischief does
remain,
The twelfth Apartment bears the Lord of
Spain ;   40
Whence I conclude, it is your Author's Lot,
To be indanger'd by a Spanish plot.
Prolo. Our Poet yet Protection hopes from
you ;
But bribes you not with any thing that's
new.
Nature is old, which Poets imitate ;
And for Wit, those that boast their own
estate
Forget *Fletcher* and *Ben* before them went,
Their Elder Brothers, and that vastly
spent :
So much, 'twill hardly be repair'd again,
Not though supply'd with all the wealth
of *Spain*.   50
This Play is *English*, and the growth your
own ;
As such it yields to *English* Plays alone.
He could have wish'd it better for your
Sakes,
But that in Plays he finds you love Mis-
takes :
Besides, he thought it was in vain to mend
What you are bound in Honour to defend ;

That *English* wit, how e'r despis'd by
some,
Like *English* valour, still may overcome.

EPILOGUE.

The *Wilde Gallant* has quite play'd out his
Game ;
He's marry'd now, and that will make him
tame.
Or if you think Marriage will not reclaim him,
The Critiques swear they'll damn him, but
they'll tame him.
Yet, though our Poet's threatened most by
these,
They are the only People he can please :
For he, to humour them, has shown to day
That which they only like, a wretched Play.
But though his Play be ill, here have been
shown   9
The greatest Wits and Beauties of the Town ;
And his Occasion having brought you here,
You are too grateful to become severe.
There is not any Person here so mean,
But he may freely judge each Act and Scene.
But if you bid him chuse his Judges, then
He boldly names true *English* Gentlemen ;
For he ne'r thought a handsome Garb or
Dress
So great a Crime to make their Judgment less ;
And with these Gallants he these Ladies joyns,
To judge that Language their Converse re-
fines.   20
But if their Censures should condemn his
Play,
Far from disputing, he does only pray
He may *Leanders* Destiny obtain :
Now spare him, drown him when he comes
again.

PROLOGUE TO THE RIVAL LADIES.

'TIS much desir'd, you Judges of the Town
Would pass a vote to put all *Prologues* down ;
For who can show me, since they first were
writ,
They e'r converted one hard-harted Wit ?
Yet the World's mended well; in former Days
Good *Prologues* were as scarce as now good
Plays.

For the reforming Poets of our Age
In this first Charge spend their poetique
rage.
Expect no more when once the *Prologue's*
done ;
The wit is ended ere the *Play's* begun.   10
You now have Habits, Dances, Scenes, and
Rhymes,
High Language often, ay, and Sense some-
times.

As for a clear Contrivance, doubt it not ;
They blow out Candles to give Light to th'
Plot.
And for Surprize, two Bloody-minded Men
Fight till they dye, then rise and dance again.
Such deep Intrigues you're welcome to this
Day :
But blame your Selves, not him who writ the
Play.
Though his Plot's dull as can be well desir'd,
Wit stiff as any you have e'r admir'd,   20
He's bound to please, not to write well, and
knows
There is a mode in Playes as well as Cloaths ;
Therefore, kind Judges—

A Second Prologue enters.

2.   Hold ! would you admit
For Judges all you see within the Pit ?

1. Whom would he then except, or on what
Score ?
2. All who (like him) have writ ill Plays
before ;
For they, like Thieves condemn'd, are hang-
men made
To execute the Members of their Trade.
All that are writing now he would disown,
But then he must except—ev'n all the
Town ;   30
All Chol'rique losing Gamesters, who in
spight
Will damn to Day, because they lost last
Night ;
All Servants, whom their Mistress' Scorn
upbraids,
All Maudlin Lovers, and all slighted Maids,
All who are out of Humour or severe,
All that want Wit, or hope to find it here.

PROLOGUE AND EPILOGUE TO THE INDIAN EMPEROR.

PROLOGUE.

ALMIGHTY critiques ! whom our *Indians* here
Worship, just as they do the Devil—for fear;
In Rev'rence to your Power, I come this day,
To give you timely warning of our Play.
The Scenes are old, the Habits are the same
We wore last Year, before the *Spaniards*
came.
Our Prologue, th' old-cast too
For to observe the new it should at least
Be spoke by some ingenious Bird or Beast. 9
Now, if you stay, the Blood that shall be shed
From this poor Play be all upon your Head.
We neither promise you one Dance or Show ;
Then Plot and Language, they are wanting
too.
But you, kind Wits, will those light Faults
excuse,
Those are the common Frailties of the *Muse* ;
Which who observes, he buys his Place too
dear ;
For 'tis your Business to be cozen'd here.
These wretched Spies of Wit must then con-
fess,
They take more Pains to please themselves
the less.

Grant us such Judges, *Phœbus*, we request,
As still mistake themselves into a Jest ;   21
Such easy Judges that our Poet may
Himself admire the Fortune of his Play ;
And arrogantly, as his Fellows do,
Think he writes well, because he pleases
you.
This he conceives not hard to bring about,
If all of you would join to help him out :
Would each Man take but what he under-
stands,
And leave the rest upon the Poet's Hands.

EPILOGUE.

Spoken by a Mercury.

To all and singular in this full Meeting,
Ladies and Gallants, *Phœbus* sends me
greeting.
To all his Sons, by whate'er Title known,
Whether of Court, of Coffee-house, or Town ;
From his most mighty Sons, whose Confi-
dence
Is plac'd in lofty Sound and humble Sense,
Even to his little Infants of the Time,
Who write new Songs and trust in Tune and
Rhyme;
Be't known, that *Phœbus* (being daily griev'd
To see good Frays condemn'd and bad
receiv'd)   10

THE INDIAN EMPEROR, 1665.   Prologue 7–9.
These lines are not in all copies.
9 spoke] spoke, *1665.*

Ordains your Judgment upon every Cause
Henceforth be limited by wholesome Laws.
He first thinks fit no Sonnetteer advance
His Censure farther than the Song or Dance.
Your Wit burlesque may one Step higher climb,
And in his Sphere may judge all dogrel Rhyme ;
All proves, and moves, and loves, and honours too ;
All that appears high Sense, and scarce is low.

As for the Coffee-wits, he says not much ;
Their proper Business is to damn the *Dutch*.
For the great Dons of Wit ————   21
Phœbus gives them full Privilege alone
To damn all others, and cry up their own.
Last, for the Ladies, 'tis *Apollo's* Will,
They should have power to save, but not to kill ;
For Love and he long since have thought it fit,
Wit live by Beauty, Beauty reign by Wit.

PROLOGUE TO SECRET LOVE, OR THE MAIDEN QUEEN.

FIRST PROLOGUE.

1
HE who writ this, not without Pains and Thought,
From *French* and *English* Theaters has brought
Th' exactest Rules by which a Play is wrought,

2
The Unities of Action, Place, and Time ;
The Scenes unbroken ; and a mingled chime
Of *Johnsons* Humour with *Corneilles* rhyme.

3
But while dead colours he with care did lay,
He fears his Wit or Plot he did not weigh,
Which are the living Beauties of a Play.   9

4
Plays are like Towns, which, howe're fortifi'd
By Engineers, have still some weaker side,
By the o'reseen Defendant unespy'd.

5
And with that Art you make approaches now;
Such skilful fury in Assaults you show,
That every Poet without shame may bow.

6
Ours therefore humbly would attend your doom,
If, Souldier-like, he may have Terms to come
With flying colours and with beat of Drum.
The Prologue goes out, and stayes while a Tune is play'd, after which he returnes again.

SECOND PROLOGUE.

I had forgot one half, I do protest,
And now am sent again to speak the rest.   20
He bows to every great and noble Wit ;⎫
But to the little Hectors of the Pit ⎬
Our Poet's sturdy, and will not submit.⎭
He'll be before-hand with 'em, and not stay
To see each peevish Critick stab his Play ;
Each Puny Censor, who, his skill to boast,
Is cheaply witty on the Poets Cost.
No Criticks Verdict should, of right, stand good,
They are excepted all, as men of blood ;
And the same Law should shield him from their fury,   30
Which has excluded Butchers from a Jury.
You'd all be Wits ————
But writing's tedious, and that way may fail ;
The most compendious Method is to rail ;
Which you so like, you think your selves ill us'd,
When in smart Prologues you are not abus'd,
A civil Prologue is approv'd by no man ;
You hate it as you do a Civil woman.
Your Fancy's pall'd, and liberally you pay
To have it quicken'd, e're you see a Play.   40
Just as old Sinners, worn from their delight,
Give money to be whip'd to appetite.
But what a Pox keep I so much ado
To save our Poet ? he is one of you ;
A Brother Judgment, and, as I hear say,
A cursed Critick as e'er damned a Play.

SECRET LOVE, 1667.   Prologue 6 *Johnsons*]
Here and elsewhere editors correct to Jonson's.

6 with *Corneilles*] *Bell wrongly inserted* old *between these words*.

Good salvage Gentlemen, your own kind
　　spare ;
He is, like you, a very Wolf or Bear ;
Yet think not he'll your ancient rights invade,
Or stop the course of your free damning
　　trade ;　　　　　　　　　　　　　　50
For he (he vows) at no Friend's Play can sit,
But he must needs find fault, to show his Wit ;

Then, for his sake, ne'er stint your own
　　delight ;
Throw boldly, for he sets to all that write ;
With such he ventures on an even lay,
For they bring ready money into Play.
Those who write not, and yet all Writers nick,
Are Bankrupt Gamesters, for they damn on
　　Tick.

PROLOGUE AND EPILOGUE TO THE WILD GALLANT,

REVIVED.

PROLOGUE.

As some raw Squire, by tender Mother bred,
Till one and Twenty keeps his Maidenhead ;
(Pleas'd with some Sport, which he alone
　　does find,
And thinks a Secret to all Humane kind,)
Till mightily in Love, yet half afraid,
He first attempts the gentle Dairymaid :
Succeeding there, and, led by the renown
Of *Whetstones Park*, he comes at length to
　　Town :
Where enter'd by some School-fellow or
　　Friend,　　　　　　　　　　　　　　9
He grows to break Glass-Windows in the end:
His Valour too, which with the Watch began,
Proceeds to duell, and he kills his Man.
By such Degrees, while Knowledge he did
　　want,
Our unfletch'd Author writ a *Wild Gallant*.
He thought him monstrous leud (I'll lay my
　　Life)
Because suspected with his Landlords Wife ;
But, since his Knowledge of the Town began,
He thinks him now a very civil Man ;
And, much asham'd of what he was before,
Has fairly play'd him at three Wenches more.
'Tis some amends his Frailties to confess ;　21
Pray pardon him his want of Wickedness.
He's towardly, and will come on apace ;
His frank Confession shows he has some
　　Grace.
You balk'd him when he was a young
　　Beginner,
And almost spoyl'd a very hopeful Sinner ;
But if once more you slight his weak
　　indeavour,
For ought I know, he may turn taile for ever.

THE WILD GALLANT, REVIVED, 1667.　Prologue, 14 unfletch'd] *The editors give* unfledged

EPILOGUE.

Of all Dramatique Writing, Comick Wit,
As 'tis the best, so 'tis most hard to hit.
For it lies all in level to the Eye,
Where all may judge, and each Defect may
　　spye.
Humour is that which every Day we meet,
And therefore known as every publick Street;
In which, if e'r the Poet go astray,
You all can point, 'twas there he lost his
　　Way,
But what's so common to make pleasant
　　too,
Is more than any Wit can always do.　　10
For 'tis, like *Turkes* with Hen and Rice to
　　treat,
To make Regalio's out of common Meat.
But, in your Diet, you grow Salvages :
Nothing but humane Flesh your Taste can
　　please ;
And as their Feasts with slaughter'd Slaves
　　began,
So you, at each new Play, must have a
　　Man.
Hither you come, as to see Prizes fought ;
If no Blood's drawn, you cry, the Prize is
　　naught.
But Fooles grow wary now ; and, when they
　　see
A Poet eyeing round the Company,　　20
Straight each Man for himself begins to
　　doubt ;
They shrink like Seamen when a Press comes
　　out.
Few of 'em will be found for publick Use,
Except you charge an Oph upon each
　　House,
Like the Train-Bands, and every man ingage
For a sufficient Fool to serve the Stage.

And when with much adoe you get him
  there,
Where he in all his Glory should appear,
Your Poets make him such rare Things to
  say,
That he's more Wit than any Man ith' Play :
But of so ill a mingle with the rest,   31
As when a Parrat's taught to break a Jest.
Thus, aiming to be fine, they make a Show,
As tawdry Squires in country Churches do.
Things well consider'd, 'tis so hard to
  make
A Comedy, which should the knowing
  take,
That our dull Poet, in despair to please,
Does humbly beg by me his writ of ease.

'Tis a Land-tax, which he's too poor to
  pay ;
You therefore must some other Impost lay. 40
Would you but change for serious Plot and
  Verse
This motley garniture of Fool and Farce,
Nor scorn a Mode, because 'tis taught at
  home,
Which does, like Vests, our Gravity become,
Our Poet yields you should this Play
  refuse :
As Tradesmen by the change of Fashions
  lose
With some content their Fripperies of
  France,
In Hope it may their staple Trade advance.

PROLOGUE AND EPILOGUE TO SIR MARTIN MAR-ALL,
OR THE FEIGNED INNOCENCE.

PROLOGUE.

FOOLS, which each man meets in his Dish
  each Day,
Are yet the great Regalio's of a Play ;
In which to Poets you but just appear,
To prize that highest which cost them so
  dear :
Fops in the Town more easily will pass ;
One story makes a statutable Ass ;
But such in Plays must be much thicker
  sown,
Like yolks of Eggs, a dozen beat to one.
Observing Poets all their walks invade,
As men watch Woodcocks gliding through
  a Glade :   10
And when they have enough for Comedy,
They stow their several Bodies in a Pye :
The Poet's but the Cook to fashion it,
For, Gallants, you yourselves have found the
  Wit.
To bid you welcome would your bounty
  wrong ;
None welcome those who bring their Chear
  along.

EPILOGUE.

As country Vicars, when the Sermon's done,
Run hudling to the Benediction ;
Well knowing, though the better sort may
  stay,
The Vulgar Rout will run unblesst away :
So we, when once our Play is done, make
  haste
With a short Epilogue to close your taste.
In thus withdrawing, we seem mannerly ;
But, when the Curtain's down we peep and
  see
A Jury of the Wits, who still stay late,   9
And in their Club decree the poor Plays fate ;
Their Verdict back is to the Boxes brought,
Thence all the Town pronounces it their
  thought.
Thus, Gallants, we like *Lilly* can foresee ;
But if you ask us what our doom will be,
We by to morrow will our Fortune cast,
As he tells all things when the Year is past.

SIR MARTIN MAR-ALL, 1667.   Epilogue 2
hudling] *Scott gives* headlong

PROLOGUE AND EPILOGUE TO THE TEMPEST.

PROLOGUE.

As when a Tree's cut down, the secret root
Lives under ground, and thence new
    Branches shoot,
So from old *Shakespear's* honoured dust this
    day
Springs up and buds a new reviving Play :
Shakespear, who (taught by none) did first
    impart
To *Fletcher* Wit, to labouring *Johnson* Art ;
He Monarch-like, gave those his subjects
    law,
And is that Nature which they paint and
    draw.
Fletcher reach'd that which on his heights
    did grow,   9
Whilst *Johnson* crept and gather'd all below.
This did his Love, and this his Mirth digest :
One imitates him most, the other best.
If they have since out-writ all other men,
'Tis with the drops which fell from *Shake-
    spear's* Pen.
The Storm which vanish'd on the Neighbring
    shore
Was taught by *Shakespear's* Tempest first to
    roar.
That Innocence and Beauty, which did smile
In *Fletcher*, grew on this *Enchanted Isle*.
But *Shakespear's* Magick could not copy'd be;
Within that Circle none durst walk but he. 20
I must confess 'twas bold, nor would you now
That liberty to vulgar Wits allow,
Which works by Magick supernatural things;
But *Shakespear's* pow'r is sacred as a King's.
Those Legends from old Priest-hood were
    receiv'd,

And he then writ, as People then believ'd.
But if for *Shakespear* we your grace implore,
We for our Theatre shall want it more ;
Who by our dearth of Youths are forc'd t'
    employ
One of our Women to present a Boy.   30
And that's a transformation you will say
Exceeding all the Magick in the Play.
Let none expect in the last Act to find
Her Sex transform'd from Man to Woman-
    kind.
What e're she was before the Play began,
All you shall see of her is perfect Man.
Or, if your fancy will be farther led
To find her Woman, it must be abed.

EPILOGUE.

Gallants, by all good Signs it does appear
That Sixty Seven's a very damning Year,
For Knaves aboard, and for ill Poets here.

Among the Muses there's a gen'ral Rot ;
The Rhyming Monsieur and the *Spanish* Plot,
Defie or court, all's one, they go to Pot.

The Ghosts of Poets walk within this place,
And haunt us Actors wheresoe're we pass,
In Visions bloodier than King *Richard's* was.

For this poor Wretch, he has not much to say,
But quietly brings in his Part o' th' Play, 11
And begs the Favour to be damn'd to-day.

He sends me only like a Sh'riffs man here
To let you know the Malefactor's neer,
And that he means to dye *en cavalier.*

For, if you shou'd be gracious to his Pen,
Th' Example will prove ill to other Men,
And you'll be troubled with 'em all agen.

PROLOGUE TO ALBUMAZAR.

To say this Comedy pleas'd long ago
Is not enough to make it pass you now.
Yet, Gentlemen, your Ancestors had wit,
When few Men censur'd, and when fewer
    writ ;

And *Johnson* (of those few the best) chose this
As the best Model of his Master-piece.
Subtle was got by our *Albumazar*,
That *Alchymist* by his *Astrologer* ;
Here he was fashion'd, and we may suppose
He lik'd the fashion well who wore the
    Cloaths.   10

THE TEMPEST, 1667. Published in 1670.
17 Innocence] innocence *1670.*
    Beauty] beauty *1670.*
34 and 36 Man] man *1670.*
Epilogue 3 aboard] *Some editors wrongly
give* abroad
    13 Sh'riffs] *The editors print* Sheriff's

ALBUMAZAR, 1668.   Reprinted in *Coven.
Garden Drollery*, 1672.   The play is by Tomkis.
Prologue 9 we may] I should *1672.*
    10 lik'd the] likes my *1672.*
    who wore the] that wears my *1672.*

But *Ben* made nobly his what he did Mould ;
What was another's Lead, becomes his Gold:
Like an unrighteous Conqueror he Reigns,
Yet rules that well, which he unjustly Gains.
But this our Age such Authors does afford,
As make whole Plays, and yet scarce write
    one word ;
Who, in this Anarchy of Wit, rob all,
And what's their Plunder, their Possession
    call :
Who, like bold Padders, scorn by Night to
    prey,
But rob by Sun-shine, in the Face of Day: 20
Nay scarce the common Ceremony use
Of Stand, Sir, and deliver up your Muse ;
But knock the Poet down, and, with a Grace,
Mount *Pegasus* before the Owner's Face.
Faith, if you have such Country *Toms* abroad,
'Tis time for all true Men to leave that Road.
Yet it were modest, could it but be said,
They strip the Living, but these rob the
    Dead ;
Dare with the Mummies of the Muses play,
And make Love to them the *Ægyptian*
    way ;   30

Or, as a Rhiming Author would have said,
Join the Dead Living to the Living Dead.
Such Men in Poetry may claim some Part ;
They have the Licence, tho' they want the
    Art ;
And might, where Theft was prais'd, for
    Laureats stand,
Poets, not of the Head, but of the Hand.
They make the Benefits of others' studying,
Much like the Meals of Politick *Jack-Pudding*,
Whose dish to challenge no Man has the
    Courage ;
'Tis all his own, when once h' has spit i' the
    Porridge.   40
But, Gentlemen, you're all concern'd in this ;
You are in Fault for what they do amiss :
For they their Thefts still undiscovered
    think,
And durst not steal, unless you please to
    wink.
Perhaps, you may award by your Decree,
They shou'd refund,—but that can never be ;
For should you Letters of Reprisal seal,
These Men write that which no Man else
    would steal.

PROLOGUE AND EPILOGUE TO AN EVENING'S LOVE,
OR THE MOCK ASTROLOGER.

PROLOGUE.

When first our Poet set himself to write,
Like a young Bridegroom on his Wedding-
    night,
He laid about him, and did so bestir him,
His Muse could never lye in quiet for him :
But now his Honey-moon is gone and past,
Yet the ungrateful drudgery must last,
And he is bound, as civil Husbands do,
To strain himself, in complaisance to you :
To write in pain, and counterfeit a Bliss,
Like the faint smackings of an after-Kiss. 10
But you, like Wives ill pleas'd, supply his
    want;
Each Writing *Monsieur* is a fresh gallant :

And though, perhaps, 'twas done as well
    before,
Yet still there's something in a new Amour.
Your several Poets work with several Tools,
One gets you Wits, another gets you Fools :
This pleases you with some by-stroke of Wit
This finds some cranny that was never hit.
But should these janty Lovers daily come
To do your Work, like your good Man at
    home,   20
Their fine small-timber'd Wits would soon
    decay;
These are Gallants but for a Holiday.
Others you had, who oftner have appear'd,
Whom for meer impotence you have
    cashier'd :

12 becomes] became *1672*.
28 strip] stript *1672*.   these] they *1672*.
33 Such Men] Yet such *1672*.
35 Such as in *Sparta* weight for Laurels stand
1672.
37 the Benefits] their Benefit *1672*.

39 Whose Broth to claim there's no one has the
Courage *1672*.
40 when once] after *1672*.
45-46 *omitted 1672*.
An Evening's Love, 1668.
10 smackings] *Edd. give* smacking

Such as at first came on with Pomp and
  Glory,
But, over-straining, soon fell flat before ye.
Their useless weight with patience long was
  borne,
But at the last you threw 'em off with scorn.
As for the Poet of this present night,   ⎫
Though now he claims in you an Hus-   ⎬
  bands right,   30 ⎪
He will not hinder you of fresh delight.   ⎭
He, like a Seaman, seldom will appear,
And means to trouble home but thrice a year;
That only time from your Gallants he'll
  borrow;
Be kind to day, and Cuckold him to morrow.

EPILOGUE.

My Part being small, I have had time to day
To mark your various censures of our Play.
First, looking for a Judgement or a Wit,
Like *Jews*, I saw 'em scatter'd through the
  Pit ;
And where a lot of Smilers lent an Ear
To one that talk'd, I knew the Foe was there.
The Club of jests went round ; he, who had
  none,
Borrow'd o' th' next, and told it for his own.
Among the rest, they kept a fearful stir,
In whisp'ring that he stole th' *Astrologer* ; 10
And said, betwixt a *French* and *English* Plot,
He eased his halfe-tir'd Muse, on Pace and
  Trot.
Up starts a *Mounsieur*, new come o'er, and
  warm
In the *French* stoop, and the pull-back o' th'
  Arm :

Morbleu dit il, and cocks, I am a Rogue,
But he has quite spoil'd the fein'd *Astrologue*.
'Pox, says another, here's so great a stir
With a Son of a Whore, Farce that's regular,
A Rule, where nothing must *decorum* shock !
Dam'me, 'ts as dull as Dining by the Clock. 20
An Evening ! why the Devil should we be
  vext,
Whether he gets the Wench this night or
  next ?
When I heard this, I to the Poet went,   ⎫
Told him the House was full of Discontent, ⎬
And ask'd him what excuse he could invent. ⎭
He neither swore nor storm'd, as Poets do,
But, most unlike an Author, vow'd 'twas
  true ;
Yet said, he used the *French* like Enemies,
And did not steal their Plots, but made 'em
  Prize.
But should he all the pains and charges
  count   30
Of taking 'em, the Bill so high wou'd mount,
That, like Prize-Goods, which through the
  Office come,
He should have had 'em much more cheap at
  home.
He still must write, and, Banquier-like, each
  Day
Accept new Bills, and he must break, or pay.
When through his hands such sums must
  yearly run,
You cannot think the Stock is all his own.
His haste his other errors might excuse,
But there's no mercy for a guilty Muse ;
For, like a Mistress, she must stand or fall, 40
And please you to a height, or not at all.

PROLOGUE AND EPILOGUE TO TYRANNICK LOVE, OR THE ROYAL MARTYR.

PROLOGUE.

SELF-LOVE (which never rightly understood)
Makes Poets still conclude their Plays are
  good,
And Malice in all Criticks raigns so high,
That for small Errors, they whole Plays
  decry ;

So that to see this fondness, and that spite,
You'd think that none but Mad-men judge
  or write.
Therefore our Poet, as he thinks not fit
T' impose upon you what he writes for Wit
So hopes that, leaving you your censures ⎫
  free,   ⎬
You equal Judges of the whole will be : 10 ⎪
They judge but half, who only faults will see. ⎭
Poets, like Lovers, should be bold and dare,
They spoil their business with an over-care ;

TYRANNICK LOVE, 1669. *The editors make
nonsense by printing the first line thus :*
  Self-love, which, never rightly understood,

And he, who servilely creeps after sence,
Is safe, but ne're will reach an Excellence.
Hence 'tis, our Poet, in his conjuring,
Allow'd his Fancy the full scope and swing.
But when a Tyrant for his Theme he had,
He loos'd the Reins, and bid his Muse run
    mad ;
And though he stumbles in a full career, 20
Yet rashness is a better fault than fear.
He saw his way ; but in so swift a pace,
To chuse the ground might be to lose the
    race.
They then, who of each trip th' advantage
    take,
Find but those Faults, which they want Wit
    to make.

EPILOGUE.

Spoken by MRS. ELLEN *when she was to be
carried off dead by the Bearers.*

TO THE BEARER. Hold ! are you mad ? you
    damn'd, confounded Dog !
I am to rise, and speak the Epilogue.
TO THE AUDIENCE. I come, kind Gentlemen,
    strange news to tell ye ;
I am the Ghost of poor departed *Nelly.*
Sweet Ladies, be not frighted ; I'le be civil ;
I'm what I was, a little harmless Devil.
For, after death, we Sprights have just such
    Natures,
We had, for all the World, when humane
    Creatures ;

And, therefore, I, that was an Actress here,
Play all my Tricks in Hell, a Goblin there. 10
Gallants, look to 't, you say there are no
    Sprights ;
But I'll come dance about your Beds at
    nights ;
And faith you'll be in a sweet kind of
    taking,
When I surprise you between sleep and
    waking.
To tell you true, I walk, because I dye
Out of my Calling, in a Tragedy.
O Poet, damn'd dull Poet, who could prove
So senseless, to make *Nelly* dye for Love !
Nay, what's yet worse, to kill me in the
    prime
Of *Easter*-term, in Tart and Cheese-cake
    time !   20
I'le fit the Fopp ; for I'le not one word
    say,
T' excuse his godly, out of fashion Play;
A Play, which, if you dare but twice sit out,
You'll all be slander'd, and be thought
    devout.
But, farewel, Gentlemen, make haste to me,
I'm sure e're long to have your company.
As for my Epitaph when I am gone,
I'le trust no Poet, but will write my own.

Here *Nelly* lies, who, though she lived a
    Slater'n,
Yet dy'd a Princess, acting in *S.Cathar'n.* 30

PROLOGUE AND EPILOGUE TO THE CONQUEST OF GRANADA BY THE SPANIARDS.

PROLOGUE

Spoken by MRS. ELLEN GWYN *in a broad-
brimmed hat and waist-belt.*

THIS jeast was first of t' other houses making,
And, five times try'd, has never fail'd of
    taking ;
For 'twere a shame a Poet shoud be kill'd
Under the shelter of so broad a shield.
This is that hat, whose very sight did win yee
To laugh and clap as though the Devil were
    in yee.

THE CONQUEST OF GRANADA, 1670. Published
in 1672. The originals are careless in the use of
capitals.

As then for *Nokes,* so now I hope you'l be
So dull, to laugh once more for love of me.
I'll write a Play, says one, for I have got
A broad-brim'd hat and wastbelt towards
    a Plot.   10
Sayes t' other, I have one more large than
    that.
Thus they out-write each other—with a hat.
The brims still grew with every Play they
    writ ;
And grew so large, they cover'd all the wit.
Hat was the Play ; 'twas language, wit,
    and Tale ;
Like them that find Meat, drink, and cloth
    in Ale.

What dulness do these Mungrill-wits confess,
When all their hope is acting of a dress !
Thus, two the best Comedians of the Age
Must be worn out with being Blocks o' th'
    Stage :   20
Like a young Girl, who better things has
    known,
Beneath their Poets Impotence they groan.
See now what Charity it was to save !
They thought you lik'd what onely you for-
    gave ;
And brought you more dull sence, dull sence
    much worse
Than brisk gay Non-sence, and the heavyer
    Curse.
They bring old Ir'n and glass upon the Stage,
To barter with the Indians of our Age.
Still they write on, and like great Authors⎫
    show ;   29 ⎪
But 'tis as Rowlers in wet gardens grow ⎬
Heavy with dirt, and gath'ring as they   ⎪
    goe.   ⎭
May none, who have so little understood,
To like such trash, presume to praise what's
    good !
And may those drudges of the Stage, whose
    fate
Is, damn'd dull farce more dully to translate,
Fall under that excise the State thinks fit
To set on all French wares, whose worst is
    wit.
French Farce, worn out at home, is sent
    abroad ;
And, patch'd up here, is made our English
    mode.   39
Henceforth, let Poets, 'ere allow'd to write,
Be search'd, like Duellists before they fight,
For wheel-broad hats, dull Humour, all that
    chaffe,
Which makes you mourn, and makes the
    Vulgar laugh :
For these, in Playes, are as unlawful Arms,
As, in a Combat, Coats of Mayle, and Charms.

EPILOGUE.

Success, which can no more than beauty last,
Makes our sad Poet mourn your favours
    past ;
For, since without desert he got a name,
He fears to loose it now with greater shame.

Fame, like a little Mistriss of the Town,
Is gaind with ease ; but then she's lost as
    soon ;
For, as those taudry Misses, soon or late,
Jilt such as keep 'em at the highest rate,
(And oft the Lacquey, or the Brawny Clown,
Gets what is hid in the loose body'd gown ;)
So, Fame is false to all that keep her long ;
And turns up to the Fop that's brisk and
    young.   12
Some wiser Poet now would leave Fame
    first ;
But elder wits are, like old Lovers, curst :
Who, when the vigor of their Youth is
    spent,
Still grow more fond as they grow impotent.
This, some years hence, our Poets case may
    prove ;
But yet, he hopes, he's young enough to love.
When forty comes, if ere he live to see
That wretched, fumbling age of poetry ; 20
'Twill be high time to bid his Muse adieu :
Well he may please him self, but never you.
Till then, he'l do as well as he began,
And hopes you will not finde him less a man.
Think him not duller for this years delay ;⎫
He was prepar'd, the women were away ; ⎪
And men, without their parts, can hardly⎬
    play.   ⎭
If they, through sickness, seldome did⎫
    appear,   ⎬
Pity the Virgins of each Theatre !   ⎭
For, at both houses, 'twas a sickly year ! 30
And pity us, your servants, to whose cost,
In one such sickness, nine whole Months are
    lost.
Their Stay, he fears, has ruin'd what he
    writ :
Long waiting both disables love and wit.
They thought they gave him Leisure to do
    well ;
But, when they forc'd him to attend, he
    fell !
Yet, though he much has faild, he begs to
    day
You will excuse his unperforming Play :
Weakness sometimes great passion does
    express ;
He had pleas'd better, had he lov'd you
    less.   40

Prologue. 42 Humour] *Some editors wrongly give* Honour

Epilogue 21 'Twill] T'will *1672.*
32 Months] Mon'ths *1672.*

PROLOGUE AND EPILOGUE TO THE SECOND PART OF THE CONQUEST OF GRANADA BY THE SPANIARDS.

PROLOGUE.

THEY who write Ill, and they who ne'r durst write,
Turn Critiques out of meer Revenge and Spight :
A *Play-house* gives 'em Fame ; and up there starts,
From a mean Fifth-rate Wit, a Man of Parts.
(So Common Faces on the Stage appear ;
We take 'em in, and they turn Beauties here.)
Our Authour fears those Critiques as his Fate ;
And those he Fears, by consequence, must Hate,
For they the Trafficque of all Wit invade,
As Scriv'ners draw away the Bankers Trade.
Howe're, the Poet's safe enough to day ;   11
They cannot censure an unfinish'd Play.
But, as when Vizard Masque appears in Pit,
Straight every Man who thinks himself a Wit
Perks up ; and, managing his Comb with grace,
With his white Wigg sets off his Nut-brown Face ;
That done, bears up to th' prize, and views each Limb,
To know her by her Rigging and her Trimm ;
Then, the whole noise of Fops to wagers go,
Pox on her, 't must be she ; and *Damm'ee* no :
Just so, I Prophecy, these Wits to-day   21
Will blindly guess at our imperfect Play :
With what new Plots our Second Part is fill'd,
Who must be kept alive, and who be kill'd.
And as those Vizard Masques maintain that Fashion,
To soothe and tickle sweet Imagination ;
So, our dull Poet keeps you on with Masquing ;
To make you think there's something worth your asking :
But when 'tis shown, that which does now delight you
Will prove a Dowdy, with a Face to fright you.   30

EPILOGUE.

They who have best succeeded on the Stage,
Have still conform'd their Genius to their Age.
Thus *Jonson* did Mechanique humour show
When men were dull, and conversation low.
Then, Comedy was faultless, but 'twas course ;
Cobbs Tankard was a Jest, and *Otter's* horse.
And as their Comedy, their Love was mean ;
Except, by chance, in some one labour'd Scene,
Which must attone for an ill-written play,
They rose, but at their height could seldome stay.   10
Fame then was cheap, and the first commer sped ;
And they have kept it since, by being dead,
But, were they now to write, when Critiques weigh
Each Line, and ev'ry Word, throughout a Play,
None of 'em, no, not *Jonson* in his height,
Could pass, without allowing grains for weight.
Think it not envy, that these truths are told ;
Our Poet's not malicious, though he's bold.
'Tis not to brand 'em that their faults are shown,
But by their errours to excuse his own.   20
If Love and Honour now are higher rais'd,
'Tis not the Poet, but the Age is prais'd.
Wit's now ariv'd to a more high degree ;
Our native Language more refin'd and free ;
Our Ladies and our men now speak more wit
In conversation, than those Poets writ.
Then, one of these is, consequently, true ;
That what this Poet writes comes short of you,
And imitates you ill (which most he fears)
Or else his writing is not worse than theirs.
Yet, though you judge (as sure the Critiques will)   31
That some before him writ with greater skill,
In this one praise he has their fame surpast,
To please an Age more Gallant than the last.

PROLOGUE.

Spoken on the First Day of the Kings House acting after the Fire.

So shipwrackt Passengers escape to Land,
So look they, when on the bare Beach they
    stand,
Dropping and cold, and their first fear scarce
    o'er,
Expecting Famine on a Desart Shore.
From that hard Climate we must wait for
    Bread,
Whence ev'n the Natives, forc'd by hunger,
    fled.
Our Stage does humane Chance present to
    view,
But ne'er before was seen so sadly true :
You are chang'd too, and your Pretence to
    see
Is but a Nobler Name for Charity.   10
Your own Provisions furnish out our Feasts,
While you, the Founders, make your selves
    the guests.
Of all Mankind beside Fate had some Care,)
But for poor Wit no portion did prepare ; |
'Tis left a Rent Charge to the Brave and   (
    Fair.   )

You cherish'd it, and now its Fall you
    mourn,
Which blind unmanner'd Zelots make their
    scorn,
Who think that Fire a Judgment on the
    Stage,
Which spar'd not Temples in its furious
    Rage.
But as our new-built City rises higher, 20)
So from old Theatres may new aspire,   >
Since Fate contrives Magnificence by Fire.)
Our great Metropolis does far surpass
Whate'er is now, and equals all that was :
Our Wit as far does Foreign Wit excel,
And, like a King, shou'd in a Palace
    dwell.
But we with Golden Hopes are vainly
    fed,
Talk high, and entertain you in a shed :
Your Presence here (for which we humbly
    sue)
Will grace Old Theatres, and build up
    New.   30

PROLOGUE TO ARVIRAGUS AND PHILICIA ; REVIVED.

WITH sickly Actors and an old House too,
We're match'd with glorious Theatres and
    new,
And with our Ale-house scenes and Cloaths
    bare worn
Can neither raise old Plays nor new adorn.
If all these Ills could not undo us quite,
A brisk *French* Troop is grown your dear
    delight ;
Who with broad bloudy Bills call you each
    day
To laugh and break your Buttons at their
    Play ;
Or see some serious Piece, which we presume
Is fall'n from some incomparable plume ; 10
And therefore, *Messieurs*, if you'll do us
    Grace,
Send Lacquies early to preserve your Place.

We dare not on your Priviledge intrench,
Or ask you why you like 'em ? They are
    French.
Therefore some go with Courtesie exceeding,
Neither to hear nor see, but show their
    Breeding :
Each Lady striving to out-laugh the rest ;
To make it seem they understood the Jest.
Their Countrymen come in, and nothing
    pay,
To teach us *English* where to clap the play :
Civil, *Igad* ; Our Hospitable Land   21
Bears all the Charge, for them to under-
    stand :
Mean time we languish, and neglected lye,
Like Wives, while you keep better Company;
And wish for our own sakes, without a
    Satyr,
You'd less good Breeding or had more good
    Nature.

PROLOGUE AFTER THE FIRE.   Text from the
Miscellanies of 1692.   Variants from *Covent
Garden Drollery*, 1672.
4 on] from *1672*.
10 for] of *1672*.

ARVIRAGUS AND PHILICIA.   Text from the
Miscellanies of 1684.   The play is by Carlell.

PROLOGUE, *for the Women,*

When they Acted at the Old Theatre *in* Lincoln's Inn Fields.

WERE none of you, Gallants, e'er driven so
    hard,
As when the poor kind Soul was under guard,
And could not do't at home, in some By-
    street
To take a Lodging, and in private meet ?
Such is our Case ; We can't appoint our
    House,
The Lovers old and wonted Rendezvous,
But hither to this trusty Nook remove ;
The worse the Lodging is, the more the Love.
For much good Pastime, many a dear sweet
    hug
Is stol'n in Garrets, on the humble Rugg, 10
Here's good Accommodation in the Pit ;
The Grave demurely in the midst may sit,

And so the hot *Burgundian* on the Side
Ply Vizard Masque, and o'er the Benches
    stride :
Here are convenient upper Boxes too, ⎫
For those that make the most triumphant ⎬
    show ; ⎪
All that keep Coaches must not sit below. ⎭
There, Gallants, you betwixt the Acts
    retire,
And at dull Plays have something to
    admire :   19
We, who look up, can your Addresses mark,
And see the Creatures coupled in the Ark :
So we expect the *Lovers, Braves, and Wits* ;
The gaudy House with Scenes will serve for
    Cits.

PROLOGUE AND EPILOGUE TO THE MAIDEN QUEEN, OR SECRET LOVE,

When acted by the Women only.

PROLOGUE.

Spoken by MRS. BOUTELL, *in man's clothes.*

WOMEN like us (passing for Men) you'l
    cry,
Presume too much upon your Secresie.
There's not a Fop in Town but will pretend,
To know the Cheat himself, or by his
    Friend.
Then make no words on't, Gallants, 'tis e'en
    true,
We are condemn'd to look, and strut, like
    you.
Since we thus freely our hard Fate confess,
Accept us, these bad Times, in any Dress.
You'll find the sweet on't, now old Panta- ⎫
    loons ⎪
Will go as far, as formerly new Gowns ; 10 ⎬
And from your own cast Wigs expect no ⎪
    Frowns. ⎭

The Ladies we shall not so easily please.
They'l say what impudent bold things are
    these,
That dare provoke, yet cannot do us
    right,
Like Men, with huffing Looks, that dare not
    fight.
But this reproach our Courage must not ⎫
    daunt, ⎪
The BravestSouldier may a Weapon want, ⎬
Let Her that doubts us, still send Her ⎪
    Gallant. ⎭
Ladies, in us you'l Youth and Beauty
    find,
All Things, but one, according to your
    Mind.   20
And when your Eyes and Ears are feasted
    here,
Rise up, and make out the short Meal else-
    where.

PROLOGUE FOR THE WOMEN. Text from the
same, except as noted.
  1 Were] Where *1684 : a misprint.*
17 Coaches] *Bell wrongly printed* Couches

THE MAIDEN QUEEN, 1672. Text from *Covent
Garden Drollery,* 1672, where many of the stops
are wrong, but as the text had not Dryden's
authority the errors are not here noted.

EPILOGUE.

Spoken by MRS. REEVE, *in man's clothes.*

What think you, Sirs, was't not all well
  enough ?
Will you not grant that we can strut, and
  huff ?
Men may be proud ; but faith, for ought
  I see,
They neither walk, nor cock, so well as we ;
And for the fighting part, we may in time
Grow up to swagger in heroick Rhime ;
For though we cannot boast of equal Force,
Yet at some Weapons Men have still the
  worse.
Why should not then we Women act alone, ⎫
Or whence are Men so necessary grown? 10 ⎬
Our's are so old, they are as good as none. ⎭
Some who have tri'd 'em, if you'l take
  their Oaths,
Swear they're as arrant Tinsell as their
  Cloaths.

Imagine us but what we represent,
And we could e'en give you as good Content.
Our Faces, Shapes,—all's better than you
  see,
And for the rest, they want as much as we.
Oh, would the higher Pow'rs be kind to us,
And grant us to set up a female House.
Wee'l make ourselves to please both Sexes
  then,   20
To the Men Women, to the Women Men.
Here we presume, our Legs are no ill Sight,
And they will give you no ill Dreams at
  Night.
In Dreams both Sexes must their Passions
  ease,
You make us then as civil as you please.
This would prevent the Houses joyning too,
At which we are as much displeas'd as
  you ;
For all our Women most devoutly swear, ⎫
Each would be rather a poor Actress here ⎬
Than to be made a Mamamouchi there. 30 ⎭

PROLOGUE AND EPILOGUE TO MARRIAGE-A-LA-MODE.

PROLOGUE.

LORD, how reform'd and quiet are we grown,
Since all our Braves and all our Wits are
  gone :
Fop-corner now is free from Civil War,
White-Wig and Vizard-Mask no longer jar.
France, and the Fleet have swept the Town
  so clear,
That we can Act in peace, and you can hear.
Those that durst fight are gone to get renown ;
And those that durst not, blush to stand in
  Town.
'Twas a sad sight, before they march'd ⎫
  from home,   ⎪
To see our Warriours, in Red Wastecoats, ⎬
  come,   10 ⎪
With hair tuck'd up, into our Tireing-room. ⎭
But 'twas more sad to hear their last Adieu
The Women sob'd, and swore they would be
  true ;

And so they were, as long as e're they ⎫
  cou'd ;   ⎪
But powerful *Guinnee* cannot be withstood, ⎬
And they were made of Playhouse flesh ⎪
  and bloud.   ⎭
Fate did their Friends for double Use
  ordain ;
In Wars abroad, they grinning Honour gain,
And Mistresses, for all that stay, maintain.
Now they are gone, 'tis dead Vacation here,
For neither Friends nor Enemies appear. 21
Poor pensive Punk now peeps ere Plays
  begin,
Sees the bare Bench, and dares not venture
  in ;
But manages her last Half-crown with care,
And trudges to the *Mall*, on foot, for Air.
Our City Friends so far will hardly roam,
They can take up with Pleasures nearer
  home ;
And see gay Shows with gaudy Scenes else-
  where :   28
For we presume they seldom come to hear.

MARRIAGE-A-LA-MODE, 1672. Printed in *Covent Garden Drollery*, 1672, and with the play. 1673.
Prologue 4 Vizard-Mask] *Christie*: Vizard Masks *1672*: Vizard make *1673*.
7-8 *omitted 1673*.
9 march'd] *1673* : went *1672*.

16 Playhouse] Play house *1673*.
26 roam] *1672* : come *1673*.
28 with] *1672* : and *1673*.

But they have now ta'n up a glorious Trade,
And cutting *Moorcraft* struts in Masquerade.
There's all our hope, for we shall show to day
A Masquing Ball, to recommend our Play ;
Nay, to endear 'em more, and let 'em see
We scorn to come behind in Courtesie,
We'll follow the new Mode which they begin,
And treat 'em with a Room, and Couch
within :
For that's one way, how e're the Play fall
short,
T' oblige the Town, the City, and the Court.

EPILOGUE.

Thus have my Spouse and I inform'd the
Nation,
And led you all the way to Reformation ;
Not with dull Morals, gravely writ, like those
Which men of easy Phlegme with care com-
pose,
Your Poets, of stiff Words and limber sense,
Born on the confines of indifference :
But by Examples drawn, I dare to say,
From most of you who hear, and see the Play
There are more *Rhodophils* in this Theatre,
More *Palamedes*, and some few Wives, I fear :
But yet too far our Poet would not run ;   11
Though 'twas well offer'd, there was nothing
done.

He would not quite the Woman's frailty
bare,
But stript 'em to the waste, and left 'em
there :
And the men's faults are less severely
shown,
For he considers that himself is one.
Some stabbing Wits, to bloudy Satyr bent,
Would treat both Sexes with less comple-
ment :
Would lay the Scene at home ; of Husbands
tell,
For Wenches taking up their Wives i' th'
Mell ;   20
And a brisk bout, which each of them did
want,
Made by mistake of Mistris and Gallant.
Our modest Authour thought it was enough
To cut you off a Sample of the stuff :
He spared my shame, which you, I'm sure,
would not,
For you were all for driving on the Plot :
You sigh'd when I came in to break the sport,
And set your teeth when each design fell
short.
To Wives, and Servants all good wishes lend,
But the poor Cuckold seldom finds a friend.
Since therefore, Court and Town will take
no pity,   31
I humbly cast myself upon the City.

PROLOGUE AND EPILOGUE TO THE ASSIGNATION,
OR LOVE IN A NUNNERY.

PROLOGUE.

PROLOGUES, like Bells to Churches, toul
you in
With Chimeing Verse, till the dull Playes
begin ;
With this sad difference though, of Pit and
Pue ;
You damn the *Poet*, but the *Priest* damns
you.
But Priests can treat you at your own
expence,
And, gravely, call you Fools, without Offence

Poets, poor Devils, have ne'er your Folly
shown,
But, to their Cost, you prov'd it was their
own :   8
For, when a Fop's presented on the Stage,
Straight all the Coxcombs in the Town ingage ;
For his deliverance and revenge they joyn,
And grunt, like Hogs, about their Captive
Swine.
Your Poets daily split upon this shelf :
You must have Fools, yet none will have
himself.
Or, if in kindness, you that leave would give,
No man could write you at that rate you live :

MARRIAGE-A-LA-MODE. Prologue. 31 *Moorcraft*] Morrcraft *1673.*

THE ASSIGNATION, 1672. Published in 1673.

For some of you grow Fops with so much
   haste,
Riot in nonsence, and commit such waste,
'Twould Ruine Poets should they spend so
   fast.
He who made this observed what Farces
   hit,   20
And durst not disoblige you now with wit.
But, Gentlemen, you overdo the Mode ;
You must have Fools out of the common
   Rode.
Th'unnatural strain'd Buffoon is only taking ;
No Fop can please you now of Gods own
   making.
Pardon our Poet, if he speaks his Mind ;
You come to Plays with your own Follies
   lin'd :
Small Fools fall on you, like small showers,
   in vain ;
Your own oyl'd Coats keep out all common
   rain.
You must have Mamamouchi, such a Fop
As would appear a Monster in a Shop ;   31
He'll fill your Pit and Boxes to the brim,
Where, Ram'd in Crowds, you see your selves
   in him.
Sure there's some spell our Poet never knew,
In hullibabilah de, and Chu, chu, chu;
But Marabarah sahem most did touch you;
That is, Oh how we love the Mamamouchi !
Grimace and habit sent you pleas'd away;
You damn'd the poet, and cried up the Play.
   This Thought had made our Author more
      uneasie,   40
But that he hopes I'm Fool enough to
   please ye.

But here's my grief,—though Nature, joined
   with Art,
Have cut me out to act a Fooling Part,
Yet, to your Praise, the few wits here will
   say,
'Twas imitating you taught *Haynes* to Play.

EPILOGUE.

Some have expected, from our Biils to-day,
To find a *Satyre* in our *Poet's Play*.
The *Zealous Rout* from *Coleman-street* did run,
To see the Story of the *Fryer* and *Nun*,
Or Tales, yet more Ridiculous to hear,
Vouch'd by their Vicar of Ten pounds a year;
Of Nuns who did against Temptation Pray,
And Discipline laid on the pleasant Way :
Or that, to please the Malice of the Town,
Our *Poet* should in some close Cell have
   shown   10
Some Sister, Playing at Content alone.
This they did hope ; the other Side did
   fear ;
And both, you see, alike are Couzen'd here.
Some thought the Title of our Play to blame ;
They liked the thing, but yet abhorr'd the
   Name :
Like modest *Puncks*, who all you ask afford,
But, for the *World*, they would not name
   that word.
Yet, if you'll credit what I heard him say,
Our *Poet* meant no Scandal in his *Play* ;
His Nuns are good which on the Stage are
   shown,   20
And, sure, behind our *Scenes* you'll look for
   none.

PROLOGUE AND EPILOGUE TO
AMBOYNA, OR THE CRUELTIES OF THE DUTCH
TO THE ENGLISH MERCHANTS.

PROLOGUE.

As needy Gallants in the Scriv'ners hands
Court the rich Knave that gripes their Mort-
   gag'd Lands,
The first fat Buck of all the Season's sent,
And Keeper takes no Fee in Complement;

The doteage of some *Englishmen* is such,
To fawn on those who ruine them, the *Dutch*.
They shall have all rather than make a War
With those who of the same Religion are.
The *Streights*, the *Guiney* Trade, the Herrings
   too,   9
Nay, to keep friendship, they shall pickle you.
Some are resolv'd not to find out the Cheat,
But Cuckold-like, love him who does the
   Feat :

   AMBOYNA, 1673. Prologue 10 keep friendship]
Christie, I do not know from what source, gives
preserve them

What injuries soe'r upon us fall,
Yet still the same Religion answers all :
Religion wheedled you to Civil War,
Drew *English* Blood, and *Dutchmens* now
    wou'd spare.
Be gull'd no longer ; for you'l find it true,
They have no more Religion, faith—then
    you ;
Interest's the God they worship in their
    State ;   19
And you, I take it, have not much of that.
Well, Monarchys may own Religions name,
But States are Atheists in their very frame.
They share a sin, and such proportions fall
That, like a stink, 'tis nothing to 'em all.
How they love *England*, you shall see this
    day :
No Map shows *Holland* truer then our Play :
Their Pictures and Inscriptions well we know ;
We may be bold one Medal sure to show.
View then their Falshoods, Rapine, Cruelty ;
And think what once they were they still
    would be :   30
But hope not either Language, Plot, or Art ;
'Twas writ in haste, but with an *English*
    Heart :
And lest hope Wit ; in *Dutchmen* that would
    be
As much improper as would Honesty.

EPILOGUE.

A Poet once the *Spartan's* led to fight,
And made 'em conquer in the Muses right :
So would our Poet lead you on this day,
Showing your tortur'd Fathers in his Play.
To one well born th' affront is worse and more,
When he's abus'd and baffled by a Bore :
With an ill Grace the *Dutch* their mischiefs do,
They've both ill Nature and ill Manners too.
Well may they boast themselves an antient
    Nation,
For they were bred e're Manners were in
    fashion :   10
And their new Commonwealth has set 'em free,
Onely from Honour and Civility.
Venetians do not more uncouthly ride,
Than did their Lubber-State Mankind be-
    stride ;
Their Sway became 'em with as ill a Meen,
As their own Paunches swell above their Chin :
Yet is their Empire no true Growth but
    Humour,
And onely two Kings' touch can cure the
    Tumor.
As *Cato* did his *Affricque* Fruits display,
So we before your Eies their *Indies* lay :   20
All loyal *English* will like him conclude,
Let *Cæsar* Live, and *Carthage* be subdu'd !

PROLOGUE AND EPILOGUE TO THE UNIVERSITY
OF OXFORD.

PROLOGUE.

Spoken by MR. HART *at the acting of the
Silent Woman,*

WHAT *Greece*, when learning flourish'd, onely
    knew,
(*Athenian* Judges,) you this day renew.
Here too are Annual Rites to *Pallas* done,
And here Poetique prizes lost or won.
Methinks I see you crown'd with Olives sit,
And strike a sacred Horrour from the Pit.
A Day of Doom is this of your Decree,
Where even the Best are but by Mercy free : }
A Day which none but *Johnson* durst have
    wish'd to see.

PROLOGUE AND EPILOGUE TO THE UNIVERSITY
OF OXFORD, 1673. Printed in 1684, again in 1692.

Here they who long have known the usefull
    Stage   10
Come to be taught themselves to teach the
    Age.
As your Commissioners our Poets go,
To cultivate the Virtue which you sow ;
In your *Lycaeum* first themselves refin'd,
And delegated thence to Humane kind.
But as Embassadours, when long from
    home,
For new Instructions to their Princes
    come ;
So Poets who your Precepts have forgot,
Return, and beg they may be better taught :
Follies and Faults else-where by them are
    shown,   20
But by your Manners they correct their own.

Th' illiterate Writer, Emperique like, applies
To Minds diseas'd, unsafe, chance Remedies :
The Learn'd in Schools, where Knowledge
first began,
Studies with Care th' Anatomy of Man ;
Sees Vertue, Vice, and Passions in their
Cause,
And Fame from Science, not from Fortune,
draws.
So Poetry, which is in *Oxford* made
An Art, in *London* onely is a Trade.
There haughty Dunces, whose unlearned
Pen   30
Could ne'er spell Grammar, would be reading
Men.
Such build their Poems the *Lucretian* way ;
So many Huddled Atoms make a Play,
And if they hit in Order by some Chance,
They call that Nature which is Ignorance.
To such a Fame let mere Town-Wits
aspire,
And their gay Nonsense their own Citts
admire.
Our Poet, could he find Forgiveness here,
Would wish it rather than a *Plaudit* there.
He owns no Crown from those *Prætorian*
Bands,   40
But knows *that* Right is in this Senates
Hands.
Not impudent enough to hope your Praise, ⎫
Low at the Muses Feet, his Wreath he lays, ⎬
And, where he took it up, resigns his Bays. ⎭
Kings make their Poets whom themselves
think fit.
But 'tis your Suffrage makes Authentique
Wit.

EPILOGUE.

Spoken by MR. HART.

No poor *Dutch* Peasant, wing'd with all his
Fear,
Flies with more haste, when the *French* Arms
draw near,
Than we with our Poetique Train come
down,
For Refuge hither from th' infected Town ;
Heaven for our Sins this Summer has thought
fit
To visit us with all the Plagues of Wit.

A *French* Troop first swept all things in
its way ;
But those hot *Monsieurs* were too quick to
stay ;
Yet, to our Cost, in that short time, we find
They left their Itch of Novelty behind.   10
Th' *Italian* Merry-Andrews took their
place,
And quite debauch'd the Stage with lewd
Grimace :
Instead of Wit and Humours, your Delight
Was there to see two Hobby-horses fight,
Stout *Scaramoucha* with Rush Lance rode in,
And ran a Tilt at Centaure *Arlequin.*
For Love you heard how amorous Asses
bray'd,
And Cats in Gutters gave their Serenade.
Nature was out of Countenance, and each
Day
Some new-born Monster shewn you for a
Play.   20
But when all fail'd, to strike the Stage
quite dumb,
Those wicked Engines, call'd Machines, are
come.
Thunder and Lightning now for Wit are
play'd.
And shortly Scenes in *Lapland* will be lay'd :
Art Magique is for Poetry profest,
And Cats and Dogs, and each obscener Beast
To which *Ægyptian* Dotards once did bow,
Upon our *English* Stage are worshipp'd now.
Witchcraft reigns there, and raises to Renown
Macbeth, the *Simon Magus* of the town.   30
Fletcher's despis'd, your *Johnson* out of
Fashion,
And Wit the onely Drug in all the Nation.
In this low Ebb our Wares to you are ⎫
shown,   ⎪
By you those Staple Authours Worth is ⎬
known ;   ⎪
For Wit's a Manufacture of your own. ⎭
When you, who only can, their scenes have
prais'd,
We'll boldly back, and say their Price is
rais'd.

Epilogue 30 the *Simon*] and Simon *1692, and
most editors. Christie wrongly ascribes the
error to Broughton.*

PROLOGUE AND EPILOGUE *Spoken at the opening of the New House,*
MARCH 26, 1674.

PROLOGUE.

A Plain built House, after so long a stay,
Will send you half unsatisfi'd away ;
When, fall'n from your expected Pomp, you find
A bare convenience only is designed.
You, who each Day can Theatres behold,
Like *Nero's* Palace, shining all with Gold,
Our mean ungilded Stage will scorn, we fear,
And for the homely Room, disdain the Chear.
Yet now cheap Druggets to a Mode are
   grown,
And a plain Suit (since we can make but
   one)   10
Is better than to be by tarnisht gawdry
   known.
They, who are by your Favours wealthy
   made,
With mighty Sums may carry on the Trade :
We, broken Banquiers, half destroy'd by
   Fire,
With our small Stock to humble Roofs
   retire ;
Pity our Loss, while you their Pomp
   admire.
For Fame and Honour we no longer strive ;
We yield in both, and only beg to live ;
Unable to support their vast Expense,
Who build and treat with such Magnificence,
That, like th' Ambitious Monarchs of the
   Age,   21
They give the Law to our Provincial Stage.
Great Neibours enviously promote Excess,
While they impose their Splendor on the
   less ;
But only Fools, and they of vast Estate,
Th' extremity of Modes will imitate,
The dangling Knee-fringe and the Bib-
   cravat.
Yet if some Pride with want may be allow'd,
We in our plainness may be justly proud ;
Our Royal Master will'd it should be so; 30
Whate'er he's pleased to own can need no
   show ;

That sacred Name gives Ornament and
   Grace ;
And, like his Stamp, makes basest Mettals
   pass.
'Twere Folly now a stately Pile to raise,
To build a Play-house, while you throw down
   Plays ;
Whilst Scenes, Machines, and empty *Opera's*
   reign,
And for the Pencil you the Pen disdain ;
While Troops of famish'd *Frenchmen* hither
   drive,
And laugh at those upon whose Alms they
   live :   39
Old *English* Authors vanish, and give place
To these new Conqu'rors of the *Norman*
   Race.
More tamely than your Fathers you submit ;
You're now grown Vassals to 'em in your Wit.
Mark, when they play, how our fine Fops
   advance
The Mighty Merits of these Men of *France*,
Keep time, cry *Ben*, and humour the
   Cadence.
Well, please your selves; but sure 'tis under-
   stood,
That *French* Machines have ne'er done
   England good.
I would not prophesie our Houses Fate ;
But while vain Shows and Scenes you over-
   rate,   50
'Tis to be feared ——
That, as a Fire the former House o'erthrew,
Machines and Tempests will destroy the new.

EPILOGUE.

Though what our Prologue said was sadly
   true,
Yet, Gentlemen, our homely House is new.
A Charm that seldom fails with wicked
   you.
A Country Lip may have the Velvet touch :
Tho' she's no Lady, you may think her
   such :
A strong Imagination may do much.

PROLOGUE AND EPILOGUE AT THE OPENING,
1674. First printed in 1684.

Prologue 46 *Ben*] *Many editions give Bon*

But you, loud Sirs, who thro' your Curls
    look big,
Criticks in plume and white vallancy Wig,
Who lolling on our foremost Benches sit,
And still charge first, (the true forlorn of
    Wit)   10
Whose favours, like the Sun, warm where
    you roul,
Yet you, like him, have neither heat nor
    Soul ;
So may your Hats your Foretops never
    press,
Untouch'd your Ribbons, sacred be your
    Dress ;
So may you slowly to old Age advance,
And have th' Excuse of Youth for Ignorance;
So may Fop corner full of Noise remain,
And drive far off the dull, attentive Train;
So may your Midnight Scowrings happy
    prove,
And Morning Batt'ries force your way to
    love ;   20
So may not *France* your Warlike Hands
    recal,
But leave you by each other's Swords to fall,
As you come here to ruffle Vizard Punk,
When sober rail, and roar when you are
    drunk.

But to the Wits we can some Merit plead,
And urge what by themselves has oft been
    said :
Our House relieves the Ladies from the
    frights
Of ill-pav'd Streets, and long dark Winter
    Nights ;
The *Flanders* Horses from a cold bleak Road,
Where Bears in Furs dare scarcely look
    abroad ;   30
The Audience from worn Plays and Fustian
    Stuff
Of Rhime, more nauseous than three Boys
    in Buff.
Though in their House the Poets Heads
    appear,
We hope we may presume their Wits are here.
The best which they reserv'd they now
    will play,
For, like kind Cuckcolds, tho' w' have not
    the way
To please, we'll find you abler Men who
    may.
If they shou'd fail, for last Recruits we
    breed
A Troop of frisking Monsiers to succeed.
(You know the *French* sure Cards at time
    of need.)   40

PROLOGUE AND EPILOGUE TO THE UNIVERSITY
OF OXFORD.

PROLOGUE.

Spoken by MR. HART.

POETS, your Subjects, have their Parts
    assign'd,
T' unbend and to divert their Sov'reign's
    Mind :
When, tyr'd with following Nature, you
    think fit
To seek repose in the cool shades of Wit,
And from the sweet Retreat, with Joy survey
What rests, and what is conquer'd, of the
    way.
Here, free your selves from Envy, Care, and
    Strife,
You view the various Turns of humane Life ;

PROLOGUE AND EPILOGUE TO THE UNIVERSITY
OF OXFORD, 1674. Printed twice over in the
Miscellanies of 1684.

Safe in our Scene, through dangerous Courts
    you go,
And undebauch'd the Vice of Cities know. 10
Your Theories are here to Practice brought,
As in Mechanick Operations wrought ;
And Man, the little World, before you set,
As once the Sphere of Chrystal Shew'd the
    Great.
Blest sure are you above all Mortal Kind,
If to your Fortunes you can suit your
    Mind ;
Content to see, and shun, those ills we show,
And Crimes, on Theatres alone, to know.
With joy we bring what our dead Authors
    writ,
And beg from you the value of their Wit : 20
That *Shakespear's, Fletcher's,* and great *John-
son's* Claim
May be renew'd from those who gave them
    Fame.

None of our living Poets dare appear ;
For Muses so severe are worshipt here
That, conscious of their Faults, they shun
   the Eye,
And, as Prophane, from sacred Places fly,
Rather than see th' offended God, and dye.
We bring no Imperfections, but our own ;
Such Faults as made are by the Makers
   shown,
And you have been so kind that we may
   boast, 30
The greatest Judges still can pardon most.
Poets must stoop, when they would please
   our Pit,
Debas'd even to the Level of their Wit ;
Disdaining that which yet they know will
   take,
Hating themselves what their Applause must
   make.
But when to Praise from you they would
   aspire,
Though they like Eagles mount, your *Jove*
   is higher.
So far your Knowledge all their Pow'r tran-
   scends,
As what *should* be beyond what *Is*, extends.

EPILOGUE.

Spoken by MRS. MARSHALL.

Oft has our Poet wisht, this happy Seat
Might prove his fading Muses last Retreat :
I wonder'd at his Wish, but now I find
He sought for quiet, and content of mind ;
Which noisefull Towns and Courts can never
   know,

And onely in the shades, like Laurels, grow.
Youth, e'er it sees the World, here studies
   Rest,
And Age, returning thence, concludes it best.
What wonder if we court that happiness,
Yearly to share, which hourly you possess ;
Teaching ev'n you, while the vext World we
   show, 11
Your Peace to value more, and better know
'Tis all we can return for favours past,
Whose holy Memory shall ever last,
For Patronage from him whose care presides
O'er every noble Art, and every Science
   guides :
Bathurst, a name the learn'd with reverence
   know,
And scarcely more to his own *Virgil* owe ;
Whose Age enjoys but what his Youth
   deserv'd, 19
To rule those Muses whom before he serv'd.
His Learning, and untainted Manners too,
We find (*Athenians*) are deriv'd to you ;
Such Antient Hospitality there rests
In yours, as dwelt in the first *Grecian*
   Breasts,
Whose kindness was Religion to their
   Guests.
Such Modesty did to our Sex appear,
As had there been no Laws we need not
   fear,
Since each of you was our Protector here.
Converse so chast, and so strict Vertue
   shown,
As might *Apollo* with the Muses own. 30
Till our return, we must despair to find
Judges so just, so knowing, and so kind.

PROLOGUE AND EPILOGUE TO AURENG-ZEBE

PROLOGUE.

OUR Author by experience finds it true,
'Tis much more hard to please himself than
   you ;
And out of no feign'd Modesty, this day,
Damns his laborious Trifle of a Play;
Not that its worse than what before he writ,
But he has now another taste of Wit;

And, to confess a Truth (though out of
   Time,)
Grows weary of his long-loved Mistris Rhyme.
Passion's too fierce to be in Fetters bound, 9
And Nature flies him like Enchanted Ground:
What Verse can do he has perform'd in this,
Which he presumes the most correct of his;
But spite of all his pride, a secret shame
Invades his Breast at *Shakespear's* sacred
   name :

Epilogue 4 sought for] *One version has here*
sought

AURENG-ZEBE, 1675. Published in 1676.

Aw'd when he hears his Godlike *Romans*
rage,
He in a just despair would quit the Stage ;
And to an Age less polish'd, more unskill'd,
Does with disdain the foremost Honours
yield.
As with the greater Dead he dares not strive,
He wou'd not match his Verse with those
who live :   20
Let him retire, betwixt two Ages cast,
The first of this, and hindmost of the last.
A losing Gamester, let him sneak away;
He bears no ready Money from the Play.
The Fate which governs Poets, thought it fit,
He shou'd not raise his Fortunes by his Wit.
The Clergy thrive, and the litigious Bar ;
Dull Heroes fatten with the Spoils of War:
All Southern Vices, Heav'n be prais'd, are
here ;
But Wit's a Luxury you think too dear.   30
When you to cultivate the Plant are loth,
'Tis a shrewd sign 'twas never of your
growth :
And Wit in Northern Climates will not blow,
Except, like *Orange-trees*, 'tis hous'd from
Snow.
There needs no care to put a Play-house
down,
'Tis the most desart place of all the Town :
We and our Neighbours, to speak proudly,
are
Like Monarchs, ruin'd with expensive War ;
While, like wise *English*, unconcern'd you
sit,
And see us play the Tragedy of Wit.   40

EPILOGUE.

A pretty task ! and so I told the Fool,
Who needs would undertake to please by
Rule :
He thought that, if his Characters were good,
The Scenes entire, and freed from noise and
bloud ;
The Action great, yet circumscrib'd by Time,
The Words not forc'd, but sliding into
Rhime,
The Passions rais'd and calm'd by just
Degrees,
As Tides are swell'd, and then retire to Seas ;

He thought in hitting these his bus'ness
done,
Though he perhaps has fail'd in ev'ry one : 10
But, after all, a Poet must confess,
His Art's, like Physick, but a happy ghess.
Your Pleasure on your Fancy must depend :
The Lady's pleas'd, just as she likes her
Friend.
No Song ! no Dance ! no Show ! he fears
you'l say :
You love all naked Beauties, but a Play.
He much mistakes your methods to delight;)
And, like the *French*, abhors our Target-
fight :
But those damn'd Dogs can never be i' th'
right.
True *English* hate your Monsieur's paltry
Arts,   20
For you are all Silk-weavers, in your hearts.
Bold *Brittons*, at a brave Bear-garden Fray,
Are rouz'd ; and, clatt'ring Sticks, cry, *Play,
play, play.*
Meantime, your filthy Forreigner will stare,
And mutter to himself, *Ha gens Barbare* !
And, Gad, 'tis well he mutters ; well for him ;
Our Butchers else would tear him limb from
limb.
'Tis true, the time may come, your Sons may
be
Infected with this *French* civility :
But this in After-ages will be done :   30
Our Poet writes a hundred years too soon.
This Age comes on too slow, or he too fast ;
And early Springs are subject to a blast !
Who would excel, when few can make a Test
Betwixt indiff'rent Writing and the best ?
For Favours cheap and common, who wou'd
strive,
Which, like abandoned Prostitutes, you
give ?
Yet scatter'd here and there, I some behold,
Who can discern the Tinsel from the Gold :
To these he writes ; and, if by them allow'd,
'Tis their Prerogative to rule the Crowd. 41
For he more fears (like a presuming Man)
Their Votes who cannot judge, than theirs
who can.

Epilogue 18 and 29 *French*] French *1676.*
22 *Brittons*] Brittons *1676.*
25 *gens*] *Saintsbury conjectures* gent

EPILOGUE TO CALISTO, OR THE CHASTE NYMPH.

Intended to have been spoken by the LADY HENRIETTA MARIA WENTWORTH, *when* Calisto *was Acted at Court.*

As *Jupiter* I made my Court in vain ;
I'll now assume my Native shape again.
I'm weary to be so unkindly us'd,
And would not be a God to be refus'd.
State grows uneasie when it hinders Love ;
A glorious Burden, which the wise remove.
Now, as a Nymph, I need not sue, nor try
The force of any lightning but the Eye.
Beauty and Youth more than a God command ;
No *Jove* could e'er the force of these withstand. 10
'Tis here that Sovereign Power admits dispute,
Beauty sometimes is justly absolute.
Our sullen *Catoes*, whatsoe'er they say,
Even while they frown and dictate Laws, obey.
You, mighty Sir, our bonds more easie make,
And gracefully what all must suffer take ;
Above those forms the Grave affect to wear,
For 'tis not to be wise to be severe.

True wisdom may some gallantry admit,
And soften business with the charms of wit.
These peaceful Triumphs with your Cares you bought, 21
And from the midst of fighting Nations brought.
You only hear it thunder from afar,
And sit in peace the Arbiter of War :
Peace, the loath'd Manna, which hot Brains despise,
You knew its worth, and made it early prize :
And in its happy leisure sit and see
The promises of more felicity.
Two glorious Nymphs of your one God-like line,
Whose Morning Rays like Noontide strike and shine ; 30
Whom you to suppliant Monarchs shall dispose,
To bind your Friends and to disarm your Foes.

EPILOGUE TO THE MAN OF MODE, OR SIR FOPLING FLUTTER.

MOST Modern Wits such monstrous Fools have shown,
They seem not of heav'ns making, but their own.
Those Nauseous Harlequins in Farce may pass ;
But there goes more to a substantial Ass !
Something of man must be expos'd to View,
That, Gallants, they may more resemble you.
Sir *Fopling* is a Fool so nicely writ,
The Ladies wou'd mistake him for a Wit ;
And, when he sings, talks lowd, and cocks, wou'd cry,
I vow methinks he's pretty Company ! 10

So brisk, so gay, so travail'd, so refin'd !
As he took pains to graff upon his kind.
True Fops help Natures work, and go to school,
To file and finish god-A'mighty's fool.
Yet none Sir *Fopling* him, or him can call ;
He's Knight o' th' Shire, and represents ye all.
From each he meets he culls whate're he can,
Legion's his name, a people in a Man.
His bulky folly gathers as it goes,
And, rolling o're you, like a Snow-ball growes. 20
His various Modes from various Fathers follow ;
One taught the Toss, and one the new *French* Wallow ;

CALISTO. Printed in 1684 but not assigned to Dryden till 1704. The play is by Crowne.

THE MAN OF MODE, 1676. The play is by Etherege.

His Sword-knot this, his Crevat this design'd ;
And this the yard long Snake he twirls behind.
From one the sacred Perriwig he gain'd,
Which Wind ne'er blew, nor touch of Hat prophan'd.
Another's diving Bow he did adore,
Which with a shog casts all the hair before,
Till he with full Decorum brings it back,
And rises with a Water Spaniel shake.   30
As for his Songs (the Ladies dear Delight)
Those sure he took from most of you who Write.
Yet every man is safe from what he fear'd ;
For no one fool is hunted from the herd.

PROLOGUE TO CIRCE.

Were you but half so wise as you're severe,
Our youthfull Poet shou'd not need to fear ;
To his green years your Censures you would suit,
Not blast the Blossom, but expect the Fruit.
The Sex that best does pleasure understand
Will alwayes chuse to err on t'other hand.
They check not him that's aukard in delight,
But clap the young Rogues Cheek, and set him right.
Thus heartn'd well, and flesh't upon his Prey,
The youth may prove a man another day.   10
Your *Ben* and *Fletcher*, in their first young flight,
Did no *Volpone*, no *Arbaces* write ;
But hopp'd about, and short Excursions made
From Bough to Bough, as if they were afraid,
And each were guilty of some *Slighted Maid*.

Shakespear's own Muse her *Pericles* first bore ;
The Prince of *Tyre* was elder than the *Moore*.
'Tis miracle to see a first good Play ;
All Hawthorns do not bloom on *Christmas-day*.
A slender Poet must have time to grow,   20
And spread and burnish as his Brothers do.
Who still looks lean, sure with some *pox* is curst,
But no Man can be *Falstaff*-fat at first,
Then damn not, but indulge his stew'd Essays,
Encourage him, and bloat him up with Praise,
That he may get more bulk before he dies,
He's not yet fed enough for Sacrifice.
Perhaps, if now your Grace you will not grudge,
He may grow up to write, and you to judge.

EARLIER VERSION OF PROLOGUE TO CIRCE.

Were you but half so wise as y' are severe,
Our youthful Poet shou'd not need to fear ;
To his green years your Censures you wou'd suit,
Not blast the Blossom, but expect the Fruit.
The Sex that best does pleasure understand
Will alwayes chuse to err on t'other hand.
They check not him that's Aukward in delight,
But clap the young Rogues Cheek, and set him right.

Thus heartn'd well, and flesh't upon his Prey,
The youth may prove a man another day.   10
For your own sakes, instruct him when he's out,
You'll find him mend his work at every bout.
When some young lusty Thief is passing by,
How many of your tender Kind will cry,
A proper Fellow ! pity he should dye !
He might be sav'd, and thank us for our pains,
There's such a stock of Love within his Veins.

CIRCE, 1677. Two versions of this Prologue. The play is by Charles Davenant.
12 no] *Scott and others wrongly give* nor no
15 were] *Scott and others wrongly give* was

24 stew'd] *This can hardly be right. Scott and others give* rude   *Dr. Aldis Wright conjectured* sterv'd *and this may well be right.*

These Arguments the Women may persuade,
But move not you, the Brothers of the Trade,
Who, scattering your Infection through
    the Pit,   20
With aking Hearts and empty Purses sit,
To take your dear five Shillings worth of
    Wit.
The Praise you give him in your kindest mood
Comes dribling from you, just like drops of
    Blood ;
And then you clap so civilly, for fear
The loudness might offend your Neighbours
    ear,

That we suspect your Gloves are lin'd
    within,
For silence sake, and Cotten'd next the
    skin.
From these Usurpers we appeal to you,
The only knowing, only judging few ;   30
You, who in private have this Play allow'd,
Ought to maintain your Suffrage to the
    Crowd.
The Captive, once submitted to your
    Bands,
You should protect from Death by Vulgar
    hands.

PROLOGUE AND EPILOGUE TO ALL FOR LOVE, OR THE WORLD WELL LOST.

PROLOGUE.

WHAT Flocks of Critiques hover here to-day,
As Vultures wait on Armies for their Prey,
All gaping for the Carcase of a Play !)
With croaking Notes they bode some dire
    event,
And follow dying Poets by the scent.
Ours gives himself for gone; y' have watch'd
    your Time ;
He fights this day unarm'd, without his
    Rhyme,
And brings a Tale which often has been told,
As sad as *Dido's*, and almost as old.
His Heroe, whom you Wits his Bully call, 10
Bates of his Mettle, and scarce rants at all ;
He's somewhat lewd, but a well-meaning
    mind,
Weeps much, fights little, but is wondrous
    kind ;
In short, a Pattern and Companion fit
For all the keeping *Tonyes* of the Pit.
I cou'd name more : A Wife, and Mistress
    too,
Both (to be plain) too good for most of
    you ;
The Wife well-natur'd, and the Mistress
    true.
  Now, Poets, if your fame has been his
    Care,
Allow him all the Candour you can spare. 20

A brave Man scorns to quarrel once a
    day,
Like Hectors in at ev'ry petty fray.
Let those find fault whose Wit's so very
    small,
They've need to show that they can think
    at all.
Errors, like Straws, upon the surface flow ;
He who would scarch for Pearls must dive
    below.
Fops may have leave to level all they can,
As Pigmies wou'd be glad to lop a Man.
Half-wits are Fleas, so little and so light,
We scarce cou'd know they live, but that
    they bite.   30
But, as the rich, when tir'd with daily
    Feasts,
For Change become their next poor Tenants
    Ghests ;
Drink hearty Draughts of Ale from plain
    brown Bowls,
And snatch the homely Rasher from the
    Coals :
So you, retiring from much better Cheer,
For once may venture to do penance
    here.
And since that plenteous Autumn now is
    past,
Whose Grapes and Peaches have indulg'd
    your Taste,
Take in good Part from our poor Poets
    boord
Such rivell'd Fruits as Winter can afford. 40

EPILOGUE.

Poets, like Disputants, when Reasons fail,
Have one sure Refuge left, and that's to
   rail.
Fop, Coxcomb, Fool, are thunder'd through
   the Pit,
And this is all their Equipage of Wit.
We wonder how the Devil this diff'rence
   grows,
Betwixt our Fools in Verse, and yours in
   Prose:
For, 'Faith, the Quarrel rightly under-
   stood,
'Tis *Civil War* with their own Flesh and
   Blood.
The thread-bare Author hates the gawdy
   Coat,
And swears at the Guilt Coach, but swears
   afoot: 10
For 'tis observ'd of ev'ry Scribling Man,
He grows a Fop as fast as e'er he can;
Prunes up, and asks his Oracle the Glass,
If Pink or Purple best become his Face.

For our poor Wretch, he neither rails nor
   prays,
Nor likes your Wit just as you like his Plays;
He has not yet so much of Mr. *Bays.*
He does his best; and if he cannot please,
Wou'd quietly sue out his *Writ of Ease.*
Yet, if he might his own grand Jury call, 20
By the Fair Sex he begs to stand or fall.
Let *Cæsar's* Pow'r the Mens Ambition move,
But grace you him, who lost the World for
   Love!
Yet if some antiquated Lady say,
The last Age is not copy'd in his Play;
Heav'n help the man who for that face must
   drudge,
Which only has the wrinkles of a Judge.
Let not the Young and Beauteous join with
   those;
For shou'd you raise such numerous Hosts of
   Foes,
Young Wits and Sparks he to his aid must
   call;   30
'Tis more than one Man's work to please
   you all.

EPILOGUE TO MITHRIDATES, KING OF PONTUS.

You've seen a Pair of faithful Lovers
   die:
And much you care, for most of you will
   cry,
'Twas a just Judgment on their Constancy.
For, Heaven be thank'd, we live in such an
   Age,
When no man dies for Love, but on the
   Stage:
And ev'n those Martyrs are but rare in
   Plays;
A cursed sign how much true Faith
   decays:
Love is no more a violent desire;
'Tis a meer Metaphor, a painted Fire.
In all our Sex, the name examin'd well, 10
Is Pride to gain, and Vanity to tell.

In Woman, 'tis of subtil int'rest made;
Curse on the Punk that made it first a
   Trade!
She first did Wits Prerogative remove,
And made a Fool presume to prate of
   Love.
Let Honour and Preferment go for Gold,
But glorious Beauty is not to be sold;
Or, if it be, 'tis at a rate so high,
That nothing but adoring it shou'd buy.
Yet the rich Cullies may their boasting
   spare;   20
They purchase but sophisticated Ware.
'Tis Prodigality that brys deceit,
Where both the Giver, and the Taker
   cheat.
Men but refine on the old Half-Crown
   way;
And Women fight, like *Swizzers,* for their Pay.

MITHRIDATES, 1678.   The play is by Lee.

PROLOGUE AND EPILOGUE TO THE KIND KEEPER, OR MR. LIMBERHAM.

PROLOGUE

TRUE Wit has seen its best Days long ago ;
It ne'er look'd up since we were dipt in Show,
When sense in dogrel Rhymes and Clouds
    was lost,
And Dulness flourish'd at the Actors' Cost.
Nor stopt it here ; when Tragedy was done,
Satire and Humour the same Fate have run,
And Comedy is sunk to Trick and Pun.
Now our machining Lumber will not sell,
And you no longer care for Heav'n or Hell ;
What Stuff will please you next, the Lord
    can tell.   10
Let them, who the Rebellion first began
To Wit, restore the Monarch if they can ;
Our Author dares not be the first bold Man.
He, like the prudent Citizen, takes care
To keep for better Marts his staple Ware ;
His Toys are good enough for *Sturbridge* Fair.
Tricks were the Fashion ; if it now be spent,
'Tis time enough at Easter to invent ;
No man will make up a new Suit for Lent.
If now and then he takes a small Pretence, 20
To forage for a little Wit and Sense,
Pray pardon him, he meant you no Offence,
Next summer, *Nostradamus* tells, they say,
That all the Criticks shall be shipp'd away.
And not enow be left to damn a Play.
To every Sail beside, good Heav'n, be
    kind ;
But drive away that Swarm with such a
    Wind
That not one Locust may be left behind !

EPILOGUE.

Spoken by LIMBERHAM.

I beg a Boon, that, e're you all disband,
Some one would take my Bargain off my
    hand ;
To keep a Punk is but a common evil ;
To find her false, and Marry,— that's the
    Devil.
Well, I ne're acted Part in all my life,
But still I was fobb'd off with some such Wife
I find the Trick ; these Poets take no pity
Of one that is a Member of the City.
We Cheat you lawfully, and in our Trades ;
You Cheat us basely with your Common
    Jades.   10
Now I am Married, I must sit down by it ;
But let me keep my Dear-bought Spouse in
    quiet :
Let none of you Damn'd *Woodalls* of the Pit
Put in for Shares to mend our breed in Wit ;
We know your Bastards from our Flesh and
    Blood,
Not one in ten of yours e're comes to good.
In all the Boys their Fathers Vertues shine,
But all the Female Fry turn *Pugs*, like mine.
When these grow up, Lord, with what Ram-
    pant Gadders
Our Counters will be throng'd, and Roads
    with Padders.   20
This Town two Bargains has, not worth one
    farthing,
A *Smithfield* Horse, and Wife of *Covent-
    Garden.*

PROLOGUE TO THE TRUE WIDOW.

HEav'n save ye Gallants, and this hopeful
    Age,
Y' are welcome to the downfal of the Stage :
The Fools have labour'd long in their
    Vocation ;
And Vice (the Manufacture of the Nation)
O'erstocks the Town so much, and thrives
    so well,
That Fopps and Knaves grow Druggs, and
    will not sell.

In vain our Wares on Theaters are shown,
When each has a Plantation of his own.
His Cruse ne'r fails ; for whatsoe're he
    spends,
There's still God's Plenty for himself and
    friends.   10

THE TRUE WIDOW, 1678. The play is by
Shadwell. The Prologue was reprinted in 1690
with Aphra Behn's *The Widow Ranter.*
    9 Cruse] *Editors till Christie absurdly give*
Cause

THE KIND KEEPER, 1678.

Shou'd Men be rated by Poetick Rules,
Lord, what a Poll would there be rais'd from
    Fools !
Mean time poor Wit prohibited must lye,
As if 'twere made some *French* Commodity.
Fools you will have, and rais'd at vast
    expence,
And yet as soon as seen, they give offence.
Time was, when none wou'd cry that Oaf
    was mee,
But now you strive about your Pedigree.
Bauble and Cap no sooner are thrown down,
But there's a Muss of more than half the
    Town.   20
Each one will challenge a Child's part at
    least ;
A sign the Family is well increas'd :

Of Forreign Cattle there's no longer
    need,
When w'are supply'd so fast with *English*
    Breed.
Well ! Flourish, Countrymen ; drink, swear,
    and roar ;
Let every free-born Subject keep his
    Whore,
And wandring in the Wilderness about,
At end of 40 years not wear her out.·
But when you see these Pictures, let none
    dare
To own beyond a Limb, or single share ; 30
For where the Punk is common, he's a
    Sot
Who needs will father what the Parish
    got.

PROLOGUE AND EPILOGUE TO ŒDIPUS.

PROLOGUE.

WHEN *Athens* all the *Græcian* State did guide,
And *Greece* gave Laws to all the World beside;
Then *Sophocles* with *Socrates* did sit,
Supreme in Wisdom one, and one in Wit :
And Wit from Wisdom differ'd not in those,
But as 'twas Sung in Verse or said in Prose.
Then *Œdipus*, on crowded Theaters
Drew all admiring Eyes and listning Ears :
The pleas'd Spectator shouted every Line,
The noblest, manliest, and the best Design !
And every Critick of each learned Age   11
By this just Model has reform'd the Stage.
Now, should it fail, (as Heav'n avert our
    fear !)
Damn it in silence, lest the World should hear.
For were it known this Poem did not please,
You might set up for perfect Salvages :
Your Neighbours would not look on you as
    men :
But think the Nation all turned *Picts* agen.
Faith, as you manage matters, 'tis not fit
You should suspect your selves of too much
    Wit.   20
Drive not the jeast too far, but spare this
    piece ;
And for this once be not more Wise than
    Greece.

See twice ! Do not pell-mell to Damning fall,
Like true-born *Brittains*, who ne're think
    at all :
Pray be advis'd ; and though at *Mons* you
    won,
On pointed Cannon do not always run.
With some Respect to antient Wit proceed,
And take the four first Councils for your
    Creed.
But, when you lay Tradition wholly by, ⎫
And on the private Spirit alone relye,   30 ⎬
You turn Fanaticks in your Poetry. ⎭
If, notwithstanding all that we can say, ⎫
You needs will have your pen'worths of ⎪
    the Play, ⎬
And come resolv'd to Damn, because you ⎪
    pay, ⎭
Record it, in memorial of the Fact,
The first Play bury'd since the Wollen Act.

EPILOGUE.

WHAT *Sophocles* could undertake alone,
Our Poets found a Work for more than one ;
And therefore Two lay tugging at the piece,
With all their force, to draw the pondrous
    Mass from *Greece* ;
A weight that bent ev'n *Seneca's* strong
    Muse,
And which *Corneille's* Shoulders did refuse :

ŒDIPUS, 1678. Published in 1679.
Prologue 1 State] *Edd. give* states

Prologue 28 four first] *Christie and others
wrongly give* first four

So hard it is th' *Athenian* Harp to string !
So much two Consuls yield to one just King.
Terrour and Pity this whole Poem sway ;
The mightiest Machines that can mount
   a Play ;   10
How heavy will those Vulgar Souls be found,
Whom two such Engines cannot move from
   Ground !
When *Greece* and *Rome* have smil'd upon
   this Birth,
You can but damn for one poor spot of Earth ;
And when your Children find your judgment
   such,
They'll scorn their Sires, and wish them-
   selves born *Dutch* ;
Each haughty Poet will infer with ease,
How much his Wit must under-write to
   please.
As some strong Churle would brandishing
   advance
The monumental Sword that conquer'd
   France,   20

So you by judging this your judgments
   teach,
Thus far you like, that is, thus far you reach.
Since then the Vote of full two Thousand
   years
Has Crown'd this Plot, and all the Dead are
   theirs,
Think it a Debt you pay, not Alms you
   give,
And in your own defence let this Play live.
Think 'em not vain, when *Sophocles* is
   shown,
To praise his worth, they humbly doubt their
   own.
Yet as weak States each other's pow'r
   assure,
Weak Poets by Conjunction are secure. 30
Their Treat is what your Pallats rellish most,
Charm ! Song ! and Show ! a Murder and
   a Ghost !
We know not what you can desire or hope,
To please you more, but burning of a *Pope*.

PROLOGUE AND EPILOGUE TO TROILUS AND CRESSIDA, OR TRUTH FOUND TOO LATE.

PROLOGUE.

Spoken by MR. BETTERTON, *representing
the Ghost of* SHAKSPEAR.

SEE, my lov'd *Britons*, see your *Shakespeare*
   rise,
An awfull Ghost confess'd to human Eyes !
Unnam'd, methinks, distinguish'd I had
   been
From other Shades by this eternal Green,
About whose Wreaths the vulgar Poets strive,
And with a Touch, their wither'd Bays
   revive.
Untaught, unpractis'd, in a barbarous Age,
I found not, but created first the Stage.
And if I drain'd no *Greek* or *Latin* Store,
'Twas that my own Abundance gave me
   more.   10
On foreign Trade I needed not rely,
Like fruitfull *Britain*, rich without Supply.
In this my rough-drawn Play, you shall
   behold
Some Master-strokes, so manly and so bold

That he, who meant to alter, found 'em such
He shook ; and thought it Sacrilege to touch.
Now, where are the Successors to my Name ?
What bring they to fill out a Poets Fame ?
Weak, short-liv'd Issues of a feeble Age ;
Scarce living to be Christen'd on the Stage !
For Humour Farce, for Love they Rhyme
   dispence,   21
That tolls the Knell for their departed Sence.
Dulness might thrive in any Trade but this :
'Twould recommend to some fat Benefice.
Dulness, that in a Playhouse meets Disgrace,
Might meet with Reverence in its proper
   place.
The fulsome Clench that nauseats the town
Wou'd from a Judge or Alderman go down !
Such Virtue is there in a Robe and Gown !
And that insipid Stuff which here you hate,
Might somewhere else be call'd a grave
   Debate ;   31
Dulness is decent in the Church and State.
But I forget that still 'tis understood,
Bad Plays are best decry'd by showing good :

ŒDIPUS, 1678. Epilogue 9 Pity] pity *1678.*
10 mount] *Christie wrongly gives* move

TROILUS AND CRESSIDA, 1679. The original
text is careless in the use of capitals.

Sit silent then, that my pleas'd Soul may see
A Judging Audience once, and worthy me :
My faithful Scene from true Records shall
   tell,
How *Trojan* Valour did the *Greek* excell ;
Your great Forefathers shall their Fame
   regain,
And *Homers* angry Ghost repine in vain. 40

EPILOGUE.

Spoken by THERSITES.

These cruel Critiques put me into Passion,
For in their lowring Looks I reade Damna-
   tion :
You expect a Satyr, and I seldom fail ;
When I'm first beaten, 'tis my Part to rail.
You *British* Fools of the old *Trojan* Stock,
That stand so thick one cannot miss the
   Flock,
Poets have cause to dread a keeping Pit,
When Womens Cullyes come to judge of Wit.
As we strew Rats-bane when we Vermine
   fear,
'Twere worth our Cost to scatter Fool-bane
   here ;   10

And after all our judging Fops were serv'd,
Dull Poets too shou'd have a Dose reserv'd,
Such Reprobates as, past all Sence of
   Shaming,
Write on, and nere are satisfy'd with
   Damming,
Next, those, to whom the Stage does not
   belong
Such whose Vocation onely is to Song,
At most to Prologue ; when for Want of
   Time
Poets take in for Journeywork in Rhime.
But I want Curses for those mighty Shoales
Of scribling *Chlorisses*, and *Phillis* Fools : 20
Those Ophs should be restrain'd, during their
   Lives,
From Pen and Ink, as Madmen are from
   Knives :
I cou'd rayl on, but 'twere a Task as vain
As Preaching Truth at *Rome*, or Wit in
   Spain :
Yet to huff out our Play was worth my
   trying ;
John Lilbourn scap'd his Judges by defying.
If guilty, yet I'm sure oth'Churches Blessing,
By suffering for the Plot, without confessing.

PROLOGUE TO CÆSAR BORGIA, SON OF POPE ALEXANDER THE SIXTH.

Th' unhappy man who once has trail'd a
   Pen,
Lives not to please himself, but other
   men ;
Is always drudging, wasts his Life and
   Blood,
Yet only eats and drinks what you think
   good.
What praise soe're the Poetry deserve,
Yet every Fool can bid the Poet starve.
That fumbling Lecher to revenge is bent,
Because he thinks himself or Whore is
   meant :
Name but a Cuckold, all the City swarms ;
From *Leaden-hall* to *Ludgate* is in Arms.   10
Were there no fear of *Antichrist* or *France*,
In the best times poor Poets live by chance.

Either you come not here, or, as you grace
Some old acquaintance, drop into the place,
Careless and qualmish with a yawning Face.
You sleep o're Wit, and by my troth you
   may ;
Most of your Talents lye another way.
You love to hear of some prodigious Tale,
The Bell that tolled alone, or *Irish* Whale.
News is your Food, and you enough provide,
Both for your selves and all the World
   beside.   21
One Theatre there is of vast resort,
Which whilome of Requests was called the
   Court.
But now the great *Exchange* of News 'tis
   hight,
And full of hum and buzz from Noon till
   Night :
Up Stairs and down you run, as for a Race,
And each Man wears three Nations in his
   Face.

CÆSAR BORGIA, 1680.   The play is by Lee.
12 best] *Editors till Christie wrongly give*
blest
times] *The editors wrongly give* time

So big you look, tho' Claret you retrench,
That, arm'd with bottled Ale, you huff the
    French.
But all your Entertainment still is fed   30
By Villains in our own dull Island bred :
Would you return to us, we dare engage
To show you better Rogues upon the Stage.
You know no Poison but plain Rats-bane
    here ;
Death's more refind, and better bred else-
    where.

They have a civil way in *Italy*
By smelling a perfume to make you dye,
A Trick would make you lay your Snuff-
    box by.
Murder's a Trade—so known and practis'd
    there,
That 'tis Infallible as is the Chair ―― 40
But mark their Feasts, you shall behold
    such Pranks ;
The Pope says Grace, but 'tis the Devil gives
    Thanks.

THE PROLOGUE AT OXFORD, 1680.

THespis, the first Professor of our Art,
At Country Wakes, Sung Ballads in a Cart.
To prove this true, if *Latin* be no Trespass,
Dicitur et Plaustris vexisse Poemata Thespis.
But *Eschylus*, says *Horace* in some Page,
Was the first Mountebank e'er trod the Stage ;
Yet *Athens* never knew your learned Sport
Of tossing Poets in a *Tennis-Court*.
But 'tis the Talent of our *English* Nation
Still to be plotting some new Reformation ;
And few years hence, if anarchy go on,   11
Jack Presbyter will here erect his Throne,
Knock out a Tub with Preaching once a Day.
And every Prayer be longer than a Play.
Then all you Heathen Wits shall go to pot
For disbelieving of a Popish plot :

Nor should we want the Sentence to
    depart
Ev'n in our first Original, a Cart.
Occham, Dun Scotus, must though learn'd go
    down,
As chief Supporters of the Triple Crown. 20
And *Aristotle* for destruction ripe :
Some say he call'd the Soul an Organ-pipe,
Which, by some little help of Derivation,
Shall thence be call'd a Pipe of Inspiration.
Your wiser Judgments further penetrate
Who late found out one Tare amongst the
    Wheat,
This is our Comfort : none e'er cried us
    down
But who disturb'd both Bishop and a Crown.

PROLOGUE TO THE LOYAL GENERAL.

IF yet there be a few that take delight ⎫
In that which reasonable Men should write, ⎬
To them Alone we Dedicate this Night. ⎭
The Rest may satisfie their curious Itch
With City Gazets, or some Factious Speech,
Or what-ere Libel, for the Publick Good,
Stirs up the Shrove-tide Crew to Fire and
    Blood.

Remove your Benches, you apostate Pit,
And take Above, twelve penny-worth of Wit ;
Go back to your dear Dancing on the Rope, 10
Or see what's worse, the Devil and the Pope !
The Plays that take on our Corrupted Stage,
Methinks, resemble the distracted Age ;

16 *After this line in 1684 this couplet :*
Your Poets shall be us'd like Infidels,
And worst the Author of the *Oxford Bells.*
17 want] scape *1684.*
18 *After this line in 1684 these couplets :*
No Zealous Brother there would want a Stone,
To maul Us Cardinals, and pelt Pope *Joan.*
Religion, Learning, Wit, would be supprest,
Rags of the Whore, and Trappings of the Beast.
19. *This line in 1684 thus :*
Scot, *Swarez, Tom of Aquin,* must go down.
21 *Aristotle*] Aristotle's *1684.*
24 thence be call'd] then be prov'd *1684.*
25-28. *Omitted 1684.*
THE LOYAL GENERAL, 1680. The play is by Tate.

CÆSAR BORGIA, 1680.
    31 our] *Some editors wrongly give* your
41 Feasts] *Some editors wrongly give* Feast
THE PROLOGUE AT OXFORD, 1680. The text as
given with Nat. Lee's tragedy of *Sophonisba*, for
which the Prologue was written. The variants
below are from the version in the *Miscellany
Poems.*
2 in] from *1684.*
5 *Eschylus*] Escalus *1684.*
6 e'er] that *1684.*   11 go] goes *1684.*
12 will] shall *1684.*   15 you] your *1684.*

Noise, Madness, all unreasonable Things,
That strike at Sense, as Rebels do at Kings!
The stile of Forty One our Poets write, 16
And you are grown to judge like Forty Eight.
Such Censures our mistaking Audience make,
That 'tis almost grown scandalous to take.
They talk of Feavours that infect the Brains;
But Non-sence is the new Disease that reigns.
Weak Stomachs, with a long Disease opprest,
Cannot the Cordials of strong Wit digest;
Therefore thin Nourishment of Farce ye
choose, 24
Decoctions of a Barly-water Muse:

A Meal of Tragedy wou'd make ye Sick,
Unless it were a very tender Chick.
Some Scenes in Sippets would be worth our
time:
Those wou'd go down; some Love that's
poach'd in Rime:
If these shou'd fail —— 30
We must lie down, and, after all our cost,
Keep Holy-day, like Water-men in Frost;
Whilst you turn Players on the Worlds
great Stage,
And Act your selves the Farce of your own
Age.

PROLOGUE TO THE SPANISH FRYAR, OR THE DOUBLE DISCOVERY.

Now, Luck for us, and a kind hearty Pit,
For he who pleases, never failes of Wit.
Honour is yours:
And you, like Kings at City Treats, bestow it;
The Writer kneels, and is bid rise a Poet.
But you are fickle Sovereigns, to our Sorrow;
You dubb to day, and hang a man tomorrow:
You cry the same Sense up, and down again,
Just like brass Money once a year in *Spain*:
Take you i' th' mood, what e'er base metal
come, 10
You coin as fast as Groats at *Bromingam*;
Though 'tis no more like Sense in ancient
Plays
Than *Rome's* religion like St. *Peter's* days.
In short, so swift your Judgments turn and
wind,
You cast our fleetest Wits a mile behind.
'Twere well your Judgments but in Plays did
range,
But ev'n your Follies and Debauches change
With such a Whirl, the Poets of your Age
Are tyr'd, and cannot score 'em on the Stage,
Unless each Vice in short-hand they indite, 20
Ev'n as notcht Prentices whole Sermons
write.
The heavy *Hollanders* no Vices know, ⎞
But what they us'd a hundred years ago; ⎟
Like honest Plants, where they were stuck, ⎟
they grow; ⎠

They cheat, but still from cheating Sires they
come;
They drink, but they were christen'd first in
Mum.
Their patrimonial Sloth the *Spaniards* keep,
And *Philip* first taught *Philip* how to sleep.
The *French* and we still change; but here's
the Curse,
They change for better, and we change for
worse; 30
They take up our old trade of Conquering,
And we are taking theirs, to dance and sing:
Our Fathers did for change to *France* repair,
And they for change will try our *English* Air.
As Children, when they throw one Toy away,
Straight a more foolish Gugaw comes in play;
So we, grown penitent, on serious thinking,
Leave Whoring, and devoutly fall to Drink-
ing.
Scowring the Watch grows out of fashion
wit;
Now we set up for Tilting in the Pit, 40
Where 'tis agreed by Bullies, chicken-
hearted,
To fright the Ladies first, and then be parted.
A fair attempt has twice or thrice been made,
To hire Night-murth'rers, and make Death
a Trade.
When Murther's out, what Vice can we
advance?
Unless the new-found Pois'ning Trick of
France:
And when their art of *Rats-bane* we have
got,
By way of thanks, we'll send 'em o'er our
Plot.

THE SPANISH FRYAR, 1681. Published in 1682.
4 Kings at City Treats,] Kings, at City Treats
1682.
11 *Bromingam*] *The editors print* Birming-
ham
12-13 *Omitted in the 2nd edition, 1686*.

EPILOGUE TO TAMERLANE THE GREAT.

LADIES, the Beardless Author of this Day
Commends to you the Fortune of his Play.
A Woman Wit has often grac'd the Stage,
But he's the first Boy-Poet of our Age
Early as is the Year his Fancies blow,
Like young *Narcissus* peeping through the
    Snow ;
Thus *Cowley* blossom'd soon, yet Flourish'd
    long,
This is as forward, and may prove as
    strong.
Youth with the Fair should always Favour
    find,   9
Or we are damn'd Dissemblers of our kind.
What's all this Love they put into our
    Parts ?
'Tis but the pit-a-pat of Two Young
    Hearts.

Shou'd Hag and Gray-beard make such
    tender moan,
Faith, you'd e'en trust 'em to themselves
    alone,
And cry, let's go, here's nothing to be
    done.
Since Love's our Business, as 'tis your
    Delight,
The Young, who best can practise, best can
    Write.
What though he be not come to his full Pow'r ?
He's mending and improving every Hour.
You sly She-Jockies of the Box and Pit   20
Are pleas'd to find a hot unbroken Wit,
By management he may in time be made,
But there's no hopes of an old batter'd Jade ;
Faint and unnerv'd he runs into a Sweat,
And always fails you at the Second Heat.

A PROLOGUE.

GALLANTS, a bashful Poet bids me say
He's come to lose his Maidenhead to-day.
Be not too fierce, for he's but green of *Age*,
And ne're till now debauch'd upon the
    Stage.
He wants the suff'ring part of Resolution,
And comes with blushes to his Execution.
E're you deflow'r his Muse, he hopes the
    Pit
Will make some Settlement upon his Wit.
Promise him well, before the Play begin ;
For he wou'd fain be cozen'd into Sin.   10
'Tis not but that he knows you mean to fail ;)
But, if you leave him after being frail,   }
He'll have, at least, a fair Pretence to rail ;)
To call you base, and swear you us'd him ill,
And put you in the new Deserters Bill :
Lord, what a Troop of perjur'd Men we see ;
Enough to fill another Mercury !
But this the Ladies may with patience
    brook :
Their's are not the first Colours you forsook !
He wou'd be loth the *Beauties* to offend ; 20
But if he shou'd, he's not too old to mend.

He's a young Plant, in his first Year of
    bearing,
But his Friend swears he will be worth the
    reering.
His Gloss is still upon him, tho' 'tis true
He's yet unripe, yet take him for the blue.
You think an *Apricot* half green is best ;
There's sweet and sour ; and one side good
    at least.
Mango's and Limes, whose Nourishment is
    little,
Tho' not for Food, are yet preserv'd for
    Pickle.   29
So this green Writer may pretend, at least,
To whet your Stomachs for a better Feast.
He makes this Difference in the Sexes too ;
He sells to Men, he gives himself to you.
To both he wou'd contribute some delight ;
A mere Poetical Hermaphrodite,
Thus he's equipp'd, both to be woo'd and)
    woo ;   }
With *Arms* offensive, and defensive too ; }
'Tis hard, he thinks, if neither part will do.)

TAMERLANE THE GREAT, 1681.   The play is by
Charles Saunders.

A PROLOGUE. Published in the *Miscellanies*
of 1603.
28 Limes] Berries *in posthumous editions.*

PROLOGUE AND EPILOGUE TO THE PRINCESS OF CLEVES.

PROLOGUE.

LADIES! (I hope there's none behind to hear,)
I long to whisper something in your Ear,
A Secret, which does much my Mind perplex:
There's Treason in the Play against our Sex.
A Man that's false to Love, that vows and
    cheats,
And kisses every living thing he meets !
A Rogue in Mode, I dare not speak too broad,
One that does something to the very Bawd.
Out on him, Traytor, for a filthy Beast ! 9
Nay, and he's like the pack of all the rest :
None of 'em stick at mark ; They all deceive.
Some *Jew* has changed the Text, I half
    believe ;
Their *Adam* cozen'd our poor Grandame *Eve*.
To hide their Faults they rap out Oaths, and
    tear ;
Now tho' we lye, we're too well-bred to
    swear.
So we compound for half the Sin we owe,
But men are dipt for Soul and Body too ;
And, when found out, excuse themselves,
    Pox cant 'em,
With Latin stuff, *perjuria ridet Amantum*.
I'm not Book Learn'd, to know that word in
    vogue, 20
But I suspect 'tis Latin for a Rogue.
I'm sure, I never heard that Schritch-Owl
    hollow'd
In my poor Ears, but Separation follow'd.
How can not perjur'd Villains e'er be saved ?
Achitophel's not half so false to *David*.
With Vows and soft Expressions to allure,
They stand, like Foremen of a Shop,
    demure :
No sooner out of sight, but they are gadding,
And for the next new Face ride out a padding.
Yet, by their Favour, when they have bin
    kissing, 30
We can perceive the ready Mony missing.
Well ! we may rail ; but 'tis as good e'en
    wink ;
Something we find, and something they will
    sink.

But, since they're at renouncing, 'tis our
    Parts
To trump their Diamonds, & they trump
    our Hearts.

EPILOGUE.

A Qualm of Conscience brings me back agen,
To make amends to you bespatter'd Men.
We Women love like Cats, that hide their
    Joys
By growling, squaling, and a hideous Noise.
I rail'd at wild young Sparks ; but without
    lying,
Never was Man worse thought on for high-
    flying.
The Prodigal of Love gives each her Part,
And Squandring shows at least a noble Heart.
I've heard of Men, who, in some lewd Lam-
    poon,
Have hir'd a Friend to make their Valour
    known. 10
That Accusation straight this Question brings,
What is the Man that does such naughty
    things ?
The Spaniel Lover, like a sneaking Fop,
Lies at our Feet ; he's scarce worth taking
    up,
Tis true, such Heroes in a Play go far ;
But Chamber Practice is not like the Bar.
When Men such vile, such feint Petitions
    make,
We fear to give, because they fear to take ;
Since Modesty's the Virtue of our Kind,
Pray let it be to our own Sex confin'd. 20
When Men usurp it from the Female Nation,
'Tis but a Work of Supererogation——
We show'd a Princess in the Play, 'tis true,
Who gave her *Cæsar* more than all his due ;
Told her own Faults ; but I shou'd much
    abhor
To choose a Husband for my Confessor.
You see what Fate follow'd the Saint-like
    Fool,
For telling Tales from out the Nuptial School.
Our Play a merry Comedy had prov'd, 29
Had she confess'd as much to him she lov'd.
True *Presbyterian*-Wives the *means* wou'd
    try :
But damn'd Confessing is flat Popery.

THE PRINCESS OF CLEVES, 1681. Text from
the *Miscellanies* of 1684. The play is by Lee.
  Prologue 13 Their] *Editors till Christie give*
There

PROLOGUE TO THE UNIVERSITY OF OXFORD.

THE fam'd *Italian* Muse, whose Rhymes advance
Orlando, and the *Paladins* of *France*,
Records that, when our Wit and Sense is flown,
'Tis lodg'd within the Circle of the Moon
In Earthen Jars, which one, who thither soar'd,
Set to his Nose, snufft up, and was restor'd.
What e're the Story be, the Moral's true ;
The Wit we lost in Town we find in you.
Our Poets their fled Parts may draw from hence,
And fill their windy Heads with sober Sense.
When *London* Votes with *Southwark's* disagree,   11
Here may they find their long-lost Loyalty,
Here busie Senates, to th' old Cause inclin'd,
May snuff the Votes their Fellows left behind :

Your Country Neighbours, when their Grain grows dear,
May come, and find their *last Provision* here ;
Whereas we cannot much lament our Loss,
Who neither carried back nor brought one Cross.
We look'd what Representatives wou'd bring,
But they help'd us, just as they did the King.
Yet we despair not ; for we now lay forth   21
The *Sybill's* Books to those who know their Worth ;
And tho the first was Sacrific'd before,
These Volumes doubly will the price restore.
Our Poet bade us hope this Grace to find,
To whom by long Prescription you are kind.
He, whose undaunted Muse with Loyal Rage
Has never spar'd the Vices of the Age,
Here finding nothing that his Spleen can raise,
Is forced to turn his Satire into Praise.   30

PROLOGUE TO THE UNIVERSITY OF OXFORD.

DISCORD and Plots, which have undone our Age,
With the same ruine have o'erwhelmed the Stage.
Our House has suffered in the common Woe,
We have been troubled with *Scotch* Rebels too.
Our brethren are from *Thames* to *Tweed* departed,
And of our Sisters all the kinder-hearted
To *Edenborough* gone, or coached or carted.
With bonny Blewcap there they act all night
For *Scotch* half-crown, in *English* Threepence hight.
One Nymph, to whom fat *Sir John Falstaff's* lean,   10
There with her single Person fills the Scene.
Another, with long Use and Age decay'd,
Div'd here old Woman, and rose there a Maid.
Our trusty Door-keepers of former time
There strut and swagger in Heroique Rhyme.
Tack but a copper Lace to drugget Suit,
And there's a Heroe made without Dispute ;

And that which was a Capon's tayl before
Becomes a plume for *Indian* emperor.
But all his Subjects, to express the Care   20
Of Imitation, go, like *Indians*, bare ;
Lac'd Linen there would be a dangerous Thing ;
It might perhaps a new Rebellion bring ;
The *Scot* who wore it wou'd be chosen King.
But why should I these Renegades describe,
When you yourselves have seen a lewder Tribe ?
Teag has been here, and to this learned Pit
With *Irish* Action slandered *English* Wit ;
You have beheld such barbarous *Macs* appear
As merited a second Massacre ;   30
Such as like *Cain* were branded with Disgrace,
And had their Country stampt upon their Face.
When Strollers durst presume to pick your purse,
We humbly thought our broken Troop not worse.
How ill soe'er our Action may deserve,
Oxford's a place where Wit can never sterve.

FIRST PROLOGUE TO THE UNIV. OF OXFORD, 1681. Text from the *Miscellanies* of 1693.

SECOND PROLOGUE, 1681. Text from the *Miscellanies* of 1684.

PROLOGUE TO THE UNIVERSITY OF OXFORD.

THO' Actors cannot much of Learning
    boast,
Of all who want it, we admire it most :
We love the Praises of a learned Pit,
As we remotely are ally'd to Wit.
We speak our Poet's Wit, and trade in
    Ore,
Like those who touch upon the Golden
    Shore ;
Betwixt our Judges can distinction make,
Discern how much and why our Poems
    take ;
Mark if the Fools, or Men of Sense, rejoice ;
Whether th' Applause be only Sound or
    Voice.   10
When our Fop Gallants, or our City Folly,
Clap over-loud, it makes us melancholy :
We doubt that Scene which does their
    wonder raise,
And for their Ignorance contemn their
    Praise.
Judge then, if we who act and they who
    write
Shou'd not be proud of giving you delight.
London likes grosly ; but this nicer Pit
Examines, fathoms, all the Depths of Wit ;

The ready Finger lays on every Blot ;
Knows what shou'd justly please, and what
    shou'd not.   20
Nature her self lyes open to your view,
You judge by her what draught of her is
    true,
Where Out-lines false, and Colours seem too
    faint,
Where Bunglers dawb, and where true Poets
    Paint.
But by the sacred Genius of this Place,
By every Muse, by each Domestick Grace,
Be kind to Wit, which but endeavours well,
And, where you judge, presumes not to
    excel.
Our Poets hither for Adoption come,
As Nations su'd to be made free of *Rome* : 30
Not in the suffragating Tribes to stand,
But in your utmost, last, Provincial Band.
If his Ambition may those Hopes pursue,
Who with Religion loves your Arts and you,
Oxford to him a dearer Name shall be,
Than his own Mother University.
Thebes did his green unknowing Youth in-
    gage,
He chuses *Athens* in his riper Age.

PROLOGUE.

TO THE UNHAPPY FAVOURITE.

SPOKEN TO THE KING AND THE QUEEN AT THEIR COMING TO THE HOUSE.

WHEN first the Ark was landed on the
    Shore,
And Heav'n had vowed to curse the Ground
    no more,
When Tops of Hills the longing Patriark
    saw,
And the new Scene of Earth began to draw,
The Dove was sent to View the Waves
    Decrease,
And first brought back to Man the Pledge of
    Peace.
'Tis needless to apply, when those appear

Who bring the Olive, and who Plant it here
We have before our Eyes the Royal Dove,
Still Innocence is Harbinger to Love.   10
The Ark is open'd to dismiss the Train,
And people with a better Race the Plain.
Tell me, you Pow'rs, why should vain Man
    pursue
With endless Toyl each object that is new,
And for the seeming Substance leave the
    true ?
Why should he quit for Hopes his certain
    good,
And loath the Manna of his daily food ?

PROLOGUE TO THE UNIV. OF OXFORD. Text
from the *Miscellanies* of 1684.

THE UNHAPPY FAVOURITE, 1682. Printed in
the *Miscellanies* of 1684 and with the play, which
is by Banks, in 1685.

Must *England* still the Scene of Changes be,
Tost and Tempestuous like our Ambient
   Sea ?
Must still our Weather and our Wills agree ?
Without our Blood our Liberties we
   have ; 21
Who that is Free would fight to be a
   Slave ?
Or what can Wars to after Times Assure,
Of which our Present Age is not secure ?
All that our Monarch would for us Ordain
Is but t' injoy the Blessings of his Reign.

Our Land's an *Eden* and the Main's our
   Fence,
While we preserve our State of Innocence :
That lost, then Beasts their Bruital Force
   employ,
And first their Lord and then themselves
   destroy. 30
What Civil Broils have cost we knew too well;
Oh ! let it be enough that once we fell,
And every Heart conspire, with every
   Tongue,
Still to have such a King, and this King Long.

EPILOGUE TO THE UNHAPPY FAVOURITE,
OR THE EARL OF ESSEX.

WE act by Fits and Starts, like drowning
   Men,
But just peep up, and then Dop down again.
Let those who call us Wicked change their
   Sence,
For never Men liv'd more on Providence.
Not Lott'ry Cavaliers are half so poor,
Nor Broken Cits, nor a Vacation Whore ;
Not Courts, nor Courtiers living on the Rents
Of the three last ungiving Parliaments ;
So wretched, that, if *Pharaoh* could Divine,
He might have spar'd his Dream of Seven
   lean Kine, 10
And chang'd his Vision for the Muses Nine.
The *Comet* which, they say, portends a Dearth
Was but a Vapour drawn from *Play-house*
   Earth,
Pent there since our last Fire, and *Lilly* sayes,
Foreshows our change of State and thin
   Third-dayes.
'Tis not our want of Wit that keeps us poor,
For then the Printers Press would suffer
   more.
Their Pamphleteers each Day their Venom
   spit ;
They thrive by Treason, and we starve by
   Wit. 19

Confess the truth, which of you has not laid
Four Farthings out to buy the
   Hatfield Maid ?   *To the*
Or, what is duller yet and more *upper*
   does spite us,   *Gallery.*
Democritus his Wars with *Heraclitus* ?
These are the Authors that have run us
   down,
And Exercise you Critticks of the Town.
Yet these are Pearls to your *Lampooning*
   Rhimes,
Y' abuse your selves more dully than the
   Times.
Scandal, the Glory of the *English* Nation,
Is worn to Raggs, and Scribled out of
   Fashion ;
Such harmless Thrusts as if like Fencers
   Wise, 30
You had agreed your Play before their
   Prize.
Faith, you may hang your Harps upon the
   Willows,
'Tis just like Children when they box with
   Pillows.
Then put an end to Civil Wars for
   shame,
Let each Knight Errant who has wrong'd a
   Dame
Throw down his Pen and give her if he
   can,
The satisfaction of a Gentleman.

EPILOGUE TO THE UNHAPPY FAVOURITE.
2 Dop] *Editors till Christie give* pop
18 each Day their Venom] their Venom daily
1685.

PROLOGUE.

TO HIS ROYAL HIGHNESS UPON HIS FIRST APPEARANCE AT THE DUKE'S THEATRE SINCE HIS RETURN FROM SCOTLAND.

IN those cold Regions which no Summers
      chear,
When brooding darkness covers half the year,
To hollow Caves the shivering Natives go,
Bears range abroad and hunt in tracks of
      Snow ;
But when the tedious Twilight wears away
And Stars grow paler at the approach of Day,
The longing crowds to frozen Mountains run,
Happy who first can see the glimmering Sun ;
The surly Salvage Off-spring disappear ;
And curse the bright Successor of the Year.
Yet though rough Bears in covert seek⎫
      defence,   11 ⎪
White Foxes stay with seeming Innocence ; ⎬
That crafty kind with day-light can dis- ⎪
      pense.   ⎭
Still we are throng'd so full with *Reynard's*
      race
That Loyal Subjects scarce can find a place :
Thus modest Truth is cast behind the Crowd,
Truth speaks too Low, Hypocrisie too Loud.
Let them be first to flatter in success ;
Duty can stay, but Guilt has need to press.
Once, when true Zeal the Sons of God did call,
To make their solemn show at Heaven's
      White-hall,   21
The fawning Devil appear'd among the rest
And made as good a Courtier as the best.

The friends of *Job*, who rail'd at him before,
Came Cap in hand when he had three times
      more.
Yet, late Repentance may perhaps be true ;
Kings can forgive, if Rebels can but sue.
A Tyrant's Pow'r in rigour is exprest :
The Father yearns in the true Prince's breast.
We grant an Ore'grown Whig no grace can
      mend,   30
But most are Babes that know not they
      offend.
The Crowd, to restless motion still enclin'd,
Are clouds that rack according to the wind.
Driv'n by their Chiefs, they storms of Hail-
      stones pour,
Then mourn, and soften to a silent showre.
O welcome to this much offending land
The Prince that brings forgiveness in his
      hand !
Thus Angels on glad messages appear ;
Their first Salute commands us not to fear :
Thus Heav'n, that cou'd constrain us to⎫
      obey,   40 ⎪
(With rev'rence if we might presume to ⎬
      say,)   ⎪
Seems to relax the rights of Sov'reign ⎭
      sway,
Permits to Man the choice of Good and Ill,
And makes us Happy by our own Free-will.

PROLOGUE

TO THE DUCHESS ON HER RETURN FROM SCOTLAND.

WHEN factious Rage to cruel Exile drove
The Queen of Beauty, and the Court of Love,
The Muses droop'd with their forsaken Arts,
And the sad Cupids broke their useless Darts.
Our fruitful Plains to Wilds and Deserts
      turn'd,
Like *Eden's* Face when banish'd Man it
      mourned :
Love was no more when Loyalty was gone,
The great Supporter of his awful Throne.

Love could no longer after Beauty stay,⎫
But wander'd northward to the Verge of⎪
      Day,   ⎬
As if the Sun and he had lost their ⎪
      Way.   11⎭
But now the illustrious Nymph, return'd
      again,
Brings every Grace triumphant in her Train :
The wondering Nereids, though they rais'd
      no Storm,
Foreslow'd her Passage to behold her Form ;

PROLOGUE TO HIS ROYAL HIGHNESS, 1682.
2 When] *Editors till Christie give* Where
33 rack] *Editors till Christie give* tack

PROLOGUE TO THE DUCHESS, 1682. Text from
the *Miscellanies* of 1693.

Some cried a *Venus*, some a *Thetis* past,
But this was not so fair nor that so chaste.
Far from her Sight flew Faction, Strife, and
    Pride,
And Envy did but look on her, and died.
Whate'er we suffer'd from our sullen Fate, 20
Her Sight is purchased at an easy rate :
Three gloomy Years against this Day were set,
But this one mighty Sum has clear'd the debt.
Like *Joseph's* Dream, but with a better
    Doom ;
The Famine past, the Plenty still to come.
For her the weeping Heavens become serene,
For her the Ground is clad in cheerful green,
For her the Nightingales are taught to sing,
And Nature has for her delay'd the Spring.
The Muse resumes her long-forgotten Lays,
And Love, restor'd, his ancient Realm sur-
    veys,
                    31

Recalls our Beauties and revives our Plays ;
His waste Dominions peoples once again,
And from her Presence dates his second
    Reign.
But awful Charms on her fair Forehead sit,
Dispensing what she never will admit ;
Pleasing yet cold, like *Cynthia's* silver Beam,
The People's Wonder and the Poet's Theme.
Distemper'd Zeal, Sedition, canker'd Hate
No more shall vex the Church and tear the
    State ;   40
No more shall Faction civil Discords move,
Or only Discords of too tender Love :
Discord like that of Music's various Parts,
Discord that makes the Harmony of
    Hearts,
Discord that only this Dispute shall bring,
Who best shall love the Duke and serve the
    King.

PROLOGUE AND EPILOGUE TO THE LOYAL BROTHER, OR THE PERSIAN PRINCE.

PROLOGUE.

POETS, like Lawful Monarchs, rul'd the
    Stage,
Till Criticks, like Damn'd Whiggs, debauch'd
    our Age.
Mark how they jump ; Criticks wou'd regu-
    late
Our Theatres, and Whiggs reform our State ;
Both pretend love, and both (Plague rot
    'em) hate.
The Critick humbly seems Advice to bring,
The fawning Whigg Petitions to the King ;
But ones Advice into a Satyr slides,
T' other's Petition a Remonstrance hides.
These will no Taxes give, and those no
    Pence ;   10
Criticks wou'd starve the Poet, Whiggs the
    Prince.
The critick all our Troops of friends discards ;
Just so the Whigg wou'd fain pull down the
    Guards.
Guards are illegal that drive foes away,
As watchful Shepherds that fright beasts of
    prey.

THE LOYAL BROTHER, 1682. The play is by
Southern.

Kings who Disband such needless Aids as
    these
Are safe—as long as e're their Subjects
    please ;
And that would be till next Queen *Besses*
    night,
Which thus grave penny Chroniclers indite.
Sir *Edmond-berry* first, in woful wise   20
Leads up the show, and Milks their Maudlin
    Eyes.
There's not a Butcher's Wife but Dribs her
    part,
And pities the poor Pageant from her heart ;
Who, to provoke Revenge, rides round the
    Fire,
And with a civil congee does retire :
But guiltless blood to ground must never
    fall :
There's *Antichrist* behind, to pay for all.
The Punk of *Babylon* in Pomp appears,
A lewd Old Gentleman of seventy years ;
Whose Age in vain our Mercy wou'd implore,
For few take Pity on an Old-cast Whore. 31
The Devil, who brought him to the shame,
    takes part ;
Sits cheek by jowl in black to chear his heart,
Like Thief and Parson in a *Tiburn-Cart.*

The word is given, and with a loud Huzzaw
The Miter'd Moppet from his Chair they
    draw :
On the slain Corps contending Nations
    fall :
Alas, what's one poor Pope among 'em
    all !
He burns; now all true hearts your Triumphs
    ring,
And next (for fashion) cry, *God save the*
    King.   40
A needful Cry in midst of such Alarms,
When Forty thousand Men are up in
    Arms.
But after he's once sav'd, to make amends,⎱
In each succeeding Health they Damn his ⎰
    Friends :
So God begins, but still the Devil ends.
What if some one inspir'd with Zeal shou'd
    call,
Come, let's go cry, God save him at *White-*
    hall ?
His best Friends wou'd not like this over-
    care,
Or think him e're the safer for that
    pray'r.   49
Five praying Saints are by an Act allow'd,
But not the whole Church-Militant in
    crowd ;
Yet, should Heav'n all the true Petitions⎱
    drain   ⎰
Of *Presbyterians* who wou'd Kings maintain,
Of Forty thousand five wou'd scarce
    remain.

EPILOGUE.

A Virgin Poet was serv'd up to day,
Who till this Hour ne're cackl'd for a Play.
He's neither yet a Whigg nor Tory-Boy,⎱
But, like a Girl, whom several wou'd ⎰
    enjoy,
Begs leave to make the best of his own
    natural Toy.
Were I to play my callow Author's game,
The King's House wou'd instruct me by the
    Name :
There's Loyalty to one ; I wish no more ;
A Commonwealth sounds like a common
    Whore.

Let Husband or Gallant be what they will,
One part of Woman is true Tory still.   11
If any factious spirit should rebell,
Our Sex with ease can every rising quell.
Then, as you hope we shou'd we shou'd your failings
    hide,
An honest Jury for our play provide.
Whiggs at their Poets never take offence ;
They save dull Culpritts who have Murtherd
    Sense.
Though Nonsense is a nauseous heavy
    Mass,
The Vehicle called faction makes it
    pass ;
Faction in Play's the Commonwealths man's
    bribe,   20
The leaden Farthing of the Canting
    Tribe :
Though void in payment Laws and Statutes
    make it,
The Neighbourhood, that knows the Man,
    will take it.
'Tis Faction buys the Votes of half the
    Pit ;
Theirs is the Pension-Parliament of wit.
In City-Clubs their venom let 'em vent ;
For there 'tis safe, in its own Element.
Here, where their Madness can have no
    pretence,
Let 'em forget themselves an hour in
    sense.
In one poor Isle, why should two Factions⎱
    be ?   30⎰
Small diff'rence in your Vices I can see :
In Drink and Drabs both Sides too well
    agree.
Wou'd there were more Preferments in the
    Land ;
If Places fell, the Party could not stand.
Of this damn'd Grievance ev'ry Whigg com-
    plains ;
They grunt like Hogs till they have got their
    Grains.
Mean time you see what Trade our Plots ad-
    vance :
We send each Year good Money into
    France ;
And they that know what Merchandise we
    need,
Send o're true Protestants to mend our
    breed.   40

Prologue 36 Moppet] *Editors till Christie give*
Poppet

Epilogue 29 in] *The editors give* of

PROLOGUE AND EPILOGUE TO THE KING AND QUEEN,

AT THE OPENING OF THEIR THEATRE UPON THE UNION OF THE TWO
COMPANIES IN 1682.

PROLOGUE.

SINCE Faction ebbs, and Rogues grow out of
 Fashion,
Their penny-Scribes take care t' inform the
 Nation
How well men thrive in this or that Planta-
 tion :
How *Pennsylvania's* Air agrees with Quakers,
And *Carolina's* with Associators :
Both e'en too good for Madmen and for
 Traitors.
Truth is, our Land with Saints is so run o'er,
And every Age produces such a store,
That now there's need of two *New-Englands*
 more.
What's this, you'll say, to Us and our Voca-
 tion ?   10
Only thus much, that we have left our
 Station,
And made this Theatre our new Plantation.
The Factious Natives never cou'd agree ;
But aiming, as they call'd it, to be Free,
Those Play-house Whiggs set up for
 Property.
Some say they no Obedience paid of late,
But would new Fears and Jealousies create,
'Till topsy-turvy they had turned the State.
Plain Sense, without the Talent of Fore-
 telling,
Might guess 'twould end in down-right
 knocks and quelling ;   20
For seldom comes there better of Rebelling.
When Men will, needlessly, their Freedom
 barter
For lawless Pow'r, sometimes they catch a
 Tartar ;
(There's a damned word that rhimes to this,
 call'd Charter.)
But since the Victory with Us remains,
You shall be call'd to Twelve in all our
 gains,
(If you'll not think Us sawcy for our Pains.)

───────────────

TO THE KING AND QUEEN, 1682. Text of 1683.

Old men shall have good old Plays to delight
 'em :
And you, fair Ladies and Galants, that
 slight 'em,
We'll treat with good new Plays, if our new
 Wits can write 'em.   30
We'll take no blundering Verse, no fustian
 Tumour,
No dribling Love from this or that Presumer,
No dull fat Fooll shamm'd on the Stage for
 humour.
For, faith, some of 'em such vile stuff have
 made,
As none but Fools or Fairies ever Play'd ;
But 'twas,as Shop-men say, to force a Trade.
We've giv'n you Tragedies all sense defying ;
And singing men in woeful Metre dying ;
This 'tis when heavy Lubbers will be flying.
All these disasters we well hope to weather ;
We bring you none of our old Lumber
 hether ;   41
Whigg Poets and Whigg Sheriffs may hang
 together.

EPILOGUE.

New Ministers, when first they get in place,
Must have a care to please ; and that's our
 Case :
Some Laws for public Welfare we design,
If you, the Power supream, will please to
 join.
There are a sort of Pratlers in the Pit,
Who either have, or who pretend to Wit ;
These noisy Sirs so loud their Parts rehearse,
That oft the Play is silenc'd by the Farce :
Let such be dumb, this penalty to shun,
Each to be thought my Lady's eldest Son. 10
But stay ; methinks some Vizard Mask I see
Cast out her Lure from the mid Gallery :
About her all the fluttering Sparks are
 rang'd ;
The Noise continues, though the Scene is
 chang'd :
Now growling, sputt'ring, wauling, such a
 clutter,
'Tis just like Puss defendant in a Gutter ;

Fine Love, no doubt ; but ere two days are o'er ye,
The Surgeon will be told a woful story.
Let Vizard Mask her naked Face expose,
On pain of being thought to want a Nose : 20
Then for your laqueys, and your Train beside,
(By whate'er Name or Title dignify'd,)
They roar so loud, you'd think behind the Stairs
Tom Dove, and all the Brotherhood of Bears :
They're grown a Nuisance, beyond all Disasters ;
We've none so great but their unpaying Masters.
We beg you, Sirs, to beg your Men that they
Would please to give you leave to hear the Play.
Next, in the Play-house, spare your precious Lives ;
Think, like good *Christians*, on your *bearns* and *wives* ;   30
Think on your Souls ; but by your lugging forth,
It seems you know how little they are worth.

If none of these will move the warlike Mind,
Think on the helpless Whore you leave behind.
We beg you, last, our Scene-room to forbear
And leave our Goods and Chattels to our Care.
Alas, our Women are but washy Toys,
And wholly taken up in Stage Employs :
Poor willing Tits they are : but yet I doubt
This double Duty soon will wear them out.
Then you are watch'd besides with jealous Care :   41
What if my Lady's Page should find you there ?
My Lady knows t' a tittle what there's in ye ;
No passing your gilt Shilling for a Guinea.
Thus, Gentlemen, we have summ'd up in short
Our Grievances, from Country, Town, and Court :
Which humbly we submit to your good pleasure ;
But first Vote Money, then redress at leasure.

PROLOGUE AND EPILOGUE TO THE DUKE OF GUISE.

PROLOGUE.

Spoken by Mr. SMITH.

OUR Play's a Parallel : The Holy League
Begot our Cov'nant ; Guisards got the Whigg :
Whate'er our hot-brain'd Sheriffs did advance
Was like our Fashions, first produc'd in *France* ;
And, when worn out, well scour'd, and banish'd there,
Sent over, like their godly Beggars, here.
Cou'd the same Trick, twice play'd, our Nation gull ?
It looks as if the Devil were grown dull ;
Or serv'd us up in Scorn his broken Meat,
And thought we were not worth a better Cheat.   10
The fulsome Cov'nant, one wou'd think in Reason,
Had given us all our Bellys-full of Treason ;

And yet, the Name but chang'd, our nasty Nation
Chaws its own Excrement, th' Association.
'Tis true, we have not learn'd their pois'ning way,
For that's a mode but newly come in play ;
Besides, Your Drug's uncertain to prevail, ⎫
But your True Protestant can never fail ⎬
With that compendious Instrument, a Flail. ⎭
Go on, and bite, ev'n though the Hook lies bare,   20
Twice in one Age expel the lawful Heir,
Once more decide Religion by the Sword ;
And purchase for us a new Tyrant Lord.
Pray for your King, but yet your Purses spare ;
Make Him not Two-Pence richer by your Prayer.
To show you love Him much, chastise Him more,
And make Him very Great, and very Poor.
Push Him to Wars, but still no Pence advance ;

Let Him lose *England*, to recover *France*. 29
Cry Freedom up with Popular noisie Votes,
And get enough to cut each other's Throats,
Lop all the Rights that fence your Monarch's
   Throne ;
For fear of too much Pow'r, pray leave Him
   none.
A noise was made of Arbitrary Sway ;
But in Revenge, you Whiggs have found
   a way,
An Arbitrary Duty now to pay.
Let His own Servants turn, to save their
   stake,
Glean from His Plenty, and His Wants for-
   sake ;
But let some *Judas* near His Person stay,
To swallow the last Sop, and then betray.
Make *London* independant of the Crown ; 41
A Realm a part ; the Kingdom of the Town.
Let *Ignoramus* juries find no Traytors,
And *Ignoramus* Poets scribble Satyrs.
And, that your meaning none may fail to
   scan,
Do what in Coffee-houses you began ;
Pull down the Master, and Set up the Man.

EPILOGUE.

Spoken by Mrs. COOKE.

Much Time and Trouble this poor Play has
   cost ;
And faith, I doubted once the Cause was lost.
Yet no one Man was meant, nor Great nor
   Small ;
Our Poets, like frank Gamesters, threw at
   All.
They took no single Aim :——
But, like bold Boys, true to their Prince and
   hearty,
Huzza'd, and fired Broad-sides at the whole
   Party.
Duels are Crimes ; but, when the Cause is
   right,
In Battel every Man is bound to fight.
For what should hinder Me to sell my
   Skin,   10
Dear as I cou'd, if once my Hand were in ?
Se defendendo never was a Sin.
'Tis a fine World, my Masters, right or
   wrong,
The Whiggs must talk, and Tories hold their
   Tongue.
They must do all they can——

But We, Forsooth, must bear a Christian
   mind,
And fight, like Boys, with one Hand ty'd
   behind ;
Nay, and when one Boy's down, 'twere
   wond'rous wise
To cry, Box fair, and give him time to
   rise.
When Fortune favours, none but Fools will
   dally ;   20
Would any of you Sparks, if *Nan* or *Mally*
Tipp'd you th' inviting Wink, stand, shall I,
   shall I ?
A *Trimmer* cry'd (that heard me tell this
   Story),
Fie, Mistress *Cooke* ! Faith, you're too rank
   a Tory !
Wish not Whiggs hang'd, but pity their hard
   Cases ;
You Women love to see Men make wry
   Faces.——
Pray, Sir, said I, don't think me such
   a *Jew* ;
I say no more, but give the Dev'l his due.——
Lenitives, says he, best suit with our Con-
   dition.
Jack Ketch, says I, 's an excellent Physi-
   cian.   30
I love no Bloud.—Nor I, Sir, as I breath ;
But hanging is a fine dry kind of Death.
We *Trimmers* are for holding all things
   even.——
Yes—just like him that hung 'twixt Hell
   and Heaven.——
Have we not had Men's Lives enow
   already ? '——
Yes sure :—but you're for holding all
   things steddy.
Now since the Weight hangs all on one side,
   Brother,
You *Trimmers* shou'd, to poize it, hang on
   t' other.
Damn'd Neuters, in their middle way of
   steering,
Are neither Fish nor Flesh nor good Red-
   Herring :   40
Not Whiggs, nor Tories they : nor this, nor
   that ;
Not Birds, nor Beasts ; but just a kind of
   Bat :
A Twilight Animal ; true to neither Cause,
With Tory Wings, but Whiggish Teeth and
   Claws.

ANOTHER EPILOGUE.

*Intended to have been spoken to the Play
before it was forbidden last summer.*

Two Houses join'd, two Poets to a Play?⎫
You noisy Whigs will sure be pleas'd to-day;⎬
It looks so like two Shrieves the City Way.⎭
But since our Discords and Divisions cease,
You, *Bilboa*-gallants, learn to keep the
    Peace ;
Make here no Tilts ; let our poor Stage⎫
    alone ;   ⎬
Or if a decent Murder must be done,   ⎭
Pray take a civil Turn to Marybone.
If not, I swear we'll pull up all our Benches ;
Not for your Sakes, but for our Orange-
    wenches :   10
For you thrust wide sometimes, and many
    a Spark,
That misses one, can hit the other Mark.
This makes our Boxes full ; for men of
    Sense
Pay their four Shillings in their own Defence:
That safe behind the Ladies they may
    stay,
Peep o'er the Fan, and judge the bloody
    Fray.
But other Foes give Beauty worse Alarms ;
The *posse-poetarum's* up in Arms :
No Woman's Fame their libels has escap'd ;
Their Ink runs Venom, and their Pens are
    clapp'd.   20

When Sighs and Prayers their ladies cannot
    move,
They rail, write Treason, and turn Whigs to
    love.
Nay, and I fear they worse Designs advance,
There's a damn'd Love-trick new brought
    o'er from *France.*
We charm in vain, and dress, and keep
    a Pother,
While those false Rogues are ogling one
    another.
All Sins besides admit some Expiation ;
But this against our Sex is plain Damnation.
They join for Libels too, these Women-
    haters ;
And as they club for Love, they club for
    Satyres ;   30
The best on't is they hurt not : for they wear
Stings in their Tails ; their only Venom's
    there.
'Tis true, some shot at first the Ladies hit,
Which able Marksmen made and Men of Wit:
But now the Fools give Fire, whose Bounce
    is louder ;
And yet, like mere Train-bands, they shoot
    but Powder.
Libels, like Plots, sweep all in their first
    Fury ;
Then dwindle like an ignoramus Jury :
Thus Age begins with towzing and with
    tumbling,
But grunts, and groans, and ends at last in
    fumbling.   40

EPILOGUE TO CONSTANTINE THE GREAT.

Our Hero's happy in the Plays Conclusion ;
The holy Rogue at last has met Confusion ;
Though *Arius* all along appeared a Saint,
The last Act showed him a true Protestant.
Eusebius (for you know I read *Greek* Authors)
Reports, that, after all these Plots and
    Slaughters,
The Court of *Constantine* was full of Glory,
And every *Trimmer* turn'd Addressing *Tory.*
They follow'd him in Herds as they were
    mad :
When *Clause* was King, then all the World
    was glad.   10

Whiggs kept the places they possest before,
And most were in a way of getting more ;
Which was as much as saying, Gentlemen,
Here's Power and Money to be Rogues
    again.
Indeed, there were a sort of peaking Tools,
Some call 'em Modest, but I call 'em Fools ;
Men much more Loyal, tho' not half so loud ;
But these poor Devils were cast behind the
    Croud.
For bold Knaves thrive without one grain of
    Sense,
But good Men starve for want of Impudence.

Another Epilogue. Text from the original
broadsheet, 1682.

Constantine the Great, 1684. The play is
by Lee.

Besides all these, there were a sort of Wights, 21
(I think my Author calls them *Teckelites*),
Such hearty Rogues against the King and Laws,
They favour'd even a foreign Rebel's Cause,
When their own damn'd Design was quash'd and aw'd ;
At least they gave it their good Word abroad.
As many a Man, who for a quiet Life
Breeds out his Bastard, not to nose his Wife,
Thus ore their Darling Plot these *Trimmers* cry, 29
And, tho' they cannot keep it in their Eye,
They bind it Prentice to *Count Teckely*.
They believe not the last Plot ; may I be curst,
If I believe they e'er believ'd the first.

No wonder their own Plot no Plot they think,
The Man that makes it never smells the Stink.
And now it comes into my Head, I'll tell
Why these damn'd *Trimmers* lov'd the *Turks* so well.
The Original *Trimmer*, though a Friend to no Man,
Yet in his Heart ador'd a pretty Woman ;
He knew that *Mahomet* laid up for ever 40
Kind Black-eyed Rogues for every true Believer ;
And, which was more than mortal Man e'er tasted,
One Pleasure that for threescore Twelve-months lasted.
To turn for this, may surely be forgiven :
Who'd not be circumcis'd for such a Heaven ?

PROLOGUE TO DISAPPOINTMENT, OR THE MOTHER IN FASHION.

Spoken by Mr. BETTERTON.

How comes it, Gentlemen, that, now-a-days,
When all of you so shrewdly judge of Plays,
Our Poets tax you still with want of Sence ?
All Prologues treat you at your own Ex-pence.
Sharp Citizens a wiser way can go ;
They make you Fools, but never call you so.
They, in good Manners, seldom make a slip,
But treat a Common Whore with Ladyship :
But here each sawcy Wit at Random writes,
And uses Ladies as he uses Knights. 10
Our Author, Young and Grateful in his Nature,
Vows that from him no Nymph deserves a Satyr.
Nor will he ever Draw—I mean his Rhime
Against the sweet Partaker of his Crime.
Nor is he yet so bold an Undertaker
To call MEN Fools, 'tis railing at their MAKER.
Besides, he fears to split upon that Shelf ;
He's young enough to be a FOP himself :

And, if his Praise can bring you all A-bed,
He swears such hopeful Youth no Nation ever bred. 20
Your Nurses, we presume, in such a Case,
Your Father chose, because he lik'd the Face ;
And often they supply'd your Mother's place.
The Dry Nurse was your Mother's ancient Maid,
Who knew some former Slip she ne'er betray'd.
Betwixt 'em both, for Milk and Sugar-Candy,
Your sucking Bottles were well stor'd with Brandy.
Your Father, to initiate your discourse,
Meant to have taught you first to swear and curse, 29
But was prevented by each careful Nurse.
For, leaving Dad and Mam, as names too common,
They taught you certain parts of Man and Woman.

CONSTANTINE THE GREAT, 1684. 28 nose] noise *1702 and edd. till Christie*.
DISAPPOINTMENT, 1684. Text from the original of 1684. The play is by Southern. The Epilogue is printed in some editions as Dryden's. It was rightly rejected by Christie on the ground of its ascription in the collected edition of Southern's plays to the Hon. John Stafford. It has escaped the notice of editors that the same ascription is made in the original edition of the play. The statement that the Prologue was spoken by Better-ton is omitted by the editors.

I pass your Schools, for there when first
   you came,
You wou'd be sure to learn the Latin
   name.
In Colledges, you scorn'd their Art of thinking,
But learn'd all Moods and Figures of good
   Drinking :
Thence come to Town, you practise Play, to
   know
The Vertues of the High Dice and the Low.
Each thinks himself a SHARPER most pro-
   found :
He cheats by Pence, is cheated by the
   Pound.   40
With these perfections, and what else he ⎫
   gleans, |
The SPARK sets up for Love behind our ⎬
   Scenes, |
Hot in pursuit of Princesses and Queens. ⎭
There, if they know their Man, with cunning
   Carriage,
Twenty to one but it concludes in Marriage.
He hires some homely Room, Love's Fruits
   to gather,
And Garret-high rebells against his Father :
But he once dead——

Brings her in Triumph, with her Portion,
   down,
A Twillet, Dressing-Box, and Half a
   Crown.
Some Marry first, and then they fall to
   Scowring,   51
Which is, Refining Marriage into Whoring.
Our Women batten well on their good
   Nature,
All they can rap and rend for the dear
   Creature.
But while abroad so liberal the DOLT is,
Poor SPOUSE at Home as Ragged as a
   Colt is.
Last, some there are, who take their first
   Degrees
Of Lewdness in our middle Galleries ;
The Doughty BULLIES enter Bloody
   Drunk,   59
Invade and grabble one another's PUNK ;
They Caterwoul, and make a dismal Rout,
Call SONS of WHORES, and strike, but
   ne're lug out :
Thus, while for *Paultry Punk* they roar and
   stickle,
They make it *Bawdier* than a Conventicle.

PROLOGUE AND EPILOGUE TO ALBION AND ALBANIUS.

PROLOGUE.

FULL twenty years and more, our lab'ring
   Stage
Has lost, on this incorrigible age :
Our Poets, the *John Ketches* of the Nation,
Have seem'd to lash yee ev'n to excoriation :
But still no sign remains ; which plainly notes
You bore like Hero's or you brib'd like *Oates*.
What can we do, when mimicking a Fop,
Like beating Nut-trees, makes a larger Crop ?
Faith, we'll e'en spare our pains, and to
   content you,
We'll fairly leave you what your Maker
   meant you.   10
Satyre was once your Physick, Wit your
   Food :
One nourisht not, and t' other drew no Blood.
Wee now prescribe, like Doctors in despair,
The Diet your weak appetites can bear.
Since hearty Beef and Mutton will not do,

Here's Julep dance, Ptisan of Song and show :
Give you strong Sense, the Liquor is too
   heady ;
You're come to farce, that's Asses' Milk,
   already.
Some hopeful Youths there are of callow Wit,
Who one day may be Men, if Heav'n think fit ;
Sound may serve such, ere they to Sense are
   grown ;   21
Like leading strings, till they can walk alone.
But yet, to keep our Friends in count'nance,
   know,
The Wise *Italians* first invented show :
Thence into *France* the Noble Pageant past ;
'Tis *England's* Credit to be cozn'd last.
Freedom and Zeal have chous'd you o'er ⎫
   and o'er ; |
'Pray give us leave to bubble you once ⎬
   more ; |
You never were so cheaply fool'd before. ⎭
We bring you change, to humour your
   Disease ;   30
Change for the Worse has ever used to please :

DISAPPOINTMENT 35 their] *edd. give* the
ALBION AND ALBANIUS, 1685.

Then 'tis the mode of *France*, without whose Rules
None must presume to set up here for Fools :
In *France*, the oldest Man is always young, ⎫
Sees *Opera's* daily, learns the Tunes so long, ⎬
Till Foot, Hand, Head, keep Time with ⎭
ev'ry Song.
Each sings his part, echoing from Pit and Box,
With his hoarse Voice, half Harmony, half Pox.
Le plus grand Roy du Monde, is always ringing ;
They show themselves good Subjects by their singing.   40
On that Condition, set up every Throat ;
You Whiggs may sing, for you have chang'd your Note.
Cits and Citesses, raise a joyful Strain,
'Tis a good Omen to begin a Reign :
Voices may help your Charter to restoring,
And get by singing, what you lost by roaring.

EPILOGUE.

After our *Æsop's* Fable shown to day,
I come to give the Moral of the play.
Feign'd Zeal, you saw, set out the speedier pace ;
But, the last Heat, *Plain Dealing* won the Race :
Plain Dealing for a Jewel has been known ;
But ne'er till now the Jewel of a Crown.
When Heav'n made Man, to show the work Divine,
Truth was his Image, stampt upon the Coin :
And, when a King is to a God refin'd,
On all he says and does, he stamps his Mind.   10
This proves a Soul without allay, and pure ;
Kings, like their Gold, should every touch endure.
To dare in Fields is Valour ; but how few
Dare be so thoroughly Valiant to be true ?
The Name of Great let other Kings affect :
He's Great indeed, the Prince that is direct.
His Subjects know him now, and trust him more,
Than all their Kings, and all their Laws before.
What safety could their publick Acts afford ?
Those he can break, but cannot break his Word.   20
So great a Trust to him alone was due ;
Well have they trusted whom so well they knew.
The Saint, who walk'd on Waves, securely trod,
While he believ'd the beckning of his God ;
But, when his Faith no longer bore him out,
Began to sink, as he began to doubt.
Let us our native Character maintain,
'Tis of our Growth to be sincerely plain.
T' excel in Truth we Loyally may strive,
Set Privilege against Prerogative :   30
He Plights his Faith, and we believe him just :
His Honour is to Promise, ours to Trust.
Thus *Britain's* Basis on a Word is laid,
As by a Word the World it self was made.

PROLOGUE AND EPILOGUE TO DON SEBASTIAN.

PROLOGUE.

Spoken by a Woman.

THE Judge remov'd, tho he's no more My Lord,
May plead at Bar, or at the Council-Board :
So may cast Poets write ; there's no Pretension,
To argue loss of Wit from loss of Pension.
Your looks are cheerful ; and in all this place
I see not one that wears a damning face.
The *British* Nation is too brave to show

Ignoble vengeance on a vanquish'd foe.
At least be civil to the Wretch imploring ;
And lay your Paws upon him without roaring :
Suppose our Poet was your foe before,   11
Yet now, the bus'ness of the Field is o'er ;
'Tis Time to let your Civil Wars alone,
When Troops are into Winter-quarters gone.
Jove was alike to *Latian* and to *Phrygian* ;
And you well know, a Play's of no Religion.
Take good advice, and please your selves this Day
No matter from what hands you have the Play.
Among good Fellows ev'ry health will pass,
That serves to carry round another glass : 20

When with full bowls of *Burgundy* you dine,
Tho at the Mighty Monarch you repine,
You grant him still most Christian, in his
  Wine.
  Thus far the Poet ; but his brains grow
    Addle,
And all the rest is purely from this Noddle.
You've seen young Ladies at the Senate
  door
Prefer Petitions, and your grace implore ;
However grave the Legislators were,
Their Cause went ne're the worse for being
  fair.   29
Reasons as weak as theirs, perhaps I bring ;
But I cou'd bribe you with as good a thing,
I heard him make advances of good Nature,
That he for once, wou'd sheath his cutting
  Satyr :
Sign but his Peace, he vows he'll ne'er
  again
The Sacred Names of Fops and Beaus pro-
  fane.
Strike up the Bargain quickly ; for I swear,
As Times go now, he offers very fair.
Be not too hard on him with Statutes
  neither ;
Be kind ; and do not set your Teeth
  together,
To stretch the Laws, as Coblers do their
  Leather.   40
Horses by Papists are not to be ridden,
But sure the Muses Horse was ne're for-
  bidden ;
For in no Rate-Book it was ever found
That *Pegasus* was valued at Five-pound :
Fine him to dayly Drudging and Inditing ;
And let him pay his Taxes out in Writing.

EPILOGUE.

Spoken betwixt Antonio *and* Morayma.

Mor. I Quak'd at heart for fear the Royal
  Fashion
Shou'd have seduc'd Us two to Seperation :
To be drawn in, against our own desire,
Poor I to be a Nun, poor You a Fryar.
  Ant. I trembled when the Old Man's hand
    was in,
He would have prov'd we were too near of
  kin,

Discovering old Intrigues of Love, like
  t'other,
Betwixt my Father and thy sinful Mother;
To make Us Sister Turk and Christian
  Brother.
  Mor. Excuse me there ; that League
    shou'd have been rather   10
Betwixt your Mother and my *Mufti*-Father ;
'Tis for my own and my Relations Credit
Your Friends shou'd bear the Bastard, mine
  shou'd get it.
  Ant. Suppose us two, *Almeyda* and
    Sebastian,
With Incest prov'd upon us :——
  Mor.   Without Question,
Their Conscience was too queazy of diges-
  tion.
  Ant. Thou woud'st have kept the Councell
    of thy Brother
And sinn'd till we repented of each other.
  Mor. Beast as you are, on Natures Laws
    to trample !   19
'Twere fitter that we follow'd their Example.
And since all Marriage in Repentance ends,
'Tis good for us to part while we are Friends.
To save a Maids Remorses and Confusions,
E'en leave me now, before We try Con-
  clusions.
  Ant. To copy their Example first make
    certain
Of one good hour, like theirs, before our
  parting ;
Make a debauch o're Night of Love and
  Madness ;
And marry, when we wake, in sober sadness.
  Mor. I'le follow no new Sects of your
    inventing.
One Night might cost me nine long months
  repenting :   30
First wed, and, if you find that Life a Fetter,
Dye when you please, the sooner Sir the better:
My wealth wou'd get me love e're I cou'd
  ask it :
Oh there's a strange Temptation in the
  Casket :
All these Young Sharpers would my grace
  importune,
And make me thundring Votes of Lives and
  Fortune.

Prologue 35 Beaus] *The editors mostly print*
Beaux

Epilogue 36 Votes] *The editors impertinently*
change this into Vows
Lives] *The editors give* Life

PROLOGUE TO THE PROPHETESS.

WHAT *Nostradame*, with all his Art, can guess
The Fate of our approaching *Prophetess* ?
A Play, which, like a Prospective set right,
Presents our vast Expences close to Sight ;
But turn the Tube, and there we sadly view
Our distant Gains, and those uncertain too ;
A sweeping Tax, which on our selves we raise,
And all, like you, in hopes of better Days.
When will our Losses warn us to be Wise ?
Our Wealth decreases, and our Charges rise.
Money, the sweet Allurer of our Hopes,   11
Ebbs out in Oceans, and comes in by Drops.
We raise new Objects to provoke Delight,
But you grow sated ere the second Sight.
False Men, ev'n so you serve your Mistresses;
They rise three Stories in their Tow'ring
      Dress ;
And, after all, you Love not long enough
To pay the Rigging, ere ycu leave 'em off.·
Never content with what you had before,
But true to Change, and *English* Men all o'er.
Now Honour calls you hence ; and all your
      Care   21
Is to provide the horrid Pomp of War.
In Plume and Scarf, Jack-Boots and *Bilbo*
      Blade
Your Silver goes, that shou'd support our
      Trade.
Go, unkind Heroes, leave our Stage to mourn,
'Till rich from vanquish'd Rebels you return;
And the fat Spoils of *Teague* in Triumph draw,
His Firkin-Butter and his Usquebaugh.

Go, Conqu'rors of your Male and Female
      Foes ;
Men without Hearts, and Women without
      Hose.   30
Each bring his Love a *Bogland* Captive
      home ;
Such proper Pages will long Trains become :
With Copper Collars, and with Brawny
      Backs,
Quite to put down the Fashion of our Blacks.
Then shall the Pious Muses pay their Vows,
And furnish all their Laurels for your Brows ;
Their tuneful Voice shall rise for your De-
      lights ;
We want not Poets fit to sing your Flights.
But you, bright Beauties, fo whose only sakc
Those Doughty Knights such Dangers under-
      take,   40
When they with happy Gales are gone away, ⎞
With your propitious Presence grace our ⎟
      Play, ⎟
And with a Sigh their Empty Seats survey ; ⎠
Then think, on that bare Bench my servant
      sate,
I see him Ogle still, and hear him Chat ;
Selling facetious Bargains, and propounding
That witty Recreation, called Dum-founding.
Their Loss with Patience we will try to bear,
And wou'd do more, to see you often here ;
That our dead Stage, reviv'd by your fair
      Eyes,   50
Under a Female Regency may rise.

PROLOGUE AND EPILOGUE TO AMPHITRYON, OR THE TWO SOSIAS.

PROLOGUE.

Spoken by Mrs. BRACEGIRDLE.

THE lab'ring Bee, when his sharp Sting is
      gone,
Forgets his golden Work, and turns a Drone :
Such is a Satyr, when you take away
That Rage in which his Noble Vigour lay.

What gain you, by not suffering him to teize
      ye ?
He neither can offend you now, nor please ye.
The Honey-Bag and Venome lay so near, ⎞
That both, together, you resolv'd to tear ; ⎟
And lost your Pleasure, to secure your Fear. ⎠
How can he show his Manhood, if you bind
      him   10
To box, like Boys, with one hand ty'd
      behind him ?

THE PROPHETESS, 1690. This is Fletcher's
play transformed into an opera.
  3 Prospective] *Editors till Christie wrongly
give* Perspective

AMPHITRYON, 1690. Published in 1691. The
original text has many false stops.

This is plain Levelling of Wit ; in which
The Poor has all th' advantage, not the
Rich.
The Blockhead stands excus'd, for wanting
Sense ;
And Wits turn Blockheads in their own
defence.
Yet, though the Stages Traffick is undone,
Still *Julian's* interloping Trade goes on :
Though Satyr on the Theatre you smother,
Yet in Lampoons, you Libel one another.
The first produces still, a second Jig ;   20
You whip 'em out, like School-boys, till they
gig :
And, with the same Success, we Readers
guess,
For ev'ry one still dwindles to a less ;
And much good Malice is so meanly drest,
That we wou'd laugh, but cannot find the
Jest.
If no Advice your Rhiming Rage can
stay,
Let not the Ladies suffer in the Fray.
Their tender Sex is priviledg'd from War ;
'Tis not like Knights, to draw upon the
Fair.
What Fame expect you from so mean a
Prize ?   30
We wear no murd'ring Weapons, but our
Eyes.
Our Sex, you know, was after yours de-
sign'd;
The last Perfection of the Makers Mind ;
Heav'n drew out all the Gold for us, and
left your Dross behind.
Beauty, for Valours best Reward, He
chose ;
Peace, after War ; and after Toil, Repose.
Hence, ye Prophane, excluded from our
sights ;
And, charm'd by Day, with Honour's vain
delights,
Go, make your best of solitary Nights.
Recant betimes, 'tis prudence to submit; 40
Our Sex is still your Overmatch in Wit :
We never fail, with new, successful Arts,
To make fine Fools of you, and all your
Parts.

EPILOGUE.

Spoken by PHÆDRA, *Mrs.* MOUNTFORT.

I'm thinking (and it almost makes me
mad)
How sweet a time those Heathen Ladies
had.
Idolatry was ev'n their Gods' own trade :
They Worshipt the fine Creatures they had
made.
Cupid was chief of all the Deities ;
And Love was all the fashion, in the
Skies.
When the sweet Nymph held up the Lilly
hand,
Jove, was her humble Servant, at Command.
The Treasury of Heav'n was ne're so bare,
But still there was a Pension for the Fair. 10
In all his Reign, Adultry was no Sin ;
For *Jove* the good Example did begin.
Mark too, when he usurp'd the Husband's
name,
How civilly he sav'd the Ladies fame.
The secret Joys of Love he wisely hid ;
But you, Sirs, boast of more than e'er you
did.
You teize your Cuckolds ; to their face tor-
ment 'em :
But *Jove* gave his, new Honours to content
'em,
And, in the kind Remembrance of the
Fair,
On each exalted Son, bestowed a Star.   20
For these good deeds, as by the date
appears,
His Godship flourish'd full Two thousand
Years.
At last, when He and all his Priests grew old,
The Ladies grew in their devotion cold ;
And that false Worship would no longer
hold.
Severity of Life did next begin ;
(And always does, when we no more can Sin.)
That Doctrine, too, so hard, in Practice, lyes,
That the next Age may see another rise.   29
Then, Pagan Gods may, once again, suc-
ceed ;
And *Jove*, or *Mars*, be ready, at our need,
To get young Godlings ; and, so, mend
our breed.

PROLOGUE TO MISTAKES, OR THE FALSE REPORT.

Enter Mr. Bright.

Gentlemen, we must beg your pardon ; here's no Prologue to be had to day ; our New Play is like to come on, without a Frontispiece ; as bald as one of you young Beaux without your Perriwig. I left our young Poet sniveling and sobbing behind the Scenes, and cursing somebody that has deceiv'd him.

Enter Mr. Bowen.

Hold your prating to the Audience: Here's honest Mr. *Williams* just come in, half mellow, from the *Rose-Tavern.* He swears he is inspir'd with Claret, and will come on, and that *Extempore* too, either with a Prologue of his own, or something like one : O here he comes to his Tryal, at all Adventures ; for my part, I wish him a good Deliverance.

[*Exeunt Mr.* Bright *and Mr.* Bowen.

Enter Mr. Williams.

Save ye, sirs, save ye ! I am in a hopefull ⎫
  way. ⎪
I shou'd speak something, in Rhyme, now, ⎬
  for the Play : ⎪
But the duce take me, if I know what to say ! ⎭
I'le stick to my Friend the Authour, that
  I can tell ye,
To the last drop of Claret in my belly.
So far I'me sure 'tis Rhyme—that needs no
  granting :
And, if my verses feet stumble—you see my
  own are wanting.
Our young Poet has brought a piece of ⎫
  work, ⎪
In which though much of Art there does not ⎬
  lurk, ⎪
It may hold out three days—And that's ⎪
  as long as *Cork.*   10 ⎭

But, for this Play—(which, till I have done,
  we show not.)
What may be its fortune—By the Lord—
  I know not.
This I dare swear, no malice here is writ ;
'Tis Innocent of all things—ev'n of Wit.
He's no high Flyer—he makes no sky
  Rockets,
His Squibbs are only levell'd at your
  Pockets ;
And if his Crackers light among your pelf,
You are blown-up ; if not, then he's blown-
  up himself.
By this time, I'm something recover'd of my
  fluster'd madness :
And, now, a word or two in sober sadness. 20
Ours is a Common Play : and you pay
  down
A common Harlots price—just half a
  Crown.
You'l say, I play the Pimp on my Friends ⎫
  score ; ⎪
But since 'tis for a Friend, your gibes give ⎬
  o're, ⎪
For many a Mother has done that before. ⎭
How's this ? you cry : an Actor write ?—
  we know it ;
But *Shakespear* was an Actor, and a Poet
Has not great *Johnson's* learning often
  fail'd,
But *Shakespear's* greater Genius still pre-
  vail'd ?   29
Have not some writing Actors, in this Age
Deserv'd and found Success upon the
  Stage ?
To tell the truth, when our old Wits are tir'd.
Not one of us but means to be inspir'd.
Let your kind presence grace our homely ⎫
  cheer ; ⎪
Peace and the Butt is all our bus'ness here ; ⎬
So much for that ;—and the Devil take ⎪
  small beer. ⎭

Mistakes, 1690. The play is by Joseph Harris. | 26 this? you cry :] this, you cry ? *1690.*

PROLOGUE AND EPILOGUE TO KING ARTHUR, OR THE BRITISH WORTHY.

PROLOGUE TO THE OPERA.

Spoken by Mr. BETTERTON.

SURE there's a dearth of Wit in this dull Town,
When silly Plays so savourly go down ;
As, when Clipp'd Money passes, 'tis a sign
A Nation is not over-stock'd with Coin.
Happy is he, who in his own Defence,
Can write just level to your humble Sence ;
Who higher than your Pitch can never go ;
And doubtless, he must creep, who Writes below.
So have I seen, in Hall of Knight, or Lord,
A weak Arm throw on a long Shovel-Board ;
He barely lays his Piece, bar Rubs and Knocks,   11
Secur'd by Weakness not to reach the Box.
A feeble Poet will his Bus'ness do, ⎫
Who, straining all he can, comes up to you: ⎬
For, if you like your Selves, you like him too. ⎭
An Ape his own Dear Image will embrace ;
An ugly *Beau* adores a Hatchet Face :
So, some of you, on pure instinct of Nature,
Are led, by Kind, t' admire your fellow Creature.   19
In fear of which, our House has sent this Day,
T' insure our New-Built-Vessel, call'd a Play ;
No sooner Nam'd, than one crys out, These Stagers
Come in good time, to make more Work for Wagers.
The Town divides, if it will take or no ; ⎫
The Courtiers Bet, the Cits, the Merchants too ; ⎬
A sign they have but little else to do. ⎭
Betts at the first were Fool-Traps ; where the Wise
Like Spiders, lay in Ambush for the Flies ;
But now they're grown a common Trade for all, ⎫
And Actions by the News-Book Rise and Fall ;   30 ⎬
Wits, Cheats, and Fops are free of Wager-Hall. ⎭

One Policy as far as *Lyons* carries ;
Another, nearer home sets up for *Paris*.
Our Betts, at last, wou'd ev'n to *Rome* extend,
But that the Pope has proved our Trusty Friend.
Indeed, it were a Bargain, worth our Money,
Cou'd we insure another *Ottobuoni*.
Among the rest there are a sharping Sett,
That Pray for us, and yet against us Bett :
Sure Heav'n it self is at a loss to know   40
If these wou'd have their Pray'rs be heard, or no :
For, in great Stakes, we piously suppose,
Men Pray but very faintly they may lose.
Leave off these Wagers ; for, in Conscience Speaking,
The City needs not your new Tricks for Breaking :
And if you Gallants lose, to all appearing
You'll want an Equipage for Volunteering ;
While thus, no Spark of Honour left within ye,
When you shou'd draw the Sword, you draw the Guinea.

THE EPILOGUE.

Spoke by Mrs. BRACEGIRDLE.

I'VE had to-day a Dozen *Billet-Doux*
From *Fops*, and *Wits*, and *Cits*, and *Bow-street Beaux* :
Some from *Whitehal*, but from the *Temple* more :
A *Covent-Garden* Porter brought me four.
I have not yet read all : But, without feigning,
We *Maids* can make shrewd Ghesses at your Meaning.
What if, to shew your Styles, I read 'em here ? ⎫
Me thinks I hear one cry, *Oh Lord, forbear :* ⎬
No, Madam, no ; by Heav'n, that's too severe. ⎭
Well then, be safe   10 ⎫
But swear henceforwards to renounce all Writing, ⎬
And take this Solemn Oath of my inditing,— ⎬
As you love Ease and hate Campaigns and Fighting. ⎭

KING ARTHUR, 1691.
Prologue 2 savourly] savourily *Scott* : favourably *Bell*.

Yet, Faith, 'tis just to make some few
    Examples :
What if I shew'd you one or two for Samples ?
    Pulls one out.] Heres, one desires my
    Ladyship to meet
At the kind Couch above in *Bridges-Street.*
Oh Sharping Knave ! That wou'd have you
    know what,
For a Poor Sneaking Treat of *Chocolat.*
    Pulls out another.] Now, in the Name of
    Luck, I'll break this open,   20
Because I Dreamt last Night I had a Token ;
The Superscription is exceeding pretty,
To the Desire of all the Town and City.
Now, *Gallants*, you must know, this precious
    Fop
Is Foreman of a Haberdashers-Shop :
One who devoutly cheats, demure in
    Carriage,
And courts me to the Holy Bands of
    Marriage ;

But, with a *Civil Inuendo* too,
My Overplus of Love shall be for you.
    Reads.]   *Madam, I swear your Looks are
    so Divine,*   30
*When I set up, your Face shall be my
    Sign ;*
*Tho Times are hard—to show how I Adore
    you,*
*Here's my whole Heart, and half a Guinea for
    you.*
But, have a Care of Beaux ; *They're false, my
    Honey ;*
*And, which is worse, have not one Rag of
    Money.*
See how Maliciously the Rogue would
    wrong ye !
But I know better Things of some among ye.
My wisest way will be to keep the Stage,
And trust to the Good Nature of the Age :
And he that likes the Musick and the Play 40
Shall be my Favourite Gallant to-day.

PROLOGUE AND EPILOGUE TO CLEOMENES, THE SPARTAN HEROE.

PROLOGUE

Spoken by Mr. MOUNTFORD.

I THINK, or hope at least, the Coast is clear ;
That none but Men of Wit and Sense are
    here ;
That our Bear-Garden Friends are all away,
Who bounce with Hands and Feet, and cry,
    Play, Play,
Who, to save Coach-Hire, trudge along the
    Street,
Then print our matted Seats with dirty Feet;
Who, while we speak, make Love to Orange-
    Wenches,
And between Acts stand strutting on the
    Benches ;
Where got a Cock-horse, making vile
    Grimaces,
They to the Boxes show their Booby Faces.
A Merry-Andrew such a Mob will serve, 11
And treat 'em with such Wit as they
    deserve :

Let 'em go people *Ireland*, where there's
    need
Of such new Planters, to repair the Breed ;
Or to *Virginia* or *Jamaica* steer,
But have a Care of some *French* Privateer ;
For, if they should become the Prize of
    Battle,
They'll take 'em, black and white, for *Irish*
    Cattle.
Arise, true Judges, in your own Defence,
Controul those Foplings, and declare for
    Sense :   20
For, should the Fools prevail, they stop not
    there,
But make their next Descent upon the Fair.
Then rise, ye Fair ; for it concerns you most,
That Fools no longer should your Favours
    boast :
'Tis time you should renounce 'em, for we
    find
They plead a senseless Claim to Woman-kind :
Such Squires are only fit for Country-Towns,
To stink of Ale and dust a Stand with Clowns;
Who, to be chosen for the Land's Protectors,
Tope and get drunk before their wise Electors.

CLEOMENES, 1692. The Prologue and Epilogue
were not printed with the first edition of the
play.

DR.   K

Let not Farce-Lovers your weak Choice
upbraid, 31
But turn 'em over to the Chamber-maid.
Or, if they come to see our Tragick Scenes,
Instruct them what a *Spartan* Heroe means :
Teach 'em how manly Passions ought to
move,
For such as cannot Think can never Love ;
And, since they needs will judge the Poet's
Art,
Point 'em with Fescu's to each shining part.
Our Author hopes in you ; but still in Pain,
He fears your Charms will be employ'd in
vain. 40
You can make Fools of Wits, we find each
Hour ;
But to make Wits of Fools is past your Pow'r.

EPILOGUE.

Spoken by Mrs. BRACEGIRDLE.

This day, the Poet, bloodily inclin'd,
Has made me die, full sore against my Mind !
Some of you naughty Men, I fear, will cry,
Poor Rogue ! would I might teach thee how
to die !
Thanks for your Love ; but I sincerely say,
I never mean to die your wicked way.
Well, since it is decreed all Flesh must go,
(And I am Flesh, at least, for aught you
know,)
I first declare, I die with pious Mind,
In perfect Charity with all Mankind. 10
Next, for my Will :——I have in my Dispose
Some certain Moveables would please you
Beaux ;

As, first, my Youth ; for, as I have been told,
Some of you, modish Sparks, are devilish
old.
My Chastity I need not leave among ye :
For to suspect old Fops were much to wrong
ye.
You swear you're Sinners ; but for all your
Haste,
Your Misses shake their Heads, and find you
chaste.
I give my Courage to those bold Commanders,
That stay with us, and dare not go for
Flanders. 20
I leave my Truth (to make his Plot more
clear)
To Mr. *Fuller,* when he next shall swear.
I give my Judgment, craving all your
Mercies,
To those that leave good Plays, for damn'd
dull Farces.
My small Devotion let the Gallants share,
That come to ogle us at Evening Pray'r.
I give my Person——let me well consider,
Faith e'en to him that is the fairest Bidder ;
To some rich Hunks, if any be so bold
To say those dreadful Words, *To have and
hold.* 30
But stay——to give, and be bequeathing
still,
When I'm so poor, is just like *Wickham's*
Will :
Like that notorious Cheat, vast Sums I give,
Only that you may keep me while I live.
Buy a good Bargain, Gallants, while you
may ;
I'll cost you but your Half-a-Crown a Day.

EPILOGUE TO HENRY II., KING OF ENGLAND, WITH THE DEATH OF ROSAMOND.

THUS you the sad Catastrophe have seen,
Occasion'd by a Mistress and a Queen.
Queen *Eleanor* the proud was *French*, they
say ;
But *English* Manufacture got the Day.
Jane Clifford was her Name, as Books aver :
Fair *Rosamond* was but her *Nom de Guerre.*
Now tell me, Gallants, wou'd you lead your
Life
With such a Mistress, or with such a Wife ?

If one must be your Choice, which d'ye
approve,
The Curtain-Lecture or the Curtain-Love ? 10
Wou'd ye be godly with perpetual Strife,
Still drudging on with homely *Joan* your
Wife,
Or take your Pleasure in a wicked way,
Like honest Whoring *Harry* in the Play ?
I guess your Minds ; The Mistress wou'd be
taking,
And nauseous Matrimony sent a packing.

HENRY II, 1693. The play is by John Bancroft,
published in 1693.

15 taking] *Some editions wrongly give* taken

The Devil's in ye all; Mankind's a Rogue,
You love the Bride, but you detest the Clog:
After a Year, poor Spouse is left i' th' lurch;
And you, like *Haynes*, return to Mother-Church.   20
Or, if the Name of Church comes cross your mind,
Chapels of Ease behind our Scenes you find.
The Play-house is a kind of Market-place;
One chaffers for a Voice, another for a Face;

Nay, some of you, I dare not say how many,
Would buy of me a Pen'worth for your Pony.
Even this poor Face (which with my Fan I hide)
Would make a shift my Portion to provide,
With some small Perquisites I have beside.
Though for your Love, perhaps, I should not care,   30
I could not hate a Man that bids me fair.
What might ensue, 'tis hard for me to tell;
But I was drench'd to day for loving well,
And fear the Poyson that would make me swell.

PROLOGUE AND EPILOGUE TO LOVE TRIUMPHANT, OR NATURE WILL PREVAIL.

PROLOGUE.

Spoken by Mr. BETTERTON.

As, when some Treasurer lays down the Stick,
Warrants are Sign'd for ready Mony thick,
And many desperate Debentures paid,
Which never had been, had his Lordship staid:
So now, this Poet, who forsakes the Stage,
Intends to gratifie the present Age.
One Warrant shall be Sign'd for every Man;
All shall be Wits that will; and *Beaux* that can:
Provided still, this Warrant be not shown,
And you be Wits but to your selves alone; 10
Provided too; you rail at one another:
For there's no one Wit, will allow a Brother;
Provided also; that you spare this Story,
Damn all the Plays that e're shall come before ye.
If one by chance prove good in half a score,
Let that one pay for all, and Damn it more.
For if a good one scape among the Crew,
And you continue Judging as you do,
Every bad Play will hope for Damning too.
You might Damn this, if it were worth your pains,   20
Here's nothing you will like; no fustian Scenes,
And nothing too of—you know what he means.

No double *Entendrès*, which you Sparks allow.
To make the Ladies look—they know not how;
Simply as 'twere, and knowing both together.
Seeming to fan their Faces in cold Weather
But here's a Story, which no Books relate,
Coin'd from our own Old Poet's Addle-Pate
The Fable has a Moral too, if sought:
But let that go; for, upon second Thought,   30
He fears but few come hither to be Taught.
Yet if you will be profited, you may;
And he would Bribe you too, to like his Play.
He Dies, at least to us, and to the Stage,
And what he has he leaves this Noble Age.
He leaves you, first, all Plays of his Inditing,
The whole Estate which he has got by Writing.
The Beaux may think this nothing but vain Praise;
They'l find it something, the Testator says:
For half their Love is made from scraps of Plays.   40
To his worst Foes, he leaves his Honesty;
That they may thrive upon't as much as he.
He leaves his Manners to the Roaring Boys,
Who come in Drunk and fill the House with noise.
He leaves to the dire Critiques of his Wit
His Silence and Contempt of all they Writ.
To *Shakespear's* Critique he bequeaths the Curse,
To find his faults; and yet himself make worse;

A precious Reader in Poetique Schools,
Who by his own Examples damns his
　　Rules.　　　　　　　　　　　　　50
Last, for the Fair, he wishes you may be
From your dull Critiques, the Lampooners
　free.
Tho' he pretends no Legacy to leave you,
An Old Man may at least good wishes give
　you.
Your Beauty names the Play ; and may it
　prove,
To each, an Omen of Triumphant Love.

EPILOGUE.

Now, in good Manners, nothing shou'd be
　sed
Against this Play, because the Poet's
　dead.
The Prologue told us of a Moral here :
Wou'd I cou'd find it, but the Devil knows
　where.
If in my Part it lyes, I fear he means
To warn us of the Sparks behind our
　Scenes.
For, if you'll take it on *Dalinda's* Word,
'Tis a hard Chapter to refuse a Lord.
The Poet might pretend this Moral too,
That when a Wit and Fool together woo, 10
The Damsel (not to break an Ancient Rule)
Shou'd leave the Wit, and take the Wealthy
　Fool.

This he might mean ; but there's a Truth
　behind,
And, since it touches none of all our Kind
But Masks and Misses, faith, I'le speak my
　Mind.
What if he Taught our Sex more cautious
　Carriage,
And not to be too Coming before Marriage ;
For fear of my Misfortune in the Play,
A Kid brought home upon the Wedding day !
I fear there are few *Sancho's* in the Pit, 20
So good as to forgive and to forget,
That will, like him, restore us into Favour,
And take us after on our good Behaviour.
Few, when they find the Mony Bag is rent,
Will take it for good Payment on content.
But in the Telling, there the difference is,
Sometimes they find it more than they cou'd
　wish.
Therefore be warn'd, you Misses and you
　Masks,
Look to your hits, nor give the first that asks.
Tears, Sighs, and Oaths, no truth of Passion
　prove ;　　　　　　　　　　　　30
True Settlement alone, declares true Love.
For him that Weds a Puss, who kept her first,
I say but little, but I doubt the worst :
The Wife, that was a Cat, may mind her
　house,
And prove an Honest and a Careful Spouse ;
But, faith, I wou'd not trust her with a
　Mouse.

EPILOGUE TO THE HUSBAND HIS OWN CUCKOLD.

Spoken by Mrs. BRACEGIRDLE.

LIKE some raw Sophister that mounts the
　Pulpit,
So trembles a young Poet at a full Pit.
Unus'd to Crowds, the Parson quakes for
　fear,
And wonders how the Devil he durst come
　there ;
Wanting three Talents needful for the
　Place,
Some Beard, some Learning, and some little
　Grace.

Nor is the Puny Poet void of Care ;
For Authors, such as our new Authors are,
Have not much Learning, nor much Wit to
　spare ;
And as for Grace, to tell the Truth, there's
　scarce one,　　　　　　　　　　10
But has as little as the very Parson :
Both say they Preach and Write for your
　Instruction ;
But 'tis for a Third Day, and for Induction.
The difference is, that tho' you like the
　Play,
The Poet's Gain is ne'er beyond his Day.

LOVE TRIUMPHANT, 1694.
Epilogue 1 shou'd] *Christie and other editors
absurdly give* shall
10 woo,] woo ; *1694.*

THE HUSBAND HIS OWN CUCKOLD, 1696. The
play is by John Dryden the younger.

But with the Parson 'tis another Case,
He, without Holiness, may rise to
   Grace ;
The Poet has one disadvantage more,
That if his Play be dull, he 's Damn'd all
   o'er,
Not only a damn'd Blockhead, but damn'd
   Poor.   20
But Dullness well becomes the Sable Gar-
   ment ;
I warrant that ne'er spoil'd a Priest's Pre-
   ferment :
Wit's not his Business, and as Wit now
   goes,
Sirs, 'tis not so much yours as you suppose,
For you like nothing now but nauseous
   Beaux.

You laugh not, Gallants, as by proof appears,
At what his Beauship says, but what he
   wears ;
So 'tis your Eyes are tickled, not your Ears.
The Taylor and the Furrier find the Stuff,
The Wit lies in the Dress and monstrous Muff.
The Truth on't is, the Payment of the Pit   31
Is like for like, Clipt Money for Clipt Wit.
You cannot from our absent Author hope
He should equip the Stage with such a Fop
Fools Change in *England*, and new Fools
   arise ;
For, tho' th' Immortal Species never dies,
Yet ev'ry Year new Maggots make new
   Flies.
But where he lives abroad, he scarce can find
One Fool, for Million that he left behind.

PROLOGUE AND EPILOGUE

ON THE OCCASION OF A REPRESENTATION FOR DRYDEN'S BENEFIT,
MARCH 25, 1700.

PROLOGUE.

How wretched is the Fate of those who
   write !
Brought muzl'd to the Stage, for fear they
   bite ;
Where, like *Tom Dove*, they stand the
   Common Foe,
Lugg'd by the *Critique*, Baited by the *Beau*.
Yet, worse, their Brother Poets damn the
   Play,
And Roar the loudest, tho' they never pay.
The Fops are proud of Scandal, for they cry,
At every lewd, low Character,—That's I.
He who writes Letters to himself wou'd
   Swear,
The World forgot him if he was not there.   10
What shou'd a Poet do ? 'Tis hard for One
To pleasure all the Fools that wou'd be
   shown :
And yet not Two in Ten will pass the Town.
Most Coxcombs are not of the Laughing kind ;
More goes to make a Fop, than Fops can
   find.
   Quack *Maurus*, tho' he never took Degrees
In either of our Universities,

Yet to be shown by some kind Wit he looks,
Because he plai'd the Fool, and writ Three
   Books.
But if he wou'd be worth a Poet's Pen,   20
He must be more a Fool, and write again :
For all the former Fustian stuff he wrote
Was Dead-born Doggrel, or is quite forgot ;
His Man of *Uz*, stript of his *Hebrew* Robe,
Is just the Proverb, and *As poor as Job*.
One would have thought he could no longer
   Jog ;
But *Arthur* was a level, *Job's* a Bog.
There, tho' he crept, yet still he kept in
   sight ;
But here, he founders in, and sinks down-
   right.
Had he prepar'd us, and been dull by Rule,
Tobit had first been turned to Ridicule ;   31
But our bold *Britton*, without Fear or Awe,
O'er-leaps at once the whole Apocrypha ;
Invades the Psalms with Rhymes, and leaves
   no room
For any Vandal *Hopkins* yet to come.
   But when, if, after all, this Godly Geer
Is not so Senceless as it would appear ?
Our Mountebank has laid a deeper Train ;
His Cant, like *Merry Andrew's* Noble Vein,
Cat-call's the Sects to draw 'em in again.

At leisure Hours in Epique Song he deals, 41
Writes to the rumbling of his Coaches
    Wheels ;
Prescribes in hast, and seldom kills by rule,
But rides Triumphant between Stool and
    Stool.
    Well, let him go ; 'tis yet too early day
To get himself a Place in Farce or Play ;
We know not by what Name we should
    Arraign him,
For no one Category can contain him ;
A Pedant, canting Preacher, and a Quack,
Are load enough to break one Asses Back : 50
At last, grown wanton, he presum'd to write, ⎫
Traduc'd Two Kings, their kindness to re- ⎪
    quite ;   ⎬
One made the Doctor, and one dubb'd the   ⎪
    Knight.   ⎭

EPILOGUE.

Perhaps the Parson stretch'd a point too far,
When with our *Theatres* he wag'd a War.
He tells you, that this very Moral Age
Receiv'd the first Infection from the Stage ;
But sure, a banisht Court, with Lewdness
    fraught,
The Seeds of open Vice returning brought.
Thus lodg'd, (as Vice by great Example
    thrives,)
It first debauch'd the Daughters and the
    Wives.
London, a fruitful Soil, yet never bore
So plentiful a Crop of Horns before.   10
The Poets, who must live by Courts or
    starve,
Were proud, so good a Government to serve ;
And, mixing with Buffoons and Pimps pro-
    fain,
Tainted the Stage for some small Snip of
    Gain ;

For they, like *Harlots*, under *Bawds* profess't,
Took all the ungodly pains, and got the
    least.
Thus did the thriving Malady prevail ;
The Court it's Head, the Poets but the Tail.
The Sin was of our Native Growth, 'tis
    true ;
The Scandall of the Sin was wholly new. 20
Misses there were, but modestly conceal'd ;
White-hall the naked *Venus* first reveal'd,
Who standing as at *Cyprus* in her Shrine,
The Strumpet was ador'd with Rites Divine.
E're this, if Saints had any Secret Motion,
'Twas Chamber Practice all, and Close Devo-
    tion.
I pass the Peccadillo's of their time ;
Nothing but open Lewdness was a Crime.
A *Monarch's* Blood was venial to the Nation,
Compar'd with one foul Act of Fornication.
Now, they wou'd Silence us, and shut the
    Door   31
That let in all the barefac'd Vice before.
As for reforming us, which some pretend, ⎫
That Work in *England* is without an end ; ⎪
Well we may change, but we shall never   ⎬
    mend.   ⎭
Yet, if you can but bear the present Stage,
We hope much better of the coming Age.
What wou'd you say, if we should first begin ⎫
To Stop the Trade of Love behind the Scene : ⎬
Where *Actresses* make bold with married   ⎪
    Men ?   40⎭
For while abroad so prodigal the *Dolt* is,
Poor Spouse at Home as ragged as a Colt is.
In short, we'll grow as Moral as we can,
Save, here and there, a Woman or a Man ;
But neither you, nor we, with all our pains,
Can make clean work ; there will be some
    Remains,
While you have still your *Oats*, and we our
    Hains.

FABLES

Ancient and *Modern* ;

Tranſlated into VERSE,

FROM

Homer, Ovid,
Boccace, & Chaucer :

WITH

ORIGINAL POEMS.

By Mr *DRYDEN.*

*Nunc ultrò ad Cineres ipſius & oſſa parentis
(Haud equidem ſine mente, reor, ſine numine divum)
Adſumus.* Virg. Æn. lib. 5.

LONDON:

Printed for *Jacob Tonſon,* within *Gray's Inn Gate* next
Gray's Inn Lane. MDCC.

TO
HIS GRACE
THE
DUKE OF ORMOND.

My Lord,—Some Estates are held in *England* by paying a Fine at the change of every Lord : I have enjoy'd the Patronage of your Family, from the time of your excellent Grandfather to this present Day. I have dedicated the Lives of *Plutarch* to the first Duke ; and have celebrated the Memory of your Heroick Father. Tho' I am very short of the Age of *Nestor*, yet I have liv'd to a third Generation of your House ; and by your Grace's Favour am admitted still to hold from you by the same Tenure.

I am not vain enough to boast that I have deserv'd the value of so Illustrious a Line but my Fortune is the greater, that for three Descents they have been pleas'd to distinguish my Poems from those of other Men, and have accordingly made me their peculiar Care May it be permitted me to say, That as your Grandfather and Father were cherish'd and adorn'd with Honours by two successive Monarchs, so I have been esteem'd and patronis'd by the Grandfather, the Father, and the Son, descended from one of the most Ancient, most Conspicuous, and most Deserving Families in *Europe*.

'Tis true, that by delaying the Payment of my last Fine, when it was due by your Grace's Accession to the Titles and Patrimonies of your House, I may seem in rigour of Law to have made a forfeiture of my Claim ; yet my Heart has always been devoted to your Service ; and since you have been graciously pleas'd, by your permission of this Address, to accept the tender of my Duty, 'tis not yet too late to lay these Poems at your Feet.

The World is sensible that you worthily succeed not only to the Honours of your Ancestors, but also to their Virtues. The long Chain of Magnanimity, Courage, easiness of Access, and desire of doing Good, even to the Prejudice of your Fortune, is so far from being broken in your Grace, that the precious Metal yet runs pure to the newest Link of it which I will not call the last, because I hope and pray it may descend to late Posterity And your flourishing Youth, and that of your excellent Dutchess, are happy Omens of my Wish.

'Tis observ'd by *Livy* and by others, That some of the noblest *Roman* Families retain'd a resemblance of their Ancestry, not only in their Shapes and Features, but also in their Manners, their Qualities, and the distinguishing Characters of their Minds : Some Lines were noted for a stern, rigid Virtue, salvage, haughty, parcimonious, and unpopular Others were more sweet, and affable ; made of a more pliant Past, humble, courteous and obliging ; studious of doing charitable Offices, and diffusive of the Goods which they enjoy'd. The last of these is the proper and indelible Character of your Grace's Family God Almighty has endu'd you with a Softness, a Beneficence, an attractive Behaviour winning on the Hearts of others ; and so sensible of their Misery, that the Wounds of Fortune seem not inflicted on them, but on your self. You are so ready to redress, that you almost prevent their Wishes, and always exceed their Expectations : As if what was yours, was not your own, and not given you to possess, but to bestow on wanting Merit. But this is a Topick which I must cast in Shades, lest I offend your Modesty which is so far from being ostentatious of the Good you do, that it blushes even to have it known : And therefore I must leave you to the Satisfaction and Testimony of your own Conscience, which, though it be a silent Panegyrick, is yet the best.

You are so easy of Access that *Poplicola* was not more, whose Doors were open'd on the Outside to save the people even the common Civility of asking entrance ; where all were equally admitted ; where nothing that was reasonable was deny'd, where Misfortune was a powerful Recommendation, and where (I can scarce forbear saying) that Want it self was a powerful Mediator, and was next to Merit.

The History of *Peru* assures us, That their *Inca's*, above all their Titles, esteem'd that the highest, which called them Lovers of the Poor : A Name more glorious than the *Felix, Pius*, and *Augustus* of the *Roman* Emperors ; which were Epithets of Flattery, deserv'd by few of them ; and not running in a Blood like the perpetual Gentleness and inherent Goodness of the *Ormond* Family.

Gold, as it is the purest, so it is the softest and most ductile of all Metals : Iron, which is the hardest, gathers Rust, corrodes its self ; and is therefore subject to Corruption : It was never intended for Coins and Medals, or to bear the Faces and Inscriptions of the Great. Indeed 'tis fit for Armour, to bear off Insults, and preserve the Wearer in the Day of Battle ; but the Danger once repell'd, it is laid aside by the Brave, as a Garment 10 too rough for civil Conversation ; a necessary Guard in War, but too harsh and cumbersome in Peace, and which keeps off the embraces of a more human Life.

For this reason, my Lord, though you have Courage in a heroical Degree, yet I ascribe it to you but as your second Attribute : Mercy, Beneficence, and Compassion, claim Precedence, as they are first in the divine Nature. An intrepid Courage, which is inherent in your Grace, is at best but a Holiday-kind of Virtue, to be seldom exercis'd, and never but in Cases of Necessity ; Affability, Mildness, Tenderness, and a Word, which I would fain bring back to its original Signification of Virtue, I mean good Nature, are of daily use : They are the Bread of Mankind and Staff of Life : Neither Sighs, nor Tears, nor Groans, nor Curses of the vanquish'd follow Acts of Compassion, and of Charity : But 20 a sincere Pleasure and Serenity of Mind, in him who performs an Action of Mercy, which cannot suffer the Misfortunes of another, without redress ; lest they should bring a kind of Contagion along with them, and pollute the Happiness which he enjoys.

Yet since the perverse Tempers of Mankind, since Oppression on one side, and Ambition on the other, are sometimes the unavoidable Occasions of War ; that Courage, that Magnanimity, and Resolution, which is born with you, cannot be too much commended : And here it grieves me that I am scanted in the pleasure of dwelling on many of your Actions : But αἰδέομαι Τρῶας is an Expression which *Tully* often uses, when he would do what he dares not, and fears the Censure of the *Romans*.

I have sometimes been forc'd to amplify on others ; but here, where the Subject is so 30 fruitful that the Harvest overcomes the Reaper, I am shorten'd by my Chain, and can only see what is forbidden me to reach : Since it is not permitted me to commend you according to the extent of my Wishes, and much less is it in my Power to make my Commendations equal to your Merits.

Yet in this Frugality of your Praises, there are some Things which I cannot omit, without detracting from your Character. You have so form'd your own Education, as enables you to pay the Debt you owe your Country, or, more properly speaking, both your Countries : Because you were born, I may almost say in Purple at the Castle of *Dublin*, when your Grandfather was Lord-Lieutenant, and have since been bred in the Court of *England*.

If this Address had been in Verse, I might have call'd you, as *Claudian* calls *Mercury*, 40 *Numen commune, Gemino faciens commercia mundo.* The better to satisfy this double Obligation, you have early cultivated the Genius you have to Arms, that when the service of *Britain* or *Ireland* shall require your Courage and your Conduct, you may exert them both to the Benefit of either Country. You began in the Cabinet what you afterwards practis'd in the Camp ; and thus both *Lucullus* and *Cæsar* (to omit a crowd of shining *Romans*) form'd them selves to the War by the Study of History, and by the examples of the greatest Captains, both of *Greece* and *Italy*, before their time. I name those two Commanders in particular, because they were better read in Chronicle than any of the *Roman* Leaders ; and that *Lucullus* in particular, having only the Theory of War from Books, was thought fit, without Practice, to be sent into the Field against the most 50 formidable Enemy of *Rome*. *Tully* indeed was call'd the learn'd Consul in derision; but then, he was not born a Soldier : His Head was turn'd another way : When he read the Tactics, he was thinking on the Bar, which was his Field of Battle. The Knowledge of Warfare is thrown away on a General who dares not make use of what he knows. I commend it only in a Man of Courage and of Resolution : in him it will direct his Martial Spirit, and teach him the way to the best Victories, which are those that are least bloody, and which, tho' atchieved by the Hand, are managed by the Head. Science distinguishes a Man of Honour from one of those Athletick Brutes whom undeservedly we call Heroes. Curs'd be the Poet, who first honour'd with that Name a meer *Ajax*, a Man-killing Ideot. The *Ulysses* of *Ovid* upbraids his Ignorance, that he understood not the Shield for which he pleaded : There was engraven on it, Plans of Cities, and Maps of Countries, which *Ajax* could not comprehend, but look'd on them as stupidly as his Fellow-Beast the Lion. But 10 on the other side, your Grace has given your self the Education of his Rival ; you have studied every Spot of Ground in *Flanders*, which for these ten Years past has been the Scene of Battles and of Sieges. No wonder if you perform'd your part with such Applause on a Theater which you understood so well.

If I design'd this for a Poetical Encomium, it were easy to enlarge on so copious a Subject ; but confining my self to the Severity of Truth, and to what is becoming me to say, I must not only pass over many Instances of your Military Skill, but also those of your assiduous Diligence in the War, and of your personal bravery, attended with an ardent Thirst of Honour ; a long train of Generosity ; Profuseness of doing Good ; a Soul unsatisfy'd with all it has done ; and an unextinguish'd Desire of doing more. But all this is Matter 20 for your own Historians ; I am, as *Virgil* says, *Spatiis exclusus iniquis*.

Yet not to be wholly silent of all your Charities, I must stay a little on one Action, which preferr'd the Relief of Others, to the Consideration of your Self. When, in the Battle of *Landen*, your Heat of Courage (a Fault only pardonable to your Youth) had transported you so far before your Friends, that they were unable to follow, much less to succour you ; when you were not only dangerously, but in all appearance mortally wounded ; when in that desperate Condition you were made Prisoner, and carried to *Namur*, at that time in Possession of the *French* ; then it was, my Lord, that you took a considerable Part of what was remitted to you of your own Revenues, and as a memorable Instance of your Heroick Charity, put it into the Hands of Count *Guiscard*, who was Governor of the 30 Place, to be distributed among your Fellow-Prisoners. The *French* Commander, charm'd with the greatness of your Soul, accordingly consign'd it to the Use for which it was intended by the Donor: By which means the Lives of so many miserable Men were sav'd, and a comfortable Provision made for their Subsistance, who had otherwise perish'd, had not you been the Companion of their Misfortune : or rather sent by Providence, like another *Joseph*, to keep out Famine from invading those, whom in Humility you called your Brethren. How happy was it for those poor Creatures that your Grace was made their Fellow-Sufferer ? And how glorious for You, that you chose to want, rather than not relieve the Wants of others ? The Heathen Poet, in commending the charity of *Dido* to the *Trojans*, spoke like a Christian : *Non ignara mali, miseris succurrere disco*. All 40 men, even those of a different Interest, and contrary Principles, must praise this Action, as the most eminent for Piety, not only in this degenerate Age, but almost in any of the former ; when Men were made *de meliore luto* ; when Examples of Charity were frequent, and when there were in being, *Teucri, pulcherrima proles, Magnanimi heroes, nati melioribus annis*. No Envy can detract from this : it will shine in History ; and like Swans, grow whiter the longer it endures : and the Name of ORMOND will be more celebrated in his Captivity than in his greatest Triumphs.

But all Actions of your Grace are of a piece ; as Waters keep the Tenour of their Fountains : your Compassion is general, and has the same Effect as well on Enemies as Friends. 'Tis so much in your Nature to do Good, that your Life is but one continued Act of placing 50 Benefits on many, as the Sun is always carrying his Light to some Part or other of the World : And were it not that your Reason guides you where to give, I might almost say that you could not help bestowing more, than is consisting with the Fortune of a private Man, or with the Will of any but an *Alexander*.

What Wonder is it then, that being born for a Blessing to Mankind, your suppos'd Death in that Engagement, was so generally lamented through the Nation ? The Concernment for it was as universal as the Loss : And though the Gratitude might be counterfeit in some ; yet the Tears of all were real : Where every man deplor'd his private Part in that Calamity, and even those who had not tasted of your Favours, yet built so much on the Fame of your Beneficence, that they bemoan'd the Loss of their Expectations.

This brought the untimely Death of your Great Father into fresh remembrance ; as if the same Decree had pass'd on two short successive Generations of the Virtuous ; and I repeated to my self the same Verses, which I had formerly apply'd to him: *Ostendunt terris hunc tantum fata, nec ultra Esse sinunt.*   10

But to the Joy not only of all good Men, but of Mankind in general, the unhappy Omen took not place. You are still living to enjoy the Blessings and Applause of all the Good you have perform'd, the Prayers of Multitudes whom you have oblig'd, for your long Prosperity, and that your Power of doing generous and charitable Actions may be as extended as your Will ; which is by none more zealously desir'd than by

Your Grace's most humble,

most oblig'd, and most

obedient servant,

JOHN DRYDEN.

PREFACE.   20

'TIS with a Poet as with a Man who designs to build, and is very exact, as he supposes, in casting up the Cost beforehand : But, generally speaking, he is mistaken in his Account, and reckons short of the Expense he first intended : He alters his Mind as the Work proceeds, and will have this or that Convenience more, of which he had not thought when he began. So has it hapned to me ; I have built a House, where I intended but a Lodge : Yet with better Success than a certain Nobleman, who, beginning with a Dog-kennil never liv'd to finish the Palace he had contriv'd.

From translating the First of *Homer's Iliads* (which I intended as an Essay to the whole Work) I proceeded to the Translation of the Twelfth Book of *Ovid's Metamorphoses*, because it contains, among other Things, the Causes, the Beginning, and Ending of the *Trojan* 30 War : Here I ought in reason to have stopp'd ; but the speeches of *Ajax* and *Ulysses* lying next in my way, I could not balk 'em. When I had compass'd them, I was so taken with the former Part of the Fifteenth Book (which is the Master-piece of the whole *Metamorphoses*) that I enjoyn'd myself the pleasing Task of rendring it into *English*. And now I found by the Number of my Verses, that they began to swell into a little Volume ; which gave me an Occasion of looking backward on some Beauties of my Author, in his former Books : There occur'd to me the Hunting of the Boar, *Cinyras* and *Myrrha*, the good-natured story of *Baucis* and *Philemon*, with the rest, which I hope I have translated closely enough, and given them the same Turn of Verse which they had in the Original ; and this, I may say without vanity, is not the Talent of every Poet : He who has arriv'd 40 the nearest to it is the Ingenious and Learned *Sandys*, the best Versifier of the former Age ; if I may properly call it by that Name, which was the former Part of this concluding Century. For *Spenser* and *Fairfax* both flourished in the reign of Queen *Elizabeth* ; Great Masters in our Language ; and who saw much farther into the Beauties of our Numbers, than those who immediately followed them. *Milton* was the Poetical son of *Spencer*, and Mr. *Waller* of *Fairfax* ; for we have our Lineal Descents and Clans, as well as other Families : *Spencer* more than once insinuates, that the Soul of *Chaucer* was transfus'd

PREFACE TO THE FABLES AND DEDICATION TO THE DUTCHESS OF ORMOND. Text from the original and only contemporary edition, 1700.

into his Body ; and that he was begotten by him Two hundred years after his Decease. *Milton* has acknowledg'd to me, that *Spencer* was his Original ; and many besides my self have heard our famous *Waller* own, that he deriv'd the Harmony of his Numbers from the *Godfrey of Bulloign*, which was turned into *English* by Mr. *Fairfax*. But to return : Having done with *Ovid* for this time, it came into my mind, that our old *English* poet, *Chaucer*, in many Things resembled him, and that with no disadvantage on the Side of the Modern Author, as I shall endeavour to prove when I compare them : And as I am, and always have been, studious to promote the Honour of my Native Country, so I soon resolved to put their Merits to the Trial, by turning some of the *Canterbury* Tales into our
10 Language, as it is now refin'd : For by this means, both the Poets being set in the same light, and dress'd in the same *English* Habit, Story to be compared with Story, a certain Judgment may be made betwixt them by the Reader, without obtruding my Opinion on him : Or if I seem partial to my Country-man and Predecessor in the Laurel, the Friends of Antiquity are not few : And besides many of the Learn'd, *Ovid* has almost all the *Beaux*, and the whole Fair Sex, his declar'd Patrons. Perhaps I have assum'd somewhat more to my self than they allow me ; because I have adventur'd to sum up the Evidence : But the Readers are the Jury ; and their Privilege remains entire to decide according to the Merits of the Cause : Or, if they please to bring it to another Hearing before some other Court. In the mean time, to follow the Thrid of my Discourse (as Thoughts, according
20 to Mr. *Hobbs*, have always some Connexion), so from *Chaucer* I was led to think on *Boccace*, who was not only his Contemporary, but also pursu'd the same Studies ; wrote Novels in Prose, and many Works in Verse ; particularly is said to have invented the Octave Rhyme, or *Stanza* of Eight Lines, which ever since has been maintain'd by the Practice of all *Italian* Writers, who are, or at least assume the Title of, *Heroick Poets*: He and *Chaucer*, among other Things, had this in common, that they refin'd their Mother-Tongues ; but with this difference, that *Dante* had begun to file their Language, at least in Verse, before the time of *Boccace*, who likewise receiv'd no little Help from his Master *Petrarch :* But the Reformation of their Prose was wholly owing to *Boccace* himself, who is yet the Standard of Purity in the *Italian* Tongue ; though many of his Phrases are become obsolete, as in
30 process of Time it must needs happen. *Chaucer* (as you have formerly been told by our learn'd Mr. *Rhymer*) first adorn'd and amplified our barren Tongue from the *Provencall*, which was then the most polish'd of all the Modern Languages : But this Subject has been copiously treated by that great Critick, who deserves no little Commendation from us his Countrymen. For these Reasons of Time and Resemblance of Genius in *Chaucer* and *Boccace*, I resolv'd to join them in my present Work ; to which I have added some Original Papers of my own, which whether they are equal or inferiour to my other Poems, an Author is the most improper Judge ; and therefore I leave them wholly to the Mercy of the Reader : I will hope the best, that they will not be condemn'd ; but if they should, I have the Excuse of an old Gentleman, who mounting on Horseback before some Ladies,
40 when I was present, got up somewhat heavily, but desir'd of the Fair Spectators that they would count Fourscore and eight before they judg'd him. By the Mercy of God, I am already come within Twenty Years of his Number, a Cripple in my Limbs ; but what Decays are in my Mind, the Reader must determine. I think my self as vigorous as ever in the Faculties of my Soul, excepting only my Memory, which is not impair'd to any great degree ; and if I lose not more of it, I have no great reason to complain. What Judgment I had increases rather than diminishes ; and Thoughts, such as they are, come crowding in so fast upon me, that my only Difficulty is to chuse or to reject ; to run them into Verse or to give them the other harmony of Prose, I have so long studied and practis'd both, that they are grown into a Habit, and become familiar to me. In short, though
50 I may lawfully plead some part of the old Gentleman's Excuse, yet I will reserve it till I think I have greater need, and ask no Grains of Allowance for the Faults of this my present Work, but those which are given of course to Humane Frailty. I will not trouble my Reader with the shortness of Time in which I writ it, or the several Intervals of Sickness :

They who think too well of their own Performances are apt to boast in their Prefaces how little Time their Works have cost them, and what other Business of more importance interfer'd : but the Reader will be as apt to ask the Question, Why they allow'd not a longer Time to make their Works more perfect, and why they had so despicable an Opinion of their Judges as to thrust their indigested Stuff upon them, as if they deserv'd no better ?

With this Account of my present Undertaking I conclude the first Part of this Discourse : in the second Part, as at a second Sitting, though I alter not the Draught, I must touch the same Features over again, and change the Dead-colouring of the Whole. In general I will only say, that I have written nothing which savours of Immorality or Profaneness ; at least, I am not conscious to my self of any such Intention. If there happen to be 10 found an irreverent Expression, or a Thought too wanton, they are crept into my Verses through my Inadvertency ; If the Searchers find any in the Cargo, let them be stav'd or forfeited, like Counterbanded Goods ; at least, let their Authors be answerable for them, as being but imported Merchandise, and not of my own Manufacture. On the other Side, I have endeavour'd to chuse such Fables, both Ancient and Modern, as contain in each of them some instructive Moral, which I could prove by Induction, but the Way is tedious ; and they leap foremost into sight, without the Reader's Trouble of looking after them. I wish I could affirm with a safe Conscience, that I had taken the same Care in all my former Writings ; for it must be own'd, that supposing Verses are never so beautiful or pleasing, yet if they contain any thing which shocks Religion, or Good Manners, 20 they are at best, what *Horace* says of good Numbers without good sense, *Versus inopes rerum, nugæque canoræ*: Thus far, I hope, I am Right in Court, without renouncing to my other Right of Self-defence, where I have been wrongfully accus'd, and my Sense wire-drawn into Blasphemy or Bawdry, as it has often been by a Religious Lawyer, in a late Pleading against the Stage ; in which he mixes Truth with Falsehood, and has not forgotten the old Rule of calumniating strongly, that something may remain.

I resume the Thrid of my Discourse with the first of my Translations, which was the First *Iliad* of *Homer*. If it shall please God to give me longer Life, and moderate Health, my Intentions are to translate the whole Ilias ; provided still, that I meet with those Encouragements from the Publick, which may enable me to proceed in my Undertaking 30 with some Chearfulness. And this I dare assure the World before-hand, that I have found by Trial, *Homer* a more pleasing Task than *Virgil* (though I say not the Translation will be less laborious). For the *Grecian* is more according to my Genius than the *Latin* Poet. In the Works of the two Authors we may read their Manners and natural Inclinations, which are wholly different. *Virgil* was of a quiet, sedate Temper ; *Homer* was violent, impetuous, and full of Fire. The chief Talent of *Virgil* was Propriety of Thoughts, and Ornament of Words : *Homer* was rapid in his Thoughts, and took all the Liberties both of Numbers and of Expressions, which his Language, and the Age in which he liv'd allow'd him. *Homer's* Invention was more copious, *Virgil's* more confin'd : So that if *Homer* had not led the Way, it was not in *Virgil* to have begun Heroick Poetry : For, 40 nothing can be more evident, than that the *Roman* Poem is but the Second Part of the *Ilias ;* a Continuation of the same Story : And the Persons already form'd : The Manners of *Æneas*, are those of *Hector* superadded to those which *Homer* gave him. The Adventures of *Ulysses* in the *Odysseis*, are imitated in the first Six Books of *Virgil's Æneis :* and though the Accidents are not the same (which would have argu'd him of a servile, copying, and total Barrenness of Invention), yet the Seas were the same in which both the *Heroes* wander'd ; and *Dido* cannot be deny'd to be the Poetical Daughter of *Calypso*. The Six latter books of *Virgil's* Poem are the Four and twenty *Iliads* contracted : A Quarrel occasion'd by a Lady, a Single Combate, Battels fought, and a Town besieg'd. I say not this in derogation to *Virgil*, neither do I contradict any thing which I have formerly 50 said in his just Praise : for his *Episodes* are almost wholly of his own Invention ; and the

13 Counterbanded] *Some editors wrongly give* contrabanded

Form which he has given to the Telling, makes the Tale his own, even though the Original Story had been the same. But this proves, however, that *Homer* taught *Virgil* to design : And if Invention be the first Vertue of an Epick Poet, then the *Latin* Poem can only be allow'd the second Place. Mr. *Hobbs*, in the Preface to his own bald Translation of the *Ilias* (studying Poetry as he did Mathematicks, when it was too late), Mr. *Hobbs*, I say, begins the Praise of *Homer* where he should have ended it. He tells us, that the first Beauty of an Epick Poem consists in Diction, that is, in the Choice of Words, and Harmony of Numbers ; Now, the Words are the Colouring of the Work, which in the Order of Nature is last to be consider'd. The Design, the Disposition, the Manners, and the Thoughts are all before it : Where any of those are wanting or imperfect, so much wants or is imperfect in the Imitation of Humane Life ; which is in the very Definition of a Poem. Words indeed, like glaring Colours, are the first Beauties that arise, and strike the Sight : but if the Draught be false or lame, the Figures ill dispos'd, the Manners obscure or inconsistent, or the Thoughts unnatural, then the finest Colours are but Dawbing, and the Piece is a beautiful Monster at the best. Neither *Virgil* nor *Homer* were deficient in any of the former Beauties ; but in this last, which is Expression, the *Roman* poet is at least equal to the *Grecian*, as I have said elsewhere ; supplying the poverty of his Language by his Musical Ear, and by his Diligence. But to return : Our two Great Poets, being so different in their Tempers, one Cholerick and Sanguin, the other Phlegmatick and Melancholick : that which makes them excel in their several Ways is, that each of them has follow'd his own natural Inclination, as well in Forming the Design as in the Execution of it. The very *Heroes* show their Authors : *Achilles* is hot, impatient, revengeful, *Impiger, iracundus, inexorabilis, acer,* &c. *Æneas* patient, considerate, careful of his People and merciful to his Enemies ; ever submissive to the Will of Heaven, *quo fata trahunt retrahuntque sequamur.* I could please my self with enlarging on this Subject, but am forc'd to defer it to a fitter Time. From all I have said I will only draw this Inference, That the Action of *Homer* being more full of Vigour than that of *Virgil,* according to the Temper of the Writer, is of consequence more pleasing to the Reader. One warms you by Degrees ; the other sets you on fire all at once, and never intermits his Heat. 'Tis the same Difference which *Longinus* makes betwixt the effects of eloquence in *Demosthenes,* and *Tully.* One persuades ; the other commands. You never cool while you read *Homer,* even not in the Second Book (a graceful Flattery to his Countrymen) ; but he hastens from the Ships, and concludes not that Book till he has made you an Amends by the violent playing of a new Machine. From thence he hurries on his Action with Variety of Events, and ends it in less Compass than Two months. This Vehemence of his, I confess, is more suitable to my Temper : and therefore I have translated his First Book with greater Pleasure than any Part of *Virgil* ; But it was not a Pleasure without Pains : The continual Agitations of the Spirits, must needs be a Weaking of any Constitution, especially in Age ; and many Pauses are required for Refreshment betwixt the Heats ; the *Iliad* of its self being a third part longer than all *Virgil's* Works together.

   This is what I thought needful in this Place to say of *Homer.* I proceed to *Ovid,* and *Chaucer* ; considering the former only in relation to the latter. With *Ovid* ended the Golden Age of the *Roman* Tongue : From *Chaucer* the purity of the *English* Tongue began, The Manners of the Poets were not unlike : Both of them were well-bred, well-natur'd, amorous, and Libertine, at least in their Writings, it may be also in their Lives. Their Studies were the same, Philosophy and Philology. Both of them were knowing in Astronomy, of which *Ovid's* Books of the *Roman* Feasts, and *Chaucer's* Treatise of the *Astrolabe,* are sufficient Witnesses. But *Chaucer* was likewise an Astrologer, as were *Virgil, Horace, Persius,* and *Manilius.* Both writ with wonderful Facility and Clearness : neither were great Inventors : For *Ovid* only copied the *Grecian* Fables ; and most of *Chaucer's* Stories were taken from his *Italian* Contemporaries or their Predecessors : *Boccace* his *Decameron* was first publish'd ; and from thence our *Englishman* has borrow'd many of his *Canterbury* Tales; Yet that of *Palamon* and *Arcite* was written, in all probability, by some *Italian* Wit, in a former Age, as I shall prove hereafter : The Tale of *Grizild* was the invention of *Petrarch* ; by him sent to *Boccace* ; from whom it came to *Chaucer* : *Troïlus* and *Cressida* was also written by a *Lombard* Author ; but much amplified by our *English* translatour, as well as beautified ; the Genius of our Countrymen in general being rather to improve an Invention, than to invent themselves ; as is evident not only in our Poetry, but in many of our Manufactures. I find I have anticipated already, and taken up from *Boccace* before I come to him ; But there is so much less behind ; and I am of the Temper of most Kings, *who love to be in debt*, are all for present Money, no matter how they pay it afterwards : Besides, the Nature of a preface is Rambling ; never wholly out of the Way, nor in it. This I have learn'd from the Practice of honest *Montaign*, 10 and return at my pleasure to *Ovid* and *Chaucer*, of whom I have little more to say. Both of them built on the Inventions of other Men ; yet since *Chaucer* had something of his own, as *The Wife of Baths Tale, The Cock and the Fox*, which I have translated, and some others, I may justly give our Countryman the Precedence in that Part ; since I can remember nothing of *Ovid* which was wholly his. Both of them understood the Manners, under which Name I comprehend the Passions, and, in a larger Sense, the Descriptions of Persons, and their very Habits. For an Example, I see *Baucis* and *Philemon* as perfectly before me, as if some ancient Painter had drawn them ; and all the Pilgrims in the *Canterbury* Tales, their Humours, their Features, and the very Dress, as distinctly as if I had supp'd with them at the Tabard in *Southwark ;* Yet even there too the Figures 20 in *Chaucer* are much more lively, and set in a better Light : which though I have not Time to prove, yet I appeal to the Reader, and am sure he will clear me from Partiality. The Thoughts and Words remain to be consider'd, in the Comparison of the two Poets ; and I have sav'd my self one half of that Labour, by owning that *Ovid* liv'd when the *Roman* Tongue was in its Meridian ; *Chaucer*, in the Dawning of our Language : Therefore that Part of the Comparison stands not on an equal Foot, any more than the Diction of *Ennius* and *Ovid*, or of *Chaucer*, and our present *English*. The Words are given up as a Post not to be defended in our Poet, because he wanted the Modern Art of Fortifying. The Thoughts remain to be consider'd : And they are to be measur'd only by their Propriety ; that is, as they flow more or less naturally from the Persons describ'd, on such and such Occasions. 30 The Vulgar Judges, which are Nine Parts in Ten of all Nations, who call Conceits and Jingles Wit, who see *Ovid* full of them, and *Chaucer* altogether without them, will think me little less than mad for preferring the *Englishman* to the *Roman* : Yet, with their leave, I must presume to say, that the Things they admire are only glittering Trifles, and so far from being Witty, that in a serious Poem they are nauseous, because they are unnatural. Wou'd any Man, who is ready to die for Love, describe his passion like *Narcissus* ? Wou'd he think of *inopem me copia fecit*, and a Dozen more of such Expressions, pour'd on the Neck of one another, and signifying all the same Thing ? If this were Wit, was this a Time to be witty, when the poor Wretch was in the Agony of Death ? This is just *John Littlewit* in *Bartholomew Fair*, who had a Conceit (as he tells you) left him in his Misery ; a miserable 40 Conceit. On these Occasions the Poet shou'd endeavour to raise Pity ; but instead of this, *Ovid* is tickling you to laugh. *Virgil* never made use of such Machines, when he was moving you to commiserate the Death of *Dido* : He would not destroy what he was building. *Chaucer* makes *Arcite* violent in his Love, and unjust in the Pursuit of it : Yet when he came to die, he made him think more reasonably : He repents not of his Love, for that had alter'd his Character ; but acknowledges the Injustice of his Proceedings, and resigns *Emilia* to *Palamon*. What would *Ovid* have done on this Occasion ? He would certainly have made *Arcite* witty on his Death-bed. He had complain'd he was farther off from Possession, by being so near, and a thousand such Boyisms, which *Chaucer* rejected as below the Dignity of the Subject. They who think otherwise, would, by the same Reason, 50 prefer *Lucan* and *Ovid* to *Homer* and *Virgil*, and *Martial* to all Four of them. As for the Turn of Words, in which *Ovid* particularly excels all Poets ; they are sometimes a Fault, and sometimes a Beauty, as they are used properly or improperly ; but in strong

Passions always to be shunn'd, because Passions are serious, and will admit no Playing. The *French* have a high Value for them ; and I confess, they are often what they call Delicate, when they are introduced with Judgment ; but *Chaucer* writ with more Simplicity, and follow'd Nature more closely, than to use them. I have thus far, to the best of my Knowledge, been an upright Judge betwixt the Parties in Competition, not medling with the Design nor the Disposition of it ; because the Design was not their own, and in the disposing of it they were equal. It remains that I say somewhat of *Chaucer* in particular.

In the first place, As he is the father of *English* Poetry, so I hold him in the same Degree
10 of Veneration as the *Grecians* held *Homer*, or the *Romans Virgil :* He is a perpetual Fountain of good Sense ; learn'd in all Sciences ; and therefore speaks properly on all Subjects : As he knew what to say, so he knows also when to leave off ; a Continence which is practis'd by few Writers, and scarcely by any of the Ancients, excepting *Virgil* and *Horace*. One of our late great Poets is sunk in his Reputation because he cou'd never forgo any conceit which came in his way ; but swept like a Drag-net, great and small. There was plenty enough, but the Dishes were ill-sorted ; whole pyramids of Sweet-meats, for Boys and Women ; but little of solid Meat, for Men : All this proceeded not from any want of Knowledge, but of Judgment ; neither did he want that in discerning the Beauties and Faults of other Poets ; but only indulg'd himself in the Luxury of Writing ; and perhaps
20 knew it was a Fault, but hop'd the Reader would not find it. For this Reason, though he must always be thought a great Poet, he is no longer esteem'd a good Writer : and for Ten Impressions which his Works have had in so many successive Years, yet at present a hundred Books are scarcely purchas'd once a Twelve month : For as my last Lord *Rochester* said, though somewhat profanely, *Not being of God, he could not stand.*

Chaucer follow'd Nature every where ; but was never so bold to go beyond her : And there is a great Difference of being *Poeta* and *nimis Poeta,* if we may believe *Catullus,* as much as betwixt a modest Behaviour and Affectation. The Verse of *Chaucer,* I confess, is not Harmonious to us ; but 'tis like the Eloquence of one whom *Tacitus* commends, it was *auribus istius temporis accommodata ;* they who liv'd with him, and some time after
30 him, thought it Musical ; and it continues so even in our Judgment, if compar'd with the Numbers of *Lidgate* and *Gower,* his Contemporaries : there is the rude Sweetness of a *Scotch* Tune in it, which is natural and pleasing, though not perfect. 'Tis true, I cannot go so far as he who publish'd the last Edition of him ; for he would make us believe the Fault is in our Ears, and that there were really Ten Syllables in a Verse where we find but Nine : But this opinion is not worth confuting ; 'tis so gross and obvious an Errour, that common Sense (which is a Rule in every thing but Matters of Faith and Revelation) must convince the Reader, that Equality of Numbers in every Verse which we call *Heroick,* was either not known, or not always practis'd in *Chaucer's* Age. It were an easie Matter to produce some thousands of his Verses, which are lame for want of half a foot, and
40 sometimes a whole one, and which no pronunciation can make otherwise. We can only say, that he liv'd in the Infancy of our Poetry, and that nothing is brought to Perfection at the first. We must be Children before we grow Men. There was an *Ennius,* and in process of Time a *Lucilius,* and a *Lucretius,* before *Virgil* and *Horace ;* even after *Chaucer* there was a *Spencer,* a *Harrington,* a *Fairfax,* before *Waller* and *Denham* were in being : And our Numbers were in their Nonage till these last appear'd. I need say little of his Parentage, Life, and Fortunes : they are to be found at large in all the Editions of his Works. He was employ'd abroad and favoured by *Edward* the Third, *Richard* the Second, and *Henry* the Fourth, and was Poet, as I suppose, to all Three of them. In *Richard's* time, I doubt, he was a little dipt in the Rebellion of the Commons ; and being Brother-
50 in-Law to *John of Ghant,* it was no wonder if he follow'd the Fortunes of that Family ;

---

14 forgo any conceit] forgive any conceit *1700. This can hardly be right, though most editors print it without comment. Christie, also without comment, prints* forego

and was well with *Henry* the Fourth when he had depos'd his Predecessor. Neither is it to be admir'd, that *Henry*, who was a wise as well as a valiant Prince, who claim'd by Succession, and was sensible that his Title was not sound, but was rightfully in *Mortimer*, who had married the Heir of *York* ; it was not to be admir'd, I say, if that great Politician should be pleas'd to have the greatest Wit of those Times in his Interests, and to be the Trumpet of his Praises. *Augustus* had given him the Example, by the Advice of *Mecænas*, who recommended *Virgil* and *Horace* to him ; whose Praises help'd to make him popular while he was alive, and after his Death have made him Precious to Posterity. As for the Religion of our Poet, he seems to have some little Byas towards the Opinions of *Wickliff*, after *John of Gaunt* his Patron ; somewhat of which appears in the Tale of *Piers Plowman* : 10 Yet I cannot blame him for inveighing so sharply against the Vices of the Clergy in his Age : Their Pride, their Ambition, their Pomp, their Avarice, their Worldly Interest, deserv'd the Lashes which he gave them, both in that, and in most of his *Canterbury Tales* : Neither has his Contemporary *Boccace*, spar'd them. Yet both those Poets lived in much esteem with good and holy Men in Orders : For the Scandal which is given by particular Priests, reflects not on the Sacred Function. *Chaucer's Monk*, his *Chanon*, and his *Fryar* took not from the Character of his *Good Parson*. A Satyrical Poet is the Check of the Laymen on bad Priests. We are only to take care, that we involve not the Innocent with the Guilty in the same Condemnation. The Good cannot be too much honour'd, nor the Bad too coursely us'd : For the Corruption of the Best, becomes the Worst. When a 20 Clergy-man is whipp'd, his Gown is first taken off, by which the Dignity of his Order is secur'd : If he be wrongfully accus'd, he has his Action of Slander ; and 'tis at the Poet's Peril, if he transgress the Law. But they will tell us, that all kind of Satire, though never so well deserv'd by particular Priests, yet brings the whole Order into Contempt. Is then the Peerage of *England* anything dishonour'd, when a peer suffers for his Treason ? If he be libell'd, or any way defam'd, he has his *Scandalum Magnatum* to punish the Offendor. They who use this kind of Argument, seem to be conscious to themselves of somewhat which has deserv'd the Poet's Lash ; and are less concern'd for their Publick Capacity, than for their private : At least there is Pride at the bottom of their Reasoning. If the Faults of Men in Orders are only to be judg'd among themselves, they are all in some sort 30 Parties : For, since they say the Honour of their Order is concern'd in every Member of it, how can we be sure, that they will be impartial Judges ? How far I may be allow'd to speak my Opinion in this Case, I know not : But I am sure a Dispute of this Nature caused Mischief in abundance betwixt a King of *England* and an Archbishop of *Canterbury* ; one standing up for the Laws of his Land, and the other for the Honour (as he called it), of God's Church ; which ended in the Murther of the Prelate, and in the whipping of his Majesty from Post to Pillar for his Penance. The Learn'd and Ingenious Dr. *Drake* has sav'd me the Labour of inquiring into the Esteem and Reverence which the Priests have had of old : and I would rather extend than diminish any part of it : Yet I must needs say, that when a Priest provokes me without any Occasion given him, I have no 40 Reason, unless it be the Charity of a *Christian*, to forgive him : *Prior læsit* is Justification sufficient in the Civil Law. If I answer him in his own Language, Self-defence, I am sure, must be allow'd me ; and if I carry it farther, even to a sharp Recrimination, somewhat may be indulged to Humane Frailty. Yet my Resentment has not wrought so far but that I have follow'd *Chaucer* in his Character of a Holy Man, and have enlarg'd on that Subject with some Pleasure, reserving to my self the Right, if I shall think fit hereafter, to describe another sort of Priests, such as are more easily to be found than the Good Parson ; such as have given the last Blow to Christianity in this Age, by a Practice so contrary to their Doctrine. But this will keep cold till another time. In the mean while, I take up *Chaucer* where I left him. He must have been a Man of a most 50 wonderful comprehensive Nature, because, as it has been truly observ'd of him, he has taken into the Compass of his *Canterbury Tales* the various Manners and Humours (as we now call them) of the whole *English* Nation in his Age. Not a single Character has

escap'd him. All his Pilgrims are severally distinguish'd from each other : and not only in their Inclinations, but in their very Phisiognomies and Persons. *Baptista Porta* could not have describ'd their Natures better, than by the Marks which the Poet gives them. The Matter and Manner of their Tales, and of their Telling are so suited to their different Educations, Humours and Callings, that each of them would be improper in any other Mouth. Even the grave and serious Characters are distinguish'd by their several sorts of Gravity : Their Discourses are such as belong to their Age, their Calling, and their Breeding ; such as are becoming of them, and of them only. Some of his Persons are Vicious, and some vertuous ; some are unlearn'd or (as *Chaucer* calls them) Lewd, and some are
10 Learn'd. Even the Ribaldry of the Low Characters is different : The *Reeve*, the *Miller*, and the *Cook* are several Men, and distinguish'd from each other, as much as the mincing Lady Prioress and the broad-speaking gap-toothed Wife of *Bathe*. But enough of this : There is such a Variety of Game springing up before me, that I am distracted in my Choice, and know not which to follow. 'Tis sufficient to say, according to the Proverb, that here is God's Plenty. We have our Fore-fathers and Great Grandames all before us, as they were in *Chaucer's* Days ; their general Characters are still remaining in Mankind, and even in *England*, though they are called by other Names than those of *Moncks* and *Fryars*, and *Chanons*, and *Lady Abbesses*, and *Nuns* : For Mankind is ever the same, and nothing lost out of Nature, though every thing is alter'd. May I have leave to do myself the
20 Justice (since my Enemies will do me none, and are so far from granting me to be a good Poet that they will not allow me so much as to be a Christian, or a Moral Man), may I have leave, I say, to inform my Reader, that I have confin'd my Choice to such Tales of *Chaucer* as savour nothing of Immodesty. If I had desir'd more to please than to instruct, the *Reve*, the *Miller*, the *Shipman*, the *Merchant*, the *Sumner*, and, above all, the *Wife of Bathe*, in the Prologue to her Tale, would have procur'd me as many Friends and Readers, as there are *Beaux* and Ladies of Pleasure in the Town. But I will no more offend against Good Manners : I am sensible, as I ought to be, of the Scandal I have given by my loose Writings ; and make what Reparation I am able by this Publick Acknowledgment. If anything of this Nature, or of Profaneness, be crept into these Poems, I am so far from
30 defending it, that I disown it. *Totum hoc indictum volo. Chaucer* makes another manner of Apologie for his broad-speaking, and *Boccace* makes the like ; but I will follow neither of them. Our Country-man, in the end of his Characters, before the *Canterbury Tales*, thus excuses the Ribaldry, which is very gross in many of his Novels :

> But first, I pray you of your courtesy,
> That ye ne arrete it nought my villany,
> Though that I plainly speak in this mattere
> To tellen you her words, and eke her chere :
> Ne though I speak her words properly,
> For this ye knowen as well as I,
> Who shall tellen a tale after a man
> He mote rehearse as nye as ever he can
> Everich word of it been in his charge,
> All speke he, never so rudely, ne large.
> Or else he mote tellen his tale untrue,
> Or feine things, or find words new :
> He may not spare, altho he were his brother,
> He mote as well say o word as another.
> Christ *spake himself full broad in holy writ,*
> And well I wote no villany is it,
> Eke Plato *saith, who so can him rede,*
> The words mote been cousin to the dede.

Yet if a Man should have enquir'd of *Boccace* or of *Chaucer*, what need they had of introducing such Characters, where obscene Words were proper in their Mouths, but very undecent to be heard, I know not what Answer they could have made : For that Reason, such Tales shall be left untold by me. You have here a *Specimen* of *Chaucer's* Language, which is so obsolete, that his Sense is scarce to be understood ; and you have likewise more than one Example of his unequal Numbers, which were mention'd before. Yet many of his Verses consist of Ten Syllables, and the Words not much behind our present *English* : As, for Example, these two lines, in the Description of the Carpenter's Young Wife :

> *Wincing she was, as is a jolly Colt,*
> *Long as a Mast, and upright as a Bolt.*

I have almost done with *Chaucer*, when I have answer'd some Objections relating to 10 my present Work. I find some People are offended that I have turned these Tales into modern *English*, because they think them unworthy of my Pains, and look on *Chaucer* as a dry, old-fashion'd Wit, not worth reviving. I have often heard the late Earl of *Leicester* say, that Mr. *Cowley* himself was of that opinion ; who having read him over at my Lord's Request, declared he had no Taste of him. I dare not advance my Opinion against the Judgment of so great an Author : But I think it fair, however, to leave the Decision to the Publick : Mr. *Cowley* was too modest to set up for a Dictatour ; and being shock'd perhaps with his old Style, never examin'd into the depth of his good Sense. *Chaucer*, I confess, is a rough Diamond ; and must first be polish'd e'er he shines. I deny not likewise, that, living in our early Days of Poetry, he writes not always of a piece ; but 20 sometimes mingles trivial Things with those of greater Moment. Sometimes also, though not often, he runs riot, like *Ovid*, and knows not when he has said enough. But there are more great Wits beside *Chaucer*, whose Fault is their Excess of Conceits, and those ill sorted. An Author is not to write all he can, but only all he ought. Having observ'd this Redundancy in *Chaucer* (as it is an easie Matter for a Man of ordinary Parts to find a Fault in one of greater) I have not ty'd myself to a Literal Translation ; but have often omitted what I judged unnecessary, or not of Dignity enough to appear in the Company of better Thoughts. I have presum'd farther in some Places ; and added somewhat of my own where I thought my Author was deficient, and had not given his Thoughts their true Lustre, for want of Words in the Beginning of our Language. And to this I was 30 the more embolden'd, because (if I may be permitted to say it of my self) I found I had a Soul congenial to his, and that I had been conversant in the same Studies. Another Poet, in another Age, may take the same Liberty with my Writings ; if at least they live long enough to deserve Correction. It was also necessary sometimes to restore the Sense of *Chaucer*, which was lost or mangled in the Errors of the Press. Let this Example suffice at present : in the Story of *Palamon* and *Arcite*, where the Temple of *Diana* is describ'd, you find these Verses in all the Editions of our Author :

> *There saw I* Danè, *turned unto a Tree,*
> *I mean not the Goddess* Diane,
> *But* Venus *daughter, which that hight* Danè. 40

Which after a little Consideration I knew was to be reform'd into this Sense, that *Daphne*, the Daughter of *Peneus*, was turn'd into a Tree. I durst not make thus bold with *Ovid* ; lest some future *Milbourn* should arise, and say, I varied from my Author, because I understood him not.

But there are other Judges who think I ought not to have translated *Chaucer* into *English*, out of a quite contrary Notion : They suppose there is a certain Veneration due to his old Language ; and that it is little less than Profanation and Sacrilege to alter it. They are farther of opinion, that somewhat of his good Sense will suffer in this Transfusion, and much of the Beauty of his Thoughts will infallibly be lost, which appear with more Grace in their old Habit. Of this Opinion was that excellent Person whom I mention'd, the late Earl of *Leicester*, who valu'd *Chaucer* as much as Mr. *Cowley* despis'd him. My 50

---

23 beside *Chaucer*] *Most editors give* besides *Chaucer*

Lord dissuaded me from this Attempt (for I was thinking of it some Years before his Death) and his Authority prevail'd so far with me as to defer my Undertaking while he liv'd, in deference to him : Yet my Reason was not convinc'd with what he urg'd against it. If the first End of a Writer be to be understood, then as his Language grows obsolete, his Thoughts must grow obscure : *multa renascuntur quæ nunc cecidere ; cadentque quæ nunc sunt in honore vocabula, si volet usus, quem penes arbitrium est et jus et norma loquendi.* When an ancient Word for its Sound and Significancy deserves to be reviv'd, I have that reasonable Veneration for Antiquity, to restore it. All beyond this is Superstition. Words are not like Land-marks, so sacred as never to be remov'd : Customs are chang'd, and
10 even Statutes are silently repeal'd, when the Reason ceases for which they were enacted. As for the other Part of the Argument, that his Thoughts will lose of their original Beauty, by the innovation of Words ; in the first place, not only their Beauty, but their Being is lost, where they are no longer understood, which is the present Case. I grant, that something must be lost in all Transfusion, that is, in all Translations ; but the Sense will remain, which would otherwise be lost, or at least be maim'd, when it is scarce intelligible ; and that but to a few. How few are there who can read *Chaucer*, so as to understand him perfectly ! And if imperfectly, then with less Profit, and no Pleasure. 'Tis not for the Use of some old *Saxon* Friends that I have taken these Pains with him : Let them neglect my Version, because they have no need of it. I made it for their sakes who understand
20 Sense and Poetry as well as they ; when that Poetry and Sense is put into Words which they understand. I will go farther, and dare to add, that what Beauties I lose in some Places, I give to others which had them not originally : But in this I may be partial to my self ; let the Reader judge, and I submit to his Decision. Yet I think I have just Occasion to complain of them, who, because they understand *Chaucer*, would deprive the greater part of their Countrymen of the same Advantage, and hoord him up, as Misers do their Grandam Gold, only to look on it themselves, and hinder others from making use of it. In sum, I seriously protest, that no Man ever had, or can have, a greater Veneration for *Chaucer* than my self. I have translated some part of his Works, only that I might perpetuate his Memory, or at least refresh it, amongst my Countrymen. If I have alter'd
30 him anywhere for the better, I must at the same time acknowledge, that I could have done nothing without him : *Facile est inventis addere*, is no great Commendation ; and I am not so vain to think I have deserv'd a greater. I will conclude what I have to say of him singly, with this one Remark : A Lady of my Acquaintance, who keeps a kind of Correspondence with some Authors of the Fair Sex in *France*, has been inform'd by them, that *Mademoiselle de Scudery*, who is as old as *Sibyl*, and inspir'd like her by the same God of Poetry, is at this time translating *Chaucer* into modern *French*. From which I gather, that he has been formerly translated into the old *Provençall* (for, how she should come to understand Old *English*, I know not). But the Matter of Fact being true, it makes me think, that there is something in it like Fatality ; that, after certain Periods of Time, the Fame
40 and Memory of Great Wits should be renew'd, as *Chaucer* is both in *France* and *England*. If this be wholly Chance, 'tis extraordinary ; and I dare not call it more, for fear of being tax'd with Superstition.

Boccace comes last to be consider'd, who, living in the same Age with *Chaucer*, had the same Genius, and follow'd the same Studies. Both writ Novels, and each of them cultivated his Mother-Tongue. But the greatest Resemblance of our two Modern Authors being in their familiar Style, and pleasing way of relating Comical Adventures, I may pass it over, because I have translated nothing from *Boccace* of that Nature. In the serious Part of Poetry, the Advantage is wholly on *Chaucer's* Side ; for though the *English-man* has borrow'd many Tales from the *Italian*, yet it appears, that those of *Boccace* were
50 not generally of his own making, but taken from Authors of former Ages, and by him only modell'd : So that what there was of invention in either of them, may be judg'd equal. But *Chaucer* has refin'd on *Boccace*, and has mended the Stories which he has borrow'd, in his way of telling ; though Prose allows more Liberty of Thought, and the Expression

is more easie, when unconfin'd by Numbers. Our Countryman carries Weight, and yet wins the Race at disadvantage. I desire not the Reader should take my Word; and therefore I will set two of their Discourses on the same Subject, in the same Light, for every Man to judge betwixt them. I translated *Chaucer* first; and amongst the rest, pitch'd on The Wife of *Bath's* Tale; not daring, as I have said, to adventure on her Prologue; because it is too licentious: There *Chaucer* introduces an old Woman of mean Parentage, whom a youthful Knight of Noble Blood was forc'd to marry, and consequently loath'd her: The Crone being in bed with him on the wedding Night, and finding his Aversion, endeavours to win his Affection by Reason, and speaks a good Word for her self, (as who could blame her?) in hope to mollifie the sullen Bridegroom. She takes her Topiques from 10 the Benefits of Poverty, the Advantages of old Age and Ugliness, the Vanity of Youth, and the silly Pride of Ancestry and Titles without inherent Vertue, which is the true Nobility. When I had clos'd *Chaucer*, I return'd to *Ovid*, and translated some more of his Fables; and by this time had so far forgotten The Wife of *Bath's* Tale, that, when I took up *Boccace*, unawares I fell on the same Argument of preferring Vertue to Nobility of Blood, and Titles, in the Story of *Sigismonda*; which I had certainly avoided for the Resemblance of the two Discourses, if my Memory had not fail'd me. Let the Reader weigh them both; and if he thinks me partial to *Chaucer*, 'tis in him to right *Boccace*.

I prefer in our Countryman, far above all his other Stories, the Noble Poem of *Palamon* and *Arcite*, which is of the Epique kind, and perhaps not much inferiour to the *Ilias* or 20 the *Æneis*: The Story is more pleasing than either of them, the Manners as perfect, the Diction as poetical, the Learning as deep and various; and the Disposition full as artful: only it includes a greater length of time; as taking up seven years at least; but *Aristotle* has left undecided the Duration of the Action; which yet is easily reduc'd into the Compass of a year, by a Narration of what preceded the Return of *Palamon* to *Athens*. I had thought for the Honour of our Nation, and more particularly for his, whose Laurel, tho' unworthy, I have worn after him, that this Story was of *English* Growth and *Chaucer's* own: But I was undeceiv'd by *Boccace*; for casually looking on the End of his seventh *Giornata*, I found *Dioneo* (under which name he shadows himself) and *Fiametta* (who represents his Mistress, the natural Daughter of *Robert*, King of *Naples*) of whom these 30 Words are spoken. *Dioneo e Fiametta gran pezza cantarono insieme d' Arcita e di Pala mone:* by which it appears that this Story was written before the time of *Boccace;* but the Name of its Author being wholly lost, *Chaucer* is now become an Original; and I question not but the Poem has receiv'd many Beauties by passing through his Noble Hands. Besides this Tale, there is another of his own Invention, after the manner of the *Provencalls*, called *The Flower and the Leaf*; with which I was so particularly pleas'd, both for the Invention and the Moral; that I cannot hinder my self from recommending it to the Reader.

As a Corollary to this Preface, in which I have done Justice to others, I owe somewhat to my self: not that I think it worth my time to enter the Lists with one *M*—— or 40 one *B*——, but barely to take notice, that such Men there are who have written scurrilously against me, without any Provocation. *M*——, who is in Orders, pretends amongst the rest this Quarrel to me, that I have fallen foul on Priesthood; If I have, I am only to ask Pardon of good Priests, and am afraid his part of the Reparation will come to little. Let him be satisfied that he shall not be able to force himself upon me for an Adversary. I contemn him too much to enter into Competition with him. His own Translations of *Virgil* have answer'd his Criticisms on mine. If (as they say, he has declar'd in print) he prefers the Version of *Ogilby* to mine, the World has made him the same Compliment: For 'tis agreed on all hands, that he writes even below *Ogilby*: That, you will say, is not easily to be done; but what cannot *M*—— bring about? I am satisfy'd, however, 50 that while he and I live together, I shall not be thought the worst Poet of the Age. It looks as if I had desir'd him underhand to write so ill against me: But upon my honest word I have not brib'd him to do me this Service, and am wholly guiltless of his Pamphlet.

'Tis true I should be glad if I could persuade him to continue his good Offices, and write such another Critique on any thing of mine: For I find by Experience he has a great Stroke with the Reader, when he condemns any of my Poems, to make the World have a better Opinion of them. He has taken some Pains with my Poetry; but no body will be persuaded to take the same with his. If I had taken to the Church (as he affirms, but which was never in my Thoughts) I should have had more Sense, if not more Grace, than to have turn'd myself out of my Benefice by writing Libels on my Parishioners. But his Account of my Manners and my Principles, are of a Piece with his Cavils and his Poetry: And so I have done with him for ever.

10   As for the City Bard or Knight Physician, I hear his Quarrel to me is, that I was the Author of *Absalom* and *Achitophel*, which he thinks is a little hard on his Fanatique Patrons in *London*.

But I will deal the more civilly with his two Poems, because nothing ill is to be spoken of the Dead: And therefore peace be to the *Manes* of his *Arthurs*. I will only say, that it was not for this Noble Knight that I drew the plan of an Epick Poem on King *Arthur*, in my Preface to the Translation of *Juvenal*. The Guardian Angels of Kingdoms were Machines too ponderous for him to manage; and therefore he rejected them, as *Dares* did the Whirl-bats of *Eryx*, when they were thrown before him by *Entellus*: Yet from that Preface he plainly took his Hint: For he began immediately upon the Story;
20   though he had the Baseness not to acknowledge his Benefactor, but in stead of it, to traduce me in a Libel.

I shall say the less of Mr. *Collier*, because in many Things he has tax'd me justly; and I have pleaded Guilty to all Thoughts and Expressions of mine, which can be truly argu'd of Obscenity, Profaneness, or Immorality; and retract them. If he be my Enemy, let him triumph; if he be my Friend, as I have given him no Personal Occasion to be otherwise, he will be glad of my Repentance. It becomes me not to draw my Pen in the Defence of a bad Cause, when I have so often drawn it for a good one. Yet it were not difficult to prove, that in many Places he has perverted my Meaning by his Glosses; and interpreted my Words into Blasphemy and Baudry, of which they were not guilty. Besides
30   that, he is too much given to Horse-play in his Raillery; and comes to Battel, like a Dictatour from the Plough. I will not say, *The zeal of God's House has eaten him up*; but I am sure it has devour'd some Part of his Good Manners and Civility. It might also be doubted, whether it were altogether Zeal, which prompted him to this rough manner of Proceeding; perhaps it became not one of his Function to rake into the Rubbish of Ancient and Modern Plays; a Divine might have employ'd his Pains to better purpose than in the Nastiness of *Plautus* and *Aristophanes*; whose Examples, as they excuse not me, so it might be possibly suppos'd, that he read them not without some Pleasure. They who have written Commentaries on those Poets, or on *Horace, Juvenal*, and *Martial*, have explain'd some Vices, which without their Interpretation had been unknown to
40   Modern Times. Neither has he judg'd impartially betwixt the former Age and us.

There is more Baudry in one Play of *Fletcher's*, called *The Custom of the Country*, than in all ours together. Yet this has been often acted on the Stage in my remembrance. Are the Times so much more reform'd now, than they were Five and twenty Years ago? If they are, I congratulate the Amendment of our Morals. But I am not to prejudice the Cause of my Fellow-Poets, though I abandon my own Defence: They have some of them answer'd for themselves, and neither they nor I can think Mr. *Collier* so formidable an Enemy, that we should shun him. He has lost Ground at the latter end of the Day, by pursuing his Point too far, like the Prince of *Conde* at the Battel of *Senneph*: From immoral Plays, to no Plays; *ab abusu ad usum, non valet consequentia*. But being a Party, I am not to
50   erect myself into a Judge. As for the rest of those who have written against me, they are such Scoundrels, that they deserve not the least Notice to be taken of them. *B*——— and *M*——— are only distinguish'd from the Crowd by being remember'd to their Infamy.

Demetri, Teque Tigelli
Discipularum inter jubeo plorare cathedras.

TO

HER GRACE

THE

DUTCHESS

OF

ORMOND,

WITH THE FOLLOWING POEM OF

PALAMON AND ARCITE

FROM

CHAUCER.

TO

HER GRACE

THE

DUTCHESS

OF

ORMOND.

MADAM

The Bard who first adorn'd our Native
    Tongue
Tun'd to his *British* Lyre this ancient Song :
Which *Homer* might without a Blush reherse,
And leaves a doubtful Palm in *Virgil's*
    Verse :
He match'd their Beauties, where they most
    excell ;
Of Love sung better, and of Arms as well.
  Vouchsafe, Illustrious *Ormond*, to behold
What Pow'r the Charms of Beauty had of
    old ;
Nor wonder if such Deeds of Arms were done,
Inspir'd by two fair Eyes that sparkled like
    your own.   10
If *Chaucer* by the best Idea wrought,
And Poets can divine each other's Thought,
The fairest Nymph before his Eyes he set ;
And then the fairest was *Plantagenet* ;
Who three contending Princes made her
    Prize,
And rul'd the Rival-Nations with her Eyes :
Who left Immortal Trophies of her Fame,
And to the Noblest Order gave the Name.

Like Her, of equal Kindred to the Throne.
You keep her Conquests, and extend your
    own :   20
As when the Stars, in their Etherial Race,
At length have roll'd around the Liquid
    Space,
At certain Periods they resume their Place,
From the same Point of Heav'n their Course
    advance,
And move in Measures of their former Dance;
Thus, after length of Ages, she returns,
Restor'd in you, and the same Place adorns :
Or you perform her Office in the Sphere,
Born of her Blood, and make a new Platonick
    Year.
  O true *Plantagenet*, O Race Divine,   30
(For Beauty still is fatal to the Line,)
Had *Chaucer* liv'd that Angel-Face to view,
Sure he had drawn his *Emily* from You ;
Or had You liv'd to judge the doubtful Right,
Your Noble *Palamon* had been the Knight :
And Conqu'ring *Theseus* from his Side had
    sent
Your Gen'rous Lord, to guide the *Theban*
    Government

Time shall accomplish that; and I shall see
A *Palamon* in him, in You an *Emily*.
    Already have the Fates your Path pre-
        par'd,   40
And sure Presage your future Sway declar'd:
When Westward, like the Sun, you took
    your Way,
And from benighted *Britain* bore the Day,
Blue *Triton* gave the Signal from the Shore,
The ready *Nereids* heard, and swam before
To smooth the Seas; a soft *Etesian* Gale
But just inspir'd, and gently swell'd the Sail;
Portunus took his Turn, whose ample Hand
Heav'd up the lighten'd Keel, and sunk the
    Sand,   49
And steer'd the sacred Vessel safe to Land.
The Land, if not restrain'd, had met Your
    Way,
Projected out a Neck, and jutted to the Sea.
Hibernia, prostrate at your Feet, ador'd
In You the Pledge of her expected Lord;
Due to her Isle; a venerable Name;
His Father and his Grandsire known to
    Fame;
Aw'd by that House, accustom'd to com-
    mand,
The sturdy *Kerns* in due subjection stand,
Nor hear the Reins in any Foreign Hand.
    At Your Approach, they crowded to the
        Port;   60
And scarcely Landed, You create a Court:
As *Ormond's* Harbinger, to You they run,
For *Venus* is the Promise of the *Sun*.
    The Waste of Civil Wars, their Towns
        destroy'd,
Pales unhonour'd, *Ceres* unemploy'd,
Were all forgot; and one Triumphant Day
Wip'd all the Tears of three Campaigns away.
Blood, Rapines, Massacres, were cheaply
    bought,   68
So mighty Recompense Your Beauty brought.
As when the Dove returning bore the Mark
Of Earth restor'd to the long-lab'ring Ark,
The Relicks of Mankind, secure of Rest,
Op'd every Window to receive the Guest,
And the fair Bearer of the Message bless'd;
So, when You came, with loud repeated Cries,
The Nation took an Omen from your Eyes,
And God advanc'd his Rainbow in the Skies,
To sign inviolable Peace restor'd;
The Saints with solemn Shouts proclaim'd
    the new accord.

    When at Your second Coming You appear,
(For I foretell that Millenary Year)   81
The sharpen'd Share shall vex the Soil no
    more,
But Earth unbidden shall produce her Store:
The Land shall laugh, the circling Ocean
    smile,
And Heav'n's Indulgence bless the Holy Isle.
    Heav'n from all Ages has reserv'd for You
That happy Clime, which Venom never
    knew;
Or if it had been there, Your Eyes alone
Have Pow'r to chase all Poyson, but their
    own.   89
    Now in this Interval, which Fate has cast
Betwixt Your Future Glories and Your Past,
This Pause of Pow'r, 'tis *Irelands* Hour to
    mourn;
While *England* celebrates Your safe Return,
By which You seem the Seasons to command,
And bring our Summers back to their for-
    saken Land.
    The Vanquish'd Isle our Leisure must
        attend,
Till the Fair Blessing we vouchsafe to send;
Nor can we spare You long, though often
    we may lend.
The Dove was twice employ'd abroad, before
The World was dry'd; and she return'd no
    more.   100
Nor dare we trust so soft a Messenger,
New from her Sickness, to that Northern Air;
Rest here a while, Your Lustre to restore,
That they may see You, as You shone before;
For yet, th' Eclipse not wholly past, You
    wade
Thro' some Remains and Dimness of a Shade.
    A Subject in his Prince may claim a Right,
Nor suffer him with Strength impair'd to
    fight;
Till Force returns, his Ardour we restrain,
And curb his Warlike Wish to cross the Main.
    Now past the Danger, let the Learn'd
        begin   111
Th' Enquiry, where Disease could enter in;
How those malignant Atoms forc'd their
    Way,
What in the Faultless Frame they found to
    make their Prey?
Where ev'ry Element was weigh'd so well,
That Heav'n alone, who mix'd the Mass,
    could tell
Which of the Four Ingredients could rebel;

And where, imprison'd in so sweet a Cage,
A Soul might well be pleas'd to pass an Age.
  And yet the fine Materials made it weak ;
Porcelain by being Pure, is apt to break. 121
Ev'n to Your Breast the Sickness durst ⎫
  aspire,   ⎪
And forc'd from that fair Temple to retire, ⎬
Profanely set the Holy Place on Fire.   ⎭
In vain Your Lord, like young *Vespasian*,
  mourn'd,
When the fierce Flames the Sanctuary burn'd,
And I prepar'd to pay in Verses rude
A most detested Act of Gratitude :
Ev'n this had been Your Elegy, which now
Is offer'd for Your Health, the Table of my
  Vow.   130
  Your Angel sure our *Morley's* Mind in-
  spir'd,
To find the Remedy Your Ill requir'd ;
As once the *Macedon*, by *Jove's* Decree,
Was taught to dream an Herb for Ptolomee :
Or Heav'n, which had such Over-cost
  bestow'd
As scarce it could afford to Flesh and
  Blood,
So lik'd the Frame, he would not work anew,
To save the Charges of another You.
Or by his middle Science did he steer, ⎫
And saw some great contingent Good ⎪
  appear,   140 ⎬
Well worth a Miracle to keep You here, ⎪
And for that End preserv'd the precious ⎭
  Mould,
Which all the Future *Ormonds* was to hold ;

And meditated, in his better Mind
An Heir from You who may redeem the
  failing Kind.
  Bless'd be the Power which has at once
  restor'd
The Hopes of lost Succession to Your Lord ;
Joy to the first, and last of each Degree, ⎫
Vertue to Courts, and, what I long'd to see, ⎬
To You the Graces, and the Muse to me. ⎭
  O daughter of the Rose, whose Cheeks
  unite   151
The diff'ring Titles of the Red and White ;
Who Heav'ns alternate Beauty well display,
The Blush of Morning, and the Milky Way ;
Whose Face is Paradise, but fenc'd from Sin :
For God in either Eye has placed a Cherubin.
  All is Your Lord's alone ; ev'n absent, He
Employs the Care of Chast *Penelope*.
For him You waste in Tears Your Widow'd
  Hours,
For him Your curious Needle paints the
  Flow'rs ;   160
Such Works of Old Imperial Dames were
  taught,
Such for *Ascanius*, fair *Elisa* wrought.
  The soft Recesses of Your Hours improve
The Three fair Pledges of Your Happy Love :
All other Parts of Pious Duty done,
You owe Your *Ormond* nothing but a son,
To fill in future Times his Father's Place,
And wear the Garter of his Mother's Race.

145 who] *Derrick and editors till Christie
wrongly give* which

PALAMON

AND

ARCITE:

OR

The Knight's Tale

FROM

CHAUCER

In Three Books.

BOOK I.

In Days of old, there liv'd, of mighty Fame
A valiant Prince; and *Theseus* was his Name:
A Chief, who more in Feats of Arms excell'd
The Rising nor the Setting Sun beheld.
Of *Athens* he was Lord ; much Land he won,
And added Foreign Countrys to his Crown.
In *Scythia* with the Warriour Queen he strove,
Whom first by Force he conquer'd, then by
 Love ;
He brought in Triumph back the beauteous
 Dame,
With whom her Sister, fair *Emilia*, came. 10
With Honour to his Home let *Theseus* ride, ⎫
With Love to Friend, and Fortune for his ⎬
 Guide, ⎭
And his victorious Army at his Side.
I pass their warlike Pomp, their proud Array,
Their Shouts, their Songs, their Welcome on
 the Way :
But, were it not too long, I would recite ⎫
The Feats of *Amazons*, the fatal Fight ⎬
Betwixt the hardy Queen and *Heroe* Knight. ⎭
The Town besieg'd, and how much Blood it
 cost
The Female Army, and th' *Athenian* Host ;
The Spousals of *Hippolita* the Queen ; 21
What Tilts, and Turneys at the Feast were
 seen ;
The Storm at their Return, the Ladies Fear :
But these and other Things I must forbear.

PALAMON AND ARCITE. The text is that of the
first and only contemporary edition, 1700, except
for the variants here noted. There are some false
stops in the original.

The Field is spacious I design to sow,
With Oxen far unfit to draw the Plow :
The Remnant of my Tale is of a length
To tire your Patience, and to waste my
 Strength ;
And trivial Accidents shall be forborn,
That others may have time to take their
 Turn ; 30
As was at first enjoin'd us by mine Host :
That he whose Tale is best, and pleases ⎫
 most, ⎬
Should win his Supper at our common Cost. ⎭
 And therefore where I left, I will pursue ⎫
This ancient Story, whether false or true, ⎬
In hope it may be mended with a new. ⎭
The Prince I mention'd, full of high Renown,
In this Array drew near th' *Athenian* Town ;
When, in his Pomp and utmost of his Pride,
Marching, he chanc'd to cast his Eye aside,
And saw a Quire of mourning Dames, who
 lay 41
By Two and Two across the common Way :
At his Approach they rais'd a rueful Cry,
And beat their Breasts, and held their Hands
 on high,
Creeping and crying, till they seiz'd at last
His Coursers Bridle and his Feet embrac'd.
Tell me, said *Theseus*, what and whence you
 are,
And why this Funeral Pageant you prepare ?
Is this the Welcome of my worthy Deeds, 49
To meet my Triumph in Ill-omen'd Weeds ?
Or envy you my Praise, and would destroy
With Grief my Pleasures, and pollute my Joy?
Or are you injur'd, and demand Relief ?
Name your Request, and I will ease your
 Grief.

The most in Years of all the Mourning
  Train
Began ; (but sounded first away for Pain)
Then scarce recover'd, spoke : Nor envy we
Thy great Renown, nor grudge thy Victory ;
Tis thine, O King, th' Afflicted to redress,
And Fame has fill'd the World with thy
  Success :   60
We wretched Women sue for that alone,
Which of thy Goodness is refus'd to none :
Let fall some Drops of Pity on our Grief,
If what we beg be just, and we deserve
  Relief :
For none of us, who now thy Grace implore,
But held the Rank of Sovereign Queen
  before ;
Till, thanks to giddy Chance, which never
  bears
That Mortal Bliss should last for length of
  Years,
She cast us headlong from our high Estate,
And here in hope of thy Return we wait : 70
And long have waited in the Temple nigh,
Built to the gracious Goddess *Clemency*.
But rev'rence thou the Pow'r whose Name it
  bears,
Relieve th' Oppressed, and wipe the Widows
  Tears.
I, wretched I, have other Fortune seen,
The Wife of *Capaneus*, and once a Queen :
At *Thebes* he fell ; curs'd be the fatal Day !
And all the rest thou seest in this Array,
To make their Moan their Lords in Battel lost,
Before that Town besieg'd by our Confed'rate
  Host :   80
But *Creon*, old and impious, who commands
The *Theban* City, and usurps the Lands,
Denies the Rites of Fun'ral Fires to those
Whose breathless Bodies yet he calls his
  Foes.
Unburn'd, unbury'd, on a Heap they lie ;
Such is their Fate, and such his Tyranny ;
No Friend has leave to bear away the Dead,
But with their Lifeless Limbs his Hounds are
  fed.
At this she shriek'd aloud, the mournful
  Train
Echo'd her Grief, and grov'ling on the Plain,

With Groans, and Hands upheld, to move
  his Mind,   91
Besought his Pity to their helpless Kind !
The Prince was touch'd, his Tears began
  to flow,
And, as his tender Heart would break in two,
He sigh'd ; and could not but their Fate
  deplore,
So wretched now, so fortunate before.
Then lightly from his lofty Steed he flew,
And raising one by one the suppliant Crew,
To comfort each, full solemnly he swore,
That by the Faith which Knights to Knight-
  hood bore,   100
And what e'er else to Chivalry belongs,
He would not cease, till he reveng'd their
  Wrongs :
That *Greece* should see perform'd what he
  declar'd,
And cruel *Creon* find his just Reward.
He said no more, but shunning all Delay
Rode on ; nor enter'd *Athens* on his Way ;
But left his Sister and his Queen behind,
And wav'd his Royal Banner in the Wind :
Where in an *Argent* Field the God of War
Was drawn triumphant on his Iron Carr ;
Red was his Sword, and Shield, and whole
  Attire,   111
And all the Godhead seem'd to glow with
  Fire ;
Ev'n the Ground glitter'd where the Stan-
  dard flew,
And the green Grass was dy'd to sanguine
  Hue.
High on his pointed Lance his Pennon bore
His *Cretan* Fight, the conquer'd *Minotaure* :
The Soldiers shout around with generous
  Rage,
And in that Victory, their own presage.
He prais'd their Ardour, inly pleas'd to see
His Host, the Flow'r of *Grecian* Chivalry. 120
All Day he march'd ; and all th' ensuing
  Night ;
And saw the City with returning Light.
The Process of the War I need not tell,
How *Theseus* conquer'd, and how *Creon* fell :
Or after, how by Storm the Walls were won,
Or how the Victor sack'd and burn'd the
  Town ;
How to the Ladies he restor'd again
The Bodies of their Lords in Battel slain ;

---

56 sounded] i. e. swoon'd *The form is genuine
and was used by Goldsmith. Many editors
wrongly give* swooned *and Christie gives*
swounded
89 shriek'd] skriek'd *1700*.

103 he] de *1700: a misprint*.

And with what ancient Rites they were
    interr'd ;
All these to fitter time shall be deferr'd : 130
I spare the Widows Tears, their woful Cries,
And Howling at their Husbands Obsequies ;
How *Theseus* at these Fun'rals did assist,
And with what Gifts the mourning Dames
    dismiss'd.
    Thus when the Victor Chief had *Creon*
    slain,
And conquer'd *Thebes*, he pitch'd upon the
    Plain
His mighty Camp, and when the Day
    return'd,
The Country wasted and the Hamlets burn'd ;
And left the Pillagers, to Rapine bred,
Without Controul to strip and spoil the
    Dead.   140
    There, in a Heap of Slain, among the rest
Two youthful Knights they found beneath
    a Load oppress'd
Of slaughter'd Foes, whom first to Death
    they sent,
The Trophies of their Strength, a bloody
    Monument.
Both fair, and both of Royal Blood they
    seem'd,
Whom Kinsmen to the Crown the Heralds
    deem'd ;
That Day in equal Arms they fought for
    Fame ;
Their Swords, their Shields, their Surcoats
    were the same.
Close by each other laid they press'd the
    Ground,
Their manly Bosoms pierc'd with many
    a griesly Wound ;   150
Nor well alive nor wholly dead they were,
But some faint Signs of feeble Life appear :
The wandring Breath was on the Wing to
    part,
Weak was the Pulse, and hardly heav'd the
    Heart.
These two were Sisters Sons ; and *Arcite* one,
Much fam'd in Fields, with valiant *Palamon*.
From These their costly Arms the Spoilers
    rent,
And softly both convey'd to *Theseus* Tent :
Whom, known of *Creon's* Line and cur'd
    with Care,   159
He to his City sent as Pris'ners of the War,
Hopeless of Ransom, and condemn'd to lie
In Durance, doom'd a lingring Death to die.

This done, he march'd away with warlike
    Sound,
And to his *Athens* turn'd with Laurels
    crown'd,
Where happy long he liv'd, much lov'd,
    and more renown'd.
But in a Tow'r, and never to be loos'd.
The woful captive Kinsmen are enclos'd.
    Thus Year by Year they pass, and Day by
    Day,
Till once ('twas on the Morn of chearful *May*)
The young *Emilia*, fairer to be seen   170
Than the fair Lilly on the Flow'ry Green,
More fresh than *May* her self in Blossoms
    new,
(For with the rosie Colour strove her Hue)
Wak'd, as her Custom was, before the Day,
To do th' Observance due to sprightly *May* :
For sprightly *May* commands our Youth to
    keep
The Vigils of her Night, and breaks their
    sluggard Sleep :
Each gentle Breast with kindly Warmth she
    moves ;
Inspires new Flames, revives extinguish'd
    Loves.
In this Remembrance *Emily* e'er day   180
Arose, and dress'd her self in rich Array ;
Fresh as the Month, and as the Morning
    fair :
Adown her Shoulders fell her Length of
    Hair :
A Ribband did the braided Tresses bind,
The rest was loose, and wanton'd in the
    Wind :
Aurora had but newly chas'd the Night,
And purpl'd o'er the Sky with blushing Light,
When to the Garden-walks he took her way,
To sport and trip along in Cool of Day,
And offer Maiden Vows in Honour of the
    May.   190
    At ev'ry Turn she made a little Stand,
And thrust among the Thorns her Lilly hand
To draw the Rose ; and ev'ry Rose she drew,
She shook the Stalk, and brush'd away the
    Dew :
Then party-colour'd Flow'rs of white and red
She wove, to make a Garland for her Head :
This done, she sung and caroll'd out so clear,
That Men and Angels might rejoice to hear.
Ev'n wondring *Philomel* forgot to sing,
And learn'd from Her to welcome in the
    Spring.   200

The Tow'r, of which before was mention
    made,
Within whose Keep the captive Knights were
    laid,
Built of a large Extent, and strong withal,
Was one Partition of the Palace Wall :
The Garden was enclos'd within the Square
Where young *Emilia* took the Morning-Air.
  It happen'd *Palamon*, the Pris'ner Knight,
Restless for Woe, arose before the Light,
And with his Jaylor's leave desir'd to breathe
An Air more wholesom than the Damps
    beneath.   210
This granted, to the Tow'r he took his way,
Cheer'd with the Promise of a glorious Day :
Then cast a languishing Regard around,
And saw with hateful Eyes the Temples
    crown'd
With golden Spires, and all the Hostile
    Ground.
He sigh'd, and turned his Eyes, because he
    knew
'Twas but a larger Jayl he had in view :
Then look'd below, and from the Castles
    height
Beheld a nearer and more pleasing Sight ;
The Garden, which before he had not seen,
In Spring's new Livery clad of White and
    Green,   221
Fresh Flow'rs in wide *Parterres*, and shady
    Walks between.
This view'd, but not enjoy'd, with Arms
    across
He stood, reflecting on his Country's Loss ;
Himself an Object of the Publick Scorn,
And often wish'd he never had been born.
At last (for so his Destiny requir'd)
With walking giddy, and with thinking tir'd,
He thro' a little Window cast his Sight,
Tho' thick of Bars, that gave a scanty Light :
But ev'n that Glimmering serv'd him to
    descry   231
Th' inevitable Charms of *Emily*.
  Scarce had he seen, but, seiz'd with sudden
    Smart,
Stung to the Quick, he felt it at his Heart ;
Struck blind with overpowering Light he
    stood,
Then started back amaz'd, and cry'd aloud.
  Young *Arcite* heard ; and up he ran with
    haste,
To help his Friend, and in his Arms em-
    brac'd ;

And ask'd him why he look'd so deadly wan,
And whence, and how, his change of Cheer
    began ?   240
Or who had done th' offence ? But if, said he,
Your Grief alone is hard Captivity ;
For Love of Heav'n, with Patience undergo
A cureless Ill, since Fate will have it so :
So stood our *Horoscope* in Chains to lie,
And *Saturn* in the Dungeon of the Sky,
Or other baleful Aspect, rul'd our Birth,
When all the friendly Stars were under Earth :
Whate'er betides, by Destiny 'tis done ;
And better bear like Men, than vainly seek
    to shun,   250
Nor of my bonds, said *Palamon* again,
Nor of unhappy Planets I complain ;
But when my mortal Anguish caus'd my Cry,
The Moment I was hurt thro' either Eye ;
Pierc'd with a Random-shaft, I faint away,
And perish with insensible Decay :
A Glance of some new Goddess gave the
    Wound,
Whom, like *Acteon*, unaware I found.   258
Look how she walks along yon shady Space ;
Not *Juno* moves with more Majestick Grace,
And all the *Cyprian* Queen is in her face.
If thou art *Venus*, (for thy Charms confess
That Face was form'd in Heaven) nor art
    thou less ;
Disguis'd in Habit, undisguis'd in Shape,
O help us Captives from our Chains to scape ;
But if our Doom be past in Bonds to lie
For Life, and in a loathsom Dungeon die ;
Then be thy Wrath appeas'd with our Dis-
    grace,
And show Compassion to the *Theban* Race,
Oppress'd by Tyrant Pow'r ! While yet he
    spoke,   270
Arcite on *Emily* had fix'd his Look ;
The fatal Dart a ready Passage found,
And deep within his Heart infix'd the Wound :
So that if *Palamon* were wounded sore,
Arcite was hurt as much as he, or more :
Then from his inmost Soul he sigh'd, and
    said,
The Beauty I behold has struck me dead :
Unknowingly she strikes, and kills by chance ;
Poyson is in her Eyes, and Death in ev'ry
    Glance.
O, I must ask ; nor ask alone, but move 280
Her Mind to Mercy, or must die for Love.
  Thus *Arcite* : And thus *Palamon* replies,
(Eager his Tone, and ardent were his Eyes.)

Speak'st thou in earnest, or in jesting Vein?)
Jesting, said *Arcite*, suits but ill with Pain. }
It suits far worse, (said *Palamon* again,   )
And bent his Brows) with Men who Honour
    weigh,
Their Faith to break, their friendship to
    betray ;   288
But worst with Thee, of Noble Lineage born,
My Kinsman, and in Arms my Brother sworn.
Have we not plighted each our holy Oath,
That one shou'd be the Common Good of
    both ?
One Soul shou'd both inspire, and neither
    prove
His Fellows Hindrance in pursuit of Love ?
To this before the Gods we gave our Hands,
And nothing but our Death can break the
    Bands.
This binds thee, then, to farther my Design,
As I am bound by Vow to farther thine :
Nor canst, nor dar'st thou, Traytor, on the
    Plain   299
Appeach my Honour, or thy own maintain,
Since thou art of my Council, and the Friend
Whose Faith I trust, and on whose Care
    depend :
And would'st thou court my Ladies Love,
    which I
Much rather than release, would chuse to die?
But thou, false *Arcite*, never shalt obtain,
Thy bad Pretence; I told thee first my
    Pain :
For first my Love began e'er thine was born ;
Thou, as my Council, and my Brother sworn,
Art bound t'assist my Eldership of Right,
Or justly to be deemd a perjur'd Knight. 310
    Thus *Palamon* : But *Arcite* with disdain
In haughty Language thus reply'd again :
Forsworn thy self : The Traytor's odious
    Name
I first return, and then disprove thy Claim.
If Love be Passion, and that Passion nurst
With strong Desires, I lov'd the Lady first.
Canst thou pretend Desire, whom Zeal in-
    flam'd
To worship, and a Pow'r Cœlestial nam'd ?
Thine was Devotion to the Blest above,
I saw the Woman, and desir'd her Love ; 320
First own'd my Passion, and to thee com-
    mend
Th' important Secret, as my chosen Friend.
Suppose (which yet I grant not) thy Desire
A Moment elder than my Rival Fire ;

Can Chance of seeing first thy Title prove ?
And know'st thou not, no Law is made for
    Love ?
Law is to Things which to free Choice relate ;
Love is not in our Choice, but in our Fate :
Laws are but positive : Loves Pow'r we see
Is Natures Sanction, and her first Decree. 330
Each Day we break the Bond of Humane
    Laws
For Love, and vindicate the Common Cause.
Laws for Defence of Civil Rights are plac'd,
Love throws the Fences down, and makes
    a general Waste :
Maids, Widows, Wives, without distinction
    fall ;
The sweeping Deluge, Love, comes on and
    covers all.
If then the Laws of Friendship I transgress,)
I keep the Greater, while I break the Less ; }
And both are mad alike, since neither can |
    possess.   )
Both hopeless to be ransom'd, never more
To see the Sun, but as he passes o'er.   341
Like Esop's Hounds contending for the Bone,
Each pleaded Right, and wou'd be lord
    alone ;
The fruitless Fight continu'd all the Day,
A Cur came by and snatch'd the Prize away.
As Courtiers therefore justle for a Grant,
And when they break their Friendship, plead
    their Want,
So thou, if Fortune will thy Suit advance,
Love on ; nor envy me my equal Chance :
For I must love, and am resolv'd to try 350
My Fate, or failing in th' Adventure die.
    Great was their Strife, which hourly was
    renew'd,
Till each with mortal Hate his Rival view'd :
Now Friends no more, nor walking Hand in
    Hand ;
But when they met, they made a surly Stand;
And glar'd like angry Lions as they pass'd,
And wish'd that every Look might be their
    last.
    It chanc'd at length, *Perithous* came
    t' attend
This worthy *Theseus*, his familiar Friend :

---

312 The *first edition began a new paragraph
here. This was a mistake, but it led some editors
to suppose that Arcite's speech ended with the
words* passes o'er. *In fact it goes down to* in th'
Adventure die, *but the lines are not quite grammatical.*

Their Love in early Infancy began,   360
And rose as Childhood ripen'd into Man.
Companions of the War; and lov'd so well,⎫
That when one dy'd, as ancient Stories tell,⎬
His Fellow to redeem him went to Hell. ⎭
    But to pursue my Tale ; to welcome
        home
His Warlike Brother, is *Perithous* come :
Arcite of *Thebes* was known in Arms long
        since,
And honour'd by this young *Thessalian*
    Prince.
Theseus, to gratifie his Friend and Guest,
Who made our *Arcite's* Freedom his Request,
Restor'd to Liberty the Captive Knight,   371
But on these hard Conditions I recite :
That if hereafter *Arcite* shou'd be found
Within the Compass of *Athenian* Ground,
By Day or Night, or on whate'er Pretence,
His Head shou'd pay the Forfeit of th'
    Offence.
To this *Perithous* for his Friend agreed,
And on his Promise was the Pris'ner freed.
    Unpleas'd and pensive hence he takes his
        way,
At his own Peril ; for his Life must pay.
Who now but *Arcite* mourns his bitter
    Fate,   381
Finds his dear Purchase, and repents too
    late ?
What have I gain'd, he said, in Prison pent,
If I but change my Bonds for Banishment ?
And banish'd from her Sight, I suffer more
In Freedom than I felt in Bonds before ;
Forc'd from her Presence and condemn'd to
    live :
Unwelcom Freedom and unthank'd Reprieve:
Heav'n is not but where *Emily* abides,   389
And where she's absent, all is Hell besides.
Next to my Day of Birth, was that accurst
Which bound my Friendship to *Perithous*
    first :
Had I not known that Prince, I still had
    been
In Bondage, and had still *Emilia* seen :
For tho' I never can her Grace deserve,
'Tis Recompense enough to see and serve.
O *Palamon*, my Kinsman and my Friend,
How much more happy Fates thy Love
    attend !

Thine is th' Adventure ; thine the Victory :
Well has thy Fortune turn'd the Dice for
    thee :   400
Thou on that Angels Face maist feed thy
    Eyes,
In Prison, no ; but blissful Paradise !
Thou daily seest that Sun of Beauty shine,
And lov'st at least in Loves extreamest Line.
I mourn in Absence, Loves Eternal Night;⎫
And who can tell but since thou hast her ⎪
    Sight,   ⎬
And art a comely, young, and valiant   ⎪
    Knight,   ⎭
Fortune (a various Pow'r) may cease to
    frown,
And by some Ways unknown thy Wishes
    crown :
But I, the most forlorn of Humane Kind,   410
Nor Help can hope, nor Remedy can find ;
But doom'd to drag my loathsom Life in
    Care,
For my Reward, must end it in Despair.
Fire, Water, Air, and Earth, and Force of
    Fates
That governs all, and Heav'n that all
    creates,
Nor Art, nor Natures Hand can ease my
    Grief ;
Nothing but Death, the Wretches last
    Relief :
Then farewel Youth, and all the Joys that
    dwell
With Youth and Life, and Life it self, fare-
    well.
    But why, alas ! do mortal Men in vain   420
Of Fortune, Fate, or Providence complain ?
God gives us what he knows our Wants
    require,
And better Things than those which we
    desire :
Some pray for Riches ; Riches they obtain ;
But watch'd by Robbers, for their Wealth
    are slain :
Some pray from Prison to be freed ; and
    come
When guilty of their Vows, to fall at home ;
Murder'd by those they trusted with their
    Life,
A favour'd Servant, or a Bosom Wife.
Such dear-bought Blessings happen ev'ry
    Day,   430
Because we know not for what Things to
    pray.

----

377 To this *Perithous* for his Friend] To this,
Perithous for his Friend, *1700.*

Like drunken Sots about the Streets we
 roam
Well knows the Sot he has a certain Home ;
Yet knows not how to find th' uncertain
 Place,
And blunders on, and staggers ev'ry Pace.
Thus all seek Happiness ; but few can find,
For far the greater Part of Men are blind.
This is my Case, who thought our utmost
 Good
Was in one Word of Freedom understood :
The fatal Blessing came : From Prison free,
I starve abroad, and lose the Sight of
 Emily.   441
 Thus *Arcite* : but if *Arcite* thus deplore
His Suff'rings, *Palamon* yet suffers more.
For when he knew his Rival freed and
 gone,
He swells with Wrath ; he makes outrageous
 Moan :
He frets, he fumes, he stares, he stamps the
 Ground ;
The hollow Tow'r with Clamours rings
 around :
With briny Tears he bath'd his fetter'd
 Feet,
And dropp'd all o'er with Agony of Sweat.
Alas! he cry'd, I, Wretch, in Prison pine, 450
Too happy Rival, while the Fruit is thine :
Thou liv'st at large, thou draw'st thy Native
 Air,
Pleas'd with thy Freedom, proud of my
 Despair :
Thou may'st, since thou hast Youth and
 Courage join'd,
A sweet Behaviour, and a solid Mind,
Assemble ours, and all the *Theban* Race,
To vindicate on *Athens* thy Disgrace ;
And after (by some Treaty made) possess
Fair *Emily*, the Pledge of lasting Peace.
So thine shall be the beauteous Prize, while I
Must languish in Despair, in Prison die. 461
Thus all th'Advantage of the Strife is thine,
Thy portion double Joys, and double Sorrows
 mine.
 The Rage of Jealousie then fir'd his Soul,
And his Face kindl'd like a burning Coal :
Now cold Despair, succeeding in her stead,
To livid Paleness turns the glowing Red.
His Blood scarce Liquid, creeps within his
 Veins,
Like Water which the freezing Wind con-
 strains.

Then thus he said ; Eternal Deities   470
Who rule the World with absolute Decrees,
And write whatever Time shall bring to
 pass
With Pens of Adamant on Plates of Brass ;
What is the Race of Humane Kind your
 Care
Beyond what all his Fellow-Creatures are ?
He with the rest is liable to Pain,
And like the Sheep, his Brother-Beast, is
 slain.
Cold, Hunger, Prisons, Ills without a Cure,
All these he must, and guiltless oft, endure :
Or does your Justice, Pow'r, or Prescience
 fail,   480
When the Good suffer and the Bad prevail ?
What worse to wretched Vertue could befall,
If Fate, or giddy Fortune govern'd all ?
Nay, worse than other Beasts is our Estate :
Them, to pursue their Pleasures you create ;
We, bound by harder Laws, must curb our
 Will,
And your Commands, not our Desires
 fulfil :
Then when the Creature is unjustly slain,
Yet, after Death at least, he feels no
 Pain ;
But Man in Life surcharg'd with Woe before,
Not freed when dead, is doom'd to suffer
 more.   491
A Serpent shoots his Sting at unaware ;
An ambush'd Thief forelays a Traveller ;
The Man lies murder'd, while the Thief and
 Snake,
One gains the Thickets, and one thrids the
 Brake.
This let Divines decide ; but well I know,
Just, or unjust, I have my Share of Woe :
Through *Saturn* seated in a luckless Place,
And *Juno's* Wrath, that persecutes my
 Race ;
Or *Mars* and *Venus* in a Quartil, move 500
My Pangs of Jealousie for *Arcite's* Love.
 Let *Palamon* oppress'd in Bondage mourn,
While to his exil'd Rival we return.
By this the Sun, declining from his Height,
The Day had shortned to prolong the Night :
The lengthen'd Night gave length of Misery
Both to the Captive Lover, and the Free :
For *Palamon* in endless Prison mourns,
And *Arcite* forfeits Life if he returns. 509
The Banish'd never hopes his Love to see,
Nor hopes the Captive Lord his Liberty :

'Tis hard to say who suffers greater Pains,
One sees his Love, but cannot break his
  Chains :
One free, and all his Motions uncontroul'd,
Beholds whate'er he wou'd, but what he
  wou'd behold.
Judge as you please, for I will haste to tell
What Fortune to the banish'd Knight befel.
When *Arcite* was to *Thebes* return'd again,
The Loss of her he lov'd renew'd his Pain ;
What could be worse than never more to see
His Life, his Soul, his charming *Emily* ? 521
He rav'd with all the Madness of Despair,
He roar'd, he beat his Breast, he tore his
  Hair.
Dry Sorrow in his stupid Eyes appears,
For wanting Nourishment, he wanted Tears :
His Eye-balls in their hollow Sockets sink,
Bereft of Sleep ; he loaths his Meat and
  Drink :
He withers at his Heart, and looks as wan
As the pale spectre of a murder'd Man : 529
That Pale turns Yellow, and his Face receives
The faded Hue of sapless Boxen Leaves ;
In solitary Groves he makes his Moan,
Walks early out, and ever is alone.
Nor mix'd in Mirth, in youthful Pleasure
  shares,
But sighs when Songs and Instruments he
  hears.
His Spirits are so low, his Voice is drown'd, }
He hears as from afar, or in a Swound,   }
Like the deaf Murmurs of a distant Sound : }
Uncomb'd his locks, and squalid his Attire,
Unlike the Trim of Love and gay Desire ;
But full of museful Mopings, which pre-
  sage   541
The loss of Reason, and conclude in Rage.
  This when he had endur'd a Year and
  more,
Now wholly chang'd from what he was
  before,
It happen'd once, that, slumbring as he lay,
He dreamt (his Dream began at Break of
  Day)
That *Hermes* o'er his Head in Air appear'd,
And with soft Words his drooping Spirits
  cheer'd :
His Hat adorn'd with Wings disclos'd the God,
And in his Hand he bore the Sleep-com-
  pelling Rod ;   550
Such as he seem'd, when at his Sire's Com-
  mand,

On *Argus* Head he laid the Snaky Wand ;
Arise, he said, to conqu'ring *Athens* go,
There Fate appoints an End of all thy Woe.
The fright awaken'd *Arcite* with a Start,
Against his Bosom bounc'd his heaving
  Heart ;
But soon he said, with scarce-recover'd
  Breath,
And thither will I go to meet my Death,
Sure to be slain ; but Death is my Desire,
Since in *Emilia's* Sight I shall expire.   560
By chance he spy'd a Mirrour while he spoke,
And gazing there beheld his alter'd Look ;
Wondring, he saw his Features and his Hue
So much were chang'd, that scarce himself he
  knew.
A sudden Thought then starting in his Mind,
Since I in *Arcite* cannot *Arcite* find,
The World may search in vain with all their
  Eyes,
But never penetrate through this Disguise.
Thanks to the Change which Grief and Sick-
  ness give,
In low Estate I may securely live,   570
And see unknown my Mistress Day by Day.
He said, and cloth'd himself in course Array ;
A lab'ring Hind in shew : Then forth he went,
And to the *Athenian* Tow'rs his Journey
  bent :
One Squire attended in the same Disguise,
Made conscious of his Master's Enterprize.
Arriv'd at *Athens*, soon he came to Court,
Unknown, unquestion'd in that thick Resort ;
Proff'ring for Hire his Service at the Gate,
To drudge, draw Water, and to run or wait.
So fair befel him, that for little Gain   581
He serv'd at first *Emilia's* Chamberlain ;
And, watchful all Advantages to spy,
Was still at Hand, and in his Master's Eye ;
And as his Bones were big, and Sinews strong,
Refus'd no Toil that could to Slaves belong ;
But from deep Wells with Engines Water
  drew,
And us'd his Noble Hands the Wood to hew.
He pass'd a Year at least attending thus
On *Emily*, and call'd *Philostratus*.   590
But never was there Man of his Degree
So much esteem'd, so well belov'd as he.
So gentle of Condition was he known,
That through the Court his Courtesie was
  blown :
All think him worthy of a greater Place,
And recommend him to the Royal Grace ;

That exercis'd within a higher Sphere,
His Vertues more conspicuous might appear.
Thus by the general Voice was *Arcite* prais'd,
And by Great *Theseus* to high Favour rais'd;
Among his Menial Servants first enroll'd, 601
And largely entertain'd with Sums of Gold :
Besides what secretly from *Thebes* was
    sent,
Of his own Income, and his Annual Rent.

This well employ'd, he purchas'd Friends
    and Fame,
But cautiously conceal'd from whence it
    came.
Thus for three Years he liv'd with large
    Increase,
In Arms of Honour, and Esteem in Peace ;
To *Theseus* Person he was ever near,   609
And *Theseus* for his Vertues held him dear.

The End of the First Book.

PALAMON AND ARCITE : OR, THE KNIGHT'S TALE.

BOOK II.

WHILE *Arcite* lives in Bliss, the Story turns
Where hopeless *Palamon* in Prison mourns.
For six long Years immur'd, the captive
    Knight
Had dragg'd his Chains, and scarcely seen
    the Light :
Lost Liberty, and Love at once he bore ;
His Prison pain'd him much, his Passion
    more :
Nor dares he hope his Fetters to remove,
Nor ever wishes to be free from Love.
    But when the sixth revolving Year was run,
And *May* within the *Twins* received the Sun,
Were it by Chance, or forceful Destiny,   11
Which forms in Causes first whate'er shall be,
Assisted by a Friend one Moonless Night,
This *Palamon* from Prison took his flight :
A pleasant Beverage he prepar'd before
Of Wine and Honey mix'd, with added Store
Of *Opium* ; to his Keeper this he brought,
Who swallow'd unaware the sleepy Draught,
And snor'd secure till Morn, his Senses bound
In Slumber, and in long Oblivion drown'd.
Short was the Night, and careful *Palamon* 21
Sought the next Covert e'er the rising Sun.
A thick spread Forest near the City lay,
To this with lengthened Strides he took
    his Way,
(For far he cou'd not fly, and fear'd the
    Day :)
Safe from Pursuit, he meant to shun the
    Light,
Till the brown Shadows of the friendly Night
To *Thebes* might favour his intended Flight.
When to his Country come, his next Design
Was all the *Theban* Race in Arms to join,   30

And war on *Theseus*, till he lost his Life,
Or won the Beauteous *Emily* to Wife.
Thus while his thoughts the lingring Day
    beguile,
To gentle *Arcite* let us turn our Style ;
Who little dreamt how nigh he was to Care,
Till treacherous Fortune caught him in the
    Snare.
The Morning-Lark, the Messenger of Day,
Saluted in her Song the Morning gray ;
And soon the Sun arose with Beams so bright,
That all th' Horizon laugh'd to see the joyous
    Sight ;   40
He with his tepid Rays the Rose renews,
And licks the dropping Leaves, and dries the
    Dews ;
When *Arcite* left his Bed, resolv'd to pay
Observance to the Month of merry *May*,
Forth on his fiery Steed betimes he rode,
That scarcely prints the Turf on which he
    trod :
At ease he seem'd, and pransing o'er the
    Plains,
Turn'd only to the Grove his Horse's Reins,
The Grove I nam'd before ; and lighting
    there,
A Woodbind Garland sought to crown his
    Hair ;   50
Then turned his Face against the rising Day,
And rais'd his Voice to welcom in the *May*.
    For thee, sweet Month, the Groves green
    Liv'ries wear :
If not the first, the fairest of the Year :
For thee the Graces lead the dancing Hours,
And Nature's ready Pencil paints the Flow'rs:

---

42 dropping] *Warton and others wrongly give*
drooping

When thy short Reign is past, the Fev'rish
    Sun
The sultry Tropick fears, and moves more
    slowly on.
So may thy tender Blossoms fear no Blite,
Nor Goats with venom'd Teeth thy Tendrils
    bite,   60
As thou shalt guide my wandring Feet to
    find
The fragrant Greens I seek, my Brows to
    bind.

His Vows address'd, within the Grove he
    stray'd,
Till Fate, or Fortune, near the Place con-
    vey'd
His Steps where secret *Palamon* was laid.
Full little thought of him the gentle Knight,
Who flying Death had there conceal'd his
    Flight,
In Brakes and Brambles hid, and shunning
    Mortal Sight ;
And less he knew him for his hated Foe,
But fear'd him as a Man he did not know. 70
But as it has been said of ancient Years,
That Fields are full of Eyes, and Woods have
    Ears ;
For this the Wise are ever on their Guard,
For, Unforeseen, they say, is unprepar'd.
Uncautious *Arcite* thought himself alone,
And less than all suspected *Palamon*,
Who, listning, heard him, while he search'd
    the Grove,
And loudly sung his Roundelay of Love :
But on the sudden stopp'd, and silent stood,
(As Lovers often muse, and change their
    Mood ;)   80
Now high as Heav'n, and then as low as Hell,
Now up, now down, as Buckets in a Well :
For *Venus*, like her Day, will change her
    Cheer,
And seldom shall we see a *Friday* clear.
Thus *Arcite* having sung, with alter'd Hue
Sunk on the Ground, and from his Bosom
    drew
A desp'rate Sigh, accusing Heav'n and Fate,
And angry *Juno's* unrelenting Hate.
Curs'd be the Day when first I did appear ;
Let it be blotted from the Calendar,   90
Lest it pollute the Month, and poison all
    the Year.
Still will the jealous Queen pursue our
    Race ?
Cadmus is dead, the *Theban* City was :

Yet ceases not her Hate : For all who come
From *Cadmus* are involv'd in *Cadmus* Doom.
I suffer for my Blood : Unjust Decree !
That punishes another's Crime on me.
In mean Estate I serve my mortal Foe,
The Man who caus'd my Countrys Overthrow
This is not all ; for *Juno*, to my Shame,   100
Has forc'd me to forsake my former Name ;
Arcite I was, *Philostratus* I am.
That side of Heav'n is all my Enemy :
Mars ruin'd *Thebes* ; his Mother ruin'd me.
Of all the Royal Race remains but one
Beside my self, th' unhappy *Palamon*,
Whom *Theseus* holds in Bonds, and will not
    free ;
Without a Crime, except his Kin to me.
Yet these, and all the rest I cou'd endure ;
But Love's a Malady without a Cure :   110
Fierce Love has pierc'd me with his fiery
    Dart,
He fries within, and hisses at my Heart.
Your Eyes, fair *Emily*, my Fate pursue ;
I suffer for the rest, I die for you.
Of such a Goddess no Time leaves Record,
Who burn'd the Temple where she was
    ador'd :
And let it burn, I never will complain,
Pleas'd with my Suff'rings, if you knew my
    Pain.

At this a sickly Qualm his Heart assail'd,
His Ears ring inward, and his Senses fail'd.
No Word miss'd *Palamon* of all he spoke, 121
But soon to deadly Pale he changed his Look :
He trembl'd ev'ry Limb, and felt a Smart,
As if cold Steel had glided through his Heart ;
Nor longer staid, but starting from his Place,
Discover'd stood, and shew'd his hostile Face :
False Traytor, *Arcite*, Traytor to thy Blood,
Bound by thy sacred Oath to seek my Good,
Now art thou found forsworn for *Emily* ;
And dar'st attempt her Love, for whom I die.
So hast thou cheated *Theseus* with a Wile,
Against thy Vow, returning to beguile   132
Under a borrow'd Name : As false to me,
So false thou art to him who set thee free
But rest assur'd, that either thou shalt die,
Or else renounce thy Claim in *Emily* :
For though unarm'd I am, and (freed by
    Chance)
Am here without my Sword, or pointed
    Lance,

---

112 fries] fires *1713 and others wrongly.*

Hope not, base Man, unquestion'd hence to
    go,
For I am *Palamon*, thy mortal Foe.   140
    Arcite, who heard his Tale and knew the
    Man,
His sword unsheath'd, and fiercely thus
    began :
Now, by the Gods who govern Heav'n above,
Wert thou not weak with Hunger, mad with
    Love,
That Word had been thy last, or in this
    Grove
This Hand should force thee to renounce thy
    Love.
The Surety which I gave thee I defie ;   ⎫
Fool, not to know that Love endures no Tie, ⎬
And *Jove* but laughs at Lovers Perjury. 149 ⎭
Know, I will serve the fair in thy despight ;
But since thou art my Kinsman, and a Knight,
Here, have my Faith, to-morrow in this
    Grove
Our Arms shall plead the Titles of our Love :
And Heaven so help my Right, as I alone
Will come, and keep the Cause and Quarrel
    both unknown ;
With Arms of Proof both for my self and thee;
Chuse thou the best, and leave the worst to
    me.
And, that at better Ease thou maist abide,
Bedding and Clothes I will this Night provide,
And needful Sustenance, that thou maist be
A Conquest better won, and worthy me. 161
His Promise *Palamon* accepts ; but pray'd,
To keep it better than the first he made.
Thus fair they parted till the Morrows Dawn;
For each had laid his plighted Faith to Pawn.
Oh Love ! Thou sternly dost thy Pow'r ⎫
    maintain,   ⎪
And wilt not bear a Rival in thy Reign,   ⎬
Tyrants and thou all Fellowship disdain. ⎭
This was in *Arcite* prov'd and *Palamon* :
Both in Despair, yet each would love alone.
Arcite return'd, and, as in Honour ty'd, 171
His Foe with Bedding, and with Food sup-
    ply'd ;
Then, e'er the Day, two Suits of Armour
    sought,
Which born before him on his Steed he
    brought :
Both were of shining Steel, and wrought so
    pure
As might the Strokes of two such Arms
    endure.

Now, at the Time, and in th' appointed Place.
The Challenger, and Challeng'd, Face to Face,
Approach ; each other from afar they knew,
And from afar their Hatred chang'd their
    Hue.   180
So stands the *Thracian* Heardsman with his
    Spear,
Full in the Gap, and hopes the hunted Bear,
And hears him rustling in the Wood, and sees
His Course at Distance by the bending Trees:
And thinks, Here comes my mortal Enemy,
And either he must fall in Fight, or I :
This while he thinks, he lifts aloft his Dart ; ⎫
A gen'rous Chillness seizes ev'ry Part ;   ⎬
The Veins pour back the Blood, and fortifie   ⎪
    the Heart.   ⎭
    Thus pale they meet ; their Eyes with
    Fury burn ;   190
None greets ; for none the Greeting will
    return ;
But in dumb Surliness, each arm'd with Care
His Foe profest, as Brother of the War ;
Then both, no Moment lost, at once advance
Against each other, arm'd with Sword and
    Lance :
They lash, they foin, they pass, they strive
    to bore
Their Corslets, and the thinnest Parts explore.
Thus two long Hours in equal Arms they
    stood,
And wounded, wound; till both were bath'd
    in Blood ;
And not a Foot of Ground had either got, 200
As if the World depended on the Spot.
Fell *Arcite* like an angry Tyger far'd,
And like a Lion *Palamon* appear'd :
Or as two Boars whom Love to Battel draws,
With rising Bristles and with froathy Jaws,
Their adverse Breasts with Tusks oblique
    they wound ;
With Grunts and Groans the Forest rings
    around.
So fought the Knights, and fighting must
    abide,
Till Fate an Umpire sends their Diff'rence to
    decide.   209
The Pow'r that ministers to God's Decrees,
And executes on Earth what Heav'n foresees,
Called Providence, or Chance, or Fatal Sway,
Comes with resistless Force, and finds or
    makes her Way.
Nor Kings, nor Nations, nor united Pow'r
One Moment can retard th' appointed Hour.

And some one Day, some wondrous Chance appears,
Which happen'd not in Centuries of Years:
For sure, whate'er we Mortals hate or love,
Or hope, or fear, depends on Pow'rs above:
They move our Appetites to Good or Ill, 220
And by Foresight necessitate the Will.
In *Theseus* this appears; whose youthful Joy
Was Beasts of Chase in Forests to destroy;
This gentle Knight, inspir'd by jolly *May*, ⎫
Forsook his easie Couch at early Day, ⎬
And to the Wood and Wilds pursu'd his ⎭
      Way.
Beside him rode *Hippolita* the Queen,
And *Emily* attir'd in lively Green,
With Horns, and Hounds, and all the tuneful Cry,
To hunt a Royal Hart within the Covert
      nigh: 230
And, as he follow'd *Mars* before, so now
He serves the Goddess of the Silver Bow.
The way that *Theseus* took was to the Wood,
Where the two Knights in cruel Battel stood:
The Laund on which they fought, th' ap-
      pointed Place
In which th' uncoupl'd Hounds began the
      Chace.
Thither forth-right he rode to rowse the Prey,
That shaded by the Fern in Harbour lay;
And thence dislodg'd, was wont to leave the
      Wood   239
For open Fields, and cross the Crystal Flood.
Approach'd, and looking underneath the Sun,
He saw proud *Arcite*, and fierce *Palamon*,
In mortal Battel doubling Blow on Blow.
Like Lightning flam'd their Fauchions to
      and fro,
And shot a dreadful Gleam; so strong they
      strook,
There seem'd less Force requir'd to fell an
      Oak:
He gaz'd with Wonder on their equal Might,
Look'd eager on, but knew not either Knight:
Resolv'd to learn, he spurr'd his fiery Steed
With goring Rowels, to provoke his Speed.
The Minute ended that began the Race, 251
So soon he was betwixt 'em on the Place;
And with his Sword unsheath'd, on Pain of
      Life
Commands both Combatants to cease their
      Strife:
Then with imperious Tone pursues his Threat;
What are you? Why in Arms together met?

How dares your Pride presume against my
      Laws,
As in a listed Field to fight your Cause?
Unask'd the Royal Grant; no Marshal by,
As Knightly Rites require; nor Judge to
      try?   260
Then *Palamon*, with scarce recover'd Breath,
Thus hasty spoke; We both deserve the
      Death,
And both wou'd die; for look the World
      around,
A Pair so wretched is not to be found.
Our Life's a Load; encumber'd with the
      Charge,
We long to set th' imprison'd Soul at large.
Now, as thou art a Sovereign Judge, decree ⎫
The rightful Doom of Death to him and me, ⎬
Let neither find thy Grace, for Grace is ⎭
      Cruelty.
Me first, O kill me first, and cure my Woe;
Then sheath the Sword of Justice on my
      Foe: 271
Or kill him first, for when his Name is
      heard,
He foremost will receive his due Reward.
Arcite of *Thebes* is he; thy mortal Foe,
On whom thy Grace did Liberty bestow,
But first contracted, that, if ever found
By Day or Night upon th' *Athenian* Ground,
His Head should pay the Forfeit: See
      return'd
The perjur'd Knight, his Oath and Honour
      scorn'd.   279
For this is he, who, with a borrow'd Name
And profer'd Service, to thy Palace came,
Now call'd *Philostratus*: retain'd by thee, ⎫
A Traytor trusted, and in high Degree ⎬
Aspiring to the Bed of beauteous *Emily*. ⎭
My Part remains, from *Thebes* my Birth
      I own,
And call myself th' unhappy *Palamon*.
Think me not like that Man; since no Dis-
      grace
Can force me to renounce the Honour of my
      Race.
Know me for what I am: I broke thy
      Chain,
Nor promis'd I thy Pris'ner to remain: 290
The Love of Liberty with Life is giv'n,
And Life it self th' inferiour Gift of Heaven.
Thus without Crime I fled; but farther
      know,
I with this *Arcite* am thy mortal Foe:

Then give me Death, since I thy Life pursue ;
For Safeguard of thy self, Death is my Due.
More would'st thou know ? I love bright
    Emily,
And for her sake and in her Sight will
    die :
But kill my Rival too ; for he no less   ⎫
Deserves ; and I thy righteous Doom will ⎪
    bless,   300 ⎬
Assur'd that what I lose, he never shall ⎪
    possess.   ⎭
To this reply'd the stern *Athenian* Prince,
And sow'rly smild, In owning your Offence
You judge your self, and I but keep record
In place of Law, while you pronounce the
    Word.
Take your Desert, the Death you have
    decreed ;
I seal thy Doom, and ratifie the Deed.
By *Mars*, the Patron of my Arms, you die.
  He said ; dumb Sorrow seiz'd the Standers
    by.   309
The Queen, above the rest, by Nature good,
(The Pattern form'd of perfect Womanhood)
For tender Pity wept : When she began,
Through the bright Quire th' infectious
    Vertue ran.
All dropt their Tears, ev'n the contended
    Maid ;
And thus among themselves they softly said :
What Eyes can suffer this unworthy Sight !
Two Youths of Royal Blood, renown'd in
    Fight,
The Mastership of Heav'n in Face and Mind,
And Lovers, far beyond their faithless Kind :
See their wide streaming Wounds ; they
    neither came   320
From Pride of Empire, nor desire of Fame :
Kings fight for Kingdoms, Madmen for
    Applause :
But Love for Love alone ; that crowns the
    Lover's Cause.
This Thought, which ever bribes the beau-
    teous Kind,
Such Pity wrought in ev'ry Ladies Mind,
They left their Steeds, and prostrate on the
    Place,
From the fierce King, implor'd th' Offenders
    Grace.

He paus'd a while, stood silent in his Mood,
(For yet his Rage was boiling in his Blood)
But soon his tender Mind th' Impression felt.
(As softest Metals are not slow to melt   331
And Pity soonest runs in gentle Minds :)
Then reasons with himself ; and first he finds
His Passion cast a Mist before his Sense,
And either made, or magnifi'd th' Offence.
Offence ! of what ? to whom ? Who judg'd
    the Cause ?
The Pris'ner freed himself by Natures Laws ;
Born free, he sought his Right : The Man
    he freed
Was perjur'd, but his Love excus'd the Deed :
Thus pond'ring, he look'd under with his
    Eyes,   340
And saw the Womens Tears, and heard their
    Cries ;
Which mov'd Compassion more : He shook
    his Head,
And softly sighing to himself, he said,
  Curse on th' unpard'ning Prince, whom
    Tears can draw
To no Remorse ; who rules by Lions Law ;
And deaf to Pray'rs, by no Submission
    bow'd,
Rends all alike ; the Penitent, and Proud :
At this with look serene he rais'd his Head ;
Reason resum'd her Place, and Passion fled :
Then thus aloud he spoke : The Pow'r of
    Love,   350
In Earth, and Seas, and Air, and Heav'n
    above,
Rules, unresisted, with an awful Nod ;
By daily Miracles declar'd a God :
He blinds the Wise, gives Eye-sight to the
    Blind ;
And moulds and stamps anew the Lover's
    Mind.
Behold that *Arcite*, and this *Palamon*,
Freed from my Fetters, and in Safety gone,
What hinder'd either in their Native Soil
At ease to reap the Harvest of their Toil ?
But Love, their Lord, did otherwise ordain,
And brought 'em, in their own Despite again,
To suffer Death deserv'd ; for well they
    know   362
'Tis in my Pow'r, and I their deadly Foe.
The Proverb holds, That to be wise and love,
Is hardly granted to the Gods above.
See how the Madmen bleed : Behold the Gains
With which their Master, Love, rewards
    their Pains :

---

295 pursue ;] pursue, *1700*.
321 From] *Warton and others wrongly give*
For
  323 Love for] love for *1700*.

For sev'n long Years, on Duty ev'ry Day,
Lo their Obedience, and their Monarch's
    Pay :   369
Yet, as in Duty bound, they serve him on,
And ask the Fools, they think it wisely done :
Nor Ease nor Wealth nor Life it self regard,
For 'tis their Maxim, Love is Love's Reward.
This is not all ; the Fair, for whom they
    strove
Nor knew before, nor could suspect their
    Love,
Nor thought, when she beheld the Fight
    from far,
Her Beauty was th' Occasion of the War.
But sure a gen'ral Doom on Man is past,
And all are Fools and Lovers, first or last :
This both by others and my self I know,
For I have serv'd their Sovereign, long ago ;
Oft have been caught within the winding
    Train   382
Of Female Snares, and felt the Lover's
    Pain,
And learn'd how far the God can Humane
    Hearts constrain.
To this Remembrance, and the Pray'rs of
    those
Who for th' offending Warriors interpose,
I give their forfeit Lives ; on this accord,
To do me Homage as their Sov'reign Lord ;
And as my Vassals, to their utmost Might,
Assist my Person, and assert my Right. 390
This freely sworn, the Knights their Grace
    obtain'd ;
Then thus the King his secret Thoughts
    explain'd :
If Wealth, or Honour, or a Royal Race,
Or each, or all, may win a Ladies Grace,
Then either of you Knights may well deserve
A Princess born ; and such is she you serve :
For Emily is Sister to the Crown,
And but too well to both her Beauty known :
But shou'd you combat till you both were
    dead,
Two Lovers cannot share a single Bed : 400
As, therefore, both are equal in Degree,
The Lot of both be left to Destiny.
Now hear th' Award, and happy may it prove
To her, and him who best deserves her Love.
Depart from hence in peace, and free as Air,
Search the wide World, and where you please
    repair ;
But on the Day when this returning Sun
To the same Point through ev'ry sign has run,

Then each of you his Hundred Knights shall
    bring
In Royal Lists, to fight before the King ; 410
And then, the Knight, whom Fate or happy
    Chance
Shall with his Friends to Victory advance,
And grace his Arms so far in equal Fight,
From out the Bars to force his Opposite,
Or kill, or make him Recreant on the Plain,
The Prize of Valour and of Love shall gain ;
The vanquish'd Party shall their Claim
    release,
And the long Jars conclude in lasting Peace.
The Charge be mine t' adorn the chosen
    Ground,
The Theatre of War, for Champions so
    renown'd ;   420
And take the Patrons Place of either
    Knight,
With Eyes impartial to behold the Fight ;
And Heav'n of me so judge, as I shall
    judge aright.
If both are satisfi'd with this Accord,
Swear by the Laws of Knighthood on my
    Sword.
Who now but Palamon exults with joy ?
And ravish'd Arcite seems to touch the Sky :
The whole assembl'd Troop was pleas'd as
    well,
Extol'd the Award, and on their Knees they
    fell
To bless the gracious King. The Knights
    with Leave   430
Departing from the Place, his last Commands
    receive ;
On Emily with equal Ardour look,
And from her Eyes their Inspiration took :
From thence to Thebes old Walls pursue
    their Way,
Each to provide his Champions for the Day.
    It might be deem'd, on our Historian's
    Part,
Or too much Negligence, or Want of Art,
If he forgot the vast Magnificence
Of Royal Theseus, and his large Expence.
He first enclos'd for Lists a level Ground, 440
The whole Circumference a Mile around :
The Form was Circular ; and all without
A Trench was sunk, to Moat the Place about.
Within, an Amphitheatre appear'd,
Rais'd in Degrees ; to sixty Paces rear'd :

   429 Extol'd] *Derrick and editors before Chris-*
tie wrongly give Extol

That when a Man was plac'd in one Degree,
Height was allow'd for him above to see.
   Eastward was built a Gate of Marble
      white ;
The like adorn'd the Western opposite.
A nobler Object than this Fabrick was,   450
Rome never saw ; nor of so vast a Space.
For, rich with Spoils of many a conquer'd
      Land,
All Arts and Artists *Theseus* could command;
Who sold for Hire, or wrought for better
      Fame :
The Master-Painters, and the Carvers came.
So rose within the Compass of the Year
An Ages Work, a glorious Theatre.
Then, o'er its Eastern Gate was rais'd above
A Temple, sacred to the Queen of Love ;
An Altar stood below : On either Hand 460
A Priest with Roses crown'd, who held
      a Myrtle Wand.
   The Dome of *Mars* was on the Gate
      oppos'd,
And on the North a Turret was enclos'd,
Within the Wall, of Alabaster white,
And crimson Coral, for the Queen of Night,
Who takes in Sylvan Sports her chaste
      Delight.
   Within these Oratories might you see
Rich Carvings, Pourtraitures, and Imagery :
Where ev'ry Figure to the Life express'd
The Godhead's Pow'r to whom it was
      address'd.   470
In *Venus* Temple on the Sides were seen
The broken Slumbers of inamour'd Men ;
Pray'rs that ev'n spoke and Pity seemed
      to call,
And issuing Sighs that smoak'd along the
      Wall ;
Complaints and hot Desires, the Lover's Hell,
And scalding Tears, that wore a Channel
      where they fell ;
And all around were Nuptial Bonds, the
      Ties
Of Loves Assurance, and a Train of Lies,
That, made in Lust, conclude in Perjuries.
Beauty, and Youth, and Wealth, and
      Luxury,   480
And spritely Hope, and short-enduring Joy ;
And Sorceries, to raise th' Infernal Pow'rs,
And Sigils fram'd in Planetary Hours ;
Expense, and After-thought, and idle Care,
And Doubts of motley Hue, and dark De-
      spair ;

Suspicions, and Fantastical Surmise,
And Jealousie suffus'd, with Jaundice in her
      Eyes ;
Discolouring all she view'd, in Tawney
      dress'd ;
Down-look'd, and with a Cuckow on her Fist.
Oppos'd to her, on t' other side advance 490
The costly Feast, the Carol, and the Dance,
Minstrels, and Musick, Poetry, and Play,
And Balls by night, and Turnaments by Day.
All these were painted on the Wall, and
      more ;
With Acts, and Monuments of Times before ;
And others added by Prophetick Doom,
And Lovers yet unborn, and Loves to come :
For there th' *Idalian* mount, and *Citheron*,
The Court of *Venus*, was in Colours drawn :
Before the Palace-gate, in careless Dress, 500
And loose Array, sat Portress Idleness ;
There, by the Fount, *Narcissus* pin'd alone;
There *Samson* was ; with wiser *Solomon*,
And all the mighty Names by Love undone:
Medea's Charms were there ; *Circean* Feasts,
With Bowls that turn'd inamoured Youth
      to Beasts.
Here might be seen, that Beauty, Wealth,
      and Wit,
And Prowess, to the Pow'r of Love submit ;
The spreading Snare for all Mankind is laid ;
And Lovers all betray, and are betray'd. 510
The Goddess self, some noble Hand had
      wrought ;
Smiling she seem'd, and full of pleasing
      Thought :
From Ocean as she first began to rise,
And smooth'd the ruffl'd Seas, and clear'd
      the Skies ;
She trode the Brine, all bare below the
      Breast,
And the green Waves but ill conceal'd the
      Rest ;
A Lute she held ; and on her Head was seen
A Wreath of Roses red and Myrtles green ;
Her Turtles fann'd the buxom Air above ;
And, by his Mother, stood an Infant-Love :
With Wings unfledg'd ; his Eyes were
      banded o'er ;   521
His Hands a Bow, his Back a Quiver bore,
Supply'd with Arrows bright and keen,
      a deadly Store.

------

506 Youth] *The edd. give* youths

But in the Dome of mighty *Mars* the Red
With diff'rent Figures all the Sides were
    spread :
This Temple, less in Form, with equal Grace
Was imitative of the first in *Thrace* :
For that cold Region was the lov'd Abode,
And Sovereign Mansion of the Warriour-God.
The Landscape was a Forest wide and bare ;
Where neither Beast nor Humane Kind
    repair ;   531
The Fowl, that scent afar, the Borders fly,
And shun the bitter Blast, and wheel about
    the Sky.
A Cake of Scurf lies baking on the Ground,
And prickly Stubs, instead of Trees, are found;
Or Woods with Knots, and Knares deform'd
    and old,
Headless the most, and hideous to behold :
A ratling Tempest through the Branches
    went,
That stripp'd 'em bare, and one sole way
    they bent.
Heav'n froze above, severe, the Clouds con-
    geal,   540
And through the Crystal Vault appear'd the
    standing Hail.
Such was the Face without, a Mountain stood
Threatning from high, and overlook'd the
    Wood :
Beneath the lowring Brow, and on a Bent,
The Temple stood of *Mars* Armipotent ;
The Frame of burnish'd Steel, that cast a
    glare
From far, and seem'd to thaw the freezing
    Air.
A streight, long Entry to the Temple led,
Blind with high Walls ; and Horrour over
    Head :
Thence issu'd such a Blast, and hollow Rore,
As threaten'd from the Hinge, to heave the
    Door ;   551
In, through that Door, a Northern Light
    there shone ;
'Twas all it had, for Windows there were
    none.
The Gate was Adamant ; Eternal Frame !
Which, hew'd by *Mars* himself, from *Indian*
    Quarries came,
The Labour of a God ; and all along
Tough Iron Plates were clench'd to make
    it strong.
A Tun about was ev'ry Pillar there ;
A polish'd Mirrour shone not half so clear.

There saw I how the secret Fellon wrought,
And Treason lab'ring in the Traytor's
    Thought ;   561
And Midwife Time the ripen'd Plot to
    Murder brought.
There, the Red Anger dar'd the Pallid Fear ;
Next stood Hypocrisie, with holy Lear :
Soft, smiling, and demurely looking down,
But hid the Dagger underneath the Gown :
Th' assassinating Wife, the Houshold Fiend ;
And far the blackest there, the Traytor-
    Friend.
On t' other side there stood Destruction
    bare ;
Unpunish'd Rapine, and a Waste of War, 570
Contest, with sharpen'd Knives in Cloysters
    drawn,
And all with Blood bespread the holy Lawn.
Loud Menaces were heard, and foul Disgrace,
And bawling Infamy, in Language base ;
Till Sense was lost in Sound, and Silence
    fled the Place.
The Slayer of Himself yet saw I there,
The Gore congeal'd was clotter'd in his Hair :
With Eyes half clos'd, and gaping Mouth
    he lay,
And grim, as when he breath'd his sullen
    Soul away.
In midst of all the Dome, Misfortune sat, 580
And gloomy Discontent, and fell Debate,
And Madness laughing in his ireful Mood ;
And arm'd Complaint on Theft ; and Cries
    of Blood.
There was the murder'd Corps, in Covert
    laid,
And Violent Death in thousand Shapes dis-
    play'd :
The City to the Soldier's Rage resign'd :
Successless Wars, and Poverty behind :
Ships burnt in Fight, or forc'd on Rocky
    Shores,
And the rash Hunter strangled by the Boars :
The new-born Babe by Nurses overlaid ;
And the Cook caught within the raging Fire
    he made.   591
All ills of *Mars* his Nature, Flame and
    Steel :
The gasping Charioteer, beneath the Wheel
Of his own Car ; the ruin'd House that falls
And intercepts her Lord betwixt the Walls :
The whole Division that to *Mars* pertains,
All Trades of Death that deal in Steel for
    Gains,

Were there: The Butcher, Armourer, and
　　Smith,
Who forges sharpen'd Fauchions, or the
　　Scythe.　　　　　　　　　　　　　599
The scarlet Conquest on a Tow'r was plac'd,
With Shouts, and Soldiers Acclamations
　　grac'd:
A pointed Sword hung threatning o'er his
　　Head,
Sustain'd but by a slender Twine of Thred.
There saw I *Mars* his *Ides*, the *Capitol*,
The Seer in vain foretelling *Cæsar's* Fall;
The last *Triumvirs*, and the Wars they move,
And *Antony*, who lost the World for Love.
These, and a thousand more, the Fane adorn;
Their Fates were painted e'er the Men were
　　born,　　　　　　　　　　　　　609
All copied from the Heav'ns, and ruling Force
Of the Red Star, in his revolving Course.
The Form of *Mars* high on a Chariot stood,
All sheath'd in Arms, and gruffly look'd the
　　God:
Two Geomantick Figures were
　　display'd
Above his Head, a *Warriour
　　and a Maid,
One when Direct, and one when
　　Retrograde.

　　*Rubeus, &
　　Puella.*

　Tir'd with Deformities of Death, I haste
To the third Temple of *Diana* chaste;
A Sylvan Scene with various Greens was
　　drawn,
Shades on the Sides, and on the midst
　　a Lawn:　　　　　　　　　　　　620
The Silver*Cynthia*, with her Nymphs around,
Pursu'd the flying Deer, the Woods with
　　Horns resound:
Calistho there stood manifest of Shame,
And, turn'd a Bear, the Northern Star be-
　　came:
Her Son was next, and, by peculiar Grace
In the cold Circle held the second Place:
The Stag *Acteon* in the Stream had spy'd
The naked Huntress, and, for seeing, dy'd;
His Hounds, unknowing of his Change,
　　pursue
The Chace, and their mistaken Master slew.

Peneian Daphne too was there to see,　631
Apollo's Love before, and now his Tree:
Th' adjoining Fane th' assembl'd *Greeks*
　　express'd,
And hunting of the *Caledonian* beast.
Oenides Valour, and his envy'd Prize;
The fatal Pow'r of *Atalanta's* Eyes;
Diana's Vengeance on the Victor shown,
The Murdress Mother, and consuming Son;
The *Volscian* Queen extended on the Plain;
The Treason punish'd, and the Traytor slain.
The rest were various Huntings, well
　　design'd,　　　　　　　　　　　641
And Salvage Beasts destroy'd, of ev'ry Kind:
The graceful Goddess was array'd in Green;
About her Feet were little Beagles seen,
That watch'd with upward Eyes the Motions
　　of their Queen.
Her Legs were Buskin'd, and the Left before,
In act to shoot, a Silver Bow she bore,
And at her Back a painted Quiver wore.
She trod a wexing Moon, that soon wou'd
　　wane,
And drinking borrowed Light, be fill'd
　　again;　　　　　　　　　　　　　650
With down-cast Eyes, as seeming to survey
The dark Dominions, her alternate Sway.
Before her stood a Woman in her Throws,
And call'd *Lucina's* Aid, her Burden to
　　disclose.
All these the Painter drew with such
　　Command,
That Nature snatch'd the Pencil from his
　　Hand,
Asham'd and angry that his Art could feign
And mend the Tortures of a Mothers Pain.
Theseus beheld the Fanes of ev'ry God,
And thought his mighty Cost was well
　　bestow'd:　　　　　　　　　　　660
So Princes now their Poets should regard;
But few can write, and fewer can reward.
　The Theater thus rais'd, the Lists enclos'd,
And all with vast Magnificence dispos'd,
We leave the Monarch pleased, and haste to
　　bring
The Knights to combate; and their Arms
　　to sing.

The End of the Second Book.

615 side note. *Rubeus*] *Christie reports* Rubens *as the reading of 1700.　My copy has* Rubeus
634 *Caledonian*] i. e. Calydonian

PALAMON AND ARCITE: OR, THE KNIGHT'S TALE.

BOOK III.

THE Day approach'd when Fortune shou'd
    decide
Th' important Enterprize, and give the
    Bride ;
For now, the Rivals round the World had
    sought,
And each his Number, well appointed,
    brought.
The Nations far and near contend in Choice,
And send the Flow'r of War by Publick
    Voice ;
That after, or before, were never known
Such Chiefs ; as each an Army seem'd alone :
Beside the Champions ; all of high Degree,
Who Knighthood lov'd, and Deeds of
    Chivalry,   10
Throng'd to the Lists, and envy'd to behold,
The Names of others, not their own, inroll'd.
Nor seems it strange ; for ev'ry Noble
    Knight
Who loves the Fair, and is endu'd with
    Might,
In such a Quarrel wou'd be proud to fight.
There breaths not scarce a Man on *British*
    Ground
(An Isle for Love and Arms of old renown'd)
But would have sold his Life to purchase
    Fame,
To *Palamon* or *Arcite* sent his Name ;
And had the Land selected of the best,   20
Half had come hence, and let the World
    provide the rest.
A hundred Knights with *Palamon* there
    came,
Approv'd in Fight, and Men of Mighty
    Name ;
Their Arms were sev'ral, as their Nations
    were,
But furnish'd all alike with Sword and Spear.
Some wore Coat-armour, imitating Scale ;
And next their Skins were stubborn Shirts
    of Mail.
Some wore a Breastplate and a light Juppon,
Their Horses cloth'd with rich Caparison ;
Some for Defence would Leathern Bucklers
    use,   30
Of folded Hides ; and others Shields of
    Pruce.

One hung a Poleax at his Saddle-bow,
And one a heavy Mace, to stun the Foe :
One for his Legs and Knees provided well,
With *Jambeux* arm'd, and double Plates
    of Steel :
This on his Helmet wore a Ladies Glove,
And that a Sleeve embroider'd by his Love.
   With *Palamon*, above the rest in Place,
Lycurgus came, the surly King of *Thrace* ;
Black was his Beard, and manly was his
    Face :   40
The Balls of his broad Eyes roll'd in his head,
And glar'd betwixt a Yellow and a Red ;
He look'd a Lion with a gloomy Stare,
And o'er his Eye-brows hung his matted
    Hair ;
Big-bon'd and large of Limbs, with Sinews
    strong,
Broad-shoulder'd, and his Arms were round
    and long.
Four Milk-white Bulls (the *Thracian* Use
    of old)
Were yok'd to draw his Car of burnish'd
    Gold.
Upright he stood, and bore aloft his Shield,
Conspicuous from afar, and over-look'd the
    Field   50
His Surcoat was a Bear-skin on his Back ;
His Hair hung long behind, and glossy
    Raven-black.
His ample Forehead bore a Coronet
With sparkling Diamonds, and with Rubies
    set :
Ten Brace, and more, of Greyhounds, snowy
    fair,
And tall as Stags, ran loose, and cours'd
    around his Chair,
A Match for Pards in Flight, in grappling
    for the Bear :
With Golden Muzzles all their Mouths were
    bound,
And Collars of the same their Necks
    surround.
Thus thro' the Fields *Lycurgus* took his
    way ;   60
His hundred Knights attend in Pomp and
    proud Array.
   To match this Monarch, with strong
    Arcite came
Emetrius, king of *Inde*, a mighty Name,

On a Bay Courser, goodly to behold,
The Trappings of his Horse emboss'd with
  barb'rous Gold.
Not *Mars* bestrode a Steed with greater
  Grace ;
His Surcoat o'er his Arms was Cloth of
  Thrace,
Adorn'd with Pearls, ali Orient, round, and
  great ;
His Saddle was of Gold, with Emeralds set.
His Shoulders large a Mantle did attire, 70
With Rubies thick, and sparkling as the
  Fire ;
His Amber-colour'd Locks in Ringlets run,
With graceful Negligence, and shone against
  the Sun.
His Nose was aquiline, his eyes were blue,
Ruddy his Lips, and fresh and fair his Hue :
Some sprinkled Freckles on his Face were
  seen,
Whose dusk set off the Whiteness of the
  Skin :
His awful Presence did the Crowd surprize,
Nor durst the rash Spectator meet his
  Eyes,
Eyes that confess'd him born for Kingly
  Sway, 80
So fierce, they flash'd intolerable Day.
His Age in Nature's youthful Prime appeared,
And just began to bloom his yellow Beard.
Whene'er he spoke, his Voice was heard
  around,
Loud as a Trumpet, with a Silver Sound.
A Laurel wreath'd his Temples, fresh, and
  green,
And Myrtle-sprigs, the Marks of Love, were
  mix'd between.
Upon his Fist he bore, for his Delight,
An Eagle well reclaim'd, and Lilly-white.
  His hundred Knights attend him to the
  War, 90
All arm'd for Battel ; save their Heads were
  bare.
Words, and Devices blaz'd on ev'ry Shield,
And pleasing was the Terrour of the Field.
For Kings, and Dukes, and Barons you⎫
  might see,   ⎪
Like sparkling Stars, though diff'rent in⎬
  Degree,   ⎪
All for th' Increase of Arms, and Love of⎭
  Chivalry.
Before the King, tame Leopards led the Way,
And Troops of Lions innocently play.

So *Bacchus* through the conquer'd *Indies*
  rode,
And Beasts in Gambols frisk'd before their
  honest God. 100
  In this Array the War of either side
Through *Athens* pass'd with Military Pride.
At Prime, they entered on the *Sunday* Morn ;
Rich Tap'stry spread the Streets, and
  Flowers the Posts adorn.
The Town was all a Jubilee of Feasts ;
So *Theseus* will'd, in Honour of his Guests ;
Himself with open Arms the Kings embrac'd,
Then all the rest in their Degrees were grac'd.
No Harbinger was needful for the Night,
For ev'ry House was proud to lodge a
  Knight. 110
  I pass the Royal Treat, nor must relate
The Gifts bestow'd, nor how the Champions
  sate ;
Who first, who last, or how the Knights
  address'd
Their Vows, or who was fairest at the Feast ;
Whose Voice, whose graceful Dance did most
  surprise,
Soft am'rous Sighs, and silent Love of Eyes.
The Rivals call my Muse another Way,
To sing their Vigils for th' ensuing Day.
'Twas ebbing Darkness, past the Noon of
  Night : 119
And *Phospher* on the Confines of the Light,
Promis'd the Sun; ere Day began to spring,⎫
The tuneful Lark already stretch'd her⎪
  Wing,   ⎬
And flick'ring on her Nest, made short⎪
  Essays to sing.   ⎭
  When wakeful *Palamon*, preventing Day,⎫
Took, to the Royal Lists, his early way, ⎬
To *Venus* at her Fane, in her own House,⎭
  to pray.
There, falling on his Knees before her Shrine,
He thus implor'd with Pray'rs her Pow'r
  divine.
Creator *Venus*, genial Pow'r of Love,
The Bliss of Men below, and Gods above,
Beneath the sliding Sun thou runn'st thy
  Race, 131
Dost fairest shine, and best become thy
  Place.

---

104 Posts] Pots *1700. Dr. Saintsbury pre-*
fers this misprint, but cf. Cymon and Iph. 561.
          'the Streets were throng'd around,
The Palace open'd, and the Posts were crown'd.'

For thee the Winds their Eastern Blasts
forbear,
Thy Month reveals the Spring, and opens all
the Year.
Thee, Goddess, thee the Storms of Winter
fly,
Earth smiles with Flow'rs renewing; laughs
the Sky,
And Birds to Lays of Love their tuneful
Notes apply.
For thee the Lion loaths the Taste of Blood,
And roaring hunts his Female through the
Wood ;
For thee the Bulls rebellow through the
Groves,   140
And tempt the Stream, and snuff their absent
Loves.
'Tis thine, whate'er is pleasant, good, or
fair ;
All Nature is thy Province, Life thy Care ;
Thou mad'st the World, and dost the World
repair.
Thou gladder of the mount of *Cytheron*,
Increase of *Jove*, Companion of the Sun,
If e'er *Adonis* touch'd thy tender Heart,
Have pity, Goddess, for thou know'st the
Smart :   148
Alas ! I have not Words to tell my Grief ;
To vent my Sorrow wou'd be some Relief :
Light Suff'rings give us Leisure to complain ;
We groan, but cannot speak, in greater Pain.
O Goddess, tell thy self what I would say,
Thou know'st it, and I feel too much to pray.
So grant my Suit, as I enforce my Might,
In Love to be thy Champion, and thy Knight,
A Servant to thy Sex, a Slave to thee,
A foe profess'd to barren Chastity.
Nor ask I Fame or Honour of the Field,
Nor chuse I more to vanquish, than to yield :
In my Divine *Emilia* make me blest,   161
Let Fate, or partial Chance, dispose the rest :
Find thou the Manner, and the Means pre-
pare ;
Possession, more than Conquest, is my Care.
Mars is the Warriour's God ; in him it lies
On whom he favours, to confer the Prize ;
With smiling Aspect you serenely move
In your fifth Orb, and rule the Realm of
Love.
The Fates but only spin the courser Clue,
The finest of the Wooll is left for you.   17

Spare me but one small portion of the Twine,
And let the Sisters cut below your Line :
The rest among the Rubbish may they
sweep,
Or add it to the Yarn of some old Miser's
Heap.
But if you this ambitious Pray'r deny,
(A Wish, I grant, beyond Mortality,)
Then let me sink beneath proud *Arcite*':
Arms,
And I once dead, let him possess her Charms.
Thus ended he ; then, with Observance
due,
The sacred Incence on her Altar threw : 180
The curling Smoke mounts heavy from the
Fires ;
At length it catches Flame, and in a Blaze
expires ;
At once the gracious Goddess gave the Sign,
Her Statue shook, and trembl'd all the
Shrine :
Pleas'd *Palamon* the tardy *Omen* took ;
For, since the Flames pursued the trailing
Smoke,
He knew his Boon was granted ; but the
Day
To distance driv'n, and Joy adjourn'd with
long Delay
  Now Morn with Rosie Light had streak'd
the Sky,
Up rose the Sun, and up rose *Emily*   190
Address'd her early Steps to *Cynthia's* Fane,
In State attended by her Maiden Train,
Who bore the Vests that Holy Rites require,
Incence, and od'rous Gums, and cover'd Fire.
The plenteous Horns with pleasant Mead
they crown,
Nor wanted aught besides in Honour of the
Moon.
Now while the Temple smoak'd with hallow'd
Steam,
They wash the Virgin in a living Stream ;
The secret Ceremonies I conceal :
Uncouth ; perhaps unlawful to reveal : 200
But such they were as Pagan Use requir'd,
Performed by Women when the Men retir'd,
Whose Eyes profane their chast mysterious
Rites
Might turn to Scandal, or obscene Delights.
Well-meaners think no Harm ; but for the
rest,
Things sacred they pervert, and Silence is
the best.

Her shining Hair, uncomb'd, was loosly
   spread,
A Crown of Mastless Oak adorn'd her Head
When to the Shrine approach'd, the spotless
   Maid
Had kindling Fires on either Altar laid : 210
(The Rites were such as were observ'd of old,
By *Statius* in his *Theban* Story told.)
Then kneeling with her Hands across her
   Breast,
Thus lowly she preferr'd her chast Request.
  O Goddess, Haunter of the Woodland
   Green,
To whom both Heav'n and Earth and Seas
   are seen ;
Queen of the nether Skies, where half the
   Year
Thy Silver Beams descend, and light the
   gloomy Sphere ;
Goddess of Maids, and conscious of our
   Hearts,
So keep me from the Vengeance of thy
   Darts,   220
Which *Niobe's* devoted Issue felt,
When hissing through the Skies the feather'd
   Deaths were dealt :
As I desire to live a Virgin-life,
Nor wear the Name of Mother or of Wife.
Thy Votress from my tender Years I am,
And love, like thee, the Woods and Sylvan
   Game.
Like Death, thou know'st, I loath the ⎫
   Nuptial State,   ⎪
And Man, the Tyrant of our Sex, I hate, ⎬
A lowly Servant, but a lofty Mate.   ⎭
Where Love is Duty on the Female Side, 230
On theirs mere sensual Gust, and sought
   with surly Pride.
Now by thy triple Shape, as thou art seen
In Heav'n, Earth, Hell, and ev'ry where a
   Queen,
Grant this my first Desire; let Discord cease,
And make betwixt the Rivals lasting Peace :
Quench their hot Fire, or far from me
   remove
The Flame, and turn it on some other Love.
Or if my frowning Stars have so decreed,
That one must be rejected, one succeed,
Make him my Lord, within whose faithful
   Breast   240
Is fix'd my Image, and who loves me best.
But oh ! ev'n that avert ! I chuse it not,
But take it as the least unhappy Lot.

A Maid I am, and of thy Virgin-Train ;
Oh, let me still that spotless Name retain !
Frequent the Forests, thy chast Will obey,
And only make the Beasts of Chace my Prey !
  The Flames ascend on either Altar clear,
While thus the blameless Maid address'd her
   Pray'r.
When lo ! the burning Fire that shone so
   bright   250
Flew off, all sudden, with extinguish'd Light,
And left one Altar dark, a little space ;
Which turn'd self-kindl'd, and renew'd the
   Blaze :
That other Victour-Flame a Moment stood
Then fell, and lifeless left th' extinguish'd
   Wood ;
For ever lost, th' irrevocable Light
Forsook the blackning Coals, and sunk to
   Night :
At either End it whistled as it flew,   ⎫
And as the Brands were green, so dropp'd ⎬
   the Dew ;   ⎪
Infected as it fell with Sweat of Sanguin Hue. ⎭
  The Maid from that ill *Omen* turned her
   Eyes,   261
And with loud Shrieks and Clamours rent
   the Skies,
Nor knew what signifi'd the boding Sign,
But found the Pow'rs displeas'd, and fear'd
   the Wrath Divine.
  Then shook the Sacred Shrine, and sudden
   Light
Sprung through the vaulted Roof, and made
   the Temple bright.
The Pow'r, behold ! the Power in Glory
   shone,
By her bent Bow and her keen Arrows
   known ;
The rest, a Huntress issuing from the Wood,
Reclining on her Cornel Spear she stood. 270
Then gracious thus began ; Dismiss thy
   Fear,
And Heav'ns unchang'd Decrees attentive
   hear :
More pow'rful Gods have torn thee from my
   Side,
Unwilling to resign, and doom'd a Bride :
The two contending Knights are weigh'd
   above ;
One *Mars* protects, and one the Queen of
   Love :

---

254 That] *Derrick wrongly gives* The

But which the Man is in the Thund'rer's
   Breast,
This he pronounc'd, 'tis he who loves thee
   best.
The Fire that once extinct, reviv'd again
Foreshews the Love allotted to remain. 280
Farewell ! she said, and vanish'd from the
   Place ;
The Sheaf of Arrows shook, and rattl'd in
   the Case.
Agast at this, the Royal Virgin stood,
Disclaim'd, and now no more a Sister of the
   Wood :
But to the parting Goddess thus she pray'd:
Propitious still, be present to my Aid,
Nor quite abandon your once favour'd
   Maid.
Then sighing she return'd ; but smil'd be-
   twixt,
With Hopes, and Fears, and Joys with
   Sorrows mixt.
   The next returning Planetary Hour   290
Of *Mars*, who shar'd the Heptarchy of Pow'r,
His Steps bold *Arcite* to the Temple bent,
T' adore with Pagan Rites the Pow'r Armi-
   potent :
Then prostrate, low before his Altar lay,
And rais'd his manly Voice, and thus began
   to pray.
Strong God of Arms, whose Iron Scepter
   sways
The freezing North, and *Hyperborean* seas,
And *Scythian* Colds, and *Thracia's* Wintry
   Coast,
Where stand thy Steeds, and thou art
   honour'd most :
There most, but ev'ry where thy Pow'r is
   known,   300
The Fortune of the Fight is all thy own :
Terrour is thine, and wild Amazement flung
From out thy Chariot, withers ev'n the
   Strong,
And Disarray and shameful Rout ensue,
And Force is added to the fainting Crew.
Acknowledg'd as thou art, accept my Prayer,
If ought I have atchiev'd deserve thy Care :
If to my utmost Pow'r with Sword and
   Shield
I dar'd the Death, unknowing how to yield,
And falling in my Rank, still kept the
   Field :   310

Then let my Arms prevail, by thee sustain'd,
That *Emily* by Conquest may be gain'd.
Have pity on my Pains ; nor those un-
   known
To *Mars*, which, when a Lover, were his own.
Venus, the Publick Care of all above,
Thy stubborn Heart has softned into Love :
Now by her Blandishments and pow'rful
   Charms,
When yielded, she lay curling in thy Arms,
Ev'n by thy Shame, if Shame it may be
   call'd,
When *Vulcan* had thee in his net inthrall'd ;
O envy'd Ignominy, sweet Disgrace,   321
When ev'ry god that saw thee, wish'd thy
   Place !
By those dear Pleasures, aid my Arms in
   Fight,
And make me conquer in my Patron's
   Right :
For I am young, a Novice in the Trade,
The Fool of Love, unpractis'd to persuade ;
And want the soothing Arts that catch the
   Fair,
But, caught my self, lie strugling in the
   Snare ;
And she I love, or laughs at all my Pain
Or knows her Worth too well ; and pays me
   with Disdain.   330
For sure I am, unless I win in Arms,
To stand excluded from *Emilia's* Charms :
Nor can my Strength avail, unless by thee
Endu'd with force I gain the Victory :
Then for the Fire which warm'd thy gen'rous
   Heart,
Pity thy Subject's Pains and equal Smart
So be the Morrows Sweat and Labour mine,
The Palm and Honour of the Conquest
   thine :
Then shall the War, and stern Debate, and
   Strife
Immortal, be the Bus'ness of my Life ;   340
And in thy Fane, the dusty Spoils among,
High on the burnish'd Roof, my Banner
   shall be hung ;
Rank'd with my Champions Bucklers, and
   below,
With Arms revers'd, th' Atchievements of
   my Foe :
And while these Limbs the vital Spirit
   feeds,
While Day to Night, and Night to Day
   succeeds,

---

293 adore] *Christie wrongly gives* adorn

Thy smoaking Altar shall be fat with Food
Of Incence and the grateful Steam of Blood ;
Burnt Off'rings Morn and Ev'ning shall be
thine,
And Fires eternal in thy Temple shine.   350
This Bush of yellow Beard, this Length of
Hair,
Which from my Birth inviolate I bear,
Guiltless of Steel, and from the Razour free,
Shall fall a plenteous Crop, reserv'd for thee.
So may my Arms with Victory be blest,
I ask no more ; let Fate dispose the rest.
    The Champion ceas'd ; there follow'd in
the Close
A hollow Groan ; a murm'ring Wind arose,
The Rings of Ir'n, that on the Doors were
hung,
Sent out a jarring Sound, and harshly rung
The bolted Gates flew open at the Blast,   361
The Storm rush'd in ; and Arcite stood
agast :
The Flames were blown aside, yet shone
they bright,
Fann'd by the Wind, and gave a ruffl'd
Light.
    Then from the Ground a Scent began to
rise,
Sweet-smelling as accepted Sacrifice :
This Omen pleas'd, and as the Flames aspire,
With od'rous Incence Arcite heaps the Fire
Nor wanted Hymns to Mars or Heathen
Charms :
At length the nodding Statue clash'd his
Arms,   370
And with a sullen Sound, and feeble Cry,
Half sunk, and half pronounc'd the Word of
Victory.
For this, with Soul devout, he thank'd the
God,
And, of Success secure, return'd to his
Abode.
    These Vows thus granted, rais'd a Strife
above,
Betwixt the God of War, and Queen of Love.
She granting first, had Right of Time to
plead ;   377
But he had granted too, nor would recede.
Jove was for Venus ; but he fear'd his Wife,
And seem'd unwilling to decide the Strife ;
Till Saturn from his Leaden Throne arose,
And found a Way the Diff'rence to compose:

Though sparing of his Grace, to Mischief
bent,
He seldom does a Good with good Intent.
Wayward, but wise ; by long Experience
taught,
To please both Parties, for ill Ends, he
sought :
For this Advantage Age from Youth has
won,
As not to be outridden, though outrun.
By Fortune he was now to Venus Trin'd,
And with stern Mars in Capricorn was
join'd :   390
Of him disposing in his own Abode,
He sooth'd the Goddess, while he gull'd the
God :
Cease, Daughter, to complain ; and stint the
Strife ;
Thy Palamon shall have his promis'd Wife :
And Mars, the Lord of Conquest, in the
Fight
With Palm and Laurel shall adorn his Knight.
Wide is my Course, nor turn I to my Place
Till Length of Time, and move with tardy
Pace.
Man feels me, when I press th' Etherial
Plains ;   399
My Hand is heavy, and the Wound remains.
Mine is the Shipwreck in a Watry Sign ;
And in an Earthy, the dark Dungeon mine.
Cold shivering Agues, melancholy Care,   ⎫
And bitter blasting Winds, and poison'd Air, ⎪
Are mine, and wilful Death, resulting from ⎬
Despair.   ⎭
The throtling Quinsey 'tis my Star appoints,
And Rheumatisms I send to rack the Joints:
When Churls rebel against their Native
Prince,
I arm their Hands, and furnish the Pretence ;
And housing in the Lion's hateful Sign,   410
Bought Senates, and deserting Troops are
mine.
Mine is the privy Pois'ning ; I command
Unkindly Seasons, and ungrateful Land.
By me Kings Palaces are push'd to Ground,
And Miners, crush'd beneath their Mines
are found.
'Twas I slew Samson, when the Pillar'd Hall
Fell down, and crush'd the Many with the
Fall.

My Looking is the Sire of Pestilence,
That sweeps at once the People and the
    Prince.
Now weep no more, but trust thy Grandsire's
    Art ;   420
Mars shall be pleas'd, and thou perform
    thy Part.
'Tis ill, though diff'rent your Complexions
    are,
The Family of Heav'n for Men should war.
Th' Expedient pleas'd, where neither lost
    his Right :
Mars had the Day, and Venus had the
    Night.
The Management they left to Chronos Care.
Now turn we to th' Effect, and sing the War.
  In Athens all was Pleasure, Mirth, and
    Play,
All proper to the Spring, and spritely May :
Which every Soul inspir'd with such Delight,
'Twas Justing all the Day, and Love at
    Night.   431
Heav'n smil'd, and gladded was the Heart
    of Man ;
And Venus had the World, as when it first
    began.
At length in Sleep their Bodies they com-
    pose,
And dreamt the future Fight, and early rose.
  Now scarce the dawning Day began to
    spring,
As at a Signal giv'n, the Streets with
    Clamours ring :
At once the Crowd arose; confus'd and high, ⎫
Even from the Heav'n was heard a shouting ⎪
    Cry ;   439 ⎬
For Mars was early up, and rowz'd the Sky. ⎭
The Gods came downward to behold the
    Wars,
Sharpning their Sights, and leaning from
    their Stars.
The Neighing of the gen'rous Horse was
    heard,
For Battel by the busie Groom prepar'd :
Rustling of Harness, ratling of the Shield,
Clatt'ring of Armour, furbish'd for the
    Field.
Crowds to the Castle mounted up the
    Street ;
Batt'ring the Pavement with their Coursers
    Feet :

The greedy Sight might there devour the
    Gold
Of glittring Arms, too dazling to behold : 450
And polish'd Steel that cast the View aside,
And Crested Morions, with their Plumy
    Pride.
Knights, with a long Retinue of their Squires,
In gawdy Liv'ries march, and quaint Attires.
One lac'd the Helm, another held the Lance :
A third the shining Buckler did advance.
The Courser paw'd the Ground with restless
    Feet,
And snorting foam'd, and champ'd the
    Golden Bit.
The Smiths and Armourers on Palfreys ride, ⎫
Files in their Hands, and Hammers at their ⎪
    Side,   460 ⎬
And nails for loosen'd Spears, and Thongs ⎪
    for Shields provide.   ⎭
The Yeomen guard the Streets, in seemly
    Bands ;
And Clowns come crowding on, with Cudgels
    in their Hands.
  The Trumpets, next the Gate, in order
    plac'd,
Attend the Sign to sound the Martial Blast :
The Palace-yard is fill'd with floating Tides,
And the last Comers bear the former to
    the Sides.
The Throng is in the midst : The common
    Crew
Shut out, the Hall admits the better Few.
In Knots they stand, or in a Rank they
    walk,   470
Serious in Aspect, earnest in their Talk :
Factious, and fav'ring this or t'other Side,
As their strong Fancies, and weak Reason
    guide :
Their Wagers back their Wishes : Numbers
    hold
With the fair freckl'd King, and Beard of
    Gold :
So vig'rous are his Eyes, such Rays they
    cast,
So prominent his Eagles Beak is plac'd.
But most their Looks on the black Monarch
    bend,
His rising Muscles, and his Brawn commend ;
His double-biting Ax, and beamy Spear, 480
Each asking a Gygantick Force to rear.
All spoke as partial Favour mov'd the
    mind ;
And safe themselves, at others Cost divin'd.

Wak'd by the Cries, th' *Athenian* Chief
arose,
The Knightly Forms of Combate to dispose ;
And passing through th' obsequious Guards,
he sate
Conspicuous on a Throne, sublime in State ;
There, for the two contending Knights he
sent :
Arm'd *Cap-a-pe*, with Rev'rence low they
bent ;
He smil'd on both, and with superiour Look
Alike their offer'd Adoration took.   491
The People press on ev'ry Side to see
Their awful Prince, and hear his high
Decree.
Then signing to their Heralds with his
Hand,
They gave his Orders from their lofty Stand.
Silence is thrice enjoin'd ; then thus aloud
The King at Arms bespeaks the Knights and
listning Crowd.
Our Sovereign Lord has ponder'd in his
Mind
The Means to spare the Blood of gentle
Kind ;
And of his Grace and in-born Clemency 500
He modifies his first severe Decree ;
The keener Edge of Battel to rebate,
The Troops for Honour fighting, not for
Hate.
He wills, not Death shou'd terminate their
Strife,
And Wounds, if Wounds ensue, be short of
Life ;
But issues, e'er the Fight, his dread Com-
mand,
That Slings afar, and Ponyards Hand to
Hand,
Be banish'd from the Field ; that none shall
dare
With shortned Sword to stab in closer War ;
But in fair Combate fight with manly
Strength   510
Nor push with biting Point, but strike at
length.
The Turney is allow'd but one Career,
Of the tough Ash, with the sharp-grinded
Spear.
But Knights unhors'd may rise from off the
Plain,
And fight on Foot, their Honour to regain.
Nor, if at Mischief taken, on the Ground
Be slain, but Pris'ners to the Pillar bound,

At either Barrier placed ; nor (Captives
made,)
Be freed, or arm'd anew the Fight invade :
The Chief of either side, bereft of Life, 520
Or yielded to his Foe, concludes the Strife.
Thus dooms the Lord : Now valiant Knights
and young,
Fight each his fill with Swords and Maces
long.
The Herald ends : The vaulted Firma-
ment
With loud Acclaims, and vast Applause is
rent :
Heav'n guard a Prince so gracious and so
good,
So just, and yet so provident of Blood !
This was the gen'ral Cry. The Trumpets
sound,
And Warlike Symphony is heard around.
The marching Troops through *Athens* take
their Way,   530
The great Earl-Marshal orders their Array.
The Fair from high the passing Pomp behold;
A Rain of Flow'rs is from the Windows roll'd.
The Casements are with Golden Tissue
spread,
And Horses Hoofs, for Earth, on silken
Tap'stry tread.
The King goes midmost, and the Rivals ride
In equal Rank, and close his either Side.
Next after these, there rode the Royal Wife,
With *Emily*, the Cause, and the Reward of
Strife.
The following Cavalcade, by Three and
Three,   540
Proceed by Titles marshall'd in Degree.
Thus through the Southern Gate they take
their Way,
And at the Lists arriv'd e'er Prime of Day.
There, parting from the King, the Chiefs
divide,
And wheeling East and West, before their
Many ride.
Th' *Athenian* Monarch mounts his Throne
on high,
And after him the Queen, and *Emily* :
Next these, the Kindred of the Crown are
grac'd
With nearer Seats, and Lords by Ladies
plac'd.
Scarce were they seated, when with Clamours
loud   550
In rush'd at once a rude promiscuous Crowd,

The Guards, and then each other overbare,
And in a Moment throng the spacious
    Theatre.
Now chang'd the jarring Noise to Whispers
    low,
As Winds forsaking Seas more softly blow ;
When at the Western Gate, on which the
    Car
Is plac'd aloft, that bears the God of War,
Proud *Arcite* entring arm'd before his Train
Stops at the Barrier, and divides the Plain.
Red was his Banner, and display'd abroad
The bloody Colours of his Patron God. 561
    At that self-moment enters *Palamon*
The Gate of *Venus*, and the Rising Sun ;
Wav'd by the wanton Winds, his Banner
    flies,
All maiden White, and shares the peoples
    Eyes.
From East to West, look all the World
    around,
Two Troops so match'd were never to be
    found :
Such Bodies built for Strength, of equal Age,
In Stature siz'd ; so proud an Equipage :
The nicest Eye cou'd no Distinction make,
Where lay th' Advantage, or what Side to
    take.   571
    Thus rang'd, the Herald for the last pro-
    claims
A Silence, while they answer'd to their
    Names :
For so the King decreed, to shun with Care
The Fraud of Musters false, the common
    Bane of War.
The Tale was just, and then the Gates were
    clos'd ;
And Chief to Chief, and Troop to Troop
    oppos'd.
The Heralds last retir'd, and loudly cry'd,
The Fortune of the Field be fairly try'd.
    At this the Challenger, with fierce Defie
His Trumpet sounds ; the Challeng'd makes
    Reply :   581
With Clangour rings the Field, resounds
    the vaulted Sky.
Their Vizors closed, their Lances in the
    Rest,
Or at the Helmet pointed, or the Crest ;
They vanish from the Barrier, speed the
    Race,
And spurring see decrease the middle
    Space.

A Cloud of Smoke envellops either Host,
And all at once the Combatants are lost :
Darkling they join adverse, and shock un-
    seen,
Coursers with Coursers justling, Men with
    Men :   590
As lab'ring in Eclipse, a while they stay,
Till the next Blast of Wind restores the Day.
They look anew : The beauteous Form of
    Fight
Is chang'd, and War appears a grizly Sight.
Two Troops in fair Array one moment
    show'd,
The next, a Field with fallen Bodies strow'd :
Not half the Number in their Seats are
    found,
But Men and Steeds lie grov'ling on the
    Ground.
The points of Spears are stuck within the
    Shield,
The Steeds without their Riders scour the
    Field.   600
The Knights unhors'd, on Foot renew the
    Fight ;
The glitt'ring Fauchions cast a gleaming
    Light ;
Hauberks and Helms are hew'd with many
    a Wound ;
Out spins the streaming Blood, and dies the
    Ground.
The mighty Maces with such Haste descend,
They break the Bones, and make the solid
    Armour bend.
This thrusts amid the Throng with furious
    Force ;
Down goes, at once, the Horseman and the
    Horse :
That Courser stumbles on the fallen Steed,
And floundring, throws the Rider o'er his
    Head.   610
One rolls along, a Foot-ball to his Foes ;
One with a broken Truncheon deals his
    Blows.
This halting, this disabl'd with his Wound,
In Triumph led, is to the Pillar bound,
Where by the King's Award he must abide :
There goes a Captive led on t'other Side.
By Fits they cease ; and leaning on the
    Lance,
Take Breath a while, and to new Fight
    advance.
    Full oft the Rivals met, and neither spar'd
His utmost Force, and each forgot to ward.

The Head of this was to the Saddle bent, 621
That other backward to the Crupper sent :
Both were by Turns unhors'd ; the jealous Blows
Fall thick and heavy, when on Foot they close.
So deep their Fauchions bite, that ev'ry Stroke
Pierc'd to the Quick ; and equal Wounds they gave and took.
Born far asunder by the Tides of men,
Like Adamant and Steel they met agen.
   So when a Tyger sucks the Bullock's Blood,
A famish'd Lion issuing from the Wood 630
Roars Lordly fierce, and challenges the Food.
Each claims Possession, neither will obey,
But both their Paws are fasten'd on the Prey ;
They bite, they tear ; and while in vain they strive,
The Swains come arm'd between, and both to Distance drive.
   At length, as Fate foredoom'd, and all things tend
By Course of Time to their appointed End ;
So when the Sun to West was far declin'd,
And both afresh in mortal Battel join'd,
The strong *Emetrius* came in *Arcite's* Aid,
And *Palamon* with Odds was overlaid : 641
For turning short, he struck with all his Might
Full on the Helmet of th' unwary Knight.
Deep was the Wound ; he stagger'd with the Blow,
And turn'd him to his unexpected Foe ;
Whom with such Force he struck, he fell'd him down,
And cleft the Circle of his Golden Crown.
But *Arcite's* Men, who now prevail'd in Fight,
Twice Ten at once surround the single Knight :
O'erpower'd at length, they force him to the Ground, 650
Unyielded as he was, and to the Pillar bound ;
And king *Lycurgus*, while he fought in Vain
His Friend to free, was tumbl'd on the Plain.

622 That] *Derrick, Christie, and others wrongly give* The

Who now laments but *Palamon*, compell'd
No more to try the Fortune of the Field !
And worse than Death, to view with hateful Eyes
His Rival's Conquest, and renounce the Prize !
   The Royal Judge on his Tribunal plac'd,
Who had beheld the Fight from first to last,
Bad cease the War ; pronouncing from on high 660
Arcite of *Thebes* had won the beauteous *Emily*.
The Sound of Trumpets to the Voice reply'd,
And round the Royal Lists the Heralds cry'd,
Arcite of *Thebes* has won the beauteous Bride.
   The People rend the Skies with vast Applause ;
All own the Chief, when Fortune owns the Cause.
Arcite is own'd ev'n by the Gods above,
And conqu'ring *Mars* insults the Queen of Love.
So laugh'd he when the rightful *Titan* fail'd,
And *Jove's* usurping Arms in Heav'n prevail'd. 670
Laugh'd all the Pow'rs who favour Tyranny ;
And all the Standing Army of the Sky.
But *Venus* with dejected Eyes appears,
And weeping, on the Lists, distill'd her Tears ;
Her Will refus'd, which grieves a Woman most,
And, in her Champion foil'd, the Cause of Love is lost.
Till *Saturn* said, Fair Daughter, now be still,
The blustring Fool has satisfi'd his Will ;
His Boon is given ; his Knight has gain'd the Day,
But lost the Prize, th' Arrears are yet to pay. 680
Thy Hour is come, and mine the Care shall be
To please thy Knight, and set thy Promise free.
   Now while the Heralds run the Lists around,
And *Arcite, Arcite,* Heav'n and Earth resound,
A Miracle (nor less it could be call'd)
Their Joy with unexpected Sorrow pall'd.

The Victor Knight had laid his Helm aside,
Part for his Ease, the greater part for Pride :
Bare-headed, popularly low he bow'd,
And paid the Salutations of the Crowd ;   690
Then spurring, at full speed, ran endlong on
Where *Theseus* sat on his Imperial Throne ;
Furious he drove, and upward cast his
  Eye,
Where next the Queen was plac'd his
  Emily ;
Then passing, to the Saddle-bow he bent,
A sweet Regard the gracious Virgin lent :
(For Women to the Brave an easie Prey,
Still follow Fortune, where she leads the
  Way :)
Just then, from Earth sprung out a flashing
  Fire,
By *Pluto* sent, at *Saturn's* bad Desire :   700
The startling Steed was seiz'd with sudden
  Fright,
And, bounding, o'er the Pummel cast the
  Knight :
Forward he flew, and pitching on his Head,
He quiver'd with his Feet, and lay for Dead.
Black was his Count'nance in a little Space,
For all the Blood was gather'd in his Face.
Help was at Hand ; they rear'd him from
  the Ground,
And from his cumbrous Arms his Limbs
  unbound ;
Then lanc'd a Vein, and watch'd returning
  Breath ;
It came, but clogg'd with Symptoms of his
  Death.   710
The Saddle-bow the Noble Parts had prest,
All bruis'd and mortifi'd his Manly Breast.
Him still entrancd, and in a Litter laid,
They bore from Field, and to his Bed con-
  vey'd.
At length he wak'd ; and, with a feeble Cry,
The Word he first pronounc'd was *Emily*.
  Mean time the King, though inwardly he
  mourn'd,
In Pomp triumphant to the Town return'd,
Attended by the Chiefs who fought the Field,
(Now friendly mix'd, and in one Troop
  compell'd ;)   720
Compos'd his Looks to counterfeited Cheer,
And bade them not for *Arcite's* Life to fear.
But that which gladded all the Warriour
  Train,
Though most were sorely wounded, none
  were slain.

The Surgeons soon despoil'd 'em of their Arms,
And some with Salves they cure, and some
  with Charms ;
Foment the Bruises, and the Pains asswage
And heal their inward Hurts with Sov'reign
  Draughts of Sage.
The King in Person visits all around,   729
Comforts the Sick, congratulates the Sound ;
Honours the Princely Chiefs, rewards the rest,
And holds for thrice three Days a Royal
  Feast.
None was disgrac'd ; for Falling is no Shame;
And Cowardice alone is Loss of Fame.
The vent'rous Knight is from the Saddle
  thrown,
But 'tis the Fault of Fortune, not his own.
If Crowds and Palms the conqu'ring Side
  adorn,
The Victor under better Stars was born :
The brave Man seeks not popular Applause,
Nor overpower'd with Arms, deserts his
  Cause ;   740
Unsham'd, though foil'd, he does the best
  he can ;
Force is of Brutes, but Honour is of Man.
  Thus *Theseus* smil'd on all with equal
  Grace,
And each was set according to his Place.
With Ease were reconcil'd the diff'ring Parts,
For Envy never dwells in Noble Hearts.
At length they took their Leave, the Time
  expir'd ;
Well pleas'd ; and to their sev'ral Homes
  retir'd.
  Mean while, the Health of *Arcite* still
  impairs ;
From Bad proceeds to Worse, and mocks the
  Leeches Cares :   750
Swoln is his Breast, his inward Pains in-
  crease ;
All Means are us'd, and all without Success.
The clotted Blood lies heavy on his Heart,
Corrupts, and there remains in spite of Art :
Nor breathing Veins nor Cupping will
  prevail ;
All outward Remedies and inward fail :
The Mold of Natures Fabrick is destroy'd,
Her Vessels discompos'd, her Vertue void :
The Bellows of his Lungs begins to swell :⎫
All out of frame is ev'ry secret Cell,   760⎬
Nor can the Good receive, nor Bad expel. ⎭

---

753 clotted] *Edd. give* clottered

Those breathing Organs thus within opprest,
With Venom soon distend the Sinews of his
    Breast.
Nought profits him to save abandon'd Life,
Nor Vomits upward Aid, nor downward
    Laxatife.
The midmost Region batter'd, and destroy'd,
When Nature cannot work, th' Effect of
    Art is void.
For Physick can but mend our crazie State,
Patch an old Building, not a new create.
Arcite is Doom'd to die in all his Pride, 770
Must leave his Youth, and yield his beau-
    teous Bride,
Gain'd hardly, against Right, and un-
    enjoy'd.
When 'twas declar'd, all Hope of Life was
    past,
Conscience, that of all Physick works the
    last,
Causd him to send for *Emily* in haste.
With her, at his Desire, came *Palamon* ;
Then, on his Pillow rais'd, he thus begun.
No Language can express the smallest part
Of what I feel, and suffer in my Heart, 779
For you, whom best I love and value most ;
But to your Service I bequeath my Ghost ;
Which, from this mortal Body when unty'd,
Unseen, unheard, shall hover at your Side ;
Nor fright you waking, nor your Sleep offend,
But wait officious, and your Steps attend.
How I have lov'd, excuse my faltring Tongue,
My Spirit's feeble, and my Pains are strong:
This I may say, I only grieve to die,
Because I lose my charming *Emily*.
To die, when Heav'n had put you in my
    Pow'r ;   790
Fate could not chuse a more malicious Hour !
What greater Curse cou'd envious Fortune
    give,
Than just to die when I began to live !
Vain Men, how vanishing a Bliss we crave,
Now warm in Love, now with'ring in the
    Grave !
Never, O never more to see the Sun !
Still dark, in a damp Vault, and still alone !
This Fate is common ; but I lose my Breath
Near Bliss, and yet not bless'd before my
    Death.
Farewell ; but take me dying in your Arms,
'Tis all I can enjoy of all your Charms : 801
This Hand I cannot but in Death resign ;
Ah, could I live ! But while I live 'tis mine.

I feel my End approach, and thus em-
    brac'd
Am pleas'd to die ; but hear me speak my
    last.
Ah ! my sweet Foe, for you, and you alone,
I broke my Faith with injur'd *Palamon*.
But Love the Sense of Right and Wrong
    confounds ;
Strong Love and proud Ambition have no
    Bounds.
And much I doubt, shou'd Heav'n my Life
    prolong,   810
I shou'd return to justifie my Wrong ;
For while my former Flames remain within,
Repentance is but want of Pow'r to Sin.
With mortal Hatred I pursu'd his Life,
Nor he nor you were guilty of the Strife ;
Nor I, but as I lov'd ; Yet all combin'd,
Your Beauty, and my Impotence of Mind,
And his concurrent Flame, that blew my
    Fire ;
For still our Kindred Souls had one Desire.
He had a Moments Right in point of Time ;
Had I seen first, then his had been the
    Crime.   821
Fate made it mine, and justified his Right ;
Nor holds this Earth a more deserving
    Knight
For Vertue, Valour, and for Noble Blood,
Truth, Honour, all that is compriz'd in Good;
So help me Heav'n, in all the World is none
So worthy to be lov'd as *Palamon*.
He loves you too ; with such a holy Fire,
As will not, cannot but with Life expire :
Our vow'd Affections both have often
    try'd,   830
Nor any Love but yours could ours divide,
Then by my Loves inviolable Band,
By my long Suff'ring, and my short Com-
    mand,
If e'er you plight your Vows when I am gone,
Have pity on the faithful *Palamon*.
    This was his last ; for Death came on
    amain,
And exercis'd below his Iron Reign ;
Then upward, to the Seat of Life he goes ;
Sense fled before him, what he touch'd he
    froze :
Yet cou'd he not his closing Eyes withdraw,
Though less and less of *Emily* he saw : 841
So, speechless, for a little space he lay ;
Then grasp'd the Hand he held, and sigh'd
    his Soul away.

But whither went his Soul, let such relate
Who search the Secrets of the future State :
Divines can say but what themselves believe;
Strong Proofs they have, but not demonstra-
    tive :
For, were all plain, then all Sides must agree,
And Faith it self be lost in Certainty.
To live uprightly then is sure the best ; 850
To save our selves, and not to damn the rest.
The soul of *Arcite* went, where Heathens go,
Who better live than we, though less they
    know.

  In *Palamon* a manly Grief appears ;
Silent, he wept, asham'd to show his Tears.
Emilia shriek'd but once ; and then,
    oppress'd
With Sorrow, sunk upon her Lovers Breast :
Till *Theseus* in his Arms convey'd with Care
Far from so sad a Sight, the swooning Fair.
'Twere Loss of Time her Sorrow to relate; ⎫
Ill bears the Sex a youthful Lover's ⎪
    Fate,   861 ⎬
When just approaching to the Nuptial State: ⎭
But like a low-hung Cloud, it rains so fast,
That all at once it falls, and cannot last.
The Face of Things is chang'd, and *Athens* now,
That laugh'd so late, becomes the Scene of
    Woe :
Matrons and Maids, both Sexes, ev'ry State,
With Tears lament the Knight's untimely
    Fate.
Not greater Grief in falling *Troy* was seen
For *Hector's* Death ; but *Hector* was not
    then.   870
Old Men with Dust deform'd their hoary
    Hair,
The Women beat their Breasts, their Cheeks
    they tear.
Why would'st thou go, with one consent
    they cry,
When thou hadst Gold enough, and *Emily* !
Theseus himself, who shou'd have cheer'd
    the Grief
Of others, wanted now the same Relief.
Old *Egeus* only could revive his Son,
Who various Changes of the World had
    known,
And strange Vicissitudes of Humane Fate,
Still alt'ring, never in a steady State : 880

Good after Ill and after Pain, Delight,
Alternate, like the Scenes of Day and Night.
Since ev'ry Man who lives is born to die,
And none can boast sincere Felicity,
With equal Mind, what happens, let us bear,
Nor joy, nor grieve too much for Things
    beyond our Care.
Like Pilgrims to th' appointed Place we
    tend ;
The World's an Inn, and Death the Journeys
    End.
Ev'n Kings but play ; and when their Part
    is done,
Some other, worse or better, mount the
    Throne.   890
With words like these the Crowd was satis-
    fi'd ;
And so they would have been, had *Theseus*
    dy'd.
But he, their King, was lab'ring in his Mind, ⎫
A fitting Place for Fun'ral Pomps to find, ⎬
Which were in Honour of the Dead design'd. ⎭
And, after long Debate, at last he found
(As Love it self had mark'd the Spot of
    Ground)
That Grove for ever green, that conscious
    Lawnd,
Where he with *Palamon* fought Hand to
    Hand :
That where he fed his amorous Desires 900
With soft Complaints, and felt his hottest
    Fires,
There other Flames might waste his Earthly
    Part,
And burn his Limbs, where Love had burn'd
    his Heart.
  This once resolv'd, the Peasants were
    enjoin'd
Sere Wood, and Firs, and dodder'd Oaks to
    find.
With sounding Axes to the Grove they go,
Fell, split, and lay the Fewel on a Row,
Vulcanian Food : A Bier is next prepar'd,
On which the lifeless Body should be rear'd,
Cover'd with Cloth of Gold, on which was
    laid   910
The Corps of *Arcite*, in like Robes array'd.
White Gloves were on his Hands, and on
    his Head
A Wreath of Laurel, mix'd with Myrtle,
    spread.

---

844 Soul,] *Christie and others wrongly give*
Soul?

869 Not] *Warton and others wrongly give*
Nor

907 on] *Christie wrongly gives* in

A Sword keen-edg'd within his Right he held,
The warlike Emblem of the conquer'd Field:
Bare was his manly Visage on the Bier;
Menac'd his Countenance; ev'n in Death
severe.
Then to the Palace-Hall they bore the
Knight,
To lie in solemn State, a Publick Sight.
Groans, Cries, and Howlings fill the Crowded
Place,   920
And unaffected Sorrow sat on ev'ry Face.
Sad *Palamon* above the rest appears,
In Sable Garments, dew'd with gushing
Tears:
His Aubourn Locks on either Shoulder
flow'd,
Which to the Fun'ral of his Friend he vow'd:
But *Emily*, as Chief, was next his Side,
A Virgin-Widow and a *Mourning Bride*.
And that the Princely Obsequies might be
Perform'd according to his high Degree,
The Steed, that bore him living to the Fight, ⎫
Was trapp'd with polish'd Steel, all shining ⎪
bright,   931 ⎬
And cover'd with th' Atchievements of the ⎪
Knight.   ⎭
The Riders rode abreast, and one his Shield,
His Lance of Cornel-wood another held;
The third his Bow, and, glorious to behold,
The costly Quiver, all of burnish'd Gold.
The Noblest of the *Grecians* next appear,
And weeping, on their Shoulders bore the
Bier;
With sober Pace they march'd, and often
staid,
And through the Master-Street the Corps
convey'd.   940
The Houses to their Tops with Black were
spread,
And ev'n the Pavements were with Mourn-
ing hid.
The Right-side of the Pall old *Egeus* kept,
And on the Left the Royal *Theseus* wept;
Each bore a Golden Bowl of Work Divine,
With Honey fill'd, and Milk, and mix'd
with ruddy Wine.
Then *Palamon*, the Kinsman of the Slain,
And after him appear'd th' Illustrious Train:
To grace the Pomp came *Emily* the Bright,
With cover'd Fire, the Fun'ral Pile to
light.   950
With high Devotion was the Service made
And all the Rites of Pagan-Honour paid:

So lofty was the Pile, a *Parthian* Bow,
With Vigour drawn, must send the Shaft
below.
The Bottom was full twenty Fathom broad,
With crackling Straw beneath in due Pro-
portion strow'd.
The Fabrick seem'd a Wood of rising Green,
With Sulphur and Bitumen cast between,
To feed the Flames: The Trees were ⎫
unctuous Fir,   959 ⎪
And Mountain-Ash, the Mother of the ⎪
Spear;   ⎬
The Mourner Eugh and Builder Oak were ⎪
there: ⎭
The Beech, the swimming Alder, and the ⎫
Plane,   ⎪
Hard Box, and Linden of a softer Grain, ⎬
And Laurels, which the Gods for Conqu'ring ⎪
Chiefs ordain.   ⎭
How they were rank'd shall rest untold
by me,
With nameless Nymphs that lived in ev'ry
Tree;
Nor how the Dryads and the Woodland
Train,
Disherited, ran howling o'er the Plain:
Nor how the Birds to Foreign Seats repair'd,
Or Beasts that bolted out, and saw the
Forest bar'd: 970
Nor how the Ground now clear'd with
gastly Fright
Beheld the sudden Sun, a Stranger to the
Light.
The Straw, as first I said, was laid below;
Of Chips and Sere-wood was the second Row;
The third of Greens, and Timber newly fell'd;
The fourth high Stage the fragrant Odours
held,
And Pearls, and precious Stones, and rich
Array;
In midst of which, embalm'd, the Body lay.
The Service sung, the Maid with mourning
Eyes
The Stubble fir'd; the smouldring Flames
arise: 980
This Office done, she sunk upon the Ground;
But what she spoke, recover'd from her
Swoond,
I want the Wit in moving Words to dress;
But by themselves the tender Sex may guess.

961 Eugh] *The editors print* Yew   *Dryden's*
was a Westminster spelling, probably Busby's;
    ᶜ Oxford Historical Society, vol. xxxii, p. 294.

While the devouring Fire was burning fast,
Rich Jewels in the Flame the Wealthy cast ;
And some their Shields, and some their
Lances threw,
And gave the Warriour's Ghost a Warriour's
Due.
Full Bowls of Wine, of Honey, Milk and
Blood
Were pour'd upon the Pile of burning
Wood, 990
And hissing Flames receive, and hungry
lick the Food.
Then thrice the mounted Squadrons ride
around
The Fire, and *Arcite's* Name they thrice
resound :
Hail, and Farewell, they shouted thrice
amain,
Thrice facing to the Left, and thrice they
turn'd again :
Still, as they turn'd, they beat their
clatt'ring Shields ;
The Women mix their Cries ; and Clamour
fills the Fields.
The warlike Wakes continu'd all the Night,
And Fun'ral Games were played at new-
returning Light :
Who naked wrestl'd best, besmear'd with
Oil, 1000
Or who with Gantlets gave or took the
Foil,
I will not tell you, nor wou'd you attend ;
But briefly haste to my long Stories End.
I pass the rest ; the Year was fully
mourn'd,
And *Palamon* long since to *Thebes* return'd :
When, by the *Grecians* general Consent,
At *Athens Theseus* held his Parliament ;
Among the Laws that pass'd, it was decreed,
That conquer'd *Thebes* from Bondage shou'd
be freed ;
Reserving Homage to th' *Athenian* throne,
To which the Sov'reign summon'd *Pala-
mon*. 1011
Unknowing of the Cause, he took his Way,
Mournful in Mind, and still in Black Array,
The Monarch mounts the Throne, and,
plac'd on high,
Commands into the Court the beauteous
Emily :

988 the] *Derrick and Warton wrongly give*
their

So call'd, she came ; the Senate rose, and
paid
Becoming Rev'rence to the Royal Maid.
And first, soft Whispers through th' Assembly
went ;
With silent Wonder then they watch'd th'
Event ;
All hush'd, the King arose with awful Grace ;
Deep Thought was in his Breast, and
Counsel in his Face. 1021
At length he sigh'd ; and having first
prepar'd
Th' attentive Audience, thus his Will
declar'd.
The Cause and Spring of Motion, from
above
Hung down on Earth the Golden Chain of
Love :
Great was th' Effect, and high was his Intent,
When Peace among the jarring Seeds he
sent ;
Fire, Flood, and Earth, and Air by this were
bound,
And Love, the common Link, the new
Creation crown'd.
The Chain still holds ; for though the Forms
decay, 1030
Eternal Matter never wears away :
The same First Mover certain Bounds has
plac'd,
How long those perishable Forms shall last ;
Nor can they last beyond the Time assign'd
By that All-seeing and All-making Mind :
Shorten their Hours they may ; for Will is
free,
But never pass th' appointed Destiny.
So Men oppress'd, when weary of their
Breath,
Throw off the Burden, and subborn their
Death.
Then, since those Forms begin, and have
their End, 1040
On some unalter'd Cause they sure depend :
Parts of the Whole are we, but God the
Whole,
Who gives us Life, and animating Soul.
For Nature cannot from a Part derive
That Being, which the Whole can only give :
He perfect, stable ; but imperfect We,
Subject to Change, and diff'rent in Degree ;
Plants, Beasts, and Man ; and, as our
Organs are,
We more or less of his Perfection share.

But, by a long Descent, th' Etherial Fire
Corrupts ;   and Forms, the mortal Part,
   expire.   1051
As he withdraws his Vertue, so they pass,
And the same Matter makes another Mass :
This Law th' Omniscient Pow'r was pleas'd
   to give,
That ev'ry Kind should by Succession live ;
That Individuals die, his Will ordains ;
The propagated Species still remains.
The Monarch Oak, the Patriarch of the Trees,
Shoots rising up, and spreads by slow
   Degrees ;
Three Centuries he grows, and three he stays,
Supreme in State ;   and in three more
   decays :   1061
So wears the paving Pebble in the Street,
And Towns and Tow'rs their fatal Period
   meet :
So Rivers, rapid once, now naked lie,
Forsaken of their Springs ; and leave their
   Channels dry.
So Man, at first a Drop, dilates with Heat,
Then form'd, the little Heart begins to beat ;
Secret he feeds, unknowing in the Cell ;
At length, for Hatching ripe, he breaks the
   Shell,   1069
And struggles into Breath, and cries for Aid ;
Then, helpless, in his Mother's Lap is laid.
He creeps, he walks, and, issuing into Man,
Grudges their Life from whence his own
   began :
Retchless of Laws, affects to rule alone,
Anxious to reign, and restless on the Throne ;
First vegetive, then feels, and reasons last ;
Rich of Three Souls, and lives all three to
   waste.
Some thus ; but thousands more in Flow'r
   of Age :
For few arrive to run the latter Stage.
Sunk in the first, in Battel some are slain,
And others whelm'd beneath the stormy
   Main.   1081
What makes all this, but *Jupiter* the King,
At whose Command we perish, and we
   spring ?
Then 'tis our best, since thus ordain'd to die,
To make a Vertue of Necessity.
Take what he gives, since to rebel is vain ;
The Bad grows better, which we well sustain :
And cou'd we chuse the Time, and chuse
   aright,
Tis best to die, our Honour at the height.

When we have done our Ancestors no
   Shame,   1090
But serv'd our Friends, and well secur'd our
   Fame ;
Then should we wish our happy Life to close,
And leave no more for Fortune to dispose :
So should we make our Death a glad Relief
From future Shame, from Sickness, and from
   Grief :
Enjoying while we live the present Hour,
And dying in our Excellence, and Flow'r.
Then round our Death-bed every Friend
   shou'd run,
And joy us of our Conquest, early won ;
While the malicious World, with envious
   Tears,   1100
Shou'd grudge our happy End, and wish it
   Theirs.
Since then our *Arcite* is with Honour dead, ⎫
Why shou'd we mourn, that he so soon is   ⎬
   freed,   ⎭
Or call untimely, what the Gods decreed ?
With Grief as just a Friend may be deplor'd,
From a foul Prison to free Air restor'd.
Ought he to thank his Kinsman, or his Wife,
Cou'd Tears recall him into wretched Life !
Their Sorrow hurts themselves ;   on him
   is lost ;
And worse than both, offends his happy
   Ghost.   1110
What then remains, but after past Annoy
To take the good Vicissitude of Joy ?
To thank the gracious Gods for what they
   give,
Possess our Souls, and, while we live, to live ?
Ordain we then two Sorrows to combine,
And in one Point th' Extremes of Grief to
   join ;
That thence resulting Joy may be renewed,
As jarring Notes in Harmony conclude.
Then I propose that *Palamon* shall be
In Marriage join'd with beauteous *Emily* ;
For which already I have gained the
   Assent   1121
Of my free People in full Parliament.
Long Love to her has borne the faithful
   Knight,
And well deserv'd, had Fortune done him
   Right :
'Tis Time to mend her Fault ; since *Emily*
By *Arcite's* Death from former Vows is free :

1099 joy us] *Warton and others absurdly give*
joyous

If you, Fair Sister, ratifie the Accord,
And take him for your Husband, and your
   Lord.
'Tis no Dishonour to confer your Grace
On one descended from a Royal Race : 1130
And were he less, yet Years of Service
   past
From grateful Souls exact Reward at last :
Pity is Heav'n's and yours ; Nor can she
   find
A Throne so soft as in a Womans Mind.
He said ; she blush'd ; and as o'eraw'd by
   Might,
Seem'd to give *Theseus* what she gave the
   Knight.
Then turning to the *Theban*, thus he said :
Small Arguments are needful to persuade
Your Temper to comply with my Com-
   mand ;
And speaking thus, he gave *Emilia's* Hand.

Smil'd *Venus*, to behold her own true
   Knight   1141
Obtain the Conquest, though he lost the
   Fight,
And bless'd with Nuptial Bliss the sweet
   laborious Night.
Eros, and *Anteros*, on either Side,
One fir'd the Bridegroom, and one warm'd
   the Bride ;
And long-attending *Hymen* from above
Showr'd on the Bed the whole *Idalian* Grove.
All of a Tenour was their After-Life,
No Day discolour'd with Domestick Strife ;
No Jealousie, but mutual Truth believ'd,
Secure Repose, and Kindness undeceiv'd.
Thus Heavn, beyond the Compass of his
   Thought,   1152
Sent him the Blessing he so dearly bought.
   So may the Queen of Love long Duty bless,
And all true Lovers find the same Success.

The End of the Third Book.

THE COCK AND THE FOX: OR, THE TALE OF THE NUN'S PRIEST.

There liv'd, as Authors tell, in Days of
   Yore,
A Widow, somewhat old, and very poor :
Deep in a Cell her Cottage lonely stood,
Well thatch'd, and under covert of a Wood.
   This Dowager, on whom my Tale I found,
Since last she laid her Husband in the
   Ground,
A simple sober Life in patience led,
And had but just enough to buy her Bread :
But Huswifing the little Heav'n had lent,
She duly paid a Groat for Quarter-Rent ; 10
And pinch'd her Belly, with her Daughters
   two,
To bring the Year about with much ado.
   The Cattel in her Homestead were three
   Sows,
An Ewe called *Mally*, and three brinded
   Cows.

Her Parlor-Window stuck with Herbs around
Of sav'ry Smell ; and Rushes strewed the
   Ground.
A Maple-Dresser in her Hall she had,
On which full many a slender Meal she made :
For no delicious Morsel pass'd her Throat ;
According to her Cloth she cut her Coat : 20
No paynant Sawce she knew, no costly Treat,
Her Hunger gave a Relish to her Meat :
A sparing Diet did her Health assure ;
Or sick, a Pepper-Posset was her Cure.
Before the Day was done, her Work she sped,
And never went by Candle-light to Bed ;
With Exercise she sweat ill Humors out ;
Her Dancing was not hinder'd by the Gout.
Her Poverty was glad ; her Heart content,
Nor knew she what the Spleen or Vapors
   meant.   30

1128 Lord.] *Some editors print* Lord, *The full stop of the original seems right.*
THE COCK AND THE FOX. Text from the original and only contemporary edition, 1700. There are some very false stops in the original.

3 Cell] *This can hardly be right. Chaucer's word is* Dale. *Bell conjectured* Dell, *and this may be right.*
11] Daughters] Daughter 1700. *A misprint.*
21 paynant] *Dryden elsewhere uses the form* poynant, *and perhaps it should be restored here.*

Of Wine she never tasted through the
     Year,
But White and Black was all her homely
     Chear ;
Brown Bread, and Milk (but first she
     skim'd her bowls)
And Rashers of sindg'd Bacon on the Coals.
On Holy-Days, an Egg or two at most ;
But her Ambition never reach'd to roast.
    A Yard she had with Pales enclos'd about,
Some high, some low, and a dry Ditch
     without.
Within this Homestead, liv'd without a Peer,
For crowing loud, the noble Chanticleer : 40
So hight her Cock, whose singing did surpass
The merry Notes of Organs at the Mass.
More certain was the crowing of a Cock
To number Hours, than is an Abbey-clock ;
And sooner than the Mattin-Bell was rung,
He clap'd his Wings upon his Roost, and
     sung :
For when Degrees fifteen ascended right,
By sure Instinct he knew 'twas One at
     Night.
High was his Comb, and Coral-red withal,
In dents embattel'd like a Castle-Wall ; 50
His Bill was Raven-black, and shon like Jet,
Blue were his Legs, and Orient were his Feet:
White were his Nails, like Silver to behold,
His Body glitt'ring like the burnish'd Gold.
    This gentle Cock, for solace of his Life,
Six Misses had beside his lawful Wife ;
Scandal, that spares no King, tho' ne'er so
     good,
Says, they were all of his own Flesh and
     Blood :
His Sisters both by Sire, and Mother's Side,
And sure their Likeness show'd them near
     ally'd.   60
But make the worst, the Monarch did no
     more
Than all the *Ptolomey's* had done before :
When Incest is for Int'rest of a Nation,
'Tis made no Sin by Holy Dispensation.
Some Lines have been maintain'd by this
     alone,
Which by their common Ugliness are known.
    But passing this as from our Tale apart,
Dame Partlet was the Soveraign of his Heart:
Ardent in Love, outragious in his Play,
He feather'd her a hundred times a Day ; 70
And she, that was not only passing fair,
But was withal discreet, and debonair,

Resolv'd the passive Doctrin to fulfil,
Tho' loath, and let him work his wicked
     Will :
At Board and Bed was affable and kind,
According as their Marriage-Vow did bind,
And as the Churches Precept had enjoin'd.
Ev'n since she was a Sennight old, they say
Was chast, and humble to her dying Day,
Nor Chick nor Hen was known to dis-
     obey.   80
    By this her Husband's Heart she did
     obtain ;
What cannot Beauty join'd with Virtue gain !
She was his only Joy, and he her Pride :
She, when he walk'd, went pecking by his
     Side ;
If, spurning up the Ground, he sprung a
     Corn,
The Tribute in his Bill to her was born.
But oh ! what Joy it was to hear him sing
In Summer, when the Day began to spring,
Stretching his Neck, and warbling in his
     Throat,
Solus cum Sola, then was all his Note. 90
For in the Days of Yore, the Birds of Parts
Were bred to Speak, and Sing, and learn the
     lib'ral Arts.
    It happ'd that perching on the Parlor
     beam
Amidst his Wives he had a deadly Dream,
Just at the Dawn, and sigh'd, and groan'd
     so fast,
As every Breath he drew would be his last.
Dame Partlet, ever nearest to his Side,
Heard all his piteous Moan, and how he cry'd
For help from Gods and Men : And sore
     aghast
She peck'd and pull'd, and waken'd him at
     last.   100
Dear Heart, said she, for Love of Heav'n
     declare
Your Pain, and make me Partner of your
     Care.
You groan, Sir, ever since the Morning-light,
As something had disturb'd your noble
     Spright.
    And, Madam, well I might, said Chanti-
     cleer.
Never was *Shrovetide*-Cock in such a Fear.
Ev'n still I run all over in a Sweat,
My Princely Senses not recover'd yet.
For such a Dream I had of dire Portent,
That much I fear my Body will be shent :

It bodes I shall have Wars and woful
    Strife,   111
Or in a loathsom Dungeon end my Life.
Know, Dame, I dreamt within my troubl'd
    Breast,
That in our Yard I saw a murd'rous Beast,
That on my Body would have made Arrest.
With waking Eyes I ne'er beheld his Fellow,
His Colour was betwixt a Red and Yellow:
Tipp'd was his Tail, and both his pricking
    Ears
With black; and much unlike his other
    Hairs:
The rest, in Shape a Beagle's Whelp through-
    out,   120
With broader Forehead, and a sharper Snout:
Deep in his Front were sunk his glowing
    Eyes,
That yet, methinks, I see him with Surprize.
Reach out your Hand, I drop with clammy
    Sweat,
And lay it to my Heart, and feel it beat.
    Now fy for Shame, quoth she, by Heav'n
    above,
Thou hast for ever lost thy Ladies Love.
No Woman can endure a Recreant Knight,
He must be bold by Day, and free by Night:
Our Sex desires a Husband or a Friend, 130
Who can our Honour and his own defend;
Wise, Hardy, Secret, lib'ral of his Purse;
A Fool is nauseous, but a Coward worse:
No bragging Coxcomb, yet no baffled Knight.
How dar'st thou talk of Love, and dar'st not
    Fight?
How dar'st thou tell thy Dame thou art
    affer'd?
Hast thou no manly Heart, and hast a Beard?
    If ought from fearful Dreams may be
    divin'd,
They signify a Cock of Dunghill-kind.
All Dreams, as in old *Gallen* I have read, 140
Are from Repletion and Complexion bred;
From rising Fumes of indigested Food,
And noxious Humors that infect the Blood:
And sure, my Lord, if I can read aright,
These foolish Fancies you have had to Night
Are certain Symptoms (in the canting Style)
Of boiling Choler and abounding Bile:
This yellow Gaul that in your Stomach floats,
Ingenders all these visionary Thoughts.

When Choler overflows, then Dreams are
    bred   150
Of Flames, and all the Family of Red;
Red Dragons, and red Beasts in Sleep we
    view;
For Humors are distinguish'd by their Hue.
From hence we Dream of Wars and Warlike
    Things,
And Wasps and Hornets with their double
    Wings.
Choler adust congeals our Blood with fear;
Then black Bulls toss us, and black Devils
    tear.
In sanguine airy Dreams aloft we bound;
With Rhumes oppress'd, we sink in Rivers
    drown'd.
    More I could say, but thus conclude my
    Theme,   160
The dominating Humour makes the Dream.
Cato was in his time accounted Wise,
And he condemns them all for empty Lies.
Take my Advice, and when we fly to Ground
With Laxatives preserve your Body sound,
And purge the peccant Humors that abound.
I should be loath to lay you on a Bier;
And though there lives no 'Pothecary near,
I dare for once prescribe for your Disease,
And save long Bills, and a damn'd Doctor's
    Fees.   170
    Two Soveraign Herbs, which I by practise
    know,
Are both at hand (for in our Yard they
    grow;)
On Peril of my Soul shall rid you wholly
Of yellow Choler, and of Melancholy:
You must both Purge, and Vomit; but obey,
And for the Love of Heav'n make no delay.
Since hot and dry in your Complexion join,
Beware the Sun when in a vernal Sign;
For when he mounts exalted in the Ram,
If then he finds your Body in a Flame, 180
Replete with Choler, I dare lay a Groat,
A Tertian Ague is at least your Lot.
Perhaps a Fever (which the Gods forefend)
May bring your Youth to some untimely End.
And therefore, Sir, as you desire to live,
A Day or two before your Laxative,
Take just three Worms, nor under nor above,
Because the Gods unequal Numbers love,
These Digestives prepare you for your Purge,
Of Fumetery, Centaury, and Spurge, 190

---

119 With] *Warton and others wrongly give*
Were

187 under] *over 1700. A slip of the pen.*

And of Ground-Ivy add a Leaf, or two,
All which within our Yard or Garden grow.
Eat these, and be, my Lord, of better Cheer ;
Your Father's Son was never born to fear.
  Madam, quoth he, Grammercy for your
    Care,
But *Cato*, whom you quoted, you may spare ;
'Tis true, a wise, and worthy Man he seems,
And (as you say) gave no belief to Dreams :
But other Men of more Authority,
And, by th' Immortal Powers as wise as He,
Maintain, with sounder Sense, that Dreams
    forebode ;   201
For *Homer* plainly says they come from God.
Nor *Cato* said it : But some modern Fool
Impos'd in *Cato's* Name on Boys at School.
  Believe me, Madam, Morning Dreams fore-
    show
Th' Events of Things, and future Weal or
    Woe :
Some Truths are not by Reason to be try'd,
But we have sure Experience for our Guide.
An ancient Author, equal with the best,
Relates this Tale of Dreams among the rest.
  Two Friends, or Brothers, with devout
    Intent,   211
On some far Pilgrimage together went.
It happen'd so that, when the Sun was down,
They just arriv'd by twilight at a Town ;
That Day had been the baiting of a Bull,
'Twas at a Feast, and ev'ry Inn so full,
That no void Room in Chamber, or on
    Ground,
And but one sorry Bed was to be found,
And that so little it would hold but one,
Though till this Hour they never lay alone.
  So were they forc'd to part ; one stay'd
    behind,   221
His Fellow sought what Lodging he could
    find :
At last he found a Stall where Oxen stood,
And that he rather chose than lie abroad,
'Twas in a farther Yard without a Door ;
But, for his ease, well litter'd was the Floor.
His Fellow, who the narrow Bed had kept,
Was weary, and without a Rocker slept :
Supine he snor'd ; but in the Dead of Night,
He dreamt his Friend appear'd before his
    Sight,   230
Who, with a ghastly Look and doleful Cry,
Said, Help me, Brother, or this Night I die :
Arise, and help, before all Help be vain,
Or in an Oxes Stall I shall be slain.

Rowz'd from his Rest, he waken'd in a
    Start,
Shiv'ring with Horror, and with aking
    Heart :
At length to cure himself by Reason tries ;
'Tis but a Dream, and what are Dreams
    but Lies ?
So thinking chang'd his Side, and closed
    his Eyes.
His Dream returns ; his Friend appears
    again :   240
The Murd'rers come, now help, or I am
    slain :
'Twas but a Vision still, and Visions are
    but vain.
  He dreamt the third : But now his Friend
    appear'd,
Pale, naked, pierc'd with Wounds, with
    Blood besmear'd :
Thrice warn'd, awake, said he ; Relief is late,
The Deed is done ; but thou revenge my
    Fate :
Tardy of Aid, unseal thy heavy Eyes,
Awake, and with the dawning Day arise :
Take to the Western Gate thy ready way,
For by that Passage they my Corps convey :
My Corps is in a Tumbril laid ; among   251
The Filth and Ordure, and enclos'd with
    Dung.
That Cart arrest, and raise a common Cry,
For sacred hunger of my Gold I die ;
Then show'd his grisly Wounds ; and last
    he drew
A piteous Sigh ; and took a long Adieu.
  The frighted Friend arose by break of Day,
And found the Stall where late his Fellow lay.
Then of his impious Host inquiring more,
Was answer'd that his Guest was gone
    before :   260
Muttring, he went, said he, by Morning-light,
And much complain'd of his ill Rest by
    Night.
This rais'd Suspicion in the Pilgrim's Mind ;
Because all Hosts are of an evil Kind,
And oft, to share the Spoil, with Robbers
    join'd.
  His Dream confirm'd his Thought : with
    troubled look
Straight to the Western-Gate his Way he
    took ;
There, as his Dream foretold, a Cart he found,
That carry'd Compost forth to dung the
    Ground.

This when the Pilgrim saw, he stretch'd his
 Throat,   270
And cry'd out Murther with a yelling Note.
My murther'd Fellow in this Cart lies dead,
Vengeance and Justice on the Villain's
 Head.
You, Magistrates, who sacred Laws dispense,
On you I call to punish this Offence.
 The Word thus giv'n, within a little Space
The Mob came roaring out, and throng'd the
 Place.
All in a trice they cast the Cart to Ground, ⎫
And in the Dung the murther'd Body found; ⎪
Though breathless, warm, and reeking from ⎬
 the Wound.   280 ⎭
Good Heav'n, whose darling Attribute we
 find
Is boundless Grace, and Mercy to Mankind,
Abhors the Cruel ; and the Deeds of Night
By wond'rous Ways reveals in open Light :
Murther may pass unpunish'd for a time,
But tardy Justice will o'ertake the Crime
And oft a speedier pain the Guilty feels,
The Hue and Cry of Heav'n pursues him
 at the Heels,
Fresh from the Fact; as in the present Case; ⎫
The Criminals are seiz'd upon the Place: 290 ⎬
Carter and Host confronted Face to Face. ⎭
Stiff in denial, as the Law appoints,
On Engins they distend their tortur'd
 Joints :
So was confession forc'd, th' Offence was
 known,
And publick Justice on th' Offenders done.
 Here may you see that Visions are to
 dread ;
And in the Page that follows this I read
Of two young Merchants, whom the hope
 of Gain
Induc'd in Partnership to cross the Main :
Waiting till willing Winds their Sails ⎫
 supply'd,   300 ⎬
Within a Trading-Town they long abide, ⎪
Full fairly situate on a Haven's side. ⎭
 One Evening it befel that looking out,
The Wind they long had wish'd was come
 about :
Well pleas'd they went to Rest ; and if the
 Gale
Till Morn continu'd, both resolv'd to sail.

But as together in a Bed they lay,
The younger had a Dream at break of Day.
A Man, he thought, stood frowning at his ⎫
 side,   309 ⎬
Who warn'd him for his Safety to provide, ⎪
Not put to Sea, but safe on Shore abide. ⎭
I come, thy Genius, to command thy stay ; ⎫
Trust not the Winds, for fatal is the Day, ⎬
And Death unhop'd attends the watry way. ⎭
 The Vision said : And vanish'd from his
 Sight ;
The Dreamer waken'd in a mortal Fright ;
Then pull'd his drowzy Neighbour, and
 declar'd
What in his Slumber he had seen, and heard.
His Friend smil'd scornful, and, with proud
 contempt,
Rejects as idle what his Fellow dreamt. 320
Stay, who will stay : For me no Fears
 restrain,
Who follow *Mercury* the God of Gain :
Let each Man do as to his Fancy seems,
I wait not, I, till you have better Dreams.
Dreams are but Interludes, which Fancy
 makes ;
When Monarch-Reason sleeps, this Mimick
 wakes :
Compounds a Medley of disjointed Things,
A Mob of Coblers and a Court of Kings :
Light Fumes are merry, grosser Fumes are
 sad ;
Both are the reasonable Soul run mad : 330
And many monstrous Forms in Sleep we
 see,
That neither were, nor are, nor e'er can be.
Sometimes, forgotten Things long cast
 behind
Rush forward in the Brain, and come to
 mind.
The Nurses Legends are for Truths receiv'd,
And the Man dreams but what the Boy
 believ'd.
 Sometimes we but rehearse a former Play, ⎫
The Night restores our Actions done by ⎬
 Day ;   ⎪
As Hounds in sleep will open for their Prey. ⎭
In short, the Farce of Dreams is of a piece,
Chimera's all ; and more absurd, or less. 341
You, who believe in Tales, abide alone,
What e'er I get this Voyage is my own.
 Thus while he spoke he heard the shouting
 Crew
That call'd aboard and took his last adieu.

The Vessel went before a merry Gale,
And for quick Passage put on ev'ry Sail :
But when least fear'd, and ev'n in open Day,
The Mischief overtook her in the way :
Whether she sprung a Leak, I cannot find,
Or whether she was overset with Wind ;   351
Or that some Rock below, her bottom rent ;
But down at once with all her Crew she went ;
Her Fellow Ships from far her Loss de-
    scry'd ;
But only she was sunk, and all were safe
    beside.
By this Example you are taught again,
That Dreams and Visions are not always vain :
But if, dear Partlet, you are yet in doubt,
Another Tale shall make the former out.
    Kenelm, the Son of Kenulph, Mercia's
    King,   360
Whose holy Life the Legends loudly sing,
Warn'd, in a Dream, his Murther did foretel
From Point to Point as after it befel :
All Circumstances to his Nurse he told,
(A Wonder, from a Child of sev'n Years old)
The Dream with Horror heard, the good old
    Wife
From Treason counsell'd him to guard his
    Life :
But close to keep the Secret in his Mind,
For a Boy's Vision small Belief would find.
The pious Child, by Promise bound, obey'd,
Nor was the fatal Murther long delay'd :   371
By Quenda slain, he fell before his time,
Made a young Martyr by his Sister's Crime.
The Tale is told by venerable Bede,
Which, at your better leisure, you may
    read.
    Macrobius too relates the Vision sent
To the great Scipio with the fam'd event ;
Objections makes, but after makes Replies,
And adds, that Dreams are often Prophecies.
    Of Daniel you may read in Holy⎫
    Writ,   380 ⎬
Who, when the King his Vision did forget, ⎪
Cou'd Word for Word the wond'rous⎭
    Dream repeat.
Nor less of Patriarch Joseph understand,
Who by a Dream inslav'd th' Egyptian Land,
The Years of Plenty and of Dearth foretold,
When for their Bread, their Liberty they
    sold.
Nor must th' exalted Buttler be forgot,
Nor he whose Dream presag'd his hanging
    Lot.

And did not Crœsus the same Death
    foresee,
Rais'd in his Vision on a lofty Tree ?   390
The wife of Hector in his utmost Pride,
Dreamt of his Death the Night before he
    dy'd :
Well was he warn'd from Battle to refrain ;⎫
But Men to Death decreed are warn'd in⎪
    vain :   ⎬
He dar'd the Dream, and by his fatal Foe⎪
    was slain.   ⎭
    Much more I know, which I forbear to
    speak,
For see the ruddy Day begins to break :
Let this suffice, that plainly I foresee
My Dream was bad, and bodes Adversity :
But neither Pills nor Laxatives I like,   400
They only serve to make a well-man sick :
Of these his Gain the sharp Phisician makes,
And often gives a Purge, but seldom takes :
They not correct, but poyson all the Blood,
And ne'er did any but the Doctors good.
Their Tribe, Trade, Trinkets, I defy them all,
With ev'ry work of 'Pothecary's Hall.
    These melancholy Matters I forbear ;
But let me tell Thee, Partlet mine, and
    swear,
That when I view the Beauties of thy Face,
I fear not Death, nor Dangers, nor Dis-
    grace :   411
So may my Soul have Bliss, as when I spy
The Scarlet Red about thy Partridge Eye,
While thou art constant to thy own true⎫
    Knight,   ⎬
While thou art mine, and I am thy delight,⎪
All Sorrows at thy Presence take their⎭
    flight.
For true it is, as in Principio,
Mulier est hominis confusio.
Madam, the meaning of this Latin is,   419
That Woman is to Man his Soveraign Bliss.
For when by Night I feel your tender Side,
Though for the narrow Perch I cannot ride,
Yet I have such a Solace in my Mind,
That all my boding Cares are cast behind :
And ev'n already I forget my Dream.
He said, and downward flew from off the
    Beam,
For Day-light now began apace to spring,
The Thrush to whistle, and the Lark to sing.
Then crowing clap'd his Wings, th' appointed
    call,
To chuck his Wives together in the Hall.   430

By this the Widow had unbarr'd the Door,
And Chanticleer went strutting out before,
With Royal Courage, and with Heart so light,
As shew'd he scorn'd the Visions of the Night.
Now roaming in the Yard, he spurn'd the
  Ground,
And gave to Partlet the first Grain he found.
Then often feather'd her with wanton Play,
And trod her twenty times e'er prime of Day
And took by turns and gave so much delight,
Her Sisters pin'd with Envy at the Sight. 440
  He chuck'd again, when other Corns he
  found,
And scarcely deign'd to set a Foot to
  Ground,
But swagger'd like a Lord about his Hall,
And his sev'n Wives came running at his call.
  'Twas now the Month in which the World
  began,
(If *March* beheld the first created Man :)
And since the vernal Equinox, the Sun
In *Aries* twelve Degrees, or more had run ;
When, casting up his Eyes against the Light,
Both Month, and Day, and Hour, he
  measur'd right ;   450
And told more truly, than th' Ephemeris,
For Art may err, but Nature cannot miss.
  Thus numb'ring Times, and Seasons in
  his Breast,
His second crowing the third Hour confess'd.
Then turning, said to Partlet, See, my Dear,
How lavish Nature has adorn'd the Year ;
How the pale Primrose, and blue Violet
  spring,
And Birds essay their Throats disus'd to sing:
All these are ours ; and I with pleasure see
Man strutting on two Legs, and aping
  me !   460
An unfledg'd Creature, of a lumpish frame,
Indew'd with fewer Particles of Flame :
Our Dame sits couring o'er the Kitchin-fire,
I draw fresh Air, and Nature's Works
  admire :
And ev'n this Day, in more delight abound,
Than, since I was an Egg, I ever found.
  The time shall come when Chanticleer shall
  wish
His Words unsaid, and hate his boasted Bliss:
The crested Bird shall by Experience know,⎫
Jove made not him his Master-piece below ;⎬
And learn the latter end of Joy is Woe. 471⎭
The Vessel of his Bliss to Dregs is run,
And Heav'n will have him tast his other Tun.

Ye Wise, draw near, and hearken to my
  Tale,
Which proves that oft the Proud by Flatt'ry
  fall ;
The Legend is as true I undertake
As *Tristram* is, and *Launcelot* of the Lake :
Which all our Ladies in such rev'rence hold,
As if in Book of Martyrs it were told.
  A Fox full fraught with seeming Sanctity,
That fear'd an Oath, but like the Devil,
  would lie,   481
Who look'd like Lent, and had the holy Leer,
And durst not sin before he say'd his Pray'r :
This pious Cheat, that never suck'd the⎫
  Blood,   ⎪
Nor chaw'd the Flesh of Lambs, but when⎬
  he cou'd,   ⎪
Had pass'd three Summers in the neigh-⎭
  b'ring Wood ;
And musing long whom next to circumvent,
On Chanticleer his wicked Fancy bent ;
And in his high imagination cast,
By Stratagem to gratify his Tast.   490
  The Plot contriv'd, before the break of
  Day,
Saint *Reynard* through the Hedge had made
  his way ;
The Pale was next, but proudly, with a
  bound
He lept the Fence of the forbidden Ground :
Yet fearing to be seen, within a Bed
Of Coleworts he conceal'd his wily Head ;
Then sculk'd till Afternoon, and watch'd
  his time,
(As Murd'rers use) to perpetrate his Crime.
  O Hypocrite, ingenious to destroy,
O Traytor, worse than *Sinon* was to *Troy* ;
O vile Subverter of the *Gallick* Reign, 501
More false than *Gano* was to *Charlemaign* !
O Chanticleer, in an unhappy Hour
Did'st thou forsake the Safety of thy Bow'r :
Better for Thee thou had'st believ'd thy
  Dream,
And not that Day descended from the Beam!
  But here the Doctors eagerly dispute :
Some hold Predestination absolute :
Some Clerks maintain, that Heav'n at first
  foresees,
And in the virtue of Foresight decrees. 510
If this be so, then Prescience binds the Will,
And Mortals are not free to Good or Ill
For what he first foresaw, he must ordain
Or its eternal Prescience may be vain

As bad for us as Prescience had not bin :
For first, or last, he's Author of the Sin.
And who says that, let the blaspheming Man
Say worse ev'n of the Devil, if he can.
For how can that Eternal Pow'r be just
To punish Man, who Sins because he must ?
Or, how can He reward a vertuous Deed, 521
Which is not done by us ; but first decreed ?
  I cannot boult this Matter to the Bran,
As *Bradwardin* and holy *Austin* can :
If Prescience can determine Actions so
That we must do, because he did foreknow
Or that foreknowing, yet our Choice is free,
Not forc'd to Sin by strict necessity ;
This strict necessity they simple call,
Another sort there is, conditional.   530
The first so binds the Will that Things fore-
       known
By Spontaneity, not Choice, are done.
Thus Galley-Slaves tug willing, at their Oar, ⎫
Content to work, in prospect of the Shore ; ⎬
But wou'd not work at all, if not con- ⎪
       strain'd before.   ⎭
That other does not Liberty constrain,
But Man may either act, or may refrain.
Heav'n made us Agents free to Good or Ill,
And forc'd it not, tho' he foresaw the Will.
Freedom was first bestow'd on human
       Race,   540
And Prescience only held the second place.
  If he could make such Agents wholly free,
I not dispute ; the Point 's too high for me ;
For Heav'n's unfathom'd Pow'r what Man
       can sound,
Or put to his Omnipotence a Bound ?
He made us to his Image all agree ;   ⎫
That Image is the Soul, and that must be, ⎬
Or not the Maker's Image, or be free.   ⎭
  But whether it were better Man had been
By Nature bound to Good, not free to Sin,
I wave, for fear of splitting on a Rock.   551
The Tale I tell is only of a Cock ;
Who had not run the hazard of his Life
Had he believ'd his Dream, and not his Wife:
For Women, with a mischief to their Kind,
Pervert, with bad Advice, our better Mind.
A Woman's Counsel brought us first to Woe,
And made her Man his Paradice forego,
Where at Heart's ease he liv'd, and might
       have bin
As free from Sorrow as he was from Sin. 560

For what the Devil had their Sex to do,
That, born to Folly, they presum'd to know,
And could not see the Serpent in the Grass ?
But I my self presume, and let it pass.
  Silence in times of Suff'ring is the best,
'Tis dang'rous to disturb a Hornet's Nest.
In other Authors you may find enough,
But all they say of Dames is idle Stuff.
Legends of lying Wits together bound,
The Wife of *Bath* would throw 'em to the
       Ground :   570
These are the words of Chanticleer, not mine,
I honour Dames, and think their Sex divine.
  Now to continue what my Tale begun.
Lay Madam Partlet basking in the Sun,
Breast-high in Sand : Her Sisters, in a row,
Enjoyed the Beams above, the Warmth
       below.
The Cock, that of his Flesh was ever free,
Sung merrier than the Mermaid in the Sea :
And so befel, that as he cast his Eye
Among the Colworts on a Butterfly,   580
He saw false *Reynard* where he lay full low,
I need not swear he had no list to Crow :
But cry'd, Cock, Cock, and gave a suddain
       Start,
As sore dismaid and frighted at his Heart.
For Birds and Beasts, inform'd by Nature,
       know
Kinds opposite to theirs, and fly their Foe.
So, Chanticleer, who never saw a Fox,
Yet shun'd him as a Sailor shuns the Rocks.
  But the false Loon, who cou'd not work
       his Will
By open Force, employed his flatt'ring Skill :
I hope, my Lord, said he, I not offend, 591
Are you afraid of me that am your Friend ?
I were a Beast indeed to do you wrong,
I, who have lov'd and honour'd you so long :
Stay, gentle Sir, nor take a false Alarm,
For, on my Soul, I never meant you harm.
I come no Spy, nor as a Traytor press,
To learn the Secrets of your soft Recess :
Far be from *Reynard* so prophane a Thought,
But by the Sweetness of your Voice was
       brought :   600
For, as I bid my Beads. by chance I heard
The Song as of an Angel in the Yard :
A Song that wou'd have charm'd th' infernal
       Gods,
And banish'd Horror from the dark Abodes :

---

534 *Content*] Consent *1700*.

599 so] to *1700*.

Had *Orpheus* sung it in the neather Sphere,
So much the Hymn had pleas'd the Tyrant's
Ear,
The Wife had been detain'd, to keep the
Husband there.

My Lord, your Sire familiarly I knew,
A Peer deserving such a Son, as you :
He, with your Lady-Mother (whom Heav'n
rest) 610
Has often grac'd my House, and been my
Guest
To view his living Features does me good,
For I am your poor Neighbour in the Wood ;
And in my Cottage shou'd be proud to see
The worthy Heir of my Friend's Family.

But since I speak of Singing let me say,
As with an upright Heart I safely may,
That, save your self, there breaths not on
the Ground
One like your Father for a Silver sound.
So sweetly wou'd he wake the Winter-day,
That Matrons to the Church mistook
their way, 621
And thought they heard the merry Organ
play.
And he to raise his Voice with artful Care,
(What will not Beaux attempt to please
the Fair ?)
On Tiptoe stood to sing with greater Strength,
And stretch'd his comely Neck at all the
length :
And while he pain'd his Voice to pierce the
Skies,
As Saints in Raptures use, would shut his
Eyes,
That the sound striving through the narrow
Throat,
His winking might avail, to mend the Note.
By this, in Song, he never had his Peer, 631
From sweet *Cecilia* down to Chanticleer :
Not *Maro's* Muse, who sung the mighty Man,
Nor *Pindar's* heav'nly Lyre, nor *Horace*
when a Swan.

Your Ancestors proceed from Race divine :
From *Brennus* and *Belinus* is your Line ;
Who gave to sov'raign *Rome* such loud
Alarms,
That ev'n the Priests were not excus'd from
Arms.

Besides, a famous Monk of modern times,
Has left of Cocks recorded in his Rhimes, 640
That of a Parish-Priest the Son and Heir
(When Sons of Priests were from the
Proverb clear)
Affronted once a Cock of noble Kind,
And either lam'd his Legs, or struck him
blind ;
For which the Clerk his Father was disgrac'd,
And in his Benefice another plac'd.
Now sing, my Lord, if not for love of me,
Yet for the sake of sweet Saint Charity ;
Make Hills and Dales, and Earth and
Heav'n rejoice,
And emulate your Father's Angel-voice. 650

The Cock was pleas'd to hear him speak
so fair,
And proud beside, as solar People are ;
Nor cou'd the Treason from the Truth descry,
So was he ravish'd with this Flattery :
So much the more as from a little Elf,
He had a high Opinion of himself :
Though sickly, slender, and not large of
Limb,
Concluding all the World was made for
him.

Ye Princes, rais'd by Poets to the Gods,
And *Alexander'd* up in lying Odes, 660
Believe not ev'ry flatt'ring Knave's report,
There's many a *Reynard* lurking in the
Court ;
And he shall be receiv'd with more regard
And list'ned to, than modest Truth is
heard.

This Chanticleer, of whom the Story sings,
Stood high upon his Toes, and clap'd his
Wings ;
Then stretch'd his Neck, and wink'd with
both his Eyes,
Ambitious, as he sought th' Olympick
Prize.
But while he pain'd himself to raise his Note,
False *Reynard* rush'd, and caught him by the
Throat. 670
Then on his Back he laid the precious Load,
And sought his wonted shelter of the Wood ;
Swiftly he made his way, the Mischief done,
Of all unheeded, and pursu'd by none.

Alas, what stay is there in human State,
Or who can shun inevitable Fate ?
The Doom was written, the Decree was past,
E'er the Foundations of the World were
cast !

605 *Orpheus*] Orphans *1700. A ludicrous misprint.
627 pain'd] *Derrick, Warton,* and *others
wrongly give* strain'd

In *Arles* though the Sun exalted stood,
His Patron-Planet to procure his good ; 680
Yet *Saturn* was his mortal Foe, and he
In *Libra* rais'd, oppos'd the same Degree :
The Rays both good and bad, of equal Pow'r,
Each thwarting other, made a mingled Hour.
On *Friday*-morn he dreamt this direful Dream,
Cross to the worthy Native, in his Scheme !
Ah blissful Venus, Goddess of Delight,
How cou'dst thou suffer thy devoted Knight,
On thy own Day, to fall by Foe oppress'd,
The wight of all the World who serv'd thee best ?   690
Who true to Love, was all for Recreation,
And minded not the Work of Propagation.
Gaufride, who could'st so well in Rhime complain
The Death of *Richard* with an Arrow slain,
Why had not I thy Muse, or thou my Heart,
To sing this heavy Dirge with equal Art !
That I like thee on *Friday* might complain ;
For on that Day was *Ceur de Lion* slain.
  Not louder Cries, when *Ilium* was in Flames,
Were sent to Heav'n by woful *Trojan* Dames,   700
When *Pyrrhus* toss'd on high his burnish'd Blade,
And offer'd *Priam* to his Father's Shade,
Than for the Cock the widow'd Poultry made.
Fair Partlet first, when he was born from sight,
With soveraign Shrieks bewail'd her Captive Knight :
Far lowder than the *Carthaginian* Wife,
When *Asdrubal* her Husband lost his Life,
When she beheld the smouldring Flames ascend,
And all the *Punick* Glories at an end :
Willing into the Fires she plung'd her Head,
With greater Ease than others seek their Bed.   711
Not more aghast the Matrons of Renown,
When Tyrant *Nero* burn'd th' Imperial Town,
Shriek'd for the downfal in a doleful Cry,
For which their guiltless Lords were doom'd to die.
  Now to my Story I return again :
The trembling Widow, and her Daughters twain,

This woful cackling Cry with Horror heard,
Of those distracted Damsels in the Yard ;
And starting up, beheld the heavy Sight, 720
How *Reynard* to the Forest took his Flight,
And cross his Back, as in triumphant Scorn,
The Hope and Pillar of the House was born.
  The Fox, the wicked Fox, was all the Cry,
Out from his House ran ev'ry Neighbour nigh :
The Vicar first, and after him the Crew,
With Forks and Staves the Fellon to pursue.
Ran *Coll* our Dog, and *Talbot* with the Band,
And *Malkin*, with her Distaff in her Hand :
Ran Cow and Calf, and Family of Hogs, 730
In Panique Horror of pursuing Dogs ;
With many a deadly Grunt and doleful Squeak
Poor Swine, as if their pretty Hearts would break.
The Shouts of Men, the Women in dismay,
With Shrieks augment the Terror of the Day.
The Ducks, that heard the Proclamation cry'd,
And fear'd a Persecution might betide,
Full twenty Mile from Town their Voyage take,
Obscure in Rushes of the liquid Lake.
The Geese fly o'er the Barn ; the Bees in Arms,   740
Drive headlong from their Waxen Cells in Swarms.
Jack Straw at *London*-stone with all his Rout
Struck not the City with so loud a Shout ;
Not when with English Hate they did pursue
A French Man, or an unbelieving *Jew* :
Not when the Welkin rung with one and all ;
And Echoes bounded back from *Fox's* Hall ;
Earth seem'd to sink beneath, and Heav'n above to fall.
With Might and Main they chas'd the murd'rous Fox,
With brazen Trumpets, and inflated Box,
To kindle *Mars* with military Sounds, 751
Nor wanted Horns t' inspire sagacious Hounds.
  But see how Fortune can confound the Wise,
And when they least expect it, turn the Dice.
The Captive Cock, who scarce cou'd draw his Breath,
And lay within the very Jaws of Death,

Yet in this Agony his Fancy wrought,
And Fear supply'd him with this happy
   Thought :
Yours is the Prize, victorious Prince, said he,
The Vicar my defeat, and all the Village
   see, 760
Enjoy your friendly Fortune while you may,
And bid the Churls that envy you the Prey,
Call back their mungril Curs, and cease their
   Cry,
See, Fools, the shelter of the Wood is nigh,
And Chanticleer in your despight shall die.
He shall be pluck'd and eaten to the
   Bone.
'Tis well advis'd, in Faith it shall be done ;
This *Reynard* said : but as the Word he
   spoke,
The Pris'ner with a Spring from Prison
   broke :
Then stretch'd his feather'd Fans with all
   his might, 770
And to the neighb'ring Maple wing'd his
   flight.
  Whom when the Traytor safe on Tree
   beheld,
He curs'd the Gods, with Shame and Sorrow
   fill'd ;
Shame for his Folly ; Sorrow out of time,
For Plotting an unprofitable Crime :
Yet mast'ring both, th' Artificer of Lies
Renews th' Assault, and his last Batt'ry
   tries.
  Though I, said he, did ne'er in Thought
   offend,
How justly may my Lord suspect his
   Friend !
Th' appearance is against me, I confess, 780
Who seemingly have put you in Distress :
You, if your Goodness does not plead my
   Cause,
May think I broke all hospitable Laws,
To bear you from your Palace-yard by
   Might,
And put your noble Person in a Fright :
This, since you take it ill, I must repent,
Though Heav'n can witness with no bad
   intent
I practis'd it, to make you taste your Cheer,
With double Pleasure, first prepared by fear.

So loyal Subjects often seize their
   Prince, 790
Forc'd (for his Good) to seeming Violence,
Yet mean his sacred Person not the least
   Offence.
Descend ; so help me *Jove* as you shall find
That *Reynard* comes of no dissembling Kind.
  Nay, quoth the Cock ; but I beshrew us
   both,
If I believe a Saint upon his Oath :
An honest Man may take a Knave's Advice,
But Idiots only will be couzen'd twice :
Once warn'd is well bewar'd: No flattering
   lies
Shall sooth me more to sing with winking
   Eyes, 800
And open Mouth, for fear of catching Flies.
Who Blindfold walks upon a Rivers brim,
When he should see, has he deserv'd to
   swim ?
Better, Sir Cock, let all Contention cease,
Come down, said *Reynard*, let us treat of
   Peace.
A Peace with all my Soul, said Chanticleer ;
But, with your Favour, I will treat it here :
And least the Truce with Treason should be
   mixt,
'Tis my concern to have the Tree betwixt.

THE MORAL

  In this plain Fable you th' Effect may see
Of Negligence, and fond Credulity : 811
And learn besides of Flatt'rers to beware,
Then most pernicious when they speak too
   fair.
The Cock and Fox, the Fool and Knave
   imply ;
The Truth is moral, though the Tale a Lie.
Who spoke in Parables, I dare not say ;
But sure, he knew it was a pleasing way,
Sound Sense, by plain Example, to convey.
And in a Heathen Author we may find,
That Pleasure with Instruction should be
   join'd : 820
So take the Corn, and leave the Chaff be-
   hind.

---

798 will] *Christie and others give* may
799 No] *Christie wrongly gives* not

THE FLOWER AND THE LEAF; OR, THE LADY IN THE ARBOUR.

A VISION.

Now turning from the wintry Signs, the Sun
His Course exalted through the Ram had run :
And whirling up the Skies, his Chariot drove
Through *Taurus,* and the lightsome Realms of Love,
Where *Venus* from her Orb descends in Show'rs
To glad the Ground, and paint the Fields with Flow'rs :
When first the tender Blades of Grass appear,
And Buds that yet the blast of *Eurus* fear,
Stand at the door of Life ; and doubt to cloath the Year ;
Till gentle Heat, and soft repeated Rains 10
Make the green Blood to dance within their Veins :
Then, at their Call, embolden'd out they come,
And swell the Gems, and burst the narrow Room ;
Broader and broader yet, their Blooms display,
Salute the welcome Sun, and entertain the Day.
Then from their breathing Souls the Sweets repair
To scent the Skies, and purge th' unwholesome Air :
Joy spreads the Heart, and with a general Song,
Spring issues out, and leads the jolly Months along.
     In that sweet Season, as in Bed I lay, 20
And sought in Sleep to pass the Night away,
I turned my weary Side, but still in vain,
Tho' full of youthful Health, and void of Pain :
Cares I had none to keep me from my Rest,
For Love had never enter'd in my Breast ;
I wanted nothing Fortune could supply,
Nor did she Slumber till that hour deny :

I wonder'd then, but after found it true,
Much Joy had dry'd away the balmy Dew :
Sea's wou'd be Pools without the brushing Air, 30
To curl the Waves ; and sure some little Care
Shou'd weary Nature so, to make her want repair.
     When Chaunticleer the second Watch had sung,
Scorning the Scorner Sleep from Bed I sprung.
And dressing, by the Moon, in loose Array
Pass'd out in open Air, preventing Day,
And sought a goodly Grove, as Fancy led my way.
Strait as a Line in beauteous Order stood
Of Oaks unshorn a venerable Wood ;
Fresh was the Grass beneath, and ev'ry Tree, 40
At distance planted in a due degree,
Their branching Arms in Air with equal space
Stretch'd to their Neighbours with a long Embrace :
And the new Leaves on ev'ry Bough were seen,
Some ruddy-colour'd, some of lighter green.
The painted Birds, Companions of the Spring,
Hopping from Spray to Spray, were heard to sing ;
Both Eyes and Ears receiv'd a like Delight,
Enchanting Musick, and a charming Sight.
On *Philomel* I fix'd my whole Desire ; 50
And list'n'd for the Queen of all the Quire ;
Fain would I hear her heav'nly Voice to sing ;
And wanted yet an Omen to the Spring.
     Attending long in vain ; I took the way
Which through a Path, but scarcely printed, lay ;
In narrow Mazes oft it seemed to meet,
And look'd as lightly press'd by Fairy Feet.

THE FLOWER AND THE LEAF. Text from the first and only contemporary edition, 1700, except or variants noted.

57 look'd as lightly press'd] look'd, **as lightly** press'd, *1700.*

Wandring I walk'd alone, for still methought
To some strange End so strange a Path was
    wrought :
At last it led me where an Arbour stood, 60
The sacred Receptacle of the Wood :
This Place unmark'd though oft I walk'd
    the Green,
In all my Progress I had never seen :
And seiz'd at once with Wonder and
    Delight,
Gaz'd all arround me, new to the transport-
    ing Sight.
'Twas bench'd with Turf, and, goodly to
    be seen,
The thick young Grass arose in fresher
    Green :
The Mound was newly made, no Sight cou'd
    pass
Betwixt the nice Partitions of the Grass ;
The well-united Sods so closely lay ; 70
And all arround the Shades defended it
    from Day.
For Sycamours with Eglantine were spread,
A Hedge about the Sides, a Covering over
    Head.
And so the fragrant Brier was wove between,
The Sycamour and Flow'rs were mix'd with
    Green,
That Nature seem'd to vary the Delight ;
And satisfy'd at once the Smell und Sight.
The Master Work-man of the Bow'r was
    known
Through Fairy-Lands, and built for *Oberon* ;
Who twining Leaves with such Proportion
    drew, 80
They rose by Measure, and by Rule they
    grew ;
No Mortal Tongue can half the Beauty tell,
For none but Hands divine could work so
    well.
Both Roof and Sides were like a Parlour
    made,
A soft Recess, and a cool Summer Shade ;
The Hedge was set so thick, no Foreign
    Eye
The Persons plac'd within it could espy ;
But all that pass'd without with Ease was
    seen,
As if nor Fence nor Tree was plac'd between.
'Twas border'd with a Field ; and some was
    plain 90
With Grass ; and some was sow'd with
    rising Grain.

That (now the Dew with Spangles deck'd
    the Ground,)
A sweeter spot of Earth was never found.
I look'd, and look'd, and still with new
    Delight ;
Such Joy my Soul, such Pleasures fill'd my
    Sight :
And the fresh Eglantine exhal'd a Breath ;
Whose Odours were of Pow'r to raise from
    Death.
Nor sullen Discontent nor anxious Care,
Ev'n tho' brought thither, could inhabit
    there :
But thence they fled as from their mortal
    Foe ; 100
For this sweet Place cou'd only Pleasure
    know.
    Thus as I mus'd, I cast aside my Eye,
And saw a Medlar-Tree was planted nigh.
The spreading Branches made a goodly
    Show,
And full of opening Blooms was ev'ry
    Bough :
A Goldfinch there I saw with gawdy Pride
Of painted Plumes, that hopp'd from side
    to side,
Still pecking as she pass'd ; and still she
    drew
The Sweets from ev'ry Flower, and suck'd
    the Dew : 109
Suffic'd at length, she warbled in her Throat,
And tun'd her Voice to many a merry Note,
But indistinct, and neither Sweet nor Clear,
Yet such as sooth'd my Soul, and pleas'd
    my Ear.
    Her short Performance was no sooner
    try'd,
When she I sought, the Nightingale reply'd :
So sweet, so shrill, so variously she sung,
That the grove eccho'd, and the Valleys
    rung :
And I so ravish'd with her heav'nly Note
I stood intranc'd, and had no room for
    Thought, 119
But all o'er-pow'r'd with Extasy of Bliss,
Was in a pleasing Dream of Paradice ;
At length I wak'd ; and looking round the
    Bow'r
Search'd every Tree, and pry'd on ev'ry
    Flow'r,

120 o'er-pow'r'd] o'er-pou'r'd *1700*. *Probably
a misprint.*

If anywhere by chance I might espy
The rural Poet of the Melody :
For still methought she sung not far away ;
At last I found her on a Lawrel Spray,
Close by my Side she sate, and fair in Sight,
Full in a Line, against her opposite ;
Where stood with Eglantine the Lawrel
    twin'd :   130
And both their native Sweets were well con-
    join'd.
   On the green Bank I sat, and listen'd long ;
(Sitting was more convenient for the Song !)
Nor till her Lay was ended could I move,
But wish'd to dwell for ever in the Grove.
Only methought the time too swiftly pass'd,
And ev'ry Note I fear'd would be the last.
My Sight, and Smell, and Hearing were
    employ'd,
And all three Senses in full Gust enjoy'd.
And drew alone did all the rest surpass, 140
The sweet Possession of the Fairy Place ;
Single, and conscious to my Self alone
Of Pleasures to th' excluded World unknown.
Pleasures which nowhere else, were to be
    found,
And all *Elysium* in a spot of Ground.
   Thus while I sat intent to see and hear,
And drew Perfumes of more than vital Air,
All suddenly I heard th' approaching sound
Of vocal Musick, on th' enchanted Ground :
An Host of Saints it seem'd, so full the⎫
    Quire ;   150 ⎪
As if the Bless'd above did all conspire,   ⎬
To join their Voices, and neglect the Lyre. ⎭
At length there issu'd from the Grove
    behind
A fair Assembly of the Female Kind :
A Train less fair, as ancient Fathers tell,
Seduc'd the Sons of Heaven to rebel.
I pass their Forms, and ev'ry charming
    Grace,
Less than an Angel would their Worth
    debase :
But their Attire like Liveries of a kind,
All rich and rare is fresh within my Mind.
In Velvet white as Snow the Troop was
    gown'd,   161
The Seams with sparkling Emeralds set
    around ;

Their Hoods and Sleeves the same : And
    purfled o'er
With Diamonds, Pearls, and all the shining
    store
Of Eastern Pomp : Their long descending
    Train
With Rubies edg'd, and Saphires, swept the
    Plain :
High on their Heads, with Jewels richly set
Each Lady wore a radiant Coronet.
Beneath the Circles, al the Quire was grac'd
With Chaplets green on their fair Foreheads
    plac'd,   170
Of Lawrel some, of Woodbine many more ;
And Wreaths of *Agnus castus* others bore :
These last, who with those Virgin Crowns
    were dress'd,
Appear'd in higher Honour than the rest.
They danc'd around, but in the midst was⎫
    seen   ⎪
A Lady of a more majestique Mien ;   ⎬
By Stature, and by Beauty mark'd their   ⎪
    Sovereign Queen.   ⎭
   She in the midst began with sober Grace ;
Her Servants Eyes were fix'd upon her Face,
And as she mov'd or turn'd, her Motions
    view'd,   180
Her Measures kept, and Step by Step
    pursu'd.
Methought she trod the Ground with
    greater Grace,
With more of Godhead shining in her Face ;
And as in Beauty she surpass'd the Quire,
So, nobler than the rest, was her Attire.
A crown of ruddy Gold inclos'd her Brow,
Plain without Pomp, and Rich without
    a Show :
A Branch of *Agnus castus* in her Hand
She bore aloft (her Scepter of Command ;)
Admir'd, ador'd by all the circling Crowd,
For wheresoe'er she turn'd her Face, they
    bow'd :   191
And as she danc'd, a Roundelay she sung,
In honour of the Lawrel, ever young :
She rais'd her Voice on high, and sung⎫
    so clear,   ⎪
The Fawns came scudding from the Groves ⎬
    to hear :   ⎪
And all the bending Forest lent an Ear.   ⎭
At ev'ry Close she made, th' attending
    Throng
Reply'd, and bore the Burden of the
    Song :

157 Forms] *Christie wrongly gives* form
159 kind,] *Christie omitted the comma, but no
doubt of* a kind *means 'of one kind', i.e. uniform.*

So just, so small, yet in so sweet a Note,
It seem'd the Musick melted in the Throat.
　Thus dancing on, and singing as they
　　danc'd, 201
They to the middle of the Mead advanc'd:
Till round my Arbour, a new Ring they
　made,
And footed it about the secret Shade :
O'erjoy'd to see the jolly Troop so near,
But somewhat aw'd I shook with holy Fear ;
Yet not so much, but that I noted well
Who did the most in Song, or Dance excel.
　Not long I had observ'd, when from afar
I heard a suddain Symphony of War ; 210
The neighing Coursers, and the Soldiers cry,
And sounding Trumps that seem'd to tear
　the Sky.
I saw soon after this, behind the Grove
From whence the Ladies did in order move,
Come issuing out in Arms a Warrior-Train,
That like a Deluge pour'd upon the Plain :
On barbed Steeds they rode in proud Array,
Thick as the College of the Bees in *May*,
When swarming o'er the dusky Fields they
　fly,
New to the Flow'rs, and intercept the Sky.
So fierce they drove, their Coursers were so
　fleet, 221
That the Turf trembled underneath their
　Feet.
　To tell their costly Furniture were long,
The Summers Day wou'd end before the
　Song :
To purchase but the Tenth of all their Store
Would make the mighty *Persian* Monarch
　poor.
Yet what I can, I will ; before the rest
The Trumpets issu'd in white Mantles dress'd:
A numerous Troop, and all their Heads ⎫
　around　　　　　　　　　　　　　　　⎪
With Chaplets green of Cerrial-Oak were ⎬
　crown'd, 230　　　　　　　　　　　　⎪
And at each Trumpet was a Banner bound; ⎭
Which waving in the Wind display'd at large
Their Master's Coat of Arms, and Knightly
　Charge.
Broad were the Banners, and of snowy Hue,
A purer Web the Silk-worm never drew.
The chief about their Necks the Scutcheons
　wore,
With Orient Pearls and Jewels pouder'd o'er:

Broad were their Collars too, and ev'ry one
Was set about with many a costly Stone.
Next these of Kings at Arms a goodly Train,
In proud Array came prancing o'er the
　Plain : 241
Their Cloaks were Cloth of Silver mix'd with
　Gold,
And Garlands green arround their Temples
　roll'd :
Rich Crowns were on their royal Scutcheons
　plac'd,
With Saphires, Diamonds, and with Rubies
　grac'd :
And as the Trumpets their appearance
　made,
So these in Habits were alike array'd ;
But with a Pace more sober, and more slow :
And twenty, Rank in Rank, they rode a-row.
The Pursevants came next, in number more ;
And like the Heralds each his Scutcheon
　bore : 251
Clad in white Velvet all their Troop they led,
With each an Oaken Chaplet on his Head.
　Nine royal Knights in equal Rank succeed,
Each Warrior mounted on a fiery Steed :
In golden Armour glorious to behold ;
The Rivets of their Arms were nail'd with
　Gold.
Their Surcoats of white Ermin-Fur were
　made ;
With Cloth of Gold between that cast a
　glitt'ring Shade.
The Trappings of their Steeds were of the
　same ; 260
The golden Fringe ev'n set the Ground on
　flame,
And drew a precious Trail : A Crown divine
Of Lawrel did about their Temples twine.
　Three Henchmen were for ev'ry Knight
　　assign'd,
All in rich Livery clad, and of a kind :
White Velvet, but unshorn, for Cloaks they
　wore,
And each within his Hand a Truncheon bore:
The foremost held a Helm of rare device ;
A Prince's Ransom wou'd not pay the
　Price. 269
The second bore the Buckler of his Knight, ⎫
The third of Cornel-Wood a Spear upright, ⎬
Headed with piercing Steel, and polish'd ⎪
　bright.　　　　　　　　　　　　　　⎭

---

229 Troop] *Christie wrongly gives* group　　　253 Oaken] *Christie wrongly gives* open

Like to their Lords their Equipage was seen,
And all their Foreheads crown'd with Gar-
    lands green.
    And after these came arm'd with Spear
    and Shield
An Host so great as cover'd all the Field :
And all their Foreheads, like the Knights
    before,
With Lawrels ever green were shaded o'er,
Or Oak, or other Leaves of lasting kind,
Tenacious of the Stem and firm against the
    Wind.   280
Some in their Hands, besides the Lance and
    Shield.
The Boughs of Woodbind or of Hauthorn
    held,
Or Branches for their mistique Emblems
    took,
Of Palm, of Lawrel, or of Cerrial Oak.
    Thus marching to the Trumpets lofty
    Sound,
Drawn in two Lines adverse they wheel'd
    around,
And in the middle Meadow took their
    Ground.
Among themselves the Turney they divide
In equal Squadrons rang'd on either side.
Then turn'd their Horses Heads, and Man
    to Man,   290
And Steed to Steed oppos'd, the Justs
    began.
They lightly set their Lances in the rest,
And, at the Sign, against each other press'd
They met, I sitting at my Ease beheld
The mix'd Events, and Fortunes of the Field.
Some broke their Spears, some tumbled
    Horse and Man,
And round the Fields the lighten'd Coursers
    ran.
An Hour and more like Tides, in equal sway
They rush'd, and won by turns, and lost
    the Day :
At length the Nine (who still together held)
Their fainting Foes to shameful Flight
    compell'd,   301
And with resistless Force, o'er-ran the Field.
Thus, to their Fame, when finish'd was the
    Fight,
The Victors from their lofty Steeds alight :

Like them dismounted all the Warlike Train,
And two by two proceeded o'er the Plain :
Till to the fair Assembly they advanc'd,
Who near the secret Arbour sung and danc'd.
    The Ladies left their Measures at the
    Sight,
To meet the Chiefs returning from the
    Fight,   310
And each with open Arms embrac'd her
    chosen Knight.
Amid the Plain a spreading Lawrel stood,
The Grace and Ornament of all the Wood :
That pleasing Shade they sought, a soft
    Retreat
From suddain *April* Show'rs, a Shelter from
    the Heat.
Her leavy Arms with such extent were spread,
So near the Clouds was her aspiring Head,
That Hosts of Birds that wing the liquid Air,
Perch'd in the Boughs, had nightly Lodging
    there.
And Flocks of Sheep beneath the Shade
    from far   320
Might hear the ratling Hail, and wintry War ;
From Heav'ns Inclemency here found
    retreat,
Enjoy'd the cool, and shun'd the scorching
    Heat :
A hundred Knights might there at Ease
    abide ;
And ev'ry Knight a Lady by his side :
The Trunk it self such Odours did bequeath
That a Moluccan Breeze to these was
    common Breath.
The Lords, and Ladies here approaching,
    paid
Their Homage, with a low Obeisance made :
And seem'd to venerate the sacred Shade.
These Rites perform'd, their Pleasures they
    pursue,   331
With Songs of Love, and mix with Measures
    new ;
Around the holy Tree their Dance they
    frame,
And ev'ry Champion leads his chosen Dame.
    I cast my Sight upon the farther Field,
And a fresh Object of Delight beheld :
For from the Region of the West I heard
New Musick sound, and a new Troop
    appear'd ;

---

297 Coursers] Courses *1700*. *A misprint.*
298 Tides, in equal sway] *Christie gives* tides
in equal sway
   301 Flight] Fight *1700*. *A misprint.*

---

332 Measures] *Derrick wrongly gives* pleasures

Of Knights, and Ladies mix'd a jolly Band,
But all on Foot they march'd, and Hand in
   Hand. 340
The Ladies dress'd in rich Symarrs were
   seen
Of *Florence* Satten, flower'd with White and
   Green,
And for a Shade betwixt the bloomy
   Gridelin.
The Borders of their Petticoats below
Were guarded thick with Rubies on a-row ;
And ev'ry Damsel wore upon her Head
Of Flow'rs a Garland blended White and
   Red.
Attir'd in Mantles all the Knights were seen
That gratify'd the View with chearful Green:
Their Chaplets of their Ladies Colours were
Compos'd of White and Red, to shade their
   shining Hair. 351
Before the merry Troop the Minstrels play'd,
All in their Master's Liveries were array'd,
And clad in Green, and on their Temples
   wore
The Chaplets White and Red their Ladies
   bore.
Their Instruments were various in their
   kind,
Some for the Bow, and some for breathing
   Wind :
The Sawtry, Pipe, and Hautbois noisy band,
And the soft Lute trembling beneath the
   touching Hand.
A Tuft of Dasies on a flow'ry Lay 360
They saw, and thitherward they bent their
   way :
To this both Knights and Dames their
   Homage made,
And due Obeisance to the Daisy paid.
And then the Band of Flutes began to play,
To which a Lady sung a Virelay ;
And still at ev'ry close she wou'd repeat
The Burden of the Song, *The Daisy is so*
sweet.
The Daisy is so sweet when she begun,
The Troop of Knights and Dames con-
   tinu'd on.
The Concert and the Voice so charm'd my
   Ear, 370
And sooth'd my Soul, that it was Heav'n
   to hear.

360 Lay] *This is the Northamptonshire spell-*
ing, wrongly taken by Dr. Saintsbury for a
misprint and given by him and Christie as lea

But soon their Pleasure pass'd : At Noon
   of Day
The Sun with sultry Beams began to play :
Not *Syrius* shoots a fiercer Flame from high,
When with his pois'nous Breath he blasts
   the Sky :
Then droop'd the fading Flow'rs (their
   Beauty fled)
And clos'd their sickly Eyes, and hung the
   Head ;
And, rivell'd up with Heat, lay dying in
   their Bed.
The Ladies gasp'd, and scarcely could
   respire ;
The Breath they drew, no longer Air, but
   Fire ; 380
The fainty Knights were scorch'd ; and
   knew not where
To run for Shelter, for no Shade was near.
And after this the gath'ring Clouds amain
Pour'd down a Storm of rattling Hail and
   Rain ;
And lightning flashed betwixt : The Field,
   and Flow'rs,
Burnt up before, were bury'd in the Show'rs.
The Ladies, and the Knights no Shelter nigh,
Bare to the Weather, and the wintry Sky,
Were dropping wet, disconsolate, and wan,
And through their thin Array receiv'd the
   Rain. 390
  While those in White, protected by the
   Tree,
Saw pass the vain Assault, and stood from
   Danger free.
But as Compassion mov'd their gentle Minds,
When ceas'd the Storm, and silent were the
   Winds,
Displeas'd at what, not suff'ring they had
   seen,
They went to chear the Faction of the Green.
The Queen in white Array before her Band,
Saluting, took her Rival by the Hand ;
So did the Knights and Dames, with courtly
   grace
And with Behaviour sweet their Foes em-
   brace. 400
Then thus the Queen with Lawrel on her
   Brow :
Fair Sister, I have suffer'd in your Woe :
Nor shall be wanting ought within my Pow'r
For your Relief in my refreshing Bow'r.
That other answer'd with a lowly Look,
And soon the gracious Invitation took

For ill at ease both she and all her Train
The scorching Sun had born, and beating
  Rain.
Like Courtesy was us'd by all in White,
Each Dame a Dame receiv'd, and ev'ry
  Knight a Knight.   410
The Lawrel-Champions with their Swords
  invade
The neighb'ring Forests where the Justs were
  made,
And Serewood from the rotten Hedges
  took,
And Seeds of Latent-Fire from Flints pro-
  voke :
A chearful Blaze arose, and by the Fire
They warm'd their frozen Feet, and dry'd
  their wet Attire.
Refresh'd with Heat the Ladies sought
  around
For virtuous Herbs which gathered from the
  ground
They squeez'd the Juice ; and cooling
  Ointment made,
Which on their Sun-burnt Cheeks, and their
  chapt Skins they laid :   420
Then sought green Salads, which they bad
  'em eat,
A Soveraign Remedy for inward Heat.
  The Lady of the Leaf ordain'd a Feast,
And made the Lady of the Flow'r her Guest :
When lo, a Bow'r ascended on the Plain,
With suddain Seats adorn'd, and large for
  either Train.
This Bow'r was near my pleasant Arbour
  plac'd,
That I could hear and see whatever pass'd
The Ladies sat, with each a Knight between,
Distinguish'd by their Colours White and
  Green ;   430
The vanquish'd Party with the Victors
  join'd,
Nor wanted sweet Discourse, the Banquet
  of the Mind.
Mean time the Minstrels play'd on either
  side
Vain of their Art, and for the Mast'ry vy'd
The sweet Contention lasted for an Hour,
And reach'd my secret Arbour from the
  Bow'r.
  The Sun was set ; and Vesper to supply
His absent Beams, had lighted up the Sky ;
When *Philomel*, officious all the Day
To sing the Service of th' ensuing *May*,   440

Fled from her Lawrel Shade, and wing'd
  her Flight
Directly to the Queen array'd in White :
And hopping sate familiar on her Hand,
A new Musitian, and increas'd the Band.
  The Goldfinch, who to shun the scalding
    Heat,
  Had chang'd the Medlar for a safer Seat,
  And hid in Bushes scap'd the bitter Show'r,
  Now perch'd upon the Lady of the Flow'r ;
  And either Songster holding out their
    Throats,
  And folding up their Wings renew'd their
    Notes :   450
As if all Day, preluding to the Fight,
They only had rehears'd, to sing by Night.
The Banquet ended, and the Battle done,
They danc'd by Star-light and the friendly
  Moon :
And when they were to part, the Laureat
  Queen
Supply'd with Steeds the Lady of the
  Green,
Her, and her Train conducting on the way
The Moon to follow, and avoid the Day.
  This when I saw, inquisitive to know
The secret Moral of the Mystique Show,   460
I started from my Shade, in hopes to find
Some Nymph to satisfy my longing Mind :
And as my fair Adventure fell, I found
A Lady all in White, with Lawrel crown'd,
Who clos'd the Rear and softly pac'd along,
Repeating to her self the former Song.
With due respect my Body I inclin'd,
As to some Being of Superiour Kind,
And made my Court, according to the Day,
Wishing her Queen and Her a happy *May*.
Great Thanks my Daughter, with a gracious
  Bow   471
She said ; and I who much desir'd to know
Of whence she was, yet fearful how to break
My Mind, adventur'd humbly thus to speak
Madam, Might I presume and not offend,
So may the Stars and shining Moon attend
Your Nightly Sports, as you vouchsafe to⎫
  tell,   ⎪
What Nymphs they were who mortal ⎬
  Forms excel,   ⎪
And what the Knights who fought in listed⎭
  Fields so well.
  To this the Dame reply'd : Fair daughter
    know,   480
That what you saw, was all a Fairy Show :

And all those airy Shapes you now behold
Were humane Bodies once, and cloath'd with
earthly Mold.
Our Souls, not yet prepar'd for upper Light,
Till Doomsday wander in the Shades of
Night ;
This only Holiday of all the Year,
We priviledg'd in Sun-shine may appear :
With Songs and Dance we celebrate the Day,
And with due Honours usher in the *May*.
At other Times we reign by Night alone, 490
And posting through the Skies pursue the
Moon :
But when the Morn arises, none are found ;
For cruel *Demogorgon* walks the round,
And if he finds a Fairy lag in Light,
He drives the Wretch before ; and lashes
into Night.
  All Courteous are by Kind ; and ever proud
With friendly Offices to help the Good.
In every Land we have a larger Space
Than what is known to you of mortal Race ;
Where we with Green adorn our Fairy
Bow'rs, 500
And even this Grove unseen before, is ours.
Know farther ; Ev'ry Lady cloath'd in
White,
And crown'd with Oak and Lawrel ev'ry
Knight,
Are Servants to the Leaf, by Liveries known
Of Innocence ; and I myself am one.
Saw you not Her so graceful to behold,
In white Attire, and crown'd with Radiant
Gold ?
The Soveraign Lady of our Land is She,
Diana call'd, the Queen of Chastity : 509
And, for the spotless Name of Maid she bears,
That *Agnus castus* in her Hand appears ;
And all her Train with leavy Chaplets
crown'd
Were for unblam'd Virginity renown'd
But those the chief and highest in Command
Who bear those holy Branches in their
Hand :
The Knights adorned with Lawrel-Crowns,
  are they,
Whom Death nor Danger ever cou'd dis-
  may,
Victorious Names, who made the World
  obey :
Who while they liv'd, in Deeds of Arms
  excell'd,
And after Death for Deities were held. 520

But those who wear the Woodbine on their
Brow
Were Knights of Love, who never broke
their Vow :
Firm to their plighted Faith, and ever free
From Fears and fickle Chance, and Jealousy.
The Lords and Ladies, who the Woodbine
bear,
As true as *Tristram* and *Isotta* were.
  But what are those said I, th' unconquered
Nine,
Who crown'd with Lawrel-Wreaths, in
golden Armour shine ?
And who the Knights in Green, and what
the Train 529
Of Ladies dress'd with Daisies on the Plain ?
Why both the Bands in Worship disagree,
And some adore the Flow'r, and some the
Tree ?
  Just is your Suit, fair daughter, said the
Dame,
Those lawrell'd Chiefs were Men of mighty
Fame ;
Nine Worthies were they call'd of diff'rent
Rites,
Three Jews, three Pagans, and three
Christian Knights.
These, as you see, ride foremost in the Field, ⎫
As they the foremost Rank of Honour held, ⎬
And all in Deeds of Chivalry excell'd.   ⎭
Their Temples wreath'd with Leafs, that
still renew ;   540
For deathless Lawrel is the Victor's due.
Who bear the Bows were Knights in *Arthur's*
Reign,
Twelve they, and twelve the Peers of *Charle-
main* :
For Bows the Strength of brawny Arms imply
Emblems of Valour, and of Victory.
Behold an Order yet of newer Date
Doubling their Number, equal in their State ;
Our *England's* Ornament, the Crown's
Defence,
In Battle brave, Protectors of their Prince
Unchang'd by Fortune, to their Soveraign
true,   550
For which their manly Legs are bound with
Blue.
These, of the Garter call'd, of Faith un- ⎫
stain'd,   ⎬
In fighting Fields the Lawrel have obtain'd, ⎬
And well repaid these Honours which they ⎭
gain'd.

The Lawrel-Wreaths were first by *Cæsar* worn,
And still they *Cæsar's* Successors adorn :
One Leaf of this is Immortality,
And more of Worth, than all the World can buy.

 One Doubt remains, said I, the Dames in Green,
What were their Qualities, and who their Queen ?   560
Flora commands, said she, those Nymphs and Knights,
Who liv'd in slothful Ease, and loose Delights :
Who never Acts of Honour durst pursue,
The Men inglorious Knights, the Ladies all untrue :
Who nurs'd in Idleness, and train'd in Courts,
Pass'd all their precious Hours in Plays, and Sports,
Till Death behind came stalking on, unseen,
And wither'd (like the Storm) the freshness of their Green.
These, and their Mates, enjoy the present Hour,
And therefore pay their Homage to the Flow'r.   570
But Knights in Knightly Deeds should persevere,
And still continue what at first they were ;
Continue, and proceed in Honour's fair Career.
No room for Cowardise, or dull Delay ;
From Good to Better they should urge their way.
For this with golden Spurs the Chiefs are grac'd,
With pointed Rowels arm'd to mend their haste ;
For this with lasting Leaves their Brows are bound,
For Lawrel is the Sign of Labour crown'd ;
Which bears the bitter Blast, nor shaken falls to Ground :   580
From Winter-Winds it suffers no decay,
For ever fresh and fair, and ev'ry Month is *May*.

Ev'n when the vital Sap retreats below,
Ev'n when the hoary Head is hid in Snow ;
The Life is in the Leaf, and still between
The Fits of falling Snows, appears the streaky Green.
Not so the Flow'r which lasts for little space,
A short-liv'd Good, and an uncertain Grace ;
This way and that the feeble Stem is driv'n,
Weak to sustain the Storms, and Injuries of Heav'n.   590
Prop'd by the Spring, it lifts aloft the Head,
But of a sickly Beauty, soon to shed ;
In Summer living, and in Winter dead.
For Things of tender Kind for Pleasure made
Shoot up with swift Increase, and suddain are decay'd.

 With humble Words, the wisest I could frame,
And profer'd Service I repaid the Dame :
That of her Grace she gave her Maid to know
The secret meaning of this moral Show.
And she to prove what Profit I had made 600
Of mystique Truth, in Fables first convey'd,
Demanded, till the next returning *May*,
Whether the Leaf or Flow'r I would obey ?
I chose the Leaf ; she smil'd with sober Chear,
And wish'd me fair Adventure for the Year,
And gave me Charms and Sigils, for defence
Against ill Tongues that scandal Innocence :
But I, said she, my Fellows must pursue,
Already past the Plain, and out of view.

 We parted thus ; I homeward sped my way, 610
Bewilder'd in the Wood till Dawn of Day :
And met the merry Crew who danc'd about the *May*.
Then late refresh'd with Sleep I rose to write
The visionary Vigils of the Night.
Blush, as thou may'st, my little Book for Shame,
Nor hope with homely Verse to purchase Fame ;
For such thy Maker chose ; and so design'd
Thy simple Style to suit thy lowly Kind.

THE WIFE OF BATH HER TALE.

In Days of Old, when *Arthur* fill'd the Throne,
Whose Acts and Fame to Foreign Lands
  were blown,
The King of Elfs and little fairy Queen
Gamboll'd on Heaths, and danc'd on ev'ry
  Green ;
And where the jolly Troop had led the
  Round,
The Grass unbidden rose, and mark'd the
  Ground.
Nor darkling did they dance, the Silver
  Light
Of *Phœbe* serv'd to guide their Steps
  aright,
And, with their Tripping pleas'd, prolong'd
  the Night.
Her Beams they follow'd, where at full
  she plaid,   10
Nor longer than she shed her Horns they
  staid,
From thence with airy Flight to Foreign
  Lands convey'd.
Above the rest our *Britain* held they dear,
More solemnly they kept their Sabbaths
  here,
And made more spacious Rings, and revell'd
  half the Year.
  I speak of ancient Times ; for now the
  Swain
Returning late may pass the Woods in vain,
And never hope to see the nightly Train :
In vain the Dairy now with Mints is dress'd,
The Dairy-Maid expects no Fairy Guest, 20
To skim the Bowls and after pay the Feast.
She sighs, and shakes her empty Shoes in
  vain,
No Silver Penny to reward her Pain :
For Priests with Pray'rs, and other godly
  Geer,
Have made the merry Goblins disappear ;
And where they plaid their merry Pranks
  before,
Have sprinkled Holy Water on the Floor :
And Fry'rs that through the wealthy
  Regions run
Thick as the Motes, that twinkle in the Sun,

Resort to Farmers rich, and bless their
  Halls   30
And exorcise the Beds, and cross the Walls :
This makes the Fairy Quires forsake the
  Place,
When once 'tis hallow'd with the Rites of
  Grace :
But in the Walks, where wicked Elves have
  been,
The Learning of the Parish now is seen,
The Midnight Parson posting o'er the Green
With Gown tuck'd up to Wakes ; for
  Sunday next
With humming Ale encouraging his Text ;
Nor wants the holy Leer to Country-Girl
  betwixt.
From Fiends and Imps he sets the Village
  free,   40
There haunts not any Incubus, but He.
The Maids and Women need no Danger fear
To walk by Night, and Sanctity so near :
For by some Haycock or some shady Thorn
He bids his Beads both Even-song and Morn.
  It so befel in this King *Arthur's* Reign,
A lusty Knight was pricking o'er the Plain ;
A Bachelor he was, and of the courtly Train.
It happen'd as he rode, a Damsel gay   49
In Russet-Robes to Market took her way ;
Soon on the Girl he cast an amorous Eye,
So strait she walk'd, and on her Pasterns
  high :
If seeing her behind he lik'd her Pace,
Now turning short he better lik'd her Face.
He lights in hast, and, full of Youthful
  Fire,
By Force accomplish'd his obscene Desire
This done away he rode, not unespy'd,
For swarming at his Back the Country
  cry'd ;
And once in view they never lost the Sight,
But seiz'd, and pinion'd brought to Court
  the Knight.   60
  Then Courts of Kings were held in high
  Renown,
E'er made the common Brothels of the
  Town ;
There, Virgins honourable Vows receiv'd,
But chast as Maids in Monasteries liv'd :

THE WIFE OF BATH'S TALE. Text from the
original and only contemporary edition, 1700.
7 dance] *Some editors wrongly give* glance

60 Court] court *1700*.

The King himself to Nuptial Ties a Slave,
No bad Example to his Poets gave ;
And they not bad, but in a vicious Age
Had not to please the Prince debauch'd the
    Stage.
    Now what shou'd *Arthur* do ? He lov'd
    the Knight,
But Soveraign Monarchs are the Source of
    Right :   70
Mov'd by the Damsels Tears and common
    Cry,
He doom'd the brutal Ravisher to die.
But fair *Geneura* rose in his Defence,
And pray'd so hard for Mercy from the
    Prince ;
That to his Queen the King th' Offender
    gave,
And left it in her Pow'r to Kill or Save :
This gracious Act the Ladies all approve,
Who thought it much a Man shou'd die for
    Love ;
And with their Mistress join'd in close⎫
    Debate,   ⎪
(Covering their Kindness with dissembled ⎬
    Hate ;)   80 ⎪
If not to free him, to prolong his Fate.   ⎭
At last agreed, they call'd him by consent
Before the Queen and Female Parliament.
And the fair Speaker, rising from her Chair
Did thus the Judgment of the House declare.
    Sir Knight, tho' I have ask'd thy Life,
    yet still
Thy Destiny depends upon my Will :
Nor hast thou other Surety than the Grace
Not due to thee from our offended Race.
But as our Kind is of a softer Mold,   90
And cannot Blood without a Sigh behold,
I grant the Life ; reserving still the
    Pow'r
To take the Forfeit when I see my Hour ;
Unless thy Answer to my next Demand
Shall set Thee free from our avenging
    Hand ;
The Question, whose Solution I require,
Is what the Sex of Women most desire ?
In this Dispute thy Judges are at Strife ;
Beware, for on thy Wit depends thy Life
Yet (lest surpriz'd, unknowing what to say,
Thou damn thy self) we give thee farther
    Day :   101
A Year is thine to wander at thy Will :
And learn from others, if thou want'st the
    Skill.

But, not to hold our Proffer [as] in Scorn,
Good Sureties will we have for thy return ;
That at the time prefix'd thou shalt obey,
And at thy Pledges Peril keep thy Day.
    Woe was the Knight at this severe
    Command !
But well he knew 'twas bootless to with-
    stand :
The Terms accepted as the Fair ordain, 110
He put in Bail for his return again ;
And promis'd Answer at the Day assign'd,
The best, with Heav'n's Assistance, he could
    find.
    His Leave thus taken, on his Way he went ⎫
With heavy Heart, and full of Discontent, ⎬
Misdoubting much, and fearful of th' Event. ⎭
'Twas hard the Truth of such a Point to find,
As was not yet agreed among the Kind.
Thus on he went ; still anxious more and
    more,
Ask'd all he met ; and knock'd at ev'ry
    Door ;   120
Enquir'd of Men ; but made his chief
    Request
To learn from Women what they lov'd the
    best.
They answer'd each according to her Mind,
To please her self, not all the Female Kind.
One was for Wealth, another was for Place :
Crones old and ugly, wish'd a better Face ;
The Widow's Wish was oftentimes to Wed ;
The wanton Maids were all for Sport a Bed.
Some said the Sex were pleas'd with hand-
    som Lies,
And some gross Flatt'ry lov'd without
    disguise :   130
Truth is, says one, he seldom fails to win
Who Flatters well ; for that's our darling Sin.
But long Attendance, and a duteous Mind,
Will work ev'n with the wisest of the Kind.
One thought the Sexes prime Felicity
Was from the Bonds of Wedlock to be
    free ;

---

104 Proffer [as] in Scorn] Proffer in Scorn *1700.
*A word has dropt out in the printing. Warton
gives* proffer'd turn in scorn *and is followed by
Scott and Saintsbury, but the conjecture has
little to recommend it. Christie gives* proffer for
in scorn, *a reading which Saintsbury justly
stigmatises as meaningless. The conjecture in
the text is mine. The added word makes no
appreciable difference in the sense, and the same
word, though no editor seems to have noticed the
fact, has dropt out in* 543 *below.*

Their Pleasures, Hours, and Actions all
    their own,
And uncontroll'd to give Account to none.
Some wish a Husband-Fool; but such are
    curst,
For Fools perverse, of Husbands are the
    worst: 140
All Women wou'd be counted Chast and
    Wise,
Nor should our Spouses see, but with our
    Eyes;
For Fools will prate; and tho' they want
    the Wit
To find close Faults, yet open Blots will hit:
Tho' better for their Ease to hold their
    Tongue,
For Womankind was never in the Wrong.
So Noise ensues, and Quarrels last for Life;
The Wife abhors the Fool, the Fool the Wife.
And some Men say, that great Delight
    have we,
To be for Truth extoll'd, and Secrecy: 150
And constant in one Purpose still to dwell;
And not our Husband's Counsels to reveal.
But that's a Fable: for our Sex is frail,
Inventing rather than not tell a Tale.
Like leaky Sives no Secrets we can hold:
Witness the famous Tale that *Ovid* told.
  Midas the King, as in his Book appears,
By *Phœbus* was endow'd with Asses Ears,
Which under his long Locks, he well con-
    ceal'd   159
(As Monarch's Vices must not be reveal'd),
For fear the People have 'em in the Wind,
Who long ago were neither Dumb nor Blind;
Nor apt to think from Heav'n their Title
    springs,
Since *Jove* and *Mars* left off begetting Kings.
This *Midas* knew; and durst communicate
To none but to his Wife, his Ears of State;
One must be trusted, and he thought her fit,
As passing prudent; and a parlous Wit.
To this sagacious Confessor he went,
And told her what a Gift the Gods had sent;
But told it under Matrimonial Seal,   171
With strict Injunction never to reveal.
The Secret heard she plighted him her Troth,
(And sacred sure is every Woman's Oath)
The royal Malady should rest unknown
Both for her Husband's Honour and her
    own:
But ne'ertheless she pin'd with Discontent;
The Counsel rumbled till it found a vent.

The Thing she knew she was oblig'd to hide;⎫
By Int'rest and by Oath the Wife was ty'd;⎪
But if she told it not, the Woman dy'd. 181⎪
Loath to betray a Husband and a Prince,⎬
But she must burst, or blab; and no⎪
    pretence⎪
Of Honour ty'd her Tongue from Self-⎭
    defence.
A marshy Ground commodiously was near,
Thither she ran, and held her Breath for
    fear,
Lest if a Word she spoke of any Thing,
That Word might be the Secret of the King.
Thus full of Counsel to the Fen she went,
Grip'd all the way, and longing for a vent:
Arriv'd, by pure Necessity compell'd,   191
On her majestick mary-bones she kneel'd:
Then to the Waters-brink she laid her Head,
And, as a Bittour bumps within a Reed,
To thee alone, O Lake, she said, I tell
(And as thy Queen command thee to con-
    ceal)
Beneath his Locks the King my Husband
    wears
A goodly Royal pair of Asses Ears:
Now I have eas'd my Bosom of the Pain
Till the next longing Fit return again! 200
  Thus through a Woman was the Secret
    known;
Tell us, and in effect you tell the Town:
But to my Tale: The knight with heavy
    Cheer,
Wandring in vain, had now consum'd the
    Year:
One Day was only left to solve the Doubt,
Yet knew no more than when he first set
    out.
But home he must: And as th' Award had
    been,
Yield up his Body Captive to the Queen.
In this despairing State he hap'd to ride,
As Fortune led him, by a Forest-side: 210
Lonely the Vale, and full of Horror stood,
Brown with the shade of a religious Wood:
When full before him at the Noon of night,
(The Moon was up, and shot a gleamy Light)
He saw a Quire of Ladies in a round,
That featly footing seem'd to skim the
    Ground:
Thus dancing Hand in Hand, so light they
    were,
He knew not where they trod, on Earth or
    Air.

At speed he drove, and came a suddain
Guest,
In hope where many Women were, at least,
Some one by chance might answer his
Request.   221
But faster than his Horse the Ladies flew,
And in a trice were vanish'd out of view.
One only Hag remain'd : But fowler far
Than Grandame Apes in *Indian* Forests are :
Against a wither'd Oak she lean'd her
weight,
Prop'd on her trusty Staff, not half upright,
And drop'd an awkard Court'sy to the
Knight.
Then said, What make you, Sir, so late
abroad
Without a Guide, and this no beaten Road ?
Or want you aught that here you hope to
find,   231
Or travel for some Trouble in your Mind ?
The last I guess ; and, if I read aright,
Those of our Sex are bound to serve a
Knight :
Perhaps good Counsel may your Grief
asswage,
Then tell your pain : For Wisdom is in Age.
To this the Knight : Good Mother, wou'd
you know
The secret Cause and Spring of all my
Woe ?
My Life must with to Morrow's Light expire,
Unless I tell, what Women most desire: 240
Now cou'd you help me at this hard Essay,
Or for your inborn Goodness, or for Pay :
Yours is my Life, redeem'd by your Advice,
Ask what you please, and I will pay the
Price :
The proudest Kerchief of the Court shall
rest
Well satisfy'd of what they love the best.
Plight me thy Faith, quoth she : That what
I ask
Thy Danger over, and perform'd the Task ;
That shalt thou give for Hire of thy Demand;
Here take thy Oath, and seal it on my
Hand ;   250
I warrant thee, on Peril of my Life,
Thy Words shall please both Widow, Maid,
and Wife.

More Words there needed not to move the
Knight,
To take her Offer, and his Truth to plight.
With that she spread her Mantle on the
Ground,
And first enquiring whether he was bound,
Bade him not fear, tho' long and rough the
Way,
At Court he should arrive e'er break of Day
His Horse should find the way without
a Guide.
She said: With Fury they began to ride, 260
He on the midst, the Beldam at his Side.
The Horse, what Devil drove I cannot tell,
But only this, they sped their Journey well :
And all the way the Crone inform'd the
Knight,
How he should answer the Demand aright.
To Court they came: The News was
quickly spread
Of his returning to redeem his Head.
The Female Senate was assembled soon,
With all the Mob of Women in the Town :
The Queen sate Lord Chief Justice of the
Hall,   270
And bad the Cryer cite the Criminal.
The Knight appear'd ; and Silence they
proclaim,
Then first the *Culprit* answer'd to his Name ;
And after Forms of Laws, was last requir'd
To name the Thing that Women most desir'd.
Th' Offender, taught his Lesson by the
way,
And by his Counsel order'd what to say,
Thus bold began ; My Lady Liege, said he,
What all your Sex desire is *Soveraignty*.
The Wife affects her Husband to command ;
All must be hers, both Mony, House, and
Land.   281
The Maids are Mistresses ev'n in their Name ;
And of their Servants full Dominion claim,
This, at the Peril of my Head, I say
A blunt plain Truth, the Sex aspires to
sway,
You to rule all ; while we, like Slaves,
obey.
There was not one, or Widow, Maid, or
Wife,
But said the Knight had well deserv'd his
Life.

Ev'n fair *Geneura*, with a Blush confess'd,
The Man had found what Women love the
best.   290
Upstarts the Beldam, who was there
unseen,
And Reverence made, accosted thus the
Queen.
My Liege, said she, before the Court arise,
May I poor Wretch find Favour in your Eyes,
To grant my just Request : 'Twas I who
taught
The Knight this Answer, and inspir'd his
Thought.
None but a Woman could a Man direct
To tell us Women, what we most affect.
But first I swore him on his Knightly Troth,
(And here demand performance of his
Oath)   300
To grant the Boon that next I should desire ;
He gave his Faith, and I expect my Hire :
My Promise is fulfill'd : I sav'd his Life,
And claim his Debt, to take me for his Wife.
The Knight was ask'd, nor cou'd his Oath
deny,
But hop'd they would not force him to
comply.
The Women, who would rather wrest the
Laws,
Than let a Sister-Plaintiff lose the Cause,
(As Judges on the Bench more gracious are,
And more attent to Brothers of the Bar) 310
Cry'd, one and all, the Suppliant should
have Right,
And to the Grandame-Hag adjudg'd the
Knight.
    In vain he sigh'd, and oft with Tears
desir'd
Some reasonable Sute might be requir'd.
But still the Crone was constant to her Note ;
The more he spoke, the more she stretch'd
her Throat.
In vain he proffer'd all his Goods, to save
His Body, destin'd to that living Grave.
The liquorish Hag rejects the Pelf with
scorn :
And nothing but the Man would serve her
turn.   320
Not all the Wealth of Eastern Kings, said
she,
Have Pow'r to part my plighted Love, and
me ;
And . Old, and Ugly as I am, and Poor ;
Yet never will I break the Faith I swore ;

For mine thou art by Promise, during Life,
And I thy loving and obedient Wife.
    My Love ! Nay, rather my Damnation
Thou,
Said he : Nor am I bound to keep my Vow :
The Fiend thy Sire has sent thee from below,
Else how cou'dst thou my secret Sorrows
know ?   330
Avaunt, old Witch, for I renounce thy Bed: ⎫
The Queen may take the Forfeit of my ⎪
Head,   ⎬
E'er any of my Race so foul a Crone shall ⎪
wed.   ⎭
    Both heard, the Judge pronounc'd against
the Knight ;
So was he Marry'd in his own despight ;
And all Day after hid him as an Owl,
Not able to sustain a Sight so foul.
Perhaps the Reader thinks I do him wrong
To pass the Marriage-Feast and Nuptial
Song :
Mirth there was none, the Man was *a-la-
mort*,   340
And little Courage had to make his Court.
To Bed they went, the Bridegroom and the
Bride :
Was never such an ill-pair'd Couple ty'd.
Restless he toss'd, and tumbled to and fro,
And rowl'd, and wriggled further off ; for
Woe.
The good old Wife lay smiling by his Side,
And caught him in her quiv'ring Arms, and
cry'd,
When you my ravish'd Predecessor saw, ⎫
You were not then become this Man of ⎪
Straw ;   ⎬
Had you been such, you might have scap'd ⎪
the Law.   350 ⎭
Is this the Custom of King *Arthur's* Court ?
Are all Round-Table Knights of such a sort ?
Remember I am she who sav'd your Life,
Your loving, lawful, and complying Wife :
Not thus you swore in your unhappy Hour,
Nor I for this return employ'd my Pow'r.
In time of Need I was your faithful Friend ;
Nor did I since, nor ever will offend.
Believe me, my lov'd Lord, 'tis much un-
kind ;
What Fury has possessed your alter'd
Mind ?   360
Thus on my Wedding-night—Without Pre-
tence—
Come, turn this way, or tell me my Offence.

If not your Wife, let Reasons Rule persuade,
Name but my Fault, amends shall soon be
    made.
    Amends! Nay, that's impossible, said he,
What change of Age, or Ugliness can be!
Or could *Medea's* Magick mend thy Face, ⎫
Thou art descended from so mean a Race, ⎬
That never Knight was match'd with such ⎪
    Disgrace. ⎭
What wonder, Madam, if I move my Side,
When, if I turn, I turn to such a Bride? 371
    And is this all that troubles you so sore!
And what the Devil cou'dst thou wish me
    more?
Ah *Benedicite*, reply'd the Crone:
Then cause of just Complaining have you
    none.
The Remedy to this were soon apply'd,
Wou'd you be like the Bridegroom to the
    Bride.
But, for you say a long descended Race,
And Wealth, and Dignity, and Pow'r, and
    Place,
Make Gentlemen, and that your high
    Degree   380
Is much disparag'd to be match'd with me;
Know this, my Lord, Nobility of Blood
Is but a glitt'ring, and fallacious Good:
The Nobleman is he whose noble Mind
Is fill'd with inborn Worth, unborrow'd
    from his Kind.
The King of Heav'n was in a Manger laid;
And took his Earth but from an humble
    Maid:
Then what can Birth, or mortal Men bestow,
Since Floods no higher than their Fountains
    flow?
We who for Name, and empty Honour strive,
Our true Nobility from him derive.   391
Your Ancestors, who puff your Mind with
    Pride,
And vast Estates to mighty Titles ty'd,
Did not your Honour, but their own advance,
For Virtue comes not by Inheritance.
If you tralineate from your Father's Mind,
What are you else but of a Bastard-kind?
Do, as your great Progenitors have done,
And by their virtues prove your self their
    Son.
No Father can infuse, or Wit or Grace;   400
A Mother comes across, and marrs the Race.
A Grandsire or a Grandame taints the Blood;
And seldom three Descents continue Good.

Were Virtue by Descent, a noble Name
Could never villanize his Father's Fame:
But, as the first the last of all the Line,
Wou'd like the Sun ev'n in Descending
    shine.
Take Fire, and bear it to the darkest House
Betwixt King *Arthur's* Court and *Caucasus*,
If you depart, the Flame shall still remain,
And the bright Blaze enlighten all the
    Plain;   411
Nor, till the Fewel perish, can decay,
By Nature form'd on Things combustible to
    prey.
Such is not Man, who mixing better Seed
With worse, begets a base, degenerate Breed:
The Bad corrupts the Good, and leaves
    behind
No trace of all the great Begetter's Mind.
The Father sinks within his Son, we see,
And often rises in the third Degree;
If better Luck, a better Mother give: 420
Chance gave us being, and by Chance we
    live.
Such as our Atoms were, ev'n such are we, ⎫
Or call it Chance, or strong Necessity. ⎬
Thus, loaded with dead weight, the Will is ⎪
    free. ⎭
And thus it needs must be: For Seed con-
    join'd
Lets into Nature's Work th' imperfect
    Kind:
But Fire, th' enliv'ner of the general Frame,
Is one, its Operation still the same.
Its Principle is in it self: While ours
Works, as Confederate's War, with mingled
    Pow'rs: 430
Or Man, or Woman, which soever fails:
And, oft, the Vigour of the Worse prevails.
Æther with Sulphur blended alters hue,
And casts a dusky gleam of *Sodom* blue.
Thus in a Brute, their ancient Honour ends,
And the fair Mermaid in a Fish descends:
The Line is gone; no longer Duke or Earl;
But by himself degraded turns a Churl.
Nobility of Blood is but Renown ⎫
Of thy great Fathers by their Virtue ⎬
    known,   440 ⎪
And a long trail of Light, to thee descend- ⎭
    ing down.
If in thy Smoke it ends, their Glories shine;
But Infamy and Villanage are thine.
Then what I said before, is plainly show'd,
That true Nobility proceeds from God:

Nor left us by Inheritance, but giv'n
By Bounty of our Stars, and Grace of
    Heaven.
Thus from a Captive *Servius Tullus* rose,
Whom for his Virtues, the first *Romans*
    chose:
Fabritius from their Walls repell'd the Foe,
Whose noble Hands had exercis'd the
    Plough.   451
From hence, my Lord, and Love, I thus
    conclude,
That tho' my homely Ancestors were rude,
Mean as I am, yet I may have the Grace
To make you Father of a generous Race:
And Noble then am I, when I begin,
In Virtue cloath'd, to cast the Rags of Sin:
If Poverty be my upbraided Crime,
And you believe in Heav'n; there was a
    time,   459
When He, the great Controller of our Fate
Deign'd to be Man, and lived in low Estate;
Which he who had the World at his dispose,
If Poverty were Vice, wou'd never choose.
Philosophers have said, and Poets sing,
That a glad Poverty's an honest Thing.
Content is Wealth, the Riches of the Mind;
And happy He who can that Treasure find,
But the base Miser starves amidst his Store,⎫
Broods on his Gold, and griping still at ⎬
    more   ⎭
Sits sadly pining, and believes he's Poor.⎭
The ragged Beggar, tho' he wants
    Relief,   471
Has not to lose, and sings before the Thief.
Want is a bitter, and a hateful Good,
Because its Virtues are not understood.
Yet many Things, impossible to Thought,
Have been by Need to full Perfection
    brought:
The daring of the Soul proceeds from thence,
Sharpness of Wit, and active Diligence:
Prudence at once, and Fortitude it gives,
And if in patience taken mends our Lives;
For ev'n that Indigence that brings me
    low   481
Makes me my self and Him above to know.
A Good which none would challenge, few
    would choose,
A fair Possession, which Mankind refuse.

If we from Wealth to Poverty descend,
Want gives to know the Flatt'rer from the
    Friend.
If I am Old, and Ugly, well for you,
No leud Adult'rer will my Love pursue;
Nor Jealousy, the Bane of marry'd Life,
Shall haunt you, for a wither'd homely Wife:
For Age, and Ugliness, as all agree,   491
Are the best Guards of Female Chastity.
  Yet since I see your Mind is Worldly bent,
I'll do my best to further your Content.
And therefore of two Gifts in my dispose,
Think e'er you speak, I grant you leave to
    choose:
Wou'd you I should be still Deform'd, and
    Old,
Nauseous to Touch, and Loathsome to
    Behold;
On this Condition, to remain for life
A careful, tender and obedient Wife,   500
In all I can contribute to your Ease,
And not in Deed, or Word, or Thought dis-
    please?
Or would you rather have me Young and
    Fair,
And take the Chance that happens to your
    share?
Temptations are in Beauty, and in Youth,
And how can you depend upon my Truth?
Now weigh the Danger with the doubtful
    Bliss,
And thank your self, if ought should fall
    amiss.
  Sore sigh'd the Knight, who this long
    Sermon heard;
At length considering all, his Heart he
    chear'd,   510
And thus reply'd, My Lady, and my Wife,
To your wise Conduct I resign my Life:
Choose you for me, for well you understand
The future Good and Ill, on either Hand:
But if an humble Husband may request,
Provide, and order all Things for the best;
Your's be the Care to profit, and to please:
And let your Subject-Servant take his Ease.
  Then thus in Peace, quoth she, concludes
    the Strife,
Since I am turn'd the Husband, you the
    Wife: 520
The Matrimonial Victory is mine,
Which having fairly gain'd, I will resign;
Forgive if I have said, or done amiss,
And seal the Bargain with a Friendly Kiss:

---

448 *Tullus*] Editors print *Tullius, but the
error is Dryden's.*
472 not] *Editors give* nought, *perhaps rightly.*

I promis'd you but one Content to share.
But now I will become both Good, and Fair.
No Nuptial Quarrel shall disturb your Ease,
The Business of my Life shall be to please :
And for my Beauty that, as Time shall try ;
But draw the Curtain first, and cast your
　Eye.　　　　　　　　　　　　530
　He look'd, and saw a Creature heav'nly
　　Fair,
In bloom of Youth, and of a charming Air.
With Joy he turn'd, and seiz'd her Iv'ry
　Arm ;
And like *Pygmalion* found the Statue warm.
Small Arguments there needed to prevail,
A Storm of Kisses pour'd as thick as Hail.

Thus long in mutual Bliss they lay em-
　braced,
And their first Love continu'd to the last :
One Sun-shine was their Life ; no Cloud
　between ;
Nor ever was a kinder Couple seen.　　540
　And so may all our Lives like their's be
　　led ;
Heav'n send the Maids young Husbands,
　fresh in Bed :
May Widows Wed as often as they can,
And ever for the better change their Man.
And some devouring Plague pursue their
　Lives,
Who will not well be govern'd by their Wives.

THE CHARACTER OF A GOOD PARSON.

IMITATED FROM CHAUCER AND INLARG'D.

A Parish-Priest was of the Pilgrim-Train ;
An Awful, Reverend, and Religious Man.
His Eyes diffus'd a venerable Grace,
And Charity it self was in his Face.
Rich was his Soul, though his Attire was
　poor ;
(As God had cloath'd his own Embassador;)
For such, on Earth, his bless'd Redeemer
　bore.
Of Sixty Years he seem'd ; and well might
　last
To Sixty more, but that he liv'd too fast ;
Refin'd himself to Soul, to curb the Sense ; 10
And made almost a Sin of Abstinence.
Yet, had his Aspect nothing of severe,
But such a Face as promis'd him sincere.
Nothing reserv'd or sullen was to see,
But sweet Regards ; and pleasing Sanctity:
Mild was his Accent, and his Action free.
With Eloquence innate his Tongue was
　arm'd ;
Tho' harsh the Precept, yet the Preacher
　charm'd ;
For, letting down the golden Chain from high,
He drew his Audience upward to the Sky : 20

And oft, with holy Hymns, he charm'd their
　Ears
(A　Musick　more　melodious　than　the
　Spheres.)
For *David* left him, when he went to rest,
His Lyre ; and after him, he sung the best.
He bore his great Commission in his Look :
But sweetly temper'd Awe, and soften'd all
　he spoke.
He preach'd the Joys of Heav'n and Pains
　of Hell ;
And warn'd the Sinner with becoming Zeal;
But on Eternal Mercy lov'd to dwell.
He taught the Gospel rather than the Law :
And forc'd himself to drive ; but lov'd to
　draw.　　　　　　　　　　　31
For Fear but freezes Minds ; but Love, like
　Heat,
Exhales the Soul sublime, to seek her
　Native Seat.
　To Threats, the stubborn Sinner oft is
　　hard,
Wrap'd in his Crimes, against the Storm
　prepar'd ;
But, when the milder Beams of Mercy
　play,
He melts, and throws his cumb'rous Cloak
　away.

543 often as they] often they *1700. The correction was silently made in the second edition, and,
as no editor has really collated the first, the
omission has never been noticed. See note on
104 above.

Lightnings and Thunder (Heav'ns Artillery)
As Harbingers before th' Almighty fly :
Those, but proclaim his Stile, and disappear ;
The stiller Sound succeeds ; and God is there.   41
  The Tythes, his Parish freely paid, he took ;
But never Su'd ; or Curs'd with Bell and Book.
With Patience bearing wrong ; but off'ring none :
Since every Man is free to lose his own.
The Country-Churles, according to their Kind,
(Who grudge their Dues, and love to be behind,)
The less he sought his Off'rings, pinch'd the more ;
And prais'd a Priest, contented to be Poor.
  Yet, of his little, he had some to spare,   50
To feed the Famish'd, and to cloath the Bare :
For Mortify'd he was to that degree,
A poorer than himself, he wou'd not see
True Priests, he said, and Preachers of the Word,
Were only Stewards of their Soveraign Lord,
Nothing was theirs ; but all the publick Store,
Intrusted Riches to relieve the Poor.
Who, shou'd they steal, for want of his Relief
He judg'd himself Accomplice with the Thief.
  Wide was his Parish ; not contracted close
In Streets, but here and there a straggling House ;   61
Yet still he was at Hand, without Request
To serve the Sick ; to succour the Distress'd :
Tempting, on Foot, alone, without affright,
The Dangers of a dark, tempestuous Night.
  All this the good old Man perform'd alone,
Nor spar'd his pains ; for Curate he had none.
Nor durst he trust another with his Care ;
Nor rode himself to *Pauls*, the publick Fair,
To chaffer for Preferment with his Gold,   70
Where Bishopricks, and *sine Cures* are sold.
But duly watch'd his Flock, by Night and Day ;
And from the prowling Wolf, redeem'd the Prey,
And hungry sent the wily Fox away.

The Proud he tam'd, the Penitent he chear'd :
Nor to rebuke the rich Offender fear'd.
His Preaching much, but more his Practice wrought ;
(A living Sermon of the Truths he taught ;)
For this by Rules severe his Life he squar'd :
That all might see the Doctrin which they heard.   80
For Priests, he said, are Patterns for the rest :
(The Gold of Heav'n, who bear the God Impress'd :)
But when the precious Coin is kept unclean,
The Soveraign's Image is no longer seen.
If they be foul, on whom the People trust,
Well may the baser Brass contract a rust.
  The Prelate for his Holy Life he priz'd ;
The worldly Pomp of Prelacy despis'd.
His Saviour came not with a gawdy Show,
Nor was his Kingdom of the World below.   90
Patience in Want, and Poverty of Mind, ⎫
These Marks of Church and Churchmen he ⎬
  design'd,   ⎭
And living taught ; and dying left behind.
The Crown he wore was of the pointed Thorn:
In Purple he was Crucify'd, not born.
They who contend for Place and high Degree,
Are not his Sons, but those of *Zebadee*.
  Not, but he knew the Signs of Earthly Pow'r
Might well become St. *Peter's* Successor ;
The Holy Father holds a double Reign,   100
The Prince may keep his Pomp ; the Fisher must be plain.
  Such was the Saint ; who shone with every Grace :
Reflecting, *Moses*-like, his Maker's Face.
God saw his Image lively was express'd ;
And his own Work, as in Creation, bless'd.
  The Tempter saw him too, with envious Eye,
And, as on *Job*, demanded leave to try.
He took the time when *Richard* was depos'd,
And High and Low with happy *Harry* clos'd.
This Prince, tho' great in Arms, the Priest withstood,   110
Near tho' he was, yet not the next of Blood.
Had *Richard* unconstrain'd, resign'd the ⎫
  Throne,   ⎬
A King can give no more than is his own :   ⎬
The Title stood entail'd, had *Richard* had ⎭
  a Son.

Conquest, an odious Name, was laid aside,
Where all submitted, none the Battle try'd.
The senseless Plea of Right by Providence,
Was, by a flatt'ring Priest, invented since :
And lasts no longer than the present sway ;
But justifies the next who comes in play. 120
  The People's Right remains ; let those who dare
Dispute their Pow'r, when they the Judges are.
  He join'd not in their Choice ; because he knew
Worse might, and often did from Change ensue.
Much to himself he thought ; but little spoke :
And, Undepriv'd, his Benefice forsook.

Now, through the Land, his Cure of Souls he stretch'd,
And like a Primitive Apostle preach'd.
Still Chearful ; ever Constant to his Call ;
By many follow'd ; Lov'd by most, Admir'd by All. 130
With what he beg'd, his Brethren he reliev'd;
And gave the Charities himself receiv'd ;
Gave, while he Taught ; and Edify'd the more,
Because he shew'd by Proof, 'twas easy to be Poor.
  He went not, with the Crowd, to see a Shrine ;
But fed us by the way, with Food divine.
  In deference to his Virtues, I forbear
To show you, what the rest in Orders were
This Brillant is so Spotless, and so Bright,
He needs no Foyl : But shines by his own proper Light. 140

SIGISMONDA AND GUISCARDO.

FROM BOCCACE.

WHILE *Norman Tancred* in *Salerno* reign'd,
The Title of a Gracious Prince he gain'd ;
Till turn'd a Tyrant in his latter Days,
He lost the Lustre of his former Praise,
And from the bright Meridian where he stood
Descending, dipp'd his Hands in Lovers Blood.
  This Prince, of Fortunes Favour long possess'd,
Yet was with one fair Daughter only bless'd ;
And bless'd he might have been with her alone :
But oh ! how much more happy, had he none ! 10
She was his Care, his Hope, and his Delight,
Most in his Thought, and ever in his Sight :
Next, nay beyond his Life, he held her dear ;
She liv'd by him, and now he liv'd in her.
For this, when ripe for Marriage, he delay'd
Her Nuptial Bands, and kept her long a Maid,
As envying any else should share a Part
Of what was his, and claiming all her Heart.

At length, as Publick Decency requir'd,
And all his Vassals eagerly desir'd, 20
With Mind averse, he rather underwent
His Peoples Will than gave his own Consent
So was she torn, as from a Lover's Side,
And made almost in his despite a Bride.
  Short were her Marriage-Joys ; for in the Prime
Of Youth, her Lord expir'd before his time ;
And to her Father's Court in little space }
Restor'd anew, she held a higher Place ; }
More lov'd, and more exalted into Grace. }
This Princess fresh and young, and fair, and wise, 30
The worship'd Idol of her Father's Eyes,
Did all her Sex in ev'ry Grace exceed,
And had more Wit beside than Women need.
Youth, Health, and Ease, and most an }
  amorous Mind, }
To second Nuptials had her Thoughts }
  inclin'd ; }
And former Joys had left a secret Sting }
behind. }

---

129 Brillant] *The editors wrongly print* Brilliant

SIGISMONDA AND GUISCARDO. Text from the original and only contemporary edition, 1700.

But, prodigal in ev'ry other Grant,
Her Sire left unsupply'd her only Want;
And she, betwixt her Modesty and Pride,
Her Wishes, which she could not help, would
    hide.   40
   Resolv'd at last to lose no longer Time,
And yet to please her self without a Crime,
She cast her Eyes around the Court, to find
A worthy Subject suiting to her Mind,
To him in holy Nuptials to be ty'd,
A seeming Widow, and a secret Bride.
Among the Train of Courtiers, one she found
With all the Gifts of bounteous Nature
    crown'd,
Of gentle Blood; but one whose niggard
    Fate
Had set him far below her high Estate; 50
Guiscard his Name was call'd, of blooming
    Age,
Now Squire to Tancred, and before his Page;
To him, the Choice of all the shining Crowd,
Her Heart the noble Sigismonda vow'd.
   Yet hitherto she kept her Love conceal'd,
And with close Glances ev'ry Day beheld
The graceful Youth; and ev'ry Day
    increas'd
The raging Fire that burn'd within her
    Breast;
Some secret Charm did all his Acts attend,
And what his Fortune wanted, hers could
    mend;   60
Till, as the Fire will force its outward way,
Or, in the Prison pent, consume the Prey;
So long her earnest Eyes on his were set,
At length their twisted Rays together met;
And he, surpriz'd with humble Joy, survey'd
One sweet Regard, shot by the Royal Maid:
Not well assur'd, while doubtful Hopes he
    nurs'd,
A second Glance came gliding like the first;
And he, who saw the Sharpness of the Dart,
Without Defence receiv'd it in his Heart. 70
In Publick though their Passion wanted
    Speech,
Yet mutual Looks interpreted for each:
Time, Ways, and Means of Meeting were
    deny'd,
But all those Wants ingenious Love supply'd.
Th' inventive God, who never fails his Part,
Inspires the Wit, when once he warms the
    Heart.
   When Guiscard next was in the Circle seen,
Where Sigismonda held the Place of Queen,

A hollow Cane within her Hand she brought,
But in the Concave had enclos'd a Note; 80
With this she seem'd to play, and, as in
    sport,
Toss'd to her Love, in presence of the Court;
Take it, she said; and when your Needs
    require,
This little Brand will serve to light your Fire.
He took it with a Bow, and soon divin'd
The seeming Toy was not for nought
    design'd:
But when retir'd, so long with curious Eyes
He view'd the Present, that he found the
    Prize.
Much in little writ; and all convey'd   ⎫
With cautious Care, for fear to be be- ⎪
    tray'd   90 ⎬
By some false Confident or Fav'rite Maid. ⎭
The Time, the Place, the Manner how to
    meet,
Were all in punctual Order plainly writ:
But since a Trust must be, she thought it ⎫
    best   ⎪
To put it out of Laymens Pow'r at least, ⎬
And for their solemn Vows prepar'd a   ⎪
    Priest.   ⎭
  Guiscard (her secret purpose understood)
With Joy prepar'd to meet the coming Good;
Nor Pains nor Danger was resolv'd to
    spare,   99
But use the Means appointed by the Fair.
  Near the proud Palace of Salerno stood
A Mount of rough Ascent, and thick with
    Wood;
Through this a Cave was dug with vast
    Expence,
The Work it seem'd of some suspicious
    Prince,
Who, when abusing Pow'r with lawless
    Might,
From Publick Justice would secure his
    Flight.
The Passage made by many a winding Way,
Reach'd ev'n the Room in which the Tyrant
    lay.
Fit for his purpose, on a lower Floor
He lodg'd, whose Issue was an Iron Door,
From whence, by Stairs descending to the
    Ground,   111
In the blind Grot a safe Retreat he found.
Its Outlet ended in a Brake o'ergrown
With Brambles, choak'd by Time, and now
    unknown.

A Rift there was, which from the Mountains
    Height
Convey'd a glimm'ring and malignant Light,
A Breathing-place to draw the Damps away,
A Twilight of an intercepted Day.
The Tyrants Den, whose Use, though lost to
    Fame,
Was now th' Apartment of the Royal Dame ;
The Cavern, only to her Father known, 121
By him was to his Darling-Daughter shown.
  Neglected long she let the Secret rest,
Till Love recall'd it to her lab'ring Breast,
And hinted as the Way by Heav'n design'd
The Teacher, by the Means he taught, to
    blind.
What will not Women do, when Need inspires
Their Wit, or Love their Inclination fires !
Though Jealousie of State th' Invention
    found,
Yet Love refin'd upon the former Ground.
That Way, the tyrant had reserv'd, to fly 131
Pursuing Hate, now serv'd to bring two
    Lovers nigh.
  The Dame, who long in vain had kept
    the Key,
Bold by Desire, explor'd the secret Way ;
Now try'd the Stairs, and wading through
    the Night,
Search'd all the deep Recess, and issu'd into
    Light.
All this her Letter had so well explain'd,
Th' instructed Youth might compass what
    remain'd ;
The Cavern-mouth alone was hard to find,
Because the Path disus'd, was out of mind :
But in what Quarter of the Cops it lay, 141
His Eye by certain Level could survey :
Yet (for the Wood perplex'd with Thorns
    he knew)
A Frock of Leather o'er his Limbs he drew ;
And thus provided, search'd the Brake
    around,
Till the choak d Entry of the Cave he found.
  Thus, all prepar'd, the promis'd Hour
    arrived,
So long expected, and so well contriv'd :
With Love to Friend, th' impatient Lover
    went,
Fenc'd from the Thorns, and trod the deep
    Descent. 150
The conscious Priest, who was suborn'd
    before,
Stood ready posted at the Postern-door ;

The Maids in distant Rooms were sent to
    rest,
And nothing wanted but th' invited Guest.
He came, and, knocking thrice, without
    delay,
The longing Lady heard, and turn'd the Key;
At once invaded him with all her Charms,
And the first Step he made, was in her Arms :
The Leathern Out-side, boistrous as it was,
Gave way, and bent beneath her strict
    Embrace : 160
On either Side the Kisses flew so thick,
That neither he nor she had Breath to speak.
The holy Man amaz'd at what he saw,
Made haste to sanctifie the Bliss by Law ;
And mutter'd fast the Matrimony o're,
For fear committed Sin should get before.
His Work perform'd, he left the Pair alone,
Because he knew he could not go too soon ;
His Presence odious, when his Task was done.
What Thoughts he had beseems not me
    to say, 170
Though some surmise he went to fast and
    pray,
And needed both, to drive the tempting
    Thoughts away.
  The Foe once gone, they took their full
    Delight ;
'Twas restless Rage, and Tempest all the
    night :
For greedy Love each Moment would employ,
And grudg'd the shortest Pauses of their Joy.
  Thus were their Loves auspiciously begun,
And thus with secret Care were carried on,
The Stealth it self did Appetite restore,
And look'd so like a Sin, it pleas'd the more.
  The Cave was now become a common
    Way, 181
The Wicket, often open'd, knew the Key :
Love rioted secure, and long enjoy'd,
Was ever eager, and was never cloy'd.
  But as Extremes are short, of Ill and Good,
And Tides at highest Mark regorge the
    Flood ;
So Fate, that could no more improve their
    Joy,
Took a malicious Pleasure to destroy.
  Tancred, who fondly lov'd, and whose
    Delight 189
Was plac'd in his fair Daughters daily Sight
Of Custom, when his State-Affairs were done,
Would pass his pleasing Hours with her
    alone :

And, as a Father's Privilege allow'd,
Without Attendance of th' officious Crowd.
  It happen'd once, that when in Heat of
      Day
He try'd to sleep, as was his usual Way,
The balmy Slumber fled his wakeful Eyes,
And forc'd him, in his own despite, to rise :
Of Sleep forsaken, to relieve his Care,
He sought the Conversation of the Fair ; 200
But with her Train of Damsels she was gone,
In shady Walks the scorching Heat to shun :
He would not violate that sweet Recess,
And found besides a welcome Heaviness
That seiz'd his Eyes ; and Slumber, which
      forgot
When call'd before to come, now came
      unsought.
From Light retir'd, behind his Daughters
      Bed,
He for approaching Sleep compos'd his
      Head ;
A Chair was ready, for that Use design'd,
So quilted that he lay at ease reclin'd ; 210
The Curtains closely drawn, the Light to
      skreen,
As if he had contriv'd to lie unseen :
Thus cover'd with an artificial Night,
Sleep did his Office soon, and seal'd his Sight.
  With Heav'n averse, in this ill-omen'd
      Hour
Was *Guiscard* summon'd to the secret Bow'r,
And the fair Nymph, with Expectation fir'd,
From her attending Damsels was retir'd :
For, true to Love, she measur'd Time so
      right
As not to miss one Moment of Delight. 220
The Garden, seated on the level Floor,
She left behind, and locking ev'ry Door,
Thought all secure ; but little did she know,
Blind to her Fate, she had inclos'd her Foe.
Attending *Guiscard* in his Leathern Frock
Stood ready, with his thrice-repeated
      Knock :
Thrice with a doleful Sound the jarring
      Grate
Rung deaf, and hollow, and presag'd their
      Fate.
The Door unlock'd, to known Delight they
      haste,   229
And panting in each other's Arms, embrac'd,
Rush to the conscious Bed, a mutual Freight,
And heedless press it with their wonted
      Weight.

The sudden Bound awak'd the sleeping
      Sire,
And shew'd a Sight no Parent can desire :
His opening Eyes at once with odious View
The Love discover'd, and the Lover knew :
He would have cry'd ; but hoping that he
      dreamt,
Amazement ty'd his Tongue, and stopp'd th'
      Attempt.
Th' ensuing Moment all the Truth declar'd, ⎫
But now he stood collected, and prepar'd ; ⎪
For Malice and Revenge had put him on ⎬
      his Guard.   241 ⎭
So, like a Lion that unheeded lay, ⎫
Dissembling Sleep, and watchful to betray, ⎬
With inward Rage he meditates his Prey. ⎭
The thoughtless Pair, indulging their Desires,
Alternate kindl'd and then quench'd their
      Fires ;
Nor thinking in the Shades of Death they ⎫
      play'd, ⎪
Full of themselves, themselves alone sur- ⎬
      vey'd, ⎪
And, too secure, were by themselves ⎪
      betray'd. ⎭
Long time dissolv'd in Pleasure thus they
      lay,   250
Till Nature could no more suffice their Play :
Then rose the Youth, and through the Cave
      again
Return'd ; the Princess mingl'd with her
      Train.
  Resolv'd his unripe Vengeance to defer,
The Royal Spy, when now the Coast was
      clear,
Sought not the Garden, but retir'd unseen,
To brood in secret on his gather'd Spleen,
And methodize Revenge : To Death he
      griev'd ;
And, but he saw the Crime, had scarce
      believ'd.
Th' Appointment for th' ensuing Night he ⎫
      heard ;   260 ⎪
And therefore in the Cavern had prepar'd ⎬
Two brawny Yeomen of his trusty Guard. ⎭
  Scarce had unwary *Guiscard* set his Foot
Within the farmost Entrance of the Grot,
When these in secret Ambush ready lay,
And rushing on the sudden, seiz'd the Prey :
Encumber'd with his Frock, without defence, ⎫
An easie Prize, they led the Pris'ner thence, ⎬
And, as commanded, brought before the ⎪
      Prince ⎭

The gloomy Sire, too sensible of Wrong 270
To vent his Rage in Words, restrain'd his
   Tongue ;
And only said, Thus Servants are preferr'd
And trusted, thus their Sov'reigns they
   reward.
Had I not seen, had not these Eyes receiv'd
Too clear a Proof, I could not have
   believ'd.
   He paus'd, and choak'd the rest. The
     Youth, who saw
His forfeit Life abandon'd to the Law,
The Judge th' Accuser, and th' Offence to
   him,
Who had both Pow'r and Will t' avenge the
   Crime ; 279
No vain Defence prepar'd, but thus reply'd,
The Faults of Love by Love are justify'd ;
With unresisted Might the Monarch reigns,
He levels Mountains, and he raises Plains,
And, not regarding Diff'rence of Degree,
Abas'd your Daughter, and exalted me.
   This bold Return with seeming Patience
     heard,
The Pris'ner was remitted to the Guard.
The sullen Tyrant slept not all the Night,
But lonely walking by a winking Light,
Sobb'd, wept, and groan'd, and beat his
   wither'd Breast, 290
But would not violate his Daughters Rest ;
Who long expecting lay, for Bliss prepar'd,
Listning for Noise, and griev'd that none
   she heard ;
Oft rose, and oft in vain employ'd the Key,⎫
And oft accus'd her Lover of Delay, ⎬
And pass'd the tedious Hours in anxious ⎪
   Thoughts away. ⎭
   The Morrow came ; and at his usual Hour
Old *Tancred* visited his Daughters Bow'r ;
Her Cheek (for such his Custom was) he
   kiss'd,
Then blessed her kneeling, and her Maids
   dismiss'd. 300
The Royal Dignity thus far maintain'd,
Now left in private, he no longer feign'd ;
But all at once his Grief and Rage appear'd,
And Floods of Tears ran trickling down his
   Beard.
   O *Sigismonda*, he began to say ; ⎫
Thrice he began, and thrice was forc'd to ⎪
   stay, ⎬
Till Words with often trying found their ⎪
   Way ; ⎭

I thought, O *Sigismonda*, (But how blind
Are Parents Eyes their Childrens Faults to
   find !) 309
Thy Vertue, Birth, and Breeding were above
A mean Desire, and vulgar sense of Love :
Nor less than Sight and Hearing could⎫
   convince ⎪
So fond a Father, and so just a Prince, ⎬
Of such an unforeseen, and unbeliev'd ⎪
   Offence. ⎭
Then what indignant Sorrow must I have,
To see thee lie subjected to my Slave !
A Man so smelling of the Peoples Lee,
The Court receiv'd him first for Charity ;
And since with no Degree of Honour grac'd,
But only suffer'd where he first was
   plac'd : 320
A grov'ling Insect still ; and so design'd
By Natures Hand, nor born of Noble Kind :
A Thing by neither Man nor Woman priz'd,
And scarcely known enough to be despis'd :
To what has Heav'n reserv'd my Age ? Ah !
   why
Should Man, when Nature calls, not chuse
   to die,
Rather than stretch the Span of Life, to find
Such Ills as Fate has wisely cast behind,
For those to feel, whom fond Desire to live
Makes covetous of more than Life can give !
Each has his Share of Good ; and when 'tis
   gone, 331
The Guest, though hungry, cannot rise too
   soon.
But I, expecting more, in my own wrong
Protracting Life, have liv'd a Day too long.
If Yesterday cou'd be recall'd again,
Ev'n now would I conclude my happy Reign :
But 'tis too late, my glorious Race is run,
And a dark Cloud o'ertakes my setting Sun.
Hadst thou not lov'd, or loving sav'd the
   Shame,
If not the Sin, by some Illustrious Name, 340
This little Comfort had reliev'd my Mind,
'Twas Frailty, not unusual to thy Kind :
But thy low Fall beneath thy Royal Blood
Shews downward Appetite to mix with Mud :
Thus not the least Excuse is left for thee,
Nor the least Refuge for unhappy me.
   For him I have resolv'd : whom by
     Surprize
I took, and scarce can call it, in Disguise ;
For such was his Attire, as, with Intent
Of Nature, suited to his mean Descent : 350

The harder Question yet remains behind, ⎫
What Pains a Parent and a Prince can find ⎬
To punish an Offence of this degenerate ⎮
    Kind. ⎭
  As I have lov'd, and yet I love thee more
Than ever Father lov'd a Child before ;
So, that Indulgence draws me to forgive :
Nature, that gave thee Life, would have
    thee live,
But, as a Publick Parent of the State,
My Justice, and thy Crime, requires thy
    Fate.
Fain would I chuse a middle Course to
    steer ;   360
Nature's too kind, and Justice too severe :
Speak for us both, and to the Balance bring
On either side, the Father, and the King.
Heav'n knows, my Heart is bent to favour
    thee ;
Make it but scanty weight, and leave the
    rest to me.
  Here stopping with a Sigh, he pour'd a
    Flood
Of Tears, to make his last Expression good.
  She who had heard him speak, nor saw
    alone
The secret Conduct of her Love was known,
But he was taken who her Soul possess'd, 370
Felt all the Pangs of Sorrow in her Breast :
And little wanted, but a Womans Heart
With Cries, and Tears had testifi'd her
    Smart :
But in-born Worth, that Fortune can
    controul,
New strung, and stiffer bent her softer Soul ;
The *Heroine* assum'd the Womans Place,
Confirmed her Mind, and fortifi'd her Face :
Why should she beg, or what cou'd she
    pretend,
When her stern Father had condemned her
    Friend !
Her Life she might have had ; but her
    Despair   380
Of saving his, had put it past her Care :
Resolv'd on Fate, she would not lose her
    Breath,
But rather than not die, sollicit Death.
Fix'd on this Thought, she, not as Women
    use,
Her Fault by common Frailty would excuse ;
But boldly justifi'd her Innocence,
And while the Fact was own'd, deny'd th'
    Offence :

Then with dry Eyes, and with an open Look,
She met his Glance mid-way, and thus un-
    daunted spoke.   389
  Tancred, I neither am dispos'd to make
Request for Life, nor offer'd Life to take ;
Much less deny the Deed ; but least of all
Beneath pretended Justice weakly fall.
My Words to sacred Truth shall be confin'd,
My Deeds shall shew the Greatness of my
    Mind.
That I have lov'd, I own ; that still I love,
I call to Witness all the Pow'rs above :
Yet more I own ; To *Guiscard's* Love I give
The small remaining Time I have to live ;
And if beyond this Life Desire can be, 400
Not Fate it self shall set my Passion free.
  This first avow'd ; nor Folly warp'd my
    Mind,
Nor the frail Texture of the Female Kind
Betray'd my Vertue : For too well I knew
What Honour was, and Honour had his due :
Before the Holy Priest my Vows were ty'd,
So came I not a Strumpet, but a Bride ;
This for my Fame, and for the Publick Voice :
Yet more, his Merits justify'd my Choice ;
Which had they not, the first Election
    thine,   410
That Bond dissolv'd, the next is freely mine :
Or grant I err'd, (which yet I must deny,)
Had Parents Pow'r ev'n second Vows to tie,
Thy little Care to mend my Widow'd Nights ⎫
Has forc'd me to recourse of Marriage-Rites, ⎬
To fill an empty Side, and follow known ⎮
    Delights. ⎭
What have I done in this, deserving Blame ?
State-Laws may alter : Nature's are the
    same
Those are usurp'd on helpless Woman-kind,
Made without our Consent, and wanting
    Pow'r to bind.   420
  Thou, *Tancred*, better should'st have
    understood,
That, as thy Father gave thee Flesh and
    Blood,
So gav'st thou me : Not from the Quarry
    hew'd,
But of a softer Mould, with Sense endu'd ;
Ev'n softer than thy own, of suppler Kind,
More exquisite of Taste, and more than man
    refin'd.
Nor need'st thou by thy Daughter to be told,
Though now thy spritely Blood with Age
    be cold,

Thou hast been young ; and canst remember
   still,
That when thou hadst the Pow'r, thou hadst
   the Will ;   430
And from the past Experience of thy Fires,
Canst tell with what a Tide our strong
   Desires
Come rushing on in Youth, and what their
   Rage requires.
   And grant thy Youth was exercis'd in
      Arms,
When Love no Leisure found for softer
   Charms,
My tender Age in Luxury was train'd,
With idle Ease and Pageants entertain'd ;
My Hours my own, my Pleasures un-
   restrain'd.
So bred, no wonder if I took the Bent
That seem'd ev'n warranted by thy Consent ;
For, when the Father is too fondly kind, 441
Such Seed he sows, such Harvest shall he find.
Blame then thy self, as Reason's Law
   requires,
(Since Nature gave, and thou foment st my
   Fires ;)
If still those Appetites continue strong,
Thou mayest consider I am yet but young
Consider too, that having been a Wife,
I must have tasted of a better Life,
And am not to be blam'd, if I renew,
By lawful Means, the Joys which then
   I knew.   450
Where was the Crime, if Pleasure I procur d,
Young, and a Woman, and to Bliss inur'd ?
That was my Case, and this is my Defence ;
I pleas'd my self, I shunned Incontinence,
And, urg'd by strong Desires, indulg'd
   my Sense.
   Left to my self, I must avow, I strove
From publick Shame to screen my secret
   Love,
And, well acquainted with thy Native
   Pride,
Endeavour'd, what I could not help, to
   hide,
For which a Womans Wit an easie Way
   supply'd.   460
How this, so well contriv'd, so closely laid,
Was known to thee, or by what Chance
   betray'd,
Is not my Care : To please thy Pride alone
I could have wish'd it had been still un-
   known.

Nor took I *Guiscard* by blind Fancy led,
Or hasty Choice, as many Women wed ;
But with delib'rate Care, and ripen'd
   Thought,
At Leisure first design'd, before I wrought :
On him I rested after long Debate,
And not without consid'ring, fix'd my Fate :
His Flame was equal, though by mine
   inspir'd :   471
(For so the Diff'rence of our Birth requir'd :)
Had he been born like me, like me his Love
Had first begun, what mine was forc'd to
   move :
But thus beginning, thus we persevere ;
Our Passions yet continue what they were,
Nor length of Trial makes our Joys the
   less sincere.
   At this my Choice, though not by thine
      allow'd,
(Thy Judgment herding with the common
   Crowd)
Thou tak'st unjust Offence ; and, led by
   them,   480
Dost less the Merit than the Man esteem.
Too sharply, *Tancred*, by thy Pride betray'd,
Hast thou against the Laws of Kind in-
   veigh'd ;
For all th' Offence is in Opinion plac'd,
Which deems high Birth by lowly Choice
   debas'd.
This Thought alone with Fury fires thy
   Breast,
(For Holy Marriage justifies the rest)
That I have sunk the Glories of the State,
And mix'd my Blood with a Plebeian Mate :
In which I wonder thou shouldst oversee
Superiour Causes, or impute to me   491
The Fault of Fortune, or the Fates Decree.
Or call it Heav'ns Imperial Pow'r alone,
Which moves on Springs of Justice, though
   unknown ;
Yet this we see, though order'd for the best,
The Bad exalted, and the Good oppress'd ;
Permitted Laurels grace the Lawless Brow,
Th' Unworthy rais'd, the Worthy cast below.
   But leaving that : Search we the secret
      Springs,
And backward trace the Principles of
   Things ;   500
There shall we find, that when the World
   began,
One common Mass compos'd the Mould of
   Man ;

One Paste of Flesh on all Degrees bestow d,
And kneaded up alike with moistning Blood.
The same Almighty Pow'r inspir'd the Frame
With kindl'd Life, and form'd the Souls the same :
The Faculties of Intellect, and Will,
Dispens'd with equal Hand, dispos'd with equal Skill,
Like Liberty indulg'd with Choice of Good or Ill.
Thus born alike, from Vertue first began 510
The Diff'rence that distinguish'd Man from Man :
He claim'd no Title from Descent of Blood,
But that which made him Noble, made him Good :
Warm'd with more Particles of Heav'nly Flame,
He wing'd his upward Flight, and soar'd to Fame ;
The rest remain'd below, a Tribe without a Name.
  This Law, though Custom now diverts the Course,
As Natures Institute, is yet in Force ;
Uncancell'd, tho disus'd : And he, whose Mind
Is Vertuous, is alone of Noble Kind ; 520
Though poor in Fortune, of Celestial Race ;
And he commits the Crime, who calls him Base.
  Now lay the Line ; and measure all thy Court,
By inward Vertue, not external Port,
And find whom justly to prefer above
The Man on whom my Judgment plac'd my Love :
So shalt thou see his Parts, and Person shine,
And thus compar'd, the rest a base degen'rate Line.
Nor took I, when I first survey'd thy Court,
His Valour or his Vertues on Report ; 530
But trusted what I ought to trust alone,
Relying on thy Eyes, and not my own ;
Thy Praise (and Thine was then the Publick Voice)
First recommended *Guiscard* to my Choice :
Directed thus by thee, I look'd, and found
A Man, I thought, deserving to be crowned !
First by my Father pointed to my Sight,
Nor less conspicuous by his Native Light :

His Mind, his Meen, the Features of his Face,
Excelling all the rest of Humane Race : 540
These were thy Thoughts, and thou could'st judge aright,
Till Int'rest made a Jaundice in thy Sight.
  Or shou'd I grant thou didst not rightly see ;
Then thou wert first deceiv'd, and I deceiv'd by thee.
But if thou shalt alledge, through Pride of Mind,
Thy Blood with one of base Condition join'd,
'Tis false ; for 'tis not Baseness to be Poor ;
His Poverty augments thy Crime the more ;
Upbraids thy Justice with the scant Regard
Of Worth : Whom Princes praise, they shou'd reward. 550
Are these the Kings entrusted by the Crowd
With Wealth, to be dispens'd for Common Good ?
The People sweat not for their King's Delight,
T' enrich a Pimp, or raise a Parasite ;
Theirs is the Toil; and he who well has serv'd
His Country, has his Countrys Wealth deserv'd.
  Ev'n mighty Monarchs oft are meanly born,
And Kings by Birth to lowest Rank return ;
All subject to the Pow'r of giddy Chance,
For Fortune can depress, or can advance :
But true Nobility is of the Mind, 561
Not giv'n by Chance, and not to Chance resign'd.
  For the remaining Doubt of thy Decree,
What to resolve, and how dispose of me,
Be warn'd to cast that useless Care aside,
My self alone will for my self provide.
If in thy doting, and decrepit Age,
Thy Soul, a Stranger in thy Youth to Rage,
Begins in cruel Deeds to take Delight,
Gorge with my Blood thy barb'rous Appetite ; 570
For I so little am dispos'd to pray
For Life, I would not cast a Wish away.
Such as it is, th' Offence is all my own ;
And what to *Guiscard* is already done,
Or to be done, is doom'd by thy Decree,
That, if not executed first by thee,
Shall on my Person be perform'd by me.

Away, with Women weep, and leave me
here,
Fix'd, like a Man to die, without a Tear ;
Or save, or slay us both this present
Hour,   580
'Tis all that Fate has left within thy Pow'r.
   She said : Nor did her Father fail to find,
In all she spoke, the Greatness of her Mind ;
Yet thought she was not obstinate to die,
Nor deem'd the Death she promis'd was so
nigh :
Secure in this Belief, he left the Dame,
Resolv'd to spare her Life, and save her
Shame ;
But that detested Object to remove,
To wreak his Vengeance, and to cure her
Love.
   Intent on this, a secret Order sign'd   590
The Death of *Guiscard* to his Guards
enjoin'd :
Strangling was chosen, and the Night the
Time ;
A mute Revenge, and blind as was the
Crime :
His faithful Heart, a bloody Sacrifice,
Torn from his Breast, to glut the Tyrant's
Eyes,
Clos'd the severe Command : For, (Slaves
to pay)
What Kings decree the Soldier must obey :
Wag'd against Foes, and, when the Wars
are o'er,
Fit only to maintain Despotick Pow'r :
Dang'rous to Freedom, and desir'd alone 600
By Kings, who seek an Arbitrary Throne.
Such were these Guards ; as ready to have
slain
The Prince himself, allur'd with greater gain:
So was the Charge perform'd with better Will,
By Men inur'd to Blood, and exercis'd in Ill.
   Now, though the sullen Sire had eas'd⎱
his Mind,   ⎱
The Pomp of his Revenge was yet behind, ⎰
A Pomp prepar'd to grace the Present he ⎰
design'd.   ⎰
A Goblet rich with Gems, and rough with
Gold,
Of Depth, and Breadth, the precious Pledge
to hold,   610

With cruel Care he chose : The hollow Part
Inclos'd, the lid conceal'd the Lover's Heart :
Then of his trusted Mischiefs one he sent,
And bad him with these Words the Gift
present :
Thy Father sends thee this, to cheer thy
Breast,
And glad thy Sight with what thou lov'st the
best,
As thou hast pleas'd his Eyes, and joy'd his
Mind,
With what he lov'd the most of Humane
Kind.
   E'er this the Royal Dame, who well had
weigh'd
The Consequence of what her Sire had said,
Fix'd on her Fate, against th' expected
Hour,   621
Procur'd the Means to have it in her Pow'r :
For this she had distill'd, with early Care,
The Juice of Simples, friendly to Despair,
A Magazine of Death ; and thus prepar'd,
Secure to die, the fatal Message heard :
Then smil'd severe ; nor with a troubl'd
Look,
Or trembling hand, the Fun'ral Present took;
Ev'n kept her Count'nance, when the Lid
remov'd
Disclos'd the Heart, unfortunately lov'd :
She needed not be told within whose
Breast   631
It lodg'd ; the Message had explain'd the
rest.
Or not amaz'd, or hiding her Surprize,
She sternly on the Bearer fix'd her Eyes ;
Then thus ; Tell *Tancred*, on his Daughters
part,
The Gold, though precious, equals not the
Heart :
But he did well to give his best ; and I,
Who wish'd a worthier Urn, forgive his
Poverty.
   At this she curb'd a Groan, that else had
come,
And pausing, view'd the Present in the
Tomb :   640
Then to the Heart ador'd devoutly glew'd
Her Lips, and raising it, her Speech renew'd :
Ev'n from my Day of Birth, to this, the
Bound
Of my unhappy Being, I have found
My Father's Care and Tenderness express'd :
But this last Act of Love excels the rest :

---

579 Fix'd, like a Man to die, without a Tear ;]
Christie wrongly gives Fixed like a man, to die
without a tear ;

For this so dear a Present, bear him back
The best Return that I can live to make.
　The Messenger dispatch'd, again she
　　view'd
The lov'd Remains, and sighing, thus
　pursu'd :　　　　　　　　　　　　650
Source of my Life, and Lord of my Desires,
In whom I liv'd, with whom my Soul ex-
　pires ;
Poor Heart, no more the Spring of Vital
　Heat,
Curs'd be the Hands that tore thee from thy
　Seat !
The Course is finish'd, which thy Fates
　decreed,
And thou, from thy Corporeal Prison freed :
Soon hast thou reach'd the Goal with
　mended Pace,
A World of Woes dispatch'd in little space :
Forc'd by thy Worth, thy Foe in Death
　become
Thy Friend, has lodg'd thee in a costly
　Tomb ;　　　　　　　　　　　　　660
There yet remain'd thy Fun'ral Exequies,
The weeping Tribute of thy Widows Eyes ;
And those, indulgent Heav'n has found the
　way
That I, before my Death, have leave to pay
My Father ev'n in Cruelty is kind,　　　⎫
Or Heaven has turn'd the Malice of his　⎬
　Mind　　　　　　　　　　　　　　⎭
To better Uses than his Hate design'd ;
And made th' Insult, which in his Gift
　appears,
The Means to mourn thee with my pious
　Tears ;
Which I will pay thee down, before I go, 670
And save my self the Pains to weep below,
If Souls can weep ; though once I meant
　to meet
My Fate with Face unmov'd, and Eyes un-
　wet,
Yet since I have thee here in narrow
　Room,
My Tears shall set thee first afloat within
　thy Tomb :
Then (as I know thy Spirit hovers nigh)
Under thy friendly Conduct will I fly
To Regions unexplor'd, secure to share　⎫
Thy State ;　nor Hell shall Punishment　⎬
　appear ;　　　　　　　　　　　　⎭
And Heav'n is double Heav'n, if thou art
　there.　　　　　　　　　　　　　680

She said : Her brim-full Eyes, that ready
　stood,
And only wanted Will to weep a Flood,
Releas'd their watry Store, and pour'd
　amain,
Like Clouds low hung, a sober Show'r of
　Rain ;
Mute solemn Sorrow, free from Female
　Noise,
Such as the Majesty of Grief destroys :
For, bending o'er the Cup, the Tears she shed
Seem'd by the Posture to discharge her
　Head,
O'er-fill'd before ;　and oft (her Mouth
　apply'd
To the cold Heart) she kiss'd at once, and
　cry'd.　　　　　　　　　　　　　690
Her Maids, who stood amaz'd, nor knew the
　Cause
Of her Complaining, nor whose Heart it was ;
Yet all due Measures of her Mourning kept,
Did Office at the Dirge, and by Infection
　wept ;
And oft enquir'd th' Occasion of her Grief,
(Unanswer'd but by Sighs) and offer'd vain
　Relief.
At length, her Stock of Tears already shed,
She wip'd her Eyes, she rais'd her drooping
　Head,
And thus pursu'd : O ever faithful Heart,
I have perform'd the Ceremonial Part, 700
The Decencies of Grief ; It rests behind,
That, as our Bodies were, our Souls be join'd :
To thy whate'er abode, my Shade convey,
And as an elder Ghost, direct the way.
She said ; and bad the Vial to be brought,
Where she before had brew'd the deadly
　Draught :
First pouring out the med'cinable Bane,
The Heart, her Tears had rins'd, she bath'd
　again ;
Then down her Throat the Death securely
　throws,
And quaffs a long Oblivion of her Woes. 710
　This done, she mounts the Genial Bed, and
　　there,
(Her Body first compos'd with honest Care,)
Attends the welcom Rest ; Her Hands yet
　hold
Close to her Heart, the Monumental Gold ;
Nor farther Word she spoke, but clos'd
　her Sight,
And quiet, sought the Covert of the Night.

The Damsels, who the while in Silence
mourn'd,
Not knowing, nor suspecting Death suborn'd,
Yet, as their Duty was, to *Tancred* sent,
Who, conscious of th' Occasion, fear'd th'
Event.　　　　720
Alarm'd, and with presaging Heart he came
And drew the Curtains, and expos'd the
Dame
To loathsom Light ; then with a late Relief
Made vain Efforts to mitigate her Grief.
She, what she could, excluding Day, her
Eyes
Kept firmly seal'd, and sternly thus replies :
Tancred, restrain thy Tears unsought by
me,
And Sorrow, unavailing now to thee :
Did ever Man before afflict his Mind,
To see th' Effect of what himself design'd ?
Yet, if thou hast remaining in thy Heart　731
Some Sense of Love, some unextinguish'd
Part
Of former Kindness, largely once profess'd,⎫
Let me by that adjure thy harden'd Breast, ⎬
Not to deny thy Daughters last Request : ⎭
The secret Love which I so long enjoy'd,
And still conceal'd, to gratifie thy Pride,

Thou hast disjoin'd ; but, with my dying
Breath,
Seek not, I beg thee, to disjoin our Death :
Where-e'er his Corps by thy Command is
laid,　　　　740
Thither let mine in publick be convey'd ;
Expos'd in open View, and Side by Side,
Acknowledg'd as a Bridegroom and a Bride.
　The Prince's Anguish hinder'd his Reply :
And she, who felt her Fate approaching
nigh,
Seiz'd the cold Heart, and heaving to her
Breast,
Here, precious Pledge, she said, securely rest.
These Accents were her last ; the creeping
Death
Benum'd her Senses first, then stopp'd her
Breath.
　Thus she for Disobedience justly dy'd ; 750
The Sire was justly punish'd for his Pride ;
The Youth, least guilty, suffer'd for th'
Offence
Of Duty violated to his Prince ;
Who late repenting of his cruel Deed,
One common Sepulcher for both decreed ;
Intomb'd the wretched Pair in Royal State,
And on their Monument inscrib'd their Fate.

THEODORE AND HONORIA.

OF all the Cities in *Romanian* Lands,
The chief, and most renown'd *Ravenna*
stands :
Adorn'd in ancient Times with Arms and Arts,
And rich Inhabitants, with generous Hearts.
But *Theodore* the Brave, above the rest,
With Gifts of Fortune, and of Nature
bless'd,
The foremost Place, for Wealth and Honour
held,
And all in Feats of Chivalry excell'd.
　This noble Youth to Madness lov'd a
Dame,
Of high Degree, *Honoria* was her Name ; 10
Fair as the Fairest, but of haughty Mind,
And fiercer than became so soft a kind ;
Proud of her Birth ;` (for equal she had
none ;)
The rest she scorn'd ; but hated him alone.

His Gifts, his constant Courtship, nothing
gain'd ;
For she, the more he lov'd, the more dis-
dain'd :
He liv'd with all the Pomp he cou'd devise,⎫
At Tilts and Turnaments obtain'd the Prize, ⎬
But found no favour in his Ladies Eyes : ⎭
Relentless as a Rock, the lofty Maid　　20
Turn'd all to Poyson that he did, or said :
Nor Pray'rs, nor Tears, nor offer'd Vows⎫
could move ;　　　　　　　　　　　　 ⎪
The Work went backward ; and the more ⎬
he strove　　　　　　　　　　　　　 ⎪
T' advance his Sute, the farther from her ⎭
Love.
　Weary'd at length, and wanting Remedy,
He doubted oft, and oft resolv'd to die.
But Pride stood ready to prevent the Blow,
For who would die to gratify a Foe ?
His generous Mind disdain'd so mean a Fate ;
That pass'd, his next Endeavour was to
Hate.　　　　　30

THEODORE AND HONORIA. Text from the original and only contemporary edition, 1700.

But vainer that Relief than all the rest ;
The less he hop'd, with more Desire possessed ;
Love stood the Siege, and would not yield his Breast.
Change was the next, but change deceiv'd his Care,
He sought a Fairer, but found none so Fair.
He would have worn her out by slow degrees,
As Men by Fasting starve th' untam'd Disease :
But present Love requir'd a present Ease.
Looking he feeds alone his famish'd Eyes,
Feeds lingring Death, but, looking not, he dies.   40
Yet still he chose the longest way to Fate,
Wasting at once his Life, and his Estate.
  His Friends beheld, and pity'd him in vain,
For what Advice can ease a Lover's Pain !
Absence, the best Expedient they could find
Might save the Fortune, if not cure the Mind :
This Means they long propos'd, but little gain'd,
Yet after much pursuit, at length obtain'd.
  Hard, you may think it was, to give consent,
But, struggling with his own Desires, he went ;   50
With large Expence, and with a pompous Train,
Provided, as to visit France or Spain,
Or for some distant Voyage o'er the Main.
But Love had clipp'd his Wings, and cut him short,
Confin'd within the purlieus of his Court :
Three Miles he went, nor farther could retreat ;
His Travels ended at his Country-Seat :
To Chassis pleasing Plains he took his way,
There pitch'd his Tents, and there resolv'd to stay.
  The Spring was in the Prime ; the neighb'ring Grove   60
Supply'd with Birds, the Choristers of Love :
Musick unbought, that minister'd Delight
To Morning-walks, and lull'd his Cares by Night :
There he discharg'd his Friends ; but not th' Expence
Of frequent Treats, and proud Magnificence.

He liv'd as Kings retire, though more at large,
From publick Business, yet with equal Charge ;
With House, and Heart still open to receive ;
As well content, as Love would give him leave :
He would have liv'd more free ; but many a Guest,   70
Who could forsake the Friend, pursu'd the Feast.
  It happ'd one Morning, as his Fancy led,
Before his usual Hour, he left his Bed ;
To walk within a lonely Lawn, that stood
On ev'ry side surrounded by the Wood :
Alone he walk'd, to please his pensive Mind,
And sought the deepest Solitude to find :
'Twas in a Grove of spreading Pines he stray'd ;
The Winds, within the quiv'ring Branches plaid,
And Dancing-Trees a mournful Musick made.   80
The Place it self was suiting to his Care,
Uncouth and Salvage as the cruel Fair.
He wander'd on, unknowing where he went,
Lost in the Wood, and all on Love intent :
The Day already half his Race had run,
And summon'd him to due Repast at Noon,
But Love could feel no Hunger but his own.
  While list'ning to the murm'ring Leaves he stood,
More than a Mile immers'd within the Wood,
At once the Wind was laid ; the whisp'ring sound   90
Was dumb ; a rising Earthquake rock'd the Ground :
With deeper Brown the Grove was overspred,
A sudden Horror seiz'd his giddy Head,
And his Ears tinckled, and his Colour fled.
Nature was in alarm ; some Danger nigh
Seem'd threaten'd, though unseen to mortal Eye :
Unus'd to fear, he summon'd all his Soul,
And stood collected in himself, and whole :
Not long : For soon a Whirlwind rose around,   99
And from afar he heard a screaming sound,
As of a Dame distress'd, who cry'd for Aid,
And fill'd with loud Laments the secret Shade.

A Thicket close beside the Grove there
stood,
With Breers and Brambles choak'd, and
dwarfish Wood:
From thence the Noise: Which now
approaching near
With more distinguish'd Notes invades his
Ear:
He rais'd his Head, and saw a beauteous
Maid,
With Hair dishevell'd issuing through the
Shade;
Stripp'd of her Cloaths, and e'en those
Parts reveal'd
Which modest Natuie keeps from Sight
conceal'd.   110
Her Face, her Hands, her naked Limbs were
torn,
With passing through the Brakes, and
prickly Thorn:
Two Mastiffs gaunt and grim, her Flight
pursu'd,
And oft their fasten'd Fangs in Blood
embru'd:
Oft they came up, and pinch'd her tender
Side,
Mercy, O Mercy, Heav'n, she ran, and cry'd;
When Heav'n was nam'd, they loos'd their
Hold again,
Then sprung she forth, they follow'd her
amain.
Not far behind, a Knight of swarthy Face,
High on a Coal-black Steed pursu'd the
Chace;   120
With flashing Flames his ardent Eyes were
fill'd,
And in his Hands a naked Sword he held:
He chear'd the Dogs to follow her who fled,
And vow'd Revenge on her devoted Head.
As Theodore was born of noble Kind,
The Brutal Action rowz'd his manly Mind:
Mov'd with unworthy Usage of the Maid,
He, though unarm'd, resolv'd to give her
Aid.
A Saplin Pine he wrench'd from out the
Ground,
The readiest Weapon that his Fury found.
Thus, furnish'd for Offence, he cross'd the
way   131
Betwixt the graceless Villain, and his Prey.

The Knight came thund'ring on, but from
afar
Thus in imperious Tone forbad the War:
Cease, Theodore, to proffer vain Relief,
Nor stop the vengeance of so just a Grief;
But give me leave to seize my destin'd
Prey,
And let eternal Justice take the way:
I but revenge my Fate; disdain'd, betray'd,
And suff'ring Death for this ungrateful
Maid.   140
He say'd, at once dismounting from the
Steed;
For now the Hell-hounds with superiour
Speed
Had reach'd the Dame, and fast'ning on her
Side,
The Ground with issuing Streams of Purple
dy'd.
Stood Theodore surpriz'd in deadly Fright,
With chatt'ring Teeth, and bristling Hair
upright;
Yet arm'd with inborn Worth, What e'er,
said he,
Thou art, who know'st me better than I
thee;
Or prove thy rightful Cause, or be defy'd.
The Spectre, fiercely staring, thus reply'd.
    Know, Theodore, thy Ancestry I claim, 151
And Guido Cavalcanti was my Name.
One common Sire our Fathers did beget,
My Name and Story some remember yet:
Thee, then a Boy, within my Arms I laid,
When for my Sins I lov'd this haughty
Maid;
Not less ador'd in Life, nor serv'd by Me,
Than proud Honoria now is lov'd by Thee.
What did I not her stubborn Heart to gain?
But all my Vows were answer'd with Dis-
dain;   160
She scorn'd my Sorrows, and despis'd my
Pain.
Long time I dragg'd my Days in fruitless
Care,
Then loathing Life, and plung'd in deep
Despair,
To finish my unhappy Life, I fell
On this sharp Sword, and now am damn'd
in Hell.
    Short was her Joy; for soon th' insulting
Maid
By Heav'n's Decree in the cold Grave was
laid,

And as in unrepenting Sin she dy'd,
Doom'd to the same bad Place, is punish'd
    for her Pride ;
Because she deem'd I well deserv'd to die,
And made a Merit of her Cruelty.   171
There, then, we met ; both try'd, and both
    were cast,
And this irrevocable Sentence pass'd ;
That she whom I so long pursu'd in vain,
Should suffer from my Hands a lingring
    Pain :
Renew'd to Life, that she might daily die,
I daily doom'd to follow, she to fly ;
No more a Lover but a mortal Foe,
I seek her Life (for Love is none below :)
As often as my Dogs with better speed   180
Arrest her Flight, is she to Death decreed :
Then with this fatal Sword on which I dy'd,
I pierce her open'd Back or tender Side,
And tear that harden'd Heart from out her
    Breast,
Which, with her Entrails, makes my hungry
    Hounds a Feast.
Nor lies she long, but as her Fates ordain, \
Springs up to Life, and fresh to second Pain, }
Is sav'd to Day, to Morrow to be slain. /
    This, vers'd in Death, th' infernal Knight
    relates,
And then for Proof fulfill'd their common
    Fates ;   190
Her Heart and Bowels through her Back he
    drew,
And fed the Hounds that help'd him to
    pursue.
Stern look'd the Fiend, as frustrate of his
    Will,
Not half suffic'd, and greedy yet to kill.
And now the Soul expiring through the
    Wound,
Had left the Body breathless on the Ground,
When thus the grisly Spectre spoke again :
Behold the Fruit of ill-rewarded Pain :
As many Months as I sustain'd her Hate,
So many Years is she condemn'd by Fate 200
To daily Death ; and ev'ry several Place,
Conscious of her Disdain, and my Disgrace,
Must witness her just Punishment ; and be
A Scene of Triumph and Revenge to me.
As in this Grove I took my last Farewel,
As on this very spot of Earth I fell,

As *Friday* saw me die, so she my Prey
Becomes ev'n here, on this revolving Day.
    Thus while he spoke, the Virgin from the
    Ground
Upstarted fresh, already clos'd the Wound,
And unconcern'd for all she felt before,   211
Precipitates her Flight along the Shore :
The Hell-hounds, as ungorg'd with Flesh
    and Blood
Pursue their Prey, and seek their wonted
    Food :
The Fiend remounts his Courser ; mends his
    Pace,
And all the Vision vanish'd from the Place.
    Long stood the noble Youth oppress'd \
    with Awe |
And stupid at the wond'rous Things he saw -
Surpassing common Faith ; transgressing |
    Nature's Law.   /
He would have been asleep, and wish'd to
    wake,   220
But Dreams, he knew, no long Impression
    make,
Though strong at first : If Vision, to what \
    end, |
But such as must his future State portend ? }
His Love the Damsel, and himself the |
    Fiend.   /
But yet reflecting that it could not be
From Heav'n, which cannot impious Acts
    decree,
Resolv'd within him self to shun the Snare
Which hell for his Distruction did prepare ;
And as his better Genius should direct
From an ill Cause to draw a good effect. 230
    Inspir'd from Heav'n he homeward took
    his way,
Nor pall'd his new Design with long delay ;
But of his Train a trusty Servant sent,
To call his Friends together at his Tent.
They came, and usual Salutations paid,
With Words premeditated thus he said :
What you have often counsell'd, to remove
My vain pursuit of unregarded Love ;
By Thrift my sinking Fortune to repair,
Tho' late, yet is at last become my Care : 240
My Heart shall be my own ; my vast Expence
Reduc'd to bounds, by timely Providence :
This only I require ; invite for me
Honoria, with her Father's Family,
Her Friends, and mine ; the Cause I shall
    display,
On *Friday* next, for that's th' appointed **Day.**

Well pleas'd were all his Friends, the
   Task was light ;
The Father, Mother, Daughter they invite
Hardly the Dame was drawn to this repast ;
But yet resolv'd, because it was the last. 250
The Day was come ; the Guests invited
   came,
And, with the rest, th' inexorable Dame :
A Feast prepar'd with riotous Expence,
Much Cost, more Care, and most Magnifi-
   cence.
The Place ordain'd was in that haunted
   Grove
Where the revenging Ghost pursu'd his Love:
The Tables in a proud Pavilion spread,
With Flow'rs below, and Tissue overhead :
The rest in rank ; *Honoria* chief in place
Was artfully contriv'd to set her Face   260
To front the Thicket and behold the Chace.
The Feast was serv'd ; the time so well
   forecast,
That just when the Dessert, and Fruits were
   plac'd,
The Fiend's Alarm began ; the hollow sound
Sung in the Leaves, the Forest shook
   around,
Air blacken'd ; rowl'd the Thunder ;
   groan'd the ground.
   Nor long before the loud Laments arise,
Of one distress'd, and Mastiffs mingled Cries;
And first the Dame came rushing through
   the Wood,
And next the famish'd Hounds that sought
   their Food   270
And grip'd her Flanks, and oft essay'd their
   Jaws in Blood.
Last came the Fellon on the Sable Steed,
Arm'd with his naked Sword, and urg'd his
   Dogs to speed :
She ran, and cry'd ; her Flight directly
   bent,
(A Guest unbidden) to the fatal Tent,
The Scene of Death, and Place ordain'd for
   Punishment.
Loud was the Noise, aghast was every Guest,
The Women shriek'd, the Men forsook the
   Feast ;
The Hounds at nearer distance hoarsely
   bay'd ;
The Hunter close pursu'd the visionary
   Maid,   280
She rent the Heav'n with loud Laments,
   imploring Aid.

The Gallants, to protect the Ladies right,
Their Fauchions brandish'd at the grisly
   Spright ;
High on his Stirups, he provok'd the Fight.
Then on the Crowd he cast a furious Look,
And wither'd all their Strength before he
   strook :
Back on your Lives ; let be, said he, my
   Prey,
And let my Vengeance take the destin'd way.
Vain are your Arms, and vainer your
   Defence,
Against th' eternal Doom of Providence : 290
Mine is th' ungrateful Maid by Heav'n
   design'd :
Mercy she would not give, nor Mercy shall
   she find.
At this the former Tale again he told
With thund'ring Tone, and dreadful to
   behold :
Sunk were their Hearts with Horror of the
   Crime,
Nor needed to be warn'd a second time,
But bore each other back ; some knew the
   Face,
And all had heard the much lamented Case
Of him who fell for Love, and this the fatal
   Place.
   And now th' infernal Minister advanc'd,
Seiz'd the due Victim, and with Fury
   lanch'd   301
Her Back, and piercing through her inmost
   Heart,
Drew backward, as before, th' offending part.
The reeking Entrails next he tore away,
And to his meagre Mastiffs made a Prey :
The pale Assistants on each other star'd,
With gaping Mouths for issuing Words
   prepar'd ;
The still-born sounds upon the Palate hung,
And dy'd imperfect on the faltring Tongue.
The Fright was general ; but the Female
   Band   310
(A helpless Train) in more Confusion stand ;
With horror shuddring, on a heap they run,
Sick at the sight of hateful Justice done ;
For Conscience rung th' Alarm, and made
   the Case their own.
   So spread upon a Lake, with upward Eye,
A plump of Fowl behold their Foe on high ;
They close their trembling Troop ; and all
   attend
On whom the sowsing Eagle will descend.

But most the proud *Honoria* fear'd th'
    Event,
And thought to her alone the Vision sent. 320
Her Guilt presents to her distracted Mind ⎫
Heav'n's Justice, *Theodore's* revengeful ⎬
    Kind, ⎪
And the same Fate to the same Sin assign'd; ⎭
Already sees her self the Monster's Prey,
And feels her Heart, and Entrails torn away.
'Twas a mute Scene of Sorrow, mix'd with
    fear ;
Still on the Table lay th' unfinished Cheer ;
The Knight, and hungry Mastiffs stood
    around,
The mangled Dame lay breathless on the
    Ground ;
When on a suddain reinspired with Breath,
Again she rose, again to suffer Death ; 331
Nor stay'd the Hell-hounds, nor the Hunter
    stay'd,
But follow'd, as before, the flying Maid :
Th' Avenger took from Earth th' avenging
    Sword,
And mounting light as Air, his Sable Steed
    he spurr'd :
The Clouds dispell'd, the Sky resum'd her
    Light,
And Nature stood recover'd of her Fright.
  But Fear, the last of Ills, remain'd behind,
And Horror heavy sat on ev'ry Mind.
Nor *Theodore* incourag'd more his Feast, 340
But sternly look'd, as hatching in his Breast
Some deep Design, which when *Honoria*
    view'd
The fresh Impulse her former Fright
    renew'd :
She thought her self the trembling Dame
    who fled,
And him the grisly Ghost that spurr'd th'
    infernal Steed :
The more dismay'd, for when the Guests ⎫
    withdrew, ⎪
Their courteous Host saluting all the Crew ⎬
Regardless passed her o'er ; nor grac'd ⎪
    with kind adieu. ⎭
That sting infix'd within her haughty Mind, ⎫
The downfal of her Empire she divin'd ; 350 ⎬
And her proud Heart with secret Sorrow ⎪
    pin'd. ⎭
Home as they went, the sad Discourse ⎫
    renew'd ⎬
Of the relentless Dame to Death pursu'd, ⎪
And of the Sight obscene so lately view'd ; ⎭

None durst arraign the righteous Doom she
    bore,
Ev'n they who pity'd most yet blam'd her
    more :
The Parallel they needed not to name,
But in the Dead they damn'd the living
    Dame.
  At ev'ry little Noise she look'd behind,
For still the Knight was present to her
    Mind : 360
And anxious oft she started on the way,
And thought the Horseman-Ghost came
    thundring for his Prey.
Return'd, she took her Bed with little
    Rest,
But in short Slumbers dreamt the Funeral
    Feast :
Awak'd, she turned her Side ; and slept ⎫
    again, ⎪
The same black Vapors mounted in her ⎬
    Brain, ⎪
And the same Dreams return'd with ⎭
    double Pain.
  Now forc'd to wake because afraid to
    sleep
Her Blood all Fever'd, with a furious Leap
She sprung from Bed, distracted in her
    Mind, 370
And fear'd, at ev'ry Step, a twitching
    Spright behind.
Darkling and desp'rate, with a stagg'ring
    pace,
Of Death afraid, and conscious of Disgrace ;
Fear, Pride, Remorse, at once her Heart
    assail'd,
Pride put Remorse to flight, but Fear pre-
    vail'd.
Friday, the fatal Day, when next it came,
Her Soul forethought the Fiend would
    change his Game,
And her pursue, or *Theodore* be slain,
And two Ghosts join their Packs to hunt
    her o'er the Plain.
  This dreadful Image so possess'd her
    Mind, 380
That, desp'rate any Succour else to find,
She ceas'd all farther Hope ; and now began
To make reflection on th' unhappy Man.
Rich, Brave, and Young, who past expres-
    sion lov'd,
Proof to Disdain ; and not to be remov'd :
Of all the Men respected, and admir'd,
Of all the Dames, except her self, desir'd :

Why not of her ? Preferr'd above the rest
By him with Knightly Deeds, and open
   Love profess'd ?
So had another been ; where he his Vows
   address'd.   390
This quell'd her Pride, yet other Doubts
   remain'd,
That once disdaining she might be dis-
   dain'd :
The Fear was just, but greater Fear prevail'd,
Fear of her Life by hellish Hounds assail'd :
He took a low'ring leave ; but who can tell
What outward Hate might inward Love
   conceal ?
Her Sexes Arts she knew, and why not then
Might deep dissembling have a place in Men ?
Here Hope began to dawn ; resolv'd to try,
She fix'd on this her utmost Remedy ; 400
Death was behind, but hard it was to die.
'Twas time enough at last on Death to call ;
The Precipice in sight, a Shrub was all,
That kindly stood betwixt to break the
   fatal fall.
  One Maid she had, belov'd above the rest :
Secure of her, the Secret she confess'd :
And now the chearful Light her Fears
   dispell'd,
She with no winding turns the Truth con-
   ceal'd,
But put the Woman off, and stood reveal'd :

With Faults confess'd commission'd her
   to go,   410
If Pity yet had place, and reconcile her
   Foe.
The welcom Message made, was soon
   receiv'd ;
'Twas what he wish'd, and hop'd, but scarce
   believ'd ;
Fate seem'd a fair occasion to present,
He knew the Sex, and fear'd she might
   repent,
Should he delay the moment of Consent.
There yet remain'd to gain her Friends
   (a Care
The modesty of Maidens well might spare ;)
But she with such a Zeal the Cause em-
   brac'd,
(As Women where they will, are all in
   hast,)   420
That Father, Mother, and the Kin beside,
Were overborn by Fury of the Tide :
With full consent of all, she chang'd her
   State,
Resistless in her Love, as in her Hate.
  By her Example warn'd, the rest beware ;
More Easy, less Imperious, were the Fair ;
And that one Hunting which the Devil
   design'd,
For one fair Female, lost him half the
   Kind.

CYMON AND IPHIGENIA.

FROM BOCCACE.

Poeta loquitur,

OLD as I am, for Ladies Love unfit,
The Pow'r of Beauty I remember yet,
Which once inflam'd my Soul, and still
   inspires my Wit.
If Love be Folly, the severe Divine
Has felt that Folly, tho' he censures mine ;
Pollutes the Pleasures of a chast Embrace,
Acts what I write, and propagates in Grace
With riotous Excess, a Priestly Race :
Suppose him free, and that I forge th'
   offence,   9
He shew'd the way, perverting first my Sense :

In Malice witty, and with Venom fraught,
He makes me speak the Things I never
   thought.
Compute the Gains of his ungovern'd Zeal ;
Ill sutes his Cloth the Praise of Railing well !
The World will think that what we loosly
   write,
Tho' now arraign'd, he read with some
   delight ;
Because he seems to chew the Cud again,
When his broad Comment makes the Text
   too plain,

403 sight, a] sight : A *1700.*
413 what he] *Warton and others wrongly give*
to be

CYMON AND IPHIGENIA.
1 Ladies] *Chrissie and Saintsbury give* lady's
Some editors give ladies' *There can be no
doubt that the word is genitive plural: cf.
Horace, Car.* iii. 26. 1.

And teaches more in one explaining Page,
Than all the double Meanings of the Stage.
What needs he Paraphrase on what we
  mean ?   21
We were at worst but Wanton ; he's
  Obscene.
I, nor my fellows, nor my Self excuse ;
But Love's the Subject of the Comick Muse :
Nor can we write without it, nor would you
A Tale of only dry Instruction view ;
Nor Love is always of a vicious Kind,
But oft to virtuous Acts inflames the Mind,
Awakes the sleepy Vigour of the Soul,
And, brushing o'er, adds Motion to the
  Pool.   30
Love, studious how to please, improves our
  Parts,
With polish'd Manners, and adorns with
  Arts.
Love first invented Verse, and form'd the
  Rhime,
The Motion measur'd, harmoniz'd the
  Chime ;
To lib'ral Acts inlarg'd the narrow-Soul'd,
Soften'd the Fierce, and made the Coward
  Bold :
The World when wast, he Peopled with
  increase,
And warring Nations reconcil'd in Peace.
Ormond, the first, and all the Fair may find ⎫
In this one Legend to their Fame design'd, ⎪
When Beauty fires the Blood, how Love ⎬
  exalts the Mind.   41 ⎭
IN that sweet Isle, where Venus keeps her
  Court,
And ev'ry Grace, and all the Loves resort ;
Where either Sex is form'd of softer Earth,
And takes the bent of Pleasure from their
  Birth ;
There liv'd a Cyprian Lord, above the rest
Wise, Wealthy, with a num'rous Issue blest.
But as no Gift of Fortune is sincere,
Was only wanting in a worthy Heir :
His eldest Born a goodly youth to view 50
Excell'd the rest in Shape, and outward
  Shew ;
Fair, Tall, his Limbs with due Proportion
  join'd,
But of a heavy, dull, degenerate Mind.
His Soul bely'd the Features of his Face ;
Beauty was there, but Beauty in disgrace.
A clownish Mien, a Voice with rustick sound,
And stupid Eyes, that ever lov'd the Ground.

He looked like Nature's Error ; as the Mind ⎫
And Body were not of a Piece design'd, ⎪
But made for two, and by mistake in one ⎬
  were join'd.   60 ⎭
The ruling Rod, the Father's forming
  Care,
Were exercis'd in vain, on Wit's despair ;
The more inform'd the less he understood,
And deeper sunk by flound'ring in the
  Mud.
Now scorn'd of all, and grown the publick
  Shame,
The people from Galesus changed his name,
And Cymon call'd, which signifies a Brute ;
So well his Name did with his Nature sute.
His Father, when he found his Labour
  lost,
And Care employ'd that answer'd not the
  Cost,   70
Chose an ungrateful Object to remove,
And loath'd to see what Nature made him
  love ;
So to his Country-Farm the Fool confin'd :
Rude Work well suted with a rustick Mind.
Thus to the Wilds the sturdy Cymon went,
A Squire among the Swains, and pleas'd
  with Banishment.
His Corn, and Cattle, were his only Care,
And his supreme Delight a Country-Fair.
  It happen'd on a Summers Holiday, ⎫
That to the Greenwood-shade he took his ⎪
  way ;   80 ⎬
For Cymon shunn'd the Church, and us'd ⎪
  not much to Pray. ⎭
His Quarter Staff, which he cou'd ne'er for-
  sake,
Hung half before, and half behind his Back.
He trudg'd along unknowing what he
  sought,
And whistled as he went, for want of
  Thought.
  By Chance conducted, or by Thirst con-
  strain'd,
The deep Recesses of the Grove he gain'd ;
Where, in a Plain, defended by the Wood, ⎫
Crept through the matted Grass a Chrystal ⎪
  Flood, ⎬
By which an Alabaster Fountain stood: 90 ⎭
And on the Margin of the Fount was laid
(Attended by her Slaves) a sleeping Maid
Like Dian and her Nymphs, when, tir'd
  with Sport,
To rest by cool Eurotas they resort :

The Dame herself the Goddess well ex-
press'd,
Not more distinguish'd by her Purple Vest,
Than by the charming Features of her Face,
And ev'n in Slumber a superiour Grace :
Her comely Limbs compos'd with decent Care, 99
Her Body shaded with a slight Cymarr ;
Her Bosom to the view was only bare :
Where two beginning Paps were scarcely spy'd
For yet their Places were but signify'd :
The fanning Wind upon her Bosom blows,
To meet the fanning Wind the Bosom rose;
The fanning Wind, and purling Streams continue her repose.
    The Fool of Nature, stood with stupid Eyes
And gaping Mouth, that testify'd Surprize,
Fix'd on her Face, nor cou'd remove his Sight,
New as he was to Love, and Novice in Delight : 110
Long mute he stood, and leaning on his Staff,
His Wonder witness'd with an Ideot laugh ;
Then would have spoke, but by his glimmer-
ing Sense
First found his want of Words, and fear'd
Offence :
Doubted for what he was he should be
known,
By his Clown-Accent and his Country-Tone.
Through the rude Chaos thus the running Light
Shot the first Ray that pirc'd the Native Night :
Then Day and Darkness in the Mass were mix'd,
Till gather'd in a Globe, the Beams were fix'd : 120
Last shon the Sun who, radiant in his Sphere
Illumin'd Heav'n, and Earth, and rowl'd around the Year.
So Reason in this Brutal Soul began :
Love made him first suspect he was a Man ;
Love made him doubt his broad barbarian Sound ;
By Love his want of Words and Wit he found ;
That sense of want prepar'd the future way
To Knowledge, and disclos'd the promise of a Day.

What not his Father's Care, nor Tutor's Art
Cou'd plant with Pains in his unpolish'd Heart, 130
The best Instructor Love at once inspir'd,
As barren Grounds to Fruitfulness are fir'd ;
Love taught him Shame, and Shame with Love at Strife
Soon taught the sweet Civilities of Life ;
His gross material Soul at once could find
Somewhat in her excelling all her Kind :
Exciting a Desire till then unknown,
Somewhat unfound, or found in her alone.
This made the first Impression in his Mind,
Above, but just above, the Brutal Kind. 140
For Beasts can like, but not distinguish too.
Nor their own liking by reflection know ;
Nor why they like or this, or t'other Face,
Or judge of this or that peculiar Grace ;
But love in gross, and stupidly admire ;
As Flies allur'd by Light, approach the Fire.
Thus our Man-Beast advancing by degrees
First likes the whole, then sep'rates what he sees ;
On sev'ral Parts a sev'ral Praise bestows,
The ruby Lips, the well-proportion'd Nose,
The snowy Skin, in Raven-glossy Hair, 151
The dimpled Cheek, the Forehead rising fair,
And ev'n in Sleep it self a smiling Air.
From thence his Eyes descending view'd the rest,
Her plump round Arms, white Hands, and heaving Breast.
Long on the last he dwelt, though ev'ry part
A pointed Arrow sped to pierce his Heart.
    Thus in a trice a Judge of Beauty grown,
(A Judge erected from a Country-Clown)
He long'd to see her Eyes in Slumber hid,
And wish'd his own cou'd pierce within the Lid : 161
He wou'd have wak'd her, but restrain'd his Thought,
And Love new-born the first good Manners taught.
An awful Fear his ardent Wish withstood,
Nor durst disturb the Goddess of the Wood ;
For such she seem'd by her celestial Face,
Excelling all the rest of human Race :

---

139 in] *The editors wrongly give* on

And Things divine, by common Sense he
  knew,
Must be devoutly seen at distant view :
So checking his Desire, with trembling
  Heart   170
Gazing he stood, nor would, nor could depart;
Fix'd as a Pilgrim wilder'd in his way,
Who dares not stir by Night for fear to
  stray ;
But stands with awful Eyes to watch the
  dawn of Day.
  At length awaking, *Iphigene* the fair
(So was the Beauty call'd who caus'd his
  Care)
Unclos'd her eyes, and double Day reveal'd,
While those of all her Slaves in Sleep were
  seal'd.
    The slavering Cudden, prop'd upon his
  Staff,
Stood ready gaping with a grinning Laugh,
To welcome her awake, nor durst begin 181
To speak, but wisely kept the Fool within.
Then she : What make you *Cymon* here
  alone ?
(For *Cymon's* name was round the Country
  known,
Because descended of a noble Race,
And for a Soul ill sorted with his Face.)
  But still the Sot stood silent with Surprize,
With fix'd regard on her new open'd Eyes,
And in his Breast receiv'd th' invenom'd
  Dart,
A tickling Pain that pleas'd amid the Smart.
But conscious of her Form, with quick
  distrust   191
She saw his sparkling Eyes, and fear'd his
  brutal Lust :
This to prevent, she wak'd her sleepy Crew,
And rising hasty took a short Adieu.
  Then *Cymon* first his rustick Voice essay'd,
With proffer'd Service to the parting Maid
To see her safe ; his Hand she long deny'd,
But took at length, asham'd of such a Guide.
So *Cymon* led her home, and leaving there,
No more wou'd to his Country Clowns
  repair,   200
But sought his Father's House, with better
  Mind,
Refusing in the Farm to be confin'd.
  The Father wonder'd at the Son's return,
And knew not whether to rejoice or mourn ;
But doubtfully receiv'd, expecting still
To learn the secret Causes of his alter'd Will.

Nor was he long delay'd : the first Request
He made, was, like his Brothers to be dress'd,
And, as his Birth requir'd, above the rest.
  With ease his Sute was granted by his Syre,
Distinguishing his Heir by rich Attire : 211
His Body thus adorn'd, he next design'd
With lib'ral Arts to cultivate his Mind ;
He sought a Tutor of his own accord,
And study'd Lessons he before abhorr'd.
  Thus the Man-Child advanc'd, and learned
  so fast,
That in short time his Equals he surpass'd :
His brutal Manners from his Breast exil'd,
His Mien he fashion'd, and his Tongue he
  fil'd ;
In ev'ry Exercise of all admir'd,   220
He seem'd, nor only seem'd but was in-
  spir'd :
Inspir'd by Love, whose Business is to
  please ;
He Rode, he Fenc'd, he moved with grace-
  ful Ease,
More fam'd for Sense, for courtly Carriage
  more,
Than for his brutal Folly known before.
  What then of alter'd *Cymon* shall we say,
But that the Fire which choak'd in Ashes lay,
A Load too heavy for his Soul to move,
Was upward blown below, and brush'd away
  by Love ?
Love made an active Progress through his
  Mind,   230
The dusky Parts he clear'd, the gross refin'd ;
The drowsy wak'd ; and as he went im-
  press'd
The Maker's Image on the human Beast.
Thus was the Man amended by Desire,
And, tho' he lov'd perhaps with too much
  Fire,
His Father all his Faults with Reason scan'd,
And lik'd an error of the better Hand ;
Excus'd th' excess of Passion in his Mind,
By Flames too fierce, perhaps too much
  refin'd :   239
So *Cymon*, since his Sire indulg'd his Will,
Impetuous lov'd, and would be *Cymon* still ;
Galesus he disown'd, and chose to bear
The Name of Fool confirm'd, and Bishop'd
  by the Fair.

---

233 Beast] *All the English editors change
this word into* Breast, *a most thoughtless and
ludicrous error.*

To *Cipseus* by his Friends his Sute he mov'd,
Cipseus the Father of the Fair he lov'd:
But he was pre-ingag'd by former Ties,
While *Cymon* was endeav'ring to be wise
And *Iphigene*, oblig'd by former Vows,
Had giv'n her Faith to wed a Foreign Spouse:
Her Sire and She to *Rhodian Pasimond*, 250
Tho' both repenting, were by Promise bound,
Nor could retract; and thus, as Fate decreed,
Tho' better lov'd, he spoke too late to speed.
  The Doom was past, the Ship already sent
Did all his tardy Diligence prevent:
Sigh'd to her self the fair unhappy Maid,
While stormy *Cymon* thus in secret said:
The time is come for *Iphigene* to find
The Miracle she wrought upon my Mind:
Her Charms have made me Man, her ravish'd Love 260
In rank shall place me with the Bless'd above.
For mine by Love, by Force she shall be mine,
Or Death, if Force should fail, shall finish my Design.
  Resolv'd he said: And rigg'd with speedy Care
A Vessel strong, and well equipp'd for War.
The secret Ship with chosen Friends he stor'd,
And bent to die, or conquer, went aboard.
Ambush'd he lay behind the *Cyprian* Shore,
Waiting the Sail that all his Wishes bore; 270
Nor long expected, for the following Tide
Sent out the hostile Ship and beauteous Bride.
  To *Rhodes* the Rival Bark directly steer'd,
When *Cymon* sudden at her Back appear'd,
And stop'd her Flight: Then standing on his Prow
In haughty Terms he thus defy'd the Foe:
Or strike your Sails at Summons, or prepare
To prove the last Extremities of War.
Thus warn'd, the *Rhodians* for the Fight provide;
Already were the Vessels Side by Side,
These obstinate to save, and those to seize the Bride. 280
But *Cymon* soon his crooked Grapples cast,
Which with tenacious hold his Foes embrac'd,
And arm'd with Sword and Shield, amid the Press he pass'd.

Fierce was the Fight, but hast'ning to his Prey,
By force the furious Lover freed his way:
Himself alone dispers'd the *Rhodian* Crew,
The Weak disdain'd, the Valiant overthrew;
Cheap Conquest for his following Friends remain'd,
He reap'd the Field, and they but only glean'd. 289
  His Victory confess'd, the Foes retreat,
And cast their Weapons at the Victor's Feet.
Whom thus he chear'd: O *Rhodian* Youth, I fought
For Love alone, nor other Booty sought;
Your Lives are safe; your Vessel I resign.
Yours be your own, restoring what is mine:
In *Iphigene* I claim my rightful Due,
Rob'd by my Rival, and detain'd by you:
Your *Pasimond* a lawless Bargain drove,
The Parent could not sell the Daughters Love;
Or if he cou'd, my Love disdains the Laws,
And like a King by Conquest gains his Cause; 301
Where Arms take place, all other Pleas are vain;
Love taught me Force, and Force shall Love maintain.
You, what by Strength you could not keep, release,
And at an easy Ransom buy your Peace.
  Fear on the conquer'd Side soon sign'd th' Accord,
And *Iphigene* to *Cymon* was restor'd:
While to his Arms the blushing Bride he took,
To seeming Sadness she compos'd her Look;
As if by Force subjected to his Will, 310
Tho' pleas'd, dissembling, and a Woman still.
And, for she wept, he wip'd her falling Tears,
And pray'd her to dismiss her empty Fears;
For yours I am, he said, and have deserv'd
Your Love much better, whom so long I serv'd,
Than he to whom your formal Father ty'd
Your Vows; and sold a Slave, not sent a Bride.
Thus while he spoke, he seiz'd the willing Prey,
As *Paris* bore the *Spartan* Spouse away:
Faintly she scream'd, and ev'n her Eyes confess'd 320
She rather would be thought, than was distress'd.

Who now exults but *Cymon* in his Mind? ⎫
Vain hopes and empty Joys of human Kind, ⎬
Proud of the present, to the future blind! ⎭
Secure of Fate, while *Cymon* plows the Sea,
And steers to *Candy* with his conquer'd Prey,
Scarce the third Glass of measur'd Hours
   was run,
When like a fiery Meteor sunk the Sun,
The Promise of a Storm ; the shifting Gales
Forsake by Fits and fill the flagging Sails :
Hoarse Murmurs of the Main from far were
   heard,   331
And Night came on, not by degrees prepar'd,
But all at once ; at once the Winds arise,
The Thunders roul, the forky Lightning flies
In vain the Master issues out Commands,
In vain the trembling Sailors ply their
   Hands ;
The Tempest unforeseen prevents their Care,
And from the first they labour in despair.
The giddy Ship betwixt the Winds and
   Tides,
Forc'd back and forwards, in a Circle rides,
Stun'd with the diff'rent Blows ; then shoots
   amain   341
Till counterbuff'd she stops, and sleeps again.
Not more aghast the proud Archangel fell,
Plung'd from the height of Heav'n to
   deepest Hell,
Than stood the Lover of his Love possess'd
Now curs'd the more, the more he had been
   bless'd ;
More anxious for her Danger than his own,
Death he defies ; but would be lost alone.
  Sad *Iphigene* to Womanish Complaints
Adds pious Pray'rs, and wearies all the
   Saints ;   350
Ev'n if she could, her Love she would
   repent,
But since she cannot, dreads the Punish-
   ment :
Her forfeit Faith, and *Pasimond* betray'd,
Are ever present, and her Crime upbraid.
She blames herself, nor blames her Lover
   less ;
Augments her Anger as her Fears increase ;
From her own Back the Burden would
   remove,
And lays the Load on his ungovern'd Love,
Which interposing durst in Heav'n's despight
Invade, and violate another's Right :   360
The Pow'rs incens'd awhile deferr'd his Pain,
And made him Master of his Vows in vain :

But soon they punish'd his presumptuous ⎫
   Pride ;   ⎬
That for his daring Enterprize she dy'd, ⎬
Who rather not resisted, than comply'd. ⎭
  Then impotent of Mind, with alter'd Sense,
She hugg'd th' Offender, and forgave th'
   Offence,
Sex to the last : Mean time with Sails
   declin'd
The wand'ring Vessel drove before the Wind:
Toss'd, and retoss'd, aloft, and then alow ; ⎫
Nor Port they seek, nor certain Course ⎬
   they know,   371 ⎬
But ev'ry moment wait the coming Blow. ⎭
Thus blindly driv'n, by breaking Day they
   view'd
The Land before 'em, and their Fears
   renew'd ;
The Land was welcome, but the Tempest
   bore
The threaten'd Ship against a rocky Shore.
  A winding Bay was near ; to this they
   bent,
And just escap'd ; their Force already spent.
Secure from Storms, and panting from the
   Sea,
The Land unknown at leisure they survey ;
And saw (but soon their sickly Sight with-
   drew)   381
The rising Tow'rs of *Rhodes* at distant view ;
And curs'd the hostile Shoar of *Pasimond*,
Sav'd from the Seas, and shipwreck'd on
   the Ground.
  The frighted Sailors try'd their Strength
   in vain
To turn the Stern, and tempt the stormy
   Main ;
But the stiff Wind withstood the lab'ring
   Oar,
And forc'd them forward on the fatal Shoar !
The crooked Keel now bites the *Rhodian*
   Strand,
And the Ship moor'd, constrains the Crew
   to land :   390
Yet still they might be safe, because un-
   known ;
But as ill Fortune seldom comes alone,
The Vessel they dismiss'd was driv'n before,
Already shelter'd on their Native Shoar ;
Known each, they know : But each with
   change of Chear ;
The vanquish'd side exults ; the Victors
   fear ;

Not them but theirs, made Pris'ners ere
   they Fight,
Despairing Conquest and depriv'd of Flight.
The Country rings around with loud
   Alarms,
And raw in Fields the rude Militia swarms ;
Mouths without Hands ; maintain'd at vast
   Expence,					401
In Peace a Charge, in War a weak Defence ;
Stout once a Month they march, a blust'ring
   Band,
And ever, but in times of Need, at hand ;
This was the Morn when issuing on the
   Guard,
Drawn up in Rank and File they stood
   prepar'd
Of seeming Arms to make a short essay,
Then hasten to be Drunk, the Business of
   the Day.
The Cowards would have fled, but that
   they knew
Themselves so many, and their Foes so few ;
But crowding on, the last the first impel ; 411
Till overborn with weight the *Cyprians* fell.
Cymon inslav'd, who first the War begun,
And *Iphigene* once more is lost and won.
Deep in a Dungeon was the Captive cast,
Depriv'd of Day, and held in Fetters fast :
His Life was only spar'd at their Request,
Whom taken he so nobly had releas'd :
But *Iphigenia* was the Ladies Care,
Each in their turn address'd to treat the ⎫
   Fair ;					420 ⎬
While *Pasimond* and his, the Nuptial Feast ⎭
   prepare.
Her secret Soul to *Cymon* was inclin'd, ⎫
Butshemust sufferwhat herFates assign'd; ⎬
So passive is the Church of Womankind. ⎭
What worse to *Cymon* could his Fortune deal,
Rowl'd to the lowest Spoke of all her Wheel ?
It rested to dismiss the downward weight,
Or raise him upward to his former height ;
The latter pleas'd ; and Love (concern'd the
   most)
Prepar'd th' amends, for what by Love he
   lost.					430
The Sire of *Pasimond* had left a Son,
Thoughyounger,yet forCourage early known,
Ormisda call'd, to whom, by Promise ty'd,
A *Rhodian* Beauty was the destin'd Bride :
Cassandra was her Name, above the rest
Renown'd for Birth, with Fortune amply
   bless'd.

Lysymachus who rul'd the *Rhodian* State,
Was then by choice their annual Magistrate :
He lov'd *Cassandra* too with equal Fire,
But Fortune had not favour'd his Desire ;
Cross'd by her Friends, by her not dis-
   approv'd,					441
Nor yet preferr'd, or like *Ormisda* lov'd :
So stood th' Affair : Some little Hope
   remain'd,
That should his Rival chance to lose, he
   gain'd.
Meantime young *Pasimond* his Marriage
   press'd,
Ordain'd the Nuptial Day, prepar'd the
   Feast ;
And frugally resolv'd (the Charge to shun, ⎫
Whichwould bedoubleshould hewedalone) ⎬
To join his Brother's Bridal with his own. ⎭
Lysymachus oppress'd with mortal Grief
Receiv'd the News, and study'd quick Re-
   lief :					451
The fatalDayapproach'd: IfForce wereus'd,
The Magistrate his publick Trust abus'd ;
To Justice liable, as Law requir'd,
For when his Office ceas'd, his Pow'r ex-
   pir'd :
While Pow'r remain'd, the Means were in
   his Hand
By Force to seize, and then forsake theLand:
Betwixt Extreams he knew not how to
   move,
A Slave to Fame, but more a Slave to Love :
Restraining others, yet himself not free,
Made impotent by Pow'r, debas'd by
   Dignity !					461
Both Sides he weigh'd : But after much
   Debate,
The Man prevail'd above the Magistrate.
Love never fails to master what he finds, ⎫
But works a diff'rent way in diff'rent ⎬
   Minds,   ⎪
The Fool enlightens, and the Wise he ⎭
   blinds.
This Youth proposing to possess, and scape,
Began in Murder, to conclude in Rape :
Unprais'd by me, tho' Heav'n sometime
   may bless
An impious Act with undeserv'd Success :
The Great, it seems, are priviledg'd alone 471
To punish all Injustice but their own.
But here I stop, not daring to proceed, ⎫
Yet blush to flatter an unrighteous Deed : ⎬
For Crimes are but permitted, not decreed. ⎭

Resolv'd on Force, his Wit the Pretor
    bent
To find the Means that might secure th'
    event ;
Nor long he labour'd, for his lucky Thought
In Captive *Cymon* found the Friend he
    sought.
Th' Example pleas'd : The Cause and Crime
    the same ;   480
An injur'd Lover, and a ravish'd Dame.
How much he durst he knew by what he
    dar'd,
The less he had to lose, the less he car'd
To menage loathsom Life when Love was
    the Reward.
    This ponder'd well, and fix'd on his Intent,
In depth of Night he for the Pris'ner sent ;
In secret sent, the publick View to shun,
Then with a sober Smile he thus begun :
The Pow'rs above, who bounteously bestow
Their Gifts and Graces on Mankind be-
    low,   490
Yet prove our Merit first, nor blindly give
To such as are not worthy to receive :
For Valour and for Virtue they provide
Their due Reward, but first they must be
    try'd :
These fruitful Seeds within your Mind they
    sow'd ;
'Twas yours t' improve the Talent they
    bestow'd ;
They gave you to be born of noble Kind,
They gave you Love to lighten up your Mind
And purge the grosser Parts ; they gave you
    Care
To please, and Courage to deserve the Fair.
    Thus far they try'd you, and by Proof
    they found   501
The Grain intrusted in a grateful Ground :
But still the great Experiment remain'd,
They suffer'd you to lose the Prize you
    gain'd ;
That you might learn the Gift was theirs
    alone,
And when restor'd, to them the Blessing
    own.
Restor'd it soon will be ; the Means pre-
    par'd,
The Difficulty smooth'd, the Danger shar'd :
Be but your self, the Care to me resign,
Then *Iphigene* is yours, *Cassandra* mine. 510
Your Rival *Pasimond* pursues your Life,
Impatient to revenge his ravish'd Wife.

But yet not his ; to Morrow is behind,
And Love our Fortunes in one Band has
    join'd :
Two Brothers are our Foes, *Ormisda* mine,
As much declar'd, as *Pasimond* is thine :
To Morrow must their common Vows be
    ty'd :
With Love to Friend, and Fortune for our
    Guide,
Let both resolve to die, or each redeem a
    Bride.
    Right I have none, nor hast thou much
    to plead ;   520
'Tis Force when done must justify the Deed :
Our Task perform'd we next prepare for
    Flight :
And let the Losers talk in vain of Right :
We with the Fair will sail before the Wind,
If they are griev'd, I leave the Laws behind.
Speak thy Resolves ; if now thy Courage
    droop,
Despair in Prison, and abandon Hope ;
But if thou dar'st in Arms thy Love regain,
(For Liberty without thy Love were vain :)
Then second my Design to seize the Prey,
Or lead to second Rape, for well thou know'st
    the way.   531
    Said *Cymon*, overjoy'd, Do Thou propose
The Means to Fight, and only shew the Foes;
For from the first, when Love had fir'd my
    Mind,
Resolv'd I left the Care of Life behind.
    To this the bold *Lysymachus* reply'd,
Let Heav'n be neuter and the Sword decide :
The Spousals are prepar'd, already play
The Minstrels, and provoke the tardy Day :
By this the Brides are wak'd, their Grooms
    are dress'd ;   540
All *Rhodes* is summon'd to the Nuptial
    Feast,
All but my self, the sole unbidden Guest.
Unbidden though I am, I will be there,
And, join'd by thee, intend to joy the Fair.
    Now hear the rest ; when Day resigns
    the Light,
And chearful Torches guild the jolly Night ;
Be ready at my Call, my chosen few
With Arms administer'd shall aid thy Crew.
Then entring unexpected will we seize
Our destin'd Prey, from Men dissolv'd in
    ease,   550
By Wine disabled, unprepar'd for Fight,
And hast'ning to the Seas suborn our Flight :

The Seas are ours, for I command the Fort,
A Ship well man'd, expects us in the Port:
If they, or if their Friends the Prize contest,
Death shall attend the Man who dares resist.
    It pleas'd! The Pris'ner to his Hold
      retir'd,
His Troop with equal Emulation fir'd,
All fix'd to Fight, and all their wonted
      Work requir'd.
    The Sun arose; the Streets were throng'd
      around,   560
The Palace open'd, and the Posts were
    crown'd:
The double Bridegroom at the Door attends
Th' expected Spouse, and entertains the
    Friends:
They meet, they lead to Church; the Priests
    invoke
The Pow'rs, and feed the Flames with
    fragrant Smoke:
This done they Feast, and at the close of
    Night
By kindled Torches vary their Delight,
These lead the lively Dance, and those the
    brimming Bowls invite.
    Now, at th' appointed Place and Hour
    assign'd,
With Souls resolv'd the Ravishers were
    join'd: 570
Three Bands are form'd: The first is sent
    before
To favour the Retreat and guard the Shore:
The second at the Palace-gate is plac'd,
And up the lofty Stairs ascend the last:
A peaceful Troop they seem with shining
    Vests,
But Coats of Male beneath secure their
    Breasts.
    Dauntless they enter, *Cymon* at their
    Head,
And find the Feast renew'd, the Table spread:
Sweet Voices mix'd with instrumental
    Sounds
Ascend the vaulted Roof, the vaulted Roof
    rebounds.   580
When like the Harpies rushing through the
    Hall
The suddain Troop appears, the Tables fall,
Their smoaking Load is on the Pavement
    thrown;
Each Ravisher prepares to seize his own:
The Brides invaded with a rude Embrace
Shreek out for Aid, Confusion fills the Place:

Quick to redeem the Prey their plighted
    Lords
Advance, the Palace gleams with shining
    Swords.
    But late is all Defence; and Succour vain;
The Rape is made, the Ravishers remain:
Two sturdy Slaves were only sent before   591
To bear the purchas'd Prize in Safety to the
    Shore.
The Troop retires, the Lovers close the rear,
With forward Faces not confessing Fear:
Backward they move, but scorn their Pace
    to mend,
Then seek the Stairs, and with slow hast
    descend.
    Fierce *Pasimond*, their passage to pre-
      vent,
Thrust full on *Cymon's* Back in his descent,
The Blade return'd unbath'd, and to the
      Handle bent: 599
Stout *Cymon* soon remounts, and cleft in two
His Rival's Head with one descending Blow:
And as the next in rank *Ormisda* stood,
He turn'd the Point; The sword inur'd to
    Blood
Bor'd his unguarded Breast, which pour'd
    a purple Flood.
    With vow'd Revenge the gath'ring Crowd
    pursues,
The Ravishers turn Head, the Fight renews;
The Hall is heap'd with Corps; the sprinkled
    Gore
Besmears the Walls, and floats the Marble
    Floor.
Dispers'd at length the drunken Squadron
    flies,
The Victors to their Vessel bear the Prize;
And hear behind loud Groans, and lament-
    able Cries.   611
    The Crew with merry Shouts their
    Anchors weigh,
Then ply their Oars, and brush the buxom
    Sea,
While Troops of gather'd *Rhodians* croud
    the Key.
What should the People do, when left alone?
The Governor, and Government are gone;
The publick Wealth to Foreign Parts con-
    vey'd;
Some Troops disbanded, and the rest unpaid.
Rhodes is the Soveraign of the Sea no more;
Their Ships unrigg'd, and spent their Naval
    Store;   620

They neither could defend, nor can pursue,
But grind their Teeth, and cast a helpless
    view :
In vain with Darts a distant War they try,
Short, and more short the missive Weapons
    fly.
Mean while the Ravishers their Crimes enjoy,
And flying Sails, and sweeping Oars employ :
The Cliffs of *Rhodes* in little space are lost ;
Jove's Isle they seek ; nor *Jove* denies his
    Coast.
    In safety landed on the *Candian* Shore,
With generous Wines their Spirits they
    restore ;   630

There *Cymon* with his *Rhodian* Friend
    resides,
Both Court, and Wed at once the willing
    Brides.
A War ensues, the *Cretans* own their Cause,
Stiff to defend their hospitable Laws :
Both Parties lose by turns ; and neither
    wins,
Till Peace propounded by a Truce begins.
The Kindred of the Slain forgive the Deed,
But a short Exile must for Show precede ;
The Term expir'd, from *Candia* they
    remove ;   639
And happy each at Home enjoys his love.

TRANSLATIONS OF LATIN HYMNS
AND
MINOR MISCELLANIES.

VENI, CREATOR SPIRITUS.

TRANSLATED IN PARAPHRASE.

CREATOR Spirit, by whose aid
The World's Foundations first were laid,
Come, visit ev'ry pious Mind ;
Come, pour thy Joys on Human Kind ;
From Sin, and Sorrow set us free ;
And make thy Temples worthy Thee.
    O, Source of uncreated Light,
The Father's promis'd *Paraclite* !
Thrice Holy Fount, thrice Holy Fire,
Our Hearts with Heav'nly Love inspire ;   10
Come, and thy Sacred Unction bring
To Sanctifie us, while we sing !
    Plenteous of Grace, descend from high,
Rich in thy sev'n-fold Energy !
Thou strength of his Almighty Hand,
Whose Pow'r does Heav'n and Earth com-
    mand :
Proceeding Spirit, our Defence,
Who do'st the Gift of Tongues dispence, }
And crown'st thy Gift with Eloquence !

    Refine and purge our Earthy Parts ;   20
But, oh, inflame and fire our Hearts !
Our Frailties help, our Vice controul ;
Submit the Senses to the Soul ;
And when Rebellious they are grown,
Then, lay thy hand, and hold 'em down.
    Chace from our Minds th' Infernal Foe ;
And Peace, the fruit of Love, bestow ;
And, lest our Feet shou'd step astray,
Protect, and guide us in the way.
    Make us Eternal Truths receive,   30
And practise, all that we believe :
Give us thy self, that we may see
The Father and the Son, by thee.
    Immortal Honour, endless Fame,
Attend th' Almighty Father's Name :
The Saviour Son be glorify'd,
Who for lost Man's Redemption dy'd :
And equal Adoration be,
Eternal *Paraclete*, to thee.

VENI CREATOR.   Text from the original in *Examen Poeticum*, 1693.

TE DEUM.

THEE, Sovereign God, our grateful Accents
    praise ;
We own thee Lord, and bless thy wondrous
    ways ;
To thee, Eternal Father, Earth's whole
    Frame
With loudest Trumpets sounds immortal
    Fame.
Lord God of Hosts ! for thee the heav'nly
    Pow'rs
With sounding Anthems fill the vaulted
    Tow'rs.
Thy Cherubims thrice Holy, Holy, Holy cry ; ⎫
Thrice Holy, all the Seraphims reply,   ⎬
And thrice returning Echoes endless Songs ⎪
    supply.   ⎭
Both Heav'n and Earth thy Majesty dis-
    play ;   10
They owe their Beauty to thy glorious
    Ray.
Thy Praises fill the loud Apostles' Quire :
The Train of Prophets in the Song conspire.
Legions of Martyrs in the Chorus shine,
And vocal Blood with vocal Musick join.
By these thy Church, inspir'd by heav'nly
    Art,
Around the World maintains a second Part,
And tunes her sweetest Notes, O God, to
    thee,
The Father of unbounded Majesty ;
The Son, ador'd Co-partner of thy Seat,   20
And equal everlasting *Paraclete.*

Thou King of Glory, Christ, of the Most
    High
Thou co-eternal filial Deity ;
Thou who, to save the World's impending
    Doom,
Vouchsaf'dst to dwell within a Virgin's
    Womb ;
Old Tyrant Death disarm'd, before thee flew
The Bolts of Heav'n, and back the Foldings
    drew,
To give access, and make thy faithful way ;
From God's right Hand thy filial Beams
    display.
Thou art to judge the Living and the Dead ;
Then spare those Souls for whom thy Veins
    have bled.   31
O take us up amongst thy blest above,
To share with them thy everlasting Love
Preserve, O Lord ! thy People, and enhance
Thy Blessing on thine own Inheritance.
For ever raise their Hearts, and rule their
    ways,
Each Day we bless thee, and proclaim thy
    Praise ;
No Age shall fail to celebrate thy Name,
No Hour neglect thy everlasting Fame.
Preserve our Souls, O Lord, this Day from
    Ill ;   40
Have Mercy on us, Lord, have Mercy still :
As we have hop'd, do thou reward our Pain ;
We've hop'd in thee, let not our Hope be
    vain.

HYMN FOR THE NATIVITY OF ST. JOHN BAPTIST,
24TH JUNE.

O SYLVAN Prophet ! whose eternal Fame
Echoes from *Judah's* Hills and *Jordan's*
    Stream,
The Musick of our Numbers raise,
And tune our Voices to thy Praise.

A Messenger from high *Olympus* came
To bear the Tidings of thy Life and Name,
And told thy Sire each Prodigy
That Heav'n design'd to work in thee.

Hearing the News, and doubting in Surprize,
His faltering Speech in fetter'd Accent dy's ;
But Providence, with happy Choice,
In thee restor'd thy Father's Voice.

In the Recess of Nature's dark Abode,
Though still enclos'd, yet knewest thou thy
    God ;
Whilst each glad Parent told and blest
The Secrets of each other's Breast.

TE DEUM.   First printed as Dryden's by Scott
from a Roman Catholic *Primer* of Hymns, 1706.
    HYMN FOR THE NATIVITY OF ST. JOHN. Printed
with an incorrect title by Scott from the same.
The title was corrected by Saintsbury, who adds

other verses from the *Primer.*   There is no proof
that these are Dryden's, and in any case, since the
compilers of Hymn Books often deal immorally
with their texts, it seems best not to publish what
may be spurious and is certainly corrupt.

LINES IN A LETTER TO HIS LADY COUSIN, HONOR DRIDEN,

WHO HAD GIVEN HIM A SILVER INKSTAND, WITH A SET OF WRITING MATERIALS, 1655.

FOR since 'twas mine, the white hath lost
its Hiew,
To show twas n'ere it selfe but whilst in
you,
The virgin Waxe hath blush'd it selfe to red
Since it with mee hath lost its Maydenhead.

You, Fairest Nymph, are Waxe: Oh may
you bee
As well in Softnesse as in Purity !
Till Fate and your own happy Choice reveale
Whom you so farre shall bless to make your
Seale.

LINES PRINTED UNDER THE ENGRAVED PORTRAIT OF MILTON,

IN TONSON'S FOLIO EDITION OF THE 'PARADISE LOST,' 1688.

THREE Poets, in three distant Ages born,
Greece, Italy, and *England* did adorn.
The first in Loftiness of Thought surpass'd,
The next in Majesty, in both the last :
The Force of Nature could no farther go ;
To make a third she join'd the former two.

IMPROMPTU LINES ADDRESSED TO HIS COUSIN, MRS. CREED,

IN A CONVERSATION AFTER DINNER ON THE ORIGIN OF NAMES.

So much Religion in your Name doth dwell,
Your Soul must needs with Piety excel.
Thus Names, like [   ] Pictures drawn
of old,
Their owners' Nature and their Story told.
Your Name but half expresses, for in you
Belief and Practice do together go.

My Pray'rs shall be, while this short Life
endures,
These may go Hand in Hand, with you and
yours ;
Till Faith hereafter is in Vision drown'd,
And Practice is with endless Glory
crown'd.   10

FRAGMENT OF A CHARACTER OF JACOB TONSON,

HIS PUBLISHER.

WITH leering Looks, Bull-fac'd, and freckl'd fair,
With two left Legs, and *Judas*-colour'd Hair,
And frowzy Pores that taint the ambient Air.

LINES IN A LETTER. Text from the original as printed.
LINES ON MILTON. Text from the original of 1688.
IMPROMPTU LINES. Text first printed by Malone.

SONGS FROM THE PLAYS.

SONG OF AERIAL SPIRITS,
FROM
THE INDIAN QUEEN.

Poor Mortals that are clog'd with Earth
    below
    Sink under Love and Care,
    While we that dwell in Air
Such heavy Passions never know.
    Why then shou'd Mortals be
    Unwilling to be free
    From Blood, that sullen Cloud
    Which shining Souls does shroud ?
    Then they'l shew bright,
    And like us light,   10
When leaving Bodies with their Care
    They slide to us and Air.

HYMN TO THE SUN, FROM THE SAME.

You to whom Victory we owe,
    Whose glories rise
    By sacrifice
And from our fates below,
Never did your Altars shine
Feasted with Blood so near divine.
    Princes to whom we bow,
    As they to you,
Thus you can ravish from a throne,
And by their loss of pow'r declare your
    own.   10

FROM THE INDIAN EMPEROR.

I look'd and saw within the Book of Fate,
    When many Days did lower,
    When lo one happy hour
Leapt up, and smil'd to save thy sinking
    State ;
    A day shall come when in thy pow'r
    Thy cruel Foes shall be
    Then shall thy Land be free
    And then in Peace shall Raign :
But take, O take that opportunity,
Which once refus'd will never come again.

FROM THE SAME

Ah fading joy, how quickly art thou past !
    Yet we thy ruine haste :
As if the Cares of Humane Life were few,
    We seek out new,
And follow Fate that does too fast pursue.

See how on ev'ry Bough the Birds express
    In their sweet notes their happiness.
    They all enjoy and nothing spare ;
But on their Mother Nature lay their care:
Why then should Man, the Lord of all
    below,   10
    Such troubles chuse to know,
As none of all his Subjects undergo ?

Hark, hark, the Waters fall, fall, fall
    And with a Murmuring sound
    Dash, dash, upon the ground,
        To gentle slumbers call.

FROM THE MAIDEN QUEEN.

I Feed a Flame within which so torments me
That it both pains my heart, and yet con-
    tents me :
'Tis such a pleasing smart and I so love it,
That I had rather die, then once remove it.

Yet he for whom I grieve shall never know it,
My tongue does not betray, nor my eyes
    shew it :
Not a sigh not a tear my pain discloses,
But they fall silently like dew on Roses.

Thus to prevent my love from being cruel,
My heart's the sacrifice as 'tis the fuel : 10
And while I suffer thus to give him quiet,
My faith rewards my love, tho he deny it.

On his eyes will I gaze, and there delight
    me ;
Where I conceal my love, no frown can
    fright me :
To be more happy I dare not aspire ;
Nor can I fall more low, mounting no higher.

FROM THE INDIAN EMPEROR.
4 thy] the *some edd.*

FROM THE SAME.
5 that does] *Some editors give* which would

From Sir Martin Marr-All.

He. Make ready fair Lady to night,
  And stand at the Door below,
    For I will be there
    To receive you with Care,
  And to your true Love you shall go.

She. And when the Stars twinckle so bright,
  Then down to the Door will I creep,
    To my Love will I flye,
    E'er the jealous can spye,
  And leave my old daddy asleep.   10

From the Same (*after* Voiture).

  Blind Love, to this hour,
Had never like me, a Slave under his Pow'r.
    Then blest be the Dart
    That he threw at my heart,
  For nothing can prove
A joy so great as to be wounded with love.

    My Days and my Nights
Are fill'd to the purpose with sorrows and
    frights ;
  From my heart still I sigh,
  And my Eyes are ne'r dry,   10
    So that, *Cupid* be prais'd.
I am to the top of Love's happiness rais'd.

  My Soul's all on fire
So that I have the pleasure to dote and
    desire,
  Such a pretty soft pain,
  That it tickles each vein,
    'Tis the dream of a smart,
Which makes me breathe short when it
    beats at my heart.

    Somctimes in a Pet,
When I am despis'd, I my freedom would
    get ;   20
  But straight a sweet smile
  Does my anger beguile,
    And my heart does recall,
Then the more I do struggle the lower I fall.

    Heaven does not impart
Such a grace as to love unto ev'ry one's
    heart ;
  For many may wish
  To be wounded, and miss.
    Then blest be loves Fire,
And more blest her Eyes that first taught
    me desire.   30

From an Evening's Love.

You charm'd me not with that fair face
  Though it was all Divine :
To be anothers is the Grace,
  That makes me wish you mine.
The Gods and Fortune take their part
  Who like young Monarchs fight ;
And boldly dare invade that Heart
  Which is anothers right.
First mad with hope we undertake
  To pull up ev'ry Bar ;   10
But once possess'd we faintly make
  A dull defensive War.
Now ev'ry Friend is turn'd a foe
  In hope to get our store ;
And passion makes us Cowards grow
  Which made us brave before.

From the Same.

After the pangs of a desperate Lover,
  When day and night I have sigh'd all
    in vain,
Ah what a Pleasure it is to discover
  In her eyes pity, who causes my pain !

When with unkindness our Love at a
    stand is,
  And both have punish'd our selves with
    the pain,
Ah what a pleasure the touch of her
    hand is,
  Ah what a pleasure to press it again !

When the denial comes fainter and fainter,
  And her Eyes give what her tongue
    does deny,   10
Ah what a trembling I feel when I ven-
    ture,
  Ah what a Trembling does usher my
    joy !

When, with a Sigh, she accords me the
    blessing,
  And her Eyes twinkle 'twixt pleasure
    and pain ;
Ah what a joy 'tis, beyond all Express-
    ing,
  Ah what a joy to hear, shall we again !

FROM THE SAME.

CALM was the Even, and clear was the Sky,
 And the new-budding Flowers did spring,
When all alone went *Amyntas* and I
 To hear the sweet Nightingal sing ;
I sate, and he laid him down by me ;
 But scarcely his breath he could draw ;
For when with a fear, he began to draw
   near,
 He was dash'd with A ha ha ha ha !

He blush'd to himself, and lay still for
   a while,
 And his modesty curb'd his desire ; 10
But straight I convinc'd all his fear with
   a smile,
 Which added new Flames to his Fire.
O *Sylvia*, said he, you are cruel,
 To keep your poor Lover in awe ;
Then once more he prest with his hand to
   my brest
 But was dash'd with A ha ha ha ha.

I knew 'twas his passion that caus'd all his
   fear ;
 And therefore I pity'd his Case :
I whisper'd him softly, there's no body here
 And laid my Cheek close to his Face : 20
But as he grew bolder and bolder,
 A Shepheard came by us and saw ;
And just as our bliss we began with a Kiss,
 He laugh'd out with A ha ha ha ha.

FROM THE SAME.

Damon. *Celimena*, of my heart
 None shall e're bereave you :
 If with your good leave I may
 Quarrel with you once a day
 I will never leave you.

Celimena. Passion's but an empty name
 Where respect is wanting :
 Damon, you mistake your aim ;
 Hang your Heart and burn your Flame,
 If you must be ranting. 10

Damon. Love as dull and muddy is,
 As decaying Liquor :
 Anger sets it on the Lees,
 And refines it by degrees,
 Till it works it quicker

Celimena. Love by Quarrels to beget
 Wisely you endeavour ;
 With a grave Physitian's wit,
 Who to cure an Ague fit
 Put me in a Feavor. 20

Damon. Anger rouzes Love to fight,
 And his only bait is,
 'Tis the spurre to dull delight,
 And is but an eager Bite,
 When desire at height is.

Celimena. If such drops of heat can fall
 In our wooing weather
 If such drops of heat can fall
 We shall have the Devil and all
 When we come together. 30

FROM TYRANNICK LOVE

You pleasing Dreams of Love and sweet
   delight,
Appear before this slumbring Virgins sight :
Soft visions set her free
From mournful piety.
Let her sad thoughts from Heav'n retire ;
And let the Melancholy Love
Of those remoter joys above
Give place to your more sprightly fire.
Let purling streams be in her fancy seen ;
And flowry Meads, and Vales of chearful
   green : 10
And in the midst of deathless Groves
Soft smiling wishes ly,
And smiling hopes fast by,
And just beyond 'em ever Laughing Loves.

FROM THE SAME.

AH how sweet it is to love,
Ah how gay is young desire !
And what pleasing pains we prove
When we first approach Loves fire !
 Pains of Love be sweeter far
 Than all other pleasures are.

Sighs which are from Lovers blown,
Do but gently heave the Heart :
Ev'n the tears they shed alone
Cure, like trickling Balm, their smart. 10
 Lovers when they lose their breath
 Bleed away in easie death

Love and Time with reverence use,
Treat 'em like a parting friend :
Nor the golden gifts refuse
Which in youth sincere they send :
    For each year their price is more,
    And they less simple than before.

Love like Spring-tides full and high
Swells in ev'ry youthful vein :   20
But each Tide does less supply,
Till they quite shrink in again
    If a flow in Age appear,
    'Tis but rain, and runs not clear.

FROM THE CONQUEST OF GRANADA.

1

WHEREVER I am, and whatever I doe,
  My *Phillis* is still in my mind :
When angry I mean not to *Phillis* to goe,
  My Feet of themselves the way find :
Unknown to my self I am just at her door,
And when I would raile, I can bring out no
    more,
  Than *Phillis* too fair and unkind !

2

When *Phillis* I see, my Heart bounds in
    my Breast,
  And the Love I wou'd stifle is shown :
But asleep, or awake, I am never at Rest
  When from my Eyes *Phillis* is gone !
Sometimes a sad Dream does delude my
    sad mind,
But, alas, when I wake and no *Phillis* I find
  How I sigh to my self all alone.

3

Should a King be my Rival in her I adore
  He should offer his Treasure in vain :
O let me alone to be happy and poor,
  And give me my *Phillis* again :
Let *Phillis* be mine, and but ever be kind
I could to a Desart with her be confin'd,
  And envy no Monarch his Raign.

4

Alas, I discover too much of my Love,
  And she too well knows her own power !
She makes me each day a new Martyrdom
    prove,
  And makes me grow jealous each hour :
But let her each minute torment my poor mind
I had rather love *Phillis* both False and
    Unkind,
  Than ever be freed from her Pow'r.

SONG OF THE ZAMBRA DANCE,
FROM
THE CONQUEST OF GRANADA.

1

BENEATH a Myrtle shade
Which Love for none but happy Lovers
    made,
I slept, and straight my Love before me
    brought
Phillis the object of my waking thought ;
Undres'd she came my flames to meet,
While Love strow'd flow'rs beneath her
    feet ;
Flow'rs, which so press'd by her, became
    more sweet.

2

From the bright Visions Head
A careless vail of Lawn was loosely spread :
From her white temples fell her shaded hair,
Like cloudy sunshine not too brown nor fair :
Her hands, her lips did love inspire ;
Her ev'ry grace my heart did fire :
But most her eyes which languish'd with
    desire.

3

Ah, Charming fair, said I,
How long can you my bliss and yours deny ?
By Nature and by love this lonely shade
Was for revenge of suffring Lovers made :
Silence and shades with love agree :
Both shelter you and favour me ;
You cannot blush because I cannot see.

4

No, let me dye, she said,
Rather than loose the spotless name of
    Maid :
Faintly methought she spoke, for all the while
She bid me not believe her, with a smile.
Then dye, said I, she still deny'd :
And is it thus, thus, thus she cry'd
You use a harmless Maid, and so she dy'd !

5

I wak'd, and straight I knew
I lov'd so well it made my dream prove true :
Fancy, the kinder Mistress of the two,
Fancy had done what *Phillis* wou'd not do !
Ah, Cruel Nymph, cease your disdain,
While I can dream you scorn in vain ;
Asleep or waking you must ease my pain.

FROM THE SAME, PART II.

I

He. How unhappy a Lover am I
　　　While I sigh for my *Phillis* in vain ;
　　All my Hopes of Delight
　　Are another man's Right,
　　　Who is happy while I am in pain !

2

She. Since her Honour allows no Relief,
　　　But to pity the pains which you
　　　　bear,
　　'Tis the best of your Fate,
　　(In a hopeless Estate,)
　　　To give o're and betimes to despair.

3

He. I have try'd the false Med'cine in
　　　　vain ;
　　　For I wish what I hope not to win :
　　From without, my desire
　　Has no Food to its Fire,
　　　But it burns and consumes me
　　　　within.

4

She. Yet at least 'tis a pleasure to know
　　　That you are not unhappy alone :
　　For the Nymph you adore
　　Is as wretched and more,
　　　And accounts all your suff'rings her
　　　　own.

5

He. O ye Gods, let me suffer for both ;
　　　At the Feet of my *Phillis* I'le lye :
　　I'll resign up my Breath,
　　And take Pleasure in Death,
　　　To be pity'd by her when I dye.

6

She. What her Honour deny'd you in
　　　　Life
　　　In her Death she will give to your
　　　　Love :
　　Such a Flame as is true
　　After Fate will renew,
　　　For the Souls to meet closer above.

FROM THE SAME, PART II.
4.5 accounts] counts *some edd.*

FROM MARRIAGE A-LA-MODE.

I

WHY should a foolish Marriage Vow
　　Which long ago was made,
Oblige us to each other now
　　When Passion is decay'd ?
We lov'd, and we lov'd, as long as we cou'd,
　　Till our Love was lov'd out in us both :
But our Marriage is dead, when the Pleasure
　　is fled :
　　'Twas Pleasure first made it an Oath.

2

If I have Pleasures for a Friend,
　　And farther Love in store,
What Wrong has he whose Joys did end,
　　And who cou'd give no more ?
'Tis a madness that he
Shou'd be jealous of me,
Or that I shou'd bar him of another :
For all we can gain is to give our selves pain,
When neither can hinder the other.

FROM THE SAME.

I

WHILST *Alexis* lay prest
　　In her Arms he lov'd best,
With his hands round her neck,
　　And his head on her breast,
He found the fierce pleasure too hasty to
　　stay,
And his soul in the tempest just flying away.

2

When *Cælia* saw this,
With a sigh, and a kiss,
She cry'd, Oh my dear, I am robb'd of my
　　bliss ;
'Tis unkind to your Love, and unfaithfully
　　done,
To leave me behind you, and die all alone.

3

The Youth, though in haste,
And breathing his last,
In pity dy'd slowly, while she dy'd more
　　fast ;
Till at length she cry'd, Now, my dear, now
　　let us go,
Now die, my *Alexis*, and I will die too

4

Thus intranc'd they did lie,
Till *Alexis* did try
To recover new Breath, that again he might
    die :
Then often they di'd ; but the more they
    did so,
The Nymph dy'd more quick, and the
    Shepherd more slow.

FROM THE ASSIGNATION.

LONG betwixt Love and fear *Phillis* tor-
    mented
Shun'd her own wish yet at last she con-
    sented :
But loath that day shou'd her Blushes
    discover,
    Come, gentle Night She said,
    Come quickly to my aid,
    And a poor Shamefac'd Maid
    Hide from her Lover.

Now cold as Ice I am, now hot as Fire,
I dare not tell my self my own desire ;
But let Day fly away, and let Night haste
    her   10
    Grant ye kind Powers above,
    Slow Hours to parting Love,
    But when to Bliss we move,
    Bid 'em fly faster.

How sweet it is to Love when I discover
That Fire which burns my Heart warming
    my Lover ;
'Tis Pity Love so true shou'd be mistaken :
    But if this Night he be
    False or unkinde to me,
    Let me dye ere I see   20
    That I'm forsaken.

EPITHALAMIUM, FROM AMBOYNA.

THE Day is come, I see it rise,
Betwixt the Bride's and Bridegroom's Eyes,
That Golden day they wish'd so long
Love pick'd it out amidst the throng ;
He destin'd to himself this Sun,
And took the Reins and drove him on ;
In his own Beams he drest him bright,
Yet bid him bring a better night.

The day you wish'd arriv'd at last,
You wish as much that it were past,   10
One Minute more and night will hide
The Bridegroom and the blushing Bride.
The Virgin now to Bed do's goe :
Take care oh Youth, she rise not soe ;
She pants and trembles at her doom
And fears and wishes thou wou'dst come.

The Bridegroom comes, He comes apace
With Love and Fury in his Face ;
She shrinks away, He close pursues,
And Pray'rs and Threats at once do's use ; 20
She softly sighing begs delay,
And with her hand, puts his away,
Now out aloud for help she cryes,
And now despairing shuts her Eyes.

SONG OF THE SEA FIGHT,
FROM THE SAME.

WHO ever saw a noble sight,
That never view'd a brave Sea Fight ?
Hang up your bloody Colours in the Aire,
Up with your Fights and your Nettings
    prepare,
Your Merry Mates chear with a lusty bold
    spright,
Now each Man his brindice and then to the
    Fight.
St. George, St. George, we cry,
The shouting Turks reply.
Oh now it begins, and the Gunroom grows hot
Plie it with Culverin and with small shot ; 10
Heark do's it not Thunder ? no 'tis the Guns
    roar
The Neighbouring Billows are turn'd into
    Gore.
Now each Man must resolve to dye,
For here the Coward cannot flye.
Drums and Trumpets toll the Knell,
And Culverins the Passing Bell
Now now they Grapple and now board a Main,
Blow up the Hatches, they're off all again :
Give 'em a broadside, the Dice run at all,
Down comes the Mast and Yard, and tack-
    lings fall ;   20
She grows giddy now like blind fortunes
    wheel ;
She sinks there she sinks she turns up her
    Keel,
Who ever beholds so noble a sight
As this so brave, so bloody Sea Fight.

From THE KIND KEEPER.

Song from the Italian.

By a dismal Cypress lying,
Damon cry'd, all pale and dying,
Kind is Death that ends my pain,
But cruel She I lov'd in vain.
The Mossy Fountains
Murmure my trouble,
And hollow Mountains
My groans redouble :
Every Nymph mourns me,
Thus while I languish ;   10
She only scorns me,
Who caus'd my anguish.
No Love returning me, all my hope denying ;
By a dismal Cypress lying,
Like a *Swan*, so sung he dying :
Kind is Death that ends my pain,
But cruel She I lov'd in vain.

From ŒDIPUS.

SONG TO APOLLO.

Phœbus, God belov'd by men ;
At thy dawn, ev'ry Beast is rouz'd in his
        Den ;
At thy Setting, all the Birds of thy absence
        complain,
And we dye, all dye till the morning comes
        again,
Phœbus, God belov'd by men !
Idol of the Eastern Kings,
Awful as the God who flings
His Thunder round, and the Lightning
        wings ;
God of Songs, and *Orphean* Strings,
Who to this mortal bosom brings   10
All harmonious heav'nly Things !
Thy drouzie Prophet to revive,
Ten thousand thousand forms before him
        drive ;
With Chariots and Horses all o' Fire awake
        him,
Convulsions, and Furies, and Prophesies
        shake him :
Let him tell it in Groans, tho' he bend with
        the load,
Tho' he burst with the weight of the terrible
        God.

From TROILUS AND CRESSIDA.

Can Life be a Blessing,
    Or worth the possessing,
Can Life be a blessing if Love were away ?
    Ah no ! though our Love all Night keep
        us waking,
And though he torment us with Cares all
        the Day,
    Yet he sweetens he sweetens our Pains in
        the taking,
There's an Hour at the last, there's an Hour
    to repay.

2

In ev'ry possessing,
    The ravishing Blessing,
In ev'ry possessing the Fruit of our Pain,
Poor Lovers forget long Ages of Anguish,
What e're they have suffer'd and done to
        obtain ;
    'Tis a Pleasure, a Pleasure to sigh and
        to languish,
When we hope, when we hope to be happy
    again.

From THE SPANISH FRYAR.

I

Farwell ungratefull Traytor,
    Farwell my perjur'd Swain,
Let never injur'd Creature
    Believe a Man again.
The Pleasure of Possessing
Surpasses all Expressing,
But 'tis too short a Blessing,
    And Love too long a Pain.

II

'Tis easie to deceive us
    In Pity of your Pain,
But when we love you leave us
    To rail at you in vain.
Before we have descry'd it,
There is no Bliss beside it,
But she that once has try'd it
    Will never love again.

III

The Passion you pretended
  Was onely to obtain
But when the Charm is ended
  The Charmer you disdain.
Your Love by ours we measure
Till we have lost our Treasure,
But dying is a Pleasure,
  When Living is a Pain.

SONG BETWIXT A SHEPHERD AND
A SHEPHERDESS,
FROM
THE DUKE OF GUISE.

Shepherdess. Tell me *Thirsis*, tell your
    Anguish,
  Why you Sigh, and why you Languish ;
  When the Nymph whom you Adore,
  Grants the Blessing of Possessing,
  What can Love and I do more ?

Shepherd. Think it's Love beyond all
    Measure,
  Makes me faint away with Pleasure ;
  Strength of Cordial may destroy,
  And the Blessing of possessing
  Kills me with Excess of Joy.   10

Shepherdess. Thirsis, how can I believe
    you ?
  But confess and I'le forgive you ;
  Men are false, and so are you ;
  Never Nature fram'd a Creature
  To enjoy, and yet be true.

Shepherd. Mine's a Flame beyond expiring,
  Still possessing, still desiring,
    Fit for Love's imperial Crown ;
  Ever shining, and refining,
    Still the more 'tis melted down.   20

Chorus together. Mine's a Flame beyond
    expiring,
  Still possessing, still desiring,
    Fit for Love's imperial Crown ;
  Ever shining, and refining,
    Still the more 'tis melted down.

FROM AMPHITRYON.
I

Celia, that I once was blest
Is now the Torment of my Brest ;
Since to curse me, you bereave me
Of the Pleasures I possest :
Cruel Creature, to deceive me !
First to love, and then to leave me.

II

Had you the Bliss refus'd to grant,
Then I had never known the want :
But possessing once the Blessing,
Is the Cause of my Complaint :
Once possessing is but tasting ;
'Tis no Bliss that is not lasting.

III

Celia now is mine no more ;
But I am hers and must adore :
Nor to leave her will endeavour ;
Charms, that captiv'd me before,
No Unkindness can dissever :
Love that's true, is Love for ever.

FROM THE SAME.
I

FAIR *Iris* I love and hourly I dye,
But not for a Lip nor a languishing Eye ·
She's fickle and false, and there I agree ;
For I am as false and as fickle as she :
We neither believe what either can say ;
And, neither believing, we neither betray.

II

'Tis civil to swear and say Things of course ;
We mean not the taking for better or worse.
When present we love, when absent agree ;
I think not of *Iris,* nor *Iris* of me :
The Legend of Love no Couple can find
So easie to part, or so equally join'd.

PASTORAL DIALOGUE FROM THE
SAME.
I

Thyrsis. Fair *Iris* and her Swain
    Were in a shady Bow'r ;
  Where *Thyrsis* long in vain
    Had sought the Shepherd's hour ·
At length his Hand advancing upon her
    snowy Breast,
  He said, O kiss me longer,
  And longer yet and longer,
    If you will make me Blest.

II

Iris.   An easie yielding Maid
        By trusting is undone ;
Our Sex is oft betray'd,
        By granting Love too soon.
If you desire to gain me, your Suff'rings to
        redress ;
Prepare to love me longer,
        And longer yet, and longer,
        Before you shall possess.

III

Thyrsis.   The little Care you show,
        Of all my Sorrows past,
Makes Death appear too slow,
        And Life too long to last.
Fair *Iris* kiss me kindly, in pity of my
        Fate ;
And kindly still, and kindly,
        Before it is too late.

IV

Iris.   You fondly Court your Bliss,
        And no Advances make ;
'Tis not for Maids to kiss,
        But 'tis for Men to take.
So you may kiss me kindly, and I will
        not rebell ;
But kindly still, and kindly,
        But Kiss me not and tell.

V

A RONDEAU

Chorus.   Thus at the Height we love and
        live,
        And fear not to be poor :
We give, and give, and give, and give,
        Till we can give no more :
But what to day will take away,
        To Morrow will restore.
Thus at the heighth we love and live,
        And fear not to be poor.

FROM KING ARTHUR.

Man sings

Oh SIGHT, the Mother of Desires,
    What Charming Objects dost thou yield !
'Tis sweet, when tedious Night expires,
    To see the Rosie Morning guild
    The Mountain-Tops and paint the Field !

But when *Clorinda* comes in Sight,
She makes the Summers Day more bright ;
And when she goes away, 'tis Night.

Chorus.   When fair *Clorinda* comes in
    Sight, &c.

Woman sings

'Tis sweet the Blushing Morn to view ;   10
And Plains adorn'd with Pearly Dew :
    But such cheap Delights to see,
        Heaven and Nature
        Give each Creature ;
    They have Eyes, as well as we.
This is the Joy, all Joys above,
        To see, to see,
        That only she,
That only she we love !   19

Chorus.   This is the Joy, all Joys above, &c.

Man sings

And, if we may discover,
What Charms both Nymph and Lover,
    'Tis, when the Fair at Mercy lies,
With Kind and Amorous Anguish,
To Sigh, to Look, to Languish,
    On each others Eyes !

Chorus of all Men and Women

And if we may discover, &c.

FROM THE SAME.

I

How happy the Lover,
    How easie his Chain,
    How pleasing his Pain !
How sweet to discover
    He sighs not in vain.
For Love ev'ry Creature
Is form'd by his Nature ;
No Joys are above
The Pleasures of Love.

2

In vain are our Graces,
    In vain are your Eyes,
    If Love you despise ;
When Age furrows Faces,
    'Tis time to be wise.
Then use the short Blessing,
That flies in Possessing :
No Joys are above
The Pleasures of Love.

SONG OF ÆOLUS, FROM THE SAME.

YE blust'ring Brethren of the Skies,
  Whose Breath has ruffled all the Watry
    Plain,
Retire, and let *Britannia* rise,
  In Triumph o'er the Main.
Serene and Calm, and void of Fear,
The Queen of Islands must appear:
Serene and Calm, as when the Spring
The New-Created World began,
And Birds on Boughs did softly sing,
  Their peaceful Homage paid to Man,   10
While *Eurus* did his Blasts forbear
In Favour of the Tender Year.
Retreat, rude Winds, Retreat,
To Hollow Rocks, your Stormy Seat;
There swell your Lungs, and vainly, vainly
  threat.

SONG OF PAN AND NEREIDE, FROM
THE SAME.

ROUND thy Coasts, Fair Nymph of *Britain*,
  For thy Guard our Waters flow:
Proteus all his Herds admitting
  On thy Greens to Graze below.
Foreign Lands thy Fishes Tasting
Learn from thee Luxurious Fasting.

I

For Folded Flocks, on Fruitful Plains,
The Shepherds and the Farmers Gains,
  Fair *Britain* all the world outvyes;
And *Pan*, as in *Arcadia* reigns
  Where Pleasure mixt with Profit lyes.

2

Though *Jasons* Fleece was Fam'd of old,
The *British* Wool is growing Gold;
  No Mines can more of Wealth supply:
It keeps the Peasant from the Cold,
  And takes for Kings the *Tyrian* Dye.

FROM THE SAME.

Comus. Your Hay it is Mow'd, and your
    Corn is Reap'd;
  Your Barns will be full, and your
    Hovels heap'd:
  Come, my Boys, come;
  Come, my Boys, come;
And merrily Roar out Harvest Home.
Chorus. Come, my Boys, come, &c.

1 *Man.* WE ha' cheated the Parson, we'll
    cheat him agen,
For why shou'd a Blockhead ha' One in
    Ten?
  One in Ten,
  One in Ten,
For why shou'd a Blockhead ha' One in
    Ten?

2 For Prating so long like a Book-learn'd
    Sot,
Till Pudding and Dumplin burn to Pot
    Burn to Pot,
  Burn to Pot,
Till Pudding and Dumplin burn to Pot.
Chorus. Burn to Pot, &c.

3 We'll toss off our Ale till we canno'
    stand,
And Hoigh for the Honour of old *England*:
  Old *England*,
  Old *England*,
And Hoigh for the Honour of Old *England*.
Chorus. Old *England*, &c.

SONG OF VENUS, FROM THE SAME.

I

FAIREST Isle, all Isles Excelling,
  Seat of Pleasures, and of Loves;
Venus here will chuse her Dwelling,
  And forsake her *Cyprian* Groves.

2

Cupid, from his Fav'rite Nation,
  Care and Envy will Remove;
Jealousy that poysons Passion,
  And Despair that dies for Love.

3

Gentle Murmurs, sweet Complaining,
  Sighs that blow the Fire of Love;
Soft Repulses, kind Disdaining,
  Shall be all the Pains you prove.

4

Ev'ry Swain shall pay his Duty,
  Grateful ev'ry Nymph shall prove;
And as these Excel in Beauty,
  Those shall be Renown'd for Love.

From CLEOMENES

No, no, poor suff'ring Heart, no Change
  endeavour,
Choose to sustain the smart, rather than
  leave her;
My ravish'd Eyes behold such Charms
  about her,
I can dye with her, but not live without
  her
One tender Sigh of hers to see me Languish,
Will more than pay the price of my past
  Anguish:
Beware, O cruel Fair, how you smile on me,
'Twas a kind look of yours that has undone
  me.

2

Love has in store for me one happy
  Minute,
And She will end my pain who did begin it;
Then no day void of Bliss, or Pleasure
  leaving,
Ages shall slide away without perceiving:
Cupid shall guard the Door the more to
  please us,
And keep out Time and Death, when they
  would seize us:
Time and Death shall depart, and say in
  flying,
Love has found out a way to Live by Dying.

SONG OF JEALOUSIE,
FROM
LOVE TRIUMPHANT.

1

WHAT State of Life can be so blest
As Love, that warms a Lover's Breast?
Two Souls in one, the same desire
To grant the Bliss, and to require!
But if in Heav'n a Hell we find,
'Tis all from thee,
O Jealousie!
Thou Tyrant, Tyrant Jealousie,
Thou Tyrant of the Mind!

2

All other ills, tho sharp they prove,
Serve to refine, and perfect Love:
In absence, or unkind disdain,
Sweet Hope relieves the Lover's pain:
But ah, no Cure but Death we find
To set us free
From Jealousie:
O Jealousie!
Thou Tyrant, Tyrant Jealousie,
Thou Tyrant of the Mind.

3

False in thy Glass all Objects are,
Some set too near, and some too far:
Thou art the Fire of endless Night
The Fire that burns, and gives no Light.
All Torments of the Damn'd we find
In only thee
O Jealousie!
Thou Tyrant, Tyrant Jealousie
Thou Tyrant of the Mind!

SONG FOR A GIRL, FROM THE SAME.

1

YOUNG I am, and yet unskill'd
How to make a Lover yield:
How to keep, or how to gain,
When to love; and when to feign.

2

Take me, take me, some of you,
While I yet am Young and True;
E're I can my Soul disguise;
Heave my Breasts, and roul my Eyes.

3

Stay not till I learn the way,
How to Lye, and to Betray:
He that has me first, is blest,
For I may deceive the rest.

4

Cou'd I find a blooming Youth,
Full of Love, and full of Truth,
Brisk, and of a janty mean
I shou'd long to be Fifteen.

TRANSLATIONS.

[PREFACE TO SYLVAE

OR THE SECOND PART OF POETICAL MISCELLANIES: 1685.]

For this last half Year I have been troubled with the disease (as I may call it) of Translation; the cold Prose fits of it (which are always the most tedious with me) were spent in the History of the League; the hot (which succeeded them) in this Volume of Verse Miscellanies. The truth is, I fancied to my self, a kind of ease in the change of the Paroxism; never suspecting but the humour wou'd have wasted itself in two or three Pastorals of Theocritus, and as many Odes of Horace. But finding, or at least thinking I found, something that was more pleasing in them than my ordinary productions, I encourag'd myself to renew my old acquaintance 10 *with Lucretius and Virgil; and immediately fix'd upon some parts of them, which had most affected me in the reading. These were my natural Impulses for the undertaking: But there was an accidental motive which was full as forcible, and God forgive him who was the occasion of it. It was my Lord Roscommon's Essay on Translated Verse; which made me uneasie till I tried whether or no I was capable of following his Rules, and of reducing the speculation into practice. For many a fair Precept in Poetry is like a seeming Demonstration in the Mathematicks, very specious in the Diagram, but failing in the Mechanick Operation. I think I have generally observ'd his instructions; I am sure my reason is sufficiently convinc'd both of their truth and usefulness; which, in other words, is to confess no less a vanity, than to pretend that I have at least in some places made Examples to his Rules. Yet withall, I must* 20 *acknowledge, that I have many times exceeded my Commission; for I have both added and omitted, and even sometimes very boldly made such expositions of my Authors, as no Dutch Commentator will forgive me. Perhaps, in such particular passages, I have thought that I discover'd some beauty yet undiscovered by those Pedants, which none but a Poet could have found. Where I have taken away some of their Expressions, and cut them shorter, it may possibly be on this consideration, that what was beautiful in the Greek or Latin, would not appear so shining in the English; and where I have enlarg'd them, I desire the false Criticks would not always think that those thoughts are wholly mine, but that either they are secretly in the Poet, or may be fairly deduc'd from him; or at least, if both those considerations should fail, that my own is of a piece with his, and that if he were living, and an Englishman, they* 30 *are such as he wou'd probably have written.*

For, after all, a Translator is to make his Author appear as charming as possibly he can, provided he maintains his Character, and makes him not unlike himself. Translation is a kind of Drawing after the Life, where every one will acknowledge there is a double sort of likeness, a good one and a bad. 'Tis one thing to draw the Out-lines true, the Features like, the Proportions exact, the Colouring it self perhaps tolerable, and another thing to make all these graceful, by the posture, the shadowings, and chiefly by the Spirit which animates the whole. I cannot, without some indignation, look on an ill Copy of an excellent Original. Much less can I behold with patience Virgil, Homer, and some others, whose beauties I have been endeavouring all my Life to imitate, so abused, as I may say, to their Faces, by a botching 40 *Interpreter. What English Readers, unacquainted with Greek or Latin, will believe me, or any other Man, when we commend those Authors, and confess we derive all that is pardonable in us from their Fountains, if they take those to be the same Poets, whom our Ogleby's have Translated? But I dare assure them, that a good Poet is no more like himself, in a dull Translation, than his Carcass would be to his living Body. There are many, who understand*

Greek and Latin, and yet are ignorant of their Mother Tongue. The proprieties and delicacies of the English are known to few : 'tis impossible even for a good Wit to understand and practise them, without the help of a liberal Education, long Reading, and digesting of those few good Authors we have amongst us, the knowledge of Men and Manners, the freedom of habitudes and conversation with the best company of both Sexes ; and, in short, without wearing off the rust which he contracted, while he was laying in a stock of Learning. Thus difficult it is to understand the purity of English, and critically to discern not only good Writers from bad, and a proper stile from a corrupt, but also to distinguish that which is pure in a good Author, from that which is vicious and corrupt in him. And for want of all these requisites, or the
10   greatest part of them, most of our ingenious young Men take up some cry'd up English Poet for their Model, adore him, and imitate him, as they think, without knowing wherein he is defective, where he is Boyish and trifling, wherein either his thoughts are improper to his Subjects, or his Expressions unworthy of his Thoughts, or the turn of both is unharmonious.

Thus it appears necessary that a Man shou'd be a nice Critick in his Mother Tongue, before he attempts to Translate a foreign Language. Neither is it sufficient, that he be able to Judge of Words and Stile ; but he must be a Master of them too : He must perfectly understand his Authors Tongue, and absolutely command his own : So that, to be a thorow Translator, he must be a thorow Poet. Neither is it enough to give his Authors sence in good English, in Poetical expressions, and in Musical numbers ; For, though all these are exceeding difficult
20   to perform, there yet remains a harder task ; and 'tis a secret of which few Translators have sufficiently thought. I have already hinted a word or two concerning it ; that is, the maintaining the Character of an Author, which distinguishes him from all others, and makes him appear that individual Poet, whom you wou'd interpret. For example, not only the thoughts, but the Style and Versification of Virgil and Ovid, are very different : Yet I see, even in our best Poets, who have Translated some parts of them, that they have confounded their several Talents ; and, by endeavouring only at the sweetness and harmony of Numbers, have made them both so much alike, that if I did not know the Originals, I should never be able to Judge by the Copies, which was Virgil, and which was Ovid. It was objected against a late noble Painter, that he drew many graceful Pictures, but few of them were like. And this happen'd to him, because
30   he always studied himself, more than those who sat to him. In such Translatours I can easily distinguish the hand which performed the Work, but I cannot distinguish their Poet from another. Suppose two Authors are equally sweet, yet there is as great distinction to be made in sweetness, as in that of Sugar, and that of Honey. I can make the difference more plain, by giving you (if it be worth knowing) my own method of proceeding, in my Translations out of four several Poets in this volume—Virgil, Theocritus, Lucretius, and Horace. In each of these, before I undertook them, I consider'd the Genius and distinguishing Character of my Author. I looked on Virgil, as a succinct and grave Majestick writer ; one who weigh'd not only every thought, but every Word and Syllable : who was still aiming to crowd his sence into as narrow a compass as possibly he cou'd ; for which reason he is so very Figurative,
40   that he requires (I may almost say) a Grammar apart to construe him. His Verse is every where sounding the very thing in your Ears, whose sence it bears : yet the Numbers are perpetually varied, to increase the delight of the Reader ; so that the same sounds are never repeated twice together. On the contrary, Ovid and Claudian, though they Write in Styles differing from each other, yet have each of them but one sort of Musick in their Verses. All the versification and little variety of Claudian is included within the compass of four or five Lines, and then he begins again in the same tenour ; perpetually closing his sence at the end of a Verse, and that Verse commonly which they call golden, or two Substantives and two Adjectives, with a Verb betwixt them to keep the peace. Ovid with all his sweetness, has as little variety of Numbers and sound as he : He is always, as it were, upon the Hand-gallop, and his Verse
50   runs upon Carpet ground. He avoids, like the other, all Synalæpha's, or cutting off one Vowel when it comes before another, in the following word : So that minding only smoothness, he

---

38 *Syllable : who*] Syllable. Who *1685.*

wants both Variety and Majesty. But to return to Virgil : *though he is smooth where smoothness is requir'd, yet he is so far from affecting it, that he seems rather to disdain it ; frequently makes use of Synalœpha's, and concludes his sence in the middle of his Verse. He is every where above conceits of Epigrammatick Wit, and gross Hyperboles : He maintains Majesty in the midst of plainess ; he shines, but glares not ; and is stately without ambition, which is the vice of* Lucan. *I drew my definition of Poetical Wit from my particular consideration of him : For propriety of thoughts and words are only to be found in him ; and, where they are proper, they will be delightful. Pleasure follows of necessity, as the effect does the cause ; and therefore is not to be put into the definition. This exact propriety of* Virgil *I particularly regarded, as a great part of his Character ; but must confess to my shame, that I have not* 10 *been able to Translate any part of him so well, as to make him appear wholly like himself. For where the Original is close, no Version can reach it in the same compass.* Hannibal Caro's, *in the* Italian, *is the nearest, the most Poetical, and the most Sonorous of any Translation of the* Æneids : *yet, though he takes the advantage of blank Verse, he commonly allows two lines for one of* Virgil, *and does not always hit his sence.* Tasso *tells us, in his Letters, that* Sperone Speroni, *a great* Italian *Wit, who was his Contemporary, observed of* Virgil *and* Tully ; *that the* Latin *Oratour endeavoured to imitate the Copiousness of* Homer, *the* Greek *poet ; and that the* Latine *Poet made it his business to reach the conciseness of* Demosthenes, *the* Greek *Oratour.* Virgil *therefore, being so very sparing of his words, and leaving so much to be imagined by the Reader, can never be translated as he ought, in any modern Tongue. To make* 20 *him Copious, is to alter his Character ; and to Translate him Line for Line is impossible ; because the* Latin *is naturally a more succinct Language than either the* Italian, Spanish, French, *or even than the* English *(which, by reason of its Monosyllables, is far the most compendious of them.)* Virgil *is much the closest of any* Roman *Poet, and the* Latin *Hexameter has more Feet than the* English *Heroick.*

Besides all this, an Author has the choice of his own thoughts and words, which a Translatour has not ; he is confin'd by the sence of the Inventor to those expressions which are the nearest to it : So that Virgil, *studying brevity, and having the command of his own Language, could bring those words into a narrow compass, which a Translatour cannot render without Circumlocutions. In short, they, who have call'd him the torture of Grammarians, might also* 30 *have called him the plague of Translatours ; for he seems to have studied not to be Translated. I own that, endeavouring to turn his* Nisus *and* Euryalus *as close as I was able, I have performed that* Episode *too literally ; that, giving more scope to* Mezentius *and* Lausus, *that Version, which has more of the Majesty of* Virgil, *has less of his conciseness ; and all that I can promise for myself is only that I have done both better than* Ogleby, *and perhaps as well as* Caro. *So that, methinks, I come like a Malefactor, to make a Speech upon the Gallows, and to warn all other Poets, by my sad example, from the Sacrilege of Translating* Virgil. *Yet, by considering him so carefully as I did before my attempt, I have made some faint resemblance of him ; and, had I taken more time, might possibly have succeeded better ; but never so well, as to have satisfied myself.*

He who excels all other Poets in his own Language, were it possible to do him right, must 40 *appear above them in our Tongue ; which, as my Lord* Roscommon *justly observes, approaches nearest to the* Roman *in its Majesty : Nearest indeed, but with a vast interval betwixt them. There is an inimitable grace in* Virgils *words, and in them principally consists that beauty which gives so unexpressible a pleasure to him who best understands their force. This Diction of his, I must once again say, is never to be Copied ; and, since it cannot, he will appear but lame in the best Translation. The turns of his Verse, his breakings, his propriety, his numbers, and his gravity, I have as far imitated as the poverty of our Language and the hastiness of my performance wou'd allow. I may seem sometimes to have varied from his sence ; but I think the greatest variations may be fairly deduc'd from him ; and where I leave his Com-* 50 *mentators, it may be I understand him better : At least I Writ without consulting them in many places. But two particular lines in* Mezentius *and* Lausus *I cannot so easily excuse ; they are indeed remotely allied to* Virgil's *sence ; but they are too like the trifling tenderness of* Ovid

*and were printed before I had consider'd them enough to alter them : The first of them I have
forgotten, and cannot easily retrieve, because the Copy is at the Press : the second is this ;*

When *Lausus* dy'd, I was already slain.

*This appears pretty enough at first sight ; but I am convinc'd for many reasons, that the
expression is too bold ; that* Virgil *wou'd not have said it, though* Ovid *wou'd.   The Reader
may pardon it, if he please, for the freeness of the confession ; and instead of that, and the
former, admit these two Lines, which are more according to the Author :*

Nor ask I Life, nor fought with that design ;
As I had us'd my Fortune, use thou thine.

10 *Having with much ado got clear of* Virgil, *I have, in the next place, to consider the genius
of* Lucretius, *whom I have translated more happily in those parts of him which I undertook.
If he was not of the best age of* Roman *Poetry, he was at least of that which preceded it ; and
he himself refin'd it to that degree of perfection, both in the Language and the thoughts, that
he left an easy task to* Virgil ; *who as he succeeded him in time, so he Copy'd his excellencies :
for the method of the* Georgicks *is plainly deriv'd from him.   Lucretius had chosen a Subject
naturally crabbed ; he therefore adorn'd it with Poetical descriptions, and Precepts of Morality,
in the beginning and ending of his Books.   Which you see* Virgil *has imitated with great
success, in those four Books, which in my opinion, are more perfect in their kind than 'even
his Divine Æneids.   The turn of his Verse he has likewise follow'd, in those places which*
20 Lucretius *has most labour'd, and some of his very lines he has transplanted into his own Works,
without much variation.   If I am not mistaken, the distinguishing Character of* Lucretius
(*I mean of his Soul and Genius) is a certain kind of noble pride, and positive assertion of
his Opinions.   He is every where confident of his own reason, and assuming an absolute
command, not only over his vulgar Reader, but even his Patron* Memmius.   *For he is
always bidding him attend, as if he had the Rod over him, and using a Magisterial
authority, while he instructs him.   From his time to ours, I know none so like him
as our Poet and Philosopher of* Malmsbury.   *This is that perpetual Dictatorship, which
is exercis'd by* Lucretius ; *who, though often in the wrong, yet seems to deal* bonâ fide
with his Reader, and tells him nothing but what he thinks : in which plain sincerity,
30 *I believe, he differs from our* Hobbs, *who cou'd not but be convinc'd, or at least doubt
of some eternal Truths, which he has oppos'd.   But for* Lucretius, *he seems to disdain all
manner of Replies, and is so confident of his cause, that he is beforehand with his Antagonists ;
Urging for them whatever he imagin'd they cou'd say, and leaving them, as he supposes, without
an objection for the future ; all this too, with so much scorn and indignation, as if he were
assur'd of the Triumph, before he entered into the lists.   From this sublime and daring Genius
of his, it must of necessity come to pass, that his thoughts must be Masculine, full of argumenta-
tion, and that sufficiently warm.   From the same fiery temper proceeds the loftiness of his
Expressions, and the perpetual torrent of his Verse, where the barrenness of his Subject does
not too much constrain the quickness of his Fancy.   For there is no doubt to be made, but that*
40 *he cou'd have been every where as Poetical, as he is in his Descriptions, and in the Moral
part of his Philosophy, if he had not aim'd more to instruct, in his Systeme of Nature, than
to delight.   But he was bent upon making* Memmius *a* Materialist, *and teaching him to defie
an invisible power : In short, he was so much an Atheist, that he forgot sometimes to be a Poet.
These are the considerations which I had of that Author, before I attempted to translate some
parts of him.   And accordingly I lay'd by my natural Diffidence and Scepticism for a while,
to take up that Dogmatical way of his, which, as I said, is so much his Character, as to make
him that individual Poet.   As for his Opinions concerning the mortality of the Soul, they are
so absurd, that I cannot, if I wou'd, believe them.   I think a future state demonstrable even
by natural Arguments ; at least, to take away rewards and punishments, is only a pleasing*
50 *prospect to a Man, who resolves beforehand not to live morally.   But on the other side, the
thought of being nothing after death is a burthen unsupportable to a vertuous Man, even though*

a Heathen. We naturally aim at happiness, and cannot bear to have it confin'd to the shortness of our present Being, especially when we consider, that vertue is generally unhappy in this World and vice fortunate : so that 'tis hope of Futurity alone that makes this Life tolerable, in expectation of a better. Who wou'd not commit all the excesses, to which he is prompted by his natural inclinations, if he may do them with security while he is alive, and be uncapable of punishment after he is dead! if he be cunning and secret enough to avoid the Laws, there is no band of morality to restrain him : for Fame and Reputation are weak ties : many men have not the least sence of them : Powerful men are only aw'd by them, as they conduce to their interest, and that not always, when a passion is predominant : and no Man will be contain'd within the bounds of duty, when he may safely transgress them. These are my 10 *thoughts abstractedly, and without entering into the Notions of our Christian Faith, which is the proper business of Divines.*

But there are other Arguments in this Poem (which I have turned into English*) not belonging to the Mortality of the Soul, which are strong enough to a reasonable Man, to make him less in love with Life, and consequently in less apprehensions of Death. Such as are the natural Satiety proceeding from a perpetual enjoyment of the same things ; the inconveniences of old age, which make him uncapable of corporeal pleasures ; the decay of understanding and memory, which render him contemptible, and useless to others. These, and many other reasons, so pathetically urged, so beautifully express'd, so adorn'd with examples, and so admirably rais'd by the* Prosopopeia *of* Nature, *who is brought in speaking to her Children, with so much* 20 *authority and vigour, deserve the pains I have taken with them, which I hope have not been unsuccessful, or unworthy of my Author. At least I must take the liberty to own, that I was pleased with my own endeavours, which but rarely happens to me ; and that I am not dissatisfied upon the review of any thing I have done in this Author.*

'Tis true, there is something, and that of some moment, to be objected against my Englishing *the Nature of Love, from the fourth book of* Lucretius *; and I can less easily answer why I Translated it, than why I thus Translated it. The Objection arises from the Obscenity of the Subject ; which is aggravated by the too lively and alluring delicacy of the Verses. In the first place, without the least Formality of an excuse, I own it pleas'd me : and let my enemies make the worst they can of this Confession : I am not yet so secure from that passion, but* 30 *that I want my Authors Antidotes against it. He has given the truest and most Philosophical account both of the Disease and Remedy, which I ever found in any Author : For which reasons I Translated him. But it will be ask'd why I turned him into this luscious* English, *(for I will not give it a worse word :) Instead of an answer, I wou'd ask again of my Supercilious Adversaries, whether I am not bound, when I translate an author, to do him all the right I can, and to Translate him to the best advantage? If, to mince his meaning, which I am satisfi'd was honest and instructive, I had either omitted some part of what he said, or taken from the strength of his expression, I certainly had wrong'd him ; and that freeness of thought and words being thus cashier'd in my hands, he had no longer been* Lucretius. *If nothing of this kind be to be read, Physicians must not study nature, Anatomies must not be* 40 *seen, and somewhat I cou'd say of particular passages in Books, which, to avoid prophaneness, I do not name. But the intention qualifies the act ; and both mine and my Authors were to instruct as well as please. 'Tis most certain that barefac'd Bawdery is the poorest pretence to wit imaginable : If I shou'd say otherwise, I should have two great authorities against me: The one is the Essay on Poetry, which I publickly valu'd before I knew the Author of it, and with the commendation of which my Lord* Roscommon *so happily begins his Essay on Translated Verse : The other is no less than our admir'd* Cowley, *who says the same thing in other words : For in his Ode concerning Wit, he writes thus of it :*

> Much less can that have any place,
> At which a Virgin hides her Face :
> Such dross the fire must purge away ; 'tis just 50
> The Author blush, there, where the Reader must.

Here indeed Mr. Cowley *goes farther than the Essay; for he asserts plainly, that obscenity has no place in Wit: the other only says, 'tis a poor pretence to it, or an ill sort of Wit, which has nothing more to support it than bare-faced Ribaldry; which is both unmannerly in it self, and fulsome to the Reader. But neither of these will reach my case: For in the first place, I am only the Translatour, not the Inventor; so that the heaviest part of the censure falls upon* Lucretius, *before it reaches me; in the next place, neither he nor I have us'd the grossest words, but the cleanliest Metaphors we cou'd find, to palliate the broadness of the meaning; and, to conclude, have carried the Poetical part no farther, than the philosophical exacted. There is one mistake of mine which I will not lay to the Printer's* 10 *charge, who has enough to answer for in false pointings: 'tis in the word* Viper: *I wou'd have the verse run thus,*

The Scorpion, Love, must on the wound be bruis'd.

There are a sort of blundering half-witted people, who make a great deal of noise about a Verbal slip; though Horace *wou'd instruct them better in true criticism:* Non ego paucis Offendor maculis, quas aut incuria fudit, Aut humana parum cavit natura. *True judgment in Poetry, like that in Painting, takes a view of the whole together, whether it be good or not; and where the beauties are more than the Faults, concludes for the Poet against the little Judge; 'tis a sign that malice is hard driven, when 'tis forc'd to lay hold on a Word or Syllable; to arraign a Man is one thing, and to cavil at him is another. In the midst of an* 20 *ill natur'd Generation of Scriblers, there is always Justice enough left in Mankind to protect good Writers: And they too are oblig'd, both by humanity and interest, to espouse each other's cause against false Criticks, who are the common Enemies. This last consideration puts me in mind of what I owe to the Ingenious and Learned translatour of* Lucretius; *I have not here design'd to rob him of any part of that commendation, which he has so justly acquir'd by the whole Author, whose Fragments only fall to my Portion. What I have now perform'd, is no more than I intended above twenty years ago: The ways of our Translation are very different; he follows him more closely than I have done, which became an Interpreter of the whole Poem: I take more liberty, because it best suited with my design, which was to make him as pleasing as I could. He had been too voluminous, had he us'd my method in* 30 *so long a work; and I had certainly taken his, had I made it my business to Translate the whole. The preference then is justly his: and I joyn with* Mr. Evelyn *in the confession of it, with this additional advantage to him, that his Reputation is already establish'd in this Poet, mine is to make its Fortune in the World. If I have been any where obscure, in following our common Author, or if* Lucretius *himself is to be condemn'd, I refer my self to his excellent Annotations, which I have often read, and always with some new pleasure.*

My Preface begins already to swell upon me, and looks as if I were afraid of my Reader, by so tedious a bespeaking of him: and yet I have Horace *and* Theocritus *upon my hands; but the* Greek *Gentleman shall quickly be dispatch'd, because I have more business with the* 40 Roman.

That which distinguishes Theocritus *from all other Poets, both* Greek *and* Latin, *and which raises him even above* Virgil *in his Eclogues, is the inimitable tenderness of his passions, and the natural expression of them in words so becoming of a Pastoral. A simplicity shines through all he writes: he shows his Art and Learning by disguising both. His Shepherds never rise above their Country Education in their complaints of Love: There is the same difference betwixt him and* Virgil, *as there is betwixt* Tasso's Aminta *and the Pastor* Fido *of* Guarini. Virgils *Shepherds are too well read in the Philosophy of* Epicurus *and of* Plato; *and* Guarini's *seem to have been bred in Courts: but* Theocritus *and* Tasso *have taken theirs*

9-12 *There is one ... bruis'd*] This passage is omitted by some editors, who nevertheless do **not** make the correction of the text which it enjoins.

from Cottages and Plains. It was said of Tasso, *in relation to his similitudes,* Mai esce del Bosco : *That he never departed from the Woods, that is, all his comparisons were taken from the Country.* The same may be said of our Theocritus ; *he is softer than* Ovid, *he touches the passions more delicately, and performs all this out of his own Fond, without diving into the Arts and Sciences for a supply.* Even his Dorick Dialect has an incomparable sweetness in its Clownishness, like a fair Shepherdess in her Country Russet, talking in a Yorkshire Tone. This was impossible for Virgil to imitate ; because the severity of the Roman Language denied him that advantage. Spencer has endeavour'd it in his Shepherds Calendar ; but neither will it succeed in English ; for which reason I forebore to attempt it. For Theocritus writ to Sicilians, who spoke that Dialect ; and I direct this part of my Translations to our 10 Ladies, who neither understand nor will take pleasure in such homely expressions. I proceed to Horace.

Take him in parts, and he is chiefly to be consider'd in his three different Talents, as he was a Critick, a Satyrist, and a Writer of Odes. His Morals are uniform, and run through all of them ; For let his Dutch Commentatours say what they will, his Philosophy was Epicurean ; and he made use of Gods and providence only to serve a turn in Poetry. But since neither his Criticisms (which are the most instructive of any that are written in this Art) nor his Satyrs (which are incomparably beyond Juvenals, if to laugh and rally is to be preferr'd to railing and declaiming), are no part of my present undertaking, I confine my self wholly to his Odes. These are also of several sorts : some of them are Panegyrical, others Moral, 20 the rest Jovial, or (if I may so call them) Bacchanalian. As difficult as he makes it, and as indeed it is, to imitate Pindar, yet in his most elevated flights, and in the sudden changes of his Subject with almost imperceptible connexions, that Theban Poet is his Master. But Horace is of the more bounded Fancy, and confines himself strictly to one sort of Verse, or Stanza, in every Ode. That which will distinguish his Style from all other Poets, is the Elegance of his Words, and the numerousness of his Verse ; there is nothing so delicately turn'd in all the Roman Language. There appears in every part of his diction, or, (to speak English) in all his Expressions, a kind of noble and bold Purity. His Words are chosen with as much exactness as Virgils ; but there seems to be a greater Spirit in them. There is a secret Happiness attends his Choice, which in Petronius is called Curiosa Felicitas, and which I suppose he 30 had from the Feliciter audere of Horace himself. But the most distinguishing part of all his Character seems to me to be his Briskness, his Jollity, and his good Humour : and those I have chiefly endeavour'd to Coppy ; his other Excellencies, I confess, are above my Imitation. One Ode, which infinitely pleas'd me in the reading, I have attempted to translate in Pindarique Verse : 'tis that which is inscrib'd to the present Earl of Rochester, to whom I have particular Obligations, which this small testimony of my gratitude can never pay. 'Tis his Darling in the Latine, and I have taken some pains to make it my Master-Piece in English : for which reason I took this kind of verse, which allows more Latitude than any other. Every one knows it was introduced into our Language, in this age, by the happy Genius of Mr. Cowley. The seeming easiness of it has made it spread ; but it has not been consider'd enough, to be so 40 well cultivated. It languishes in almost every hand but his, and some very few, (whom to keep the rest in countenance) I do not name. He, indeed, has brought it as near Perfection as was possible in so short a time. But if I may be allowed to speak my Mind modestly, and without Injury to his sacred Ashes, somewhat of the Purity of the English, somewhat of more equal Thoughts, somewhat of sweetness in the Numbers, in one Word, somewhat of a finer turn and more Lyrical Verse is yet wanting. As for the Soul of it, which consists in the Warmth and Vigor of Fancy, the masterly Figures, and the copiousness of Imagination, he has excelld all others in this kind. Yet, if the kind it self be capable of more Perfection, though rather in the Ornamental parts of it, than the Essential. what Rules

---

3 *said of our* Theocritus] said, *of our* Theocritus 1685.
4 *Fond*] Wantonly altered by most editors into *Fund* See N. E. D.
9 *attempt it. For*] *attempt it, for 1685.*

*of Morality or respect have I broken, in naming the defects, that they may hereafter be amended ?
Imitation is a nice point, and there are few Poets who deserve to be Models in all they write.
Miltons Paradice Lost is admirable ; but am I therefore bound to maintain, that there are
no flats amongst his Elevations, when 'tis evident he creeps along sometimes, for above an
Hundred lines together ? cannot I admire the height of his Invention, and the strength of
his expression, without defending his antiquated words, and the perpetual harshness of their
sound ? 'Tis as much commendation as a Man can bear, to own him excellent ; all beyond
it is Idolatry. Since Pindar was the Prince of Lyrick Poets, let me have leave to say, that
in imitating him, our numbers shou'd, for the most part, be Lyrical : For variety, or rather*
10 *where the Majesty of thought requires it, they may be stretch'd to the English Heroick of five
Feet, and to the French Alexandrine of Six. But the ear must preside, and direct the Judgment to the choice of numbers : Without the nicety of this, the Harmony of Pindarick Verse
can never be compleat : the cadency of one line must be a rule to that of the next ; and the
sound of the former must slide gently into that which follows ; without leaping from one extream
into another. It must be done like the shadowings of a Picture, which fall by degrees into
a darker colour. I shall be glad, if I have so explain'd my self as to be understood ; but if
I have not, quod nequeo dicere, & sentio tantùm, must be my excuse. There remains
much more to be said on this subject ; but, to avoid envy, I will be silent. What I have said
is the general Opinion of the best Judges, and in a manner has been forc'd from me, by seeing*
20 *a noble sort of Poetry so happily restor'd by one Man, and so grossly copied by almost all the
rest : A musical eare, and a great genius, if another Mr. Cowley cou'd arise, in another age
may bring it to perfection. In the mean time,*

—— Fungar vice cotis, acutum
Reddere quæ ferrum valet, expers ipsa secandi.

*I hope it will not be expected from me, that I shou'd say any thing of my fellow undertakers
in this Miscellany. Some of them are too nearly related to me, to be commended without
suspicion of partiality : Others I am sure need it not ; and the rest I have not perus'd.
To conclude, I am sensible that I have written this too hastily and too loosely : I fear I have
been tedious, and, which is worse, it comes out from the first draught, and uncorrected. This*
30 *I grant is no excuse ; for it may be reasonably urg'd, why did he not write with more leisure,
or, if he had it not (which was certainly my case), why did he attempt to write on so nice a
subject ? The objection is unanswerable ; but in part of recompence, let me assure the Reader,
that, in hasty productions, he is sure to meet with an Authors present sence, which cooler thoughts
would possibly have disguis'd. There is undoubtedly more of spirit though not of judgment,
in these uncorrect Essays, and consequently, though my hazard be the greater, yet the Readers
pleasure is not the less.*

John Dryden.

4 *an Hundred*] Most edd. give *a hundred*
24 expers ipsa secandi] *Some edd. correct the quotation, printing* exsors.

TRANSLATIONS FROM THEOCRITUS

AMARYLLIS;

OR, THE THIRD IDYLLIUM OF THEOCRITUS, PARAPHRAS'D.

To *Amaryllis* Love compells my way,
My browzing *Goats* upon the Mountains
    stray :
O *Tityrus*, tend them well, and see them fed ⎱
In Pastures fresh, and to their watring led ; ⎰
And 'ware the Ridgling with his butting ⎰
    head. ⎰
Ah, beauteous Nymph, can you forget your
    Love,
The conscious *Grottos*, and the shady Grove ;
Where stretcht at ease your tender Limbs
    were laid,
Your nameless Beauties nakedly display'd ?
Then I was call'd your darling, your
    desire,   10
With Kisses such as set my Soul on fire :
But you are chang'd, yet I am still the
    same ;
Myheart maintains for both a double Flame;
Griev'd, but unmov'd, and patient of your
    scorn :
So faithfull I, and you so much forsworn !
I dye, and Death will finish all my pain ;
Yet e'er I dye, behold me once again :
Am I so much deform'd, so chang'd of late ?
What partial Judges are our Love and Hate !
Ten Wildings have I gather'd for my Dear ;
How ruddy like your Lips their streaks
    appear !   21
Far off you view'd them with a longing Eye
Upon the topmost branch (the Tree was
    high ;)
Yet nimbly up, from bough to bough I
    swerv'd,
And for to Morrow have Ten more reserv'd.
Look on me Kindly, and some pity shew,
Or give me leave at least to look on you.
Some God transform me by his Heavenly
    pow'r
Ev'n to a *Bee* to buzz within your Bow'r,

The winding Ivy-chaplet to invade,   30
And folded Fern, that your fair Forehead
    shade.
Now to my cost the force of Love I find ;
The heavy hand he bears on humane kind.
The Milk of *Tygers* was his Infant food, ⎱
Taught from his tender years the tast of ⎰
    blood ; ⎰
His Brother whelps and he ran wild about ⎰
    the wood. ⎰
Ah nymph, train'd up in his Tyrannick
    Court,
To make the suff'rings of your Slaves your
    sport !
Unheeded Ruine ! treacherous delight !
O polish'd hardness, soften'd to the sight ! 40
Whose radiant Eyes your Ebon Brows adorn,
Like Midnight those, and these like break
    of Morn !
Smile once again, revive me with your
    Charms :
And let me dye contented in your Arms.
I would not ask to live another Day,
Might I but sweetly Kiss my Soul away.
Ah, why am I from empty Joys debarr'd ?
For Kisses are but empty, when Compar'd !
I rave, and in my raging fit shall tear
The Garland which I wove for you to wear,
Of Parsley with a wreath of Ivy bound, 51
And border'd with a Rosie edging round.
What pangs I feel, unpity'd and unheard !
Since I must dye, why is my Fate deferr'd !
I strip my Body of my Shepherds Frock :
Behold that dreadfull downfall of a Rock,
Where yon old *Fisher* views the Waves from
    high !
'Tis that Convenient leap I mean to try.
You would be pleas'd to see me plunge to
    shoar,
But better pleas'd if I should rise no more. 60
I might have read my Fortune long agoe,
When, seeking my success in Love to know,
I try'd th' infallible Prophetique way,
A Poppy leaf upon my palm to lay ;

AMARYLLIS. Text from the original edition of
1692.
   5 'ware] w'are *1692.*
   butting] *The editors absurdly give* budding

I struck, and yet no lucky crack did follow,
Yet I struck hard, and yet the leaf lay
    hollow.
And, which was worse, if any worse cou'd
    prove.
The withring leaf foreshew'd your withring
    Love.
Yet farther (Ah, how far a Lover dares !)
My last recourse I had to Seive and Sheeres ;
And told the Witch *Agreo* my disease,   71
(*Agreo*, that in Harvest us'd to lease ;
But Harvest done, to Chare-work did aspire ;
Meat, drink, and Two-pence was her daily
    hire ;)
To work she went, her Charms she mutter'd
    o'er,
And yet the resty Seive wagg'd ne'er the
    more ;
I wept for Woe, the testy Beldame swore,
And foaming with her God, foretold my
    Fate ;
That I was doom'd to Love, and you to
    Hate.
A milk-white Goat for you I did provide ;
Two milk-white Kids run frisking by her
    side,   81
For which the Nut-brown Lass, *Erithacis*,
Full often offer'd many a savoury Kiss.
Hers they shall be, since you refuse the price,
What madman would o'erstand his Market
    twice !
My right Eye itches, some good-luck is
    near,
Perhaps my *Amaryllis* may appear ;
I'll set up such a Note as she shall hear.
What Nymph but my melodious Voice would
    move ?
She must be Flint, if she refuse my Love. 90
Hippomenes, who ran with Noble strife
To win his Lady, or to lose his Life,
(What shift some men will make to get
    a Wife !)
Threw down a Golden Apple in her way ;
For all her haste she could not chuse but
    stay :

------

81 milk-white] milk-whit *1693*.

Renown said run ; the glitt'ring Bribe
    cry'd hold ;
The Man might have been hang'd, but for
    his Gold.
Yet some suppose 'twas Love (some few
    indeed,)
That stopt the fatal fury of her Speed :
She saw, she sigh'd ; her nimble Feet
    refuse   100
Their wonted Speed, and she took pains to
    lose.
A Prophet some, and some a Poet cry,
(No matter which, so neither of them lye)
From steepy *Othrys* top to *Pylus* drove
His herd ; and for his pains enjoy'd his
    Love :
If such another Wager shou'd be laid,
I'll find the Man, if you can find the Maid.
Why name I Men, When Love extended
    finds
His pow'r on high, and in Celestial Minds ?
Venus the Shepherd's homely habit took,
And manag'd something else besides the
    Crook ;   111
Nay, when *Adonis* dy'd, was heard to roar,
And never from her heart forgave the
    Boar.
How blest is fair *Endymion* with his Moon,
Who sleeps on Latmos top from Night to
    Noon !
What *Jason* from *Medea's* Love possest,
You shall not hear, but know 'tis like the
    rest.
My aking Head can scarce support the
    pain ;
This cursed Love will surely turn my Brain :
Feel how it shoots, and yet you take no
    Pity,   120
Nay then 'tis time to end my doleful Ditty.
A clammy Sweat does o'er my Temples
    creep ;
My heavy Eyes are urg'd with Iron sleep :
I lay me down to gasp my latest Breath,
The Wolves will get a Breakfast by my
    Death ;
Yet scarce enough their hunger to supply,
For Love has made me Carrion e'er I dye.

THE EPITHALAMIUM OF HELEN AND MENELAUS.

FROM THE EIGHTEENTH IDYLLIUM OF THEOCRITUS.

TWELVE *Spartan* Virgins, noble, young, and
   fair,
With Violet wreaths adorn'd their flowing
   hair ;
And to the pompous Palace did resort,
Where *Menelaus* kept his Royal Court.
There hand in hand a comely Quire they led; ⌉
To sing a blessing to his Nuptial Bed,   ⌋
With curious Needles wrought, and painted
   Flow'rs bespread.

Joves beauteous Daughter now his Bride
   must be,
And *Jove* himself was less a God than he :
For this their artful hands instruct the Lute
   to sound,   10
Their feet assist their hands, and justly
   beat the ground.
This was their Song : Why, happy Bride-
   groom, why,
E're yet the Stars are kindl'd in the Skie,
E're twilight shades, or Ev'ning dews are
   shed,
Why dost thou steal so soon away to Bed ?
Has *Somnus* brush'd thy Eye-lids with his ⌉
   Rod,   ⌇
Or do thy Legs refuse to bear their Load ⌇
With flowing bowles of a more generous ⌇
   God ?   ⌋
If gentle Slumber on thy Temples creep,
(But naughty Man thou dost not mean to
   sleep)   20
Betake thee to thy Bed, thou drowzy Drone,
Sleep by thy self, and leave thy Bride alone :
Go, leave her with her Maiden Mates to play
At sports more harmless, till the break of
   day :
Give us this Evening : thou hast Morn and
   Night,
And all the year before thee, for delight.
O happy Youth ! to thee, among the crowd
Of Rival Princes, *Cupid* sneez'd aloud ;
And every lucky *Omen* sent before,   29
To meet thee landing on the *Spartan* shore.
Of all our *Heroes* thou canst boast alone,
That *Jove*, when e're he Thunders, calls
   thee Son.

Betwixt two Sheets thou shalt enjoy her ⌉
   bare,   ⌇
With whom no *Grecian* Virgin can compare ⌇
So soft, so sweet, so balmy, and so fair. ⌋
A Boy like thee would make a Kingly line :
But oh, a Girl like her must be divine.
Her equals we, in years, but not in face,
Twelve score *Virago's* of the *Spartan* Race,
While naked to *Eurota's* banks we bend,
And there in manly exercise contend,   41
When she appears, are all eclips'd and lost,
And hide the beauties that we made our
   boast.
So, when the Night and Winter disappear,
The Purple morning, rising with the year,
Salutes the spring, as her Celestial eyes
Adorn the World, and brighten all the Skies :
So beauteous *Helen* shines among the rest,
Tall, slender, straight, with all the Graces
   blest.
As Pines the Mountains, or as Fields the
   Corn,   50
Or as *Thessalian* Steeds the Race adorn ;
So Rosie colour'd *Helen* is the pride
Of *Lacedemon*, and of *Greece* beside.
Like her no Nymph can willing Ozyers bend ⌉
In basket-works, which painted streaks ⌇
   commend :   ⌇
With *Pallas* in the Loombs she may contend. ⌋
But none, ah ! none can animate the Lyre,
And the mute strings with Vocal Souls
   inspire :
Whether the Learn'd *Minerva* be her Theam,
Or chaste *Diana* bathing in the Stream ; 60
None can record their Heavenly praise so
   well
As *Helen*, in whose eyes ten thousand
   Cupids dwell.
O fair, O Graceful ! yet with Maids inroll'd,
But whom to morrow's Sun a Matron shall
   behold !
Yet e're to morrow's Sun shall show his ⌉
   head,   ⌇
The dewy paths of meadows we will tread. ⌇
For Crowns and Chaplets to adorn thy   ⌇
   head.   ⌋

EPITHALAMIUM OF HELEN AND MENELAUS.
Text from the original of 1685 except as noted.

36 Boy like thee] Boy, like thee, *1685.*
40 *Eurota's*] *Eurotas' would be more accurate.*

Where all shall weep, and wish for thy return,
As bleating Lambs their absent Mother mourn.
Our Noblest Maids shall to thy Name bequeath   70
The boughs of *Lotos*, form'd into a wreath.
This Monument, thy Maiden beauties due,
High on a Plane tree shall be hung to view :
On the smooth rind the Passenger shall see
Thy Name ingrav'd, and worship *Helens* Tree :
Balm, from a Silver box distill'd around
Shall all bedew the roots, and scent the sacred ground.
The balm, 'tis true, can aged Plants prolong,
But *Helens* name will keep it ever young.
Hail Bride, hail Bridegroom, son in Law to *Jove* !   80
With fruitful joys *Latona* bless your Love !

Let *Venus* furnish you with full desires,
Add vigour to your wills, and fuel to your fires !
Almighty *Jove* augment your wealthy store,
Give much to you, and to his Grandsons more !
From generous Loyns a generous Race will spring,
Each Girl, like her, a Queen ; each Boy, like you, a King.
Now sleep if sleep you can ; but while you rest,
Sleep close, with folded arms, and breast to breast :
Rise in the morn ; but oh before you rise,   90
Forget not to perform your morning Sacrifice.
We will be with you e're the crowing Cock
Salute the light, and struts before his feather'd Flock.
Hymen, oh *Hymen*, to thy Triumphs run,
And view the mighty spoils thou hast in Battle won.

THE DESPAIRING LOVER,

FROM THE TWENTY-THIRD IDYLLIUM OF THEOCRITUS.

WITH inauspicious love, a wretched Swain
Pursu'd the fairest Nimph of all the Plain ;
Fairest indeed, but prouder far than fair,
She plung'd him hopeless in a deep despair :
Her heav'nly form too haughtily she priz'd,
His person hated, and his Gifts despis'd ;
Nor knew the force of *Cupids* cruel darts,
Nor fear'd his awful power on human hearts ;
But either from her hopeless Lover fled,
Or with disdainful glances shot him dead.   10
No kiss, no look, to cheer the drooping Boy ;
No word she spoke, she scorn'd ev'n to deny.
But, as a hunted Panther casts about
Her glaring eyes, and pricks her list'ning ears to scout,
So she, to shun his Toyls, her cares imploy'd,
And fiercely in her savage freedom joy'd.
Her mouth she writh'd, her forehead taught to frown,
Her eyes to sparkle fires to Love unknown :

Her sallow Cheeks her envious mind did show,
And every feature spoke aloud the curstness of a Shrew.   20
Yet cou'd not he his obvious Fate escape ;
His love still drest her in a pleasing shape ;
And every sullen frown, and bitter scorn,
But fann'd the fuel that too fast did burn.
Long time, unequal to his mighty pain,
He strove to curb it, but he strove in vain :
At last his woes broke out, and begg'd relief
With tears, the dumb petitioners of grief :
With Tears so tender, as adorn'd his Love,
And any heart, but only hers, wou'd move.   30
Trembling before her bolted doors he stood,
And there pour'd out th' unprofitable flood :
Staring his eyes, and haggard was his look ;
Then, kissing first the threshold, thus he spoke.
     Ah Nymph more cruel than of humane Race,
Thy Tygress heart belies thy Angel Face !

THE DESPAIRING LOVER.   Text from the original of 1685.

Too well thou show'st thy Pedigree from Stone :
Thy Grandames was the first by *Pyrrha* thrown :
Unworthy thou to be so long desir'd ;
But so my Love, and so my Fate requir'd. 40
I beg not now (for 'tis in vain) to live ;
But take this gift, the last that I can give.
This friendly Cord shall soon decide the strife
Betwixt my ling'ring Love and loathsome life :
This moment puts an end to all my pain ;
I shall no more despair, nor thou disdain.
Farewel, ungrateful and unkind ! I go
Condemn'd by thee to those sad shades below.
I go th' extreamest remedy to prove,
To drink Oblivion, and to drench my Love :
There happily to lose my long desires :   51
But ah, what draught so deep to quench my Fires ?
Farewell, ye never-opening Gates, ye Stones,
And Threshold guilty of my Midnight Moans:
What I have suffer'd here ye know too well ;
What I shall do the gods and I can tell.
The Rose is fragrant, but it fades in time :
The Violet sweet, but quickly past the prime;
White Lillies hang their heads, and soon decay,
And whiter Snow in minutes melts away : 60
Such is your blooming youth, and withering so :
The time will come, it will, when you shall know
The rage of Love ; your haughty heart shall burn
In Flames like mine, and meet a like return.
Obdurate as you are, oh ! hear at least
My dying prayers, and grant my last request.
When first you ope your doors, and, passing by,
The sad ill Omend Object meets your Eye,
Think it not lost, a moment if you stay ;
The breathless wretch, so made by you, survey :   70
Some cruel pleasure will from thence arise,
To view the mighty ravage of your Eyes.
I wish (but oh ! my wish is vain I fear)
The kind Oblation of a falling Tear :
Then loose the knot, and take me from the place,
And spread your Mantle o'er my grizly Face ;

Upon my livid Lips bestow a kiss
O envy not the dead, they feel not bliss !
Nor fear your kisses can restore my breath;
E'en you are not more pittiless than death.
Then for my Corps a homely Grave provide,
Which Love and me from publick Scorn may hide,   82
Thrice call upon my Name, thrice beat your Breast,
And hayl me thrice to everlasting rest :
Lastlet my Tomb this sad Inscription bear: ⎫
A wretch whom Love has kill'd lies buried ⎬
 here ;   ⎭
Oh, Passengers, *Amintas* Eyes beware.
  Thus having said, and furious with his Love,
He heav'd with more than humane force to move
A weighty Stone (the labour of a Team) 90
And rais'd from thence he reach'd the Neighbouring Beam :
Around its bulk a sliding knot he throws,
And fitted to his Neck the fatal noose :
Then spurning backward, took a swing, 'till death
Crept up, and stopp'd the passage of his Breath.
The bounce burst ope the door ; the Scornful Fair
Relentless lookt, and saw him beat his quivering feet in Air,
Nor wept his fate, nor cast a pitying eye,
Nor took him down, but brusht regardless by :
And, as she pass'd, her chance or fate was such,   100
Her Garments toucht the dead, polluted by the touch.
Next to the dance, thence to the Bath did move ;
The bath was sacred to the God of Love ;
Whose injur'd Image, with a wrathful Eye,
Stood threatning from a Pedestal on high :
Nodding a while, and watchful of his blow,
He fell ; and falling crusht th' ungrateful Nymph below :
Her gushing Blood the Pavement all besmear'd ;
And this her last expiring Voice was heard ;
  Lovers, farewell, revenge has reacht my scorn ;   110
Thus warn'd, be wise, and love for love return.

TRANSLATIONS FROM LUCRETIUS.

LUCRETIUS

THE BEGINNING OF THE FIRST BOOK.

DElight of Humane kind, and Gods above,
Parent of *Rome* ; Propitious Queen of Love,
Whose vital pow'r, Air, Earth, and Sea
　　supplies,
And breeds what e'r is born beneath the
　　rowling Skies :
For every kind, by thy prolifique might,
Springs, and beholds the Regions of the
　　light.
Thee, Goddess, thee the clouds and tem-
　　pests fear,
And at thy pleasing presence disappear :
For thee the Land in fragrant Flow'rs is⎫
　　drest ;　　　　　　　　　　　　　　 ⎬
For thee the Ocean smiles,and smooths her⎪
　　wavy breast ;　　　　　　　　　10 ⎪
And Heav'n it self with more serene and⎬
　　purer light is blest.　　　　　　 ⎭
For when the rising Spring adorns the Mead,
And a new Scene of Nature stands display'd,
When teeming Budds, and chearful greens
　　appear,
And Western gales unlock the lazy year :
The joyous Birds thy welcome first express ;
Whose native Songs thy genial fire confess ;
Then salvage Beasts bound o're their
　　slighted food,
Strook with thy darts, and tempt the
　　raging floud.
All Nature is thy Gift ; Earth, Air,⎫
　　and Sea :　　　　　　　　20 ⎬
Of all that breaths, the various progeny,⎪
Stung with delight, is goaded on by thee.⎭
O're barren Mountains, o're the flowery⎫
　　Plain,　　　　　　　　　　　　 ⎬
The leafy Forest, and the liquid Main⎬
Extends thy uncontroul'd and boundless⎪
　　reign. ·　　　　　　　　　　　 ⎭
Through all the living Regions dost thou
　　move,
And scatter'st, where thou goest, the kindly
　　seeds of Love : ·

FROM LUCRETIUS. Text from the original of
1685.

Since then the race of every living thing
Obeys thy pow'r ; since nothing new can
　　spring
Without thy warmth, without thy influence
　　bear,　　　　　　　　　　　　　30
Or beautiful, or lovesome can appear ;
Be thou my ayd ; My tuneful Song
　　inspire,
And kindle with thy own productive fire ;
While all thy Province, Nature, I survey,⎫
And sing to *Memmius* an immortal lay ⎬
Of Heav'n, and Earth,and every where thy⎪
　　wondrous power display :　　　　 ⎭
To *Memmius*, under thy sweet influence
　　born,
Whom thou with all thy gifts and graces
　　dost adorn.
The rather then assist my Muse and me,
Infusing Verses worthy him and thee.　40
Mean time on Land and Sea let barb'rous
　　discord cease,
And lull the listning world in universal
　　peace
To thee Mankind their soft repose must
　　owe ;
For thou alone that blessing canst bestow ;
Because the brutal business of the War
Is manag'd by thy dreadful Servant's care ;
Who oft retires from fighting fields, to
　　prove
The pleasing pains of thy eternal Love :
And panting on thy breast supinely lies,
While with thy heavenly form he feeds his
　　famish'd eyes ;　　　　　　　　50
Sucks in with open lips thy balmy breath,
By turns restor'd to life, and plung'd in
　　pleasing death.
There while thy curling limbs about him
　　move,
Involv'd and fetter'd in the links of Love,
When wishing all, he nothing can deny,
Thy Charms in that auspicious moment
　　try ;
With winning eloquence our peace implore,
And quiet to the weary World restore.

LUCRETIUS

THE BEGINNING OF THE SECOND BOOK.

Suave Mari magno, &c.

'Tis pleasant, safely to behold from shore
The rowling Ship, and hear the Tempest
  roar :
Not that anothers pain is our delight ;
But pains unfelt produce the pleasing sight.
'Tis pleasant also to behold from far
The moving Legions mingled in the War :
But much more sweet thy lab'ring steps⎫
  to guide   ⎪
To Vertues heights, with wisdom well⎬
  supply'd,   ⎪
And all the *Magazins* of Learning fortifi'd :⎭
From thence to look below on humane
  kind,   10
Bewilder'd in the Maze of Life, and blind :
To see vain fools ambitiously contend
For Wit and Pow'r ; their last endeavours
  bend
T' outshine each other, waste their time
  and health
In search of honour, and pursuit of wealth.
O wretched man ! in what a mist of Life,
Inclos'd with dangers and with noisie strife,
He spends his little Span ; And overfeeds
His cramm'd desires with more than nature
  needs !
For Nature wisely stints our appetite, 20
And craves no more than undisturb'd
  delight :
Which minds unmix'd with cares, and fears,
  obtain ;
A Soul serene, a body void of pain.
So little this corporeal frame requires ;
So bounded are our natural desires,
That wanting all, and setting pain aside,
With bare privation sence is satisfied.
If Golden Sconces hang not on the Walls,
To light the costly Suppers and the Balls ;
If the proud Palace shines not with the
  state   30
Of burnish'd Bowls, and of reflected Plate ;
If well tun'd Harps, nor the more pleasing
  sound
Of Voices, from the vaulted roofs rebound ;
Yet on the grass, beneath a poplar shade,
By the cool stream our careless limbs are
  lay'd ;

With cheaper pleasures innocently bless'd,
When the warm Spring with gaudy flow'rs
  is dress'd.
Nor will the rageing Feavours fire abate,
With Golden Canopies and Beds of State :
But the poor Patient will as soon be sound 40
On the hard mattrass, or the Mother ground.
Then since our Bodies are not eas'd the
  more
By Birth, or Pow'r, or Fortunes wealthy
  store,
'Tis plain, these useless toyes of every
  kind
As little can relieve the lab'ring mind :
Unless we could suppose the dreadful sight
Of marshall'd Legions moving to the fight,
Cou'd, with their sound and terrible array,
Expel our fears, and drive the thoughts of
  death away ;
But, since the supposition vain appears, 50
Since clinging cares, and trains of inbred
  fears,
Are not with sounds to be affrighted thence,
But in the midst of Pomp pursue the
  Prince,
Not aw'd by arms, but in the presence
  bold,
Without respect to Purple, or to Gold ;
Why shou'd not we these pageantries
  despise ;
Whose worth but in our want of reason
  lies ?
For life is all in wandring errours led ;
And just as Children are surpriz'd with
  dread,
And tremble in the dark, so riper years 60
Ev'n in broad daylight are possest with
  fears ;
And shake at shadows fanciful and vain,
As those which in the breasts of Children
  reign.
These bugbears of the mind, this inward
  Hell,
No rayes of outward sunshine can dispel ;
But nature and right reason must display
Their beames abroad, and bring the dark-
  some soul to day.

THE LATTER PART OF THE THIRD BOOK OF LUCRETIUS;
AGAINST THE FEAR OF DEATH.

What has this Bugbear Death to frighten Man,
If Souls can die, as well as Bodies can ?
For, as before our Birth we felt no Pain,
When Punique arms infested Land and Main,
When Heaven and Earth were in confusion hurl'd,
For the debated Empire of the World,
Which aw'd with dreadful expectation lay,
Sure to be Slaves, uncertain who shou'd sway :
So, when our mortal frame shall be disjoyn'd,
The lifeless Lump uncoupled from the mind,
From sense of grief and pain we shall be free ;   11
We shall not feel, because we shall not *Be*.
Though Earth in Seas, and Seas in Heav'n were lost,
We shou'd not move, we only shou'd be tost.
Nay, ev'n suppose when we have suffer'd Fate,
The Soul cou'd feel, in her divided state,
What's that to us ? for we are only we
While Souls and Bodies in one frame agree.
Nay, tho' our Atoms shou'd revolve by chance,
And matter leape into the former dance ;   20
Tho' time our life and motion cou'd restore,
And make our Bodies what they were before,
What gain to us wou'd all this bustle bring ?
The new-made Man wou'd be another thing ;
When once an interrupting pause is made,
That individual Being is decay'd.
We, who are dead and gone, shall bear no part
In all the pleasures, nor shall feel the smart,
Which to that other Mortal shall accrew,
Whom, of our Matter Time shall mould anew.   30
For backward if you look, on that long space
Of Ages past, and view the changing face
Of Matter, tost and variously combin'd
In sundry shapes, 'tis easie for the mind
From thence t' infer, that Seeds of things have been
In the same order as they now are seen :
Which yet our dark remembrance cannot trace,
Because a pause of Life, a gaping space,

Has come betwixt, where memory lies dead,
And all the wandring motions from the sense are fled.   40
For whosoe're shall in misfortunes live,
Must *Be*, when those misfortunes shall arrive ;
And since the Man who *Is* not, feels not woe,
(For death exempts him and wards off the blow,
Which we, the living, only feel and bear)
What is there left for us in Death to fear ?
When once that pause of life has come between,
'Tis just the same as we had never been.
And therefore if a Man bemoan his lot,
That after death his mouldring limbs shall rot,   50
Or flames, or jaws of Beasts devour his Ass,
Know, he's an unsincere, unthinking Ass.
A secret Sting remains within his mind,
The fool is to his own cast offals kind.
He boasts no sense can after death remain ; ⎫
Yet makes himself a part of life again ;   ⎬
As if some other He could feel the pain.   ⎭
If, while he live, this Thought molest his head,
What Wolf or Vulture shall devour me dead,
He wasts his days in idle grief, nor can   60
Distinguish 'twixt the Body and the Man ;
But thinks himself can still himself survive :
And what when dead he feels not, feels alive.
Then he repines that he was born to die,
Nor knows in death there is no other He,
No living He remains his grief to vent,
And o're his senseless Carcass to lament.
If after death 'tis painful to be torn
By Birds and Beasts, then why not so to burn,
Or drench'd in floods of honey to be soak'd,
Imbalm'd to be at once preserv'd and choak'd ;   71
Or on an ayery Mountains top to lie,
Expos'd to cold and Heav'ns inclemency ;
Or crowded in a Tomb to be opprest
With Monumental Marble on thy breast ?
But to be snatch'd from all the household joys,
From thy Chast Wife, and thy dear prattling Boys,

Whose little arms about thy Legs are cast,
And climbing for a Kiss prevent their
Mothers hast,
Inspiring secret pleasure thro' thy Breast,
All these shall be no more: Thy Friends
opprest   81
Thy Care and Courage now no more shall
free ;
Ah Wretch ! thou cry'st, ah ! miserable me ;
One woful day sweeps children, friends, and
wife,
And all the brittle blessings of my life !
Add one thing more, and all thou say'st is
true ;
Thy want and wish of them is vanish'd too :
Which, well consider'd, were a quick relief,
To all thy vain imaginary grief.
For thou shalt sleep, and never wake again,
And, quitting life, shalt quit thy living
pain.   91
But we, thy friends, shall all those sorrows find,
Which in forgetful death thou leav'st
behind ;
No time shall dry our tears, nor drive thee
from our mind.
The worst that can befall thee, measur'd
right,
Is a sound slumber, and a long good night.
Yet thus the Fools, that would be thought
the Wits,
Disturb their mirth with melancholy fits :
When healths go round, and kindly brimmers
flow,
'Till the fresh Garlands on their foreheads
glow,   100
They whine, and cry, Let us make haste
to live,
Short are the joys that humane Life can give.
Eternal Preachers, that corrupt the draught,
And pall the God, that never thinks, with
thought ;
Ideots with all that Thought, to whom the
worst
Of death is want of drink, and endless
thirst,
Or any fond desire as vain as these.
For, e'en in sleep, the body, wrapt in ease,
Supinely lies, as in the peaceful grave,
And wanting nothing, nothing can it crave.
Were that sound sleep eternal, it were
death ;   111
Yet the first Atoms then, the seeds of breath,

Are moving near to sense ; we do but shake
And rouze that sense, and straight we are
awake.
Then death to us, and deaths anxiety
Is less than nothing, if a less could be.
For then our Atoms, which in order lay,
Are scatter'd from their heap, and puff'd
away,
And never can return into their place,
When once the pause of Life has left an
empty space.   120
And last, suppose Great Natures Voice
shou'd call
To thee, or me, or any of us all,
What dost thou mean, ungrateful Wretch,
thou vain,
Thou mortal thing, thus idly to complain,
And sigh and sob, that thou shalt be no
more ?
For if thy Life were pleasant heretofore,
If all the bounteous Blessings, I cou'd give,
Thou hast enjoy'd, if thou hast known to
live,
And Pleasure not leak'd through thee like
a Seive,
Why dost thou not give thanks as at a
plenteous feast,   130
Cram'd to the throat with life, and rise
and take thy rest ?
But if my blessings thou hast thrown away,
If indigested joys pass'd thro', and wou'd
not stay,
Why dost thou wish for more to squander
still ?
If Life be grown a load, a real ill,
And I wou'd all thy cares and labours end,
Lay down thy burden fool, and know thy
friend.
To please thee, I have empti'd all my
store,
I can invent, and can supply no more ;
But run the round again, the round I ran
before.   140
Suppose thou art not broken yet with years,
Yet still the self same Scene of things
appears,
And wou'd be ever, coud'st thou ever live ;
For Life is still but Life, there's nothing
new to give.
What can we plead against so just a Bill ?
We stand convicted, and our cause goes ill.
But if a wretch, a man opprest by fate,
Shou'd beg of Nature to prolong his date,

She speaks aloud to him with more disdain,
Be still, thou Martyr fool, thou covetous
    of pain.   150
But if an old decrepit Sot lament ;
What thou ((She cryes) who hast outliv'd
    content !
Dost thou complain, who hast enjoy'd my
    store ?
But this is still th' effect of wishing more.
Unsatisfy'd with all that Nature brings ;
Loathing the present, liking absent things ;
From hence it comes, thy vain desires, at
    strife
Within themselves, have tantaliz'd thy Life.
And ghastly death appear'd before thy
    sight,
E're thou hadst gorg'd thy Soul & Senses
    with delight.   160
Now leave those joys, unsuiting to thy age,
To a fresh Comer, and resign the Stage ;
Is Nature to be blam'd if thus she chide ?
No sure ; for 'tis her business to provide
Against this ever-changing Frames decay,
New things to come, and old to pass away.
One Being, worn, another Being makes ;
Chang'd, but not lost ; for Nature gives and
    takes :
New Matter must be found for things to
    come,
And these must waste like those, and follow
    Natures doom.   170
All things, like thee, have time to rise and
    rot ;
And from each other's ruin are begot :
For Life is not confin'd to him or thee :
'Tis giv'n to all for use, to none for Property.
Consider former Ages past and gone,
Whose Circles ended long ere thine begun,
Then tell me Fool, what part in them thou
    hast ?
Thus may'st thou judge the future by the
    past.
What horrour seest thou in that quiet state,
What Bugbear Dreams to fright thee after
    Fate ?   180
No Ghost, no Gobblins, that still passage
    keep ;
But all is there serene, in that eternal Sleep.
For all the dismal Tales that Poets tell,
Are verify'd on Earth, and not in Hell.
No *Tantalus* looks up with fearful eye,
Or dreads th' impending Rock to crush him
    from on high :

But fear of Chance on earth disturbs our
    easie hours,
Or vain imagin'd wrath of vain imagin'd
    Pow'rs.
No *Tityus* torn by Vultures lies in Hell ;
Nor cou'd the Lobes of his rank liver swell
To that prodigious Mass, for their eternal
    meal :   191
Not tho' his monstrous Bulk had cover'd
    o're
Nine spreading Acres, or nine thousand
    more ;
Not tho' the Globe of earth had been the
    Gyants floor
Nor in eternal torments could he lie :
Nor could his Corps sufficient food supply.
But he's the *Tityus*, who by love opprest,
Or Tyrant Passion preying on his breast,
And ever anxious Thoughts, is robb'd
    of rest.
The *Sisiphus* is he, whom noise and strife 200
Seduce from all the soft retreats of life,
To vex the Government, disturb the Laws :
Drunk with the Fumes of popular Applause,
He courts the giddy Crowd to make him
    great,
And sweats & toils in vain, to mount the
    sovereign Seat.
For still to aim at Pow'r and still to fail,
Ever to strive, and never to prevail,
What is it, but, in reason's true account
To heave the Stone against the rising
    Mount ?
Which urg'd, and labour'd, and forc'd up
    with pain,   210
Recoils, & rowls impetuous down, and
    smoaks along the plain.
Then still to treat thy ever-craving mind
With ev'ry blessing, and of ev'ry kind,
Yet never fill thy rav'ning appetite ;
Though years and seasons vary thy delight,
Yet nothing to be seen of all the store,
But still the Wolf within thee barks for
    more ;
This is the Fables Moral, which they tell
Of fifty foolish Virgins damn'd in Hell
To leaky Vessels, which the Liquor spill ; 220
To Vessels of their Sex, which none cou'd
    ever fill.
As for the Dog, the Furies, and their Snakes
The gloomy Caverns, and the burning Lakes,
And all the vain infernal trumpery,
They neither are, nor were, nor e're can be.

But here on Earth, the guilty have in view
The mighty Pains to mighty mischiefs
   due ;
Racks, Prisons, Poisons, the *Tarpeian* Rock,
Stripes, Hangmen, Pitch, and suffocating
   Smoak ;
And last, and most, if these were cast
   behind,   230
Th' avenging horrour of a Conscious mind,
Whose deadly fear anticipates the blow,
And sees no end of Punishment and woe ;
But looks for more, at the last gasp of
   breath :
This makes an Hell on Earth, and Life a
   death.
Mean time when thoughts of death disturb
   thy head ;
Consider, *Ancus* great and good is dead ;
Ancus thy better far, was born to die ;
And thou, dost thou bewail mortality ?
So many Monarchs with their mighty
   State,   240
Who rul'd the World, were over-rul'd by
   fate.
That haughty King, who lorded o're the
   Main,
And whose stupendous Bridge did the wild
   Waves restrain,
(In vain they foam'd, in vain they threatned
   wreck,
While his proud Legions march'd upon their
   back :)
Him death, a greater Monarch, overcame ;
Nor spar'd his guards the more, for their
   immortal name.
The *Roman* chief, the *Carthaginian* dread,
Scipio, the Thunder Bolt of War, is dead,
And like a common Slave, by fate in
   triumph led.   250
The Founders of invented Arts are lost ;
And Wits who made Eternity their boast.
Where now is *Homer*, who possest the
   Throne ?
Th' immortal Work remains, the mortal
   Author's gone.
Democritus, perceiving age invade,
His Body weakn'd, and his mind decay'd,
Obey'd the summons with a cheerful face ;
Made hast to welcom death, and met him
   half the race.

254 mortal] *By a most absurd error the*
English editors change this into immortal

That stroke ev'n *Epicurus* cou'd not bar,
Though he in Wit surpass'd Mankind,
   as far   260
As does the midday Sun the midnight Star.
And thou, dost thou disdain to yield thy
   breath,
Whose very Life is little more than
   Death ?
More than one half by Lazy sleep possest ;
And when awake, thy Soul but nods at best,
Day-Dreams and sickly thoughts revolv-
   ing in thy breast
Eternal troubles haunt thy anxious mind,
Whose cause and cure thou never hop'st to
   find ;
But still uncertain, with thyself at strife,
Thou wander'st in the *Labyrinth* of
   Life.   270
O ! if the foolish race of man, who find
A weight of cares still pressing on their
   mind,
Cou'd find as well the cause of this
   unrest,
And all this burden lodg'd within the
   breast ;
Sure they wou'd change their course, nor
   live as now,
Uncertain what to wish or what to vow.
Uneasie both in Countrey and in Town,
They search a place to lay their burden
   down.
One, restless in his Palace, walks abroad,
And vainly thinks to leave behind the
   load :   280
But straight returns ; for he's as restless
   there ;
And finds there's no relief in open Air.
Another to his *Villa* wou'd retire,
And spurs as hard as if it were on fire ,
No sooner enter'd at his Country door,
But he begins to stretch, and yawn, and
   snore ;
Or seeks the City which he left before.
Thus every man o're works his weary Will,
To shun himself, and to shake off his ill :
The shaking Fit returns, and hangs upon
   him still.   290
No prospect of repose, nor hope of ease ;
The Wretch is ignorant of his disease ;
Which known wou'd all his fruitless trouble
   spare ;
For he wou'd know the World not worth
   his care ;

Then wou'd he search more deeply for the cause ;
And study Nature well, and Natures Laws :
For in this moment lies not the debate,
But on our future, fix'd, Eternal State ;
That never changing state, which all must keep,
Whom Death has doom'd to everlasting sleep.   300
Why are we then so fond of mortal Life,
Beset with dangers, and maintain'd with strife ?
A Life, which all our care can never save ;
One Fate attends us ; and one common Grave.
Besides, we tread but a perpetual round ; ⎫
We ne're strike out, but beat the former ⎬
   ground,   ⎪
And the same Maukish joyes in the same ⎪
   track are found.   ⎭

For still we think an absent blessing best, ⎫
Which cloys, and is no blessing when ⎪
   possest ;   ⎬
A new arising wish expells it from the ⎪
   Breast.   310 ⎭
The Feav'rish thirst of Life increases still ;
We call for more and more, and never have our fill ;
Yet know not what to-morrow we shall try,
What dregs of life in the last draught may lie :
Nor, by the longest life we can attain,
One moment from the length of death we ⎫
   gain ;   ⎬
For all behind belongs to his Eternal ⎪
   reign.   ⎭
When once the Fates have cut the mortal Thred,
The Man as much to all intents is dead,
Who dyes to day, and will as long be so, 320
As he who dy'd a thousand years ago.

FROM LUCRETIUS—BOOK THE FIFTH.

Tum porrò puer, &c.

Thus like a Sayler by a Tempest hurl'd
A shore, the Babe is shipwrack'd on the World :
Naked he lies, and ready to expire ;
Helpless of all that humane wants require :
Expos'd upon unhospitable Earth,
From the first moment of his hapless Birth.
Straight with forebodeing cryes he fills the Room ;
(Too true presages of his future doom.)
But Flocks, and Herds, and every Savage Beast,
By more indulgent Nature are increas'd, 10

They want no Rattles for their froward mood,
Nor Nurse to reconcile them to their food,
With broken words ; nor Winter blasts they fear,
Nor change their habits with the changing year :
Nor, for their safety, Citadels prepare ;
Nor forge the wicked Instruments of War :
Unlabour'd Earth her bounteous treasure grants,
And Nature's lavish hand supplies their common wants.

BOOK IV. *It is impossible to reprint this piece.*

BOOK V. 18 hand] hands *1685. A misprint.*

TRANSLATIONS FROM HORACE.

THE THIRD ODE OF THE FIRST BOOK OF HORACE;

Inscrib'd to the Earl of Roscommon, on his Intended Voyage to IRELAND.

So may th' auspicious Queen of Love,
And the Twin Stars, (the Seed of *Jove*,)
And he who rules the rageing wind,
To thee, O sacred Ship, be kind ;
And gentle Breezes fill thy Sails,
Supplying soft *Etesian* Gales :
As thou, to whom the Muse commends
The best of Poets and of Friends,
Dost thy committed Pledge restore,
And land him safely on the shore ;   10
And save the better part of me,
From perishing with him at Sea.
Sure he, who first the passage try'd,   )
In harden'd Oak his heart did hide,   }
And ribs of Iron arm'd his side ;   )
Or his at least, in hollow wood
Who tempted first the briny Floud :
Nor fear'd the winds contending roar,
Nor billows beating on the Shoar ;
Nor *Hyades* portending Rain ;   20
Nor all the Tyrants of the Main.
What form of death cou'd him affright,
Who unconcern'd, with steadfast sight,
Cou'd veiw the Surges mounting steep,
And monsters rolling in the deep !
Cou'd thro' the ranks of ruin go,
With Storms above, and Rocks below !
In vain did Natures wise command

Divide the Waters from the Land,
If daring Ships, and Men prophane,   30
Invade th' inviolable Main ;
Th' eternal Fences overleap,
And pass at will the boundless deep.
No toyl, no hardship can restrain
Ambitious Man, inur'd to pain ;
The more confin'd, the more he tries,
And at forbidden quarry flies.
Thus bold *Prometheus* did aspire,
And stole from heav'n the seed of Fire :
A train of Ills, a ghastly crew,   40
The Robber's blazing track persue ;
Fierce Famine, with her Meagre face,
And Feavours of the fiery Race,
In swarms th' offending Wretch surround
All brooding on the blasted ground :
And limping Death, lash'd on by Fate
Comes up to shorten half our date.
This made not *Dedalus* beware,
With borrow'd wings to sail in Air :
To Hell *Alcides* forc'd his way,   50
Plung'd thro' the Lake, and snatch'd the
        Prey.
Nay scarce the Gods, or heav'nly Climes,
Are safe from our audacious Crimes ;
We reach at *Jove's* Imperial Crown,
And pull th' unwilling thunder down.

THE NINTH ODE OF THE FIRST BOOK OF HORACE

I

Behold yon Mountains hoary height,
  Made higher with new Mounts of Snow ;
Again behold the Winters weight
  Oppress the lab'ring Woods below :
And Streams, with Icy fetters bound,
Benum'd and crampt to solid Ground.

II

With well-heap'd Logs dissolve the cold,
  And feed the genial hearth with fires ;
Produce the Wine, that makes us bold,
  And sprightly Wit and Love inspires :   10
For what hereafter shall betide,
God, if 'tis worth his care, provide.

TRANSLATIONS FROM HORACE. ODES I. iii.
Text from the original of 1685.

ODES I. ix.   Text from the original of 1684.

III

Let him alone, with what he made,
  To toss and turn the World below ;
At his command the storms invade ;
  The winds by his Commission blow ;
Till with a Nod he bids 'em cease,
And then the Calm returns, and all is
  peace.

IV

To morrow and her works defie,
  Lay hold upon the present hour,   20
And snatch the pleasures passing by,
  To put them out of Fortunes pow'r :
Nor love, nor love's delights disdain ;
Whate're thou get'st to day is gain.

V

Secure those golden early joyes,
  That Youth unsowr'd with sorrow bears,
E're with'ring time the taste destroyes,
  With sickness and unwieldy years !
For active sports, for pleasing rest,
This is the time to be possest ;   30
The best is but in season best.

VI

The pointed hour of promis'd Bliss,
  The pleasing whisper in the dark,
The half unwilling willing kiss,
  The laugh that guides thee to the mark,
When the kind Nymph wou'd coyness feign,
And hides but to be found again ;
These, these are joyes the Gods for Youth
  ordain.

THE TWENTY-NINTH ODE OF THE THIRD BOOK OF HORACE;

PARAPHRASED IN PINDARICK VERSE, AND INSCRIBED TO THE RIGHT HON. LAURENCE EARL OF ROCHESTER.

I

DESCENDED of an ancient Line,
That long the *Tuscan* Scepter sway'd,
Make haste to meet the generous Wine,
  Whose piercing is for thee delay'd :
The rosie wreath is ready made ;
  And artful hands prepare
The fragrant *Syrian* Oyl, that shall perfume
  thy hair.

II

When the Wine sparkles from a far,
  And the well-natur'd Friend cries, come
  away ;
Make haste, and leave thy business and
  thy care :   10
No mortal int'rest can be worth thy stay.

III

Leave for a while thy costly Country Seat ;
  And, to be Great indeed, forget
The nauseous pleasures of the Great :
  Make haste and come :

Come, and forsake thy cloying store ;
  Thy Turret that surveys, from high,
The smoke, and wealth, and noise of *Rome*;
  And all the busie pageantry
That wise men scorn, and fools adore : 20
Come, give thy Soul a loose, and taste the
  pleasures of the poor.

IV

Sometimes 'tis grateful to the Rich, to try
A short vicissitude, and fit of Poverty :
  A savoury Dish, a homely Treat,
  Where all is plain, where all is neat,
Without the stately spacious Room,
The *Persian* Carpet, or the *Tyrian* Loom,
Clear up the cloudy foreheads of the Great.

V

The Sun is in the Lion mounted high ;
    The *Syrian* Star   30
    Barks from afar,
  And with his sultry breath infects the Sky ;
The ground below is parch'd, the heav'ns
    above us fry.
The Shepheard drives his fainting Flock
  Beneath the covert of a Rock,
  And seeks refreshing Rivulets nigh

ODES I. ix. 32 pointed] *i.e.* appointed, *which editors print.*
ODES III. xxix. Text from the original of 1685.
Title. THIRD] *All the English editors wrongly change this into* FIRST
11 be] *by* 1685. *A misprint.*

The *Sylvans* to their shades retire,
Those very shades and streams new shades
    and streams require,
And want a cooling breeze of wind to fan
    the raging fire.

VI

Thou, what befits the new Lord May'r, 40
And what the City Faction dare,
And what the *Gallique* arms will do,
And what the Quiverbearing foe,
    Art anxiously inquisitive to know :
But God has, wisely, hid from humane sight
    The dark decrees of future fate ;
And sown their seeds in depth of night ;
He laughs at all the giddy turns of State ;
When Mortals search too soon, and fear too
    late.

VII

Enjoy the present smiling hour ;   50
    And put it out of Fortunes pow'r :
The tide of bus'ness, like the running
    stream,
Is sometimes high, and sometimes low,
A quiet ebb, or a tempestuous flow,
    And alwayes in extream.
Now with a noiseless gentle course
    It keeps within the middle Bed ;
Anon it lifts aloft the head,
And bears down all before it with impetuous
    force :
    And trunks of Trees come rowling
      down,   60
    Sheep and their Folds together drown :
Both House and Homested into Seas are
    borne ;
And Rocks are from their old foundations
    torn,
And woods, made thin with winds, their
    scatter'd honours mourn.

VIII

Happy the Man, and happy he alone,
He, who can call to day his own :
    He who, secure within, can say,
To morrow do thy worst, for I have
    liv'd to-day.

---

41 Faction] *All the English editors wrongly
give* Factions

Be fair, or foul, or rain, or shine,
The joys I have possest, in spight of
    fate, are mine.   70
Not Heav'n it self upon the past has
    pow'r ;
But what has been, has been, and I have
    had my hour.

IX

Fortune, that with malicious joy
    Does Man her slave oppress,
Proud of her Office to destroy,
    Is seldome pleas'd to bless :
Still various, and unconstant still,
But with an inclination to be ill.
    Promotes, degrades, delights in
      strife,
    And makes a Lottery of life.   80
I can enjoy her while she's kind ;
But when she dances in the wind,
    And shakes the wings, and will not
      stay,
I puff the Prostitute away :
The little or the much she gave, is quietly
    resign'd :
Content with poverty, my Soul I arm ;
And Vertue, tho' in rags, will keep me
    warm.

X

    What is't to me,
Who never sail in her unfaithful Sea,
    If Storms arise, and Clouds grow
      black ;   90
If the Mast split, and threaten wreck ?
Then let the greedy Merchant fear
    For his ill gotten gain ;
And pray to Gods that will not hear,
While the debating winds and billows
    bear
    His Wealth into the Main
For me, secure from Fortunes blows
(Secure of what I cannot lose,)
In my small Pinnace I can sail,
Contemning all the blustring roar ;   100
    And running with a merry gale,
With friendly Stars my safety seek
Within some little winding Creek ;
    And see the storm a shore.

THE SECOND EPODE OF HORACE.

How happy in his low degree,
How rich in humble Poverty, is he,
Who leads a quiet country life !
Discharg'd of business, void of strife,
And from the gripeing Scrivener free.
(Thus, e're the Seeds of Vice were sown,
  Liv'd Men in better Ages born,
Who Plow'd, with Oxen of their own,
  Their small paternal field of Corn.)
Nor Trumpets summon him to War   10
  Nor drums disturb his morning Sleep,
Nor knows he Merchants gainful care,
  Nor fears the dangers of the deep.
The clamours of contentious Law,
  And Court and state, he wisely shuns,
Nor brib'd with hopes, nor dar'd with
    awe,
  To servile Salutations runs ;
But either to the clasping Vine
  Does the supporting Poplar Wed,
Or with his pruneing hook disjoyn   20
  Unbearing Branches from their Head,
  And grafts more happy in their stead :
Or climbing to a hilly steep,
  He views his Herds in Vales afar,
Or Sheers his overburden'd Sheep,
  Or mead for cooling drink prepares
  Of Virgin honey in the Jars.
Or in the now declining year,
  When bounteous *Autumn* rears his head,
He joyes to pull the ripen'd Pear,   30
  And clustring Grapes with purple spread.
The fairest of his fruit he serves,
  Priapus thy rewards :
Sylvanus too his part deserves,
  Whose care the fences guards.
Sometimes beneath an ancient Oak,
  Or on the matted grass he lies :
No God of Sleep he need invoke ;
  The stream, that o're the pebbles flies,
  With gentle slumber crowns his Eyes.   40
The Wind, that Whistles through the
    sprays,
  Maintains the consort of the Song ;
And hidden Birds, with native layes,
  The golden sleep prolong.

EPODE II. Text from the original of 1685.

But when the blast of Winter blows,
  And hoary frost inverts the year,
Into the naked Woods he goes,
  And seeks the tusky Boar to rear,
  With well mouth'd hounds and pointed
    Spear.
Or spreads his subtile Nets from sight   50
  With twinckling glasses to betray
The Larkes that in the Meshes light,
  Or makes the fearful Hare his prey.
Amidst his harmless easie joys
  No anxious care invades his health,
Nor Love his peace of mind destroys,
  Nor wicked avarice of Wealth.
But if a chast and pleasing Wife,
To ease the business of his Life,
Divides with him his houshold care,   60
Such as the Sabine *Matrons* were,
Such as the swift *Apulians* Bride,
  Sunburnt and Swarthy tho' she be,
Will fire for Winter Nights provide,
  And without noise will oversee
  His Children and his Family,
And order all things till he come,
Sweaty and overlabour'd, home ;
If she in pens his Flocks will fold,
  And then produce her Dairy store,   70
With Wine to drive away the cold,
  And unbought dainties of the poor ;
Not Oysters of the *Lucrine* Lake
  My sober appetite wou'd wish,
  Nor *Turbet*, or the Foreign Fish
That rowling Tempests overtake,
  And hither waft the costly dish.
Not *Heathpout*, or the rarer Bird,
  Which *Phasis*, or *Ionia* yields,
More pleasing morsels wou'd afford   80
  Than the fat Olives of my fields ;
Than Shards or Mallows for the pot,
  That keep the loosen'd Body sound
Or than the Lamb, that falls by Lot,
  To the just Guardian of my ground.
Amidst these feasts of happy Swains,
  The jolly Shepheard smiles to see
His flock returning from the Plains ;
  The farmer is as pleas'd as he,
To view his Oxen, sweating smoak,   90
Bear on their Necks the loosen'd Yoke :

To look upon his menial Crew,
  That sit around his cheerful hearth,
And bodies spent in toil renew
  With wholesome Food and Country
    Mirth.
This *Morecraft* said within himself;

Resolv'd to leave the wicked Town;
  And live retir'd upon his own;
He call'd his Mony in:
  But the prevailing love of pelf   100
  Soon split him on the former shelf,
And put it out again.

TRANSLATIONS FROM HOMER.

THE FIRST BOOK OF *HOMER'S ILIAS*.

THE ARGUMENT.

CHRYSES, *Priest of* Apollo, *brings Presents to the* Grecian *Princes, to ransom his Daughter* Chryseis, *who was Prisoner in the Fleet.* Agamemnon, *the General, whose Captive and Mistress the young Lady was, refuses to deliver her, threatens the Venerable Old Man, and dismisses him with Contumely.—The Priest craves Vengeance of his God; who sends a Plague among the* Greeks: *which occasions* Achilles, *their Great Champion, to summon a Council of the Chief Officers: He encourages* Calchas, *the High Priest and Prophet, to tell the Reason, why the Gods were so much incensed against them.*—Calchas *is fearful of provoking* Agamemnon, *till* Achilles *engages to protect him: Then, embolden'd by the* Heroe, *he accuses the General as the Cause of all, by detaining the Fair Captive, and refusing the Presents offer'd for her Ransom. By this Proceeding,* Agamemnon *is oblig'd, against his Will, to restore* Chryseis, *with Gifts, that he might appease the Wrath of* Phœbus; *but at the same time, to revenge himself on* Achilles, *sends to seize his Slave* Briseis. Achilles, *thus affronted, complains to his Mother* Thetis; *and begs her to revenge his Injury, not only on the General, but on all the Army, by giving Victory to the* Trojans, *till the ungrateful King became sensible of his Injustice. At the same time, he retires from the Camp into his Ships, and withdraws his aid from his Countrymen. Thetis prefers her Son's Petition to Jupiter, who grants her Sute.* Juno *suspects her Errand, and quarrels with her Husband, for his Grant; till* Vulcan *reconciles his Parents with a Bowl of Nectar, and sends them peaceably to Bed.*

THE wrath of *Peleus* Son, O Muse, resound;
Whose dire Effects the *Grecian* Army found:
And many a Heroe, King, and hardy
    Knight,
Were sent, in early Youth, to Shades of
    Night:
Their Limbs a Prey to Dogs and Vultures
    made;
So was the Sov'reign Will of *Jove* obey'd:
From that ill-omen'd Hour when Strife begun,
Betwixt *Atrides* Great, and *Thetis* God-like
    Son.
What Pow'r provok'd, and for what Cause,
    relate,
Sow'd, in their Breasts, the Seeds of stern
    Debate: 10
Jove's and *Latona's* Son his Wrath express'd,
In Vengeance of his violated Priest,
Against the King of Men; who swoln with
    Pride,
Refus'd his Presents, and his Pray'rs deny'd.
For this the God a swift Contagion spread
Amid the Camp, where Heaps on Heaps lay
    dead.
For Venerable *Chryses* came to buy,
With Gold and Gifts of Price, his Daughter's
    Liberty.
Suppliant before the Grecian chiefs he stood;
Awful, and arm'd with Ensigns of his God:

THE FIRST BOOK OF HOMER'S ILIAS. The text from the original edition of 1700. The text is given with fair accuracy in most editions. In the original there are some obvious misprints and some false stops.

1 *Peleus*] *Peleu's 1700.*

Bare was his hoary Head ; one holy Hand 21
Held forth his Laurel Crown, and one his
  Sceptre of Command.
His Suit was common ; but above the rest,
To both the Brother-Princes thus address'd :
Ye Sons of *Atreus*, and ye *Grecian* Pow'rs,
So may the Gods who dwell in Heav'nly
  Bow'rs
Succeed your Siege, accord the Vows you
  make,
And give you *Troys* Imperial Town to take ;
So, by their happy Conduct, may you come
With Conquest back to your sweet Native
  Home ; 30
As you receive the Ransom which I bring,
(Respecting *Jove*, and the far-shooting
  King,)
And break my Daughters Bonds, at my
  desire ;
And glad with her Return her grieving Sire.
  With Shouts of loud Acclaim the *Greeks*
  decree
To take the Gifts, to set the Damsel free.
The King of Men alone with Fury burn'd ;
And haughty, these opprobrious Words
  return'd :
Hence, Holy Dotard, and avoid my Sight,
E'er Evil intercept thy tardy Flight : 40
Nor dare to tread this interdicted Strand, ⎫
Lest not that idle Sceptre in thy Hand, ⎬
Nor thy God's Crown, my vow'd Revenge ⎭
  withstand.
Hence on thy Life : The Captive-Maid is
  mine ;
Whom not for Price or Pray'rs I will resign :
Mine she shall be, till creeping Age and Time
Her Bloom have wither'd, and consum'd her
  Prime :
Till then my Royal Bed she shall attend ;
And having first adorn'd it, late ascend :
This, for the Night ; by Day, the Web and ⎫
  Loom 50 ⎪
And homely Household-task, shall be her ⎬
  Doom, ⎪
Far from thy lov'd Embrace, and her sweet ⎪
  Native Home. ⎭
He said : The helpless Priest reply'd no
  more,
But sped his Steps along the hoarse-resound-
  ing Shore :
Silent he fled ; secure at length he stood,
Devoutly curs'd his Foes, and thus invok'd
  his God.

O Source of Sacred Light, attend my
  Pray'r,
God with the Silver Bow, and Golden Hair ;
Whom *Chrysa, Cilla, Tenedos* obeys,
And whose broad Eye their happy Soil
  surveys ; 60
If, *Smintheus*, I have pour'd before thy
  Shrine
The Blood of Oxen, Goats, and ruddy Wine,
And Larded Thighs on loaded Altars laid,
Hear, and my just Revenge propitious aid,
Pierce the proud *Greeks*, and with thy Shafts
  attest
How much thy pow'r is injured in thy
  Priest.
  He pray'd, and *Phœbus* hearing, urg'd his
  Flight,
With fury kindled, from *Olympus* Height ;
His Quiver o'er his ample Shoulders threw ;
His Bow twang'd, and his Arrows rattl'd as
  they flew. 70
Black as a stormy Night, he rang'd around
The Tents, and compass'd the devoted
  Ground.
Then with full Force his deadly Bowe he
  bent,
And Feather'd Fates among the Mules and
  Sumpters sent,
Th' Essay of Rage, on faithful Dogs the
  next ;
And last, in Humane Hearts his Arrows
  fix'd.
The God nine Days the *Greeks* at Rovers
  kill'd,
Nine Days the Camp with Fun'ral Fires was
  fill'd ;
The tenth, *Achilles*, by the Queens Com-
  mand,
Who bears Heav'ns awful Sceptre in her
  Hand, 80
A Council summon'd : for the Goddess
  griev'd
Her favour'd Hoast shou'd perish unreliev'd.
  The Kings assembled, soon their Chief
  inclose ;
Then from his Seat the Goddess-born arose,
And thus undaunted spoke : What now
  remains,
But that once more we tempt the watry
  Plains,
And wandring homeward, seek our Safety
  hence,
In Flight at least if we can find Defence ?

Such Woes at once encompass us about,
The Plague within the Camp, the Sword
    without.   90
Consult, O King, the Prophets of th' Event:
And whence these Ills, and what the Gods
    intent,
Let them by Dreams explore ; for Dreams
    from *Jove* are sent.
What want of offer'd Victims, what Offence
In Fact committed cou'd the Sun incense,
To deal his deadly Shafts ? What may
    remove
His settled Hate, and reconcile his Love ?
That he may look propitious on our Toils ;
And hungry Graves no more be glutted with
    our Spoils.
    Thus to the King of Men the Hero spoke,
Then *Calchas* the desir'd Occasion took : 101
Calchas the sacred Seer, who had in view
Things present and the past ; and Things
    to come foreknew,
Supream of *Augurs*, who by *Phœbus* taught,
The *Grecian* Pow'rs to *Troy's* Destruction
    brought.
Skill'd in the secret Causes of their Woes,
The Reverend Priest in graceful Act arose :
And thus bespoke *Pelides :* Care of *Jove*,
Favour'd of all th' Immortal Pow'rs above ;
Wou'dst thou the Seeds deep sown of Mis-
    chief know,   110
And why, provok'd *Apollo* bends his bow ?
Plight first thy Faith, inviolably true,
To save me from those Ills, that may
    ensue.
For I shall tell ungrateful Truths, to those
Whose boundless Pow'rs of Life and Death
    dispose.
And Sov'reigns, ever jealous of their State,
Forgive not those whom once they mark for
    Hate ;
Ev'n tho' th' Offence they seemingly digest,
Revenge, like Embers, rak'd within their
    Breast,
Bursts forth in Flames ; whose unresisted
    Pow'r   120
Will seize th' unwary Wretch, and soon
    devour.
Such, and no less is he, on whom depends
The sum of Things ; and whom my Tongue
    of force offends.
Secure me then from his foreseen Intent,
That what his Wrath may doom, thy Valour
    may prevent.

    To this the stern *Achilles* made Reply :
Be bold ; and on my plighted Faith rely,
To speak what *Phœbus* has inspir'd thy
    Soul
For common Good ; and speak without con-
    troul.
His Godhead I invoke, by him I swear, 130
That while my Nostrils draw this vital Air,
None shall presume to violate those Bands ;
Or touch thy Person with unhallow'd
    Hands :
Ev'n not the King of Men that all com-
    mands.
    At this, resuming Heart, the Prophet said :
Nor Hecatombs unslain, nor Vows unpaid,
On *Greeks*, accurs'd, this dire Contagion
    bring ;
Or call for Vengeance from the Bowyer King ;
But he the Tyrant, whom none dares
    resist,   139
Affronts the Godhead in his injur'd Priest :
He keeps the Damsel Captive in his Chain,
And Presents are refus'd, and Pray'rs pre-
    ferr'd in vain.
For this th' avenging Pow'r employs his
    Darts ;
And empties all his Quiver in our Hearts :
Thus will persist, relentless in his ire,
Till the fair Slave be render'd to her Syre :
And Ransom-free restor'd to his Abode,
With Sacrifice to reconcile the God :
Then he, perhaps, atton'd by Pray'r, may
    cease
His Vengeance justly vow'd, and give the
    Peace.   150
    Thus having said, he sate : Thus an-
    swer'd then
Upstarting from his Throne, the King of
    Men,
His Breast with Fury fill'd, his Eyes with Fire ;
Which rowling round, he shot in Sparkles
    on the Sire :
Augur of Ill, whose Tongue was never found
Without a Priestly Curse or boding Sound ;
For not one bless'd Event foretold to me
Pass'd through that Mouth, or pass'd un-
    willingly.
And now thou dost with Lies the Throne
    invade,
By Practice harden'd in thy sland'ring
    Trade.   160

136 Hecatombs] *The editors give* Hecatomb

Obtending Heav'n, for what e'er Ills befal ;
And sputtring under specious Names thy
Gall.
Now *Phœbus* is provok'd ; his Rites and
Laws
Are in his Priest profan'd, and I the Cause :
Since I detain a Slave, my Sov'reign Prize ;
And sacred Gold, your Idol-God, despise.
I love her well : And well her Merits claim,
To stand preferr'd before my *Grecian* Dame :
Not *Clytemnestra's* self in Beauties Bloom
More charm'd, or better ply'd the various
Loom :   170
Mine is the Maid ; and brought in happy
Hour
With every Household-grace adorn'd, to
bless my Nuptial Bow'r.
Yet shall she be restor'd ; since publick⎫
Good   ⎪
For private Int'rest ought not to be with-⎬
stood,   ⎪
To save th' Effusion of my People's Blood.⎭
But Right requires, if I resign my own,
I shou'd not suffer for your sakes alone ;
Alone excluded from the Prize I gain'd,
And by your common Suffrage have obtain'd
The Slave without a Ransom shall be sent :
It rests for you to make th' Equivalent. 181
    To this the fierce *Thessalian* Prince reply'd:
O first in Pow'r, but passing all in Pride,
Griping, and still tenacious of thy Hold,
Would'st thou the *Grecian* Chiefs, though
largely Sould,
Shou'd give the Prizes they had gain'd before,
And with their Loss thy Sacrilege restore ?
Whate'er by force of Arms the Soldier got,
Is each his own, by dividend of Lot :
Which to resume, were both unjust, and
base ;   190
Not to be borne but by a servile Race.
But this we can : If *Saturn's* Son bestows
The Sack of *Troy*, which he by Promise
owes ;
Then shall the conquering *Greeks* thy Loss
restore,
And with large Int'rest make th' advantage
more.
    To this *Atrides* answer'd, Though thy
Boast
Assumes the foremost Name of all our
Host,
Pretend not, mighty Man, that what is mine,
Controll'd by thee, I tamely shou'd resign.

Shall I release the Prize I gain'd by
Right,   200
In taken Towns, and many a bloody Fight,
While thou detain'st *Briseis* in thy Bands,
By priestly glossing on the God's Commands?
Resolve on this, (a short Alternative)
Quit mine, or, in Exchange, another give ;
Else I, assure thy Soul, by Sov'reign Right
Will seize thy Captive in thy own Despight.
Or from stout *Ajax*, or *Ulysses*, bear
What other Prize my Fancy shall prefer :
Then softly murmur, or aloud complain, 210
Rage as you please, you shall resist in vain.
But more of this, in proper Time and Place ;
To Things of greater Moment let us pass.
A Ship to sail the sacred Seas prepare ;⎫
Proud in her Trim ; and put on board the⎪
Fair,   ⎬
With Sacrifice and Gifts, and all the Pomp⎪
of Pray'r.   ⎭
The Crew well chosen, the Command shall⎫
be   ⎪
In *Ajax* ; or if other I decree,   ⎬
In *Creta's* King, or *Ithacus*, or, if I please⎪
in Thee :   ⎭
Most fit thy self to see perform'd th' Intent⎫
From which my Pris'ner from my Sight is⎪
sent ;   221⎬
(Thanks to thy pious Care) that *Phœbus*⎪
may relent.   ⎭
    At this, *Achilles* roul'd his furious Eyes,
Fix'd on the King askant ; and thus replies :
O, Impudent, regardful of thy own,
Whose thoughts are center'd on thy self
alone,
Advanc'd to Sovereign Sway, for better Ends
Than thus like abject Slaves to treat thy
Friends.
What *Greek* is he, that urg'd by thy Command,
Against the *Trojan* Troops will lift his
Hand ?   230
Not I : Nor such inforc'd Respect I owe ;
Nor *Pergamus* I hate, nor *Priam* is my Foe.
What Wrong from *Troy* remote, cou'd I⎫
sustain,   ⎪
To leave my fruitful Soil, and happy Reign,⎬
And plough the Surges of the stormy⎪
Main ?   ⎭
Thee, frontless Man, we follow'd from afar ;
Thy Instruments of Death, and Tools of War.
Thine is the Triumph ; ours the Toil alone :
We bear thee on our Backs, and mount thee
on the Throne.

For thee we fall in Fight ; for thee redress
Thy baffled Brother ; not the Wrongs of
   Greece.   241
And now thou threaten'st with unjust
   Decree,
To punish thy affronting Heav'n, on me.
To seize the Prize which I so dearly bought ;
By common Suffrage giv'n, confirm'd by
   Lot.
Mean Match to thine : For still above the
   rest,
Thy hook'd rapacious Hands usurp the best.
Though mine are first in Fight, to force the
   Prey ;
And last sustain the Labours of the Day.
Nor grudge I thee the much the *Grecians*
   give ;   250
Nor murm'ring take the little I receive.
Yet ev'n this little, thou, who woud'st in-
   gross
The whole, Insatiate, envy'st as thy Loss.
Know, then, for *Phthya* fix'd is my return : ⎫
Better at home my ill-paid Pains to mourn, ⎬
Than from an Equal here sustain the publick ⎭
   Scorn.
  The King, whose Brows with shining
   Gold were bound,
Who saw his Throne with scepter'd Slaves
   encompass'd round,
Thus answer'd stern : Go, at thy Pleasure,
   go :
We need not such a Friend, nor fear we such
   a Foe.   260
There will not want to follow me in Fight :
Jove will assist, and *Jove* assert my Right.
But thou of all the Kings (his Care below)
Art least at my Command, and most my Foe.
Debates, Dissentions, Uproars are thy Joy ;
Provok'd without Offence, and practis'd to
   destroy.
Strength is of Brutes ; and not thy Boast
   alone ;
At least 'tis lent from Heav'n ; and not thy
   own.
Fly then, ill-manner'd, to thy Native Land,
And there, thy Ant-born *Myrmidons* com-
   mand.   270
But mark this Menace ; since I must resign
My black-ey'd Maid, to please the Pow'rs
   divine :
(A well-rigg'd Vessel in the Port attends,
Mann'd at my Charge, commanded by my
   Friends)

The Ship shall waft her to her wish'd Abode,
Full fraught with holy Bribes to the far-
   shooting God.
This thus dispatch'd, I owe my self the Care,
My Fame and injur'd Honour to repair :
From thy own Tent, proud Man, in thy
   despight,   279
This Hand shall ravish thy pretended Right.
Briseis shall be mine, and thou shalt see, ⎫
What odds of awful Pow'r I have on thee : ⎬
That others at thy cost may learn the ⎭
   diff'rence of degree.
  At this th' Impatient Hero sowrly smil'd.
His Heart, impetuous in his Bosom boil'd,
And justled by two Tides of equal sway,
Stood, for a while, suspended in his way.
Betwixt his Reason and his Rage untam'd ;
One whisper'd soft, and one aloud reclaim'd :
That only counsell'd to the safer side ; 290
This to the Sword his ready Hand apply'd.
Unpunish'd to support th' Affront was hard :
Nor easy was th' Attempt to force the
   Guard.
But soon the Thirst of Vengeance fir'd his
   Blood :
Half shone his Faulchion, and half sheath'd
   it stood.
  In that nice Moment, *Pallas*, from above,
Commission'd by th' Imperial Wife of *Jove*,
Descended swift : (the white-arm'd Queen
   was loath
The Fight shou'd follow ; for she favour'd
   both :)   299
Just as in Act he stood, in Clouds inshrin'd,
Her Hand she fasten'd on his Hair behind ;
Then backward by his yellow Curls she
   drew ;
To him and him alone confess'd in view.
Tam'd by superiour Force, he turn'd his Eyes
Aghast at first, and stupid with Surprize :
But by her sparkling Eyes, and ardent Look,
The Virgin-Warrior known, he thus bespoke.
  Com'st thou, Celestial, to behold my
   Wrongs ?
Then view the Vengeance which to Crimes
   belongs.
  Thus He. The blue-ey'd Goddess thus
   rejoin'd :   310
I come to calm thy turbulence of Mind,
If Reason will resume her soveraign Sway,
And, sent by *Juno*, her Commands obey.

---

309 Then] *Edd. give* To

Equal she loves you both, and I protect :
Then give thy Guardian Gods their due
    respect ;
And cease Contention ; be thy Words severe,
Sharp as he merits : But the Sword forbear.
An Hour unhop'd already wings her way,
When he his dire Affront shall dearly pay :
When the proud King shall sue, with trebble
    Gain,   320
To quit thy Loss, and conquer thy Disdain.
But thou, secure of my unfailing Word,
Compose thy swelling Soul ; and sheath the
    Sword.
    The Youth thus answer'd mild ; Auspi-
    cious Maid,
Heaven's will be mine, and your Commands
    obey'd.
The Gods are just, and when subduing Sense,
We serve their Pow'rs, provide the Recom-
    pence.
He said ; with surly Faith believ'd her
    Word,
And, in the Sheath, reluctant, plung'd the
    Sword.
Her Message done, she mounts the bless'd
    Abodes,   330
And mix'd among the Senate of the Gods.
    At her Departure his Disdain return'd :
The Fire she fan'd, with greater Fury
    burn'd ;
Rumbling within till thus it found a Vent :
Dastard, and Drunkard, Mean and Insolent :
Tongue-valiant Hero, Vaunter of thy Might,
In Threats the foremost, but the lag in
    Fight ;
When did'st thou thrust amid the mingled
    Preace,
Content to bid the War aloof in Peace ?
Arms are the Trade of each *Plebeyan* soul ;
'Tis Death to fight ; but Kingly to con-
    troul.   341
Lord-like at ease, with arbitrary Pow'r,
To peel the Chiefs, the People to devour.
These, Traitor, are thy Tallents ; safer far
Than to contend in Fields, and Toils of War.
Nor coud'st thou thus have dar'd the com-
    mon Hate,
Were not their Souls as abject as their State.
But, by this Scepter, solemnly I swear,
(Which never more green Leaf or growing
    Branch shall bear :

Torn from the Tree, and giv'n by *Jove* to
    those   350
Who Laws dispence and mighty Wrongs
    oppose)
That when the *Grecians* want my wonted
    Aid,
No Gift shall bribe it, and no Pray'r per-
    suade.
When *Hector* comes, the Homicide, to wield
His conquering Arms, with Corps to strow
    the Field,
Then shalt thou mourn thy Pride ; and late
    confess
My Wrong repented, when 'tis past
    Redress.
He said : And with Disdain, in open view,
Against the Ground his golden Scepter
    threw ;
Then sate : with boiling Rage *Atrides*
    burn'd :   360
And Foam betwixt his gnashing Grinders
    churn'd.
    But from his Seat the *Pylian* Prince
    arose,
With Reas'ning mild, their Madness to com-
    pose :
Words, sweet as Hony, from his Mouth
    distill'd ;
Two Centuries already he fulfill'd ;
And now began the third ; unbroken yet :
Once fam'd for Courage ; still in Council
    great.
    What worse, he said, can *Argos* undergo,
What can more gratify the *Phrygian* Foe,
Than these distemper'd Heats ? If both the
    Lights   370
Of *Greece* their private Int'rest disunites !
Believè a Friend, with thrice your Years
    increas'd,
And let these youthful Passions be repress'd :
I flourish'd long before your Birth ; and
    then ⎫
Liv'd equal with a Race of braver Men, ⎬
Than these dim Eyes shall e'er behold agen. ⎭
Ceneus and *Dryas*, and, excelling them,
Great *Theseus*, and the Force of greater
    Polypheme.
With these I went, a Brother of the War,
Their Dangers to divide ; their Fame to
    share.   380
Nor idle stood with unassisting Hands,
When salvage Beasts, and Men's more sal-
    vage Bands,

339 bid] *Dryden's spelling* of bide

Their virtuous Toil subdued: yet those
I sway'd,
With pow'rful Speech: I spoke, and they
obey'd.
If such as those, my Councils cou'd reclaim,
Think not, young Warriors, your diminish'd
Name
Shall lose of Lustre, by subjecting Rage
To the cool Dictates of experienc'd Age.
Thou, King of Men, stretch not thy sove-
reign Sway
Beyond the Bounds free Subjects can obey:
But let *Pelides* in his Prize rejoice,   391
Atchiev'd in arms, allow'd by publick Voice.
Nor Thou, brave Champion, with his Pow'r
contend,
Before whose Throne ev'n Kings their
lower'd Scepters bend.
The Head of Action He, and Thou the Hand,
Matchless thy Force; but mightier his
Command:
Thou first, O king, release the rights of
Sway;
Pow'r, self-restrain'd, the People best obey.
Sanctions of Law from Thee derive their
Source;
Command thy Self, whom no Commands
can force.   400
The Son of *Thetis* Rampire of our Host,
Is worth our Care to keep; nor shall my
Pray'rs be lost.
    Thus *Nestor* said, and ceas'd: *Atrides*
broke
His Silence next; but ponder'd e'er he
spoke.
Wise are thy Words, and glad I would obey,
But this proud Man affects Imperial Sway.
Controlling Kings, and trampling on our
State
His Will is Law; and what he wills is Fate.
The Gods have giv'n him Strength: But
whence the Style,
Of lawless Pow'r assum'd, or Licence to
revile?   410
    Achilles cut him short; and thus reply'd:
My Worth allow'd in Words, is in effect
deny'd.
For who but a Poltron, possess'd with Fear,
Such haughty Insolence can tamely bear?
Command thy Slaves: My freeborn Soul
disdains
A Tyrant's Curb; and restiff breaks the
Reins.

Take this along; that no Dispute shall rise
(Though mine the Woman) for my ravish'd
Prize:
But, she excepted, as unworthy Strife,
Dare not, I charge thee dare not, on thy
Life,   420
Touch ought of mine beside, by Lot my due,
But stand aloof, and think profane to view:
This Fauchion, else, not hitherto withstood,
These hostile Fields shall fatten with thy
Blood.
    He said; and rose the first: the Council
broke;
And all their grave Consults dissolv'd in
Smoke.
The Royal Youth retir'd, on Vengeance
bent,
Patroclus follow'd silent to his Tent.
    Mean time, the King with Gifts a Vessel
stores;
Supplies the Banks with twenty chosen
Oars: 430
And next, to reconcile the shooter God,
Within her hollow Sides the Sacrifice he
stow'd:
Chryseis last was set on board; whose
Hand
Ulysses took, intrusted with Command;
They plow the liquid Seas; and leave the
less'ning Land.
Atrides then his outward Zeal to boast,
Bade purify the Sin-polluted Host.
With perfect Hecatombs the God they
grac'd;
Whose offer'd Entrails in the Main were cast.
Black Bulls, and bearded Goats on Altars
lie;   440
And clouds of sav'ry stench involve the
Sky.
These Pomps the Royal Hypocrite design'd
For Shew: But harbour'd Vengeance in his
Mind:
Till holy Malice, longing for a Vent,
At length, discover'd his conceal'd Intent.
Talthybius, and *Eurybates* the just,
Heralds of Arms, and Ministers of Trust,
He call'd; and thus bespoke: Haste hence
your way;
And from the Goddess-born demand his
Prey.
If yielded, bring the Captive: If deny'd,
The King (so tell him) shall chastise his
Pride: 451

And with arm'd Multitudes in Person come
To vindicate his Pow'r, and justify his
   Doom.
   This hard Command unwilling they
      obey,
And o'er the barren Shore pursue their way,
Where quarter'd in their Camp, the fierce
   Thessalians lay.
Their Sov'reign seated on his Chair, they
   find ;
His pensive Cheek upon his Hand reclin'd,
And anxious Thoughts revolving in his
   Mind.
With gloomy Looks he saw them entring in
Without Salute : Nor durst they first
   begin,   461
Fearful of rash Offence and Death foreseen.
He soon the Cause divining, clear'd his Brow ;
And thus did liberty of Speech allow.
   Interpreters of Gods and Men, be bold
Awful your Character, and uncontroll'd :
Howe'er unpleasing be the News you bring,
I blame not you, but your Imperious King.
You come, I know, my Captive to demand ;
Patroclus, give her to the Herald's Hand.
But you, authentick Witnesses I bring,   471
Before the Gods, and your ungrateful King,
Of this my Manifest : That never more
This Hand shall combate on the crooked
   Shore :
No, let the Grecian Pow'rs oppress'd in
   Fight,
Unpity'd perish in their Tyrants Sight.
Blind of the future, and by Rage misled,
He pulls his Crimes upon his People's Head.
Forc'd from the Field in Trenches to con-
   tend,
And his Insulted Camp from foes defend. 480
He said, and soon, obeying his Intent,
Patroclus brought Briseis from her Tent ;
Then to th' intrusted Messengers resign'd :
She wept, and often cast her Eyes behind ;
Forc'd from the Man she lov'd : They led
   her thence,
Along the Shore a Pris'ner to their Prince.
   Sole on the barren Sands the suff'ring
      Chief
Roar'd out for Anguish, and indulg'd his
   Grief ;
Cast on his Kindred Seas a stormy Look,
And his upbraided Mother thus bespoke. 490
   Unhappy Parent of a short-liv'd Son,
Since Jove in Pity by thy Pray'rs was won

To grace my small Remains of Breath with
   Fame,
Why loads he this imbitter'd Life with
   Shame ?
Suff'ring his King of Men to force my Slave,
Whom well deserv'd in War, the Grecians
   gave.
   Set by old Ocean's side the Goddess
      heard ;
Then from the sacred Deep her Head she
   rear'd :
Rose like a Morning-mist ; and thus begun
To soothe the Sorrows of her plaintive Son.
Why cry's my Care, and why conceals his
   Smart ?   501
Let thy afflicted Parent share her part.
   Then sighing from the bottom of his
      Breast,
To the Sea-Goddess thus the Goddess-born
   address'd.
Thou know'st my Pain, which telling but
   recals :
By Force of Arms we raz'd the Theban
   Walls ;
The ransack'd City, taken by our Toils,
We left, and hither brought the golden
   Spoils :
Equal we shar'd them ; but before the rest,
The proud Prerogative had seiz'd the best.
Chryseis was the greedy Tyrant's Prize, 511
Chryseis, rosy-cheek'd, with charming Eyes.
Her Syre, Apollo's Priest, arriv'd to buy
With proffer'd Gifts of Price, his Daughter's
   Liberty.
Suppliant before the Grecians Chiefs he stood,
Awful, and arm'd with Ensigns of his God :
Bare was his hoary Head, one holy Hand
Held forth his Lawrel-Crown, and one, his
   Scepter of Command.
His suit was common, but above the rest
To both the Brother-Princes was address'd.
With Shouts of loud Acclaim the Greeks
   agree   521
To take the Gifts, to set the Pris'ner free.
Not so the Tyrant, who with scorn the
   Priest
Receiv'd, and with opprobrious Words dis-
   miss'd.
The good old Man, forlorn of human Aid,
For Vengeance to his heav'nly Patron
   pray'd :
The Godhead gave a favourable Ear,
And granted all to him he held so dear ;

In an ill Hour his piercing Shafts he sped ;
And Heaps on Heaps of slaughter'd *Greeks*
lay dead,   530
While round the Camp he rang'd : At
length arose
A Seer who well divin'd ; and durst disclose
The Source of all our Ills : I took the Word ;
And urg'd the sacred Slave to be restor'd,
The God appeas'd : The swelling Monarch
storm'd :
And then the Vengeance vow'd, he since
perform'd :
The *Groohs* 'tis true, their Ruin to prevent,
Have to the Royal Priest his Daughter
sent ;
But from their haughty King his Heralds
came,
And seiz'd by his command, my Captive
Dame,   540
By common Suffrage given ; but, thou, be
won,
If in thy Pow'r, t' avenge thy injur'd Son :
Ascend the Skies ; and supplicating move
Thy just Complaint to Cloud-compelling
Jove.
If thou by either Word or Deed hast wrought
A kind remembrance in his grateful
Thought,
Urge him by that : For often hast thou said
Thy Pow'r was once not useless in his Aid,
When He who high above the Highest reigns,
Surpriz'd by Traytor-Gods, was bound in
Chains.   550
When *Juno*, *Pallas*, with Ambition fir'd,
And his blue Brother of the Seas conspir'd,
Thou freed'st the Soveraign from unworthy
Bands,
Thou brought'st *Briareus* with his hundred
Hands,
(So call'd in Heav'n, but mortal Men below
By his terrestrial Name, *Ægeon* know :
Twice stronger than his Syre, who sate above
Assessor to the Throne of thundring *Jove*.)
The Gods, dismay'd at his approach, with-
drew,
Nor durst their unaccomplish'd Crime pur-
sue.   560
That Action to his grateful Mind recal :
Embrace his Knees, and at his Footstool
fall :
That now if ever, he will aid our Foes ;
Let *Troy's* triumphant Troops the Camp in-
close :

Ours beaten to the Shore, the Siege forsake ;
And what their King deserves with him par-
take ;
That the proud Tyrant at his proper Cost,
May learn the Value of the Man he lost.
To whom the Mother-Goddess thus
reply'd,
Sigh'd ere she spoke, and while she spoke
she cry'd,   570
Ah wretched me ! by Fates averse decreed
To bring thee forth with Pain, with care to
breed !
Did envious Heav'n not otherwise ordain, ⎫
Safe in thy hollow Ships thou shou'd'st   ⎬
remain ;   ⎭
Nor ever tempt the fatal Field again.
But now thy Planet sheds his pois'nous
Rays :
And short, and full of Sorrow are thy Days.
For what remains, to Heav'n I will ascend,
And at the Thund'rer's Throne thy Suit com-
mend.
Till then, secure in Ships, abstain from
Fight ;   580
Indulge thy Grief in Tears, and vent thy
Spight.
For yesterday the Court of Heav'n with
Jove
Remov'd : 'Tis dead Vacation now above.
Twelve Days the Gods their solemn Revels
keep,
And quaff with blameless *Ethiops* in the
Deep.
Return'd from thence, to Heav'n my Flight
I take,
Knock at the brazen Gates, and Providence
awake,
Embrace his Knees, and suppliant to the
Sire,
Doubt not I will obtain the grant of thy
desire.
She said : And parting left him on the
place,   590
Swoln with Disdain, resenting his Disgrace :
Revengeful Thoughts revolving in his Mind,
He wept for Anger and for Love he pin'd.
Mean time with prosperous Gales, *Ulysses*
brought
The Slave, and Ship with Sacrifices fraught,
To *Chrysa's* Port : Where entring with the
Tide,
He drop'd his Anchors, and his Oars he
ply'd.

Furl'd every Sail, and drawing down the
   Mast,
His Vessel moor'd ; and made with Haulsers
   fast.   599
Descending on the Plain, ashore they bring
The Hecatomb to please the shooter King.
The Dame before an Altars holy Fire
Ulysses led ; and thus bespoke her Sire.
  Reverenc'd be thou, and be thy God
   ador'd :
The King of Men thy Daughter has restor'd ;
And sent by me with Presents and with
   Pray'r ;
He recommends him to thy pious Care ;
That *Phœbus* at thy Sute his Wrath may
   cease,
And give the penitent Offenders Peace.
  He said, and gave her to her Father's
   Hands,   610
Who glad receiv'd her, free from servile
   Bands.
This done, in Order they with sober
   Grace,
Their gifts around the well-built Altar
   place.
Then wash'd, and took the Cakes ; while
   Chryses stood
With Hands upheld, and thus invok'd his
   God.
  God of the Silver Bow, whose Eyes⎫
   survey   ⎪
The sacred *Cilla*, thou whose awful Sway, ⎬
Chrysa the bless'd, and *Tenedos* obey : ⎭
Now hear, as thou before my Pray'r hast
   heard,
Against the *Grecians*, and their Prince, pre-
   ferr'd :   620
Once thou hast honour'd, honour once again
Thy Priest ; nor let his second Vows be
   vain ;
But from th' afflicted Host and humbled
   Prince
Avert thy Wrath, and cease thy Pestilence.
Apollo heard, and, conquering his Disdain,
Unbent his Bow and *Greece* respir'd again.
  Now when the solemn Rites of Pray'r were
   past,
Their salted Cakes on crackling Flames they
   cast.
Then, turning back, the Sacrifice they sped :
The fatted Oxen slew, and flea'd the Dead,

Chopp'd off their nervous Thighs, and next
   prepar'd   631
T' involve the lean in Cauls, and mend with
   Lard.
Sweet-breads and Collops were with Skewers
   prick'd
About the Sides ; inbibing what they deck'd.
The Priest with holy Hands was seen to tine
The cloven Wood, and pour the ruddy Wine,
The Youth approach'd the Fire, and as it
   burn'd
On five sharp Broachers rank'd, the Roast
   they turn'd ;
These Morsels stay'd their stomachs ; then
   the rest
They cut in Legs and Fillets for the Feast ;
Which drawn and serv'd, their Hunger they
   appease   641
With sav'ry Meat, and set their Minds at ease.
  Now when the rage of Eating was repell'd,
The Boys with generous Wine the Goblets
   fill'd.
The first Libations to the Gods they pour :
And then with Songs indulge the Genial
   Hour,
Holy Debauch ! till Day to Night they bring,
With Hymns and Pæans to the Bowyer
   King.
At Sun-set to their Ship they make return,
And snore secure on Decks, till rosy Morn.
  The Skies with dawning Day were purpled
   o'er ;   651
Awak'd, with lab'ring Oars they leave the
   Shore :
The Pow'r appeas'd, with Winds suffic'd the
   Sail,
The bellying Canvass strutted with the
   Gale ;
The Waves indignant roar with surly Pride,
And press against the Sides, and beaten off
   divide.
They cut the foamy way, with Force impell'd
Superiour, till the *Trojan* Port they held :
Then hauling on the Strand, their Gally
   moor,
And pitch their Tents along the crooked
   Shore.   660
  Mean time the Goddess-born in secret
   pin'd ;
Nor visited the Camp, nor in the Council
   join'd,

---

530 flea'd] i. e. flay'd *as edd. print.*
              659 moor] Moor *1700.*

But, keeping close, his gnawing Heart he fed
With Hopes of Vengeance on the Tyrant's
Head :
And wish'd for bloody Wars and mortal
Wounds,
And of the *Greeks* oppress'd in Fight, to hear
the dying Sounds.
  Now, when twelve Days compleat had
  run their Race,
The Gods bethought them of the Cares
belonging to their place.
Jove at their Head ascending from the Sea,
A shoal of puny Pow'rs attend his way. 670
Then *Thetis* not unmindful of her Son
Emerging from the Deep, to beg her Boon,
Pursu'd their Track ; and waken'd from
his Rest,
Before the Soveraign stood a Morning
Guest.
Him in the Circle but apart, she found :
The rest at awful Distance stood around.
She bow'd, and e'er she durst her Sute
begin,
One Hand embrac'd his Knees, one prop'd
his Chin.
Then thus. If I, Celestial Sire, in aught
Have serv'd thy Will, or gratify'd thy
Thought,   680
One glimpse of Glory to my Issue give ;
Grac'd for the little time he has to live.
Dishonour'd by the King of Men he stands :
His rightful Prize is ravish'd from his Hands.
But thou, O Father, in my Son's Defence,
Assume thy Pow'r, assert thy Providence.
Let *Troy* prevail, till *Greece* th' Affront has
paid
With doubled Honours ; and redeem'd his
Aid.
  She ceas'd, but the consid'ring God was
  mute :   689
Till she, resolv'd to win, renew'd her Sute :
Nor loos'd her Hold, but forc'd him to
reply,
Or grant me my Petition, or deny :
Jove cannot fear : then tell me to my Face
That I, of all the Gods am least in Grace.
This I can bear : The Cloud-compeller
mourn'd,
And sighing first, this Answer he return'd :
  Know'st thou what Clamors will disturb
  my Reign,
What my stun'd Ears from *Juno* must sus-
tain ?

In Council she gives Licence to her Tongue,
Loquacious, Brawling, ever in the wrong.
And now she will my partial Pow'r up-
braid,   701
If alienate from *Greece*, I give the *Trojans* Aid.
But thou depart, and shun her jealous
Sight,
The Care be mine, to do *Pelides* right.
Go then, and on the Faith of *Jove* rely,
When nodding to thy Sute, he bows the Sky.
This ratifies th' irrevocable Doom :
The Sign ordain'd, that what I will shall
come :
The Stamp of Heav'n, and Seal of Fate : He
said,
And shook the sacred Honours of his Head.
With Terror trembled Heav'ns subsiding
Hill :   711
And from his shaken Curls Ambrosial Dews
distil.
The Goddess goes exulting from his Sight,
And seeks the Seas profound ; and leaves
the Realms of Light.
  He moves into his Hall : The Pow'rs
  resort,
Each from his House to fill the Sovraign's
Court.
Nor waiting Summons, nor expecting stood ;
But met with Reverence, and receiv'd the
God.
He mounts the Throne ; and *Juno* took her
place :
But sullen Discontent sate lowring on her
Face.   720
With jealous Eyes, at distance she had
seen,
Whisp'ring with *Jove* the Silver-footed
Queen ;
Then, impotent of Tongue (her Silence
broke)
Thus turbulent in rattling Tone she spoke :
  Author of Ills, and close Contriver *Jove*,
Which of thy Dames, what Prostitute of
Love,
Has held thy Ear so long, and begg'd so hard
For some old Service done, some new Re-
ward ?
Apart you talk'd, for that's your special
Care,   729
The Consort never must the Council share.
One gracious Word is for a Wife too much :
Such is a Marriage-Vow, and *Jove's* own
Faith is such.

DR.   P

Then thus the Sire of Gods, and Men
  below :
What I have hidden, hope not thou to
  know.
Ev'n Goddesses are Women : And no Wife
Has Pow'r to regulate her Husband's Life :
Counsel she may ; and I will give thy Ear
The Knowledge first, of what is fit to hear.
What I transact with others, or alone,
Beware to learn ; nor press too near the
  Throne.   740
  To whom the Goddess with the charming
    Eyes :
What hast thou said, O Tyrant of the Skies !
When did I search the Secrets of thy
  Reign,
Though priviledg'd to know, but priviledg'd
  in vain ?
But well thou dost, to hide from common
  Sight
Thy close Intrigues, too bad to bear the
  Light.
Nor doubt I, but the Silver-footed Dame,
Tripping from Sea, on such an Errand came
To grace her Issue, at the *Grecians* Cost,
And for one peevish Man destroy an Host.
  To whom the Thund'rer made this stern
    Reply ;   751
My Household Curse, my lawful Plague,
  the Spy
Of *Jove's* Designs, his other squinting Eye ;
Why this vain prying, and for what avail ?
Jove will be Master still, and *Juno* fail.
Shou'd thy suspicious Thoughts divine
  aright,
Thou but becom'st more odious to my
  Sight,
For this Attempt : uneasy Life to me
Still watch'd, and importun'd, but worse for
  thee.
Curb that impetuous Tongue, before too
  late   760
The Gods behold, and tremble at thy
  Fate ;
Pitying, but daring not, in thy Defence,
To lift a Hand against Omnipotence.
  This heard, the Imperious Queen sate
    mute with Fear :
Nor further durst incense the gloomy
  Thunderer.
Silence was in the Court at this Rebuke :
Nor cou'd the Gods abash'd, sustain their
  Sov'reigns Look.

The Limping Smith observ'd the sadden'd
  Feast,
And hopping here and there (himself a Jest)
Put in his Word, that neither might
  offend ;   770
To *Jove* obsequious, yet his Mother's Friend.
What End in Heav'n will be of civil War,
If Gods of Pleasure will for Mortals jar ?
Such Discord but disturbs our Jovial Feast ;
One Grain of Bad embitters all the best.
Mother, tho' wise your self, my Counsel
  weigh ;
'Tis much unsafe my Sire to disobey
Not only you provoke him to your Cost,
But Mirth is marr'd, and the good Chear is
  lost.
Tempt not his heavy Hand ; for he has
  Pow'r   780
To throw you Headlong, from his Heav'nly
  Tow'r.
But one submissive Word, which you let fall,
Will make him in good Humour with us All.
  He said no more but crown'd a Bowl,
    unbid :
The laughing Nectar overlook'd the Lid :
Then put it to her Hand ; and thus pursued :
This cursed Quarrel be no more renew'd.
Be, as becomes a Wife, obedient still ;
Though griev'd, yet subject to her Hus-
  band's Will.
I would not see you beaten ; yet affraid   790
Of *Jove's* superiour Force, I dare not aid.
Too well I know him, since that hapless
  Hour
When I, and all the Gods employ'd our
  Pow'r
To break your Bonds : Me by the Heel he
  drew ;
And o'er Heav'n's Battlements with Fury
  threw.
All Day I fell ; My flight at Morn begun,
And ended not but with the setting Sun.
Pitch'd on my Head, at length the *Lemnian*-
  Ground
Receiv'd my batter'd Skull, the *Sinthians*
  heal'd my Wound.
  At *Vulcan's* homely Mirth his Mother
    smil'd,   800
And smiling took the Cup the Clown had
  filled.
The Reconciler Bowl went round the Board,
Which empty'd, the rude Skinker still
  restor'd.

Louds Fits of Laughter seiz'd the Guests, to see
The limping God so deft at his new Ministry.
The Feast continued till declining Light :
They drank, they laugh'd, they lov'd, and then 'twas Night.
Nor wanted tuneful Harp, nor vocal Quire ;
The Muses sung ; *Apollo* touch'd the Lyre.

Drunken at last, and drowsy they depart,
Each to his House ; Adorn'd with labour'd Art 811
Of the lame Architect : The thund'ring God
Ev'n he withdrew to rest, and had his Load.
His swimming Head to needful Sleep apply'd ;
And *Juno* lay unheeded by his Side.

THE | LAST PARTING | OF | HECTOR | AND ANDROMACHE.

FROM | THE SIXTH BOOK | OF *Homer's* ILIADS.

THE ARGUMENT.

Hector, *returning from the Field of Battel, to visit* Helen *his Sister-in-Law, and his Brother* Paris, *who had fought unsuccessfully hand to hand with* Menelaus, *from thence goes to his own Palace to see his wife* Andromache, *and his Infant Son* Astyanax. *The description of that Interview is the subject of this translation.*

THus having said, brave *Hector* went to see
His Virtuous Wife, the fair Andromache.
He found her not at home ; for she was gone
(Attended by her Maid and Infant Son,)
To climb the steepy Tow'r of *Ilion* :
From whence with heavy Heart she might survey
The bloody business of the Dreadful day.
Her mournful Eyes she cast around the Plain,
And sought the Lord of her Desires in vain.
But he, who thought his peopled Palace bare, 10
When she, his only Comfort, was not there,
Stood in the Gate, and ask'd of ev'ry one,
Which way she took, and whither she was gone :
If to the Court, or, with his Mother's Train,
In long Procession to *Minerva's* Fane ?
The Servants answer'd, neither to the Court
Where *Priam's* Sons and Daughters did resort,

Nor to the Temple was she gone, to move ;
With Prayers the blew-ey'd Progeny of *Jove*
But, more solicitous for him alone, 20
Than all their safety, to the Tow'r was gone,
There to survey the Labours of the Field,
Where the *Greeks* conquer, and the *Trojans* yield.
Swiftly she pass'd, with Fear and Fury wild ;
The Nurse went lagging after with the Child.
This heard, the Noble *Hector* made no stay ;
Th' admiring Throng divide, to give him way :
He pass'd through every Street, by which he came,
And at the Gate he met the mournful Dame.
His Wife beheld him, and with eager pace, 30
Flew to his *Arms*, to meet a dear Embrace :
His Wife, who brought in Dow'r *Cilicia's* Crown,
And in her self a greater Dow'r alone :
Aëtion's Heyr, who on the Woody Plain
Of *Hippoplacus* did in *Thebe* reign.
Breathless she flew, with Joy and Passion wild ;
The Nurse came lagging after with her Child.
The *Royal Babe* upon her *Breast* was laid ;
Who, like the Morning Star, his beams display'd.
Scamandrius was his Name which *Hector* gave, 40
From that fair Flood which *Ilion's* Wall did lave :
But him *Astyanax* the *Trojans* call,
From his great Father who defends the Wall.

HECTOR AND ANDROMACHE. Text from the original of 1603.
I do not follow the use of italics in this piece, but, as it seems to be Dryden's, it is here retained.

34 *Aëtion*] Saintsbury *prints* Ætion *and by mistake attributes the error to Dryden.*

35 *Hippoplacus*] *The form is bad, but even that which is given by the editors,* Hypoplacus, *is not correct in this place.*

37 her] *Some editors wrongly give the*

Hector beheld him with a silent Smile :
His tender Wife stood weeping by, the while :
Prest in her own, his Warlike hand she took,
Then sigh'd, and thus Prophetically spoke.
Thy dauntless Heart (which I foresee too late,)
Too daring Man, will urge thee to thy Fate :
Nor dost thou pity, with a Parent's mind,
This helpless Orphan whom thou leav'st behind ;   51
Nor me, th' unhappy Partner of thy *Bed* ;
Who must in Triumph by the *Greeks* be led :
They seek thy Life ; and, in unequal Fight,
With many will oppress thy single Might :
Better it were for miserable me
To die, before the Fate which I foresee.
For ah what comfort can the World bequeath
To *Hector's* Widow, after *Hector's* death ?
Eternal Sorrow and perpetual Tears 60
Began my Youth, and will conclude my Years :
I have no Parents, Friends, nor Brothers left ;
By stern *Achilles* all of Life bereft.
Then when the Walls of *Thebes* he o'rethrew,
His fatal Hand my Royal Father slew ;
He slew *Aëtion,* but despoil'd him not ;
Nor in his hate the Funeral Rites forgot ;
Arm'd as he was he sent him whole below,
And reverenc'd thus the Manes of his Foe :
A Tomb he rais'd ; the Mountain Nymphs around   70
Enclos'd with planted Elms the Holy Ground.
My sev'n brave *Brothers* in one fatal Day
To Death's dark Mansions took the mournful way ;
Slain by the same *Achilles,* while they keep
The bellowing Oxen and the bleating Sheep.
My Mother, who the Royal Scepter sway'd,
Was Captive to the cruel Victor made,
And hither led ; but hence redeem'd with Gold,
Her Native Country did again behold,
And but beheld : for soon *Diana's* Dart 80
In an unhappy Chace transfix'd her Heart.

But thou, my *Hector,* art thy self alone
My Parents, Brothers, and my Lord in one
O kill not all my Kindred o're again,
Nor tempt the Dangers of the dusty Plain ;
But in this Tow'r, for our Defence, remain.
Thy Wife and Son are in thy Ruin lost :
This is a Husband's and a Father's Post.
The *Scæan* Gate commands the Plains below ;   89
Here marshal all thy Souldiers as they go ;
And hence, with other Hands, repel the Foe.
By yon wild Fig-tree lies their chief ascent,
And thither all their Pow'rs are daily bent ;
The two *Ajaces* have I often seen,
And the wrong'd Husband of the *Spartan* Queen :
With him his greater *Brother* ; and with these
Fierce *Diomede* and bold *Meriones* :
Uncertain if by *Augury,* or chance,
But by this easie rise they all advance ;
Guard well that Pass, secure of all beside.
To whom the Noble *Hector* thus reply'd. 101
That and the rest are in my daily care ;
But, shou'd I shun the Dangers of the War,
With scorn the *Trojans* wou'd reward my Pains,
And their proud Ladies with their sweeping Trains.
The *Grecian* Swords and Lances I can bear
But loss of Honour is my only Fear.
Shall *Hector,* born to War, his *Birth-right* yield,
Belie his Courage, and forsake the Field ?
Early in rugged *Arms* I took delight ; 110
And still have been the foremost in the Fight :
With dangers dearly have I bought Renown,
And am the Champion of my Father's Crown.
And yet my mind forebodes, with sure presage,
That *Troy* shall perish by the *Grecian* Rage.
The fatal Day draws on, when I must fall ;
And Universal Ruine cover all.
Not *Troy* it self, tho' built by Hands Divine,
Nor *Priam,* nor his People, nor his Line,
My Mother, nor my *Brothers* of Renown, 120
Whose Valour yet defends th' unhappy Town,
Not these, nor all their Fates which I foresee,
Are half of that concern I have for thee.

---

64 o'rethrew] *The editors, not noticing that* Thebes *is here made disyllabic to distinguish it from the Bæotian town, wrongly give* overthrew

I see, I see thee, in that fatal Hour,
Subjected to the Victor's cruel Pow'r;
Led hence a Slave to some insulting Sword,
Forlorn and trembling at a Foreign Lord;
A spectacle in *Argos*, at the Loom,
Gracing with *Trojan* Fights a *Grecian* Room;
Or from deep Wells, the living Stream to
take,   130
And on thy weary Shoulders bring it back.
While, groaning under this laborious Life,
They insolently call thee *Hector's* Wife;
Upbraid thy *Bondage* with thy Husband's
name;
And from my Glory propagate thy Shame.
This when they say, thy Sorrows will en-
crease
With anxious thoughts of former Happi-
ness;
That he is dead who cou'd thy wrongs
redress.
But I, opprest with Iron Sleep before,
Shall hear thy unavailing Cries no more. 140
He said,
Then, holding forth his *Arms*, he took his
Boy,
(The Pledge of Love, and other hope of
Troy;
The fearful Infant turn'd his Head away,
And on his Nurse's Neck reclining lay,
His unknown Father shunning with affright,
And looking back on so uncouth a sight;
Daunted to see a Face with Steel o're-spread,
And his high Plume, that nodded o're his
Head.
His Sire and Mother smil'd with silent
Joy;   150
And *Hector* hasten'd to relieve his *Boy*;
Dismiss'd his burnish'd Helm, that shone
afar,
(The Pride of Warriours, and the Pomp of
War:)
Th' *Illustrious Babe*, thus reconcil'd, he
took:
Hugg'd in his *Arms*, and kiss'd, and thus he
spoke.
    Parent of Gods and Men, propitious *Jove*,
And you bright Synod of the Pow'rs above;
On this my Son your Gracious Gifts bestow;
Grant him to live, and great in *Arms* to
grow,   159

To reign in *Troy*, to Govern with Renown,
To shield the People, and assert the Crown:
That, when hereafter he from War shall come,
And bring his *Trojans* Peace and Triumph
home,
Some aged Man, who lives this act to see,
And who in former times remember'd me,
May say the Son in Fortitude and Fame
Out-goes the Mark; and drowns his Father's
Name:
That at these words his Mother may rejoyce,
And add her Suffrage to the publick Voice.
    Thus having said,   170
He first with suppliant Hands the Gods
ador'd:
Then to the Mother's *Arms* the Child
restor'd:
With Tears and Smiles she took her Son
and press'd
Th' Illustrious Infant to her fragrant *Breast*.
He, wiping her fair Eyes, indulg'd her Grief,
And eas'd her Sorrows with this last Relief.
    My Wife and Mistress, drive thy fears
away,
Nor give so bad an Omen to the Day:
Think not it lies in any *Grecian's* Pow'r,
To take my Life before the fatal Hour. 180
When that arrives, nor good nor bad can fly
Th' irrevocable Doom of Destiny.
Return, and, to divert thy thoughts at
home,
There task thy Maids, and exercise the
Loom,
Employ'd in Works that Womankind
become.
The Toils of War, and Fears of Chivalry
Belong to Men, and most of all to me.
At this, for new Replies he did not stay,
But lac'd his Crested Helm, and strode
away.   189
    His lovely Consort to her House return'd,
And looking often back in silence mourn'd:
Home when she came, her secret Woe she
vents,
And fills the Palace with her loud Laments;
These loud Laments her ecchoing Maids
restore,
And *Hector*, yet alive, as dead deplore.

---

162 War] *Some editors wrongly give* Wars

[THE DEDICATION TO EXAMEN POETICUM, 1693.]

TO THE

RIGHT HONOURABLE

MY

LORD RADCLIFFE.

My Lord,

THese Miscellany Poems, are by many Titles yours. The first they claim from your acceptance of my Promise to present them to you; before some of them were yet in being. The rest are deriv'd from your own Merit, the exactness of your Judgment in Poetry, and the candour of your Nature; easie to forgive some trivial faults, when they come accompanied with countervailing Beauties. But after all, though these are your equitable claims to a Dedication from other Poets, yet I must acknowledge a Bribe in the case, which is your particular liking of my Verses. 'Tis a vanity common to all Writers, to over-value their own Productions; and 'tis better for me to own this failing in my self, than the World to do it for me. For what other Reason have I spent my Life in so unprofitable a Study? Why am I grown Old, in seeking so barren a Reward as Fame! The same Parts and Application, which have made me a Poet, might rais'd me to any Honours of the Gown, which are often given to Men of as little Learning and less Honesty than my self. No Government has ever been, or ever can be, wherein Time-servers and Blockheads will not be uppermost. The Persons are only chang'd, but the same juglings in State, the same Hypocrisie in Religion, the same Self-Interest, and Mis-mannagement, will remain for ever. Blood and Mony will be lavish'd in all Ages, only for the Preferment of new Faces, with old Consciences. There is too often a Jaundise in the Eyes of Great Men; they see not those whom they raise in the same Colours with other Men. All whom they affect, look Golden to them; when the Gilding is only in their own distemper'd Sight. These Considerations have given me a kind of Contempt for those who have risen by unworthy ways. I am not asham'd to be Little, when I see them so Infamously Great. Neither, do I know, why the Name of Poet should be Dis-honourable to me, if I am truly one, as I hope I am; for I will never do any thing, that shall dishonour it. The Noticns of Morality are known to all Men; None can pretend Ignorance of those Idea's which are In-born in Mankind: and if I see one thing, and practise the contrary, I must be Disingenuous, not to acknowledge a clear Truth, and Base, to Act against the light of my own Conscience. For the Reputation of my Honesty, no Man can question it, who has any of his own: For that of my Poetry, it shall either stand by its own Merit; or fall for want of it. Ill Writers are usually the sharpest Censors; For they (as the best Poet, and the best Patron said), When in the full perfection of decay, turn Vinegar, and come again in Play. Thus the corruption of a Poet is the Generation of a Critick: I mean of a Critick in the general acceptation of this Age; for formerly they were quite another Species of Men. They were Defenders of Poets, and Com-mentators on their Works: to Illustrate obscure Beauties; to place some passages in a better light; to redeem others from malicious Interpretations: to help out an Author's Modesty, who is not ostentatious of his Wit; and, in short, to shield him from the Ill-

---

DEDICATION TO EXAMEN POETICUM, 1693.   11 accompanied with] accompanied, with *1693.*
26 Considerations have] Considerations, have *1693.*   37 Poet is] Poet, is *1693.*

Nature of those Fellows, who were then call'd *Zoili* and *Momi*, and now take upon themselves the Venerable Name of Censors. But neither *Zoilus*, nor he who endeavour'd to defame *Virgil*, were ever Adopted into the Name of Criticks by the *Ancients*: what their Reputation was then, we know; and their Successours in this Age deserve no better. Are our Auxiliary Forces turn'd our Enemies? Are they, who, at best, are but Wits of the Second Order, and whose only Credit amongst Readers is what they obtain'd by being subservient to the Fame of Writers; are these become Rebels of Slaves, and Usurpers of Subjects; or to speak in the most Honourable Terms of them, are they from our Seconds, become Principals against us? Does the Ivy undermine the Oke, which supports its weakness? What labour wou'd it cost them to put in a better Line, than the worst of those which they expunge in a True Poet? *Petronius*, the greatest Wit perhaps of all the *Romans*, yet when his Envy prevail'd upon his Judgment, to fall on *Lucan*, he fell himself in his attempt: He perform'd worse in his Essay of the Civil War, than the Authour of the *Pharsalia*; and avoiding his Errours, has made greater of his own. *Julius Scaliger* wou'd needs turn down *Homer*, and Abdicate him after the possession of Three Thousand Years: Has he succeeded in his Attempt? He has indeed shown us some of those Imperfections in him, which are incident to Humane Kind; But who had not rather be that *Homer* than this *Scaliger*? You see the same Hypercritick, when he endeavours to mend the beginning of *Claudian* (a faulty Poet, and Living in a Barbarous Age), yet how short he comes of him, and substitutes such Verses of his own as deserve the *Ferula*. What a Censure has he made of *Lucan*, that he rather seems to Bark than Sing! Wou'd any but a Dog, have made so snarling a Comparison? One wou'd have thought he had Learn'd Latin, as late as they tell us he did Greek. Yet he came off with a *pace tuâ*, by your good leave, *Lucan*; he call'd him not by those outrageous Names, of Fool, Booby, and Blockhead: He had somewhat more of good Manners, than his Successours, as he had much more Knowledge. We have two sorts of those Gentlemen in our Nation: Some of them proceeding with a seeming moderation and pretence of Respect, to the Dramatick Writers of the last Age, only scorn and vilifie the present Poets, to set up their Predecessours. But this is only in appearance; for their real design is nothing less, than to do Honour to any Man, besides themselves. *Horace* took notice of such men in his age: —— *Non Ingeniis favet ille Sepultis; Nostra sed impugnat; nos nostraque lividus odit.* 'Tis not with an ultimate intention to pay Reverence to the Manes of *Shakespear*, *Fletcher*, and *Ben Johnson*, that they commend their Writings, but to throw Dirt on the Writers of this Age: Their *Declaration* is one thing, and their Practice is another. By a seeming veneration to our Fathers, they wou'd thrust out us their Lawful Issue, and Govern us themselves, under a specious pretence of Reformation. If they could compass their intent, what wou'd Wit and Learning get by such a change? If we are bad Poets, they are worse; and when any of their woful pieces come abroad, the difference is so great betwixt them and good Writers, that there need no Criticisms on our part to decide it. When they describe the Writers of this Age, they draw such monstrous figures of them, as resemble none of us: Our pretended Pictures are so unlike, that it is evident we never sate to them: they are all Grotesque; the products of their wild Imaginations, things out of Nature, so far from being Copy'd from us, that they resemble nothing that ever was, or ever can be. But there is another sort of Insects, more venomous than the former. Those who manifestly aim at the destruction of our Poetical Church and State. Who allow nothing to their Country-Men, either of this or of the former Age. These attack the Living by raking up the Ashes of the Dead; well knowing that if they can subvert their Original Title to the Stage, we who claim under them, must fall of course. Peace be to the Venerable Shades of *Shakespear* and *Ben Johnson*: None of the Living will presume to have any competition with them: as they were our Predecessours, so they were our

Masters. We Trayl our Plays under them, but, (as at the Funerals of a *Turkish* Emperour) our Ensigns are furl'd or dragg'd upon the ground, in Honour to the Dead ; so we may lawfully advance our own, afterwards, to show that we succeed : If less in Dignity, yet on the same Foot and Title, which we think too we can maintain against the Insolence of our own Janizaries. If I am the Man, as I have Reason to believe, who am seemingly Courted, and secretly Undermined : I think I shall be able to defend my self, when I am openly Attacqu'd. And to shew besides, that the *Greek* Writers only gave us the Rudiments of a Stage which they never finish'd : that many of the Tragedies in the former Age amongst us, were without Comparison beyond those of *Sophocles*
10 and *Euripides*. But at present, I have neither the leisure nor the means for such an Undertaking. 'Tis ill going to Law for an Estate, with him who is in possession of it, and enjoys the present Profits, to feed his Cause. But the *quantum mutatus* may be remembered in due time. In the mean while, I leave the World to judge, who gave the Provocation.

This, my Lord, is, I confess, a long digression, from *Miscellany Poems* to *Modern Tragedies* : But I have the ordinary excuse of an Injur'd Man, who will be telling his Tale unseasonably to his Betters. Though at the same time, I am certain you are so good a Friend, as to take a Concern in all things which belong to one who so truly Honours you. And besides, being yourself a Critick of the Genuine sort, who have Read the best Authours in their
20 own Languages, who perfectly distinguish of their several Merits, and in general prefer them to the Moderns, yet, I know, you judge for the *English* Tragedies, against the *Greek* and *Latin*, as well as against the *French, Italian* and *Spanish,* of these latter Ages. Indeed there is a vast difference betwixt arguing like *Perault*, in behalf of the *French* Poets, against *Homer* and *Virgil*, and betwixt giving the *English* Poets their undoubted due of excelling *Æschylus, Euripides,* and *Sophocles.* For if we, or our greater Fathers, have not yet brought the *Drama* to an absolute Perfection, yet at least we have carried it much farther than those Ancient *Greeks* ; who, beginning from a *Chorus,* cou'd never totally exclude it, as we have done ; who find it an unprofitable incumbrance, without any necessity of Entertaining it amongst us ; and without the possibility of establishing it here, unless
30 it were supported by a Publick Charge. Neither can we accept of those Lay Bishops, as some call them, who, under pretence of reforming the Stage, wou'd intrude themselves upon us, as our Superiours, being indeed incompetent Judges of what is Manners, what Religion, and least of all, what is Poetry and Good Sense. I can tell them in behalf of all my Fellows, that when they come to Exercise a Jurisdiction over us, they shall have the Stage to themselves, as they have the Lawrel. As little can I grant, that the *French* Dramatick Writers excel the *English* : Our authours as far surpass them in Genius, as our Souldiers Excel theirs in Courage : 'tis true, in Conduct they surpass us either way : Yet that proceeds not so much from their greater Knowledge, as from the difference of Tasts in the two Nations. They content themselves with a thin Design, without Episodes, and
40 manag'd by few Persons. Our Audience will not be pleas'd, but with variety of Accidents, an Underplot, and many Actours. They follow the Ancients too servilely, in the Mechanick Rules, and we assume too much License to our selves, in keeping them only in view, at too great a distance. But if our Audience had their Tasts, our Poets could more easily comply with them, than the *French* Writers cou'd come up to the Sublimity of our Thoughts, or to the difficult variety of our Designs. However it be, I dare establish it for a Rule of Practice on the Stage, that we are bound to please those whom we pretend to Entertain ; and that at any price, Religion and Good Manners only excepted. And I care not much, if I give this handle to our bad Illiterate Poetasters, for the defence of their SCRIPTIONS, as they call them. There is a sort of Merit in delighting the Spectatours ; which is a

---

8 finish'd : that] finish'd. That *1693*.   23 difference betwixt] difference, betwixt *1693*.
38 Tasts in the two Nations] *Some editors wrongly give* Taste   48 handle to] handle, to
1693.

Name more proper for them, than that of Auditours. Or else *Horace* is in the wrong. when he commends *Lucilius* for it. But these common places I mean to treat at greater leisure. In the mean time, submitting that little I have said, to your Lordship's Approbation, or your Censure, and chusing rather to Entertain you this way, as you are a judge of writing, than to oppress your Modesty with other Commendations ; which, though they are your due, yet wou'd not be equally receiv'd, in this Satirical, and Censorious Age. That which cannot without Injury be deny'd to you, is the easiness of your Conversation, far from Affectation or Pride : not denying even to Enemies their just Praises. And this, if I wou'd dwell on any Theme of this Nature, is no vulgar Commendation to your Lordship. Without Flattery, my Lord, you have 10 it in your Nature, to be a Patron and Encourager of Good Poets, but your Fortune has not yet put into your hands the opportunity of expressing it. What you will be hereafter, may be more than guessed, by what you are at present. You maintain the Character of a Nobleman, without that Haughtiness which generally attends too many of the Nobility, and when you converse with Gentlemen, you forget not that you have been of their Order. You are Marryed to the Daughter of a King, who, amongst her other high Perfections, has deriv'd from him a Charming Behaviour, a winning Goodness, and a Majestick Person. The Muses and the Graces are the Ornaments of your Family. While the Muse sings, the Grace accompanies her Voice : even the Servants of the Muses have sometimes had the Happiness to hear her ; and to receive their Inspirations 20 from her.

    I will not give my self the liberty of going farther ; for 'tis so sweet to wander in a pleasing way, that I shou'd never arrive at my Journeys end. To keep my self from being belated in my Letter, and tiring your Attention, I must return to the place where I was setting out. I humbly Dedicate to your Lordship, my own Labours in this Miscellany : At the same time, not arrogating to myself the Priviledge of Inscribing to you the Works of others who are join'd with me in this undertaking, over which I can pretend no right. Your lady and You have done me the favour to hear me Read my Translations of *Ovid* : And you both seem'd not to be displeas'd with them. Whether it be the partiality of an Old Man to his Youngest Child, I know not : But they appear to me the best of all my 30 Endeavours in this kind. Perhaps this Poet is more easie to be Translated than some others, whom I have lately attempted : Perhaps too, he was more according to my Genius. He is certainly more palatable to the Reader, than any of the *Roman* Wits, though some of them are more lofty, some more Instructive, and others more Correct. He had Learning enough to make him equal in the best. But as his Verse came easily, he wanted the toyl of Application to amend it. He is often luxuriant both in his Fancy and Expressions, and as it has lately been observ'd, not always Natural. If Wit be pleasantry, he has it to excess ; but if it be propriety, *Lucretius*, *Horace*, and, above all, *Virgil* are his Superiours. I have said so much of him already, in my Preface to his Heroical Epistles, that there remains little to be added in this place : for my own part, I have endeavoured to Copy his Character 40 what I cou'd in this Translation, even, perhaps, farther than I shou'd have done ; to his very faults. Mr. *Chapman*, in his Translation of *Homer*, professes to have done it somewhat paraphrastically, and that on set purpose ; his Opinion being, that a good Poet is to be Translated in that manner. I remember not the Reason which he gives for it : But I suppose it is, for fear of omitting any of his Excellencies : sure I am, that if it be a Fault, 'tis much more pardonable than that of those, who run into the other extream of a litteral and close Translation, where the Poet is confin'd so streightly to his Author's Words, that he wants elbow-room to express his Elegancies. He leaves him obscure ; he leaves him Prose, where he found him Verse. And no better than thus has *Ovid* been served by the so much admir'd *Sandys*. This is at least the Idea which I have remaining 50 of his Translation ; for I never Read him since I was a Boy. They who take him upon

----

Content, from the Praises which their Fathers gave him, may inform their Judgment by Reading him again, and see (if they understand the Original) what is become of *Ovid's* Poetry, in his Version ; whether it be not all, or the greatest part of it, evaporated : but this proceeded from the wrong Judgment of the Age in which he Liv'd. They neither knew good Verse nor lov'd it ! they were Scholars, 'tis true, but they were Pedants. And for a just Reward of their Pedantick pains, all their Translations want to be Translated, into *English*.

If I flatter not my self, or if my Friends have not Flatter'd me, I have given my Author's Sense, for the most part truly : for to mistake sometimes is incident to all Men : And not
10 to follow the *Dutch* Commentatours always, may be forgiven to a Man who thinks them in the general, heavy gross-witted Fellows, fit only to gloss on their own dull Poets. But I leave a farther Satire on their Wit, till I have a better opportunity to shew how much I Love and Honour them. I have likewise attempted to restore *Ovid* to his Native sweetness, easiness, and smoothness ; and to give my Poetry a kind of Cadence, and, as we call it, a run of Verse, as like the Original, as the *English* can come up to the *Latin*. As he seldom uses any *Synalephas*, so I have endeavour'd to avoid them, as often as I cou'd : I have likewise given him his own turns, both on the Words and on the Thought ; which I cannot say are inimitable, because I have Copyed them ; and so may others, if they use the same diligence : But certainly they are wonderfully Graceful in this Poet. Since
20 I have Nam'd the *Synalepha*, which is the cutting off one Vowel, immediately before another, I will give an Example of it from *Chapman's Homer*, which lies before me ; for the benefit of those who understand not the *Latine Prosodia*. 'Tis in the first Line of the Argument to the First *Iliad*.

Apollo's *Priest to th'* Argive *Fleet doth bring*, &c.

There we see he makes it not the *Argive*, but th' *Argive*, to shun the shock of the two Vowels, immediately following each other ; but in his Second Argument, in the same Page, he gives a bad example of the quite contrary kind :

Alpha *the Pray'r of* Chryses *sings* :
The Army's Plague, the Strife of Kings.

30 In these words *the Armies, the* ending with a Vowel, and *Armies* beginning with another Vowel, without cutting off the first, which by it had been th' Armies, there remains a most horrible ill-sounding gap betwixt those Words. I cannot say that I have every where observ'd the Rule of the *Synalepha* in my Translation ; but wheresoever I have not, 'tis a fault in sound : The *French* and *Italians* have made it an inviolable Precept in their versification ; therein following the severe example of the *Latin* Poets. Our Countrymen have not yet Reform'd their Poetry so far ; but content themselves with following the Licentious practice of the *Greeks* ; who, though they sometimes use *Synalepha's*, yet make no difficulty very often, to sound one Vowel upon another ; as *Homer* does in the very first line of *Alpha*. Μῆνιν ἄειδε Θεὰ, Πηληιάδεω Ἀχιλῆ῀. 'Tis true, indeed, that in
40 the second line in these words μυρὶ' Ἀχαιοῖς, and ἄλγε ἔθηκε, the *Synalepha* in revenge is twice observed. But it becomes us, for the sake of *Euphony*, rather *Musas colere severiores*, with the *Romans*, than to give into the looseness of the *Grecians*.

I have tir'd my self, and have been summon'd by the Press to send away this Dedication, otherwise I had expos'd some other faults, which are daily committed by our *English* Poets ; which, with care and observation, might be amended. For, after all, our Language is both Copious, Significant, and Majestical, and might be reduc'd into a more harmonious sound. But, for want of Publick Encouragement, in this *Iron Age*, we are so far from

---

39 Μῆνιν] Μήνιν 1693. *This error has been carefully preserved by the editors.*

making any progress in the improvement of our Tongue, that in few years, we shall Speak and Write as Barbarously as our Neighbours.

Notwithstanding my haste, I cannot forbear to tell your Lordship, that there are two fragments of *Homer* Translated in this *Miscellany* ; one by Mr. *Congreve* (whom I cannot mention without the Honour which is due to his Excellent Parts, and that entire Affection which I bear him ;) and the other by my self. Both the Subjects are pathetical, and I am sure my Friend has added to the Tenderness which he found in the Original, and, without Flattery, surpass'd his Author. Yet I must needs say this in reference to *Homer*, that he is much more capable of exciting the Manly Passions than those of Grief and Pity. To cause Admiration, is indeed the proper and adequate design of an Epick Poem : and 10 in that he has excell'd even *Virgil*. Yet, without presuming to Arraign our Master, I may venture to affirm, that he is somewhat too Talkative, and more than somewhat too digressive. This is so manifest, that it cannot be deny'd, in that little parcel which I have Translated, perhaps too literally : There *Andromache* in the midst of her Concernment, and Fright for *Hector*, runs off her Biass, to tell him a Story of her Pedigree, and of the lamentable Death of her Father, her Mother, and her seven Brothers. The Devil was in *Hector* if he knew not all this matter, as well as she who told it him ; for she had been his Bed-fellow for many Years together : and if he knew it, then it must be confess'd, that *Homer* in this long digression, has rather given us his own Character, than that of the Fair Lady whom he Paints. His Dear Friends the Com- 20 mentators, who never fail him at a pinch, will needs excuse him, by making the present Sorrow of *Andromache*, to occasion the remembrance of all the past : But others think that she had enough to do with that Grief which now oppress'd her, without running for assistance to her Family. *Virgil*, I am confident, wou'd have omitted such a work of supererrogation. But *Virgil* had the Gift of expressing much in little, and sometimes in silence : For though he yielded much to *Homer* in Invention, he more Excell'd him in his Admirable Judgment. He drew the Passion of *Dido* for *Eneas*, in the most lively and most natural Colours imaginable. *Homer* was ambitious enough of moving pity ; for he has attempted twice on the same subject of *Hector's* death : first, when *Priam* and *Hecuba* beheld his Corps, which was drag'd after the chariot of *Achilles* ; and then in the 30 Lamentation which was made over him, when his Body was redeem d by *Priam* ; and the same Persons again bewail his death, with a Chorus of others to help the cry. But if this last excite Compassion in you, as I doubt not but it will, you are more oblig'd to the Translator than the Poet. For *Homer*, as I observ'd before, can move rage better than he can pity : He stirs up the irascible appetite, as our Philosophers call it ; he provokes to Murther, and the destruction of God's Images ; he forms and equips those ungodly Man-killers, whom we Poets, when we flatter them, call Heroes ; a race of Men who can never enjoy quiet in themselves, 'till they have taken it from all the World. This is *Homer's* Commendation, and such as it is, the Lovers of Peace, or at least of more moderate Heroism, will never Envy him. But let *Homer* and *Virgil* contend for the Prize of Honour, betwixt 40 themselves, I am satisfied they will never have a third Concurrent. I wish Mr. *Congreve* had the leisure to Translate him, and the World the good Nature and Justice to Encourage him in that Noble Design, of which he is more capable than any Man I know. The Earl of *Mulgrave* and Mr. *Waller*, two the best Judges of our Age, have assured me, that they cou'd never read over the Translation of *Chapman*, without incredible Pleasure and extreme Transport. This Admiration of theirs must needs proceed from the Author himself : For the Translator has thrown him down as low, as harsh Numbers, improper *English*, and a monstrous length of Verse cou'd carry him. What then wou'd he appear in the Harmonious Version of one of the best Writers, Living in a much better Age than was the last ? I mean for versification, and the Art of Numbers : for in the *Drama* we 50 have not arriv'd to the pitch of *Shakespear* and *Ben Johnson*. But here, my Lord, I am

36 Man-killers] Man killers *1693*.   42 Justice to] Justice, to *1693*.

forc'd to break off abruptly, without endeavouring at a Compliment in the close. This *Miscellany* is, without dispute, one of the best of the kind, which has hitherto been extant in our Tongue. At least, as Sir *Samuel Tuke* has said before me, a Modest Man may praise what is not his own. My Fellows have no need of any Protection, but I humbly recommend my part of it, as much as it deserves, to your Patronage and Acceptance, and all the rest of your Forgiveness.

> I am,
>
> *My Lord,*
>
> *Your Lordship's most*
>
> *Obedient Servant,*
>
> JOHN DRYDEN.

THE FIRST BOOK

OF

Ovid's Metamorphoses.

Of Bodies chang'd to various Forms I sing;
Ye Gods, from whom these Miracles did
spring,
Inspire my Numbers with Cœlestial heat;
Till I my long laborious Work compleat;
And add perpetual Tenour to my Rhimes,
Deduc'd from Nature's Birth, to *Cæsar's*
Times.
Before the Seas, and this Terrestrial Ball,
And Heav'ns high Canopy, that covers all,
One was the Face of Nature, if a Face;
Rather a rude and indigested Mass: 10
A lifeless Lump, unfashion'd, and unfram'd;
Of jarring Seeds; and justly Chaos nam'd.
No Sun was lighted up the World to view;
No Moon did yet her blunted Horns renew:
Nor yet was Earth suspended in the Skye;
Nor, pois'd, did on her own Foundations lye:
Nor Seas about the Shoars their Arms had
thrown;
But Earth and Air and Water were in one.
Thus Air was void of Light, and Earth
unstable,
And Waters dark Abyss unnavigable.   20
No certain Form on any was imprest;
All were confus'd, and each disturb'd the
rest.
For hot and cold were in one Body fixt,
And soft with hard, and light with heavy
mixt.

But God, or Nature, while they thus con-
tend,
To these intestine Discords put an end.
Then Earth from Air, and Seas from Earth
were driv'n,
And grosser Air sunk from Æthereal
Heav'n.
Thus disembroil'd, they take their proper
place;
The next of Kin contiguously embrace;   30
And Foes are sunder'd by a larger space.
The force of Fire ascended first on high,
And took its dwelling in the vaulted Skie:
Then Air succeeds, in lightness next to
Fire:
Whose Atoms from unactive Earth retire.
Earth sinks beneath, and draws a numerous
throng
Of pondrous, thick, unweildy Seeds along.
About her Coasts, unruly Waters roar,
And, rising on a Ridge, insult the Shoar.
Thus when the God, what ever God was he,
Had form'd the whole, and made the parts
agree,   41
That no unequal portions might be found,
He moulded Earth into a spacious round:
Then with a Breath, he gave the Winds to
blow;
And bad the congregated Waters flow.
He adds the running Springs, and standing
Lakes;
And bounding Banks for winding Rivers
makes.

Ovid's Metamorphoses, I. Text from the original of 1693.

Some part, in Earth are swallow'd up, the most
In ample Oceans, disimbogu'd, are lost.
He shades the Woods, the Vallies he re-
strains   50
With Rocky Mountains, and extends the
Plains.
  And as five Zones th' Æthereal Regions
  bind,
Five Correspondent, are to Earth assign'd :
The Sun, with Rays directly darting down,
Fires all beneath, and fries the middle Zone :
The two beneath the distant Poles complain
Of endless Winter, and perpetual Rain.
Betwixt th' extreams, two happier Climates
hold
The Temper that partakes of Hot and Cold.
The Feilds of liquid Air, inclosing all,   60
Surround the Compass of this Earthly Ball :
The lighter parts lie next the Fires above ;
The grosser near the watry Surface move :
Thick Clouds are spread, and Storms
engender there,
And Thunders Voice, which wretched
Mortals fear,
And Winds that on their Wings cold Winter
bear.
Nor were those blustring Brethren left at
large,
On Seas and Shoars their fury to dis-
charge :
Bound as they are, and circumscrib'd in
place,
They rend the World, resistless, where they
pass ;   70
And mighty Marks of Mischief leave behind ;
Such is the Rage of their tempestuous kind.
First *Eurus* to the rising Morn is sent,
(The Regions of the balmy Continent ;)
And *Eastern* Realms, where early *Persians*
run,
To greet the blest appearance of the Sun.
Westward, the wanton *Zephyr* wings his
Flight ;
Pleas'd with the Remnants of departing
light :
Fierce *Boreas* with his Off-spring issues
forth,
T' invade the frozen Waggon of the North.
While frowning *Auster* seeks the Southern
Sphere,   81
And rots with endless Rain, th' unwholesom
year.

High o're the Clouds, and empty Realms
of wind,
The God a clearer space for Heav'n design'd;
Where Fields of Light, and Liquid Æther
flow,
Purg'd from the pondrous dregs of Earth
below.
  Scarce had the Pow'r distinguish'd these,
  when streight
The Stars, no longer overlaid with weight,
Exert their Heads from underneath the
Mass,
And upward shoot, and kindle as they pass
And with diffusive Light, adorn their
Heav'nly place.   91
Then, every void of Nature to supply,
With Forms of Gods he fills the vacant Skie :
New Herds of Beasts he sends the Plains to
share ;
New Colonies of Birds, to people Air ;
And to their Oozy Beds the finny Fish repair.
A Creature of a more Exalted Kind
Was wanting yet, and then was Man
design'd :
Conscious of Thought, of more capacious
Breast,
For Empire form'd, and fit to rule the rest :
Whether with particles of Heav'nly Fire 101
The God of Nature did his Soul Inspire ;
Or Earth, but new divided from the Skie,
And, pliant, still, retain'd th' Æthereal
Energy :
Which Wise *Prometheus* temper'd into paste,
And mixt with living Streams, the Godlike
Image cast.
Thus, while the mute Creation downward
bend
Their Sight, and to their Earthy Mother tend,
Man looks aloft ; and with erected Eyes
Beholds his own Hereditary Skies.   110
From such rude Principles our Form began,
And Earth was Metamorphos'd into Man.

The Golden Age.

The Golden Age was first ; when Man
yet New,
No Rule but uncorrupted Reason knew ;
And, with a Native bent, did Good pursue.
Un-forc'd by Punishment, un-aw'd by fear,
His words were simple, and his Soul sincere :

---

108 Earthy] *Most editors wrongly give* Earthly

Needless was written Law, where none
  opprest ;
The Law of Man was written in his Breast :
No suppliant Crowds before the Judge
  appear'd :   120
No Court Erected yet, nor Cause was hear'd;
But all was safe, for Conscience was their
  Guard.
The Mountain Trees in distant prospect
  please,
E're yet the Pine descended to the Seas ;
E're Sails were spread, new Oceans to
  explore ;
And happy Mortals, unconcern'd for more,
Confin'd their Wishes to their Native
  Shoar.
No Walls were yet ; nor Fence, nor Moat
  nor Mownd ;
Nor Drum was heard, nor Trumpets angry
  Sound :
Nor Swords were forg'd ; but, void of Care
  and Crime,   130
The soft Creation slept away their time.
The teeming Earth, yet guiltless of the
  Plough,
And unprovok'd, did fruitful Stores allow :
Content with Food, which Nature freely bred,
On Wildings, and on Strawberries they fed ;
Cornels and Bramble-berries gave the rest,
And falling Acorns furnisht out a Feast.
The Flow'rs un-sown, in Fields and Meadows
  reign'd,
And *Western* Winds immortal Spring main-
  tain'd.
In following Years, the bearded Corn ensu'd
From Earth unask'd, nor was that Earth
  renew'd.   141
From Veins of Vallies, Milk and Nectar broke;
And Honey sweating through the pores of
  Oak.

The Silver Age.

But when Good *Saturne*, banish'd from
  above,
Was driv'n to Hell, the World was under
  Jove.
Succeeding times a Silver Age behold,
Excelling Brass, but more excell'd by Gold.
Then Summer, Autumn, Winter did appear ;
And Spring was but a Season of the Year.

The Sun his Annual course obliquely
  made,   150
Good days contracted, and enlarg'd the bad.
Then Air with sultry Heats began to glow,
The Wings of Winds were clogg'd with Ice
  and Snow ;
And shivering Mortals, into Houses driven,
Sought shelter from th' inclemency of Heav'n.
Those Houses, then, were Caves, or homely
  Sheds,
With twining Oziers fenc'd ; and Moss their
  Beds.
Then Ploughs, for Seed, the fruitful Furrows
  broke,
And Oxen labour'd first beneath the Yoke.

The Brazen Age.

To this next came in course the Brazen
  Age :   160
A Warlike Offspring prompt to Bloody Rage,
Not Impious yet ———

The Iron Age.

——— Hard Steel succeeded then ;
And stubborn as the Mettal, were the Men.
Truth, Modesty, and Shame, the World
  forsook :
Fraud, Avarice, and Force, their places took.
Then Sails were spread, to every Wind that
  blew ;
Raw were the Sailors, and the Depths were
  new :
Trees rudely hollow'd, did the Waves sus-
  tain ;
E're Ships in Triumph plough'd the watry
  Plain.   170
Then Land-marks limited to each his right:
For all before was common, as the light.
Nor was the Ground alone requir'd to bear
Her annual Income to the crooked share ;
But greedy Mortals, rummaging her Store,
Digg'd from her Entrails first the precious
  Oar ;
Which next to Hell the prudent Gods had
  laid ;
And that alluring ill to sight displaid.
Thus cursed Steel, and more accursed Gold,
Gave Mischief Birth, and made that Mis-
  chief bold :   180

And double death did wretched Man invade,
By Steel assaulted, and by Gold betray'd.
Now, (brandish'd Weapons glitt'ring in their
    Hands)
Mankind is broken loose from moral Bands ;
No Rights of Hospitality remain :
The Guest by him who harbour'd him, is
    slain :
The Son in Law pursues the Father's life ;
The Wife her Husband murders, he the
    Wife.
The Step-dame Poyson for the Son prepares ;
The Son inquires into his Father's years. 190
Faith flies, and Piety in Exile mourns ;
And Justice, here opprest, to Heav'n
    returns.

The Gyants War.

Nor were the Gods themselves more safe
    above ;
Against beleagur'd Heav'n, the Gyants
    move.
Hills piled on Hills, on Mountains, Moun-
    tains lie,
To make their mad approaches to the Skie.
Till *Jove*, no longer patient, took his time
T'' avenge with Thunder their audacious
    Crime :
Red Light'ning play'd along the Firmament,
And their demolish't Works to pieces rent.
Sing'd with the Flames, and with the Bolts
    transfixt, 201
With Native Earth their Blood the Monsters
    mixt ;
The Blood, indu'd with animating Heat,
Did in th' impregnant Earth, new Sons
    beget :
They, like the Seed from which they sprung,
    accurst,
Against the Gods Immortal Hatred nurst :
An Impious, Arrogant, and Cruel Brood ;
Expressing their Original from Blood.
Which when the King of Gods beheld from
    high
(Withal revolving in his Memory, 210
What he himself had found on Earth of late,
Lycaon's Guilt, and his Inhuman Treate)
He sigh'd ; nor longer with his Pity strove ;
But kindled to a Wrath becoming *Jove* ;

204 impregnant] *The editors wrongly give*
impregnate

Then, call'd a General Council of the Gods ;
Who Summon'd, Issue from their Blest
    Abodes,
And fill th' Assembly, with a shining Train.
A way there is, in Heavens expanded Plain,
Which when the Skies are clear, is seen
    below,
And Mortals, by the Name of Milky, know.
The Ground-work is of Stars ; through
    which the Road 221
Lyes open to the Thunderer's Abode.
The Gods of greater Nations dwell around,
And on the Right and Left the Palace
    bound ;
The Commons where they can, the Nobler
    sort,
With Winding-doors wide open, front the
    Court.
This Place, as far as Earth with Heav'n may
    vie,
I dare to call the *Loovre* of the Skie.
When all were plac'd, in Seats distinctly
    known,
And he, their Father, had assum'd the
    Throne, 230
Upon his Iv'ry Sceptre first he leant,
Then shook his Head, that shook the
    Firmament :
Air, Earth, and Seas, obey'd th' Almighty
    nod ;
And with a gen'ral fear, confess'd the God.
At length, with Indignation, thus he broke
His awful Silence, and the Pow'rs bespoke.
I was not more concern'd in that Debate
Of Empire, when our Universal State
Was put to hazard, and the Giant Race 239
Our Captive Skies were ready to imbrace :
For tho' the Foe was fierce, the Seeds of all
Rebellion, sprung from one Original ;
Now wheresoever ambient waters glide,
All are corrupt, and all must be destroy'd.
Let me this Holy Protestation make,
By Hell, and Hell's inviolable Lake,
I try'd whatever in the God-Head lay ; ⎫
But gangreen'd Members must be lopt ⎬
    away,   ⎭
Before the Nobler Parts are tainted to
    decay.
There dwells below, a race of Demi-Gods,
Of Nymphs in Waters, and of Fawns in
    Woods ; 251
Who, tho not worthy yet, in Heav'n to live,
Let 'em, at least, enjoy that Earth we give.

Can these be thought securely lodg'd below,
When I my self, who no Superior know,
I, who have Heav'n and Earth at my com-
    mand,
Have been attempted by *Lycaon's* Hand ?
  At this a Murmur thro' the Synod went,
And with one Voice they vote his Punish-
    ment.
Thus, when Conspiring Traytors dar'd to
    doom   260
The fall of *Cæsar*, and in him of *Rome*,
The Nations trembled, with a pious Fear ;
All anxious for their Earthly Thunderer :
Nor was their care, O *Cæsar* ! less esteem'd
By thee, than that of Heav'n for *Jove* was
    deem'd ;
Who with his Hand and Voice, did first
    restrain
Their Murmurs, then resum'd his Speech
    again.
The Gods to Silence were compos'd, and sate
With Reverence, due to his Superior State.
  Cancel your pious Cares ; already he 270
Has paid his Debt to Justice, and to me.
Yet what his Crimes, and what my Judg-
    ments were,
Remains for me thus briefly to declare.
The Clamours of this vile degenerate Age,
The Cries of Orphans, and th' Oppressor's
    Rage,
Had reach'd the Stars ; I will descend, said I,
In hope to prove this loud Complaint a Lye.
Disguis'd in Humane Shape, I Travell'd
    round
The World, and more than what I hear'd
    I found.
O're *Mænalus* I took my steepy way, 280
By Caverns infamous for Beasts of Prey.
Then cross'd *Cyllenè*, and the piny shade,
More infamous by Curst *Lycaon* made :
Dark Night had cover'd Heaven and Earth,
    before
I enter'd his Unhospitable Door.
Just at my entrance, I display'd the Sign
That somewhat was approaching of Divine.
The prostrate People pray : the Tyrant grins,
And, adding Prophanation to his Sins,
I'll try, said he, and if a God appear, 290
To prove his Deity, shall cost him dear.
'Twas late ; the Graceless Wretch my Death
    prepares,
When I shou'd soundly Sleep, opprest with
    Cares :

This dire Experiment he chose, to prove
If I were Mortal, or undoubted *Jove* ;
But first he had resolv'd to taste my Pow'r :
Not long before, but in a luckless hour
Some Legates sent from the *Molossian*
    State,
Were on a peaceful Errant come to Treat :
Of these he Murders one, he boils the Flesh,
And lays the mangl'd Morsels in a Dish : 301
Some part he Roasts ; then serves it up, so
    drest,
And bids me welcome to this Humane
    Feast.
Mov'd with Disdain, the Table I o're-turn'd ;
And with avenging Flames, the Palace
    burn'd.
The Tyrant in a fright, for shelter, gains
The Neighb'ring Fields, and scours along the
    Plains.
Howling he fled, and fain he would have
    spoke,
But Humane Voice his Brutal Tongue for-
    sook.
About his lips, the gather'd Foam he ⎫
    churns,   310
And breathing slaughters, still with Rage ⎬
    he burns,
But on the bleating Flock his fury turns. ⎭
His Mantle, now his Hide, with rugged hairs
Cleaves to his back ; a famish'd face he
    bears ;
His arms descend, his shoulders sink away,
To multiply his legs for chace of Prey.
He grows a Wolf, his hoariness remains,
And the same rage in other Members reigns.
His eyes still sparkle in a narr'wer space,
His jaws retain the grin, and violence of his
    face.   320
  This was a single ruine, but not one
Deserves so just a punishment alone.
Mankind's a Monster, and th' Ungodly
    times,
Confed'rate into guilt, are sworn to Crimes.
All are alike involv'd in ill, and all
Must by the same relentless Fury fall.
  Thus ended he ; the greater Gods assent, ⎫
By Clamours urging his severe intent ;   ⎬
The less fill up the cry for punishment.   ⎭
Yet still with pity they remember Man ; 330
And mourn as much as Heav'nly Spirits can.

---

299 Errant] *The editors print* Errand
311 slaughters] slaughter *edd.*

They ask, when those were lost of humane
  Birth,
What he wou'd do with all this waste of
  Earth :
If his dispeopl'd World he would resign
To Beasts, a mute, and more ignoble Line ;
Neglected Altars must no longer smoke,
If none were left to worship and invoke.
To whom the Father of the Gods reply'd :⎫
Lay that unnecessary fear aside :   ⎬
Mine be the care, new People to provide. ⎭
I will from wondrous Principles ordain 341
A Race unlike the first, and try my skill
  again.

  Already had he toss'd the flaming Brand,⎫
And roll'd the Thunder in his spatious ⎬
  hand ;   ⎭
Preparing to discharge on Seas and Land :⎭
But stopp'd, for fear thus violently driv'n,
The Sparks should catch his Axle-tree of
  Heav'n.
Remembring, in the Fates, a time when
  Fire
Shou'd to the Battlements of Heav'n aspire,
And all his blazing Worlds above shou'd
  burn,   350
And all th' inferiour Globe to Cinders turn.
His dire Artill'ry thus dismist, he bent
His thoughts to some securer Punishment :
Concludes to pour a Watry Deluge down ;
And what he durst not burn, resolves to
  drown.
  The Northern breath, that freezes Floods,
  he binds ;
With all the race of Cloud-dispelling Winds
The South he loos'd, who Night and Horror
  brings ;
And Foggs are shaken from his flaggy Wings.
From his divided Beard, two Streams he
  pours ;   360
His head and rhumy eyes distil in showers.
With Rain his Robe and heavy Mantle
  flow :
And lazy mists are lowring on his brow.
Still as he swept along, with his clench't fist,
He squeez'd the Clouds ; th' imprison'd
  Clouds resist :
The Skies, from Pole to Pole, with peals
  resound :
And show'rs inlarg'd come pouring on the
  ground.
Then, clad in Colours of a various dye,
Junonian Iris breeds a new supply

To feed the Clouds : Impetuous Rain de-
  scends ;   370
The bearded Corn beneath the Burden bends :
Defrauded Clowns deplore their perish'd
  grain ;
And the long labours of the Year are vain.
  Nor from his Patrimonial Heav'n alone
Is *Jove* content to pour his Vengeance down :
Aid from his Brother of the Seas he craves,
To help him with Auxiliary Waves.
The watry Tyrant calls his Brooks and
  Floods,
Who rowl from mossie Caves (their moist
  abodes ;)
And with perpetual Urns his Palace fill : 380
To whom in breif, he thus imparts his Will.
  Small exhortation needs ; your Pow'rs
  employ :
And this bad World, so *Jove* requires,
  destroy.
Let loose the Reins to all your watry Store :
Bear down the Damms, and open every door.
  The Floods, by Nature Enemies to Land,
And proudly swelling with their new Com-
  mand,
Remove the living Stones, that stopt their
  way,
And gushing from their Source, augment
  the Sea.
Then, with his Mace, their Monarch struck⎫
  the Ground :   390⎪
With inward trembling, Earth receiv'd the ⎬
  Wound ;   ⎪
And rising streams a ready passage found. ⎭
Th' expanded Waters gather on the Plain,
They flote the Fields, and over-top the Grain ;
Then rushing onwards, with a sweepy sway,
Bear Flocks, and Folds, and lab'ring Hinds
  away.
Nor safe their Dwellings were ; for, sap'd
  by Floods,
Their Houses fell upon their Household Gods.
The solid Piles, too strongly built to fall,
High o're their Heads, behold a watry
  Wall :   400
Now Seas and Earth were in confusion lost ;
A World of Waters, and without a Coast.
  One climbs a Cliff ; one in his Boat is
  born,
And Ploughs above, where late he sow'd his
  Corn.
Others o're Chimney tops and Turrets row,
And drop their Anchors on the Meads below :

Or downward driv'n, they bruise the tender
    Vine,
Or tost aloft, are knock't against a Pine.
And where of late the Kids had cropt the
    Grass,
The Monsters of the deep now take their
    place   410
Insulting Nereids on the Cities ride,
And wondring Dolphins o're the Palace
    glide.
On leaves and masts of mighty Oaks they
    brouze.
And their broad Finns entangle in the
    Boughs.
The frighted Wolf now swims amongst the
    Sheep ;
The yellow Lyon wanders in the deep :
His rapid force no longer helps the
    Boar :
The Stag swims faster, than he ran before.
The Fowls, long beating on their Wings in
    vain,
Despair of Land, and drop into the Main.
Now Hills and Vales no more distinction
    know,   421
And levell'd Nature lies oppress'd below.
The most of Mortals perish in the Flood :
The small remainder dies for want of
    Food.
A Mountain of stupendous height there
    stands
Betwixt th' *Athenian* and *Bœotian* Lands,
The bound of fruitful Fields, while Fields
    they were,
But then a Field of Waters did appear :
Parnassus is its name ; whose forky rise
Mounts through the Clouds, and mates the
    lofty Skies.   430
High on the Summet of this dubious Cliff,
Deucalion wafting, moor'd his little Skiff.
He with his Wife were only left behind
Of perish'd Man ; they two were Humane
    Kind.
The Mountain Nymphs and *Themis* they
    adore,
And from her Oracles relief implore.
The most upright of Mortal Men was he ;
The most sincere and holy Woman, she.
    When *Jupiter*, surveying Earth from
    high,
Beheld it in a Lake of Water lie,   440
That, where so many Millions lately liv'd,
But two. the best of either Sex, surviv'd,

He loos'd the Northern Wind ; fierce *Boreas*
    flies
To puff away the Clouds, and purge the
    Skies :
Serenely, while he blows, the Vapours, driven,
Discover Heav'n to Earth, and Earth to
    Heaven.
The Billows fall, while *Neptune* lays his Mace
On the rough Sea, and smooths its furrow'd
    face,
Already *Triton*, at his call appears   ⎫
Above the Waves ; a *Tyrian* Robe he   ⎪
    wears ;   450 ⎬
And in his Hand a crooked Trumpet bears.   ⎭
The Soveraign bids him peaceful Sounds
    inspire,
And give the Waves the signal to retire.
His writhen Shell he takes ; whose narrow
    vent
Grows by degrees into a large extent ;
Then gives it breath ; the blast, with
    doubling sound,
Runs the wide Circuit of the World around.
The Sun first heard it, in his early East,
And met the rattling Eccho's in the West.
The Waters, listning to the Trumpets
    roar,   460
Obey the Summons, and forsake the Shoar.
    A thin Circumference of Land appears ;
And Earth, but not at once, her visage rears,
And peeps upon the Seas from upper
    Grounds :
The Streams, but just contain'd within their
    bounds.
By slow degrees into their Channels crawl
And Earth increases as the Waters fall.
In longer time the tops of Trees appear,
Which Mud on their dishonour'd Branches
    bear.
    At length the World was all restor'd to
    view,   470
But desolate, and of a sickly hue :
Nature beheld her self, and stood aghast,
A dismal Desart, and a silent Waste.
    Which when *Deucalion*, with a piteous
    Look,
Beheld, he wept, and thus to *Pyrrha* spoke :
Oh Wife, oh Sister, oh oh all thy kind   ⎫
The best and only Creature left behind,   ⎪
By Kindred, Love, and now by Dangers   ⎬
    joyn'd ;   ⎭

448 Sea] Seas *1693*.

Of Multitudes, who breath'd the common
   Air,
We two remain ; a Species in a pair ; 480
The rest the Seas have swallow'd ; nor have
   we
Ev'n of this wretched life a certainty.
The Clouds are still above ; and, while
   I speak,
A second Deluge o're our Heads may break.
Shou'd I be snatch'd from hence, and thou
   remain,
Without relief, or Partner of thy pain,
How cou'd'st thou such a wretched Life
   sustain ?
Shou'd I be left, and thou be lost, the Sea,
That bury'd her I lov'd, shou'd bury me.
Oh cou'd our Father his old Arts inspire, 490
And make me Heir of his informing Fire,
That so I might abolisht Man retrieve,
And perisht People in new Souls might live.
But Heav'n is pleas'd, nor ought we to com-
   plain,
That we, th' Examples of Mankind remain.
He said : the careful couple joyn their
   Tears,
And then invoke the Gods, with pious
   Prayers.
Thus, in Devotion having eas'd their grief,
From Sacred Oracles they seek relief :
And to *Cephysus* Brook their way pursue :
The Stream was troubl'd, but the Foord
   they knew. 501
With living Waters in the Fountain bred,
They sprinkle first, their Garments, and
   their Head,
Then took the way which to the Temple
   led.
The Roofs were all defil'd with Moss and
   Mire,
The Desart Altars void of Solemn Fire.
Before the Gradual, prostrate they ador'd,
The Pavement kiss'd, and thus the Saint
   implor'd.
  O Righteous *Themis*, if the Pow'rs above
By Pray'rs are bent to pity, and to love ; 510
If humane Miseries can move their mind ;
If yet they can forgive, and yet be kind ;
Tell how we may restore, by second birth,
Mankind, and People desolated Earth.
Then thus the gracious Goddess, nodding,
   said ;
Depart, and with your Vestments veil your
   head :

And stooping lowly down, with loosn'd
   Zones,
Throw each behind your backs, your mighty
   Mother's bones.
Amaz'd the pair ; and mute with wonder,
   stand,
Till *Pyrrha* first refus'd the dire command.
Forbid it Heav'n, said she, that I shou'd
   tear 521
Those Holy Reliques from the Sepulchre :
They ponder'd the mysterious Words again,
For some new sence ; and long they sought
   in vain.
At length *Deucalion* clear'd his cloudy
   brow,
And said ; The dark *Ænigma* will allow
A meaning, which, if well I understand,
From Sacriledge will free the Gods Com-
   mand :
This Earth our mighty Mother is, the Stones
In her capacious Body, are her Bones. 530
These we must cast behind : with hope
   and fear,
The Woman did the new solution hear :
The Man diffides in his own Augury,
And doubts the Gods ; yet both resolve to
   try.
Descending from the Mount, they first
   unbind
Their Vests, and veil'd, they cast the Stones
   behind :
The Stones (a Miracle to Mortal View,
But long Tradition makes it pass for true)
Did first the Rigour of their Kind expell,
And suppl'd into softness as they fell ; 540
Then swell'd, and swelling, by degrees grew
   warm ;
And took the Rudiments of Humane Form ;
Imperfect shapes : in Marble such are seen,
When the rude Chizzel does the Man
   begin ;
While yet the roughness of the Stone
   remains,
Without the rising Muscles, and the Veins.
The sappy parts, and next resembling
   juice,
Were turn'd to Moisture, for the Bodies use :
Supplying humours, blood, and nourish-
   ment :
The rest, (too solid to receive a bent ;) 550
Converts to bones ; and what was once
   a vein,
Its former Name and Nature did retain.

By help of Pow'r Divine, in little space,
What the Man threw, assum'd a Manly
  face ;
And what the Wife, renew'd the Female
  Race.
Hence we derive our Nature, born to bear
Laborious life ; and harden'd into care.

The rest of Animals, from teeming Earth
Produc'd, in various Forms receiv'd their
  birth.
The native moisture, in its close retreat, 560
Digested by the Sun's Æthereal heat,
As in a kindly Womb, began to breed :
Then swell'd and quicken'd by the vital
  seed.
And some in less, and some in longer space,
Were ripen'd into form, and took a several
  face.
Thus when the *Nile* from *Pharian* Fields is
  fled,
And seeks, with Ebbing Tides, his ancient
  Bed,
The fat Manure with Heav'nly Fire is
  warm'd ;
And crusted Creatures, as in Wombs are
  form'd :
These, when they turn the Glebe, the
  Peasants find :   570
Some rude, and yet unfinish'd in their Kind :
Short of their Limbs, a lame imperfect Birth;
One half alive ; and one of lifeless Earth.
  For heat and moisture, when in Bodies
  joyn'd,
The temper that results from either Kind,
Conception makes ; and fighting, till they
  mix,
Their mingl'd Atoms in each other fix.
Thus Nature's hand the Genial Bed prepares
With Friendly Discord, and with fruitful
  Wars.
  From hence the surface of the Ground
  with Mud   580
And Slime besmear'd (the fæces of the
  Flood),
Receiv'd the Rays of Heav'n ; and sucking
  in
The Seeds of Heat, new Creatures did begin :
Some were of sev'ral sorts produc'd before ;
But of new Monsters, Earth created more.
  Unwillingly, but yet she brought to light
Thee, *Python* too, the wondring World to
  fright,
And the new Nations, with so dire a Sight.

So monstrous was his Bulk, so large a space
Did his vast Body, and long Train em-
  brace :   590
Whom *Phœbus* basking on a Bank espy'd,
E're now the God his Arrows had not try'd,
But on the trembling Deer, or Mountain Goat;
At this new Quarry he prepares to shoot.
Though every Shaft took place, he spent
  the Store
Of his full Quiver ; and 'twas long before
Th' expiring Serpent wallow'd in his Gore.
Then, to preserve the Fame of such a deed,
For *Python* slain, he *Pythian* Games decreed,
Where Noble Youths for Mastership shou'd
  strive,   600
To Quoit, to Run, and Steeds and Chariots
  drive.
The Prize was Fame : In witness of Renown,
An Oaken Garland did the Victor crown.
The Lawrel was not yet for Triumphs born,
But every Green, alike by *Phœbus* worn,
Did with promiscuous Grace, his flowing
  Locks adorn.

The Transformation of Daphne *into a Lawrel.*

  The first and fairest of his Loves was she,
Whom not blind Fortune, but the dire decree
Of angry *Cupid* forc'd him to desire :
Daphne her name, and *Peneus* was her Sire,
Swell'd with the Pride, that new Success
  attends,   611
He sees the Stripling, while his Bow he
  bends,
And thus insults him : Thou lascivious Boy,
Are Arms like these, for Children to employ ?
Know, such atchievements are my proper
  claim :
Due to my vigour and unerring aim :
Resistless are my Shafts, and *Python* late,
In such a feather'd Death, has found his fate.
Take up thy Torch, (and lay my Weapons
  by ;)
With that the feeble Souls of Lovers fry. 620
To whom the Son of *Venus* thus reply'd :
Phœbus, thy Shafts are sure on all beside ;
But mine on *Phœbus*, mine the Fame shall be
Of all thy Conquests, when I conquer thee.

613 Thou] thou *1693*.

He said, and soaring swiftly wing'd his
    flight ;
Nor stopt but on *Parnassus* airy height.
Two diff'rent Shafts he from his Quiver
    draws ;
One to repel Desire, and one to cause.
One Shaft is pointed with refulgent Gold,
To bribe the Love, and make the Lover
    bold :   630
One blunt, and tipt with Lead, whose base
    Allay
Provokes disdain, and drives desire away.
The blunted bolt against the Nymph he
    drest :
But with the sharp, transfixt *Apollo's*
    Breast.
    Th' enamour'd Deity pursues the Chace ;
The scornful Damsel shuns his loath'd
    Embrace ;
In hunting Beasts of Prey her Youth em-
    ploys ;
And *Phœbe* Rivals in her rural Joys.
With naked Neck she goes, and Shoulders
    bare,
And with a Fillet binds her flowing Hair. 640
By many Suitors sought, she mocks their
    pains,
And still her vow'd Virginity maintains.
Impatient of a Yoke, the name of Bride
She shuns, and hates the Joys she never
    try'd.
On Wilds and Woods she fixes her desire :
Nor knows what Youth and kindly Love
    inspire.
Her Father chides her oft : Thou ow'st, says
    he,
A Husband to thy self, a Son to me.
She, like a Crime, abhors the Nuptial Bed :
She glows with blushes, and she hangs her
    head.   650
Then, casting round his Neck her tender
    Arms,
Sooths him with blandishments, and filial
    Charms :
Give me, my Lord, she said, to live and die
A spotless Maid, without the Marriage tye.
'Tis but a small request ; I beg no more
Than what *Diana's* Father gave before.
The good old Sire was softn'd to consent ;
But said her Wish wou'd prove her Punish-
    ment :

For so much Youth, and so much Beauty
    joyn'd,
Oppos'd the State, which her desires de-
    sign'd.   660
    The God of light, aspiring to her Bed,
Hopes what he seeks, with flattering Fancies
    fed :
And is, by his own Oracles mis-led.
And as in empty Fields, the Stubble burns,
Or nightly Travellers, when day returns,
Their useless Torches on dry Hedges throw,
That catch the Flames, and kindle all the
    row ;
So burns the God, consuming in desire,
And feeding in his Breast a fruitless Fire :
Her well-turn'd Neck he view'd (her Neck
    was bare)   670
And on her Shoulders her dishevel'd Hair :
Oh were it comb'd, said he, with what a
    grace
Wou'd every waving Curl become her Face !
He view'd her eyes, like Heavenly Lamps
    that shone ;
He view'd her Lips, too sweet to view
    alone,
Her taper Fingers, and her panting Breast ; ⎫
He praises all he sees, and for the rest,   ⎬
Believes the Beauties yet unseen are best : ⎭
Swift as the Wind, the Damsel fled away,
Nor did for these alluring Speeches stay : 680
Stay, Nymph, he cry'd, I follow not a Foe :
Thus from the Lyon trips the trembling
    Doe :
Thus from the Wolf the frightn'd Lamb⎫
    removes,   ⎪
And, from pursuing Faulcons, fearful ⎬
    Doves ;   ⎪
Thou shunn'st a God, and shunn'st a God⎭
    that loves.
Ah lest some thorn shou'd pierce thy tender
    foot,
Or thou shou'd'st fall in flying my pursuit !
To sharp uneven ways thy steps decline ;
Abate thy speed, and I will bate of mine.
Yet think from whom thou dost so rashly
    fly ;   690
Nor basely born, nor Shepherd's Swain
    am I.
Perhaps thou know'st not my Superior
    State ;
And from that ignorance proceeds thy hate.
Me *Claros, Delphos, Tenedos* obey,
These Hands the *Patareian* Scepter sway.

The King of Gods begot me : What shall be,
Or is, or ever was, in Fate, I see.
Mine is th' invention of the charming Lyre ;
Sweet notes, and Heav'nly numbers I in-
spire.
Sure is my Bow, unerring is my Dart ;   700
But ah more deadly his, who pierc'd my
Heart.
Med'cine is mine, what Herbs and Simples
grow
In Fields and Forrests, all their Pow'rs I
know ;
And am the great Physician call'd, below.
Alas that Fields and Forrests can afford
No Remedies to heal their Love-sick Lord !
To cure the pains of Love, no Plant avails ;
And his own Physick the Physician fails.
She heard not half ; so furiously she flies,
And on her Ear th' imperfect accent dies.
Fear gave her Wings ; and as she fled, the
wind   711
Increasing spread her flowing Hair behind ;
And left her Legs and Thighs expos'd to
view ;
Which made the God more eager to pursue.
The God was young, and was too hotly
bent
To lose his time in empty Compliment :
But led by Love, and fir'd with such a sight,
Impetuously pursu'd his near delight.
As when th' impatient Greyhound slipt
from far,
Bounds o're the Glebe, to course the fearful
Hare,   720
She in her speed does all her safety lay ;
And he with double speed pursues the Prey ;
O're-runs her at the sitting turn, and licks
His Chaps in vain, and blows upon the Flix,
She scapes, and for the neighb'ring Covert
strives,
And gaining shelter, doubts if yet she lives :
If little things with great we may compare,
Such was the God, and such the flying Fair :
She urg'd by fear, her feet did swiftly
move,
But he more swiftly, who was urg'd by
Love.   730
He gathers ground upon her in the chace :
Now breaths upon her Hair, with nearer
pace ;
And just is fast'ning on the wish'd Embrace.

The Nymph grew pale, and in a mortal
fright,
Spent with the Labour of so long a Flight ;
And now despairing, cast a mournful look,
Upon the Streams of her Paternal Brook :
Oh help, she cry'd, in this extreamest
need,
If Water Gods are Deities indeed :
Gape, Earth and this unhappy Wretch
intomb :   740
Or change my form whence all my sorrows
come.
Scarce had she finish'd, when her Feet she
found
Benumm'd with cold, and fasten'd to the
Ground :
A filmy rind about her Body grows,
Her Hair to Leaves, her Arms extend to
Boughs :
The Nymph is all into a Lawrel gone,
The smoothness of her Skin remains alone.
Yet *Phœbus* loves her still, and, casting
round
Her Bole, his Arms, some little warmth he
found.   749
The Tree still panted in the unfinish'd part,
Not wholly vegetive, and heav'd her Heart.
He fix'd his Lips upon the trembling Rind ;
It swerv'd aside, and his Embrace declin'd.
To whom the God : Because thou canst not
be
My Mistress, I espouse thee for my Tree :
Be thou the prize of Honour and Renown ;
The deathless Poet, and the Poem crown.
Thou shalt the *Roman* Festivals adorn,
And, after Poets, be by Victors worn.
Thou shalt returning *Cæsar's* Triumph
grace ;   760
When Pomps shall in a long Procession pass :
Wreath'd on the Posts before his Palace
wait ;
And be the sacred Guardian of the Gate :
Secure from Thunder, and unharm'd by
Jove,
Unfading as th' immortal Pow'rs above :
And as the Locks of *Phœbus* are unshorn,
So shall perpetual green thy Boughs adorn.
The grateful Tree was pleas'd with what he
sed,
And shook the shady Honours of her Head.

717 with] *Some editors wrongly give* by

762 Posts] *By an unscholarly error some
editors give* Post

The Transformation of Io into a Heyfar.

An ancient Forrest in *Thessalia* grows ;
Which *Tempe's* pleasing Valley does in-
   close :   771
Through this the rapid *Peneus* takes his
   course ;
From *Pindus* rowling with impetuous force :
Mists from the Rivers mighty fall arise ;
And deadly damps inclose the cloudy Skies :
Perpetual Fogs are hanging o're the Wood ;
And sounds of Waters deaf the Neighbour-
   hood.
Deep, in a Rocky Cave, he makes abode :
(A Mansion proper for a mourning God.)
Here he gives Audience ; issuing out
   Decrees   780
To Rivers, his dependant Deities.
On this occasion hither they resort,
To pay their homage, and to make their
   Court.
All doubtful, whether to congratulate
His Daughter's Honour, or lament her Fate.
Sperchæus, crown'd with Poplar, first
   appears ;
Then old *Apidanus* came crown'd with
   years :
Enipeus turbulent, *Amphrisos* tame ;
And *Æas*, last with lagging Waters, came.
Then, of his Kindred Brooks a numerous
   throng   790
Condole his Loss, and bring their Urns along.
Not one was wanting of the watry Train,
That fill'd his Flood, or mingl'd with the
   Main :
But *Inachus*, who, in his Cave, alone,
Wept not another's losses, but his own.
For his dear *Io*, whether stray'd, or dead,
To him uncertain, doubtful Tears he shed.
He sought her through the World, but
   sought in vain ;
And, no where finding, rather fear'd her
   slain.
   Her, just returning from her Father's
   Brook,   800
Jove had beheld, with a desiring look ;
And, Oh fair Daughter of the Flood, he
   sed,
Worthy alone of *Jove's* Imperial Bed,

771 **pleasing**] *The editors give* pleasant

Happy, whoever shall those Charms possess ;
The King of Gods, nor is thy Lover less,
Invites thee to yon cooler Shades ; to shun
The scorching Rays of the Meridian Sun.
Nor shalt thou tempt the dangers of the
   Grove
Alone, without a Guide ; thy Guide is *Jove*.
No puny Pow'r, but he whose high Com-⎫
   mand   810⎬
Isunconfin'd,who rules the Seas and Land ;⎪
And tempers Thunder in his awful hand. ⎭
Oh fly not ; (for she fled from his Embrace,)
O'er *Lerna's* Pastures he pursu'd the Chace,
Along the Shades of the *Lyrnæan* Plain ;
At length the God, who never asks in vain,
Involv'd with Vapours, imitating Night,⎫
Both Air and Earth ; and then suppress'd⎬
   her flight,⎪
And mingling force with Love, enjoy'd the⎭
   full delight.
Mean time the Jealous *Juno*, from on high,
Survey'd the fruitful Fields of *Arcady* ; 821
And wonder'd that the mist shou'd over-run
The face of Day-light, and obscure the Sun.
No Nat'ral cause she found, from Brooks, or
   Bogs,
Or marshy Lowlands, to produce the Fogs :
Then round the Skies she sought for *Jupiter* ;
Her faithless Husband ; but no *Jove* was
   there.
Suspecting now the worst, Or I, she said,
Am much mistaken, or am much betray'd.
With fury she precipitates her flight, 830⎫
Dispels the shadows of dissembled Night,⎬
And to the day restores his native light. ⎭
Th' Almighty Leacher, careful to prevent
The consequence, foreseeing her descent
Transforms his Mistress in a trice ; and now
In *Io's* place appears a lovely Cow.
So slick her skin, so faultless was her
   make,
Ev'n *Juno* did unwilling pleasure take
To see so fair a Rival of her Love ;
And what she was, and whence, enquir'd of
   Jove :   840

813-15 *The editors go astray here. It is clear
from Ovid that the edition of 1693 is right except
for a printer's comma after* Pastures *and a semi-
colon for a comma after* Chace. *The editors
have been misled into a series of false stops and
wrong connexions which destroy the sense of the
passage.*

815 *Lyrnæan*] *The editors correct to* Lyrcæan
828 Or] or *1693*.

Of what fair Herd, and from what Pedigree ?
The God, half caught, was forc'd upon a lye ;
And said she sprung from Earth ; she took
    the word,
And begg'd the beauteous Heyfar of her
    Lord.
What should he do ? 'twas equal shame to
    Jove
Or to relinquish, or betray his Love :
Yet to refuse so slight a Gift, wou'd be
But more t' increase his Consort's Jealousie :
Thus fear, and love, by turns his heart
    assail'd ;
And stronger love had sure at length pre-
    vail'd,   850
But some faint hope remain'd, his jealous
    Queen
Had not the Mistress through the Heyfar
    seen.
The cautious Goddess, of her Gift possest,
Yet harbour'd anxious thoughts within her
    breast ;
As she who knew the falshood of her *Jove*,
And justly fear'd some new relapse of Love
Which to prevent, and to secure her care,
To trusty *Argus* she commits the Fair.
    The head of *Argus* (as with Stars the
    Skies)
Was compass'd round, and wore an hundred
    eyes.   860
But two by turns their Lids in Slumber
    steep ;
The rest on duty still their station keep ;
Nor cou'd the total Constellation sleep.
Thus, ever present, to his eyes and mind,
His Charge was still before him, tho' behind.
In Fields he suffer'd her to feed by Day,
But when the setting Sun to Night gave way,
The Captive Cow he summon'd with a call,
And drove her back, and ty'd her to the
    Stall.
On Leaves of Trees and bitter Herbs she fed,
Heav'n was her Canopy, bare Earth her
    Bed ;   871
So hardly lodg'd : and to digest her Food,
She drank from troubl'd Streams, defil'd
    with Mud.
Her woeful Story fain she wou'd have told,
With Hands upheld, but had no Hands to
    hold.
Her Head to her ungentle Keeper bow'd,
She strove to speak ; she spoke not, but she
    low'd :

Affrighted with the Noise, she look'd around,
And seem'd t' inquire the Author of the
    sound.
    Once on the Banks where often she had
    play'd,   880
(Her Father's Banks) she came, and there
    survey'd
Her alter'd Visage, and her branching head ;
And, starting, from her self she wou'd have
    fled.
Her fellow Nymphs, familiar to her eyes,
Beheld, but knew her not in this disguise.
Ev'n *Inachus* himself was ignorant ;
And in his Daughter did his Daughter want.
She follow'd where her Fellows went, as she
Were still a Partner of the Company :
They stroke her Neck ; the gentle Heyfar
    stands,   890
And her Neck offers to their stroking Hands.
Her Father gave her Grass ; the Grass she
    took ;
And lick'd his Palms, and cast a piteous
    look ;
And in the language of her eyes, she spoke.
She wou'd have told her name, and ask't
    relief,
But wanting words, in tears she tells her
    grief,
Which, with her foot she makes him under-
    stand ;
And prints the name of *Io* in the Sand.
    Ah wretched me ! her mournful Father
    cry'd ;
She, with a sigh, to wretched me reply'd :
About her Milk-white neck his arms he
    threw ;   901
And wept, and then these tender words
    ensue.
And art thou she, whom I have sought
    around
The World, and have at length so sadly
    found ?
So found is worse than lost : with mutual
    words
Thou answer'st not, no voice thy tongue
    affords :
But sighs are deeply drawn from out thy
    breast ;
And speech deny'd, by lowing is express'd.
Unknowing I, prepar'd thy Bridal Bed ;
With empty Hopes of happy Issue fed.   910
But now the Husband of a Herd must be
Thy Mate, and bell'wing Sons thy Progeny.

Oh, were I mortal, Death might bring relief !
But now my God-head but extends my
    grief ;
Prolongs my Woes, of which no end I see,
And makes me curse my Immortality.
More had he said, but fearful of her stay,
The Starry Guardian drove his Charge away,
To some fresh Pasture ; on a hilly height
He sate himself, and kept her still in sight.

The Eyes of Argus transform'd into a Peacock's Train.

Now *Jove* no longer cou'd her suff'rings
    bear :   921
But call'd in haste his airy Messenger,
The son of *Maya*, with severe decree
To kill the Keeper, and to set her free.
With all his Harness soon the God was sped ;
His flying Hat was fastned on his Head ;
Wings on his Heels were hung, and in his
    Hand
He holds the Virtue of the Snaky Wand.
The liquid Air his moving Pinions wound,
And, in the moment, shoot him on the
    ground.   930
Before he came in sight, the crafty God
His Wings dismiss'd, but still retain'd his
    Rod :
That Sleep-procuring Wand wise *Hermes*
    took,
But made it seem to sight, a Shepherd's
    Hook.
With this he did a Herd of Goats controul ;
Which by the way he met, and slily stole.
Clad like a Country Swain, he Pip'd, and
    Sung ;
And playing drove his jolly Troop along.
    With pleasure, *Argus* the Musician heeds ;
But wonders much at those new vocal
    Reeds.   940
And, Whosoe're thou art, my Friend, said
    he,
Up hither drive thy Goats, and play by me :
This Hill has browz for them, and shade for
    thee.
The God, who was with ease induc'd to
    climb,
Began Discourse to pass away the time ;
And still, betwixt, his Tuneful Pipe he plyes ;
And watch'd his Hour, to close the Keeper's
    Eyes.

With much ado, he partly kept awake ;
Not suff'ring all his Eyes repose to take :
And ask'd the Stranger, who did Reeds
    invent,   950
And whence began so rare an Instrument ?

The Transformation of Syrinx into Reeds.

Then *Hermes* thus ; A Nymph of late
    there was,
Whose Heav'nly form her Fellows did
    surpass.
The Pride and Joy of Fair *Arcadia's* plains ;
Belov'd by Deities, Ador'd by Swains :
Syrinx her Name, by *Sylvans* oft pursu'd,
As oft she did the Lustful Gods delude :
The Rural, and the Woodland Pow'rs dis-
    dain'd ;
With *Cynthia* Hunted, and her Rites main-
    tain'd ;
Like *Phœbe* clad, even *Phœbe's* self she
    seems,   960
So Tall, so Streight, such well-proportion'd
    Limbs :
The nicest Eye did no distinction know,
But that the Goddess bore a Golden Bow :
Distinguish'd thus, the sight she cheated
    too.
Descending from *Lycæus*, *Pan* admires
The Matchless Nymph, and burns with new
    Desires.
A Crown of Pine upon his Head he wore ;
And thus began her pity to implore.
But e're he thus began, she took her flight
So swift, she was already out of sight.   970
Nor staid to hear the Courtship of the God ;
But bent her course to *Ladon's* gentle
    Flood :
There by the River stopt, and, tyr'd before,
Relief from water Nymphs her Pray'rs
    implore.
Now while the Lustful God, with speedy
    pace,
Just thought to strain her in a strict Em-
    brace,
He fills his Arms with Reeds, new rising
    on the place.
And while he sighs his ill-success to find,
The tender Canes were shaken by the wind ;

And breath'd a mournful Air, unhear'd
    before ;   980
That much surprizing *Pan*, yet pleas'd him
    more.
Admiring this new Musick, Thou, he sed,
Who can'st not be the Partner of my Bed,
At least shalt be the Consort of my Mind ;
And often, often, to my Lips be joyn'd.
He form'd the Reeds, proportion'd as they
    are :
Unequal in their length, and wax'd with
    Care,
They still retain the Name of his Ungrate-
    ful Fair.

  While *Hermes* pip'd, and sung, and told
    his tale,
The Keeper's winking Eyes began to fail, 990
And drowsie slumber on the lids to creep ;
Till all the Watchman was, at length, asleep.
Then soon the God his Voice and Song
    supprest ;
And with his pow'rful Rod confirm'd his rest:
Without delay his crooked Faulchion drew,
And at one fatal stroak the Keeper slew.
Down from the Rock, fell the dissever'd
    head,
Opening its Eyes in Death, and falling bled ;
And mark'd the passage with a crimson trail:
Thus *Argus* lies in pieces, cold and pale ;
And all his hundred Eyes, with all their
    light,   1001
Are clos'd at once in one perpetual night.
These *Juno* takes, that they no more may fail,
And spreads them in her Peacock's gaudy
    tail.
  Impatient to revenge her injur'd Bed,
She wreaks her Anger on her Rival's head ;
With furies frights her from her Native Home,
And drives her gadding, round the World
    to roam :   1008
Nor ceas'd her madness and her flight, before
She touch'd the limits of the *Pharian* Shore.
At length, arriving on the Banks of *Nile*,
Weary'd with length of ways, and worn
    with toil,
She laid her down : and, leaning on her
    Knees,
Invok'd the Cause of all her Miseries :
And cast her languishing regards above,
For help from Heav'n, and her ungrateful
    Jove.

She sigh'd, she wept, she low'd ; 'twas all
    she cou'd ;
And with Unkindness seem'd to tax the God.
Last, with an humble Pray'r, she begg'd
    Repose,
Or Death at least to finish all her Woes. 1020
Jove heard her Vows, and with a flatt'ring
    look,
In her behalf, to jealous *Juno* spoke.
He cast his Arms about her Neck, and sed :
Dame, rest secure ; no more thy Nuptial Bed
This Nymph shall violate ; by *Styx* I swear,
And every Oath that binds the Thunderer.
The Goddess was appeas'd : and at the word
Was *Io* to her former shape restor'd.
The rugged Hair began to fall away ;
The Sweetness of her Eyes did only stay,
Tho' not so large ; her crooked Horns
    decrease ;   1031
The wideness of her Jaws and Nostrils cease :
Her Hoofs to Hands return, in little space :
The five long taper Fingers take their place ;
And nothing of the Heyfar now is seen,
Beside the native whiteness of the Skin.
Erected on her Feet she walks again,
And Two the duty of the Four sustain.
She tries her Tongue, her silence softly
    breaks,
And fears her former lowings when she
    speaks :   1040
A Goddess now through all th' *Egyptian*
    State ;
And serv'd by Priests, who in white Linnen
    wait.
  Her son was *Epaphus*, at length believ'd
The Son of *Jove*, and as a God receiv'd :
With Sacrifice ador'd, and publick Pray'rs,
He common Temples with his Mother shares.
Equal in years, and Rival in Renown
With *Epaphus*, the youthful *Phaeton*,
Like Honour claims, and boasts his Sire
    the Sun.
His haughty Looks, and his assuming Air
The Son of *Isis* cou'd no longer bear : 1051
Thou tak'st thy Mother's Word too far,
    said he,
And hast usurp'd thy boasted Pedigree.
Go base Pretender to a borrow'd Name.
Thus tax'd, he blush'd with anger, and with
    shame ;

---

982 Thou] thou *1693*.

1036 the] *Most editors, with characteristic dis-
regard for euphony, wrongly give* her

But shame repress'd his Rage : the daunted
    Youth
Soon seeks his Mother, and inquires the
    truth :
Mother, said he, this Infamy was thrown
By *Epaphus* on you, and me your Son. 1059
He spoke in publick, told it to my face ;
Nor durst I vindicate the dire disgrace :
Ev'n I, the bold, the sensible of wrong,
Restrain'd by Shame, was forc'd to hold my
    Tongue.
To hear an open Slander is a Curse :
But not to find an Answer, is a worse.
If I am Heav'n-begot, assert your Son ⎫
By some sure Sign ; and make my Father ⎬
    known, ⎪
To right my Honour,and redeem your own. ⎭
He said, and saying cast his arms about
Her Neck, and begg'd her to resolve the
    Doubt.   1070
'Tis hard to judge if *Climenè* were mov'd
More by his Pray'r, whom she so dearly
    lov'd,
Or more with fury fir'd, to find her
    Name
Traduc'd, and made the sport of common
    Fame.

She stretch'd her Arms to Heav'n, and fix'd
    her Eyes
On that fair Planet, that adorns the Skies ;
Now by those Beams, said she, whose holy
    Fires
Consume my Breast, and kindle my desires ;
By him who sees us both, and chears our
    sight,
By him the publick Minister of light, 1080
I swear that *Sun* begot thee : if I lye,
Let him his chearful Influence deny:
Let him no more this perjur'd Creature see ;
And shine on all the World, but only me :
If still you doubt your Mother's Innocence,
His Eastern Mansion is not far from hence ;
With little pains you to his *Levè* go,
And from himself your Parentage may know.
With joy th' ambitious Youth his Mother
    heard,   1089
And eager, for the Journey soon prepar'd.
He longs the World beneath him to survey ;
To guide the Chariot ; and to give the day :
From *Meroë's* burning Sands he bends his
    course,
Nor less in *India* feels his Father's force ;
His Travel urging, till he came in sight,
And saw the Palace by the Purple light.

MELEAGER AND ATALANTA,

OUT OF THE EIGHTH BOOK OF OVID'S METAMORPHOSES.

CONNEXION TO THE FORMER STORY.

Ovid, *having told how* Theseus *had freed*
Athens *from the Tribute of Children,* (*which
was impos'd on them by* Minos, *King of*
Creta) *by killing the* Minotaur, *here makes
a Digression to the Story of* Meleager *and*
Atalanta, *which is one of the most inartificial
Connexions in all the* Metamorphoses : *For
he only says, that* Theseus *obtain'd such Honour
from that Combate, that all* Greece *had recourse to him in their Necessities ; and,
amongst others,* Calydon, *though the Heroe
of that Country, Prince* Meleager, *was then
living.*

FROM him, the *Caledonians* sought Relief ;
Tho' valiant *Meleagrus* was their Chief.
The Cause, a Boar, who ravag'd far and
    near :
Of *Cynthia's* Wrath th' avenging Minister.
For *Oeneus* with Autumnal Plenty bless'd,
By Gifts to Heav'n his Gratitude express'd :
Cull'd Sheafs, to *Ceres* ; to *Lyæus*, Wine ; ⎫
To *Pan*, and *Pales*, offer'd Sheep and Kine ; ⎬
And Fat of Olives, to *Minerva's* shrine. 9 ⎭
Beginning from the Rural Gods, his Hand
Was lib'ral to the Pow'rs of high Command :
Each Deity in ev'ry kind was bless'd,
Till at *Diana's* Fane th' invidious Honour
    ceas'd.

MELEAGER AND ATALANTA. The text from the
original edition of 1700 except for the variants
noted. There are several mistakes in the editions.
The form 'clottered' is undoubtedly Dryden's.

In 288 it would seem that the original text is
wrongly printed. Warton gives 'Brother's Ghosts,'
which is absurd.

Wrath touches ev'n the Gods; the Queen
     of Night
Fir'd with Disdain, and jealous of her
     Right,
Unhonour'd though I am, at least, said she,
Not unreveng'd that impious Act shall be.
Swift as the Word, she sped the Boar away,
With Charge on those devoted Fields to
     prey.   19
No larger Bulls th' Ægyptian Pastures feed,
And none so large Sicilian Meadows breed:
His Eye-balls glare with Fire, suffus'd with
     Blood ;
His Neck shoots up a thick-set thorny Wood;
His bristled Back a Trench impal'd appears,
And stands erected, like a Field of Spears.
Froth fills his Chaps, he sends a grunting
     Sound,
And part he churns, and part befoams the
     Ground.
For Tusks with Indian Elephants he strove,
And Jove's own Thunder from his Mouth
     he drove.
He burns the Leaves ; the scorching Blast
     invades   30
The tender Corn, and shrivels up the Blades :
Or suff'ring not their yellow Beards to
     rear,
He tramples down the Spikes, and intercepts
     the Year.
In vain the Barns expect their promis'd
     Load,
Nor Barns at home, nor Reeks are heap'd
     abroad :
In vain the Hinds the Threshing-Floor pre-
     pare,
And exercise their Flails in empty Air.
With Olives ever-green the Ground is
     strow'd,
And Grapes ungather'd shed their gen'rous
     Blood.
Amid the Fold he rages, nor the Sheep   40
Their Shepherds, nor the Grooms their Bulls
     can keep.
From Fields to Walls the frighted Rabble
     run,
Nor think themselves secure within the
     Town :
Till Meleagros, and his chosen Crew,
Contemn the Danger, and the Praise pursue.
Fair Leda's Twins (in time to Stars decreed)
One fought on Foot, one curb'd the fiery
     Steed ;

Then issued forth fam'd Jason after These,
Who mann'd the foremost Ship that sail'd
     the Seas ;
Then Theseus, join'd with bold Perithous,
     came,   50
A single Concord in a double Name :
The Thestian Sons, Idas who swiftly ran,
And Ceneus, once a Woman, now a Man.
Lynceus, with Eagles Eyes, and Lions Heart
Leucippus, with his never-erring Dart ;
Acastus, Phileus, Phœnix, Telamon, ⎫
Echion, Lelex, and Eurytion,   ⎬
Achilles Father, and great Phocus Son ; ⎭
Dryas the Fierce, and Hippasus the Strong ;
With twice old Iolas, and Nestor then but
     young,   60
Laertes active, and Ancæus bold ;   ⎫
Mopsus the Sage, who future Things fore- ⎬
     told ;   ⎪
And t'other Seer, yet by his Wife * unsold. ⎭
A thousand others of im-   * Amphiaraus.
     mortal Fame ;
Among the rest, fair Atalanta came,
Grace of the Woods : A Diamond Buckle
     bound
Her Vest behind, that else had flow'd upon
     the Ground,
And shew'd her buskin'd Legs ; her Head
     was bare,
But for her Native Ornament of Hair ;
Which in a simple Knot was ty'd above, 70
Sweet Negligence ! unheeded Bait of Love !
Her sounding Quiver on her shoulder ty'd,
One Hand a Dart, and one a Bow supply'd.
Such was her Face, as in a Nymph display'd
A fair fierce Boy, or in a Boy betray'd
The blushing Beauties of a modest Maid.
The Caledonian Chief at once the Dame
Beheld, at once his Heart receiv'd the
     Flame,
With Heav'ns averse. O happy Youth, he
     cry'd ;   79
For whom thy Fates reserve so fair a Bride !
He sigh'd, and had no leisure more to say ; ⎫
His Honour call'd his Eyes another way,   ⎬
And forced him to pursue the now neglected ⎪
     Prey.   ⎭
There stood a Forest on a Mountains
     Brow,
Which over-look'd the shaded Plains below.
No sounding Ax presum'd those Trees to
     bite ;
Coeval with the World, a venerable Sight.

The *Heroes* there arriv'd, some spread around
The Toils; some search the Footsteps on the Ground;
Some from the Chains the faithful Dogs unbound. 90
Of Action eager, and intent in Thought,
The Chiefs their honourable Danger sought:
A Valley stood below; the common Drain
Of Waters from above, and falling Rain:
The Bottom was a moist and marshy Ground,
Whose Edges were with bending Osiers crown'd;
The knotty Bulrush next in Order stood,
And all within of Reeds a trembling Wood.
From hence the Boar was rows'd, and sprung amain
Like Lightning sudden, on the Warriour-Train; 100
Beats down the Trees before him, shakes the Ground,
The Forest echoes to the crackling Sound;
Shout the fierce Youth, and Clamours ring around.
All stood with their protended Spears prepar'd,
With broad Steel Heads the brandish'd Weapons glar'd.
The Beast impetuous with his Tusks aside
Deals glancing Wounds; the fearful Dogs divide:
All spend their Mouth aloof, but none abide.
Echion threw the first, but miss'd his Mark,
And stuck his Boar-spear on a Maples Bark. 110
Then *Jason*: and his Javelin seem'd to take,
But fail'd with over-force, and whiz'd above his Back.
Mopsus was next; but, e'er he threw, address'd
To *Phœbus*, thus: O Patron, help thy Priest:
If I adore, and ever have ador'd
Thy Pow'r Divine, thy present Aid afford;
That I may reach the Beast. The God allow'd
His Pray'r, and smiling, gave him what he cou'd:
He reach'd the Savage, but no Blood he drew,
Dian unarm'd the Javelin as it flew. 120

This chaf'd the Boar, his Nostrils Flames expire,
And his red Eye-balls roll with living Fire.
Whirl'd from a Sling, or from an Engine thrown,
Amidst the Foes, so flies a mighty Stone,
As flew the Beast: The Left Wing put to flight,
The Chiefs o'erborn, he rushes on the Right.
Eupalamos and *Pelagon* he laid
In Dust, and next to Death, but for their Fellows Aid.
Enesimus far'd worse, prepar'd to fly,
The fatal Fang drove deep within his Thigh,
And cut the Nerves: The Nerves no more sustain 131
The Bulk; the Bulk unprop'd, falls head-long on the Plain.
Nestor had fail'd the Fall of *Troy* to see,
But leaning on his Lance, he vaulted on a Tree;
Then gath'ring up his Feet, look'd down with Fear,
And thought his monstrous Foe was still too near.
Against a Stump his Tusk the Monster grinds,
And in the sharpen'd Edge new Vigour finds;
Then, trusting to his Arms, young *Othrys* found,
And ranch'd his Hips with one continu'd Wound. 140
Now *Leda's* Twins, the future Stars, appear;
White were their Habits, white their Horses were,
Conspicuous both, and both in act to throw,
Their trembling Lances brandish'd at the Foe:
Nor had they miss'd; but he to Thickets fled,
Conceal'd from aiming Spears, not pervious to the Steed.
But *Telamon* rush'd in, and happ'd to meet
A rising Root, that held his fastned Feet;
So down he fell; whom, sprawling on the Ground,
His Brother from the Wooden Gyves unbound. 150

---

91 in] *The editors wrongly give* on
108 aloof] *The editors, disregarding the sense, wrongly give* aloft

129 Enesimus] *Onesimus* 1700. *Perhaps a misprint.*

Mean time the Virgin-Huntress was not slow
T' expel the Shaft from her contracted Bow :
Beneath his Ear the fastned Arrow stood,
And from the Wound appear'd the trickling Blood.
She blush'd for Joy : But *Meleagros* rais'd
His voice with loud Applause, and the fair Archer prais'd.
He was the first to see, and first to show
His Friends the Marks of the successful Blow.
Nor shall thy Valour want the Praises due,
He said ; a vertuous Envy seiz'd the Crew.
They shout ; the Shouting animates their Hearts,   161
And all at once employ their thronging Darts :
But out of Order thrown, in Air they joyn ;
And Multitude makes frustrate the Design.
With both his Hands the proud *Anceus* takes,
And flourishes his double-biting Ax :
Then forward to his Fate, he took a Stride
Before the rest, and to his Fellows cry'd,
Give place, and mark the diff'rence, if you can,
Between a Woman-Warriour, and a Man ;
The Boar is doom'd ; nor though *Diana* lend   171
Her Aid, *Diana* can her Beast defend.
Thus boasted he ; then stretch'd, on Tiptoe stood,
Secure to make his empty Promise good.
But the more wary Beast prevents the Blow,
And upward rips the Groin of his audacious Foe.
Ancæus falls ; his Bowels from the Wound
Rush out, and clotter'd Blood distains the Ground.
Perithous, no small Portion of the War,
Press'd on, and shook his Lance ; To whom from far   180
Thus *Theseus* cry'd : O stay, my better Part,
My more than Mistress ; of my Heart, the Heart.
The Strong may fight aloof : *Anceus* try'd
His Force too near, and by presuming dy'd :
He said, and while he spake his Javelin threw,
Hissing in Air th' unerring Weapon flew ;

But on an Arm of Oak, that stood betwixt
The Marks-man and the Mark, his Lance he fixt.
Once more bold *Jason* threw, but fail'd to wound
The Boar, and slew an undeserving Hound ;
And through the Dog the Dart was nail'd to Ground.   191
Two Spears from *Meleager's* Hand were sent,
With equal Force, but various in th' Event :
The first was fix'd in Earth, the second stood
On the Boars bristled Back, and deeply drank his Blood.
Now while the tortur'd Salvage turns around,
And flings about his Foam, impatient of the Wound,
The Wounds great Author close at Hand provokes
His Rage, and plyes him with redoubled Strokes ;
Wheels as he wheels ; and with his pointed Dart   200
Explores the nearest Passage to his Heart.
Quick, and more quick he spins in giddy Gires,
Then falls, and in much Foam his Soul expires.
This Act with Shouts Heav'n high the friendly Band
Applaud, and strain in theirs the Victour Hand.
Then all approach the Slain with vast Surprize,
Admire on what a Breadth of Earth he lies ;
And scarce secure, reach out their Spears afar,
And blood their Points, to prove their Partnership of War.
But he, the conqu'ring Chief, his Foot impress'd   210
On the strong Neck of that destructive Beast ;
And gazing on the Nymph with ardent Eyes,
Accept, said he, fair *Nonacrine*, my Prize,
And, though inferiour, suffer me to join
My Labours, and my Part of Praise, with thine :

---

178 clotter'd] *The editors wrongly give* clotted   205 Victour] *The editors wrongly give* victor's

At this presents her with the Tusky Head
And Chine, with rising Bristles roughly
    spread.
Glad, she receiv'd the Gift: and seem'd
    to take
With double Pleasure, for the Giver's sake.
The rest were seiz'd with sullen Discontent,
And a deaf Murmur through the Squadron
    went: 221
All envy'd; but the *Thestyan* Brethren
    show'd
The least Respect, and thus they vent their
    Spleen aloud:
Lay down those honour'd Spoils, nor think
    to share,
Weak Woman as thou art, the Prize of War:
Ours is the Title, thine a foreign Claim,
Since *Meleagros* from our Lineage came.
Trust not thy Beauty; but restore the
    Prize,
Which he, besotted on that Face and
    Eyes,
Would rend from us: At this, inflam'd with
    Spite,   230
From her they snatch the Gift, from him the
    Givers Right.
  But soon th' impatient Prince his Fau-
    chion drew,
And cry'd, Ye Robbers of another's Due,
Now learn the Diff'rence, at your proper
    Cost,
Betwixt true Valour, and an empty Boast.
At this advanc'd, and, sudden as the Word
In proud *Plexippus* Bosom plung'd the
    Sword:
Toxeus amaz'd, and with Amazement slow,
Or to revenge, or ward the coming Blow,
Stood doubting; and, while doubting thus
    he stood,   240
Receiv'd the Steel bath'd in his Brother's
    Blood.
  Pleas'd with the first, unknown the second
    News,
Althea, to the Temples, pays their Dues
For her Son's Conquest; when at length
    appear
Her griesly Brethren stretch'd upon the
    Bier:
Pale at the sudden Sight, she chang'd her
    Cheer,

And with her Cheer her Robes; but hearing
    tell
The Cause, the Manner, and by whom they
    fell,
'Twas Grief no more, or Grief and Rage were
    One   249
Within her Soul; at last 'twas Rage alone;
Which burning upwards in succession dries
The Tears that stood consid'ring in her Eyes.
  There lay a Log unlighted on the Hearth:
When she was lab'ring in the Throws of
    Birth
For th' unborn Chief, the Fatal Sisters came,
And rais'd it up, and toss'd it on the Flame:
Then on the Rock a scanty Measure place
Of Vital Flax, and turn'd the Wheel apace;
And turning sung, To this red Brand and
    thee,
O new-born Babe, we give an equal Destiny:
So vanish'd out of View. The frighted
    Dame   261
Sprung hasty from her Bed, and quench'd
    the Flame:
The Log in secret lock'd, she kept with Care,
And that, while thus preserv'd, preserv'd
    her Heir.
This Brand she now produc'd; and first she
    strows
The Hearth with Heaps of Chips, and after
    blows,
Thrice heav'd her Hand, and heav'd, she ⎫
    thrice repress'd: ⎬
The Sister and the Mother long contest   ⎭
Two doubtful Titles in one tender Breast;
And now her Eyes and Cheeks with Fury
    glow,   270
Now pale her Cheeks, her Eyes with Pity flow;
Now lowring Looks presage approaching
    Storms,
And now prevailing Love her Face reforms:
Resolv'd, she doubts again; the Tears she
    dry'd
With burning Rage, are by new Tears sup-
    ply'd;
And as a Ship, which Winds and Waves ⎫
    assail,   ⎪
Now with the Current drives, now with the ⎬
    Gale,   ⎪
Both opposite, and neither long prevail: ⎭

---

237 *Plexippus*] *Ploxippus* 1700.   *Probably a misprint.*

253 Hearth] *The English editors thoughtlessly and wrongly give* earth
275 burning] *The English editors wantonly give* blushing

She feels a double Force, by Turns obeys
Th' imperious Tempest, and th' impetuous
   Seas: 280
So fares *Althæa's* Mind; she first relents
With Pity, of that Pity then repents:
Sister and Mother long the Scales divide,
But the Beam nodded on the Sisters side.
Sometimes she softly sigh'd, then roar'd
   aloud;
But Sighs were stifled in the Cries of
   Blood.
  The pious, impious Wretch at length
   decreed,
To please her Brother's Ghost, her Son
   shou'd bleed;
And when the Fun'ral Flames began to
   rise,
Receive, she said, a Sisters Sacrifice: 290
A Mothers Bowels burn: High in her
   Hand
Thus while she spoke, she held the fatal
   Brand;
Then thrice before the kindled Pyle she
   bow'd,
And the three Furies thrice invok'd aloud:
Come, come, revenging Sisters, come and
   view
A Sister paying her dead Brothers due:
A Crime I punish, and a Crime commit;
But Blood for Blood, and Death for Death
   is fit:
Great Crimes must be with greater Crimes
   repaid,
And second Funerals on the former laid. 300
Let the whole Houshold in one Ruine fall,
And may *Diana's* Curse o'ertake us all.
Shall Fate to happy *Oeneus* still allow ⎫
One Son, while *Thestius* stands depriv'd of ⎬
   two?   ⎪
Better three lost, than one unpunish'd go. ⎭
Take then, dear Ghosts, (while yet admitted
   new
In Hell you wait my Duty) take your
   Due:
A costly Off'ring on your Tomb is laid,
When with my Blood the Price of yours is
   paid.
  Ah! Whither am I hurried? Ah!
   forgive,   310
Ye Shades, and let your Sisters Issue live:

A Mother cannot give him Death; though
   he
Deserves it, he deserves it not from me.
  Then shall th' unpunish'd Wretch insult
   the Slain,
Triumphant live, nor only live, but reign?
While you, thin Shades, the Sport of Winds,
   are toss'd
O'er dreery Plains, or tread the burning
   Coast.
I cannot, cannot bear; 'tis past, 'tis done;
Perish this impious, this detested Son:
Perish his Sire, and perish I withal;   320
And let the Houses Heir, and the hop'd
   Kingdom fall.
  Where is the Mother fled, her pious
   Love,
And where the Pains with which ten Months
   I strove!
Ah! hadst thou dy'd, my Son, in Infant-
   years,
Thy little Herse had been bedew'd with
   Tears.
  Thou liv'st by me; to me thy Breath
   resign;
Mine is the Merit, the Demerit thine.
Thy Life by double Title I require;
Once giv'n at Birth, and once preserv'd
   from Fire:
One Murder pay, or add one Murder more,
And me to them who fell by thee restore. 331
  I wou'd, but cannot: My Son's Image
   stands
Before my Sight; and now their angry
   Hands
My Brothers hold, and Vengeance these
   exact,
This pleads Compassion, and repents the
   Fact.
  He pleads in vain, and I pronounce his
   Doom:
My Brothers, though unjustly, shall o'er-
   come.
But having paid their injur'd Ghosts their
   Due,
My Son requires my Death, and mine shall
   his pursue.
  At this, for the last time she lifts her
   Hand,   340
Averts her Eyes, and, half unwilling, drops
   the Brand.

---

281 she first] *Most editors wrongly give* first
she

317 tread] *Some editors absurdly give* dread

The Brand, amid the flaming Fewel thrown,
Or drew, or seem'd to draw, a dying Groan :
The Fires themselves but faintly lick'd their
    Prey,
Then loath'd their impious Food, and wou'd
    have shrunk away.
Just then the *Heroe* cast a doleful Cry,
And in those absent Flames began to fry.
The blind Contagion rag'd within his
    Veins ;
But he with manly Patience bore his
    Pains :
He fear'd not Fate, but only griev'd to die
Without an honest Wound, and by a Death
    so dry.   351
Happy *Ancæus*, thrice aloud he cry'd,
With what becoming Fate in Arms he dy'd !
Then call'd his Brothers, Sisters, Sire,
    around,
And her to whom his Nuptial Vows were
    bound ;
Perhaps his Mother ; a long Sigh he drew,
And his Voice failing, took his last Adieu :
For as the Flames augment, and as they
    stay
At their full Height, then languish to decay,
They rise, and sink by Fits ; at last they
    soar   360
In one bright Blaze, and then descend no
    more :
Just so his inward Heats at height, impair,
Till the last burning Breath shoots out the
    Soul in Air.
   Now lofty *Calidon* in Ruines lies ; ⎫
All Ages, all Degrees unsluice their Eyes ; ⎬
And Heaven & Earth resound with Mur- ⎪
    murs, Groans, & Cries.   ⎭
Matrons and Maidens beat their Breasts,
    and tear
Their Habits, and root up their scatter'd
    Hair.
The wretched Father, Father now no more,
With Sorrow sunk, lies prostrate on the
    Floor,   370
Deforms his hoary Locks with Dust obscene,
And curses Age, and loaths a Life pro-
    long'd with Pain.

By Steel her stubborn Soul his Mother
    freed,
And punish'd on her self her impious
    Deed.
Had I a hundred Tongues, a Wit so large
As cou'd their hundred Offices discharge ;
Had *Phœbus* all his *Helicon* bestow'd,
In all the Streams inspiring all the God ;
Those Tongues, that Wit, those Streams,
    that God, in vain
Wou'd offer to describe his Sisters pain : 380
They beat their Breasts with many a bruiz-
    ing Blow,
Till they turn'd livid, and corrupt the Snow.
The Corps they cherish, while the Corps
    remains,
And exercise and rub with fruitless Pains ;
And when to Fun'ral Flames 'tis born
    away,
They kiss the Bed on which the Body lay :
And when those Fun'ral Flames no longer
    burn,
(The Dust compos'd within a pious Urn)
Ev'n in that Urn their Brother they
    confess,
And hug it in their Arms, and to their
    Bosoms press.   390
   His Tomb is rais'd ; then, stretch'd along
    the Ground,
Those living Monuments his Tomb sur-
    round :
Ev'n to his Name, inscrib'd, their Tears
    they pay,
Till Tears and Kisses wear his Name away.
   But *Cynthia* now had all her Fury spent,
Not with less Ruine than a Race, content :
Excepting *Gorge*, perish'd all the Seed,
And * Her whom Heav'n for   *Dejanira.*
    Hercules decreed.
Satiate at last, no longer she pursu'd
The weeping Sisters ; but with Wings en-
    du'd,   400
And Horny Beaks, and sent to flit in Air ;
Who yearly round the Tomb in Feather'd
    Flocks repair.

   382 turn'd] *Some editors give* turn

BAUCIS | AND | PHILEMON.

OUT OF THE EIGHTH BOOK OF | OVID'S METAMORPHOSES.

The Author, pursuing the Deeds of Theseus, relates how He, with his friend Perithous, were invited by Achelous, the River-God, to stay with him, till his Waters were abated. Achelous entertains them with a Relation of his own Love to Perimele, who was chang'd into an Island by Neptune, at his Request. Perithous, being an Atheist, derides the Legend, and denies the Power of the Gods to work that Miracle. Lelex, another Companion of Theseus, to confirm the Story of Achelous, relates another Metamorphosis of Baucis and Philemon into Trees; of which he was partly an Eye-witness.

THUS *Achelous* ends: His Audience hear
With admiration, and admiring, fear
The Pow'rs of Heav'n ; except *Ixion's* Son,
Who laugh'd at all the Gods, believ'd in
   none :
He shook his impious Head, and thus replies,
These Legends are no more than pious Lyes :
You attribute too much to Heavenly Sway,
To think they give us Forms, and take away.
  The rest, of better Minds, their Sense
   declar'd
Against this Doctrine, and with Horrour
  heard.   10
Then *Lelex* rose, an old experienc'd Man,
And thus with sober Gravity began :
Heav'ns Pow'r is Infinite : Earth, Air, and Sea,
The Manufacture Mass, the making Pow'r
  obey :
By Proof to clear your Doubt ; In *Phrygian*
  Ground
Two neighb'ring Trees, with Walls encom-
  pass'd round,
Stand on a mod'rate Rise, with wonder
  shown,
One a hard Oak, a softer Linden one :
I saw the Place and them, by *Pittheus* sent
To *Phrygian* Realms, my Grandsire's
  Government.   20
Not far from thence is seen a Lake, the Haunt
Of Coots, and of the fishing Cormorant :

Here *Jove* with *Hermes* came ; but in
  Disguise
Of mortal Men conceal'd their Deities ;
One laid aside his Thunder, one his Rod ;
And many toilsom Steps together trod ;
For Harbour at a thousand Doors they
  knock'd,
Not one of all the thousand but was lock'd
At last an hospitable House they found,
A homely Shed ; the Roof, not far from
  Ground,   30
Was thatch'd with Reeds and Straw
  together bound.
There *Baucis* and *Philemon* liv'd, and there
Had liv'd long marry'd and a happy Pair :
Now old in Love, though little was their
  Store,
Inur'd to Want, their Poverty they bore,
Nor aim'd at Wealth, professing to be poor.
For Master or for Servant here to call,
Was all alike, where only Two were All.
Command was none, where equal Love was
  paid,
Or rather both commanded, both obey'd. 40
  From lofty Roofs the Gods repuls'd before,
Now stooping, enter'd through the little
  Door :
The Man (their hearty Welcome first
  express'd)
A common Settle drew for either Guest,
Inviting each his weary Limbs to rest.
But e'er they sat, officious *Baucis* lays
Two Cushions stuff'd with Straw, the Seat
  to raise ;
Course, but the best she had ; then rakes
  the Load
Of Ashes from the Hearth, and spreads abroad
The living Coals, and, lest they should expire,
With Leaves and Barks she feeds her Infant-
  fire :   51
It smoaks ; and then with trembling Breath
  she blows,
Till in a chearful Blaze the Flames arose.
With Brush-wood and with Chips she
  strengthens these,
And adds at last the Boughs of rotten Trees.

BAUCIS AND PHILEMON. The text from the original edition of 1700. In 160 'Crotches' is certainly Dryden's form.

48 rakes] *Most editors thoughtlessly and wrongly give* takes

The Fire thus form'd, she sets the Kettle on,
(Like burnish'd Gold the little Seether shone)
Next took the Coleworts which her Hus-
band got
From his own Ground (a small well-water'd
Spot ;)
She stripp'd the Stalks of all their Leaves ;
the best   60
She cull'd, and then with handy-care she
dress'd.
High o'er the Hearth a Chine of Bacon hung ;
Good old *Philemon* seiz'd it with a Prong,
And from the ┌ooty Rafter drew it down,
Then cut a Slice, but scarce enough for one ;
Yet a large Portion of a little Store,
Which for their Sakes alone he wish'd were
more.
This in the Pot he plung'd without delay,
To tame the Flesh, and drain the Salt away.
The Time between, before the Fire they
sat,   70
And shorten'd the Delay by pleasing Chat.
   A Beam there was, on which a Beechen
Pail
Hung by the Handle, on a driven Nail :
This fill'd with Water, gently warm'd, they ⎫
set |
Before their Guests ; in this they bath'd ⎬
their Feet, |
And after with clean Towels dry'd their ⎭
Sweat :
This done, the Host produc'd the genial Bed, ⎫
Sallow the Feet, the Borders, and the Sted, ⎬
Which with no costly Coverlet they spread ; ⎭
But course old Garments, yet such Robes as
these   80
They laid alone, at Feasts, on Holydays.
The good old Huswife tucking up her Gown,
The Table sets ; th' invited Gods lie down.
The Trivet-Table of a Foot was lame,
A Blot which prudent *Baucis* overcame,
Who thrusts beneath the limping Leg, a
Sherd,
So was the mended Board exactly rear'd :
Then rubb'd it o'er with newly-gather'd Mint,
A wholesom Herb, that breath'd a grateful
Scent.
Pallas began the Feast, where first were
seen   90
The party-colour'd Olive, Black and Green :

Autumnal Cornels next in order serv'd,
In Lees of Wine well pickl'd, and preserv'd :
A Garden-Sallad was the third Supply,
Of Endive, Radishes, and Succory :
Then Curds and Cream, the Flow'r of ⎫
Country-Fare, |
And new-laid Eggs, which *Baucis* busie ⎬
Care |
Turn'd by a gentle Fire, and roasted rear. ⎭
All these in Earthen Ware were serv'd to ⎫
Board ; |
And next in place, an Earthen Pitcher, ⎬
stor'd   100 |
With Liquor of the best the Cottage cou'd ⎭
afford.
This was the Tables Ornament and Pride,
With Figures wrought : Like Pages at his
Side
Stood Beechen Bowls ; and these were
shining clean,
Vernish'd with Wax without, and lin'd within.
By this the boiling Kettle had prepar'd,
And to the Table sent the smoaking Lard ;
On which with eager Appetite they dine,
A sav'ry Bit, that serv'd to rellish Wine :
The Wine it self was suiting to the rest, 110
Still working in the Must, and lately press'd.
The Second Course succeeds like that before,
Plums, Apples, Nuts, and of their Wintry
Store,
Dry Figs, and Grapes, and wrinkl'd Dates
were set
In Canisters, t'enlarge the little Treat
All these a Milk-white Honey-comb surround,
Which in the midst the Country Banquet
crown'd :
But the kind Hosts their Entertainment
grace
With hearty Welcom, and an open Face :
In all they did, you might discern with ease,
A willing Mind, and a Desire to please. 121
   Mean time the Beechen Bowls went round,
and still,
Though often empty'd, were observ'd to fill ;
Fill'd without Hands, and of their own
accord
Ran without Feet, and danc'd about the
Board.
Devotion seiz'd the Pair, to see the Feast
With Wine, and of no common Grape, in-
creas'd ;

---

78 Feet] *The English editors absurdly give*
foot
86 thrusts] *The English editors give* thrust

98 rear] *The editors change to* rare

And up they held their Hands, and fell to
    Pray'r,
Excusing, as they cou'd, their Country Fare.
  One Goose they had, ('twas all they cou'd
    allow)   130
A wakeful Cent'ry, and on Duty now,
Whom to the Gods for Sacrifice they vow:
Her, with malicious Zeal, the Couple view'd ;
She ran for Life, and limping they pursu'd :
Full well the Fowl perceiv'd their bad
  intent,
And wou'd not make her Masters Compli-
  ment ;
But persecuted, to the Pow'rs she flies,
And close between the Legs of *Jove* she lies.
He with a gracious Ear the Suppliant heard,
And sav'd her Life ; then what he was
  declar'd,   140
And own'd the God. The Neighbourhood,
  said he,
Shall justly perish for Impiety :
You stand alone exempted ; but obey
With speed, and follow where we lead the
  way :
Leave these accurs'd ; and to the Mountains
  Height
Ascend ; nor once look backward in your
  Flight.
  They haste, and what their tardy Feet
  deny'd,
The trusty Staff (their better Leg) supply'd.
An Arrows Flight they wanted to the Top,
And there secure, but spent with Travel,
  stop ;   150
Then turn their now no more forbidden
  Eyes ;
Lost in a Lake the floated Level lies :
A Watry Desart covers all the Plains,
Their Cot alone, as in an Isle, remains :
Wondring with weeping eyes, while they
  deplore
Their Neighbours Fate, and Country now no
  more,
Their little Shed, scarce large enough for Two,
Seems, from the Ground increas'd, in Height
  and Bulk to grow.
A stately Temple shoots within the Skies :
The Crotches of their Cot in Columns
  rise :   160

The Pavement polish'd Marble they behold,
The Gates with Sculpture grac'd, the Spires
  and Tiles of Gold.
  Then thus the Sire of Gods, with Look
  serene,
Speak thy Desire, thou only Just of Men ;
And thou, O Woman, only worthy found
To be with such a Man in Marriage bound.
  A while they whisper ; then, to *Jove*
  address'd,
Philemon thus prefers their joint Request :
We crave to serve before your sacred Shrine,
And offer at your Altars Rites Divine :   170
And since not any Action of our Life
Has been polluted with Domestick Strife,
We beg one Hour of Death ; that neither she
With Widows Tears may live to bury me,
Nor weeping I, with wither'd Arms may bear
My breathless *Baucis* to the Sepulcher.
  The Godheads sign their Suit. They run
  their Race
In the same Tenor all th' appointed Space ;
Then, when their Hour was come, while they
  relate
These past Adventures at the Temple-gate,
Old *Baucis* is by old *Philemon* seen   181
Sprouting with sudden Leaves of spritely
  Green :
Old *Baucis* look'd where old *Philemon* stood,
And saw his lengthen'd Arms a sprouting
  Wood :
New Roots their fasten'd Feet begin to bind,
Their Bodies stiffen in a rising Rind :
Then e'er the Bark above their Shoulders
  grew,
They give and take at once their last Adieu ;
At once, Farewell, O faithful Spouse, they
  said ;
At once th' incroaching Rinds their closing
  Lips invade.   190
Ev'n yet, an ancient *Tyanæan* shows
A spreading Oak, that near a Linden grows :
The Neighbourhood confirm the Prodigie,
Grave Men, not vain of Tongue, or like to
  lie.
I saw my self the Garlands on their Boughs,
And Tablets hung for Gifts of granted Vows ;
And off'ring fresher up, with pious Pray'r,
The Good, said I, are God's peculiar Care,
And such as honour Heav'n, shall heav'nly
  Honour share.

---

155 weeping] *The editors absurdly give* peeping
160 Crotches] *The editors give* crotchets

163 Look] *The editors wrongly give* Looks

THE FABLE OF IPHIS AND IANTHE,

FROM THE NINTH BOOK OF OVID'S METAMORPHOSES.

THE Fame of this, perhaps, through *Crete*
    had flown ;
But *Crete* had newer Wonders of her own,
In *Iphis* chang'd ; For near the *Gnossian*
    Bounds,
(As loud Report the Miracle resounds)
At *Phæstus* dwelt a man of honest blood,⎫
But meanly born, and not so rich as good ;⎪
Esteem'd and lov'd by all the Neighbour-⎬
    hood :⎭
Who to his Wife, before the time assign'd
For Child-Birth came, thus bluntly spoke
    his mind :
If Heav'n, said *Lygdus*, will vouchsafe to⎫
    hear,   10⎪
I have but two Petitions to prefer ;   ⎬
Short Pains for thee, for me a Son and⎪
    Heir.⎭
Girls cost as many throws in bringing forth ;
Beside, when born, the Titts are little worth :
Weak puling Things, unable to sustain
Their Share of Labour, and their Bread to
    gain.
If, therefore, thou a Creature shalt produce,
Of so great Charges, and so little Use,
(Bear Witness, Heav'n, with what reluct-
    ancy)
Her hapless Innocence I doom to dye.   20
He said, and tears the common grief display,
Of him who bade, and her who must obey.
  Yet *Telethusa* still persists, to find
Fit Arguments to move a Father's mind ;
T' extend his Wishes to a larger scope,
And in one Vessel not confine his hope.
Lygdus continues hard : her time drew near,
And she her heavy load cou'd scarcely bear ;
When slumb'ring, in the latter shades of
    Night,
Before th' approaches of returning light 30
She saw, or thought she saw, before her Bed,
A glorious Train, and *Isis* at their head :
Her Moony Horns were on her Forehead
    plac'd,
And yellow Sheaves her shining Temples
    grac'd :

IPHIS AND IANTHE. Text from the original of 1693.

A Mitre for a Crown, she wore on high ;
The Dog and dappl'd Bull were waiting by ;
Osyris, sought along the Banks of *Nile* ;
The silent God ; the Sacred Crocodile ;
And, last, a long Procession moving on,
With Timbrels, that assist the lab'ring Moon.
Her slumbers seem'd dispell'd, and, broad
    awake,   41
She heard a Voice that thus distinctly spake.
My Votary, thy Babe from Death defend,
Nor fear to save whate're the Gods will send.
Delude with Art thy Husband's dire Decree ;⎫
When danger calls, repose thy trust on me ;⎬
And know thou hast not serv'd a thankless⎪
    Deity.⎭
This Promise made ; with Night the
    Goddess fled :
With Joy the Woman wakes, and leaves her
    Bed :
Devoutly lifts her spotless hands on high ; 50
And prays the Pow'rs their Gift to ratifie.
  Now grinding pains proceed to bearing
    throws,
Till its own weight the burden did disclose.
'Twas of the beauteous Kind ; and brought
    to light
With secresie, to shun the Father's sight.
Th' indulgent Mother did her Care employ ;
And pass'd it on her Husband for a Boy.
The Nurse was conscious of the Fact alone ;
The Father paid his Vows, as for a Son ;
And call'd him *Iphis*, by a common Name,
Which either Sex with equal right may
    claim.   61
Iphis his Grandsire was : the Wife was
    pleas'd,
Of half the fraud by Fortune's favour eas'd :
The doubtful Name was us'd without deceit
And Truth was cover'd with a pious Cheat.
The Habit shew'd a Boy, the beauteous Face
With manly fierceness mingled Female grace.
  Now thirteen years of Age were swiftly⎫
    run,⎪
When the fond Father thought the time⎬
    drew on⎪
Of settling in the World his only Son. 70⎭
Ianthe was his choice ; so wondrous fair,
Her Form alone with *Iphis* cou'd compare :

A Neighbour's Daughter of his own Degree,
And not more blest with Fortunes Goods
    than he.
  They soon espous'd : for they with ease
    were joyn'd,
Who were before Contracted in the Mind.
Their Age the same, their Inclinations too ;
And bred together, in one School they grew.
Thus, fatally dispos'd to mutual fires,
They felt, before they knew, the same
    desires.   80
Equal their flame, unequal was their care :
One lov'd with Hope, one languish'd in
    Despair.
The Maid accus'd the ling'ring days alone :
For whom she thought a man, she thought
    her own.
But *Iphis* bends beneath a greater grief :
As fiercely burns, but hopes for no relief.
Ev'n her Despair adds fuel to her fire ;
A Maid with madness does a Maid desire.
And, scarce refraining tears, alas ! said she,
What issue of my love remains for me ! 90
How wild a Passion works within my
    Breast,
With what prodigious Flames am I possest !
Cou'd I the Care of Providence deserve,
Heav'n must destroy me, if it wou'd pre-
    serve.
And that's my Fate, or sure it wou'd have
    sent
Some usual Evil for my punishment :
Not this unkindly Curse ; to rage and burn,
Where Nature shews no prospect of return
Nor Cows for Cows consume with fruitless
    fire :
Nor Mares, when hot, their fellow Mares
    desire :   100
The Father of the Fold supplies his Ewes ;
The Stag through secret Woods his Hind
    pursues ;
And Birds for Mates the Males of their own
    Species chuse.
Her Females Nature guards from Female
    flame ;
And joins two Sexes to preserve the Game :
Wou'd I were nothing, or not what I am !
Crete fam'd for Monsters wanted of her
    Store,
Till my new Love produc'd one Monster
    more.
The Daughter of the Sun a Bull desir'd,
And yet ev'n then a Male a Female fir'd : 110

Her Passion was extravagantly new :
But mine is much the madder of the two.
To things impossible she was not bent,
But found the Means to compass her Intent.
To cheat his Eyes, she took a different shape ;
Yet still she gain'd a Lover, and a leap.
Shou'd all the Wit of all the World conspire,
Shou'd *Dædalus* assist my wild desire,
What Art can make me able to enjoy,
Or what can change *Ianthe* to a Boy ? 120
Extinguish then thy passion, hopeless Maid,
And recollect thy Reason for thy aid.
Know what thou art, and love as Maidens
    ought ;
And drive these Golden Wishes from thy
    thought.
Thou canst not hope thy fond desires to
    gain ;
Where Hope is wanting, Wishes are in vain.
  And yet no Guards against our Joys con-
    spire ;
No jealous Husband hinders our desire :
My Parents are propitious to my Wish
And she her self consenting to the bliss. 130
All things concur to prosper our Design :
All things to prosper any Love but mine.
And yet I never can enjoy the Fair :
'Tis past the Pow'r of Heav'n to grant my
    Pray'r.
Heav'n has been kind, as far as Heav'n can
    be ;
Our Parents with our own desires agree,
But Nature, stronger than the Gods above,
Refuses her assistance to my love.
She sets the Bar, that causes all my pain :
One Gift refus'd makes all their Bounty vain.
And now the happy day is just at hand, 141
To bind our Hearts in *Hymen's* Holy Band :
Our Hearts, but not our Bodies : thus,
    accurs'd,
In midst of water I complain of thirst.
Why com'st thou, *Juno*, to these barren
    Rites,
To bless a Bed, defrauded of delights ?
And why shou'd *Hymen* lift his Torch on
    high,
To see two Brides in cold Embraces lye ?
  Thus love-sick *Iphis* her vain Passion
    mourns :
With equal Ardour fair *Ianthe* burns : 150
Invoking *Hymen's* Name, and *Juno's* Pow'r,
To speed the work, and haste the happy
    hour.

She hopes, while *Telethusa* fears the Day ;
And strives to interpose some new Delay :
Now feigns a sickness, now is in a fright
For this bad Omen, or that boding sight.
But having done whate're she cou'd devise,
And empty'd all her Magazine of lies,
The time approach'd ; the next ensuing day
The Fatal Secret must to light betray. 160
Then *Telethusa* had recourse to Pray'r,
She and her Daughter with dishevell'd hair :
Trembling with fear, great *Isis* they ador'd ;
Embrac'd her Altar, and her aid implor'd.
  Fair Queen, who dost on fruitful *Egypt* smile,
Who sway'st the Sceptre of the *Pharian* Isle,
And sev'n-fold falls of disembogueing *Nile* ;
Relieve, in this our last distress, she said,
A suppliant Mother, and a mournful Maid.
Thou, Goddess, thou wert present to my sight ; 170
Reveal'd I saw thee, by thy own fair Light :
I saw thee in my Dream, as now I see
With all thy marks of awful Majesty :
The Glorious Train, that compass'd thee around ;
And heard the hollow Timbrels holy sound.
Thy Words I noted, which I still retain ;
Let not thy Sacred Oracles be vain.
That *Iphis* lives, that I my self am free
From shame, and punishment, I owe to thee.
On thy Protection all our hopes depend : 180
Thy Counsel sav'd us, let thy Pow'r defend.
  Her Tears pursu'd her Words, and while she spoke,
The Goddess nodded, and her Altar shook :

The Temple doors, as with a blast of wind,
Were heard to clap ; the Lunar Horns, that bind
The brows of *Isis*, cast a blaze around ;
The trembling Timbrel made a murm'ring sound.
  Some hopes these happy Omens did impart ;
Forth went the Mother with a beating Heart :
Not much in Fear, nor fully satisfi'd ; 190
But *Iphis* follow'd with a larger stride :
The whiteness of her Skin forsook her Face ;
Her looks emboldn'd, with an awful Grace :
Her Features and her Strength together grew,
And her long Hair to curling Locks withdrew.
Her sparkling Eyes with Manly Vigour shone ;
Big was her Voice, Audacious was her Tone.
The latent Parts, at length reveal'd, began
To shoot, and spread, and burnish into Man.
The Maid becomes a Youth ; no more delay 200
Your Vows, but look, and confidently pay.
Their Gifts, the Parents to the Temple bear :
The Votive Tables this Inscription wear :
Iphis, the Man, has to the Goddess paid
The Vows, that *Iphis* offer'd, when a Maid.
  Now when the Star of Day had shewn his face,
Venus and *Juno* with their Presence grace
The Nuptial Rites, and *Hymen* from above
Descended to compleat their happy Love :
The Gods of Marriage lend their mutual aid ; 210
And the warm Youth enjoys the lovely Maid.

PYGMALION | AND THE | STATUE,

OUT OF THE TENTH BOOK OF | OVID'S METAMORPHOSES.

The Propætides, *for their impudent Behaviour, being turn'd into Stone by* Venus, Pygmalion, *Prince of* Cyprus, *detested all Women for their Sake, and resolv'd never to marry : He falls in love with a Statue of his own making, which is chang'd into a Maid, whom he marries. One of his Descendants is* Cinyras, *the Father of* Myrrha ; *the Daughter incestuously loves her own Father ; for which she is changed into the Tree which bears* her Name. *These two Stories immediately follow each other, and are admirably well connected.*

Pygmalion loathing their lascivious Life,
Abhorr'd all Womankind, but most a Wife :
So single chose to live, and shunn'd to wed,
Well pleas'd to want a Consort of his Bed.
Yet fearing Idleness, the Nurse of Ill,
In Sculpture exercis'd his happy Skill ;

PYGMALION AND THE STATUE. Text from the original edition of 1700.

Argument. 10 *the Tree*] *The editors give a* Tree

And carv'd in Iv'ry such a Maid, so fair,
As Nature could not with his Art compare,
Were she to work ; but in her own Defence,
Must take her Pattern here, and copy hence.
Pleas'd with his Idol, he commends, ad-
　　mires,　　　　　　　　　　　　　　　11
Adores ; and last, the Thing ador'd, desires.
A very Virgin in her Face was seen,
And had she mov'd, a living Maid had been :
One wou'd have thought she could have
　　stirr'd ; but strove
With Modesty, and was asham'd to move.
Art hid with Art, so well perform'd the
　　Cheat,
It caught the Carver with his own Deceit :
He knows 'tis Madness, yet he must adore,
And still the more he knows it, loves the
　　more :　　　　　　　　　　　　　　　20
The Flesh, or what so seems, he touches oft,
Which feels so smooth, that he believes it
　　soft.
Fir'd with this Thought, at once he strain'd
　　the Breast,
And on the Lips a burning Kiss impress'd.
'Tis true, the harden'd Breast resists the
　　Gripe,
And the cold Lips return a Kiss unripe :
But when, retiring back, he look'd agen,
To think it Iv'ry, was a thought too mean :
So wou'd believe she kiss'd, and courting
　　more,
Again embrac'd her naked Body o'er ;　　30
And straining hard the Statue, was afraid
His Hands had made a Dint, and hurt his
　　Maid :
Explor'd her, Limb by Limb, and fear'd to
　　find
So rude a Gripe had left a livid Mark
　　behind :
With Flatt'ry now he seeks her Mind to
　　move,
And now with Gifts, (the pow'rful Bribes of
　　Love :)
He furnishes her Closet first ; and fills
The crowded Shelves with Rarities of Shells ;
Adds Orient Pearls, which from the Conchs
　　he drew,
And all the sparkling Stones of various
　　Hue :　　　　　　　　　　　　　　　40
And Parrots, imitating Humane Tongue,
And Singing-birds in Silver Cages hung ;

And ev'ry fragrant Flow'r, and od'rous
　　Green,
Were sorted well, with Lumps of Amber
　　laid between :
Rich, fashionable Robes her person Deck :
Pendants her Ears, and Pearls adorn her
　　Neck :
Her taper'd Fingers too with Rings are
　　grac'd,
And an embroider'd Zone surrounds her
　　slender Waste.
Thus like a Queen array'd, so richly dress'd,
Beauteous she shew'd, but naked shew'd the
　　best.　　　　　　　　　　　　　　　50
Then, from the Floor, he rais'd a Royal
　　Bed,
With Cov'rings of *Sydonian* Purple spread :
The Solemn Rites perform'd, her calls her
　　Bride,
With Blandishments invites her to his Side,
And as she were with Vital Sense possess'd,
Her Head did on a plumy Pillow rest.
　　The Feast of *Venus* came, a Solemn Day,
To which the *Cypriots* due Devotion pay ;
With gilded Horns the Milk-white Heifers
　　led,
Slaughter'd before the sacred Altars, bled :
Pygmalion off'ring, first approach'd the
　　Shrine,　　　　　　　　　　　　　　61
And then with Pray'rs implor'd the Pow'rs
　　Divine :
Almighty Gods, if all we Mortals want,
If all we can require, be yours to grant ;
Make this fair Statue mine, he would have⎫
　　said,　　　　　　　　　　　　　　　　⎬
But chang'd his Words for shame ; and　⎥
　　only pray'd,　　　　　　　　　　　　　⎭
Give me the Likeness of my Iv'ry Maid.
　　The Golden Goddess, present at the
　　Pray'r,
Well knew he meant th' inanimated Fair,
And gave the Sign of granting his Desire ;　70
For thrice in chearful Flames ascends the
　　Fire.
The Youth, returning to his Mistress, hies,⎫
And, impudent in Hope, with ardent Eyes,⎬
And beating Breast, by the dear Statue lies.⎭
He kisses her white Lips, renews the Bliss,
And looks and thinks they redden at the
　　Kiss :
He thought them warm before : Nor longer
　　stays,
But next his Hand on her hard Bosom lays :

32 his] *The English editors wrongly give* the

Hard as it was, beginning to relent,
It seem'd, the Breast beneath his Fingers
    bent;   80
He felt again, his Fingers made a Print,
'Twas Flesh, but Flesh so firm, it rose
    against the Dint:
The pleasing Task he fails not to renew;
Soft, and more soft at ev'ry Touch it grew;
Like pliant Wax, when chafing Hands
    reduce
The former Mass to Form, and frame for Use
He would believe, but yet is still in pain,)
And tries his Argument of Sense again, |
Presses the Pulse, and feels the leaping |
    Vein.   )
Convinc'd, o'erjoy'd, his studied Thanks and
    Praise,   90
To her who made the Miracle, he pays:

Then Lips to Lips he join'd; now freed from
    Fear,
He found the Savour of the Kiss sincere:
At this the waken'd Image op'd her
    Eyes,
And view'd at once the Light and Lover,
    with surprize.
The Goddess present at the Match she
    made,
So bless'd the Bed, such Fruitfulness con-
    vey'd,
That e'er ten Moons had sharpen'd either
    Horn,
To crown their Bliss, a lovely Boy was
    born;
Paphos his Name, who, grown to Manhood,
    wall'd   100
The City *Paphos*, from the Founder call'd.

CINYRAS | AND | MYRRHA,

OUT OF THE TENTH BOOK OF | OVID'S METAMORPHOSES.

There needs no connection of this Story
with the Former: for the Beginning of This
immediately follows the End of the Last:
The Reader is only to take notice, that Orpheus,
who relates both, was by Birth a Thracian*;*
and his Country far distant from Cyprus,
where Myrrha *was born, and from* Arabia,
whither she fled. You will see the Reason of
this Note, soon after the first Lines of this
Fable.

NOR him alone produc'd the fruitful Queen;
But *Cinyras,* who like his Sire had been
A happy Prince, had he not been a Sire.
Daughters and Fathers from my Song retire;
I sing of Horrour; and could I prevail,
You shou'd not hear, or not believe my Tale.
Yet if the Pleasure of my Song be such,
That you will hear, and credit me too much,
Attentive listen to the last Event,
And with the Sin believe the Punishment:
Since Nature cou'd behold so dire a Crime, 11
I gratulate at least my Native Clime,
That such a Land, which such a Monster
    bore,
So far is distant from our *Thracian* Shore.

Let *Araby* extol her happy Coast,
Her Cinamon and sweet *Amomum* boast,
Her fragrant Flow'rs, her Trees with \
    precious Tears, |
Her second Harvests, and her double |
    Years; |
How can the Land be call'd so bless'd that |
    Myrrha bears?   /
Not all her od'rous Tears can cleanse her
    Crime,   20
Her Plant alone deforms the happy Clime:
Cupid denies to have inflam'd thy Heart,
Disowns thy Love, and vindicates his Dart
Some Fury gave thee those infernal Pains,
And shot her venom'd Vipers in thy Veins.
To hate thy Sire, had merited a Curse;
But such an impious Love deserv'd a worse.
The Neighb'ring Monarchs, by thy Beauty led,
Contend in Crowds, ambitious of thy Bed:
The World is at thy Choice, except but
    one,   30
Except but him thou canst not chuse alone.
She knew it too, the miserable Maid,   \
E'er impious Love her better Thoughts |
    betray'd, |
And thus within her secret Soul she said:/

PYGMALION AND THE STATUE. 86 for] *The*
English editors wrongly give to

CINYRAS AND MYRRHA. Text from the
original edition of 1700.

Ah *Myrrha*! whither wou'd thy Wishes
  tend ?
Ye Gods, ye sacred Laws, my Soul defend
From such a Crime, as all Mankind detest,
And never lodg'd before in Humane Breast !
But is it Sin ? Or makes my Mind alone
Th' imagin d Sin ? For Nature makes it
  none. 40
What Tyrant then these envious Laws began,
Made not for any other Beast, but Man !
The Father-Bull his Daughter may bestride,
The Horse may make his Mother-Mare
  a Bride ;
What Piety forbids the lusty Ram,
Or more salacious Goat, to rut their Dam ?
The Hen is free to wed her Chick she bore,
And make a Husband, whom she hatch'd
  before.
All Creatures else are of a happier Kind,
Whom nor ill-natur'd Laws from Pleasure
  bind, 50
Nor Thoughts of Sin disturb their Peace
  of Mind.
But Man, a Slave of his own making lives :
The Fool denies himself what Nature gives :
Too busie Senates, with an over-care
To make us better than our Kind can bear,
Have dash'd a Spice of Envy in the Laws,
And straining up too high, have spoil'd the
  Cause.
Yet some wise Nations break their cruel
  Chains,
And own no Laws, but those which Love
  ordains :
Where happy Daughters with their Sires are
  join'd, 60
And Piety is doubly paid in Kind.
O that I had been born in such a Clime,
Not here, where 'tis the Country makes the
  Crime !
But whither wou'd my impious Fancy
  stray ?
Hence Hopes, and ye forbidden Thoughts
  away !
His Worth deserves to kindle my Desires,
But with the Love, that Daughters bear to
  Sires.
Then had not *Cinyras* my Father been,
What hinder'd *Myrrha's* Hopes to be his
  Queen ?
But the Perverseness of my Fate is such, 70
That he's not mine, because he's mine too
  much :

Our Kindred-Blood debars a better Tie ;
He might be nearer, were he not so nigh.
Eyes and their Objects never must unite,
Some Distance is requir'd to help the Sight :
Fain wou'd I travel to some Foreign Shore,
Never to see my Native Country more,
So might I to my self my self restore ;
So might my Mind these impious Thoughts
  remove,
And ceasing to behold, might cease to
  love. 80
But stay I must, to feed my famish'd Sight,
To talk, to kiss ; and more, if more I might :
More, impious Maid ! What more canst
  thou design,
To make a monstrous Mixture in thy Line,
And break all Statutes Humane and Divine?
Canst thou be call'd (to save thy wretched
  Life)
Thy Mother's Rival, and thy Father's Wife ?
Confound so many sacred Names in one,
Thy Brother's Mother, Sister to thy Son !
And fear'st thou not to see th' Infernal
  Bands, 90
Their Heads with Snakes, with Torches
  arm'd their Hands,
Full at thy Face th' avenging Brands to bear,
And shake the Serpents from their hissing
  Hair ?
But thou in time th' increasing Ill controul,
Nor first debauch the Body by the Soul ;
Secure the sacred Quiet of thy Mind,
And keep the Sanctions Nature has design'd.
Suppose I shou'd attempt, th' Attempt were
  vain ;
No Thoughts like mine his sinless Soul pro-
  fane :
Observant of the Right ; and O, that he 100
Cou'd cure my Madness, or be mad like me !
  Thus she : But *Cinyras*, who daily sees
A Crowd of Noble Suitors at his Knees,
Among so many, knew not whom to chuse,
Irresolute to grant, or to refuse.
But having told their Names, enquir'd of her,
Who pleas'd her best, and whom she would
  prefer ?
The blushing Maid stood silent with Sur-
  prize,
And on her Father fix'd her ardent Eyes,
And looking sigh'd ; and as she sigh'd,
  began 110
Round Tears to shed, that scalded as they
  ran.

The tender Sire, who saw her blush, and cry,
Ascrib'd it all to Maiden-modesty ;
And dry'd the falling Drops, and yet more kind,
He strok'd her Cheeks, and holy Kisses join'd :
She felt a secret Venom fire her Blood,
And found more Pleasure than a Daughter shou'd ;
And, ask'd again, what Lover of the Crew
She lik'd the best ; she answer'd, One like you.   119
Mistaking what she meant, her pious Will
He prais'd, and bad her so continue still :
The Word of Pious heard, she blush'd with shame
Of secret Guilt, and cou'd not bear the Name.
'Twas now the mid of Night, when Slumbers close
Our Eyes, and sooth our Cares with soft Repose ;
But no Repose cou'd wretched *Myrrha* find,
Her Body rouling, as she rould her Mind :
Mad with Desire, she ruminates her Sin,
And wishes all her Wishes o'er again :
Now she despairs, and now resolves to try ;
Wou'd not, and wou'd again, she knows not why ;   131
Stops and returns, makes and retracts the Vow ;
Fain wou'd begin, but understands not how :
As when a Pine is hew'd upon the Plains,
And the last mortal Stroke alone remains,
Lab'ring in Pangs of Death, and threatning all,
This way, and that she nods, consid'ring where to fall :
So *Myrrha's* Mind, impell'd on either Side,
Takes ev'ry Bent, but cannot long abide :
Irresolute on which she shou'd relie,   140
At last unfix'd in all, is only fix'd to die ;
On that sad Thought she rests ; resolv'd on Death,
She rises, and prepares to choak her Breath :
Then while about the Beam her Zone she ties,
Dear *Cinyras*, farewell, she softly cries ;
For thee I die, and only wish to be
Not hated, when thou know'st I die for thee :
Pardon the Crime, in pity to the Cause :
This said, about her Neck the Noose she draws.

The Nurse, who lay without, her faithful Guard,   150
Though not the Words, the Murmurs over heard,
And Sighs, and hollow Sounds : Surpriz'd with Fright,
She starts, and leaves her Bed, and springs a Light ;
Unlocks the Door, and entring out of Breath,
The Dying saw, and Instruments of Death ;
She shrieks, she cuts the Zone, with trembling haste,
And in her Arms her fainting Charge embrac'd :
Next, (for she now had leisure for her Tears)
She weeping ask'd, in these her blooming Years,   159
What unforeseen Misfortune caus'd her Care,
To loath her Life, and languish in Despair !
The Maid, with down-cast Eyes, and mute with Grief,
For Death unfinish'd, and ill-tim'd Relief,
Stood sullen to her Suit : The Beldame press'd
The more to know, and har'd her wither'd Breast ;
Adjur'd her, by the kindly Food she drew
From those dry Founts, her secret Ill to shew.
Sad *Myrrha* sigh'd, and turn'd her Eyes aside :
The Nurse still urg'd, and wou'd not be deny'd :
Nor only promis'd Secresie ; but pray'd   170
She might have leave to give her offer'd Aid.
Good-will, she said, my want of Strength supplies,
And Diligence shall give, what Age denies :
If strong Desires thy Mind to Fury move,
With Charms and Med'cines I can cure thy Love :
If Envious eyes their hurtful Rays have cast,
More pow'rful Verse shall free thee from the Blast :
If Heav'd offended sends thee this Disease,
Offended Heav'n with Pray'rs we can appease.
What then remains, that can these Cares procure ?   180
Thy House is flourishing, thy Fortune sure :
Thy careful Mother yet in Health survives,
And, to thy Comfort, thy kind Father lives.

The Virgin started at her Father's Name,
And sigh'd profoundly, conscious of the Shame:
Nor yet the Nurse her impious Love divin'd;
But yet surmis'd, that Love disturb'd her Mind:
Thus thinking, she pursu'd her Point, and laid
And lull'd within her Lap the mourning Maid;
Then softly sooth'd her thus, I guess your Grief: 190
You love, my Child; your Love shall find Relief.
My long-experienc'd Age shall be your Guide;
Rely on that, and lay Distrust aside:
No Breath of Air shall on the Secret blow,
Nor shall (what most you fear) your Father know.
Struck once again, as with a Thunder-clap,
The guilty Virgin bounded from her Lap,
And threw her Body prostrate on the Bed,
And, to conceal her Blushes, hid her Head:
There silent lay, and warn'd her with her Hand   200
To go: But she receiv'd not the Command;
Remaining still importunate to know:
Then *Myrrha* thus; Or ask no more, or go:
I prethee go, or staying spare my Shame;
What thou wou'dst hear, is impious ev'n to name.
At this, on high the Beldame holds her Hands,
And trembling, both with Age and Terrour, stands;
Adjures, and falling at her Feet intreats,
Sooths her with Blandishments, and frights with Threats,
To tell the Crime intended, or disclose   210
What Part of it she knew, if she no farther knows:
And last, if conscious to her Counsel made,
Confirms anew the Promise of her Aid.
Now *Myrrha* rais'd her Head; but soon oppress'd
With Shame, reclin'd it on her Nurses Breast;
Bath'd it with Tears, and strove to have confess'd:
Twice she began, and stopp'd; again she try'd;
The falt'ring Tongue its Office still deny'd:

At last her Veil before her Face she spread,
And drew a long preluding Sigh, and said,
O happy mother, in thy Marriage-bed! 221
Then groan'd and ceas'd; the good Old Woman shook,
Stiff were her Eyes, and ghastly was her Look:
Her hoary Hair upright with Horrour stood,
Made (to her Grief) more knowing than she wou'd:
Much she reproach'd and many Things she said,
To cure the Madness of th' unhappy Maid:
In vain: For *Myrrha* stood convict of Ill;
Her Reason vanquish'd, but unchang'd her Will:
Perverse of Mind, unable to reply,   230
She stood resolv'd or to possess, or die.
At length the Fondness of a Nurse prevail'd
Against her better Sense, and Vertue fail'd:
Enjoy, my Child, since such is thy Desire,
Thy Love, she said; she durst not say, thy Sire.
Live, though unhappy, live on any Terms:
Then with a second Oath her Faith confirms.
    The Solemn Feast of *Ceres* now was near,
When long white Linen Stoles the Matrons wear;
Rank'd in Procession walk the pious Train,
Off'ring First-fruits, and Spikes of yellow Grain: 241
For nine long Nights the Nuptial-bed they shun,
And, sanctifying Harvest, lie alone.
    Mix'd with the Crowd, the Queen forsook her Lord,
And *Ceres* Pow'r with secret Rites ador'd:
The Royal Couch now vacant for a time,
The crafty Crone, officious in her Crime,
The curst Occasion took: The King she found
Easie with Wine, and deep in Pleasures drown'd,
Prepar'd for Love: The Beldame blew the Flame,   250
Confess'd the Passion, but conceal'd the Name.
Her Form she prais'd; the Monarch ask'd her Years,
And she reply'd, The same thy *Myrrha* bears.

---

249 Pleasures] *Some editors wrongly give* Pleasure

Wine and commended Beauty fir'd his
Thought ;
Impatient, he commands her to be brought.
Pleas'd with her Charge perform'd, she hies
her home,
And gratulates the Nymph, the Task was
overcome.
Myrrha was joy'd the welcom News to hear ;
But clogg'd with Guilt, the Joy was un-
sincere :
So various, so discordant is the Mind,   260
That in our Will, a diff'rent Will we find.
Ill she presag'd, and yet pursu'd her Lust ;
For guilty Pleasures give a double Gust.
'Twas Depth of Night : *Arctophylax* had
driv'n
His lazy Wain half round the Northern
Heav'n,
When *Myrrha* hasten'd to the Crime desir'd ;
The Moon beheld her first, and first retir'd :
The Stars amaz'd, ran backward from the
Sight,
And (shrunk within their Sockets) lost their
Light.
Icarius first withdraws his holy Flame : 270
The Virgin Sign, in Heav'n the second
Name,
Slides down the Belt, and from her Station
flies,
And Night with Sable Clouds involves the
Skies.
Bold *Myrrha* still pursues her black Intent: ⎫
She stumbl'd thrice (an Omen of th'Event); ⎬
Thrice shriek'd the Fun'ral Owl, yet on she ⎭
went,
Secure of Shame, because secure of Sight ;
Ev'n bashful Sins are impudent by Night.
Link'd Hand in Hand, th' Accomplice and
the Dame,
Their Way exploring, to the Chamber
came :   280
The Door was ope, they blindly grope their
Way,
Where dark in Bed th' expecting Monarch
lay :
Thus far her Courage held, but here for-
sakes ;
Her faint Knees knock at ev'ry Step she
makes.
The nearer to her Crime, the more within
She feels Remorse, and Horrour of her Sin ;

Repents too late her criminal Desire,
And wishes, that unknown she cou'd retire.
Her, lingring thus, the Nurse (who fear'd
Delay
The fatal Secret might at length betray) 290
Pull'd forward, to compleat the Work
begun,
And said to *Cinyras*, Receive thy own :
Thus saying, she deliver'd Kind to Kind,
Accurs'd, and their devoted Bodies join'd.
The Sire, unknowing of the Crime, admits
His Bowels, and profanes the hallow'd
Sheets.
He found she trembl'd, but believ'd she ⎫
strove,   ⎬
With Maiden-Modesty, against her Love, ⎬
And sought with flatt'ring Words vain ⎭
Fancies to remove.
Perhaps he said, My Daughter, cease thy
Fears,   300
(Because the Title suited with her Years ;)
And, Father, she might whisper him agen,
That Names might not be wanting to the
Sin.
Full of her Sire, she left th' incestuous Bed,
And carry'd in her Womb the Crime she
bred :
Another, and another Night she came ;
For frequent Sin had left no Sense of Shame :
Till *Cinyras* desir'd to see her Face,
Whose Body he had held in close Embrace,
And brought a Taper ; the Revealer,
Light,   310
Expos'd both Crime, and Criminal to Sight :
Grief, Rage, Amazement, cou'd no Speech
afford,
But from the Sheath he drew th' avenging
Sword ;
The Guilty fled : The Benefit of Night,
That favour'd first the Sin, secur'd the
Flight.
Long wandring through the spacious Fields,
she bent
Her Voyage to th' *Arabian* Continent ;
Then pass'd the Region which *Panchæa*
join'd,
And flying, left the Palmy Plains behind.
Nine times the Moon had mew'd her Horns ;
at length   320
With Travel weary, unsupply'd with
Strength,
And with the Burden of her Womb oppress'd,
Sabæan Fields afford her needful Rest :

There, loathing Life, and yet of Death
afraid,
In Anguish of her Spirit, thus she pray'd.
Ye Pow'rs, if any so propitious are
T' accept my Penitence, and hear my
Pray'r,
Your Judgments, I confess, are justly sent ;
Great Sins deserve as great a Punishment :
Yet since my Life the Living will pro-
fane,   330
And since my Death the happy Dead will
stain,
A middle State your Mercy may bestow,
Betwixt the Realms above, and those below :
Some other Form to wretched *Myrrha*
give,
Nor let her wholly die, nor wholly live.
The Pray'rs of Penitents are never vain ;
At least, she did her last Request obtain ;
For while she spoke, the Ground began to
rise,
And gather'd round her Feet, her Leggs,
and Thighs ;
Her Toes in Roots descend, and spreading
wide,   340
A firm Foundation for the Trunk provide :
Her solid Bones convert to solid Wood,
To Pith her Marrow, and to Sap her
Blood :
Her Arms are Boughs, her Fingers change
their Kind,
Her tender Skin is harden'd into Rind.
And now the rising Tree her Womb invests,
Now, shooting upwards still, invades her
Breasts,
And shades the Neck ; when, weary with
Delay,
She sunk her Head within, and met it half
the Way.
And though with outward Shape she lost
her Sense,   350
With bitter Tears she wept her last Offence ;
And still she weeps, nor sheds her Tears in
vain ;
For still the precious Drops her Name
retain.
Meantime the mis-begotten Infant grows,
And, ripe for Birth, distends with deadly
Throws

The swelling Rind, with unavailing Strife,
To leave the wooden Womb, and pushes
into Life.
The Mother-Tree, as if oppress'd with
Pain,
Writhes here and there, to break the Bark,
in vain ;
And, like a Lab'ring Woman, wou'd have
pray'd,   360
But wants a Voice to call *Lucina's* Aid :
The bending Bole sends out a hollow Sound,
And trickling Tears fall thicker on the
Ground.
The mild *Lucina* came uncall'd, and stood
Beside the struggling Boughs, and heard
the groaning Wood :
Then reach'd her Midwife-Hand, to speed the
Throws,
And spoke the pow'rful Spells that Babes to
Birth disclose.
The Bark divides, the living Load to free,
And safe delivers the Convulsive Tree.
The ready Nymphs receive the crying Child,
And wash him in the Tears the Parent-
Plant distill'd.   371
They swath'd him with their Scarfs; beneath
him spread
The Ground with Herbs ; with Roses
rais'd his Head.
The lovely Babe was born with ev'ry Grace :
Ev'n Envy must have prais'd so fair a Face :
Such was his Form, as Painters when they
show
Their utmost Art, on naked Loves bestow :
And that their Arms no Diff'rence might
betray,
Give him a Bow, or his from *Cupid* take
away.   379
Time glides along, with undiscover'd haste,
The Future but a Length behind the past :
So swift are Years : The Babe, whom just
before
His Grandsire got, and whom his Sister bore ;
The Drop, the Thing which late the Tree
inclos'd,
And late the yawning Bark to Life expos'd ;
A Babe, a Boy, a beauteous Youth appears ;
And lovelier than himself at riper Years.
Now to the Queen of Love he gave Desires,
And, with her Pains, reveng'd his Mother's
Fires.

---

348 when] *The English editors wrongly give* and

CEYX | AND | ALCYONE,

OUT OF THE ELEVENTH BOOK OF OVID'S METAMORPHOSES.

CONNEXION OF THIS FABLE WITH
THE FORMER.

Ceyx, *the Son of* Lucifer, (*the Morning
Star*) *and King of* Trachin *in* Thessaly, *was
married to* Alcyone, *Daughter to* Æolus,
*God of the Winds. Both the Husband and
the Wife lov'd each other with an entire
Affection.* Dœdalion, *the Elder Brother of*
Ceyx (*whom he succeeded*) *having been
turn'd into a Falcon by* Apollo, *and* Chione,
Dædalion's *Daughter, slain by* Diana, Ceyx
prepares a Ship to sail to Claros, *there to
consult the Oracle of* Apollo, *and* (*as* Ovid
seems to intimate) *to enquire how the Anger
of the Gods might be atton'd.*

THESE Prodigies affect the pious Prince,
But more perplex'd with those that happen'd
   since,
He purposes to seek the *Clarian* God,   ⎫
Avoiding *Delphos*, his more fam'd Abode ;   ⎬
Since *Phlegyan* Robbers made unsafe the   ⎭
   Road.
Yet cou'd not he from her he lov'd so well,
The fatal Voyage, he resolv'd, conceal :
But when she saw her Lord prepar'd to part,
A deadly Cold ran shiv'ring to her Heart :
Her faded Cheeks are chang'd to Boxen Hue,
And in her Eyes the Tears are ever new : 11
She thrice assay'd to Speak ; her Accents
   hung,
And faltring dy'd unfinish'd on her Tongue,
Or vanish'd into Sighs : With long delay
Her Voice return'd ; and found the wonted
   way.
   Tell me, my Lord, she said, what Fault ⎫
      unknown   ⎪
Thy once belov'd *Alcyone* has done ?   ⎬
Whether, ah whether is thy Kindness gone! ⎭
Can *Ceyx* then sustain to leave his Wife,
And unconcern'd forsake the Sweets of Life ?
What can thy Mind to this long Journey
   move,   21
Or need'st thou absence to renew thy Love ?

Yet, if thou go'st by Land, tho' Grief possess
My Soul ev'n then, my Fears will be the less.
But ah ! be warn'd to shun the Watry Way,
The Face is frightful of the stormy Sea.
For late I saw a-drift disjointed Planks,
And empty Tombs erected on the Banks.
Nor let false Hopes to trust betray thy Mind,
Because my Sire in Caves constrains the Wind,
Can with a Breath their clam'rous Rage
   appease,
They fear his Whistle, and forsake the Seas ;
Not so, for, once indulg'd, they sweep the
   Main,
Deaf to the Call, or, hearing hear in vain :
But bent on Mischief bear the Waves before,
And not content with Seas insult the Shoar,
When Ocean, Air, and Earth, at once
   ingage,
And rooted Forrests fly before their Rage :
At once the clashing Clouds to Battle move,
And Lightnings run across the Fields above :
I know them well, and mark'd their rude
   Comport,   41
While yet a Child, within my Father's Court :
In times of Tempest they command alone,
And he but sits precarious on the Throne :
The more I know, the more my Fears
   augment,
And Fears are oft prophetick of th' Event.
But if not Fears, or Reasons will prevail,
If Fate has fix'd thee obstinate to sail,
Go not without thy Wife, but let me bear ⎫
My part of Danger with an equal share, 50 ⎬
And present, what I suffer only fear :   ⎭
Then o'er the bounding Billows shall we fly,
Secure to live together, or to die.
   These Reasons mov'd her starlike Hus-
      band's Heart,
But still he held his Purpose to depart :
For as he lov'd her equal to his Life,
He wou'd not to the Seas expose his Wife ;
Nor cou'd be wrought his Voyage to refrain,
But sought by Arguments to sooth **her** Pain ;

---

18 Whether . . . whether] *The editors print*
Whither . . . whither
51 what I suffer only fear] *Some editors alter
to* suffer what I only fear *improving the sense.*

Nor these avail'd ; at length he lights on
   one,   60
With which, so difficult a Cause he won :
My Love, so short an absence cease to fear,
For, by my Father's holy Flame, I swear,
Before two Moons their Orb with Light
   adorn,
If Heav'n allow me Life, I will return.
   This Promise of so short a stay prevails :
He soon equips the Ship, supplies the Sails,
And gives the Word to launch ; she trem-
   bling views
This pomp of Death, and parting Tears
   renews :
Last, with a Kiss, she took a long farewel, 70
Sigh'd, with a sad Presage, and swooning
   fell.
While *Ceyx* seeks Delays, the lusty Crew,
Rais'd on their Banks, their Oars in order
   drew
To their broad Breasts, the Ship with fury
   flew.
   The Queen recover'd rears her humid
   Eyes,
And first her Husband on the Poop espies
Shaking his Hand at distance on the Main ;
She took the Sign ; and shook her Hand
   again.
Still as the Ground recedes, contracts her
   View
With sharpen'd Sight, till she no longer
   knew   80
The much-lov'd Face ; that Comfort lost
   supplies
With less, and with the Galley feeds her
   Eyes ;
The Galley born from view by rising Gales,
She follow'd with her Sight the flying Sails :
When ev'n the flying Sails were seen no
   more,
Forsaken of all Sight, she left the Shoar.
   Then on her Bridal-Bed her Body
   throws,
And sought in Sleep her weary'd Eyes to
   close.
Her Husband's Pillow, and the Widow'd
   part
Which once he press'd, renew'd the former
   Smart.   90

79 contracts] *The English editors wrongly
give* retracts *and Saintsbury even annotates the
false reading.*

And now a Breeze from Shoar began to
   blow,
The Sailors ship their Oars, and cease to
   row ;
Then hoist their Yards a-trip, and all their
   Sails
Let fall, to court the Wind, and catch the
   Gales :
By this the Vessel half her Course had run,
And as much rested till the rising Sun ;
Both Shores were lost to Sight, when at the
   close
Of Day, a stiffer Gale at East arose :
The Sea grew White, the rowling Waves
   from far   99
Like Heralds first denounce the Watry War.
   This seen, the Master soon began to cry,
Strike, strike the Top-sail ; let the Main-
   sheet fly,
And furl your Sails : The Winds repel the
   sound
And in the Speaker's Mouth the Speech is
   drown'd.
Yet of their own accord, as Danger taught,
Each in his way, officiously they wrought ;
Some stow their Oars, or stop the leaky
   Sides,
Another bolder yet the Yard bestrides,
And folds the Sails ; a fourth with Labour,
   laves
Th' intruding Seas, and Waves ejects on
   Waves.   110
   In this Confusion while their Work they
   ply,
The Winds augment the Winter of the Sky,
And wage intestine Wars ; the suff'ring Seas
Are toss'd, and mingled as their Tyrants
   please.
The Master wou'd command, but in despair
Of Safety, stands amaz'd with stupid Care,
Nor what to bid, or what forbid he knows,
Th' ungovern'd Tempest to such Fury grows:
Vain is his Force, and vainer is his Skill ;
With such a Concourse comes the Flood of
   Ill :   120
The Cries of Men are mix'd with rattling
   Shrowds ;
Seas dash on Seas, and Clouds encounter
   Clouds :
At once from East to West, from Pole to
   Pole,
The forky Lightnings flash, the roaring
   Thunders roul.

Now Waves on Waves ascending scale
    the Skies,
And in the Fires above, the Water fries :
When yellow Sands are sifted from below,
The glitt'ring Billows give a golden Show :
And when the fouler bottom spews the
    Black,   129
The *Stygian* Dye the tainted Waters take :
Then frothy White appear the flatted Seas,
And change their Colour, changing their
    Disease.
Like various Fits the *Trachin* Vessel finds,
And now sublime, she rides upon the Winds;
As from a lofty Summet looks from high,
And from the Clouds beholds the neather
    Sky ;
Now from the depth of Hell they lift their
    Sight,
And at a distance see superiour Light :
The lashing Billows make a loud report,
And beat her Sides, as batt'ring Rams,
    a Fort :   140
Or as a Lyon, bounding in his way,
With Force augumented bears against his
    Prey,
Sidelong to seize ; or unappal'd with Fear
Springs on the Toils, and rushes on the Spear :
So Seas impell'd by Winds with added Pow'r
Assault the Sides, and o'er the Hatches tow'r.
    The Planks (their pitchy Cov'ring wash'd
        away)
Now yield ; and now a yawning Breach
    display :
The roaring Waters with a hostile Tide
Rush through the Ruins of her gaping Side.
Mean time in Sheets of Rain the Sky
    descends,   151
And Ocean swell'd with Waters upwards
    tends,
One rising, falling one, the Heav'ns, and Sea
Meet at their Confines, in the middle Way :
The Sails are drunk with Show'rs, and drop
    with Rain,
Sweet Waters mingle with the briny Main.
No Star appears to lend his friendly Light :
Darkness and Tempest make a double Night.
But flashing Fires disclose the Deep by
    turns,
And while the Light'nings blaze, the Water
    burns.   160

Now all the Waves their scatter'd Force
    unite,
And as a Soldier, foremost in the Fight,
Makes way for others : And an Host alone,
Still presses on, and urging gains the Town ;
So while th' invading Billows come a-brest,
The Hero tenth advanc'd before the rest,
Sweeps all before him with impetuous Sway,
And from the Walls descends upon the Prey ;
Part following enter, part remain without,
With Envy hear their Fellows conqu'ring
    Shout,   170
And mount on others Backs, in Hope to
    share
The City, thus become the Seat of War.
    An universal Cry resounds aloud,
The Sailors run in Heaps, a helpless Crowd ;
Art fails, and Courage falls, no Succour near ;
As many Waves, as many Deaths appear.
    One weeps, and yet despairs of late Relief ;
One cannot weep, his Fears congeal his
    Grief,
But stupid, with dry Eyes expects his Fate. ⎫
One with loud Shrieks laments his lost ⎪
    Estate,   180 ⎬
And calls those happy whom their Funerals ⎪
    wait.   ⎭
This Wretch with Pray'rs and Vows the
    Gods implores,
And ev'n the Sky's he cannot see, adores.
That other on his Friends his Thoughts
    bestows,
His careful Father, and his faithful Spouse.
The covetous Worlding in his anxious Mind
Thinks only on the Wealth he left behind.
    All *Ceyx* his *Alcyone* employs,
For her he grieves, yet in her absence joys :
His Wife he wishes, and wou'd still be
    near,   190
Not her with him, but wishes him with
    her :
Now with last Looks he seeks his Native
    Shoar,
Which Fate has destin'd him to see no more :
He sought, but in the dark tempestuous
    Night
He knew not whither to direct his Sight.
So whirl the Seas, such Darkness blinds the
    Sky,
That the black Night receives a deeper Dye.
    The giddy Ship ran round ; the Tempest
        tore
Her Mast, and over-board the Rudder bore

---

147 Cov'ring] *The English editors give* cover-
ings

One Billow mounts ; and with a scornful
   Brow   200
Proud of her Conquest gain'd insults the
   Waves below ;
Nor lighter falls, than if some Gyant tore
Pindus and *Athos*, with the Freight they
   bore,
And toss'd on Seas : press'd with the pon-
   drous Blow
Down sinks the Ship within th' Abyss below
Down with the Vessel sink into the Main
The many, never more to rise again.
Some few on scatter'd Planks with fruitless
   Care
Lay hold, and swim, but while they swim,
   despair.   209
   Ev'n he who late a Scepter did command
Now grasps a floating Fragment in his Hand,
And while he struggles on the stormy Main,
Invokes his Father, and his Wife's, in vain ;
But yet his Consort is his greater Care ;
Alcyone he names amidst his Pray'r,
Names as a Charm against the Waves, and
   Wind ;
Most in his Mouth, and ever in his Mind :
Tir'd with his Toyl, all hopes of Safety past,
From Pray'rs to Wishes he descends at last :
That his dead Body, wafted to the Sands,
Might have its Burial from her Friendly
   Hands.   221
As oft as he can catch a gulp of Air,
And peep above the Seas, he names the Fair ;
And ev'n when plung'd beneath, on her he
   raves,
Murm'ring *Alcyone* below the Waves :
At last a falling Billow stops his Breath,
Breaks o'er his Head, and whelms him under-
   neath.
Bright *Lucifer* unlike himself appears
That Night, his heav'nly Form obscur'd
   with Tears,
And since he was forbid to leave the Skies,
He muffled with a Cloud his mournful
   Eyes.   231
   Mean time *Alcyone* (his Fate unknown)
Computes how many Nights he had been
   gone,
Observes the waning Moon with hourly
   View,
Numbers her Age, and wishes for a new ;

Against the promis'd Time provides with
   care,
And hastens in the Woof the Robes he was
   to wear :
And for her Self employs another Loom,
New-dress'd to meet her Lord returning
   home,
Flatt'ring her Heart with Joys that never
   were to come :   240
She fum'd the Temples with an odrous
   Flame,
And oft before the sacred Altars came,
To pray for him, who was an empty Name
All Pow'rs implor'd, but far above the rest
To *Juno* she her pious Vows address'd,
Her much-lov'd Lord from Perils to protect
And safe o'er Seas his Voyage to direct :
Then pray'd that she might still possess his
   Heart,
And no pretending Rival share a part ;
This last Petition heard of all her Pray'r,   250
The rest dispers'd by Winds were lost in Air.
   But she, the Goddess of the Nuptial-Bed,
Tir'd with her vain Devotions for the Dead,
Resolv'd the tainted Hand should be
   repell'd,
Which Incense offer'd, and her Altar held :
Then *Iris* thus bespoke : Thou faithful Maid,
By whom thy Queen's Commands are well
   convey'd,
Haste to the House of Sleep, and bid the God
Who rules the Night by Visions with a Nod,
Prepare a Dream, in Figure and in Form   260
Resembling him who perish'd in the Storm :
This form before *Alcyone* present,
To make her certain of the sad Event.
   Indu'd with Robes of various Hew she
   flies,
And flying draws an Arch, (a segment of the
   Skies :)
Then leaves her bending Bow, and from the
   Steep
Descends to search the silent House of
   Sleep.
   Near the *Cymmerians*, in his dark Abode
Deep in a Cavern, dwells the drowzy God ;
Whose gloomy Mansion nor the rising
   Sun   270
Nor setting, visits, nor the lightsome Noon :
But lazy Vapors round the Region fly,
Perpetual Twilight, and a doubtful Sky ;

No crowing Cock does there his Wings
display,
Nor with his horny Bill provoke the Day :
Nor watchful Dogs, nor the more wakeful
Geese,
Disturb with nightly Noise the sacred Peace :
Nor Beast of Nature, nor the Tame are nigh,
Nor Trees with Tempests rock'd, nor human
Cry ;
But safe Repose without an Air of Breath
Dwells here, and a dumb Quiet next to
Death.   281
An Arm of *Lethe* with a gentle Flow
Arising upwards from the Rock below,
The Palace moats, and o'er the Pebbles
creeps,
And with soft Murmers calls the coming
Sleeps ;
Around its Entry nodding Poppies grow,
And all cool Simples that sweet Rest bestow ;
Night from the Plants their sleepy Virtue
drains,
And passing, sheds it on the silent Plains :
No Door there was th' unguarded House
to keep,   290
On creaking Hinges turn'd, to break his
Sleep.
  But in the gloomy Court was rais'd a Bed,
Stuff'd with black Plumes, and on an Ebon-
sted :
Black was the Cov'ring too, where lay the
God
And slept supine, his Limbs display'd
abroad :
About his Head fantastick Visions fly,
Which various Images of Things supply,
And mock their Forms, the Leaves on Trees
not more,
Nor bearded Ears in Fields, nor Sands upon
the Shore.
  The Virgin entring bright indulg'd the
Day   300
To the brown Cave, and brush'd the Dreams
away :
The God disturb'd with this new Glare of
Light
Cast sudden on his Face, unseal'd his Sight,
And rais'd his tardy Head, which sunk agen,
And sinking on his Bosom knock'd his Chin :
At length shook off himself ; and ask'd the
Dame,
(And asking yawn'd) for what intent she
came ?

To whom the Goddess thus : O sacred
Rest,
Sweet pleasing Sleep, of all the Pow'rs the
best !
O Peace of Mind, repairer of Decay,   310
Whose Balms renew the Limbs to Labours
of the Day,
Care shuns thy soft approach, and sullen
flies away !
Adorn a Dream, expressing human Form,
The Shape of him who suffer'd in the
Storm,
And send it flitting to the *Trachin* Court,
The Wreck of wretched *Ceyx* to report :
Before his Queen bid the pale Spectre
stand,
Who begs a vain Relief at *Juno's* Hand.
She said, and scarce awake her Eyes cou'd
keep,
Unable to support the Fumes of Sleep : 320
But fled returning by the way she went,
And swerv'd along her Bow with swift
ascent.
  The God uneasy till he slept again
Resolv'd at once to rid himself of Pain ;
And tho' against his Custom, call'd aloud,
Exciting *Morpheus* from the sleepy Crowd :
Morpheus of all his numerous Train ex-
press'd
The Shape of Man, and imitated best ;
The Walk, the Words, the Gesture cou'd
supply,
The Habit mimick, and the Mien bely ; 330
Plays well, but all his Action is confin'd ;
Extending not beyond our human kind.
Another Birds, and Beasts, and Dragons
apes,
And dreadful Images, and Monster shapes :
This Demon, *Icelos*, in Heav'ns high Hall
The Gods have nam'd ; but men *Phobetor*
call :
A third is *Phantasus*, whose Actions roul
On meaner Thoughts, and Things devoid
of Soul ;
Earth, Fruits and Flow'rs, he represents in
Dreams,
And solid Rocks unmov'd, and running
Streams :   340
These three to Kings, and Chiefs their Scenes
display,
The rest before th' ignoble Commons play :
Of these the chosen *Morpheus* is dispatch'd,
Which done, the lazy Monarch overwatch'd,

Down from his propping Elbow drops his
    Head,
Dissolv'd in Sleep, and shrinks within his
    Bed.
  Darkling the Demon glides for Flight
    prepar'd,
So soft that scarce his fanning Wings are
    heard.
To *Trachin*, swift as Thought, the flitting
    Shade   349
Through Air his momentary Journey made:
Then lays aside the steerage of his Wings,
Forsakes his proper Form, assumes the
    King's ;
And pale as Death despoil'd of his Array)
Into the Queen's Apartment takes his way, }
And stands before the Bed at dawn of Day:)
Unmov'd his Eyes, and wet his Beard
    appears ;
And shedding vain, but seeming real Tears;
The briny Water dropping from his Hairs ;
Then staring on her, with a ghastly Look
And hollow Voice, he thus the Queen be-
    spoke.   360
  Know'st thou not me ? Not yet unhappy
    Wife ?
Or are my Features perish'd with my Life ?
Look once again, and for thy Husband lost,
Lo all that's left of him, thy Husband's
    Ghost !
Thy Vows for my return were all in vain ;)
The stormy South o'ertook us in the Main; }
And never shalt thou see thy living Lord |
    again.   )
Bear witness Heav'n I call'd on thee in
    Death,
And while I call'd, a Billow stop'd my
    Breath :
Think not that flying Fame reports my
    Fate ;   370
I present, I appear, and my own Wreck
    relate.
Rise wretched Widow, rise, nor undeplor'd)
Permit my Ghost to pass the *Stygian* Ford : }
But rise, prepar'd, in Black, to mourn thy |
    perish'd Lord.   )
  Thus said the Player-God ; and adding
    Art
Of Voice and Gesture, so perform'd his part,

She thought (so like her Love the Shade
    appears)
That *Ceyx* spake the Words, and *Ceyx* shed
    the Tears.
She groan'd, her inward Soul with Grief
    opprest,
She sigh'd, she wept ; and sleeping beat her
    Breast :   380
Then stretch'd her Arms t' embrace his
    Body bare,
Her clasping Arms inclose but empty Air :
At this not yet awake, she cry'd, O stay,
One is our Fate, and common is our way !
So dreadful was the Dream, so loud she
    spoke,
That starting sudden up, the Slumber broke;
Then cast her Eyes around in hope to view
Her vanish'd Lord, and find the Vision true :
For now the Maids, who waited her Com-
    mands,
Ran in with lighted Tapers in their Hands.
Tir'd with the Search, not finding what she
    seeks,   391
With cruel Blows she pounds her blubber'd
    Cheeks ;
Then from her beaten Breast the Linnen tare,
And cut the golden Caull that bound her
    Hair.
Her Nurse demands the Cause ; with louder
    Cries
She prosecutes her Griefs, and thus replies.
  No more *Alcyone* ; she suffer'd Death
With her lov'd Lord, when *Ceyx* lost his
    Breath :
No Flatt'ry, no false Comfort, give me none,
My Shipwreck'd *Ceyx* is for ever gone ; 400
I saw, I saw him manifest in view,
His Voice, his Figure, and his Gestures knew:
His Lustre lost, and ev'ry living Grace,
Yet I retain'd the Features of his Face ;
Though with pale Cheeks, wet Beard, and
    dropping Hair,
None but my *Ceyx* cou'd appear so fair :
I would have strain'd him with a strict
    Embrace,
But through my arms he slip'd, and vanish'd
    from the Place :
There, ev'n just there, he stood ; and as she
    spoke
Where last the Spectre was, she cast her
    Look :   410

---

347 Darkling] *Darkling 1700. The printer*
took it for a demon's name.
367 living] *The editors wrongly give* loving

395 Cause ; with] Cause with *1700.*

Fain wou'd she hope, and gaz'd upon the Ground
If any printed Footsteps might be found.
  Then sigh'd and said : This I too well foreknew,
And my prophetick Fear presag'd too true :
'Twas what I beg'd, when with a bleeding Heart
I took my leave, and suffer'd Thee to part,
Or I to go along, or Thou to stay,
Never, ah never to divide our way !
Happier for me, that all our Hours assign'd
Together we had liv'd ; e'en not in Death disjoin'd !   420
So had my *Ceyx* still been living here,
Or with my *Ceyx* I had perish'd there :
Now I die absent, in the vast profound ;
And Me without my Self the Seas have drown'd :
The Storms were not so cruel ; should I strive
To lengthen Life, and such a Grief survive ;
But neither will I strive, nor wretched Thee
In Death forsake, but keep thee Company.
If not one common Sepulcher contains
Our Bodies, or one Urn, our last Remains,
Yet *Ceyx* and *Alcyone* shall join,   431
Their Names remember'd in one common Line.
  No farther Voice her mighty Grief affords,
For Sighs come rushing in betwixt her Words,
And stop'd her Tongue ; but what her Tongue deny'd,
Soft Tears, and Groans, and dumb Complaints supply'd.
  'Twas Morning ; to the Port she takes her way,
And stands upon the Margin of the Sea :
That Place, that very Spot of Ground she sought,
Or thither by her Destiny was brought ;   440
Where last he stood : And while she sadly said }
'Twas here he left me, lingring here delay'd }
His parting Kiss ; and there his Anchors weigh'd. }
  Thus speaking, while her Thoughts past Actions trace,
And call to mind admonish'd by the Place,
Sharp at her utmost Ken she cast her Eyes,
And somewhat floating from afar descries ;

It seem'd a Corps adrift, to distant Sight,
But at a distance who could judge aright ?
It wafted nearer yet, and then she knew   450
That what before she but surmis'd, was true :
A Corps it was, but whose it was, unknown,
Yet mov'd, howe'er, she made the Case her own :
Took the bad Omen of a shipwreck'd Man,
As for a Stranger wept, and thus began.
  Poor Wretch, on stormy Seas to lose thy Life,
Unhappy thou, but more thy widdow'd Wife !
At this she paus'd ; for now the flowing Tide
Had brought the Body nearer to the side :
The more she looks, the more her Fears increase   460
At nearer Sight ; and she's her self the less :
Now driv'n ashore, and at her Feet it lies,
She knows too much, in knowing whom she sees :
Her Husband's Corps ; at this she loudly shrieks,
'Tis he, 'tis he, she cries, and tears her Cheeks,
Her Hair, her Vest, and stooping to the Sands
About his Neck she cast her trembling Hands.
  And is it thus, O dearer than my Life,
Thus, thus return'st Thou to thy longing Wife !
She said, and to the neighb'ring Mole she strode,   470
(Rais'd there to break th' Incursions of the Flood ;)
Headlong from hence to plunge her self she springs,
But shoots along supported on her Wings ;
A Bird new-made about the Banks she plies,
Not far from Shore ; and short Excursions tries ;
Nor seeks in Air her humble Flight to raise,
Content to skim the Surface of the Seas :
Her Bill, tho' slender, sends a creaking Noise,
And imitates a lamentable Voice :
Now lighting where the bloodless Body lies,   480
She with a Funeral Note renews her Cries.

---

472 *A new paragraph* 1700.

At all her stretch her little Wings she spread,
And with her feather'd Arms embrac'd the
    Dead :
Then flick'ring to his palid Lips, she strove
To print a Kiss, the last essay of Love :
Whether the vital Touch reviv'd the Dead,
Or that the moving Waters rais'd his Head
To meet the Kiss, the Vulgar doubt alone ;
For sure a present Miracle was shown.
The Gods their Shapes to Winter-Birds
    translate,   490
But both obnoxious to their former Fate.

Their conjugal Affection still is ty'd,
And still the mournful Race is multiply'd ;
They bill, they tread ; *Alcyone* com-
    press'd
Sev'n days sits brooding on her floating
    Nest :
A wintry Queen : Her Sire at length is
    kind,
Calms ev'ry Storm, and hushes ev'ry Wind :
Prepares his Empire for his Daughter's Ease,
And for his hatching Nephews smooths the
    Seas.

ÆSACUS TRANSFORMED INTO A CORMORANT.

FROM THE ELEVENTH BOOK OF OVID'S METAMORPHOSES.

THESE some old Man sees wanton in the
    Air,
And praises the unhappy constant Pair.
Then to his Friend the long-neck'd Corm'-
    rant shews,
The former Tale reviving others Woes :
That sable Bird, he cries, which cuts the
    Flood
With slender Legs, was once of Royal
    Blood ;
His Ancestors from mighty *Tros* proceed,
The brave *Laomedon*, and *Ganymede*,
(Whose Beauty tempted *Jove* to steal the
    Boy)
And *Priam*, hapless Prince ! who fell with
    Troy.   10
Himself was *Hector's* Brother, and (had
    Fate
But giv'n this hopeful Youth a longer Date)
Perhaps had rival'd warlike *Hector's* Worth,
Tho' on the Mother's side of meaner Birth ;
Fair *Alyxothoe*, a Country Maid,
Bare *Æsacus* by stealth in *Ida's* Shade.
He fled the noisy Town, and pompous
    Court,
Lov'd the lone Hills, and simple rural
    Sport,
And seldom to the City would resort.
Yet he no rustick Clownishness profest,   20
Nor was soft Love a Stranger to his Breast :

The Youth had long the Nymph *Hesperie*
    woo'd,
Oft thro' the Thicket or the Mead pursu'd :
Her haply on her Father's Bank he spy'd,
While fearless she her silver Tresses dry'd :
Away she fled : Not Stags with half such
    Speed,
Before the prowling Wolf, scud o'er the
    Mead ;
Not Ducks, when they the safer Flood
    forsake,
Pursu'd by Hawks, so swift regain the Lake.
As fast he follow'd in the hot Career ;   30
Desire the Lover wing'd, the Virgin Fear.
A Snake unseen now pierc'd her heedless
    Foot :
Quick thro' the Veins the venom'd Juices
    shoot :
She fell, and 'scaped by Death his fierce
    Pursuit.
Her lifeless Body, frighted, he embrac'd,
And cry'd, Not this I dreaded, but thy
    Haste :
O had my Love been less, or less thy Fear !
The Victory thus bought is far too dear.
Accursed Snake ! Yet I more curs'd than
    he !
He gave the Wound ; the Cause was giv'n
    by me.   40
Yet none shall say, that unreveng'd you
    dy'd.
He spoke ; then climb'd a Cliff's o'er-
    hanging Side
And, resolute, leap'd on the foaming Tide.

ÆSACUS. Text from Garth's edition, 1717.
15 *Alyxothoe*] *The editors mostly change to*
Alexirhoe. *Saintsbury gives* Alexirrhoe, *a form
impossible in hexameters.*

Tethys receiv'd him gently on the Wave ;
The Death he sought deny'd, and Feathers
    gave.
Debarr'd the surest Remedy of Grief,
And forc'd to live, he curst th' unask'd
    Relief.
Then on his airy Pinions upward flies, ⎫
And at a second Fall successless tries ; 49 ⎬
The downy Plume a quick Descent denies. ⎭

Enrag'd, he often dives beneath the Wave,
And there in vain expects to find a
    Grave.
His ceaseless Sorrow for th' unhappy Maid
Meager'd his Look, and on his Spirits
    prey'd.
Still near the sounding Deep he lives ; his
    Name
From frequent Diving and Emerging came.

THE | TWELFTH BOOK | OF THE | METAMORPHOSES,

WHOLLY TRANSLATED.

Connection to the end of the Eleventh Book.

Æsacus, the Son of Priam, *loving a Country-Life, forsakes the Court : Living obscurely, he falls in Love with a Nymph ; who, flying from him, was kill'd by a Serpent ; for Grief of this, he would have drown'd himself ; but, by the pity of the Gods, is turned into a Cormorant.* Priam, *not hearing of* Æsacus, *believes him to be dead, and raises a Tomb to preserve his Memory. By this Transition, which is one of the finest in all* Ovid, *the Poet naturally falls into the Story of the* Trojan War, *which is summ'd up, in the present Book, but so very briefly, in many Places, that* Ovid *seems more short than* Virgil, *contrary to his usual Style. Yet the House of Fame, which is here describ'd, is one of the most beautiful Pieces in the whole* Metamorphoses. *The Fight of* Achilles *and* Cygnus, *and the Fray betwixt the* Lapythæ *and* Centaurs, *yield to no other part of this Poet : And particularly the Loves and Death of* Cyllarus *and* Hylonome, *the Male and Female* Centaur, *are wonderfully moving*

Pʀiam, to whom the Story was unknown,
As dead, deplor'd his Metamorphos'd
    Son :

A Cenotaph his Name and Title kept,
And *Hector* round the Tomb, with all his
    Brothers wept.
This pious Office *Paris* did not share ;
Absent alone ; and Author of the War,
Which, for the *Spartan* Queen, the *Grecians*
    drew
T' avenge the Rape, and *Asia* to subdue.
A thousand Ships were man'd, to sail the ⎫
    Sea :   ⎪
Nor had their just Resentments found delay, ⎬
Had not the Winds and Waves oppos'd   ⎪
    their way.   11 ⎭
At *Aulis*, with United Pow'rs they meet,
But there, Cross-winds or Calms detain'd
    the Fleet.
Now, while they raise an Altar on the
    Shore,
And *Jove* with solemn Sacrifice adore ;
A boding Sign the Priests and People see :
A Snake of size immense, ascends a Tree,
And in the leafy Summet, spy'd a Neast,
Which, o'er her Callow young, a Sparrow
    press'd.
Eight were the Birds unfledg'd ; their
    Mother flew ;   20
And hover'd round her Care ; but still in
    view :
Till the fierce Reptile first devour'd the
    Brood ;
Then siez'd the flutt'ring Dam, and drunk
    her Blood.
This dire Ostent, the fearful People view ;
Calchas alone, by *Phœbus* taught, foreknew
What Heav'n decreed : and with a smiling
    Glance,
Thus gratulates to *Greece* her happy Chance.

OVID'S METAMORPHOSES XII. The text is from the original of 1700, except as noted. The original was carelessly printed. The current texts have some ugly errors, as in 524 where Ovid's words are *Nec te pugnantem tua, Cyllare, forma redemit,* and in 826. The original has many false stops.

O *Argives*, we shall Conquer ; *Troy* is ours,
But long Delays shall first afflict our
   Pow'rs :
Nine Years of Labour, the nine Birds por-
   tend ;   30
The Tenth shall in the Town's Destruction
   end.
  The Serpent, who his Maw obscene had
   fill'd,
The Branches in his curl'd Embraces held :
But as in Spires he stood, he turn'd to
   Stone :
The stony Snake retain'd the Figure still
   his own.
  Yet not for this the Wind-bound Navy
   weigh'd,
Slack were their Sails ; and *Neptune* dis-
   obey'd.
Some thought him loath the Town shou'd
   be destroy'd,
Whose Building had his Hands divine
   employ'd :
Not so the Seer ; who knew, and known
   foreshow'd,   40
The Virgin *Phœbe* with a Virgin's Blood
Must first be reconcil'd ; the common
   Cause
Prevail'd ; and Pity yielding to the Laws,
Fair *Iphigenia* the devoted Maid
Was, by the weeping Priests, in Linnen-
   Robes array'd ;
All mourn her Fate ; but no Relief appear'd :
The Royal Victim bound, the Knife already
   rear'd :
When that offended Pow'r, who caus'd their
   Woe,
Relenting ceas'd her Wrath ; and stop'd the
   coming Blow.
A Mist before the Ministers she cast ;   50
And, in the Virgin's room, a Hind she plac'd.
Th' Oblation slain, and *Phœbe* reconcil'd,
The Storm was hush'd, and dimpled Ocean
   smil'd :
A favourable Gale arose from Shore,
Which to the Port desir'd the *Grecian*
   Gallies bore.
  Full in the midst of this Created Space,
Betwixt Heav'n, Earth, and Skies, there
   stands a Place,
Confining on all three ; with triple Bound ;
Whence all Things, though remote, are
   view'd around ;
And thither bring their Undulating Sound.

The Palace of loud Fame ; her Seat of
   Pow'r ;   61
Plac'd on the Summet of a lofty Tow'r ;
A thousand winding Entries long and wide,
Receive of fresh Reports a flowing Tide.
A thousand Crannies in the Walls are made ;
Nor Gate nor Bars exclude the busy Trade.
'Tis built of Brass the better to diffuse
The spreading Sounds, and multiply the
   News :
Where Eccho's in repeated Eccho's play :
A Mart for ever full ; and open Night and
   Day.   70
Nor Silence is within, nor Voice express,
But a deaf Noise of Sounds that never cease ;
Confus'd, and Chiding, like the hollow Roar
Of Tides, receding from th' insulted Shore :
Or like the broken Thunder, heard from far,
When *Jove* to distance drives the rowling
   War.
The Courts are fill'd with a tumultuous Din
Of Crowds, or issuing forth, or entring in :
A thorough fare of News : Where some
   devise
Things never heard ; some mingle Truth
   with Lies :   80
The troubled Air with empty Sounds they
   beat ;
Intent to hear ; and eager to repeat.
Error sits brooding there ; with added
   Train
Of vain Credulity ; and Joys as vain :
Suspicion, with Sedition join'd, are near ;
And Rumors rais'd, and Murmurs mix'd,
   and Panique Fear.
Fame sits aloft ; and sees the subject Ground,
And Seas about, and Skies above ; enquiring
   all around.
  The Goddess gives th' Alarm ; and soon
   is known   89
The *Grecian* Fleet, descending on the Town.
Fix'd on Defence the *Trojans* are not slow
To guard their Shore from an expected Foe.
They meet in Fight : By *Hector's* fatal
   Hand
Protesilaus falls ; and bites the Strand :
Which with expence of Blood the *Grecians*
   won ;
And prov'd the Strength unknown of *Priam's*
   Son.
And to their Cost the *Trojan* Leaders felt
The *Grecian* Heroes ; and what Deaths
   they dealt.

From these first Onsets, the *Sigæan* Shore
Was strew'd with Carcasses ; and stain'd
  with Gore :   100
Neptunian Cygnus Troops of *Greeks* had
  slain ;
Achilles in his Carr had scow'r'd the Plain :
And clear'd the *Trojan* Ranks : Where e'er
  he fought,
Cygnus, or *Hector*, through the Fields he
  sought :
Cyngus he found ; on him his Force
  essay'd :
For *Hector* was to the tenth Year delay'd.
His white man'd Steeds, that bow'd
  beneath the Yoke
He chear'd to Courage, with a gentle
  Stroke ;
Then urg'd his fiery Chariot on the Foe :
And rising, shook his Lance, in act to
  throw.   110
But first, he cry'd, O Youth, be proud to
  bear
Thy Death, enobled, by *Pelides* Spear.
The Lance pursu'd the Voice without delay ;
Nor did the whizzing Weapon miss the way :
But pierc'd his Cuirass, with such Fury
  sent ;
And sign'd his Bosom with a Purple Dint.
At this the Seed of *Neptune* ; Goddess-born,
For Ornament, not Use, these Arms are
  worn ;
This Helm, and heavy Buckler, I can spare ;
As only Decorations of the War :   120
So *Mars* is arm'd for Glory, not for Need.
'Tis somewhat more from *Neptune* to
  proceed,
Than from a Daughter of the Sea to spring :
Thy Sire is Mortal ; mine is Ocean's King.
Secure of Death, I shou'd contemn thy Dart,
Tho' naked, and impassible depart :
He said, and threw : The trembling⎱
  Weapon pass'd   ⎪
Through nine Bull-hides, each under other ⎬
  plac'd,   ⎪
On his broad Shield, and stuck within the⎭
  last.
Achilles wrench'd it out ; and sent again 130
The hostile Gift : The hostile Gift was vain.
He try'd a third, a tough well-chosen Spear ;
Th' inviolable Body stood sincere ;
Though *Cygnus* then did no Defence pro-
  vide,
But scornful offer'd his unshielded Side.

Not otherwise th' impatient Hero far'd,
Than as a Bull, incompass'd with a Guard
Amid the *Circus* roars : Provok'd from far
By sight of Scarlet, and a sanguine War :
They quit their Ground ; his bended Horns
  elude ;   140
In vain pursuing, and in vain pursu'd.
Before to farther Fight he wou'd advance,
He stood considering, and survey'd his
  Lance.
Doubts if he wielded not a Wooden Spear
Without a Point : He look'd, the Point was
  there.
This is my Hand, and this my Lance, he⎱
  se'd,   ⎬
By which so many thousand Foes are dead.⎭
O whether is their usual Virtue fled !
I had it once ; and the *Lyrnessian* Wall,
And *Tenedos* confess'd it in their Fall. 150
Thy Streams, *Caicus*, rowl'd a Crimson-
  Flood ;
And *Thebes* ran Red with her own Natives
  Blood.
Twice *Telephus* employ'd this piercing
  Steel,
To wound him first, and afterward to heal.
The Vigour of this Arm was never vain ;⎱
And that my wonted Prowess I retain,   ⎬
Witness these Heaps of Slaughter on the⎭
  Plain.
He said ; and, doubtful of his former
  Deeds,
To some new trial of his Force proceeds.
He chose *Menœtes* from among the rest ; 160
At him he lanch'd his Spear ; and pierc'd his
  Breast :
On the hard Earth, the *Lycian* knock'd his
  Head,
And lay supine ; and forth the Spirit fled.
  Then thus the Hero : Neither can I
  blame,
The Hand, or Javelin ; both are still the
  same.
The same I will employ against this Foe ;
And wish but with the same Success to
  throw.
So spoke the Chief ; and while he spoke he
  threw ;
The Weapon with unerring Fury flew,
At his left Shoulder aim'd : Nor Entrance
  found ;   170
But back, as from a Rock, with swift
  rebound

Harmless return'd: A bloody Mark appear'd,
Which with false Joy the flatter'd Hero
    chear'd.
Wound there was none ; the Blood that
    was in view,
The Lance before from slain *Menætes* drew
Headlong he leaps from off his lofty Car,
And in close Fight on foot renews the War.
Raging with high Disdain, repeats his
    Blows ;
Nor Shield nor Armour can their Force
    oppose ;
Huge Cantlets of his Buckler strew the
    Ground,   180
And no Defence in his bor'd Arms is found.
But on his Flesh, no Wound or Blood is
    seen ;
The Sword it self is blunted on the Skin.
   This vain Attempt the Chief no longer
    bears ;
But round his hollow Temples and his Ears
His Buckler beats : The Son of *Neptune*,
    stun'd
With these repeated Buffets, quits his
    Ground ;
A sickly Sweat succeeds ; and Shades of
    Night :
Inverted Nature swims before his Sight :
Th' insulting Victor presses on the more, 190
And treads the Steps the vanquish'd trod
    before,
Nor Rest, nor Respite gives : A Stone there
    lay
Behind his trembling Foe ; and stop'd his
    way.
Achilles took th' Advantage which he found,
O'er-turn'd, and push'd him backward on
    the Ground.
His Buckler held him under. while he press'd
With both his Knees above, his panting
    Breast ;
Unlac'd his Helm : About his Chin the Twist
He ty'd ; and soon the strangled Soul
    dismiss'd.
   With eager haste he went to strip the
    Dead   200
The vanish'd Body from his Arms was
    fled.
His Sea-God Sire t' immortalize his Fame,
Had turn'd it to the Bird that bears his
    Name.
   A Truce succeeds the Labours of this Day,
And Arms suspended with a long delay.

While *Trojan* Walls are kept with Watch
    and Ward ;
The *Greeks* before their Trenches mount the
    Guard ;
The Feast approach'd ; when to the blue-⎫
    Ey'd Maid   ⎪
His Vows for *Cygnus* slain the Victor paid, ⎬
And a white Heyfer, on her Altar laid. 210⎭
The reeking Entrails on the Fire they
    threw ;
And to the Gods the grateful Odour flew :
Heav'n had its part in Sacrifice : The rest
Was broil'd and roasted for the future
    Feast.
The chief invited Guests were set around ;⎫
And Hunger first asswag'd, the Bowls were⎪
    crown'd,   ⎬
Which in deep Draughts their Cares and ⎪
    Labours drown'd.   ⎭
The mellow Harp did not their Ears employ :
And mute was all the Warlike Symphony :
Discourse, the Food of Souls, was their
    Delight,   220
And pleasing Chat prolong'd the Summers-
    night.
The Subject, Deeds of Arms ; and Valour
    shown
Or on the *Trojan* side, or on their own.
Of Dangers undertaken, Fame atchiev'd ;
They talk'd by turns ; the Talk by turns
    reliev'd.
What Things but these, cou'd fierce *Achilles*
    tell,
Or what cou'd fierce *Achilles* hear so well ?
The last great Act perform'd, of *Cygnus*
    slain,
Did most the Martial Audience entertain :
Wondring to find a Body, free by Fate 230
From Steel ; and which could ev'n that
    Steel rebate :
Amaz'd, their Admiration they renew ;
And scarce *Pelides* cou'd believe it true.
   Then *Nestor* thus ; What once this Age
    has known,
In fated *Cygnus*, and in him alone,
These Eyes have seen in *Cæneus* long before,
Whose body not a thousand Swords cou'd
    bore.
Cæneus, in Courage, and in Strength ex-
    cell'd ;
And still his *Othrys* with his Fame is fill'd :

---

239 *Othrys*] *Othry's* 1700.

But what did most his Martial Deeds
adorn,   240
(Though since he chang'd his Sex) a Woman
born.
A Novelty so strange, and full of Fate,
His list'ning Audience ask'd him to relate.
Achilles thus commends their common Sute ;
O Father, first for Prudence in repute,
Tell, with that Eloquence, so much thy own,
What thou hast heard, or what of *Cæneus*
known :
What was he, whence his change of Sex
begun,
What Trophies, join'd in Wars with thee,
he won ?
Who conquer'd him, and in what fatal
Strife   250
The Youth without a Wound, cou'd lose his
Life ?
Neleides then ; Though tardy Age, and
Time
Have shrunk my Sinews, and decay'd my
Prime ;
Though much I have forgotten of my Store,
Yet not exhausted, I remember more.
Of all that Arms atchiev'd, or Peace de-
sign'd,
That Action still is fresher in my Mind
Than ought beside. If Reverend Age can
give
To Faith a Sanction, in my third I live.
'Twas in my second Cent'ry, I survey'd 260
Young *Cænis*, then a fair *Thessalian* Maid :
Cænis the bright was born to high Com-
mand ;
A Princess ; and a Native of thy Land,
Divine *Achilles* : every Tongue proclaim'd
Her Beauty ; and her Eyes all Hearts in-
flam'd.
Peleus, thy sire, perhaps had sought her
Bed,
Among the rest ; but he had either led
Thy Mother then, or was by Promise ty'd ;
But she to him, and all alike her Love
deny'd.
It was her Fortune once, to take her way 270
Along the sandy Margin of the Sea :
The Pow'r of Ocean view'd her as she pass'd,
And lov'd as soon as seen, by Force
embrac'd.
So Fame reports. Her Virgin-Treasure
seiz'd,
And his new Joys, the Ravisher so pleas'd,

That thus, transported, to the Nymph he
cry'd ;
Ask what thou wilt, no Pray'r shall be
deny'd.
This also Fame relates : The haughty Fair,
Who not the Rape, ev'n of a God cou'd
bear,
This Answer, proud, return'd : To mighty
Wrongs   280
A mighty Recompense, of right, belongs.
Give me no more to suffer such a Shame ;
But change the Woman, for a better Name ;
One Gift for all : She said ; and while she
spoke,
A stern, majestick, manly Tone she took.
A Man she was : And as the Godhead
swore,
To *Cæneus* turn'd, who *Cænis* was before.
To this the Lover adds without request :
No force of Steel shou'd violate his Breast.
Glad of the Gift, the new-made Warrior
goes ;   290
And Arms among the *Greeks* ; and longs for
equal Foes.
Now brave *Perithous*, bold *Ixion's* Son,
The Love of fair *Hippodame* had won.
The Cloud-begotten Race, half Men, half
Beast,
Invited, came to grace the Nuptial Feast :
In a cool Cave's recess the Treat was made,
Whose entrance Trees with spreading
Boughs o'ershade.
They sate : And summon'd by the Bride-
groom, came,
To mix with those the *Lapythæan* Name :
Nor wanted I : The Roofs with Joy
resound :   300
And *Hymen, Io Hymen*, rung around,
Rais'd Altars shone with holy Fires ; the
Bride,
Lovely her self (and lovely by her side
A Bevy of bright Nimphs, with sober Grace,)
Came glitt'ring like a Star, and took her
Place.
Her heav'nly Form beheld, all wish'd her
Joy ;
And little wanted, but in vain, their Wishes
all employ.
For One, most Brutal of the Brutal Brood,
Or whether Wine or Beauty fir'd his Blood
Or both at once ; beheld with lustful Eyes
The Bride ; at once resolv'd to make his
Prize.   311

Down went the Board ; and fastening on her
  Hair,
He seiz'd with sudden Force the frighted
  Fair.
'Twas *Eurytus* began : His bestial Kind
His Crime pursu'd ; and each as pleas'd his
  Mind,
Or her, whom Chance presented, took : The
  Feast
An Image of a taken Town express'd.
  The Cave resounds with Female Shrieks ;
    we rise,
Mad with Revenge, to make a swift Reprise
And *Theseus* first ; What Frenzy has
  possess'd   320
O *Eurytus*, he cry'd, thy brutal Breast,
To wrong *Perithous*, and not him alone,
But, while I live, two Friends conjoyn'd in
  one ?
To justify his Threat, he thrusts aside
The Crowd of Centaurs ; and redeems the
  Bride :
The Monster nought replied : For Words
  were vain ;
And Deeds cou'd only Deeds unjust main-
  tain :
But answers with his Hand ; and forward
  press'd,
With Blows redoubled, on his Face and
  Breast.
An ample Goblet stood, of antick Mold, 330
And rough with Figures of the rising Gold ;
The Hero snatch'd it up, and toss'd in
  Air,
Full at the Front of the foul Ravisher :
He falls ; and falling vomits forth a Flood
Of Wine, and Foam and Brains, and mingled
  Blood.
Half roaring, and half neighing through the
  Hall,
Arms, Arms, the double-form'd with Fury
  call ;
To wreak their Brother's Death : A Medley-
  Flight
Of Bowls and Jars, at first supply the
  Fight,
Once Instruments of Feasts, but now of
  Fate ;   340
Wine animates their Rage, and arms their
  Hate.
  Bold *Amycus*, from the robb'd Vestry
    brings
The Chalices of Heav'n ; and holy Things

Of precious Weight : A Sconce, that hung
  on high,
With Tapers fill'd, to light the Sacristy,
Torn from the Cord, with his unhallow'd
  Hand
He threw amid the *Lapythæan* Band.
On *Celadon* the Ruin fell, and left
His Face of Feature and of Form bereft :
So, when some brawny Sacrificer knocks,
Before an altar led, an offer'd Oxe,   351
His Eye-balls rooted out are thrown to
  ground :
His Nose dismantled in his Mouth is found,
His Jaws, Cheeks, Front, one undistin-
  guish'd Wound.
  This, *Belates*, th' Avenger, cou'd not
    brook :
But, by the Foot a Maple-board he took ;
And hurl'd at Amycus ; his Chin it bent
Against his Chest, and down the Centaur
  sent ;
Whom sputtring bloody Teeth, the second
  Blow
Of his drawn Sword dispatch'd to Shades
  below.   360
  Grineus was near ; and cast a furious
    Look
On the side Altar, cens'd with sacred
  Smoke,
And bright with flaming Fires : The Gods,
  he cry'd,
Have with their holy Trade, our Hands
  supply'd :
Why use we not their Gifts ? Then from the
  Floor
An Altar-Stone he heav'd, with all the Load
  it bore :
Altar and Altars freight together flew,
Where thickest throng'd the *Lapythæan*
  Crew ;
And *Broteas*, and at once, *Oryus* slew :
Oryus mother, *Mycale*, was known   370
Down from her Sphere to draw the lab'ring
  Moon.
  Exadius cry'd, Unpunish'd shall not go
This Fact, if Arms are found against the
  Foe.
He look'd about, where on a Pine were spred
The votive Horns of a Stags branching
  Head :

---

369 *Broteas*, and at once,] *Some editors
wrongly give* at once *Broteas* and

At *Grineus* these he throws ; so just they fly,
That the sharp Antlers stuck in either Eye :
Breathless and Blind he fell ; with Blood
besmear'd ;
His Eye-balls beaten out hung dangling on
his Beard.
Fierce *Rhœtus*, from the Hearth a burning
Brand   380
Selects, and whirling waves ; till, from his
Hand
The Fire took Flame ; then dash'd it from
the right,
On fair *Charaxus* Temples near the Sight :
The whistling Pest came on ; and pierc'd
the Bone,
And caught the yellow Hair, that shrievel'd
while it shone :
Caught, like dry Stubble fir'd ; or like Seer-
wood ;
Yet from the Wound ensu'd no Purple
Flood ;
But look'd a bubbling Mass of frying Blood.
His blazing Locks sent forth a crackling
Sound ;
And hiss'd, like red hot Iron within the
Smithy drown'd.   390
The wounded Warrior shook his flaming
Hair,
Then (what a Team of Horse cou'd hardly
rear)
He heaves the Threshold-Stone ; but cou'd
not throw ;
The Weight it self forbad the threaten'd
Blow ;
Which dropping from his lifted Arms, came
down,
Full on *Cometes* Head ; and crush'd his
Crown.
Nor *Rhœtus* then retain'd his Joy; but se'd ;
So by their Fellows may our Foes be sped,
Then, with redoubled Strokes he plies his
Head :
The burning Lever not deludes his Pains,
But drives the batter'd Skull within the
Brains.   401
Thus flush'd, the Conqueror, with force
renew'd,
Evagrus, Dryas, Corythus, pursu'd :
First *Corythus*, with downy Cheeks, he slew ;
Whose Fall when fierce *Evagrus* had in view,
He cry'd, What Palm is from a beardless
Prey ?
Rhœtus prevents what more he had to say ;

And drove within his Mouth the fiery Death,
Which enter'd hissing in, and choak'd his
Breath.
At *Dryas* next he flew; But weary Chance 410
No longer wou'd the same Success advance.
But while he whirl'd in fiery Circles round
The Brand, a sharpen'd Stake strong
Dryas found ;
And in the Shoulder's Joint inflicts the
Wound.
The Weapon struck ; which roaring out
with Pain
He drew ; nor longer durst the Fight main-
tain,
But turn'd his Back, for fear ; and fled
amain.
With him fled *Orneus*, with like Dread
possess'd ;
Thaumas, and *Medon*, wounded in the
Breast ;
And *Mermeros* in the late Race renown'd, 420
Now limping ran, and tardy with his
Wound.
Pholus and *Melaneus* from Fight withdrew,
And *Abas* maim'd, who Boars encountring
slew :
And *Augur Astylos*, whose Art in vain
From Fight dissuaded the four-footed
Train,
Now beat the Hoof with *Nessus* on the
Plain ;
But to his Fellow cry'd, Be safely slow,
Thy Death deferr'd is due to great *Alcides*
Bow.
Mean time strong *Dryas* urg'd his Chance
so well,
That *Lycidas, Areos, Imbreus* fell ;   430
All, one by one, and fighting Face to Face :
Crenæus fled, to fall with more Disgrace :
For, fearful, while he look'd behind, he bore
Betwixt his Nose and Front, the Blow
before.
Amid the Noise and Tumult of the Fray,
Snoring, and drunk with Wine, *Aphidas* lay.
Ev'n then the Bowl within his Hand he
kept :
And on a Bear's rough Hide securely slept.
Him *Phorbas* with his flying Dart, transfix'd ;
Take thy next Draught with *Stygian* Waters
mix'd,   440
And sleep thy fill, th' insulting Victor cry'd ;
Surpris'd with Death unfelt, the Centaur
dy'd :

The ruddy Vomit, as he breath'd his Soul,
Repass'd his Throat ; and fill'd his empty
    Bowl.
I saw *Petræus* Arms employ'd around
A well-grown Oak, to root it from the
    Ground.
This way, and that, he wrench'd the fibrous
    Bands,
The Trunk was like a Sapling in his Hands,
And still obey'd the Bent : While thus he
    stood,
Perithous Dart drove on ; and nail'd him to
    the Wood.   450
Lycus, and *Chromis* fell by him oppress'd :
Helops and *Dictys* added to the rest
A nobler Palm : *Helops* through either Ear
Transfix'd, receiv'd the penetrating Spear.
This *Dictys* saw ; and seiz'd with suddain
    Fright
Leapt headlong from the Hill of steepy
    height ;
And crush'd an Ash beneath, that cou'd not
    bear his weight.
The shatter'd Tree receives his Fall ; and
    strikes
Within his full-blown Paunch, the sharpen'd
    Spikes.
Strong *Aphareus* had heav'd a mighty Stone,
The Fragment of a Rock ; and wou'd have
    thrown ;   461
But *Theseus* with a Club of harden'd Oak,
The Cubit-bone of the bold Centaur broke ;
And left him maim'd ; nor seconded the
    Stroke.
Then leapt on tall *Bianor's* Back : (Who bore
No mortal Burden but his own, before)
Press'd with his Knees his Sides ; the
    double Man,
His Speed with Spurs increas'd, unwilling
    ran.
One Hand the Hero fasten'd on his Locks ;
His other ply'd him with repeated Strokes.
The Club rung round his Ears, and batter'd
    Brows ;   471
He falls ; and lashing up his Heels, his
    Rider throws.
The same *Herculean* Arms *Nedymnus*
    wound ;
And lay by him *Lycotas* on the Ground ;
And *Hippasus*, whose Beard his Breast
    invades ;
And *Ripheus*, haunter of the Woodland
    Shades :

And *Tereus*, us'd with Mountain Bears to
    strive ;
And from their Dens to draw th' indignant
    Beasts alive.
Demoleon cou'd not bear this hateful
    Sight,   479
Or the long Fortune of th' *Athenian* Knight :
But pull'd with all his Force, to disengage
From Earth a Pine, the Product of an Age :
The Root stuck fast : The broken Trunk he
    sent
At *Theseus* : *Theseus* frustrates his Intent,
And leaps aside, by *Pallas* warn'd, the Blow
To shun : (for so he said ; and we believ'd
    it so.)
Yet not in vain th' enormous Weight was
    cast ;
Which *Crantor's* Body sunder'd at the Waist,
Thy Father's Squire, *Achilles*, and his
    Care ;
Whom conquer'd in the *Dolopeian* War,   490
Their King, his present Ruin to prevent,
A Pledge of Peace implor'd, to *Peleus* sent.
Thy Sire, with grieving Eyes, beheld his
    Fate ;
And cry'd, Not long, lov'd *Crantor*, shalt
    thou wait
Thy vow'd Revenge. At once he said, and
    threw
His Ashen-Spear ; which quiver'd as it flew ;
With all his Force and all his Soul apply'd ;
The sharp Point enter'd in the Centaur's
    Side :
Both Hands, to wrench it out, the Monster
    join'd ;
And wrench'd it out ; but left the Steel
    behind.   500
Stuck in his Lungs it stood : Inrag'd he
    rears
His Hoofs, and down to Ground thy Father
    bears.
Thus trampled under foot, his Shield defends
His Head ; his other Hand the Lance
    protends.
Ev'n while he lay extended on the Dust,
He sped the Centaur, with one single
    Thrust.
Two more his Lance before transfix'd from
    far ;
And two his Sword had slain in closer War.

504 protends] *Some editors wrongly give*
portends

To these was added *Dorylas* : Who spread
A Bull's two goring Horns around his
    Head.   510
With these he push'd ; in Blood already
    dy'd :
Him, fearless, I approach'd ; and thus
    defy'd :
Now, Monster, now, by Proof it shall
    appear,
Whether thy Horns are sharper or my Spear.
At this, I threw : For want of other Ward,
He lifted up his Hand, his Front to guard.
His Hand it pass'd : And fix'd it to his
    Brow :
Loud Shouts of ours attend the lucky Blow.
Him *Peleus* finish'd, with a second Wound,⎫
Which through the Navel pierc'd: He reel'd⎮
    around ;   520⎬
And drag'd his dangling Bowels on the⎮
    Ground ;   ⎭
Trod what he drag'd ; and what he trod he
    crush'd :
And to his Mother-Earth, with empty Belly
    rush'd.
    Nor cou'd thy Form, O *Cyllarus*, fore-
    slow
Thy Fate ; (if Form to Monsters Men
    allow :)
Just bloom'd thy Beard, thy Beard of golden
    Hew :
Thy Locks in golden Waves, about thy
    Shoulders flew.
Sprightly thy Look : Thy Shapes in ev'ry
    part
So clean ; as might instruct the Sculptor's
    Art :
As far as Man extended : Where began 530
The Beast, the Beast was equal to the Man.
Add but a Horses Head and Neck ; and he,
O *Castor*, was a Courser worthy thee.
So was his Back proportion'd for the Seat ;
So rose his brawny Chest ; so swiftly mov'd
    his Feet.
Coal-black his Colour ; but like Jet it shone ;
His Legs and flowing Tail were White alone.
Belov'd by many Maidens of his Kind,
But fair *Hylonome* possess'd his Mind :
Hylonome, for Features, and for Face   540
Excelling all the Nymphs of double Race :

Nor less her Blandishments, than Beauty
    move ;
At once both loving, and confessing Love.
For him she dress'd : For him with female
    care
She comb'd, and set in Curls, her auborn
    Hair.
Of Roses, Violets, and Lillies mix'd
And Sprigs of flowing Rosemary betwixt
She form'd the Chaplet, that adorn'd her
    Front :
In Waters of the *Pagasæan* Fount,
And in the Streams that from the Fountain
    play,   550
She wash'd her Face ; and bath'd her twice
    a Day.
The Scarf of Furs, that hung below her Side,
Was Ermin, or the Panther's spotted Pride ;
Spoils of no common Beast : With equal
    Flame
They lov'd : Their Sylvan Pleasures were the
    same :
All Day they hunted ; And when Day expir'd,
Together to some shady Cave retir'd :
Invited to the nuptials, both repair :
And Side by Side, they both ingage in War.
Uncertain from what Hand, a flying Dart
At *Cyllarus* was sent ; which pierc'd his
    Heart.   561
The Javelin drawn from out the mortal
    Wound,
He faints with staggring Steps ; and seeks
    the Ground :
The Fair within her Arms receiv'd his Fall,
And strove his wandring Spirits to recal :
And while her Hand the streaming Blood
    oppos'd,
Join'd Face to Face, his Lips with hers
    she clos'd.
Stifled with Kisses, a sweet Death he dies ;
She fills the Fields with undistinguish'd Cries:
At least her Words were in her Clamour
    drown'd ;   570
For my stun'd Ears receiv'd no vocal Sound.
In madness of her Grief, she seiz'd the Dart
New-drawn, and reeking from her Lover's
    Heart ;
To her bare Bosom the sharp Point apply'd ;⎫
And wounded fell ; and falling by his Side,⎮
Embrac'd him in her Arms ; and thus   ⎬
    embracing, dy'd.   ⎭

Ev'n still, methinks, I see *Phæocomes* ;
Strange was his Habit ; and as odd his
   Dress.
Six Lion's Hides, with Thongs together
   fast,
His upper part defended to his Waist ; 580
And where Man ended, the continued Vest,
Spread on his Back, the Houss and Trappings
   of a Beast
A Stump too heavy for a Team to draw,
(It seems a Fable, tho' the Fact I saw ;)
He threw at *Pholon* ; the descending Blow
Divides the Skull, and cleaves his Head in
   two.
The Brains, from Nose and Mouth, and
   either Ear
Came issuing out, as through a Colender
The curdled Milk ; or from the Press the
   Whey
Driv'n down by Weights above, is drain'd
   away.   590
  But him, while stooping down to spoil the
   Slain,
Pierc'd through the Paunch, I tumbled on
   the Plain.
Then *Chthonyus* and *Teleboas* I slew :
A Fork the former arm'd ; a Dart his Fellow
   threw.
The Javelin wounded me ; (behold the Skar,)
Then was my time to seek the *Trojan*
   War ;
Then I was *Hector's* Match in open Field ;
But he was then unborn ; at least a Child ;
Now, I am nothing. I forbear to tell
By *Periphantas* how *Pyretus* fell ;   600
The Centaur by the Knight : Nor will I stay
On *Amphyx*, or what Deaths he dealt that
   Day :
What Honour with a pointless Lance he
   won,
Stuck in the front of a four-footed Man ;
What fame young *Macareus* obtain'd in
   Fight :
Or dwell on *Nessus*, now return'd from
   Flight ;
How Prophet *Mopsus* not alone devin'd,
Whose Valour equall'd his foreseeing Mind.
  Already *Cæneus*, with his conquering
   Hand,
Had slaughter'd five the boldest of their
   Band ;   610
Pyrachmus, Helymus, Antimachus,
Bromus the Brave, and stronger *Stiphelus* ;

Their Names I number'd, and remember well,
No Trace remaining, by what Wounds they
   fell.
  Latreus, the bulkiest of the double Race,
Whom the spoil'd Arms of slain *Halesus* grace,
In Years retaining still his Youthful Might,
Though his black Hairs were interspers'd
   with White,
Betwixt th' imbattled Ranks began to
   prance,
Proud of his Helm, and *Macedonian* Lance ;
And rode the Ring around ; that either
   Hoast   621
Might hear him, while he made this empty
   Boast.
And from a Strumpet shall we suffer
   Shame,
For *Cænis* still, not *Cæneus* is thy Name :
And still the Native Softness of thy Kind
Prevails ; and leaves the Woman in thy
   Mind ?
Remember what thou wert ; what price was
   paid
To change thy Sex : to make thee not a
   Maid ;
And but a Man in shew : go, Card and Spin ;
And leave the Business of the War to Men.
  While thus the Boaster exercis'd his
   Pride,   631
The fatal Spear of *Cæneus* reach'd his Side :
Just in the mixture of the Kinds it ran ;
Betwixt the neather Beast, and upper Man :
The Monster mad with Rage, and stung with
   Smart,
His Lance directed at the Hero's Heart :
It strook : But bounded from his harden'd
   Breast,
Like Hail from Tiles, which the safe House
   invest.
Nor seem'd the Stroke with more effect to
   come,
Than a small Pebble falling on a Drum. 640
He next his Fauchion try'd, in closer Fight ;
But the keen Fauchion had no Pow'r to bite.
He thrust ; the blunted Point return'd
   again :
Since downright Blows, he cry'd, and
   Thrusts are vain,
I'll prove his Side : In strong Embraces held
He prov'd his Side ; his Side the Sword
   repell'd :

------

634 Beast] Breast *1700.*

His hollow Belly eccho'd to the Stroke ;
Untouch'd his Body, as a solid Rock ;
Aim'd at his Neck at last, the Blade in
    Shivers broke.
   Th' Impassive Knight stood Idle, to
    deride   650
His Rage, and offer'd oft his naked Side :
At length, Now Monster, in thy turn, he
    cry'd,
Try thou the Strength of *Cæneus* : At the
    Word
He thrust ; and in his Shoulder plung'd the
    Sword.
Then writh'd his Hand ; and as he drove it
    down,
Deep in his Breast, made many Wounds in
    one.
   The Centaurs saw inrag'd, th' unhop'd
    Success ;
And rushing on, in Crowds, together press ;
At him, and him alone, their Darts they
    threw :
Repuls'd they from his fated Body flew. 660
Amaz'd they stood ; till *Monychus* began,
O Shame, a Nation conquer'd by a Man !
A Woman-Man ; yet more a Man is He,
Than all our Race ; and what He was, are
    We.
Now, what avail our Nerves ? The united
    Force,
Of two the strongest Creatures, Man and
    Horse,
Nor Goddess-born, nor of *Ixion's* Seed
We seem ; (a Lover built for *Juno's* Bed ;)
Master'd by this half Man. Whole Moun-
    tains throw   669
With Woods at once, and bury him below.
This only way remains. Nor need we doubt
To choak the Soul within ; though not to
    force it out.
Heap Weights, instead of Wounds : He
    chanc'd to see
Where Southern Storms had rooted up
    a Tree ;
This, raised from Earth, against the Foe
    he threw ;
Th' Example shewn, his Fellow-Brutes
    pursue.
With Forest-loads the Warrior they in-
    vade ;
Othrys and *Pelion* soon were void of Shade ;
And spreading Groves were naked Moun-
    tains made.

Press'd with the Burden, *Cæneus* pants for
    Breath ;   680
And on his Shoulders bears the Wooden
    Death.
To heave th' intolerable Weight he tries ;
At length it rose above his Mouth and Eyes :
Yet still he heaves : And strugling with
    Despair,
Shakes all aside ; and gains a gulp of Air :
A short Relief, which but prolongs his Pain ;
He faints by Fits ; and then respires again :
At last, the Burden only nods above,
As when an Earthquake stirs th' *Idæan*
    Grove.   689
Doubtful his Death : He suffocated seem'd
To most ; but otherwise our *Mopsus* deem'd
Who said he saw a yellow Bird arise
From out the Pile, and cleave the liquid
    Skies :
I saw it too, with golden feathers bright,
Nor e're before beheld so strange a Sight.
Whom *Mopsus* viewing, as it soar'd around
Our Troop, and heard the Pinions rattling
    Sound,
All hail, he cry'd, thy Countries Grace and
    Love ;
Once first of Men below ; now first of Birds
    above.
Its Author to the Story gave Belief : 700
For us, our Courage was increas'd by Grief :
Asham'd to see a single Man, pursu'd
With Odds, to sink beneath a Multitude :
We push'd the Foe ; and forc'd to shameful
    Flight,
Part fell ; and part escap'd by favour of the
    Night.
   This Tale, by *Nestor* told, did much dis-
    please
Tlepolemus, the Seed of *Hercules* :
For, often he had heard his Father say,
That he himself was present at the Fray ;
And more than shar'd the Glories of the
    Day.   710
Old Chronicle, he said, among the rest,
You might have nam'd *Alcides* at the least :
Is he not worth your Praise ? The *Pylian*
    Prince
Sigh'd ere he spoke ; then made this proud
    Defence.
My former Woes, in long Oblivion drown'd
I would have lost ; but you renew the Wound:

---

704 Flight] *Some editors absurdly give* Fight

DR.   R

Better to pass him o'er, than to relate
The Cause I have your mighty Sire to hate.
His Fame has fill'd the World, and reach'd
    the Sky ;
(Which, Oh, I wish, with Truth, I cou'd
    deny !)   720
We praise not *Hector* ; though his name, we
    know,
Is great in Arms ; 'tis hard to praise a Foe.
He, your Great Father, levell'd to the
    Ground
Messenia's Towers : Nor better Fortune
    found
Elis, and *Pylus* ; that a neighb'ring State
And this my own : Both guiltless of their
    Fate.
  To pass the rest, twelve wanting one, he
    slew,
My Brethren, who their Birth from *Neleus*
    drew.
All Youths of early Promise, had they liv'd ;
By him they perish'd : I alone surviv'd. 730
The rest were easy Conquest : But the Fate
Of *Periclymenos* is wondrous to relate.
To him our common Grandsire of the Main
Had giv'n to change his Form, and chang'd,
    resume again.
Vary'd at Pleasure, every Shape he try'd ;
And in all Beasts *Alcides* still defy'd :
Vanquish'd on Earth, at length he soar'd
    above ;
Chang'd to the Bird, that bears the Bolt of
    Jove.
The new-dissembled Eagle, now endu'd
With Beak and Pounces, *Hercules* pursu'd,
And cuff'd his manly Cheeks, and tore his
    Face ;   741
Then, safe retir'd, and tour'd in empty space.
Alcides bore not long his flying Foe :
But bending his inevitable Bow,
Reach'd him in Air, suspended as he stood ;
And in his Pinion fix'd the feather'd Wood.
Light was the Wound ; but in the Sinew
    hung
The Point : and his disabled Wing unstrung.
He wheel'd in Air, and stretch'd his Vans in
    vain ;   749
His Vans no longer cou'd his Flight sustain :
For while one gather'd Wind, one unsupply'd
Hung drooping down ; nor pois'd his other
    Side.

He fell : The Shaft that slightly was im-
    press'd,
Now from his heavy Fall with weight in-
    creas'd,
Drove through his Neck, aslant ; he spurns
    the Ground,
And the Soul issues through the Weazon's
    Wound.
  Now, brave Commander of the *Rhodian*
    Seas,
What Praise is due from me to *Hercules* ?
Silence is all the Vengeance I decree
For my slain Brothers ; but 'tis Peace with
    thee.   760
  Thus with a flowing Tongue old *Nestor*
    spoke :
Then, to full Bowls each other they provoke :
At length, with Weariness, and Wine
    oppress'd
They rise from Table ; and withdraw to
    rest.
  The Sire of *Cygnus*, Monarch of the Main,
Mean time, laments his Son, in Battle slain :
And vows the Victor's Death ; nor vows
    in vain.
For nine long Years the smoother'd Pain he
    bore ;
(*Achilles* was not ripe for Fate, before :)
Then when he saw the promis'd Hour was
    near,   770
He thus bespoke the God, that guides the
    Year.
Immortal Offspring of my Brother *Jove* ;
My brightest Nephew, and whom best I love,
Whose Hands were join'd with mine, to
    raise the Wall
Of tottring *Troy*, now nodding to her fall ;
Dost thou not mourn our Pow'r employ'd in
    vain ;
And the Defenders of our City slain ?
To pass the rest, cou'd noble *Hector* lie
Unpity'd, drag'd around his Native *Troy* ?
And yet the Murd'rer lives: Himself by far 780
A greater Plague, than all the wastful War :
He lives ; the proud *Pelides* lives to boast
Our Town destroy'd, our common Labour
    lost !
O, cou'd I meet him ! But I wish too late
To prove my Trident is not in his Fate !
But let him try (for that's allow'd) thy Dart,
And pierce his only penetrable Part.
  Apollo bows to the superiour Throne
And to his Uncle's Anger, adds his own.

---

742 tour'd] *The spelling is probably Dryden's.*

Then in a Cloud involv'd, he takes his
  Flight,   790
Where *Greeks* and *Trojans* mix'd in mortal
  Fight ;
And found out *Paris*, lurking where he stood,
And stain'd his Arrows with *Plebeyan* Blood :
Phœbus to him alone the God confess'd,
Then to the recreant Knight he thus
  address'd.
Dost thou not blush, to spend thy Shafts in
  vain
On a degenerate, and ignoble Train ?
If Fame, or better Vengeance be thy Care,
There aim : And with one Arrow, end the war.
  He said ; and shew'd from far the blazing ⎫
    Shield   800 ⎮
And Sword, which but *Achilles* none cou'd ⎬
    weild ;   ⎮
And how he mov'd a God, and mow'd the ⎮
    standing Field.   ⎭
The Deity himself directs aright
Th' invenom'd Shaft ; and wings the fatal
  Flight.
  Thus fell the foremost of the *Grecian* Name ;
And He, the base Adult'rer, boasts the Fame.
A Spectacle to glad the *Trojan* Train ;
And please old *Priam*, after *Hector* slain.
If by a Female Hand he had foreseen ⎫
He was to die, his Wish had rather been ⎮
The Lance and double Axe of the fair ⎬
    Warriour Queen.   811 ⎭

And now, the Terror of the *Trojan* Field,
The   *Grecian*   Honour, Ornament, and
  Shield,
High on a Pile th' Unconquer'd Chief is
  plac'd :
The God that arm'd him first, consum'd at
  last.
Of all the Mighty Man, the small Remains
A little Urn, and scarcely fill'd, contains.
Yet great in *Homer*, still *Achilles* lives ;
And equal to himself, himself survives.
  His Buckler owns its former Lord ; and
    brings   820
New cause of Strife betwixt contending
  Kings ;
Who Worthiest after him, his Sword to
  wield,
Or wear his Armour, or sustain his Shield.
Ev'n *Diomede* sat mute, with down-cast
  Eyes ;
Conscious of wanted Worth to win the Prize :
Nor *Menelas* presum'd these Arms to claim,
Nor He the King of Men, a greater Name.
Two Rivals only rose : *Laertes* Son,
And the vast Bulk of *Ajax Telamon* :
The King, who cherish'd each, with equal
  Love,   830
And from himself all Envy wou'd remove,
Left both to be determin'd by the Laws ;
And to the *Grecian* Chiefs transferr'd the
  Cause.

THE | SPEECHES | OF | AJAX | AND | ULYSSES :

FROM | OVID'S METAMORPHOSES,

BOOK XIII

THE Chiefs were set ; the Soldiers crown'd
  the Field :
To these the Master of the sevenfold Shield
Upstarted fierce : And kindled with Disdain
Eager to speak, unable to contain
His boiling Rage, he rowl'd his Eyes around

OVID'S METAMORPHOSES XII.   826 Menelas]
*The editors, regardless of scansion, wrongly
give* Menelaus
  THE SPEECHES OF AJAX AND ULYSSES. Text
from the original edition of 1700. In l. 157
Dryden's spelling of 'Slight' for 'Sleight' has produced in Warton's, Hooper's, and other editions
the absurd reading 'Flight'. The original has
several false stops.

The Shore, and *Grecian* Gallies hall'd
  a-ground.
Then stretching out his Hands, O *Jove*, he
  cry'd,
Must then our Cause before the Fleet be
  try'd ?
And dares *Ulysses* for the Prize contend,
In sight of what he durst not once
  defend ?   10
But basely fled that memorable Day,
When I from *Hector's* Hands redeem'd the
  flaming Prey.
So much 'tis safer at the noisy Bar
With Words to flourish than ingage in War.

By different Methods we maintain our
Right,
Nor am I made to Talk, nor he to Fight.
In bloody Fields I labour to be great;
His Arms are a smooth Tongue, and soft
deceit:
Nor need I speak my Deeds, for those you
see;
The Sun and Day are Witnesses for me, 20
Let him who fights unseen relate his own,
And vouch the silent Stars, and conscious
Moon;
Great is the Prize demanded, I confess,
But such an abject Rival makes it less;
That Gift, those Honours, he but hop'd to
gain
Can leave no room for *Ajax* to be vain:
Losing he wins, because his Name will be
Enobled by Defeat, who durst contend with
me.
Were my known Valour question'd, yet my
Blood
Without that Plea wou'd make my Title
good: 30
My Sire was *Telamon* whose Arms, employ'd
With *Hercules*, these *Trojan* Walls destroy'd;
And who before, with *Jason*, sent from
Greece,
In the first Ship brought home the Golden
Fleece;
Great *Telamon* from *Æacus* derives
His birth (th' Inquisitor of guilty Lives
In Shades below where *Sysiphus* whose Son
This Thief is thought rouls up the restless
heavy Stone,)
Just *Æacus* the King of Gods above
Begot: Thus *Ajax* is the third from *Jove*. 40
Nor shou'd I seek advantage from my
Line,
Unless (*Achilles*) it were mix'd with thine:
As next of Kin *Achilles* Arms I claim;
This Fellow wou'd ingraft a Foreign Name
Upon our Stock, and the *Sysiphian* Seed
By Fraud and Theft asserts his Father's
Breed:
Then must I lose these Arms, because I came
To fight uncall'd, a voluntary Name,
Nor shun'd the Cause, but offer'd you my
Aid,
While he long lurking was to War betray'd?
Forc'd to the Field he came, but in the
Reer; 51
And feign'd Distraction to conceal his Fear:

Till one more cunning caught him in the
Snare;
(Ill for himself) and drag'd him into War.
Now let a Hero's Arms a Coward vest,
And he who shun'd all Honours, gain the best:
And let me stand excluded from my Right
Rob'd of my Kinsman's Arms, who first
appear'd in Fight.
Better for us at home had he remain'd
Had it been true, the Madness which he
feign'd, 60
Or so believ'd; the less had been our Shame,
The less his counsell'd Crime which brands
the *Grecian* Name;
Nor *Philoctetes* had been left inclos'd
In a bare Isle to Wants and Pains expos'd,
Where to the Rocks, with solitary Groans
His Suff'rings and our Baseness he bemoans;
And wishes (so may Heav'n his Wish
fulfill)
The due Reward to him who caus'd his Ill.
Now he, with us to *Troy's* Destruction
sworn
Our Brother of the War, by whom are
borne 70
Alcides Arrows, pent in narrow Bounds
With Cold and Hunger pinch'd, and pain'd
with Wounds,
To find him Food and Cloathing must
employ
Against the Birds the Shafts due to the Fate
of *Troy*.
Yet still he lives, and lives from Treason
free,
Because he left *Ulysses* Company:
Poor *Palamede* might wish, so void of Aid,
Rather to have been left, than so to Death
betray'd.
The Coward bore the Man immortal Spight,
Who sham'd him out of Madness into Fight:
Nor daring otherwise to vent his Hate 81
Accus'd him first of Treason to the State,
And then for Proof produc'd the golden
Store,
Himself had hidden in his Tent before:
Thus of two Champions he depriv'd our
Hoast,
By Exile one, and one by Treason lost.
Thus fights *Ulysses*, thus his Fame extends,
A formidable Man, but to his Friends
Great, for what Greatness is in Words and
Sound:
Ev'n faithful *Nestor* less in both is found: 90

But that he might without a Rival reign,
He left this faithful *Nestor* on the Plain ;
Forsook his Friend ev'n at his utmost Need,
Who tir'd, and tardy with his wounded
    Steed
Cry'd out for Aid, and call'd him by his
    Name ;
But Cowardice has neither Ears nor Shame :
Thus fled the good old Man, bereft of Aid,
And for as much as lay in him, betray'd :
That this is not a Fable forg'd by me,
Like one of his, an *Ulyssean* Lie,   100
I vouch ev'n *Diomede*, who tho' his Friend
Cannot that Act excuse, much less defend :
He call'd him back aloud, and tax'd his
    Fear ;
And sure enough he heard, but durst not
    hear.
    The Gods with equal Eyes on Mortals
    look,
He justly was forsaken, who forsook :
Wanted that Succour he refus'd to lend,
Found ev'ry Fellow such another Friend :
No wonder, if he roar'd that all might hear ;
His Elocution was increas'd by Fear :   110
I heard, I ran, I found him out of Breath,
Pale, trembling, and half dead, with Fear of
    Death.
Though he had judg'd himself by his own
    Laws,
And stood condemn'd, I help'd the common
    Cause :
With my broad Buckler hid him from the
    Foe ;
(Ev'n the Shield trembled as he lay below ;)
And from impending Fate the Coward freed :
Good Heav'n forgive me for so bad a Deed !
If still he will persist, and urge the Strife,
First let him give me back his forfeit
    Life :   120
Let him return to that opprobrious Field :
Again creep under my protecting Shield :
Let him lie wounded, let the Foe be near,
And let his quiv'ring Heart confess his Fear ;
There put him in the very Jaws of Fate ;
And let him plead his Cause in that Estate :
And yet, when snatch'd from Death, when
    from below
My lifted Shield I loos'd, and let him go :
Good Heav'ns, how light he rose, with what
    a bound
He sprung from Earth, forgetful of his
    Wound ;   130

How fresh, how eager then his Feet to ply ;
Who had not Strength to stand, had Speed
    to fly !.
    Hector came on, and brought the Gods
    along ;
Fear seiz'd alike the Feeble and the Strong :
Each *Greek* was an *Ulysses* ; such a Dread
Th' approach, and e'en the sound of *Hector*
    bred :
Him, flesh'd with Slaughter, and with
    Conquest crown'd,
I met, and over-turn'd him to the Ground.
When after, matchless as he deem'd, in
    Might,
He challeng'd all our Hoast to single Fight ;
All Eyes were fix'd on me : The Lots were
    thrown ;   141
But for your Champion I was wish'd alone :
Your Vows were heard, we Fought and
    neither yield ;
Yet I return'd unvanquish'd from the
    Field.
With *Jove* to friend th' insulting *Trojan*
    came,
And menac'd us with Force, our Fleet with
    Flame :
Was it the Strength of this Tongue-valiant
    Lord,
In that black Hour, that sav'd you from the
    Sword ?
Or was my Breast expos'd alone, to brave
A thousand Swords, a thousand Ships to
    save ?   150
The hopes of your return ! And can you
    yield,
For a sav'd Fleet, less than a single Shield ?
Think it no Boast, O *Grecians*, if I deem
These Arms want *Ajax*, more than *Ajax*
    them ;
Or, I with them an equal Honour share ;
They honour'd to be worn, and I to wear.
Will he compare my Courage with his Slight ?
As well he may compare the Day with Night.
Night is indeed the Province of his Reign :
Yet all his dark Exploits no more contain⎫
Than a Spy taken, and a Sleeper slain ; 161⎬
A Priest made Pris'ner, *Pallas* made a Prey⎫
But none of all these Actions done by⎪
    Day :⎬
Nor ought of these was done, and *Diomed*⎪
    away.⎭
If on such petty Merits you confer
So vast a Prize, let each his Portion share ;

Make a just Dividend : and if not all,
The greater part to *Diomed* will fall.
But why for *Ithacus* such Arms as those,
Who naked and by Night invades his Foes ?
The glitt'ring Helm by Moonlight will
    proclaim   171
The latent Robber, and prevent his Game :
Nor could he hold his tott'ring Head up-
    right
Beneath that Motion, or sustain the Weight ;
Nor that right Arm cou'd toss the beamy
    Lance ;
Much less the left that ampler Shield
    advance ;
Pond'rous with precious Weight, and rough
    with Cost
Of the round World in rising Gold emboss'd.
That Orb would ill become his Hand to wield,
And look as for the Gold he stole the Shield ;
Which shou'd your Error on the Wretch
    bestow,   181
It would not frighten, but allure the Foe :
Why asks he, what avails him not in Fight,
And wou'd but cumber and retard his Flight,
In which his only Excellence is plac'd ?
You give him Death, that intercept his
    hast.
Add, that his own is yet a Maiden-Shield,
Nor the least Dint has suffer'd in the Field,
Guiltless of Fight : Mine batter'd, hew'd,
    and bor'd,
Worn out of Service, must forsake his Lord.
What farther need of Words our Right to
    scan ?   191
My Arguments are Deeds, let Action speak
    the Man.
Since from a Champion's Arms the Strife
    arose,
So cast the glorious Prize amid the Foes ;
Then send us to redeem both Arms and
    Shield,
And let him wear who wins 'em in the Field.
    He said : A Murmur from the Multitude,
Or somewhat like a stiffled Shout, ensu'd :
Till from his Seat arose *Laertes* Son,
Look'd down awhile, and paus'd e'er he
    begun ;   200
Then to th' expecting Audience rais'd his
    Look,
And not without prepar'd Attention spoke :
Soft was his Tone, and sober was his Face ;
Action his Words, and Words his Action
    grace.

If Heav'n, my Lords, had heard our
    common Pray'r,
These Arms had caus'd no Quarrel for an
    Heir ;
Still great *Achilles* had his own possess'd,
And we with great *Achilles* had been bless'd.
But since hard Fate, and Heav'ns severe
    Decree,
Have ravish'd him away from you and me,
(At this he sigh'd, and wip'd his Eyes, and
    drew,   211
Or seem'd to draw some Drops of kindly
    Dew)
Who better can succeed *Achilles* lost,
Than he who gave *Achilles* to your Hoast ?
This only I request, that neither He
May gain, by being what he seems to be,
A stupid Thing, nor I may lose the Prize,
By having Sense, which Heav'n to him
    denies :
Since, great or small, the Talent I enjoy'd
Was ever in the common Cause employ'd :
Nor let my Wit, and wonted Eloquence 221
Which often has been us'd in your Defence
And in my own, this only time be brought
To bear against my self, and deem'd a
    Fault.
Make not a Crime, where Nature made it
    none ;
For ev'ry Man may freely use his own.
The Deeds of long descended Ancestors
Are but by grace of Imputation ours,
Theirs in effect : but since he draws his
    Line
From *Jove*, and seems to plead a Right
    Divine,   230
From *Jove*, like him, I claim my Pedigree,
And am descended in the same degree :
My sire *Laertes* was *Arcesius* Heir,
Arcesius was the Son of *Jupiter* :
No Paricide, no banish'd Man, is known
In all my Line : Let him excuse his own.
Hermes ennobles too my Mother's Side,
By both my Parents to the Gods ally'd ;
But not because that on the Female Part
My Blood is better, dare I claim Desert, 240
Or that my Sire from Paricide is free,
But judge by Merit betwixt Him and Me :
The Prize be to the best ; provided yet,
That *Ajax* for awhile his Kin forget,
And his great Sire, and greater Uncles
    Name,
To fortify by them his feeble Claim :

Be Kindred and Relation laid aside,
And Honours Cause by Laws of Honour
    try'd :
For if he plead Proximity of Blood ;   249
That empty Title is with Ease withstood.
Peleus, the Hero's Sire, more nigh than he,
And *Pyrrhus*, his undoubted Progeny,
Inherit first these Trophies of the Field ;
To *Scyros*, or to *Phthya*, send the Shield :
And *Teucer* has an Uncle's Right ; yet he
Waves his Pretensions, nor contends with
    me.
    Then since the Cause on pure Desert is
        plac'd,
Whence shall I take my Rise, what reckon
    last ?
I not presume on ev'ry Act to dwell,
But take these few, in order as they fell. 260
Thetis, who knew the Fates, apply'd her
    Care,
To keep *Achilles* in Disguise from War ;
And till the threat'ning Influence were past,
A Woman's Habit on the Hero cast :
All Eyes were couzen'd by the borrow'd
    Vest,
And *Ajax* (never wiser than the rest)
Found no *Pelides* there : At length I came
With proffer'd Wares to this pretended
    Dame ;
She not discover'd by her Mien or Voice, 269
Betray'd her Manhood by her manly Choice ;
And while on Female Toys her Fellows look,⎫
Grasp'd in her Warlike Hand, a Javelin ⎬
    shook ;   ⎪
Whom, by this Act reveal'd, I thus bespoke :⎭
O Goddess-born ! resist not Heav'ns Decree,
The Fall of *Ilium* is reserv'd for thee ;
Then seiz'd him, and, produc'd in open
    Light,
Sent blushing to the Field the fatal Knight.
Mine then are all his Actions of the War ;
Great *Telephus* was conquer'd by my Spear,
And after cur'd : To me the *Thebans* owe,
Lesbos and *Tenedos*, their Overthrow ;   280
Syros and *Cylla* ! Not on all to dwell,
By me *Lyrnesus*, and strong *Chrysa* fell :
And since I sent the Man who *Hector*
    slew,
To me the noble *Hector's* Death is due :
Those Arms I put into his living Hand,
Those Arms, *Pelides* dead, I now demand.

When *Greece* was injur'd in the *Spartan*
    Prince,
And met at *Aulis* to revenge th' Offence,
'Twas a dead Calm, or adverse Blasts that
    reign'd,   290
And in the Port the Wind-bound Fleet
    detain'd :
Bad Signs were seen, and Oracles severe
Were daily thunder'd in our General's Ear :
That by his Daughter's Blood we must
    appease
Diana's kindled Wrath, and free the Seas.
Affection,   Int'rest,   Fame,   his   Heart
    assail'd ;
But soon the Father o'er the King prevail'd :
Bold, on himself he took the pious Crime,
As angry with the Gods, as they with him.
No Subject cou'd sustain their Sov'raign's
    Look,   300
Till this hard Enterprize I undertook :
I only durst th' Imperial Pow'r controul,
And undermin'd the Parent in his Soul ;
Forc'd him t' exert the King for common
    Good,
And pay our Ransom with his Daughters
    Blood.
Never was Cause more difficult to plead,
Than where the Judge against himself
    decreed :
Yet this I won by Dint of Argument ;   ⎫
The Wrongs his injur'd Brother underwent, ⎬
And his own office sham'd him to consent. ⎭
    'Twas harder yet to move the Mother's
        Mind,   311
And to this heavy Task was I design'd :
Reasons against her Love I knew were vain :
I circumvented whom I could not gain :
Had *Ajax* been employ'd, our slacken'd
    Sails
Had still at *Aulis* waited happy Gales.
    Arriv'd at *Troy*, your Choice was fix'd on
        me,
A fearless Envoy, fit for a bold Embassy :
Secure, I enter'd through the hostile Court,
Glitt'ring with Steel, and crowded with
    Resort :   320
There, in the midst of Arms, I plead our
    Cause,
Urge the foul Rape, and violated Laws ;
Accuse the Foes, as Authors of the Strife,
Reproach the Ravisher, demand the Wife
Priam, *Antenor*, and the wiser few,
I mov'd ; but *Paris* and his lawless Crew

Scarce held their Hands, and lifted Swords:
　But stood
In Act to quench their Impious thirst of
　Blood:
This *Menelaus* knows; expos'd to share
With me the rough Preludium of the
　War.　　　　　　　　　　　　　330
　Endless it were to tell what I have done,
In Arms, or Council, since the Siege begun:
The first Encounters pass'd, the Foe
　repell'd,
They skulk'd within the Town, we kept the
　Field.
War seem'd asleep for nine long Years, at
　length,
Both Sides resolv'd to push, we try'd our
　Strength.
Now what did *Ajax* while our Arms took
　Breath,
Vers'd only in the gross mechanick Trade of
　Death?
If you require my Deeds, with ambush'd
　Arms
I trap'd the Foe, or tir'd with false Alarms;
Secur'd the Ships, drew Lines along the
　Plain,　　　　　　　　　　　　341
The Fainting chear'd, chastis'd the Rebel-
　train,
Provided Forage, our spent Arms renew'd;
Employ'd at home, or sent abroad, the
　common Cause pursu'd.
The King, deluded in a Dream by Jove,
Despair'd to take the Town, and order'd to
　remove.
What Subject durst arraign the Pow'r
　supreme,
Producing *Jove* to justify his Dream?
Ajax might wish the Soldiers to retain
From shameful Flight, but Wishes were in
　vain:　　　　　　　　　　　　350
As wanting of effect had been his Words,
Such as of course his thundring Tongue
　affords.
But did this Boaster threaten, did he pray,⎫
Or by his own Example urge their stay?⎬
None, none of these, but ran himself away.⎭
I saw him run, and was asham'd to see;
Who ply'd his Feet so fast to get aboard as
　He?
Then speeding through the Place, I made⎫
　a stand,　　　　　　　　　　　⎬
And loudly cry'd, O base degen'rate Band,
To leave a Town already in your Hand! 360

After so long expence of Blood, for Fame,
To bring home nothing but perpetual
　Shame!
These Words, or what I have forgotten
　since,
(For Grief inspir'd me then with Eloquence)
Reduc'd their Minds, they leave the crowded
　Port,
And to their late forsaken Camp resort;
Dismay'd the Council met: This Man was
　there,
But mute, and not recover'd of his Fear.
Thersites tax'd the King, and loudly rail'd,
But his wide opening Mouth with Blows
　I seal'd.　　　　　　　　　　　370
Then, rising, I excite their Souls to Fame,
And kindle sleeping Virtue into Flame,
From thence, whatever he perform'd in
　Fight
Is justly mine, who drew him back from
　Flight.
　Which of the *Grecian* Chiefs consorts with⎫
　　Thee?　　　　　　　　　　　⎬
But *Diomede* desires my Company,　　　⎭
And still communicates his Praise with me.
As guided by a God, secure he goes,
Arm'd with my Fellowship amid the Foes:
And sure no little Merit I may boast,　　380
Whom such a Man selects from such an
　Hoast;
Unforc'd by Lots I went without Affright,
To dare with him the Dangers of the
　Night:
On the same Errand sent, we met the Spy
Of *Hector*, double tongu'd, and us'd to lie;
Him I dispatch'd, but not till undermin'd
I drew him first to tell what treacherous
　Troy design'd:
My Task perform'd, with Praise I had retir'd,
But not content with this, to greater Praise
　aspir'd;
Invaded *Rhæsus*, and his *Thracian* Crew,
And him, and his, in their own Strength,
　I slew;　　　　　　　　　　　391
Return'd a Victor, all my Vows compleat,
With the King's Chariot, in his Royal Seat:
Refuse me now his Arms, whose fiery
　Steeds
Were promis'd to the Spy for his Nocturnal
　Deeds:
And let dull *Ajax* bear away my Right,
When all his Days out-ballance this one
　Night.

Nor fought I darkling still: The Sun beheld
With slaughter'd *Lycians* when I strew'd the Field;
You saw, and counted as I pass'd along,   400
Alastor, Cromyus, Ceranos the Strong,
Alcander, Prytanis, and *Halius*,
Noemon, Charopes, and *Ennomus*,
Choon, Chersidamas ; and five beside
Men of obscure Descent, but Courage try'd :
All these this Hand laid breathless on the Ground ;
Nor want I Proofs of many a manly Wound :
All honest, all before : Believe not me ;
Words may deceive, but credit what you see.
At this he bar'd his Breast, and show'd his Scars,   410
As of a furrow'd Field, well plough'd with Wars ;
Nor is this Part unexercis'd, said he ;
That Gyant-bulk of his from Wounds is free :
Safe in his Shield he fears no Foe to try,
And better manages his Blood than I :
But this avails me not ; our Boaster strove
Not with our Foes alone, but partial *Jove*,
To save the Fleet : This I confess is true,
(Nor will I take from any Man his Due :)
But thus assuming all, he robs from you. 420
Some part of Honour to your share will fall,
He did the best indeed, but did not all.
Patroclus in *Achilles* Arms, and thought
The Chief he seem'd, with equal Ardour fought ;
Preserv'd the Fleet, repell'd the raging Fire,
And forc'd the fearful *Trojans* to retire.
But *Ajax* boasts, that he was only thought
A Match for *Hector*, who the Combat sought :
Sure he forgets the King, the Chiefs, and Me ;
All were as eager for the Fight as He :   430
He but the ninth, and, not by publick Voice,
Or ours preferr'd, was only Fortunes Choice :
They fought, nor can our Hero boast the Event,
For *Hector* from the Field unwounded went.
Why am I forc'd to name that fatal Day,
That snatch'd the Prop and Pride of *Greece* away ?

I saw *Pelides* sink, with pious Grief,
And ran in vain, alas, to his Relief ;
For the brave Soul was fled : Full of my Friend,
I rush'd amid the War, his Relicks to defend :   440
Nor ceas'd my Toil till I redeem'd the Prey,
And loaded with *Achilles*, march'd away :
Those Arms, which on these Shoulders then I bore,
'Tis just you to these Shoulders should restore.
You see I want not Nerves, who cou'd sustain
The pond'rous Ruins of so great a Man :
Or if in others equal Force you find,
None is endu'd with a more grateful Mind.
Did *Thetis* then, ambitious in her Care,
These Arms thus labour'd for her Son prepare ;   450
That *Ajax* after him the heav'nly gift should wear ?
For that dull Soul to stare, with stupid Eyes,
On the learn'd unintelligible Prize !
What are to him the Sculptures of the Shield,
Heav'ns Planets, Earth, and Oceans watry Field ?
The *Pleiads, Hyads* ; less, and greater Bear,
Undipp'd in Seas ; *Orion's* angry Star ;
Two diff'ring Cities, grav'd on either Hand ?
Would he wear Arms he cannot understand ?
Beside, what wise Objections he prepares
Against my late Accession to the Wars ?   461
Does not the Fool perceive his Argument
Is with more force against *Achilles* bent ?
For, if Dissembling be so great a Crime,
The Fault is common, and the same in him :
And if he taxes both of long delay,
My Guilt is less, who sooner came away.
His pious Mother anxious for his Life,
Detain'd her Son, and me, my pious Wife.
To them the Blossoms of our Youth were due :   470
Our riper Manhood we reserv'd for you.
But grant me guilty, 'tis not much my care,
When with so great a Man my Guilt I share :
My Wit to War the matchless Hero brought,
But by this Fool I never had been caught.
Nor need I wonder, that on me he threw
Such foul Aspersions, when he spares not you :

---

398 darkling] Darkling *1700.*

If *Palamede* unjustly fell by me,
Your Honour suffer'd in th' unjust Decree:
I but accus'd, you doom'd: And yet he
    dy'd,   480
Convinc'd of Treason, and was fairly try'd:
You heard not he was false; your Eyes
    beheld
The Traytor manifest; the Bribe reveal'd.
  That *Philoctetes* is on *Lemnos* left,
Wounded, forlorn, of human Aid bereft,
Is not my Crime, or not my Crime alone;
Defend your Justice, for the Fact's your
    own:
'Tis true, th' Advice was mine: that staying ⎫
    there   ⎬
He might his weary Limbs with rest ⎬
    repair,   ⎬
From a long Voyage free, and from a longer ⎭
    War.   490
He took the Counsel, and he lives at least;
Th' Event declares I counsell'd for the best:
Though Faith is all in Ministers of State;
For who can promise to be fortunate?
Now since his Arrows are the Fate of *Troy*,
Do not my Wit, or weak Address, employ;
Send *Ajax* there, with his persuasive Sense
To mollify the Man, and draw him thence:
But *Xanthus* shall run backward; *Ida* stand
A leafless Mountain; and the *Grecian*
    Band   500
Shall fight for *Troy*; if when my Counsels
    fail,
The Wit of heavy *Ajax* can prevail.
  Hard *Philoctetes*, exercise thy Spleen,
Against thy Fellows, and the King of Men;
Curse my devoted Head, above the rest,
And wish in Arms to meet me Breast to
    Breast:
Yet I the dang'rous Task will undertake
And either die my self, or bring thee back.
  Nor doubt the same Success, as when
    before
The *Phrygian* Prophet to these Tents I bore,
Surpriz'd by Night, and forc'd him to
    declare   511
In what was plac'd the fortune of the War;
Heav'ns dark Decrees, and Answers to
    display,
And how to take the Town, and where the
    Secret lay:
Yet this I compass'd, and from *Troy* con-
    vey'd
The fatal Image of their Guardian-Maid;

That Work was mine; for *Pallas*, though our
    Friend,
Yet while she was in *Troy*, did *Troy* defend.
Now what has *Ajax* done, or what design'd,
A noisy Nothing, and an empty Wind?   520
If he be what he promises in Show,
Why was I sent, and why fear'd he to go
Our boasting Champion thought the Task
    not light
To pass the Guards, commit himself to
    Night;
Not only through a hostile Town to pass,
But scale, with steep Ascent, the sacred
    Place;
With wand'ring Steps to search the Cittadel,
And from the Priests their Patroness to
    steal:
Then through surrounding Foes to force my
    way,
And bear in Triumph home the heav'nly
    Prey;   530
Which had I not, *Ajax* in vain had held,
Before that monst'rous Bulk, his sev'nfold
    Shield
That Night to conquer *Troy* I might be said
When *Troy* was liable to Conquest made.
  Why point'st thou to my Partner of the
    War?
Tydides had indeed a worthy share
In all my Toil, and Praise; but when thy
    Might
Our Ships protected, didst thou singly fight?
All join'd, and thou of many wert but one;
I ask'd no Friend, nor had, but him
    alone;   540
Who, had he not been well assur'd, that Art
And Conduct were of War the better part,
And more avail'd than Strength, my valiant
    Friend
Had urg'd a better Right, than *Ajax* can
    pretend:
As good at least *Euripylus* may claim,
And the more moderate *Ajax* of the Name:
The *Cretan* King, and his brave Charioteer,
And *Menelaus* bold with Sword and Spear;
All these had been my Rivals in the Shield,
And yet all these to my Pretensions yield
Thy boist'rous Hands are then of Use,
    when I   551
With this directing Head those Hands apply.
Brawn without Brain is thine: My prudent
    Care
Foresees, provides, administers the War:

Thy Province is to Fight ; but when shall be
The time to Fight, the King consults with
  me :
No dram of Judgment with thy force is
  join'd ;
Thy Body is of Profit, and my Mind.
By how much more the Ship her Safety
  owes
To him who steers, than him that only
  rows,   560
By how much more the Captain merits
  Praise
Than he who Fights, and Fighting but
  obeys ;
By so much greater is my Worth than
  thine,
Who canst but execute what I design.
What gain'st thou brutal Man, if I confess
Thy Strength superiour, when thy Wit is
  less ?
Mind is the Man : I claim my whole
  Desert
From the Mind's Vigour, and th' immortal
  part.
But you, O *Grecian* Chiefs, reward my
  Care,
Be grateful to your Watchman of the
  War :   570
For all my Labours in so long a space,
Sure I may plead a Title to your Grace :
Enter the Town ; I then unbarr'd the
  Gates,
When I remov'd their tutelary Fates.
By all our common hopes, if hopes they be
Which I have now reduc'd to Certainty ;
By falling *Troy*, by yonder tott'ring Towers,
And by their taken Gods, which now are
  ours ;
Or if there yet a farther Task remains,
To be perform'd by Prudence or by
  Pains ;   580
If yet some desperate Action rests behind,
That asks high Conduct, and a dauntless
  Mind :
If ought be wanting to the *Trojan* Doom,
Which none but I can manage and o'er-
  come,

Award those Arms I ask, by your Decree :
Or give to this what you refuse to me.
  He ceas'd : And ceasing with Respect he
  bow'd,
And with his Hand at once the fatal Statue
  show'd.
Heav'n, Air and Ocean rung, with loud
  Applause,
And by the general Vote he gain'd his
  Cause.   590
Thus Conduct won the Prize, when Courage
  fail'd,
And Eloquence o'er brutal Force prevail'd.

The Death of Ajax.

He who cou'd often, and alone withstand
The Foe, the Fire, and *Jove's* own partial
  Hand,
Now cannot his unmaster'd Grief sustain,
But yields to Rage, to Madness, and Disdain ;
Then snatching out his Fauchion, Thou,
  said He,
Art mine ; *Ulysses* lays no claim to Thee.
O often try'd, and ever trusty Sword,
Now do thy last kind Office to thy
  Lord :   600
'Tis *Ajax*, who requests thy Aid, to show
None but himself, himself cou'd overthrow :
He said, and with so good a Will to die
Did to his Breast the fatal Point apply,
It found his Heart, a way till then
  unknown,
Where never Weapon enter'd but his own.
No Hands cou'd force it thence, so fix'd it
  stood,
Till out it rush'd, expell'd by Streams of
  spouting Blood.
The fruitful Blood produc'd a Flow'r, which ⎫
  grew   ⎬
On a green Stem ; and of a Purple Hue : ⎭
Like his, whom unaware *Apollo* slew : 611
Inscrib'd in both, the Letters are the same,
But those express the Grief, and these the
  Name.

THE DEATH OF AJAX. Text from the original
edition of 1700.

THE FABLE | OF | ACIS, | POLYPHEMUS, | AND | GALATEA.

FROM THE | THIRTEENTH BOOK OF THE METAMORPHOSES.

GALATEA *relates the Story.*

Acis, the Lovely Youth, whose loss I mourn,
From *Faunus* and the Nymph *Symethis* born,
Was both his Parents pleasure : but to me
Was all that Love cou'd make a Lover be.
The Gods our Minds in mutual Bands did
  joyn :
I was his only Joy, and he was mine.
Now sixteen Summers the sweet Youth had
  seen ;
And doubtful Down began to shade his
  Chin :
When *Polyphemus* first disturb'd our Joy,
And lov'd me fiercely, as I lov'd the Boy. 10
Ask not which passion in my Soul was
  high'r,
My last Aversion, or my first Desire :
Nor this the greater was, nor that the less ;
Both were alike ; for both were in excess.
Thee, *Venus*, thee both Heav'n and Earth
  obey ;
Immense thy Pow'r, and boundless is thy
  Sway.
The *Cyclops*, who defi'd th' Æthereal Throne,
And thought no Thunder louder than his own,
The terrour of the Woods, and wilder far
Than Wolves in Plains, or Bears in Forrests
  are,   20
Th' Inhumane Host, who made his bloody
  Feasts
On mangl'd Members of his butcher'd
  Guests,
Yet felt the force of Love, and fierce Desire,
And burnt for me, with unrelenting Fire :
Forgot his Caverns, and his woolly care, ⎫
Assum'd the softness of a Lover's Air ; ⎬
And comb'd, with Teeth of Rakes, his ⎭
  rugged hair.
Now with a crooked Sythe his Beard he
  sleeks ;
And mows the stubborn Stubble of his
  Cheeks :
Now, in the Crystal Stream he looks, to
  try   30
His Simagres, and rowls his glaring eye.

His Cruelty and thirst of Blood are lost ;
And Ships securely sail along the Coast.
  The Prophet *Telemus* (arriv'd by chance
Where *Ætna's* Summets to the Seas
  advance,
Who mark'd the Tracts of every Bird that
  flew,
And sure Presages from their flying drew)
Foretold the *Cyclops*, that *Ulysses* hand
In his broad eye shou'd thrust a flaming
  Brand.
The Giant, with a scornful grin, reply'd, 40
Vain Augur, thou hast falsely prophesi'd ;
Already Love his flaming Brand has tost ;
Looking on two fair Eyes, my sight I lost.
Thus, warn'd in vain, with stalking pace
  he strode,
And stamp'd the Margine of the briny Flood
With heavy steps ; and weary, sought agen
The cool Retirement of his gloomy Den.
  A Promontory, sharp'ning by degrees,
Ends in a Wedge, and over-looks the Seas :
On either side, below, the water flows :   50
This airy walk the Giant Lover chose.
Here, on the midst he sate ; his Flocks,
  unled,
Their Shepherd follow'd, and securely fed.
A Pine so burly, and of length so vast,
That sailing Ships requir'd it for a Mast,
He wielded for a Staff ; his steps to guide :
But laid it by, his Whistle while he try'd.
A hundred Reeds, of a prodigious growth,
Scarce made a Pipe proportion'd to his
  mouth :
Which, when he gave it wind, the Rocks
  around,   60
And watry Plains, the dreadful hiss resound.
I heard the Ruffian-Shepherd rudely blow,
Where, in a hollow Cave, I sat below ;
On *Acis* bosom I my head reclin'd :
And still preserve the Poem in my mind.
  Oh lovely *Galatea*, whiter far
Than falling Snows, and rising Lillies are ;
More flowry than the Meads, as Crystal
  bright ;
Erect as Alders, and of equal heigh : :

ACIS AND GALATEA.   Text of 1693.

More wanton than a Kid, more sleek thy
   Skin   70
Than Orient Shells, that on the Shores are
   seen :
Than Apples fairer, when the boughs they
   lade ;
Pleasing, as Winter Suns or Summer Shade :
More grateful to the sight, than goodly
   Planes ;
And softer to the touch, than down of
   Swans,
Or Curds new turn'd ; and sweeter to the
   taste
Than swelling Grapes, that to the Vintage
   haste :
More clear than Ice, or running Streams,
   that stray
Through Garden Plots, but ah more swift
   than they.
   Yet, *Galatea*, harder to be broke   80
Than Bullocks, unreclaim'd to bear the
   Yoke,
And far more stubborn than the knotted
   Oak :
Like sliding Streams, impossible to hold ;
Like them fallacious ; like their Fountains,
   cold :
More warping than the Willow, to decline
My warm Embrace, more brittle than the
   Vine ;
Immoveable, and fixt in thy disdain ;
Rough, as these Rocks, and of a harder
   grain.
More violent than is the rising Flood :
And the prais'd Peacock is not half so
   proud.   90
Fierce as the Fire, and sharp as Thistles are ;
And more outragious than a Mother-Bear :
Deaf as the billows to the Vows I make ;
And more revengeful, than a trodden Snake.
In swiftness fleeter than the flying Hind,
Or driven Tempests, or the driving Wind.
All other faults with patience I can bear ;
But swiftness is the Vice I only fear.
   Yet, if you knew me well, you wou'd not
   shun
My Love, but to my wish'd Embraces run :
Wou'd languish in your turn, and court my
   stay ;   101
And much repent of your unwise delay.

My Palace, in the living Rock, is made
By Nature's hand ; a spacious pleasing
   Shade ;
Which neither heat can pierce, nor cold
   invade.
My Garden fill'd with Fruits you may behold,
And Grapes in clusters, imitating Gold ;
Some blushing Bunches of a purple hue :
And these, and those, are all reserv'd for you.
Red Strawberries, in shades, expecting
   stand,   110
Proud to be gather'd by so white a hand.
Autumnal Cornels latter Fruit provide,
And Plumbs, to tempt you, turn their
   glossy side
Not those of common kinds ; but such alone
As in *Phæacian* Orchards might have grown :
Nor Chestnuts shall be wanting to your
   Food,
Nor Garden-fruits, nor Wildings of the Wood;
The laden Boughs for you alone shall bear ;
And yours shall be the product of the Year.
   The Flocks you see, are all my own ;
   beside   120
The rest that Woods and winding Vallies
   hide ;
And those that fold'd in the Caves abide.
Ask not the numbers of my growing Store ;
Who knows how many, knows he has no
   more.
Nor will I praise my Cattel ; trust not me,
But judge your self, and pass your own
   decree :
Behold their swelling Dugs ; the sweepy
   weight
Of Ews that sink beneath the Milky fraight ;
In the warm Folds their tender Lambkins
   lye ;
Apart from Kids, that call with humane cry.
New Milk in Nut-brown Bowls is duely
   serv'd   131
For daily Drink ; the rest for Cheese
   reserv'd.
Nor are these House-hold Dainties all my
   Store :
The Fields and Forrests will afford us more;
The Deer, the Hare, the Goat, the Salvage
   Boar.
All sorts of Ven'son ; and of Birds the best ;
A pair of Turtles taken from the Nest.

---

120 The Flocks you see, are] *Most editors
wrongly print* The Flocks, you see, are

I walk'd the Mountains, and two Cubs
  I found,
(Whose dam had left 'em on the naked
  ground,)   139
So like, that no distinction cou'd be seen ;
So pretty, they were Presents for a Queen ;
And so they shall ; I took 'em both away ;
And keep, to be Companions of your Play.
  Oh raise, fair Nymph, your Beauteous
    Face above
The Waves ; nor scorn my Presents, and my
    Love.
Come, *Galatea*, come, and view my face ; ⎫
I late beheld it, in the watry Glass ;   ⎬
And found it lovelier than I fear'd it was. ⎭
Survey my towring Stature, and my Size :
Not *Jove*, the *Jove* you dream, that rules the
    Skies   150
Bears such a bulk, or is so largely spread :
My Locks (the plenteous Harvest of my
    head)
Hang o're my Manly Face ; and dangling
    down,
As with a shady Grove, my shoulders crown.
Nor think, because my limbs and body bear
A thickset underwood of bristling hair,
My shape deform'd : what fouler sight can
    be,
Than the bald Branches of a leafless Tree ?
Foul is the Steed, without a flowing Main ;
And Birds, without their Feathers, and their
    Train.   160
Wool decks the Sheep ; and Man receives
    a Grace
From bushy Limbs, and from a bearded
    Face.
My forehead with a single eye is fill'd,
Round as a Ball, and ample as a Shield.
The Glorious Lamp of Heav'n, the Radiant
    Sun,
Is Nature's eye ; and is content with one.
Add, that my Father sways your Seas, and I
Like you am of the watry Family.
I make you his, in making you my own ;
You I adore ; and kneel to you alone : 170
Jove, with his Fabled Thunder, I despise,
And only fear the lightning of your eyes.
Frown not, fair Nymph ; yet I cou'd bear to
    be
Disdain'd, if others were disdain'd with me.

But to repulse the *Cyclops*, and prefer
The Love of *Acis*, (Heav'ns) I cannot bear.
But let the Stripling please himself ; nay
    more,
Please you, tho' that's the thing I most
    abhor ;
The Boy shall find, if e're we cope in Fight,
These Giant Limbs endu'd with Giant
    Might.   180
His living Bowels, from his Belly torn,
And scatter'd Limbs, shall on the Flood be
    born :
Thy Flood, ungrateful Nymph, and fate
    shall find
That way for thee and *Acis* to be joyn'd.
For oh I burn with Love, and thy Disdain
Augments at once my Passion and my pain.
Translated *Ætna* flames within my Heart,
And thou, Inhumane, wilt not ease my
    smart.
  Lamenting thus in vain, he rose, and
    strode   189
With furious paces to the Neighb'ring Wood :
Restless his feet, distracted was his walk ;
Mad were his motions, and confus'd his
    talk.
Mad as the vanquish'd Bull, when forc'd to
    Yield
His lovely Mistress, and forsake the Field.
  Thus far unseen I saw : when, fatal
    chance
His looks directing, with a sudden glance,
Acis and I were to his sight betray'd ;
Where, nought suspecting, we securely
    play'd.
From his wide mouth a bellowing cry he
    cast ;
I see, I see, but this shall be your last. 200
A roar so loud made *Ætna* to rebound ;
And all the *Cyclops* labour'd in the sound.
Affrighted with his monstrous Voice, I fled,
And in the Neighb'ring Ocean plung'd my
    head.
Poor *Acis* turn'd his back, and, help, he cried,
Help, *Galatea*, help, my Parent Gods,
And take me dying to your deep Abodes.
The *Cyclops* follow'd : but he sent before
A Rib, which from the living Rock he tore :
Though but an Angle reach'd him of the
    Stone,   210
The mighty Fragment was enough alone
To crush all *Acis* ; 'twas too late to save,
But what the Fates allow'd to give, I gave :

---

166 is] *The editors, who may here be right,
give* she's

That *Acis* to his Lineage should return ;
And rowl, among the River Gods, his Urn.
Straight issu'd from the Stone a Stream of blood ;
Which lost the Purple, mingling with the Flood.
Then like a troubled Torrent it appear'd :
The Torrent too, in little space, was clear'd.
The Stone was cleft, and through the yawn-ing chink   220
New Reeds arose, on the new River's brink.
The Rock, from out its hollow Womb, disclos'd
A sound like Water in its course oppos'd :

When, (wondrous to behold,) full in the Flood
Up starts a Youth, and Navel high he stood.
Horns from his Temples rise ; and either Horn
Thick Wreaths of Reeds (his Native growth) adorn.
Were not his Stature taller than before,
His bulk augmented, and his beauty more,
His colour blue, for *Acis* he might pass :   230
And *Acis* chang'd into a Stream he was.
But mine no more, he rowls along the Plains
With rapid motion, and his Name retains.

OF THE PYTHAGOREAN PHILOSOPHY ;

FROM THE FIFTEENTH BOOK OF OVID'S METAMORPHOSES.

The Fourteenth Book concludes with the Death and Deification of Romulus ; The Fifteenth begins with the Election of Numa to the Crown of Rome. On this Occasion, Ovid following the Opinion of some Authors, makes Numa the Schollar of Pythagoras ; and to have begun his Acquaintance with that Philosopher at Crotona, a Town in Italy ; from thence he makes a Digression to the Moral and Natural Philosophyof Pythagoras: On both which our Author enlarges ; and which are the most learned and beautiful Parts of the Metamorphoses.

A King is sought to guide the growing State, ⎫
One able to support the Publick Weight, ⎬
And fill the Throne where *Romulus* had sat. ⎭
Renown, which oft bespeaks the Publick Voice,
Had recommended *Numa* to their Choice :
A peaceful, pious Prince ; who, not con-tent
To know the *Sabine* Rites, his Study bent
To cultivate his Mind : To learn the Laws
Of Nature, and explore their hidden Cause.

Urg'd by this Care, his Country he forsook,
And to *Crotona* thence his Journey took.   11
Arriv'd, he first enquir'd the Founder's Name
Of this new Colony ; and whence he came
Then thus a Senior of the Place replies,
(Well read, and curious of Antiquities)
'Tis said, *Alcides* hither took his way
From *Spain*, and drove along his conquer'd Prey,
Then, leaving in the Fields his grazing Cows,
He sought himself some hospitable House.
Good *Croton* entertain'd his Godlike Guest ;
While he repair'd his weary Limbs with rest.   21
The Hero, thence departing, bless'd the Place ;
And here, he said, in Times revolving Race,
A rising Town shall take its Name from thee.
Revolving Time fulfill'd the Prophecy :
For *Myscelos*, the justest Man on Earth,
Alemon's Son, at *Argos* had his Birth :
Him *Hercules*, arm'd with his Club of Oak
O'ershadow'd in a Dream, and thus bespoke ;
Go, leave thy Native Soil, and make ⎫
    Abode   30 ⎪
Where *Æsaris* rowls down his rapid Flood. ⎬
He said ; and Sleep forsook him, and the ⎪
    God. ⎭
Trembling he wak'd, and rose with anxious Heart ;
His Country Laws forbad him to depart :

OF THE PYTHAGOREAN PHILOSOPHY. Text from the original edition of 1700. The current texts have errors in ll. 118, 374, 435, and others. The alteration in l. 118 shows that the editors did not understand the text. On the other hand their substitution of ' Birth ' for ' Breath ' in l. 658 is probably right, as it improves the sense and gets rid of an intolerable rhyme.

What shou'd he do? 'Twas Death to go
    away;
And the God menac'd if he dar'd to stay:
All Day he doubted, and, when Night came
    on,
Sleep, and the same forewarning Dream
    begun:
Once more the God stood threatning o'er
    his head;
With added Curses if he disobey'd.   40
Twice warn'd, he study'd Flight; but
    wou'd convey,
At once his Person, and his Wealth away.
Thus while he linger'd, his Design was heard;
A speedy Process form'd, and Death
    declar'd.
Witness there needed none of his Offence,
Against himself the Wretch was Evidence:
Condemn'd, and destitute of human Aid,
To him, for whom he suffer'd, thus he pray'd.
    O Pow'r, who hast deserv'd in Heav'n
        a Throne,
Not giv'n, but by thy Labours made thy
    own,   50
Pity thy Suppliant, and protect his Cause,
Whom thou hast made obnoxious to the
    Laws.
    A Custom was of old, and still remains,
Which Life or Death by Suffrages ordains;
White Stones and Black within an Urn are
    cast,
The first absolve, but Fate is in the last.
The Judges to the common Urn bequeath
Their Votes, and drop the Sable Signs of
    Death;
The Box receives all Black; but pour'd
    from thence
The Stones came candid forth, the Hue of
    Innocence.   60
Thus *Alemonides* his Safety won,
Preserv'd from Death by *Alcumena's* Son:
Then to his Kinsman-God his Vows he pays,
And cuts with prosp'rous Gales th' *Ionian*
    Seas;
He leaves *Tarentum*, favour'd by the Wind,
And *Thurine* Bays, and *Temises*, behind;
Soft *Sybaris*, and all the Capes that stand
Along the Shore, he makes in sight of Land;
Still doubling, and still coasting, till he
    found   69
The Mouth of *Æsaris*, and promis'd Ground,

Then saw where, on the Margin of the
    Flood,
The Tomb that held the Bones of *Croton*
    stood:
Here, by the God's Command, he built and
    wall'd
The Place predicted; and *Crotona* call'd
Thus Fame, from time to time, delivers
    down
The sure Tradition of th' *Italian* Town.
    Here dwelt the Man divine whom *Samos*
        bore,
But now Self-banish'd from his Native
    Shore,
Because he hated Tyrants, nor cou'd bear
The Chains which none but servile Souls will
    wear: 80
He, tho' from Heav'n remote, to Heav'n
    could move,
With Strength of Mind, and tread th' Abyss
    above;
And penetrate with his interiour Light
Those upper Depths, which Nature hid from
    Sight:
And what he had observ'd, and learnt from
    thence,
Lov'd in familiar Language to dispence.
    The Crowd with silent Admiration stand,
And heard him, as they heard their God's
    Command;
While he discours'd of Heav'ns mysterious
    Laws,
The World's Original, and Nature's Cause;
And what was God, and why the fleecy
    Snows   91
In silence fell, and rattling Winds arose;
What shook the stedfast Earth, and whence
    begun
The Dance of Planets round the radiant
    Sun;
If Thunder was the Voice of angry *Jove*,
Or Clouds with Nitre pregnant burst above:
Of these, and Things beyond the common
    Reach,
He spoke, and charm'd his Audience with his
    Speech.
    He first the tast of Flesh from Tables
        drove,
And argued well, if Arguments cou'd
    move.   100
O Mortals! from your Fellow's Blood
    abstain,
Nor taint your Bodies with a Food profane:

60 forth, the] forth: The *1700.*

While Corn and Pulse by Nature are be-
　stow'd,
And planted Orchards bend their willing
　Load ;
While labour'd Gardens wholesom Herbs
　produce,
And teeming Vines afford their generous
　Juice :
Nor tardier Fruits of cruder Kind are lost,
But tam'd with Fire, or mellow'd by the
　Frost :
While Kine to Pails distended Udders bring,
And Bees their Hony redolent of Spring :
While Earth not only can your Needs
　supply.　　　　　　　　　　　　　111
But lavish of her Store, provides for Luxury ;
A guiltless Feast administers with Ease,
And without Blood is prodigal to please.
Wild Beasts their Maws with their slain
　Brethren fill ;
And yet not all, for some refuse to kill :
Sheep, Goats, and Oxen, and the nobler
　Steed,
On Browz and Corn, and flow'ry Meadows
　feed.
Bears, Tygers, Wolves, the Lion's angry
　Brood,
Whom Heaven endu'd with Principles of
　Blood,　　　　　　　　　　　　　120
He wisely sundred from the rest, to yell
In Forests, and in lonely Caves to dwell,
Where stronger Beasts oppress the weak
　by Might
And all in Prey, and Purple Feasts delight.
　O impious use ! to Nature's Laws
　oppos'd,
Where Bowels are in other Bowels clos'd :
Where, fatten'd by their Fellow's Fat, they
　thrive ;
Maintain'd by Murder, and by Death they
　live.
'Tis then for nought that Mother Earth
　provides
The Stores of all she shows, and all she
　hides,　　　　　　　　　　　　　130
If Men with fleshy Morsels must be fed,
And chaw with bloody Teeth the breathing
　Bread :
What else is this but to devour our Guests,
And barbarously renew *Cyclopean* Feasts !

We, by destroying Life, our Life sustain ;
And gorge th' ungodly Maw with Meats
　obscene.
　Not so the Golden Age, who fed on Fruit,
Nor durst with bloody Meals their Mouths
　pollute.
Then Birds in airy space might safely move,
And timerous Hares on Heaths securely
　rove :　　　　　　　　　　　　　140
Nor needed Fish the guileful Hooks to fear,
For all was peaceful ; and that Peace
　sincere.
Whoever was the Wretch (and curs'd be He)
That envy'd first our Food's simplicity ;
Th' essay of bloody Feasts on Bruits
　began,
And after forg'd the Sword to murther Man.
Had he the sharpen'd Steel alone employ'd
On Beasts of Prey that other Beasts
　destroy'd,
Or Men invaded with their Fangs and
　Paws,
This had been justify'd by Nature's Laws,
And Self-defence : But who did Feasts
　begin　　　　　　　　　　　　　151
Of Flesh, he stretch'd Necessity to Sin.
To kill Man-killers, Man has lawful Pow'r,
But not th' extended License, to devour.
　Ill Habits gather by unseen degrees,
As Brooks make Rivers, Rivers run to Seas.
The Sow, with her broad Snout for rooting
　up
Th' intrusted Seed, was judg'd to spoil the
　Crop,
And intercept the sweating Farmer's hope :
The cov'tous Churl, of unforgiving kind, 160
Th' Offender to the bloody Priest resign'd :
Her Hunger was no Plea : For that she dy'd.
The Goat came next in order, to be try'd :
The Goat had cropt the tendrills of the
　Vine :
In vengeance Laity and Clergy join,
Where one had lost his Profit, one his Wine.
Here was at least, some shadow of Offence :
The Sheep was sacrific'd on no pretence,
But meek, and unresisting Innocence.
A patient, useful Creature, born to bear 170
The warm and woolly Fleece, that cloath'd
　her Murderer,
And daily to give down the Milk she bred,
A Tribute for the Grass on which she fed.

---

118 and flow'ry] *The editors, making non-*
sense, give the flowery

160 cov'tous] covet'ous *1700*

Living, both Food and Rayment she
    supplies,
And is of least advantage when she dies.
  How did the toiling Oxe his Death
    deserve,
A downright simple Drudge, and born to
    serve ?
O Tyrant ! with what Justice canst thou
    hope
The Promise of the Year, a plenteous Crop ;
When thou destroy'st thy lab'ring Steer,
    who till'd,   180
And plough'd with Pains, thy else ungrateful
    Field ?
From his yet reeking Neck to draw the
    Yoke,
That Neck, with which the surly Clods he
    broke ;
And to the Hatchet yield thy Husband-Man,
Who finish'd Autumn, and the Spring began !
  Nor this alone ! but Heav'n it self to bribe,
We to the Gods our impious Acts ascribe :
First recompence with Death their Creatures
    Toil,
Then call the Bless'd above to share the
    Spoil :   189
The fairest Victim must the Pow'rs appease :
(So fatal 'tis sometimes too much to please !)
A purple Fillet his broad Brows adorns,
With flow'ry Garlands crown'd, and gilded
    Horns :
He hears the murd'rous Pray'r the Priest
    prefers,
But understands not, 'tis his Doom he hears :
Beholds the Meal betwixt his Temples cast,
(The Fruit and Product of his Labours
    past ;)
And in the Water views perhaps the Knife
Uplifted, to deprive him of his Life ;
Then broken up alive his Entrails sees,   200
Torn out for Priests t' inspect the God's
    Decrees.
  From whence, O mortal Men, this gust of
    Blood
Have you deriv'd, and interdicted Food ?
Be taught by me this dire Delight to shun,
Warn'd by my Precepts, by my Practice
    won :
And when you eat the well deserving Beast,
Think, on the Lab'rer of your Field you
    feast !
  Now since the God inspires me to proceed,
Be that, whate'er inspiring Pow'r, obey'd.

For I will sing of mighty Mysteries,   210
Of Truths conceal'd before, from human
    Eyes,
Dark Oracles unveil, and open all the Skies.
Pleas'd as I am to walk along the Sphere
Of shining Stars, and travel with the Year,
To leave the heavy Earth, and scale the
    height
Of *Atlas*, who supports the heav'nly weight:
To look from upper Light, and thence survey
Mistaken Mortals wandring from the way,
And wanting Wisdom, fearful for the State
Of future Things, and trembling at their
    Fate ;   220
  Those I would teach ; and by right Reason
    bring
To think of Death, as but an idle Thing.
Why thus affrighted at an empty Name,
A Dream of Darkness, and fictitious Flame ?
Vain Themes of Wit, which but in Poems
    Pass,
And Fables of a World, that never was !
What feels the Body when the Soul expires,
By time corrupted, or consum'd by Fires ?
Nor dies the Spirit, but new Life repeats
In other Forms, and only changes Seats.
  Ev'n I, who these mysterious Truths
    declare,   231
Was once *Euphorbus* in the *Trojan* War ;
My Name and Lineage I remember well,
And how in Fight by *Sparta's* King I fell.
In *Argive Juno's* Fane I late beheld
My Buckler hung on high, and own'd my
    former Shield.
  Then, Death, so call'd, is but old Matter
    dress'd
In some new Figure, and a vary'd Vest :
Thus all Things are but alter'd, nothing dies ;
And here and there th' unbodied Spirit
    flies,   240
By Time, or Force, or Sickness dispossest,
And lodges, where it lights, in Man or Beast ;
Or hunts without, till ready Limbs it find,
And actuates those according to their kind ;
From Tenement to Tenement is toss'd ;
The Soul is still the same, the Figure only
    lost :
And, as the soften'd Wax new Seals receives,
This Face assumes, and that Impression
    leaves ;
Now call'd by one, now by another Name ;
The Form is only chang'd, the Wax is still
    the same :   250

So Death, so call'd, can but the Form
    deface,
Th' immortal Soul flies out in empty space;
To seek her Fortune in some other Place.
    Then let not Picty be put to flight,
To please the taste of Glutton-Appetite ;
But suffer inmate Souls secure to dwell,
Lest from their Seats your Parents you
    expel ;
With rabid Hunger feed upon your kind,
Or from a Beast dislodge a Brother's Mind.
    And since, like *Tiphys* parting from the
    Shore,   260
In ample Seas I sail, and Depths untry'd
    before,
This let me further add, that Nature knows
No stedfast Station, but, or Ebbs, or Flows :
Ever in motion ; she destroys her old,
And casts new Figures in another Mold.
Ev'n Times are in perpetual Flux ; and run,
Like Rivers from their Fountain rowling on ;
For Time no more than Streams, is at a Stay:
The flying Hour is ever on her way ;
And as the Fountain still supplies her
    store,   270
The Wave behind impels the Wave before ;
Thus in successive Course the Minutes run,
And urge their Predecessor Minutes on,
Still moving, ever new : For former Things
Are set aside, like abdicated Kings :
And every moment alters what is done,
And innovates some Act till then unknown.
    Darkness we see emerges into Light,
And shining Suns descend to Sable Night ;
Ev'n Heav'n it self receives another die, 280
When weari'd Animals in Slumbers lie,
Of Midnight Ease : Another when the gray
Of Morn preludes the Splendor of the Day.
The Disk of *Phœbus* when he climbs on
    high,
Appears at first but as a bloodshot Eye ;
And when his Chariot downward drives to
    Bed,
His Ball is with the same Suffusion red ;
But mounted high in his Meridian Race
All bright he shines, and with a better Face :
For there, pure Particles of *Æther* flow, 290
Far from th' Infection of the World below.
    Nor equal Light th' unequal Moon adorns,
Or in her wexing or her waning Horns.
For ev'ry Day she wanes, her Face is less,
But gath'ring into Globe, she fattens at
    increase.

Perceiv'st thou not the process of the
    Year,
How the four Seasons in four Forms appear,
Resembling human Life in ev'ry Shape
    they wear ?
Spring first, like Infancy, shoots out her
    Head,
With milky Juice requiring to be fed : 300
Helpless, tho' fresh, and wanting to be led.
The green Stem grows in Stature and in Size,
But only feeds with hope the Farmer's
    Eyes ;
Then laughs the childish Year with Flourets
    crown'd,
And lavishly perfumes the Fields around,
But no substantial Nourishment receives,
Infirm the Stalks, unsolid are the Leaves.
    Proceeding onward whence the Year
    began
The Summer grows adult, and ripens into
    Man.
This Season, as in Men, is most repleat, 310
With kindly Moisture, and prolifick Heat.
    Autumn succeeds, a sober tepid Age,
Not froze with Fear, nor boiling into Rage ;
More than mature, and tending to decay,
When our brown Locks repine to mix with
    odious Grey.
    Last Winter creeps along with tardy pace,
Sour is his Front, and furrow'd is his Face.
His Scalp if not dishonour'd quite of Hair,
The ragg'd Fleece is thin, and thin is worse
    than bare.
    Ev'n our own Bodies daily change receive,
Some part of what was theirs before, they
    leave ;   321
Nor are to Day what Yesterday they were ;
Nor the whole same to Morrow will appear.
    Time was, when we were sow'd, and just
    began
From some few fruitful Drops, the promise
    of a Man ;
Then Nature's Hand (fermented as it was)
Moulded to Shape the soft, coagulated Mass ;
And when the little Man was fully form'd,
The breathless Embryo with a Spirit
    warm'd ;
But when the Mothers Throws begin to
    come,   330
The Creature, pent within the narrow Room,
Breaks his blind Prison, pushing to repair
His stiffled Breath, and draw the living
    Air ;

Cast on the Margin of the World he lies,
A helpless Babe, but by Instinct he cries.
He next essays to walk, but downward
   press'd,
On four Feet imitates his Brother Beast :
By slow degrees he gathers from the
   Ground
His Legs, and to the rowling Chair is bound ;
Then walks alone ; a Horseman now
   become,   340
He rides a Stick, and travels round the
   Room :
In time he vaunts among his Youthful
   Peers,
Strong-bon'd, and strung with Nerves, in
   pride of Years,
He runs with Mettle his first merry Stage, ⎫
Maintains the next, abated of his Rage,   ⎬
But manages his Strength, and spares his ⎭
   Age.
Heavy the third, and stiff, he sinks apace,
And tho' 'tis down-hill all, but creeps along
   the Race.
Now sapless on the verge of Death he
   stands,
Contemplating his former Feet, and Hands ;⎫
And *Milo*-like, his slacken'd Sinews sees, 351⎮
And wither'd Arms, once fit to cope with   ⎬
   Hercules,   ⎮
Unable now to shake, much less to tear the ⎮
   Trees.   ⎭
   So *Helen* wept, when her too faithful Glass
Reflected to her Eyes the ruins of her Face :
Wondring what Charms her Ravishers cou'd
   spy,
To force her twice, or ev'n but once enjoy !
Thy Teeth, devouring Time, thine, envious
   Age,
On Things below still exercise your Rage :
With venom'd Grinders you corrupt your
   Meat,   360
And then at lingring Meals, the Morsels eat.
   Nor those, which Elements we call, abide,
Nor to this Figure, nor to that, are ty'd ;
For this eternal World is said of Old
But four prolifick Principles to hold,
Four different Bodies ; two to Heaven
   ascend,
And other two down to the Center tend :
Fire first with Wings expanded mounts on
   high,
Pure, void of weight, and dwells in upper
   Sky ;

Then Air, because unclogg'd in empty
   space,   370
Flies after Fire, and claims the second Place :
But weighty Water, as her Nature guides,
Lies on the Lap of Earth, and Mother Earth
   subsides.
   All things are mix'd of these, which all
   contain,
And into these are all resolv'd again
Earth rarifies to Dew, expanded more
The subtil Dew in Air begins to soar ;
Spreads as she flies, and weary of her Name
Extenuates still, and changes into Flame ;
Thus having by Degrees Perfection won, 380
Restless they soon untwist the Web they
   spun,
And Fire begins to lose her radiant Hue,
Mix'd with gross Air, and Air descends to
   Dew ;
And Dew condensing, does her Form
   forego.
And sinks, a heavy Lump of Earth below.
   Thus are their Figures never at a stand,
But chang'd by Nature's innovating Hand ;
All Things are alter'd, nothing is destroy'd,
The shifted Scene, for some new Show
   employ'd.
   Then to be born, is to begin to be,   390
Some other Thing we were not formerly :
And what we call to Die, is not t' appear,
Or be the Thing that formerly we were.
Those very Elements, which we partake
Alive, when Dead some other Bodies make :
Translated grow, have Sense, or can dis-
   course ;
But Death on deathless Substance has no
   force.
   That Forms are chang'd, I grant, that
   nothing can
Continue in the Figure it began :
The Golden Age to Silver was debas'd : 400
To Copper that ; our Mettal came at last.
   The Face of Places, and their Forms
   decay ;
And that is solid Earth, that once was Sea :
Seas in their turn retreating from the Shore,
Make solid Land, what Ocean was before ;
And far from Strands are Shells of Fishes
   found,
And rusty Anchors fix'd on Mountain-
   Ground :

374 o'] *The editors wrongly give* with

And what were Fields before, now wash'd
    and worn
By falling Floods from high, to Valleys turn,
And crumbling still descend to level Lands ;
And Lakes, and trembling Bogs are barren
    Sands :   411
And the parch'd Desart floats in Streams
    unknown ;
Wondring to drink of Waters not her own.
  Here Nature living Fountains opes ; and
    there,
Seals up the Wombs where living Fountains
    were ;
Or Earthquakes stop their ancient Course,
    and bring
Diverted Streams to feed a distant Spring.
So *Lycus*, swallow'd up, is seen no more,
But far from thence knocks out another
    Door.
Thus *Erasinus* dives ; and blind in Earth
Runs on, and gropes his way to second
    Birth.   421
Starts up in *Argos* Meads, and shakes his
    Locks
Around the Fields, and fattens all the
    Flocks.
So *Mysus* by another way is led,
And, grown a River now disdains his Head :
Forgets his humble Birth, his Name for-
    sakes,
And the proud Title of *Caicus* takes.
Large *Amenane*, impure with yellow Sands,
Runs rapid often, and as often stands ;
And here he threats the drunken Fields to
    drown,   430
And there his Dugs deny to give their Liquor
    down.
  Anigros once did wholesome Draughts
    afford,
But now his deadly Waters are abhorr'd :
Since, hurt by *Hercules*, as Fame resounds,
The Centaurs in his current wash'd their
    Wounds.
The Streams of *Hypanis* are sweet no more,
But brackish lose the tast they had before.
Antissa, *Pharos*, *Tyre* in Seas were pent,
Once Isles, but now increase the Continent ;
While the *Leucadian* Coast, main Land
    before,   440
By rushing Seas is sever'd from the Shore.

So *Zancle* to th' *Italian* Earth was ty'd,
And Men once walk'd where Ships at
    Anchor ride ;
Till *Neptune* overlook'd the narrow way,
And in disdain pour'd in the conqu'ring Sea.
  Two Cities that adorn'd th' *Achaian*⎫
    Ground,   ⎬
Buris and *Helice*, no more are found, ⎪
But whelm'd beneath a Lake, are sunk and⎪
    drown'd ;   ⎭
And Boatsmen through the Chrystal Water
    show   449
To wond'ring Passengers the Walls below.
  Near *Trœzen* stands a Hill, expos'd in Air
To Winter-Winds, of leafy Shadows bare :
This once was level Ground : But (strange
    to tell)
Th' included Vapors, that in Caverns dwell,
Lab'ring with Cholick Pangs, and close con-
    fin'd,
In vain sought issue for the rumbling
    Wind :
Yet still they heav'd for vent, and heaving
    still
Inlarg'd the Concave, and shot up the Hill;
As Breath extends a Bladder, or the Skins
Of Goats are blown t' inclose the hoarded
    Wines :   460
The Mountain yet retains a Mountain's
    Face,
And gather'd Rubbish heals the hollow
    space.
  Of many Wonders, which I heard or knew,
Retrenching most, I will relate but few :
What, are not Springs with Qualities oppos'd
Endu'd at Seasons, and at Seasons lost ?
Thrice in a Day thine, *Ammon*, change their
    Form,
Cold at high Noon, at Morn and Evening
    warm :
Thine, *Athaman*, will kindle Wood, if thrown
On the pil'd Earth, and in the waning Moon.
The *Thracians* have a Stream, if any try 471
The tast, his harden'd Bowels petrify ;
Whate'er it touches it converts to Stones,
And makes a Marble Pavement where it
    runs.
  Crathis, and *Sybaris* her Sister Flood,
That slide through our *Calabrian* Neighbour
    Wood,
With Gold and Amber die the shining Hair,
And thither Youth resort ; (for who wou'd
    not be Fair ?)

---

435 Centaurs . . . their] *The editors, regardless
of Dryden and Ovid, give* Centaur . . . his

But stranger Virtues yet in Streams we find,
Some change not only Bodies, but the Mind :   480
Who has not heard of *Salmacis* obscene.
Whose Waters into Women soften Men ?
Of *Æthyopian* Lakes, which turn the Brain
To Madness, or in heavy Sleep constrain ?
Clytorian Streams the Love of Wine expel,
(Such is the Virtue of th' abstemious Well ;)
Whether the colder Nymph that rules the Flood
Extinguishes, and balks the drunken God ;
Or that *Melampus* (so have some assur'd)
When the mad *Prœtides* with Charms he cur'd,   490
And pow'rful Herbs, both Charms and Simples cast
Into the sober Spring, where still their Virtues last.
   Unlike Effects *Lyncestis* will produce ;
Who drinks his Waters, tho' with moderate use,
Reels as with Wine, and sees with double Sight :
His Heels too heavy, and his Head too light.
Ladon, once *Pheneos,* an *Arcadian* Stream,
(Ambiguous in th' Effects, as in the Name)
By Day is wholesom Bev'rage ; but is thought
By Night infected, and a deadly Draught.
   Thus running Rivers, and the standing Lake   501
Now of these virtues, now of those partake :
Time was (and all Things Time and Fate obey)
When fast *Ortygia* floated on the Sea ;
Such were *Cyanean* Isles, when *Tiphys* steer'd
Betwixt their Streights, and their Collision fear'd ;
They swam where now they sit ; and firmly join'd
Secure of rooting up, resist the Wind.
Nor *Ætna* vomiting sulphureous Fire
Will ever belch ; for Sulphur will expire,   510
(The Veins exhausted of the liquid Store ;)
Time was she cast no Flames ; in time will cast no more.
   For whether Earth's an Animal, and Air
Imbibes, her Lungs with Coolness to repair,
And what she sucks remits ; she still requires
Inlets for Air, and Outlets for her Fires ;

When tortur'd with convulsive Fits she shakes,
That Motion chokes the vent, till other vent she makes :
Or when the Winds in hollow Caves are clos'd,
And subtil Spirits find that way oppos'd,
They toss up Flints in Air ; the Flints that hide   521
The Seeds of Fire, thus toss'd in Air, collide,
Kindling the Sulphur, till the Fewel spent
The Cave is cool'd, and the fierce Winds relent.
Or whether Sulphur, catching Fire, feeds on
Its unctuous Parts, till all the Matter gone,
The Flames no more ascend ; for Earth supplies
The Fat that feeds them ; and when Earth denies
That Food, by length of Time consum'd, the Fire
Famish'd for want of Fewel must expire.
   A Race of Men there are, as Fame has told,   531
Who shiv'ring suffer *Hyperborean* Cold,
Till nine times bathing in *Minerva's* Lake,
Soft Feathers, to defend their naked Sides, they take.
'Tis said, the *Scythian* Wives (believe who will)
Transform themselves to Birds by Magick Skill ;
Smear'd over with an Oil of wond'rous Might,
That adds new Pinions to their airy Flight.
   But this by sure Experiment we know,
That living Creatures from Corruption grow :   540
Hide in a hollow Pit a slaughter'd Steer,
Bees from his putrid Bowels will appear ;
Who like their Parents haunt the Fields, and bring
Their Hony-Harvest home, and hope another Spring.
The Warlike-Steed is multiply'd we find,
To Wasps and Hornets of the Warrior Kind.
Cut from a Crab his crooked Claws, and hide
The rest in Earth, a Scorpion thence will glide
And shoot his Sting, his Tail in Circles toss'd
Refers the Limbs his backward Father lost.

---

541 hollow] hallow *1700.*

And Worms, that Stretch on Leaves their
   filmy Loom,   551
Crawl from their Bags, and Butterflies
   become
Ev'n Slime begets the Frog's loquacious
   Race :
Short of their Feet at first, in little Space
With Arms and Legs endu'd, long leaps they
   take,
Rais'd on their hinder part, and swim the
   Lake,
And waves repel : For Nature gives their
   Kind,
To that intent, a length of Legs behind.
   The Cubs of Bears a living lump appear,
When whelp'd, and no determin'd Figure
   wear.   560
Their Mother licks 'em into Shape, and gives
As much of Form, as she her self receives.
   The Grubs from their sexangular abode
Crawl out unfinish'd, like the Maggot's
   Brood :
Trunks without Limbs ; till time at
   Leisure brings
The Thighs they wanted, and their tardy
   Wings.
   The Bird who draws the Carr of *Juno*,
   vain
Of her crown'd Head, and of her Starry
   Train ;
And he that bears th' Artillery of *Jove*,
The strong-pounc'd Eagle ; and the billing
   Dove ;   570
And all the feather'd Kind, who cou'd
   suppose
(But that from sight the surest Sense he
   knows)
They from th' included Yolk, not ambient
   White arose.
   There are who think the Marrow of a Man,
Which in the Spine, while he was living,
   ran ;
When dead, the Pith corrupted will become
A Snake, and hiss within the hollow Tomb.
   All these receive their Birth from other
   Things ;
But from himself the *Phœnix* only springs :
Self-born, begotten by the Parent Flame 580
In which he burn'd, another and the same :
Who not by Corn or Herbs his Life sustains,
But the sweet Essence of *Amomum* drains

And watches the rich Gums *Arabia* bears,
While yet in tender Dew they drop their
   Tears.
He, (his five Centuries of life fulfill'd)
His Nest on Oaken Boughs begins to build,
Or trembling tops of Palm : and first he
   draws
The Plan with his broad Bill, and crooked
   Claws,
Nature's Artificers ; on this the Pile   590
Is form'd, and rises round, then with the
   Spoil
Of *Casia, Cynamon*, and Stems of *Nard*,
(For Softness strew'd beneath,) his Fun'ral
   Bed is rear'd :
Fun'ral and Bridal both ; and all around
The Borders with corruptless Myrrh are
   crown'd :
On this incumbent ; till ætherial Flame
First catches, then consumes the costly
   Frame ;
Consumes him too, as on the Pile he lies ;
He liv'd on Odours, and in Odours dies.
   An Infant-*Phœnix* from the former springs,
His Father's Heir, and from his tender
   Wings   601
Shakes off his Parent Dust ; his Method he
   pursues,
And the same Lease of Life on the same
   Terms renews :
When grown to Manhood he begins his
   Reign,
And with stiff Pinions can his Flight sustain,
He lightens of its Load the Tree that bore
His Father's Royal Sepulcher before,
And his own Cradle : This (with pious Care
Plac'd on his Back) he cuts the buxome Air,
Seeks the Sun's City, and his sacred Church,
And decently lays down his Burden in the
   Porch.   611
   A Wonder more amazing wou'd we find ?
Th' *Hyæna* shows it, of a double kind,
Varying the Sexes in alternate Years,
In one begets, and in another bears.
The thin *Camelion*, fed with Air, receives
The colour of the Thing to which he cleaves.
   India when conquer'd, on the conqu'ring
   God
For planted Vines the sharp-ey'd Lynx
   bestow'd,
Whose Urine, shed before it touches Earth,
Congeals in Air, and gives to Gems their
   Birth.   621

So *Coral* soft and white in Oceans Bed,
Comes harden'd up in Air, and glows with
    Red.
   All changing Species should my Song
    recite ;
Before I ceas'd, wou'd change the Day to
    Night.
Nations and Empires flourish and decay,
By turns command, and in their turns
    obey ;
Time softens hardy People, Time again
Hardens to War a soft, unwarlike Train.
Thus *Troy*, for ten long Years, her Foes
    withstood,   630
And daily bleeding bore th' expence of
    Blood :
Now for thick Streets it shows an empty ⎫
    Space,   ⎪
Or only fill'd with Tombs of her own perish'd ⎬
    Race,   ⎪
Her self becomes the Sepulcher of what she ⎪
    was.   ⎭
Mycene, Sparta, Thebes of mighty Fame,
Are vanish'd out of Substance into Name,
And *Dardan Rome*, that just begins to rise,
On *Tiber's* Banks, in time shall mate the
    Skies ;
Widening her Bounds, and working on her
    way,
Ev'n now she meditates Imperial Sway :   640
Yet this is change, but she by changing
    thrives,
Like Moons new-born, and in her Cradle
    strives
To fill her Infant-Horns ; an Hour shall
    come
When the round World shall be contain'd
    in *Rome*.
   For thus old Saws fortel, and *Helenus*
Anchises drooping Son enliven'd thus,
When *Ilium* now was in a sinking State,
And he was doubtful of his future Fate :
O Goddess-born, with thy hard Fortune
    strive,
Troy never can be lost, and thou alive. 650
Thy Passage thou shalt free through Fire
    and Sword,
And *Troy* in Foreign Lands shall be restor'd.
In happier Fields a rising Town I see,   ⎫
Greater than what e'er was, or is, or e'er ⎪
    shall be :   ⎬
And Heav'n yet owes the World a Race   ⎪
    deriv'd from Thee.   ⎭

Sages, and Chiefs of other Lineage born,
The City shall extend, extended shall
    adorn :
But from *Iulus* he must draw his Birth,
By whom thy *Rome* shall rule the conquer'd
    Earth :
Whom Heav'n will lend Mankind on Earth
    to reign,   660
And late require the precious Pledge again.
This *Helenus* to great *Æneas* told,
Which I retain, e'er since in other Mould
My Soul was cloath'd ; and now rejoice to
    view
My Country Walls rebuilt, and *Troy* reviv'd
    anew,
Rais'd by the fall : Decreed by Loss to Gain ;
Enslav'd but to be free, and conquer'd but
    to reign.
'Tis time my hard-mouth'd Coursers to
    controul,
Apt to run Riot, and transgress the Goal :
And therefore I conclude, whatever lies   670
In Earth, or flits in Air, or fills the Skies,
All suffer change, and we, that are of Soul
And Body mix'd, are Members of the whole.
Then, when our Sires, or Grandsires shall
    forsake
The Forms of Men, and brutal Figures take,
Thus hous'd, securely let their Spirits rest,
Nor violate thy Father in the Beast,
Thy Friend, thy Brother, any of thy Kin ;
If none of these, yet there's a Man within :
O spare to make a *Thyestæan* Meal,   680
T' inclose his Body, and his Soul expel.
Ill Customs by degrees to Habits rise,
Ill Habits soon become exalted Vice :
What more Advance can Mortals make in Sin
So near Perfection, who with Blood begin ?
Deaf to the Calf that lies beneath the Knife,
Looks up, and from her Butcher begs her
    Life :
Deaf to the harmless Kid, that, e'er he dies, ⎫
All Methods to procure thy Mercy tries,   ⎬
And imitates in vain thy Children's Cries.   ⎭
Where will he stop, who feeds with Household
    Bread,   691
Then eats the Poultry which before he fed ?
Let plough thy Steers ; that when they lose
    their Breath,
To Nature, not to thee, they may impute
    their Death.

_____

658 *Iulus*] *Julus* 1700. Birth] Breath 1700.

Let Goats for Food their loaded Udders lend,
And Sheep from Winter-cold thy Sides
defend;
But neither Sprindges, Nets, nor Snares
employ,
And be no more Ingenious to destroy.
Free as in Air, let Birds on Earth remain,
Not let insidious Glue their Wings constrain;
Nor opening Hounds the trembling Stag
affright, 701
Nor purple Feathers intercept his Flight;
Nor Hooks conceal'd in Baits for Fish
prepare,
Nor Lines to heave 'em twinkling up in Air.
Take not away the Life you cannot give:
For all Things have an equal right to live.

Kill noxious Creatures, where 'tis Sin to save;
This only just Prerogative we have:
But nourish Life with vegetable Food,
And shun the sacrilegious tast of Blood. 710
These Precepts by the *Samian* Sage were
taught,
Which Godlike *Numa* to the *Sabines* brought,
And thence transferr'd to *Rome*, by Gift his
own:
A willing People, and an offer'd Throne.
O happy Monarch, sent by Heav'n to bless
A Salvage Nation with soft Arts of Peace,
To teach Religion, Rapine to restrain,
Give Laws to Lust, and Sacrifice ordain:
Himself a Saint, a Goddess was his Bride,
And all the Muses o'er his Acts preside. 720

TRANSLATIONS FROM OVID'S EPISTLES.

PREFACE CONCERNING OVID'S EPISTLES.

The Life of Ovid *being already written in our language before the Translation of his* Meta-morphoses, *I will not presume so far upon myself, to think I can add any thing to Mr.* Sandys *his undertaking. The* English *reader may there be satisfied, that he flourish'd in the reign of* Augustus Cæsar; *that he was Extracted from an Ancient Family of* Roman *Knights; that he was born to the Inheritance of a Splendid Fortune; that he was design'd to the Study of the Law, and had made considerable progress in it, before he quitted that Profession, for this of* Poetry, *to which he was more naturally form'd. The Cause of his Banishment is*

10 *unknown; because he was himself unwilling further to provoke the Emperour, by ascribing it to any other reason, than what was pretended by* Augustus, *which was, the Lasciviousness of his Elegies, and his Art of Love.* 'Tis true, *they are not to be Excus'd in the severity of Manners, as being able to corrupt a larger Empire, if there were any, than that of* Rome : *yet this may be said in behalf of* Ovid, *that no man has ever treated the Passion of Love with so much Delicacy of thought, and of Expression, or search'd into the nature of it more Philo-sophically than he. And the Emperour, who condemn'd him, had as little reason as another Man to punish that fault with so much severity, if at least he were the Author of a certain Epigram, which is ascrib'd to him, relating to the cause of the first Civil War betwixt himself and* Mark Anthony *the triumvir, which is more fulsome than any passage I have met with*

20 *in our Poet. To pass by the naked familiarity of his Expressions to* Horace, *which are cited in that Author's Life, I need only mention one notorious Act of his, in taking* Livia *to his Bed, when she was not only Married, but with Child by her Husband, then living. But Deeds, it seems, may be Justified by Arbitrary Pow'r, when words are question'd in a Poet. There is another ghess of the* Grammarians, *as far from truth as the first from Reason; they will have him Banish'd for some favours, which, they say, he receiv'd from* Julia, *the Daughter of* Augustus, *whom they think he Celebrates under the Name of* Corinna *in his Elegies. But he, who will observe the Verses which are made to that Mistress, may gather from the whole contexture of them, that* Corinna *was not a Woman of the highest Quality. If* Julia *were then Married to* Agrippa, *why should our Poet make his Petition to* Isis, *for her safe delivery,*

30 *and afterwards Condole her Miscarriage; which, for ought he knew, might be by her own Husband? Or indeed how durst he be so bold to make the least discovery of such a Crime, which was no less than Capital, especially Committed against a Person of* Agrippa's *Rank? Or, if it were before her Marriage, he would surely have been more discreet, than to have published an Accident which must have been fatal to them both. But what most Confirms me against this Opinion is, that* Ovid *himself complains, that the true Person of* Corinna *was found out by the Fame of his Verses to her : which if it had been* Julia, *he durst not have own'd; and, besides, an immediate punishment must have follow'd. He seems himself more truly to have touch'd at the Cause of his Exile in those obscure verses,*

Cur aliquid vidi, cur noxia Lumina feci? &c.

40 *Namely, that he had either seen, or was Conscious to somewhat, which had procur'd him his disgrace. But neither am I satisfied, that this was the Incest of the Emperour with his own Daughter : for* Augustus *was of a nature too vindicative, to have contented himself with so small a Revenge, or so unsafe to himself, as that of simple Banishment, and would certainly have secur'd his Crimes from publick notice, by the death of him who was witness to them. Neither have Histories given us any sight into such an Action of this Emperour : nor would he (the greatest Politician of his time,) in all probability, have manag'd his Crimes with so*

Preface concerning Ovid's Epistles. Text of 1683. Some passages are omitted in several editions.

little secrecie, as not to shun the Observation of any man. It seems more probable, that Ovid
*was either the confident of some other passion, or that he had stumbled by some inadvertency
upon the privacies of* Livia, *and seen her in a Bath : For the words*

Sine veste Dianam,

agree better with Livia, *who had the Fame of Chastity, than with either of the* Julia's, *who
were both noted of incontinency. The first Verses, which were made by him in his Youth,
and recited publickly, according to the Custom, were, as he himself assures us, to* Corinna :
*his Banishment happen'd not till the age of fifty : from which it may be deduced, with probability
enough, that the love of* Corinna *did not occasion it : Nay, he tells us plainly, that his offence
was that of Errour only, not of wickedness ; and in the same Paper of Verses also, that the* 10
cause was notoriously known at Rome, *though it be left so obscure to after ages.*

But to leave *Conjectures on a Subject so incertain, and to write somewhat more Authentick
of this Poet : That he frequented the Court of* Augustus, *and was well receiv'd in it, is most
undoubted : all his Poems bear the Character of a Court, and appear to be written, as the*
French *call it,* Cavalierement : *add to this, that the Titles of many of his Elegies, and more
of his Letters in his Banishment, are address'd to persons well known to us, even at this distance,
to have been considerable in that Court.*

*Nor was his acquaintance less with the famous Poets of his age, than with the Noble men
and Ladies ; he tells you himself, in a particular account of his own Life, that* Macer, Horace,
Tibullus, Propertius, *and many others of them, were his familiar Friends, and that some of* 20
them communicated their Writings to him ; but that he had only seen Virgil.

*If the imitation of Nature be the business of a Poet, I know no Author who can justly be
compar'd with ours, especially in the Description of the passions. And, to prove this, I shall
need no other Judges than the generality of his Readers ; for all Passions being inborn with
us, we are almost equally Judges, when we are concern'd in the representation of them : Now
I will appeal to any man, who has read this Poet, whether he find not the natural Emotion of
the same Passion in himself, which the Poet describes in his feigned persons ? His thoughts,
which are the Pictures and results of those Passions, are generally such as naturally arise
from those disorderly Motions of our Spirits. Yet, not to speak too partially in his behalf,
I will confess, that the Copiousness of his Wit was such, that he often writ too pointedly for his* 30
*Subject, and made his persons speak more Eloquently than the violence of their Passion would
admit ; so that he is frequently witty out of season : leaving the imitation of Nature, and the
cooler dictates of his Judgment, for the false applause of Fancy. Yet he seems to have found
out this Imperfection in his riper age : for why else should he complain, that his* Metamorphosis
*was left unfinished ? Nothing sure can be added to the Wit of that Poem, or of the rest :
but many things ought to have been retrenched ; which I suppose would have been the business
of his Age, if his Misfortunes had not come too fast upon him. But take him uncorrected, as
he is transmitted to us, and it must be acknowledged, in spite of his* Dutch *Friends, the Commentators, even of* Julius Scaliger *himself, that* Seneca's *Censure will stand good against him ;*   40

Nescivit quod bene cessit relinquere ;

*he never knew how to give over, when he had done well, but continually varying the same sence
an hundred ways, and taking up in another place, what he had more than enough inculcated
before, he sometimes cloys his Readers instead of satisfying them ; and gives occasion to
his Translators, who dare not cover him, to blush at the nakedness of their Father. This then
is the Allay of* Ovid's *writing, which is sufficiently recompenc'd by his other Excellencies : nay,
this very fault is not without its Beauties ; for the most severe Censor cannot but be pleas'd
with the prodigality of his Wit, though at the same time he could have wish'd that the Master of
it had been a better Manager. Every thing which he does, becomes him ; and, if sometimes
he appear too gay, yet there is a secret gracefulness of youth, which accompanies his Writings,
though the stay'dness and sobriety of Age be wanting. In the most material part, which is the* 50
conduct, 'tis certain that he seldom has miscarried ; for if his Elegies be compared with those

of Tibullus *and* Propertius *his Contemporaries, it will be found, that those Poets seldom design'd before they writ ; And though the language of* Tibullus *be more polish'd, and the Learning of* Propertius, *especially in his Fourth Book, more set out to ostentation ; Yet their common practice was to look no further before them than the next Line ; whence it will inevitably follow, that they can drive to no certain point, but ramble from one Subject to another, and conclude with somewhat, which is not of a piece with their beginning :*

> Purpureus, latè qui splendeat, unus et alter
> Assuitur pannus, *as Horace says,*

though the Verses are Golden, they are but patch'd into the Garment. But our Poet has always
10 *the Goal in his Eye, which directs him in his Race : some Beautiful design, which he first establishes, and then contrives the means, which will naturally conduct it to his end. This will be Evident to Judicious Readers in this work of his Epistles of which somewhat, at least in general, will be expected.*

The Title of them in our late Editions is Epistolæ Heroidum, *the Letters of the* Heroines. *But* Heinsius *has judg'd more truly, that the* Inscription *of our Author was barely,* Epistles *; which he concludes from his cited Verses, where* Ovid *asserts this Work as his own Invention, and not borrow'd from the* Greeks, *whom (as the Masters of their Learning) the* Romans *usually did imitate. But it appears not from their writers, that any of the* Grecians *ever touch'd upon this way, which our Poet therefore justly has vindicated to himself. I quarrel not at*
20 *the word* Heroidum, *because'tis used by* Ovid *in his Art of Love :*

> Jupiter ad veteres supplex *Heroidas* ibat.

But, sure, he cou'd not be guilty of such an over-sight, to call his Work by the Name of Heroines, *when there are divers Men, or Heroes, as, namely,* Paris, Leander, *and* Acontius, *joyned in it. Except* Sabinus, *who writ some Answers to* Ovid's *Letters,*

> (Quam celer è toto rediit meus orbe *Sabinus*)

I remember not any of the Romans, *who have treated this Subject, save only* Propertius, *and that but once, in his Epistle of* Arethusa *to* Lycotas, *which is written so near the style of* Ovid, *that it seems to be but an Imitation ; and therefore ought not to defraud our Poet of the Glory of his Invention.*
30 *Concerning this work of the Epistles, I shall content my self to observe these few particulars : first, that they are generally granted to be the most perfect piece of* Ovid, *and that the Style of them is tenderly Passionate and Courtly ; two properties well agreeing with the Persons, which were* Heroines *and Lovers. Yet where the Characters were lower, as in* Œnone, *and* Hero, *he has kept close to Nature, in drawing his Images after a Country Life, though, perhaps, he has Romanized his* Grecian *Dames too much, and made them speak, sometimes, as if they had been born in the City of* Rome, *and under the Empire of* Augustus. *There seems to be no great variety in the particular Subjects which he has chosen ; Most of the Epistles being written from Ladies, who were forsaken by their Lovers : Which is the reason that many of the same thoughts come back upon us in divers Letters : But of the general Character of* Women,
40 *which is Modesty, he has taken a most becoming care ; for his amorous Expressions go no further than vertue may allow, and therefore may be read, as he intended them, by Matrons without a blush.*

Thus much concerning the Poet : Whom you find translated by divers hands, that you may at least have that variety in the English, *which the Subject denied to the Author of the* Latine. *It remains that I should say somewhat of Poetical Translations in general, and give my Opinion (with submission to better Judgments) which way of Version seems to be most proper.*

All Translation, I suppose, may be reduced to these three heads :

First, that of Metaphrase, or turning an Author Word by Word, and Line by Line, from one Language into another Thus, or near this manner, was Horace *his Art of Poetry trans-*

---

43 *Whom you find . . . of the* Latine] *This passage is omitted by some editors.*

lated by Ben Johnson. *The second way is that of Paraphrase, or Translation with Latitude, where the Author is kept in view by the Translator, so as never to be lost, but his words are not so strictly follow'd as his sense; and that too is admitted to be amplified, but not alter'd. Such is Mr.* Waller's *Translation of Virgil's Fourth Æneid. The Third way is that of Imitation, where the Translator (if now he has not lost that Name) assumes the liberty, not only to vary from the words and sence, but to forsake them both as he sees occasion; and taking only some general hints from the Original, to run division on the Ground-work, as he pleases. Such is Mr.* Cowley's *practice in turning two Odes of* Pindar, *and one of* Horace, *into* English.

Concerning the First of these Methods, our Master Horace *has given us this caution,*

> Nec verbum verbo curabis reddere, fidus   10
> Interpres——

Nor word for word too faithfully translate. As the Earl of Roscommon *has excellently render'd it. Too faithfully is indeed pedantically: 'Tis a faith, like that which proceeds from Superstition, blind and zealous. Take it in the expression of Sir* John Denham *to Sir* Rich. Fanshaw, *on his Version of the Pastor* Fido.

> That servile path thou nobly do'st decline,
> Of tracing Word by Word, and Line by Line.
> A new and nobler way thou do'st pursue,
> To make Translations and Translators too:
> They but preserve the Ashes, thou the Flame,   20
> True to his Sense, but truer to his Fame.

'Tis almost impossible to Translate verbally, and well, at the same time; for the Latin (a most Severe and Compendious Language) often expresses that in one word, which either the Barbarity, or the narrowness of modern Tongues cannot supply in more. 'Tis frequent also that the Conceit is couch'd in some Expression, which will be lost in English.

> Atque iidem Venti vela fidemque ferent.

What Poet of our Nation is so happy as to express this thought Literally in English, *and to strike Wit, or almost Sense, out of it?*

In short, the Verbal Copier is incumber'd with so many difficulties at once, that he can never disentangle himself from all. He is to consider, at the same time, the thought of his 30 *Author, and his words, and to find out the Counterpart to each in another Language; And besides this he is to confine himself to the compass of Numbers, and the Slavery of Rhime. 'Tis much like dancing on Ropes with fetter'd Legs: A man can shun a fall by using Caution, but the gracefulness of Motion is not to be expected: And when we have said the best of it, 'tis but a foolish Task; for no sober man would put himself into a danger for the Applause of scaping without breaking his Neck. We see* Ben. Johnson *could not avoid obscurity in his literal Translation of* Horace, *attempted in the same compass of Lines: nay* Horace *himself could scarce have done it to a Greek Poet:*

> Brevis esse laboro, obscurus fio.

either perspicuity or gracefulness will frequently be wanting. Horace *has, indeed, avoided* 40 *both these Rocks in his translation of the three first Lines of* Homers. Odysses, *which he has Contracted into two.*

> Dic mihi, Musa, Virum, captæ post tempora *Trojæ*
> Qui mores hominum multorum vidit & urbes.
> Muse, speak the man, who, since the Siege of *Troy,* ⎱ *Earl of*
> So many Towns, such Change of Manners saw.   ⎰ Rosc.

But then the sufferings of Ulysses, *which are a Considerable part of that Sentence, are omitted :*

["Ος μάλα πολλὰ πλάγχθη.]

    The Consideration of these difficulties, in a servile, literal, Translation, not long since made two of our Famous Wits, Sir John Denham, *and Mr.* Cowley, *to contrive another way of turning Authors into our Tongue, called, by the latter of them, Imitation. As they were Friends, I suppose they communicated their thoughts on this Subject to each other ; and, therefore, their reasons for it are little different : though the practice of one is much more moderate. I take Imitation of an Author, in their sense, to be an Endeavour of a later*
10 *Poet to write like one, who has written before him, on the same Subject : that is, not to translate his Words, or to be Confin'd to his Sense, but only to set him as a Pattern, and to write, as he supposes that Author would have done, had he liv'd in our Age, and in our Country. Yet I dare not say that either of them have carried this libertine way of rendring Authors (as Mr.* Cowley *calls it) so far as my Definition reaches. For in the Pindarick Odes, the Customs and Ceremonies of Ancient* Greece *are still preserv'd : but I know not what mischief may arise hereafter from the Example of such an innovation, when Writers of unequal parts to him, shall imitate so bold an undertaking ; to add and to diminish what we please, which is the way avow'd by him, ought only to be granted to Mr.* Cowley, *and that too only in his translation of* Pindar ; *because he alone was able to make him amends, by giving him better*
20 *of his own, when ever he refus'd his Authors thoughts.* Pindar *is generally known to be a dark Writer, to want Connexion, (I mean as to our understanding) to soar out of sight, and leave his Reader at a Gaze. So wild and ungovernable a Poet cannot be translated literally, his Genius is too strong to bear a Chain, and,* Sampson-like, *he shakes it off : A Genius so elevated and unconfin'd as Mr.* Cowley's *was but necessary to make* Pindar *speak* English, *and that was to be perform'd by no other way than Imitation. But if* Virgil, *or* Ovid, *or any regular intelligible Authors be thus us'd, 'tis no longer to be called their work, when neither the thoughts nor words are drawn from the Original : but instead of them there is something new produced, which is almost the Creation of another hand. By this way 'tis true, somewhat that is Excellent may be invented, perhaps more Excellent than*
30 *the first design ; though* Virgil *must be still excepted, when that perhaps takes place : Yet he who is inquisitive to know an Authors thoughts, will be disappointed in his expectation. And 'tis not always that a man will be contented to have a Present made him, when he expects the payment of a Debt. To state it fairly, Imitation of an Author is the most advantageous way for a Translator to shew himself, but the greatest wrong which can be done to the Memory and Reputation of the dead. Sir* John Denham (who advis'd more Liberty than he took himself,) *gives this Reason for his innovation, in his admirable Preface before the Translation of the second* Æneid. *Poetry is of so subtil a Spirit, that, in pouring out of one Language into another, it will all Evaporate ; and, if a new Spirit not added in the transfusion, there will remain nothing but a* Caput Mortuum. *I confess this Argument holds good*
40 *against a literal Translation ; but who defends it ? Imitation and verbal Version are, in my opinion, the two extreams, which ought to be avoided : and therefore when I have propos'd the mean betwixt them, it will be seen how far his Argument will reach.*

    No man is capable of translating Poetry, who, besides a Genius to that Art, is not a Master both of his Authors Language, and of his own : Nor must we understand the Language only of the Poet, but his particular turn of Thoughts and of Expression, which are the Characters that distinguish, and as it were individuate him from all other Writers. When we are come thus far, 'tis time to look into our selves, to conform our Genius to his, to give his thought either the same turn, if our tongue will bear it, or, if not, to vary but the dress, not to alter or destroy the substance. The like Care must be taken of the more outward Ornaments, the Words ; when
50 *they appear (which is but seldom) literally graceful, it were an injury to the Author that they*

---

23 Sampson-*like*] Sampson *like* 1683.

should be chang'd : But since every Language is so full of its own proprieties, that what is Beautiful in one, is often Barbarous, nay sometimes Nonsense, in another, it would be unreasonable to limit a Translator to the narrow compass of his Author's Words : 'tis enough if he chuse out some Expression which does not vitiate the Sense. I suppose he may stretch his Chain to such a Latitude, but, by innovation of thoughts, methinks he breaks it. By this means the Spirit of an Author may be transfus'd, and yet not lost : and thus 'tis plain, that the reason alledged by Sir John Denham has no farther force than to Expression : For thought, if it be translated truly, cannot be lost in another Language ; but the words that convey it to our apprehension (which are the Image and Ornament of that thought) may be so ill chosen as to make it appear in an unhandsome dress, and rob it of its native Lustre. There is therefore 10 *a Liberty to be allowed for the Expression ; neither is it necessary that Words and Lines should be confin'd to the measure of their Original. The sense of an Author, generally speaking, is to be Sacred and Inviolable. If the Fancy of Ovid be luxuriant, 'tis his character to be so ; and if I retrench it, he is no longer Ovid. It will be replied, that he receives advantage by this lopping of his superfluous Branches ; but I rejoyn, that a Translator has no such Right : when a* Painter *Copies from the life, I suppose he has no priviledge to alter Features, and Lineaments, under pretence that his Picture will look better : perhaps the Face, which he has drawn, would be more Exact, if the Eyes, or Nose were alter'd ; but 'tis his business to make it resemble the Original. In two Cases only there may a seeming difficulty arise ; that is, if the thought be notoriously trivial, or dishonest : But the same Answer* 20 *will serve for both, that then they ought not to be Translated :*

——— Et quæ
Desperes tractata nitescere posse, relinquas.

Thus I have ventur'd to give my Opinion on this Subject against the Authority of two great men, but I hope without offence to either of their Memories, for I both lov'd them living, and reverence them now they are dead. But if, after what I have urg'd, it be thought by better Judges, that the praise of a Translation consists in adding new Beauties to the piece, thereby to recompense the loss which it sustains by change of Language, I shall be willing to be taught better, and to recant. In the mean time, it seems to me, that the true reason, why we have so few versions which are tolerable, is not from the too close pursuing of the Authors Sence, but because 30 *there are so few, who have all the Talents, which are requisite for Translation, and that there is so little Praise, and so small Encouragement, for so considerable a part of Learning.*

To apply in short, what has been said, to this present Work, the Reader will here find most of the Translations, with some little Latitude or variation from the Author's Sence : That of Œnone *to* Paris, *is in Mr.* Cowley's *way of Imitation only. I was desir'd to say that the Author who is of the* Fair Sex, *understood not* Latine. *But if she does not, I am afraid she has given us occasion to be asham'd who do.*

For my own part I am ready to acknowledge that I have transgress'd the Rules which I have given ; and taken more liberty than a just Translation will allow. But so many Gentlemen whose Wit and Learning are well known being joyn'd in it, I doubt not but that their Excellencies 40 *will make you ample Satisfaction for my Errours.*

CANACE TO MACAREUS.

THE ARGUMENT.

Macareus *and* Canace, *Son and Daughter
to Æolus, God of the Winds, lov'd each other
Incestuously:* Canace *was delivered of a Son,
and committed the Babe to her Nurse, to be
secretly convey'd away. The Infant crying
out, by that means was discovered to* Æolus,
*who, inraged at the wickedness of his Children,
commanded the Babe to be exposed to Wild
Beasts on the Mountains: And withal, sent
a Sword to* Canace, *with this Message, That
her Crimes would instruct her how to use it.
With this Sword she slew her self: But
before she died, she writ the following Letter
to her Brother* Macareus, *who had taken
Sanctuary in the Temple of* Apollo.

IF streaming Blood my fatal Letter stain,
Imagine, e're you read, the Writer slain ;
One hand the Sword, and one the Pen
   imploys,
And in my lap the ready Paper lyes.
Think in this posture thou behold'st me
   Write :
In this my cruel Father wou'd delight.
O were he present, that his Eyes and Hands
Might see and urge the Death which he
   commands !
Than all his raging Winds more dreadful, he,
Unmov'd, without a Tear, my Wounds
   wou'd see.   10
Jove justly plac'd him on a stormy Throne,
His Peoples temper is so like his own.
The *North* and *South*, and each contending
   Blast,
Are underneath his wide Dominion cast :
Those he can rule; but his tempestuous Mind
Is, like his airy Kingdom, unconfin'd.
Ah ! what avail my Kindred Gods above,
That in their number I can reckon *Jove* !
What help will all my heav'nly Friends
   afford,
When to my Breast I lift the pointed Sword ?
That Hour, which joyn'd us, came before its
   time :   21
In Death we had been one without a Crime,

Why did thy Flames beyond a *Brothers*
   move ?
Why lov'd I thee with more than *Sisters*
   love ?
For I lov'd too ; and, knowing not my
   Wound,
A secret pleasure in thy Kisses found :
My Cheeks no longer did their Colour
   boast,
My Food grew loathsom, and my Strength
   I lost :
Still e're I spoke, a Sigh wou'd stop my
   Tongue ;
Short were my Slumbers, and my Nights
   were long.   30
I knew not from my Love these Griefs did
   grow,
Yet was, alas, the thing I did not know.
My wily Nurse, by long Experience found,
And first discover'd to my Soul its Wound.
'Tis Love, said she ; and then my down-
   cast eyes,
And guilty Dumbness, witness'd my Sur-
   prize.
Forc'd at the last, my shameful Pain
   I tell :
And, oh, what follow'd, we both know too
   well !
' When half denying, more than half
   content,
' Embraces warm'd me to a full Consent, 40
' Then with tumultuous Joyes my Heart
   did beat,
' And Guilt, that made them anxious, made
   them great.'
But now my swelling Womb heav'd up my
   Breast,
And rising weight my sinking Limbs opprest.
What Herbs, what Plants, did not my
   Nurse produce,
To make Abortion by their pow'rful
   Juice ?
What Med'cines try'd we not, to thee un-
   known ?
Our first Crime common ; this was mine
   alone.
But the strong Child, secure in his dark
   Cell,
With Natures vigour, did our Arts repell. 50

And now the pale-fac'd Empress of the Night
Nine times had fill'd her Orb with borrow'd
    light :
Not knowing 'twas my Labour, I complain
Of sudden Shootings, and of grinding Pain
My Throws came thicker, and my cryes in-
    creast,
Which with her hand the conscious Nurse
    supprest.
To that unhappy Fortune was I come,
Pain urg'd my Clamours, but Fear kept me
    dumb.
With inward strugling I restrain'd my Cries,
And drunk the Tears that trickled from my
    Eyes.   60
Death was in Sight, *Lucina* gave no Aid ;
And ev'n my dying had my Guilt betray'd.
Thou cam'st ; And in thy Count'nance sate
    Despair ;
Rent were thy Garments all, and torn thy
    Hair :
Yet, feigning comfort, which thou cou'dst
    not give,
(Prest in thy Arms, and whispr'ing me to
    live :)
For both our sakes, (said'st thou) preserve
    thy Life ;
Live, my dear Sister, and my dearer Wife.
Rais'd by that Name, with my last Pangs
    I strove :
Such pow'r have Words, when spoke by
    those we love.   70
The *Babe*, as if he heard what thou hadst
    sworn,
With hasty Joy sprung forward to be born.
What helps it to have weather'd out one
    Storm ?
Fear of our *Father* does another form.
High in his Hall, rock'd in a Chair of
    State,
The King with his tempestuous Council
    sate.
Through this large Room our only passage
    lay,
By which we cou'd the new-born *Babe* con-
    vey.
Swath'd in her lap, the bold Nurse bore him
    out,
With Olive branches cover'd round about ;
And, mutt'ring Pray'rs, as holy Rites she
    meant,   81
Through the divided Crowd unquestion'd
    went.

Just at the Door, th' unhappy Infant cry'd :
The Grandsire heard him, and the theft he
    spy'd.
Swift as a Whirl-wind to the Nurse he flyes,
And deafs his stormy Subjects with his cries.
With one fierce Puff he blows the leaves
    away :
Expos'd the self-discovered Infant lay.
The noise reach'd me, and my presaging
    Mind
Too soon its own approaching Woes
    divin'd.   90
Not Ships at Sea with Winds are shaken
    more,
Nor Seas themselves, when angry Tempests
    roar,
Than I, when my loud Father's Voice I hear :
The *Bed* beneath me trembled with my Fear.
He rush'd upon me, and divulg'd my Stain ;
Scarce from my Murther cou'd his hands
    refrain.
I only answer'd him with silent Tears ;
They flow'd : my Tongue was frozen up
    with Fears.
His little Grand-child he commands away,
To Mountain Wolves and every Bird of
    prey.   100
The Babe cry'd out, as if he understood,
And beg'd his Pardon with what Voice he
    cou'd.
By what Expressions can my Grief be shown ?
(Yet you may guess my Anguish by your
    own)
To see my Bowels, and, what yet was worse,
Your Bowels too, condemn'd to such a Curse !
Out went the King ; my Voice its Freedom
    found,
My Breasts I beat, my blubber'd Cheeks
    I wound.
And now appear'd the Messenger of death ;
Sad were his Looks, and scarce he drew his
    Breath,   110
To say, *Your Father sends you*—(with that
    word
His trembling hands presented me a Sword :)
*Your Father sends you this ; and lets you
    know,*
That your own Crimes the use of it will show.
Too well I know the sence those Words
    impart :
His *Present* shall be treasur'd in my heart.
Are these the Nuptial Gifts a Bride receives ?
And this the fatal Dow'r a Father gives ?

Thou God of Marriage, shun thy own Dis-
    grace,
And take thy Torch from this detested
    place: 120
Instead of that, let Furies light their brands,
And fire my Pile with their infernal Hands.
With happier Fortune may my Sisters wed ;
Warn'd by the dire Example of the dead.
For thee, poor Babe, what Crime cou'd they
    pretend ?
How cou'd thy Infant Innocence offend ?
A guilt there was ; but, Oh, that Guilt was
    mine !
Thou suffer'st for a Sin that was not thine.
Thy Mothers Grief and Crime ! but just
    enjoy'd,
Shown to my Sight, and born to be de-
    stroy'd ! 130
Unhappy Off-spring of my teeming Womb !
Drag'd head-long from thy Cradle to thy
    Tomb !

Thy un-offending Life I could not save,
Nor weeping cou'd I follow to thy Grave !
Nor on thy Tomb could offer my shorn
    Hair ;
Nor show the Grief which tender Mothers
    bear.
Yet long thou shalt not from my Arms be
    lost ;
For soon I will o'retake thy Infant Ghost.
But thou, my Love, and now my Love's
    Despair,
Perform his Funerals with paternal Care. 140
His scatter'd Limbs with my dead Body
    burn ;
And once more joyn us in the pious Urn.
If on my wounded Breast thou drop'st
    a Tear,
Think for whose sake my Breast that Wound
    did bear ;
And faithfully my last Desires fulfill,
As I perform my cruel Fathers Will.

HELEN TO PARIS.

THE ARGUMENT.

Helen, *having receiv'd the foregoing Epistle
from* Paris, *returns the following Answer :
Wherein she seems at first to chide him for
his Presumption in Writing as he had done,
which could only proceed from his low
Opinion of her Vertue : then owns herself
to be sensible of the Passion, which he had
express'd for her, tho' she much suspect
his Constancy ; and at last discovers her
Inclinations to be favourable to him. The
whole Letter showing the extream artifice of
Woman-kind.*

WHEN loose Epistles violate Chast Eyes,
She half Consents, who silently denies :
How dares a Stranger with Designs so vain,
Marriage and Hospitable Rights Prophane ?
Was it for this, your Fleet did shelter find
From swelling Seas, and ev'ry faithless
    Wind ?
(For tho a distant Country brought you
    forth,
Your usage here was equal to your Worth.)

Does this deserve to be rewarded so ?
Did you come here a Stranger or a Foe ? 10
Your partial Judgment may perhaps com-
    plain,
And think me barbarous for my just disdain ;
Ill-bred then let me be, but not unchast,
Nor my clear Fame with any Spot defac'd.
Tho in my face there's no affected Frown,
Nor in my Carriage a feign'd Niceness shown,
I keep my Honor still without a Stain,
Nor has my Love made any Coxcomb vain.
Your Boldness I with admiration see ;
What Hope had you to gain a Queen like
    me ? 20
Because a Hero forc'd me once away
Am I thought fit to be a second Prey ?
Had I been won, I had deserv'd your Blame,
But sure my part was nothing but the
    Shame.
Yet the base Theft to him no Fruit did
    bear,
I 'scap'd unhurt by any thing but Fear.
Rude force might some unwilling Kisses
    gain,
But that was all he ever could obtain.

You on such terms would nere have let me
go ;
Were he like you, we had not parted so. 30
Untouch'd the Youth restor'd me to my
Friends,
And modest Usage made me some amends.
'Tis vertue to repent a vicious Deed,
Did he repent, that *Paris* might succeed ?
Sure 'tis some Fate that sets me above
Wrongs,
Yet still exposes me to busie Tongues.
I'le not complain ; for who's displeas'd with
Love,
If it sincere, discreet, and constant prove ?
But that I fear ; not that I think you base,
Or doubt the blooming Beauties of my
Face ;   40
But all your Sex is subject to deceive,
And ours alas, too willing to believe.
Yet others yield ; and Love o'recomes the
best :
But why should I not shine above the rest ?
Fair *Leda's* Story seems at first to be
A fit example ready found for me.
But she was Cousen'd by a borrow'd shape,
And under harmless Feathers felt a Rape :
If I should yield, what reason could I use ?
By what mistake the Loving Crime excuse ?
Her fault was in her pow'rfull Lover lost ; 51
But of what *Jupiter* have I to boast ?
Tho you to Heroes and to Kings succeed,
Our Famous Race does no addition need ;
And great Alliances but useless prove
To one that comes her self from mighty *Jove*.
Go then, and boast in some less haughty
place
Your *Phrygian* blood, and *Priam's* ancient
Race ;
Which I wou'd shew I valu'd, if I durst ;
You are the fifth from *Jove*, but I the
first.   60
The Crown of *Troy* is pow'rful I confess ;
But I have reason to think ours no less.
Your Letter fill'd with promises of all,
That Men can good, and Women pleasant call,
Gives expectation such an ample field,
As wou'd move Goddesses themselves to
yield.
But if I e're offend great *Juno's* Laws,
Your self shall be the dear, the only cause :
Either my Honour I'll to death maintain,
Or follow you, without mean thoughts of
gain.   70

Not that so fair a Present I despise ;
We like the Gift, when we the giver prize.
But 'tis your Love moves me, which made
you take
Such pains, and run such hazards for my
sake ;
I have perceiv'd (though I dissembled too)
A thousand things that Love has made you
do.
Your eager Eyes would almost dazle mine,
In which (wild man) your wanton thoughts
wou'd shine,
Sometimes you'd sigh, sometimes disorder'd
stand,
And with unusual Ardor, press my hand ;
Contrive just after me to take the Glass, 81
Nor wou'd you let the least Occasion pass :
Which oft I fear'd, I did not mind alone,
And blushing sate for things which you have
done :
Then murmur'd to my self, he'll for my sake
Do any thing ; I hope 'twas no mistake.
Oft have I read within this pleasing Grove,
Under my Name, those Charming words,
I Love.
I frowning seem'd not to believe your
Flame,
But now, alas, am come to write the same.
If I were capable to do amiss,   91
I could not but be sensible of this.
For oh ! your Face has such peculiar
Charms,
That who can hold from flying to your
Arms !
But what I ne're can have without Offence,
May some blest Maid possess with innocence.
Pleasure may tempt, but Vertue more should
move ;
O Learn of me to want the thing you Love.
What you Desire is sought by all Mankind :
As you have Eyes, so others are not blind.
Like you they see, like you my Charms
adore :   101
They wish not less, but you dare venture
more.
Oh ! had you then upon our Coasts been
brought,
My Virgin Love when thousand Rivals
sought,
You had I seen, you should have had my
Voice ;
Nor could my Husband justly blame my
Choice.

For both our hopes, alas you come too late !
Another now is Master of my Fate.
More to my wish I cou'd have liv'd with you,
And yet my present Lot can undergo. 110
Cease to solicit a weak Woman's Will,
And urge not her you Love, to so much ill.
But let me live contented as I may,
And make not my unspotted Fame your
    prey.
Some Right you claim, since naked to your
    Eyes
Three Goddesses disputed Beauties prize :
One offer'd Valour, t'other Crowns ; but she
Obtain'd her Cause, who smiling promis'd
    me.
But first I am not of Belief so light,
To think such Nymphs wou'd shew you such
    a sight :   120
Yet granting this, the other part is feign'd ;
A Bribe so mean your Sentence had not
    gain'd.
With partial eyes I shou'd my self regard,
To think that *Venus* made me her reward :
I humbly am content with human Praise ;
A Goddess's Applause would Envy raise :
But be it as you say ; for, 'tis confest,
The Men, who flatter highest, please us
    best.
That I suspect it, ought not to displease ;
For Miracles are not believ'd with Ease. 130
One joy I have, that I had *Venus* voice ;
A greater yet, that you confirm'd her Choice ;
That proffer'd Laurels, promis'd Sov'raignty,
Juno and *Pallas*, you contemn'd for me.
Am I your Empire then, and your renown ?
What heart of Rock, but must by this be
    won ?
And yet bear witness, O you Pow'rs above,
How rude I am in all the Arts of Love !
My hand is yet untaught to write to Men :
This is th' Essay of my unpractis'd Pen : 140
Happy those Nymphs whom use has perfect
    made ;
I think all Crime, and tremble at a Shade.
Ev'n while I write, my fearful conscious
    Eyes
Look often back, misdoubting a surprize.
For now the Rumour spreads among the
    Croud,
At Court in whispers, but in Town aloud.
Dissemble you, what e're you hear 'em say :⎫
To leave off Loving were your better way ; ⎬
Yet if you will dissemble it, you may.   ⎭

Love secretly : the absence of my Lord 150
More Freedom gives, but does not all
    afford :
Long is his journey, long will be his stay ;
Call'd by affairs of Consequence away.
To go or not when unresolv'd he stood,
I bid him make what swift return he cou'd :
Then Kissing me, he said I recommend
All to thy Care, but most my *Trojan* Friend.
I smil'd at what he innocently said,
And only answer'd, you shall be obey'd.
Propitious Winds have borne him far from
    hence,   160
But let not this secure your Confidence.
Absent he is, yet absent he Commands :
You know the Proverb, *Princes have long
    hands*.
My Fame's my Burden : for the more I'm
    prais'd,
A juster Ground of jealousie is rais'd.
Were I less fair, I might have been more
    blest :
Great Beauty through great Danger is
    possest,
To leave me here his Venture was not hard,
Because he thought my vertue was my
    Guard.
He fear'd my Face, but trusted to my
    Life,   170
The Beauty doubted, but believ'd the Wife.
You bid me use th' Occasion while I can,
Put in our Hands by the good easie Man.
I wou'd, and yet I doubt, 'twixt Love and
    Fear ;
One draws me from you, and one brings me
    near.
Our Flames are mutual ; and my Husband's
    gone :
The Nights are long ; I fear to lie alone.
One House contains us, and weak Walls
    divide,
And you're too pressing to be long denied :
Let me not live, but every thing con-
    spires   180
To joyn our Loves, and yet my Fear retires.
You court with Words, when you should
    force imploy :
A Rape is requisite to shamefac'd Joy.
Indulgent to the Wrongs which we receive,
Our Sex can suffer what we dare not give.
What have I said ! for both of us 'twere
    best,
Our kindling fires if each of us supprest.

The Faith of Strangers is too prone to change,
And, like themselves, their wandring Passions range.
Hipsypyle, and the fond *Minoian* Maid, 190
Were both by trusting of their Ghests betray'd.
How can I doubt that other men deceive,
When you yourself did fair *Oenone* leave ?
But lest I shou'd upbraid your Treachery,
You make a Merit of that Crime to me.
Yet grant you were to faithful Love inclin'd,
Your weary *Trojans* wait but for a Wind.
Should you prevail ; while I assign the Night,
Your Sails are hoysted, and you take your Flight :
Some bawling Mariner our Love destroys,
And breaks asunder our unfinish'd Joys. 201
But I with you may leave the *Spartan* Port,
To view the *Trojan* Wealth, and *Priam's* Court :
Shown while I see, I shall expose my Fame,
And fill a foreign Country with my Shame.
In *Asia* what reception shall I find ?
And what Dishonour leave in *Greece* behind ?
What will your Brothers, *Priam*, *Hecuba*,
And what will all your modest Matrons say ?
Ev'n you, when on this Action you reflect,
My future Conduct justly may suspect ; 211
And what e're Stranger lands upon your Coast,
Conclude me, by your own Example, lost.
I from your rage a Strumpet's Name shall hear,
While you forget what part in it you bear.
You, my Crimes Author, will my Crime upbraid :
Deep under ground, Oh let me first be laid !
You boast the Pomp and Plenty of your Land,
And promise all shall be at my Command ; 219
Your *Trojan* Wealth, believe me, I despise ;
My own poor Native Land has dearer ties.
Shou'd I be injur'd on your *Phrygian* Shore,
What help of Kindred cou'd I there implore ?
Medea was by *Jasons* flatt'ry won :
I may, like her, believe, and be undon.

Plain honest Hearts, like mine, suspect no Cheat,
And Love contributes to its own Deceit.
The Ships, about whose sides loud Tempests roar,
With gentle Winds were wafted from the Shore.
Your teeming Mother dreamt a flaming Brand, 230
Sprung from her Womb, consum'd the Trojan Land.
To second this, old Prophecies conspire,
That *Ilium* shall be burnt with *Grecian* fire.
Both give me fear ; nor is it much allai'd,
That *Venus* is oblig'd our Loves to aid.
For they who lost their Cause, Revenge will take ;
And for one friend two Enemies you make.
Nor can I doubt, but shou'd I follow you,
The Sword wou'd soon our fatal Crime pursue :
A wrong so great my Husband's Rage wou'd rouze, 240
And my Relations wou'd his Cause espouse.
You boast your Strength and Courage ; but alas !
Your Words receive small credit from your Face.
Let Heroes in the Dusty Field delight,
Those Limbs were fashion'd for another Fight.
Bid *Hector* sally from the Walls of *Troy* ;
A sweeter Quarrel shou'd your Arms employ.
Yet Fears like these, shou'd not my Mind perplex,
Were I as wise as many of my Sex.
But time and you may bolder Thoughts inspire ; 250
And I perhaps may yield to your Desire.
You last demand a private Conference,
These are your Words, but I can ghess your Sense.
Your unripe Hopes their Harvest must attend :
Be Rul'd by me, and Time may be your Friend.
This is enough to let you understand ;
For now my Pen has tir'd my tender Hand :
My Woman Knows the Secret of my Heart,
And may hereafter better News impart.

[Helen to Paris *is by Dryden and the Earl of Mulgrave.*]

DIDO TO ÆNEAS.

THE ARGUMENT.

Æneas, *the Son of* Venus *and* Anchises, *having, at the Destruction of* Troy, *sav'd his Gods, his Father, and son* Ascanius, *from the Fire, put to Sea with twenty Sail of Ships : and, having been long tost with Tempests, was at last cast upon the shore of* Lybia, *where* queen Dido *(flying from the cruelty of* Pygmalion, *her Brother, who had kill'd her Husband* Sichæus) *had lately built* Carthage. *She entertain'd Æneas and his Fleet with great civility, fell passionately in Love with him, and in the end denied him not the last Favours. But* Mercury *admonishing Æneas to go in search of* Italy, (*a Kingdom promis'd him by the Gods*) *he readily prepar'd to Obey him.* Dido *soon perceiv'd it, and having in vain try'd all other means to ingage him to stay, at last in Despair writes to him as follows.*

So, on *Mæander's* banks, when death is nigh,
The Mournful *Swan* sings her own Elegie.
Not that I hope (for, oh, that hope were vain !)
By words your lost affection to regain :
But having lost what ere was worth my care,
Why shou'd I fear to lose a dying pray'r ?
'Tis then resolv'd poor *Dido* must be left,
Of Life, of Honour, and of Love bereft !
While you, with loosen'd Sails, & Vows, prepare
To seek a Land that flies the Searchers care.
Nor can my rising Tow'rs your flight restrain,   11
Nor my new Empire, offer'd you in vain.
Built Walls you shun, unbuilt you seek ; that Land
Is yet to Conquer ; but you this Command.
Suppose you Landed where your wish design'd,
Think what Reception Forreiners would find.
What People is so void of common sence,
To Vote Succession from a Native Prince ?
Yet there new Scepters and new Loves you seek ;
New Vows to plight, and plighted Vows to break.   20

When will your Tow'rs the height of *Carthage* know ?
Or when, your Eyes discern such Crowds below ?
If such a Town and Subjects you cou'd see,
Still wou'd you want a Wife who lov'd like me.
For, oh, I burn, like Fires with Incense bright :
Not holy Tapers flame with purer Light :
Æneas is my Thoughts perpetual Theme ;
Their daily Longing, and their nightly Dream.
Yet he ungrateful and obdurate still :
Fool that I am to place my Heart so ill !   30
My self I cannot to my self restore ;
Still I complain, and still I love him more.
Have pity, *Cupid*, on my bleeding Heart,
And pierce thy Brothers with an equal Dart.
I rave : nor canst thou *Venus'* offspring be,
Love's Mother could not bear a Son like thee.
From harden'd Oak, or from a Rocks cold Womb,
At least thou art from some fierce *Tygress* come ;
Or, on rough Seas, from their Foundation torn,
Got by the Winds, and in a Tempest born :
Like that, which now thy trembling Sailors fear ;   41
Like that, whose Rage should still detain thee here.
Behold how high the Foamy Billows ride !
The Winds and Waves are on the juster side.
To Winter Weather, and a stormy Sea
I'll owe, what rather I wou'd owe to thee.
Death thou deserv'st from Heav'ns avenging Laws ;
But I'm unwilling to become the Cause.
To shun my Love, if thou wilt seek thy Fate,
'Tis a dear Purchase, and a costly Hate.   50
Stay but a little, 'till the Tempest cease,
And the loud Winds are lull'd into a Peace.
May all thy Rage, like theirs, unconstant prove !
And so it will, if there be Pow'r in Love.

Know'st thou not yet what dangers Ships
  sustain ?
So often wrack'd, how dar'st thou tempt the
  Main ?
Which were it smooth, were ev'ry Wave
  asleep,
Ten thousand forms of Death are in the
  Deep.
In that abyss the Gods their Vengeance
  store,
For broken Vows of those who falsely swore.
There winged Storms on Sea-born *Venus*
  wait,   61
To vindicate the Justice of her State.
Thus, I to thee the means of Safety show ;
And, lost my self, would still preserve my
  Foe.
False as thou art, I not thy Death design :
O rather live, to be the Cause of mine !
Shou'd some avenging Storm thy Vessel
  tear,
(But Heav'n forbid my words shou'd Omen
  bear)
Then in thy Face thy perjur'd Vows would
  fly ;
And my wrong'd Ghost be present to thy
  Eye.   70
With threatning looks think thou behold'st
  me stare,
Gasping my Mouth, and clotted all my Hair.
Then shou'd fork'd Lightning and red
  Thunder fall,
What cou'dst thou say, but, I deserv'd 'em
  all.
Lest this shou'd happen, make not hast
  away ;
To shun the Danger will be worth thy Stay.
Have pity on thy Son, if not on me :
My Death alone is Guilt enough for thee.
What has his Youth, what have thy Gods
  deserv'd,
To sink in Seas, who were from fires
  preserv'd ?   80
But neither Gods nor Parent didst thou
  bear ;
(Smooth stories all, to please a Womans ear,)
False was the tale of thy Romantick life ;
Nor yet am I thy first deluded Wife.
Left to pursuing Foes *Creüsa* stai'd,
By thee, base Man, forsaken and betray'd.
This, when thou told'st me, struck my tender
  Heart,
That such Requital follow'd such Desert.

Nor doubt I but the Gods, for Crimes like
  these,
Sev'n Winters kept thee wandring on the
  Seas.   90
Thy starv'd Companions, cast ashore, I fed,
Thy self admitted to my Crown and Bed.
To harbour Strangers, succour the distrest,
Was kind enough ; but oh too kind the
  rest !
Curst be the Cave which first my Ruin
  brought,
Where, from the Storm, we common Shelter
  sought !
A dreadful howling eccho'd round the
  place :
The Mountain Nymphs, thought I, my
  Nuptials grace.
I thought so then, but now too late I know
The Furies yell'd my Funerals from below.
O Chastity and violated Fame,   101
Exact your dues to my dead Husband's
  name !
By Death redeem my reputation lost,
And to his Arms restore my guilty Ghost.
Close by my Pallace, in a Gloomy Grove,
Is rais'd a Chappel to my Murder'd Love ;
There, wreath'd with boughs and wool his
  Statue stands
The pious Monument of Artful hands.
Last Night, me thought, he call'd me from
  the dome
And thrice, with hollow Voice, cry'd, *Dido*,
  come.   110
She comes ; thy Wife thy lawful Summons
  hears ;
But comes more slowly, clogg'd with con-
  scious Fears.
Forgive the wrong I offer'd to thy Bed ;
Strong were his Charms, who my weak Faith
  misled.
His Goddess Mother, and his aged Sire,
Born on his Back, did to my Fall conspire.
Oh such he was, and is, that were he
  true,
Without a Blush I might his Love pursue.
But cruel Stars my Birth day did attend ;
And as my Fortune open'd, it must end. 120
My plighted Lord was at the Altar slain,
Whose Wealth was made my bloody
  Brothers gain.
Friendless, and follow'd by the Murd'rer's
  Hate,
To forein Countreys I remov'd my Fate ;

And here, a Suppliant, from the Natives hands
I bought the Ground on which my City stands,
With all the Coast that stretches to the Sea ;
Ev'n to the friendly Port that sheltred Thee:
Then rais'd these Walls, which mount into the Air,
At once my Neighbours wonder, and their fear.   130
For now they Arm ; and round me Leagues are made,
My scarce Establisht Empire to invade.
To Man my new built walls I must prepare,
An helpless Woman, and unskill'd in War.
Yet thousand Rivals to my Love pretend ;
And for my Person, would my Crown defend :
Whose jarring Votes in one complaint agree,
That each unjustly is disdain'd for thee.
To proud *Hyarbas* give me up a prey ;   139
(For that must follow, if thou go'st away :)
Or to my Husbands Murd'rer leave my life,
That to the Husband he may add the Wife.
Go then, since no Complaints can move thy Mind :
Go, perjur'd Man, but leave thy Gods behind.
Touch not those Gods, by whom thou art forsworn,
Who will in impious Hands no more be born.
Thy Sacrilegious worship they disdain,
And rather wou'd the *Grecian* fires sustain.
Perhaps my greatest Shame is still to come ;
And part of thee lies hid within my Womb.   150
The Babe unborn must perish by thy Hate,
And perish guiltless in his Mothers Fate.
Some God, thou say'st, thy Voyage does command ;
Wou'd the same God had barr'd thee from my Land !
The same, I doubt not, thy departure Steers,
Who kept thee out at Sea so many Years ;
While thy long Labours were a Price so great,
As thou to purchase *Troy* wouldst not repeat.
But *Tyber* now thou seek'st ; to be at best,
When there arriv'd, a poor precarious Ghest.   160
Yet it deludes thy Search : Perhaps it will
To thy Old Age lie undiscover'd still.
A ready Crown and Wealth in Dower I bring,
And, without Conqu'ring, here thou art a King.

Here thou to *Carthage* may'st transfer thy *Troy* :
Here young *Ascanius* may his Arms imploy ;
And, while we live secure in soft Repose,
Bring many Laurells home from Conquer'd Foes.
By *Cupids* Arrows, I adjure thee stay ;
By all the Gods, Companions of thy way. 170
So may thy *Trojans*, who are yet alive
Live still, and with no future Fortune strive ;
So may thy Youthful Son old Age attain,
And thy dead Fathers Bones in Peace remain ;
As thou hast Pity on unhappy me,
Who knew no Crime, but too much Love of thee.
I am not born from fierce *Achilles* Line,
Nor did my Parents against *Troy* combine.
To be thy Wife if I unworthy prove,
By some inferiour Name admit my Love. 180
To be secur'd of still possessing thee,
What wou'd I do, and what wou'd I not be !
Our *Lybian* Coasts their certain Seasons know,
When free from Tempests Passengers may go :
But now with Northern Blasts the Billows roar,
And drive the floating Sea-weed to the Shore.
Leave to my care the time to Sail away ;
When safe, I will not suffer thee to stay.
Thy weary Men wou'd be with ease content ;
Their Sails are tatter'd, and their Masts are spent.   190
If by no Merit I thy Mind can move,
What thou deny'st my Merit, give my Love.
Stay, till I learn my Loss to undergo ;
And give me time to struggle with my Woe.
If not ; Know this, I will not suffer long ;
My Life's too loathsome, and my Love too strong.
Death holds my Pen, and dictates what I say,
While cross my Lap Thy *Trojan* Sword I lay.
My Tears flow down ; the sharp Edge cuts their Flood,
And drinks my Sorrows, that must drink my bloud.   200

How well thy Gift does with my Fate agree !
My Funeral Pomp is cheaply made by thee.
To no new Wounds my Bosom I display :
The Sword but enters where Love made the
    way.
But thou, dear Sister, and yet dearer friend,
Shalt my cold Ashes to their Urn attend.

Sichæus Wife let not the Marble boast,
I lost that Title, when my Fame I lost.
This short Inscription only let it bear :
Unhappy *Dido* lies in quiet here.   210
The cause of death, & Sword by which she
    dy'd,
Æneas gave : the rest her arm supply'd.

TRANSLATIONS FROM OVID'S ART OF LOVE.

THE FIRST BOOK OF OVID'S ART OF LOVE.

IN *Cupid's* school whoe'er wou'd take Degree,
Must learn his Rudiments, by reading me.
Seamen with sailing Arts their Vessels move ;
Art guides the Chariot ; Art instructs to
    Love.
Of Ships and Chariots others know the Rule ;
But I am Master in Love's mighty School.
Cupid indeed is obstinate and wild,
A stubborn God ; but yet the God's a Child :
Easy to govern in his tender Age,
Like fierce *Achilles* in his Pupillage.   10
That Heroe, born for Conquest, trembling
    stood
Before the Centaur, and receiv'd the Rod.
As *Chyron* mollify'd his cruel Mind
With Art ; and taught his Warlike Hands
    to wind
The Silver Strings of his melodious Lyre :
So Love's fair Goddess does my Soul inspire,
To teach her softer Arts ; to soothe the
    Mind,
And smooth the rugged Breasts of Human
    Kind.
    Yet *Cupid* and *Achilles*, each with Scorn
And Rage were fill'd ; and both were
    Goddess-born.   20
The Bull, reclaim'd and yok'd, the Burden
    draws :
The Horse receives the Bit within his Jaws ;
And stubborn Love shall bend beneath my
    Sway,
Tho struling oft he strives to disobey.
He shakes his Torch, he wounds me with
    his Darts ;

But vain his Force, and vainer are his Arts.
The more he burns my Soul, or wounds my
    Sight,
The more he teaches to revenge the Spight.
    I boast no Aid the *Delphian* God affords,
Nor Auspice from the flight of chattering
    Birds ;   30
Nor *Clio*, nor her Sisters have I seen ;
As *Hesiod* saw them on the shady Green :
Experience makes my Work a Truth so
    try'd,
You may believe ; and *Venus* be my Guide.
Far hence, ye Vestals, be, who bind your
    Hair ;
And Wives, who Gowns below your Ankles
    wear.
I sing the Brothels loose and unconfin'd, ⎫
Th' unpunishable Pleasures of the Kind ; ⎬
Which all a-like, for Love, or Mony find. ⎭
    You, who in *Cupid's* Rolls inscribe your
    Name,   40
First seek an Object worthy of your Flame ;
Then strive, with Art, your Lady's Mind to
    gain :
And, last, provide your Love may long
    remain.
On these three Precepts all my Work shall
    move :
These are the Rules and Principles of Love.
    Before your Youth with Marriage is
    opprest,
Make choice of one who suits your Humour
    best :
And such a Damsel drops not from the
    Sky ;
She must be sought for with a curious Eye.

OVID'S ART OF LOVE. TEXT OF 1709.

The wary Angler, in the winding Brook, 50
Knows what the Fish, and where to bait his
  Hook.
The Fowler and the Hunts-man know by
  Name
The certain Haunts and Harbour of their
  Game.
So must the Lover beat the likeliest Grounds;
Th' Assemblies where his quarry most
  abounds.
Nor shall my Novice wander far astray ;
These Rules shall put him in the ready Way.
Thou shalt not sail around the Continent,
As far as *Perseus*, or as *Paris* went :
For *Rome* alone affords thee such a Store, 60
As all the World can hardly shew thee
  more.
The Face of Heav'n with fewer Stars is
  crown'd,
Than Beauties in the *Roman* Sphere are
  found.
Whether thy Love is bent on blooming
  Youth,
On dawning Sweetness, in unartful Truth ;
Or courts the juicy Joys of riper Growth ;
Here mayst thou find thy full Desires in
  both.
Or if Autumnal Beauties please thy Sight
(An Age that knows to give, and take
  Delight ;)
Millions of Matrons of the graver Sort,   70
In common Prudence, will not balk the
  Sport.
  In Summer Heats thou needst but only go
To *Pompey's* cool and shady *Portico* ;
Or *Concord's* Fane ; or that Proud Edifice,
Whose Turrets near the bawdy Suburb rise :
Or to that other *Portico*, where stands
The cruel Father, urging his Commands,
And fifty Daughters wait the Time of Rest,
To plunge their Ponyards in the Bride-
  groom's Breast :
Or *Venus* Temple ; where, on Annual
  Nights,   80
They mourn *Adonis* with *Assyrian* Rites.
Nor shun the *Jewish* Walk, where the foul
  drove,
On Sabbaths, rest from every thing but
  Love.
Nor *Isis* Temple ; for that sacred Whore
Makes others, what to *Jove* she was before.

And if the Hall itself be not bely'd,
Ev'n there the Cause of Love is often try'd ;
Near it at least, or in the Palace Yard,
From whence the noisy Combatants are
  heard.
The crafty Counsellors, in formal Gown, 90
There gain another's Cause, but lose their
  own.
There Eloquence is nonplust in the Sute ;
And Lawyers, who had Words at Will, are
  mute.
Venus, from her adjoyning Temple, smiles,
To see them caught in their litigious Wiles.
Grave Senators lead home the Youthful
  Dame,
Returning Clients, when they Patrons came.
But above all, the Play-House is the Place ;
There's Choice of Quarry in that narrow
  Chace.
There take thy Stand, and sharply looking
  out,   100
Soon mayst thou find a Mistress in the Rout,
For Length of Time, or for a single Bout.
The Theatres are Berries for the Fair ;
Like Ants on Mole-hills, thither they repair ;
Like Bees to Hives, so numerously they
  throng,
It may be said, they to that Place belong.
Thither they swarm, who have the publick
  Voice :
There choose, if Plenty not distracts thy
  Choice.
To see and to be seen, in Heaps they run ;
Some to undo, and some to be undone. 110
  From *Romulus* the Rise of Plays began,
To his new Subjects a commodious Man ;
Who, his unmarried Soldiers to supply,
Took care the Common-Wealth should
  multiply :
Providing *Sabine* Women for his Braves,
Like a true King, to get a Race of Slaves.
His Play-House not of *Parian* Marble made,
Nor was it spread with purple Sayls for shade.
The Stage with Rushes, or with Leaves they
  strew d :   119
No Scenes in Prospect, no machining God.
On Rows of homely Turf they sate to see,
Crown'd with the Wreaths of every common
  Tree.
There, while they sat in rustick Majesty,
Each Lover had his Mistress in his Eye ;
And whom he saw most suiting to his Mind,
For Joys of matrimonial Rape design'd.

Scarce cou'd they wait the *Plaudit* in their
    Haste ;
But, e're the Dances and the Song were past,
The Monarch gave the Signal from his
    Throne ;
And rising, bad his merry Men fall on.   130
The Martial Crew, like Soldiers ready prest,
Just at the Word (the Word too was the
    Best)
With joyful Cries each other animate ;
Some choose, and some at Hazzard seize their
    Mate.
As Doves from Eagles, or from Wolves the
    Lambs,
So from their lawless Lovers fly the Dames.
Their Fear was one, but not one Face of⎫
    Fear ;   ⎬
Some rend the lovely Tresses of their Hair ;
Some shriek, and some are struck with⎭
    dumb Despair.
Her absent Mother one invokes in vain ;⎫
One stands amaz'd, not daring to com- ⎪
    plain ;   141⎬
The nimbler trust their Feet, the slow ⎪
    remain.⎭
But nought availing, all are Captives led,
Trembling and Blushing to the Genial Bed.
She who too long resisted, or deny'd,⎫
The lusty Lover made by Force a Bride ;⎪
And, with superiour Strength, compell'd⎬
    her to his Side.⎭
Then sooth'd her thus!—My Soul's far better
    Part,
Cease weeping, nor afflict thy tender Heart :
For what thy Father to thy Mother was,   150
That Faith to thee, that solemn Vow I pass !
    Thus *Romulus* became so popular ;
This was the Way to thrive in Peace and
    War ;
To pay his Army, and fresh Whores to
    bring :
Who wou'd not fight for such a gracious
    King !
Thus Love in Theaters did first improve ;
And Theaters are still the Scene of Love :
Nor shun the Chariots, and the Courser's
    Race ;
The *Circus* is no inconvenient Place.
No need is there of talking on the Hand ;   160
Nor Nods, nor Signs, which Lovers under-
    stand.
But boldly next the fair your Seat provide ;
Close as you can to hers ; and Side by Side.

Pleas'd or unpleas'd, no matter ; crowding
    sit :
For so the Laws of publick Shows permit.
Then find Occasion to begin Discourse ;
Enquire, whose Chariot this, and whose
    that Horse ?
To whatsoever Side she is inclin'd,
Suit all your Inclinations to her Mind ;
Like what she likes ; from thence your
    Court begin ;   170
And whom she favours, wish that he may
    win.
But when the Statues of the Deities,⎫
In Chariots roll'd, appear before the Prize ;⎬
When *Venus* comes, with deep Devotion⎪
    rise.⎭
If Dust be on her Lap, or Grains of Sand,
Brush both away with your officious Hand.
If none be there, yet brush that nothing
    thence ;
And still to touch her Lap make some
    Pretence.
Touch any thing of hers ; and if her Train⎫
Sweep on the Ground, let it not sweep in⎬
    vain ;   180⎪
But gently take it up, and wipe it clean ;⎭
And while you wipe it, with observing
    Eyes,
Who knows but you may see her naked
    Thighs !
Observe, who sits behind her ; and beware,
Dest his incroaching Knee shou'd press the
    Fair.
Light Service takes light Minds : For some
    can tell
Of Favours won, by laying Cushions well :
By Fanning Faces some their Fortune meet ;
And some by laying Footstools for their
    Feet.
These Overtures of Love the *Circus* gives ;
Nor at the Sword-play less the Lover
    thrives :   191
For there the Son of *Venus* fights his Prize ;
And deepest Wounds are oft receiv'd from
    Eyes.
One, while the Crowd their Acclamations
    make,
Or while he Betts, and puts his Ring to
    Stake,
Is struck from far, and feels the flying Dart ;
And of the Spectacle is made a Part.
    Cæsar wou'd represent a Naval Fight,
For his own Honour, and for *Rome's* Delight.

From either Sea the Youths and Maidens
  come ;   200
And all the World was then contain'd in
  Rome !
In this vast Concourse, in this Choice of
  Game,
What *Roman* Heart but felt a foreign Flame?
Once more our Prince prepares to make us
  glad ;
And the remaining East to Rome will add.
Rejoice, ye *Roman* Souldiers, in your Urn ;
Your Ensigns from the *Parthians* shall
  return ;
And the slain *Crassi* shall no longer mourn.
A youth is sent those trophies to demand ;
And bears his father's thunder in his
  hand :   210
Doubt not th' Imperial Boy in Wars unseen ;
In Childhood all of *Cæsar's* Race are Men.
Celestial Seeds shoot out before their Day,
Prevent their Years, and brook no dull
  Delay.
Thus Infant *Hercules* the Snakes did press,
And in his Cradle did his Sire confess.
Bacchus a Boy, yet like a Hero fought,
And early Spoils from conquer'd *India*
  brought.
Thus you your Father's Troops shall lead to
  Fight,
And thus shall vanquish in your Father's
  Right.   220
These Rudiments you to your Lineage owe ;
Born to increase your Titles as you grow.
Brethren you had, Revenge your Brethren
  slain ;
You have a Father, and his Rights maintain.
Arm'd by your Country's Parent, and your
  own,
Redeem your Country, and restore his
  Throne.
Your Enemies assert an impious Cause ;
You fight both for divine and humane Laws.
Already in their Cause they are o'ercome :
Subject them too, by Force of Arms, to
  Rome.   230
Great Father *Mars* with greater *Cæsar* joyn,
To give a prosperous *Omen* to your Line :
One of you is, and one shall be divine.
I prophesy you shall, you shall o'ercome :
My Verse shall bring you back in Triumph
  Home.
Speak in my Verse, exhort to loud Alarms :
O were my Numbers equal to your Arms.

Then will I sing the *Parthians* Overthrow ;
Their Shot averse sent from a flying Bow :
The *Parthians*, who already flying fight, 240
Already give an *Omen* of their Flight.
O when will come the Day, by Heav'n
  design'd,
When thou, the best and fairest of Mankind,
Drawn by white Horses shalt in Triumph
  ride,
With conquer'd Slaves attending on thy
  Side ;
Slaves, that no longer can be safe in Flight;
O glorious Object, O surprizing Sight,
O Day of Publick Joy, too good to end in
  Night !
On such a Day, if thou, and, next to thee,
Some Beauty sits the Spectacle to see : 250
If she enquire the Names of conquer'd Kings,
Of Mountains, Rivers, and their hidden
  Springs,
Answer to all thou know'st ; and, if need be,
Of things unknown seem to speak know-
  ingly ;
This is *Euphrates*, crown'd with Reeds ; and
  there
Flows the swift *Tigris* with his Sea-green
  Hair.
Invent new Names of things unknown
  before ;
Call this *Armenia*, that the *Caspian* Shore ;
Call this a *Mede*, and that a *Parthian* Youth ;
Talk probably ; no Matter for the Truth. 260
In Feasts, as at our Shows, new Means
  abound ;
More Pleasure there, than that of Wine is
  found.
The *Paphian* Goddess there her Ambush
  lays ;
And Love betwixt the Horns of *Bacchus*
  plays :
Desires encrease at ev'ry swilling Draught ;
Brisk Vapours add new Vigour to the
  Thought.
There *Cupid's* purple Wings no Flight
  afford ;
But wet with Wine, he flutters on the
  Board.
He shakes his Pinnions, but he cannot move;
Fix'd he remains, and turns a Maudlin Love.
Wine warms the Blood, and makes the
  Spirits flow ;   271
Care flies, and Wrinkles from the Forehead
  go :

Exalts the Poor, Invigorates the Weak ;
Gives Mirth and Laughter, and a Rosy
  Cheek.
Bold Truths it speaks ; and, spoken, dares
  maintain ;
And brings our old Simplicity again.
Love sparkles in the Cup, and fills it higher :
Wine feeds the Flames, and Fuel adds to
  Fire.
But choose no Mistress in thy drunken Fit ;
Wine gilds too much their Beauties and their
  Wit.   280
Nor trust thy Judgment when the Tapers
  dance ;
But sober, and by Day, thy Sute advance.
By Day-Light *Paris* judg'd the beauteous
  Three ;
And for the fairest did the Prize decree.
Night is a Cheat, and all Deformities
Are hid, or lessen'd in her dark Disguise.
The Sun's fair Light each Error will confess,
In Face, in Shape, in Jewels, and in Dress.
  Why name I ev'ry Place where Youths
    abound ?
'Tis Loss of Time, and a too fruitful Ground.
The *Bajan* Baths, where Ships at Anchor
  ride,   291
And wholesome Streams from Sulphur
  Fountains glide ;
Where wounded Youths are by Experience
  taught,
The Waters are less healthful than they
  thought :
Or *Dian's* Fane, which near the Suburb lies,
Where Priests, for their Promotion, fight
  a Prize.
That Maiden Goddess is Love's mortal Foe
And much from her his Subjects undergo.
  Thus far the sportful Muse, with Myrtle
    bound,
Has sung where lovely Lasses may be
  found.   300
Now let me sing, how she who wounds your
  Mind,
With Art, may be to cure your Wounds
  inclin'd.
Young Nobles, to my Laws Attention lend ;
And all you Vulgar of my School, attend.
  First then believe, all Women may be
    won ;
Attempt with Confidence, the Work is done.
The Grasshopper shall first forbear to sing
In Summer Season, or the Birds in Spring,

Than Women can resist your flattering Skill :
Ev'n She will yield, who swears she never
  will.   310
To Secret Pleasure both the Sexes move ;
But Women most, who most dissemble Love.
'Twere best for us, if they wou'd first declare,
Avow their Passion, and submit to Prayer.
The Cow by lowing tells the Bull her Flame :
The neighing Mare invites her Stallion to the
  Game.
Man is more temp'rate in his Lust than they,
And more than Women, can his Passion sway.
Biblis, we know, did first her Love declare,
And had Recourse to Death in her De-
  spair.   320
Her Brother She, her Father *Myrrha* sought,
And lov'd ; but lov'd not as a Daughter
  ought.
Now from a Tree she stills her odorous Tears,
Which yet the Name of her who shed 'em
  bears.
  In *Ida's* shady Vale a Bull appear'd,
White as the Snow, the fairest of the Herd ;
A Beauty Spot of black there only rose,   }
Betwixt his equal Horns and ample Brows : }
The Love and Wish of all the *Cretan* Cows. }
The Queen beheld him as his Head he
  rear'd ;   330
And envy'd ev'ry Leap he gave the Herd.
A Secret Fire she nourish'd in her Breast,
And hated ev'ry Heifer he caress'd.
A Story known, and known for true, I tell ;
Nor *Crete*, though lying, can the Truth con-
  ceal.
She cut him Grass ; (so much can Love
  command)
She strok'd, she fed him with her Royal
  Hand :
Was pleas'd in Pastures with the Herd to
  rome ;
And *Minos* by the Bull was overcome.
  Cease Queen, with Gemms t' adorn thy
    beauteous Brows ;   340
The Monarch of thy Heart no Jewel knows.
Nor in thy Glass compose thy Looks and
  Eyes :
Secure from all thy Charms thy Lover lies :
Yet trust thy Mirrour, when it tells thee true ;
Thou art no Heifer to allure his View.
Soon wouldst thou quit thy Royal Diadem
To thy fair Rivals, to be horn'd like them.
If *Minos* please, no Lover seek to find ;
If not, at least seek one of humane Kind.

The wretched Queen the *Cretan* Court
forsakes ;   350
In Woods and Wilds her Habitation makes :
She curses ev'ry beauteous Cow she sees ;
Ah, why dost thou my Lord and Master
please !
And think'st, ungrateful Creature as thou
art,
With frisking awkwardly, to gain his Heart.
She said ; and straight commands, with
frowning Look,
To put her, undeserving, to the Yoke ;
Or feigns some holy Rites of Sacrifice,
And sees her Rival's Death with joyful
Eyes :
Then, when the Bloody Priest has done his
Part,   360
Pleas'd, in her Hand she holds the beating
Heart ;
Nor from a scornful Taunt can scarce refrain;
Go, Fool, and strive to please my Love again.
    Now she would be *Europa*—*Io*, now ;
(One bore a Bull ; and one was made a
Cow.)
Yet she at last her Brutal Bliss obtain'd,
And in a woodden Cow the Bull sustain'd ;
Fill'd with his Seed, accomplish'd her
Desire ;
Till, by his Form, the Son betray'd the Sire.
If *Atreus* Wife to Incest had not run,   370
(But ah, how hard it is to love but one !)
His Coursers *Phœbus* had not driv'n away,
To shun that Sight, and interrupt the Day.
Thy Daughter, *Nisus*, pull'd thy purple
Hair,
And barking Sea-Dogs yet her Bowels tear.
At Sea and Land *Atrides* sav'd his Life,
Yet fell a Prey to his adult'rous Wife.
Who knows not what Revenge *Medea*
sought,
When the slain Offspring bore the Father's
Fault ?
Thus *Phœnix* did a Woman's Love bewail :
And thus *Hippolitus* by *Phœdra* fell.   381
These Crimes revengeful Matrons did com-
mit :
Hotter their Lust, and sharper is their Wit.
Doubt not from them an easie Victory :
Scarce of a thousand Dames will one deny.
All Women are content that Men shou'd
woo ;
She who complains, and She who will not
do.

Rest then secure, whate'er thy Luck may
prove,
Not to be hated for declaring Love :
And yet how can'st thou miss, since Woman-
kind   390
Is frail and vain, and still to Change in-
clin'd ?
Old Husbands and stale Gallants they
despise ;
And more another's than their own, they
prize.
A larger Crop adorns our Neighbour's Field ;
More Milk his Kine from swelling Udders
yield.
    First gain the Maid ; By her thou shalt
be sure
A free Access, and easie to procure :
Who knows what to her Office does belong,
Is in the Secret, and can hold her Tongue.
Bribe her with Gifts, with Promises, and
Pray'rs ;   400
For her good Word goes far in Love
Affairs.
The Time and fit Occasion leave to her,
When she most aptly can thy Sute prefer.
The Time for Maids to fire their Lady's
Blood,
Is, when they find her in a merry Mood.
When all things at her Wish and Pleasure
move :
Her heart is open then, and free to Love.
Then Mirth and Wantonness to Lust betray,
And smooth the Passage to the Lover's
Way.
Troy stood the Siege, when fill'd with anxious
Care :   410
One merry Fit concluded all the War.
    If some fair Rival vex her jealous Mind,
Offer thy Service to revenge in Kind,
Instruct the Damsel, while she combs her
Hair,
To raise the Choler of that injur'd Fair :
And sighing, make her Mistress understand,
She has the Means of Vengeance in her
Hand.
Then, naming thee, thy humble Suit prefer ;
And swear thou languishest and dy'st for
her.
Then let her lose no Time, but push at all ;
For Women soon are rais'd, and soon they
fall.   421
Give their first Fury Leisure to relent,
They melt like Ice, and suddenly repent.

T' enjoy the Maid, will that thy Suit
    advance ?
'Tis a hard Question, and a doubtful Chance.
One Maid, corrupted, bawds the better for't ;
Another for her self wou'd keep the Sport.
Thy Bus'ness may be further'd or delay'd :
But by my Counsel, let alone the Maid :
Ev'n tho she shou'd consent to do the
    Feat,   430
The Profit's little, and the Danger great.
I will not lead thee through a rugged Road ;
But where the Way lies open, safe, and
    broad.
Yet if thou find'st her very much thy
    Friend,
And her good Face her Diligence commend :
Let the fair Mistress have thy first Embrace,
And let the Maid come after in her Place.
    But this I will advise, and mark my
        Words,
For 'tis the best Advice my Skill affords :
If needs thou with the Damsel wilt begin ;
Before th' Attempt is made, make sure to
    win :   441
For then the Secret better will be kept ;
And she can tell no Tales when once she's
    dipt.
'Tis for the Fowlers Interest to beware,
The Bird intangled shou'd not scape the
    Snare.
The Fish, once prick'd, avoids the bearded
    Hook,
And spoils the Sport of all the neighb'ring
    Brook.
But if the Wench be thine, she makes thy
    Way ;
And, for thy Sake, her Mistress will betray ;
Tell all she knows, and all she hears her
    say.   450
Keep well the Counsel of thy faithful Spy :
So shalt thou learn whene'er she treads
    awry.
    All things the Stations of their Seasons
        keep ;
And certain Times there are to sow and
    reap.
Ploughmen and Sailors for the Season stay, ⎫
One to plough Land, and one to plough   ⎬
    the Sea :   ⎭
So shou'd the Lover wait the lucky Day.
Then stop thy Suit ; it hurts not thy
    Design :
But think another Hour she may be thine.

And when she celebrates her Birth at home, ⎫
Or when she views the publick shows of   ⎬
    Rome,   461   ⎭
Know, all thy Visits then are troublesome.
Defer thy Work, and put not then to Sea,
For that's a boding and a stormy Day.
Else take thy Time, and, when thou canst,
    begin :
To break a Jewish Sabbath, think no Sin :
Nor ev'n on superstitious Days abstain ;
Not when the Romans were at Allia slain.
Ill Omens in her Frowns are understood ;
When She's in humour, ev'ry Day is good.
But than her Birth-day seldom comes a ⎫
    worse ;   471   ⎬
When Bribes and Presents must be sent of ⎪
    course ;   ⎬
And that's a bloody Day, that costs thy   ⎪
    Purse.   ⎭
Be stanch ; yet Parsimony will be vain :
The craving Sex will still the Lover drain.
No Skill can shift 'em off, nor Art remove ;
They will be Begging, when they know we
    Love.
The Merchant comes upon th' appointed
    Day,
Who shall before thy Face his Wares dis-
    play.
To chuse for her she craves thy kind
    Advice ;   480
Then begs again, to bargain for the Price :
But when she has her Purchase in her
    Eye,
She hugs thee close, and kisses thee to buy.
'Tis what I want, and 'tis a Pennorth too ;
In many years I will not trouble you.
If you complain you have no ready Coin ;
No matter, 'tis but Writing of a Line,
A little Bill, not to be paid at Sight ;
(Now curse the Time when thou wert taught
    to Write)
She keeps her Birth-day ; you must send
    the Chear ;   490
And she'll be Born a hundred times a year
With daily Lies she dribs thee into Cost ;
That Ear-ring dropt a Stone, that Ring is
    lost.
They often borrow what they never pay ;
What e'er you lend her, think it thrown
    away.
Had I ten Mouths and Tongues to tell
    each Art,
All wou'd be weary'd e'er I told a Part.

By Letters, not by Words, thy Love begin ;
And Foord the dangerous Passage with thy Pen.
If to her Heart thou aim'st to find the way,
Extreamly Flatter, and extreamly Pray. 501
Priam by Pray'rs did *Hector's* Body gain ;
Nor is an Angry God invok'd in vain.
With promis'd Gifts her easy Mind bewitch ;
For ev'n the Poor in promise may be Rich.
Vain Hopes a while her Appetite will stay ;
'Tis a deceitful, but commodious way.
Who gives is Mad, but make her still believe
'Twill come, and that's the cheapest way to give.
Ev'n barren Lands fair promises afford ; 510
But the lean Harvest cheats the starving Lord.
Buy not thy first Enjoyment ; lest it prove
Of bad example to thy future Love :
But get it *gratis* ; and she'll give thee more,
For fear of losing what she gave before.
The losing Gamester shakes the Box in vain,
And Bleeds, and loses on, in hopes to gain.
Write then, and in thy Letter, as I said,
Let her with mighty Promises be fed.
Cydippe by a Letter was betray'd, 520
Writ on an Apple to th' unwary Maid.
She read herself into a Marriage Vow ;
(And ev'ry Cheat in Love the Gods allow.)
Learn Eloquence, ye noble Youth of *Rome* ;
It will not only at the Bar o'ercome :
Sweet words the People and the Senate move ;
But the chief end of Eloquence is Love.
But in thy Letter hide thy moving Arts ;
Affect not to be thought a Man of Parts.
None but vain Fools to simple Women Preach ; 530
A learned Letter oft has made a Breach.
In a familiar Style your Thoughts convey,
And Write such things, as Present you wou'd say ;
Such words as from the Heart may seem to move :
'Tis Wit enough to make her think you Love.
If Seal'd she sends it back, and will not read :
Yet hope, in time, the business may succeed.
In time the Steer will to the Yoke submit ;
In time the restiff Horse will bear the Bit.
Ev'n the hard Plough-share use will wear away ; 540
And stubborn Steel in length of time decay.

Water is soft, and Marble hard ; and yet
We see soft Water through hard Marble Eat.
Though late, yet *Troy* at length in Flames expir'd ;
And ten years more *Penelope* had tir'd.
Perhaps, thy Lines unanswer'd she retain'd ;
No matter ; there's a Point already gain'd :
For she who Reads, in time will Answer too ;
Things must be left by just degrees to grow.
Perhaps she Writes, but Answers with disdain, 550
And sharply bids you not to Write again :
What she requires, she fears you shou'd accord ;
The Jilt wou'd not be taken at her word.
Mean time, if she be carried in her Chair,
Approach ; but do not seem to know she's there.
Speak softly, to delude the Standers by ;
Or, if aloud, then speak ambiguously.
If Sauntring in the Portico she Walk,
Move slowly too ; for that's a time for talk :
And sometimes follow, sometimes be her guide : 560
But when the Croud permits, go side by side
Nor in the *Play-House* let her sit alone :
For she's the *Play-House* and the *Play* in one.
There thou may'st ogle, or by signs advance
Thy suit, and seem to touch her Hand by chance.
Admire the Dancer who her liking gains,
And pity in the *Play* the Lover's pains ;
For her sweet sake the loss of time despise ;
Sit while she sits, and when she rises rise.
But dress not like a Fop ; nor curle your Hair, 570
Nor with a Pumice make your body bare.
Leave those effeminate and useless toys
To *Eunuchs*, who can give no solid joys.
Neglect becomes a Man : this *Theseus* found :
Uncurl'd, uncomb'd, the Nymph his Wishes Crown'd.
The rough *Hippolitus* was *Phædra's* care ;
And *Venus* thought the rude *Adonis* fair.
Be not too Finical ; but yet be clean ;
And wear well-fashion'd Cloaths, like other Men.
Let not your Teeth be yellow, or be foul ;
Nor in wide Shoes your Feet too loosely roul. 581
Of a black Muzzel, and long Beard beware ;
And let a skilful Barber cut your Hair :

Your Nailes be pick'd from filth, and even
par'd ;
Nor let your nasty Nostrils bud with Beard.
Cure your unsav'ry Breath, gargle your
Throat,
And free your Arm-pits from the Ram and
Goat.
Dress not, in short, too little, or too much ;
And be not wholly *French*, nor wholly
Dutch.   589
   Now *Bacchus* calls me to his jolly Rites :
Who wou'd not follow, when a God invites ?
He helps the Poet, and his Pen inspires,
Kind and indulgent to his former Fires.
   Fair *Ariadne* wander'd on the shore,
Forsaken now ; and *Theseus* Loves no more :
Loose was her Gown, dishevel'd was her
Hair ;
Her Bosom naked, and her Feet were bare :
Exclaiming, in the Waters brink she stood ;
Her briny Tears augment the briny Flood.
She shreik'd, and wept, and both became
her Face :   600
No posture cou'd that Heav'nly form
disgrace.
She beat her Breast : The Traytor's gone,
said she,
What shall become of poor forsaken me ?
What shall become——she had not time for
more,
The sounding Cymbals ratled on the Shore.
She swoons for fear, she falls upon the
Ground ;
No vital heat was in her body found.
The *Mimallonian* Dames about her stood ;
And scudding *Satyrs* ran before their God.
Silenus on his Ass did next appear,   610
And held upon the Mane (the God was clear)
The drunken *Syre* pursues ; the Dames retire ;
Sometimes the drunken Dames pursue the
drunken Syre.
At last he topples over on the Plain ;
The *Satyrs* laugh, and bid him rise again.
And now the God of Wine came driving on,
High on his Chariot by swift *Tygers* drawn,
Her Colour, Voice, and Sense forsook the
fair ;
Thrice did her trembling Feet for flight
prepare,   619
And thrice affrighted did her flight forbear.

She shook, like leaves of Corn when Tempests
blow
Or slender Reeds that in the Marshes grow.
To whom the God—Compose thy fearful
Mind ;
In me a truer Husband thou shalt find.
With Heav'n I will endow thee ; and thy
Star
Shall with propitious Light be seen afar,
And guide on Seas the doubtful Mariner.
He said ; and from his Chariot leaping light ;
Lest the grim *Tygers* shou'd the Nymph
affright,
His brawny Arms around her wast he
threw ;   630
(For Gods, what ere they will, with ease
can do :)
And swiftly bore her thence : th' attending
throng
Shout at the Sight, and sing the *Nuptial*
song.
Now in full bowls her Sorrow she may steep :
The Bridegroom's Liquor lays the Bride
asleep.
   But thou, when flowing Cups in Triumph
ride,
And the lov'd Nymph is seated by thy side ;
Invoke the God, and all the mighty Pow'rs,
That Wine may not defraud thy Genial hours.
Then in ambiguous Words thy suit prefer ;
Which she may know were all addrest to
her,   641
In liquid purple Letters write her Name,
Which she may read, and reading find thy
Flame.
Then may your Eyes confess your mutual
Fires ;
(For Eyes have Tongues, and glances tell
desires)
Whene'er she Drinks, be first to take the
Cup ;
And where she laid her Lips, the Blessing sup.
When she to Carving does her Hand ad-
vance,
Put out thy own, and touch it as by
chance.   649
Thy service ev'n her Husband must attend :
(A Husband is a most convenient Friend.)
Seat the fool Cuckold in the highest place :
And with thy Garland his dull Temples
grace.

595 Loves] *The editors wrongly give* loved
598 in] *The editors give* on

653 thy] *The editors nonsensically give* the

Whether below, or equal in degree,
Let him be Lord of all the Company ;
And what he says, be seconded by Thee.
'Tis common to deceive through friendships
    Name :
But common though it be, 'tis still to
    blame :
Thus Factors frequently their Trust betray,
And to themselves their Masters gains con-
    vey.   660
Drink to a certain Pitch, and then give o're ;
Thy Tongue and Feet may stumble, drinking
    more.
Of drunken Quarrels in her sight beware ;
Pot Valour only serves to fright the Fair.
Eurytion justly fell, by Wine opprest,
For his rude Riot at a Wedding-Feast.
Sing, if you have a Voice ; and show your
    Parts
In Dancing, if endu'd with Dancing Arts.
Do any thing within your power to please ;
Nay, ev'n affect a seeming Drunkenness ;
Clip every word ; and if by chance you
    speak   671
Too home ; or if too broad a Jest you
    break ;
In your excuse the Company will joyn,
And lay the Fault upon the Force of Wine.
True Drunkenness is subject to offend ;
But when 'tis feign'd, 'tis oft a Lover's
    Friend.
Then safely you may praise her beauteous
    Face,
And call him Happy, who is in her grace.
Her Husband thinks himself the Man de-
    sign'd ;
But curse the Cuckold in your secret Mind.
When all are risen, and prepare to go,   681
Mix with the Croud, and tread upon her Toe.
This is the proper time to make thy
    Court ;
For now she's in the Vein, and fit for
    Sport ;
Lay Bashfulness, that rustick Virtue, by ;
To manly Confidence thy Thoughts apply.
On Fortune's Foretop timely fix thy hold ;
Now speak and speed, for *Venus* loves the
    old.
No Rules of Rhetorick here I need afford :
Only begin, and trust the following word ;
It will be Witty of its own accord.   691
    Act well the Lover, let thy Speech abound
In dying words, that represent thy Wound.

Distrust not her belief ; she will be mov'd ;
All women think they merit to be lov'd.
    Sometimes a Man begins to Love in Jest,
And, after, feels the Torments he profest.
For your own sakes be pitiful ye Fair ;
For a feign'd Passion may a true prepare.
By Flatteries we prevail on Woman-kind ;
As hollow Banks by Streams are under-
    min'd.   701
Tell her, her Face is Fair, her Eyes are
    Sweet
Her Taper Fingers praise, and little Feet.
Such Praises ev'n the Chast are pleas'd to
    hear ;
Both Maids and Matrons hold their Beauty
    dear.
    Once naked *Pallas* with *Jove's* Queen ap-
        pear'd ;
And still they grieve that *Venus* was pre-
    fer'd.
Praise the proud Peacock, and he spreads
    his Train ;
Be silent, and he pulls it in again.
Pleas'd is the Courser in his rapid Race ; 710
Applaud his Running, and he mends his
    pace.
But largely promise, and devoutly swear ;
And, if need be, call ev'ry God to hear.
Jove sits above, forgiving with a Smile
The Perjuries that easy Maids beguile.
He swore to *Juno* by the *Stygian* Lake :
Forsworn, he dares not an Example make,
Or punish Falshood, for his own dear
    sake.
'Tis for our Int'rest that the Gods shou'd
    be ;
Let us believe 'em : I believe, they see, 720
And both reward, and punish equally.
Not that they live above like lazy Drones,
Or Kings below, supine upon their Thrones.
Lead then your Lives as present in their
    sight ;
Be Just in Dealings, and defend the right ;
By Fraud betray not, nor Oppress by Might.
But 'tis a Venial Sin to Cheat the Fair ;
All Men have Liberty of Conscience there.
On cheating Nymphs a Cheat is well de-
    sign'd ;
'Tis a prophane and a deceitful Kind. 730
    'Tis said, that *Ægypt* for nine Years was
    dry,
Nor *Nile* did Floods, nor Heav'n did Rain
    supply.

A Foreigner at length inform'd the King,
That slaughter'd Guests would kindly Mois-
    ture bring.
The King reply'd, On thee the Lot shall fall,
Be thou, my Guest, the Sacrifice for all.
Thus *Phalaris*, *Perillus* taught to low,
And made him season first the brazen Cow.
A rightful Doom, the Laws of Nature cry,
'Tis, the Artificers of Death should die. 740
Thus justly Women suffer by Deceit ;
Their Practice authorizes us to cheat.
Beg her, with Tears, thy warm Desires to
    grant ;
For Tears will pierce a Heart of Adamant.
If Tears will not be squeez'd, then rub your
    Eye,
Or noint the Lids, and seem at least to cry.
Kiss, if you can : Resistance if she make,
And will not give you Kisses, let her take.
Fie, fie, you naughty Man, are Words of
    Course ;   749
She struggles but to be subdu'd by Force.
Kiss only soft, I charge you, and beware,
With your hard Bristles not to brush the
    Fair.
He who has gain'd a Kiss, and gains no
    more,
Deserves to lose the Bliss he got before.
If once she kiss, her Meaning is exprest ;
There wants but little Pushing for the rest.
Which if thou dost not gain, by Strength
    or Art,
The Name of Clown then suits with thy
    Desert ;
'Tis downright Dulness, and a shameful
    Part.
Perhaps, she calls it Force ; but, if she
    'scape,   760
She will not thank you for th' omitted Rape.
The Sex is cunning to conceal their Fires ;
They would be forc'd, ev'n to their own
    Desires.
They seem t' accuse you, with a down-cast
    Sight,
But in their Souls confess you did them
    right.
Who might be forc'd, and yet untouch'd
    depart,
Thank with their Tongues, but curse you
    with their Heart.

Fair *Phœbe* and her Sister did prefer,
To their dull Mates, the noble Ravisher.
    What *Deidamia* did, in Days of Yore, 770
The Tale is old, but worth the reading
    o'er.
When *Venus* had the golden Apple gain'd,
And the just Judge fair *Hellen* had obtain'd :
When she with Triumph was at *Troy*
    receiv'd,
The *Trojans* joyful while the *Grecians*
    griev'd :
They vow'd Revenge of violated Laws,
And *Greece* was arming in the Cuckold's
    Cause :
Achilles, by his Mother warn'd from War,
Disguis'd his Sex, and lurk'd among the
    Fair,
What means *Eacides* to spin and sow ? 780
With Spear, and Sword, in Field thy Valour
    show ;
And, leaving this, the Nobler *Pallas* know.
Why dost thou in that Hand the Distaff
    wield,
Which is more worthy to sustain a Shield ?
Or with that other draw the woolly Twine,
The same the Fates for *Hector's* Thread
    assign ?
Brandish thy Fauchion in thy pow'rful
    Hand,
Which can alone the pond'rous Lance com-
    mand.
In the same Room by chance the Royal
    Maid
Was lodg'd, and, by his seeming Sex
    betray'd,   790
Close to her Side the Youthful Heroe laid.
I know not how his Courtship he began ;
But, to her Cost, she found it was a Man.
'Tis thought she struggled ; but withal 'tis
    thought,
Her Wish was to be conquer'd, when she
    fought.
For when disclos'd, and hast'ning to the
    Field,
He laid his Distaff down, and took the
    Shield,
With Tears her humble Suit she did prefer,
And thought to stay the grateful Ravisher.
She sighs, she sobs, she begs him not to
    part :   800
And now 'tis Nature, what before was Art.
She strives by Force her Lover to detain,
And wishes to be ravish'd once again.

This is the Sex ; they will not first begin,
But, when compell'd, are pleas'd to suffer Sin.
Is there, who thinks that Women first should woo ;
Lay by thy Self-Conceit, thou foolish Beaux.
Begin, and save their Modesty the Shame ;
'Tis well for thee, if they receive thy Flame.
'Tis decent for a Man to speak his Mind ; 810
They but expect th' Occasion to be kind.
Ask, that thou may'st enjoy ; she waits for this ;
And on thy first Advance depends thy Bliss.
Ev'n *Jove* himself was forc'd to sue for Love ;
None of the Nymphs did first sollicit *Jove*.
But if you find your Pray'rs encrease her Pride,
Strike Sail awhile, and wait another Tide.
They fly when we pursue ; but make Delay,
And when they see you slacken, they will stay.
Sometimes it profits to conceal your End ;
Name not your self her Lover, but her Friend.   821
How many skittish Girls have thus been caught ?
He prov'd a Lover, who a Friend was thought.
Sailors by Sun and Wind are swarthy made ;
A tann'd Complexion best becomes their Trade.
'Tis a Disgrace to Ploughmen to be fair ;
Bluff Cheeks they have, and weather-beaten Hair.
Th' ambitious Youth, who seeks an Olive Crown,
Is Sun-burnt with his daily Toil, and brown.
But if the Lover hopes to be in Grace, 830
Wan be his Looks, and meager be his Face.
That Colour, from the Fair, Compassion draws :
She thinks you sick, and thinks herself the Cause.
Orion wander'd in the Woods for Love, ⎫
His Paleness did the Nymphs to Pity move; ⎬
His ghastly Visage argu'd hidden Love. ⎭
Nor fail a Night-Cap, in full Health, to wear ;
Neglect thy Dress, and discompose thy Hair.

All things are decent, that in Love avail.
Read long by Night, and study to be pale :
Forsake your Food, refuse your needful Rest ;   841
Be miserable, that you may be blest.
Shall I complain, or shall I warn you ⎫
most ?   ⎪
Faith, Truth, and Friendship in the World ⎬
are lost ;   ⎪
A little and an empty Name they boast. ⎭
Trust not thy Friend, much less thy Mistress praise :
If he believe, thou may'st a Rival raise.
'Tis true, *Patroclus*, by no Lust mis-led,
Sought not to stain his dear Companion's Bed.
Nor *Pylades Hermione* embrac'd ;   850
Ev'n *Phædra* to *Perithous* still was chaste.
But hope not thou, in this vile Age, to find
Those rare Examples of a faithful Mind.
The Sea shall sooner with sweet Hony flow ;
Or from the Furzes Pears and Apples grow.
We Sin with Gust, we love by Fraud to gain :
And find a Pleasure in our Fellows Pain.
From Rival Foes you may the Fair defend ;
But would you ward the Blow, beware your Friend.
Beware your Brother, and your next of Kin ;   860
But from your Bosom Friend your Care begin.
Here I had ended, but Experience finds,
That sundry Women are of sundry Minds ;
With various Crochets fill'd, and hard to please ;
They therefore must be caught by various Ways.
All things are not produc'd in any Soil ;
This Ground for Wine is proper, that for Oil.
So 'tis in Men, but more in women-kind : ⎫
Diff'rent in Face, in Manners, and in Mind : ⎬
But wise Men shift their Sails with ev'ry ⎪
Wind :   870 ⎭
As changeful *Proteus* vary'd oft his Shape,
And did in sundry Forms and Figures 'scape ;
A running Stream, a standing Tree became,
A roaring Lyon, or a bleating Lamb.
Some Fish with Harpons, some with Darts are strook,
Some drawn with Nets, some hang upon the Hook :

So turn thy self ; and, imitating them,
Try sev'ral Tricks, and change thy Strata-
gem.
One Rule will not for diff'rent Ages hold ;
The Jades grow cunning, as they grow more
old.   880
Then talk not Bawdy to the bashful Maid ;
Bug words will make her Innocence afraid.

Nor to an ign'rant Girl of Learning speak ;
She thinks you conjure, when you talk in
Greek
And hence 'tis often seen, the Simple
shun
The Learn'd, and into vile Embraces run.
  Part of my Task is done, and part to do ;
But here 'tis time to rest my self and you.

FROM OVID'S AMOURS.

BOOK I.   ELEG. I.

FOR mighty Wars I thought to Tune my
Lute,
And make my Measures to my Subject suit.
Six Feet for ev'ry Verse the Muse design'd : }
But *Cupid*, laughing, when he saw my Mind, }
From ev'ry Second Verse a Foot purloin'd. }
Who gave Thee, Boy, this Arbitrary sway, }
On Subjects, not thy own, Commands to lay, }
Who *Phœbus* only and his Laws obey ? }
'Tis more absurd than if the *Queen of Love*
Should in *Minerva's* arms to Battel move ;
Or Manly *Pallas* from that Queen should
take   11
Her Torch, and o're the dying Lover shake.
In fields as well may *Cynthia* sow the Corn,
Or *Ceres* wind in Woods the Bugle Horn.
As well may *Phœbus* quit the trembling
String,
For Sword and Shield ; and *Mars* may learn
to Sing.
Already thy Dominions are too large ;
Be not ambitious of a Foreign Charge.

If thou wilt Reign e're all, and ev'ry where,
The God of Musick for his Harp may fear. 20
Thus when with soaring Wings I seek
Renown,
Thou pluck'st my Pinnions, and I flutter
down.
Cou'd I on such mean Thoughts my Muse
employ,
I want a Mistress or a Blooming Boy.
Thus I complain'd : his Bow the Stripling
bent,
And chose an Arrow fit for his Intent.
The Shaft his purpose fatally pursues ;
Now, Poet, there's a Subject for thy Muse.
He said, (too well, alas, he knows his Trade,)
For in my Breast a Mortal Wound he
made.   30
Far hence, ye proud *Hexameters*, remove,
My Verse is pac'd and tramel'd into love.
With Myrtle Wreaths my thoughtful brows
inclose,
While in unequal Verse I sing my Woes.

FROM OVID'S AMOURS.

BOOK I.   ELEG. IV.

*To his Mistress, whose Husband is invited
to a Feast with them.   The Poet instructs her
how to behave **herself** in his Company.*

YOUR husband will be with us at the
Treat ;
May that be the last Supper he shall Eat.
And am poor I, a Guest invited there,
Only to see, while he may touch the Fair ?

To see you Kiss and Hug your nauseous
Lord,
While his leud Hand descends below the
Board ?
Now wonder not that *Hippodamia's* Charms,
At such a sight, the *Centaurs* urg'd to Arms ;
That in a rage they threw their Cups aside,
Assail'd the Bridegroom, and wou'd force
the Bride.   10

OVID'S ART OF LOVE.   882 Bug] *The editors
give* Broad
OVID'S AMOURS, I. I. and I. IV.   Text of 1704.

I. IV. 3 poor I, a Guest] *The editors delete the
comma and thereby give a sense other than
Ovid's and Dryden's.*

I am not half a Horse, (I would I were :)
Yet hardly can from you my Hands forbear.
Take then my Counsel ; which observ'd,
 may be
Of some Importance both to you and me.
Be sure to come before your Man be there ;
There's nothing can be done ; but come
 howe're.
Sit next him (that belongs to Decency ;)
But tread upon my Foot in passing by.
Read in my Looks what silently they speak,
And slily, with your Eyes, your Answer
 make.   20
My Lifted Eye-brow shall declare my Pain ;
My Right-Hand to his fellow shall complain ;
And on the Back a Letter shall design ;
Besides a Note that shall be Writ in Wine.
When e're you think upon our last Embrace,
With your Fore-finger gently touch your
 Face.
If any Word of mine offend my Dear,
Pull, with your Hand, the Velvet of your
 Ear.
If you are pleas'd with what I do or say,
Handle your Rings, or with your Fingers
 play.   30
As Suppliants use at Altars, hold the Boord,
Whene're you wish the Devil may take
 your Lord.
When he fills for you, never touch the
 Cup ;
But bid th' officious Cuckold drink it up.
The Waiter on those Services employ ;
Drink you, and I will snatch it from the
 Boy :
Watching the part where your sweet Mouth
 hath been,
And thence, with eager Lips, will suck it in.
If he, with Clownish Manners, thinks it fit
To taste, and offer you the nasty Bit, 40
Reject his greazy Kindness, and restore
Th' unsav'ry Morsel he had chew'd before.
Nor let his Arms embrace your Neck, nor
 rest
Your tender Cheek upon his hairy Breast.
Let not his Hand within your Bosom stray,
And rudely with your pretty Bubbies play.
But above all, let him no Kiss receive ;
That's an Offence I never can forgive.

Do not, O do not that sweet Mouth resign,
Lest I rise up in Arms, and cry, 'Tis mine. 50
I shall thrust in betwixt, and void of Fear
The manifest Adult'rer will appear.
These things are plain to Sight ; but more
 I doubt
What you conceal beneath your Petticoat.
Take not his Leg between your tender
 Thighs,
Nor, with your Hand, provoke my Foe to
 rise.
How many Love-Inventions I deplore,
Which I, my self, have practis'd all before ?
How oft have I been forc'd the Robe to lift
In Company ; to make a homely shift 60
For a bare Bout, ill huddled o're in hast,
While o're my side the Fair her Mantle cast.
You to your Husband shall not be so kind ;
But, lest you shou'd, your Mantle leave
 behind.
Encourage him to Tope ; but Kiss him not,
Nor mix one drop of Water in his Pot.
If he be Fuddled well, and Snores apace
Then we may take Advice from Time and
 Place.
When all depart, when Complements are
 loud,
Be sure to mix among the thickest Crowd
There I will be, and there we cannot miss, 71
Perhaps to Grubble, or at least to Kiss
Alas, what length of Labour I employ,
Just to secure a short and transient Joy !
For Night must part us : and when Night
 is come,
Tuck'd underneath his Arm he leads you
 Home.
He locks you in ; I follow to the Door,
His Fortune envy, and my own deplore.
He kisses you, he more than kisses too ;
Th' outrageous Cuckold thinks it all his due.
But, add not to his Joy, by your consent, 81
And let it not be giv'n, but only lent.
Return no Kiss, nor move in any sort ;
Make it a dull and a malignant Sport.
Had I my Wish, he shou'd no Pleasure take,
But slubber o're your Business for my sake.
And what e're Fortune shall this Night
 befal,
Coax me to-morrow, by forswearing all.

FROM OVID'S AMOURS.

BOOK II. ELEG. XIX.

IF for thy self thou wilt not watch thy
    Whore,
Watch her for me, that I may love her
    more.
What comes with ease, we nauseously receive,
Who, but a Sot, wou'd scorn to love with
    leave ?
With hopes and fears my Flames are blown
    up higher ;
Make me despair, and then I can desire.
Give me a Jilt to tease my Jealous mind ;
Deceits are Vertues in the Female kind.
Corinna my Fantastick humour knew,
Play'd trick for trick, and kept her self still
    new :   10
She, that next night I might the sharper
    come,
Fell out with me, and sent me fasting
    home ;
Or some pretence to lye alone would take,
Whene'er she pleas'd her head and teeth
    wou'd ake :
Till having won me to the highest strain,
She took occasion to be sweet again.
With what a Gust, ye Gods, we then im-
    brac'd !
How every kiss was dearer than the last !
  Thou whom I now adore, be edify'd,
Take care that I may often be deny'd.   20
Forget the promis'd hour, or feign some
    fright,
Make me lye rough on Bulks each other
    Night.
These are the Arts that best secure thy
    reign,
And this the Food that must my Fires
    maintain.
Gross easie Love does like gross diet, pall,
In squeasie Stomachs Honey turns to Gall.
Had *Danae* not been kept in brazen Tow'rs,
Jove had not thought her worth his Golden
    Show'rs.

When *Juno* to a Cow turn'd *Io's* Shape, 29
The Watchman helpt her to a second Leap.
Let him who loves an easie Whetstone
    Whore.
Pluck leaves from Trees, and drink the
    Common Shore.
The Jilting Harlot strikes the surest blow,
A truth which I by sad Experience know.
The kind poor constant Creature we despise,
Man but pursues the Quarry while it flies.
  But thou dull Husband of a Wife too fair,
Stand on thy Guard, and watch the pretious
    Ware ;
If creaking Doors, or barking Dogs thou
    hear,
Or Windows scratcht, suspect a Rival there.
An Orange-wench wou'd tempt thy Wife
    abroad ;   41
Kick her, for she's a Letter-bearing Bawd ;
In short, be Jealous as the Devil in Hell ;
And set my Wit on work to cheat thee well.
The sneaking City Cuckold is my Foe,
I scorn to strike, but when he Wards the
    blow.
Look to thy hits, and leave off thy Con-
    niving,
I'll be no Drudge to any Wittall living ;
I have been patient, and forborn thee long,
In hope thou wou'dst not pocket up thy
    wrong :   50
If no Affront can rouse thee, understand
I'll take no more Indulgence at thy hand.
What, ne'er to be forbid thy House, and
    Wife !
Damn him who loves to lead so dull a life.
Now I can neither sigh, nor whine, nor pray,
All those occasions thou hast ta'ne away.
Why art thou so incorrigibly Civil ?
Doe somewhat I may wish thee at the
    Devil.
For shame be no Accomplice in my Treason,
A Pimping Husband is too much in reason.
  Once more wear horns, before I quite
      forsake her,   61
In hopes whereof I rest thy Cuckold-maker.

OVID'S AMOURS, II. XIX.   Text from the
original of 1692.

[TRANSLATIONS FROM JUVENAL.]

THE FIRST SATYR.

ARGUMENT of the first Satyr.

The Poet gives us first a kind of humorous Reason for his Writing : That being provok'd by hearing so many ill Poets rehearse their Works, he does himself Justice on them, by giving them as bad as they bring. But since no man will rank himself with ill Writers, 'tis easie to conclude, that if such Wretches cou'd draw an Audience, he thought it no hard matter to excel them, and gain a greater esteem with the Publick. Next he informs us more openly, why he rather addicts himself to Satyr, than any other kind of Poetry. And here he discovers that it is not so much his indignation to ill Poets, as to ill Men, which has prompted him to write. He therefore gives us a summary and general view of the Vices and Follies reigning in his time. So that this first Satyr is the natural Groundwork of all the rest. Herein he confines himself to no one Subject, but strikes indifferently at all Men in his way : In every following Satyr he has chosen some particular Moral which he wou'd inculcate ; and lashes some particular Vice or Folly, (An Art with which our Lampooners are not much acquainted.) But our Poet being desirous to reform his own Age, and not daring to attempt it by an Overt act of naming living Persons, inveighs onely against those who were infamous in the times immediately preceding his, whereby he not only gives a fair warning to Great Men, that their Memory lies at the mercy of future Poets and Historians, but also with a finer stroke of his Pen, brands ev'n the living, and personates them under dead mens Names.

I have avoided as much as I cou'd possibly the borrow'd Learning of Marginal Notes and Illustrations, and for that reason have Translated this Satyr somewhat largely. And freely own (if it be a fault) that I have likewise omitted most of the Proper Names, because I thought they wou'd not much edifie the Reader. To conclude, if in two or three places I have deserted all the Commentators, 'tis because I thought they first deserted my Author, or at least have left him in so much obscurity, that too much room is left for guessing.

THE | FIRST SATYR.

Still shall I hear, and never quit the Score,
Stun'd with hoarse ¹*Codrus Theseid*, o're
   and o're ?
Shall this man's Elegies and t'other's Play
Unpunish'd Murther a long Summer's day ?
Huge ²*Telephus*, a formidable page,
Cries Vengeance ; and ³*Orestes's* bulky rage,
Unsatisfy'd with Margins closely writ,
Foams o're the Covers, and not finish'd yet.
No Man can take a more familiar note
Of his own Home, than I of *Vulcan's*
   Grott,   10
Or⁴*Mars his Grove*,or hollow winds that blow
From *Ætna's* top, or tortur'd Ghosts below.
I know by rote the Fam'd Exploits of *Greece* ;
The *Centaurs* fury, and the Golden Fleece ;
Through the thick shades th' Eternal Scribler
   bauls ;
And shakes the Statues on their Pedestals.
The ⁵best and worst on the same Theme
   employs
His Muse, and plagues us with an equal noise.
Provok'd by these Incorrigible Fools,
I left declaiming in pedantick Schools ;   20
Where, with Men-boys, I strove to get
   Renown,
Advising ⁶*Sylla* to a private Gown.
But, since the World with Writing is pos-
   sest,
I'll versifie in spite ; and do my best
To make as much waste Paper as the rest.
But why I lift aloft the Satyrs Rod,
And tread the Path which fam'd ⁷*Lucilius*
   trod,
Attend the Causes which my Muse have led :
When Sapless Eunuchs mount the Marriage-
   bed,
When ⁸Mannish *Mevia*, that two-handed
   Whore,   30
Astride on Horse-back hunts the *Tuscan* Boar;

TRANSLATIONS FROM JUVENAL. Text from the original edition, 1693. The current texts have several bad errors, especially in VI. 79 7 and 861, and X. 517.

When all our Lords are by his Wealth
    outvy'd,
Whose [9] Razour on my callow-beard was
    try'd ;
When I behold the Spawn of conquer'd *Nile
Crispinus* [10] both in Birth and Manners vile,
Pacing in pomp, with Cloak of *Tyrian* dye,
Chang'd oft a day for needless Luxury ;
And finding oft occasion to be fan'd,
Ambitious to produce his Lady-hand ;
Charg'd [11] with light Summer-rings his fingers
    sweat,   40
Unable to support a Gem of weight :
Such fulsom Objects meeting every where,
'Tis hard to write, but harder to forbear.
    To view so lewd a Town, and to refrain,
What Hoops of Iron cou'd my Spleen con-
    tain !
When [12] pleading *Matho*, born abroad for Air,
With his Fat Paunch fills his new fashion'd
    Chair,
And after him the Wretch in Pomp con-
    vey'd,
Whose Evidence his Lord and Friend be-
    tray'd,
And but the wish'd Occasion does attend 50 ⎫
From the poor Nobles the last Spoils to   ⎪
    rend,   ⎬
Whom ev'n Spies dread as their Superiour ⎪
    Fiend,   ⎭
And bribe with Presents, or, when Presents
    fail,
They send their prostituted Wives for bail :
When Night-performance holds the place
    of Merit,
And Brawn and Back the next of Kin dis-
    herit ;
For such good Parts are in Preferment's
    way,
The Rich Old Madam never fails to pay ;
Her Legacies by Nature's Standard giv'n,
One gains an Ounce, another gains Eleven :
A dear-bought Bargain, all things duly
    weigh'd,   61
For which their thrice Concocted Blood is
    paid.
With looks as wan, as he who in the Brake
At unawares has trod upon a Snake ;
Or play'd [13] at *Lions* a declaiming Prize,
For which the Vanquish'd *Rhetorician* Dyes.

What Indignation boils within my Veins, ⎫
When perjur'd Guardians, proud with   ⎪
    Impious Gains,   ⎬
Choak up the Streets, too narrow for their ⎪
    Trains !   ⎭
Whose Wards by want betray'd, to Crimes
    are led   70
Too foul to Name, too fulsom to be read !
When he who pill'd his Province scapes the
    Laws,
And keeps his Money though he lost his
    Cause :
His Fine begg'd off, contemns his Infamy,
Can rise at twelve, and get him Drunk e're
    three :
Enjoys his Exile, and, Condemn'd in vain,
Leaves thee, [14] prevailing Province, to com-
    plain !
    Such Villanies rous'd [15]*Horace* into Wrath
And 'tis more Noble to pursue his Path,
Than an Old Tale of *Diomede* to repeat, 80 ⎫
Or lab'ring after *Hercules* to sweat,   ⎬
Or wandring in the winding Maze of *Creet* ; ⎭
Or with the winged Smith aloft to fly,
Or flutt'ring Perish with his foolish Boy.
    With what Impatience must the Muse be-
    hold
The Wife by her procuring Husband sold ?
For though the Law makes Null th' Adul-
    terer's Deed
Of Lands to her, the Cuckold may succeed ;
Who being taught Eyes up to the Cieling
    throws,   89
And sleeps all over but his wakeful Nose.
When he dares hope a Colonel's Command,
Whose Coursers kept, ran out his Father's
    Land ;
Who yet a Stripling *Nero's* Chariot drove, ⎫
Whirl'd o're the Streets, while his vain   ⎬
    Master strove   ⎪
With boasted Art to please his [16] Eunuch- ⎭
    Love.
Wou'd it not make a modest Author dare
To draw his Table-Book within the Square,
And fill with Notes, when lolling at his
    ease,
Mecenas-like, [17] the happy Rogue he sees
Born by Six weary'd Slaves in open View,
Who Cancell'd an old Will, and forg'd
    a New ;   101
Made wealthy at the small expence of
    Signing
With a wet Seal, and a fresh Interlining ?

---

58 pay;] *The editors delete the semi-colon, but
are probably wrong.*

The Lady, next, requires a lashing Line,
Who squeez'd a Toad into her Husband's
    Wine :
So well the fashionable Med'cine thrives,
That now 'tis Practis'd ev'n by Country
    Wives :
Poys'ning without regard of Fame or Fear :
And spotted Corps are frequent on the Bier.
Wou'dst thou to Honours and Preferments
    climb,   110
Be bold in Mischief, dare some mighty Crime,
Which Dungeons, Death, or Banishment
    deserves :
For Virtue is but dryly Prais'd, and Sterves.
Great Men, to great Crimes, owe their⎫
    Plate Embost, |
Fair Palaces, and Furniture of Cost ;   ⎬
And high Commands : A Sneaking Sin is |
    lost.   ⎭
Who can behold that rank Old Letcher
    keep
His Son's Corrupted Wife, [18] and hope to
    sleep ?
Or that Male-Harlot, or that unfledg'd Boy,
Eager to Sin, before he can enjoy ?   120
If Nature cou'd not, Anger would indite
Such woeful stuff as I or S——ll write.
    Count from the time, since Old [19] Deu-
        calion's Boat,
Rais'd by the Flood, did on Parnassus Float ;
And scarcely Mooring on the Cliff, implor'd
An Oracle how Man might be restor'd ;
When soften'd Stones and Vital Breath
    ensu'd,
And Virgins Naked were by Lovers View'd ;
What ever since that Golden Age was done,
What Humane Kind desires, and what they
    shun,   130
Rage, Passions, Pleasures, Impotence of
    Will,
Shall this Satyrical Collection fill.
    What Age so large a Crop of Vices bore,
Or when was Avarice extended more ?
When were the Dice with more Profusion
    thrown ?
The well fill'd Fob not empty'd now alone,
But Gamesters for whole Patrimonies play ;
The Steward brings the Deeds which must
    convey
The lost Estate : What more than Madness
    reigns,
When one short sitting many Hundreds
    Drains,   140

And not enough is left him to supply   ⎫
Board-Wages, or a Footman's Livery ?   ⎬
    What Age so many Summer-Seats did see?⎭
Or which of our Forefathers far'd so well
As on seven Dishes, at a private Meal ?
Clients of Old were Feasted ; now a poor
Divided Dole is dealt at th' outward Door ;
Which by the Hungry Rout is soon dis-
    patch'd :
The Paltry Largess, too, severely watch'd
E're given ; and ev'ry Face observ'd with
    Care,   150
That no intruding Guest Usurp a share.
Known, you Receive : The Cryer calls⎫
    aloud |
Our Old Nobility of Trojan Blood,   ⎬
Who gape among the Croud for their |
    precarious Food.   ⎭
The Prætors, and the Tribunes Voice is heard ;
The Freedman justles and will be preferr'd ;
First come, first serv'd, he Cries ; and I,
    in spight
Of your Great Lordships, will Maintain my
    Right.
Tho born a Slave, tho [20] my torn Ears are
    bor'd,   159
'Tis not the Birth, tis Mony makes the Lord.
The Rents of Five fair Houses I receive ;
What greater Honours can the Purple give ?
The [21] Poor Patrician is reduc'd to keep
In Melancholly Walks a Grazier's Sheep :
Not [22] Pallas nor Licinius had my Treasure ;
Then let the Sacred Tribunes wait my
    leasure.
Once a Poor Rogue, 'tis true, I trod the
    Street,
And trudg'd to Rome upon my Naked Feet :
Gold is the greatest God ; though yet we see
No Temples rais'd to Mony's Majesty,   170
No Altars fuming to her Pow'r Divine,
Such as to Valour, Peace, and Virtue Shine,
And Faith, and Concord : [23] where the⎫
    Stork on high |
Seems to Salute her Infant Progeny,   ⎬
Presaging Pious Love with her Auspicious |
    Cry.   ⎭
    But since our Knights and Senators
        account
To what their sordid begging Vails amount,
Judge what a wretched share the Poor
    attends,
Whose whole Subsistence on those Alms
    depends !

Their Household-Fire, their Rayment, and
   their Food, 180
Prevented [24] by those Harpies ; when a
   wood
Of Litters thick besiege the Donor's Gate,
And begging Lords, and teeming Ladies
   wait
The promis'd Dole : Nay some have learn'd
   the trick
To beg for absent persons ; feign them sick,
Close mew'd in their Sedans, for fear of air :⎫
And for their Wives produce an empty ⎪
   Chair.   ⎬
This is my Spouse : Dispatch her with her ⎪
   share.   ⎭
'Tis [25] *Galla* : Let her Ladyship but peep :
No, Sir, 'tis pity to disturb her sleep. 190
  Such fine Employments our whole days
   divide :
The Salutations of the Morning-tide
Call up the Sun ; those ended, to the Hall
We wait the Patron, hear the Lawyers baul ;
Then [26] to the Statues ; where amidst the⎫
   Race   ⎪
Of Conqu'ring *Rome*, some *Arab* shews ⎬
   his Face   ⎪
Inscrib'd with Titles, and profanes the⎭
   place ;
Fit to be piss'd against, and somewhat more.
The Great Man, home conducted, shuts his
   door ;
Old Clients, weary'd out with fruitless
   care, 200
Dismiss their hopes of eating, and despair :
Though much against the grain, forc'd to⎫
   retire,   ⎬
Buy Roots for Supper, and provide a Fire.⎭
  Mean time his Lordship lolls within at
   ease,
Pamp'ring his Paunch with Foreign
   Rarities ;
Both Sea and Land are ransack'd for the
   Feast ;
And his own Gut the sole invited Guest.
Such Plate, such Tables, Dishes dress'd so
   well,
That whole Estates are swallow'd at a Meal.
Ev'n Parasites are banish'd from his
   Board : 210
(At once a sordid and luxurious Lord :)
Prodigious Throat, for which whole Boars
   are drest ;
(A Creature form'd to furnish out a Feast.)

But present Punishment pursues his Maw,
When surfeited and swell'd, the Peacock
   raw
He bears into the Bath ; whence want of
   Breath,
Repletions, Apoplex, intestate Death.
His Fate makes Table-talk, divulg'd with
   scorn,
And he, a Jeast, into his Grave is born.
  No Age can go beyond us : Future
   Times 220
Can add no farther to the present Crimes.
Our Sons but the same things can wish
   and do ;
Vice is at stand, and at the highest flow. ⎫
Then Satyr spread thy Sails ; take all ⎬
   the winds can blow. ⎭
Some may, perhaps, demand what Muse can
   yield
Sufficient strength for such a spacious Field ?
From whence can be deriv'd so large a Vein,
Bold Truths to speak, and spoken to
   maintain ;
When God-like Freedom is so far bereft
The Noble Mind, that scarce the Name is
   left ? 230
E're *Scandalum Magnatum* was begot,
No matter if the Great forgave or not
But if that honest license now you take, ⎫
If, into Rogues Omnipotent you rake, ⎬
Death is your Doom, impail' d upon a Stake :⎭
Smear'd o're with Wax, and set on fire, to
   light
The Streets, and make a dreadful blaze by
   night.
  Shall They, who drench'd three Uncles in
   a draught
Of poys'nous Juice, be then in Triumph
   brought,
Make Lanes among the People where⎫
   they go, 240 ⎪
And, mounted high on downy Chariots, ⎬
   throw   ⎪
Disdainful glances on the Crowd below ?⎭
Be silent, and beware, if such you see ;
'Tis Defamation but to say, That's He !
  Against [27] bold *Turnus* the Great *Trojan*
   Arm,
Amidst their strokes the Poet gets no harm :
Achilles may in Epique Verse be slain,
And none of all his *Myrmidons* complain :
Hylas may drop his Pitcher, none will cry ;
Not if he drown himself for company : 250

But when *Lucilius* brandishes his Pen,
And flashes in the face of Guilty Men,
A cold Sweat stands in drops on ev'ry part ;
And Rage succeeds to Tears, Revenge to Smart.

Muse, be advis'd ; 'tis past consid'ring time
When enter'd once the dangerous Lists of Rhime :
Since none the Living-Villains dare implead,
Arraign them in the Persons of the Dead.

The End of the First Satyr.

NOTES TO THE FIRST SATYR.

[1] *Codrus*, or it may be *Cordus*, a bad Poet who wrote the Life and Actions of *Theseus*.

[2] *Telephus*, the Name of a Tragedy.

[3] *Orestes*, another Tragedy.

[4] *Mars his Grove*. Some Commentators take this Grove to be a Place where Poets were us'd to repeat their Works to the People, but more probably both this and *Vulcan's* Grott or Cave, and the rest of the Places and Names here mention'd, are only meant for the Common Places of *Homer* in his *Iliads* and *Odysses*.

[5] *The best and worst* ; that is, the best and the worst Poets.

[6] *Advising Sylla*, &c. This was one of the Themes given in the Schools of Rhetoricians, in the deliberative kind ; Whether *Sylla* should lay down the Supreme Power of Dictatorship, or still keep it.

[7] *Lucilius*, the first Satyrist of the *Romans*, who wrote long before *Horace*.

[8] *Mevia*, a Name put for any Impudent or Mannish Woman.

[9] *Whose Razour*, &c. *Juvenal's* Barber now grown Wealthy.

[10] *Crispinus*, an *Egyptian* Slave ; now by his Riches transform'd into a Nobleman.

[11] *Charg'd with light Summer Rings*, &c. The *Romans* were grown so Effeminate in *Juvenal's* time, that they wore light Rings in the Summer, and heavier in Winter.

[12] *Matho*, a famous Lawyer, mention'd in other Places by *Juvenal* and *Martial*.

[13] *At Lyons* ; a City in France, where Annual Sacrifices and Games were made in Honour of *Augustus Cæsar*.

[14] *Prevailing Province*, &c. Here the Poet complains that the Governours of Provinces being accus'd for their unjust Exactions, though they were condemned at their Tryals, yet got off by Bribery.

[15] *Horace*, who wrote Satyrs : 'Tis more Noble, says our Author, to imitate him in that way, than to write the Labours of *Hercules*, the Sufferings of *Diomedes* and his Followers, or the Flight of *Dedalus* who made the Labyrinth, and the Death of his Son *Icarus*.

[16] *His Eunuch-Love*. *Nero* Marry'd *Sporus* an Eunuch ; though it may be the Poet meant *Nero's* Mistress in Man's Apparel.

[17] *Mecenas-like* : *Mecenas* is often Tax'd by *Seneca* and others for his Effeminacy.

[18] *And hope to sleep* : The Meaning is, that the very consideration of such a Crime will hinder a Virtuous Man from taking his Repose.

[19] *Deucalion* and *Pyrrha*, when the World was drown'd, escap'd to the top of Mount *Parnassus*, and were commanded to restore Mankind by throwing Stones over their Heads : The Stones he threw became Men, and those she threw became Women.

[20] *Though my torn Ears are bor'd* : The Ears of all Slaves were bor'd as a Mark of their Servitude ; which Custom is still usual in the *East-Indies*, and in other Parts, even for whole Nations, who bore Prodigious holes in their Ears, and wear vast Weights at them.

[21] *The poor Patrician* ; the poor Nobleman.

[22] *Pallas* or *Licinius*. *Pallas*, a Slave freed by *Claudius Cæsar*, and rais'd by his Favour to great Riches. *Licinius* was another Wealthy Freedman, belonging to *Augustus*.

[23] *Where the Stork on high*, &c. Perhaps the Storks were us'd to build on the top of the Temple dedicated to *Concord*.

[24] *Prevented by those Harpies* : He calls the *Roman* Knights, &c., Harpies, or Devourers : In those Days the Rich made Doles intended for the Poor : But the Great were either so Covetous, or so Needy, that they came in their Litters to demand their shares of the Largess ; and thereby prevented and consequently starv'd the Poor.

[25] *'Tis Galla*, &c. The meaning is, that Noblemen wou'd cause empty Litters to be carried to the Giver's Door, pretending their Wives were within them : *'Tis Galla*, that is, my Wife : the next words *Let her Ladyship but peep*, are of the Servant who distributes the Dole ; Let me see her, that I may be sure she is within the Litter. The Husband answers, she is asleep, and to open the Litter would disturb her Rest.

[26] *Next to the Statues*, &c. The Poet here tells you how the Idle pass'd their time ; in going first to the Levees of the Great, then to the Hall, that is, to the Temple of *Apollo*, to hear the Lawyers plead, then to the Market-place of *Augustus*, where the Statues of the Famous *Romans* were set in Ranks on Pedestals : Amongst which Statues were seen those of Foreigners, such as *Arabs*, &c. who for no desert, but only on the Account of their Wealth, or Favour, were plac'd amongst the Noblest.

[27] *Against bold* Turnus, &c. A Poet may safely write an Heroick Poem, such as that of *Virgil*, who describes the Duel of *Turnus* and *Æneas* ; or of *Homer*, who writes of *Achilles* and *Hector* ; or the death of *Hylas* the *Catamite* of *Hercules* ; who stooping for Water dropt his Pitcher, and fell into the Well after it. But 'tis dangerous to write Satyr like *Lucilius*.

THE THIRD SATYR.

ARGUMENT | *of the* | *Third Satyr.*

The Story of this Satyr speaks it self.
Umbritius, the suppos'd Friend of Juvenal,
and himself a Poet, is leaving Rome ; *and*
retiring to Cumæ. *Our Author accompanies*
him out of Town. Before they take leave of
each other, Umbritius *tells his Friend the*
Reasons which oblige him to lead a private life,
in an obscure place. He complains that an
honest man cannot get his bread at Rome.
That none but Flatterers make their Fortunes
there : that Grecians *and other Foreigners*
raise themselves by those sordid Arts which he
describes, and against which he bitterly inveighs.
He reckons up the several Inconveniences which
arise from a City life ; and the many Dangers
which attend it. Upbraids the Noblemen with
Covetousness, for not Rewarding good Poets ;
and arraigns the Government for starving them.
The great Art of this Satyr is particularly
shown, in Common Places ; and drawing in
as many Vices, as cou'd naturally fall into
the compass of it.

THE | THIRD SATYR.

GRIEV'D tho I am, an Ancient Friend to
  lose,
I like the Solitary Seat he chose :
In quiet ¹ *Cumæ* fixing his Repose :
Where, far from Noisy *Rome* secure he Lives,
And one more Citizen to *Sybil* gives ;
The road to ² *Bajæ*, and that soft Recess
Which all the Gods with all their Bounty bless.
Tho I in ³ *Prochyta* with greater ease
Cou'd live, than in a Street of Palaces.
What Scene so Desart, or so full of Fright, 10
As tow'ring Houses tumbling in the Night,
And *Rome* on Fire beheld by its own Blazing
  Light ?
But worse than all, the clatt'ring Tiles ;
  and worse
Than thousand Padders, is the Poet's Curse.
Rogues that ⁴ in Dog-days cannot Rhime
  forbear :
But without Mercy read, and make you hear.
  Now while my Friend, just ready to
  depart,
Was packing all his Goods in one poor Cart ;

He stopp'd a little at the Conduit-Gate,
Where ⁵ *Numa* modell'd once the *Roman*
  State, 20
In Mighty Councels with his Nymph ⁶retir'd:
Though now the Sacred Shades and Founts
  are hir'd
By Banish'd Jews, who their whole Wealth
  can lay
In a small Basket, on a Wisp of Hay ;
Yet such our Avarice is, that every Tree
Pays for his Head ; not Sleep it self is
  free :
Nor Place, nor Persons now are Sacred
  held,
From their own Grove the Muses are ex-
  pell'd.
Into this lonely Vale our Steps we bend,
I and my sullen discontented Friend : 30
The Marble Caves, and Aquæducts we view ;
But how Adult'rate now, and different from
  the true !
How much more Beauteous had the Foun-
  tain been
Embellish't with her first Created Green,
Where Crystal Streams through living Turf
  had run,
Contented with an Urn of Native Stone !
  Then thus *Umbricius* (with an Angry
  Frown,
And looking back on this degen'rate Town,)
Since Noble Arts in *Rome* have no support,
And ragged Virtue not a Friend at Court, 40
No Profit rises from th' ungrateful Stage,
My Poverty encreasing with my Age,
'Tis time to give my just Disdain a vent,
And, Cursing, leave so base a Government.
Where ⁷ *Dedalus* his borrow'd Wings laid
  by,
To that obscure Retreat I chuse to fly :
While yet few furrows on my Face are seen,
While I walk upright, and Old Age is green,
And ⁸ *Lachesis* has somewhat left to spin.
Now, now 'tis time to quit this cursed
  place, 50
And hide from Villains my too honest Face :
Here let ⁹ *Arturius* live, and such as he ;
Such Manners will with such a Town agree.

---

21 Nymph] Nymphs *1693. The misprint is*
implicitly corrected in Dryden's note.

Knaves who in full Assemblies have the knack
Of turning Truth to Lies, and White to Black ;
Can hire large Houses, and oppress the Poor
By farm'd Excise ; can cleanse the Common-shoare ;
And rent the Fishery ; can bear the dead;
And teach their Eyes dissembled Tears to shed,
All this for Gain ; for Gain they sell their very Head.　60
These Fellows (see what Fortune's pow'r can do)
Were once the Minstrels of a Country Show :
Follow'd the Prizes through each paltry Town,
By Trumpet-Cheeks and Bloated Faces known.
But now, grown rich, on drunken Holy-days,
At their own Costs exhibit Publick Plays ;
Where influenc'd by the Rabble's bloody will,
With [10] Thumbs bent back, they popularly kill.
From thence return'd, their sordid Avarice rakes
In Excrements again, and hires the Jakes. 70
Why hire they not the Town, not ev'ry thing,
Since such as they have Fortune in a String ?
Who, for her pleasure, can her Fools advance ;
And toss 'em topmost on the Wheel of Chance.
What's Rome to me, what bus'ness have I there,
I who can neither Lye, nor falsely Swear ?
Nor Praise my Patron's undeserving Rhimes,
Nor yet comply with him, nor with his Times ;
Unskill'd in Schemes by Planets to foreshow,
Like Canting Rascals, how the Wars will go :
I neither will, nor can Prognosticate　81
To the young gaping Heir, his Father's Fate :
Nor in the Entrails of a Toad have pry'd,
Nor carry'd Bawdy Presents to a Bride :
For want of these Town Virtues, thus, alone,
I go conducted on my way by none :
Like a dead Member from the Body rent ;
Maim'd, and unuseful to the Government.

Who now is lov'd, but he who loves the Times,
Conscious of close Intrigues, and dipt in Crimes ;　90
Lab'ring with Secrets which his Bosom burn,
Yet never must to publick light return ?
They get Reward alone who can Betray :
For keeping honest Counsels none will pay.
He who can [11] Verres, when he will, accuse,
The Purse of Verres may at Pleasure use :
But let not all the Gold which [12] Tagus hides,
And pays the Sea in Tributary Tides,
Be Bribe sufficient to corrupt thy Breast ;
Or violate with Dreams thy peaceful rest.
Great Men with jealous Eyes the Friend behold,　101
Whose secrecy they purchase with their Gold.
　I haste to tell thee, nor shall Shame oppose,
What Confidents our Wealthy Romans chose:
And whom I most abhor : To speak my Mind,
I hate, in Rome, a Grecian Town to find :
To see the Scum of Greece transplanted here,
Receiv'd like Gods, is what I cannot bear.
Nor Greeks alone, but Syrians here abound,
Obscene [13] Orontes, diving under Ground, 110
Conveys [14] his Wealth to Tyber's hungry Shoars,
And fattens Italy with Foreign Whores :
Hether their crooked Harps and Customs come ;
All find Receipt in Hospitable Rome.
The Barbarous Harlots crowd the Publick Place :
Go Fools, and purchase an unclean Embrace ;
The painted Mitre court, and the more painted Face.
Old [15] Romulus,and Father Mars look down,
Your Herdsman Primitive, your homely Clown　119
Is turn'd a Beau in a loose tawdry Gown.
His once unkem'd, and horrid Locks, behold
Stilling sweet Oyl ; his Neck inchain'd with Gold :
Aping the Foreigners, in ev'ry Dress ;
Which, bought at greater cost, becomes him less.
Mean time they wisely leave their Native Land,
From Sicyon, Samos, and from Alaband, .

And *Amydon*, to *Rome* they Swarm in Shoals:
So Sweet and Easie is the Gain from Fools.
Poor Refugies at first, they purchase here:
And, soon as Denizen'd, they domineer: 130
Grow to the Great, a flatt'ring Servile Rout:
Work themselves inward, and their Patrons out.
Quick Witted, Brazen-fac'd, with fluent Tongues,
Patient of Labours, and dissembling Wrongs
Riddle me this, and guess him if you can,
Who bears a Nation in a single Man?
A Cook, a Conjuror, a Rhetorician,
A Painter, Pedant, a Geometrician,
A Dancer on the Ropes, and a Physician.
All things the hungry *Greek* exactly knows:
And bid him go to Heav'n, to Heav'n he goes. 141
In short, no *Scythian, Moor,* or *Thracian* born,
But [16] in that Town which Arms and Arts adorn.
Shall he be plac'd above me at the Board,
In Purple Cloath'd, and lolling like a Lord?
Shall he before me sign, whom t' other Day
A small-craft Vessel hither did convey;
Where, stow'd with Prunes, and rotten Figs, he lay?
How little is the Priviledge become
Of being born a Citizen of *Rome*! 150
The *Greeks* get all by fulsom Flatteries;
A most peculiar Stroke they have at Lies.
They make a Wit of their Insipid Friend;
His blobber-Lips, and beetle-Brows commend;
His long Crane Neck, and narrow Shoulders Praise;
You'd think they were describing *Hercules.*
A creaking Voice for a clear Trebble goes;
Tho harsher than a Cock that Treads and Crows.
We can as grosly praise; but, to our Grief,
No Flatt'ry but from *Grecians* gains belief.
Besides these Qualities, we must agree 161
They Mimick better on the Stage than we
The Wife, the Whore, the Shepherdess they play,
In such a Free, and such a Graceful way,
That we believe a very Woman shown,
And fancy something underneath the Gown.

But not [17] *Antiochus*, nor *Stratocles*,
Our Ears and Ravish'd Eyes can only please:
The Nation is compos'd of such as these.
All *Greece* is one Commedian: Laugh, and they 170
Return it louder than an Ass can bray:
Grieve, and they Grieve; if you Weep silently,
There seems a silent Eccho in their Eye:
They cannot *Mourn* like you; but they can Cry.
Call for a Fire, their Winter Cloaths they take:
Begin but you to shiver, and they shake:
In Frost and Snow, if you complain of Heat,
They rub th' unsweating Brow, and Swear they Sweat.
We live not on the Square with such as these:
Such are our Betters who can better please:
Who Day and Night are like a Looking-Glass; 181
Still ready to reflect their Patron's Face.
The Panegyrick Hand, and lifted Eye,
Prepar'd for some new Piece of Flattery.
Ev'n Nastiness, Occasions will afford;
They praise a belching, or well-pissing Lord.
Besides, there's nothing Sacred, nothing free
From bold Attempts of their rank Leachery
Through the whole Family their labours run;
The Daughter is debauch'd, the Wife is won: 190
Nor scapes the Bridegroom, or the blooming Son.
If none they find for their lewd purpose fit,
They with the Walls and very Floors commit.
They search the Secrets of the House, and so
Are worshipp'd there, and fear'd for what they know.
  And, now we talk of *Grecians*, cast a view
On what, in Schools, their Men of Morals do;
A rigid [18] Stoick his own Pupil slew.
A Friend, against a Friend, of his own Cloath,
Turn'd Evidence, and murther'd on his Oath. 200
What room is left for *Romans*, in a Town
Where *Grecians* rule, and Cloaks control the Gown?

Some [19] *Diphilus*, or some *Protogenes*,
Look sharply out, our Senators to seize :
Engross 'em wholly, by their Native Art,
And fear no Rivals in their Bubbles heart :
One drop of Poison in my Patron's Ear,
One slight suggestion of a senseless fear,
Infus'd with cunning, serves to ruine me ;
Disgrac'd, and banish'd from the Family.
In vain forgotten Services I boast ;   211
My long dependance in an hour is lost :
Look round the World, what Country will
      appear,
Where Friends are left with greater ease than
      here ?
At *Rome* (nor think me partial to the
      Poor)
All Offices of ours are out of Door :
In vain we rise, and to their Levees run ;
My Lord himself is up, before, and gone :
The Praetor bids his Lictors mend their
      pace,
Lest his Collegue outstrip him in the Race :
The childless Matrons are, long since,
      awake ;   221
And for Affronts the tardy Visits take.
'Tis frequent, here, to see a free-born Son
On the left-hand of a Rich Hireling run :
Because the wealthy Rogue can throw away,
For half a Brace of Bouts, a Tribune's pay
But you, poor Sinner, tho you love the
      Vice,
And like the Whore, demurr upon the Price :
And, frighted with the wicked Sum, forbear
To lend a hand, and help her from the
      Chair.   230
   Produce a Witness of unblemish'd life,
Holy as *Numa*, or as *Numa's* Wife,
Or [20] him who bid th' unhallow'd Flames
      retire ;
And snatch'd the trembling Goddess from
      the Fire.
The Question is not put how far extends
His Piety, but what he yearly spends :
Quick, to the Bus'ness ; how he Lives and
      Eats ;
How largely Gives ; how splendidly he
      Treats :
How many thousand Acres feed his Sheep,
What are his Rents, what Servants does he
      keep ?   240
Th' Account is soon cast up ; the Judges
      rate
Our Credit in the Court. by our Estate.

Swear by our Gods, or those the *Greeks*
      adore,
Thou art as sure Forsworn, as thou art Poor :
The Poor must gain their Bread by Perjury ;
And even the Gods, that other Means deny,
In Conscience must absolve 'em, when
      they lye.
   Add, that the Rich have still a Gibe in
      store ;
And will be monstrous witty on the Poor :
For the torn Surtout and the tatter'd Vest,
The Wretch and all his Wardrobe are a
      Jest :   251
The greasie Gown, sully'd with often turning,
Gives a good hint, to say The Man's in
      Mourning :
Or if the Shoo be ript, or patches put,
He's wounded ! see the Plaister on his
      Foot.
Want is the Scorn of ev'ry Wealthy Fool ;
And Wit in Rags is turn'd to Ridicule.
   Pack hence, and from the Cover'd
      Benches rise,
(The Master of the Ceremonies cries)
This is no place for you, whose small Estate
Is not the Value of the settled Rate :   261
The Sons of happy Punks, the Pandars
      Heir,
Are priviledg'd to sit in triumph there,
To clap the first, and rule the Theatre.
Up to the Galleries, for shame, retreat :
For, by the [21] *Roscian* Law, the Poor can
      claim no Seat.
Who ever brought to his rich Daughter's
      Bed
The Man that poll'd but Twelve-pence for
      his Head ?
Who ever nam'd a poor Man for his Heir,
Or call'd him to assist the Judging Chair ?
The Poor were wise, who by the Rich
      oppress'd,   271
Withdrew, and sought a Sacred Place of
      Rest.
Once they did well, to free themselves from
      Scorn ;
But had done better never to return.
Rarely they rise by Virtues aid, who lie
Plung d in the depth of helpless Poverty.
   At *Rome* 'tis worse ; where House-rent
      by the Year,
And Servants Bellies cost so Dev'llish dear ;
And Tavern Bills run high for hungry
      Chear.

To drink or eat in Earthen Ware we scorn,
Which cheaply Country Cupboards does
   adorn : 281
And coarse blue Hoods on Holydays are worn.
Some distant parts of *Italy* are known,
Where [22] none, but only dead Men, wear a
   Gown :
On Theatres of Turf, in homely State,
Old Plays they act, old Feasts they Cele-
   brate :
The same rude Song returns upon the Crowd,
And, by Tradition, is for Wit allow'd.
The Mimick Yearly gives the same Delights ;
And in the Mother's Arms the Clownish
   Infant frights. 290
Their Habits (undistinguish'd by degree)
Are plain, alike ; the same Simplicity,
Both on the Stage, and in the Pit, you see.
In his white Cloak the Magistrate appears ;
The Country Bumpkin the same Liv'ry wears.
But here, Attir'd beyond our Purse we go,
For useless Ornament and flaunting Show :
We take on trust, in Purple Robes to shine ;
And Poor, are yet Ambitious to be fine.
This is a common Vice, tho all things
   here 300
Are sold, and sold unconscionably dear.
What will you give that [23] *Cossus* may but
   view
Your Face, and in the Crowd distinguish you ;
May take your Incense like a gracious God ;
And answer only with a Civil Nod ?
To please our Patrons, in this vicious Age,
We make our Entrance by the Fav'rite Page :
Shave his first down, and when he Polls his
   Hair,
The Consecrated Locks to Temples bear :
Pay Tributary Cracknels, which he sells ; 310
And, with our Offerings, help to raise his Vails.
Who fears, in Country Towns, a House's
   fall,
Or to be caught betwixt a riven Wall ?
But we Inhabit a weak City here ;
Which Buttresses and Props but scarcely bear :
And 'tis the Village Masons daily Calling,
To keep the World's Metropolis from falling,
To cleanse the Gutters, and the Chinks to close ;
And, for one Night, secure his Lord's Repose.
At *Cumæ* we can sleep, quite round the
   Year, 320
Nor Falls, nor Fires, nor Nightly Dangers fear ;
While rolling Flames from *Roman* Turrets fly,
And the pale Citizens for Buckets cry.

Thy Neighbour has remov'd his Wretched
   Store,
(Few Hands will rid the Lumber of the Poor)
Thy own third Story smoaks ; while thou,
   supine,
Art drench'd in Fumes of undigested Wine.
For if the lowest Floors already burn,
Cock-lofts and Garrets soon will take the Turn.
Where [24] thy tame Pigeons next the Tiles were
   bred, 330
Which in their Nests unsafe, are timely fled.
   [25] *Codrus* had but one Bed, so short to boot,
That his short Wife's short Legs hung
   dangling out ;
His Cup-board's Head six Earthen Pitchers
   grac'd,
Beneath 'em was his Trusty Tankard plac'd :
And, to support this Noble Plate, there lay
A bending Chiron cast from honest Clay :
His few Greek Books a rotten Chest con-
   tain'd,
Whose Covers much of mouldiness com-
   plain'd : 339
Where Mice and Rats devour'd Poetick Bread,
And with Heroick Verse luxuriously were fed.
'Tis true, poor *Codrus* nothing had to boast,
And yet poor *Codrus* all that Nothing lost ;
Beg'd naked through the Streets of wealthy
   Rome ;
And found not one to feed, or take him
   home.
   But if the Palace of *Arturius* burn,
The Nobles change their Cloaths, the Matrons
   mourn ;
The City Prætor will no Pleadings hear ;
The very Name of Fire we hate and fear :
And look agast, as if the *Gauls* were here.
While yet it burns, th' officious Nation
   flies, 351
Some to condole, and some to bring supplies :
One sends him Marble to rebuild, and one
White naked Statues of the *Parian* Stone,
The Work of *Polyclete*, that seem to live ;
While others, Images for Altars give ;
One Books and Skreens, and *Pallas* to the
   Brest ;
Another Bags of Gold, and he gives best.
Childless *Arturius*, vastly rich before,
Thus by his Losses multiplies his Store : 360
Suspected for Accomplice to the Fire,
That burnt his Palace but to build it higher.
   But, cou'd you be content to bid adieu
To the dear Play-house, and the Players too,

Sweet Country Seats are purchas'd ev'ry
where,
With Lands and Gardens, at less price, than
here
You hire a darksom Doghole by the year.
A small Convenience, decently prepar'd,
A shallow Well, that rises in your yard,
That spreads his easie Crystal Streams
around,   370
And waters all the pretty spot of Ground.
There, love the Fork ; thy Garden cultivate,
And give thy frugal Friends [26] a *Pythagorean*
Treat.
'Tis somewhat to be Lord of some small
Ground ;
In which a Lizard may, at least, turn round.
'Tis frequent, here, for want of sleep to
dye ;
Which Fumes of undigested Feasts deny ;
And, with imperfect heat, in languid
Stomachs fry.
What House secure from noise the poor can
keep,
When ev'n the Rich can scarce afford to
sleep ?   380
So dear it costs to purchase Rest in *Rome* ;
And hence the sources of Diseases come.
The Drover who his Fellow-drover meets,
In narrow passages of winding Streets :
The Waggoners, that curse their standing
Teams,
Would wake ev'n drowsie *Drusus* from his
Dreams.
And yet the Wealthy will not brook delay ;
But sweep above our Heads, and make their
way ;
In lofty Litters born, and read and write,
Or sleep at ease : The Shutters make it
Night.   390
Yet still he reaches, first, the Publick Place :
The prease before him stops the Client's pace.
The Crowd that follows, crush his panting
sides,
And trip his heels ; he walks not, but he
rides.
One Elbows him, one justles in the Shole :
A Rafter breaks his Head, or Chairman's
Pole :
Stockin'd with loads of fat Town-dirt he
goes ;
And some Rogue-Souldier, with his Hob-
nail'd Shoos,
Indents his Legs behind in bloody rows.

See with what Smoke our Doles we cele-
brate :   400
A hundred Ghests, invited, walk in state :
A hundred hungry Slaves, with their *Dutch*
Kitchins wait.
Huge Pans the Wretches on their heads must
bear ;
Which scarce [27] Gygantick *Corbulo* cou'd rear :
Yet they must walk upright beneath the load;
Nay run, and running blow the sparkling
flames abroad.
Their Coats, from botching newly brought,
are torn ;
Unwieldy Timber-trees, in Waggons born,
Stretch'd at their length, beyond their
Carriage lye ;
That nod, and threaten ruin from on high.
For, should their Axel break, its over-
throw   411
Wou'd crush, and pound to dust, the Crowd
below ;
Nor Friends their Friends, nor Sires their
Sons cou'd know :
Nor Limbs, nor Bones, nor Carcass wou'd
remain :
But a mash'd heap, a Hotchpotch of the Slain.
One vast destruction ; not the Soul alone,
But Bodies, like the Soul, invisible are flown.
Mean time, unknowing of their Fellows Fate,
The Servants wash the Platter, scour the
Plate,
Then blow the Fire, with puffing Cheeks,
and lay   420
The Rubbers, and the Bathing-sheets dis-
play ;
And oyl them first ; and each is handy in
his way.
But he, for whom this busie care they take,
Poor Ghost, is wandring by the Stygian Lake :
Affrighted with [28] the Ferryman's grim Face ;
New to the Horrours of that uncouth place ;
His passage begs with unregarded Pray'r :
And wants two Farthings to discharge his Fare.
Return we to the Dangers of the Night ;
And, first, behold our Houses dreadful height:
From whence come broken Potsherds
tumbling down ;   431
And leaky Ware, from Garret Windows
thrown :
Well may they break our Heads, that mark
the flinty Stone.

403 heads] *Some editors give* head

'Tis want of Sence to sup abroad too late ;
Unless thou first hast settled thy Estate.
As many Fates attend, thy Steps to meet,
As there are waking Windows in the Street.
Bless the good Gods, and think thy chance
    is rare
To have a Piss-pot only for thy share.
    The scouring Drunkard, if he does not
    fight   440
Before his Bed-time, takes no rest that
    Night,
Passing the tedious Hours in greater pain
Than stern *Achilles*, when his Friend was
    slain :
'Tis so ridiculous, but so true withall,
A Bully cannot sleep without a Braul :
Yet tho his youthful Blood be fir'd with
    Wine,
He wants not Wit, the Danger to decline :
Is cautious to avoid the Coach and Six,
And on the Lacquies will no Quarrel fix
His Train of Flambeaus, and Embroider'd
    Coat   450
May Priviledge my Lord to walk secure on
    Foot.
But me, who must by Moon-light homeward
    bend,
Or lighted only with a Candle's end,
Poor me he fights, if that be fighting, where
He only Cudgels, and I only bear.
He stands, and bids me stand : I must
    abide ;
For he's the stronger, and is Drunk beside.
    Where did you whet your Knife to Night,
    he cries,
And shred the Leeks that in your Stomach
    rise ?
Whose windy Beans have stuff't your Guts,
    and where   460
Have your black Thumbs been dipt in
    Vinegar ?
With what Companion Cobler have you fed,
On old Ox-cheeks, or He-Goats tougher
    Head ?
What, are you Dumb ? Quick with your
    Answer, quick,
Before my Foot Salutes you with a Kick.

Say, in what nasty Cellar, under Ground,
Or what Church-Porch, your Rogueship may
    be found ?
Answer, or Answer not, 'tis all the same :
He lays me on, and makes me bear the blame.
Before the Bar, for beating him, you come ;
This is a Poor Man's Liberty in *Rome*.   471
You beg his Pardon ; happy to retreat
With some remaining Teeth, to chew your
    Meat.
    Nor is this all ; for, when Retir'd, you think
To sleep securely ; when the Candles wink,
When every Door with Iron Chains is barr'd,
And roaring Taverns are no longer heard ;
The Ruffian Robbers by no Justice aw'd,
And unpaid cut-Throat Soldiers, are abroad ;
Those Venal Souls, who, harden'd in each ill
To save Complaints and Prosecution, kill. 481
Chas'd from their Woods and Bogs, the ⎫
    Padders come   ⎪
To this vast City, as their Native Home ;   ⎬
To live at ease, and safely sculk in *Rome*. ⎭
    The Forge in Fetters only is employ'd ;
Our Iron Mines exhausted and destroy'd
In Shackles ; for these Villains scarce allow
Goads for the Teams, and Plough-shares for
    the Plough.
Oh happy Ages of our Ancestours,   489
Beneath the Kings and Tribunitial Pow'rs!
One Jayl did all their Criminals restrain ;
Which, now, the Walls of *Rome* can scarce
    contain.
    More I cou'd say, more Causes I cou'd show
For my departure ; but the Sun is low :
The Waggoner grows weary of my stay ;
And whips his Horses forwards on their way.
    Farewell ;   and when, like me, o're-
    whelm'd with care.
You to your own *Aquinum* shall repair,
To take a mouthful of sweet Country air,
Be mindful of your Friend ; and send me
    word,   500
What Joys your Fountains and cool Shades
    afford :
Then, to assist your Satyrs, I will come ;
And add new Venom, when you write of
    Rome.

The End of the Third Satyr.

NOTES TO THE THIRD SATYR.

[1] *Cumæ*, a small City in *Campania*, near *Puteoli*, or *Puzzolo* as it is call'd. The Habitation of the *Cumæan Sybil*.

[2] *Bajæ*; Another little Town in *Campania*, near the sea : A pleasant Place.

[3] *Prochyta* : A small Barren Island belonging to the Kingdom of *Naples*.

[4] *In Dog-days*. The Poets in *Juvenal's* time us'd to rehearse their Poetry in August.

[5] *Numa*. The second King of *Rome* ; who made their Laws, and instituted their Religion.

[6] *Nymph*. *Ægeria*, a Nymph, or Goddess ; with whom *Numa* feigned to converse by Night ; and to be instructed by her, in modelling his Superstitions.

[7] *Where* Dædalus, &c. Meaning at *Cumæ*.

[8] *Lachesis* ; one of the three Destinies, whose Office was to spin the Life of every Man : as it was of *Clotho* to hold the Distaff, and *Atropos* to cut the Thread.

[9] *Arturius*. Any debauch'd wicked Fellow who gains by the times.

[10] *With Thumbs bent back*. In a Prize of Sword-Players, when one of the Fencers had the other at his Mercy, the Vanquished Party implored the Clemency of the Spectators. If they thought he deserv'd it not, they held up their Thumbs and bent them backwards, in sign of Death.

[11] *Verres*, Prætor in *Sicily*, Contemporary with *Cicero* ; by whom accus'd of oppressing the Province, he was Condemn'd : His Name is us'd here for any Rich Vicious Man.

[12] *Tagus* ; a famous River in *Spain*, which discharges it self into the Ocean near *Lisbone* in *Portugal*. It was held of old to be full of Golden Sands.

[13] *Orontes*, the greatest River of *Syria*. The Poet here puts the River for the Inhabitants of *Syria*.

[14] *Tyber* ; the River which runs by *Rome*.

[15] *Romulus* ; First King of *Rome*, son of *Mars*, as the Poets feign : the first *Romans* were originally Herdsmen.

[16] *But in that Town*, &c. He means *Athens* ; of which *Pallas* the Goddess of Arms and Arts was Patroness.

[17] *Antiochus, and Stratocles*, two Famous *Grecian* Mimicks, or Actors in the Poet's time.

[18] *A Rigid Stoick*, &c. *Publius Egnatius* a Stoick falsly accus'd *Bareas Soranus*, as *Tacitus* tells us.

[19] *Diphilus* and *Protogenes*, &c. Were *Grecians* living in *Rome*.

[20] *Or him who bid*, &c. *Lucius Metellus*, the High Priest ; who when the Temple of *Vesta* was on Fire sav'd the *Palladium*.

[21] *For by the* Roscian *Law*, &c. *Roscius* a Tribune, who order'd the Distinction of Places in Publick Shows betwixt the Noblemen of *Rome* and the *Plebeians*.

[22] *Where none but only dead Men*, &c. The meaning is that Men in some parts of *Italy* never wore a Gown (the usual Habit of the *Romans*) till they were bury'd in one.

[23] *Cossus* is here taken for any great Man.

[24] *Where thy tame Pidgeons*, &c. The *Romans* us'd to breed their tame Pidgeons in their Garrets.

[25] *Codrus*, a Learned Man, very poor : by his Books suppos'd to be a Poet. For, in all probability, the Heroick Verses here mention'd, which Rats and Mice devour'd, were *Homer's* Works.

[26] *A Pythagorean Treat* : He means Herbs, Roots, Fruits, and Sallads.

[27] *Gygantick Corbulo*. *Corbulo* was a Famous General in *Nero's* time, who Conquer'd *Armenia*, and was afterwards put to death by that Tyrant, when he was in *Greece*, in reward of his great Services. His Stature was not only tall above the ordinary Size, but he was also proportionably strong.

[28] *The Ferry-Man's*, &c. *Charon*, the Ferry-Man of Hell, whose Fare was a Half-penny for every Soul.

[29] *Stern* Achilles. The Friend of *Achilles* was *Patroclus* who was slain by *Hector*.

[30] *Beneath the Kings*, &c. Rome was Originally Rul'd by Kings ; till for the Rape of *Lucretia* *Tarquin* the proud was expell'd. After which it was Govern'd by two Consuls, Yearly chosen : but they oppressing the People, the Commoners Mutiny'd, and procur'd Tribunes to be created ; who defended their Priviledges, and often oppos'd the Consular Authority and the Senate.

[31] *Aquinum* was the Birth-place of *Juvenal*.

---

20 bid] bad *1693, but see the text.*
24 thy] the *1693, but see the text.*

THE SIXTH SATYR.

ARGUMENT | *of the* | *Sixth Satyr.*

This Satyr, of almost double length to any of the rest, is a bitter invective against the fair Sex. 'Tis indeed, a Common-place, from whence all the Moderns have notoriously stollen their sharpest Raileries. In his other Satyrs, the Poet has only glanc'd on some particular Women, and generally scourg'd the Men. But this he reserv'd wholly for the Ladies. How they had offended him I know not : But upon the whole matter he is not to be excus'd for imputing to all, the Vices of some few amongst them. Neither was it generously done of him, to attack the weakest as well as the fairest part of the Creation : Neither do I know what Moral he cou'd reasonably draw from it. It could not be to avoid the whole Sex, if all had been true which he alledges against them : for that had been to put an end to Humane Kind. And to bid us beware of their Artifices, is a kind of silent acknowledgment, that they have more wit than Men : which turns the Satyr upon us, and particularly upon the Poet ; who thereby makes a Complement, where he meant a Libel. If he intended only to exercise his Wit, he has forfeited his Judgment, by making the one half of his Readers his mortal Enemies : And amongst the Men, all the happy Lovers, by their own Experience, will disprove his Accusations. The whole World must allow this to be the wittiest of his Satyrs ; and truly he had need of all his parts, to maintain, with so much violence, so unjust a Charge. I am satisfied he will bring but few over to his Opinion : And on that Consideration chiefly I ventur'd to translate him. Though there wanted not another Reason, which was, that no one else would undertake it : at least, Sir C. S. who cou'd have done more right to the Author, after a long delay, at length absolutely refus'd so ungrateful an employment : And every one will grant, that the Work must have been imperfect and lame, if it had appeared without one of the Principal Members belonging to it. Let the Poet therefore bear the blame of his own Invention ; and let me satisfie the World, that I am not of his Opinion. Whatever his Roman *Ladies were, the* English *are free from all his Imputations.*

They will read with Wonder and Abhorrence the Vices of an Age, which was the most Infamous of any on Record. They will bless themselves when they behold those Examples, related of Domitian's *time : they will give back to Antiquity those Monsters it produc'd : And believe with reason, that the Species of those Women is extinguish'd ; or at least that they were never here propagated. I may safely therefore proceed to the Argument of a Satyr, which is no way relating to them : And first observe, that my Author makes their Lust the most Heroick of their Vices : The rest are in a manner but digression. He skims them over ; but he dwells on this : when he seems to have taken his last leave of it, on the sudden he returns to it : 'tis one Branch of it in* Hippia, *another in* Messalina, *but Lust is the main Body of the Tree. He begins with this Text in the first line, and takes it up with Intermissions to the end of the Chapter. Every Vice is a Loader, but that's a Ten. The Fillers, or intermediate Parts, are their Revenge ; their Contrivances of secret Crimes ; their Arts to hide them ; their Wit to excuse them ; and their Impudence to own them, when they can no longer be kept secret. Then the Persons to whom they are most addicted, and on whom they commonly bestow the last Favours : as Stage-Players, Fidlers, Singing-Boys, and Fencers. Those who pass for Chast amongst them, are not really so ; but only for their vast Dowries, are rather suffer'd, than lov'd by their own Husbands. That they are Imperious, Domineering, Scolding Wives : Set up for Learning and Criticism in Poetry, but are false Judges. Love to speak* Greek, *(which was then the Fashionable Tongue, as* French *is now with us.) That they plead Causes at the Bar, and play Prizes at the Bear-Garden. That they are Gossips and News-Mongers: Wrangle with their Neighbours abroad, and beat their Servants at home. That they lie-in for new Faces once a Month ; are sluttish with their Husbands in private ; and Paint and Dress in Publick for their Lovers. That they deal with* Jews, Diviners, *and Fortune-tellers : Learn the Arts of Miscarrying, and Barrenness. Buy Children, and produce them for their own. Murther their Husbands Sons, if they stand in their way to his Estate, and make their Adulterers his Heirs. From hence the Poet proceeds to shew the Occasions of all these Vices, their Original, and how they were introduced in* Rome, *by Peace, Wealth, and Luxury. In conclusion, if we will take the word of our malicious Author ; Bad Women are the general standing Rule ; and the Good, but some few exceptions to it.*

THE | SIXTH SATYR.

IN ¹ *Saturn's* Reign, at Nature's Early Birth,
There was that Thing call'd Chastity on Earth ;
When in a narrow Cave, their common shade,
The Sheep the Shepherds and their Gods were laid :
When Reeds and Leaves, and Hides of Beasts were spread
By Mountain Huswifes for their homely Bed,
And Mossy Pillows rais'd, for the rude Husband's head.
Unlike the Niceness of our Modern Dames,
(Affected Nymphs with new affected Names :)
The *Cynthia's* and the *Lesbia's* of our Years,
Who for a Sparrow's Death dissolve in Tears.						11
Those first unpolisht Matrons, Big and Bold,
Gave Suck to Infants of Gygantick Mold ;
Rough as their Savage Lords who Rang'd the Wood,
And ²fat with Akorns Belcht their windy Food.
For when the World was Bucksom, fresh, and young,
Her Sons were undebauch'd, and therefore strong ;
And whether Born in kindly Beds of Earth,
Or strugling from the Teeming Oaks to Birth,
Or from what other Atoms they begun,				20
No Sires they had, or if a Sire the Sun.
Some thin Remains of Chastity appear'd
Ev'n ³under *Jove*, but *Jove* without a Beard :
Before the servile *Greeks* had learnt to Swear
By Heads of Kings ; while yet the Bounteous Year

Her common Fruits in open Plains expos'd,
E're thieves were fear'd, or Gardens were enclos'd.
At length ⁴uneasie Justice upwards flew,
And both the Sisters to the Stars withdrew ;
From that Old *Æra* Whoring did begin,		30
So Venerably Ancient is the Sin.
Adult'rers next invade the Nuptial State,
And Marriage-Beds creak'd with a Foreign Weight ;
All other Ills did Iron times adorn ;
But Whores and Silver in one Age were Born.
	Yet thou, they say, for Marriage do'st provide :
Is this an Age to Buckle with a Bride ?
They say thy Hair the Curling Art is taught,
The Wedding-Ring perhaps already bought :
A Sober Man like thee to change his Life ! 40
What Fury wou'd possess thee with a Wife ?
Art thou of ev'ry other Death bereft,
No Knife, no Ratsbane, no kind Halter left ?
(For every Noose compar'd to Hers is cheap)
Is there no City-Bridge from whence to leap ?
Would'st thou become her Drudge, who dost enjoy
A better sort of Bedfellow, thy Boy ?
He keeps thee not awake with nightly Brawls,
Nor with a beg'd Reward, thy Pleasure palls;
Nor with insatiate heavings calls for more,
When all thy Spirits were drain'd out before.				51
But still *Ursidius* Courts the Marriage-Bait,
Longs for a Son, to settle his Estate,
And takes no Gifts, tho every gapeing Heir
Wou'd gladly Grease the Rich Old Batchelour.
What Revolution can appear so strange,
As such a Leacher, such a Life to change ?
A rank, notorious Whoremaster, to choose
To thrust his Neck into the Marriage-Noose !
He who so often in a dreadful fright			60
Had in a Coffer 'scap'd the jealous Cuckold's sight,
That he, to Wedlock dotingly betray'd,
Should hope, in this lewd Town, to find a Maid !
The Man's grown Mad : To ease his Frantick Pain,
Run for the Surgeon ; breathe the middle Vein :

But let a Heyfer with gilt Horns be led
To *Juno*, Regent of the Marriage-Bed,
And let him every Deity adore,
If his new Bride prove not an arrant
    Whore,
In Head and Tail, and every other Pore. 70
On [5]*Ceres* feast, restrain'd from their de-
    light,
Few Matrons, there, but Curse the tedious
    Night:
Few whom their Fathers dare Salute, such
    Lust
Their Kisses have, and come with such a
    Gust.
With Ivy now Adorn thy Doors, and Wed;
Such is thy Bride, and such thy Genial Bed.
Think'st thou one Man is for one Woman
    meant?
She, sooner, with one Eye wou'd be content
    And yet, 'tis nois'd, a Maid did once
        appear
In some small Village, tho Fame says not
    where: 80
'Tis possible; but sure no Man she found;
'Twas desart, all, about her Father's Ground:
And yet some Lustful God might there
    make bold;
Are [6]*Jove* and *Mars* grown impotent and
    old?
Many a fair Nymph has in a Cave been
    spread,
And much good Love, without a Feather-
    Bed.
Whither wou'dst thou to chuse a Wife resort,
The Park, the Mall, the Play-house, or the
    Court?
Which way soever thy Adventures fall,
Secure alike of Chastity in all.   90
    One sees a Dancing-Master Capring high,
And Raves, and Pisses, with pure Extasie:
Another does, with all his Motions, move,
And Gapes, and Grins as in the feat of
    Love:
A third is Charm'd with the new Opera
    Notes,
Admires the Song, but on the Singer Doats:
The Country Lady in the Box appears,
Softly She Warbles over all she hears;
And sucks in Passion, both at Eyes and
    Ears.
    The rest, (when now the long Vacation's
        come,   100
The noisie Hall and Theatres grown dumb)

Their Memories to refresh, and chear their
    hearts,
In borrow'd Breaches act the Players parts.
The Poor, that scarce have wherewithal
    to eat,
Will pinch, to make the Singing-Boy a Treat.
The Rich, to buy him, will refuse no price;
And stretch his Quail-pipe, till they crack
    his Voice.
Tragedians, acting Love, for Lust are
    sought:
(Tho but the Parrots of a Poet's Thought.)
The Pleading Lawyer, tho for Counsel us'd,
In Chamber-practice often is refus'd.   111
Still thou wilt have a Wife, and father Heirs;
(The product of concurring Theatres.)
Perhaps a Fencer did thy Brows adorn,
And a young Sword-man to thy Lands is
    born.
    Thus *Hippia* loath'd her old Patrician
        Lord,
And left him for a Brother of the Sword:
To wondring [7]*Pharos* with her Love she
    fled,
To show one Monster more than *Africk* bred:
Forgetting House and Husband, left
    behind,   120
Ev'n Children too; she sails before the
    wind;
False to 'em all, but constant to her Kind.
But, stranger yet, and harder to conceive,
She cou'd the Play-house and the Players
    leave.
Born of rich Parentage, and nicely bred,
She lodg'd on Down, and in a Damask Bed;
Yet, daring now the Dangers of the Deep,
On a hard Mattress is content to sleep.
E're this, 'tis true, she did her Fame expose:
But that, great Ladies with great Ease can
    lose.   130
The tender Nymph cou'd the rude Ocean
    bear:
So much her Lust was stronger than her
    Fear.
But, had some honest Cause her Passage
    prest,
The smallest hardship had disturb'd her
    brest:
Each Inconvenience makes their Virtue cold;
But Womankind, in Ills, is ever bold.
Were she to follow her own Lord to Sea,
What doubts and scruples wou'd she raise
    to stay?

Her Stomach sick, and her head giddy
grows ;
The Tar and Pitch are nauseous to her
Nose.   140
But in Love's Voyage nothing can offend ;
Women are never Sea-sick with a Friend.
Amidst the Crew, she walks upon the boord ;⎫
She eats, she drinks, she handles every Cord : ⎬
And, if she spews, 'tis thinking of her Lord.⎭
Now ask, for whom her Friends and Fame
she lost ?
What Youth, what Beauty cou'd th' Adul-
t'rer boast ?
What was the Face, for which she cou'd
sustain
To be call'd Mistress to so base a Man ?
The Gallant, of his days had known the⎫
best :   150⎪
Deep Scars were seen indented on his ⎬
breast :   ⎪
And all his batter'd Limbs requir'd their⎪
needful rest.   ⎭
A Promontory Wen, with griesly grace,
Stood high, upon the Handle of his Face :
His blear Eyes ran in gutters to his Chin :
His Beard was Stubble, and his Cheeks
were thin.
But 'twas his Fencing did her Fancy move :
'Tis Arms and Blood and Cruelty they love.
But should he quit his Trade, and sheath his
Sword,
Her Lover wou'd begin to be her Lord. 160
This was a private Crime ; but you shall
hear
What Fruits the Sacred Brows of Monarchs
bear :
The [8] good old Sluggard but began to snore,
When from his side up rose th' Imperial
Whore :
She who preferr'd the Pleasures of the
Night
To Pomps, that are but impotent delight ;
Strode from the Palace, with an eager pace,
To cope with a more Masculine Embrace ;
Muffled she march'd, like *Juno* in a Clowd,
Of all her Train but one poor Wench
allow'd,   170
One whom in Secret Service she cou'd trust ;
The Rival and Companion of her Lust.
To the known Brothel-house she takes her⎫
way ;   ⎬
And for a nasty Room gives double pay ; ⎪
That Room in which the rankest Harlot lay.⎭

Prepar'd for fight, expectingly she lies,
With heaving Breasts, and with desiring
Eyes :
Still as one drops, another takes his place,
And baffled still succeeds to like disgrace.
At length, when friendly darkness is ex-
pir'd,   180
And every Strumpet from her Cell retir'd,
She lags behind, and lingring at the Gate,
With a repining Sigh, submits to Fate :
All Filth without, and all a Fire within,
Tir'd with the Toyl, unsated with the Sin,
Old *Cæsar's* Bed the modest Matron seeks ;
The steam of Lamps still hanging on her
Cheeks,
In Ropy Smut : thus foul, and thus bedight,
She brings him back the Product of the
Night.
Now should I sing what Poisons they
provide ;   190
With all their Trumpery of Charms beside ;
And all their Arts of Death : it would be
known
Lust is the smallest Sin the Sex can own.
Cæsinia, still, they say, is guiltless found ⎫
Of ev'ry Vice, by her own Lord Renown'd : ⎬
And well she may, she brought ten thousand⎪
Pound.   ⎭
She brought him wherewithal to be call'd
chaste ;
His Tongue is ty'd in Golden Fetters fast
He Sighs, Adores, and Courts her every
Hour ;
Who wou'd not do as much for such a
Dower ?   200
She writes Love-Letters to the Youth in
Grace ;
Nay tips the wink before the Cuckold's Face ;
And might do more ; Her Portion makes it
good ;
Wealth [9] has the Priviledge of Widow-hood.
These Truths with his Example you dis-
prove,
Who with his Wife is monstrously in Love :
But know him better ; for I heard him Swear,
'Tis not that She's his Wife, but that She's
Fair.   208
Let her but have three wrinkles in her Face,
Let her Eyes Lessen, and her Skin unbrace,
Soon you will hear the Saucy Steward say,
Pack up with all your Trinkets, and away ;
You grow Offensive both at Bed and Board :
Your Betters must be had to please my Lord.

Meantime She's absolute upon the Throne;
And knowing time is Precious, loses none :
She must have Flocks of Sheep, with Wool
    more Fine
Than Silk, and Vinyards of the Noblest
    Wine :
Whole Droves of Pages for her Train she
    Craves :
And sweeps the Prisons for attending
    Slaves.   220
In short, whatever in her Eyes can come,
Or others have abroad, she wants at home.
When Winter shuts the Seas, and fleecy
    Snows
Make Houses white, she to the Merchant goes ;
Rich Crystals of the Rock She takes up there,
Huge *Agat* Vases, and old *China* Ware :
Then [10]*Berenice's* Ring her Finger proves,
More Precious made by her incestuous Loves:
And infamously Dear : A Brother's Bribe,
Ev'n God's Annointed, and of *Judah's* Tribe:
Where barefoot they approach the Sacred
    Shrine,   231
And think it only Sin, to feed on Swine.
  But is none worthy to be made a Wife
In all this Town ? Suppose her free from
    strife,
Rich, Fair, and Fruitful, of Unblemish'd
    Life ;
Chast as the *Sabines*, whose prevailing
    Charms
Dismiss'd their Husbands, and their Brothers
    Arms.
Grant her, besides, of Noble Blood, that ran
In Ancient Veins, e're Heraldry began :
Suppose all these, and take a Poet's word,
A Black Swan is not half so Rare a Bird. 241
A Wife, so hung with Virtues, such a freight,
What Mortal Shoulders cou'd support the
    weight !
Some Country Girl, scarce to a Curtsey
    bred,
Wou'd I much rather than [11]*Cornelia* Wed:
If Supercilious, Haughty, Proud, and Vain,
She brought her Father's Triumphs in her
    Train.
Away with all your *Carthaginian* State,
Let vanquish'd *Hannibal* without Doors
    wait,
Too burly and too big to pass my narrow
    Gate.   250
  Oh [12]*Pæan*, cries *Amphion*, bend thy Bow
Against my Wife, and let my Children go

But sullen *Pæan* shoots at Sons and Mothers
    too.
His *Niobe* and all his Boys he lost ;
Ev'n her who did her num'rous Offspring
    boast,
As Fair and Fruitful as the Sow that carry'd
The [13]Thirty Pigs at one large Litter
    Farrow'd.
  What Beauty or what Chastity can bear
So great a Price, if stately and severe
She still insults, and you must still adore ?
Grant that the Hony's much, the Gall is
    more.   261
Upbraided with the Virtues she displays,
Sev'n Hours in Twelve, you loath the Wife
    you Praise :
Some Faults, tho small, intolerable grow ;
For what so Nauseous and Affected too,
As those that think they due Perfection want,
Who have not learnt to Lisp the [14]*Grecian*
    Cant ?
In *Greece*, their whole Accomplishments
    they seek :
Their Fashion, Breeding, Language, must
    be *Greek* :
But Raw in all that does to *Rome* belong,
They scorn to cultivate their Mother
    Tongue.   271
In *Greek* they flatter, all their Fears they
    speak,
Tell all their Secrets ; nay, they Scold in
    Greek :
Ev'n in the Feat of Love, they use that
    Tongue.
Such Affectations may become the Young ;
But thou, Old Hag, of Threescore Years and
    Three,
Is shewing of thy Parts in *Greek* for thee ?
Ζωὴ καὶ ψυχή ! All those tender words
The Momentary trembling Bliss affords,
The kind soft Murmurs of the private
    Sheets,   280
Are Bawdy, while thou speak'st in publick
    Streets.
Those words have Fingers ; and their force
    is such,
They raise the Dead, and mount him with
    a touch.
But all Provocatives from thee are vain :
No blandishment the slacken'd Nerve can
    strain.

278 ψυχή] ψυχὴ *1693.*

If then thy Lawful Spouse thou canst not love,
What reason shou'd thy Mind to Marriage move ?
Why all the Charges of the Nuptial Feast,
Wine and Deserts and Sweet-meats to digest ?
Th' indoweing Gold that buys the dear Delight,   290
Giv'n for thy first and only happy Night ?
If thou art thus Uxoriously inclin'd,
To bear thy Bondage with a willing mind,
Prepare thy Neck, and put it in the Yoke :
But for no mercy from thy Woman look.
For tho, perhaps, she loves with equal Fires,
To Absolute Dominion she aspires ;
Joys in the Spoils, and Triumphs o'er thy Purse ;
The better Husband makes the Wife the worse.
Nothing is thine to give, or sell, or buy, 300 ⎫
All Offices of Ancient Friendship dye ;   ⎬
Nor hast thou leave to make a Legacy.   ⎭
By [15] thy Imperious Wife thou art bereft
A Priviledge, to Pimps and Panders left ;
Thy Testament's her Will ;   Where she ⎫
prefers   ⎬
Her Ruffians, Drudges, and Adulterers,   ⎬
Adopting all thy Rivals for thy Heirs.   ⎭
    Go [16]drag that Slave to Death ; [17] your Reason, why
Shou'd the poor Innocent be doom'd to Dye ?
What proofs ? for, when Man's Life is in debate,   310
The Judge can ne're too long deliberate.
Call'st [18] thou that Slave a Man ? the Wife replies :
Prov'd, or unprov'd, the Crime, the Villain Dies.
I have the Soveraign Pow'r to save or kill ;
And give no other Reason but my Will.
    Thus the She-Tyrant Reigns, till pleas'd with change,
Her wild Affections to New Empires Range :
Another Subject-Husband she desires ;
Divorc'd from him, she to the first retires,
While the last Wedding-Feast is scarcely o're,   320
And Garlands hang yet green upon the Door.

So still the Reck'ning rises ; and appears
In total Sum, Eight Husbands in Five Years.
The Title for a Tomb-Stone might be fit ;
But that it wou'd too commonly be writ.
    Her Mother Living, hope no quiet Day; ⎫
She sharpens her, instructs her how to ⎬
Flea   ⎬
Her Husband bare, and then divides the ⎬
Prey.   ⎭
She takes Love-Letters, with a Crafty smile,
And, in her Daughter's Answer, mends the stile.   330
In vain the Husband sets his watchful Spies ;
She Cheats their cunning, or she bribes their Eyes.
The Doctor's call'd ; the Daughter, taught the Trick,
Pretends to faint ; and in full Health is Sick.
The Panting Stallion, at the Closet-Door,
Hears the Consult, and wishes it were o're.
Can'st thou, in Reason, hope, a Bawd so known
Shou'd teach her other Manners than her own ?
Her Int'rest is in all th' Advice she gives :
'Tis on the Daughter's Rents the Mother lives.   340
No Cause is try'd at the Litigious Bar,
But Women Plaintiffs or Defendants are,
They form the Process, all the Briefs they ⎫
write,   ⎬
The Topicks furnish, and the Pleas indite ; ⎬
And teach the Toothless Lawyer how to ⎬
Bite.   ⎭
    They turn Virago's too ; the Wrastler's toyl
They try, and Smear their Naked Limbs with Oyl :
Against the Post, their wicker Shields they crush,
Flourish the Sword, and at the Plastron push
Of every Exercise the Mannish Crew   350
Fulfils the Parts, and oft Excels us too ;
Prepar'd not only in feign'd Fights t' engage,
But rout the Gladiators on the Stage.
What sence of shame in such a Breast can lye,
Inur'd to Arms, and her own Sex to fly ?
Yet to be wholly Man she wou'd disclaim ; ⎫
To quit her tenfold Pleasure at the Game, ⎬
For frothy Praises, and an Empty Name.   ⎭
Oh what a decent Sight 'tis to behold
All thy Wife's Magazine by Auction sold !

---

291 thy] *Some editors give* their
308 your] *Some editors give* you

The Belt, the crested Plume, the several
     Suits   361
Of Armour, and the Spanish Leather Boots !
Yet these are they, that cannot bear the heat
Of figur'd Silks, and under Sarcenet sweat.
Behold the strutting *Amazonian* Whore,
She stands in Guard with her right Foot
     before :
Her Coats Tuck'd up ; and all her Motions
     just,
She stamps, and then Cries, hah at ev'ry
     thrust :
But laugh to see her, tyr'd with many a bout,
Call for the Pot, and like a Man Piss out. 370
The Ghosts of Ancient *Romans*, shou'd they
     rise,
Wou'd grin to see their Daughters play
     a Prize.
   Besides, what endless Brawls by Wifes
     are bred :
The Curtain-Lecture makes a Mournful Bed.
Then, when she has thee sure within the
     Sheets,
Her Cry begins, and the whole Day repeats.
Conscious of Crimes her self, she teyzes first ;
Thy Servants are accus'd ; thy Whore is
     curst :
She Acts the jealous, and at Will she cries ;
For Womens Tears are but the sweat of
     Eyes.   380
Poor Cuckold-Fool, thou think'st that Love
     sincere,
And suck'st between her Lips, the falling
     Tear :
But search her Cabinet, and thou shalt find
Each Tiller there with Love Epistles lin'd.
Suppose her taken in a close embrace,   ⎫
This you wou'd think so manifest a Case,   ⎬
No Rhetorick could defend, no Impudence   ⎭
     outface :
And yet even then she Cries the Marriage
     Vow
A mental Reservation must allow ;
And there's a silent bargain still imply'd, ⎫
The Parties shou'd be pleas'd on either   ⎪
     side :   391 ⎬
And both may for their private needs   ⎪
     provide.   ⎭
Tho Men your selves, and Women us you
     call,
Yet *Homo* is a Common Name for all.

There's nothing bolder than a Woman
     Caught ;
Guilt gives 'em Courage to maintain their
     Fault.
   You ask from whence proceed these
     monstrous Crimes ?
Once Poor, and therefore Chast, in former
     times,
Our Matrons were : No Luxury found room
In low-rooft Houses, and bare Walls of Lome ;
Their Hands with Labour hard'ned while
     'twas Light,   401
And Frugal sleep supply'd the quiet Night,
While pinch't with want, their Hunger held
     'em straight ;
When ¹⁹*Hannibal* was Hov'ring at the Gate :
But wanton now, and lolling at our Ease,
We suffer all th' invet'rate ills of Peace,
And wastful Riot ; whose Destructive
     Charms
Revenge the vanquish'd World, of our Vic-
     torious Arms.
No Crime, no Lustful Postures are unknown ;
Since Poverty, our Guardian-God, is gone :
Pride, Laziness, and all Luxurious Arts,   411
Pour like a Deluge in, from Foreign Parts :
Since Gold Obscene, and Silver found the ⎫
     way,   ⎪
Strange Fashions with strange Bullion to ⎬
     convey,   ⎪
And our plain simple Manners to betray. ⎭
   What care our Drunken Dames to whom
     they spread ?
Wine no distinction makes of Tail or Head.
Who lewdly Dancing at a Midnight-Ball,
For hot Eringoes, and Fat Oysters call :
Full Brimmers to their Fuddled Noses
     thrust ;   420
Brimmers the last Provocatives of Lust,
When Vapours to their swimming Brains
     advance,
And double Tapers on the Tables dance.
   Now think what Bawdy Dialogues they
     have,
What *Tullia* talks to her confiding Slave,
At Modesty's old Statue : when by Night
They make a stand, and from their Litters
     light ;
The Good Man early to the Levee goes,
And treads the Nasty Paddle of his Spouse.
The Secrets of the ²⁰Goddess nam'd the
     Good,   430
Are even by Boys and Barbers understood :

Where the Rank Matrons, Dancing to the
Pipe,
Gig with their Bums, and are for Action
ripe ;
With Musick rais'd, they spread abroad their
Hair ;
And toss their Heads like an enamour'd
Mare :
Laufella lays her Garland by, and proves
The mimick Leachery of Manly Loves.
Rank'd with the Lady, the cheap Sinner
lies ;
For here not Blood, but Virtue gives the
prize.   439
Nothing is feign'd in this Venereal Strife ;
'Tis downright Lust, and Acted to the
Life.
So full, so fierce, so vigorous, and so strong,
That, looking on, wou'd make old [21] *Nestor*
Young.
Impatient of delay, a general sound,
An universal Groan of Lust goes round ;
For then, and only then, the Sex sincere
is found.
Now is the time of Action ; now begin,
They cry, and let the lusty Lovers in.
The Whoresons are asleep ; Then bring the
Slaves
And Watermen, a Race of strong-back'd
Knaves.   450
I wish, at least, our Sacred Rites were free
From those Pollutions of Obscenity :
But 'tis well known [22] what Singer, how
disguis'd,
A lewd audacious Action enterpriz'd :
Into the Fair with Women mixt, he went,
Arm'd with a huge two-handed Instrument ;
A grateful Present to those holy Quires,
Where the Mouse guilty of his Sex retires :
And even Male-Pictures modestly are vaild ;
Yet no Profaneness on that Age pre-
vail'd ;   460
No Scoffers at Religious Rites were found :
Tho now, at every Altar they abound.
I hear your cautious Counsel, you wou'd
say,
Keep close your Women under Lock and Key :
But, who shall keep those Keepers ? Women,
nurst
In Craft, begin with those, and Bribe 'em
first.

The Sex is turn'd all Whore ; they Love the
Game :
And Mistresses, and Maids, are both the
same.
  The poor *Ogulnia*, on the Poet's day,
Will borrow Cloaths, and Chair, to see the
Play :   470
She, who before had Mortgag'd her Estate,
And Pawn'd the last remaining piece of
Plate.
Some are reduc'd their utmost Shifts to try :
But Women have no shame of Poverty.
They live beyond their stint ; as if their
store
The more exhausted, wou'd increase the
more :
Some Men, instructed by the Lab'ring Ant,
Provide against th' Extremities of want ;
But Womankind, that never knows a mean,
Down to the Dregs their sinking Fortune
drain :   480
Hourly they give, and spend, and wast, and
wear :
And think no Pleasure can be bought too
dear.
  There are, who in soft Eunuchs place
their Bliss ;
To shun the scrubbing of a Bearded Kiss ;
And scape Abortion ; but their solid joy
Is [23] when the Page, already past a Boy,
Is Capon'd late ; and to the Guelder shown
With his two Pounders to Perfection grown.
When all the Navel-string cou'd give,
appears ;
All but the Beard ; and that's the Barber's
loss, not theirs.   490
Seen from afar, and famous for his ware,
He struts into the Bath, among the Fair :
Th' admiring Crew to their Devotions fall ;
And, kneeling, on their [24] new *Priapus* call.
Kerv'd for his Lady's use, and with her lies ;
And let him drudge for her, if thou art wise,
Rather than trust him with thy Fav'rite
Boy ;
He proffers Death in proffering to enjoy.
  If Songs they love, the Singer's Voice they
force
Beyond his Compass till his Quail-Pipe's
hoarse ;   500
His Lute and Lyre with their embrace is
worn ;
With Knots they trim it, and with Gems
adorn :

---

461 were] *Some editors nonsensically give* are

Run over all the Strings, and Kiss the Case ;
And make Love to it, in the Master's place.
　A certain Lady once, of high Degree,
To *Janus* Vow'd, and *Vesta's* Deity,
That ²⁵ *Pollio* might, in Singing, win the Prize ;
Pollio the Dear, the Darling of her Eyes :
She Pray'd, and Brib'd ; what cou'd she more have done
For a Sick Husband, or an onely Son ? 510
With her Face veil'd, and heaving up her hands,
The shameless Supplaint at the Altar stands ;
The Forms of Pray'r she solemnly pursues ;
And, pale with Fear, the offer'd Entrails views.
Answer, ye Pow'rs: For, if you heard her Vow,
Your Godships, sure, had little else to do.
　This is not all ; for ²⁶ Actors they implore :
An Impudence unknown to Heav'n before.
Th' ²⁷ *Aruspex*, tir'd with this Religious Rout,
Is forc'd to stand so long, he gets the Gout.
But suffer not thy Wife abroad to roam, 521
If she loves Singing, let her Sing at home ;
Not strut in Streets, with *Amazonian* pace ;
For that's to Cuckold thee, before thy Face.
　Their endless Itch of News comes next in play ;
They vent their own ; and hear what others say.
Know what in *Thrace*, or what in *France* is done ;
Th' Intrigues betwixt the Stepdam and the Son.
Tell who Loves who, what Favours some partake :
And who is Jilted for another's sake.　530
What pregnant Widow, in what month was made ;
How oft she did, and doing, what she said.
　She, first, beholds the raging Comet rise :
Knows whom it threatens, and what Lands destroys.
Still for the newest News she lies in wait ;
And takes Reports, just ent'ring at the Gate.
Wrecks, Floods, and Fires ; what-ever she can meet,
She spreads ; and is the *Fame* of every Street.
This is a Grievance ; but the next is worse ;
A very Judgment, and her Neighbours Curse :　540

For, if their barking Dog disturb her ease,
No Pray'r can bind her, no Excuse appease.
Th' unmanner'd Malefactor is Arraign'd ;
But first the Master, who the Curr Maintain'd,
Must feel the scourge : By Night she leaves her Bed ;
By Night her Bathing Equipage is led,
That Marching Armies a less noise create ;
She moves in Tumult, and she Sweats in State.
Mean while, her Guests their Appetites must keep ;
Some gape for Hunger, and some gasp for Sleep.　550
At length she comes, all flush'd, but e're⎫
　she sup,　　　　　　　　　　　　　　　　⎬
Swallows a swinging Preparation-Cup ;　⎬
And then, to clear her Stomach, spews it up.⎭
The Deluge-Vomit all the Floor o'reflows,
And the sour savour nauseates every Nose.
She Drinks again ; again she spews a Lake ;
Her wretched Husband sees, and dares not speak :
But mutters many a Curse, against his Wife ;
And Damns himself, for chusing such a Life.
　But of all Plagues, the greatest is untold ;
The Book-Learn'd Wife in *Greek* and *Latin* bold.　561
The Critick-Dame, who at her Table sits :⎫
Homer and *Virgil* quotes, and weighs their⎬
　Wits ;　　　　　　　　　　　　　　　　　　⎭
And pities *Didoes* Agonizing Fits.
She has so far th' ascendant of the Board,
The Prating Pedant puts not in one Word :
The Man of Law is Non-plust, in his Sute ;
Nay every other Female Tongue is mute.
Hammers, and beating Anvils, you won'd swear,
And ²⁸ *Vulcan* with his whole Militia there.
Tabours ²⁹ and Trumpets cease ; for she alone　571
Is able to Redeem the lab'ring Moon.
Ev'n Wit's a burthen, when it talks too long :
But she, who has no Continence of Tongue,
Should walk in Breeches, and shou'd wear a Beard ;
And mix among the Philosophick Herd.
O what a midnight Curse has he, whose side
Is pester'd with a ³⁰ Mood and Figure Bride !
Let mine, ye Gods, (if such must be my Fate)
No Logick Learn, nor History Translate ;

But rather be a quiet, humble Fool :   581
I hate a Wife, to whom I go to School,
Who climbs the Grammar-Tree, distinctly
    knows
Where Noun, and Verb, and Participle
    grows
Corrects her Country Neighbour; and, a Bed,
For breaking [31]*Priscian's*, breaks her Hus-
    band's Head.
  The Gawdy Gossip, when she's set agog,
In Jewels drest, and at each Ear a Bob,
Goes flaunting out, and, in her trim of
    Pride,
Thinks all she says or does, is justifi'd.   590
When Poor, she's scarce a tollerable Evil ;
But Rich, and Fine, a Wife's a very Devil.
  She duely, once a Month, renews her Face ;
Mean time, it lies in Dawb, and hid in
    Grease ;
Those are the Husband's Nights ; she craves
    her due,
He takes fat Kisses, and is stuck in Glue.
But, to the Lov'd Adult'rer when she
    steers,
Fresh from the Bath, in brightness she
    appears :
For him the Rich *Arabia* sweats her Gum ; ⎫
And precious Oyls from distant *Indies*   ⎪
    come :   600 ⎬
How Haggardly so e're she looks at home. ⎭
Th' Eclipse then vanishes ; and all her Face
Is open'd, and restor'd to ev'ry Grace,
The Crust remov'd, her Cheeks as smooth
    as Silk,
Are polish'd with a wash of Asses Milk ;
And, shou'd she to the farthest *North* be
    sent,
A train [32] of these attend her Banishment.
But, hadst thou seen her Plaistred up before,
'Twas so unlike a Face, it seem'd a Sore.
  'Tis worth our while to know what all
    the day   610
They do, and how they pass their time
    away,
For, if o're-night the Husband has been ⎫
    slack,   ⎪
Or counterfeited Sleep, and turn'd his   ⎬
    Back,   ⎪
Next day, be sure, the Servants go to   ⎭
    wrack.
The Chamber-Maid and Dresser, are call'd
    Whores ;
The Page is stript, and beaten out of Doors

The whole House suffers for the Master's
    Crime :
And he himself is warn'd to wake another
    time.
  She hires Tormentors, by the Year ; she
    Treats
Her Visitours, and talks ; but still she beats,
Beats while she Paints her Face, surveys
    her Gown,   621
Casts up the days Account, and still beats
    on :
Tir'd out, at length, with an outrageous
    Tone,
She bids 'em, in the Devil's Name, begone.
Compar'd with such a Proud, Insulting
    Dame,
Sicilian [33] Tyrants may renounce their
    Name.
For, if she hasts abroad to take the Ayr,
Or goes to *Isis* Church (the Bawdy-House
    of Pray'r)
She hurries all her Handmaids to the Task ;
Her Head, alone, will twenty Dressers ask.
Psecas, the chief, with Breast and Shoulders
    bare,   631
Trembling, considers every Sacred Hair ;
If any Stragler from his Rank be found,
A pinch must, for the Mortal Sin, compound.
Psecas is not in Fault : But, in the Glass,
The Dame's Offended at her own ill Face.
That Maid is Banish'd ; and another Girl
More dextrous, manages the Comb, and Curl;
The rest are summon'd, on a point so nice ;
And first, the Grave Old Woman gives
    Advice.   640
The next is call'd, and so the turn goes
    round,
As each for Age, or Wisdom, is Renown'd :
Such Counsel, such delib'rate care they take,
As if her Life and Honour lay at stake :
With Curls on Curls, they build her Head
    before
And mount it with a Formidable Tow'r [34].
A Gyantess she seems ; but, look behind,
And then she dwindles to the Pigmy kind.
Duck-leg'd, short-wasted, such a Dwarf
    she is,
That she must rise on Tip-toes for a Kiss.
Mean while, her Husband's whole Estate
    is spent ;   651
He may go bare, while she receives his Rent.

  637 That] *The editors wrongly give* The

She minds him not ; she lives not as a Wife,
But like a Bawling Neighbour, full of Strife :
Near him, in this alone, that she extends
Her Hate to all his Servants and his Friends.
 Bellona's Priests, an Eunuch at their
     Head,
About the Streets a mad Procession lead ;
The [35] Venerable Guelding, large, and high,
O'relooks the Herd of his inferiour Fry. 660
His awkward Clergy-Men about him prance ;
And beat the Timbrels to their Mystick
     Dance.
Guiltless of Testicles, they tear their Throats,
And squeak, in Treble, their Unmanly Notes.
Mean while, his Cheeks the Myter'd Prophet
     swells,
And Dire Presages of the Year foretels
Unless with Eggs (his Priestly hire) they
     hast
To Expiate, and avert th' Autumnal blast.
And [36] add beside a murrey-colour'd Vest,
Which, in their places, may receive the
     Pest :   670
And, thrown into the Flood, their Crimes
     may bear,
To purge th' unlucky Omens of the Year.
Th' Astonisht Matrons pay, before the rest ;
That Sex is still obnoxious to the Priest.
  Through yce they beat, and plunge into
     the Stream,
If so the God has warn'd 'em in a Dream.
Weak in their Limbs, but in Devotion⎫
     strong,   ⎪
On their bare Hands and Feet they crawl⎬
     along   ⎪
A whole Fields length, the Laughter of the⎭
     Throng.
Should *Io* (*Io's* Priest I mean) Command 680
A Pilgrimage to *Meroe's* burning Sand,
Through Desarts they wou'd seek the secret
     Spring ;
And Holy Water, for Lustration, bring.
How can they pay their Priests too much
     respect,
Who Trade with Heav'n, and Earthly Gains
     neglect ?
With him, Domestick Gods Discourse by
     Night ;
By Day, attended by his Quire in white,
The Bald-pate Tribe runs madding through
     the Street,
And Smile to see with how much ease they
     Cheat.

The Ghostly Syre forgives the Wife's De-
     lights,   690
Who Sins, through Frailty, on forbidden
     Nights ;
And Tempts her Husband in the Holy
     Time,
When Carnal Pleasure is a Mortal Crime.
The Sweating Image shakes its Head ; but he
With Mumbled Pray'rs Attones the Deity.
The Pious Priesthood the Fat Goose receive,
And they once Brib'd the Godhead must
     forgive.
  No sooner these remove, but full of Fear,
A Gypsie Jewess whispers in your Ear,
And begs an Alms : An High-priest's⎫
     Daughter she,   700 ⎬
Vers'd in their *Talmud*, and Divinity ;   ⎭
And Prophesies beneath a shady Tree.
Her Goods a Basket, and old Hay her Bed,
She strouls, and, Telling Fortunes, gains her
     Bread :
Farthings and some small Monys, are her
     Fees ;
Yet she Interprets all your Dreams for
     these.
Foretels th' Estate, when the Rich Unckle
     Dies,
And sees a Sweet-heart in the Sacrifice. 708
Such Toys, a Pidgeons Entrails can disclose :
Which yet th' *Armenian Augur* far outgoes :
In Dogs, a Victim more obscene, he rakes ;
And Murder'd Infants, for Inspection, takes :
For Gain, his Impious Practice he pursues ;
For Gain, will his Accomplices accuse.
  More Credit, yet, is to [37] *Chaldeans* giv'n ;
What they foretell, is deem'd the Voice of
     Heav'n.
Their Answers, as from *Hammon's* Altar,
     come ;
Since now the *Delphian* Oracles are dumb.
And Mankind, ignorant of future Fate,
Believes what fond Astrologers relate. 720
  Of these the most in vogue is he, who sent
Beyond Seas, is return'd from Banishment,
His Art who to [38] Aspiring *Otho* sold ;
And sure Succession to the Crown foretold.
For his Esteem is in his Exile plac'd ;
The more Believ'd, the more he was Dis-
     grac'd.
No Astrologick Wizard Honour gains,
Who has not oft been Banisht, or in Chains.
He gets Renown, who, to the Halter near,
But narrowly escapes, and buys it dear. 730

From him your Wife enquires the Planets
   Will,
When the black *Jaundies* shall her Mother
   Kill :
Her Sister's and her Unckle's end, wou'd
   know :
But, first, consults his Art, when you shall go.
And, what's the greatest Gift that Heav'n
   can give,
If, after her, th' Adulterer shall live.
She neither knows nor cares to know the
   rest ;
If ³⁹ *Mars* and *Saturn* shall the World infest;
Or *Jove* and *Venus* with their Friendly Rays,
Will interpose, and bring us better days. 740
  Beware the Woman, too, and shun her
   Sight,
Who in these Studies does her self Delight.
By whom a greasie Almanack is born,
With often handling, like chaft Amber, worn:
Not now consulting, but consulted, she
Of the Twelve Houses, and their Lords, is
   free.
She, if the Scheme a fatal Journey show,
Stays safe at Home, but lets her Husband go.
If but a Mile she Travel out of Town,
The Planetary Hour must first be known, 750
And lucky moment ; if her Eye but akes
Or itches, its Decumbiture she takes.
No Nourishment receives in her Disease,
But what the Stars and ⁴⁰ *Ptolomy* shall
   please.
The middle sort, who have not much
   to spare,
To Chiromancers cheaper Art repair,
Who clap the pretty Palm, to make the
   Lines more fair.
But the Rich Matron, who has more to give,
Her Answers from the ⁴¹ *Brachman* will
   receive :
Skill'd in the Globe and Sphere, he Gravely
   stands, 760
And, with his Compass, measures Seas and
   Lands.
  The Poorest of the Sex have still an Itch
To know their Fortunes, equal to the Rich.
The Dairy-Maid enquires, if she shall take
The trusty Taylor, and the Cook forsake.
  Yet these, tho Poor, the Pain of Child-bed
   bear ;
And, without Nurses, their own Infants rear :
You seldom hear of the Rich Mantle spread
For the Babe born in the great Lady's Bed.

Such is the Pow'r of Herbs ; such Arts
   they use 770
To make them Barren, or their Fruit to lose.
But thou, whatever Slops she will have
   bought,
Be thankful, and supply the deadly Draught:
Help her to make Manslaughter ; let her
   bleed,
And never want for Savin at her need.
For, if she holds till her nine Months be run,
Thou may'st be Father ⁴² to an *Æthiop's* Son.
A Boy, who ready gotten to thy hands,
By Law is to Inherit all thy Lands :
One of that hue, that shou'd he cross the
   way, 780
His ⁴³ Omen wou'd discolour all the day.
  I pass the Foundling by, a Race unknown,
At Doors expos'd, whom Matrons make
   their own :
And into Noble Families advance
A Nameless Issue, the blind work of Chance.
Indulgent Fortune does her Care employ,
And, smiling, broods upon the Naked Boy :
Her Garment spreads, and laps him in the
   Fold,
And covers, with her Wings, from nightly
   Cold :
Gives him her Blessing ; puts him in a way ;
Sets up the Farce, and laughs at her own
   Play. 791
Him she promotes ; she favours him alone,
And makes Provision for him, as her own.
  The craving Wife the force of Magick
   tries,
And Philters for th' unable Husband buys :
The Potion works not on the part design'd ;
But turns his Brain, and stupifies his Mind.
The sotted Moon-Calf gapes, and staring on,
Sees his own Business by another done :
A long Oblivion, a benumning Frost, 800
Constrains his Head ; and Yesterday is lost :
Some nimbler Juice would make him foam,
   and rave,
Like that *Cæsonia* ⁴⁴ to her *Caius* gave :
Who, plucking from the Forehead of the Fole
His Mother's Love, infus'd it in the Bowl :
The boiling Blood ran hissing in his Veins,
Till the mad Vapour mounted to his Brains.
The ⁴⁵ Thund'rer was not half so much on
   Fire,
When *Juno's* Girdle kindled his Desire.

---

797 Brain] *Some editors wrongly give* Brains

What Woman will not use the Poys'ning Trade,   810
When *Cæsar's* Wife the Precedent has made ?
Let [46] *Agrippina's* Mushroom be forgot,
Giv'n to a Slav'ring, Old, unuseful Sot ;
That only clos'd the driveling Dotard's Eyes,
And sent his Godhead downward to the Skies.
But this fierce Potion calls for Fire and Sword ;
Nor spares the Commons, when it strikes the Lord :
So many Mischiefs were in one combin'd ;
So much one single Poys'ner cost Mankind.
  If Stepdames seek their Sons in Law to kill,   820
'Tis Venial Trespass ; let them have their Will :
But let the Child, entrusted to the Care
Of his own Mother, of her Bread beware :
Beware the Food she reaches with her Hand ;
The Morsel is intended for thy Land.
Thy Tutour be thy Taster, e're thou Eat ;
There's Poyson in thy Drink, and in thy Meat.
  You think this feign'd ; the Satyr in a Rage
Struts in the Buskins of the Tragick Stage,
Forgets his Bus'ness is to Laugh and Bite ;
And will, of Deaths, and dire Revenges Write.   831
Wou'd it were all a Fable, that you Read ;
But [47] *Drymon's* Wife pleads Guilty to the Deed.
I (she confesses,) in the Fact was caught ;
Two Sons dispatching, at one deadly Draught.

What Two, Two Sons, thou Viper, in one day ?
Yes, sev'n, she cries, if sev'n were in my way.
Medea's [48] Legend is no more a Lye ;
Our Age adds Credit to Antiquity.
Great Ills, we grant, in former times did Reign,   840
And Murthers then were done : but not for Gain.
Less Admiration to great Crimes is due,
Which they Through Wrath, or through Revenge pursue.
For, weak of Reason, impotent of Will,
The Sex is hurri'd headlong into Ill :
And, like a Cliff from its foundations torn,
By raging Earthquakes, into Seas is born.
But those are Fiends, who Crimes from thought begin,
And, cool in Mischief, meditate the Sin.
They Read th' Example of a Pious Wife,   850
Redeeming, with her own, her Husband's Life ;
Yet, if the Laws did that Exchange afford,
Would save their Lapdog sooner than their Lord.
  Where e're you walk, the [49] *Belides* you meet ;
And [50] *Clytemnestra's* grow in ev'ry Street :
But here's the difference ; *Agamemnon's* Wife
Was a gross Butcher, with a bloody Knife ;
But Murther, now, is to perfection grown,
And subtle Poysons are employ'd alone :
Unless some Antidote prevents their Arts,   860
And lines with Balsom all the Noble parts :
In such a case, reserv'd for such a need,
Rather than fail, the Dagger does the Deed.

861 Noble] *The editors wrongly give* Nobler

The End of the Sixth Satyr.

NOTES TO THE SIXTH SATYR.

[1] In the Golden Age : when *Saturn* Reign'd.
[2] *Fat with Acorns* : Acorns were the Bread of Mankind, before Corn was found.
[3] *Under Jove*. When *Jove* had driven his Father into Banishment, the Silver Age began, according to the Poets.
[4] *Uneasie Justice*, &c. The Poet makes Justice and Chastity Sisters ; and says that they fled to Heaven together, and left Earth for ever.

[5] *Ceres Feast*. When the *Roman* Women were forbidden to bed with their Husbands.
[6] *Jove* and *Mars*. Of whom more Fornicating Stories are told, than any of the other Gods.
[7] *Wondring Pharos*. She fled to Egypt ; which wonder'd at the Enormity of her Crime.
[8] He tells the Famous Story of *Messalina*, Wife to the Emperor *Claudius*.
[9] *Wealth has the Priviledge*, &c. His meaning

is, that a Wife who brings a large Dowry may do what she pleases, and has all the Priviledges of a Widow.

¹⁰ *Berenice's Ring.* A Ring of great Price, which *Herod Agrippa* gave to his Sister *Berenice.* He was King of the *Jews,* but Tributary to the *Romans.*

¹¹ *Cornelia.* Mother to the *Gracchi,* of the Family of the *Cornelii* ; from whence *Scipio* the *Affrican* was descended, who Triumph'd over *Hannibal.*

¹² *O Pæan,* &c. He alludes to the known Fable of *Niobe* in *Ovid. Amphion* was her Husband : *Pæan* is *Apollo,* who with his Arrows killed her Children, because she boasted that she was more fruitful than *Latona, Apollo's* Mother.

¹³ *The thirty Pigs,* &c. He alludes to the white Sow in *Virgil,* who farrow'd thirty Pigs.

¹⁴ *The Grecian Cant*: Women then learnt Greek, as ours speak *French.*

¹⁵ All the *Romans,* even the most Inferiour, and most Infamous Sort of them, had the Power of making Wills.

¹⁶ *Go drag that Slave,* &c. These are the words of the Wife.

¹⁷ *Your Reason why,* &c. The Answer of the Husband.

¹⁸ *Call'st thou that Slave a Man?* The Wife again.

¹⁹ *Hannibal.* A Famous *Carthaginian* Captain ; who was upon the point of Conquering the *Romans.*

²⁰ *The good Goddess.* At whose Feasts no Men were to be present.

²¹ *Nestor.* Who lived three hundred Years.

²² *What Singer,* &c. He alludes to the Story of *P. Clodius,* who, disguis'd in the Habit of a Singing Woman, went into the House of *Cæsar,* where the Feast of the Good Goddess was Celebrated ; to find an opportunity with *Cæsar's* Wife *Pompeia.*

²³ He taxes Women with their loving Eunuchs, who can get no Children ; but adds, that they only love such Eunuchs, as are guelded when they are already at the Age of Manhood.

²⁴ *Priapus.* The God of Lust.

²⁵ *Pollio.* A Famous Singing Boy.

²⁶ That such an Actor whom they love might obtain the Prize.

²⁷ *Th' Aruspex.* He who inspects the Entrails of the Sacrifice, and from thence, foretels the Successor.

²⁸ *Vulcan.* The God of Smiths.

²⁹ *Tabours and Trumpets,* &c. The Ancients thought that with such sounds they cou'd bring the Moon out of her Eclipse.

³⁰ *A mood and figure bride.* A Woman who has learn'd Logick.

³¹ A Woman-Grammarian, who corrects her

Husband for speaking false Latin, which is call'd breaking *Priscian's* Head.

³² *A Train of these.* That is, of she Asses.

³³ *Sicilian Tyrants.* Are grown to a Proverb in Latin, for their Cruelty.

³⁴ This dressing up the Head so high, which we call a Tow'r, was an Ancient way amongst the *Romans.*

³⁵ *Bellona's* Priests were a sort of Fortune-tellers ; and the High Priest an Eunuch.

³⁶ *And add beside,* &c. A Garment was given to the Priest, which he threw into the River ; and that, they thought, bore all the Sins of the People, which were drown'd with it.

³⁷ *Chaldeans* are thought to have been the first Astrologers.

³⁸ *Otho* succeeded *Galba* in the Empire ; which was foretold him by an Astrologer.

³⁹ *Mars* and *Saturn* are the two Unfortunate Planets ; *Jupiter* and *Venus,* the two Fortunate.

⁴⁰ *Ptolemy.* A Famous Astrologer, an *Egyptian.*

⁴¹ The *Brachmans* are *Indian* Philosophers, who remain to this day ; and hold, after *Pythagoras,* the Translation of Souls from one body to another.

⁴² *to an Æthiop's son.* His meaning is, help her to any kind of Slops, which may cause her to miscarry ; for fear she may be brought to Bed of a black-moor, which thou, being her Husband, art bound to Father ; and that Bastard may by Law, Inherit thy Estate.

⁴³ *His Omen,* &c. The *Romans* thought it ominous to see a Black-moor in the Morning, if he were the first Man they met.

⁴⁴ *Cæsonia,* Wife to *Caius Caligula,* the great Tyrant : 'Tis said she gave him a Love-Potion, which flying up into his Head, distracted him ; and was the occasion of his committing so many Acts of Cruelty.

⁴⁵ *The Thunderer,* &c. The Story is in *Homer* ; where *Juno* borrow'd the Girdle of *Venus,* call'd *Cestos* ; to make *Jupiter* in love with her, while the *Grecians* and *Trojans* were fighting, that he might not help the latter.

⁴⁶ *Agrippina* was the Mother of the Tyrant *Nero,* who Poyson'd her Husband *Claudius,* that *Nero* might Succeed, who was her Son, and not *Britannicus,* who was the Son of *Claudius,* by a former Wife.

⁴⁷ The Widow of *Drymon* Poison'd her Sons, that they might Succeed to their Estate : This was done either in the Poet's time, or just before it.

⁴⁸ *Medea,* out of Revenge to *Jason,* who had forsaken her, kill'd the Children which she had by him.

⁴⁹ *the Belides.* Who were fifty Sisters, Marry'd to fifty young Men, their Cousin-Germans ; and kill'd them all on their Wedding-Night, excepting *Hipermnestra,* who sav'd her Husband *Linus.*

⁵⁰ *Clytemnestra.* The Wife of *Agamemnon,* who, in favour to her adulterer *Egysthus,* was consenting to his Murther.

27 *Aruspex*] Auruspex *1693.*

THE TENTH SATYR.

ARGUMENT | of the | Tenth Satyr.

The Poet's Design, in this Divine Satyr, is to represent the various Wishes and Desires of Mankind ; and to set out the Folly of 'em. He runs through all the several Heads of Riches, Honours, Eloquence, Fame for Martial Atchievements, Long-Life, and Beauty ; and gives Instances, in Each, how frequently they have prov'd the Ruin of those that Own'd them. He concludes therefore, that since we generally chuse so ill for our selves, we shou'd do better to leave it to the Gods, to make the choice for us. All we can safely ask of Heaven lies within a very small Compass. 'Tis but Health of Body and Mind.—*And if we have these, 'tis not much matter what we want besides : For we have already enough to make us Happy.*

THE | TENTH SATYR.

Look round the Habitable World, how few
Know their own Good ; or knowing it, pursue.
How void of Reason are our Hopes and Fears !
What in the Conduct of our Life appears
So well design'd, so luckily begun,
But, when we have our wish, we wish undone ?
Whole Houses, of their whole Desires possest,
Are often Ruin'd, at their own Request.
In Wars, and Peace, things hurtful we require,
When made Obnoxious to our own Desire. 10
With Laurels some have fatally been Crown'd ;
Some who the depths of Eloquence have found,
In that unnavigable Stream were Drown'd.
The [1] Brawny Fool, who did his Vigour boast,
In that Presumeing Confidence was lost :
But more have been by Avarice opprest,
And Heaps of Money crouded in the Chest :
Unwieldy Sums of Wealth, which higher mount
Than Files of Marshall'd Figures can account.

To which the Stores of *Crœsus*, in the Scale,
Wou'd look like little Dolphins, when they sail 21
In the vast Shadow of the *British* Whale.
For this, in *Nero's* Arbitrary time,
When Virtue was a Guilt, and Wealth a Crime,
A Troop of Cut-Throat Guards were sent, to seize
The Rich Mens Goods, and gut their Palaces :
The Mob, Commission'd by the Government,
Are seldom to an Empty Garret sent.
The Fearful Passenger, who Travels late,
Charg'd with the Carriage of a Paltry Plate, 30
Shakes at the Moonshine shadow of a Rush ;
And sees a Red-Coat rise from every Bush :
The Beggar Sings, ev'n when he sees the place
Beset with Thieves, and never mends his pace.
Of all the Vows, the first and chief Request
Of each, is to be Richer than the rest :
And yet no doubts the Poor Man's Draught controul,
He dreads no Poison in his homely Bowl,
Then fear the deadly Drug, when Gems Divine
Enchase the Cup, and sparkle in the Wine. 40
Will you not now, the pair of Sages praise,
Who the same End pursu'd, by several Ways ?
One pity'd, one contemn'd the Woful Times :
One laugh'd at Follies, one lamented Crimes :
Laughter is easie ; but the Wonder lies,
What stores of Brine supplyd the Weepers Eyes.
Democritus cou'd feed his Spleen, and shake
His sides and shoulders till he felt 'em ake ;
Tho in his Country Town no Lictors were,
Nor Rods nor Ax nor Tribune did appear ; 50
Nor all the Foppish Gravity of show,
Which cunning Magistrates on Crowds bestow :
What had he done, had he beheld, on high
Our *Prætor* seated, in Mock Majesty ;
His Charriot rowling o're the Dusty place
While, with dumb Pride, and a set formal Face,

He moves, in the dull Ceremonial track,
With *Jove's* Embroyder'd Coat upon his
   back :
A Sute of Hangings had not more opprest
His Shoulders, than that long, Laborious
   Vest.   60
A heavy Gugaw, (call'd a Crown) that spred
About his Temples, drown'd his narrow
   Head :
And wou'd have crush'd it, with the Massy
   Freight,
But that a sweating Slave sustain'd the
   weight :
A Slave in the same Chariot seen to ride,
To mortifie the mighty Madman's Pride.
Add now th' Imperial Eagle, rais'd on high,
With Golden Beak (the Mark of Majesty)
Trumpets before, and on the Left and Right,
A Cavalcade of Nobles, all in White :   70
In their own Natures false, and flatt'ring
   Tribes,
But made his Friends, by Places and by
   Bribes.
  In his own Age, *Democritus* cou'd find
Sufficient cause to laugh at Humane kind :
Learn from so great a Wit ; a Land of Bogs
With Ditches fenc'd, a Heaven Fat with Fogs,
May form a Spirit to sway the State ;
And make the Neighb'ring Monarchs fear
   their Fate.
  He laughs at all the Vulgar Cares and Fears;
At their vain Triumphs, and their vainer
   Tears :   80
An equal Temper in his Mind he found,
When Fortune flatter'd him, and when she
   frown'd.
'Tis plain from hence that what our Vows
   request,
Are hurtful things, or Useless at the best.
  Some ask for Envy'd Pow'r ; which
   publick Hate
Pursues, and hurries headlong to their Fate:
Down go the Titles ; and the Statue
   Crown'd,
Is by base Hands in the next River Drown'd.
The Guiltless Horses, and the Chariot Wheel,
The same Effects of Vulgar Fury feel :   90
The Smith prepares his Hammer for the
   Stroke,
While the Lung'd Bellows hissing Fire
   provoke ;

Sejanus,[2] almost first of *Roman* Names,
The great *Sejanus* crackles in the Flames :
Form'd in the Forge, the Pliant Brass is ⎫
   laid   ⎪
On Anvils ; and of Head and Limbs are ⎬
   made   .   ⎪
Pans, Cans, and Pispots, a whole Kitchin ⎪
   Trade.   ⎭
  Adorn your Doors with Laurels ; and
   a Bull
Milk white, and large, lead to the Capitol ;
Sejanus with a Rope is drag'd along,   100
The Sport and Laughter of the giddy Throng!
Good Lord, they Cry, what *Ethiop* Lips
   he has,
How foul a Snout, and what a hanging Face!
By Heav'n, I never cou'd endure his sight ;
But say, how came his Monstrous Crimes
   to Light ?
What is the Charge, and who the Evidence
(The Saviour of the Nation and the Prince ?)
Nothing of this ; but our Old *Cæsar* sent
A Noisie Letter to his Parliament :
Nay, Sirs, if *Cæsar* writ, I ask no more, 110
He's Guilty: and the Question's out of Door.
How goes the Mob ? (for that's a Mighty
   thing.)
When the King's Trump, the Mob are for
   the King :
They follow Fortune, and the Common Cry
Is still against the Rogue Condemn'd to Dye.
  But the same very Mob, that Rascal crowd,
Had cry'd *Sejanus*, with a Shout as loud ;
Had his Designs (by Fortune's favour Blest)
Succeeded, and the Prince's Age opprest,
But long, long since, the Times have chang'd
   their Face,   120
The People grown Degenerate and base ;
Not suffer'd now the Freedom of their choice,
To make their Magistrates, and sell their
   Voice.
  Our Wise Fore-Fathers, Great by Sea and
   Land,
Had once the Pow'r and absolute Command ;
All Offices of Trust, themselves dispos'd ;
Rais'd whom they pleas'd, and whom they
   pleas'd, Depos'd.
But we, who give our Native Rights away,
And our Inslav'd Posterity betray,
Are now reduc'd to beg an Alms, and go 130
On Holidays to see a Puppet show.

---

76 Heaven] Heav'n *1693*.   102 *Ethiop*] Ethiop *1693*.

There was a Damn'd Design, crys one, no
    doubt ;
For Warrants are already Issued out :
I met *Brutidius* in a Mortal fright ;
He's dipt for certain, and plays least in sight :
I fear the Rage of our offended Prince,
Who thinks the Senate slack in his defence !
Come let us haste, our Loyal Zeal to show,
And spurn the Wretched Corps of *Cæsar's*
    Foe :   139
But let our Slaves be present there, lest they
Accuse their Masters, and for Gain betray.
    Such were the Whispers of those jealous
    Times,
About *Sejanus* Punishment, and Crimes.
    Now tell me truly, wou'dst thou change
    thy Fate
To be, like him, first Minister of State ?
To have thy Levees Crowded with resort
Of a depending, gaping, servile Court :
Dispose all Honours of the Sword and Gown,
Grace with a Nod, and Ruin with a Frown :
To hold thy Prince in Pupill-Age, and sway
That Monarch, whom the Master'd World
    obey ?   151
While he, intent on secret Lusts alone,
Lives to himself, abandoning the Throne ;
Coopt³ in a narrow Isle, observing Dreams
With flattering Wisards, and erecting
    Schemes !
I wellbelieve, thou wou'd'st be Great as he ;
For every Man's a Fool to that Degree ;
All wish the dire Prerogative to kill ;
Ev'n they wou'd have the Pow'r, who want
    the Will :
But wou'dst thou have thy Wishes under-
    stood,   160
To take the Bad together with the Good ?
Wou'dst thou not rather choose a small
    Renown,
To be the May'r of some poor Paltry Town,
Bigly to Look, and Barb'rously to speak ;
To pound false Weights, and scanty Measures
    break ?
Then, grant we that *Sejanus* went astray,
In ev'ry Wish, and knew not how to pray :
For he who grasp'd the World's exhausted
    Store,
Yet never had enough, but wish'd for more,
Rais'd a Top-heavy Tower, of monst'rous
    height,   170
Which Mouldr'ing, crush'd him underneath
    the Weight.

    What did the mighty *Pompey's* Fall beget ?
And ruin'd ⁴him, who Greater than the
    Great,
The stubborn Pride of *Roman* Nobles broke ;
And bent their Haughty Necks beneath
    his Yoke ?
What else but his immoderate Lust of
    Pow'r,
Pray'rs made, and granted in a Luckless
    Hour ?
For few Usurpers to the Shades descend
By a dry Death, or with a quiet End
    The Boy, who scarce has paid his Entrance
    down   180
To his proud Pedant, or declin'd a Noun,
(So small an Elf, that when the days are
    foul,
He and his Satchel must be born to School,)
Yet prays, and hopes, and aims at nothing
    less,
To ⁵prove a *Tully*, or *Demosthenes* :
But both those Orators, so much renown'd,
In their own Depths of Eloquence were
    Drown'd :
The Hand and Head were never lost, of
    those   188
Who dealt in Dogrel, or who punn'd in Prose:
Fortune ⁶ foretun'd the dying Notes of Rome:
Till I, thy Consul sole, consol'd thy doom.
His Fate had crept below the lifted Swords,
Had all his Malice been to Murther words.
I rather would be *Mævius*, Thrash for
    Rhimes
Like his, the scorn and scandal of the Times,
Than ⁷that Philippique, fatally Divine,
Which is inscrib'd the Second, should be
    Mine.
    Nor he, the Wonder of the *Grecian* throng,
Who drove them with the Torrent of his
    Tongue,
Who shook the Theaters, and sway'd the
    State   200
Of *Athens*, found a more Propitious Fate.
Whom, born beneath a boding Horoscope,
His Sire, the Blear-Ey'd *Vulcan* of a Shop,
From *Mars* his Forge, sent to *Minerva's*
    Schools,
To learn th' unlucky Art of wheedling Fools.
    With Itch of Honour, and Opinion, Vain,
All things beyond their Native worth we
    strain :
The⁸ Spoils of War, brought to *Feretrian Jove*
An empty Coat of Armour hung above

The Conquerors Chariot, and in Triumph
born,   210
A Streamer from a boarded Gally torn,
A Chap-faln Beaver loosely hanging by
The cloven Helm, an Arch of Victory,
On whose high Convex sits a Captive Foe,
And sighing casts a Mournful Look below ;
Of ev'ry Nation, each Illustrious Name,
Such Toys as these have cheated into Fame :
Exchanging solid Quiet, to obtain
The Windy satisfaction of the Brain.
    So much the Thirst of Honour Fires the
Blood ;   220
So many wou'd be Great, so few be Good.
For who wou'd Virtue for her self regard,
Or Wed, without the Portion of Reward ?
Yet this Mad Chace of Fame, by few pursu'd,
Has drawn Destruction on the Multitude :
This Avarice of Praise in Times to come,
Those long Inscriptions, crowded on the
Tomb,
Shou'd some Wild Fig-Tree take her Native
bent,
And heave below the gaudy Monument,
Wou'd crack the Marble Titles, and dis-
perse   230
The Characters of all the lying Verse.
For Sepulchres themselves must crumbling
fall
In Times Abyss, the common Grave of all.
    Great *Hannibal* within the Ballance lay ;
And tell how many Pounds his Ashes weigh ;
Whom *Affrick* was not able to contain,
Whose length runs Level with th' *Atlantick*
main,
And wearies fruitful *Nilus*, to convey
His Sun-beat Waters by so long a way ;
Which *Ethiopia's* double Clime divides, 240
And Elephants in other Mountains hides.
Spain first he won, the *Pyræneans* past,
And steepy *Alps*, the Mounds that Nature cast:
And with Corroding Juices, as he went,
A passage through the living Rocks he rent.
Then, like a Torrent, rowling from on high,
He pours his head-long Rage on *Italy* ;
In three Victorious Battels overrun ;
Yet still uneasie, Cries, There's nothing done,
Till, level with the Ground, their Gates are
laid ;   250
And *Punick* Flags on *Roman* Tow'rs displaid.

233 Times] times *1693*.
249 Cries, There's] Cries there's *1693*.

Ask what a Face belong'd to this high
Fame ;
His Picture scarcely wou'd deserve a Frame :
A Sign-Post Dawber wou'd disdain to paint
The one-Ey'd Heroe on his Elephant.
Now what's his End, O Charming Glory, say
What rare fifth Act, to Crown this huffing
Play ?
In one deciding Battel overcome,
He flies, is banisht from his Native home :
Begs refuge in a Foreign Court, and there 260
Attends, his mean Petition to prefer ;
Repuls'd by surly Grooms, who wait before
The sleeping Tyrant's interdicted Door.
    What wondrous sort of Death has
        Heav'n design'd,
Distinguish'd from the Herd of Humane
        Kind,
For so untam'd, so turbulent a Mind !
Nor Swords at hand, nor hissing Darts afar,
Are doom'd t' Avenge the tedious bloody
War,
But Poyson, drawn through a Rings hollow
plate,   269
Must finish him ; a sucking Infant's Fate.
Go, climb the rugged *Alps*, Ambitious fool,
To please the Boys, and be a Theme at
School.
    One World suffis'd not *Alexander's* Mind ;
Coop't up, he seem'd in Earth and Seas con-
fin'd :
And, strugling, stretch'd his restless Limbs
about
The narrow Globe, to find a passage out.
Yet, enter'd in the ⁹Brick-built Town, he
try'd
The Tomb, and found the strait dimensions
wide :
"Death only this Mysterious Truth unfolds,
"The mighty Soul, how small a Body holds.
    Old *Greece* ¹⁰ a Tale of *Athos* wou'd
make out,   281
Cut from the Continent, and Sail'd about ;
Seas hid with Navies, Chariots passing o're
The Channel, on a Bridge from shore to
shore.
Rivers, whose depth no sharp beholder sees,
Drunk at an Armies Dinner, to the Lees ;
With a long Legend of Romantick things,
Which, in his Cups, the Bowsy Poet sings.
But how did he return, this haughty Brave
Who whipt the Winds, and made the Sea
his Slave ?   290

(Tho' *Neptune* took unkindly to be bound ;)
And *Eurus* never such hard usage found
In his *Eolian* Prisons under ground ;)
What God so mean, ev'n[11] he who points
   the way,
So Merciless a Tyrant to Obey !
But how return'd he, let us ask again ?
In a poor Skiff he pass'd the bloody Main,
Choak'd with the slaughter'd Bodies of
   his Train.
For Fame he pray'd, but let th' Event
   declare
He had no mighty penn'worth of his Pray'r.
   Jove, grant me length of Life, and Years
    good store   301
Heap on my bending Back, I ask no more.
Both Sick and Healthful, Old and Young,
   conspire
In this one silly, mischievous desire.
Mistaken Blessing, which Old Age they call,
'Tis a long, nasty, darksom Hospital,
A ropy Chain of Rhumes ; a Visage rough,
Deform'd, Unfeatur'd, and a Skin of Buff.
A stitch-fal'n Cheek, that hangs below the
   Jaw ;
Such Wrinckles, as a skillful Hand wou'd
   draw   310
For an old Grandam Ape, when, with a
   Grace,
She sits at squat, and scrubs her Leathern
   Face.
   In Youth, distinctions infinite abound ;
No Shape, or Feature, just alike are found ;
The Fair, the Black, the Feeble, and the
   Strong ;
But the same foulness does to Age belong,
The self same Palsie, both in Limbs, and
   Tongue.
The Skull and Forehead one Bald Barren
   plain ;
And Gums unarm'd to Mumble Meat in
   vain :
Besides th' Eternal Drivel, that supplies 320
The dropping Beard, from Nostrils, Mouth,
   and Eyes.
His Wife and Children loath him, and,
   what's worse,
Himself does his offensive Carrion Curse !
Flatt'rers forsake him too ; for who would
   kill
Himself, to be Remember'd in a Will ?
His taste, not only pall'd to Wine and Meat,
But to the Relish of a Nobler Treat.

The limber Nerve, in vain provok'd to rise,
Inglorious from the Field of Battel flies :
Poor Feeble Dotard, how cou'd he advance
With his Blew head-piece, and his broken
   Lance ?   331
Add, that endeavouring still without effect
A Lust more sordid justly we suspect.
   Those Senses lost, behold a new defeat,
The Soul, dislodging from another seat.
What Musick, or Enchanting Voice, can chear
A Stupid, Old, Impenetrable Ear ?
No matter in what Place, or what Degree
Of the full Theater he sits to see ;
Cornets and Trumpets cannot reach his Ear :
Under an Actor's Nose he's never near. 341
  His Boy must bawl, to make him under-
   stand
The Hour o' th' Day, or such a Lord's at
   hand :
The little Blood that creeps within his Veins,
Is but just warm'd in a hot Feaver's pains.
In fine, he wears no Limb about him sound :
With Sores and Sicknesses beleaguer'd
   round :
Ask me their Names, I sooner cou'd relate
How many Drudges on Salt *Hippia* wait ;
What Crowds of Patients the Town Doctor
   kills,   350
Or how, last fall, he rais'd the Weekly Bills.
What Provinces by *Basilus* were spoil'd,
What Herds of Heirs by Guardians are
   beguil'd :
How many bouts a Day that Bitch has try'd ;
How many Boys that Pedagogue can ride !
What Lands and Lordships for their Owners
   know
My Quondam Barber, but his worship now.
   This Dotard of his broken Back complains,
One his Legs fail, and one his Shoulder
   pains :
Another is of both his Eyes bereft ;   360
And Envies who has one for Aiming left.
A Fifth with trembling Lips expecting stands ;
As in his Child-hood, cram'd by others hands ;
One, who at sight of Supper open'd wide
His Jaws before, and Whetted Grinders
   try'd ;
Now only Yawns, and waits to be supply'd :
Like a young Swallow, when with weary
   Wings
Expected Food her fasting Mother brings.

---

359 Shoulder pains] Shoulders pain *1693*.

His loss of Members is a heavy Curse,
But all his Faculties decay'd, a worse ! 370
His Servants Names he has forgotten quite ;
Knows not his Friend who supp'd with him
    last Night.
Not ev'n the Children, he Begot and Bred ;
Or his Will knows 'em not : For, in their
    stead,
In Form of Law, a common Hackney Jade,
Sole Heir, for secret Services, is made :
So lewd, and such a batter'd Brothel Whore,
That she defies all Commers, at her Door.
Well, yet suppose his Senses are his own,
He lives to be chief Mourner for his Son : 380
Before his Face his Wife and Brother burns ;
He Numbers all his Kindred in their Urns.
These are the Fines he pays for living long ;
And dragging tedious Age, in his own
    wrong :
Griefs always Green, a House-hold still in ⎫
    Tears,   ⎪
Sad Pomps, a Threshold throng'd with   ⎬
    daily Biers ;   ⎪
And Liveries of Black for Length of Years. ⎭
    Next to the Raven's Age, the *Pylian*[12] King
Was longest liv'd of any two leg'd thing ;
Blest, to Defraud the Grave so long, to
    Mount   390
His [13] Numbred Years, and on his Right Hand
    Count ;
Three Hundred Seasons, guzling Must of
    Wine :
But, hold a while, and hear himself Repine
At Fates Unequal Laws ; and at the Clue
Which, [14] Merciless in length, the midmost
    Sister drew.
When his Brave Son upon the Fun'ral Pyre
He saw extended, and his Beard on Fire ;
He turn'd, and Weeping, ask'd his Friends,
    what Crime
Had Curs'd his Age to this unhappy Time ?
Thus Mourn'd old *Peleus* for *Achilles*
    slain,   400
And thus *Ulysses's* Father did complain.
    How Fortunate an End had *Priam* made,
Among his Ancestors a mighty shade,
While *Troy* yet stood ; When *Hector* with
    the Race
Of Royal Bastards, might his Funeral Grace:
Amidst the Tears of *Trojan* Dames inurn'd,
And by his Loyal Daughters truly mourn'd.

Had Heaven so Blest him, he had Dy'd before
The fatal Fleet to *Sparta Paris* bore.
But mark what Age produc'd ; he liv'd
    to see   410
His Town in Flames, his falling Monarchy :
In fine, the feeble Syre, reduc'd by Fate,
To change his Scepter for a Sword, too late,
His [15] last Effort before *Jove's* Altar tries
A Souldier half, and half a Sacrifice :
Falls like an Oxe, that waits the coming
    blow ;
Old and unprofitable to the Plough.
    At [16] least, he Dy'd a Man, his Queen
    surviv'd,
To Howl, and in a barking Body liv'd.
    I hasten to our own ; Nor will relate 420
Great [17] *Mithridates*, and Rich [18] *Crœssus* Fate ;
Whom *Solon* wisely Counsell'd to attend
The Name of Happy, till he knew his End.
That *Marius* was an Exile, that he fled,
Was ta'ne, in Ruin'd *Carthage* beg'd his
    Bread,
All these were owing to a Life too long:
For whom had *Rome* beheld so Happy,
    Young !
High in his Chariot and with Lawrel Crown'd,
When he had led the *Cimbrian* Captives
    round
The *Roman* Streets ; descending from his
    State,   430
In that Blest Hour he should have beg'd
    his Fate ;
Then, then, he might have dy'd of all admir'd,
And his Triumphant Soul with Shouts
    expir'd.
    Campania,[19] Fortunes Malice to prevent,
To *Pompey* an indulgent Feavour sent ;
But publick Pray'rs impos'd on Heav'n,
    to give
Their much Lov'd Leader an unkind Re-
    prieve.
The Cities Fate and his, conspir'd to save
The Head, reserv'd for an *Egyptian* Slave.
Cethegus,[20] tho a Traytor to the State, 440
And Tortur'd, scap'd this Ignominious Fate :
And *Sergius*,[21] who a bad Cause bravely
    try'd,
All of a Piece, and undiminish'd Dy'd.
    To *Venus*, the fond Mother makes a Pray'r,
That all her Sons and Daughters may be
    Fair :

---

386 Pomps, a] Pomps : A *1693*.

435 Feavour] Favour *1693*.

True, for the Boys a Mumbling Vow she
  sends ;
But, for the Girls, the Vaulted Temple rends :
They must be finish'd Pieces : 'Tis allow'd
Diana's Beauty made *Latona* Proud ;
And pleas'd, to see the Wond'ring People
  Pray   450
To the New-rising Sister of the Day.
  And yet *Lucretia's* Fate wou'd bar that
  Vow :
And fair [22] *Virginia* wou'd her Fate bestow
On *Rutila ;* and change her Faultless Make
For the foul rumple of Her Camel back.
  But, for his Mother's Boy, the Beau,
  what frights
His Parents have by Day, what Anxious
  Nights !
Form join'd with Virtue is a sight too rare :
Chast is no Epithete to sute with Fair.
Suppose the same Traditionary strain   460
Of Rigid Manners in the House remain ;
Inveterate Truth, an Old plain *Sabine's*
  Heart ;
Suppose that Nature, too, has done her part ;
Infus'd into his Soul a sober Grace,
And blusht a Modest Blood into his Face,
(For Nature is a better Guardian far,
Than Snwcy Pedants, or dull Tutors are :)
Yet still the Youth must ne're arrive at
  Man ;
(So much Almighty Bribes and Presents can:)
Ev'n with a Parent, where Perswasions fail,
Mony is impudent, and will prevail.   471
  We never Read of such a Tyrant King,
Who guelt a boy deform'd, to hear him Sing.
Nor *Nero*, in his more Luxurious Rage,
E're made a Mistress of an ugly Page :
Sporus, his Spouse, nor Crooked was, nor⎫
  Lame,   ⎪
With Mountain Back, and Belly, from the⎬
  Game   ⎪
Cross-barr'd : But both his Sexes well⎭
  became.
Go, boast your *Springal*, by his Beauty Curst
To Ills ; nor think I have declar'd the worst :
His Form procures him Journey-Work ;
  a strife   481
Betwixt Town-Madams and the Merchant's
  Wife :
Guess, when he undertakes this publick War,
What furious Beasts offended Cuckolds are.
  Adult'rers are with Dangers round beset ;
Born under *Mars*, they cannot scape the Net ;

And from Revengeful Husbands oft have
  try'd
Worse handling, than severest Laws pro-
  vide :
One stabs ; one slashes ; one, with Cruel Art,
Makes *Colon* suffer for the Peccant part. 490
  But your *Endymion*, your smooth, Smock-
  fac'd boy,
Unrivall'd, shall a Beauteous Dame enjoy :
Not so : One more Salacious, Rich, and Old,
Out-bids, and buys her Pleasure for her
  Gold :
Now he must Moil, and Drudge, for one he
  loaths,
She keeps him High, in Equipage, and
  Cloaths :
She Pawns her Jewels, and her Rich Attire,
And thinks the Workman worthy of his
  Hire :
In all things else immoral, stingy, mean ;
But, in her Lusts, a Conscionable Quean. 500
  She may be handsom, yet be Chast, you
  say ;
Good Observator, not so fast away :
Did it not cost the [23] Modest Youth his Life,
Who shun'd th' embraces of his Father's
  Wife ?
And was not [24] t'other Stripling forc'd⎫
  to fly,   ⎪
Who, coldly, did his Patron's Queen deny,⎬
And pleaded Laws of Hospitality ?⎭
The Ladies charg'd 'em home, and turn'd
  the Tail :
With shame they redn'd, and with spight
  grew Pale.
'Tis Dang'rous to deny the longing Dame ;
She loses Pity, who has lost her Shame. 511
  Now [25] *Silius* wants thy Counsel, give
  Advice ;
Wed *Cæsar's* Wife, or Dye ; the Choice is
  nice.
Her Comet-Eyes she darts on ev'ry Grace ;
And takes a fatal liking to his Face.
Adorn'd with Bridal Pomp she sits in
  State ;
The Publick Notaries and *Auspex* wait :⎫
The Genial Bed is in the Garden drest :⎪
The Portion paid, and ev'ry Rite express'd,⎬
Which in a *Roman* Marriage is profest. 520⎭

---

508 Tail i.e. Tale.
517 *Auspex*] *The editors, ignoring Juvenal
as well as Dryden's text, give* Haruspex

'Tis no stol'n Wedding, this ; rejecting awe,
She scorns to Marry, but in Form of Law :
In this moot case, your Judgment : To
  refuse
Is present Death, besides the Night you lose.
If you consent, 'tis hardly worth your pain ;
A day or two of Anxious Life you gain :
Till lowd Reports through all the Town
  have past,
And reach the Prince : For Cuckolds hear
  the last.
Indulge thy Pleasure, Youth, and take thy
  swing ;
For not to take, is but the self same thing ;
Inevitable Death before thee lies ;   531
But looks more kindly through a Ladies
  Eyes.
  What then remains ? Are we depriv'd
  of Will,
Must we not Wish, for fear of wishing Ill ?
Receive my Counsel, and securely move ;
Intrust thy Fortune to the Pow'rs above.
Leave them to manage for thee, and to grant
What their unerring Wisdom sees thee want :
In Goodness as in Greatness they excel ;
Ah that we lov'd our selves but half so
  well !   540

We, blindly by our headstrong Passions led,
Are hot for Action, and desire to Wed ;
Then wish for Heirs : But to the Gods
  alone
Our future Offspring, and our Wives are
  known ;
Th' audacious Strumpet, and ungracious
  Son.
  Yet not to rob the Priests of pious Gain,
That Altars be not wholly built in vain ;
Forgive the Gods the rest, and stand confin'd
To Health of Body, and Content of Mind :
A Soul, that can securely Death defie,   550
And count it Nature's Priviledge, to Dye ;
Serene and Manly, harden'd to sustain
The load of Life, and Exercis'd in Pain :
Guiltless of Hate, and Proof against Desire ;
That all things weighs, and nothing can
  admire :
That dares prefer the Toils of *Hercules*
To Dalliance, Banquet, and Ignoble ease.
  The Path to Peace is Virtue : What I
  show,
Thy Self may freely on Thy Self bestow :
Fortune was never Worshipp'd by the
  Wise ;   560
But, set aloft by Fools, Usurps the Skies.

The End of the Tenth Satyr.

NOTES TO THE TENTH SATYR.

[1] *Milo*, of *Crotona*, who, for a Tryal of his strength, going to rend an Oak, perish'd in the Attempt : For his Arms were caught in the Trunk of it, and he was devour'd by Wild Beasts.

[2] *Sejanus* was *Tiberius's* first Favourite, and while he continu'd so had the highest Marks of Honour bestow'd on him : Statues and Triumphal Chariots were every where erected to him ; but as soon as he fell into Disgrace with the Emperor, these were all immediately dismounted, and the Senate and Common People insulted over him as meanly, as they had fawn'd on him before.

[3] The island of *Capreæ*, which lies about a League out at Sea from the *Campanian* Shore, was the Scene of *Tiberius's* Pleasures in the latter part of his Reign. There he liv'd for some Years with Diviners, Soothsayers, and worse Company— And from thence dispatch'd all his Orders to the Senate.

[4] *Julius Cæsar*, who got the better of *Pompey*, that was stil'd *the Great.*

[5] *Demosthenes* and *Tully* both dyed for their Oratory. *Demosthenes* gave himself Poyson to avoid being carried to *Antipater*, one of *Alexander's* Captains, who had then made himself Master of *Athens*. *Tully* was Murther'd by

M. Antony's Order, in Return for those Invectives he had made against him.

[6] The Latin of this Couplet is a Famous Verse of *Tully's*, in which he sets out the Happiness of his own Consulship ; Famous for the Vanity, and the ill Poetry of it. For *Tully* as he had a good deal of the one, so he had no great share of the other.

[7] The Orations of *Tully* against *M. Antony* were stil'd by him *Philippics*, in imitation of *Demosthenes*, who had given that name before to those he made against *Philip* of *Macedon*.

[8] This is a Mock-account of a *Roman* Triumph.

[9] *Babylon*, where *Alexander* dy'd.

[10] *Xerxes* is represented in History after a very Romantick Manner, affecting Fame beyond Measure, and doing the most Extravagant things to compass it. Mount *Athos* made a Prodigious Promontory in the *Ægæan* Sea : He is said to have cut a Channel through it, and to have Sail'd round it. He made a Bridge of Boats over the *Hellespont* where it was three Miles broad : And order'd a Whipping for the Winds and Seas, because they had once crossed his Designs, as we have a very solemn account of it in *Herodotus*. But, after all these vain Boasts, he was shamefully

beaten by *Themistocles* at *Salamis*; and return'd home, leaving most of his Fleet behind him.

¹¹ *Mercury*, who was a God of the lowest size, and employ'd always in Errands between Heaven and Hell. And Mortals us'd him accordingly: For his statues were anciently plac'd, where Roads met, with Directions on the Fingers of 'em, pointing out the several ways to Travellers.

¹² *Nestor*, King of *Pylos*, who was 300 Years old, according to *Homer's* account; at least, as he is understood by his Expositors.

¹³ The Ancients counted by their Fingers. Their *Left* Hands serv'd 'em till they came up to an Hundred, after that they used their *Right*, to express all greater Numbers.

¹⁴ The *Fates* were three Sisters, which had all some peculiar business assign'd 'em by the Poets in relation to the Lives of Men. The First held the Distaff; the Second spun the Thread; and the Third cut it.

¹⁵ Whilst *Troy* was Sacking by the *Greeks*, Old King *Priam* is said to have Buckled on his Armour to oppose 'em; which he had no sooner done, but he was met by *Pyrrhus*, and slain before the Altar of *Jupiter*, in his own Palace, as we have the Story finely told in *Virgil's 2d Æneid*.

¹⁶ *Hecuba*, his Queen, escap'd the Swords of the *Grecians*, and outliv'd him. It seems she behav'd her self so fiercely and uneasily to her Husband's Murtherers while she liv'd, that the Poets thought fit to turn her into a *Bitch*, when she dy'd.

¹⁷ *Mithridates*, after he had disputed the empire of the world, for forty years together, with the Romans, was at last depriv'd of life and empire by *Pompey* the Great.

¹⁸ *Cræsus*, in the midst of his Prosperity, making his Boast to *Solon* how Happy he was, receiv'd this Answer from the Wise Man: That no One could pronounce himself Happy till he saw what his End should be. The truth of this *Cræsus* found, when he was put in Chains by *Cyrus*, and condemned to die.

¹⁹ *Pompey*, in the midst of his Glory, fell into a Dangerous Fit of Sickness at *Naples*. A great many Cities then made Publick Supplications for him. He Recover'd, was beaten at *Pharsalia*, fled to *Ptolomy*, King of *Ægypt*, and, instead of receiving Protection at his Court, had his Head struck off by his Order, to please *Cæsar*.

²⁰ *Cethegus* was one that conspir'd with *Catiline*, and was put to Death by the Senate.

²¹ *Catiline* dy'd fighting.

²² *Virginia* was kill'd by her own Father, to prevent her being expos'd to the Lust of *Appius Claudius*, who had Ill Designs upon her. The Story at large is in *Livy's* Third Book; and 'tis a remarkable one, as it gave occasion to the putting down the Power of the *Decemviri*, of whom *Appius* was one.

²³ *Hippolytus*, the Son of *Theseus*, was lov'd by his Mother in Law *Phædria*. But he not complying with her, she procur'd his Death.

²⁴ *Bellerophon*, the Son of King *Glaucus*, residing some time at the Court of *Pætus*, King of the *Argives*, the Queen, *Sthenobœa*, fell in Love with him. But he refusing her, she turn'd the Accusation upon Him, and he narrowly scap'd *Pætus's* Vengeance.

²⁵ *Messalina*, Wife to the Emperor *Claudius*, Infamous for her Lewdness. She set her Eyes upon *C. Silius*, a fine Youth; forc'd him to quit his own Wife, and Marry her with all the Formalities of a Wedding, whilst *Claudius Cæsar* was Sacrificing at *Hostia*. Upon his Return, he put both *Silius* and her to Death.

THE SIXTEENTH SATYR.

ARGUMENT | *of the | Sixteenth Satyr*.

The Poet in this Satyr proves, that the Condition of a Souldier is much better than that of a Countryman. First, because a Countryman, however Affronted, Provok'd, and Struck himself, dares not strike a Souldier: Who is only to be judg'd by a Court-Martial: And by the Law of Camillus, which obliges him not to Quarrel without the Trenches, he is also assur'd to have a speedy hearing, and quick dispatch: Whereas, the Townsman or Peasant is delaid in his suit by frivolous Pretences, and not sure of Justice when he is heard in the Court. The Souldier is also priviledg'd to make a Will, and to give away his Estate, which he got in War, to whom he pleases,

without Consideration of Parentage or Relations, which is deny'd to all other Romans. This Satyr was written by Juvenal when he was a Commander in Egypt: *'tis certainly his, tho I think it not finish'd. And if it be well observ'd, you will find he intended an Invective against a standing Army.*

THE | SIXTEENTH SATYR.

WHAT vast Prerogatives, my *Gallus*, are
Accrewing to the mighty Man of War!
For, if into a lucky Camp I light,
Tho raw in Arms, and yet afraid to Fight,
Befriend me, my good Stars, and all goes right :)

One Happy Hour is to a Souldier better,
Than Mother [1]*Juno's* recommending Letter,
Or *Venus*, when to *Mars* she wou'd prefer
My Suit, and own the Kindness done to Her.
   See what Our Common Priviledges are: 10
As first no Sawcy Citizen shall dare
To strike a Souldier, nor when struck, resent
The wrong, for fear of farther Punishment :
Not tho his Teeth are beaten out, his Eyes
Hang by a String, in Bumps his Fore-head
   rise,
Shall He presume to mention his Disgrace,
Or Beg amends for his demolish'd Face.
A Booted Judge shall sit to try his Cause,
Not by the Statute, but by Martial-Laws ;
Which old *Camillus*[2] order'd, to confine 20
The Brawls of Souldiers to the Trench and
   Line :
A Wise Provision ; and from thence 'tis
   clear,
That Officers a Souldiers Cause shou'd
   hear :
And taking cognizance of Wrongs receiv'd,
An Honest Man may hope to be reliev'd.
So far 'tis well : But with a General cry,
The Regiment will rise in Mutiny,
The Freedom of Their Fellow Rogue demand,
And, if refus'd, will threaten to Disband.
Withdraw thy Action, and depart in
   Peace ;   30
The Remedy is worse than the Disease :
This Cause is worthy [3]him, who in the
   Hall
Wou'd for his Fee, and for his Client
   bawl :
But wou'dst Thou Friend who hast two Legs
   alone,
(Which Heav'n be prais'd, Thou yet may'st
   call Thy own,)
Wou'dst Thou to run the Gauntlet these
   expose
To a whole Company of [4]Hob-nail'd Shoos ?
Sure the good Breeding of Wise Citizens
Shou'd teach 'em more good Nature to
   their Shins.
   Besides, whom can'st Thou think so
   much thy Friend,   40
Who dares appear thy Business to defend ?
Dry up thy Tears, and Pocket up th'
   Abuse,
Nor put thy Friend to make a bad excuse :
The Judge cries out, Your Evidence pro-
   duce.

Will He, who saw the Souldier's Mutton
   Fist,
And saw Thee maul'd, appear within the
   List ;
To witness Truth ? When I see one so
   Brave,
The Dead, think I, are risen from the Grave ;
And with their long Spade Beards and
   Matted Hair,
Our honest Ancestors are come to take
   the Air.   50
Against a Clown, with more security,
A Witness may be brought to swear a Lye,
Than, tho his Evidence be Full and Fair,
To vouch a Truth against a Man of War.
   More Benefits remain, and claim'd as
   Rights,
Which are a standing Armies Perquisites.
If any Rogue vexatious Suits advance
Against me for my known Inheritance,
Enter by Violence my Fruitful Grounds,
Or take the Sacred Land-Mark from my
   Bounds,   60
Those Bounds which with Procession and
   with Pray'r,
And [5]Offer'd Cakes, have been my Annual
   care :
Or if my Debtors do not keep their day,
Deny their Hands, and then refuse to pay ;
I must with Patience all the Terms attend,
Among the common Causes that depend
Till mine is call'd ; and that long look'd
   for day
Is still encumber'd with some new delay :
Perhaps [6]the Cloath of State is only spred,
Some of the *Quorum* may be Sick a Bed ; 70
That Judge is Hot, and do'ffs his Gown,
   while this
O're night was Bowsy, and goes out to
   Piss :
So many Rubs appear, the time is gone
For hearing, and the tedious Suit goes on :
But Buff, and Belt-Men never know these
   Cares,
No Time, nor Trick of Law, their Action
   Bars :
Their Cause They to an easier Issue put :
They will be heard, or They lug out, and cut.
   Another Branch of their Revenue still
Remains beyond their boundless Right
   to kill,   80
Their [7]Father yet alive, impow'r'd to make
   a Will.

For, what their Prowess Gain'd, the Law
   declares
Is to themselves alone, and to their
   Heirs:
No share of that goes back to the begettor,
But if the Son fights well, and Plunders
   better,
Like stout *Coranus*, his old shaking Sire
Does a Remembrance in his Will desire:

Inquisitive of Fights, and longs in vain
To find him in the Number of the Slain:
But still he lives, and rising by the War, 90
Enjoyes his Gains, and has enough to spare:
For 'tis a Noble General's prudent part
To cherish Valour, and reward Desert:
Let him be dawb'd with Lace, live High,
   and Whore;
Sometimes be Lowzy, but be never Poor.

The End of the Sixteenth Satyr.

NOTES TO THE SIXTEENTH SATYR.

[1] *Juno* was Mother to *Mars* the God of War:
Venus was his Mistress.

[2] *Camillus* (who being first Banish'd by his
ungrateful Countrymen the *Romans*, afterwards
return'd, and freed them from the *Gaules*,) made
a Law, which prohibited the Souldiers from
Quarrelling without the Camp, lest upon that
pretence they might happen to be absent when
they ought to be on Duty.

[3] *This Cause is worthy him*, &c. The Poet
Names a *Modenese* Lawyer, whom he calls
Vagellius; who was so Impudent that he would
Plead any Cause, right or wrong, without Shame
or Fear.

[4] *Hob-nail'd Shoos*. The *Roman* Souldiers wore
Plates of Iron under their Shoos, or stuck them
with Nails; as Countrymen do now.

[5] Land-Marks were us'd by the *Romans*,
almost in the same manner as now: And as we
go once a Year in Procession, about the Bounds
of Parishes, and renew them, so they offer'd Cakes
upon the Stone or Land-Mark.

[6] The Courts of Judicature were hung and
spread, as with us: But spread only before the
Hundred Judges were to sit and judge Publick
Causes, which were call'd by *Lot*.

[7] The *Roman* Souldiers had the Priviledge of
making a Will, in their Father's Life-time; Of
what they had purchac'd in the Wars, as being no
part of their Patrimony. By this Will they had
Power of excluding their own Parents, and giving
the Estate so gotten to whom they pleas'd.
Therefore, says the Poet, *Coranus* (a Souldier
Contemporary with *Juvenal*, who had rais'd his
Fortune by the Wars) was Courted by his own
Father, to make him his Heir.

THE
SATIRES
OF
Aulus Persius Flaccus
Made ENGLISH
BY
MR DRYDEN.

Sæpius in Libro memoratur Persius uno
Quam levis in tota Marsus Amazonide. MART.

ARGUMENT | OF THE | PROLOGUE | TO THE | FIRST SATYR

The Design of the Authour was to conceal his Name and Quality. He liv'd in the dangerous Times of the Tyrant Nero ; and aims particularly at him, in most of his Satyrs. For which Reason, though he was a Roman Knight, and of a plentiful Fortune, he would appear in this Prologue but a Beggarly Poet, who Writes for Bread. After this, he breaks into the Business of the first Satyr; which is chiefly to decry the Poetry then in Fashion, and the Impudence of those who were endeavouring to pass their Stuff upon the World.

PROLOGUE | TO THE | FIRST SATYR.

I NEVER did on cleft [1] *Pernassus* dream,
Nor taste the sacred *Heliconian* Stream ;
Nor can remember when my Brain inspir'd,
Was, by the Muses, into madness fir'd.
My share in Pale [2] *Pyrene* I resign ;
And claim no part in all the Mighty Nine.
Statues,[3] with winding Ivy crown'd, belong
To nobler Poets, for a nobler Song :
Heedless of Verse, and hopeless of the Crown,
Scarce half a Wit, and more than half a Clown,   10
Before the [4] Shrine I lay my rugged Numbers down.
Who taught the Parrot Human Notes to try,
Or with a Voice endu'd the chatt'ring Pye?

PERSIUS. Text from the original edition, 1693. The current texts have divers errors, the worst in V. 11.

'Twas witty Want, fierce Hunger to appease :
Want taught their Masters, and their Masters these.
Let Gain, that gilded Bait, be hung on high,
The hungry Witlings have it in their Eye ;
Pies, Crows, and Daws, Poetick Presents bring :
You say they squeak ; but they will swear they Sing.

ARGUMENT | OF THE | FIRST SATYR.

I need not repeat, that the chief aim of the Authour is against bad Poets, in this Satyr. But I must add, that he includes also bad Orators, who began at that Time (as Petronius in the beginning of his Book tells us) to enervate Manly Eloquence, by Tropes and Figures, ill plac'd, and worse apply'd. Amongst the Poets, Persius covertly strikes at Nero ; some of whose Verses he recites with Scorn and Indignation. He also takes notice of the Noblemen and their abominable Poetry, who, in the Luxury of their Fortune, set up for Wits, and Judges. The Satyr is in Dialogue, betwixt the Authour and his Friend or Monitor ; who dissuades him from this dangerous attempt of exposing Great Men. But Persius, who is of a free Spirit, and has not forgotten that Rome *was once a Commonwealth, breaks through all those difficulties, and boldly Arraigns the false Judgment of the Age in which he Lives. The Reader may observe that our Poet was a Stoick Philosopher ; and that all his Moral Sentences, both here and in all the rest of his Satyrs, are drawn from the Dogma's of that Sect.*

THE
FIRST SATYR.

*In Dialogue betwixt the Poet
and his friend or Monitor.*

PERSIUS.

How anxious are our Cares, and yet how
    vain
The bent of our desires !

FRIEND.

                    Thy Spleen contain :
For none will read thy Satyrs.

PERSIUS.

This to me ?

FRIEND.

None ; or what's next to none, but two
    or three.
'Tis hard, I grant.

PERSIUS.

'Tis nothing ; I can bear
That paltry Scriblers have the Publick Ear :
That this vast universal Fool, the Town,
Shou'd cry up [1] *Labeo's* Stuff, and cry me
    down.   10
They damn themselves ; nor will my Muse
    descend
To clap with such, who Fools and Knaves
    commend :
Their Smiles and Censures are to me the
    same :
I care not what they praise, or what they
    blame.
In full Assemblies let the Crowd prevail :
I weigh no Merit by the common Scale.
The Conscience is the Test of ev'ry Mind ;
Seek not thy self, without thy self, to find.
But where's that *Roman* ?—Somewhat I
    wou'd say,
But Fear ;—let Fear, for once, to Truth
    give way.   20
Truth lends the Stoick Courage : when I look
On Humane Acts, and read in Nature's Book,
From the first Pastimes of our Infant Age,
To elder Cares, and Man's severer Page ;
When stern as Tutors, and as Uncles hard,
We lash the Pupil, and defraud the Ward :
Then, then I say,—or wou'd say, if I durst—
But thus provok'd, I must speak out, or
    burst.

FRIEND.

Once more forbear.

PERSIUS.

I cannot rule my Spleen ;   30
My scorn Rebels, and tickles me within.
First, to begin at Home, our Authors write
In lonely Rooms, secur'd from publick sight ;
Whether in Prose, or Verse, 'tis all the same :
The Prose is Fustian, and the Numbers lame.
All Noise, and empty Pomp, a storm of
    words,
Lab'ring with sound, that little Sence affords.
They [2] Comb, and then they order ev'ry ⎫
    Hair :   ⎪
A Gown, or White, or Scour'd to whiteness, ⎬
    wear :   ⎪
A Birth-day Jewel bobbing at their Ear.   ⎭
Next, gargle well their Throats ; and thus
    prepar'd,   41
They mount, a God's Name, to be seen and
    heard,
From their high Scaffold, with a Trumpet
    Cheek,
And Ogling all their Audience e're they
    speak.
The nauseous Nobles, ev'n the Chief of *Rome*,
With gaping Mouths to these Rehearsals
    come,
And pant with Pleasure, when some lusty
    line
The Marrow pierces, and invades the Chine.
At open fulsom Bawdry they rejoice,   49
And slimy Jests applaud with broken Voice.
Base Prostitute, thus dost thou gain thy
    Bread ?
Thus dost thou feed their Ears, and thus art
    fed ?
At his own filthy stuff he grins and brays :
And gives the sign where he expects their
    praise.
    Why have I Learn'd, say'st thou, if thus
    confin'd,
I choak the Noble Vigour of my Mind ?
Know, my wild [3] Fig-Tree, which in Rocks
    is bred,
Will split the Quarry, and shoot out the
    Head.
Fine Fruits of Learning ! Old Ambitious
    Fool,   59
Dar'st thou apply that Adage of the School ;
As if 'tis nothing worth that lies conceal'd,
And *Science is not Science till Reveal'd* ?

Oh, but 'tis Brave to be Admir'd, to see
The Crowd, with pointing Fingers, cry,
    That's he :
That's he, whose wondrous Poem is become
A Lecture for the Noble Youth of *Rome* !
Who, by their Fathers, is at Feasts Re-
    nown'd ;
And often quoted, when the Bowls go round.
Full gorg'd and flush'd, they wantonly
    Rehearse ;
And add to Wine the Luxury of Verse.   70
One, clad in Purple, not to lose his time,
Eats, and recites some lamentable Rhime :
Some Senceless *Phyllis*, in a broken Note,
Snuffling at Nose, or croaking in his Throat :
Then Graciously the mellow Audience Nod :
Is not th' Immortal Authour made a God ?
Are not his Manes blest, such Praise to have ?
Lies not the Turf more lightly on his Grave ?
And Roses (while his lowd Applause they Sing)
Stand ready from his Sepulcher to spring ?
    All these, you cry, but light Objections
        are ;   81
Meer Malice, and you drive the Jest too far.
For does there Breathe a Man, who can reject
A general Fame, and his own Lines neglect ?
In ⁴ Cedar Tablets worthy to appear,
That need not Fish, or Franckincense to ⎫
    fear ?   ⎬
    Thou, whom I make the adverse part to ⎭
        bear,
Be answer'd thus : If I, by chance, succeed
In what I Write, (and that's a chance indeed;)
Know, I am not so stupid, or so hard,   90
Not to feel Praise, or Fame's deserv'd Reward:
But this I cannot grant, that thy Applause
Is my Works ultimate, or only Cause.
Prudence can ne're propose so mean a prize ;
For mark what Vanity within it lies.
Like *Labeo's* Iliads, in whose Verse is found
Nothing but trifling care, and empty sound :
Such little Elegies as Nobles Write,
Who wou'd be poets, in *Apollo's* spight.
Them and their woful Works the Muse defies:
Products of Citron ⁵ Beds and Golden
    Canopies.   101
To give thee all thy due, thou hast the⎫
    Heart   ⎪
To make a Supper, with a fine dessert ; ⎬
And to thy threed-bare Friend, a cast old⎪
    Sute impart.   ⎭

Thus Brib'd, thou thus bespeak'st him,
    Tell me Friend
(For I love Truth, nor can plain Speech
    offend,)
What says the World of me and of my Muse ?
    The Poor dare nothing tell but flatt'ring
        News :
But shall I speak ? thy Verse is wretched
    Rhyme ;
And all thy Labours are but loss of time. 110
Thy strutting Belly swells, thy Paunch is high;
Thou Writ'st not, but thou Pissest Poetry.
    All Authours to their own defects are blind;
Hadst thou but, *Janus* ⁶ like, a Face behind,
To see the people, what splay-Mouths they
    make ;
To mark their Fingers, pointed at thy back :
Their Tongues loll'd out, a foot beyond the
    pitch,
When most athirst, of an *Apulian* Bitch :
But Noble Scriblers are with Flatt'ry fed ;
For none dare find their faults, who Eat
    their Bread.   120
    To pass the Poets of Patrician Blood,
What is't the common Reader takes for good ?
The Verse in fashion is, when Numbers flow,
Soft without Sence, and without Spirit slow :
So smooth and equal, that no sight can find
The Rivet, where the polish'd piece was join'd.
So even all, with such a steady view,
As if he shut one Eye to level true.
Whether the Vulgar Vice his Satyr stings,
The Peoples Riots, or the Rage of Kings, 130
The gentle Poet is alike in all ;
His Reader hopes no rise, and fears no fall.

FRIEND.

Hourly we see some Raw Pin-feather'd
    thing
Attempt to mount, and Fights, and Heroes
    sing ;
Who, for false quantities, was whipt at School
Butt' other day, and breaking Grammar Rule,
Whose trivial Art was never try'd, above
The bare description of a Native Grove :
Who knows not how to praise the Country⎫
    store,   ⎪
The Feasts, the Baskets, nor the fatted   ⎬
    Bore ;   140 ⎪
Nor paint the flowry Fields, that paint   ⎭
    themselves before.

---

74 or] *The editors give* and   ¹⁰5 Tell] tell *1693.*

Where *Romulus* was Bred, and *Quintius* Born,
Whose shining Plough-share was in Furrows
   worn,
Met by his trembling Wife, returning Home,
And Rustically Joy'd, as Chief of *Rome*:
She wip'd the Sweat from the Dictator's ⎫
   Brow;
And o're his Back, his Robe did rudely ⎬
   throw;
The Lictors bore, in State, their Lord's ⎭
   Triumphant Plough.
Some love to hear the Fustian Poet roar;
And some on Antiquated Authours pore:
Rummage for Sense; and think those only
   good   151
Who labour most, and least are understood.
When thou shalt see the Blear-Ey'd Fathers
   teach
Their Sons, this harsh and mouldy sort of
   Speech;
Or others new affected ways to try,
Of wanton smoothness, Female Poetry;
One would enquire, from whence this motley
   Stile
Did first our *Roman* Purity defile:
For our Old Dotards cannot keep their Seat;
But leap and catch at all that's obsolete. 160
Others, by Foolish Ostentation led,
When call'd before the Bar, to save their
   Head,
Bring trifling Tropes, instead of solid Sence:
And mind their Figures more than their
   Defence,
Are pleas'd to hear their thick-scull'd
   Judges cry,
Well mov'd, oh finely said, and decently!
Theft (says th' Accuser) to thy Charge I lay,
O *Pedius*! What does gentle *Pedius* say?
Studious to please the Genius of the Times,
With Periods,[8] Points, and Tropes, he slurs
   his Crimes: 170
" He Robb'd not, but he Borrow'd from the
   Poor;
" And took but with intention to restore.
He lards with flourishes his long Harangue;
'Tis fine, say'st thou; What, to be Prais'd
   and Hang?
Effeminate *Roman*, shall such Stuff prevail
To tickle thee, and make thee wag thy Tail?
Say, shou'd a Shipwrack'd Saylor sing his woe,
Wou'dst thou be mov'd to pity, or bestow

An Alms? What's more prepost'rous than
   to see
A Merry Beggar? Mirth in misery?   180

PERSIUS.

He seems a Trap, for Charity, to lay:
And cons, by Night, his Lesson for the day.

FRIEND.

But to raw Numbers, and unfinished Verse,
Sweet sound is added now, to make it Terse:
" 'Tis tagg'd with Rhyme, like [9]*Berecynthian*
   Atys,
" The mid part chimes with Art, which never
   flat is.
" The Dolphin brave, that cut the liquid
   Wave,
" Or He who in his line, can chine the long-
   rib'd *Apennine*.

PERSIUS.

All this is Dogrel Stuff:

FRIEND.

What if I bring   190
A Nobler Verse? *Arms and the Man*[10] *I sing*.

PERSIUS.

Why name you *Virgil* with such Fops as
   these?
He's truly great, and must for ever please.
Not fierce, but awful is his Manly Page;
Bold is his Strength, but sober is his Rage.

FRIEND.

What Poems think you soft? and to be
   read
With languishing regards, and bending Head?

PERSIUS.

" Their crooked Horns [11] the *Mimallonian*
   Crew
" With Blasts inspir'd; and *Bassaris* who
   slew
" The scornful Calf, with Sword advanc'd on
   high,   200
" Made from his Neck his haughty Head to
   fly.
" And *Mænas*, when with Ivy-bridles ⎫
   bound,
" She led the spotted Lynx, then *Evion* ⎬
   rung around;
" *Evion* from Woods and Floods repair- ⎭
   ing Ecchos sound.

---

174 What, to] what to *1693*.
DR·   U

187 cut] *Editors give* cuts

Cou'd such rude Lines a *Roman* Mouth
become,
Were any Manly Greatness left in *Rome*?
Mænas[12] and *Atys* in the Mouth were bred;
And never hatch'd within the lab'ring Head:
No Blood, from bitten Nails, those Poems
drew:
But churn'd, like Spettle, from the Lips
they flew.   210

FRIEND.

'Tis Fustian all; 'tis execrably bad:
But if they will be Fools, must you be mad?
Your Satyrs, let me tell you, are too fierce;
The Great will never bear so blunt a Verse.
Their Doors are barr'd against a bitter flout:
Snarl, if you please, but you shall snarl
without.
Expect such Pay as railing Rhymes deserve,
Y'are in a very hopeful way to sterve.

PERSIUS.

Rather than so, uncensur'd let 'em be
All, all is admirably well, for me.   220
My harmless Rhyme shall scape the dire
disgrace
Of Common-shores, and ev'ry pissing-place.
Two [13] painted Serpents shall, on high,
appear;
'Tis Holy Ground; you must not Urine here.
This shall be writ to fright the Fry away,
Who draw their little Bawbles, when they
play.
[14] Yet old *Lucilius* never fear'd the times,
But lash'd the City, and dissected Crimes.
Mutius and *Lupus* both by Name he brought;
He mouth'd em, and betwixt his Grinders
caught.   230
Unlike in method, with conceal'd design,
Did crafty *Horace* his low Numbers joyn:
And, with a sly insinuating Grace,
Laugh'd at his Friend, and look'd him in
the Face:
Would raise a Blush, where secret Vice he
found;
And tickle, while he gently prob'd the
Wound.
With seeming Innocence the Crowd beguil'd;
But made the desperate Passes, when he
smil'd.
Could he do this, and is my Muse con-
troll'd

By Servile Awe? Born free, and not be
bold?   240
At least, I'll dig a hole within the Ground;
And to the trusty Earth commit the sound:
The Reeds shall tell you what the poet Fears,
King [15] Midas *has a Snout, and Asses Ears.*
This mean conceit, this darling Mystery,
Which thou think'st nothing, Friend, thou
shalt not buy,
Nor will I change, for all the flashy Wit,
That flatt'ring *Labeo* in his Iliads writ.

Thou, if there be a thou, in this base Town,
Who dares, with angry *Eupolis*,[16] to frown;
He, who, with bold *Cratinus*, is inspir'd   251
With Zeal, and equal Indignation fir'd;
Who, at enormous Villany, turns pale,
And steers against it with a full-blown Sail,
Like *Aristophanes*; let him but smile
On this my honest Work, tho writ in
homely Stile:
And if two Lines or three in all the Vein
Appear less drossy, read those Lines again.
May they perform their Author's just Intent,
Glow in thy Ears, and in thy Breast fer-
ment.   260
But from the reading of my Book and me,
Be far ye Foes of Virtuous Poverty:
Who [17] Fortune's fault upon the Poor can
throw;
Point at the tatter'd Coat, and ragged Shooe:
Lay Nature's failings to their Charge, and
jeer
The dim week Eye-sight, when the Mind
is clear.
When thou thy self, thus insolent in State,
Art but, perhaps, some Country Magistrate;
Whose Pow'r extends no farther than to
speak
Big on the Bench, and scanty Weights to
break.   270
Him, also, for my Censor I disdain,
Who thinks all Science, as all Virtue vain;
Who counts Geometry, and Numbers, Toys;
And [18] with his Foot the Sacred Dust
destroys:
Whose Pleasure is to see a Strumpet tear
A Cynicks Beard, and lug him by the Hair.
Such, all the Morning, to the Pleadings run;⎱
But when the Bus'ness of the Day is done, ⎰
On Dice, and Drink, and Drabs, they spend⎱
their Afternoon.   ⎰

EXPLANATORY NOTES.

PROLOGUE.

[1] *Pernassus*, and *Helicon*, were Hills Consecrated to the Muses; and the suppos'd place of their abode. *Pernassus* was forked on the top; and from *Helicon* ran a Stream; the Spring of which was call'd the Muses Well.

[2] *Pyrene*, a Fountain in Corinth; Consecrated also to the Muses.

[3] Statues, &c. The Statues of the Poets were Crown'd with Ivy about their Brows.

[4] Before the Shrine; that is, before the Shrine of *Apollo*, in his Temple at *Rome*, call'd the *Palatine.*

THE FIRST SATYR

[1] *Labeo's* Stuff. Nothing is remaining of *Atticus Labeo* (so he is call'd by the Learned *Casaubon*). Nor is he mention'd by any other Poet besides *Persius*: *Casaubon* from an old Commentator on *Persius* says that he made a very Foolish Translation of *Homer's Iliads.*

[2] *They Comb*, &c. He describes a Poet preparing himself to Rehearse his Works in Publick: which was commonly perform'd in *August.* A Room was hir'd or lent by some Friend: a Scaffold was rais'd and a Pulpit plac'd for him, who was to hold forth; who borrow'd a new Gown or scour'd his old one; and Adorn'd his Ears with Jewels, &c.

[3] *My wild Fig-Tree*: Trees of that kind grow wild in many parts of *Italy*, and make their way through Rocks: Sometimes splitting the Tombstones.

[4] The *Romans* wrote on Cedar, and Cypress Tables, in regard of the duration of the Wood: Ill Verses might justly be afraid of Franckincense; for the Papers in which they were Written were fit for nothing but to wrap it up.

[5] *Products of Citron Beds*, &c. Writings of Noblemen, whose Bedsteds were of the Wood of *Citron.*

[6] *Janus like*, &c. *Janus* was the first King of *Italy*; who refug'd *Saturn*, when he was expell'd by his Son *Jupiter* from *Creet*; (or as we now call it *Candia*.) From his Name the first Month of the Year is call'd *January.* He was Pictur'd with two Faces, one before, and one behind; as regarding the past time and the future. Some of the Mythologists think he was *Noah*, for the Reason given above.

[7] *Where Romulus*, &c. He speaks of the Country in the foregoing Verses, the Praises of which are the most easie Theme for Poets, but

which a bad Poet cannot Naturally describe. Then he makes a digression to *Romulus*, the first King of *Rome*, who had a Rustical Education, and enlarges upon *Quintius Cincinnatus*, a *Roman* Senator, who was call'd from the Plough to be Dictator of *Rome.*

[8] *In Periods*, &c. *Persius* here names Antitheses, or seeming Contradictions: which in this place are meant for Rhetorical flourishes, as I think, with *Casaubon.*

[9] *Berecynthian Atys; or Attin*, &c. Foolish Verses of *Nero*, which the Poet repeats; and which cannot be Translated properly into *English.*

[10] *Arms and the Man*, &c. The first line of *Virgil's* Æneids.

[11] *Their Crooked Horns*, &c. Other Verses of *Nero* that were meer bombast: I only Note that the Repetition of these and the former Verses of *Nero* might justly give the Poet a caution to conceal his Name.

[12] *Mænas* and *Atys.* Poems on the *Mænades*, who were Priestesses of *Bacchus*; and of *Atys*, who made himself an Eunuch, to attend on the Sacrifices of *Cybele*, call'd *Berecynthia* by the Poets: she was Mother of the Gods.

[13] *Two Painted Serpents*, &c. Two Snakes twin'd with each other were painted on the Walls by the Ancients, to shew the place was Holy.

[14] *Yet old* Lucilius, &c. *Lucilius* wrote long before *Horace*, who imitates his manner of Satyr, but far excels him, in the design.

[15] *King* Midas, &c. The Story is vulgar, that *Midas*, King of *Phrygia*, was made judge betwixt *Apollo* and *Pan*, who was the best Musician; he gave the Prize to *Pan*; and *Apollo* in revenge gave him Asses Ears. He wore his Hair long to hide them; but his Barber discovering them, and not daring to divulge the secret, dug a hole in the ground, and whisper'd into it: the place was marshy, and when the Reeds grew up, they repeated the words which were spoken by the Barber. By *Midas* the Poet meant *Nero.*

[16] *Eupolis* and *Cratinus*, as also *Aristophanes*, mention'd afterwards, were all *Athenian* Poets, who wrote that sort of Comedy, which was call'd the old Comedy, where the People were Nam'd, who were Satyriz'd by those Authors.

[17] *Who Fortunes fault*, &c. The People of *Rome* in the time of *Persius* were apt to scorn the *Grecian* Philosophers, particularly the Cinicks and Stoicks, who were the poorest of them.

[18] *And with his foot*, &c. Arithmetick and Geometry were Taught on floors which were strew'd with dust or sand, in which the Numbers and Diagrams were made and drawn, which they might strike out again at Pleasure.

THE
SECOND SATYR

Dedicated to his Friend PLOTIUS | MACRINUS, *on his Birth-day.*

THE ARGUMENT.

This Satyr contains a most Grave, and Philosophical Argument, concerning Prayers and Wishes. Undoubtedly it gave occasion to Juvenal's *Tenth Satyr ; And both of them had their Original from one of* Plato's *dialogues, called the second* Alcibiades. *Our Author has induc'd it with great mastery of Art, by taking his rise from the Birth-day of his Friend ; on which occasions, Prayers were made, and sacrifices offer'd to the Native.* Persius *commending the Purity of his Friend's Vows, descends to the Impious and Immoral Requests of others. The Satyr is divided into three parts. The first is the Exordium to* Macrinus, *which the Poet confines within the compass of four Verses. The second relates to the matter of the Prayers and Vows, and an enumeration of those things, wherein Men commonly Sinn'd against right Reason, and Offended in their Requests. The Third part consists in shewing the repugnancies of those Prayers and Wishes, to those of other Men, and inconsistencies, with themselves. He shews the Original of these Vows, and sharply inveighs against them : and Lastly, not only corrects the false Opinion of Mankind concerning them, but gives the True Doctrine of all Addresses made to Heaven, and how they may be made acceptable to the Pow'rs above, in excellent Precepts, and more worthy of a Christian than a Heathen.*

LET this auspicious Morning be exprest
With a white [1]Stone, distinguish'd from the
    rest :
White as thy Fame, and as thy Honour
    clear ;
And let new Joys attend on thy new added
    year.
Indulge thy Genius, and o'reflow thy Soul,
Till thy Wit sparkle, like the chearful Bowl.
Pray ; for thy Pray'rs the Test of Heav'n
    will bear ;
Nor need'st thou take the Gods aside, to
    hear :

While others, ev'n the Mighty Men of *Rome*,
Big swell'd with Mischief, to the Temples
    come ;   10
And in low Murmurs, and with costly Smoak,
Heav'n's Help, to prosper their black Vows,
    invoke.
So boldly to the Gods Mankind reveal,
What from each other they, for shame, con-
    ceal.
    Give me Good Fame, ye Pow'rs, and make
    me Just :
Thus much the Rogue to Publick Ears will
    trust :
In private then :—When wilt thou, mighty
    Jove,
My Wealthy Uncle from this World remove ?
Or—O thou Thund'rer's son, great [2]*Hercules*,
That once thy bounteous Deity wou'd
    please   20
To guide my Rake, upon the chinking sound
Of some vast Treasure, hidden under-
    ground !
    O were my Pupil fairly knock'd o' th'
    head ;
I should possess th' Estate, if he were dead !
He's so far gone with Rickets, and with th'
    Evil,
That one small Dose wou'd send him to
    the Devil.
    This is my Neighbour *Nerius* his third
    Spouse,
Of whom in happy time he rids his House.
But my Eternal Wife!—Grant Heav'n I may
Survive to see the Fellow of his Day !   30
Thus, that thou may'st the better bring
    about
Thy Wishes, thou art wickedly devout :
In *Tiber* ducking thrice, by break of day,
To wash th' Obscenities of [3]Night away.
But prithee tell me, ('tis a small Request)
With what ill thoughts of *Jove* art thou
    possest ?
Wou'dst thou prefer him to some Man ?
    Suppose
I dip'd among the worst, and *Staius* chose ?

---

30 his] *Some editors wrongly give this*

Which of the two wou'd thy wise Head declare
The trustier Tutor to an Orphan Heir ? 40
Or, put it thus :—Unfold to *Staius*, straight,
What to *Jove's* Ear thou didst impart of late :
He'll stare, and, O Good *Jupiter* ! will cry ;
Can'st thou indulge him in this Villany ?
And think'st thou, *Jove* himself, with patience, then,
Can hear a Pray'r condemn'd by wicked men ?
That, void of Care, he lolls supine in state,
And leaves his Bus'ness to be done by Fate ?
Because his Thunder splits some burly Tree,
And is not darted at thy House and Thee ?
Or that his Vengeance falls not at the time, 51
Just at the Perpetration of thy Crime ;
And makes Thee a sad Object of our Eyes,
Fit for *Ergenna's* Pray'r and Sacrifice ?
What well-fed Off'ring to appease the God,
What pow'rful Present to procure a Nod,
Hast thou in store ? What Bribe hast thou prepar'd,
To pull him, thus unpunish'd, by the Beard?
Our Superstitions with our life begin :
Th' Obscene old Grandam, or the next of Kin, 60
The New-born Infant from the Cradle takes,
And first of Spettle a Lustration makes :
Then in the Spawl her Middle Finger dips,
Anoints the Temples, Forehead, and the Lips,
Pretending force of Witchcraft to prevent,
By virtue of her nasty Excrement.
Then dandles him with many a mutter'd Pray'r,
That Heav'n wou'd make him some rich Miser's Heir,
Lucky to Ladies, and, in time, a King,
Which to insure, she adds a length of Navel-string. 70
But no fond Nurse is fit to make a Pray'r :
And *Jove*, if *Jove* be wise, will never hear ;
Not tho' she prays in white, with lifted hands :
A Body made of Brass the Crone demands
For her lov'd Nurseling, strung with Nerves of Wire,
Tough to the last, and with no toil to tire :

---

65 Witchcraft] *The editors strangely give*
Magic

Unconscionable Vows ! which when we use,
We teach the Gods, in Reason, to refuse.
Suppose They were indulgent to thy Wish :
Yet the fat Entrails, in the spatious Dish, 80
Wou'd stop the Grant : The very overcare,
And nauseous pomp, wou'd hinder half the Pray'r.
Thou hop'st with Sacrifice of Oxen slain
To compass Wealth, and bribe the God of Gain,
To give thee Flocks and Herds, with large increase ;
Fool ! to expect 'em from a Bullock's Grease !
And think'st, that when the fatten'd Flames aspire,
Thou seest th' accomplishment of thy desire !
Now, now, my bearded Harvest gilds the plain,
The scanty Folds can scarce my Sheep contain, 90
And show'rs of Gold come pouring in amain !
Thus dreams the Wretch, and vainly thus dreams on,
Till his lank Purse declares his Money gone.
Shou'd I present thee with rare figur'd Plate,
Or Gold as rich in Workmanship as Weight ;
O how thy rising heart wou'd throb and beat,
And thy left side, with trembling pleasure, sweat !
Thou measur'st by thy self the Pow'rs Divine ;
Thy Gods are burnish'd Gold, and Silver is their Shrine.
Thy puny Godlings of inferior Race, 100
Whose humble Statues are content with Brass,
Should some of These, in Visions purg'd from fleam,
Foretel Events, or in a Morning Dream ;
Ev'n those thou wou'dst in Veneration hold ;
And, if not Faces, give 'em Beards of Gold.
The Priests, in Temples, now no longer care
For *Saturn's* Brass, or *Numa's* Earthen-ware ;
Or Vestal Urns, in each Religious Rite :
This wicked Gold has put 'em all to flight.
O Souls, in whom no heav'nly Fire is found, 110
Fat Minds, and ever groveling on the ground !
We bring our Manners to the blest Abodes,

And think what pleases us, must please the Gods.
Of Oyl and *Casia* one th' Ingredients takes,
And, of the Mixture, a rich Ointment makes :
Another finds the way to dye in Grain :
And make ⁹ *Calabrian* Wool receive the *Tyrian* Stain :
Or from the Shells their Orient Treasure takes,
Or, for their golden Ore, in Rivers rakes ;
Then melts the Mass : All these are Vanities ! 120
Yet still some Profit from their Pains may rise :
But tell me, Priest, if I may be so bold,
What are the Gods the better for this Gold ?

The Wretch that offers from his wealthy Store
These Presents, bribes the Pow'rs to give him more :
As maids ¹⁰ to *Venus* offer Baby-Toys,
To bless the Marriage-Bed with Girls and Boys.
But let us for the Gods a Gift prepare,
Which the Great Man's great Chargers cannot bear :
A Soul, where Laws both Humane and Divine, 130
In Practice more than Speculation shine :
A genuine Virtue, of a vigorous kind,
Pure in the last recesses of the Mind :
When with such Off'rings to the Gods I come,
A ¹¹ Cake, thus giv'n, is worth a Hecatomb.

The End of the Second Satyr.

NOTES TO THE SECOND SATYR.

¹ *White Stone.* The *Romans* were us'd to mark their Fortunate Days, or any thing that luckily befell 'em, with a White Stone which they had from the Island *Creta* ; and their Unfortunate with a Coal.

² *Hercules* was thought to have the Key and Power of bestowing all hidden Treasure.

³ The Antients thought themselves tainted and polluted by Night it self, as well as bad Dreams in the Night, and therefore purifi'd themselves by washing their Heads and Hands every Morning ; which Custom the *Turks* observe to this day.

⁴ When any one was Thunderstruck, the Soothsayer (who is here call'd *Ergenna*) immediately repair'd to the place to expiate the displeasure of the Gods, by sacrificing two Sheep.

⁵ The Poet laughs at the superstitious Ceremonies, which the Old Women made use of in their Lustration or Purification Days, when they nam'd their Children, which was done on the Eighth day to Females and on the Ninth to Males.

⁶ *In Visions purg'd from Fleam,* &c. It was the Opinion both of *Grecians* and *Romans* that the Gods, in Visions or Dreams, often reveal'd to their Favourites a Cure for their Diseases, and sometimes those of others. Thus *Alexander* dreamt of an Herb which cur'd *Ptolomy.* These Gods were principally *Apollo* and *Esculapius* ; but, in after times, the same Virtue and Good-will was attributed to *Isis* and *Osiris.* Which brings to my remembrance an odd passage in Sir *Tho. Brown's Religio Medici,* or in his vulgar Errours ; the sense whereof is, *That we are beholding, for many of our Discoveries in Physick, to the courteous Revelation of Spirits.* By the Expression of *Visions purg'd from Phlegm* our Author means such Dreams or Visions as proceed not from Natural Causes, or Humours of the Body ; but such as are sent from Heaven, and are therefore certain Remedies.

⁷ *For Saturn's Brass,* &c. Brazen Vessels, in which the Publick Treasure of the *Romans* was kept. It may be the Poet means only old Vessels which were all call'd Κρόνια, from the Greek Name of *Saturn.* Note also that the *Roman* Treasury was in the Temple of *Saturn.*

⁸ *Numa's Earthen-ware.* Under *Numa,* the second King of *Rome,* and for a long time after him, the Holy Vessels for Sacrifice were of Earthen Ware : according to the Superstitious Rites, which were introduc'd by the same *Numa* : Tho' afterwards, when *Memmius* had taken *Corinth,* and *Paulus Æmilius* had conquer'd *Macedonia,* Luxury began amongst the *Romans,* and then their Utensils of Devotion were of Gold and Silver, &c.

⁹ *And make* Calabrian *Wooll,* &c. The Wooll of Calabria was of the finest sort in *Italy,* as *Juvenal* also tells us. The *Tyrian Stain* is the Purple Colour dy'd at *Tyrus,* and I suppose, but dare not positively affirm, that the richest of that Dye was nearest our Crimson, and not Scarlet, or that other Colour more approaching to the Blue. I have not room to justifie my Conjecture.

¹⁰ *As maids to* Venus, &c. Those *Baby-Toys* were little Babies, or Poppets, as we call them ; in Latin *Pupæ* ; which the girls, when they came to the Age of puberty, or Child-bearing, offer'd to *Venus* ; as the Boys at Fourteen or Fifteen years of age offer'd their *Bullæ,* or Bosses.

¹¹ *A Cake thus given,* &c. A Cake of Barley, or course Wheat-meal, with the Bran in it : The meaning is that God is pleas'd with the pure and spotless heart of the Offerer ; and not with the Riches of the offering. *Laberius* in the Fragments of his *Mimes* has a Verse like this : *Puras Deus, non plenas, aspicit Manus.*—What I had forgotten before, in its due place, I must here tell the Reader : That the first half of this Satyr was translated by one of my Sons, now in Italy : But I thought so well of it, that I let it pass without any Alteration.

7 Treasure] Treasures 1700.

THE THIRD SATYR.

ARGUMENT | OF THE | THIRD SATYR.

Our Author has made two Satyrs concerning Study; the First and the Third: the First related to Men; This to Young Students, whom he desir'd to be educated in the Stoick Philosophy: He himself sustains the Person of the Master, or Præceptor, in this admirable Satyr. Where he upbraids the Youth of Sloth, and Negligence in learning. Yet he begins with one Scholar reproaching his Fellow Students with late rising to their Books. After which he takes upon him the other part, of the Teacher. And addressing himself particularly to Young Noblemen, tells them, That, by reason of their High Birth, and the Great Possessions of their Fathers, they are careless of adorning their Minds with Precepts of Moral Philosophy: And withall, inculcates to them the Miseries which will attend them in the whole Course of their Life, if they do not apply themselves betimes to the Knowledge of Virtue, and the End of their Creation, which he pathetically insinuates to them. The Title of this satyr, in some Ancient Manuscripts, was The Reproach of Idleness; tho in others of the Scholiasts 'tis inscribed, Against the Luxury and Vices of the Rich. In both of which the Intention of the Poet is pursued; but principally in the former.

I remember I translated this Satyr, when I was a *Kings-Scholar* at *Westminster* School, for a *Thursday* Nights *Exercise*; and believe that it, and many other of my *Exercises* of this nature, in *English Verse*, are still in the hands of my *Learned Master*, the Reverend Doctor *Busby*.

THE THIRD SATYR

Is this thy daily course? The glaring Sun ⎫
Breaks in at ev'ry Chink: The Cattle run ⎬
To Shades, and Noon-tide Rays of Summer ⎭
  shun.
Yet plung d in Sloth we lye; and snore supine,
As fill d with Fumes of undigested Wine.
  This grave Advice some sober Student
    bears;
And loudly rings it in his Fellows Ears.

The yawning Youth, scarce half awake, essays
His lazy Limbs and dozy Head to raise:
Then rubs his gummy Eyes, and scrubs his
  Pate;   10
And cries I thought it had not been so late:
My Cloaths; make haste: why when! if
  none be near,
He mutters first, and then begins to swear:
And brays aloud, with a more clam'rous note,
Than an *Arcadian* Ass can stretch his throat.
  With much ado, his Book before him laid,
And ¹ Parchment with the smoother side
  display'd;
He takes the Papers; lays 'em down agen;
And, with unwilling Fingers, tries the Pen:
Some peevish quarrel straight he strives to
  pick,   20
His Quill writes double, or his Ink's too
  thick;
Infuse more water; now 'tis grown so thin
It sinks, nor can the Character be seen.
O Wretch, and still more wretched ev'ry
  day!
Are Mortals born to sleep their lives away?
Go back to what thy Infancy began,
Thou who wert never meant to be a Man:
Eat Pap and Spoon-meat; for thy Guwgaws
  cry:
Be sullen, and refuse the Lullaby.
No more accuse thy Pen: but charge the
  Crime   30
On Native Sloth, and negligence of time.
Think'st thou thy Master, or thy Friends,
  to cheat?
Fool, 'tis thy self, and that's a worse deceit.
Beware the publick Laughter of the Town;
Thou spring'st a Leak already in thy Crown.
A flaw is in thy ill-bak'd Vessel found;
'Tis hollow, and returns a jarring sound.
  Yet, thy moist Clay is pliant to Command;
Unwrought, and easie to the Potter's hand:
Now take the Mold; now bend thy Mind
  to feel   40
The first sharp Motions of the Forming
  Wheel.
  But thou hast Land; a Country Seat,
    secure
By a just Title; costly Furniture;
A ² Fuming-Pan thy *Lares* to appease:
What need of Learning when a Man's at ease?

If this be not enough to swell thy Soul,
Then please thy Pride, and search the Herald's Roll,
Where thou shalt find thy famous Pedigree
Drawn [3] from the Root of some old *Thuscan* Tree ;
And thou, a Thousand off, a Fool of long Degree ;   50
Who, clad in [4] Purple, canst thy Censor greet;
And, loudly, call him Cousin, in the Street.
  Such Pageantry be to the People shown ;
There boast thy Horse's Trappings, and thy own :
I know thee to thy Bottom ; from within
Thy shallow Centre, to thy outmost Skin :
Dost thou not blush to live so like a Beast,
So trim, so dissolute, so loosely drest ?
  But 'tis in vain : The Wretch is drench'd too deep ;
His Soul is stupid, and his Heart asleep ;   60
Fatten'd in Vice ; so callous, and so gross,
He sins, and sees not ; senseless of his Loss.
Down goes the Wretch at once, unskill'd to swim,
Hopeless to bubble up, and reach the Water's Brim.
  Great Father of the Gods, when, for our Crimes,
Thou send'st some heavy Judgment on the Times ;
Some Tyrant-King, the Terrour of his Age,
The Type, and true Vicegerent of thy Rage ;
Thus punish him : Set Virtue in his Sight,
With all her Charms adorn'd ; with all her Graces bright :   70
But set her distant, make him pale to see
His Gains out-weigh'd by lost Felicity !
  Sicilian [5] Tortures and the Brazen Bull,
Are Emblems, rather than express the Full
Of what he feels : Yet what he fears, is more :
The [6] Wretch, who sitting at his plenteous Board,
Look'd up, and view'd on high the pointed Sword
Hang o'er his Head, and hanging by a Twine,
Did with less Dread, and more securely Dine.
Ev'n in his Sleep he starts, and fears the Knife,   80
And, trembling, in his Arms, takes his Accomplice Wife :
Down, down he goes ; and from his Darling-Friend
Conceals the Woes his guilty Dreams portend.

When I was young, I, like a lazy Fool,
Wou'd blear my Eyes with Oyl to stay from School :
Averse from Pains, and loath to learn the Part
Of *Cato*, dying with a dauntless Heart :
Though much my Master that stern Virtue prais'd,
Which, o'er the Vanquisher, the Vanquish'd rais'd ;
And my pleas'd Father came, with Pride, to see   90
His Boy defend the *Roman* Liberty.
  But then my Study was to Cog the Dice,
And dext'rously to throw the lucky Sice :
To shun Ames-Ace, that swept my Stakes away ;
And watch the Box, for fear they shou'd convey
False Bones, and put upon me in the Play.
Careful, besides, the Whirling Top to whip,
And drive her giddy, till she fell asleep.
  Thy Years are ripe, nor art thou yet to learn
What's Good or Ill, and both their Ends discern :   100
Thou,[7] in the Stoick Porch, severely bred,
Hast heard the *Dogma's* of great *Zeno* read :
Where on the Walls, by [8] *Polignotus* Hand,
The Conquer'd *Medians* in Trunk-Breeches stand :
Where the Shorn Youth to Midnight-Lectures rise,
Rous'd from their Slumbers, to be early wise :
Where the coarse Cake, and homely Husks of Beans,
From pamp'ring Riot the young Stomach weans :
And [9] where the *Samian* Y directs thy Steps to run
To Virtue's Narrow Steep, and Broad-way Vice to shun.   110
And yet thou snor'st ; thou draw'st thy Drunken Breath,
Sour with Debauch ; and sleep'st the Sleep of Death.
Thy Chaps are fallen, and thy Frame disjoyn'd :
Thy Body as dissolv'd as is thy Mind.
  Hast thou not, yet, propos'd some certain End,
To which thy Life, thy ev'ry Act may tend ?

---

103 Where] *Some editors wrongly give* There

Hast thou no Mark, at which to bend thy Bow?
Or like a Boy pursu'st the Carrion Crow
With Pellets, and with Stones from Tree to
    Tree :
A fruitless Toil, and livest *Extempore* ?   120
    Watch the Disease in time : For, when
        within
The Dropsy rages, and extends the Skin,
In vain for *Hellebore* the patient Cries,
And Fees the Doctor ; but too late is wise :
Too late, for Cure, he proffers half his
    Wealth :
Conquest and *Guibbons* cannot give him
    Health.
    Learn Wretches ; learn the Motions of ⎞
        the Mind,   ⎟
Why you were made, for what you were ⎬
    design'd ;   ⎟
And the great Moral End of Humane Kind. ⎠
Study thy self, What Rank, or what degree
The wise Creator has ordain'd for thee :   131
And all the Offices of that Estate
Perform ; and with thy Prudence guide thy
    Fate.
    Pray justly, to be heard : Nor more desire
Than what the Decencies of Life require.
Learn what thou ow'st thy Country, and thy
    Friend ;
What's requisite to spare, and what to spend :
Learn this ; and after, envy not the store
Of the Greaz'd Advocate, that Grinds the
    Poor :
Fat [10] Fees from the defended *Umbrian*
    draws ;   140
And only gains the wealthy Clients Cause ;
To whom the [11] *Marsians* more Provision send,
Than he and all his Family can spend.
Gammons, that give a relish to the taste,
And potted Fowl, and Fish come in so fast,
That, e're the first is out, the second stinks :
And mouldy Mother gathers on the brinks.
    But, here, some Captain of the Land, or
        Fleet,
Stout of his hands, but of a Souldiers Wit :
Cries, I have sense to serve my turn, in store ;
And he's a Rascal who pretends to more.
Dammee, what-e're those Book-learn'd
    Blockheads say,   152
Solon's the veriest Fool in all the Play.
Top-heavy Drones, and always looking down
(As over-Ballasted within the Crown !)
Mutt'ring, betwixt their Lips, some Mystick
    thing,

Which, well examin'd, is flat Conjuring,
Mere Madmen's Dreams : For, what the ⎞
    Schools have taught   ⎟
Is only this, that nothing can be brought ⎬
From nothing ; and what is, can ne're ⎟
    be turn'd to nought.   160 ⎠
Is it for this they study ? to grow pale,
And miss the Pleasures of a Glorious Meal ?
For this, in Rags accouter'd, they are seen,
And made the May-game of the publick
    spleen ?
    Proceed, my Friend, and rail : But hear
        me tell
A story, which is just thy Parallel.
    A Spark, like thee, of the Man-killing Trade,
Fell sick ; and thus to his Physician said :
Methinks I am not right in ev'ry part ;
I feel a kind of trembling at my Heart :   170
My Pulse unequal, and my Breath is strong :
Besides, a filthy Fur upon my Tongue.
The Doctor heard him, exercis'd his skill :
And, after, bad him for four Days be still.
Three Days he took good Counsel, and began
To mend, and look like a recov'ring Man :
The fourth he cou'd not hold from Drink ;
    but sends
His Boy to one of his old trusty Friends :
Adjuring him, by all the Pow'rs Divine, ⎞
To pity his Distress, who cou'd not Dine ⎬
Without a Flaggon of his healing Wine. ⎠
He drinks a swilling Draught : And, lin'd
    within,   182
Will supple, in the Bath, his outward skin :
Whom shou'd he find, but his Physician there,
Who, wisely, bad him once again beware.
Sir, you look Wan, you hardly draw your
    Breath ;
Drinking is Dangerous, and the Bath is Death :
'Tis Nothing, says the Fool : But, says the
    friend,
This Nothing, Sir, will bring you to your end.
Do I not see your Dropsy-Belly swell ?   190
Your yellow Skin ?—No more of that ; I'm
    well.
I have already Buried two or three ⎞
That stood betwixt a fair Estate and me, ⎬
And, Doctor, I may live to Bury thee. ⎠
Thou tell'st me, I look ill ; and thou look'st
    worse.
I've done, says the Physician ; take your
    Course.

---

188 But] but *1693*.

The laughing Sot, like all unthinking Men,
Baths and gets Drunk; then Baths and
Drinks again:
His Throat half throtled with Corrupted
Fleam,
And breathing through his Jaws a belching
steam: 200
Amidst his Cups with fainting shiv'ring
seiz'd,
His Limbs dis-jointed, and all o're diseas'd,
His hand refuses to sustain the bowl:
And his Teeth chatter, and his Eye-balls
rowl:
Till, with his Meat, he vomits out his Soul:
Then, Trumpets, Torches, and a tedious Crew
Of Hireling Mourners, for his Funeral due.
Our Dear departed Brother lies in State,
His Heels [12] stretch'd out, and pointing to
the Gate:
And Slaves, now manumis'd, on their dead
Master wait.   210
They hoyst him on the Bier, and deal the
Dole;
And there's an end of a Luxurious Fool.
  But, what's thy fulsom Parable to me?
My Body is from all Diseases free:
My temperate Pulse does regularly beat;
Feel, and be satisfi'd, my Hands and Feet:
These are not cold, nor those Opprest with
heat.
Or lay thy hand upon my Naked Heart,
And thou shalt find me Hale in ev'ry part.

I grant this true: But, still, the deadly
wound   220
Is in thy Soul; 'Tis there thou art not sound.
Say, when thou seest a heap of tempting
Gold,
Or a more tempting Harlot do'st behold;
Then, when she casts on thee a side-long
glance,
Then try thy Heart; and tell me if it Dance.
  Some Course cold Salade is before thee
set;
Bread, with the Bran perhaps, and broken
Meat;
Fall on, and try thy Appetite to eat.
These are not Dishes for thy dainty Tooth:
What, hast thou got an Ulcer in thy Mouth?
Why stand'st thou picking? Is thy Pallat
sore?   231
That Bete, and Radishes will make thee roar?
Such is th' unequal Temper of thy Mind;
Thy Passions in extreams, and unconfin'd:
Thy Hair so bristles with unmanly Fears,
As Fields of Corn, that rise in bearded Ears.
And, when thy Cheeks with flushing Fury
glow,
The rage of boyling Caldrons is more slow;
When fed with fuel and with flames below.
With foam upon thy Lips, and sparkling
Eyes,   240
Thou say'st and do'st in such outrageous wise:
That mad Orestes,[13] if he saw the show,
Wou'd swear thou wert the Madder of the Two.

The End of the Third Satyr.

NOTES TO THE THIRD SATYR.

[1] *And Parchment*, &c. The Students us'd to write their Notes on Parchments; the inside, on which they wrote, was white; the other side was Hairy, and commonly Yellow. *Quintilian* re-proves this Custom, and advises rather Table-books, lin'd with Wax, and a Stile, like that we use in our Vellum Table-books, as more easie.

[2] *A Fuming-Pan*, &c. Before eating, it was Customary, to cut off some part of the Meat, which was first put into a Pan, or little Dish; then into the Fire; as an Offering to the Household Gods; this they called a *Libation.*

[3] *Drawn from the Root*, &c. The *Thuscans* were accounted of most Ancient Nobility. *Horace* observes this in most of his compliments to *Mecenas*, who was deriv'd from the Old Kings of *Tuscany*, now the Dominion of the Great Duke.

[4] *Who Clad in Purple*, &c. The Roman Knights, attir'd in the Robe call'd *Trabea*, were

2 Fuming] Fumeing *1693.*

summon'd by the Censor to appear before him, and to salute him in passing by, as their Names were call'd over. They led their Horses in their hand. See more of this in *Pompey's* Life written by *Plutarch.*

[5] *Sicilian Tortures*, &c. Some of the *Sicilian* Kings were so great tyrants, that the Name is become Proverbial. The Brazen Bull is a known Story of *Phalaris*, one of those Tyrants; who when *Perillus*, a famous Artist, had presented him with a Bull of that Metal hollow'd within, which, when the Condemn'd Person was inclos'd in it, wou'd render th' sound of a Bull's roaring, caus'd the Workman to make the first Experiment. *Docuitq; suum mugire Juvencum.*

[6] *The Wretch, who sitting*, &c. He alludes to the Story of *Damocles*, a Flatterer of one of those *Sicilian* Tyrants, namely *Dionysius. Damocles* had infinitely extoll'd the Happiness of Kings. *Dionysius*, to convince him of the contrary, invited him to a Feast, and cloath'd him in

Purple; But caus'd a Sword with the point downward, to be hung over his Head, by a Silken Twine; which when he perceiv'd, he cou'd Eat nothing of the Delicates that were set before him.

[7] *Thou, in the Stoick Porch,* &c. The Stoicks taught their Philosophy under a *Porticus,* to secure their Scholars from the Weather. *Zeno* was the Chief of that Sect.

[8] *Polygnotus.* A famous painter; who drew the Pictures of the *Medes* and *Persians,* Conquer'd by *Miltiades, Themistocles,* and other *Athenian* Captains, on the Walls of the *Portico,* in their Natural Habits.

[9] *And where the Samian Y,* &c. *Pithagoras* of *Samos* made the allusion of the Y, or Greek Upsilon, to Vice and Virtue. One side of the Letter, being broad, Characters Vice, to which the ascent is wide and easie. The other side represents Virtue; to which the Passage is strait

and difficult: And perhaps our Saviour might also allude to this, in those Noted words of the Evangelist, *The Way to Heaven,* &c.

[10] *Fat Fees,* &c. Casaubon here Notes, that among all the *Romans* who were brought up to Learning, few besides the Orators, or Lawyers, grew Rich.

[11] The *Martians* and *Umbrians* were the most Plentiful of all the Provinces in *Italy.*

[12] *His Heels stretch'd out,* &c. The *Romans* were Buried without the City; for which Reason the Poet says that the Dead man's heels were stretch'd out towards the Gate.

[13] *That Mad Orestes. Orestes* was son to *Agamemnon* and *Clitemnestra. Orestes* to revenge his Fathers Death slew both *Ægysthus* and his *Mother* : For which he was punish'd with Madness by the *Eumenides,* or Furies, who continually haunted him.

THE FOURTH SATYR.

ARGUMENT | OF THE | FOURTH SATYR.

Our Author, living in the time of Nero, was Contemporary and Friend to the Noble Poet Lucan; both of them were sufficiently sensible, with all Good Men, how Unskilfully he manag'd the Commonwealth: And perhaps might guess at his future Tyranny, by some Passages, during the latter part of his first five years; tho he broke not out, into his great Excesses, while he was restrain'd by the Counsels and Authority of Seneca. Lucan has not spar'd him in the Poem of his Pharsalia: for his very Complement look'd asquint, as well as Nero. Persius has been bolder, but with Caution likewise. For here, in the Person of young Alcibiades, he arraigns his Ambition of meddling with State Affairs, without Judgment or Experience. 'Tis probable that he makes Seneca, in this Satyr, sustain the part of Socrates, under a borrow'd Name. And, withal, discovers some secret Vices of Nero, concerning his Lust, his Drunkenness, and his Effeminacy, which had not yet arriv'd to publick Notice. He also reprehends the Flattery of his Courtiers, who endeavour'd to make all his Vices pass for Virtues. Covetousness was undoubtedly none of his Faults; but it is here described as a Veil cast over the True Meaning of the Poet, which was to Satyrize his Prodigality and Voluptuousness: to which he makes a transition. I find no Instance in History of that Emperor's

being a Pathique, though Persius seems to brand him with it. From the two dialogues of Plato, both call'd Alcibiades, the Poet took the Arguments of the Second and Third Satyr, but he inverted the order of them: For the Third Satyr is taken from the first of those Dialogues.

The Commentatours before Casaubon were ignorant of our Author's secret meaning; and thought he had only written against Young Noblemen in General, who were too forward in aspiring to publick Magistracy: But this Excellent Scholiast has unravell'd the whole Mystery: And made it apparent, that the Sting of this Satyr was particularly aim'd at Nero.

THE FOURTH SATYR.

WHO-E'RE thou art, whose forward years are bent
On State-Affairs, to guide the Government;
Hear, first, what [1]Socrates of old has said
To the lov'd Youth, whom he, at *Athens* bred.
 Tell me, thou Pupil to great [2]*Pericles,*
Our second hope, my *Alcibiades,*
What are the grounds, from whence thou dost prepare
To undertake so young, so vast a Care?
Perhaps thy Wit: (A Chance not often heard,
That Parts and Prudence shou'd prevent
        the Beard:)   10
'Tis seldom seen that Senators so young
Know when to speak, and when to hold
        their Tongue.

Sure thou art born to some peculiar Fate ;
When the mad People rise against the State,
To look them into Duty ; and command
An awful Silence with thy lifted hand.
Then to bespeak 'em thus : *Athenians*, know
Against right Reason all your Counsels go ;
This is not Fair ; nor Profitable that ;
Nor t'other Question Proper for Debate.   20
But thou, no doubt, can'st set the business right,
And give each Argument its proper weight :
Know'st, with an equal hand, to hold the
      Scale :
See'st where the Reasons pinch, and where
      they fail,
And where Exceptions, o're the general
      Rule, prevail.
And, taught by Inspiration, in a trice,
Can'st [3]punish Crimes, and brand offending
      Vice.   [as these,
   Leave ; leave to fathom such high points
Nor be ambitious, e're thy time, to please :
Unseasonably Wise, till Age, and Cares,   30
Have form'd thy Soul, to manage Great
      Affairs.
Thy Face, thy Shape, thy Outside, are but
      vain ;
Thou hast not strength such Labours to
      sustain :
Drink [4]*Hellebore*, my Boy, drink deep, and
      purge thy brain.
   What aim'st thou at, and whither tends
      thy Care,
In what thy utmost Good? Delicious Fare;
And, then, to Sun thy self in open air.
   Hold, hold; are all thy empty Wishes such?
A good old Woman wou'd have said as much.
But thou art nobly born ; 'tis true ; go boast
Thy Pedigree, the thing thou valu'st most :
Besides thou art a Beau : What's that, my
      Child ?   42
A Fop, well drest, extravagant, and wild :
She that cries Herbs, has less impertinence ;
And, in her Calling, more of common sense.
   None, none descends into himself, to find
The secret Imperfections of his Mind :
But ev'ry one is Eagle-ey'd, to see
Another's Faults, and his Deformity.   49
Say, do'st thou know [5]*Vectidius* ? Who,
      the Wretch   [stretch ;
Whose Lands beyond the *Sabines* largely

Cover the Country, that a sailing Kite
Can scarce o'reflye 'em in a day and night ;
Him, do'st thou mean, who, spight of all
      his store,
Is ever Craving, and will still be Poor ?
Who cheats for Half-pence, and who doffs
      his Coat,
To save a Farthing in a Ferry-Boat ?
Ever a Glutton, at another's Cost,
But in whose Kitchin dwells perpetual Frost?
Who eats and drinks with his Domestick
      Slaves ;   60
A verier Hind than any of his Knaves ?
Born with the Curse and Anger of the Gods,
And that indulgent Genius he defrauds ?
At Harvest-home, and on the Sheering-Day,
When he shou'd [6]Thanks to *Pan* and *Pales*
      pay,
And better *Ceres* ; trembling to approach
The little Barrel, which he fears to broach :
He 'says the Wimble, often draws it back,
And deals to thirsty Servants but a smack.
To a short Meal, he makes a tedious Grace, 70
Before the Barly Pudding comes in place :
Then, bids fall on ; himself, for saving
      charges,
A peel'd slic'd Onyon eats, and tipples
      Verjuice.
   Thus fares the Drudge : But thou, whose
      life's a Dream
Of lazy Pleasures, tak'st a worse Extream.
'Tis all thy bus'ness, bus'ness how to shun ;
To bask thy naked Body in the Sun ;
Suppl'ng thy stiffen'd Joints with fragrant
      Oyl :
Then, in thy spacious Garden, walk a while,
To suck the Moisture up, and soak it in : 80
And this, thou think'st, but vainly think'st,
      unseen.
But, know, thou art observ'd : And there
      are those   [sins expose.
Who, if they durst, would all thy secret
The [7]depilation of thy modest part :
Thy *Catamite*, the Darling of thy Heart,
His Engine-hand, and ev'ry leuder Art.
When prone to bear, and patient to receive,
Thou tak'st the pleasure which thou canst
      not give.
With odorous Oyl thy head and hair are sleek ;
And then thou kemb'st the Tuzzes on thy
      Cheek :   90

Of these thy Barbers take a costly care,
While thy salt Tail is overgrown with hair.
Not all thy Pincers, nor unmanly Arts,
Can smooth the roughness of thy shameful
  parts.
Not *five, the strongest that the *Circus*
  breeds,
From the rank Soil can root those wicked
  Weeds :
Though suppled first with Soap, to ease thy
  pain,
The stubborn Fern springs up, and sprouts
  again.
  Thus others we with Defamations wound,
While they stab us ; and so the Jest goes
  round.   100
Vain are thy Hopes, to scape censorious
  Eyes ;
Truth will appear, through all the thin Dis-
  guise :
Thou hast an Ulcer which no Leach can heal,
Though thy broad Shoulder-belt the Wound
  conceal.
Say thou art sound and hale in ev'ry part,
We know, we know thee rotten at thy heart.
We know thee sullen, impotent, and proud :
Nor canst thou cheat thy ⁹Nerve, who
  cheat'st the Croud.

But when they praise me, in the Neigh-
  bourhood,   109
When the pleas'd People take me for a God,
Shall I refuse their Incense ? Not receive
The loud Applauses which the Vulgar give ?
If thou do'st Wealth, with longing Eyes,
  behold ;
And, greedily, art gaping after Gold ;
If some alluring Girl, in gliding by,   ⎫
Shall tip the wink, with a lascivious Eye,   ⎬
And thou, with a consenting glance, reply ;   ⎭
If thou, thy own Sollicitor become,
And bid'st arise the lumpish *Pendulum* :
If thy lewd Lust provokes an empty storm,
And prompts to more than Nature can
  perform ;   121
If, with thy ¹⁰Guards, thou scour'st the
  Streets by night,
And do'st in Murthers, Rapes, and Spoils
  delight ;
Please not thy self, the flatt'ring Crowd to
  hear ;
'Tis fulsom stuff, to feed thy itching Ear.
Reject the nauseous Praises of the Times :
Give thy base Poets back their cobbled
  Rhymes :
Survey thy ¹¹Soul, not what thou do'st appear,
But what thou art ; and find the Beggar there.

The End of the Fourth Satyr.

NOTES TO THE FOURTH SATYR.

¹ **Socrates**, whom the Oracle of *Delphos* prais'd as the wisest Man of his Age, liv'd in the time of the *Peloponnesian* War. He, finding the Uncertainty of Natural Philosophy, appli'd himself wholly to the Moral. He was Master to *Xenophon* and *Plato*, and to many of the *Athenian* Young Noblemen ; amongst the rest to *Alcibiades*, the most lovely Youth then living ; Afterwards a Famous Captain, whose Life is written by *Plutarch*.

² **Pericles** was Tutor, or rather Overseer of the Will of *Clinias*, Father to *Alcibiades*. While *Pericles* liv'd, who was a wise Man, and an Excellent Orator, as well as a Great General, the *Athenians* had the better of the War.

³ *Can'st punish Crimes*, &c. That is by Death. When the Judges would Condemn a Malefactor, they cast their Votes into an Urn ; as according to the Modern Custom, a Ballotting-Box. If the Suffrages were mark'd with Θ they signify'd the Sentence of Death to the Offendor, as being the first Letter of Θάνατος, which in English is Death.

⁴ *Drink Hellebore*, &c. The Poet wou'd say, that such an ignorant Young Man, as he here describes, is fitter to be govern'd himself, than to

govern others. He therefore advises him to drink *Hellebore*, which purges the Brain.

⁵ *Say, dost thou know* Vectidius, &c. The Name of *Vectidius* is here us'd Appellatively to signifie any Rich Covetous Man ; though perhaps there might be a Man of that Name then living. I have Translated this passage paraphrastically, and loosely : And leave it to those to look on, who are not unlike the Picture.

⁶ *When He shou'd thanks*, &c. *Pan* the God of Shepherds, and *Pales* the Goddess presiding over rural Affairs ; whom *Virgil* invocates in the beginning of his Second *Georgique*. I give the Epithete of *Better* to *Ceres*, because she first taught the Use of Corn for Bread, as the Poets tell us ; Men, in the first rude Ages, feeding only on Acorns or Mast instead of Bread.

⁷ [Note suppressed.]

⁸ *Not five the Strongest*, &c. The Learned *Holiday*, (who has made us amends for his bad Poetry in this and the rest of these Satyrs with his excellent Illustrations,) here tells us, from good Authority, that the Number Five does not allude to the *Five Fingers* of one Man, who us'd them all in taking off the Hairs before mention'd ; but

to *Five Strong Men,* such as were skillful in the five robust Exercises then in Practice at *Rome,* and were perform'd in the *Circus,* or publick place, ordain'd for them. These five he reckons up in this manner. 1. The *Cæstus,* or Whirlbatts, describ'd by *Virgil,* in his fifth Eneid: And this was the most dangerous of all the rest. The 2d was the *Foot-race.* The Third the *Discus,* like the throwing a weighty Ball, a sport now us'd in *Cornwall,* and other parts of *England:* We may see it daily practis'd in Red-Lyon-Fields. The Fourth was the *Saltus,* or Leaping: And the fifth *Wrastling Naked* and besmear'd with Oyl. They who were Practis'd in these five Manly Exercises were call'd Πένταθλοι.

9 [Note suppressed.]

10 *If, with thy Guards,* &c. *Persius* durst not have been so bold with *Nero,* as I dare now; and therefore there is only an intimation of that in him, which I publickly speak; I mean of *Nero's* walking the Streets by Night in disguise; and committing all sorts of Outrages: For which he was sometimes well beaten.

11 *Survey thy Soul,* &c. That is, look into thy self, and examine thy own Conscience, there thou shalt find, that how wealthy soever thou appear'st to the World, yet thou art but a Beggar: because thou art destitute of all Virtues, which are the Riches of the Soul. This also was a Paradox of the Stoick School.

THE FIFTH SATYR.

ARGUMENT | OF THE | FIFTH SATYR.

The judicious Casaubon, *in his Proem to this Satyr, tells us, that* Aristophanes, *the Grammarian, being ask'd, what poem of* Archilochus *his Iambicks he preferr'd before the rest; answer'd, the longest. His Answer may justly be apply'd to this Fifth Satyr; which, being of a greater length than any of the rest, is also, by far, the most instructive. For this Reason I have selected it from all the others, and inscribed it to my Learned Master,* Doctor Busby; *to whom I am not only oblig'd myself for the best part of my own Education, and that of my two Sons, but have also receiv'd from him the first and truest Taste of* Persius. *May he be pleased to find in this Translation, the Gratitude, or at least some small Acknowledgment of his unworthy Scholar, at the distance of 42 Years, from the time when I departed from under his Tuition.*

This Satyr consists of two distinct Parts: The first contains the Praises of the Stoick philosopher Cornutus, *Master and Tutor to our* Persius. *It also declares the Love and Piety of* Persius, *to his well-deserving Master; And the Mutual Friendship which continu'd betwixt them, after* Persius *was now grown a Man. As also his Exhortation to Young Noblemen, that they would enter themselves into his Institution. From hence he makes an artful Transition into the second Part of his Subject: Wherein he first complains of the Sloath of Scholars, and afterwards persuades them to the pursuit of their true Liberty: Here our Author excellently Treats that Paradox of the Stoicks, which affirms, that the*

Wise or Virtuous Man is only Free, and that all Vicious Men are Naturally Slaves. And, in the Illustration of this Dogma, he takes up the remaining part of this inimitable Satyr.

THE FIFTH SATYR.

Inscrib'd to The Reverend Dr. Busby.

The Speakers Persius *and* Cornutus.

PERS.

OF ancient use to Poets it belongs,
To wish themselves an hundred Mouths and Tongues:
Whether to the well-lung'd Tragedians Rage
They recommend their Labours of the Stage,
Or sing the *Parthian,* when transfix'd he lies,
Wrenching the *Roman* Javelin from his thighs.

CORN.

And why wou'dst thou these mighty Morsels chuse,
Of Words unchaw'd, and fit to choak the Muse?
Let Fustian Poets with their Stuff be gone,
And suck the Mists that hang o're *Helicon;*
When 1 *Progne's* or 2 *Thyestes's* Feast they write;   11
And, for the mouthing Actor, Verse indite.
Thou neither, like a Bellows, swell'st thy Face,
As if thou wert to blow the burning Mass

11 *Progne's*] *All the English editors give* Progne. *They have consulted neither Dryden's text nor* Persius, *hardly even Dryden's note which they print.*

Of melting Ore ; nor can'st thou strain thy
  Throat,
Or murmur in an undistinguish'd Note ;
Like rowling Thunder, till it breaks the Cloud,
And rattling Nonsense is discharg'd aloud.
Soft Elocution does thy Stile renown,
And the sweet Accents of the peaceful Gown :
Gentle or sharp, according to thy choice, 21
To laugh at Follies, or to lash at Vice.
Hence draw thy Theme, and to the Stage
  permit
Raw-head and Bloody-Bones, and Hands
  and Feet,
Ragousts for *Tereus* or *Thyestes* drest ;
'Tis Task enough for thee t' expose a *Roman*
  Feast.

PERS.

'Tis not, indeed, my Talent to engage
In lofty Trifles, or to swell my Page
With Wind and Noise ; but freely to impart,
As to a Friend, the Secrets of my heart ; 30
And, in familiar Speech, to let thee know
How much I love thee, and how much I owe.
Knock on my Heart : for thou hast skill
  to find
If it sound solid, or be fill'd with Wind ;
And, thro the veil of words, thou view'st
  the naked Mind.
  For this a hundred Voices I desire,
To tell thee what an hundred Tongues wou'd
  tire ;
Yet never cou'd be worthily exprest,
How deeply thou art seated in my Breast.
  When first my ³ Childish Robe resign'd
  the charge ; 40
And left me, unconfin'd, to live at large ;
When now my golden *Bulla* (hung on high
To House-hold Gods) declar'd me past
  a Boy,
And my ⁴ white Shield proclaim'd my
  Liberty ;
When with my wild Companions, I could rowl
From Street to Street, and sin without
  controul ;
Just at that Age, when Manhood set me free,
I then depos'd my self, and left the Reins to
  thee.
On thy wise Bosom I repos'd my Head ;
And by my better ⁵ *Socrates* was bred. 50
Then, thy streight Rule set Virtue in my
  sight,
The crooked Line reforming by the right.

My Reason took the bent of thy Command,
Was form'd and polish'd by thy skilful hand :
Long Summer-days thy Precepts I reherse ;
And Winter-nights were short in our con-
  verse :
One was our Labour, one was our Repose ;
One frugal Supper did our Studies close.
  Sure on our Birth some friendly Planet
  shone :
And, as our ⁶ Souls, our Horoscope was one
Whether the ⁷ mounting Twins did Heav'n
  adorn, 61
Or with the rising Ballance ⁸ we were born ;
Both have the same Impressions from above ;
And both have ⁹ *Saturn's* rage repell'd by
  Jove.
What Star I know not, but some Star I find,
Has given Thee an Ascendant o're my Mind.

CORN.

Nature is ever various in her Frame :
Each has a different Will ; and few the
  same :
The greedy Merchants, led by lucre, run
To the parch'd *Indies*, and the rising Sun ; 70
From thence hot Pepper, and rich Drugs
  they bear,
Bart'ring for Spices their *Italian* Ware :
The lazy Glutton safe at home will keep,
Indulge his Sloth, and batten with his
  Sleep :
One bribes for high Preferments in the
  State ;
A second shakes the Box, and sits up late
Another shakes the Bed ; dissolving there,
Till knots upon his Gouty Joints appear,
And Chalk is in his crippled Fingers found ;
Rots like a Doddard Oke, and piecemeal
  falls to ground. 80
Then, his lewd Follies he wou'd late repent ;
And his past years, that in a Mist were spent.

PERS.

But thou art pale, in nightly Studies,
  grown,
To make the ¹⁰ *Stoick* Institutes thy own ;
Thou long, with studious Care, hast till'd
  our Youth,
And sown our well-purg'd Ears with wholesom Truth :

---

80 Doddard] *The editor's wrongly print*
dodder'd

From thee both old and young, with profit, learn
The bounds of Good and Evil to discern.

CORN.

Unhappy he who does this Work adjourn;
And to To Morrow would the search delay:
His lazy Morrow will be like to day.   91

PERS.

But is one day of Ease too much to borrow?

CORN.

Yes, sure: For Yesterday was once To Morrow.
That Yesterday is gone, and nothing gain'd:
And all thy fruitless days will thus be drain'd;
For thou hast more To Morrows yet to ask,
And wilt be ever to begin thy Task;
Who, like the hindmost Chariot Wheels, art curst;
Still to be near; but ne're to reach the first.
O Freedom! first Delight of Humane Kind!   100
Not that which Bondmen from their Masters find,
The [11]Priviledge of Doles; not yet t' inscribe
Their Names [12]in this or t'other *Roman* Tribe:
That false Enfranchisement, with ease is found:
Slaves are [13]made Citizens, by turning round.
How, replies one, can any be more free?
Here's *Dama*, once a Groom of low degree
Not worth a Farthing, and a Sot beside;
So true a Rogue, for lying's sake he ly'd:
But, with a turn, a Freeman he became;   110
Now [14]*Marcus Dama* is his Worship's Name:
Good Gods! who wou'd refuse to lend a Sum,
If Wealthy *Marcus* Surety will become!
Marcus is made a Judge, and for a Proof
Of certain Truth, *He said it*, is enough.
A Will is to be prov'd; put in your Claim;
'Tis clear, if [15]*Marcus* has subscrib'd his Name.
This is [16]true Liberty, as I believe;
What farther can we from our Caps receive,
Than as we please, without Control to live?   120

Not more to [17]Noble *Brutus* could belong.
Hold, says the Stoick, your Assumption's wrong:
I grant true Freedom you have well defin'd:
But living as you list, and to your mind,
Are loosely tack'd; and must be left behind.
What, since the Prætor did my Fetters loose,
And left me freely at my own dispose,
May I not live without Control or Awe,
Excepting still the [18]Letter of the Law?
Hear me with patience, while thy Mind I free   130
From those fond Notions of false Liberty:
'Tis not the Prætor's Province to bestow
True Freedom; nor to teach Mankind to know
What to our selves, or to our Friends we owe.
He cou'd not set thee free from Cares and Strife;
Nor give the Reins to a lewd vicious life:
As well he for an Ass a Harp might string,
Which is against the Reason of the thing;
For Reason still is whisp'ring in your Ear,
Where you are sure to fail, th' Attempt forbear.   140
No need of Publick Sanctions this to bind,
Which Nature has implanted in the Mind:
Not to pursue the Work, to which we're not design'd.
Unskill'd in *Hellebore*, if thou shou'd'st try
To mix it, and mistake the Quantity,
The Rules of Physick wou'd against thee cry.
The High-shoo'd Ploughman, shou'd he quit the Land,
To take the Pilot's Rudder in his hand,
Artless of Stars, and of the moving Sand,
The Gods wou'd leave him to the Waves and Wind,   150
And think all Shame was lost in Human-Kind.
Tell me, my Friend, from whence hadst thou the skill,
So nicely to distinguish Good from Ill?
Or by the sound to judge of Gold and Brass;
What piece is Tinkers Metal, what will pass?
And what thou art to follow, what to flye,
This to condemn, and that to ratifie?

---

128 or] *Some editors wrongly give* and

When to be Bountiful, and when to Spare,
But never Craving, or oppress'd with Care?
The Baits of Gifts, and Money to despise, 160
And look on Wealth with undesiring Eyes?
When thou can'st truly call these Virtues
thine,
Be Wise and Free, by Heav'n's consent
and mine.

But thou, who lately of the common strain,
Wert one of us, if still thou do'st retain
The same ill Habits, the same Follies too,
Gloss'd over only with a Saint-like show,
Then I resume the freedom which I gave,
Still thou art bound to Vice, and still a Slave.
Thou can'st not wag thy Finger, or begin 170
The least light motion, but it tends to sin.

How's this? Not wag my Finger, he replies? ⎫
No, Friend; nor fuming Gums, nor Sacrifice, ⎬
Can ever make a Madman free, or wise. ⎭
" Virtue and [19] Vice are never in one Soul:
" A Man is wholly Wise, or wholly is a Fool.
A heavy Bumpkin, taught with daily care,
Can never dance three steps with a becoming
air.

PERS.

In spight of this, my Freedom still remains.

CORN.

Free, what and fetter'd with so many
Chains?   180
Can'st thou no other Master understand
Than [20] him that freed thee by the Prætor's
Wand?
Shou'd he, who was thy Lord, command
thee now,
With a harsh Voice, and supercilious Brow,
To servile Duties, thou wou'd'st fear no
more;
The Gallows and the Whip are out of door.
But if thy Passions lord it in thy Breast,
Art thou not still a Slave, and still opprest?
Whether alone, or in thy Harlot's Lap,
When thou wou'dst take a lazy Morning's
Nap;   190
Up, up, says Avarice; thou snor'st again,
Stretchest thy Limbs, and yawn'st, but all
in vain;
The Tyrant Lucre no denyal takes;
At his Command th' unwilling Sluggard
wakes.
What must I do? he cries: What? says
his Lord:
Why rise, make ready, and go streight aboord:

With Fish, from *Euxine* Seas, thy Vessel
freight;
Flax, Castor, *Coan* Wines, the precious
Weight
Of Pepper, and *Sabean* Incense, take ⎫
With thy own hands, from the tir'd Camel's ⎪
back: 200 ⎬
And with Post-haste thy running Markets ⎪
make.   ⎭
Be sure to turn the Penny: lye and swear;
'Tis wholesom sin: But *Jove*, thou say'st,
will hear:
Swear, Fool, or starve; for the Dilemma's
even:
A Tradesman thou! and hope to go to
Heav'n?
Resolv'd for Sea, the Slaves thy Baggage
pack,
Each saddled, with his Burden on his back;
Nothing retards thy Voyage, now; unless
Thy other Lord forbids, Voluptuousness:
And he may ask this civil Question: Friend,
What do'st thou make a Shipboord? to
what end?   211
Art thou of *Bethlem's* Noble College free?
Stark, staring mad; that thou wou'dst
tempt the Sea?
Cubb'd in a Cabin, on a Mattress laid,
On a Brown *George*, with lowsie Swobbers,
fed,
Dead Wine, that stinks of the *Borrachio*, sup
From a foul Jack, or greasie Maple Cup?
Say, wou'd'st thou bear all this, to raise
thy store
From Six i' th' Hundred, to Six Hundred
more?
Indulge, and to thy Genius freely give; 220
For, not to live at ease, is not to live;
Death stalks behind thee: and each flying
Hour
Does some loose Remnant of thy Life devour.
Live, while thou liv'st: For Death will
make us all
A Name, a nothing but an Old Wife's Tale.
Speak; wilt thou Avarice, or Pleasure
chuse
To be thy Lord? Take one, and one refuse.
But both, by turns, the Rule of thee will
have;
And thou, betwixt 'em both, wilt be a Slave.
Nor think when once thou hast resisted
one,   230
That all thy Marks of Servitude are gone:

The strugling Greyhound gnaws his Leash in
  vain ;
If, when 'tis broken, still he drags the Chain.
  Says [21] *Phædria* to his Man, Believe me,
  Friend,
To this uneasie Love I'le put an End :
Shall I run out of all ? My Friends disgrace,
And be the first lewd Unthrift of my Race ?
Shall I the Neighbours Nightly rest invade
At her deaf Doors, with some vile Serenade ?
Well hast thou freed thy self, his Man
  replies ;   240
Go, thank the Gods, and offer Sacrifice.
Ah, says the Youth, if we unkindly part,
Will not the Poor fond Creature break her
  Heart ?
Weak Soul ! And blindly to Destruction led !
She break her Heart ! She'll sooner break
  your Head.
She knows her Man, and when you Rant
  and Swear,
Can draw you to her *with a single Hair*.
But shall I not return ? Now, when she
  Sues ?
Shall I my own, and her Desires refuse ?
Sir, take your Course : But my Advice is
  plain :   250
Once freed, 'tis Madness to resume your
  Chain.
  Ay ; there's the Man, who loos'd from
    Lust and Pelf,
Less to the Prætor owes, than to himself.
But write him down a Slave, who, humbly
  proud,
With Presents begs Preferments from the
  Crowd ;

That early [22] Suppliant, who salutes the
  Tribes,
And sets the Mob to scramble for his Bribes :
That some old Dotard, sitting in the Sun,
On Holydays may tell, that such a Feat
  was done :
In future times this will be counted rare. 260
  Thy Superstition too may claim a share :
When Flow'rs are strew'd, and Lamps in
  order plac'd,
And Windows with Illuminations grac'd,
On [23] *Herod's* Day ; when sparkling Bouls
  go round,
And *Tunny's* Tails in savoury Sauce are
  drown'd,
Thou mutter'st Prayers obscene ; nor do'st
  refuse
The Fasts and Sabbaths of the curtail'd *Jews*.
Then a crack'd [24] Eggshell thy sick Fancy
  frights,
Besides the Childish Fear of Walking Sprights.
Of o'regrown Guelding Priests thou art afraid :
The Timbrel, and the Squintifego Maid 271
Of *Isis*, awe thee : lest the Gods, for sin,
Shou'd, with a swelling Dropsie, stuff thy
  skin :
Unless three Garlick Heads the Curse avert,
Eaten each Morn, devoutly, next thy heart.
  Preach this among the brawny Guards,
    say'st thou,
And see if they thy Doctrine will allow :
The dull fat Captain, with a Hound's deep
  throat,
Wou'd bellow out a Laugh, in a Base Note ;
And prize a hundred *Zeno's* just as much 280
As a clipt Sixpence, or a Schilling *Dutch*.

The End of the Fifth Satyr.

NOTES TO THE FIFTH SATYR.

[1] *Progne* was Wife to *Tereus*, King of *Thracia* :
Tereus fell in Love with *Philomela*, Sister to
Progne, ravish'd her, and cut out her Tongue : In
Revenge of which, *Progne* kill'd *Itys*, her own
Son by *Tereus*, and serv'd him up at a Feast, to
be eaten by his Father.

[2] *Thyestes* and *Atreus* were Brothers, both
Kings : *Atreus*, to Revenge himself of his unnatural Brother, kill'd the Sons of *Thyestes*, and
invited him to eat them.

[3] By the Childish Robe is meant the *Prætexta*,
or first Gowns which the *Roman* Children of
Quality wore : These were Welted with Purple :
And on those Welts were fast-n'd the *Bullæ*, or
little Bells, which when they came to the Age of

Puberty were hung up and consecrated to the
Lares, or Household Gods.

[4] The first Shields which the *Roman* Youths
wore, were white, and without any Impress or
Device on them, to shew they had yet Atchiev'd
nothing in the Wars.

[5] *Socrates* by the Oracle was declar'd to be the
wisest of Mankind : He instructed many of the
Athenian Young Noblemen in Morality, and
amongst the rest *Alcibiades*.

[6] Astrologers divide the Heaven into Twelve
parts, according to the Number of the 12 Signs of
the Zodiack : The Sign or Constellation which
rises in the East, at the Birth of any Man,
is call'd the Ascendant : *Persius*, therefore,

judges that and he *Cornutus* had the same or a like Nativity.

[7] The Sign of *Gemini*.

[8] The Sign of *Libra*.

[9] Astrologers have an Axiome, that whatsoever *Saturn* ties is loos'd by *Jupiter* : They account *Saturn* to be a Planet of a Malevolent Nature, and *Jupiter* of a Propitious Influence.

[10] *Zeno* was the great Master of the Stoick Philosophy : And *Cleanthes* was second to him in Reputation : *Cornutus*, who was Master or Tutor to *Persius*, was of the same School.

[11] When a Slave was made free, he had the Priviledge of a *Roman* Born, which was to have a share in the Donatives or Doles of Bread, &c. which were Distributed by the Magistrates amongst the People.

[12] The *Roman* People was Distributed into several Tribes: He who was made free was inroll'd into some one of them, and thereupon enjoy'd the common Priviledges of a *Roman* Citizen.

[13] The Master, who intended to infranchise a Slave, carried him before the City Prætor, and turn'd him round, using these words, *I will that this Man be free.*

[14] Slaves had only one Name before their Freedom : After it they were admitted to a *Prænomen*, like our Christen'd Names ; so *Dama* is now call'd *Marcus Dama*.

[15] At the Proof of a Testament, the Magistrates were to subscribe their Names, as allowing the Legality of the Will.

[16] Slaves, when they were set free, had a Cap given them, in Sign of their Liberty.

[17] *Brutus* freed the *Roman* People from the Tyranny of the *Tarquins*, and chang'd the Form of the Government into a glorious Common-wealth.

[18] The Text of the *Roman* Laws was written in Red Letters ; which was call'd the Rubrick; Translated here, in more general words, *The Letter of the Law*.

[19] The Stoicks held this Paradox, That any one Vice, or Notorious Folly, which they call'd Madness, hinder'd a Man from being Virtuous : That

a Man was of a Piece, without a Mixture, either wholly Vicious or Good ; one Virtue or Vice, according to them, including all the rest.

[20] The Prætor held a Wand in his hand, with which he softly struck the Slave on the Head when he declar'd him free.

[21] This alludes to the Play of *Terence*, call'd the *Eunuch*, which was excellently imitated of late in *English* by Sir *Charles Sedley* : In the first Scene of that Comedy, *Phædria* was introduc'd with his Man *Pamphilus*, Discoursing, whether he shou'd leave his Mistress *Thais*, or return to her, now that she had invited him.

[22] He who sued for any Office amongst the *Romans* was called a Candidate, because he wore a white Gown : And sometimes Chalk'd it to make it appear whiter. He rose early, and went to the *Levees* of those who headed the People : Saluted also the Tribes severally, when they were gather'd together to chuse their Magistrates ; and Distributed a Largess amongst them, to engage them for their Voices: Much resembling our Elections of Parliament-Men.

[23] The Commentators are divided, what *Herod* this was, whom our Author mentions: Whether *Herod* the Great, whose Birth-day might possibly be celebrated, after his Death, by the *Herodians*, a Sect amongst the Jews, who thought him their Messiah ; or *Herod Agrippa*, living in the Author's time and after it. The latter seems the more probable opinion.

[24] The Ancients had a Superstition, contrary to ours concerning Egg-shells : They thought that if an Egg-shell were crack'd, or a Hole bor'd in the bottom of it, they were Subject to the Power of Sorcery : We as vainly break the Bottom of an Egg-shell, and cross it when we have eaten the Egg, lest some Hag shou'd make use of it in bewitching us, or sailing over the sea in it, if it were whole.

The rest of the Priests of Isis, and her one-ey'd or squinting Priestess is more largely treated in the Sixth Satyr of *Juvenal*, where the Superstitions of Women are related.

THE SIXTH SATYR.

ARGUMENT | OF THE | SIXTH SATYR.

This Sixth Satyr Treats an admirable Common-place of Moral Philosophy ; Of the true Use of Riches. They are certainly intended, by the Power who bestows them, as Instruments and Helps of living Commodiously our selves, and of Administring to the Wants of others who are oppress'd by Fortune. There are two Extreams in the Opinions of Men concerning them. One Error, though on the right hand, yet a great one, is, That they are no Helps to a Virtuous Life ; The other places all our Happiness in the Acquisi-

tion and Possession of them : and his is undoutedly, the worse Extream. The Mean betwixt these, is the Opinion of the Stoicks : Which is, That Riches may be Useful to the leading a Virtuous Life ; in case we rightly understand how to Give according to right Reason ; and how to receive what is given us by others. The Virtue of Giving Well, is call'd Liberality ; and 'tis of this Virtue that Persius *writes in this Satyr : Wherein he not only shows the lawful Use of Riches, but also sharply inveighs against the Vices which are oppos'd to it : And especially of those, which consist in the Defects of Giving or Spending, or in the Abuse of Riches. He writes to Cæsius Bassus, his Friend, and a Poet also. Enquires first of his Health and Studies; and afterwards informs him of his own, and where he is now resident. He gives an account of himself, that he is endeavouring by little and little to wear off his Vices; and particularly, that he is combating Ambition and the Desire of Wealth. He dwells upon the latter Vice; And being sensible that few Men either Desire, or Use Riches as they ought, he endeavours to convince them of their Folly; which is the main Design of the whole Satyr.*

THE
SIXTH SATYR.

To Cæsius Bassus, a Lyrick Poet.

HAS Winter caus'd thee, Friend, to change thy Seat,
And seek, in [1] *Sabine* Air, a warm retreat ?
Say, do'st thou yet the *Roman* Harp command ?
Do the Strings Answer to thy Noble hand ?
Great Master of the Muse, inspir'd to Sing
The Beauties of the first Created Spring ;
The Pedigree of Nature to rehearse ;
And sound the Maker's Work, in equal Verse.
Now,[2] sporting on thy Lyre the Loves of Youth,
Now Virtuous Age, and venerable Truth ; 10
Expressing justly *Sapho's* wanton Art
Of Odes, and *Pindar's* more Majestick part.

For me, my warmer Constitution more cold, than our *Ligurian* Winter grants;
And, therefore, to my Native Shores retir'd,
I view the Coast old *Ennius* once admir'd ;
Where Clifts on either side their points display ;
And, after, opening in an ampler way, 18
Afford the pleasing Prospect of the Bay.
'Tis worth thy while, O *Romans*, to regard
The Port of *Luna*, says our Learned Bard :
Who, in [3] a Drunken Dream, beheld his Soul
The Fifth within the Transmigrating roul ;
Which first a Peacock, then *Euphorbus* was,
Then *Homer* next, and next *Pythagoras* ;
And last of all the Line did into *Ennius* pass.

Secure and free from Business of the State ;
And more secure of what the vulgar Prate
Here I enjoy my private Thoughts ; nor care
What Rots for Sheep the *Southern* Winds prepare :   30
Survey the Neighb'ring Fields, and not repine,
When I behold a larger Crop than mine :
To see a Beggar's Brat in Riches flow,
Adds not a Wrinckle to my even Brow ;
Nor, envious at the sight, will I forbear
My plentious Bowl, nor bate my bounteous Cheer:
Nor yet unseal the Dregs of Wine that stink
Of Cask ; nor in a nasty Flaggon Drink ;
Let others stuff their Guts with homely fare :
For Men of diff'rent Inclinations are ;   40
Tho born, perhaps, beneath one common Star.
In minds and manners Twins oppos'd we see
In the same Sign, almost the same Degree :
One, Frugal, on his Birth-Day fears to dine,
Does at a Penny's cost in Herbs repine,
And hardly dares to dip his Fingers in the Brine.
Prepar'd as Priest of his own Rites to stand,
He sprinkles Pepper with a sparing hand.
His Jolly Brother, opposite in sence,
Laughs at his Thrift ; and, lavish of Expence,   50
Quaffs, Crams, and Guttles, in his own defence.
For me, I'le use my own ; and take my share ;
Yet will not Turbots for my Slaves prepare :
Nor be so nice in taste my self to know
If what I swallow be a Thrush, or no.
Live on thy Annual Income ! Spend thy store ;
And freely grind, from thy full Threshing-Floor ;
Next Harvest promises as much, or more.
Thus I wou'd live : But Friendship's holy Band,
And Offices of kindness hold my hand : 60
My [4] Friend is Shipwreck'd on the *Brutian* Strand,
His Riches in th' *Ionian* Main are lost ;
And he himself stands shiv'ring on the Coast;

61] *Brutian] The editors correct the spelling.*

Where, destitute of help, forlorn, and bare,
He wearies the Deaf Gods with Fruitless
Pray'r.
Their Images, the Relicks of the Wrack,
Torn from the Naked Poop, are tided back,
By the Wild Waves, and rudely thrown
ashore,
Lye impotent : Nor can themselves restore.
The Vessel sticks, and shows her open'd
side,   70
And on her shatter'd Mast the Mews in
Triumph ride.
From ⁵ thy new hope, and from thy growing
store,
Now lend Assistance, and relieve the Poor.
Come ; do a Noble Act of Charity ;
A Pittance of thy Land will set him free.
Let him not bear the Badges of a Wrack
Nor ⁶ beg with a blue Table on his back.
Nor tell me that thy frowning Heir will say,
'Tis mine that Wealth thou squander'st thus
away :
What is't to thee, if he neglect thy Urn, 80
Or ⁷ without Spices lets thy Body burn ?
If Odours to thy Ashes he refuse,
Or buys Corrupted *Cassia* from the *Jews* ?
All these, the wiser *Bestius* will reply,
Are empty Pomp, and Deadmen's Luxury :
We never knew this vain Expence, before
Th' effeminated *Grecians* brought it o're :
Now Toys and Trifles from their *Athens*
come ;
And Dates and Pepper have unsinnew'd
Rome.
Our sweating Hinds their Sallads, now,
defile,   90
Infecting homely Herbs with fragrant Oyl
But, to thy Fortune be not thou a Slave ;
For what hast thou to fear beyond the
Grave ?
And thou who gap'st for my Estate, draw
near ;
For I wou'd whisper somewhat in thy Ear.
Hear'st thou the News, my Friend ? th'
Express is come
With Laurell'd Letters from the Camp to
Rome ;
Cæsar ⁸ Salutes the Queen and Senate thus :
My Arms are, on the *Rhine*, Victorious.
From Mourning Altars sweep the Dust
away :   100
Cease Fasting, and proclaim a Fat Thanks-
giving Day.

The ⁹ goodly Empress, Jollily inclin'd,
Is, to the welcome Bearer, wond'rous kind :
And, setting her Goodhousewifry aside,
Prepares for all the Pageantry of Pride.
The ¹⁰ Captive *Germans*, of Gygantick size,
Are ranck'd in order, and are clad in frize :
The Spoils of Kings, and Conquer'd Camps
we boast,
Their Arms in Trophies hang, on the
Triumphal post.   109
    Now, for so many Glorious Actions done
In Foreign parts, and mighty Battels won ;
For Peace at Home, and for the publick
Wealth,
I mean to Crown a Bowl to *Cæsar's* Health :
Besides, in Gratitude for such high matters,
Know ¹¹ I have vow'd two hundred Gladiators.
Say, wou'dst thou hinder me from this
Expence ?
I Disinherit thee, if thou dar'st take Offence.
Yet more a publick Largess I design
Of Oyl and Pyes to make the People dine :
Controul me not, for fear I change my
Will ;   120
    And yet methinks I hear thee grumbling
still,
You give as if you were the *Persian* King ;
Your Land does no such large Revenues
bring.
Well ; on my Terms thou wilt not be my
Heir ;
If thou car'st little, less shall be my care :
Were none of all my Father's Sisters left
Nay, were I of my Mother's Kin bereft ;
None by an Uncle's or a Grandam's side
Yet I cou'd some adopted Heir provide.
I need but take my Journey half a day ¹³⁰ ⎫
From haughty *Rome*, and at *Aricea* stay, ⎬
Where Fortune throws poor *Manius* in my ⎪
way.   ⎭
Him will I chuse : What him, of humble
Birth,
Obscure, a Foundling, and a Son of Earth ?
Obscure ! Why prithee what am I ? I know
My Father, Grandsire, and great Grandsire
too :
If farther I derive my Pedigree,
I can but guess beyond the fourth degree.
The rest of my forgotten Ancestors
Were Sons of Earth, like him, or Sons of
Whores.   140

---

131 *Aricea*] *The editors correct the spelling*

Yet why shou'd'st thou, old covetous
  Wretch, aspire
To be my Heir, who might'st have been
  my Sire?
In Nature's Race, shou'd'st thou demand
  of me
My [12]Torch, when I in course run after thee?
Think I approach thee like the God of Gain,
With Wings on Head, and Heels, as Poets
  feign:
Thy mod'rate Fortune from my Gift
  receive;
Now fairly take it, or as fairly leave.
But take it as it is, and ask no more.
What, when thou hast embezel'd all thy
  store?   150
Where's all thy Father left? 'Tis true,
  I grant,
Some I have mortgag'd, to supply my want:
The Legacies of *Tadius* too are flown:
All spent, and on the selfsame Errand gone.
How little then to my poor share will fall?
Little indeed; but yet that little's all.
  Nor tell me, in a dying Father's tone,
Be careful still of the main chance, my Son;
Put out the Principal, in trusty hands:
Live of the Use; and never dip thy Lands:
But yet what's left for me? What's left,
  my Friend!   161
Ask that again, and all the rest I spend.
Is not my Fortune at my own Command?
Pour Oyl; and pour it with a plenteous hand,

Upon my Sallads, Boy: Shall I be fed
With sodden Nettles, and a sing'd Sow's
  head?
'Tis Holyday; provide me better Cheer;
'Tis Holyday, and shall be round the Year.
Shall I my Household Gods, and Genius,
  cheat,
To make him rich, who grudges me my
  Meat,   170
That he may loll at ease; and pamper'd high,
When I am laid, may feed on Giblet Pye?
And when his throbbing Lust extends the
  Vein,
Have wherewithall his Whores to entertain?
Shall I in homespun Cloath be clad, that he
His Paunch in triumph may before him see?
  Go Miser, go; for Lucre sell thy Soul;
Truck Wares for Wares, and trudge from
  Pole to Pole:
That Men may say, when thou art dead and
  gone,
See what a vast Estate he left his Son! 180
How large a Family of Brawny Knaves,
Well fed, and fat as [13]*Capadocian* Slaves!
Increase thy Wealth, and double all thy
  Store;
'Tis done: Now double that, and swell the
  score;
To ev'ry thousand add ten thousand more.
Then say, [14]*Chrysippus*, thou who wou'dst
  confine
Thy Heap, where I shall put an end to mine.

The End of the Sixth Satyr.

NOTES TO THE SIXTH SATYR.

[1] *AND seek in Sabine Air*, &c. All the Studious, and particularly the Poets, about the end of *August*, began to set themselves on Work; Refraining from Writing during the Heats of the Summer. They wrote by Night, and sate up the greatest part of it. For which Reason the Product of their Studies was call'd their *Elucubrations*, or Nightly Labours. They who had Country Seats retir'd to them, while they Studied: As *Persius* did to his, which was near the Port of the Moon in *Etruria*; and *Bassus* to his, which was in the Country of the *Sabines*, nearer *Rome*.

[2] *Now Sporting on thy Lyre*, &c. This proves *Cæsius Bassus* to have been a Lyrick Poet: 'Tis said of him, that by an Eruption of the Flameing Mountain *Vesuvius*, near which the greatest part of his Fortune lay, he was Burnt himself together with all his Writings.

[3] *Who, in a Drunken Dream*, &c. I call it a Drunken Dream of *Ennius*; not that my Author

in this place gives me any encouragement for the Epithete; but because *Horace*, and all who mention *Ennius*, say he was an Excessive Drinker of Wine. In a Dream, or Vision, call you it which you please, he thought it was reveal'd to him, that the Soul of *Pithagoras* was Transmigrated into him: As *Pithagoras* before him believ'd that himself had been *Euphorbus* in the Wars of *Troy*. Commentators differ in placing the order of this Soul, and who had it first. I have here given it to the Peacock, because it looks more according to the Order of Nature that it shou'd lodge in a Creature of an Inferiour Species, and so by Gradation rise to the informing of a Man. And *Persius* favours me, by saying that *Ennius* was the Fifth from the *Pithagorean* Peacock.

[4] *My Friend is Shipwreck'd on*, &c. Perhaps this is only a fine Transition of the Poet to introduce the business of the Satyr, and not that any such Accident had happen'd to one of the Friends of

Persius. But, however, this is the most Poetical Description of any in our Author: And since he and *Lucan* were so great Friends, I know not but *Lucan* might help him in two or three of these Verses, which seem to be written in his stile; certain it is that besides this Description of a Shipwreck, and two Lines more, which are at the End of the Second Satyr, our Poet has written nothing Elegantly. I will therefore Transcribe both the passages, to justifie my Opinion. The following are the last Verses saving one of the Second Satyr.

Compositum jus, fasque animi ; sanctosque recessus

Mentis, & incoctum generoso pectus honesto ·

The others are those in this present Satyr, which are subjoyn'd.

—— trabe ruptâ, Bruttia Saxa
Prendi. Amicu inops Remque omnem, surdaque vota
Condidit Ionio: Jacet ipse in Littore ; & unà
Ingentes de puppe Dei: Jamque obvia Mergis Costa vatis laceræ.

[5] *From thy new hope,* &c. The Latin is, *Nunc & de Cespite vivo, frange aliquid.* Casaubon only opposes the *Cespes vivus,* which word for word is the living Turf, to the Harvest or Annual Income; I suppose the Poet rather means, sell a piece of Land already Sown, and give the Money of it to my Friend who has lost all by Shipwreck ; That is, do not stay till thou hast Reap'd, but help him immediately, as his Wants require.

[6] *Not Beg with a Blue Table,* &c. Holiday Translates it a Green Table: The sense is the same, for the Table was painted of the Sea Colour; which the Shipwrecked Person carried on his back, expressing his Losses thereby, to excite the Charity of the Spectators.

[7] *Or without Spices,* &c. The Bodies of the Rich, before they were burnt, were Imbalm'd with Spices, or rather Spices were put into the Urn, with the Relicks of the Ashes. Our Author here Names *Cinnamon* and *Cassia,* which *Cassia* was sophisticated with *Cherry Gum* : And probably enough by the *Jews,* who Adulterate all things which they sell. But whether the Ancients were acquainted with the Spices of the *Molucca* Islands, *Ceylon,* and other parts of the *Indies* ; or whether their *Pepper* and *Cinnamon* &c. were the same with ours, is another Question. As for *Nutmegs* and *Mace,* 'tis plain that the Latin Names of them are Modern.

[8] *Cæsar salutes,* &c. The *Cæsar* here mention'd is *Caius Caligula,* who affected to Triumph over the *Germans,* whom he never Conquer'd, as he did over the *Britains* ; and accordingly sent Letters, wrapt about with Laurels, to the Senate, and the Empress *Cæsonia,* whom I here call Queen, though I know that name was not us'd amongst the *Romans* ; but the word Empress wou'd not stand in that Verse : For which reason I Adjourn'd it to another. The Dust which was to be swept away from the Altars, was either the Ashes which were left there, after the last Sacrifice for Victory, or might perhaps mean the Dust or Ashes which were left on the Altars since some former Defeat of the *Romans* by the *Germans* : After which overthrow, the Altars had been neglected.

[9] *Cæsonia,* Wife to *Caius Caligula,* who afterwards, in the Reign of *Claudius,* was propos'd, but ineffectually, to be Marry'd to him, after he had Executed *Messalina* for Adultery.

[10] *The Captive Germans,* &c. He means only such as were to pass for *Germans* in the Triumph; Large-Body'd Men, as they are still, whom the Empress Cloath'd new, with Course Garments, for the greater Ostentation of the Victory.

[11] *Know, I have vow'd Two Hundred Gladiators.* A hundred pair of Gladiators were beyond the Purse of a private Man to give ; therefore this is only a threatning to his Heir, that he cou'd do what he pleas'd with his Estate.

[12] *should'st thou demand of me my Torch,* &c. Why should'st thou, who art an Old Fellow, hope to outlive me, and be my Heir, who am much Younger. He who was first in the Course, or Race, delivered the Torch, which he carried, to him who was Second.

[13] *Well Fed, and Fat as Cappadocian Slaves.* Who were Famous for their Lustiness, and being, as we call it, in good likeing. They were set on a Stall when they were expos'd to Sale, to show the good Habit of their Body, and made to play Tricks before the Buyers, to show their Activity and Strength.

[14] *Then say, Chrysippus,* &c. *Chrysippus,* the Stoick, invented a kind of Argument, consisting of more than three Propositions, which is called *Sorites,* or a heap. But as *Chrysippus* cou'd never bring his propositions to a certain stint, so neither can a Covetous Man bring his Craving Desires to any certain Measure of Riches, beyond which he cou'd not wish for any more.

SOME PECULIAR SPELLINGS OF DRYDEN'S.

Built = Build (substantive).	Main = Mane.
But = Butt.	Oar = Ore.
Casme = Chasm.	Oph = Oaf.
Cent'ry = Sentry.	Pheretrian = Feretrian.
Course = Coarse.	President = Precedent.
Eugh = Yew.	Salvage = Savage.
Ghess = Guess.	Satyr and Satyre = Satire.
Helter = Hilter.	Throws = Throes.
Lest = Least.	Wex = Wax.
Loose = Lose.	Whether = Whither.

The others are not likely to mislead. Many of his proper names are eccentric. Greek and Roman names may sometimes owe their forms to misprints, but even Ben Jonson regularly appears as Johnson.

INDEX OF FIRST LINES

SET IN
GREAT BRITAIN
AT THE
UNIVERSITY PRESS
OXFORD
PRINTED BY
LATIMER TREND AND CO. LTD.
PLYMOUTH